World Politics

in a New Era

Steven L. Spiegel

University of California at Los Angeles

Harcourt Brace College Publishers

Fort Worth Philadelphia San Diego New York Orlando Austin San Antonio
Toronto Montreal London Sydney Tokyo

To Mira, Nina, Avi

Vice President, Publisher	Ted Buchholz
Senior Acquisitions Editor	David Tatom
Developmental Editor	Fritz Schanz
Senior Project Editor	Charles J. Dierker
Senior Production Manager	Kenneth Dunaway
Electronic Publishing Coordinator	Jill Stubblefield
Art Director	Jim Taylor
Cover Art	Eric C. Westbrook

ISBN: 0-03-047574-0

Library of Congress Catalog Card Number: 93-81365

Address for Editorial Correspondence: Harcourt Brace College Publishers, 301 Commerce Street, Suite 3700, Fort Worth, TX 76102.

Address for Orders: Harcourt Brace & Company, 6277 Sea Harbor Drive, Orlando, FL 32887-6777. 1-800-782-4479, or 1-800-433-0001 (in Florida).

Printed in the United States of America

5 6 7 8 9 0 1 2 3   067   9 8 7 6 5 4 3 2

Preface

Conceived, organized, and written after the end of the Cold War, this book addresses a critical question, "What is the nature of world politics in a new era?" I embarked on this project because I could not find a book that satisfactorily serves the introductory course on world politics at UCLA. I searched in vain for a volume that deals comprehensively with all major aspects of post–Cold War international politics: history, economics, military strategy, theory, major global issues, and fundamental ideas about the patterns of contemporary international relations.

In writing this book, I have tried to address these issues through a variety of unifying themes. These include the contrasting dynamics between globalization and fragmentation, and between cooperation and conflict. Although interdependence and increased communications are yielding new areas of unimagined contact and collaboration between peoples, there are also continuing trends in world politics that yield fragmentation, conflict, violence, and chaos. Why is current international politics distinguished by these countervailing pressures? This book attempts to provide answers.

Aside from its themes, another distinguishing feature of this book is its "building block" organization. In teaching the introductory course, I have found that students often do not have the background necessary to integrate the variety of theories, facts, and issues that are covered in this course. Thus, this book is organized to first provide concrete basics (history, economics, and global issues) and then progressively move toward more abstract and theoretical topics (security, policy, levels of analysis). This is a reversal of the organization presented in many other textbooks. Here, the later theoretical chapters use the earlier descriptive chapters ("building blocks") as a base to illustrate the application of the abstract and theoretical topics, thus enabling the student to better comprehend the usefulness of theory at a more advanced level.

However, this book has been written so that instructors can use its contents in an order different from that in the table of contents. A course could be designed so that the theoretical material at the end of the book could be used initially. Alternatively, a course could be organized around an early analysis of history, followed by the theoretical material, and then the chapters on global issues. Because the materials in this book are integrated and cross-referenced, an instructor need not pursue the precise order of presentation used here.

In approaching the subject matter, I strove to provide comprehensiveness. Although many instructors may wish to use ancillary volumes, my aim was to provide an entire course in a single book. Thus, after the introduction, the book begins with three history chapters that describe international politics from 1648 to 1991. In this process, I discuss the origins of the modern international system (Chapter Two), the two World Wars (Chapter Three), and the Cold War (Chapter Four). This section is admittedly European-oriented, but the following chapters emphasize the non-European context of world politics. Chapter Five is unique for an introductory book. It addresses imperialism and colonialism, and emphasizes that much of international politics in recent centuries has been about the formation and disintegration of empires, and of their impact on the Third World. Chapter Six follows with a discussion of regional politics and conflict in the developing world. Although regional politics resulted in part as a consequence of the imperial tradition, I have tried to show in Chapters Five and Six how the Third World is developing and operating on its own terms.

The next four chapters deal with two other "building blocks"—economics and global issues. The basic concepts of global economics are set forth in Chapter Seven, with a brief description of the evolution of the modern international economic system. Chapter Eight follows with an examination of North-South economic relations. Similarly, Chapter Nine covers international law and organizations, and it is followed by the Chapter Ten review of global issues critical to comprehending world politics in the post–Cold War era. These include population, migration, food and hunger, the environment, drugs, terrorism, energy, and natural resources. After fundamental chapters on security and deterrence on the one hand (Chapter Eleven), and power on the other (Chapter Twelve), we reach the pinnacle of exploration of current world politics by examining in separate chapters the three levels of analysis: systems, domestic, and individual (Chapters 13, 14, and 15).

Finally, Chapter Sixteen addresses the most difficult issue of all—the future of international politics. In particular, this chapter explains why tension between globalization and fragmentation has occurred and why there is more conflict within and among lesser powers than within and among the greater powers. This chapter serves, then, as the culmination of all previously incorporated materials.

Throughout this book, a variety of paradigms are covered, including idealism and realism, modernization and dependency theories, feminist theory, the impact of interdependence, and neoliberal explanations for why cooperation is possible even within an anarchic world. Numerous non-European events and perspectives are stressed, including Third World complaints about Western dominance of the international economic system. There is also a heavy emphasis on the continuing impact of ethnic conflict in world politics.

Such a comprehensive tableau could not be presented without features in addition to the printed text. Each chapter opens with a vignette consisting of an interesting quote designed to draw students into the issues and capture the subject on a human level. Each chapter also includes a chronology that outlines the major events relating to the chapter's topics. "What Would You Do?" boxes provide a critical-thinking component that asks the student to assume the role of a decision maker and to resolve a dilemma after analyzing countervailing arguments and options. "At A Glance" boxes summarize complex phenomena and issues, and provide a hook for major points in different sections of the chapters. In addition, miscellaneous boxes spotlight important international events and colorful personalities, and also focus on precise points of complex conflicts and theories. Bold-faced key terms appear in text where initially mentioned, and in a glossary at the end of the book. Numerous, high-quality maps are provided, as are photographs, tables, figures, and cartoons. Each chapter ends with a "Principal Points" section, a numbered summary that highlights the major concepts and ideas of that chapter. Through these elements, I hope students will be better equipped to absorb and comprehend the various topics in an introductory course.

ACKNOWLEDGMENTS

I have been assisted by a unique team of individuals who made this book possible by serving as research and writing assistants, editors, feature analysts, and as a focus group for testing chapters and concepts. If my role was sometimes analogous to that of an orchestra conductor in this effort, the first violinist would certainly be Fred Wehling, who assumed the task of refining drafts, integrating chapters, and helping to place the book in next-to-final form. Fred deserves a good deal of the credit for the humor and clarity this volume tries to convey. Gregory V. Larkin was an early advisor who helped immensely in the conceptualization of the North-South material. Stephen Ruken worked on integrating reviewer comments and recommendations when the second draft had been completed. Steven Lobell was a good-natured, hard-working analyst on the economics, security, and systems chapters. Paul Williams did basic research and initial draft work on several chapters, and in particular concentrated on wrapping up the "What Would You Do?" features. Sydney Mintzer contributed critically to the economics chapter at a point when it threatened to delay the volume. Several others contributed their talents, including Gitty Amini Cannon (coordination and proofing), Julie Taylor (coordination), Kristen Williams (international law and organization), Maria Sampanis (economics), Neal Jesse (early research), David Pervin (history), Juliann Allison (ecopolitics), Alan Kessler (economics), and Stephan De Spiegeliere (security). All of these graduate students deserve my lasting gratitude and respect.

UCLA has a marvelous undergraduate volunteer student research assistant program. I benefitted from an exceptional group that helped enormously in a variety of tasks. Elizabeth Matthews worked for two years on everything from photos and cartoons to the review of page proof, which took up much of her summer of 1994. Christopher McDonald integrated the photo and cartoon notebook, and he designed and prepared early versions of most of the "At A Glance" boxes. Elena Garcia contributed her talents on the vignettes and helped valiantly in the review of page proof. I am grateful to MichaelAnne Cahill for her work in page proof and coordinating efforts. Elizabeth Vanalek specialized in researching the vignettes. David Glaes did particular work on maps. Other stellar researchers to whom I am most grateful include Victoria Samson, Mark Habib, Michael Chan, Paul Young Choi, Fernando Vicente, Brian Hicks, Jonathan Golden, Yuchi Sung, Christina Anderson, Linda Nguyen, Ellen Shin, Sung Woo, Darren Sigal, Golareh Hamid, Michael Fitzsimmons, Brian Harpuder, Daiana Cipollone, and Chang Chung.

David Tatom, political science editor of Harcourt Brace, convinced me to undertake this task. He was a stern taskmaster—always reminding me about deadlines and difficulties, but always holding out the light at the end of the tunnel as well. I am also indebted to Fritz Schanz for his guidance and contribution to the content and features. As a Harcourt Brace developmental editor, he probably knows more about the state of undergraduate education in international relations these days than anyone else I know. Charles Dierker served as project editor, and I am grateful for his perseverance and patience. My thanks also go to electronic publishing coordinator Jill Stubblefield.

My wife, Fredi, kept insisting the project could be completed when I was not so sure. Her love, vision, and encouragement guided me through the many obstacles I confronted in trying to finish a multifaceted volume consisting of so many diverse features. Our children, Mira, Nina, and Avi, are all either in college or beyond now. Their stories about their own trials in a variety of educational settings helped to remind me what it is like to be a student reading a textbook in an introductory course. They became my teachers in this enterprise, and in return it is only appropriate that this book should be dedicated to them.

I have been educated in this enterprise by more than one generation. Many years ago Claire Spiegel awakened my interest in international politics by providing a home in which debate and discussion of prominent issues could flourish.

In addition, I would like the thank the following reviewers: Charles Bailiff, St. Petersburg Junior College; Al Balboni, Clark County Community College; Ralph Carter, Texas Christian University; Vida Davoudi, North Harris Community College–Kingwood; Mark Denham, University of Toledo; Albert F. Eldridge, Duke University; Larry Elowitz, Georgia College; Bob Evanson, University of Missouri–Kansas City; Michael Gilbert, Pensacola Junior College; Ernest Greco, University of Massachusetts–Boston; Beau Grosscup, Cal State–Chico; Bill Kelley, Auburn; Phil Kelly, Emporia State University; Timothy J. Lomperis, Duke University; Michael Mastanduno, Dartmouth College; David Meyers, University of North Carolina–Greensboro; Ed Mihalkanin, Southwest Texas State University; Karen Mingst, University of Kentucky; James Mitchell, Cal State–Northridge; George Modelski, University of Washington; Susan Northcutt, University of South Florida; Joann Paine, Southern Illinois University at Carbondale; Warren Phillips, University of Maryland–College Park; Greg Raymond, Boise State University; Carolyn Rhodes, Utah State University; Henry Shockley, Boston University; Randolph Siverson, University of California–Davis; Bridgett Starkey, West Virginia University; Donald Sylvan, Ohio State University; and James Larry Taulbee, Emory.

I hope readers find the book useful in providing new perspectives on the emergence of world politics in a new era. It was only when I began preparing this manuscript that I realized how complex this new era has become. I found that many old methods, approaches, and notions really do not work anymore. A new, comprehensive conception is necessary, and it is that conception I have tried to provide. I hope this new vision will influence students, scholars, and policy makers as we all attempt to deal with challenges and opportunities no one thought possible even a decade ago.

Table of Contents

Chapter 3
The World Wars   77

Part III
The Legacy of European Domination

Chapter 5
The Emergence of North-South Relations:
Imperialism and Its Legacy

Part IV
The Economic Dimension in International Politics   281

Chapter 7
The World Economy   283

Part VI
The Security Dimension in World Politics

Chapter 11
Security

Chapter 12
Power   547

Maps

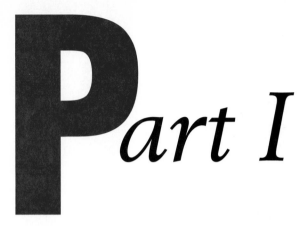

Introduction

Chapter 1

World Affairs in Our Lives

In more ways than we realize, our lives have become internationalized. The news media have played a significant role in narrowing the information gap between nations. Simply by turning on a television, we can witness a war, a riot, an earthquake, a military coup, a rebellion, a sports event, a parade, or an election thousands of miles away in a distant part of the world, live via satellite. In the next few days, you may eat pizza, egg rolls, tacos, crepes, falafel, and hamburgers, each reflecting the food and culture of very different people. We may purchase a car thinking we are buying an American or Japanese product, but it may be composed of parts produced in various countries. Shoppers can cash traveler's checks at American Express offices in Italy, Greece, Israel, India, Brazil, Venezuela, or Singapore and can buy General Motors automobiles manufactured or assembled in one of thirty-four countries, including Brazil, Finland, Kenya, Tunisia, South Korea, or Poland. Their counterparts in Australia, Canada, Malaysia, the Philippines, or Taiwan can buy Wrigley's chewing gum or Johnson & Johnson medical and surgical products. In Moscow you can eat at the largest McDonald's in the world; or you can sample the food at Taco Bell in London, or eat pizza at the Shakey's in Osaka. A few years ago, the author traveled from Los Angeles to London to Tel Aviv within a few days. The radio in the taxi that picked him up at each airport played Bobby McFerrin's popular song, "Don't Worry, Be Happy."

POPULAR IMAGES OF WORLD POLITICS

It's a Small World, After All

International politics today is ever present in our lives. From the obvious impact of news agencies and trade to the more subtle influence of cultural exchange, internationalism is as much a factor today as nationalism was in the past. Many readers may have visited either Disney World in Florida or Disneyland in California, or perhaps Tokyo Disneyland or even Euro Disney near Paris. One of the attractions, entitled "It's a Small World," involves a boat trip through a variety of cultures. Along the riverbank, singing and dancing dolls dressed in a myriad of traditional costumes represent the earth's cultural diversity. As the music plays, the rider visits far-off lands and is told, "It's a world of laughter, a world of tears/It's a world of hopes and a world of fears/There's so much that we share/That it's time we're aware/It's a small world after all."[1] The rider departs amidst fond farewells in several languages—*adios, ciao, auf Wiedersehen, say-onara.* Upon disembarking from this ten-minute journey, he or she may feel uplifted and reassured that the world is a happy place where people are sympathetic with each other and united despite their differences. This message encapsulates one particular understanding of the world in which the normal condition is one of harmony and accord, where people are naturally good and kind. From this perspective on international politics, cooperation is normal, understanding between people is easy once we get to know one another, and disputes are superficial anomalies that can be resolved amicably.

Lest the reader believe that this understanding of the world is reserved for the fantasies of Disney, we can also cite other examples in popular culture. For example, during the Ethiopian famine of 1985—which was caused not only by large-scale drought, but also by political factors, including civil war and authoritarian

Well-known celebrities record the song "We Are the World" in 1985. The group USA for Africa used proceeds from the recording to aid victims of African famine.
Source: © JetSet/Sygma.

rule—a song was written as a rallying cry for popular worldwide assistance. "We Are the World" expresses a sense of humanitarian universalism with verses that remind people of a shared sense of responsibility and an obligation to render assistance when others face the life or death agonies of famine. Inherent in its message is the notion that people can and ultimately must understand and accommodate each other.

The British singer Sting expressed similar notions when he wrote his song "Russians" in the 1980s, at the height of a particularly cold phase of the Cold War between the United States and the former Soviet Union. The words express the notion that we are essentially the same, that "we share the same biology/Regardless of ideology."[2] Sting calls on us to empathize with the problems faced by individuals in both societies rather than concentrating on the preoccupations of the leaders of states with their political "hang-ups" and controversies. This idealistic view of the world is taken to its ultimate conclusion in the famous song, "Imagine," by John Lennon, in which he expresses a view that is wistfully anti-state, anti-church, anti-political, anti-international structure: "Imagine there's no countries/It isn't hard to do/Nothing to kill or die for/And no religion too."[3] Lennon's lyrics evoke the image of a unified world of blissful anarchy in which all are one, living in harmony.

Star Wars

A very different view of the world is also present in popular culture. Movies such as *Star Wars* and *Rambo* depict an inherent conflict between good and evil. This perspective is the exact opposite of the idealistic view in which conflicts are resolvable by peaceful means and all people are naturally sympathetic with one another. In this "Star Wars" view of the world, evil persons create conflicts and seek to defeat the forces of truth, justice, and (in the American imagination) the American Way. (The Soviet film *Solo Voyage*, produced in response to *Rambo*, features the heroic acts of a Russian commando fighting evil American agents in Afghanistan.) The Star Wars approach holds that world politics is fundamentally a struggle between evil states and good states. Tension in the world is created by evil states that seek to gain at the expense of weaker nations. When a conflict arises, one nation (or a group of nations) must be at fault. Wars do not start because of the situation in which states find themselves, but rather because of the aggressive intentions of evil states or leaders.

Former President Ronald Reagan's view of the world seemed to follow this line of thinking. During Reagan's presidency he labeled the Soviet Union the "Evil Empire." From his perspective, the USSR sought to destroy democracy in Europe and America. The "good guys" had to defend against this threat by standing firm politically and increasing their military power. Sizable U.S. military budgets were justified using this type of rationale throughout the Cold War. When Soviet President Mikhail Gorbachev adopted less confrontational policies in the late 1980s, Reagan claimed that America's vigilance and military strength had caused the USSR to give up and reform its evil ways. From this

"I'M WILLING TO DISCUSS THE ARMS RACE WHENEVER THOSE RUSSIAN DEVILS ARE!"

Ronald Reagan offered a stark "good guys versus the bad guys" view of the world when he character-ized the Soviet Union as the Evil Empire.

Source: Copyright, 1984, Los Angeles Times Syndicate. Reprinted by permission.

perspective, when the USSR collapsed at the end of 1991, the "good guys" finally won, but the possibility of new threats to world peace arising from other "bad guys" remained.

These two views represented in popular culture suggest either that the natural order of humanity is harmonious, or that history is a conflict between the forces of light and those of darkness. We will see these views recurring in the sources of conflict and cooperation in international relations, the causes of war and peace, and the functioning of world politics. These contrasting interpretations are necessitated by the fact that there is no automatic order in the international system. In domestic politics, there are legal norms that are enforceable on individuals. In world politics, however, no one rules over states.

TERMINOLOGY

We should take an opportunity to define some important terms used throughout this book. All the states of the world, including the international organizations to which they belong, compose the **international system.** **World politics** refers to the competition for and exercise of power and authority in the international system, while the broader term *international relations* refers to the totality of interactions among states and nonstate actors. Obviously, world politics and international relations are closely related, but they are not entirely synonymous; a performance by a Nigerian dance troupe in Toronto and the opening of a McDonald's in Jakarta are part of international relations, but not of world politics. *Foreign policy* refers to the actions and positions on issues taken by an individual state regarding other states or groups outside its boundaries.

ANARCHY VERSUS AUTHORITY

Consider the differences between behavior in the jungle and on the football field. Both are arenas of intense competition and often violent conflict. On the gridiron, football players are supervised by referees, and the athletes abide by specific rules of the game. If they break a rule, a penalty will be assessed. They can attempt to score at will, but only within the confines of accepted patterns of behavior. In the jungle, by contrast, there are no referees and no rules. The survival of the fittest is the law of nature, and there is no higher authority than instinct and the struggle between predator and prey.

Similarly, the unique characteristic that makes international politics so complex is that it takes place in an environment of **anarchy.** There is no world government or higher authority policing nation-states. This is the fundamental difference between international and domestic politics. In domestic politics, there is a system that establishes law and order of some kind. While this system may be different for each state, each government in its own way provides enforcement of laws to maintain a more or less orderly society.

When we think of domestic politics we might think of a centralized government with a large bureaucracy. This bureaucracy is the machine that runs the everyday business of government. A leader such as a prime minister or a president is to ensure that the government functions properly. A country also usually has a set of laws, as well as a constitution. These laws guide and constrain the behavior of its citizens. Even in a totalitarian regime, where individuals do not have rights, a system of authority prevails. In a democracy, authority to govern is granted through the means of popular elections and political campaigns. In the United States, for example, a presidential election occurs every four years. Billboards dot the landscape, and interviews, endorsements, and commercials are transmitted incessantly from television and radio. In any national political system, order arises because of laws and authorities that enforce those laws, namely the courts and the police. If you disobey laws, there is always a possibility that you will be caught and punished.

In the international system, however, states worry less about "being caught," as there are no "police" to enforce the laws of international politics. Saddam Hussein, in deciding to invade and annex Kuwait, mistakenly calculated that his actions would not result in any significant response from the rest of the world, or at least he thought he could handle whatever protests emerged. Sometimes other nations, or groups of nations, such as the United Nations (UN), choose to act as police, as happened in the case of the Iraqi invasion of Kuwait, yet there is no certainty that this will occur. Examples of successful aggression include the United States' mining of Nicaragua's harbors in 1984, China's forcible absorption of Tibet in 1950, the Soviets' assumption of control of the Baltic states in 1940, the Indian takeover of the tiny Portuguese enclave of Goa in 1961, and the Vietnamese capture of Cambodia in 1978. As is so often the case in international politics, aggression is in the eye of the beholder. In each of these examples, some believed that the military action was justified. Thus international action against aggression often resembles vigilante justice, where innocents are harmed in clumsy attempts to find and punish the guilty.

The Security Dilemma

This anarchic nature of world politics leads to a situation known as the **security dilemma.** The security dilemma arises when a state feels insecure and decides that its best policy is to increase its military strength. Its objective in so doing is not to enhance its aggressive power, but only to increase its ability to defend against attack. Unfortunately, a neighboring country may then feel threatened by this increase of armaments near its border. The second state, fearing that it has been made more vulnerable by the increase in the first state's military power, initiates a military buildup of its own. As more and more states witness this increase in military potential, they consider themselves threatened by the possibility of aggressive action. An unintended spiral thus occurs, where every nation grows more and more insecure and seeks to stay equal to its neighbors in military strength.

This unfortunate situation arises despite the fact that none of the states involved intends to threaten the security of its neighbors. Each state, acting in its own self-interest, helps to create a potentially dangerous buildup of weapons. We recently witnessed this effect of the anarchic world system during the Cold War between the United States and the former Soviet Union from 1945 to 1990 (described in Chapter Four) and in the Arab-Israeli disputes of the post–World War II period (outlined in Chapter Six). The security dilemma explains how conflicts can arise even when states do not harbor aggressive intentions toward one another.

Of course, some people with a "Star Wars" view believe that the Americans or the Soviets, the Arabs or the Israelis, did or do indeed have aggressive intentions toward their adversaries. But, to those who believe in the security dilemma, conflict occurs not because states are fundamentally antagonistic, but because of the conditions in which they find themselves. That is, conflict stems from an anarchic world where the possibility of aggression is ever present. States hope for the best, but expect the worst, and thus arm themselves as a precautionary measure. Nations all seek power over one another, and must either conquer or die. The popular film series about the British spy-hero James Bond similarly suggests a world where nations that are basically good must sometimes resort to intrigue, subterfuge, and controlled force in order to survive and prevail against evil. In the same vein, many Cold War era movies such as *The Spy Who Came in from the Cold*, in which innocent people are used as pawns and sacrificed in order to save a reprehensible but indispensable British spy behind the Iron Curtain, present an image of world politics in which the ends sometimes justify the means—that is, it is necessary to commit sins in order to overcome evil. (The security dilemma and its effects are discussed further in Chapter Eleven.)

Common Interests and Cooperation under Anarchy

Even in an anarchic world dominated by the security dilemma, however, there is far more cooperation than conflict between nations. Because wars and crises make the headlines and catch our attention, it is easy to overlook the fact that relations between states are usually positive and friendly, and rarely lead to violence. The national interests that all states pursue will frequently conflict with the goals and interests of other states, but the leaders know that they are more likely to attain their goals through cooperation and reciprocal behavior. As a result, states, in interacting with one another, establish rules and norms that reinforce cooperation.

One such time-honored norm is that of diplomatic immunity. One of the reasons the seizure of the American Embassy in Teheran in 1979 by the Iranian revolutionary guards caused outrage in the United States and elsewhere is that it violated this time-honored principle. According to international law, the U.S. Embassy was considered American territory and therefore off-limits to foreign aggression. Iran decided against voluntarily complying with international norms of conduct and took over the embassy. If all states took the representatives of nations with whom they had relations hostage, normal diplomatic interchange could not exist. Chapter Nine describes how states develop the practice of diplomatic immunity and other norms of cooperative behavior.

Similarly, no country has all the resources or products that it requires. As Chapter Seven shows, many states specialize or have particular products they can produce more efficiently than other countries. If states could not trade products or resources they have in surplus for those they do not produce or possess, all would be poorer. Thus, states find that they have complementary economic interests and realize that cooperation can provide mutual benefits. In international politics, it often pays to cooperate in such areas as diplomatic and economic relations. Trade provides gains for all sides. Diplomatic relations are useful to all states. Most states realize that they would have difficulty pursuing their own interests without economic relations and diplomatic exchanges.

States also share common problems. Pollution in the air or water affects many countries. The accident at the nuclear reactor in Chernobyl in 1986 in the former

Soviet Union increased the radiation over many nearby countries. Pollution of a river like the Rhine or the Danube that runs through several countries affects many neighbors downstream. Use of fossil fuels produces carbon dioxide, which alters the earth's atmosphere and may cause temperatures around the globe to increase. Many industrial chemicals adversely affect the ozone layer, which protects the earth from harmful radiation. Because many nations derive short-term economic benefits from ignoring pollution regulations or chopping down forests for wood products, environmental degradation is a global problem about which nations must cooperate in order to solve. (Chapter Ten surveys environmental concerns, drug trafficking, terrorism, and other global issues.)

Therefore, although the nature of international politics is anarchic and encourages conflict, the nature of some of the problems that governments face encourages cooperation. The security dilemma does not prevent nations from working together to address concerns that affect them all. Simply put, nations need each other. Benjamin Franklin's remark about the leaders of the American Revolution is even more applicable to the states in the contemporary international system: "We must indeed all hang together, or, most assuredly, we shall all hang separately." Order in the international arena is thus established not through enforcement, as is the case in the domestic arena, but rather through reciprocal compliance by nations explicitly or tacitly adhering to agreements.

COOPERATION VERSUS CONFLICT

Given the anarchy of international politics, cooperation and conflict are frequently intertwined. In theory, since World War II there has been a concerted effort in economic matters to promote and establish an international trading order to the benefit of all involved. As noted in Chapter Five, however, many countries in the Third World have resented the economic success of the West and have argued that it has been achieved in large measure by exploitation of their resources without adequate or fair remuneration. For example, a South American country may feel that U.S. firms exercise excessive control over its natural resources, such as copper in Chile or oil in Peru. Countries of the former communist bloc, after decades of imposed isolation from this trading order, are attempting to integrate themselves into the global economy. Many of these states have begun to model themselves after the capitalist democracies, but these moves are bringing domestic political and ethnic conflicts to the forefront. The effects of cooperation are thus not invariably positive; cooperation itself may cause tensions in other sectors of international affairs.

As nations modernize and society becomes more complex, states begin to interact more frequently with other states for a variety of reasons and in a variety of ways, such as in trade and diplomacy. Economies become linked to those of other states. This pattern of linkage is called **interdependence.** For most industrial countries, foreign trade has become increasingly more important to their economies as their exports have grown faster than their **GNP (gross**

national product, the total sum of all goods and services produced by a nation) for at least the last two decades. Perhaps more significant is the dependence of many countries on foreign sources of raw materials. Japan's reliance on imports for practically all of its energy needs, especially petroleum, has influenced its foreign policy towards oil-producing states. Manufacturers in the United States, Japan, and the **European Union** are also dependent on foreign supplies of minerals like bauxite, manganese, and chromium.[4]

Economies are further connected by foreign investment. Multinational corporations such as Ford, Sony, Philips, and BASF have vested interests in the stability of the world economy; their investments in factories, offices, and other business expenses in countries ranging from Australia and Japan to Pakistan and Venezuela depend on friendly and stable diplomatic and economic relations being maintained. The sums of money involved in international trade and finance are truly staggering. In all, the U.S. government and private American investors owned more than $2 trillion in foreign assets at the end of 1991, while the total of Japanese, British, Dutch, and other foreign assets in the United States approached $2.5 trillion.[5] As states become more intertwined in their relations with other states, they develop greater stakes in international cooperation even though their specific economic interests may conflict.

Cooperation and conflict also coexist when nations are confronted by an event of paramount proportions, namely war. In these instances, cooperation between states emerges. In World War II, the United States, Great Britain, and the Soviet Union worked together to prevent the Nazis from conquering all of Europe. The formation of NATO (North Atlantic Treaty Organization) by the United States, Canada, and European nations in 1949 arose from post–World War II apprehensions concerning possible Soviet aggression. This perceived threat prompted former World War II allies and enemies alike to cooperate against a new common adversary.

Therefore, although world politics is anarchic, it is not disorderly. Order exists in the international system and constrains the behavior of states. While there is no world government to enforce laws, if states violate international rules, this can lead to negative outcomes that far outweigh any potential gains from such behavior. Thus many states that could easily conquer their weaker neighbors do not do so because they fear retaliation or political or moral isolation from the international community.

DOMESTIC FACTORS IN INTERNATIONAL RELATIONS

Other constraints on the actions of states and leaders are rooted in domestic politics. The U.S. antiwar movement impeded the ability of both the Johnson and Nixon administrations to conduct military operations in Vietnam as they pleased. Even the former Soviet Union's military actions in Afghanistan were restricted by domestic popular discontent with the uncertainty of prolonged combat in that forlorn country. Indeed, the Afghan War was a factor in the collapse of Soviet communism. Another famous example of domestic politics limiting the ability to act in the international arena was the widespread pacifism in Britain and France prior to World War II. This pacifism interfered with the British and French governments' abilities to counter the rise of Hitler. The popularity of isolationism in the United States during this period played a similar role.

Additionally, modern communications make it easier for citizens to obtain the information necessary to question their leaders' policies. In the highly complex environment in which we live today, we can fly to another country in a few hours, call overseas and transmit documents in an instant. Communication is cheaper and easier than before. Satellite coverage allows us to watch events around the world as they are happening. The Vietnam War was the first conflict seen on television, with full reports of the gore and uncertainty of combat. The result was a devastating decline in support for the war in the United States and in support of American policy generally. More recently, the Tiananmen Square Massacre in China, when students who were demonstrating in favor of democracy were gunned down (while other protesters faxed reports of repression to the outside world), had a temporarily devastating impact on China's ability to pursue its diplomatic and economic goals, because widespread revulsion against the bloodshed led nations like the United States to modify their relations with the

A man stands passively before a convoy of Chinese army tanks on the Avenue of Eternal Peace in Beijing on June 2, 1989. The next day government troops attacked pro-democracy demonstrators in Tianamen Square.
Source: © Reuters/Bettman.

Chinese government. The Persian Gulf War in the Middle East affected hundreds of millions of people around the world because they could see and experience it. When a CNN (Cable News Network) journalist wearing a gas mask reported impending SCUD missile attacks on Saudi Arabia and Israel during the Gulf War, viewers felt as if they were the victims. (Some Americans even bought gas masks out of fear that the United States would suffer terrorist attacks.)

Thus we see that international relations are a confusing blend of both the domestic and the international, and of cooperation and conflict. On the one hand, the nature of world politics is an anarchic system where no higher authority can enforce laws upon the individual states. On the other hand, cooperation and order emerge from mutual interests, international institutions, and constraints on action.

WHO PARTICIPATES IN INTERNATIONAL POLITICS?

The primary type of actor in international relations today is the **nation-state** around which the world is organized. The nation-state is a relatively new idea whose origins are rooted in the American and French revolutions at the end of the eighteenth century. A **state** is an independent political entity with institutions and an authority in a specific territory. A **nation** is a group of people who view themselves as having a common heritage, a common destiny, and a sense of mutual identification based on language, history, and culture. The nation-state fuses these two concepts; it is a state structure in which a nation resides and that exists (ideally) to protect and promote the interests of that nation. Modern examples of nation-states include France, Turkey, Japan, and Brazil. The concept of the nation-state is directly related to much of the conflict in international politics for the last two hundred years, and still accounts for much of the continuing conflict today. Throughout history, many bitter conflicts have arisen when nations (such as Greece, Poland, and Croatia) attempted to create their own states, and when states (such as Germany, North Korea, and Serbia) sought to unify all members of a nation. For these reasons, more will be said about the definition and origin of the nation-state in Chapter Two.

While the nation-state is the basic organizing principle of world politics, **nationalism** (the belief that a nation should have its own state) is one of the main motivating factors. National groups such as the French-speaking Quebecois in Canada, the Kurds, the Tibetans, and the Muslim Slavs in Bosnia all claim the right to "self-determination," or to have their own independent states. The situation is reversed in numerous African countries. When European states controlled much of Africa, they divided territories according to their convenience without reference to the interests or history of indigenous peoples. We therefore see conflicts in many African states due to the colonial powers' arbitrarily cutting borders across ethnic boundaries, such as the Yoruba in Benin and Nigeria, the Somali in Somalia and Ethiopia, and the Swazi in Swaziland and South Africa (see Chapters Five and Six).

While the nation-state is the primary actor in the international arena, other entities exist that can influence world politics. These may be grouped into the two broad categories of **intergovernmental organizations (IGOs)** and **nongovernmental organizations (NGOs).** IGOs, as the name implies, are groups of states or governments organized for a common purpose, while NGOs are groups not directly related to governments but organized to take an active part in international affairs. (IGOs, NGOs, and a whole alphabet soup of other non-state actors on the world stage are discussed further in Chapter Nine.)

IGOs can provide a diplomatic and legal framework for political interaction among nations (in which case they are usually termed international organizations) or they may be designed to foster cooperation in specific fields such as trade, security, health, transportation, arms control, and human rights. Some examples are the **United Nations,** the best-known and most important international organization; the **Organization of Petroleum Exporting Countries (OPEC)** and the **Organization for Economic Cooperation and Development (OECD),** which are primarily economic organizations but which frequently have political goals as well; the **North Atlantic Treaty Organization (NATO),** which is a defense alliance; and the **International Atomic Energy Agency (IAEA),** which monitors nuclear weapons proliferation and the safety of nuclear power plants.

The impact that IGOs have in the international arena ranges from minimal to quite substantial, depending on their cohesion and resources. For example, the regulation of oil prices by the OPEC nations in 1973 raised oil prices, created economic hardship in both the Third World and industrialized countries, and had a considerable political impact on world affairs due to Western demands for and dependence on oil. By contrast, the UN offers a forum for dialogue on controversial issues that in some circumstances leads to conflict resolution, and the UN Security Council can dispatch peacekeeping forces to areas of conflict—if UN member states agree to supply the troops and finance their operations. However, many UN resolutions are often ignored by states that do not agree with them. Institutions affiliated with the UN, such as the World Health Organization (WHO), the Food and Agriculture Organization (FAO), and the United Nations Relief and Works Agency (UNRWA) also provide inter-nation services in particular areas such as health care, famine relief, and protection for refugees.

NGOs come in a wide variety of types. **Multinational corporations (MNCs)** are one type. With the increasing world interdependence and a liberal international economic order that supports free trade (trade without tariffs or similar barriers), the twentieth century has seen the rise of multinational corporations as international participants. Although they may be based in one particular nation, referred to as the MNC's home country, they have operations and production plants in many other nations, or host countries. Famous examples include IBM, the Mitsubishi group, Shell Oil, Volkswagen, Coca-Cola, ICI, and General Motors. Their influence over governments and in the international arena is generated by their financial resources and economic power, which are often quite extensive.

Terrorist groups are extremist political factions that use violence to achieve political gains. This category encompasses groups that may be legitimized by other nations but are not part of the official arms of governments. Examples include the Hezbollah and the Irish Republican Army (IRA), as well as groups operating only as violent militarists, such as the Red Brigades in Italy and Peru's Sendero Luminoso (Shining Path). Often, these groups exert influence by frightening civilians with the threat and practice of violence in order to persuade others to support their political aims.

Often terrorists are supported by states, or governments, many times serving the goals of those states. For example, competing factions of the Palestine Liberation Organization (PLO) who oppose the peace process are actively sponsored and housed by various radical Arab regimes. Iran's active participation throughout the Middle East has included its sponsorship of hostage-taking in the 1980s, and its support of various local Islamic fundamentalist groups. North Korea is another state accused of supporting acts of terrorism like the bombing of a Korean Air Lines jet in 1987. Not to be overlooked is the role of the former USSR in providing arms, training, and other means of support for terrorist groups such as those operating in the Middle East. When these groups engage in terrorist activity, they further the goals of individual states and their quest for power in the region. The difference between terrorism and resistance to conquest is often a matter of perspective; one side's "terrorists" may be another's "freedom fighters."

Various other types of organizations also play a role in world politics. These include the news media, the Catholic church, Greenpeace, Amnesty International, the International Olympic Organizing Committee, and the International Committee of the Red Cross. From time to time, these organizations can influence international relations that deal with their specific interests. For example, Greenpeace's active pursuit of antiwhaling laws has contributed to negotiations between Japan, the former USSR, and the United States over whaling practices in the Pacific Ocean. The Vatican seeks to improve the human condition through religious teaching and moral persuasion, but it engages in some political activity as well. For example, it placed its own kind of sanctions against the white-dominated South African regime, denouncing apartheid as a moral evil and refusing to include the country on the Pope's itinerary. Amnesty International lobbies for an end to capital punishment and focuses publicity on individuals who are victimized by their governments, sometimes resulting in their release from prison.

The news media draw attention to particular states, personalities, and problems. By raising global awareness of specific concerns, the media can bring issues to the forefront of national and international political debate and can affect the perceptions of millions toward specific events. When Mikhail Gorbachev resigned the presidency of the now defunct USSR in December 1991, the event was covered by teams of journalists, relayed instantly around the world, followed by hours of commentary, background reports, and speculation on the impact the event would have on world politics. One news service executive even provided a pen when Gorbachev's failed.

ALL THE WORLD'S A STAGE: GEOGRAPHY

Familiarity with the world map helps to remind us that small countries often get big headlines while little is heard about many large nations. The world's geography can be examined in terms of any number of variables, including terrain, climate, resources, vegetation, population, or nationality. Glances at different types of maps can bring different aspects of the international system to our attention. A look at Map 1.1 shows how the globe's land surface has been divided into nation-states. However, a look at the earth from space eliminates national boundaries altogether, presenting the world as a single globe with a common living environment shared by all its inhabitants.

Important distinctions that may be obscured in a view from space come into focus when we take a closer look at specific areas; in policy-making and the popular imagination, all parts of the world are not created equal.[6] We might start by looking at North America, an area familiar to most of us, which consists of Canada, the United States, Mexico, Central America, and the Caribbean. These areas together comprise 9.36 million square miles, or 16 percent of the earth's land surface. To the south, the twelve countries of South America are almost 12 percent of that surface, or about 6.9 million square miles. Africa, a continent comprising fifty-one countries, is across the Atlantic and is much larger than South America. Its 11.7 million square miles are 20 percent of the earth's total land area. Together, Africa and South America cover almost a third of the earth's surface, yet we hear relatively little about events in these areas.

By contrast, the land area of Europe is tiny, comprising only 3.3 percent of the total land area, if we exclude the countries that formerly comprised the USSR. Yet the amount of attention this small part of the earth receives, culturally and politically, might lead us to anticipate a much larger size. Historically, Europe was the center of world politics for centuries, although its size was quite small compared to the lands bordering its territory on the east. Taken as a unit, the territory of the former USSR was almost 15 percent of the world's land area, as large as South America and Europe combined. As an indication of how large the area was, eleven time zones were covered by its territory. There is an old saying about Russia, which comprises 76 percent of the former USSR, that summarizes its huge size: "Russia is not a country, but a world."

Excluding the Asiatic parts of the old USSR, Asia still has 18.2 percent of the earth's land area (otherwise it contains 30 percent). This part of Asia is dominated by China, a country about the size of the United States; India, which is about twice the size of Alaska; and off the coast, Japan, slightly smaller than California. Australia, New Zealand, Micronesia, and Polynesia, which comprise another 5.6 percent of the world's land area, benefit from their location as island nations, which has helped insulate them from some of the security problems affecting their continental neighbors.

Glancing at a map can show us how the size and location of various countries have influenced their interests and actions in the international arena. Yet, if we readjusted our map to reflect population or wealth rather than territory, we would have a totally different impression of the world in which we live. The reader is encouraged now to look at Maps 8.1 and 8.2 on pages 342 and 350. Map 8.1 portrays the continents according to their share of the world's wealth as measured by GNP. Map 8.2 shows the world as it would look if it were drawn proportionally according to each continent's population. These maps show a remarkable contrast between the concentration of the world's population and that of its wealth. As we have already seen on the conventional map, Asia has almost one-third of the world's land mass, but it appears even more vast when its 3.13 billion people, or 57.8 percent of the total world inhabitants, are represented in the population map. China alone is home for more than 1 billion people, or 21 percent of the world's inhabitants, while India is home for 883 million people or 16.3 percent of the world's population. These billions of people occupy a much smaller spot on the map depicting their share of the world's wealth. Asia, not including the areas of the former USSR, accounts for only 23 percent of the world's GNP. This figure still includes Japan and the oil-rich Middle Eastern countries; the combined GNP of Japan, Saudi Arabia, Kuwait, and the United Arab Emirates alone total 15 percent of the world's GNP. The rest of populous Asia's share, including such countries as Iran, China, India, and Pakistan, is only 8 percent, but that number is likely to grow in the future.

Africa's 654 million inhabitants, 12 percent of the world's population, have plenty of room on their large continent, but they must get along on less than 2 percent of the world's wealth; comparing the size of the continent on the three maps shows just how tiny this is relative to Africa's land area and population. Across the Atlantic, South America has less than half the residents of Africa, or about 5.5 percent of the world's population, but a slightly larger share of the world's wealth, about 3 percent of the world total GNP. Together, the continents of Africa, Asia, and South America cover almost two-thirds of the world's land mass and are home to over three-quarters of the world's population, but comprise only 28 percent of the world's wealth. On the other hand, Australia and New Zealand are sparsely populated, with 0.4 percent, or just over 21.2 million people, living in an area much larger than India, and with 1.4 percent of the world's wealth. Although their population is less than one-tenth that of South America, Australia and New Zealand's share of GNP is almost half that of South America's.

In contrast, geographically tiny Europe looks bigger when drawn relative to its 13 percent of the world's population (including the European part of the former USSR). The continent appears dramatically larger when depicted in terms of GNP; if the former USSR is excluded, Europe has 29.3 percent of the world's GNP; if included, Europe accounts for 41.6 percent. Thus, economically, Europe dwarfs continents much larger and more populated than itself.

About 436 million people (8 percent of the world's population) reside in North America, which makes the continent much smaller on the population map than its territory would indicate. At the same time, North America holds a dramatically larger place on the GNP map, since the continent holds 29 percent of the world's wealth. The U.S. GNP alone is more than $5.7 trillion, much larger than the total GNP of all of Africa and South America combined. Seeing the

Map 1.1   Political Map of the World, 1994

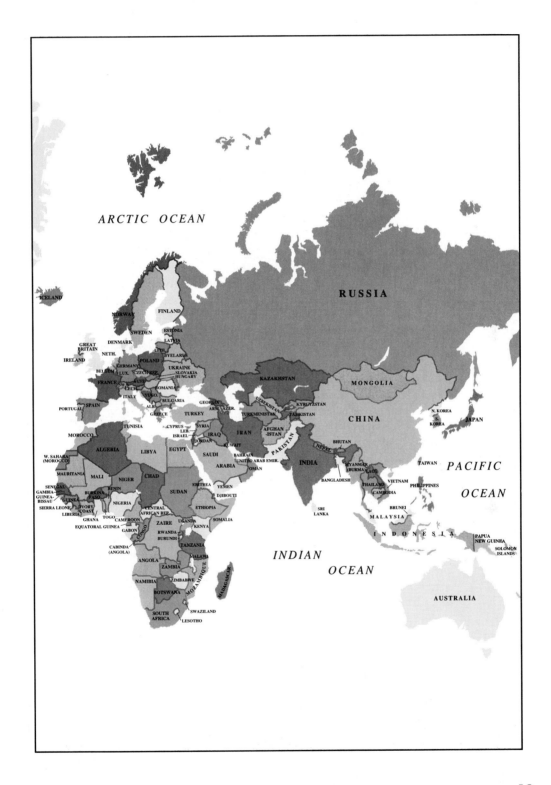

ARCTIC OCEAN

ICELAND

NORWAY
FINLAND
SWEDEN
ESTONIA
DENMARK
LATVIA
GREAT
BRITAIN
NETH.
LITH.
BYELARUS
IRELAND
POLAND
GERMANY
UKRAINE
BELGIUM
LUX.
CZECH REP.
SLOVAKIA
FRANCE
SWITZ.
AUSTRIA
HUNGARY
LIECH.
ITALY
ROMANIA
PORTUGAL
SPAIN
YUGO.
BULGARIA
ALB.
GREECE
TURKEY
TUNISIA
CYPRUS
LEB.
SYRIA
ISRAEL
IRAQ
JORDAN
KUWAIT

RUSSIA

KAZAKHSTAN

MONGOLIA

GEORGIA
ARM. AZER.
UZBEKISTAN
KYRGYZSTAN
TURKMENISTAN
TAJIKISTAN
AFGHAN-
ISTAN
IRAN
PAKISTAN

CHINA

N. KOREA
S.
KOREA
JAPAN

MOROCCO

W. SAHARA
(MOROCCO)

ALGERIA

LIBYA

EGYPT

BAHRAIN
UNITED ARAB EMIR.
OMAN

SAUDI
ARABIA

BHUTAN
NEPAL

INDIA

TAIWAN

PACIFIC

OCEAN

MAURITANIA

MALI

NIGER

CHAD

SENEGAL
GAMBIA
GUINEA-
BISSAU
SIERRA LEONE
LIBERIA

BURKINA
FASO
GUINEA

IVORY
COAST
GHANA

BENIN

NIGERIA

TOGO

CAMEROON

SUDAN

ERITREA
DJIBOUTI

YEMEN

ETHIOPIA

SRI
LANKA

BANGLADESH

MYANMAR
(BURMA)
LAOS

THAILAND

VIETNAM

CAMBODIA

PHILIPPINES

BRUNEI

MALAYSIA

EQUATORAL GUINEA

CENTRAL
AFRICAN REP.

GABON

CONGO

ZAIRE

UGANDA

RWANDA
BURUNDI

KENYA

SOMALIA

INDONESIA

PAPUA
NEW GUINEA

SOLOMON
ISLANDS

CABINDA
(ANGOLA)

TANZANIA

INDIAN

ANGOLA

ZAMBIA

MALAWI

OCEAN

NAMIBIA

ZIMBABWE

BOTSWANA

MOZAMBIQUE

MADAGASCAR

AUSTRALIA

SOUTH
AFRICA

SWAZILAND

LESOTHO

19

world according to variances in GNP, population, and territory allows us a greater understanding of how these factors affect the roles states play in the realm of international relations. The impact of a state's size, location, resources, and population on its foreign policies will be discussed further in the survey of the components of power in Chapter Twelve.

LEVELS OF ANALYSIS IN INTERNATIONAL RELATIONS

A state's geography obviously has a major impact on that state's relations with its neighbors and on its actions and influence in the global political arena, so much so that the term geopolitics is used to describe the effect of geographic factors in international affairs. But, obviously, geography is not destiny in world politics, as states that are small in terms of area, population, or GNP can affect events in a big way. This leads us to ponder a question: exactly what does determine how a state will act in the international system? As the chapters in this book will show, there is little that is either exact or predictable about world politics. Although analysts of international affairs can rarely find definitive explanations for historical events or current policies, they can at least tell us where to look. The plethora of factors influencing world politics may be grouped into **levels of analysis,** which may be thought of as categories of variables that can help us decide where to search for explanations of world affairs. Chapters Thirteen, Fourteen, and Fifteen will discuss levels of analysis in more detail, but it may be useful to briefly introduce them here before the book embarks on a survey of events and issues in international politics.

Experts in the field of international relations disagree on the number of levels of analysis. (This should begin to give you an idea of how little they agree on anything else.) It is most convenient for the purposes of this book to assign the various influences on state behavior to one of three levels: the international systemic, the domestic, or the individual.[7] The international systemic level (the systemic level, for short) claims that states are essentially similar. They are moved by the situation in which they find themselves and react to similar situations in the same way as others. Thus, it doesn't matter how the state is organized or who is in charge. Present any state with an external challenge and it will react in a particular, prescribed manner.

The systemic level covers factors which come into play in the interactions between states. These include the number of major political actors in the system and their strengths and weaknesses relative to one another (often referred to as the **balance of power**), the rules and norms that govern the relations between states, as well as geography, international organizations, and similar influences operating "above" or "outside" specific nation-states. In general, these factors exert an impact on all states in the system; the impact on each state may vary, but the nature of the influence is the same for the entire system. For example, the United Nations influences all countries, although it may have a different impact on stronger states than on weaker states. Moreover, a system cannot have more than one structure at the same time. For example, it cannot simultaneously be **bipolar** (dominated by two actors of relatively equal power that overshadow all the rest) and **multipolar** (containing several more or less equal actors). (These concepts will be discussed further in Chapter Thirteen.)

In many ways, the systemic level considers the ways in which factors common to all states prompt them to behave similarly toward one another. By contrast, the **domestic level** deals with influences that operate *within* nation-states and thus examines how different attributes of states lead them to act differently. The domestic level looks at individual nations' political and economic systems, government structure, bureaucracy, history, and culture. Analysis from the domestic level considers how each state's unique characteristics give it a particular orientation toward or outlook on world politics and how these traits define a state's specific interests, goals, and concerns. Chapter Fourteen will examine how the features of a state that distinguish it from other actors in the international system can cause it to relate to other states in a manner different from what an analysis at the systemic level might lead us to expect.

Just as states share universal characteristics while possessing unique features, people are alike in many important ways and very different in others. The **individual level** concentrates on people both as members of the human species and as personalities with their own fortes and foibles. This level considers what role, if any, "human nature" plays in world affairs and whether or not it can be changed to make the world a less conflictual and violent place. Chapter Fifteen notes that while traditional discussions of "human" nature have really focused on the nature of men rather than both men and women, feminist theory provides new perspectives on the relationship between human characteristics and the international system. The chapter then examines how individual leaders' backgrounds, experiences, styles of leadership, and personal goals and beliefs can affect the decisions they make regarding their countries' foreign policies. All too often, these decisions must be made under extremely stressful conditions, and the individual level explores how situations of confrontation and crisis can affect the decision-making process. Chapter Fifteen will therefore attempt to put a human face on world politics by looking at how leaders and the citizens they lead can shape international relations.

The three levels of analysis will be examined in more detail in Chapters Thirteen, Fourteen, and Fifteen. For now, it is most important to remember that levels of analysis are basically categories of explanations for the actions of states in the international system. Taken together, they provide an organizational scheme for theories of international relations. As such, they help analysts to formulate and test explanations for the behavior of states and nonstate actors in the international system. The levels do this by indicating what sort of data is most relevant to a particular theory and identifying the competing explanations an analyst must contend with in order to prove his or her case. They can also help us to understand events by classifying the plethora of factors that may have prompted a state to take an action or a leader to make a decision. The *At a Glance* box, "Levels of Analysis" on the next page summarizes the main features of the three levels of analysis.

AT A GLANCE

LEVELS OF ANALYSIS

Systemic (See Chapter 13)

Basic Explanation for State Actions
All states are essentially similar. State behavior results from the operation of the international system.

Examples of Theories
Balance of power
Long cycle
Hegemonic stability
Security dilemma

Types of Data Considered
Military strength
Nuclear deterrence
Gross national product (GNP)
Number of major powers

Domestic (See Chapter 14)

Basic Explanation for State Actions
All states are unique. State behavior is an outgrowth of a state's characteristic features.

Examples of Theories
Peace among democracies
Military-industrial complex
Bureaucratic politics

Types of Data Considered
Form of government
Political institutions
Economic structure
Ideology
History
Culture
Public opinion

Individual (See Chapter 15)

Basic Explanation for State Actions
State behavior is determined by decisions made by individual leaders.

Examples of Theories
Cognitive theories
Attribution theory
Crisis decision making
Operational code

Types of Data Considered
Leadership style
Leaders' beliefs, goals, and values
Generational experience
Personal relationships

THEMES AND CONTROVERSIES

Regardless of whether one concludes that the most important influences on world politics are found at the systemic, domestic, or individual level of analysis, the history of international relations has a puzzling and often depressing regularity to it. Periods of peace alternate with destructive wars; conflicts of economic interest wax and wane; political issues that were believed put to rest in one era resurface again in another. Part of the reason why we can sometimes observe cycles or patterns in international affairs is that many of the same problems crop up in the relations between different states, and many of the disputes that are central to the making of all nations' foreign policies have never been satisfactorily resolved. Opposition between contending perspectives on international politics and economics is a recurring theme in both the history of interactions between states and in contemporary debates over foreign policy. Before embarking on an examination of world politics past and present, it may be helpful to outline a few of the major controversies that, in different forms and with reference to various specific issues, have animated the theory and practice of international relations for many years.

Perhaps the most fundamental controversy in world affairs is the clash between **realism** and **idealism.** In general terms, realists believe that the security dilemma cannot be completely overcome. From this perspective, international security is a **zero-sum game,** because any increase in one state's power, no matter how well-intentioned, threatens the interests of other states to some degree. Therefore, states have no choice but to "look out for number one" by seeking power and independence in order to protect their vital interests. This viewpoint promotes policies that seek to maximize a nation's security and power in a cold, cruel world in which all other states have no choice but to do the same; such a policy course is commonly termed **realpolitik,** literally the "policy of realism." Idealists, on the other hand, refuse to believe that the security dilemma is inescapable. The fact that states do cooperate shows that cooperation is possible, and suggests that the right conditions can foster greater cooperation. The game of international relations may not always be zero-sum; interdependence may make it necessary and possible for countries to collaborate in order to solve common problems. If the structure of the international system, or human nature, leads to recurrent conflict, perhaps either or both can be improved in order to create an environment more favorable to cooperation.

A related dispute exists between **internationalism** and **isolationism.** Internationalists conclude that states have no choice but to participate actively in world politics in order to pursue their basic interests. Regardless of whether the world is fundamentally conflictual or harmonious, problems in one part of the globe, if left unchecked, can eventually spread to every corner, so states ignore the outside world at their peril. Essentially, therefore, internationalists believe that regardless of geography, no state is an island. Nations must open their doors and minds to the world for security, economic, political, or moral reasons, whether they like it or not. Isolationists, on the other hand, regard engagement with other nations as an inherently risky enterprise that affords more dangers than opportunities. Because the world is such a complex and unpredictable place, and each state's resources are limited, it is better to concentrate on solving problems at home and improving the welfare of one's fellow citizens. Isolationists, therefore, generally counsel "live and let live" in foreign policy. They argue that the best course is to keep the national nose out of another nations' business and thank other countries to do the same.

Two other fundamental controversies center around economic issues. The most common difference of opinion on a state's external economic affairs is the opposition between **free trade** and **protectionism.** Advocates of free trade argue that removal of all trade barriers will allow each state to produce goods and services most efficiently, according to its **comparative advantage.** If trade is unhindered by tariffs, import quotas, and other restrictions, products will flow freely between nations, world prices will be lower, resources will be allocated more efficiently by the free market, and everyone will be better off. Supporters of protectionism, or managed trade, counter that this would allow other states to drive key industries out of business by undercutting the prices of domestically produced goods. After disposing of the competition, and in the process eliminating good jobs in the targeted industry, foreign companies could then raise prices at will and squeeze excess profits out of domestic consumers. To avoid this, protectionists argue, trade barriers should be erected to protect important industries and high-paying jobs, even if this means that consumers will have to pay higher prices or pay for subsidies with increased taxes. (For more on these issues, see Chapters Seven and Eight.)

Conflicts between advocates of free trade and supporters of protected or managed trade have been waged for centuries. A more modern economic controversy that arose in the wake of the Industrial Revolution (see Chapter Two) stems from the antagonism between **capitalism** and **socialism.** To oversimplify (as has been done for all of the viewpoints considered in this section), capitalists believe that the means of production of goods and services should be owned privately, so that the desire for profit will lead to greater efficiency and thus benefit consumer and producer alike. The free market, according to this viewpoint, will reward productivity, and the world economic system will become more productive as a result. Socialists, in contrast, contend that productive assets should be owned collectively (which in practice means by the state) in order to maximize the benefits to society. Economic rewards should be allocated according to human need rather than corporate greed, so that wealth may be distributed more equally. In terms of international trade, free-market capitalism would tend to benefit industrialized nations (which use capital and labor most efficiently), while socialism would tend to benefit states that export natural resources and labor (which, on average, have greater populations and suffer more from poverty).

These disputes have taken many forms over the centuries. Idealists argued after World War I that creating a strong League of Nations would prevent another catastrophic world war, while realists argued that the League could not stop nations from seeking to maximize their power in pursuit of their own security and prosperity (see Chapters Three and Nine). Isolationists were determined that Americans should shed "no blood for oil" and not attempt to drive Iraqi forces out of Kuwait in 1991, while many internationalists contended that the United States must oppose Saddam Hussein by sanctions or even force in order to give collective security and a "new world order" a chance to succeed (Chapter Thirteen). Britain sought to open world markets to free trade in the nineteenth century, while many continental powers erected tariff barriers (Chapters Two and Seven). Proponents of a New International Economic Order in the 1960s argued that Northern capitalism was destroying the economies and societies of Southern developing countries and demanded a global redistribution of wealth (see Chapter Eight). One of the reasons why these controversies have not been resolved is that they are in large measure irresoluble. Arguments and analyses used in support of all of them ultimately depend on perceptions and assumptions, and reasonable people continue to disagree about them. The reader cannot expect that this book (or any other) will present a resolution of these disputes, but should expect

AT A GLANCE

OPPOSING THEMES

Realism
The security dilemma cannot be completely over-come. International security is a zero-sum game. This viewpoint is also known as realpolitik.

Idealism
The security dilemma is not inescapable, and cooperation is possible. The right conditions can foster greater cooperation.

Internationalism
States have no choice but to participate actively in world politics. Problems in one part of the globe, if left unchecked, can eventually spread to every corner. No state is an island.

Isolationism
Engagement with other nations is inherently risky. The world is a complex and unpredictable place. It is better to concentrate on one's own problems and not those of others.

Free Trade
The removal of all trade barriers will allow each state to produce goods and services most prof-itably. Products will flow freely between nations, prices will be lower, resources will be allocated more efficiently, and everyone will be better off.

Protectionism
Trade barriers should be erected to protect important industries and high-paying jobs. Con-sumers will have to pay higher prices or pay for subsidies with increased taxes.

Capitalism
In society, the means of production of goods and services should be privately owned. The desire for profit will lead to greater efficiency and thus benefit consumer and producer alike. The free market will reward productivity. As a result, the world economic system will become more productive. Industrialized nations will benefit from this system.

Socialism
Productive assets should be owned collectively (which in practice means by the state) in order to maximize the benefits to society. Economic rewards should be allocated according to human need rather than corporate greed, so that wealth may be distributed more equally. States that export natural resources and labor will benefit from this system.

to encounter them repeatedly as recurring themes in the making of foreign pol-icy and the conduct of world politics. The *At a Glance* box "Opposing Themes" summarizes these themes and controversies.

CONCLUSION: THE CONTEMPORARY INTERNATIONAL ARENA—GLOBALIZATION AND FRAGMENTATION

Because of the nature of nation-states, advanced communications technology, and economic interdependence, there is a tension today between the opposing tendencies toward globalization and fragmentation. On the one hand, the world seems to be shrinking with every year. You can turn on your television and watch an American football team playing a game in Tokyo. You can talk to people around the world instantly, and modern transportation allows you to be anywhere almost overnight. You can use VCRs or computers manufactured in distant lands, eat fruit or vegetables grown thousands of miles away, take brief vacations in faraway exotic resorts, and your financial future can be determined in part by decisions of governments in Paris or Singapore. Regions that were isolated just a few years ago, such as the Amazon River in South America, the remote forests of Siberia, and parts of the Indonesian archipelago, are now readily accessible.

The media can report on events in other nations that in the past would either have gone unnoticed or would have been reviewed days afterward. In particular, CNN is an international service that provides information simultaneously around the world to a growing global elite that watches the same news programs, wears the same clothes, and eats the same food. Recall Peter Arnett's reporting of the U.S. bombing of Baghdad in January 1991. Recall, too, reports about the aborted coup in the former USSR that August. We experienced these events as if they were happening in our backyard. Compare this immediacy to Hawaiian television broadcasts when, as late as the early 1970s, Hawaiians received only day-old news about world events. If you lived in Honolulu in 1974, the most up-to-date news about the Watergate proceedings were always a day or two late on television. By contrast, on the talk show "Larry King Live," people call with questions from all over the world. A typical hour may include participants from Vancouver, New York, Hong Kong, and Amsterdam.

Thus, travel, communications, and high technology have reduced the size of the world map, both practically and psychologically. As the USSR collapsed, people in the West could see the gripping events unfolding on their television screens, accompanied by constant reminders of the effects on their own lives. The old superpower threat might have collapsed, we were told by Russian and American analysts, but the control of nuclear weapons was now more uncertain and diffused. But other signs of globalization are not so easily dramatized. Rising unity in Western Europe means a more powerful political partner and economic competitor on the world stage, in part through the ever increasing maze of economic entanglements among the advanced industrial nations. And globalization means an easier time for criminals, as the large volume of travel and trade among countries makes trafficking in drugs and arms, as well as movement of terrorists, more difficult to monitor.

Those who believed that progress toward "one world" would cure the world's conflicts and tensions have been proven wrong. Instead, the constant homogenization process of globalization, creating one culture and shared experiences for hundreds of millions of people, creates a backlash in the form of a fragmentation process. Ironically, it seems that peoples around the world have been frightened by increased communication and consolidation of world affairs. They seek to retain their own identities in order to resist the possibility of everyone becoming alike. Thus we have a fragmentation process in which states are breaking up as in Yugoslavia, Ethiopia, and the former Soviet Union, where

In world politics, stronger states often use local conflicts as an arena in which to fight their own battles by proxy.
Source: © Jerry Robinson, © Cartoonists & Writers Syndicate.

the divisions are irreparable, and in other cases, such as India, divisions seem incipient. Even proverbially calm and stable Canada has a long-standing separatist movement in French-speaking Quebec. Europe is filled with groups that seek autonomy, including Basques in Spain, Hungarians in Romania, and Bretons and Corsicans in France.

Thus, current world politics is transfixed by two countervailing processes. Even as globalization continues, divisive tendencies may be omnipresent. Interdependence coexists with constant conflict. The advanced technology that makes globalization possible also aggravates tensions. International politics is ripe with contradictions that deepen the complexity of, and the fascination with, the processes that we address in this volume.

To understand these dynamic complexities, we will embark on an exploration of world politics that is based on a building-block approach. First, we will present the historical background essential for understanding international relations. Part II of the text (Chapters Two through Four) outlines the history of world politics from the rise of the nation-state in the seventeenth century to the end of the Cold War in 1990. Part III (Chapters Five and Six) examines the parallel evolution of the relationship between the industrialized North and the developing South and considers the conflicts and challenges faced by the developing world.

Once we have examined the historical record, we will step back and consider the operation of the international system. Accordingly, Part IV (Chapters Seven and Eight) gives a basic introduction to international economics. Moving on to a higher level of abstraction, Part V (Chapters Nine and Ten) presents key concerns that supersede problems specific to nation-states. Chapter Nine discusses international law and organizations, setting out the "rules of the game" of international politics, while Chapter Ten surveys contemporary global issues on which states frequently disagree but cannot resolve without cooperation. Continuing a higher level of abstraction in Part VI, Chapters Eleven and Twelve proceed to explore the dynamics of security and power, which, for better or worse, are the overriding concerns of all participants in world politics.

After considering these issues and concepts, we will be ready to examine theories of international relations, grouped into levels of analysis in Part VII (Chapters Thirteen through Fifteen). These levels offer explanations for why the patterns of cooperation and conflict observed in earlier chapters occur as they do. Finally, in Part VIII (Chapter Sixteen), we will utilize all of the tools and information provided in earlier material to speculate on the future of world politics in a new and uncertain era.

Essentially, this book's approach to international relations may be likened to a newspaper article. Parts II and III give the basic historical information necessary for understanding the "story" of world politics—answering the initial journalistic questions of *who, what,* and *where.* Parts IV, V, and VI then examine *how* things happen in the international system—how states determine their goals and priorities, how they attempt to achieve their aims, and how they resolve, through fair means or foul, the conflicts that inevitably occur. Following this, Part VII tackles the complex and controversial question of *why* things happen the way they do in world politics, presenting theories from the systemic, domestic, and individual levels of analysis. The last chapter of our story, which looks at the future of international politics, attempts to take on the most difficult question of all, the one that is both most mysterious and most urgent: what next?

International politics is changing rapidly in our day, and technological and political developments are accelerating the rate of change. The world is coming together, and flying apart, faster than ever before. These changes create dangers and opportunities for all of us, but it isn't always easy to tell the two apart. Many readers of this book may be wondering how developments on the international scene will affect their lives: Should I be worried that a Japanese auto maker is planning to open a plant in my home town, or should I apply for a job there? Will the North American Free Trade Agreement (NAFTA) create or destroy American jobs? Can an international convention to reduce carbon emissions stop global warming, or is climate change really not a problem? Will my company be able to sell its products in the European Union, or will it face insurmountable nontariff barriers? Will terrorists strike my hometown if the United States bombs a suspected Iraqi nuclear weapons laboratory?

The answers to such questions are not in this book—but the historical background, theoretical concepts, and analytical tools that one must have in order to attempt to answer them *are* here. The purpose of this text is to help readers develop the skills necessary to make sense of a complex and constantly changing world. It is hoped that readers will use the information and ideas presented here to make their own analyses of the ongoing events that shape world politics and increasingly affect our lives.

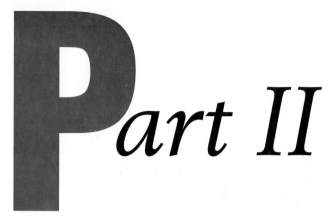

Part II

The History of World Politics

Chapter 2

Origins of the Modern International System

On the evening of June 15, 1866, I was with the Prussian premier in the garden of the foreign office on the Wilhelmstrasse in Berlin, and with us was the English ambassador Lord Loftus. When it struck midnight Bismarck rose from his chair and solemnly proclaimed, "The war has begun! At this hour Prussian troops are marching into Hanover, Saxony, and the Electorate of Hesse—long live the king!" Without batting an eyelash, the English ambassador said that Europe would never tolerate such an invasion, whereupon I heard Bismarck reply, "Who is Europe?"

Wilhelm J. C. E. Steiber, *The Chancellor's Spy: The Revelations of the Chief of Bismarck's Secret Service*, trans. by Jan Van Heurek (New York: Grove Press, 1979), p. 108.

The transformation of world politics in the eighteenth and nineteenth centuries culminated in the cynical realism demonstrated by Prussia's leader, Otto von Bismarck, in this 1866 story describing the outbreak of war with Austria. Gone were the lofty ideals of equality, liberty, and fraternity. They were replaced by a calculating posture the monarchs of the eighteenth century could only have admired. How had European politics changed—and yet oddly retained a degree of continuity? We will answer this question in the course of reviewing developments from 1648 to 1890 in the following pages.

The central term in the expression "international relations" is "nation," but the nation-state has not always been the central focus of world politics. In fact, before the seventeenth century, the nation-state as we know it did not exist. The change in the nature of world politics from relations between rulers to relations between nations was a historical development of tremendous importance. It had a powerful impact not only on politics, security, and commerce, but on every field of human endeavor. As the system of nation-states is now the primary organizational structure of the world, the time and place where it originated is the logical point from which to begin our study of world politics. This chapter will

Major Events in the International System, 1648–1882:

1648: Peace of Westphalia ends Thirty Years' War and inaugurates modern nation-state system.

1661: Louis XIV begins 54-year personal rule of France.

1689–1725: Rule of Peter the Great in Russia.

1699: Austrian armies acquire Hungary from Ottoman Empire.

1701–1714: War of the Spanish Succession checks French expansion in Europe and prevents France from acquiring Spanish possessions in North America.

1721: Treaty of Nystadt, between Russia and Sweden, definitively establishes Russia as a European power.

1740–1748: War of the Austrian Succession establishes Prussia as a major power in central and eastern Europe.

1756–1763: Seven Years' War occurs; Austria fails to defeat Prussia; most of French territory in North America ceded to Britain; British secure domination in India.

1776–1783: American Revolution occurs; United States gains independence from Britain.

1789–1799: French Revolution occurs; France is declared a Republic; Louis XVI is executed.

1795: Poland is partitioned out of existence as an independent state by Russia, Prussia, and Austria.

1799: Napoléon Bonaparte seizes power in France.

1803–1815: Napoleonic Wars occur; Napoléon becomes emperor of the French, establishes temporary French domination of continental Europe, but

outline the development of the nation-state from its beginnings in seventeenth-century Europe, through its expansion throughout the world in the eighteenth and nineteenth centuries, and to the point which many regard as its zenith, the eve of the twentieth century.

The sovereign nation-state originated in Europe and subsequently spread to other parts of the globe, making the European nation-state system the blueprint for the rest of the world. This fact requires the historical chapters of this book to concentrate heavily on Europe. The European focus of the history of seventeenth- through nineteenth-century international relations presented in this book should not be construed to mean that nothing important was happening outside Europe during this period—far from it. Chapter Four will show how Europe was eclipsed after 1945 as the center of world politics, and Chapters Five and Six will discuss political and economic developments in the wider world throughout the period covered in Chapters Two through Four. For better or worse, however, Europe set the pattern for the organization of and interaction among nation-states that persists to the present day. Any examination of how world politics came to attain its present form must begin in Europe.

POLITICS BEFORE NATIONS

Politics has existed as long as human beings have, but the nation as we know it has not. From earliest times until the seventeenth century, political entities were basically defined by the power of ruling elites and/or by religion. Territory was not divided into independent countries with precisely demarcated, recognized boundaries, but into a variety of constantly shifting and often ambiguous units, including city-states, duchies, principalities, kingdoms, or empires. In this complex and confusing situation, the area over which a ruler could exercise authority was usually determined in practice by the ability of his or her soldiers to keep the forces of other rulers out. Rulers of smaller political

after failure of Russian and Spanish campaigns is defeated and exiled.
1810–1825: Latin Americans gain independence from Spain.
1814–1815: Congress of Vienna draws up territorial settlement and establishes Concert of Europe.
1822: Brazil gains independence from Portugal.
1830: Greece and Belgium become independent.
1848: Revolutions occur throughout Europe; Second Republic is proclaimed in France, led by Louis Napoléon.

1853–1856: Crimean War demonstrates weaknessess of Concert of Europe.
1861: Italian states are unified in kingdom of Italy.
1864: Prussia and Austria defeat Denmark in war created by the Schleswig-Holstein crisis.
1866: Austro-Prussian War occurs.
1867: North German Confederation is formed.
1868: Meiji Restoration begins modernization of Japan.
1869: Suez Canal opens.
1870–1871: Franco-Prussian War

occurs; Germany is unified; France cedes Alsace and Lorraine to Germany.
1871–1890: Bismarck's system of Austrian alliances maintains fragile peace in Europe.
1878: Congress of Berlin ends Russo-Turkish War and outlines temporary Balkan settlement; Bulgaria becomes autonomous; Montenegro, Serbia and Romania recognized as independent; Austria-Hungary occupies Bosnia and Herzegovina.
1882: New wave of European colonialism begins, especially in Africa.

units, such as city-states, counties, or duchies, often owed allegiance to the rulers of larger principalities or kingdoms and were granted title over their lands in return for promises of money or military service. This arrangement was known as the feudal system. Local authorities often owed varying degrees of allegiance or types of service to more than one ruler; and these multiple divided political loyalties led to bitter struggles over territory.

Leaders could sometimes point to laws or treaties to legitimize their control over a territory, but these were rarely universally recognized and were often imprecise. With no central authority to adjudicate legal disputes and enforce judgments, such international laws as existed were usually worth less than the parchment they were written on. (Shakespeare's play, *Henry V,* and the modern drama, *The Lion in Winter,* brilliantly depict how the complexities of inheritance and passionate disputes over land often led to intrigue, violence, and war in the Middle Ages.) As a result, there was hardly any globalization and a great deal of fragmentation while the feudal order prevailed in Europe and similar arrangements governed the rest of the world.

Of course, a leader's territorial claims could be greatly strengthened if he could plausibly claim that God was on his side. This was relatively easier to do before the seventeenth century than it is now, because religious authorities played a much more active role in politics. The Roman Catholic Church controlled a substantial amount of territory directly, recognized one European monarch as head of the Holy Roman Empire (which was intended to unite all Christian lands but usually was confined to what is now Austria and Germany), and could legitimize or terminate claims to land by papal writ. Empires throughout history have frequently claimed religious backing for their right to rule. The Roman emperors and Muslim caliphs were religious officers as well as secular leaders, and the emperors of China based their authority on the "Mandate of Heaven." Spiritual and temporal leaders alike could claim the right to intervene in or conquer neighboring lands for religious reasons, which offered a convenient pretext for expanding territorial holdings. Sacred authority often meant little without profane power, however, and Niccolò Machiavelli's notorious "how to" guide to power politics, *The Prince*, was aimed at "Princes of the Church" as well as budding secular tyrants. (It was also designed to show that while kings and princes had no choice but to act ruthlessly, democratic leaders were capable of acting in the interests of the people.)

With leaders of church and state acting as Machiavelli described, it was not surprising that the inhabitants of the crazy quilt of territories usually did not feel any special loyalty to their rulers, even when they could be sure who their leaders were. There was little sense of connection between rulers and ruled, and no concept of national identity, save perhaps in those few areas (usually city-states) that were organized as republics, such as pre-imperial Rome or medieval Venice. Individuals felt and swore loyalty to individual kings or princes or to God rather than to nations, the very idea of which (other than as the place of one's birth) was meaningless. It was much easier to think of one's self as a citizen of a city with precisely delineated boundaries, common interests, and walls for mutual protection, than to feel loyalty toward an ill-defined and frequently invaded country whose rules could change with marriages and murders. There were no constitutions, and rulers rarely felt bound by laws. They could demand taxes at will, without reference to any law (which was how the legend of Robin Hood got started). In the absence of enforceable laws and treaties, foreign rulers could demand taxes or tribute as well—there was no concept of national sovereignty defined as the inviolable authority of a legitimate government within the territory of a state.

With no rules or conventions to regulate commerce, trade was a very risky business, and ruinous taxation was often a greater danger than piracy or shipwreck. The fact that each of the many picturesque castles overlooking the Rhine River imposed tolls on boat traffic in the Middle Ages illustrates the political and economic fragmentation of the period. Nevertheless, the potential rewards of trade were great, particularly after explorers such as DaGama, Columbus, and Magellan discovered sea routes to East Asia and the "New World" of North and South America. The expansion of seagoing trade in the fifteenth and sixteenth centuries began to convince many Europeans that the confusing and fragmented feudal order was stifling commerce and economic development.[1] A major political and social upheaval would be required, however, before a more stable system could be established.

THIRTY YEARS' WAR AND PEACE OF WESTPHALIA

That upheaval was the Reformation, the Protestant revolt against the religious authority of the Roman Catholic Church, which began in the early sixteenth century. Through the writings of Luther, Calvin, Zwingli, and other Protestant theologians, the Reformation created a spiritual challenge to the Catholic church's religious domination of Western Europe. Political leaders exploited this religious schism to further their own ambitions. One example was Henry VIII of

PUCK.

This 1891 political cartoon depicts the end of divine rights for kings and queens, as they are set to plunge off a cliff labeled "human rights."

Source: © Puck.

England, who in 1534 created the Church of England and declared himself as its head. The claims of authority over most of Europe asserted by the pope and the Holy Roman emperors became more burdensome to European kings as these monarchs expanded their realms of authority. Worried that religious fragmentation and growing autonomy of secular European leaders were undermining their spiritual and political authority, popes and emperors sought to crush these challenges, and the challenges and repressions culminated in the Thirty Years' War (1618–1648).

This war was a catastrophic conflict that wiped out more than a third of Europe's population; nearly 8 million people died from the devastation it caused. Originally sparked off by the religious conflict between Catholics and Protestants within the German lands of the Holy Roman Empire and the revolt of the Protestant estates of Bohemia against Prussia's Ferdinand II (then Catholic king of Bohemia), the war came to involve the military forces of Austria, England, France, the Netherlands, Spain, and Sweden. Religion did not provide the major motivation for most of these combatants, who were far more interested in preserving their own political power.

After many bloody battles, horrendous massacres, and sudden shifts in alliances, the Thirty Years' War finally ended with the signing of the **Peace of Westphalia** in 1648. This treaty established two important principles regarding the relations between states, **sovereignty** and **collective security,** both of which remain the foundations of contemporary international politics. First, the treaty established that states are to be sovereign in their internal affairs. In an obvious blow to the church, this meant that kings could decide domestic policy, such as the official religion within their domains, free from outside interference. Second, in attempting to establish a system of collective security, the treaty provided that whenever a state displayed blatant aggression toward another, all states were to unite in opposition to the offender in order to restore the status quo. The events in the Persian Gulf in 1990–1991 show how these principles are still important to contemporary international relations. In reaction to Iraq's invasion of Kuwait, global condemnation focused on Iraq's destruction of Kuwait's independence. However, while the United Nations sanctioned the use of military force in order to restore Kuwait's sovereignty, it refused to intervene in Iraq's domestic affairs.

The principle of sovereignty recognized in the Peace of Westphalia represents an essential element in the creation of the modern nation-state. The idea that political legitimacy could derive from secular legal authority rather than from divine sanction paved the way for the development of constitutional government. The high cost of waging the Thirty Years' War also aided in the creation of the modern nation-state because it forced monarchs to consolidate control over their territories in order to extract greater resources from their respective populations. This need required levying higher taxes, for example, and enforcing their collection. Tasks such as these usually mandated the creation of a more efficient and stable state organization—that is, a centralized bureaucracy. Increasingly, with the rise in importance of trade and manufacture (most of which would today be called "cottage industry"), the cooperation of a variety of institutions outside the church and state (especially banks and trade guilds) became more important for the functioning of a country's military and economy. In order to rule effectively, monarchs could no longer keep their entire ruling apparatus inside their castles and occasionally send out soldiers to knock the peasants' heads together, but had to either respond to or suppress the demands of the citizens. In other words, the focus of state activity shifted from kingship to government. The agony of the Thirty Years' War and its conclusion with the Peace of Westphalia thus inaugurated the modern nation-state.

The imperfections of the peace soon became apparent, however. Although the Peace of Westphalia established sovereignty and collective security as key principles of international law, these principles contradict each other. In an anarchic world (that is, one in which there is no world government), sovereignty dictates that actors must look out for their own interests first and foremost, as no power can compel others to come to their aid. If self-interest motivates nation-states, then achieving a consensus among states with conflicting interests becomes increasingly difficult, as the interests of one state often fail to mesh well with those of others. For example, rather than trying to judge "objectively" which state is the aggressor after the onset of war, states frequently side with those belligerents who best serve their interests. Shifting alliances and ongoing conflict often result, making international relations inherently complicated. These complex and contradictory forces rose to the forefront of European politics in the eighteenth century.

EIGHTEENTH-CENTURY EUROPE

Much as they do today, the opposing forces of globalization and fragmentation contributed to conflict in the eighteenth century. Innovations in sea transport and finance accelerated the spread of European influence into Asia, Africa, and the Americas. The European states' desire to secure greater control of their overseas trading routes manifested itself in colonialism, which led to armed conflict among the most active colonizers: Spain, Portugal, England, the Netherlands, and France. While globalization brought the people of the world into closer contact, fragmentation first occurred in the political center of the newly emerging European system. In central and eastern Europe, the disintegration of the Holy Roman Empire and the gradual weakening of the Ottoman Empire meant that new actors, mainly Prussia and Russia, emerged to challenge Austria, which had been the dominant power in the region. (See Map 2.1.) European states became less isolated from one another and from the rest of the world, and more and more, European politics became an integrated system in which developments in one area affected events in other nations.

International and Domestic Politics in the Eighteenth Century

A few characteristics of eighteenth-century Europe had profound effects on international relations. The first of these was social stratification. Autocratic monarchs ruled most of the European states, with the exception of the Netherlands and Britain, and despite all their rivalries, these monarchs had more in common with one another than with their own subjects. All of the rulers spoke French, practiced

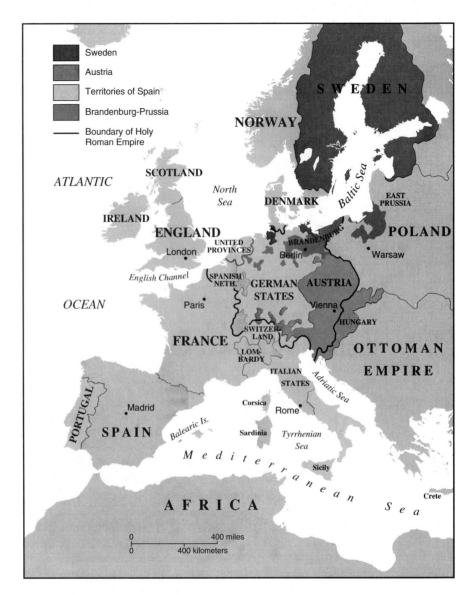

Map 2.1   **Europe in 1648**

Christianity (save for the Ottomans), and were often related by blood or marriage. As a consequence, virtually every aspect of their lives was subject to an elaborate set of rules and mores. They enjoyed a luxurious life with sumptuous balls and feasts, complete with strict codes of conduct concerning who sat where at the table and who danced with whom. The aristocracy proudly patronized music and the arts while many of their subjects worked hard and lived miserably.[2]

The novel, play, and film *Dangerous Liaisons* depict the life-styles, mores, and mind-set of many eighteenth-century aristocrats, all of which were quite different from those of ordinary Europeans.

The common culture of the European rulers did not keep their states from fighting one another, but it did contribute to keeping wars more circumscribed than later conflicts among modern nation-states. In general, eighteenth-century war was limited, fought by limited means for limited objectives. The expense of maintaining standing armies and the difficulty of supplying troops over long distances meant that armies could not engage in sustained combat for long periods, so most campaigns were short and sharp. States rarely fought to annihilate one another, and were usually willing to sue for and negotiate peace when their immediate territorial objectives were achieved. Another factor restrained the scope and destructiveness of eighteenth-century warfare: Sometimes monarchs, such as Britain's William III (who was actually Dutch) and Russia's Catherine the Great (who was born a German princess), ascended to the thrones of foreign countries. Since most rulers were related to one another and could marry only within their class, monarchs had an overriding interest in maintaining the legitimacy of the institution of monarchy by not completely destroying any ruling family or toppling crowned heads from their thrones.

Domestic conditions also often restricted the foreign policy-making latitude of a monarch. The inability to extract sufficient resources (namely taxes) from the populace limited a monarch's capability to wage war. The general populace consisted of peasants engaged in subsistence agriculture, which made tax collection inherently difficult and inefficient. (As in medieval times, taxes were often collected in kind—that is, in heads of livestock or bushels of grain rather than in money.) Since life was centered on the village, peasants often did not identify with the monarch's personal objectives and therefore had little incentive to sacrifice for the state. War drained the royal treasuries. To fight their wars, rulers generally relied on mercenaries, hired soldiers who often came from foreign states (like the Hessians hired by the British crown to fight rebellious American colonists). It was common for officers to serve wherever they could find opportunities for profit or adventure, regardless of the nationality of the troops they commanded or the monarch they served; late in his career, American naval hero John Paul Jones sailed for the Tsar of Russia. Mercenary armies required great expenditures to hire and supply, and entire units would desert if not paid on time or if the enemy offered a better deal. Monarchs therefore had to husband their resources carefully, and wars often resembled chess games, decided by maneuver or positioning rather than intense combat.

Because of the keen competition for power and influence among states, and the fact that monarchs could not always extract enough resources out of the domestic population to match or prevail over their rivals, these rulers often resorted to obtaining resources through expansion, either in Europe itself or overseas through colonization. States gained or lost extensive territories through war or diplomacy, but rarely were completely conquered or ceased to exist. The principal exception to this rule was Poland. Prussia, Russia, and Austria divided Poland among themselves three times, in 1772, 1793, and 1795; in the last partition Poland disappeared entirely. Given the close relationship between territory and power, any gain by one state would lead its competitors to seek compensation, frequently at the expense of weaker states. However, the lack of sophistication of available weaponry and battlefield techniques usually prevented conflicts from being particularly decisive or destructive.[3]

Despite these political, economic, and technological limitations, most eighteenth-century rulers could conduct foreign policy unhindered by democratic controls or the interests of the general population. As a result, the personalities and ambitions of the autocrats and their top advisors figured prominently in the policies pursued by individual states. A change of rulers could lead a country to reverse alliances, go to war, or sue for peace. Not surprisingly, kings and queens, especially Louis XIV of France (the "Sun King"), Prussia's Frederick II ("the Great"), and Russia's Catherine II (also called "the Great"), are famous for how they conducted their countries' policies in this period. All monarchs sought to increase their power through territorial expansion, increased repression at home, or alliances with other monarchs, which marriage or installing a relative on the throne of another state helped to accomplish. The fear that another ruler would gain enough power and territory to dominate all of Europe dwarfed the other worries of a monarch, except perhaps the fear of widespread popular revolt. Throughout much of the century, the state that seemed most capable of dominating Europe was France.

Great Powers

While the status of individual states fluctuated constantly during the eighteenth century, at no point did fewer than four **great powers** compete against one another. The international system during this period was therefore multipolar (containing more than two major actors). Not dependent on other states for security and militarily and economically stronger than other countries, the great powers played a major role in the security calculations of other countries. Only other great powers could threaten a great power militarily or challenge it politically, and most great powers could exert considerable influence beyond their own borders. In modern parlance, they possessed capabilities for **power projection** that less powerful countries could not match.

The exact qualifications for great-power status have always been imprecisely defined (see Chapter Twelve for more details). It is nevertheless generally agreed that to be a great power, a state needs a relatively large territory and population, a well-organized military, and a strong economy. To have only one of these attributes without the others means that the state cannot sustain its influence in the international system for very long. For example, seventeenth-century Holland, in spite of its prosperous economy, had the misfortune of being located next to much larger France and having to compete with England for overseas trade. Similarly, despite Sweden's wealth and capable army and navy at the end of the Thirty Years' War, its small population prevented it from maintaining great-power status after the early eighteenth century.

States possessing all of the necessary factors of power, on the other hand, could exercise political influence for long periods. Russia, though isolated and undeveloped at the start of the eighteenth century, became a great power as the century progressed, largely because of its huge population and vast natural resources. Austria controlled extensive territories with a large population, particularly after the Hapsburg armies acquired Hungary from the Ottomans in 1699. Beginning in the mid-seventeenth century, England became a major player in world politics because of its strong economy, powerful navy, and extensive empire. (England's status as an island nation also aided it in its quest for power and security, because it could depend on the "wooden walls" of the Royal Navy for defense without having to maintain a large and expensive standing army.) Spain also had an extensive overseas empire that reached its zenith in the 1500s and 1600s, while France had a large population and abundant wealth beginning in the seventeenth century.[4]

The influence of each great power upon the others linked their fates together. The elimination of any one power by another could threaten the interests, and possibly even the survival, of others. Therefore, most major powers sought to prevent the domination of the continent by any single state. In other words, the great powers tried to preserve a **balance of power** by allying with weaker powers against stronger states in order to protect themselves from present and future threats. Furthermore, alliances fluctuated constantly and unpredictably. They proved to be fragile and of short duration, and usually did not form until after a war had already been initiated. For instance, the common interests of England and Austria led to those countries repeatedly allying in the first half of the century. This coalition broke down in the 1750s as Austria and France grew increasingly concerned about the rise of Prussia, and in 1756 an Austro-French alliance faced England and Prussia. The multipolar nature of the eighteenth century meant, as we shall see, that alliances shifted often and wars were frequent, although limited in scope. As was touched on earlier, the intensity of conflict was restricted by the "common culture" among monarchs, the limited capabilities of the available technology, and the use of a large number of mercenaries to fill out standing armies. Despite these hindrances, the great powers managed to involve themselves in three major wars during the course of the eighteenth century. As one might expect from monarchs, two of these were provoked by dynastic struggles.

"World Wars" of the Eighteenth Century

The eighteenth century saw three major wars resulting from the way the great powers responded to one another's attempts to dominate Europe.[5] While these wars resulted primarily from European conflicts, a small portion of the fighting took place outside of Europe as well. These struggles thus may be considered the first global wars, though unlike their twentieth-century counterparts, they were limited in their scope and objectives. The eighteenth century began with the War of the Spanish Succession (1701–1714), the bloodiest conflict since the Thirty Years' War. As the name implies, the War of the Spanish Succession developed

WHAT WOULD YOU DO?

You are the king of France in the late 1770s. During the last decade, Britain's King George III imposed highly unpopular taxes on the American colonists in order to pay for the expenses Britain incurred fighting your forces during the Seven Years' War, which ended in 1763. You have gradually received word from overseas that these taxes have stirred unrest among the colonists, and that the British crown's use of troops to quell this incipient rebellion has succeeded in transforming it into a full-blown war of independence. You are trying to decide whether to assist the colonists by declaring war on Britain.

By declaring war, you can aid the colonists by forcing the British government to move its redcoats to other military fronts. Winning such a war would also force the British crown to concede important overseas

out of a controversy over who would inherit the Spanish throne when King Charles II of Spain died without an heir. King Louis XIV of France, with Spanish support, attempted to crown his grandson Philip as king of Spain, but he was opposed by the "Grand Alliance" of Austria, Britain, and the Netherlands, which was later joined by Portugal and other states. (In most eighteenth-century wars, you can't tell the players without a scorecard.) While neither side could decisively defeat the other, the terms of the treaties that concluded the fighting favored the Grand Alliance, and thus both France and Spain made territorial and trade concessions to Britain and Austria.

Another major conflict erupted in 1740, when the death of the Austrian King Charles VI, who was also the Holy Roman emperor, severely weakened Vienna's power. The ensuing confusion provided the opportunity for King Frederick II of Prussia, better known as Frederick the Great, to seize the prosperous territory of Silesia from Austria. The other great powers were alarmed at this action, not because Prussia had only a vague historical claim to Silesia (rulers had started wars on flimsier pretenses before), but because Frederick had violated a treaty that pledged to uphold the integrity of Austrian possessions.[6]

Frederick dismissed the indignation of the other European monarchs as so much hypocrisy. He saw himself as a master of realpolitik, which we saw in Chapter One is a view of world politics that holds that in the anarchic international system, states have no choice but to preserve their vital interests through whatever means are available. Like many leaders before and since, Frederick the Great used diplomacy when possible and war when necessary to achieve his goals and protect his state's interests. He summarized his policies succinctly and frankly: "If we can gain something by being honest, we will be it, and if we have to deceive, we will be cheats."[7]

When the time came for the Great Powers to put up or shut up on the issue, the Prussian takeover of Silesia was supported by France and Spain, but territories to you. Territorial concessions could yield valuable riches to fill your greatly depleted royal treasury (this is important because it is getting more difficult to increase your resources by taxing the peasantry), brighten your waning glory abroad, and quell growing unrest at home.

However, even if victory is achieved against the British, you may drain your already depleted treasury to the point of bankruptcy. Thus, even victory abroad may not increase your people's love for you and your royal house. If you lose this war, you probably will ensure bankruptcy of the royal treasury and darken the glory of your reign. You face a tough decision. You need a victory over Britain to fill your coffers and increase domestic popularity without risking greater losses to both.

What would you do?

opposed by England and Austria. The result was the War of the Austrian Succession (1740–1748), which was fought in the Americas and Asia as well as in Europe. Yet another stalemate resulted from the fighting. The Treaty of Aix-la-Chapelle in 1748 called for a general return to the *status quo ante bellum* (how things were before the war), but Prussia retained control of Silesia. The fact that "upstart" Prussia had successfully challenged Austria's dominant position in Germany, however, put the stability of central Europe under a cloud.

Eight years later, in a move which demonstrated how rapidly alliances could shift during the eighteenth century, Austria realigned itself with France and Russia, leaving Britain (whose naval power could do Prussia little good in continental Europe) as Prussia's only major-power ally. Prussia was thus surrounded by enemies, who took advantage of the situation to launch the Seven Years' War (1756–1763), the war known in North America as the French and Indian War. Combined attacks by Austria, France, and Russia put Prussian forces on the defensive, but superior organization and the military genius of Frederick the Great won Prussia some spectacular victories. While Prussia fought its adversaries to a standstill in Europe, England concentrated on attacking French possessions in the West Indies, Canada, and India. In the peace settlements that followed, France regained some of the overseas possessions it had lost during the war, but England was established as the dominant power in India and North America, where it was awarded all of Canada.

At the end of the Seven Years' War, England, France, and Russia had important interests both within and outside Europe, but Prussia and Austria were solely European powers. During the war, Britain had severely weakened France's position on the Continent and eclipsed France in the competition for empire. The reduction in the threat posed by France led Britain to devote less energy to European affairs in order to tend to domestic concerns. In addition, although it had won vast territories in North America and Asia, Britain's colonial affairs would soon become increasingly troublesome.

ADAM SMITH AND THE FREE MARKET

Two events occurred in 1776 that were destined to transform the world. One was the Declaration of Independence by Britain's American colonies; the other was the publication of *An Inquiry into the Nature and Causes of the Wealth of Nations* by the Scottish economist Adam Smith (1723–1790). Smith outlined the classical model of economics that laid the foundations for capitalism as we know it today. Before he developed his theories, most states thought trade was a zero-sum game—that is, one party to an exchange (either the buyer or the seller) would gain, but the other would lose, so the objective of trade was basically to gain profits by cheating one's trading partners. This view of trade, known as **mercantilism,** led many countries to put up economic walls

(such as the Navigation Acts, which restricted trade with and caused much political dissension in the American colonies) to protect themselves from the supposedly predatory practices of foreign traders. Under mercantilism, many European nations sought to colonize and dominate many areas outside Europe in order to monopolize trade in goods that could not be produced in Europe, such as spices from Indonesia and silk and tea from China.

Smith, however, endorsed the idea of the free market. He believed strongly in the effectiveness of market forces and proved that trade could benefit both the buyer and the seller, enriching everyone. Moreover, he insisted that governments remove themselves from economic matters, arguing for a policy of **laissez faire** (essentially

Aftermath of War and Prelude to Revolution

At first, Paris had no realistic means of directly challenging England's gains in North America because of British control of the seas under King George III. Meanwhile, the American colonists grew resentful of Britain's efforts to retire its war debt by increasing tax levies on its colonies. Much of the "taxation without representation" decried by Americans in the 1760s and 1770s was levied to pay for the Seven Years' War, and so helped to make the resulting British supremacy in North America short-lived. With the start of the American War of Independence in 1776, France saw a golden opportunity to weaken England. By assisting the rebels, France sought to shift the balance of power in its favor. Paris assisted the colonists by providing them money and arms and by engaging in active military support. This forced England to divert resources to other fronts and made the resupply of its forces in North America more difficult.

The Treaty in Paris in 1783, which recognized an independent United States of America, also forced Britain to concede several other overseas possessions to France. These losses weakened Britain's position in North America, which was even more precarious because the new United States now represented a threat to Britain's remaining colony of Canada. This Peace of Versailles might "leave well enough alone") on trade and business. The idea that interference in the markets by government benefited the economy, Smith argued, was a destructive illusion; the market would bring the best outcome for all.

Smith also believed that persons had natural rights with which governments should not interfere. *The Wealth of Nations* not only argued for free trade, but contended that states should confine themselves to providing national defense, a judicial system for property rights and contracts, and maintaining public works and an infrastructure (roads, post offices, and so on). People would not invest unless property was secure, Smith held, so governments must protect property rights. The free play of market forces is beneficial to all, Smith concluded, as in the long run markets are the most efficient and productive means of allocating resources.

Smith's arguments gained credence as his economic predictions proved accurate. First Britain and later many other nations came to favor the free-trade policies he advocated. Many point to the collapse of the Communist political and economic systems in Eastern Europe and the former USSR in the late 1980s and early 1990s as further proof of his conviction that the free market is superior to state management of the economy. Adam Smith is considered to be the founder of the study of political economy. His main argument was that politics should have as little to do with economics as possible.

thus have represented a major victory for Paris, but France's triumph would prove pyrrhic. The war with Britain had postponed important domestic reforms and dramatically escalated government debt. (The king's grandfather, Louis XIV, had severe debt problems as well; huge budget deficits were a problem for European monarchs long before they became a headache for American presidents.) When King Louis XVI sought to impose new taxes to bring down the debt, a political and financial crisis broke out in France. Within a few years, this crisis erupted into a revolution that would transform not only French politics and society, but the concept of the nation-state and the relations between them as well.

FRENCH REVOLUTION AND NAPOLEONIC WARS

Throughout the eighteenth century, France was the most powerful state in Europe. More populous than any nation except Russia, France was often led by ambitious and highly capable kings and its government was usually well organized for administration at home and the exercise of its influence abroad. As a result, French domination over the European continent remained a worrisome possibility for the other great powers during the 1700s. At various times, England, Austria, Prussia, and Spain tried to prevent a decisive French victory in Europe. Although the supremacy of the British navy weakened France in Asia and the Americas, its European position remained strong. France's global influence did not come without a price, however, and by the end of the century the tremendous costs of maintaining France's military and international political power caused a severe social and economic crisis that culminated in the French Revolution of 1789. One of the most momentous events in world history, the Revolution and the conflicts that followed represented a radical departure from the rule of autocratic monarchy (the *ancien régime*) and from the balance of power that defined eighteenth-century European politics.

French Revolution

The immediate cause of the French Revolution was the debilitating debt accumulated by France during the American War of Independence. In May 1789, in order to gain support for increased taxation, King Louis XVI called a meeting of the Estates-General (the Parliament), which represented the nobility, clergy, and townspeople, but had not met since 1614. The nobility and clergy, who controlled the meeting, sought not just to prevent a deterioration of their own status in French society, but to enhance those positions at the expense of royal power. They were willing to relinquish their privileged immunity from taxation only if they could enlarge their say in governing.

By challenging the king's authority, however, the upper classes set in motion forces beyond their control, as the politically and economically disenfranchised middle and lower classes seized the opportunity to assert their own demands. Riots and protests swept through Paris, and on July 14, 1789, a mob stormed the Bastille, a prison where many political prisoners were held. Rioting spread throughout the country, and an attempt to set up a constitutional monarchy failed to quiet protests and restore order. France was proclaimed a republic in 1792, and the king and his queen, Marie Antoinette, were guillotined in 1793.

Several political factions struggled for control of the new Republic. Radicals, such as Robespierre, demanded the sovereignty of the people, which presented a fundamental challenge to the established order in Europe. Less extreme factions called for an aristocratic republican form of government. The revolution was inspired by and sought to promote two political ideologies. One of them, liberalism, held that the power of government should reside in the people and that government should, to the greatest extent possible, allow individuals responsibility for controlling their own actions. (Eighteenth- and nineteenth-century liberals, such as the writers of America's Declaration of Independence and constitution, would probably be called "conservatives" today. They did not advocate redistribution of wealth or "big government" as do many modern liberals. The political "conservatives" in the 1700s and 1800s would today be called "monarchists" or "authoritarians.") The second ideology, **nationalism,** called for popular loyalty to focus on the nation rather than on the monarch.

This was a radical departure from previous ideas of the state and government. It was a concept of political order that, for the first time, defined a country in terms of its people rather than in terms of its rulers.[8]

The very existence of the French Republic challenged monarchical legitimacy and caused Europe's kings and emperors to fear for their thrones. France was also considered, with good reason, to be a destabilizing influence, particularly after Robespierre's Reign of Terror resulted in thousands of deaths after 1793. Even earlier, Leopold II, the Holy Roman emperor and monarch of Austria, and Prussia's King Frederick William II declared, in August 1791, that the "restoration of the monarchy in France was in the common interest of all of the European powers."[9] Although debate still surrounds the question of whether Austria and Prussia intended to act on their statements, it seemed clear to the French that these other states were hostile to the revolution and would attempt to support counterrevolutionaries in France or even invade France to save the king (who had not yet been executed) and restore the monarchy.

To respond to these foreign threats, the republic needed an army, and fast. It raised one by ordering the *levée en masse* in August 1793. This decree called for universal conscription (the draft) and the consolidation of all of France's resources under the authority of the government. Levies of troops and taxes had been commonplace since ancient times, but attempting to create an army of citizen-soldiers loyal to the nation, rather than a king, was a profound change from the use of mercenary armies by European monarchs. The truly radical development, however, was the mobilization of the entire nation's resources in defense of the vital interests of the nation, rather than paying for war out of the king's treasury to serve the king's objectives. In this sense, France's attempt to create a "nation in arms" was indeed an innovation. Although weak and inexperienced at first, by 1794 France's conscript army had more than one-half million soldiers, far outmanning its opponents. Now feeling that it had a stake in its country through the achievements of the Revolution, the French populace rallied to arms under the slogan *liberté, égalité, fraternité* ("liberty, equality, brotherhood"). In addition, the radicals in the French government declared that they would assist revolutionaries everywhere, thus making the threat to the monarchical order especially urgent. The other European powers feared the "export of revolution" throughout Europe, just as American administrations feared the export of Soviet- and Cuban-style Communist ideology to Latin America during the Cold War (see Chapter Four).

Warfare convulsed Europe for more than two decades after the French Revolution. The radical regime believed that it could compensate for its weakness at home by waging war, or that foreign expansion would enhance its domestic legitimacy. It also feared that bringing the troops back home would inevitably destabilize French politics. The conquered territories increasingly bore the costs of the war and also provided spoils to the French government. Continued French aggression led the other European powers to contain it. Yet each coalition opposing the revolution suffered from a fundamental weakness: the interests of each member state were quite different and frequently at odds. Britain, in particular, had little sympathy for the absolute monarchs whom authoritarian Austria, Prussia, and Russia were trying to restore, and the fear of republicanism did not eliminate the continental empires' old rivalries over territory. If one source of France's strength stemmed from its revolutionary form of mobilization, the other originated in the divisions among its opponents.

Napoleonic Era

The turmoil of revolution and war brought many opportunities to the daring and ambitious, and at the end of the eighteenth century no one in Europe was bolder or more ambitious than Napoléon Bonaparte. Though he began his military career as a corporal in Louis XVI's army, Napoléon became a member of the radical Jacobins and rose rapidly in rank and fame because of the ingenuity he had displayed in battle during the French Revolution. (He particularly impressed the Jacobins with his pragmatism and resolve when he stopped a riot in Paris by firing cannons into the mob.) In the wake of France's military setbacks and increased domestic disorder, Napoléon led a successful coup in 1799 and quickly seized dictatorial power.

The Revolution had laid strong military foundations for France, and now the nation would be led by a brilliant strategist and capable administrator with a vision of a Europe united under French domination. Once Napoléon completely consolidated his control of France in 1802, he then began to wage the Napoleonic Wars (1803–1815), campaigns that abandoned the eighteenth-century norms of limited war. In a deliberate return to the practices of the Roman Empire, Napoléon accepted only the complete submission and occupation of a defeated country. He made countries that remained formally independent either into satellites or allies of France. He often installed members of his own family as nominal rulers of conquered territories—one of his brothers ruled Spain, and his brother-in-law became king of Naples. Formally ratifying a status Napoléon had achieved in fact, in May 1804, the French Senate voted him Emperor Napoléon I.

His control of Europe complete, Napoléon banned the importation of British goods to the continent in 1806, creating the Continental System, a means of expanding French economic control of Europe and weakening the British. By 1810, at the height of his power, Napoléon's empire controlled Spain, western and southern Germany, most of Italy, the Netherlands, Switzerland, and the Grand Duchy of Warsaw (the Polish state that he reestablished) and maintained alliances with Austria, Denmark, Norway, and Prussia. (See Map 2.2.) France thus dominated continental Europe, but Britain retained its naval supremacy after decisively defeating the combined French and Spanish fleets at the Battle of Trafalgar in 1805.

The order Napoléon imposed changed Europe forever. The governing institutions he set up in French satellites greatly increased the efficiency of government and were much more responsive to the needs of broader segments of society than the old feudal order had ever been. Even his enemies copied Napoleonic innovations; Prussia's *landwehr* militia system (similar to the modern U.S.

Napoléon Bonaparte looks benign in this period painting. At the height of his power, however, Napoléon turned the idealistic principles of the French Revolution (Liberté, Egalité, Fraternité) into a battle cry threatening all of Europe.

Source: © Culver Pictures, Inc.

National Guard) was inspired by the *levée en masse,* and many nations to this day have legal systems based on the Napoleonic Code. Napoléon was as ruthless as any European monarch of his day, but he had tremendous energy, drive, and charisma. He literally became a legend in his own time, and he inspired works (far from all of which were flattering) by generations of Europe's creative geniuses, including Goethe, Beethoven, Victor Hugo, and Tolstoy.[10] (Inspired by Napoléon's success as a revolutionary leader, Beethoven composed his "Eroica" ["heroic"] symphony in the French emperor's honor; later, when

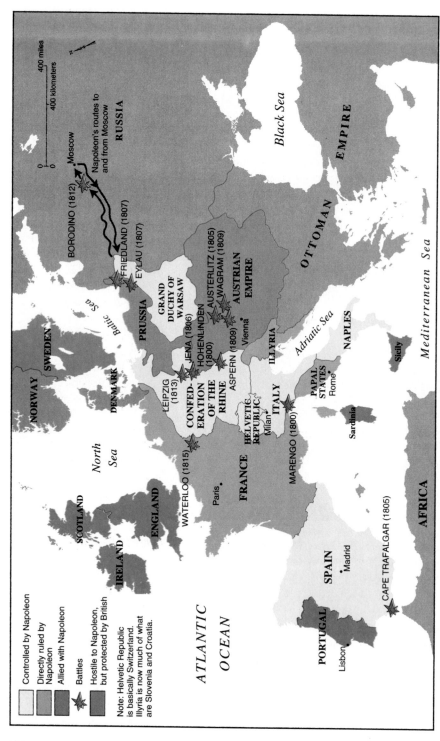

Map 2.2 Napoleonic Europe

he became disillusioned with Napoléon the dictatorial ruler, Beethoven entitled one composition "Wellington's Victory" and wrote "The Glorious Moment" to celebrate the capture of Paris by the armies of the anti-French coalition.)

Three factors, however, undermined Napoléon's power. First, while the Continental System posed a threat to Britain, it also created considerable resentment in French-controlled territories, which also profited from trade with Britain and its colonies. Second, France was unable to defeat Spain and Portugal in the long and bloody Peninsular War. Napoléon invaded Spain late in 1808 to quell a popular revolt against his brother, whom he had installed as king, and at the same time attempted to force Portugal out of its alliance with Britain and bring it into line with the anti-British Continental System. Spanish forces were weak and incompetently officered, but Britain intervened on Spain's behalf, and irregular fighters known as guerrillas (the origin of the modern term) opposed French forces at every step. By 1812 Napoléon had committed more than 300,000 troops to the conflict. During the bitter fighting, both sides committed atrocities, which the Spanish artist Goya depicted in his series of drawings, *The Disasters of War*. The endeavor drained Napoléon's resources substantially. The conflict was referred to at the time as "the Spanish ulcer," but in modern parlance it might well be called "Napoléon's Vietnam."

Third, Napoléon's boundless ambition led him to make a disastrous strategic blunder. In June 1812 Napoléon invaded Russia with an army of more than 500,000 troops. At first, his forces drove the Russians further and further east, and by September the French occupied Moscow. In retreat, however, Russian troops destroyed and burned anything that might have been useful to the conquerors in the policy of "scorched earth," and even the fall of Moscow did not cause them to submit. Overextended, far from its bases of supply, and unable to decisively defeat the Russians, Napoléon's army was forced to withdraw. As they stumbled back toward Poland, the emperor's forces were decimated by Cossack cavalry and the severe Russian winter. By the end of 1812, only 40,000 men, less than one out of ten of those who had originally invaded, crossed back into Poland. (Leo Tolstoy depicts Napoléon's attempt to capture Russia in his epic novel *War and Peace*.)

Exhausted by the fighting on two fronts (Russia and the Iberian peninsula), the French forces began to collapse. Then, France's allies and satellites turned against Napoléon. Although exhausted and reluctant to pursue Napoléon through Central Europe, Russian, Austrian, Prussian, and Swedish forces, with financial and material assistance from Britain, continued the fight. By 1814 Napoléon's armies in both the east and south retreated. In March the anti-French allies occupied Paris, and on April 6 Napoléon abdicated. The First Peace of Paris, signed on May 30, forced France to give up most of the territory it had taken since 1792 and restored Louis XVIII to the French throne.

But the Napoleonic era was not quite over. With divisions among the victorious allies and domestic instability in France, Napoléon escaped from exile on the island of Elba and returned to power in March 1815. Quickly rallying the tattered remnants of the French army, he again threatened the peace of Europe. This time, however, the allies quickly sent their armies against him. On June 18 Napoléon's final Hundred Days of glory came to an end when British, Prussian, and Dutch forces led by Generals Wellington and Blücher defeated him at Waterloo. The victorious allies then exiled him to the South Atlantic island of St. Helena, where he died in 1821.

CONCERT OF EUROPE

After Napoléon's defeat in 1814, the great powers of Europe (Austria, Prussia, Russia, England, and France) gathered in a critical meeting in Vienna to chart the future of the continent. The conference sought first and foremost to restore Europe to what it considered to be "normalcy," meaning a return to the old monarchical system. Ideological consensus, revulsion at the horrors of war, and economic exhaustion after the upheaval of the past two decades fostered cooperation among the states on forming a new international system. Prince Klemens von Metternich, chief minister of the emperor of Austria, played host at the Congress of Vienna and worked to promote his own view of a new European order. Supported solidly by British Foreign Minister Castlereagh, Prussian King Frederick William III, and Russian Czar Alexander I, Metternich firmly believed that the immediate peace and security of the other states demanded the restoration of Europe to the monarchical status quo that had preceded the French Revolution.

Largely because of Metternich's unflagging efforts and uncommon political instincts, the Grand Alliance had been able to survive the infighting that had threatened to tear it apart even before it had defeated Napoléon.[11] Czar Alexander I desired a "Holy Alliance" of all Christian powers, but the other rulers humored him while not taking his romantic ideas seriously. Defeated France was represented by the unctuous diplomat Talleyrand, who had survived both the revolution and Napoleon's downfall by knowing when it was time to switch allegiances. At the Congress, he put his political instinct to work safeguarding France's survival as a major force in Europe, and he cajoled the allies into granting Louis XVIII the succession to the French throne.[12] Talleyrand's negotiating skill helped to ensure that even in defeat, France would not lose its great-power status.

The Treaty of Vienna of 1815 was an attempt to incorporate the lessons of twenty-two years of nearly constant warfare against France by Britain, Russia, Prussia, and Austria, and reflected the leading role of Russia and Britain in the alliance that defeated Napoléon. The great powers were to contain France by establishing and guaranteeing the neutrality of buffer states, such as Switzerland, between France and the other great powers. (See Map 2.3.) Britain's demands for restoring the independence of the Netherlands and Belgium (which France had absorbed) as a unified state reinforced France's confinement. The victors also forced France to pay an indemnity, further eroding its gains from the war.

These realpolitik steps did not fully satisfy the various states that had attempted to defeat France over the years, however. Many leaders believed there would have to be cooperation among the great powers to prevent another recurrence of any such threat. They agreed to meet periodically to review developments in Europe in order to pursue their common interests and the peace of the continent. Thus the Vienna settlement established the **"Concert of Europe,"** in which the great powers sought to cooperate in the control of Europe. Comprising the Quadruple Alliance, the four other major states, Britain, Russia, Prussia, and Austria, agreed that an attack on one—by France—constituted an attack on all.

They had also learned a valuable lesson from years of war: that because domestic developments had international repercussions, they had to be contained; therefore, they agreed that the great powers could regulate domestic disturbances. In other words, they reserved the right to intervene in countries where liberalism appeared to be emerging as a threat. With the peace of Europe restored at such considerable expense, the powers sought to ensure that its repose was not again threatened. They would maintain the status quo against any possible challenge. The Concert of Europe thus became the world's first international institution designed to guarantee collective security; as such, it was a major step toward the globalization of world politics.

From the start, however, the Concert contained more discord than harmony. Despite the apparent unity among the great powers, dissension roiled just beneath the surface. Specifically, it was Russia and Austria that had demanded that the great powers agree to intervene in the domestic affairs of others should revolution threaten; Britain disagreed. In spite of Britain's opposition, the states reached a settlement. Ideologically, the British differed from the three conservative powers of the East: Austria, Prussia, and Russia. Britain was a country that had strong democratic traditions and it was gradually developing liberal ideas on trade and human rights. Although Britain sought to ensure the continued weakness of France for geopolitical reasons, British political ideas were at heart fundamentally compatible with the French Revolution's notions of liberty, equality, and fraternity and sprang from many of the same sources in the philosophy of the Enlightenment (especially the works of Locke and Montesquieu). Britain's implacable enmity with revolutionary and Napoleonic France was one of history's greatest ironies, and, along with the settlement of the Congress of Vienna, an example of the triumph of realpolitik over idealism.

STABILITY AND CHANGE IN THE NINETEENTH CENTURY

The Vienna settlement marked a restoration of the old order on two levels. First, many dethroned monarchies came back into power (most importantly, in France). Second, the dispensation of territory was again used to reward victors and punish losers. The settlement also changed past practice in that it explicitly

THE LIBERATOR

The ideas that Napoléon promulgated and the example of leadership he set continued to have great influence long after his defeat and the collapse of his empire. Many leaders who were exposed to the nationalist fervor of Napoleonic Europe attempted to supplant the old order in their countries with nationalist institutions. The unsuccessful Decembrist Revolt of 1825 was an attempt to create a constitutional monarchy in Russia, and Muhammad Ali, seeking to imitate Napoléon's example, carried out many reforms in Egypt and helped that nation win autonomy from the Ottoman Empire.

The leader who brought the fire of nationalism to Latin America was Simón Bolívar. Born in Venezuela in 1783, Bolívar

was a student in Paris when Napoléon was crowned emperor of the French in 1804. He was an eager convert to the philosophy of the Enlightenment that energized the French Revolution, and he admired Napoléon's boldness and drive, but was disappointed by the emperor's dictatorial rule. Nevertheless, he committed himself to the cause of nationalism, and vowed that he would liberate his homeland from the Spanish colonial empire.

From 1810 to 1814, Bolívar fought tirelessly for Venezuela's independence, helping to form two republican regimes (one of which gave him the title of Liberator) only to see both of them crushed by Spanish troops. Bolívar was undismayed, however, and he set forth a vision of a free community

sought to institutionalize the supremacy of particular great powers through the Concert of Europe. Despite the new accord on the future of Europe, the terms of the settlement represented a patchwork of compromises among the great powers, which were still looking out for their own interests. The restoration of the old order was more apparent than real, however, for the French Revolution had unleashed new forces of nationalism and liberalism that could not be ignored.

Nationalism in the New Europe

Nationalism, which held the self-determination of nations as its highest ideal, would increasingly threaten the established order in Europe throughout the nineteenth century. Advocates of national independence frequently supported the classical liberal ideas of the free market and individual liberty as well, which posed an additional challenge to monarchical authority. Nationalism most acutely threatened **empires,** states that encompass many ethnic and linguistic groups, or in other words, many nations. Many of these groups increasingly demanded independence from imperial rule. As a result, it became more and more difficult for the Concert of Europe to contain the political struggle between nationalism and monarchical imperialism and to of independent states from Mexico to Argentina. "A people that love freedom will in the end be free," he wrote of Latin America in 1814. "We are a microcosm of the human race. We are a world apart, confined within two oceans, young in arts and sciences, but old as a human society. We are neither Indians nor Europeans, yet we are a part of each." In a series of daring campaigns, his forces freed New Granada (now known as Colombia), Venezuela, Ecuador, and Peru from Spanish control. (Upper Peru was named Bolivia in his honor.) By 1824, Bolívar was President of Colombia and Peru, northern South America was brought together in the Union of Grand Colombia, and he proposed a cooperative alliance among all the nations of North and South America (similar to the modern Organization of American States) at the Congress of Panama in 1826.

The Liberator soon came to emulate Napoléon more closely than he intended, however. Bolívar established an authoritarian dictatorship over the countries he led and quarreled with other revolutionary leaders, and internal dissension soon split Grand Colombia apart. Beset by revolts, assassination attempts, and tuberculosis, the gallant adventurer resigned his leadership post in 1830 and died a broken man later that same year. While Bolívar the president was a failure, Bolívar the Liberator is revered throughout the Western Hemisphere as a hero of Latin American independence.

prevent the gradual dissolution of Europe's great empires. Some nationalist issues were resolved peacefully; Belgium gained independence from Holland in 1830 and Norway split from Sweden in 1905 without resorting to violent conflict. On the other hand, the prolonged disintegration of the Ottoman Empire bedeviled European politics for much of the century, and the Austrian Empire's nationality problems increasingly weakened it and seriously threatened its survival.

Nationalism also served as a unifying force, especially in Italy and Germany, which did not exist as unified political entities at the start of the nineteenth century. After the Congress of Vienna, Italy consisted of a number of independent city-states, while Austria controlled many territories such as Trieste where Italians constituted the majority of the population. Germany after 1815 was a patchwork of 39 states (down from approximately 300 in 1648) ranging in size from city-states and principalities to Austria and Prussia, which were recognized as great powers. Many German and Italian nationalists called for the unification of their respective nations into independent nation-states, and thereby greatly worried neighboring states and empires (especially Austria and France). At the start of the nineteenth century, therefore, nationalism had the potential to be a force for both unification and fragmentation, and this potential would frequently be realized as the century progressed.

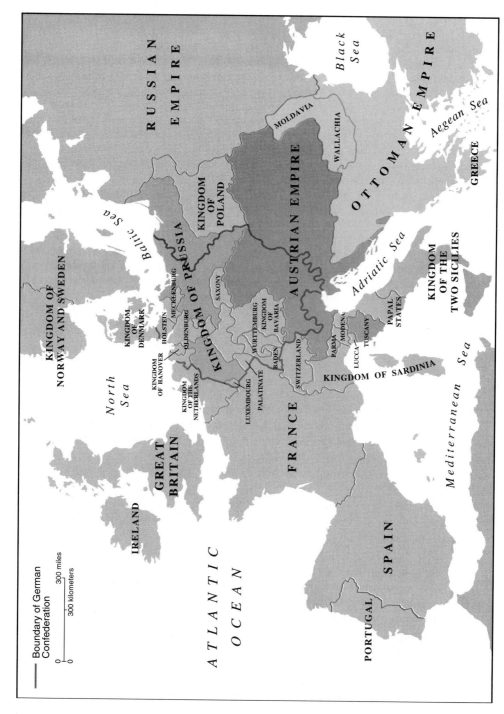

Map 2.3   Europe in 1815

Disharmony in the Concert

The years 1815–1914 were in an important sense the most peaceful in the period between 1600 and 1945. While wars continued to be fought, they were limited both in duration and geographic area. During the 99-year period after 1815, no large-scale European wars occurred. During at least the first half of the nineteenth century, the relative absence of conflict may be attributed to the exhaustion of the great powers after the French Revolution and the Napoleonic Wars. The dynasties that ruled Europe's monarchies also needed to reestablish their domestic authority and fend off the challenges of nationalism and liberalism. Their preoccupation with domestic situations left little time or resources for engaging in foreign conflicts. The system of conflict management through the Concert of Europe and the decline of Anglo-French colonial rivalry also contributed to the relative peace and stability of the first half of the nineteenth century.

Tensions arose, however, between the principle of collective security (which was one of the founding principles of the Concert of Europe) and the self-interests of the great powers. In the fifteen years following the Congress of Vienna, differing ideological and geopolitical perspectives caused independent action by the major states to replace concerted endeavors. These divisions helped France to resume a role co-equal with that of the other great powers. The conservative states of Austria, Prussia, and Russia almost always firmly opposed any challenge to the status quo. They wished to intervene in the domestic affairs of other states if liberals or nationalist movements threatened to overthrow the entrenched monarchies. Conversely, France almost always sided with the liberals. Britain shifted its allegiance, at times aligned with France and at others with the conservative states, in order to preserve the balance of power on the continent that Britain felt was vital to its security.

At the same time, political ambitions motivated each of the five great powers at the expense of ideological consistency. For example, the Concert did not function as planned during conflicts in the southern Italian state of Naples and in Spain. In the latter case, France intervened in support of the monarch, contradicting its own policies of nonintervention and liberalism in pursuit of its security and economic interests.

Perhaps the most poignant demonstration of state interest taking precedence over ideology came in the great powers' reaction to the Greek effort to secede from the Ottoman Empire, which began in earnest in 1821. Austria, too weak to take advantage of the Ottoman Empire's internal problems and fearful that its own multinational empire might erupt in revolt, worried that Russia would use the opportunity to improve its position in the Balkans. Austria thus opposed Greek independence on the principle that existing regimes and the territorial status quo should not be threatened. Although a conservative power, Russia supported Greek independence, both out of self-interest and in Orthodox Christian solidarity against the Muslim Ottomans. Britain, fearing Russian ambitions, opposed a war that would weaken the Ottoman Empire as a counterweight to Russia. (Not all Britons shared this realpolitik outlook on the conflict; the

AT A GLANCE

POLITICAL ENTITIES OVER TIME

Pre-17th Century

Territory is not divided into independent countries. Divisions are defined by the power of ruling elites and/or by religion. Feudal system is in use. Leaders are stronger if they can claim that God is on their side. Loyalty is to individual kings rather than to nations. Leaders can demand taxes at will. There are no rules to regulate commerce. Great political and economic fragmentation exists.

Late Seventeenth Century

Peace of Westphalia in 1648 establishes ideas of sovereignty and collective security. Problems result from the fact that sovereignty and collective security are contradictory principles. Yet sovereignty is important for the creation of the nation-state because leaders are forced to consolidate control over their territories. Kings can determine domestic policy, which is a blow to the church. State activity has shifted from kingship to government. All states are encouraged to unite against any aggressor state.

Eighteenth Century

Advances in transportation and finance accelerate the spread of European influence and facilitate colonialism. Social stratification prevails.

Wars are fought by limited means for limited objectives. Most nations cannot extract sufficient resources to wage major wars. Rulers rely on mercenaries. The international system is multipolar. Alliances are short-lived. A severe social and economic crisis culminates in the French Revolution of 1789. This results in ideologies of liberalism and nationalism.

Nineteenth Century

Many nations base their political systems on the Napoleonic system. The Concert of Europe is designed by the great powers to cooperate in the control of Europe. It becomes the world's first international mechanism designed to guarantee collective security. Nationalism becomes stronger. The Industrial Revolution begins. Manufacturing moves out of the home and into factories. Cities grow rapidly. War becomes deadlier because of more lethal weapons. Uneven population growth leads to domestic instability. The Bismarckian system leads Germany to a powerful position internationally.

romantic poet Lord Byron died in Greece in 1824 fighting for the Greek cause.) In 1826, after Canning replaced Castlereagh as foreign minister, Britain modified its policy and sided with Russia in supporting Greece's autonomy while allowing the country to remain technically under Turkish suzerainty (a type of feudal overlordship). The following year, France joined them, and all three destroyed the Ottoman fleet at Navarino, preventing a joint Turkish-Egyptian force from subduing Greece. Thus a strange alliance between liberal Britain and France and conservative Russia resulted in Greece gaining its independence in 1830.

A New French Revolution?

The twin fears of French power and of domestic revolution underlay the establishment of the Concert of Europe in the first place. These fears reasserted themselves with the July 1830 "revolution" in France when Louis XVIII was overthrown and replaced by a new king, Louis Philippe, who was more liberal than his predecessor. In August that same year, Belgium, which had been part of a united Netherlands under Dutch rule after 1815, rose up against the forced union with Holland, and the fear that France would take advantage of the situation heightened tensions throughout Europe. The eastern monarchs opposed Belgian efforts at independence on the principle that the Concert should preserve the territorial status quo. Yet their distance from Belgium, as well as nationalist problems in their own backyards (namely Italy and Germany), meant they had little influence over events. In January 1831 Britain and France gained the other great powers' acquiescence to Belgium's independence and recognition of its neutrality.

The year of 1830 also saw conservative Russia and Austria facing the first serious challenges from the incipient nationalism of some of their subject peoples. The liberal regime in France provided some support to these nationalist movements. While the French government made statements in support of nationalist objectives and protested Russia's harsh treatment of Polish rebels trying to regain their independence, the Tsar's forces successfully crushed the Poles in September 1831, after ten months of fighting. Thus began a series of smaller-scale rebellions and their repression, which, while frequently bloody, did not generate any serious threat to the general peace.

Industrial Revolution

In addition to ideological and political change, the nineteenth century also witnessed rapid economic change. The French Revolution was paralleled by the Industrial Revolution, which first began in Britain in the late eighteenth century. The Industrial Revolution moved manufacturing out of the home and into factories, where it became more efficient through the use of mass production and interchangeable parts. As well as radically changing the organization of industrial production, the Industrial Revolution harnessed new sources of energy, especially steam power, which enabled manufacturing to be increasingly mechanized. Beginning with textiles and food processing and expanding into the iron and steel, machine building, transportation, and communication industries, the Industrial Revolution made it possible for more people to make more things faster and better than ever before.

The Industrial Revolution changed everything. Cities grew rapidly as workers flooded in from the countryside in search of better-paying jobs. Successful investors in industry made huge sums of money, amassing fortunes that rivaled and ultimately dwarfed those of the traditional aristocracy, whose wealth was usually obtained from farming on large estates. Technology improved at a pace unsettling to many, as railroads and the telegraph allowed goods and information to move faster than had ever been dreamed possible. Families were transformed from the extended family group suited to a sedentary, agricultural way of life into what was later called the "nuclear family" of one couple and its children, which moved frequently as one or both parents sought jobs. Growing shortages of skilled workers encouraged women to enter the labor force for the first time in substantial numbers (though the radical idea of women being able to earn their own money was often slow to catch on in traditional societies). The rich enjoyed the opportunity to make unprecedented profits, though often at considerable risk; a new urban middle class of small investors, technicians, and managers flourished; and workers earned higher wages and could buy more consumer goods, but faced the possibility of unemployment if businesses lost money or failed.

The benefits of the increase in material wealth during the Industrial Revolution were numerous and widespread, but unevenly distributed, as factory owners became wealthy while many of the working poor eked out a bare existence. The rich got richer faster than ever before, and the middle classes prospered, but the living conditions of the poor were slower to improve. One British government official, Charles Dickens, was inspired by the plight of London's urban underclass to write novels, such as *Nicholas Nickleby*, *Little Dorrit*, and *Oliver Twist*, depicting the social and economic conditions of nineteenth-century England. In time, rich and poor alike would suffer from another legacy of the Industrial Revolution—deforestation and pollution.[13]

The development of industry changed war and politics as well as economics. With the increased lethality and range of weapons made possible by new technology, wars became deadlier. New types of weapons, which by the end of the nineteenth century included machine guns and long-range artillery, enabled and later required states to raise mass armies much larger than had been fielded before the industrial era. Armored steam-powered warships gave navies greater range and striking power, and naval powers raced with one another to match their adversaries' most advanced ship designs. Armies increasingly directed violence not only at military targets, but at economic and civilian ones as well, as a state's industrial capacity became a vital part of its military strength. With the growing reliance on large conscripted armies, the support of the general public became more important for the success of military campaigns, thus accelerating the entrance of a greater proportion of the population into the political arena.[14] Rulers progressively required the economic and political support of the captains of industry, labor unions, and the newly emerging mass media (newspapers) for foreign escapades as governments needed to raise more funds—and thus needed the support of financiers and the population as a whole for more expensive conflicts. Politics as well as production began to take on many modern characteristics.

Yet this increased involvement of civil society in politics did not immediately bring about greater democratization, as many liberals had hoped. The rapid pace of industrialization often led to social dislocation and turmoil. In a precursor of modern conflicts over workplace automation, "Luddites" (followers of a mythical leader named "Ned Ludd" or "King Ludd") smashed textile machinery that they feared would make their jobs obsolete. The landed aristocracy was usually less than comfortable with the rising political importance of industrial capitalists and often resented the nouveaux riches who made their money in trade and industry. The threat posed by industrialization to the established order was occasionally ameliorated by the ability of governments to focus popular attention on foreign enemies and the glory of the nation—some rulers resorted to foreign wars and colonial expansion to distract the populace from the growing trouble at home. At the same time, industrialization increased competition for markets and sources of raw materials, which provided a powerful impetus for European colonization in Asia and Africa (see Chapters Five and Six).

The spread of the Industrial Revolution slowly but inexorably changed the European system. With its origins in Britain, the Industrial Revolution was a major source of that country's strength. Industrialization spread very unevenly, depending on social and political conditions within particular countries. France industrialized slowly, Austria even more so, and Russia had barely begun the process of industrial development by the end of the nineteenth century. Prussia, on the other hand, industrialized rapidly. With increased production came increased opportunities for trade, and the Industrial Revolution increased British support for a liberal trade regime under which goods could be freely bought and sold between countries. Seagoing commerce expanded rapidly, and trade forged economic and political links among nations all over the globe. The system of free trade that Britain sought to maintain with its financial, as well as naval, strength, and the ease of international borrowing and investment throughout nineteenth-century Europe, were precursors to later economic arrangements such as the General Agreement on Tariffs and Trade (GATT) and the European Union (EU). The Industrial Revolution was thus a major impetus for the globalization of the world economy.

The uneven spread of industrialization also contributed to increased domestic instability, especially in the German states. More and more, peasants moved to the cities, where they became better organized to present their demands and to protest when their demands were ignored. This posed a threat to many ruling authoritarian regimes, which tried to preempt the challenge by focusing attention on often exaggerated foreign threats (see Chapter Fourteen). In addition, the changing domestic balance of power between rival economic interests led to increased demands for government interference in the economy—in particular, protection from imports. While these factors existed in all of the European states, they were most influential in Germany, which by mid-century would become a center of violent unrest.

Revolutions of 1848

The next major turning point in nineteenth-century European politics came when a wave of popular discontent crested in 1848. Protests, motivated by nationalist demands and the social and economic upheaval caused by the Industrial Revolution, erupted across the continent from France to Austria and Hungary. These uprisings threatened to shake the crowns off many European monarchs. While King Frederick William IV of Prussia initially promised reforms, he postponed his plans after troop confrontations with demonstrators

THE BALKANS

Be prepared to hear a lot about the Balkans in this book. This geographic expression refers to the area of southeastern Europe now consisting of Albania, Romania, Bulgaria, Greece, Yugoslavia, and the former Yugoslav states of Slovenia, Croatia, Bosnia, and Macedonia. The sheer number of nations located in this relatively small area indicates the intense political fragmentation that has plagued the region.

The Balkans are a melange of intermingled ethnic and religious groups, many of whom harbor old hatreds and quarrels with one another. Complicating the situation even further, the area has been conquered and reconquered over the centuries by many outside powers (including Austria, Russia, Turkey, and Hungary). The result has been the reinforcement of deep divisions among the many nationalities that inhabit the region. By the nineteenth century, competition

led to pitched battles in the streets of Berlin. Widespread revolts in the Austrian Empire led Emperor Ferdinand to issue a manifesto in April promising to free the Austrian peasants from all services and duties incumbent upon them. This edict helped turn the peasants to the emperor's side, but his forces proved incapable of controlling the uprisings, and the rebellion continued until it was crushed with the aid of Russian intervention in 1849.

Only in France did the revolution meet with success, in that Louis Philippe abdicated the throne and fled to England, and a provisional government proclaimed a republic. This event raised the concerns of the other monarchs, who recalled the events following 1789 all too well. The new French government did not, however, seek confrontation with the other powers. It feared that conflict would lead to conditions similar to those that had led to the radical takeover of 1790.[15] Throughout Europe, the excesses of industrial capitalism inspired an upwelling of socialism and led to the origin of communism, expressed in the writings of the German political economist Karl Marx (see Chapter Seven).

The violent events of 1848 showed that the Concert of Europe was incapable of controlling the internal threats faced by the conservative monarchies. In state after state, the urban working class rose up to demand increased political rights, which could only come at the expense of the monarchs' power. The social divisions generated by the Industrial Revolution created tensions between the rising *bourgeoisie* (the middle class of industrialists and small business owners), the landed aristocracy, and the working classes. These divisions and the spread of liberal ideas were growing in impact.[16] The revolutions of 1848 represented not only demands for greater democracy, but increasingly politically active publics demanded the revision of the 1815 settlements in order to unify nations in some cases (such as Italy and Germany) or gain their independence in others (such as Hungary and Poland).

among the declining Ottoman Empire and the Austro-Hungarian and Russian empires frequently combined with indigenous nationalism and ethnic strife to turn the Balkans into the "tinderbox" of Europe. (See Map 2.4.)

This chapter and the next will show that throughout the nineteenth and early twentieth centuries, the Balkans repeatedly exploded into violent conflict and crisis. As Chapter Four will relate, conflict in the Balkans was more or less frozen by the Cold War. With the end of that global political struggle, however, the forces of fragmentation have once again seized the Balkans with paroxysms of violence, particularly in Croatia and Bosnia. At times, it almost seems as if the flames of nationalism and ethnic hatred burn so brightly in the Balkans that those who remember the fragmentation of the past condemn the region to repeat it.

The monarchists and the landed gentry won out for the time being, largely because the liberals were not able to maintain their initial gains and were crushed with the aid of external conservative powers—especially Russia, the "Gendarme of Europe." The potential for domestic unrest to spill over into international conflicts remained, however. In the mid-nineteenth century, the Concert of Europe deliberated on the possibility and desirability of international intervention to prevent nationalist conflicts in Poland, Austria, Hungary, and elsewhere from escalating into international war. More than a century later, another collective security institution, the United Nations, would debate the same problem with regard to conflicts in Bosnia and Croatia.

A PERSPECTIVE AT MID-CENTURY

By 1850 the revolutions of 1848 had failed. The monarchist regimes in central and eastern Europe regained control of events and either destroyed or delegitimized the liberals. Since the demands of many liberal ideologues led to increased radicalism on the part of the working class, this same radicalism scared the middle classes. Willing to sacrifice political freedoms for the sake of stability, they accepted monarchical reaction and repression in many countries. Yet the stability that had been reestablished was palpably fragile, and many recognized it as only the calm before the storm. The forces of liberalism and nationalism had been released, and proved to be impossible to contain in the long run.

In the first half of the century, nationalism was feared since it threatened a revision of the territorial status quo and it was tied to liberalism. Notwithstanding the early association between liberalism and nationalism, the relative degree of fear of nationalism greatly depended on the previous history of the various

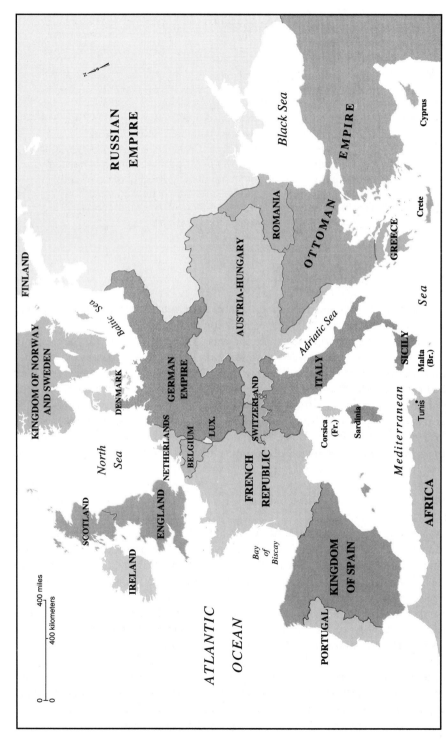

Map 2.4 Europe after German and Italian Reunification, 1872

parts of Europe. In western Europe, the state and the nation were essentially synonymous by the mid-nineteenth century, so ruling elites had little reason to fear that the extension of political rights to the working class would lead to the dissolution of the state. Germany and Italy profited from the growing force of nationalism, using it to unify their nations into single states. In central, eastern, and southern Europe, the situation was quite different. The growing strength of nationalism threatened the future of the Austrian Empire, which included Hungarians, Poles, Czechs, and others. In the Russian empire, the increased nationalist activity of the Poles, Balts, Finns, Armenians, and others subject to Russian control constituted a drain on the energies of the monarchy. It effectively suppressed any attempt at rebellion as it had the Decembrist Revolt of 1825, when liberal army officers attempted to force the Tsar to accept a constitutional monarchy. However, with the defeat of the liberals in 1848, imaginative conservatives came to the realization that they could use nationalism for their own purposes.

Crimean War

If the strength of Russia and Britain had been a stabilizing force in the first half of the century, the increased tensions between them boded ill for continued European security, as those two great powers disagreed over the future of the territories controlled by the decrepit Ottoman Empire. Meanwhile, after almost forty years of relative quiet from France, fear of the former revolutionary state had subsided. Yet the France of President Louis Napoléon Bonaparte (Napoléon Bonaparte's nephew), who took office in December of 1848, was a dissatisfied power. By restoring France to what he considered to be its proper status as a leading power in Europe, Louis Napoléon (who was crowned Emperor Napoléon III in 1852) hoped to improve his domestic legitimacy as well as gain more respect from other European nations.[17]

Seeking to demonstrate France's renewed strength, Napoléon III adroitly took advantage of the infirm Ottoman Empire. In 1852 he demanded that the keys to the Christian holy places in Jerusalem be held by Catholic rather than Orthodox clerics. This seemingly innocuous incident eventually precipitated the Crimean War (1853–1856), the first between the great powers since 1815. In 1853 Russia sent troops to occupy Moldavia and Walachia, two Turkish provinces in the Balkans. (Both areas are now part of Romania.) Britain and France intervened in order to bail out Turkey, attacking Russia in the Crimean Peninsula on the northern shore of the Black Sea. The protracted siege warfare that ensued, the futility of which is captured in Tennyson's poem "The Charge of the Light Brigade," bore little resemblance to the swift, dramatic campaigns of the Napoleonic Wars. The fighting dragged until 1856, when Russia agreed to withdraw its troops from Moldavia and Walachia, which were granted autonomy under Turkish suzerainty. While Russia's defeat spurred on some liberalizing reforms in that country, the Crimean War had little lasting impact on European politics. It did, however, demonstrate that the Concert of Europe was no longer able to maintain collective security when the interests of the great powers conflicted. Ultimately, it proved to be little more than a costly sideshow, while the main event was about to begin in central Europe.

UNIFICATION OF ITALY AND GERMANY

From 1815 to about mid-century, Britain and Russia had effectively stabilized Europe. Both counterbalanced France while Russia shared Austria's conservative revulsion to challenges to the territorial and political status quo. Their resources depleted by their exertions in the Crimean War, both Russia and Britain reduced their involvement in continental affairs. As a result, Paris obtained greater freedom of action and Vienna could no longer rely on Russia for support against nationalist demands inside Austria and in neighboring Italy and Germany.

Italian Unification

France did not delay in taking advantage of Austria's vulnerability. Napoleon III moved quickly to assist the movement for unity among the Italian city-states, or *Risorgimento*, as the Count di Cavour of Piedmont-Sardinia assumed leadership of the Italian unification movement. In July 1858 Cavour and Napoleon agreed that France would support Piedmont's cause in return for French acquisition of Nice and Savoy. In 1859 French forces intervened to push Austrian troops out of northern Italy. Nationalist troops led by Giuseppe Garibaldi won control of Sicily and Naples in 1860, paving the way for their union with Piedmont, which dominated northern Italy, and an Italian parliament proclaimed a unified kingdom of Italy in 1861.

The unification of Italy produced a profound revision of the territorial settlement of 1815. It also removed a significant source of friction between Paris and Vienna, which had previously competed for influence among the republics, principalities, and city-states of the peninsula. The new state at first was too weak to pose a major threat to either France or Austria, and provided a useful buffer between these two powers. Italy had achieved territorial unity, but remained politically divided and economically underdeveloped, and so never attained the great-power status to which its leaders aspired.

German Unification

Italy's unification left one major European nation, the Germans, still divided. In 1862 King William I of Prussia appointed Otto von Bismarck as his chancellor. The dominant personality of Europe during the second half of the nineteenth century, Bismarck was a conservative **junker** (aristocratic landlord) who sought to protect and improve the position of the monarchy, mainly in order to raise funds for a reformed army, at the expense of a liberal parliament that had limited powers. Because they had associated nationalism with liberalism since the

Otto von Bismarck created a unified Germany through three quick, carefully-calculated wars in the 1860s. The "Iron Chancellor" dominated European politics for the next 20 years.
Source: © Culver Pictures, Inc.

French Revolution, many conservatives feared that unification would threaten the status quo and their entrenched positions. Bismarck had no particular interest in German unity initially, but he gradually realized that nationalism could become the means of assuaging the masses while preserving most of the aristocracy's prerogatives and expanding Prussia's international power and prestige.

Bismarck was committed to realpolitik in foreign policy. He was only concerned with advancing the state interest by whatever means: diplomacy if possible, war if necessary. Bismarck had no qualms about resorting to military means if that would provide an opportunity to strengthen the domestic position of conservatives, the monarchy, and the army. He agreed with the German military theorist Clausewitz that "war is nothing but the continuation of politics by other means."[18] Thus, Bismarck was known as the "Iron Chancellor" for his determination to unite Germany under Prussian domination and his statement that "it is not by speeches and resolutions that the great crises of the times are decided, but by iron and blood."[19]

While serving as chancellor, Bismarck came to believe that the most practical way to unify Germany would be to exclude Austria, which was only partially German. Austria was an empire consisting of many ethnic groups, including Czechs, Slovaks, Poles, Croats, Hungarians, and diverse others. A unified Germany could never incorporate the myriad of ethnic groups in the Austrian Empire. Additionally, the prospect of a unified "greater Germany" including both Prussia and Austria would alarm the other European powers, which would probably go to war to prevent the union of the two major German states.

In 1864 the king of Denmark handed Bismarck a golden opportunity to further his goal of German unification. The Danish king, under the mistaken impression that Britain supported him, attempted to fully incorporate the autonomous duchies of Schleswig and Holstein into his kingdom. Bismarck quickly signed an alliance with Austria for the purpose of gaining control over these largely German-speaking areas, and in 1864 Austrian and Prussian forces marched in and won a quick victory. Berlin and Vienna soon fell out, however, over the agreement on joint control of the territories won from the Danes, and in June 1866 Austria broke off diplomatic relations and began to mobilize its army. Bismarck used the Austrian mobilization as a pretext for war. With superior organization, and by clever use of the emerging technologies of the railroad and telegraph, Prussia could mobilize and concentrate its forces more rapidly. This advantage proved decisive, and Prussia soundly defeated Austria within two months. In the peace settlement, Austria gave up its authority in German and Italian affairs (The Italian city of Venice, at various times part of the Austrian empire, was finally transferred to the kingdom of Italy) and the northern German states were incorporated into the Prussian-dominated North German Confederation.

Prussia's victory fundamentally challenged the previous order in central Europe. Austria's weakness forced it to accept the demands for political equality from its Hungarian provinces, and in 1867 the Austrian Empire became the "dual monarchy" of Austria-Hungary. The rapid growth in Prussia's power caused great consternation among the other great powers, but Bismarck was able to isolate France and neutralize Britain and Russia through diplomatic maneuvering. On June 14, 1870, after tensions had been exacerbated by a dispute over the succession to the Spanish throne, Bismarck leaked a telegram from Kaiser Wilhelm that the Iron Chancellor edited to make it look as if the kaiser and the French ambassador had insulted each other. Pressure for war mounted in both Vienna and Berlin, and five days later Napoléon III played right into Bismarck's hands by declaring war on Prussia.

Again making good use of new technology and its army's superior organization, Prussia rapidly defeated the French forces within a matter of weeks. Neither Britain nor any of the other great powers could come to France's aid in time. The Prussians captured Napoléon III, and after a four-month siege, took Paris as well.[20] France was forced to pay a huge indemnity and cede to Prussia the provinces of Alsace and Lorraine, which had long been part of France. While the German annexation of Alsace could be justified on nationalist grounds, as the majority of the population was German, the population of Lorraine was largely French. The loss of both troubled the French for decades thereafter.

However, by declaring the formation of the new German Empire on January 18, 1871, from the Palace of Versailles, a symbol of French power built by Louis XIV just outside Paris, Bismarck added insult to the injury of losing Alsace and Lorraine. The harsh terms and humiliation imposed on France signaled a departure from Bismarck's previous habit of tolerance toward defeated opponents, whom he well knew might be potential allies in the next conflict. He acted in deference to pressure from the kaiser and a public enraptured with victory and impatient with the subtle workings of his diplomacy. This uncharacteristic triumph of nationalism and chauvinism over realpolitik in Bismarck's policy would later cost Germany and the rest of Europe dearly. Nevertheless, in 1871 the aspirations of generations of Germans for a unified German nation-state had been realized.

The unification of Germany under the Prussian crown profoundly affected European politics and radically shifted the balance of power. Through these short wars based on rapid mobilization and decisive battles, the process of German unification influenced strategy and military organization in virtually all of the European states. It also sped the innovation of new weapons technology, including both the breech-loading rifle and machine gun, and spurred the development of railroads. (For the changes German and Italian unification brought to European political geography, see Map 2.4.) The new German Empire was now the strongest country in continental Europe. Resentment smoldered in France, but that nation was too weak to act alone and could find no allies. Austria accepted its irreversible loss of influence in Germany and turned its focus to the Balkans, a step encouraged by the demands of Hungary. Because the Crimean War blocked Russian expansion to its south, Russia increasingly focused on expanding into Asia and trying to improve its domestic economy. Finally, Britain saw little reason to involve itself on the continent as long as Belgium and the Netherlands were not threatened. Instead, it focused on strengthening its colonial and commercial empire. Thus, the achievement under Bismarck's leadership of a unified German nation was secure for the time being.

BISMARCKIAN SYSTEM

The twenty years following France's defeat in 1871 saw a succession of alliances known collectively as the **Bismarckian system.** Germany used these defensive alliances to moderate the demands of its allies, prevent the formation

DOES THE BALANCE OF POWER PROMOTE PEACE?

Both theorists and practitioners of international politics frequently use the expression *balance of power*. This term has a number of meanings, which are discussed in more detail in Chapters Eleven, Twelve, and Thirteen, but in eighteenth- and nineteenth-century Europe it usually referred to an equilibrium, or at least a rough equivalence, in the relative economic and military strengths of the great powers.

Politicians justified many actions and much expenditure by claiming that alliances, arms buildups, and almost anything else they could think of were necessary to "preserve the balance of power." In particular, when one leading great power (such as France under Louis XIV or Napoléon or the newly united Germany after 1871) threatened to outstrip the capabilities of the others to the extent that it could impose its will throughout Europe, the other major states would ally against it to prevent it from achieving domination over the Continent.

As mentioned earlier, throughout the nineteenth century Britain pursued a policy designed to ensure that no single power could dominate Europe, and all the major powers acted to counterbalance one anothers' strengths so that (it was hoped) none would feel strong enough to launch a major war.

Should they have bothered? Some international relations theorists, such as Hans Morgenthau and Morton Kaplan, argue that an equivalence of power among major states is the most effective way of preventing major war in the anarchic international system. From this viewpoint, war is caused by an *imbalance of power*—if one state or alliance feels that it can defeat its opponents, it will attempt to force them to do as it wishes and will attack if they resist.

Other analysts, however, contend that peace is maintained most effectively when a single power becomes dominant. A.F.K. Organski, George Modelski, and others (see Chapter Thirteen) argue that war becomes less frequent if the strongest power achieves **hegemony,** or recognized leadership, making the international system somewhat less anarchic. The hegemon can then impose peace on other states through economic sanctions (such as an embargo, or forcible cutoff of trade) or the threat of military force. In their view, major wars break out when the dominant power becomes too weak to fend off challengers, and its rivals launch wars with it and among themselves to see who will be the next "king of the hill." Thus, a balance of power would actually encourage war as many states would feel they had a fighting chance of coming out on top.

of coalitions of opponents that could seriously threaten its vital interests, and forestall the escalation of local conflicts into general war. A delicate balancing act performed by a master political acrobat, Bismarck's system worked splendidly for a time, but could not resolve the domestic and international conflicts that ultimately led to his downfall and his system's collapse.

Internationally, the goals of Bismarck's two major allies, Austria-Hungary and Russia, were opposed. Bismarck had been able to ally with both of these

Unfortunately, the historical evidence on whether a balance of power promotes or prevents war is supremely equivocal. When Napoleonic France dominated continental Europe militarily and imposed the Continental System to prevent trade with its rival Britain, Europe enjoyed a brief lull in the Napoleonic Wars. French hegemony soon broke down, however, as French power became overextended, and the continent plunged back into war.

During the mid- to late-nineteenth century, when British naval power was able to threaten any state with an embargo on trade, no major wars occurred, and as a result the period was referred to as the *Pax Britannica* (the "British Peace"). However, although the great powers looked to Britain for leadership, they recognized one another as ostensible equals in the Concert of Europe, and no power (including Britain) achieved military domination on the continent. Later, Bismarck's system of alliances designed to maintain a balance of power avoided large-scale war for almost twenty years, but minor conflicts were frequent and the system eventually broke down. War and peace have thus occurred under both a balance and an imbalance of power.

Given that the evidence is so inconclusive, what good, if any, does the balance of power do? While theorists will probably continue to debate this point as long as there is an international system upon which to disagree, the one behavior that appears constant among all major powers is that none will willingly allow any of the others to achieve domination. States will thus try to balance one another regardless of whether theorists recommend it. In an anarchic international system where all states face the security dilemma (see Chapter 1) and each state must look out for its own interests first, they have little choice.

This situation may not last forever; strong international institutions that can guarantee collective security may help states escape the security dilemma, and there is significant evidence that democratic states do not fight with one another, regardless of their relative power (see Chapter Fourteen). Until the world becomes less anarchic, or more democratic, however, leaders seem likely to continue to pursue a balance of power much as they did throughout the eighteenth and nineteenth centuries, whether international relations specialists approve or not.

adversaries—first with Austria-Hungary in the Dual Alliance in 1879, then with both in the Three Emperors' Alliance in 1881—but this balancing act was threatened by political developments, particularly in the Balkans. Independence movements challenged Turkish control of the Balkans, and the weakening Ottoman Empire, known as the "sick man of Europe," could neither suppress nor satisfy nationalist demands. As a result, Austria-Hungary and Russia increasingly supported various Balkan nationalist movements in a competition for territory and influence in the region. Agreements brokered by Bismarck at the Congress of Berlin in 1878 temporarily stabilized the Balkans, but issues of Austro-Hungarian and Russian competition had still failed to resolve themselves and overlapped with the tensions among the states emerging in the wake of the Ottoman Empire's disintegration.

The strategic objective of Bismarck's alliance system was to keep Germany, Austria-Hungary, and Russia together and France isolated. Bismarck's position was strengthened by disagreements between France and Britain over another part of the declining Ottoman Empire, Egypt, which Britain regarded as an area of vital interest (particularly after the opening of the Suez Canal in 1869). When France did not join with Britain in putting down an Egyptian rebellion in 1882, British troops occupied Egypt, and Britain established a de facto protectorate over the country. (It remained a nominal part of the Ottoman Empire until 1914.) This action severely alienated France and consequently removed another possible ally for Paris in its attempts to pursue its revanchist hopes against Germany. (**Revanchism** is the desire for revenge, particularly for a defeat in war.)

Seeking to reduce the tensions caused by territorial disputes between Rome and Vienna, Bismarck brought Italy into his alliance system in 1882 with the Triple Alliance between Germany, Austria-Hungary, and Italy. By 1888, however, Bismarck's system was struggling to hold itself together. Russia became increasingly distrustful of German diplomacy, which effectively prevented St. Petersburg from actively pursuing its goals in the Balkans. In its competition with Russia, Austria-Hungary grew increasingly dependent on Germany as a protector. Bismarck tried to juggle Russian and Austrian interests, but none of the great powers could control events in the Balkans, which were largely driven by the ambitions and antagonisms of the local peoples fighting for greater autonomy from Ottoman suzerainty. It was this mixture of independent action on the part of the Balkan states and the irreconcilable interests of Austria-Hungary and Russia in this region that played a major role in the decline of Bismarck's system.[21]

With formidable skill, Bismarck was able to temporarily manage the many conflicts between the interests of the great powers. Yet, by the late 1880s domestic pressures for a more assertive German policy multiplied and became more difficult to contain. The flexibility of Bismarck's policies meant that other powers were neither overly disgruntled nor particularly pleased with Germany. Once alternative sources of support became available to the dissatisfied powers, alliance with Germany looked less attractive. Meanwhile, within Germany, groups seeking protective tariffs and favoring aggressive **colonialism** increased their political clout. (Bismarck himself was not enthusiastic about German colonialism outside Europe, but his successors espoused the view that Germany needed colonies to maintain its "place in the sun" alongside the most active colonizers, France and Britain.) These internal developments affected Germany's external position, as its expanding role in world politics increasingly infringed on the established interests of the other European powers. German domestic politics eventually undermined Bismarck's position, and he was removed from office in 1890. By the time of his dismissal, most of Europe had enjoyed almost two decades of peace, but the seeds of a great-power war had been sown.

CONCLUSION: INTERNATIONAL SYSTEM ON THE EVE OF THE TWENTIETH CENTURY

Toward the end of the nineteenth century, the stability which the Concert of Europe had imposed on Europe was rapidly disappearing. Shared interests among the great powers disintegrated into local conflicts that proliferated, especially in the Balkans, serving as a constant reminder of conflicting objectives. The community of fundamental interests envisioned in the Concert of Europe, a precursor of modern political and economic globalization, was being rapidly overcome by the fragmentation caused by the conflicting interests of Europe's many nationalities. In the final analysis, Bismarck's system served only to prolong the calm before the storm.

Perhaps, however, this was all that it could have been expected to do. Institutions such as the Concert of Europe and Bismarck's alliances had proven capable of resolving conflicts between states that arose from the security dilemma or from calculations of strategic interest. But they had repeatedly shown themselves to be incapable of resolving conflicts between nations, which frequently have deep historical and cultural roots and all too often resist solution through rational compromise. These nationalist conflicts were destined to worsen as the twentieth century approached, because while some European nations, such as France, Italy, and Germany, had achieved independent statehood, many subject nations of the Austro-Hungarian, Ottoman, and Russian empires had not. Additionally, many nations in Asia and Africa were denied independence by European colonialism.

The stability of the international system in the late nineteenth century was therefore largely illusory, and the illusion was wearing thin. Europe was gradually moving toward an increasingly dangerous situation, and the spread of European power and influence throughout the globe ensured that any major conflict in Europe would threaten the peace of the entire world.

PRINCIPAL POINTS OF CHAPTER TWO

1. Generally speaking, in the period 1648–1890, great leaders such as Louis XIV, Frederick the Great, Napoléon, and Bismarck had a major impact on international politics, and the balance of power operated among the great powers to prevent a single empire from dominating Europe.

2. The concept of the sovereign nation-state was codified by the Peace of Westphalia, which ended the Thirty Years' War in 1648.

3. The period of 1648–1789 was one of competition among the primary monarchies of Europe. Wars among the great powers were frequent but limited. France made major efforts to become paramount, but the balance of power operated to block French expansion.

4. In 1789 the French Revolution challenged the European monarchies with a new wave of political ideas, including liberalism and nationalism. Nationalism holds that each nation deserves an independent state of its own.

5. After years of turmoil, Napoléon took charge of France, declared himself emperor, and embarked on a series of wars to dominate Europe and spread the ideas of the revolution.

6. With Napoléon's defeat in 1815, the major powers formed the Concert of Europe, designed to prevent the resurgence of French power and the spread of liberalism and nationalism. Ousted monarchies were returned to power.

7. The Concert of Europe established the principle of collective security and demonstrated that cooperation was possible among the great powers, but it was only partially successful. The great powers often disagreed among themselves, and the ideas of liberalism and nationalism spread.

8. Yet, major war between the great powers did not occur in the remainder of the century. Instead, violence within states over nationalism and liberalism contributed to the fragmentation of empires. France quickly returned to great-power status, and the European powers frequently disagreed over whether to intervene to prevent rebellions.

9. Globalization of European politics was accelerated by the Industrial Revolution, which led to mass production in manufacturing, new forms of transportation, growth of cities, social dislocations, domestic instability, and new and more lethal weaponry. Major political and social upheavals occurred within states, particularly the revolutions of 1848. New technology and economic imperatives pressed forward the process of globalization, and the search for colonies and additional markets began anew.

10. Bismarck, chancellor of Prussia, harnessed the conservative agenda of keeping the aristocracy in power while promoting the liberal nationalist aim of German unification. He also proved adept at diplomacy with the other great powers. Through three quick and successful wars against Denmark, Austria, and France, he united Germany in 1871 under Prussian leadership.

11. Bismarck maneuvered to maintain the stability of the European system from 1870 to 1890, but he could not contain growing opposition at home and increasing competition among the European powers.

12. The net result of the spread of nationalism in the nineteenth century was that Italy and Germany were unified, but the multinational Austrian and Ottoman (Turkish) Empires began to come apart.

13. As the twentieth century approached, industrialization, the competition between monarchy and liberalism, and nationalism combined to create a new, turbulent, and potentially explosive international political system.

Chapter 3

The World Wars

I went through selections where people next to me were taken out while I had the typhoid fever, and people next to me were yanked out that had survived already three months, four months, and they didn't take me. . . . there was no rhyme or reason for the selections, never. It was the face, the nose, something. Or a quota to fill. . . . (The Jews who went directly into the gas from the ramp . . . were the lucky ones.) not until the doors clanged shut of those gas chambers did they know what hit them. The ones that were taken out . . . at a selection after a roll call in the morning, they had to wait all day knowing . . . what was waiting for them. It was [the Nazis'] typical thoroughness. Those who were put into Block 27, which was the collection block for the daily trip, why waste food on them, why waste water on them? They were there all day long. Sometimes you would see a hand stretching out for water, water, out the barbed windows on Block 27. They would give them nothing. And these were the really . . . horrible tragic things.

Ruth R. Linden, *Making Stories, Making Selves: Feminist Reflections on the Holocaust* (Columbus: Ohio State University Press, 1993), p. 93.

In the nineteenth century, the French Revolution and the Industrial Revolution had promised better, freer, more productive lives to millions. In the first half of the twentieth century, the promise turned instead to death, destruction, and unprecedented suffering in the terrible world wars. How could these catastrophes have occurred? We will offer possible answers in the following pages.

At the start of the twentieth century, world leadership was vested in Europe. Through military power, economic strength, and colonial empires, the European great powers dominated the world's political and economic system. By the middle of the century, however, Europe was struggling to recover from catastrophic devastation, and political and economic leadership had passed from London, Paris, and Berlin to capitals thousands of miles away from Europe's center of gravity. This radical change in the structure of world politics was brought about by two horrific wars, unequaled before or since in scope or destructiveness. World War I (1914–1918) and World War II (1939–1945) were the means by

Major Events in the International System, 1894–1945

1894: France and Russia accept convention on military alliance.

1904: Anglo-French entente ends traditional enmity between Britain and France.

1904–1905: Russo-Japanese War occurs; Japan defeats Russia and becomes dominant power in northeastern Asia.

1905: First Moroccan Crisis increases Franco-German tensions.

1908: Austria annexes Bosnia and Herzegovina; crisis ensues.

1909: Turkey and Serbia recognize Austria's annexation of Bosnia and Herzegovina.

1910: Japan annexes Korea.

1911: Second Moroccan Crisis occurs.

1912–1913: Balkan Wars break Ottoman power in Europe.

1914: World War I begins, precipitated by assassination of heir to Austro-Hungarian throne, Archduke Francis Ferdinand, in Bosnia by Serbian nationalist; Central Powers (Germany and Austria-Hungary, joined later by Ottoman Empire) fight against Allies (Britain, Russia, France, Japan, Belgium, and Serbia).

1915: Italy joins Allies; Bulgaria joins Central Powers.

1917: Russian Revolution topples tsar; United States enters war on Allied side; Bolsheviks seize power in Russia.

1918: Bolsheviks end war with Central Powers; Armistice ends World War I; Germany is defeated.

1918–1920: Civil war in Russia is fought and won by Bolsheviks.

1919: Treaty of Versailles breaks up Austro-Hungarian empire, creates new states and extensive territorial changes in Europe, and imposes harsh penalties on Germany.

1920–1923: Turkish nationalists under Ataturk drive Allied forces out of Turkey; Treaty of Lausanne acknowledges abolition of Ottoman Empire and creation of republic of Turkey.

1922: USSR is created; Benito Mussolini

which the Eurocentric world order self-destructed and was replaced by a truly globalized economic and political system. The exact number of people killed in these two wars will never be known, but it certainly exceeds 55 million. This chapter will examine the causes and consequences of the world wars and their impact on world politics. Our discussion of these complex conflicts will not go into great detail on how they were fought, but will instead concentrate on why they occurred and what the fighting and the peace settlements that followed did to change the nature and structure of world politics.

Wars have always been the cause and effect of political changes, as Chapter Two has outlined. The world wars, however, were unprecedented not only in their carnage and scale, but in the degree to which they brought about political, economic, technological, and social change. They were fought not just in Europe, but in Africa, Asia, the Pacific Islands, and the Americas, and no corner of the world was sufficiently remote to remain unaffected by the conflicts and their resolution. Men were mobilized in record numbers, which meant that equally large numbers of women entered the industrial work force; this development in turn strengthened the case for women's political and social equality. Similarly, the wars' insatiable demands for workers and soldiers brought ethnic and racial minorities into the military and the industrial economy, bringing to the forefront social tensions that could be resolved only by the extension of political and civil rights.

The ramifications of the technological advances spurred on by the world wars were at first not fully comprehended either by soldiers or by military strategists. Barbed wire, invented on the American plains to fence in cattle, would be employed in Europe to confine entire armies to their trenches. The machine gun, perfected in the late nineteenth century, would become the weapon of choice in the twentieth, and dramatic developments greatly increased the ranges and firepower of artillery. World War I introduced the tank and changed the airplane from a curiosity to a tactical and strategic weapon, though the impact of

becomes prime minister of Italy and begins to institute fascist dictatorship.
1929: Stock-market crash in United States precipitates Great Depression.
1931–1932: Japan seizes Manchuria and establishes it as an independent protectorate called Manchukuo.
1933: Adolf Hitler becomes chancellor in Germany; National Socialist (Nazi) dictatorship replaces Weimar Republic.
1935: Hitler remilitarizes the Rhineland; Italy invades Ethiopia.
1936–1939: Spanish Civil War fought; fascist Francisco Franco becomes dictator of Spain.
1937: Japan invades China.
1938: Germany annexes Austria;

Munich Conference allows German annexation of Sudetenland.
1939: Germany invades Czechoslovakia; World War II begins with German invasion of Poland.
1940: German forces overrun Denmark, Norway, Netherlands, Belgium, and France, leaving Britain without allies; Italy, Hungary, and Romania join Axis powers; Battle of Britain won by the British; North African campaign begins.
1941: Bulgaria joins Axis powers; Germany conquers Yugoslavia and Greece and invades Soviet Union; Japanese attack on Pearl Harbor brings United States into war.
1942: Axis advances halted at battles of

Stalingrad (Russia), Midway (central Pacific), and El Alamein (Egypt).
1943: Allied forces drive Axis out of North Africa; Italy surrenders.
1944: Invasion of Normandy opens second front in Europe; Allied forces gain momentum in Pacific.
1945: Germany surrenders; United States drops atomic bombs on Hiroshima and Nagasaki; Japan surrenders, ending World War II.

---

both was marginal at first. These war machines would become decisive during World War II, an all-encompassing struggle that engendered a plethora of devices that now shape modern life, from the jet engine to the computer to the atomic bomb.

The two world wars thus had a deep and profound impact on almost every aspect of global civilization. An appreciation of the conditions that led to them and the legacy of their outcome is therefore necessary for an understanding of contemporary world politics. While the effects of World War I and World War II are well known, many questions remain about their causes. This chapter cannot and should not attempt to answer these questions; instead, it will outline the salient facts and contending theories about the origins, conduct, and aftermath of these catastrophic conflicts. The choice of which facts and which theories are most relevant, and the determination of whether or not these long and bloody wars could have been avoided, will be left as an exercise for the reader.

CAUSES OF WORLD WAR I

The devastation wrought by the four years of World War I has led to a continuing and at times bitter debate as to its causes. Debate also focuses on the question of responsibility for the war. In the 1919 **Treaty of Versailles,** which officially ended the war, Germany and its kaiser, Wilhelm II, were held responsible for deliberately starting it. Yet, some scholars feel that none of the states, including Germany, had intended to go to war, but were instead caught up in events beyond their control. As the diplomatic historian René Albrecht-Carrié wrote, "If the outbreak of war in [1914] may be explained as but the logical outcome of long-maturing trends and forces, it may be said with equal truth that Europe in 1914 accidentally stumbled into a catastrophe from which all her members recoiled."[1] While opinions thus differ about the causes of the Great

War, it is clear in hindsight that the complex relations among the European states prior to 1914 created the context for the crisis that arose in July 1914. The decisions made by European leaders during that crisis led to a war that none of them wanted and that would destroy the world as they knew it.

Amidst all the controversy over the origins of World War I, six factors are recognized as playing an important role in European politics and diplomacy in the years leading up to the outbreak of war in 1914:

1. The growing power of Germany.

2. The system of alliances designed to protect the security and interests of the great powers.

3. The changing balance of economic power.

4. Ascendant nationalism.

5. Heightened competition for empire within and outside of Europe.

6. The cult of the offensive—the belief that the next European war would be short and that rapid mobilization and attack would be decisive.

As this section will illustrate, all of these contending explanations for the Great War follow the same basic pattern: the potentially far-ranging impact of a political, social, or technological development was not recognized until it was too late. The significance of these developments is obvious in hindsight, but in the early years of the twentieth century, diplomatic and strategic thinking in European capitals failed to keep pace with political and economic changes. It is difficult to determine which factor contributed most to the outbreak of war in 1914, as any one of them alone would have increased tensions among the European states. Together, they overwhelmed the relative peace Europe had enjoyed in the decades after 1815.

Rise of Germany

With the stunning defeat of France in 1871 and Germany's subsequent unification (see Chapter Two), Germany took center stage in European international relations. Being at the center of Europe had both advantages and disadvantages for German diplomacy. The advantages were that Germany was well situated to expand trade, investment, and political contacts with the whole of Europe, and could concentrate its military forces rapidly to meet a threat from any direction. The disadvantage was that Germany's central location meant that it had more points of potential conflict with other states than any other great power, and thus feared encirclement by hostile neighbors. At the same time, Germany's neighbors became alarmed by Germany's growing economic and military strength—particularly France, which sought the return of Alsace and Lorraine, annexed by Germany as a result of the Franco-Prussian War.

From 1870 until 1890, when he was dismissed from office, Bismarck was able to use Germany's central position to its advantage. After 1890, however, the foundations of Bismarck's success were gradually undermined. Kaiser Wilhelm II, who came to the throne in 1888, disagreed with Bismarck's methods and felt that the chancellor had too much influence on German foreign policy, so he dismissed him at the first opportunity. As the new kaiser felt that Germany's natural affinity was with other Germans, Germany began to tie itself closer to Austria-Hungary, and Russo-German relations consequently deteriorated. The kaiser also believed, contrary to Bismarck, that Germany required a powerful navy in order to maintain its status as a great power, and Admiral Tirpitz and many other officials in Berlin concurred. Thus, after Bismarck was sacked, the way was cleared for a buildup of naval power, and in 1898 Germany initiated a rapid expansion of its fleet.

News of the ambitious German naval construction program was received with great apprehension in London. From the British perspective, there was no logical reason for Germany to construct a large fleet unless it planned to challenge the dominant position of the Royal Navy. Britain regarded its naval supremacy as absolutely necessary in order to protect the island nation from invasion and to guard its extensive overseas empire. The kaiser's policies thus heightened the security dilemma in Europe on both land and sea. By 1914 Germany was engaged in a naval arms race with Britain and, together with its ally Austria-Hungary, in a ground-forces arms race with Russia and France.[2]

Alliance System

France, tired of diplomatic isolation and intent on replacing Bismarck's system of alliances with one that better protected its interests, seized the opportunity to court Russia when antagonism between Berlin and St. Petersburg began to increase. Although reluctant at first to make an alliance, Russia agreed in 1894 to a defensive treaty with France that explicitly sought to counter the increased power of Germany.[3] This treaty put an end to Bismarck's Triple Alliance and marked the beginning of an alliance system locking the great powers into commitments to intervene if their alliance partners were threatened. The agreement was designed to make Russia and France feel more secure, but to the Germans it represented the first step in a hostile encirclement.

Germany hoped to counter the Franco-Russian alliance with closer ties to Britain, but played its diplomatic hand poorly. Ill-conceived attempts to convince Britain that it needed German support to protect its colonial empire backfired (see the section on imperialism that follows). Germany's heavy-handed policy worsened relations by arousing public opinion in both countries against an Anglo-German alliance.

One up-and-coming nation with which Britain did share strategic interests, however, was Japan. Both Britain and Japan were concerned about Russian expansion in Asia, and in 1902, the two nations signed a treaty in which they agreed to remain neutral if either country fought one other major power and to support each other should either be at war with two other powers. This Anglo-Japanese alliance presented France with a dilemma. If Japan and Russia went to war, French failure to support Russia would antagonize an ally crucial for the balance of power in Europe. If France actively assisted Russia, it would, at minimum, alienate Britain and, at most, lose a naval war to it. As France had plans for colonial expansion in North Africa, it could ill afford to antagonize Britain, and so it had to take steps to improve Anglo-French relations.

Therefore, in April 1904 the two countries signed an entente (diplomatic French for an agreement or understanding) in which France recognized British supremacy in Egypt and Britain recognized France's predominant role in Morocco. The entente bound England into an alliance with the nation that had been its perennial enemy, France, and drew London closer to another ancient British foe, Russia. England had several conflicts with Russia, especially over the Turkish Straits and Persia, but events in Europe would continue to bring the two together.

The flexible web of alliances that was set up to prevent a major war in Europe thus rigidified into a system ensuring that if two of the great powers went to war, the rest would quickly follow. None of the countries wanted a general European war, but each had its own designs and fears. Some, such as Germany, wanted to increase their influence, while others, like Austria-Hungary and Russia, sought to recapture their failing great power status. Russia, Austria-Hungary, and the Ottoman Empire were the last of the antiquated autocratic monarchies of Europe and were rapidly being eclipsed by the other great powers in terms of economic development, military strength, and political and social organization.[4] This trend became even more apparent with Russia's humiliating defeat in the Russo-Japanese War of 1904–1905, the first loss in modern times by a European power to a non-European state, which sparked off an unsuccessful but debilitating revolution in 1905. As the Russian, Ottoman, and Austrian situations became increasingly desperate, their leaders became prepared to risk anything, up to and including war, to hold on to their internal cohesion and international stature. The rigid alliance system that existed in Europe after about 1909 virtually assured that if one of the decaying empires fell into war, the other great powers would be dragged down with it.

Economic Change and Competition

The foreign and domestic political problems confronting the European powers in the late nineteenth and early twentieth centuries were compounded by the wrenching changes brought about by industrialization. Among its many other effects (see Chapter Two), the Industrial Revolution led to massive growth in Europe's population. In the first years of the new century the population was 50 million; in 1870 it was roughly 200 million, and by the eve of war in 1914 the population had soared to 300 million.[5] This population explosion generated great pressures on the economic systems of states, which had to reconcile competing demands for civilian consumption, capital investment, and military spending. Particularly in the economically and politically backward Austro-Hungarian, Russian, and Ottoman empires, it became increasingly difficult to simultaneously satisfy the resource requirements for foreign, domestic, and security policy.

The only thing that outstripped the population growth was the growth in industrial production. This growth was not evenly spread either among countries

Table 3.1   Relative Shares of World Manufacturing Output, 1880–1913

Country	1880	1900	1913
Britain	22.9%	18.5%	13.6%
United States	14.7	23.6	32.0
Germany	8.5	13.2	14.8
France	7.8	6.8	6.1
Russia	7.6	8.8	8.2
Austria-Hungary	4.4	4.4	4.4
Italy	2.5	2.4	2.4

Source: P. Barioch, "International Industrialization Levels from 1750 to 1980," *Journal of European Economic History* 11 (1982), pp. 292, 299.

or within them. Italy, Russia, and Austria-Hungary lagged behind Britain, France, and Germany in industrial development. As the twentieth century opened, Britain, as the first state to industrialize, was declining relative to late-developing states such as Germany and the United States. In 1850 Britain was the undisputed world industrial leader, and France the continental powerhouse. In that year, Britain alone accounted for over one-third of the combined manufacturing output of the great powers. During the Bismarckian period, however, Germany emerged as the most powerful continental state, and by the end of the century Germany was encroaching on Britain's lead as well, surpassing the United Kingdom in steel production and overall manufacturing.[6] During the same period, another up-and-coming power, the United States, was beginning its takeoff, and by 1914 would evolve into an industrial giant. Table 3.1, which traces the major powers' share of world manufacturing output from 1880 to 1913, gives a rough indication of how the European powers and the United States stacked up against one another in terms of economic power as European conflicts intensified.

As the industrial capacity of states grew, their ability to challenge the other great powers for political leadership grew correspondingly. As Germany's economic strength approached and then surpassed Britain's, the main objective of European alliances changed from containment of France and Russia (as had been the case in the eighteenth and early nineteenth centuries) to containment of Germany. Meanwhile, increased industrial output was intensifying competition for resources and markets. Industrialization thus heightened the potential for conflict among the great powers at the same time that it enhanced their capacity to make war.[7]

Perceptions of political power often lagged behind changes in relative economic strength, however. Prior to the outbreak of World War I, few European leaders looked to the United States as a potential counterweight to Germany or other expansionist states. Public and congressional opinion in the United States at that time ran toward isolationism, and most Americans thought it best to stay well clear of the rivalries, conflicts, and "entangling alliances" of the European powers. On both sides of the Atlantic, leaders were slow to recognize how changes in the global economic system created new dangers and opportunities and made the collective security system originally envisioned in the **Concert of Europe** increasingly difficult to manage.

Nationalism

The most powerful political doctrine of the nineteenth and early twentieth centuries was nationalism. The French Revolution largely put an end to the idea of class, religion, or locality as the primary focus of loyalty for most people. The nation-state was now the supreme focus of allegiance. Those that clung the tightest to the ideas of nationalism in the early twentieth century, however, were people whose nations did not have independent states, namely those in Eastern Europe and the Balkans. These regions were dominated by competing powers, the Russian, Austro-Hungarian, and Ottoman empires, which were convinced that suppressing nationalism within their borders was necessary for their survival as political entities. As a result, campaigns of persecution were launched against minorities who did not seem to belong to the national image. Moscow forced the Poles in its empire to conform, the Jews in eastern and central Europe were persecuted, and all over Europe attempts were made to crush nationalist forces.

One of the greatest victories for nationalism was the unification of Germany, but its effect was not limited to the creation of the German Empire. The nationalism of the various ethnic groups within the many empires of Europe became a pressing issue in the twentieth century. The empires of eastern Europe were threatened by groups demanding separation and independence. These included Poles in Prussia and the French in Alsace and Lorraine who desired freedom from the German Empire; Serbs, Czechs, Romanians, and many others from the Austro-Hungarian Empire; Finns, Poles, and Balts from the Russian Empire; and Bulgarians, Greeks, Serbs, and Arabs from the Ottoman Empire.

The empire that felt most threatened by nationalist movements was Austria-Hungary. Here was the only country in Europe that was held together not by national identity, but by the principle of personal dynastic rule. Emperor Franz Josef I had ruled over the numerous nationalities within the empire since 1848. The Hungarians and the Austrians were actually minorities in a patchwork of Slavic groups, including Poles, Czechs, Slovaks, Slovenes, Croats, and Serbs. Austria was opposed to Russian encroachment in the area and was even more concerned about further independence in the Balkans. Vienna was afraid that the independent Balkan states, especially Serbia, would stir up trouble within the empire. The various nationalities under Austrian rule longed for independence and needed little encouragement from their brethren, but many independent Balkan states supported nationalist agitation in hopes of unifying all people of their respective nationalities. In particular, the domestic problem presented by Slavic nationalism was exacerbated by the desire of Serbia, aided and abetted by Russia, to expand at Austria-Hungary's expense.

In general, empires tended to suppress nationalists within their own borders while encouraging those in neighboring empires, hoping to make political gains at the expense of their imperial rivals. This created an explosive situation in the ethnically diverse and politically fragmented Balkans, where, as will be shown later, a dispute over nationalism provided the spark that ignited the First World War.

Imperialism

Empires were not confined to Europe. By 1900 most of the world outside Europe (except the Americas) was under the domination of some European power. Nearly all of Africa had been partitioned without regard to national or ethnic boundaries, and most of Asia as well was under **de facto** if not **de jure** control by European colonial regimes.[8] (Chapter Five surveys these developments in more detail.) Since power and security depended on having control of resources, acquisition of colonies for their resources and markets was considered essential by many European leaders. But with most of the world already divided between the colonial empires, there was nowhere left to colonize. The states that felt left out of the colonial race, especially Germany, thought they deserved more, and worried that without colonies they would not be able to obtain enough raw materials or have sufficient trading partners to remain competitive with the other great powers. The breakup of the "sick man of Europe," the faltering Ottoman Empire, presented an opportunity to acquire more territory (especially in the Middle East) that some states found irresistible.

Many conflicts over colonial interests in Africa and Asia heightened tensions among the great powers in Europe. Britain and France frequently clashed over colonies and **spheres of influence** in the nineteenth century, as did Britain and Russia, but these great powers never went to war with each other over colonial disputes. As the twentieth century approached, colonial problems increased the mutual antagonism between Britain and Germany. In 1896 a conspiracy headquartered in Britain's Cape Colony (now part of South Africa) attempted to overthrow the Boer government of neighboring Transvaal, with London's knowledge. (See Chapter Five for more on the coup attempt). When the attempt failed, Kaiser Wilhelm II sent Transvaal's President Kruger a telegram congratulating him for "restoring peace and . . . maintaining the independence of the country against attacks from without."[9] The Kruger Telegram, as it came to be known, aroused public opinion in Britain against German meddling in a region that Britain saw as its rightful sphere of influence. The incident added to growing Anglo-German tensions.

Cult of the Offensive

Meanwhile, back in Europe, the improved relations between Russia and France generated great concern in Germany, especially among its top military leaders. The worst nightmare of every German leader, and of Prussian leaders before them, was the possibility of a two-front war with both Russia and France simultaneously, which would divide and thus weaken Germany's army. With the advent of new technology, it appeared that the side that could swiftly mount an effective offensive would win, offering a tempting solution to this strategic problem. In the late nineteenth and early twentieth centuries, most European strategists ascribed to this belief in what modern strategic analysts refer to as the **cult of the offensive**.[10] There were two main reasons why this became the primary strategic doctrine for European military planners. The first, as mentioned, had to do with technology. The expansion of railroads, among other technological improvements, enabled states to rapidly deploy troops to the front, and the telegraph allowed generals to receive reports and transmit orders faster, enabling them to control larger armies more effectively. Also, the breech-loading rifle and the machine gun were widely thought to increase the ability of attacking troops to concentrate their firepower at the point of assault. (For some reason, the ability of defending troops to do this as well was downplayed.)

Second, recent experience with wars in Europe seemed to indicate that the side that "landed the first blow" would win. Prussia defeated its adversaries in 1866 and 1870–1871 quickly and with relatively few casualties (see Chapter Two). Most European generals expected the next great power war to resemble the last, and accordingly based their strategies on rapid mobilization and offensives. The economic pressures inherent in maintaining a large conscript and reserve army mobilized for long periods also made striking first more attractive, as leaders could promise that the boys would be home by Christmas. The same leaders chose to ignore the experience of the American Civil War (1861–1865) and the Boer War (1899–1902), both of which were protracted struggles and, especially in the American Civil War, produced a frightening number of casualties.

The inherent dangers of the cult of the offensive were not fully realized at the time. When political and military leaders believe that war will bring great gains at little cost, war becomes more likely. States act more aggressively by increasingly challenging their neighbors through military buildups and coercive threats of war. As these neighbors grow more fearful, they, too, build up their forces and seek stronger alliances in order to better secure themselves in the event of war. Even if none of the states actually seek war, this spiral of tension makes conflicts of interest more severe and likely to lead to violence. The cult of the offensive thus enhances the security dilemma and encourages preemptive attacks, because when crises threaten to escalate into war, states have great incentives to strike first and defeat their enemies before their enemies can defeat them.

The cult of the offensive influenced the military plans of most of the European great powers. Beginning in 1892, German Chief of Staff Alfred von Schlieffen changed Germany's strategy. Previously, in the event of a two-front war with Russia and France, Germany planned to attack Russia first while German forces stood on the defensive against France. The new Schlieffen Plan called for Germany to knock out France with a fast-moving offensive, just as Prussia had done in the Franco-Prussian War, and then shift its troops by rail to the eastern front to fight the slower-moving Russian forces.

The Schlieffen Plan thus intended to utilize Germany's ability to mobilize troops and equipment faster than its adversaries to defeat first France and then Russia. To be successful, Germany had to mobilize at the first sign of Russian preparations for war, as any delay would shorten the window of opportunity for a quick victory and increase the chances of a two-front war, which would put Germany at a disadvantage. Russia and France, however, had similar plans for rapid mobilization and offensive in the event of a war with Germany. The cult of the offensive thus put the massive military machines of the great powers on a hair trigger.

PATH TO WAR

As the preceding section has outlined, there are plenty of possible explanations for *why* World War I occurred. Taken together, German expansion, the alliance system, economic competition, imperialism, nationalism, and the cult of the offensive offer more than enough reasons why Europe was pushed over the brink of war in 1914. In order to explain *how* and *when* World War I broke out, it is necessary to look at the string of crises that arose from the conflicting interests and aspirations of the great powers in the early twentieth century. There had been several regions of conflict throughout the century before 1914, but in the decade before the war, international attention was particularly focused on two areas, North Africa and the Balkans.

Moroccan Crises

At the start of the twentieth century, France was trying to draw the kingdom of Morocco under its wing in the hopes of adding it to France's African empire. In March 1905 Kaiser Wilhelm, looking for a way to break up the friendship between Britain and France and ensure German economic access to Morocco, visited Tangier in support of Moroccan independence. This catalyzed the First Moroccan Crisis, which the great powers decided to resolve at a diplomatic conference at Algeciras, Spain, in 1906. Germany's allies failed to support it at this conference, which recognized French dominance in Morocco. (In keeping with how the great powers viewed the world outside Europe, the interests of the Moroccans were given little attention.)

When French troops occupied the Moroccan capital of Fez in May 1911 to quell a revolt, Germany perceived the move (correctly) as an attempt to establish a protectorate over Morocco. To emphasize that its interests had to be taken into consideration, Germany sent a gunboat to the Moroccan port of Agadir, thereby beginning the Second Moroccan Crisis. The crisis was resolved by November with a compromise in which the Germans agreed to drop their objection to a French protectorate in Morocco in exchange for the acquisition of a slice of French colonial territory in the Congo. Nonetheless, the agreement satisfied neither France nor Germany and angered public opinion in both nations. Many people in France resented what they regarded as another humiliation of their country, while Germans regarded the incident as another denial of Germany's rightful "place in the sun." Meanwhile, taking advantage of the distraction provided by the crisis, Italy declared war on the Ottoman Empire in September 1911 and seized Tripoli (then an Ottoman domain, now the capital of Libya). In the short run, this was a sideshow for the great powers, but Italy's victory displayed the inherent weakness of the Ottoman Empire, which further encouraged nationalist demands in the Balkans.

Balkan Powder Keg Leads to July Crisis

While imperialism was heightening conflicts between the great powers in Asia and Africa, nationalism was gaining momentum in Europe. In 1908, 1912, and 1913, several crises and two wars in the Balkans created a situation of rising tensions (see Map 3.1). The heart of the problem was between German-backed Austria-Hungary and Russian-backed Serbia, which were competing for the spoils of Ottoman decline. By 1914 the stage had been set for a showdown between Austria-Hungary and Serbia.

The sequence of events that finally put out the lights of Europe is convoluted, but it is worth recounting in detail, as it is one of history's greatest tragedies. On June 28, 1914, Archduke Franz Ferdinand, heir to Austria-Hungary's crown, was assassinated while on a visit to Sarajevo (the capital of Bosnia) on a Serbian national holiday. Austria-Hungary had annexed Bosnia in 1908, but it was an area claimed by Serbia. Vienna held Serbia responsible for the assassination, and Austria's foreign minister, Count Berchtold, decided to make use of the incident as an opportunity to "settle accounts" with Serbia. Austria did not dare act without German support, however, so on July 5 the Austrian ambassador to Berlin met with Kaiser Wilhelm II to discuss the matter. Without consulting his military advisors, the kaiser not only promised Germany's support, but pressed Austria-Hungary to take quick action and capitalize on the public outcry generated by the assassination. Thus Germany, one of the strongest countries in Europe, essentially gave a blank check to the weak and unstable Austro-Hungarian Empire to deal with Serbia as it saw fit.

On July 23, Austria-Hungary issued an ultimatum to Serbia and gave Belgrade 48 hours to reply. The terms of the ultimatum were extremely harsh, and most of Europe expected that Serbia would have no choice but to reject it—as did Austria, which was simply looking for an excuse to invade Serbia. The Russian government, believing that it needed to stand firm in support of Serbia in order to preserve Russia's great-power status, resolved that Russia would not be humiliated as it had been in the Balkan crisis of 1908, when it subsequently accepted Vienna's annexation of Bosnia. When he saw the Austrian ultimatum, Russian Foreign Minister Sazanov exclaimed, "This means a European war."[11]

On July 25, Russia issued orders to prepare for the mobilization of its army. That same day, Serbia responded to the ultimatum, surprisingly accepting

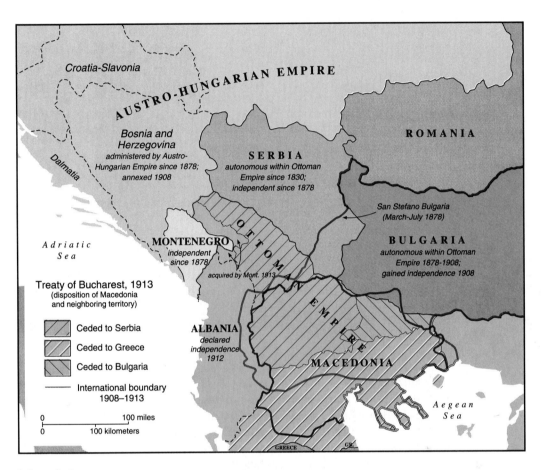

Map 3.1   The Balkans before World War I

most of Austria-Hungary's demands. Austria-Hungary, however, preferred to resolve the crisis by force. It rejected Serbia's response, broke off diplomatic relations, and, despite the fact that its army was not prepared to take action, declared war on Serbia on July 28. The following day, Tsar Nicholas ordered a partial mobilization of the Russian army directed against Austria-Hungary in an attempt to deter an attack against Serbia, but still hoped to avoid war with Germany.

In Berlin, the chief of the German General Staff, Helmuth von Moltke, wanted to mobilize the army immediately. The kaiser and chancellor, Bethmann-Hollweg, however, tried furiously to gain time for more negotiations. The kaiser wrote a note to the tsar pleading for restraint, but Tsar Nicholas was under great pressure from his own military leaders, who did not have any plans for a partial mobilization and also thought Germany was likely to intervene in any war between Russia and Austria-Hungary.[12] On July 30,

WHAT WOULD YOU DO?

You are the tsar of Russia in early August 1914. You are backing the Serbians, your Orthodox Christian brethren, whom Austria, and by extension, Germany, have threatened over the assasination of the heir to the Austrian throne on his visit to Bosnia, an Austrian province that Serbia covets. You are trying to decide whether to order full mobilization of your forces against Austria.

You are aware that mobilization may precipitate the next war. You have suggested to your military commanders that the country partially mobilize, thereby keeping its options open. If the crisis abates, you can easily demobilize; if the crisis leads to war, you will at least be partially ready. But your generals tell you that this is not possible: No one ever devised a scheme for partial mobilization; it is either all or nothing. Mobilization will threaten Germany and will likely lead to war. If you wait a few years until you are stronger industrially, you may be in a better position to fight and win.

While you have made great strides in bringing your country into the industrial age in the last twenty years (such as building more munitions factories, steel mills, and kilometers of railroads), you have also

after much vacillation, the tsar agreed to full mobilization. The next day, July 31, Germany sent Russia an ultimatum stating that Germany would be forced to mobilize against Russia if Russia moved against Austria and warned that if this occurred, "European war could scarcely be prevented."[13]

Germany also requested French assurances of neutrality in the event of a Russo-German war, but the expectation of a major war was rapidly becoming a self-fulfilling prophecy. At 3:55 A.M. on August 1, France responded to the German request by ordering a general mobilization. Five minutes later, Germany also issued orders for a general mobilization, and at 7:00 A.M. declared war on Russia.[14] The initial conflict between Austria-Hungary and Serbia had escalated into a confrontation between the continental great powers.

For each nation, mobilization was an expensive move that could not be sustained for long without causing significant economic damage. But the great powers all subscribed to the cult of the offensive described earlier—they believed that whoever attacked first would gain a decisive advantage. Belief in the power of the offensive was particularly strong in Germany, which was now faced with a two-front war. The Schlieffen Plan, which anticipated this contingency, dictated that the main French forces be circumvented, so on August 2 Germany demanded free passage for its troops through Belgium. Consistent with its neutral status, Belgium refused, but on August 3 Germany declared war on France and sent troops through Belgium anyway. Britain, which regarded Belgian neutrality as a vital interest, declared war on Germany on August 4. World War I had begun.[15]

heightened expectations on the part of the working classes for greater economic and political reform. The Japanese defeat of your armies in 1905 revealed your country's lack of military and economic preparation, and it incited a domestic revolt. You do not want to risk a repeat of this event.

On the other hand, you want to maintain your alliance with France, which opposes Germany. Your military experts tell you that if you do not mobilize your forces to thwart a possible Austrian attack against Serbia, the Austrians and their patrons, the Germans, could easily win a war. Your military officers keep saying that the first country to mobilize will win the next war. Six years ago during a similar crisis in the Balkans, you caved in and your position, and that of your clients, the Serbs, only deteriorated. If you wait too long to decide, you may appear weak and indecisive to both client and foes.

You face a dilemma. The war could be lost if you decide not to mobilize, but mobilization could lead to war. If it leads to a war that you lose, it could mean your downfall.

What would you do?

THE GREAT WAR

All of the great powers had expected a short and relatively bloodless war. Germany hoped to defeat France as rapidly as it had in 1871. Had the war been between only these two countries, Germany's hopes might have been realized, for the initial German attack threatened to take Paris. (During the First Battle of the Marne in 1914, German troops were able to see the Eiffel Tower before they were forced to retreat.) However, the assumptions of the cult of the offensive did not prove correct. The technology that seemed to favor the offense could be used even more effectively by the defense. European armies had learned to employ the machine gun, which was devastating against massive infantry offensives.

After the initial German attack failed, the armies on the western front dug in to hold their positions, and there the fighting stayed until the closing months of the war. The trench lines eventually reached more than 300 miles from the coast of Belgium to the Swiss Alps, and through most of the four years of fighting the front lines never shifted more than ten miles. On the eastern front, the initial Russian attack on Germany was halted by a spectacular German victory near Tannenberg, in eastern Prussia, and trench warfare soon set in there as well.

Instead of the quick war of maneuver that European strategists had counted on, the conflict became a **war of attrition** in which thousands of men would die fighting for advances measured in yards rather than miles.[16] During the war's major battles, the numbers of men killed for minuscule gains defy comprehension. At the

European leaders and their followers expected a quick, easy war when hostilities broke out in August 1914. Instead, troops were forced to dig elaborate trenches and erect barbed wire fortifications as the battle front became static. Horrendous casualties resulted.

Source: © UPI/Bettmann Newsphotos.

five-month Battle of the Somme in 1916, British forces gained 120 square miles at the cost of 420,000 casualties, or roughly 3500 casualties per square mile, while the Germans suffered 445,000 casualties (**casualties** refers to the total number of wounded or killed). On July 1, the first day of the British offensive, 60,000 British soldiers died (more than the number of Americans killed during the entire Vietnam conflict); 21,000 were killed in the first hour of the attack, possibly within the first few minutes.[17] Attempting to break through

defensive lines, both sides used poison gas, a new weapon that caused agoniz-
ing deaths and crippling injuries, but did not alter the stalemate. Tanks and aircraft were introduced in further attempts to generate offensive momentum, but
these military machines were still in early stages of development and had only a
marginal effect on the fighting. At sea, the fleets of British and German dreadnoughts fought only one major battle (the Battle of Jutland, in 1916), which
proved indecisive. Most of the naval war was fought between German U-boats
(submarines, another new tool of warfare) and British convoy escorts.

Italy joined the Entente Powers, France, Russia, Britain, and Serbia (collectively referred to as the Allies) in 1915, and by 1917 Montenegro, Romania,
Greece, Portugal, and Japan had joined the Allies. Germany and Austria-Hungary (the Central Powers) were joined by the Ottoman Empire in October 1914
and by Bulgaria in 1915. These new entrants to the war had little effect on the
fighting on the main eastern and western fronts, however. Fighting spread
throughout the Balkans, the Middle East, and even to German colonies in Africa
and the Pacific, but the deadlock on the primary fronts continued. The prolonged stalemate prompted peace efforts, including those initiated by U.S.
President Woodrow Wilson, who argued for ending the war with "no victor
and no vanquished." None of the peace proposals, however, could resolve the
basic problem: "Germany would not surrender territorial gains while there was
a hope of victory, while the Entente could not contemplate peace without the
restoration of French territory and Belgian independence at a minimum."[18]

While neither side was willing to make peace, the human, material, economic,
and social costs of the war were increasing for both. The fruitless slaughter and
deprivation reduced the morale of both front-line troops and the civilians at
home. In the spring of 1917 many units of the French army mutinied, and the
German army also faced disciplinary problems, including mutinies and deser-
tions. The great powers were all nearing their breaking points when, in 1917,
two dramatic developments changed the course of the war.

Russian Revolution

The war with Germany and Austria created additional pressures on the decrepit
tsarist regime in Russia. By the end of 1916, the Russian army had suffered many
defeats and more than 3.6 million casualties, with another 2.1 million Russian
soldiers taken prisoner. These losses prompted St. Petersburg to drastically
increase draft calls, which in turn increased unrest among the peasants and urban
workers. Additionally, food supplies were not getting to the cities due to an
inadequate transportation system, and inflation had skyrocketed. Finally, insufficient supplies of weapons, ammunition, and food were reaching soldiers at
the front. Strikes, mutinies, and rioting culminated in the overthrow of Nicholas
II in March 1917. The new Provisional Government, a coalition of democratic,
socialist, and communist parties headed by Alexander Kerensky, continued the
war, a decision that increasingly incurred the wrath of soldiers and the civilian
population. In November the Bolshevik (Communist) Party seized power, and

the revolutionary leader Vladimir Lenin assumed leadership on a platform of "land, bread, and peace." The Bolsheviks delivered on one plank of their platform; they signed an armistice with Germany in December, and in the March 1918 Treaty of Brest-Litovsk, the Bolshevik government signed a separate peace with Germany, relinquishing Russian claims to the Baltic States of Latvia, Lithuania, and Estonia, as well as Finland, Poland, and other territories in eastern Europe. German forces remained in occupation of the western portions of Ukraine and Russia.

United States Enters the War

With Russia eliminated from the fighting, Germany now faced a one-front war, though ironically the result was opposite to that envisioned in the Schlieffen Plan (which called for France to be defeated first). Had Germany faced only France and Britain in the west, it might have forced the Allies to sue for peace. But while Russia was leaving the war, another major power was entering on the allied side.

Neutral since 1914, the United States grew increasingly annoyed with both Britain and Germany, as the two warring powers interfered with American trade and shipping. The United States at that time was still pursuing a policy of isolationism; Washington hoped to steer clear of the tangled political conflicts that had dragged the European powers into war in 1914. (This did not stop the United States from lending billions of dollars to Britain and France to finance their war efforts, however.) America was perfectly happy to trade with other countries, including the belligerents, but few Americans saw any reason why their country should get involved in a European war.

American attitudes changed markedly, however, after Germany's January 1917 decision to launch unrestricted submarine warfare, in which ships were attacked without warning regardless of nationality. This action greatly angered the U.S. government and inflamed public opinion against Germany. Berlin was taking a calculated risk: The German high command predicted that unrestricted submarine warfare would eventually bring the United States into the war. However, they believed that they would be able to prevail in the conflict by strangling Britain's supply lines before U.S. aid or intervention could make a substantial impact. The first prediction proved true: In April 1917 the United States declared war on Germany. The second German prediction, however, was not correct. The entry of the United States provided the impetus to break the long and bloody stalemate. By the autumn of 1917 some 300,000 American troops were arriving in Europe every month, and the United States was contributing its huge productive capacity to the Allied cause.[19]

Armistice

By August 1918 the Allies successfully halted the last major German attack and went on the offensive. The number of troops America committed to the war was not large compared to the French and German armies, but U.S. entry gave the Allies a decisive advantage in industrial capability and boosted the morale of Allied soldiers and civilians. As Germany's armies were being pushed back, Berlin concluded that there was no hope of avoiding defeat, although as yet German territory had not been invaded. On October 3, Germany sought an armistice (agreement to stop fighting), which was signed on November 11, 1918.

Most wars in Europe since 1648 had been limited wars that did not cause widespread devastation or huge numbers of military and civilian casualties. World War I, however, was a **total war,** in which the whole of each involved nation's human and material resources were devoted to the conflict, and defeat threatened national survival. The destruction caused by the war was overwhelming. An estimated 8 million soldiers were killed during the war, with another 7 million permanently disabled. In addition, more than 5 million civilians were killed in Europe outside Russia, and the number of Russian civilian casualties is probably much higher.[20] An entire generation of young Europeans was all but destroyed. The agony of the war was later captured in literary works such as the poetry of Wilfred Owen, Erich Maria Remarque's novel *All Quiet on the Western Front,* and Ernest Hemingway's *A Farewell to Arms.* Stanley Kubrick's film *Paths of Glory* and Peter Weir's *Gallipoli* (named for the site of a bungled Commonwealth attempt to capture the Turkish Straits) offer powerful depictions of the physical and psychological horrors of trench warfare. The world sighed with relief when the Great War ended in 1918, but winning the peace would prove to be a struggle in itself.

VERSAILLES SETTLEMENT

With the destruction caused by the Great War fresh in their minds, the victorious Allies took upon themselves the responsibility for bringing order and stability to Europe and the rest of the world. In January 1919 the United States, Britain, France, and Italy convened the Paris Peace Conference at the palace of Versailles. The conference was attended by a number of smaller states, but neither Germany nor Austria-Hungary were invited. Since France had suffered the most during the war, it played a leading role at the conference, as did the United States, in recognition of its military and economic clout. French goals were relatively straightforward: punish Germany and take revenge not only for the losses incurred between 1914 and 1918, but also for the humiliation of 1871. Prime Minister David Lloyd George of Britain was also bent on exacting punishment to a lesser degree, but Britain and Italy, along with the smaller Balkan states, were mainly there to gain territory from the division of the fallen empires. The goals of the European conferees were thus in line with old-fashioned realpolitik as it had been practiced at the Congress of Vienna (see Chapter Two).

The goals of the United States were distinctly different. President Wilson argued that America had entered the war not out of a narrow self-interest, but in order to make the world "safe for democracy." In January 1918, before Germany's defeat, Wilson had enunciated fourteen points on which he believed the peace settlement should be based. These "Fourteen Points" called

FATHER OF THE TURKS

After World War I put an end to the decrepit Ottoman Empire, the Entente Powers attempted to contain the forces of nationalism that arose out of the empire's collapse. They failed, and the man who let the nationalist genie out of the bottle for good was Kemal Ataturk (1881–1938). Named simply Mustafa at his birth to the family of a minor government official in Salonika, Greece, he added the name Kemal at the suggestion of his math teacher and aspired to a career in the Ottoman Army. Kemal's education acquainted him with Western culture and political ideas, and he joined the secret revolutionary society of "Young Turks" that forced the Ottoman sultan to accept constitutional reforms in 1908. In the turbulent years before World War I, Mustafa Kemal organized guerrilla resistance against the Italian occupation of Tripoli in 1911 and served in the First Balkan War in 1912. His experiences in Europe's hotbed of nationalism, the Balkans, showed him firsthand how nationalist sentiments could become a powerful political force.

During World War I, Kemal led the defense of the Gallipoli Peninsula, the gateway to the Turkish Straits, against an ill-fated Allied invasion. The war's end found him in Constantinople, where the defeated Ottoman government considered accepting a British or American mandate over Turkey in order to keep the remnants of the shattered empire together. When Greek troops occupied Turkish territory in 1919, Kemal saw an opportunity to launch a nationalist revolution. Organizing a military revolt against the sultan's authority and Allied occupation, Kemal headquartered his forces in the mountain city of Ankara, which became the center of a new nationalist government. In four years of brutal fighting, Kemal's forces swept away the vestiges of the Ottoman regime and defeated the Allied occupation armies. In 1923 the Allies recognized Turkish independence in the Treaty of Lausanne, and the Republic of Turkey was proclaimed, with Mustafa Kemal as its president.

Kemal sought to drag Turkey as far into the Western world as he could. He enacted sweeping reforms of the administrative, educational, and legal systems, seeking to bring them into line with European models. While Islam remained the religion of

for open diplomacy, free trade, arms reductions, the self-determination of nations, and, perhaps most importantly, a League of Nations designed to ensure collective security. Basically, Wilson hoped to use the conference to create a new world order based on mutual respect and cooperation between nations. His position was thus an idealistic one, as it proposed a means for overcoming the security dilemma that had created so many dangerous conflicts in prewar Europe. Some of the younger delegates from Britain were also adherents to the Wilsonian crusade. But from the perspective of the European powers, particularly France and its leader Georges Clemenceau, the American proposals appeared academic and unrealistic, although they could not be ignored given the extent of American power. (For more on Wilson's role at Versailles, see Chapter Fifteen.)

most Turks, Kemal wanted the new republic to be a secular state; he disestablished Islam as a state religion and rejected the institution of Islamic law. After leading a political revolution to victory, Kemal attempted to revolutionize Turkish culture as well, encouraging the study of Western science, art, and music and the adoption of European clothes and social customs. (He shocked Islamic conservatives by promoting the scandalous idea that men and women should dance together.) At his direction, Turkey adopted the Roman alphabet and made the use of family names (which few had used in the Ottoman Empire) mandatory. In 1933 the Turkish National assembly gave Mustafa Kemal a surname appropriate for the father of his country: Ataturk, "Father of the Turks."

Unlike many other revolutionary leaders, Ataturk did not seek to break his country's links with the past, but to create a new Turkish national identity based on ethnicity rather than religion. Though many consider him a great man, he was hardly a good guy: His methods were often ruthless, democracy was conspicuously absent from the list of Western ideas he attempted to instill, and

his government suppressed Turkey's Armenian and Kurdish minorities, expelling Armenians from Turkey in the 1920s. Overall, however, Ataturk laid the foundations for a secular state that survives to this day in a region frequently convulsed with religious conflict.

Ataturk's achievements gained renewed relevance after the breakup of the Soviet Union at the end of 1991. The newly independent states of Azerbaijan, Turkmenistan, Uzbekistan, Kazakhstan, and Kyrgyzstan, preponderantly Turkic in ethnicity and Islamic in religion, quickly came under pressure to establish Islamic Republics like that in Iran (see Chapters Four and Six). A tacit struggle between Tehran and Ankara ensued as secular Turkey and militant Islamist Iran competed for influence in the potentially explosive region. Meanwhile, Turkey was attempting in the early 1990s to securely establish democracy and enter the European Union. Many leaders in Central Asia, Russia, Europe, and the United States anxiously hope that the new Turkic states will follow the example set by modern Turkey, which has demonstrated that Western ideas and Islamic traditions can coexist.

The delegates to the conference spent months arguing amongst themselves.[21] Finally, after resolving their many differences, the Allies presented Germany with a treaty. This document took Wilson's idealistic proposals and Clemenceau's vengeful demands and combined them to form a compromise that satisfied no one. The treaty called for Germany to return Alsace-Lorraine to France, cede some of its eastern territory to the recreated state of Poland, permit French and British occupation of the economically vital Saar region, and demilitarize the Rhineland (the portion of Germany bordering France). In addition, Germany was required to adhere to strict disarmament provisions that limited the size of its army; forbade it to possess submarines, tanks, or an air force; and outlawed conscription.

Consistent with the principle of national self-determination, the Austro-Hungarian Empire was divided into a number of successor states: Austria, Hungary, Czechoslovakia, and Yugoslavia (which united Serbs, Croats, Slovenes, Montenegrins, and Muslim Slavs among others in an artificial kingdom). Poland, which had been partitioned out of existence in 1795, was reunited and joined Italy and Romania in claiming other parts of the former Hapsburg Empire. Austria, most of whose population was Germanic, was forbidden from joining with Germany, and a large German population was incorporated into Czechoslovakia in an area known as the Sudetenland. (Map 3.2 shows how the Versailles Treaty redrew the map of Europe.)

Despite all the talk about self-determination of nations, the treaty granted self-determination to some nationalities but not to others; and, in particular, the doctrine was not applied to the Germans. Much to the dismay of the Arabs and the European colonies, the principle was not applied at all outside Europe. The British had promised the Arabs independence if they aided in the fight against the Ottoman Turks, but this turned out to be an empty promise, as Britain, France, and Russia had made plans to carve up the Ottoman Empire among themselves before the war had even finished.[22]

Finally, Germany was held responsible for the war and forced to pay extensive reparations to the Allies, particularly France. Germany objected to many parts of the treaty, but no clause did more to create a lasting sense of betrayal and resentment than Article 231. This article was the "war guilt" clause that held Germany and its allies wholly responsible for the war and all the damage it caused. The clause would foster rage and resentment among the German people that nationalist extremists were quick to exploit. Germany had little choice but to accept the treaty, as the Allies continued to blockade German ports and maintained large forces in position to strike at German territory until the treaty was signed.

On June 28, 1919, the five-year anniversary of the assassination of Archduke Franz Ferdinand, Germany reluctantly signed the treaty of peace. The onus of accepting the punitive treaty fell to the new Weimar Republic, which had replaced the German monarchy after the kaiser's November 1918 abdication. The signing of the peace agreement discredited the infant democratic regime in the minds of many Germans. The treaty was signed in the Hall of Mirrors at the Palace of Versailles, where in 1871 Bismarck had proclaimed the German Empire that was now no more. The "war to end all wars" was officially over, but the peace settlement created almost as many problems as it had solved.[23]

THE FALSE PEACE OF THE 1920s

Niccolò Machiavelli once noted that a victor should either conciliate his enemy or destroy him. The Treaty of Versailles accomplished neither. Germany was left scourged, humiliated, and resentful but not permanently weakened. The country lost territory, but it was not actually partitioned, and it retained most

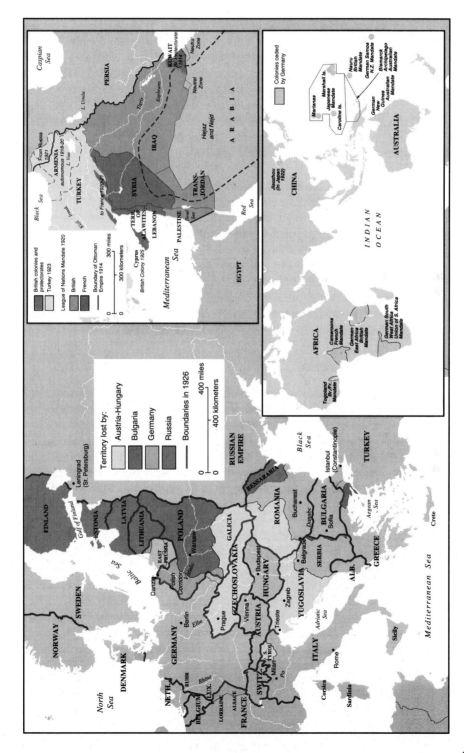

Map 3.2 Versailles Settlement, Post–World War I

Territory lost by:
- Austria-Hungary
- Bulgaria
- Germany
- Russia
- Boundaries in 1926

0 / 400 miles
0 / 400 kilometers

British colonies and protectorates
Turkey 1923
League of Nations Mandate 1920
- British
- French
— Boundary of Ottoman Empire 1914

0 / 300 miles
0 / 300 kilometers

Colonies ceded by Germany

of its industrial potential and resource base. A great many Germans felt it was unjust for Germany to be held directly responsible for the war, because (as recounted earlier in this chapter) the actions of many countries contributed to the outbreak of fighting. The reparations payments were also seen as unfair and were greatly burdensome to the German economy, which was weak and in need of extensive rebuilding. Furthermore, German armies had not been driven from France, nor had German territory been invaded; this made both the defeat and the harsh peace terms especially difficult to accept. The denial of self-determination for many ethnic Germans added to the widespread resentment of the peace settlement.

In addition, the splitting of the former Austrian Empire into a number of small states actually left Germany as the strongest Continental power, since France was virtually exhausted. These newly formed countries were weak and unable to protect themselves, and so had to rely upon the support of the great powers in order to survive as sovereign states. This left the new states vulnerable to renewed German expansion, which remained a possibility, since the Versailles Treaty did not greatly reduce Germany's economic and military potential. Disarmament and reparations, which were the harshest measures in the treaty, were left completely up to German cooperation. Allied commissions were set up to monitor German compliance, but there was nothing to back up these commissions.

A Weak League

One of the reasons why the details for enforcing the provisions of the Versailles Treaty were so feeble was the weakness of the League of Nations. The hope of establishing peace and stability through the League was thwarted by the decision of the United States not to join. The U.S. Senate refused to ratify the Treaty of Versailles. Aside from the Senate's fear of "entangling alliances," some senators demanded an amendment asserting the primacy of the U.S. Constitution, which would protect Congress's prerogative to declare war. Wilson refused to compromise, the Senate refused to ratify the treaty, and the United States remained outside the League. The absence of the United States, which had proposed and been a driving spirit of the League, left it a body without substance. Without the world's largest industrial power, the League of Nations was weakened to the point that many doubted its capability to satisfactorily resolve the many challenges to the new political order established at Versailles. The global security system Wilson envisioned thus never got off the ground.

In sum, the potential for an upsurge in German resentment, the American return to isolationism, the revolution and civil war in Russia (renamed the Union of Soviet Socialist Republics by the Bolshevik government in 1922), and the splintering of eastern Europe made the European balance of power inherently unstable. Europe became more fragmented in political, economic, and security terms than it had been before 1914.

In response to the uncertain situation, European diplomats scrambled to set up new security agreements. France established a network of defense pacts with Poland, Czechoslovakia, Romania, and Yugoslavia in an attempt to contain

Germany should the need arise. (Because the reliability of these alliances was questionable, however, France began in 1930 to build an extensive system of defensive fortifications, called the **Maginot Line,** on its border with Germany.) Britain, Italy, France, Belgium, and Germany addressed security concerns in western Europe in the Locarno Treaties of 1925, and in 1926 Germany was allowed into the League of Nations.

These international security arrangements, however, would soon be undermined by domestic developments in the various European great powers. Hoping to avoid a recurrence of the devastation that the First World War had brought to all of Europe, postwar public opinion in Britain and France was strongly against spending money on defense. The desire to avoid war at any cost was fed by a growing belief that weapons and arms races lead to war, and by reassessments of the war's origins that did not heap all of the blame on Germany. (As the earlier sections on the causes of World War I recount, there was plenty of blame to go around.) Antiwar sentiments would later guide the proponents of the policy of **appeasement,** a policy dissuading aggressors from attacking by conceding part of their demands in order to satisfy their appetite for expansion.

In contrast to the growth of pacifism in the West, many Italians and Germans, feeling cheated (for different reasons) by the outcome of World War I, increasingly turned to radical forms of nationalism as their social and economic situation led to disillusionment with democracy. In Italy, social upheaval nearly led to civil war. Fearing the possibility of a communist-inspired revolution, King Victor Emmanuel III appointed Benito Mussolini, head of the ultraconservative and nationalist Fascist party, as prime minister in 1922. Mussolini, called *Il Duce* (the leader), soon established a dictatorial regime promising to end the social and economic chaos and "make the trains run on time."[24]

Similarly, economic problems in Germany during the 1920s placed enormous strains on its fragile democratic institutions. Saddled by the Allies with crushing reparations, the German government recklessly printed money to make the payments required by the Versailles Settlement and cover its other debts. The immediate result was **hyperinflation** (an extreme, rapid, and uncontrolled rise in prices), which wiped out savings and drove millions of Germans into poverty. Housewives had to take wheelbarrows with them to do their shopping— not to carry their purchases home, but to carry enough money to buy groceries.[25] This financial disaster would soon lead many Germans to listen to extremist politicians who proposed radical solutions to the economic crisis.

The Great Depression

The already shaky global economy was dealt a crushing blow when the American stock market crashed in 1929. The crash hurled first the United States and then Europe into the Great Depression, the worst economic disaster in modern times. Banks failed, the supply of capital dried up, investments and savings vanished, and millions of workers lost their jobs. Almost overnight, international trade broke down as nations erected trade barriers to protect jobs and domestic markets. The 1930 Smoot-Hawley Tariff dramatically increased American import duties and aggravated the situation by closing off the U.S. market from industrial imports. The closing of world markets spread, further exacerbating Germany's inability to pay its war debts.[26] Unable to get new loans from America, Germany renounced payment of war reparations, which in turn led France and Britain to default on their debts. (For more on these issues, see Chapter Seven.)

The Great Depression exacerbated political and economic conflicts all over the world. The German economy, in particular, was devastated, and its political system was paralyzed. Many Germans looked for a strong hand to lead them out of the crisis, and the National Socialist (Nazi) Party, led by Adolf Hitler, offered one. In elections held from 1930 to 1933, the Nazis continuously gained seats in the Reichstag (parliament) until they controlled more seats than any other party, thus clearing the way for Hitler to become chancellor in January 1933. The man who would become the world's most infamous dictator thus came to power through the democratic process.

WHAT CAUSED WORLD WAR II?

The reasons for the outbreak of the Second World War have not been debated as extensively or enthusiastically as the causes of the First World War. In general, its origins are less complex and mysterious than those of World War I, and it is almost universally accepted that if Germany, Italy, and Japan had not pursued expansionist policies in the mid- to late 1930s, World War II might well have never occurred or at least would not have become such a massive global conflict. Nevertheless, five factors may be identified as candidates for the prime cause of World War II. Some of these factors, particularly the aforementioned expansionism on the part of Germany, Italy, and Japan and the rise of **fascism** in Europe, may have had greater influence than others, and each factor when taken individually may not have been necessary or sufficient to cause a global war. All, however, are likely to have exerted some influence on the rapid collapse of the fragile peace of the 1920s and 1930s.

The first possible reason for the outbreak of another world war was that the terms of the Versailles Treaty were too harsh. As discussed earlier, the self-determination granted to many of Europe's nationalities was not extended to the German people; many of the treaty's provisions infringed on German sovereignty; and many Germans came to support a revision of the terms of the peace, by force if necessary. On the other hand, it has been argued that a second major war occurred because the terms of the Versailles Treaty were not enforced. As the following sections will show, the European powers were reluctant to use force to compel Germany to adhere to the treaty's provisions, which may have encouraged progressively greater violations of the peace treaty. Additionally, the League of Nations never functioned as it was designed to and was severely weakened by the nonparticipation of the United States, and thus was unable to deter aggression or maintain collective security in Europe and elsewhere.

Third, the changing balance of power may have played an important role in the outbreak of a new world war. In particular, Japan, Germany, and the Soviet

Union became markedly stronger during the 1930s, which may have made conflict with the other great powers inevitable as the rising stars on the world scene challenged Britain, France, and the United States for world leadership. However, as mentioned in Chapter Two, changes in the balance of power do not always lead to war; this has led some analysts to contend that German, Italian, and Japanese expansionism was the deciding factor in the eruption of a global conflict. These states, this argument runs, decided to expand their territory and global reach in order to resolve or avoid a variety of domestic and international political problems. If Berlin, Rome, and Tokyo had chosen different solutions for their internal difficulties, war might not have resulted.

Finally, many of the same pressures that prompted the Axis powers to expand before the war prompted the rise of fascism in a number of European states and in Japan. The authoritarian and militaristic ideology of fascism was anathema to the Western democracies (as was the totalitarian communism practiced in the Soviet Union under Stalin). Perhaps if Hitler and Mussolini had not come to power, or if the Nazi party had not stamped out democracy and human rights so brutally, the great powers would have been able to resolve their differences without resorting to war.

Considering how many possible reasons there were for their outbreaks in both 1914 and 1939, the world wars may have been overdetermined. Perhaps, in both cases, the preceding peace was only an illusion waiting to be shattered. For whatever reasons, by the end of 1939 it was obvious that the so-called "war to end all wars" was nothing of the kind, and that the collective security system envisioned by the victorious allies at Versailles was a grandiose failure.

RISE OF THE THIRD REICH

Essentially, Hitler's rule can be divided into two phases.[27] In the first, roughly from 1933 to 1935, the German dictator did not seem especially threatening. During this period, many viewed Hitler as a basically reasonable leader, in spite of his Nazi party's repression of opponents, discrimination against Jews, and other antidemocratic policies. After all, under his leadership Germany was clearly getting back to work, and the poverty and suffering of most of the population were greatly alleviated. He seemed to be resolving the chaotic social and economic crisis that Germany had endured. Many dismissed his objectives as set forth in his prison memoir, *Mein Kampf* ("My Struggle"), as empty rhetoric.[28]

Hitler's ultimate goals, however, were extremely ambitious at best, and frightening at worst. Hitler sought to restore Germany to its original borders, which meant a rejection of the territorial settlement in the Versailles Treaty. After restoring its borders of 1914, Germany would then expand to include all Germans, which meant the annexation of Austria, the Sudetenland in Czechoslovakia, and the German parts of Poland before 1914. But this would still not be enough. To Hitler, the German people were the "master race," for whom the borders of even a greater Germany were insufficient. What was needed was *lebensraum* ("living space"), which necessitated expansion to the east at the

AT A GLANCE

THE WORLD WARS

World War I, 1914–1918

Nations Involved
Central Powers: Austria-Hungary, Germany, Bulgaria, Ottoman Empire, their allies
Allied Powers: British Empire, France, Russia, Serbia, Italy, United States, their allies

National Goals
Austro-Hungarian nationalism and territorial expansion. German colonial expansion for raw materials and markets. British concern for the rise of the German expansion. France sought revenge for defeat in 1870–1871. Russia wanted to protect Serbia in order to expand its line of defense against Austria and Germany.

Key Leaders
Austria-Hungary: Emperor Franz Josef
British Empire: David Lloyd George
France: Georges Clemenceau
Germany: Kaiser Wilhelm II
United States: Woodrow Wilson
Russia: Tsar Nicholas II

Causes of the War
1. The growing power of Germany
2. The system of alliances designed to protect the great powers
3. The social changes wrought by industrialization
4. Nationalist challenges to the Ottoman and Austro-Hungarian Empires
5. The impact of heightened competition for imperial gains outside of Europe on inter-European affairs
6. The belief that the next European war would be short and that rapid mobilization and attack would be decisive

Inventions
Tank, machine gun, airplane for military use, poison gas and chemical weapons, large-scale assembly-line industry, shipping (tankers)

Ideas
Cult of the offensive, nationalism, imperialism, communism in Russia

Civilian and Military Deaths
15 million

Political Results
Germany, the Ottoman Empire and the Austro-Hungarian Empire are divided into smaller nations, Communists take over Russian monarchy. The United States remains isolationist. The League of Nations is created.

Major Conferences
Versailles

Terms of Peace
Germany must limit armaments, pay reparations, admit guilt in starting the war, and treat minorities fairly. Germany is demilitarized. Germany, Austria-Hungary and the Ottoman Empire lose territories and colonies. The latter two empires collapse.

Winners
Britain, France, and the United States. Britain loses its hegemony. The United States returns to isolationism after the war.

Losers
Germany, Austria-Hungary, and the Ottoman Empire

World War II, 1939–1945

Nations Involved

Axis Powers: Germany, Italy (changed sides in 1943), Japan, their allies

Allied Powers: United States, France, Britain, USSR, their allies

National Goals

Hitler wanted to restore Germany to its former glory, purify the "master race," unify all Germans, and expand the German empire. Japan wanted access to raw materials, markets, and colonies.

Key Leaders

Germany: Adolf Hitler
Great Britain: Winston Churchill
Italy: Benito Mussolini
Soviet Union: Joseph Stalin
United States: Franklin Roosevelt
Japan: Hideki Tojo

Causes of the War

1. German, Italian, and Japanese expansionism
2. The authoritarian and militaristic ideology of fascism in these countries, led by vicious and resolute leaders
3. Changes in the economic strength of the great powers as the growth of Japan, Germany, and the Soviet Union posed a challenge to Britain, France, and the United States
4. The harsh terms of the Versailles Treaty
5. The ineffective enforcement of the Versailles Treaty

Inventions

Atomic bomb, radar, jet engine

Ideas

The "master race," blitzkrieg ("lightning war"), carpet bombing

Civilian and Military Deaths

41–49 million

Political Results

United States and the Soviet Union become superpowers. Two rival power blocs form, the Western (NATO) and the Eastern (Warsaw Pact). With the exception of East Germany, the German, Italian, and Japanese dictatorships are replaced with democracies. The League of Nations is replaced by the United Nations. The Cold War starts.

Major Conferences

Casablanca, Yalta, Potsdam

Terms of Peace

Guarantees are required against racial and religious discrimination, and fascist parties are banned. Each defeated nation has to pay reparations and limit the size of its military. Japan has the right to self-defense, to develop an economy, and to join in defense and trade agreements. Germany is divided after the war.

Winners

The Soviet Union and the United States and their allies. The United States becomes the Western hegemon while the USSR emerges as the Communist hegemon.

Losers

Germany and Japan are occupied by the Allies. Germany is divided after the war. West Germany and Japan are educated for democracy.

expense of Poles, Russians, and other Slavs, who were considered *untermenschen* ("subhumans"). These "inferior races" would be reduced to slavery, while those considered "inhuman," including Jews, Gypsies, and homosexuals, would be eliminated from the Reich. In the early years of Hitler's regime, it was never made clear how these goals were to be achieved. (Later, the Nazis decided on a "final solution" to the problem; see the section on the Holocaust.)

When Hitler came to power, however, Germany was still too weak to pursue his expansionist agenda. It was necessary to appear moderate and play on Germany's grievances stemming from the Versailles Treaty and Germans' demands for self-determination, which many considered legitimate. In 1935 Hitler received a great boost to his power and popularity when the people of the Saar region voted overwhelmingly to rejoin Germany. The holding of the **plebiscite** had been mandated in the Versailles Treaty sixteen years before, but since it occurred during Hitler's tenure he was able to take credit for it. Meanwhile, Hitler began to take steps which were forbidden by the Versailles Settlement. In 1935 compulsory conscription in Germany was reinstated, and in March of that same year Hitler revealed the previously secret existence of the *Luftwaffe*, the German air force.

Hitler thus began to openly defy the Versailles Treaty and to enter the second, more menacing phase of his regime. Encountering little international opposition thus far, he sent German troops back into the demilitarized Rhineland in 1936. Emboldened by the other European powers' failure to respond effectively, Hitler accelerated the buildup of the German military. France and Britain were well aware of this buildup, but their domestic political and economic situations constrained their ability to match Germany. In 1937 Germany spent some 23.5 percent of its national income on the military, while France spent 9.1 percent and Britain only 5.7 percent.[29] In absolute terms, the gap becomes even clearer: In the same year that Germany was spending more than $3 billion on the military, France was spending $890 million and Britain $1.2 billion.[30] In short, Germany alone spent more than France and Britain combined. (Keep in mind, however, that Germany faced a potential threat from the Soviet Union, which was also spending more than $3 billion.)

The imbalance in military expenditures contributed significantly to the continuation of the British and French policy of appeasement. Both countries sought to avoid antagonizing Hitler by agreeing to his initial demands, hoping that this would encourage him to moderate his ultimate objectives. At the time, appeasement was a popular policy; it was consistent with the widespread desire to avoid war. Concern in Paris over developments in Germany, however, led France to seek protection through cooperation with the USSR, which also had good reason to fear Germany and was alienated by Hitler's rabid anticommunism.

Growing German strength and belligerence also led to improved relations between France and Italy, because Mussolini was concerned about Hitler's ambitions towards Austria. Since the 1860s there had been some desire for German-speaking Austria to unify with Germany, but Bismarck had rejected this notion and few Austrians supported the idea at the time. In the 1930s, however, nationalist sympathies in both Germany and Austria led to demands that the two countries become unified in a single German-speaking nation. Hitler, an Austrian by birth,

Adolf Hitler addresses a Munich Nazi party meeting in November 1934. Chancellor of the Third Reich from 1933 to 1945, Hitler was perhaps the most destructive political genius in history.
Source: © Culver Pictures, Inc.

gave support to Austrian Nazis, who assassinated Austrian Chancellor Engelbert Dollfuss in July 1934 during an unsuccessful coup attempt.

China, Ethiopia, and Spain

While developments in Europe had whittled away at the new world order envisioned at Versailles, the first genuine challenge to the League of Nations' principle of collective security came not in Europe, but in Asia. By the early 1930s Japan was the only Asian country able to industrialize and avoid colonial domination by the European powers. Instead, it had embarked on an imperial course itself. Largely bereft of raw materials necessary for industrial production, Japan sought to expand its sphere of control in Asia in order to ensure their availability and guarantee markets for its goods. In addition to these economic goals, territorial expansion was advocated by the Japanese military establishment, which began to play an increasingly important role in Japan's authoritarian government.

In 1931 Japan seized Manchuria from China, and in 1932 established the nominally independent state of Manchukuo, which was actually a Japanese protectorate. The League of Nations duly condemned Japan's actions, but it was unable to impose effective economic or military sanctions, as the Soviet Union and the United States, which were not members of the League, refused to accept its recommendations. The United States feared that military sanctions against Japan might precipitate a U.S.–Japanese war in Southeast Asia, and that economic sanctions against Japan would hurt the U.S. economy at the height of the Great Depression.

In 1937, Japanese forces invaded China from Manchuria. China's weak and poorly organized army was unable to stop the Japanese advance, but continuing the offensive and garrisoning the conquered territory became an expensive burden for Japan. Temporarily shocked out of its isolationism, the United States responded by demanding that Japan withdraw from China and imposing limited sanctions. The Japanese government, heavily influenced by its army, ignored the sanctions and the condemnation of the League of Nations, and went on with the war.

The League's weakness soon became apparent in other parts of the world. Germany's increased power posed a threat to Italy, but this ironically enhanced Italy's status in Europe because France and Britain saw Mussolini's government as an important counterweight to Hitler's expansionist designs. This gave Mussolini the opening to pursue his own imperial ambitions in Abyssinia (Ethiopia), the domination of which had long been an Italian goal. (In 1896 Abyssinian troops had defeated an invading Italian force, one of only a few defeats suffered by a European power in Africa.) In October 1935 Italian troops invaded Abyssinia from their base in the neighboring Italian colony of Somaliland (now part of Somalia). When the initial attack was unsuccessful, Italian forces resorted to poison-gas attacks to bring the Abyssinians to submission. Western nations were appalled, but neither France nor Britain wanted to alienate Italy as long as Germany constituted a growing threat. Consequently, when Abyssinian Emperor Haile Selassie asked the League of Nations to halt the Italian aggression, the League imposed only limited economic sanctions. Selassie's efforts failed to stop Italy's annexation of Abyssinia. He made a final appeal to the League in 1936, but the assembled nations ignored his warning: "It was us today. It will be you tomorrow."

The League had again proven ineffective; in fact, its limited sanctions were worse than useless, as they were sufficient to alienate Italy from Britain and France. As a result, Mussolini improved relations with Germany. In 1936 Italy,

Japan, and Germany signed the Anti-Comintern Pact in which all agreed to fight communism and support each other in case of war with the Soviet Union. After discussions between Italian and German diplomats, both sides tacitly recognized Italy's sphere of influence in the Mediterranean and Germany's in central Europe.

The Spanish Civil War (1936–1939) provided another prelude to the wider conflict that was to come. Italy and Germany gave extensive assistance to the right-wing Nationalist forces, led by Francisco Franco, who were fighting against the Republican government. Hitler and Mussolini hoped that if the Nationalists won, Spain would ally with them against France. Spain also provided a proving ground for new German and Italian military hardware. The terrible destructive potential of aerial bombing was demonstrated in 1937 when German aircraft devastated the city of Guernica. (Picasso's renowned painting of the same name commemorates the atrocity.) As had been the case throughout the 1930s, the other European powers refused to take part in the conflict. The Soviet Union provided aid to the Republican forces (who counted socialists and Communists among their supporters), but all others remained steadfastly neutral. Franco's Nationalist forces won the Civil War, and though Spain remained neutral during World War II, the victory of fascism in Spain testified to the failure of isolationism and appeasement. But the worst was still yet to come.

Anschluss

German power was still growing in Europe. The next step in Hitler's plan was the fulfillment of his dream to unify all Germans. Hitler had consistently supported the Austrian Nazis and used nationalist appeals to press for unification, but the Versailles Treaty expressly forbade any such union. In 1936, Hitler had backed down on the issue of a German-Austrian union in the face of opposition from the other European powers. At that time, he even went so far as to explicitly recognize Austria's independence and provide assurances that Germany would not intervene in Austria's internal affairs. In March 1938, however, Hitler bullied the Austrian chancellor into resigning, then used his resignation as a pretext to order German troops into Austria. The *anschluss*, or annexation of Austria by Germany, was declared on March 13, and Austria ceased to exist as an independent state.

Yet again Hitler had violated the mandate of the Versailles Treaty, and once again the other great powers refused to take action. In spite of the widespread concern over Hitler's intentions, the *anschluss* was relatively easy to justify, as Austrians were arguably ethnic Germans. Besides, Hitler reassured other European leaders that his intentions were benign, and professed that all he wanted to do was to right the wrongs committed against Germany at Versailles.

Czech Crisis and Munich Conference

With the union of Austria and Germany accomplished, Hitler turned his attention to the Sudetenland, a part of Czechoslovakia inhabited by large numbers of ethnic Germans. He had encouraged the Sudeten Germans to press demands for

A scathing attack on the then-popular policy of appeasement, this 1936 cartoon appeared shortly after Hitler remilitarized the Rhineland.

Source: © David Low/Solo.

union with Germany, and the pressure on Czechoslovakia to cede the territory reached a fever pitch after the *anschluss*. In May 1938 Czechoslovakia mobilized its forces on the German border in response to reported German military troop movements. Both France and Britain cautioned Germany not to aggravate the situation, but simultaneously pressured the Czech leaders to make concessions.

Hitler was determined to force a confrontation over the Sudetenland, but Britain and France earnestly hoped to avoid one. The British foreign office explicitly warned Paris that Britain would not support France in a war over Czechoslovakia. Public opinion in Britain was still strongly opposed to involvement in another continental conflict, especially since Hitler's demands did not seem unreasonable: He was attempting to achieve self-determination for all Germans. British Prime Minister Neville Chamberlain especially made it clear that he wanted to avoid war at all costs, describing the crisis over Czechoslovakia as "a quarrel in a faraway country among people of whom we know nothing." For their part, the Soviets indicated that they would honor a treaty commitment to come to Czechoslovakia's aid, but since the treaty predicated Soviet action on French involvement, they waited for the French response. France, however, was unwilling to support Czechoslovakia without British help.

The crisis continued through the summer of 1938. Holding out one last hope to avoid war, Chamberlain proposed in September that Britain, France, Italy, and Germany meet to settle the Czech issue. Hitler, Mussolini, Chamberlain, and French Prime Minister Edouard Daladier subsequently met in Munich, Germany, where they agreed that the Sudetenland would be turned over to German control. (The Czech government was not asked for its opinion on the matter; in fact, Czechoslovakia was not even invited to participate in the conference that would decide its fate.) It appeared as if war had been averted. Upon his return to Britain, Chamberlain proclaimed that the Munich Agreement meant "peace for our time." Opposition member of Parliament Winston Churchill, on the other hand, thought the agreement would only encourage Hitler's ambitions: "The German dictator, instead of snatching the victuals from the table, has been content to have them served to him course by course."[31]

The leaders of Britain and France hoped that Hitler would now be satisfied, having incorporated virtually all German-speaking areas into the Third Reich. However, rather than achieving peace, Britain and France had merely postponed war. Czechoslovakia and the USSR had been willing to take a stand against Germany, but instead, Czech territory had been handed over to Hitler without a fight. In March 1939 German troops invaded what remained of Czechoslovakia and captured its capital, Prague.

THE APPROACH OF WAR

The invasion of Czechoslovakia proved to be a turning point in European acceptance of German aggression. First, Britain and France were outraged. Unlike Germany's annexation of Austria and the Sudetenland, the conquest of Czechoslovakia could not be justified by national self-determination. Second, London and Paris had lost a potentially helpful ally, and Czech military industries were now at Hitler's disposal. Third, neither France nor Britain had defended Czechoslovakia, even though that nation as well as the USSR had been prepared to fight. This signaled to Hitler that France and Britain were unlikely to go to war over small countries in eastern Europe. The situation was especially worrisome for Poland, which seemed the next likely target for German expansion because it included areas taken from Germany by the Treaty of Versailles. In an attempt to reassure Warsaw and deter Hitler from further aggression, in March 1939 British and French leaders pledged their assistance to Poland if Germany attacked.

While the Warsaw government felt reassured by British and French pledges, the Soviet Union remained skeptical. What could Britain and France do for Poland? Both were separated from Poland by Germany, Britain was primarily a naval power with only a small army, and France cowered behind its defensive Maginot Line with no plans to attack Germany. Absent any credible French threat to Germany in the west, French assurances to Poland were meaningless. In April 1939 the Soviet Union nevertheless began discussions with Britain and France regarding a defensive alliance against Germany. While the Western powers

THE MUNICH ANALOGY

Munich was an experience seared into the memory of all who witnessed the promises made and broken in 1938. The Munich Conference became synonymous with the discredited appeasement policy of British Prime Minister Neville Chamberlain. Adolf Hitler, Chamberlain, French Prime Minister Edouard Daladier, and Italian Prime Minister Benito Mussolini met in Munich on September 29, 1938, to resolve the crisis over the Sudetenland of Czechoslovakia. Hitler was threatening to go to war in order to annex the Czech territory where 3 million ethnic Germans lived. Chamberlain and the others sought to appease Hitler by agreeing to cede the Sudetenland to Germany, on the basis of Hitler's guarantee not to attack the remaining portion of Czechoslovakia. Chamberlain was greeted as a hero when he returned to Britain, for it was believed that war had been averted.

At the time, appeasement was a popular policy, credited with keeping Europe out of another ruinous war. Within six months,

favored such an alliance, Poland and Romania's leaders remained opposed. Remembering all too well their former domination by Russia, they refused to accept Soviet assistance if it meant bringing Soviet troops into their countries. Meanwhile, in May, Hitler and Mussolini sealed their alliance in the Pact of Steel, later known as the Rome-Berlin Axis.

Because of Soviet premier Joseph Stalin's distrust of the French and British, Moscow also began to seek improved relations with Germany. (Stalin suspected and distrusted everyone; for more on this Soviet leader, see Chapter Four.) Although initially suspicious himself of Soviet intentions, Hitler found an agreement with the Soviet Union more attractive as his plans to invade Poland progressed. When France and Britain balked at signing an agreement with the Soviet Union in deference to the objections of their eastern European allies, Stalin accepted the idea of a nonaggression pact with Germany. The Soviet-Nazi pact, also known as the Molotov-Ribbentrop Pact after the two foreign ministers (Vyacheslav Molotov of the USSR and Germany's Joachim von Ribbentrop) who negotiated it, was signed on August 23, 1939.

The world was stunned. Two leaders who espoused implacably hostile ideologies, fascism and communism, had signed an important treaty with each other. The pact served the pragmatic self-interests of both sides, however, as it temporarily alleviated the threat of a two-front war for both countries. Hitler knew that without the USSR, France and Britain lacked the military strength to invade Germany in order to protect Poland. In this regard, Hitler was following the same policy as Bismarck had before him. From Stalin's perspective, the pact gained the Soviet Union time to build up its military strength to prepare for the possibility of war with either Germany or Japan. In addition, the agreement included secret protocols that provided for the division of Poland between Germany and however, Chamberlain and his appeasement policy were thoroughly discredited when Hitler invaded the rest of Czechoslovakia. Appeasement then became a dirty word, and Munich became a metaphor for encouraging aggression by giving in to an aggressor.

In later years, leaders have referred to Munich in attempts to win support for standing firm against an opponent's challenges. During the Cold War, many policies designed to contain the Soviet Union were justified by citing the Munich analogy, most notably the decisions to send forces to counter Communist threats in Korea in 1950 and Vietnam in 1965. U.S. President George Bush invoked the Munich analogy to convince Congress to authorize the use of force against Iraq in 1991 and called Iraqi President Saddam Hussein a "new Hitler."

Ever since Munich, it appears, politicians have consistently painted their enemies as Hitlers while doing as much as they are able to avoid being remembered as Chamberlains.

the USSR and secured German consent to Soviet control of the Baltic states (Latvia, Lithuania, and Estonia) and parts of Finland and Romania.

With the signing of the Nazi-Soviet pact, Hitler no longer needed to fear war with the Soviet Union over Poland. The failure of Britain and France to support Czechoslovakia suggested that they might not support Poland either, and in any case there was little they could do to stop an invasion of Poland without Soviet help. The groundwork for Hitler's next move was thus in place. Germany attacked Poland on September 1, 1939, and France and Britain declared war on Germany two days later. Twenty-one years after the first great European war of the twentieth century had ended, the second had begun.

WORLD WAR II

Though their combined armies and navies were larger than Germany's in September 1939, the Western Allies were unprepared for the outbreak of World War II. The Allies were slow to recognize the implications of advances in military tactics and technology, but they would soon learn all too well that the use of mechanized forces and aircraft allowed advancing armies to move much faster than had been possible in the Great War.[32] In 1939 Poland was rapidly defeated, which was no real surprise given Germany's superiority in numbers and technology. The German **blitzkrieg** ("lightning war") strategy of armor and air attacks overwhelmed the obsolete Polish army; there wasn't much that horse cavalry could do against tanks. On September 17, the Soviet Union also invaded Poland and the Baltic States, as the Molotov-Ribbentrop Pact allowed. (The USSR subsequently attacked Finland on November 30.)

THE LAST LION

It would be difficult to invent a fictional character who embodied the ruling class and spirit of the British Empire as much as Sir Winston Leonard Spencer Churchill (1874–1965). The son of an American heiress and an English lord, direct descendant of the renowned eighteenth-century British general the Duke of Marlborough, Churchill nevertheless needed three attempts to pass the entrance exam to the Royal Military Academy at Sandhurst.

He craved action as a young officer, but saw less fighting as a soldier in India than he did as a war correspondent in Cuba and South Africa (where he was captured by Boer commandos, but escaped from military prison within a month). He had an equally adventurous career in politics, changing parties several times and serving as First Lord of the Admiralty during World War I. (The disastrous Allied invasion at Gallipoli was his idea.) He lost elections almost as often as he won, and once remarked, "Politics are almost as exciting as war, and quite as dangerous. In war, you can only be killed once, but in politics many times."

Churchill had a boy's impetuousness, a teenager's smugness, and an old man's arrogance throughout most of his life. In his later years, however, he suffered from alcoholism and periodic bouts of severe depression. He preferred big ideas to small details, and pursued both his causes and his avocations (painting and polo) passionately. The quality that served him best throughout his career, however, was his tenacity, which he lent to his country as prime minister in the darkest days of World War II.

When he succeeded Neville Chamberlain in that post after the debacle in France, many Britons were considering the possibility of asking Adolf Hitler for peace terms. But Churchill was convinced that accepting German domination of Europe would be tantamount to national suicide, and after the evacuation of British troops from

As Hitler had anticipated, neither France nor Britain took immediate measures to aid Poland. What ensued has come to be known as the "phony war" in which neither side actually fought. France and Britain sought only to blockade Germany and prevent it from obtaining crucial raw materials, and France made sure its Maginot fortifications were at full strength. It was not even clear whether a major confrontation would occur. In October Hitler proposed that the Western powers accept the new situation in exchange for peace, but, with Hitler's actions after Munich still in mind, the offer was rejected.

The strategy of London and Paris focused on a war of attrition. The French and British leaders believed that a Germany denied of raw materials crucial to war fighting would accept a settlement returning territory to the status quo ante. They therefore deemed it necessary to maintain control of the North Sea and the Mediterranean. Recognizing this strategy, Germany invaded Denmark and Norway in April 1940. Both were quickly defeated. In reality, there was little that Britain and France could do at this time to combat the Germans because of the lack of military preparation in the two countries.

Dunkirk his oratory rallied Britain to go on, or go down, fighting:

> We shall not flag or fail. We shall go on to the end. We shall fight in France, we shall fight on the seas and oceans, we shall fight with growing confidence and growing strength in the air, we shall defend our island, whatever the cost may be, we shall fight on the beaches, we shall fight on the landing grounds, we shall fight in the fields and in the streets, we shall fight in the hills; we shall never surrender.*

Later in 1940, during the Battle of Britain, Churchill again exhorted the nation to keep its fighting spirit:

> Let us . . . brace ourselves to our duties, and so bear ourselves that if the British Empire and its Commonwealth last for a thousand years, men will still say: "This was their finest hour."†

Churchill may have believed the Empire could last that long, but by the end of the war it was clear that British power had been eclipsed by that of the United States and the Soviet Union. Churchill argued that Britain should try to retain its empire, or at least divest itself of it slowly ("I have not become the King's First Minister in order to preside over the liquidation of the British Empire," he declared in 1942), but he was voted out of office before the war's end. (He would serve again as prime minister from 1951 to 1955.) He warned the West to beware of Soviet expansion after the war, but he believed the USSR could be contained through the same political, military, and economic means that Britain had used to contain continental threats for 150 years.

Although he is regarded as one of the greatest leaders of modern times, many of his beliefs were better suited to the period of Queen Victoria and the *Pax Britannica* than to the era of total war. In this respect, by the mid-twentieth century he was, like the British Empire, a glorious anachronism.

*Winston Churchill, *Speech on Dunkirk,* House of Commons, June 4, 1940.

†Churchill, Speech in the House of Commons, June 18, 1940.

This weakness became apparent when the war turned "real" for the British and French in May 1940. On May 10, Germany launched its blitzkrieg on France, sending its tanks through Belgium and thereby bypassing the Maginot Line. (The original German battle plan was essentially similar to the Schlieffen Plan of 1914, but a copy of the plan fell into Allied hands. Germany was forced to come up with a new scheme that surprised the Allies by sending armored divisions through the Ardennes Forest, thought to be tank-proof.) France managed to survive for five short weeks, only two weeks longer than Poland.[33]

Thus, the beginnings of both the world wars stunned strategic planners. In 1914 Germany hoped to achieve a quick victory over France as it had in 1871, but its forces soon bogged down into immobile trench warfare. In 1940 the Allies expected trench warfare and thought France would be safe behind the formidable Maginot Line, but German armies circumvented French defenses and smashed through to Paris much as they had in 1871. Confident that France was done for, Italy joined the war on Germany's side in June. (Germany and its allies were thereafter referred to as the Axis, after the Rome-Berlin Axis signed in May 1939.)

Hitler contemplated an invasion of Britain, but the English Channel remained a substantial obstacle and the British navy a formidable opponent. He decided to prepare for an invasion with demoralizing air attacks on British shipping, airfields, and cities, thus initiating the Battle of Britain between the Royal Air Force (RAF) and the German *Luftwaffe*. While inflicting heavy casualties, the air raids only strengthened the resolve of the British people, led by Churchill, who replaced Chamberlain as prime minister. The German air force was unable to win the conflict, which took place from July to October 1940. In this case, Britain's delay in rearming after World War I was a benefit: The newer British airplanes were able to outmaneuver their German counterparts. Key to the British success, however, was the new top-secret radar that warned them of the impending German attacks.[34]

Britain remained stalwart against Germany, but by the end of 1940, Hitler dominated the Continent in a manner not seen since Napoleon. Churchill tried to enforce a blockade, again as in the Napoleonic Wars, but it posed no real threat to Germany's control of the Continent. Besides, there was little to no possibility of a British invasion of Europe. In fact, despite its tenacity, Britain was rapidly nearing the end of its endurance. Germany continued to try to force a British surrender through submarine warfare, as German U-boats and surface raiders fought British naval forces in the Battle of the Atlantic.

The only hope for Britain at this dark hour was the isolationist great power across the Atlantic, the United States. The U.S. president, Franklin Delano Roosevelt, wanted to come to the aid of the British, but public and Congressional opinion prevented him from doing so. (See Chapter Fifteen for what Roosevelt was able to do to aid Britain.)

Meanwhile, a bungled Italian invasion of Greece prompted Hitler to invade the Balkans in 1941. German forces quickly overwhelmed Yugoslavia and subdued Greece, but partisan fighting would continue in those countries throughout the war. (In Yugoslavia, Croatian units organized by the Nazi occupation regime aided German forces in persecuting Serbs who cooperated with the resistance, creating a bitter legacy of ethnic violence that would tear the benighted country apart fifty years later.) After the blitzkrieg in the Balkans, Britain again stood alone, besieged by U-boats and fighting desperately in North Africa to keep German and Italian forces from capturing the strategically vital Suez Canal.

Barbarossa

The pressure on Britain, however, was ultimately relieved by Hitler's own doing. Like Napoléon, Hitler felt that a war with Russia was inevitable, and so decided to strike at the eastern colossus before it could build up its forces. On June 22, 1941, Germany launched Operation Barbarossa, the invasion of the Soviet Union. Germany's Axis partners Hungary, Romania, and Finland also joined in the attack. At first, the offensive was highly successful. In the first four months of the war, German troops killed or captured some 3 million Soviet soldiers and rapidly forced the Soviet army into retreat.

But in spite of tremendous losses, the Soviet Union was not defeated. The Germans reached the outskirts of Moscow, but the Soviets' huge territorial expanse effectively neutralized the German blitzkrieg. The same difficulties that had plagued Napoléon revisited the Nazis, including troubles with supplying troops across the great expanse of Soviet territory and especially the rigors of the great Russian winter. By 1943 the war on the eastern front thus became one of attrition in which German forces were at a disadvantage.

Pacific War

In the fall of 1941, though the situation looked bleak in Europe, it still appeared unlikely that the United States would intervene. President Roosevelt had already proposed that some economic and military aid to be sent to Britain (see Chapter Fifteen for details), but even these limited measures met with opposition in Congress. America had the potential to become a predominant military power, but it remained a basically isolationist "sleeping giant." It would not be long, however, before it received a rude awakening.

On December 7, 1941, the Japanese navy launched a surprise attack on Pearl Harbor, Hawaii, which was the principal American naval base in the Pacific. The attack was executed perfectly and sunk or put out of action most of the battleships of the U.S. Pacific Fleet.[35] The next day, the U.S. Congress declared war on Japan, but there was still some doubt as to whether America would go to war against the European Axis partners. On December 11, however, Germany and Italy, in accordance with their alliance with Japan, declared war on the United States, bringing the United States fully into the conflict.

The Japanese attack on Pearl Harbor seems inexplicable at first glance. Not only was America's gross domestic product seventeen times the size of Japan's, but it had nearly twice the population of Japan and its overall military potential was greater by a factor of ten.[36] Why would Japan attack a nation more powerful than itself? Throughout the 1930s, Japanese expansion in Asia aggravated Tokyo's relations with the United States. The United States condemned Japan's 1931 invasion of Manchuria, but took no action; in 1937, however, when Japan invaded China, the United States imposed economic sanctions. When Japan occupied French Indochina (which included Vietnam, Laos, and Cambodia) in September 1940, the Japanese leadership hoped the raw materials and strategic bases afforded by this new conquest would help bring the war in China to a speedy end. But the United States slapped Japan with an embargo on scrap metal and steel, materials sorely needed for its war effort. The costs of the war and the effects of the sanctions mounted, but from Tokyo's standpoint, withdrawal from China under foreign pressure would have been unacceptably humiliating.

By the end of 1940, therefore, Japan's leaders found themselves on the horns of a dilemma. One horn was the fact that 80 percent of Japanese oil imports came from the United States, and they feared that the United States would embargo this vital resource in an attempt to compel Japan to withdraw from China. Japan could counter this threat by invading the oil-producing Dutch East Indies (now Indonesia). But this was the other horn: It was almost certain that the United States would intervene against Japan should it expand further in Asia, particularly the Dutch East Indies.

In July 1941 Tokyo's fears came true. In a further effort to pressure Japan to pull its forces out of China, the United States halted its oil exports to Japan and froze Japanese assets in July 1941, thus restricting Japan's ability to pay for imports. Because the Japanese government still adamantly refused to end the intervention in China, war with the United States now appeared inevitable. Given this conclusion, Japan's leaders decided that their only chance to avoid total defeat was to launch a preemptive strike against U.S. naval forces, hoping that this initial blow would gain time for Japan to further build up its forces and convince the American government and people that a long, costly war would not be worth fighting.

Japan's subsequent surprise attack on Pearl Harbor was planned brilliantly and carried out masterfully. Nevertheless, it failed to achieve its primary strategic objective, as it galvanized the American public's determination to fight a war to the finish. As Japan's Admiral Isoroku Yamamoto remarked, the attack only awakened the sleeping giant.[37]

Arsenal of Democracy

The United States' entrance into the war dramatically changed its course, as had the introduction of American troops in 1917. But this change would be slow in coming, as it took time for the American economy to shift from peacetime to wartime production. Ironically, the considerable unused production capacity that existed as a result of the Depression lessened the dislocation in the United States caused by this shift. In the meantime, Germany maintained its advances in the Soviet Union and also in North Africa, while Japan increasingly took control of the Pacific. For the maximum extent of German and Italian advances during the war, see Map 3.3.

That the United States eventually fought a successful two-front war, alone in the Pacific and with Britain and the Soviet Union in Europe, indicated the extent to which it had become a world power. However, the alliance with which the United States joined was not always free of problems. Strains emerged that affected America's relations with its allies, particularly the Soviet Union. Moscow was fending off the Nazi onslaught alone and persistently called for the opening of a second front in western Europe to draw off some of the German forces. Stalin grew resentful and suspicious of American and British unwillingness to open a second front on the European continent. However, to the Americans, and especially to the British, it appeared essential that any attempt to invade Europe wait until Germany's strength was eroded. The Soviets' resentment was not soothed by the infusion of almost $11 billion of **lend-lease** aid.

The British and American leaders thought that in order to weaken Germany, its forces would first have to be driven from North Africa, and then its

Map **3.3**   Height of Axis Expansion in the European Theater

infrastructure and economy would have to be crushed by extensive bombing. Ostensibly, the latter would also destroy the German people's willingness to continue fighting. By 1943 German forces were driven from North Africa, but the bombing of Germany proved unsuccessful. Postwar analyses revealed that German production of military equipment was higher in 1944 than in 1941.[38] The bombing also failed to seriously affect civilian morale. So, in spite of the

THE HOLOCAUST

The Holocaust was the genocide of 6 million European Jews committed by the Third Reich. It was the official policy of the Nazis, who made the Jewish people the scapegoat for most of Germany's post–World War I hardships. They considered Jews, Gypsies, and homosexuals "inhuman" and likened their murder to the extermination of pests. Millions of Jews and other victims were captured, transported, enslaved, and gassed to death in concentration camps such as Auschwitz, Buchenwald, Dachau, and Bergen-Belsen.

The concentration camps had one aim: the murder of those who entered. Either one faced outright gassing, was worked to death in slave labor, or died of starvation or disease. The killings occurred on a scale unseen before in human history, using the organized and methodical techniques of mass production for murder.

Accompanying the undeniable horror of the so-called "Final Solution," Hannah Arendt has described the banality of the evil that took place.* The German railroads were paid full fare for transporting victims to the camps; and large corporations located factories near the camps to take advantage of the free forced labor. Gruesome as well were notorious medical experiments attempting to prove twisted genetic theories and the making of soap, candles, and even lampshades out of the remains of human beings. The gold

destruction of its cities, with 135,000 civilian casualties lost in the firebombing of Dresden alone, the German government continued the fight. The Western Allies became convinced that only an invasion of continental Europe could push Germany over the edge of defeat.

Second Front

Consequently, the United States and Britain invaded Italy in 1943. Few German troops were diverted to Italy, however, as the German High Command was still waiting for the main blow to fall in the west. Italy surrendered later that year. Mussolini tried to escape capture but was caught and killed by antifascist partisans, and Italy subsequently joined the Allies. Finally, on June 6, 1944 (D-Day), the United States and Britain began the liberation of France with the invasion of Normandy. Germany now fought a two-front war (actually a two and one-half-front war, counting the Mediterranean) against far superior enemies. The Allies had command of the air and were slowly progressing towards Berlin. The German defeat by now seemed a foregone conclusion, but Hitler was determined to fight to the bitter end. Indeed, the Allies wanted an unconditional surrender from their foes, believing that the Germans had not been sufficiently convinced of their defeat in World War I. Allied forces pushed on through Europe, heading for Berlin. On April 20, 1945, the Soviets reached the German capital, and the Allies met at the Elbe River on April 28. On May 8, eight days retrieved from victim's teeth also was a ghastly booty. Bodies were either buried in mass graves or were cremated in huge ovens, spreading a pall of ash over the surrounding area.

The Holocaust ended with the end of the war. None of the Allied troops who liberated the camps were prepared for what greeted them: the sight of skeleton-like prisoners and their accounts of grisly horror. The Nazi leaders responsible for this crime against humanity (with the exception of those who escaped or committed suicide) were tried and convicted after the war at a special war-crimes tribunal at Nuremberg, and all the world's nations vowed that such horrors should never be allowed to happen again. Yet part of the tragedy of the Holocaust is that while it was unique in scope, method, and its attempt to exterminate an entire people, the Jews, other genocides have also occurred in the twentieth century. From the massacre of Armenians in the Ottoman Empire during World War I to the "killing fields" of Cambodia in the 1970s, to "ethnic cleansing" in the former Yugoslavia, twentieth-century humanity has repeatedly proven itself capable of terrible crimes of hatred when the civilized world is unable or unwilling to intervene.

*Hannah Arendt, *Eichman in Jerusalem: A Report on the Banality of Evil* (New York: Penguin Books, 1977 c. 1964).

after Hitler committed suicide in his Berlin bunker, Germany unconditionally surrendered, and the Allies declared victory in Europe. Hitler's Thousand-Year Reich had collapsed within twelve years.

Uneasy Alliance

The end of the war in Europe created new political problems for the Allies. Not the least of these was resolving the question of what to do with the defeated Germany. Throughout the war a variety of conferences had been held by the main Allies in order to discuss strategy and other war concerns. Until the conflict's final stages, little thought was given to what Europe would look like after the defeat of the Axis Powers, as the immediate goal was to win the war. On this score the Allies were united. However, once the common enemy was eliminated, the wartime consensus began to break down. This became evident in the two main conferences held in 1945 at Yalta and Potsdam.[39]

Churchill, Roosevelt, and Stalin, the "Big Three" leaders, met for the final time at Yalta in the Soviet Crimea in February 1945 to address some important issues regarding postwar Europe. The most significant of these was the fate of the liberated nations of eastern Europe. It was important to the Allies, and especially to the Americans, that the countries liberated by the Soviets be granted self-determination and that they be able to choose their own (preferably democratic) governments. After all, the fate of Poland was the reason for the war in the first place.

Stalin agreed to elections in the eastern European countries, but he did not take the issue seriously. He was more concerned with Soviet security and German reparations. In both world wars Russia had been invaded through eastern Europe and hence he sought to maintain effective control over these countries so that they could never again support Germany against Russia. The Big Three also differed on the issue of war reparations, with sharp disagreement occurring between the Soviets, who demanded huge reparations, and the United States and Britain, who did not want to permanently cripple Germany. In the end, the decision was postponed until the next meeting. As will be seen in the next chapter, these hurried decisions had a fateful impact on post–World War II relations that the three leaders could not foresee.

In July 1945, shortly after the end of the war in Europe, the Allies met again to discuss the post-war settlement, this time in Potsdam, a Soviet-occupied German town near Berlin. Of the former Big Three, however, only Stalin remained. Roosevelt had suddenly died of a cerebral hemorrhage in April, leaving Vice President Harry Truman to be the new president. Churchill's Conservative party was voted out of office during the proceedings, so the new prime minister, Clement Atlee, replaced him in mid-conference. At this meeting it was confirmed that Germany was to be disarmed and that British, American, and Soviet troops would each occupy part of Germany. Berlin, located within the area to be occupied by the USSR, would also be divided among the three nations. Under pressure from Paris, Britain and the United States added France as a participant in the occupation, so Germany was divided into four zones of occupation, as was Berlin (see Map 3.4). Once again the issue of war reparations was discussed, and it was agreed that the Soviets would be able to take reparations and booty out of their own German zone of occupation and would receive a quarter of any reparations assessed in the American, British, and French zones.

The distrust brewing among the Allies was all the more apparent by the time of the Potsdam meeting. In particular, the Allies were concerned about the Soviet occupation of eastern Europe. Despite glossing over their animosity toward the Soviets during the war (to the extent that Stalin was portrayed as "Uncle Joe" to the Americans), the British, French, and Americans were wary of Moscow. Fresh on their minds were Stalin's brutal political purges and his forced collectivization of Soviet agriculture in the 1930s, which killed millions. The strains between the wartime allies were exacerbated, however, by the change in personnel at the top. Truman, Atlee, and Stalin did not have the same history of communication and cooperation that Roosevelt, Churchill, and Stalin had enjoyed.

Atomic Bomb

At Potsdam, Truman was still anxious to gain Soviet engagement in the fight against Japan. The United States had been fighting essentially alone against an implacable enemy in the Pacific throughout the war. Eventually, the United

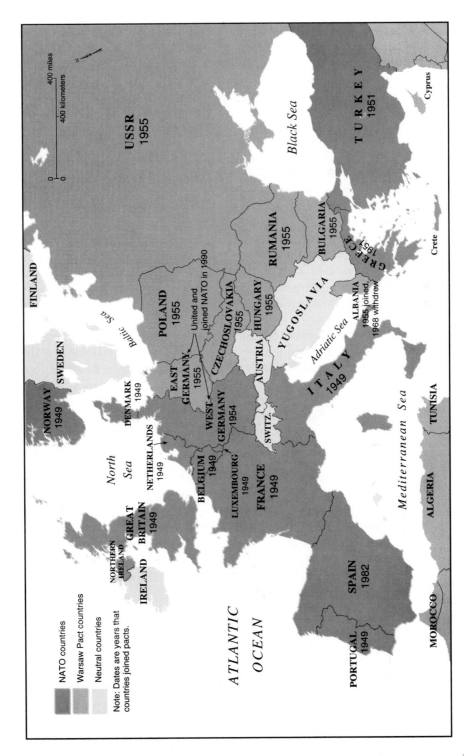

Map 3.4 Post–World War II Borders and Alliances

States gained the upper hand and secured bases from which bombing raids could be launched against the Japanese home islands. In an attempt to undermine the Japanese people's will to fight, most of Japan's major cities were extensively bombed; the firebombing of Tokyo alone killed about 200,000 people in only one week in 1945. But, as in Germany and in England, the bombing of civilians did not break the will of the Japanese, and they continued to resist.

This left the United States with a fearsome prospect: the invasion of Japan itself. President Truman recognized the political cost of transferring a large number of American troops to Asia for an invasion of Japan. With the war in Europe over, the American people were reluctant to continue fighting, and were certainly hoping to bring home their soldiers unharmed from the Pacific. Furthermore, U.S. military leaders had calculated that such an invasion would result in more than 1 million American casualties, as the Japanese could be expected to defend their home islands with ferocious tenacity. Although the Soviets would be likely to exact concessions and try to establish lasting control over whatever territory they occupied, as they had done in Europe, Truman still considered their participation in the war essential if American casualties were to be contained.

At this point, however, another option became available. Fearing that Nazi scientists were working to develop a nuclear weapon, the United States started the top-secret Manhattan Project in 1942 to produce an atomic bomb before the Germans did. This project was so secret that not even the vice president knew about it—Truman learned of the work on the atomic bomb only when he assumed the office of president upon Roosevelt's death. (For more on the Manhattan Project, see Chapter Eleven.) The German atomic bomb project never got off the ground, but on July 16, 1945, while Truman was in Potsdam, Manhattan Project scientists successfully detonated the first atomic bomb near Alamogordo, New Mexico.[40]

The development of the new weapon made Truman's dilemma much easier. If Japan were to surrender once it had seen the devastating potential of the atomic bomb, American lives would be spared. Other benefits included the saving of Japanese lives and being relieved of the disadvantages of Soviet participation in the war. But for Truman, sparing American casualties was the essential point. He therefore decided to use the new weapon.[41] On August 6, 1945, an American B-29 bomber, the *Enola Gay*, dropped the "Little Boy" atomic bomb on the Japanese city of Hiroshima. In the wake of the blinding flash and subsequent firestorm, 80,000 to 100,000 Japanese citizens were killed. The explosive force of the atomic bomb was equivalent to 14,000 tons of TNT, ten times more powerful than had been predicted. In the absence of an immediate Japanese surrender, the Soviets declared war on Japan on August 8, and a second atomic bomb (the "Fat Man") was dropped on the city of Nagasaki on August 9. The following day, the Japanese government decided to sue for peace, and Japan formally surrendered on September 2. Humankind's most terrible weapon had ended its most terrible war.

CONCLUSION: THE END OF TWO WARS—AND THE BEGINNING OF ANOTHER?

The Second World War was even more destructive than the first. It is estimated that the war killed at least 40 to 50 million people. The USSR alone suffered 7.5 to 11.5 million soldiers killed and 6 to 8 million direct civilian deaths, while the total of all Soviet war-related deaths is probably between 20 and 25 million.[42] Entire cities in Europe and Asia were destroyed by aerial bombing, ground combat, or by occupying forces as reprisals for resistance activity. Most of the combat and devastation occurred in central and eastern Europe, but the war was fought everywhere, from the frozen tundra of Lappland to the sweltering jungle of Burma, from the Aleutian Islands in the North Pacific to the estuary of the Río de la Plata in the South Atlantic. Only nine sovereign states remained neutral by the end of the war, though many nations that declared war on the Axis committed few troops to combat. World War II was truly a global war.

The experience of the war is captured in a large number of firsthand accounts by persons who participated in the war at every level, from supreme commander (Churchill's memoirs) to innocent victim *(The Diary of Anne Frank)*. World War II fiction also abounds, among which James Jones's novel set on Guadalcanal, *The Thin Red Line*, stands out as a depiction of the war from a soldier's perspective. The war spawned a myriad of films as well, but most are propagandistic or tendentious in one way or another (Hollywood spent the war perfecting the art of the propaganda film). The German film *Das Boot* (which follows the crew of an ill-fated U-boat) and the Finnish *Talvisota* (which portrays combat between Finnish and Russian forces in 1939–1940) are notable exceptions that can make the war seem all too real to modern audiences. Steven Spielberg's *Schindler's List* has provided millions with new understanding of the Holocaust. Perhaps more than any other conflict, World War II has made a lasting impression on world culture; more people know the name of Adolf Hitler than that of any other historical figure.

Together, World Wars I and II combined to fundamentally alter world politics. Except for the Soviet Union, the old empires were now gone, replaced by a growing number of states claiming to represent a particular nation. Moreover, the European powers no longer had the ability (whether they recognized it or not) to maintain their colonial holdings. The age of European political and economic domination was thus over, as the combat begun in 1914 had resulted in an astonishing process of self-destruction. One of the most important results of the Second World War was a much higher degree of globalization of world politics. The European powers and Japan had suffered staggering human and material losses from which they would need decades to recover.

At the end of the war, only the United States and the Soviet Union had the resources to contend for global leadership. It was not immediately clear, however, that the two massive powers would be adversaries. On the one hand, both nations (as well as Britain, France, and China) had seats on the newly formed Security Council of the United Nations, which was designed to facilitate cooperation among the great powers in resolving conflicts. Washington and Moscow thus recognized each other as partners in maintaining world peace just as they had been partners in victory during the world war. On the other hand, the United States and the USSR had very different political and economic systems, and their leaders espoused beliefs and values which were diametrically opposed. These political differences created a climate of mistrust that had already prompted the two countries to view each other's actions with suspicion. The world wars had decisively destroyed the old world order, but they built the foundations of a new system for resolving global issues. Whether the new order would be cooperative or conflictual, however, remained to be seen.

PRINCIPAL POINTS OF CHAPTER THREE

1. In two terrible wars in the first half of the twentieth century, Europe devastated itself and destroyed its dominant position in world politics.

2. Six main reasons are advanced for the outbreak of World War I:

    a. German expansionism.

    b. The rigid alliance system that developed in the early years of the twentieth century, with Britain, France, and Russia on one side and Germany and Austria-Hungary on the other.

    c. Changes in the relative economic strength of the great powers, as Britain's share of world industrial production declined and that of Germany, Russia, and the United States expanded.

    d. The challenge posed by nationalism to decrepit empires, especially in the Balkans.

    e. Colonial rivalries and the end of opportunities for colonial expansion.

    f. The cult of the offensive, a widespread belief that wars would be brief and the side that was first to mobilize and attack would win.

3. World War I ended with the victory of the Entente Powers (Britain, France, Italy, the United States, and their allies) over the Central Powers (Germany, Austria-Hungary, and the Ottoman Empire). The victorious allies imposed the terms of the Versailles Treaty on Germany.

4. The League of Nations was established to preserve peace through collective security, but consistently failed in this task throughout the 1930s.

5. Five factors are candidates for the primary cause of World War II:

    a. German, Italian, and Japanese expansionism.

    b. The authoritarian and militaristic ideology of fascism in these countries, led by vicious and resolute leaders.

    c. Changes in the economic strength of the great powers, as the growth of Japan, Germany, and the Soviet Union posed a challenge to Britain, France, and the United States.

    d. The terms of the Versailles Treaty being too harsh.

    e. The terms of the Versailles Treaty not being effectively enforced.

6. The Allies (Britain, France, the Soviet Union, the United States, and their allies) defeated the Axis (Germany, Italy, Japan, and their allies) in World War II.

7. At the end of World War II, the victorious United States and the Soviet Union emerged as superpowers, but conflicts between them arose immediately.

Chapter 4

The Cold War

In 1959 Vice President Richard Nixon traveled to Moscow. While there, he visited the opening of the American National Exhibition with the Russian premier, Nikita Khrushchev. The main attraction was a complete "model," six-room, ranch-style house. When the two leaders reached the kitchen, they engaged in a prolonged debate about their contrasting philosophies. To Nixon, the essence of the American way of life was a male breadwinner and a full-time female homemaker living happily—a home well-stocked with consumer goods and household appliances. "To us, diversity, the right to choose . . . is the most important thing. We don't have the decision made at the top by one government official. . . . We have many different manufacturers and many different kinds of washing machines so that the housewives have a choice. . . ."

Khrushchev countered that the Russians were proud of their hard-working women who were productive contributors to Soviet society. Implying that his country had no use for full-time housewives, he argued that his people did not have that "capitalist attitude toward women."

At another point, Khrushchev noticed Nixon admiring the young women modeling American bathing suits and sports clothes. "You are for the girls, too," he joshed with a wink. The day ended with an agreement. During a toast, Khrushchev gestured to a nearby waitress and suggested, "Let's drink to the ladies." Nixon for once concurred. "We can all drink to the ladies."

Elaine Tyler May, *Homeward Bound: American Families in the Cold War* (New York: Basic Books, 1982), pp. 16–19.

Relations between the United States and the Soviet Union in the late 1950s were far more complicated than debates about washing machines, bathing suits, and contrasting attitudes toward women. International politics during the post–World War II period was dominated by the struggle for power between the United States and the Soviet Union: the Cold War. The term describes a situation where the two superpowers were locked in an apparently intractable conflict, punctuated by crises and haunted by the danger of nuclear war, but nevertheless managed to avoid direct combat. Despite the intense and extensive competition between the two superpowers, the Cold War period, which extended roughly from 1945 to 1990, was relatively stable compared to the shifting alliances and frequent wars of earlier years.

For more than four decades, the Cold War endured through periods of rising tension followed by waves of relaxation. The particular pattern was shaped by various factors, including the personalities and beliefs of Soviet and American leaders, domestic politics, economics, and unanticipated events on the world stage. Often these events prompted each of the superpowers to take actions benefiting its own interests at its adversary's expense. This chapter begins by advancing six explanations for why the Cold War began, next traces the ebb and flow of the Cold War from its origins in the aftermath of the Second World War in 1945 to its end with the collapse of the Soviet Union in 1991, and finally concludes by discussing why the Cold War ended.

WHO OR WHAT CAUSED THE COLD WAR?

In the aftermath of World War II, the world became divided into two camps, the U.S.–led Western democracies and the Communist regimes led by the Soviet Union. Rightly or wrongly, conflicts throughout the world came to be viewed in the context of the relations between the two superpowers. The bipolar structure of the international system (meaning the system was dominated by two major powers—see Chapter Thirteen) seemed to be the culmination of an ultimate logic to world politics: from the ashes of World Wars I and II, out of a world of "Lilliputians," two giant "Gullivers" were destined to emerge.

Was this bipolar logic inescapable? Were the superpowers predestined to be hostile to each other? This question is likely to occupy students of world politics long after the Cold War itself has faded from living memory. The various explanations that have been advanced for why the Cold War began may be summarized in six main lines of argument, each of which fits into one of the images of world politics discussed in Chapter One. For some, the Cold War was a struggle between the forces of truth and justice on one side and an "evil empire" on the other; while for others, it was following the discovery of Soviet missiles in Cuba; the Cuban Missile Crisis leads to a temporary thaw in relations.

1965: U.S. forces begin large-scale intervention in Vietnam.

1967: Israel defeats Egypt, Syria, and Jordan in the Six-Day War.

1968: Soviet Union invades Czechoslovakia to thwart liberalization of Czech government; Nuclear Nonproliferation Treaty is signed.

1969: European *ostpolitik* and U.S. overtures to China herald the beginning of détente.

1972: Nixon visits China and USSR; United States and USSR sign SALT I arms limitation treaty.

1973: United States involvement in Vietnam ends after U.S. and South Vietnam sign cease-fire with North Vietnam; Arab-Israeli War leads to energy crisis.

1979: Shah of Iran is overthrown by Islamic revolution; United States and USSR sign SALT II, but it is not ratified by U.S. Senate when Soviet Union invades Afghanistan, renewing Cold War tensions.

1981–1989: United States supports anti-communist forces in Nicaragua and Afghanistan under Reagan Doctrine.

1985: Mikhail Gorbachev assumes power in the Soviet Union and inaugurates reforms.

1989: Series of revolutions in Eastern Europe replace Communist governments; Berlin Wall is dismantled.

1990: Germany is reunified.

1991: Coup intended to oust Gorbachev fails; USSR collapses, and Russia and other former Soviet republics become independent states.

---

the same dog-eat-dog world it had always been, but only the two biggest dogs were still standing. Each explanation also argues from a frame of reference provided by one of the levels of analysis of international relations presented in Chapter One. Accordingly, some contend that individual leaders were responsible (the individual level), others point to specific national characteristics of the United States or USSR (the domestic level), while still others look to the structure of the international system itself (the systemic level) for the reasons why the Cold War broke out. This section outlines the six basic explanations for the start of the Cold War.

It Was Moscow's Fault

First, the conventional American view is that the Soviet Union was primarily responsible for the Cold War. From this perspective, if the Soviets had not been bent on territorial acquisition, especially their subjugation of Eastern Europe, the United States would have retreated into its prewar position of isolationism. This explanation paints the USSR as an "evil empire" that may well have intended to conquer Western Europe as well. Without American efforts, the Soviets would have taken advantage of Western Europe's war-torn and desolate conditions to do just that. Note that this is a domestic-level argument, as it contends that the USSR was inherently aggressive and expansionistic.

According to this interpretation of the Cold War's origins, the United States was correct to adopt the policy of containing Soviet attempts to expand. Without an activist American containment policy, the Soviets would have continued to expand in Europe, the Middle East, and Asia. Particular blame is placed in this view upon the dictator Stalin, whose brutal policies and paranoid personality contributed to a sense of "encirclement" and an interest in expanding wherever possible to prevent a weakening of power. Many contemporary Russian analysts agree that Stalin's expansionist policy provoked widespread hostility toward the USSR, which contributed to its ultimate collapse. According to this argument, without Stalin's aggressive policies in the years following World War II, exemplified by Soviet actions in Eastern Europe, the Cold War would not have evolved, or at least it would not have been as vehement.

No, It Was Washington's Fault

A second interpretation of the origins of the Cold War takes the opposite position. Here the United States is to blame for the outbreak of the Cold War because it insisted on trying to expand its overseas export markets in Eastern Europe after World War II, and because it failed to comprehend the severe security problems facing the Soviet Union at the end of the war. After all, this argument goes, because the USSR suffered about 20 million deaths in the war, amounting to almost 10 percent of its population, it was understandable that the Soviets would want to protect their territory by controlling countries such as Poland, which twice within half a century had been the invasion route for Germany against Russia. Stalin thus demanded that the USSR possessed the right to have "friendly" nations on its borders. Note that this explanation is also a domestic-level analysis.

This perspective therefore contends that the United States mistook legitimate security precautions as aggressive designs and thereby initiated the Cold War, to which the Soviets were forced to react. A variant position maintains that American use of the atomic bomb at the end of World War II caused the USSR to look to its own security. It has been argued that the United States used the atomic bomb on Japan not to quickly end the war, which was already nearing its conclusion, but as a warning to the USSR not to encroach further into Asia and as a demonstration of the destructive power of the new American weapon. Though he would never admit it publicly, Stalin was very concerned by the fact that the war ended with the United States in sole possession of atomic weapons. When Truman mentioned to him at the Potsdam summit that the United States had developed a powerful new weapon (of which he had already been informed by Soviet intelligence), Stalin replied only that he hoped the United States would make good use of it. Upon his return to Moscow, however, he told Soviet military industrial officials, "You know that Hiroshima has shaken the whole world. The balance has been destroyed. Provide the bomb— it will remove a great danger from us."[1] Until Soviet science was able to fulfill Stalin's order, the American nuclear monopoly could only have exacerbated Soviet security concerns.

Ideological Conflict

A third explanation for the origins of the Cold War claims that the difference in ideologies and ways of life that the Soviet and American political systems represented was the primary cause for the conflict between these nations. According to this explanation, it would have been impossible for two potential competitors to avoid conflict when one represented an open democracy and the other a closed totalitarian system. For each, the other presented a threat of immense proportions; each saw the other as expansionist and bent on ideologically converting the world. This is another domestic-level argument, portraying the Cold War as a clash of political ideas and forms of government.

This explanation views the conflict as driven by the vast differences between capitalism and communism. Capitalism is essentially an international system. For it to properly function, it requires trading partners, open world markets, and international stability. Its essence is the private ownership of the means of production and the existence of a mobile labor force. Western democracy is anchored in the protection of individual rights and freedom. From the West, communism was perceived as monolithic, antidemocratic, and totalitarian. The Communist system rejected private property, required a centralized system of production and distribution of resources, and enforced narrow limits on individual rights such as freedom of religion, assembly, and speech. Soviet ideologues supported the explanation of ideological incompatibility, though they naturally portrayed capitalism as reprehensible.

Marxist-Leninist ideology shaped Soviet perceptions of world politics. According to socialist ideology, capitalism was the cause of war and conflict, and peace would come only with the worldwide overthrow of the capitalist system. Stalin expressed this viewpoint in a February 1946 speech declaring that "war was inevitable as long as capitalism existed."[2] Until it was eradicated, "capitalist encirclement" would threaten the gains of the 1917 revolution. Cooperation with the capitalist powers could therefore be only a temporary expedient, as a final violent struggle of socialism against capitalism would eventually come. Many Communists also sought to spread their ideology to other countries throughout the world, advocating a global Communist revolution, and viewed any Western resistance to this idea as evidence of the intent of Western governments to destroy Soviet communism.

Leadership or the Lack Thereof

A fourth explanation for the Cold War focuses on individual leaders in both the United States and the Soviet Union. In both states, according to this argument, foreign policy is ultimately the responsibility of one person, the leader. In the United States, for example, the president has considerably more leeway in foreign affairs than in domestic politics, where he competes with Congress, the Supreme Court, and special-interest groups. Consequently, his personality, beliefs, and image can have significant impact on foreign policy and the nature of interstate relations. According to this explanation, Roosevelt knew (or at least thought he knew) how to handle Stalin and believed that "if he could just have an opportunity to exert his powers of personal charm and persuasion on the Russian dictator . . . Stalin would be disarmed and his lasting friendship secured."[3] Roosevelt's intention was to demonstrate that the United States could be trusted and its commitments would be fulfilled.

However, Harry Truman, who had replaced Roosevelt upon his death in April 1945, had little experience in foreign affairs and was more suspicious of Soviet intentions. Truman, according to this line of reasoning, relied heavily on the many Roosevelt aides who were similarly suspicious of the Soviet leadership—more so than Roosevelt had been. This resulted in unnecessarily harsh

AT A GLANCE

ALTERNATIVE CAUSES OF THE COLD WAR

Soviet actions

If the Soviets had not been bent on territorial acquisition, the United States would have retreated into its prewar position of isolation. The USSR was intent on conquering Western Europe.

American actions

If the United States had not insisted on trying to expand its overseas export markets in Eastern Europe and had recognized the Soviet security dilemma, the Cold War would have been avoided. Instead, the Soviets felt that they needed Eastern Europe as a buffer. The Allies should have helped the USSR by opening a second front against Germany more quickly during World War II. According to this view, the United States used the atomic bomb on Japan to scare the Soviets out of Asia.

The behavior and interaction of Stalin and Truman

President Truman had little experience in foreign affairs and expected the worst from the Soviets. He followed a "get tough" strategy. Stalin was a brutal dictator who killed millions of his people before World War II in order to preserve his totalitarian rule at home. Western actions only increased his paranoia that his leadership was being undermined.

The competing ideologies of communism and capitalism

Capitalism is an international system that needs trading partners, open world markets, and international stability. It is based on a privatized economy, a mobile labor force, and individual rights and freedom. The Communist system

policies that strained Soviet-American relations. Examples include Truman's tough conversation with Soviet Foreign Minister Molotov a few days after he had taken office, strict Marshall Plan regulations that made it impossible and even insulting for the USSR to accept American aid, and the withholding of economic assistance.

Stalin also plays a role in this explanation. This brutal, increasingly paranoid dictator had already been responsible for the death of millions of his own citizens even before World War II started. His totalitarian rule and brutal practices at home and abroad were likely to raise fears among democracies that had just fought the most horrible war in history, which had been caused in part by their failure to respond in time to actions of a vicious autocrat. Though Stalin framed his actions in a Marxist-Leninist context, his primary concern may have been the maintenance of his own power and strength and the security of the Soviet state. But his suspicious nature, which undoubtedly magnified his perceptions of the threats to the USSR posed by Western actions immediately after World War II, led to responses by the Western powers that only reinforced his paranoia. The argument that the Cold War was primarily the fault of individual leaders therefore does not necessarily portray United States or Soviet leaders as heroes or villains; rather, it emphasizes that they were fallible human beings. Of course, consistent with this explanation, one could (and many did) blame either Truman *or* Stalin as responsible for starting the Cold War.

rejects private property, requires a centralized economic system, and adheres to a narrow definition of individual rights. Communism is designed to be spread around the world. These two ideologies are polar. Each side thought that it was right.

The United States and the USSR were the only remaining nations that were great powers

The United States and the USSR could challenge each other for global leadership, project influence around the world, and threaten the other's survival. In a bipolar system, the two leading nations inevitably oppose each other in a total confrontation.

Each side misperceived the other's actions

The Americans interpreted Soviet actions that were designed for security as Communist expansion. The Soviets misunderstood American efforts to aid its allies and trading partners as an attempt to encircle and challenge the USSR. A process of action-reaction resulted in a worldwide competition.

One World Divided by Two Superpowers Equals Conflict

A fifth explanation for the origins of the Cold War concentrates on the fact that the United States and the Soviet Union had emerged after World War II as the two dominant powers in the world. They were the only two capable of projecting influence and of challenging each other for global leadership; and ultimately, they were the only states that could threaten the other's survival. As such, they were destined to be natural adversaries. Note that this is a systemic-level argument, fitting into the **realpolitik,** or "everybody wants to rule the world," view of world politics, in which states by their very nature seek power in the international system. Accordingly, this argument holds that had Britain emerged more powerful than the USSR at the end of World War II, the Cold War would still have occurred, with London and not Moscow perceived as the main threat to American security, since only Britain would have had the capability to challenge American survival.

As Chapters Two and Three have shown, great powers have always rivaled one another throughout the history of world politics. At the end of World War II, only two superpowers remained, and it would have been unprecedented if their relations had been purely amicable. Some form of conflict between the United States and the USSR was inevitable.

The position that the Cold War started because of the great-power conflict based on the bipolar relationship that emerged after World War II is also in keeping with the security dilemma discussed in Chapters One and Eleven. The zero-sum character of the bipolar security dilemma, meaning a situation where each nation perceives the other's gain as a loss to itself, shaped the nature of the Cold War by encouraging intensive competition between the two super-powers. Thus, in 1949, when the Chinese Communists finally defeated the Nationalist party in a long, drawn-out civil war, many believed that this outcome meant that the United States "lost" China and that the Soviet Union "won" it, though it was soon shown that things were not that simple.

From this systemic perspective, there is no point in assigning blame, as the two powers became locked in conflict as a consequence of their circumstances and the structure of the postwar international system. Like two gunslingers in a Western film, the superpowers both knew that "this town ain't big enough fer the both of us," and it didn't matter who was wearing the black or the white hat.

It Was All a Misunderstanding

There is a sixth explanation for the origins of the Cold War that also fits into the systemic-level framework provided by the security dilemma. In this expla-nation, it is suggested that each side misperceived the intentions of the other. On the one hand, the United States misunderstood that Soviet actions were designed to guarantee the USSR's security in the wake of the trauma inflicted by Hitler's surprise attack and the devastation the Soviet people suffered. On the other hand, according to this argument, the Soviets also misunderstood Ameri-can interests and concerns, seeing U.S. efforts to aid its allies and trading part-ners as an attempt to encircle and challenge the USSR. Each superpower assumed the worst about its adversary.

Once the original misperceptions occurred, a process of action-reaction devel-oped in which one side's moves were countered by the other, whose actions sparked further reaction. This process led to a series of events that eventually solidified into a worldwide competition. The Cold War thus developed out of a vicious circle of mutually reinforcing misperceptions. If only both powers had comprehended the basic defensive nature of the policies of the other, the Cold War would never have occurred, or at least the competition between the super-powers would have been defused. Since the information upon which each group of leaders had to base its policies was often very limited, however, particularly with respect to its adversaries' intentions, it is not easy to see exactly how Soviet and American leaders could have broken the circle of misperception.

Who or What Was to Blame?

The reasons for the Cold War have been debated from the outset. In the late 1940s some Americans on the left of the political spectrum argued that the United States had overreacted to Soviet actions. This position was reinforced by revisionist historians in the wake of the Vietnam War who argued that the United States was guilty. By contrast, the end of the Cold War has bolstered the view of many that the Soviet Union was responsible for the conflict. With the

An ominous harbinger of the Cold War to come, this 1946 cartoon shows a growing chasm of distrust between the Russian bear and the American eagle.

Source: Copyright Los Angeles Times Syndicate.

end of Soviet aggression, these analysts argue, competition ended; the change in Soviet rather than American policy implies that the Soviet Union was at fault. These analysts are reinforced by Russian scholars in the era of ***glasnost*** (political openness) who criticize the Stalin era. Even with the new information available to historians with the recent lessening of restrictions on Soviet archives, the question of the origins of the Cold War is likely to remain an open debate for many years. The reader is invited to draw her or his own conclusion from the events and personalities involved in the conflict, to which this chapter now turns.

HEATING UP THE COLD WAR, 1945–1953

World War II ended with tensions increasing between the Soviet Union and the Western Allies, especially over the future of Eastern Europe and Germany, but the wartime allies did not immediately become bitter enemies. The prospect of impending conflict between the United States and the USSR, let alone the shape that conflict would take, was not yet apparent. Postwar events, however, soon propelled the two emerging superpowers into confrontation.

Initial Confrontations: Iran, Greece, and Turkey

During World War II, both the USSR and Britain feared the expansion of Nazi influence in the Middle East. In 1941 the Soviets and British agreed to jointly occupy Iran—the Soviets in the north and the British in the south—with the intent of protecting Iran from Nazi influence and securing supply lines to Russia during the war. The agreement specified that both Soviet and British troops were to be removed after the war. When the war ended in May 1945, the British pulled out, but Stalin refused to withdraw the Soviet troops. President Truman resolved to confront Soviet obstinacy with a "get tough" stance: A warning was dispatched to Moscow, and an aircraft carrier was sent to the eastern Mediterranean to maintain an American presence. For a time, it looked as if the wartime allies might be drawn into serious conflict less than a year after the end of World War II, but the crisis was defused in April 1946, when the Soviets pledged to leave Iran after Teheran agreed to set up a joint Iranian-Soviet oil company.

Why did Moscow retreat? According to historian Adam B. Ulam, the involvement of the American government was the primary cause. The Soviets were not willing to risk even a minor confrontation with America for fear of threatening their interests in more crucial regions.[4] Whatever the real reasoning behind the Soviet withdrawal may have been, Truman and his advisors determined that the best way to check Soviet expansion and the possibility of Soviet control of Western Europe was to directly counter Stalin's actions and stand firm against Soviet demands.

The United States and Britain hoped that a similar "get tough" stance would convince the USSR to stop allowing the newly established Communist governments in Eastern Europe to supply Communist partisans in Greece. They also wanted the USSR to cease pressuring Turkey for territorial concessions and access to the Mediterranean through the Dardanelles, since London and Washington viewed these actions as attempts to expand Soviet control into new areas.

The Iron Curtain Descends

By the end of 1945 it was clear that the USSR had firmly established itself as the dominant power in Eastern Europe. Many Western leaders, alarmed by Soviet efforts to expand into the Middle East and Mediterranean, and by the presence of massive Soviet forces in Eastern and Central Europe, began to perceive a growing

Soviet threat. In 1946, at a speech in Fulton, Missouri, Winston Churchill warned Americans that "from Stettin in the Baltic to Trieste in the Adriatic, an iron curtain has descended across the continent."[5] Using the example of Munich, he pleaded for an alliance of Western democracies to exert influence over Russia and thwart further Soviet expansion.

In early 1947 the British government informed Washington that it would no longer be able to maintain its presence in Greece and Turkey due to economic concerns and the unwillingness of the Labour government to risk British troops in foreign civil wars. The British concluded that they could not be responsible for countering Soviet advances in the region and feared that unless the United States stepped in, a power vacuum would develop and lead to dangerous consequences.

This was a dramatic change in the international system. At the end of World War II, it was widely believed that there would be three superpowers in the postwar world: the United States, the Soviet Union, and Great Britain.[6] Britain, however, had been devastated and exhausted by the effort needed to withstand the Nazi onslaught, and was consequently relinquishing political control and withdrawing its forces from India, Palestine, Iraq, Jordan, and other former colonies. The British now concluded that it was necessary to reduce their role in areas such as Greece and Turkey that were independent, but in which Britain still had important interests.

To the Truman administration, the British decision came as a shock, especially since the president believed that Greece and Turkey were still threatened by the possibility of Soviet encroachment. American officials decided the Soviet Union had to be blocked, and that the United States would have to replace the British power vacuum in the region. Many in Washington felt that Moscow was trying to pull an "end run" around Europe, and as Undersecretary of State Dean Acheson put it, "We and we alone are in a position to break up the play."[7] The Truman administration's willingness to assume greater responsibilities in world affairs marked a major turning point in the foreign policy of the traditionally isolationist United States.

Truman Doctrine

In essence, the Truman administration had decided it would have to deny the Soviets any possibility of expansion, especially in Europe. This aim would necessitate an unprecedented engagement of the United States abroad in peacetime, as it would require abandonment of its traditional isolationist stance. Yet, as Truman and his aides soon found when they began to brief Congress, to place this issue in purely realpolitik terms would not satisfy the American people. There was a strong movement in the United States to return to its prewar position of isolation. Republican Senator Arthur Vandenberg, chairman of the Senate Foreign Relations Committee, advised Truman that he would have to "scare the hell out of the American people" to make them receptive to his plans.[8] Therefore, the president rose before Congress on March 12, 1947, and introduced the **Truman Doctrine,** which some

MR. X AND CONTAINMENT

The Truman Doctrine and the Marshall Plan were based on the philosophy of containment, which was developed by George Kennan, a Soviet specialist based in the American Embassy in Moscow. His "Long Telegram" of February 1946 alerted American officials to the threat they faced from Soviet insecurities and expansion and suggested possible solutions.

In July 1947 Kennan published an article in *Foreign Affairs* under the pseudonym "X," which delineated the policy of **containment,** the basis for future American actions in the Cold War.* He argued that the Soviets threatened free institutions throughout the Western world and were determined to fulfill the Marxist-Leninist desire for worldwide revolution. "X" claimed that Soviet actions could be contained by the "joint and vigilant application of counterforce at a constantly shifting series of geographical and political points around the world."

Kennan later regretted using the term "counterforce," because he advocated

regard as an American "declaration of the Cold War." Truman's speech concentrated on the ideological conflict between freedom and totalitarianism:

> At the present moment in world history nearly every nation must choose between alternative ways of life. The choice is too often not a free one. One way of life is based upon the will of the majority, and is distinguished by free institutions, representative government, free elections, guarantees of individual liberty, freedom of speech and religion, and freedom from political oppression. The second way of life is based upon the will of a minority forcibly imposed upon the majority. It relies upon terror and oppression, a controlled press and radio, fixed elections, and the suppression of personal freedoms. I believe that it must be the policy of the United States to support free peoples who are resisting attempted subjugation by armed minorities or by outside pressures.[9]

To gain domestic support, the president thus couched his appeal for economic and financial aid to Greece and Turkey in terms of global and moral responsibility. The United States would now be called upon to help the nations of the free world gain and keep their freedom. Critics were concerned about the manner in which the Truman Doctrine was to be defined. Did this mean that the United States would intervene *anywhere* at *any time*? The president's aides had to admit that the United States would not be able to involve itself in every situation worldwide, but were unable to clarify the limits of commitment. Despite these uncertainties, Congress overwhelmingly approved the Truman Doctrine and authorized a $400 million assistance program for Greece and Turkey.

Marshall Plan

In 1947 the Truman administration was also confronting economic decline in Europe. Social and economic institutions had been demolished by the war; an economic and political, rather than military, instruments for dealing with the Soviets. This distinction would become a major controversy in the conduct of American foreign policy.

In essence, Kennan argued that the Soviets would seek to expand until counteraction from the United States forced them to retreat. Ultimately, he believed that the containment approach would cause the Soviet Union to collapse internally and force it to negotiate, a prediction that would prove accurate forty years later. Kennan's containment theory provided American decision makers with a critical vision for organizing U.S. foreign policy and remained the centerpiece of American international relations for the next four decades.

* "X" [George F. Kennan], "The Sources of Soviet Conduct," *Foreign Affairs* 20, no. 4 (July 1947), pp. 556–582.

unusually severe winter and meager harvest compounded the crisis. France and Italy were internally besieged by Communist parties, and economically exhausted Britain was retreating from its empire abroad. Winston Churchill described Europe as "a rubble heap, a charnel house, a breeding ground of pestilence and hate."[10] There was widespread fear in Washington that Communist agents would topple the governments of Western Europe in preparation for a Soviet invasion, and the war-ravaged countries would be unable to purchase American goods, which would threaten the American economy and perhaps would return the world to its prewar state of depression.

The response to this potential catastrophe was the Marshall Plan, named after Secretary of State George C. Marshall, who announced the plan in an address at Harvard University's commencement exercises as a way to "help start the European world on its way to recovery."[11] Since the United States had emerged from World War II an economic superpower, and had escaped the destruction of war at home, it was in a strong position to take this action.

The Marshall Plan, perhaps the most successful U.S. foreign policy program in history, offered American economic and military assistance to promote free-market economies within Europe. The plan was originally offered to the Soviet Union and its satellites, but in July 1948 Soviet Foreign Minister Molotov declared that the program would infringe on the sovereignty of the European states, and thus announced that Moscow would not participate. Various reports and documents declassified years later reveal that Stalin's true concerns were that American revitalization of Great Britain, France, and Germany would restore their great-power status and return the world to the pre-1939 political system. Soviet leaders feared what they perceived as America's "intention to restore the economy of Germany and Japan on the old basis, provided it is subordinated to interests of American capital."[12] Stalin believed that this would be detrimental to Soviet vital interests, especially in Eastern Europe; it represented, he thought, a threat to the security of the USSR. As a result, Marshall Plan aid, which was administered through the Economic Cooperation Act of 1948 and comprised 2.75 percent of America's gross national product, was transferred only to the democracies of the West.[13]

The Marshall Plan had three main effects. First, it revitalized European economies and restored Britain, France, and eventually Germany to major-power status (although not to the level of the United States or USSR). Second, it thwarted Communist control within the Western European countries as it helped end the economic hardships that served as a breeding ground for discontent and increased the influence of communist parties, particularly in France and Italy. Finally, it helped to create the basis for a movement toward European economic integration we now know as the European Union, and facilitated the eventual integration of West Germany into the European economy.

Stalin and Tito

In the early years of Soviet domination of Eastern Europe after World War II, Moscow allowed a considerable degree of latitude to the Communist regimes that it supported. Elections were held in several countries and noncommunist parties could compete in them, but their role was kept marginal. Communist parties that attained power largely through their own efforts rather than Soviet pressure, however, maintained a degree of independence from Moscow. As the tensions surrounding the Cold War increased, Stalin became obsessed with the possibility that these regimes could prove to be unreliable.

His fears were heightened by the growing friction between the Kremlin and the Communist government of Yugoslavia. Josip Broz Tito, the leader of Yugoslavia, had come to power with his own unique mix of **communism** and nationalism. The ethnic conflicts among the dominant Serbs and their neighbors, which had catalyzed World War I, were kept below the surface under Tito's leadership. (They would later resurface in the years after Tito's death.) Stalin became ever more concerned about Tito's independent power and legitimacy in Yugoslavia, and his challenges to Moscow's influence over the policies of East European Communist parties. As a result, Stalin began to crack down on other states in Eastern Europe in order to prevent any future, independent leaders like Tito from emerging.

Czech Coup

Against the background of dissension among Communist leaders and growing East-West suspicions, Czechoslovakia became the crucible for developments in the region and a symbol of the direction of global affairs, as it had at the Munich Conference a decade earlier. Czechoslovakia was the least Communist of the regimes that existed in Eastern Europe in early 1948. Before World War II, it had been anti-German, not anti-Soviet. Furthermore, it had been the most

Demonstrators rally beneath the balcony of Kinsky Palace in Prague, Czechoslovakia on the eve of the Communist coup in February 1948. The Czech premier later spoke, demanding Communist control of the government.
Source: © AP/Wide World Photos.

industrially advanced and democratic of the interwar eastern European regimes, and therefore had special meaning for Western leaders.

In February 1948 a Communist-engineered, Soviet-backed coup seized power in Czechoslovakia. Moscow's heavy-handed action angered the West, and convinced many that Stalin had never intended to keep the promises of open elections in Eastern Europe that he had made at the Yalta conference (see Chapter

Three). Stalin's moves in Czechoslovakia also failed to intimidate Tito, and the two Communist leaders broke publicly in June 1948. Although the West was slow to grasp the significance of Titoism, this dramatic separation showed that Communist countries were not necessarily part of one monolithic alliance that blindly followed the USSR.

Berlin Blockade

The coup in Czechoslovakia made the United States increasingly concerned with the tightening Soviet grip over Eastern Europe and Germany. As noted in Chapter Three, Germany was divided into four zones of military occupation after World War II, one each for France, the United States, Great Britain, and the USSR. An oddity of the arrangement was that Berlin, the capital of prewar Germany, was also divided among the four powers but was entirely surrounded by the Soviet zone. (See Map 4.1 for occupation zones.) All means of transportation and communication to the Western sectors of the former capital thus had to go through Soviet-occupied territory. In June 1948, ostensibly in response to a currency reform in the Western sectors of Berlin, Stalin ordered the closure of all land-access routes between Berlin and the Western occupation zones. West Berlin was isolated and surrounded by Soviet forces.

The Berlin blockade was a fateful event. Stalin would not allow the transport of food, fuel, or other basic necessities to the Western sectors; if no way could be found to supply West Berlin, the population would soon starve. Truman appeared to be forced to decide between two unpalatable alternatives: The United States could go to war against the huge Soviet army in eastern Germany to reestablish Western rights of access to Berlin, or it could allow the Soviets to control the entire city, with horrendous results for West Berliners and a major defeat for the West. Truman and his advisors, however, came up with a third option: initiating a dramatic airlift of supplies to West Berlin. "Operation Vittles," as it was called, was a colossal undertaking to supply the 2.5 million West Berliners. In total, more than 2 million tons of supplies were flown in by the airlift. At the same time, Truman moved B-29 bombers, the same type of aircraft that had dropped the two nuclear weapons on Japan in 1945, to bases in England. Stalin could have challenged the airlift, but that would have meant war with the Western allies, and he was not prepared to go so far. He halted the blockade in May 1949, though the airlift continued until September.

Stalin's attempt to use military force to gain political concessions failed. A serious crisis had passed without escalating to war. Many in the West believed that the failure of the Berlin blockade verified Kennan's prediction that the Soviets would retreat when their efforts were resolutely resisted. Meanwhile, each side proceeded with the consolidation of its parts of occupied Germany. The West backed the formation of the Federal Republic of Germany, with its capital at Bonn, and the USSR formed the Democratic German Republic, with East Berlin as its capital. Each superpower had wanted a single German state on its own terms, but both sides realized after the Berlin blockade that neither could concede all of Germany to the other. Neither side could attain its first

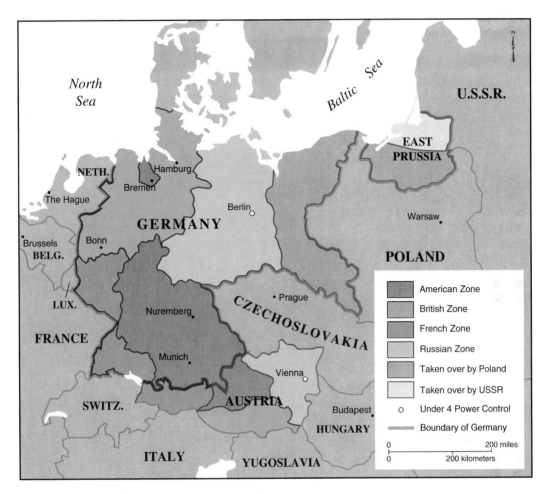

Map 4.1   A Divided Germany, Post–World War II

preference, so both settled for a divided Germany as their second choice, and the division of Germany thus took place by default.

NATO Alliance

The Berlin blockade was intended in part to thwart a Western alliance, but actually helped to speed plans for a formal security agreement to counter what the Western countries perceived as Soviet aggression. In April 1949 the North Atlantic Treaty Organization (NATO) was established. The nations of Western Europe banded together with the United States and Canada to commit themselves to resisting Soviet aggression. In joining NATO, the United States effectively renounced isolationism and accepted membership in a peacetime entangling alliance for the first time in its history.

McCARTHYISM

In an event that would have momentous consequences for world politics, the Soviet Union successfully tested an atomic bomb in the fall of 1949. This development occurred much earlier than U.S. experts had anticipated would be possible, and consequently came as a major shock. A sense developed in the West that only one reason could explain the early Soviet development of the bomb: The Communists had stolen the secret from the United States. Therefore, according to this theory, there had to be traitors in America's midst.

In February 1950, a few months after the Soviet atomic test, Senator Joseph McCarthy of Wisconsin presented a list of 205 persons whom he claimed were known by the secretary of state to be Communists but were still working in important positions in the State Department.* (He varied the numbers at subsequent hearings, sometimes citing 116 Communists, sometimes 57, sometimes 81.) McCarthy's accusations inflamed the public perception that Communist subversion put U.S. security at risk, a risk personified by traitors who would sell out the American nation to foreign Communist domination.

As **McCarthyism**—a tendency to suspect people of Communist sympathies without any evidence—swept through the country, many people's loyalties were

THE COLD WAR IN ASIA

Our account of the early Cold War years so far has concentrated on the centers of the conflict to the west and south of the Soviet Union in Europe and the Mediterranean, but conflict was also occurring in Asia. Here, in the early days of the Cold War, the centerpiece of the new competition was China.

By the end of World War II, many Americans had become quite attached to China, and they believed that Asia was actually the center of the conflict with the Soviet Union. The leader of the "Asia Firsters" was the general who had led the Allied war effort against Japan, Douglas MacArthur, who believed that Asia would "determine the course of history in the next ten thousand years" and criticized the Truman administration for concentrating too much on Europe, which he referred to as a "dying system."[14]

America's China policy dilemma became particularly acute after the war's end, when Communist forces led by Mao Zedong and the Nationalist government of Chiang Kai-shek resumed their civil war. Chiang's Nationalist party, the Kuomintang (KMT), had sunk in popularity due to rampant internal corruption and dictatorial practices. In a predicament that would recur throughout the Cold War, the United States found itself caught between the possibility of a future Communist regime viewed as a natural ally to the Soviet Union on the one hand and an unpopular and repressive right-wing government on the other. Predictably, U.S. policy took a middle position:

questioned. Professors and teachers became afraid to speak their minds. Writers, actors, and directors were "blacklisted" as Communist sympathizers and as a result became unemployable. Officials were frightened to say what they believed, and China analysts were removed from the State Department, leaving a serious deficiency in U.S. foreign policy-making for years to come. It was a bleak time in America, when some even went so far as to question whether the fundamental freedoms guaranteed in the Bill of Rights actually threatened U.S. national security by facilitating the work of Communist traitors and fellow-travelers.

In both the United States and the USSR, then, the Cold War had begun to play a major role in domestic political and economic life. Stalin, himself a Soviet version of McCarthy, began to tighten his grip, lashing out at anyone he suspected of the slightest questioning of his policies or total control. Near the end of his life he even arrested and executed his own doctors, suspecting that they were trying to murder him.

*Harold F. Gosnell, *Truman's Crises: A Political Biography of Harry S. Truman* (London: Greenwood, 1980), p. 505.

The United States offered just enough economic aid and military assistance to further alienate the Chinese Communists but not enough to have a real chance of saving the KMT. Just as predictably, this strategy failed. In October 1949 the Communists finally won the civil war and established the People's Republic of China, while the Nationalists were driven offshore to the island of Taiwan.

The American government assumed that the victory of the Chinese Communist party would mean automatic alliance with their comrades in the USSR. The Soviets did offer guidance and assistance to Mao's Communist party. However, it is now known that even during the civil war, Stalin had qualms about a Chinese Communist victory and was not averse to doing business with the Nationalists. Stalin and Mao had significant differences of opinion similar to those between Stalin and Tito. A strong China under united Communist control might represent more of a threat to Soviet interests than a weakly divided China under the Nationalists. When presented with a conflict between Communist objectives and Soviet national interests, Stalin chose the latter, establishing a pattern that his successors in the Kremlin would often follow throughout the Cold War. The inherent tensions between Soviet and Chinese interests would eventually lead to hostilities between the two communist giants. In the 1940s, however, Chinese Communists would not have the opportunity to choose between the two superpowers. American antipathy to communism would preclude any possibility of reconciliation.

NSC-68

The rapid development of the Soviet atomic bomb (which can be attributed partially to espionage, but also to a massive "crash" program in the USSR) changed the nature of the conflict. Within the American government, key figures were clearly affected by the internal tensions that had been generated by the domestic crisis and by the recent American defeats. Many officials were beginning to think more in military terms rather than concentrating on the political and economic instruments that had been the focus of Kennan's approach adopted in the Truman Doctrine and the Marshall Plan. A document, **NSC-68,** was prepared by the National Security Council (NSC) to address the question of what was to be done to counter the spread of international communism.

NSC-68 called for a major expansion of America's armed forces, adding military instrumentation to the political and economic means of containment. This approach would significantly alter the form and content of U.S. foreign policy and would eventually lead to direct American military involvement in conflicts in Korea and Vietnam. President Truman, although he agreed with the concept and principles of NSC-68, was not prepared in early 1950 to accept a major escalation in defense spending. He feared that the United States could not afford any such increase and that high military spending would ruin the economy. Unexpected developments, however, soon changed Truman's mind.

Korea: The Turning Point

The escalating pressures on both the international and domestic scenes came to a head in Korea in 1950. After the Japanese surrender that ended World War II, Korea, like Germany, was divided by the victorious allies along the thirty-eighth parallel, with the north occupied by the Soviets and the south occupied by the United States. Despite the desire for union in both halves of Korea, the United States and the USSR were unable to agree to a formula for holding elections under the auspices of the United Nations (UN). The Soviets in particular objected to a national poll, and instead held Soviet-style elections in the north, where only the Communist party had any chance of winning. At the head of the new Communist government was Kim Il-Sung, a youthful Korean Communist who had spent many years in the USSR and served as an officer in the Soviet army. (He remained in power until his death in 1994, having ruled longer than any living leader of any nation.) Confident in the loyalty of Kim's government, the USSR withdrew its occupation forces by January 1949. The United States was then under pressure to similarly withdraw from the south, which it did by the middle of that year. In early 1950, U.S. Secretary of State Acheson appeared to write off Korea when he proposed a U.S. defense perimeter in Asia that seemed to exclude the country.

An event then occurred that pushed the Cold War past the point of no return. On June 25, 1950, North Korea launched a massive surprise attack against South Korea (see Map 4.2). Although Stalin probably did not instigate the North Korean attack, he undoubtedly acquiesced in it—grossly miscalculating

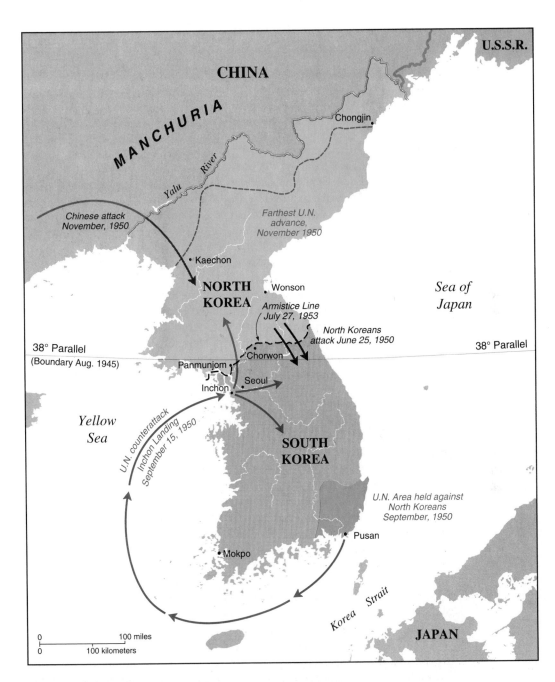

Map 4.2   The Korean War

the American reaction. This attack immediately brought to mind the lesson the
West had learned at Munich: Aggression had to be checked, or aggressors would

become bolder and more ambitious. American leaders saw the North Korean offensive as a major test of U.S. leadership and credibility in the same way that George Bush, forty years later, would call the Iraqi invasion of Kuwait a threat to world order.

Because Moscow refused to participate in the United Nations Security Council debate on Korea, the Soviets were unable to veto a U.S.–framed initiative to send UN troops to Korea. (As Chapter Nine will explain, one veto by a permanent member is sufficient to reject a UN Security Council initiative. At the time of the debate on Korea, the USSR was boycotting the Security Council to protest the assignment of China's seat on the council to Chiang's KMT government on Taiwan rather than Mao's Communist PRC.) The Security Council authorized a military response to the invasion, and a U.S.–led coalition sent forces to oppose the North Korean offensive. (The pattern would be repeated forty years later, when the UN Security Council authorized another U.S.–led coalition to intervene in Kuwait in 1991 to counteract the Iraqi invasion of that Persian Gulf sheikdom.)

There is no doubt that the intervention of the United States and its allies saved South Korea. The Communists had almost overrun South Korea until, in September, UN forces commanded by MacArthur landed at Inchon behind North Korean lines, trapping and routing the North Korean troops. MacArthur pushed for approval of his plan to liberate North Korea and "unleash" Nationalist forces on Taiwan for an attack on China itself. Truman, however, did not particularly trust MacArthur and was intent on keeping the war limited to South Korean soil. Truman allowed the general to proceed after MacArthur assured him that the Soviets and Chinese would not intervene if the United States invaded North Korea.

MacArthur was wrong. As UN forces approached the Yalu River, on the border separating Korea and China, they were engaged by Chinese armies and forced to retreat. The Chinese had indirectly warned the United States, especially through a message from the Indian ambassador to China, that they would enter the conflict if U.S. forces threatened the Chinese border, but these signals were either not clearly received or were ignored. The Communists quickly pushed the UN forces back into South Korea once again. Continued disagreements between the president and MacArthur prompted Truman to relieve MacArthur of his command in April 1951.

UN forces regained most of Korea south of the thirty-eighth parallel, and UN and Communist forces spent two more years fighting on a line near the original division between North and South Korea. When Dwight D. Eisenhower became the U.S. president in January 1953, he immediately advised the Communists that in the event that the conflict in Korea could not be resolved, the United States "intended to move decisively without inhibition in our use of [nuclear] weapons, and would no longer be responsible for confining hostilities to the Korean Peninsula."[15] This warning, and growing success on the ground by Allied forces, encouraged the Communists to agree to a cease-fire in July 1953.

DETERRENCE

During the Cold War, both superpowers practiced a policy of Mutual Assured Destruction ("MAD") in order to prevent nuclear war.

Source: © Scott Willis.

Korea was a turning point in the Cold War for several reasons. First, the war prompted the expansion of American military forces called for in NSC-68 and a similar buildup of NATO forces in Europe. Second, it stimulated American involvement in Asia, and therefore heightened the confrontation with the Soviet Union and China. Third, the Korean War solidified the bipolar competition between the United States and the Soviet Union for clients around the globe, as the United States began to view Communist actions in every part of the world as a threat to U.S. interests. This globalist view of the U.S.–Soviet conflict contrasted with Kennan's original conception of containment, in which only North America, Western and Central Europe, and the Pacific coast of Asia were seen as areas of American vital interest.

Finally, although both the United States and USSR possessed them, nuclear weapons were not used in the war and fighting was restricted to Korean territory. The conflict was thus referred to as a **limited war,** fought for limited goals by limited means, which set a pattern for restricted actions throughout the Cold War period. The Korean War thus irrevocably moved the containment effort of the West to the military sphere without escalating into actual military conflict between the superpowers. As the destructive potential of nuclear weapons made total war unthinkable, the superpowers would have to carry on their global conflict by more subtle means.

RELAXATION AND A RENEWAL OF TENSIONS, 1953–1957

This new phase began in early 1953 with Stalin's death and Dwight D. Eisenhower's accession to the presidency of the United States. As would become the case often throughout the Cold War, the domestic context of the two superpowers moved in opposing directions. In the United States, the new leadership under Eisenhower and his secretary of state, John Foster Dulles, was committed to a continued European-oriented version of American foreign policy (as opposed to the Asia-first strategy of conservative Republicans). Dulles also espoused a highly moralistic and activist view of the confrontation with international communism. He believed that the United States should attempt to "roll back" Communist gains rather than be satisfied simply with containing them in their post–World War II borders.

On the Soviet side, the top officials were preoccupied with resolving the leadership struggle that emerged with Stalin's demise. The Soviet political system lacked a constitutional means for the transfer of political power. Thus, the change from one leader to the next was a major problem in the Soviet Union at a time when the focus was on domestic issues. This was not clearly understood in Washington, leading many critics to argue that the United States missed an opportunity for breaking through the deep hostility between the United States and the USSR.

New Leaders, New Challenges

The official communiqué announcing Stalin's death to the Soviet population stressed the necessity of "prevention of any kind of disorder and panic."[16] This declaration provides a revealing insight into the disarray into which the leader's death had plunged his nation. Stalin's policies, directed toward the relentless mobilization of human and material resources and the forging of a heavy industrial base and superior military strength, to the neglect of consumer goods and agricultural production, exacted a steady toll on the Soviet people. His successors were faced with a difficult domestic agenda of improving the standard of living while departing from the terror tactics employed by Stalin. Foreign-policy issues threatened to divert the energy and resources needed for this ambitious domestic agenda. Reflective of the changes in Soviet policy in the post-Stalin era, an agreement was reached in 1955 between the major powers for the neutralization of Austria, which had been jointly occupied by the Soviets and the Western Allies after World War II.

A 1955 summit meeting in Geneva, attended by the leaders of the two superpowers, Britain, and France, at which a proposal for mutual aerial inspection was introduced by Eisenhower, signaled the culmination of this more muted phase of Soviet policy. Although this "Open Skies" proposal was not accepted by the Soviets, a cultural exchange agreement was concluded that seemed to indicate a cooling of tensions. At about the same time, Nikita Khrushchev, the key Kremlin political leader who eventually emerged after Stalin, denounced Stalin's crimes. His "secret" speech before the Twentieth Congress of the Communist party of the Soviet Union in 1956 (the full text of which was not published in the USSR until decades later) indicated potential changes in Soviet foreign and domestic policy.

Despite these positive signs, American policy-makers focused on a variety of conflictual issues around the world. In Eastern Europe, the end of the Stalin era and the promise of liberation through "rollback" by America led to rioting in East Berlin against the Communist regime in 1953, and to growing problems in Poland. As it turned out, however, the Eisenhower administration was wary of intervening in the Soviet Union's "backyard" lest it provoke a major war. This was demonstrated again in 1956, when widespread unrest in Poland brought to power a new Polish Communist regime that strove for a greater degree of autonomy from Moscow. A mass revolt that same year in Hungary also brought about a change in the government. Conceivably, Moscow might have eventually come to tolerate the new regime in Budapest, but when it announced its intention to leave the Warsaw Pact, it was smashed by Soviet forces and a more compliant Hungarian government installed. Despite previous talk of "rollback," the United States and its NATO allies did little but greet refugees streaming into the West.

In Asia the conflict between the Communist People's Republic (mainland China, the PRC) and the Nationalist Republic of China (Taiwan) after the civil war remained a source of continuing tension. The United States reinforced its relations with the Nationalist Chinese on Taiwan, not only to prevent a forceful Communist attack but also to quell the Nationalists' temptation to challenge the Communists' control on the mainland. In 1954 and 1955, air and naval incidents between the PRC and the American-backed government on Taiwan gradually intensified. After many threats and much posturing on both sides, however, the crisis temporarily abated. Nevertheless, by the mid-1950s, conflicts throughout the world confirmed that the post-Stalin era would not lead to an end to the Cold War. As would happen repeatedly, a promising prospect of relaxation in tensions was followed by renewed antagonism.

Third World

Thus, in the 1950s Moscow first began to expand its influence by establishing political ties with countries that had been previously controlled by European colonial empires, such as India, Egypt, Syria, and Indonesia. These newly independent **Third World** countries emerged on the international scene with many internal problems. Many were politically unstable and militarily and economically weak. This combination of factors created strategic uncertainties that the superpowers believed they could ignore only at peril to themselves. As a result, Third World countries were drawn into the bipolar conflict of the Cold War, which further globalized the superpower rivalry and multiplied the number of locations where Soviet and American interests collided. (These developments will be discussed in more detail in Chapter Six.)

In the early phases of the Cold War in the Third World, U.S. policy focused on intervening in countries where local nationalists, many of whom were viewed as being agents of the global Soviet Communist regime, were implementing change in their countries. In 1953 the CIA engineered a coup that overthrew Iranian Premier Mohammed Mossadegh, who sought to nationalize British-controlled oil fields in Iran, and restored the Shah to power. The following year, another CIA-backed coup ousted Guatemalan President Jacobo Arbenz, whom the United States believed to be heavily influenced and supported by Communists, and replaced him with the staunchly anticommunist Castillo Armas.

In other parts of the developing world, the United States became involved in conflicts arising from decolonization. In 1956 Egypt's President Gamal Abdel Nasser nationalized the Suez Canal, which had been owned by an Anglo-French consortium. The American government believed that the matter could be settled by negotiations, but Britain and France saw Nasser's action as directly challenging their continued influence in the Middle East. Without America's knowledge, Britain, France, and Israel secretly colluded to attack and topple Nasser's regime. Israeli forces overran the Sinai, but in order to keep up the pretense that no collusion had occurred, the British and French had to wait to move their forces into place until Egypt had refused their ultimatum. By the time they "intervened" in the conflict, a furious Eisenhower was exerting economic and diplomatic pressure on them to stop. The Soviets backed Egypt with blustering threats against Britain, France, and Israel when the crisis was abating. In the end, Nasser remained in power, the Suez Canal was blocked for many months, Britain and France were humiliated, and the United States replaced them as the major Western influence in the Middle East. (For more on the Suez Crisis and its aftermath, see Chapter Six.)

American involvement in Vietnam began in 1945 and accelerated in 1954, when Communist-led Vietminh rebels besieged and defeated French forces at Dien Bien Phu in northern Vietnam. At one time, the United States might have been tempted to support Ho Chi Minh, the leader of the Communist resistance, because he was a major anticolonialist figure who quoted from the American Declaration of Independence when he proclaimed the end of French rule in his country. But after the Korean War, the United States was preoccupied with stopping communism in Asia, vowing to permit "No More Koreas." Washington also needed France's political support in Europe, and France pressed for American support in Indochina in return. Thus, the United States backed the French, and after their defeat accepted the division of Vietnam into a Communist North and Western-backed South as a transitional measure until nationwide elections could be held. Washington quickly replaced Paris as the key sponsor of the new regime in Saigon, the capital of South Vietnam.

Nonaligned Movement

Moscow and Washington were not always able to gain influence over newly independent Third World states, as their governments often found it beneficial to play one superpower against the other. As a result, a new **Nonaligned Movement** emerged in international politics in the mid 1950s, with India's Jawaharlal Nehru, Egyptian President Nasser, and Yugoslavia's Tito in the forefront of its leadership. By playing the United States against the Soviet Union, these countries attempted to gain aid from the competing superpowers. Soviet technological advances impressed many newly independent regimes, and the Soviet model of centralized, state-controlled economic and political development was initially quite attractive to developing countries. In addition to providing an example (for a time) of a successful alternative to capitalism, the Soviets established close relations with a wide variety of Third World states, including Indonesia, Ghana, India, Egypt, Syria, Iraq, and Algeria. Moscow provided aid in the form of weapons, agricultural and industrial machinery, and military and technical advisors. During the Cold War period, educational exchange programs allowed an estimated 72,000 students from Third World countries to attend learning institutions in the USSR.

The United States, however, was wary of the Nonaligned Movement, believing that it facilitated the growth of Soviet influence in the developing world. In response, Washington stepped up military and economic assistance to states it considered more reliable as U.S. allies, such as Nicaragua, Iran, and South Vietnam—before anti–U.S. governments came to power in those nations. As a result, a considerable amount of aid flowed from both superpowers to the developing world, but not in the manner the originators of the Nonaligned Movement had intended.

TO THE BRINK AND BACK, 1957–1964

A new phase in the Cold War began with continued escalation of tension between the two superpowers. As before, this wave of confrontation ebbed and flowed as events alternatively strained and improved East-West relations.

Possibly in an attempt to test Soviet and American willingness to intervene militarily in east Asia, the Chinese Communists in 1958 resumed the shelling of two islands off the Taiwanese coast, Quemoy and Matsu. Chiang, the Chinese Nationalist leader, had placed one-third of his armed forces on these two islands in the hopes that the United States would come to their defense and provide backing for his regime. The United States threatened war, but the Soviets disappointed their Chinese allies by withholding strong support, and China eventually ceased the shelling.

Sputnik

After the Suez debacle, the Communist world appeared to the United States to be on the offensive. Mao asserted in a 1957 speech that "the international

FIDEL

Fidel Castro is one of the Cold War's most successful and influential revolutionary leaders. Born the son of a farm laborer and a household servant in 1926, Castro recalled threatening to burn the house down unless he was sent to school. He went on to earn a law degree in his native Cuba, but not before both taking part in an abortive attempt to overthrow the government of the Dominican Republic and playing minor-league baseball as part of the New York Yankees organization.

Castro spent most of his legal career doing pro bono work on behalf of Cuba's poor and attempted to fight corruption by running for political office, but he soon abandoned hope for change by constitutional means. In 1953 he and his brother Raul led an abortive attack on an army barracks in Santiago de Cuba. Castro was imprisoned by Batista's government, but was later released and went to Mexico. In 1956 he set out with eighty-one other rebels on a barely seaworthy boat to land in Cuba and join a revolt against Batista, but the expedition failed miserably, and Castro and his band retreated to the rugged Sierra Maestra to continue the fight. Waging a guerrilla war against Batista, Castro's forces never numbered more than 300, but he steadily gained support among Cuba's peasants. Finally, in late 1958, Batista's forces collapsed and a revolutionary junta led by Castro gained control of Cuba on January 1, 1959.

Once in power, Castro initiated a program of agrarian reforms. He also demanded the nationalization of U.S. property in Cuba, at first expressing willingness to compensate American owners but later confiscating foreign property. These actions

situation has reached a turning point. . . . I think the characteristic of the situation today is the East wind prevailing over the West wind."[17] In addition to gaining new allies in various Third World countries, the Soviet economy and technological progress seemed to be growing. Most spectacularly, the Soviets launched the world's first artificial satellite, Sputnik, which orbited the earth in October 1957. This accomplishment caused many in the West to fear that the Soviets had gained a major technological advantage over the United States that could be exploited for military purposes. In particular, the powerful booster rockets could carry nuclear weapons at a high speed to targets within a 4,000-mile radius. Khrushchev deliberately fed those fears, never missing an opportunity to mention the USSR's arsenal of rocket weapons, although the Soviets would not deploy missiles capable of striking the United States until 1960.[18]

Nevertheless, the Sputnik launching signaled to many that the U.S. strategic doctrine of massive retaliation against any Communist attack anywhere in the world was no longer viable, because the USSR now seemed able to strike back against American territory. The Eisenhower administration was blamed for allowing a purported "missile gap" to develop, which presidential candidate John Kennedy exploited, although it was later proved that such a gap had never existed. The Eisenhower administration had not moved to markedly and Castro's revolutionary ideology quickly soured relations between Havana and Washington, and the United States became increasingly convinced that Castro's regime was oriented toward communism. When the United States placed economic sanctions on Cuba, Castro turned to the USSR for support and eventually became Moscow's most valuable ally in the Western Hemisphere.

The clumsy attempt to overthrow his government in the Bay of Pigs fiasco in 1961 destroyed any hope of reconciliation with the United States, and there is some evidence suggesting that Castro requested Soviet missiles to defend his regime. For whatever reasons, the USSR subsequently attempted to base missiles in Cuba, which led to the Cuban Missile Crisis in 1962.

Throughout the 1970s Castro became a major proponent of revolution in the Third World, providing arms to Communist insurgents in Central America and sending Cuban troops to fight for leftist regimes in Africa. Meanwhile, the USSR sent huge subsidies to prop up Cuba's economy, donating an estimated $7 billion annually in the 1980s. After Mikhail Gorbachev came to power in Moscow and the USSR adopted less confrontational policies, many Soviets began to see Castro's Cuba as more liability than asset, and subsidies were drastically cut before the collapse of the USSR in 1991.

Unlike Communist leaders in Eastern Europe, however, Castro survived the demise of Soviet communism, and as of 1994 he was Cuba's leader and a triumphant role model to many Latin American revolutionary socialists.

change its defense policies because it was confident (with good reason) that the threat to the United States was minimal.

The psychological effect of the development of strategic missiles, however, was undeniable. For the first time, Americans were confronted with the possibility that they could become immediate victims in a nuclear war. A peace culture emerged in reaction to these developments, epitomized by the comment by renowned British philosopher Bertrand Russell that civilization was "better red than dead." Among other things, the Gaither Committee report, a presidential commission study, called for the creation of nationwide fallout shelters. This period was famous for a proliferation of antinuclear literature and art warning of the dangers inherent in destructive superpower confrontations. Nevil Shute's novel *On the Beach* tells a morose story about the last survivors of a nuclear war, while Stanley Kubrick's comedy film *Dr. Strangelove* portrays a mad American officer who brings the world to its final disaster with the help of warmongering generals and scientists.

New Tensions: Berlin and Cuba

While fear of the possibility of nuclear war and the political sting of recent Soviet gains spread throughout the West, Khrushchev felt strong enough to press the USSR's advantage. In November 1958 he suddenly announced that the Soviet Union had decided to renounce the remnants of the joint Allied occupation regime in Berlin. In subsequent notes to the United States, Britain, and France, he demanded that they withdraw their occupation forces from West Berlin, declare it a demilitarized "free city," and negotiate directly with the German Democratic Republic (East Germany) on terms of access to the city. He threatened that if the Western powers did not make an agreement with the East Germans within six months, the Soviet Union would give the German Democratic Republic control of Western military supply routes to Berlin. This action was tantamount to renouncing the post–World War II arrangements for Germany, and it revived memories of the darkest days of the Berlin blockade. With the backing of its NATO allies, the United States refused to accede to Khrushchev's demands, and Dulles replied that NATO would oppose any attempt to change the status of Berlin "if need be by military force."[19]

At the same time, a new arena of East-West conflict was emerging closer to American shores. A revolution brought Fidel Castro to power in Cuba in January 1959. Castro's forces had overthrown a much-hated dictator, Fulgencio Batista, who had maintained close ties to the United States. Washington reacted strongly to Castro's accession to power, especially when his pro-communist leanings became apparent. When the United States levied sanctions on Cuba, Castro turned to the USSR for aid. The existence of a Soviet-supported regime just ninety miles off the coast of Florida inflamed U.S. leaders and fomented fears that other countries in Latin America would follow Cuba into the Soviet camp.

Summitry

Despite Soviet technological achievements and their confident posture, it is now widely known that the USSR was much weaker in the mid and late 1950s than it appeared at the time. Though Soviet propaganda emphasized the USSR's achievements in military and space technology, U.S. intelligence, including flights of the secret U-2 spy plane over the Soviet Union, revealed to Eisenhower that American military power was still superior to Soviet capabilities. The Soviet Union and its allies also failed to catch their Western competitors in terms of gross national product, per capita income, consumption, or any other major economic indicator. In many Third World countries, although the Soviets seemed to be gaining at America's expense as they offered aid for major projects, such as Egypt's Aswan Dam, Soviet aid did not always lead to a pro-Soviet political orientation. In the Middle East, bitter disputes between pro- and anti-Nasser Arab states eroded Soviet influence in the region.[20] Additionally, the Sino-Soviet dispute, exacerbated by Moscow's refusal to assist China in developing nuclear weapons, would dominate Communist politics for the next three decades.

In this environment of apparent Communist strength and actual Soviet weakness, Khrushchev took advantage of a diplomatic opening created by the death of staunchly anticommunist Secretary of State Dulles in May 1959 to propose a meeting with Eisenhower. In September 1959 Khrushchev traveled throughout the United States, meeting the president at Camp David, mingling with

Hollywood stars such as Marilyn Monroe and Frank Sinatra, and visiting American families in San Francisco. A summit was scheduled to be held in Paris the next year, which was to be followed by a return visit by President Eisenhower to Moscow. It was hoped that major breakthroughs, such as a settlement of the Berlin issue and a nuclear test–ban treaty, would be agreed upon at the planned summits.

The U-2 Incident

This interlude of relative harmony between the two superpowers proved short-lived, however. The European allies were alarmed by the possibility that the United States might act on the German question without taking their interests into account. The conservative West German government, under Konrad Adenauer, pressed for a tough American stance at the Paris meeting. Charles de Gaulle, the French president, was also suspicious of American moves.

On May 1, 1960, the Soviets shot down a U-2 spy plane 1200 miles inside the USSR, something that American officials had believed impossible. When Washington initially denied that any overflight of Soviet airspace had occurred, Khrushchev exhibited both the wreckage of the plane and the pilot, Francis Gary Powers, who had been captured alive. As the leaders of the United States, USSR, France, and Britain gathered in Paris for the summit meeting, the premier issued threats and demanded that Eisenhower apologize for violating Soviet airspace. He added that whatever the United States did about the U-2 incident, it would be necessary for Eisenhower to cancel his scheduled visit to Russia. The president refused to apologize, and in fact blamed Soviet actions for necessitating American espionage activities. Khrushchev may have already written off the possibility of a summit before the U-2 incident, but the affair gave him an opportunity to place the blame for its collapse on the United States. In any case, the summit never took place, and the rivalry between the superpowers continued with renewed vehemence.

JFK, Cold Warrior

Eisenhower's vice president, Richard Nixon, narrowly lost the 1960 presidential election, and in 1961 John F. Kennedy (JFK) took office, committed to a more activist American foreign policy. Seeking a wider range of strategic options, the Kennedy administration instituted the doctrine of **flexible response,** which was designed to correct the shortcomings of massive retaliation. Under the new strategy, the United States would be prepared to respond in kind to Soviet moves on a variety of levels, from guerrilla war through conventional challenges to the ultimate stage of nuclear war. Rather than relying solely on nuclear deterrence, flexible response sought to increase America's credibility in dealing with a wide range of security problems by providing a correspondingly wide range of options for dealing with threats.

Committed to taking a new approach to U.S. foreign policy, the new administration had its work cut out for it. The first challenge Kennedy faced involved

WHAT WOULD YOU DO?

You are the leader of the Soviet Union in 1962. Someone in the Politburo has presented you with a risky, yet possibly golden, opportunity to extend your global influence. It involves the secret installation of missiles—capable of striking the United States—in Cuba.

If successful, the ploy could accomplish several important foreign- and domestic-policy objectives simultaneously. First, it could redress the strategic imbalance with the American capitalist ruling class and offer you a bargaining chip by which you could gain the removal of U.S. Jupiter missiles in Turkey. Second, it offers a potential means of deterring another imperialist invasion against Castro; after all, having failed miserably to oust Castro in the Bay of Pigs fiasco, the United States is even less likely to repeat this action against a nuclearized Cuba. Third, it provides a chance to convince the Chinese that "peaceful coexistence" with the U.S. imperialists does not mean you are unwilling to

redressing the supposed "missile gap." Rapid U.S. production of bombers, **intercontinental ballistic missiles (ICBMs),** and **submarine-launched ballistic missiles (SLBMs)** provided a balanced strategic triad of land-, sea-, and air-based weapons (see Chapter Eleven). Khrushchev's bluff that the USSR could outproduce the United States in missiles had now been called, since the Soviet Union had actually developed only a minimal missile capability by the early 1960s, and the strategic balance remained in America's favor throughout his tenure in the Kremlin.

Although the "missile gap" proved to be a hoax, the United States nevertheless appeared weak. In March 1961, the CIA orchestrated an invasion by Cuban insurgents at the Bay of Pigs intended to provoke a general rebellion against Castro and topple his government. The invasion was poorly planned and executed, and ended in disaster when Castro's forces easily defeated the invaders. This ham-handed attempt to unseat Castro only reinforced the image of declining American power.

Kennedy tried to counteract Soviet influence in developing countries with comprehensive programs of technical assistance (including the Peace Corps, which Kennedy created) and economic and military aid, but the United States continued to face hard choices in its policies in the Third World. Kennedy's comments on the repressive Trujillo regime in the Dominican Republic illustrated the problem:

> There are three possibilities in a descending order of preference: a decent democratic regime, a continuation of the Trujillo regime [a right-wing dictatorship], or a Castro regime. We ought to aim at the first, but we really can't renounce the second until we are sure that we can avoid the third.[21]

Meanwhile, back in Europe, tensions in Germany increased steadily. East German refugees, a high proportion of whom were professionals, intellectuals, and skilled workers, continued to flee to the west, creating a serious "brain drain" for East Germany. To stanch the flow of refugees, the East German government seize opportunities to extend Communist influence in the Third World, thereby pulling China back into your camp. Finally, it could boost your popularity at home.

On the other hand, if the ploy is unsuccessful, it could be prohibitively expensive. First, instead of treating the move as a fait accompli, as it did with the construction of the Berlin Wall, the U.S. imperialists could call your bluff and demand removal of the missiles. You are aware from intelligence reports that the U.S. president is still under tremendous pressure from the opposition Republican party to "get tough" with Castro. The United States might actually remove the missiles and Castro through a full-scale invasion and/or airstrike. Second, it could further alienate the PRC leadership and possibly increase Communist China's influence in the Third World. Finally, it could provoke a military or a party coup against you.

This is a risky decision.

What would you do?

suggested the creation of a barrier around West Berlin, and Khrushchev agreed. Without warning, on August 13, 1961, barbed wire barricades were thrown up all around the city, which were soon replaced with concrete. The Western sectors were surrounded by the Berlin Wall. The Western Allies would have had to resort to force to remove the wall, but they were unwilling to take that risk, although at one point during the crisis, U.S. and Soviet tanks confronted each other at the Brandenburg Gate on the dividing line between East and West Berlin. The U.S. government portrayed the outcome of this new Berlin crisis as a win for the West, as West Berlin remained in Allied hands, but it was never Khrushchev's intention to take over the Western sectors. Both sides could therefore claim victory, but the fact remained that Kennedy had been unable to respond effectively to a Soviet challenge.

Cuban Missile Crisis

By 1962 the United States was far ahead of the USSR in long-range missile capability, but Khrushchev may still have believed that the young American president lacked the resolve necessary to prevail in a direct confrontation. Sometime in 1962 the Soviet leader ordered offensive missiles to be secretly placed in Cuba. His motives in doing so remain unclear. He may have been trying to exploit a perceived American political weakness, to partially redress the U.S.–Soviet strategic balance, to forestall another attempt to overthrow Castro, or all of the above. Apparently, he assumed that the deployment could be kept secret until the missiles were operational, whereupon Washington would be forced to accept their presence as it had been forced to accept the sudden construction of the Berlin Wall.

Khrushchev's gamble failed, however, when U.S. intelligence discovered the missiles in October 1962, before Soviet crews could make them operational. The resulting confrontation was the most acute crisis of the Cold War. Kennedy had publicly warned Khrushchev that he could never allow the Soviet Union to station offensive weapons on Cuba. The young president, under attack by Republicans for his supposed soft policy on Cuba, could not allow the Soviets to achieve a major political victory by stationing nuclear weapons so close to American shores.

In order to compel Khrushchev to withdraw the missiles from Cuba, Kennedy and his advisors decided to impose a blockade on all shipments of weapons to the island. When he revealed the missiles' existence to the world and announced the blockade on Cuba, Kennedy demanded the removal of the missiles, warning that their use against any country in the Western Hemisphere would be regarded as an attack by the USSR against the United States. The possibility of nuclear war seemed closer during the Cuban Missile Crisis than at any other time before or since. If the USSR did not back down, the United States clearly intended to remove the missile sites by military action, which would have involved combat between Soviet and American forces.

Because the United States possessed conventional military superiority in the Caribbean region and held an indisputable advantage in strategic nuclear forces, once Khrushchev's bluff was called, he had no real choice but to back down. In exchange for the removal of the missiles, the United States promised not to invade Cuba again and to withdraw its own short-range Jupiter missiles from Turkey (a withdrawal Kennedy had previously ordered but which had not been implemented). Despite these gestures intended to avoid the humiliation of its adversary, the crisis ended with an embarrassing defeat for Moscow.[22]

The Cuban Missile Crisis had a number of important consequences. First, and paradoxically, one of the initial results of the crisis was a sudden abatement in Cold War tensions. Having confronted each other at the brink of war, both Kennedy and Khrushchev enjoyed the opportunity to reduce hostilities through a series of U.S.–Soviet agreements, including a limited nuclear test–ban treaty and the establishment of a telegraphic "Hot Line" that enabled Moscow and Washington to communicate with each other instantly in case of a crisis anywhere in the world. As Kennedy put it, "Relations with the Soviet Union could now be contained within the framework of mutual awareness of the impossibility of achieving any gains through war."[23]

Second, however, Soviet leaders set about challenging America's strategic nuclear superiority with renewed urgency. The Kremlin attempted to catch up with the United States, determined that it would never again be caught in as weak a position as it had been in the Cuban Missile Crisis. The USSR achieved strategic parity with the United States by the late 1960s, but only at tremendous cost. Moscow's strategic programs diverted vast human and material resources away from development of industry, technology, and social welfare, creating hardships and distortions that would eventually lead to the collapse of the Soviet economy and political system.

Finally, after Washington successfully demonstrated its resolve and military strength in the missile crisis, many Americans became overconfident, believing that the United States could accomplish any task in foreign policy to which it was fully committed. Whereas, in the period leading up to the Cuban Missile Crisis, the United States had overestimated Soviet power, now it was underestimating the difficulties in becoming an international police officer against communism.

INTENSIFIED COMPETITION, 1964–1968

Once again, another promising turn in the Cold War was quickly reversed. The assassination of Kennedy in November 1963 and the overthrow of Khrushchev the following year brought new teams of leaders to both capitals. Hostile tendencies that Kennedy and Khrushchev had endeavored to overcome were gradually reinforced. The new Soviet leaders, Leonid Brezhnev and Aleksey Kosygin, increased military spending (especially on strategic weapons), sustained repressive regimes in Eastern Europe, and found themselves in an intensified competition with China.

On the American side, the new president, Lyndon B. Johnson (LBJ), had little experience and, initially, not much interest in foreign policy, but was nevertheless committed to a strong anticommunist position worldwide. His administration saw both China and the USSR as dangerous threats, and these fears were reinforced by China's explosion of an atomic device in October 1964. American fears of the spread of Castroism in Latin America reached new heights. As a result, the number of authoritarian dictatorships increased, with implicit or explicit American encouragement and assistance. In April 1965 Johnson sent U.S. Marines to thwart a move that would have returned to power the elected president of the Dominican Republic, Juan Bosch, who had replaced the assassinated dictator Trujillo. Bosch had in turn been ousted by the military, but Johnson feared the instability that was accompanying the attempted return to democracy. He seemed comfortable enough with the junta that had returned that country to authoritarianism, as long as the regime could keep the Caribbean country out of the reach of communism. In Johnson's own words, "We don't propose to sit here in our rocking chair with our hands folded and let the Communists set up any government in the Western Hemisphere."[24] In the end, after American intervention, new elections were held in the Dominican Republic and a conservative president was chosen.

The Cold War had now reached a point of tragic irony. The period after the Cuban Missile Crisis boiled over with U.S. self-confidence and zeal. Rushing about from one trouble spot to another, America almost seemed destined to trip over its own power. It stumbled and fell over Vietnam.

Vietnam

In 1960 a guerrilla movement officially known as the National Liberation Front but commonly referred to as the Vietcong began to attack the American-backed government of South Vietnamese President Ngo Dinh Diem with strong support from North Vietnam. Diem's policies had alienated various sectors of the

Soldiers of the U.S. 1st Infantry wade through swampy South Vietnamese territory in October 1965. By the late 1960s, more than 500,000 U.S. troops were engaged in the Vietnam conflict.
Source: © UPI/Bettmann.

South Vietnamese population, especially in the countryside, providing opportunities for Communist influence. Kennedy had attempted to use Vietnam to show that it was possible to defeat communist-backed wars of national liberation, and he increased American military and economic aid to the South. Building upon the several hundred advisors sent by Eisenhower, Kennedy increased U.S. military personnel to 16,000 by 1963. Nevertheless, Diem's position continued to deteriorate, and he was killed in 1963 (two weeks before JFK was assassinated) in a military coup to which the United States acquiesced. A succession of generals followed as

STRATEGIC PARITY AND THE NONPROLIFERATION TREATY

The period that began in the early 1960s with joint Soviet-American moves to limit conflict ended with escalated military activity by both superpowers. Throughout the 1960s the USSR built an arsenal of nuclear weapons and missiles roughly equal to that of the United States. The only major breakthrough of the period came in 1968, with the signing of the Nuclear Nonproliferation Treaty. Three of the five nuclear powers, the United States, the USSR, and Britain (China and France initially refused to join), pledged not to employ nuclear weapons against or share nuclear weapons technology with non-nuclear states that signed the treaty. In return, the non-nuclear nations pledged not to develop nuclear weapons.

This treaty was a major achievement and certainly slowed the spread of nuclear weapons, but it could not prevent countries such as Israel, India, Pakistan, Iraq, South Africa, and North Korea from proceeding with their nuclear programs.

president, each ousted by a new military figure hoping to pursue the war more effectively and gain the spoils of power for himself.

It became clear by 1965 that stronger American intervention would be required in order to prevent a Vietcong victory in the South. President Johnson was forced to choose between withdrawal, an intermediate level of escalation, or a full-scale level of escalation. LBJ initially chose the middle option for U.S. intervention, which meant an immediate bombing campaign of the North and deployment of ground forces to protect airbases. As the war progressed, however, the administration repeatedly determined that more troops were required and continued to send more, only to conclude that still more forces were needed.

By mid-1968, 500,000 American troops were fighting in Vietnam, but the United States was no closer than before to achieving the military or political breakthrough necessary to salvage the South Vietnamese regime and permit U.S. withdrawal. American casualties mounted, eventually numbering some 58,000 deaths. The seemingly endless and fruitless intervention in Vietnam turned the American public against the war, diminished its enthusiasm for the competition with the USSR, and compromised U.S. credibility with many of its allies, especially in Europe. Meanwhile, Moscow sought to capitalize on America's diminished prestige and weakened political will to resist Soviet expansion. In order to compete with China for influence in North Vietnam, Moscow provided Hanoi with military and economic assistance. Thus, the Vietnam War enabled the Soviet Union to increase its standing throughout the Third World while the United States became vilified for conducting an ineffective campaign that resulted in more than 2.5 million military and civilian deaths.[25]

The Prague Spring

The tense period precipitated by American intervention in Vietnam reached its apex in September 1968. A new leadership in Czechoslovakia had attempted to avoid the mistakes of Hungarian rebels in 1956. Czech reformers under Alexander Dubcek reassured the Soviets of their allegiance to Communist principles, hoping to indicate to the Kremlin that they meant only to liberalize internally and posed no threat to the USSR. But to the entrenched Communist officials in power in Moscow, liberalization, even if limited to domestic affairs, was regarded as a major threat. The Soviet leadership therefore chose to crush this liberal Communist movement and brought a Soviet-backed regime to power. Brezhnev justified the invasion of Czechoslovakia by asserting that the USSR had the right to ensure the survival of any socialist regime on its borders, a formulation that became known in the West as the "Brezhnev Doctrine."

ERA OF DÉTENTE, 1969–1979

Although the United States had squandered a portion of its military advantage by assisting South Vietnam, the Soviet Union remained vulnerable to American pressure due to its conflict with China and its weak economy. After Johnson declined to run for reelection in 1968, the new Nixon administration finally recognized the depths of the Sino-Soviet dispute and the opportunities it represented for American diplomacy. When border clashes broke out between the USSR and China in April 1969, the Nixon administration used the conflict to gradually improve relations with China. This opening culminated in Nixon's dramatic visit to Beijing in February 1972. This visit increased American flexibility toward both China and the USSR, raised American hopes that Moscow and Beijing could aid the United States in extricating itself from the quagmire in Vietnam, and dramatically enhanced American leverage in dealing with the Soviets.

The new American policy toward China bore fruit for both sides. First, the two leading communist states did facilitate the American withdrawal from Vietnam to some extent. Second, the Communist government in Beijing was finally able to assume China's seat as a permanent member of the UN Security Council, which had been occupied previously by the Republic of China on Taiwan. (Later, during the Carter administration, the United States eventually broke diplomatic relations with Taiwan and established them with Beijing.) Finally, China's image in the United States was transformed from a radical, intractable regime to one with which commercial and diplomatic business was possible.

At the same time, the Nixon team attempted to transform the Soviet Union from a revisionist power to one comfortable with the status quo. In some ways, this was an unexpected course for Nixon to take, as he had begun his political career as a hard-line anticommunist. In particular, Nixon and his chief foreign-policy advisor, Henry Kissinger, sought to pursue three policies vis-a-vis the Soviet Union to augment cooperation.[26] First, they acknowledged that the USSR was a co-equal with the United States, a superpower. By doing so, the United

States recognized that the Soviets had achieved nuclear parity and would no longer be treated like a younger sibling. Second, they set out to create a number of institutions in the area of arms control and crisis management that would restrain the security dilemma and define acceptable behavior. Third, they sought to pursue a strategy of linkage politics, by linking problem areas in different parts of the world. The policy was intended to prevent the Soviets from seeking cooperation in one area and trying to gain unilateral advantages elsewhere. Instead, it encouraged cooperation and discouraged aggression through a combination of "carrots and sticks," especially economic inducements that could be extended as rewards and withdrawn as punishments. (In this respect, the Nixon-Kissinger policy was very similar to Kennan's original conception of containment discussed earlier in this chapter.)

After the opening to China and increased diplomatic pressure on the Kremlin, a U.S.–Soviet summit was convened in Moscow in May 1972. Washington was interested in using this opportunity to create a number of mutually supporting relationships with the Soviet Union. Nixon not only sought agreements for controlling the escalating arms race, but also Soviet assistance in ending the Vietnam War. The interests of the two superpowers dovetailed because Brezhnev sought access to Western technology and goods. The Kremlin's defense spending was becoming an increasing burden on the Soviet economy, which was proving increasingly unable to simultaneously maintain the USSR's massive military power and produce enough consumer goods for the population's basic needs.

The Moscow Summit, therefore, set the stage for an unprecedented series of agreements. First, Nixon and Brezhnev signed the first Strategic Arms Limitation Treaty, or SALT I. The two powers agreed to restrict the deployment of antiballistic missiles (ABMs, missiles capable of shooting down incoming missiles) and to cap the growth of strategic offensive missiles. Designed to stabilize the arms race, these agreements allowed both countries to continue developing nuclear arms, but placed temporary limitations on the number of weapons they could build. Most importantly, the agreement demonstrated that both sides finally understood that neither would gain from an ever-accelerating arms race. In addition to SALT I, a series of economic agreements were reached that would open the door to expanded trade, including large American grain sales to the USSR. An agreement on the "basic principles of mutual relations" was intended to spell out a "code of conduct" for the superpowers' interactions with each other and their respective allies.

This phase of the Cold War, which seemed again to promise a more cordial superpower relationship, became known as **détente** after the French word for relaxation of tensions. In Europe, these achievements reinforced a growing movement toward less hostile relations with the Soviet Union. Under Chancellor Willy Brandt, who had taken office in 1969, West Germany began to expand political and economic contacts with the USSR and East Germany. Brandt's *ostpolitik* ("eastern policy") signaled that Western aspirations for contact with and more independence for Eastern Europe could be more easily achieved through conciliation rather than confrontation. Earlier, de Gaulle had sought to place relations

ARCHITECT OF *OSTPOLITIK*

Willy Brandt (1913–1993) will be remembered as a European leader who made invaluable contributions to his own country, to the European Union, and to East-West relations. From the rise of the Nazi party to power in Germany in 1933 to the end of World War II in 1945, Brandt worked in exile in Norway and Sweden (where he changed his name from Karl Herbert Frahm) as a journalist. He returned to Germany after the war, and in 1957 was elected mayor of West Berlin. When the Berlin Wall was thrown up around his city in 1961, Brandt's courage inspired the citizens of the beleaguered city through the ensuing crisis.

As West Germany's foreign minister from 1966 to 1969 and chancellor from 1969 to 1974, Brandt worked to normalize relations with the Communist states of Eastern Europe. His plan for improving ties between the two Germanies and between West Germany and its eastern neighbors became known as *ostpolitik* (eastern policy). Brandt's first step as foreign minister was to reverse previous West German policy by accepting the existence of East Germany and Germany's post-1945 borders.

between Paris and Moscow on a less hostile footing. As these European initiatives had preceded the Nixon administration's openings to the USSR and China, the United States could proceed with détente with the confidence that the new American policy would be accepted by its allies in NATO.

Tensions in Détente

As détente progressed, however, it became increasingly apparent that both sides' expectations for the new superpower relationship varied significantly and that neither side fully understood the other's perspective. In the United States, détente was intended to transform the nature of superpower relations from one of confrontation to one of collaborative competition by giving the USSR a "stake in the system," which would create incentives for both powers to avoid challenging each other's interests. To the Soviet Union, however, détente meant that Cold War competition would continue, but would be conducted by new rules. From the Soviet viewpoint, there was no contradiction between détente and support for socialist or Communist "national liberation movements" throughout the Third World. Although the Soviet leaders promised to halt future aggressive actions, they still sought to make gains without directly challenging the United States, as would soon be seen clearly in the Middle East, Southeast Asia, and Africa.

The détente accords of the early 1970s also ignored domestic politics in both countries. Many Americans were uncomfortable with the idea of dealing with the USSR but ignoring its human-rights abuses. In particular, the right of

Although never formally recognizing the East German Government, he did recognize the Oder-Neisse Line as the new border between East Germany and Poland. (Following World War II, the Soviet Union moved Poland's western border about 75 miles into what had been German territory to the Oder and Western Neisse rivers.) In 1970 Brandt signed nonaggression treaties with the Soviet Union and Poland, and in 1971 he met with East German leader Walter Ulbricht to open political and trade relations between the estranged Germanies.

For his efforts to bring Eastern and Western Europe closer together, Brandt was awarded the Nobel Peace Prize in 1971. In 1974 Brandt was forced to resign as chancellor after it was revealed that one of his close assistants was an East German spy. Brandt's policies of closer integration of the European Union (EU) and improvement of ties with East Germany were continued by his successors, and ultimately came to fruition in 1990 with the reunification of Germany as part of the EU.

Soviet Jews to emigrate became a salient issue, and the Jackson-Vanik Amendment in 1975 placed limitations on the enhancement of U.S.–Soviet economic ties if the Kremlin continued to disallow Jewish emigration. Soviet leaders, for their part, viewed the linkage of trade and strategic agreements to human-rights issues as unwarranted interference in the USSR's domestic affairs.

American domestic politics were entering a turbulent period as the Vietnam War and the Watergate scandal eroded America's confidence in its leaders. The Vietnam experience made many in the United States wary of getting involved in faraway conflicts. Thus, when South Vietnam was overrun by North Vietnamese forces in the spring of 1975, the United States did not intervene. Halting Communist aggression became a secondary issue, and stopping any further disastrous foreign escapades attained primary importance. "No More Vietnams" became the slogan of the day in the 1970s. This was quite ironic, as the resolve to have "No More Koreas" in the 1950s had led to early U.S. involvement in Vietnam.

Any Soviets who might have anticipated a variety of gains in Southeast Asia, however, were probably disappointed by the emerging conflicts between Communist states. In 1975, the year of Communist victory in Vietnam, a civil war in Cambodia ended with a Chinese-backed Communist insurgency, the Khmer Rouge, in control of the country. The Khmer Rouge regime, led by Pol Pot, proved to be unspeakably brutal. It turned the country into "killing fields," carrying out a program of genocide that killed as many as 2 million people. The capital city of Phnom Penh was practically depopulated, and anyone who wore glasses risked being summarily executed as a subversive intellectual. This tyrannical regime was not ousted by the West, but was overthrown in 1978 by an invasion by the neighboring Communists in Vietnam, who promptly installed a puppet regime. This action and other conflicts led to a border war between China and Vietnam in 1979. (See Chapter Six for details.)

Escalation of conflict in the Middle East further undermined détente. In October 1973 the Soviet Union did not explicitly warn the United States of an impending attack by Syria and Egypt against Israel. Issuing a clear warning would have entailed significant political costs for the USSR, and an order from Moscow to evacuate the dependents of Soviet personnel in Egypt and Syria just before the attack may have been intended as a tacit warning, but the United States did not perceive it as such. The result was the Yom Kippur War (known also as the October War and described in Chapter Six) in which both the United States and USSR resupplied their clients with massive airlifts of arms. Washington was further antagonized when the USSR encouraged additional Arab states both to join the fray and to impose an oil embargo against the United States. In an effort to pressure the United States to end its support for Israel, Arab members of OPEC (Organization of Petroleum Exporting Countries) joined together in stopping oil shipments to the United States. The OPEC embargo caused a major energy crisis, but U.S. aid to Israel continued. U.S. and Soviet efforts to bring about a cease-fire eventually succeeded, but only after the United States placed its nuclear forces on alert in response to hints that Moscow might send troops to support Egypt.

The United States and the USSR thus continued their global competition despite détente. Moscow expanded its military presence in Cuba, Southeast Asia, and Africa, dispatching military advisors and leasing naval and air bases. In 1976 Cuban troops and Soviet military assistance were sent to aid a Soviet-backed faction in the civil war in newly independent Angola. Both the Nixon and Ford administrations continued their commitment to many Cold War–type policies in order to prevent the emergence of regimes in the Third World that threatened U.S. interests. In 1973, for example, the CIA was complicit in the violent overthrow of Chile's elected Marxist president, Salvador Allende. The United States also played by the old rules in postwar Mideast diplomacy when it left the Soviets on the sidelines in a series of limited accords between Israel and Egypt and Syria in the months which followed the October War. In many ways, détente between the United States and the Soviets more closely resembled the old Cold War than some new form of superpower relationship.

From Dialogue to Discord: The Carter Administration

The next American president, Jimmy Carter, took office in 1977 committed to improving the U.S.–Soviet relationship. Carter sought to undo the conceptual and practical assumptions inherent in American policy that had led to Vietnam in the first place. "We have fought fire with fire, never thinking that fire is better quenched with water," Carter declared.[27] The Carter administration placed more emphasis on economic factors in world politics. The energy crisis that followed the 1973 war in the Middle East led to petroleum shortages and high prices in the West. To Carter, growing international interdependence as epitomized by the energy problem seemed more central to U.S. international concerns than any threat of international communism.

Carter's foreign policy was decidedly more attuned to human-rights questions throughout the world than previous American policy had been. Human-rights issues became an important part of the Conference on Security and Cooperation in Europe (CSCE), which first convened in 1975 in Helsinki and later became a permanent international organization. The conference accepted many long-held Soviet positions on political issues in return for Soviet promises to abide by agreements that guaranteed human rights for the citizens of all participating countries. The Kremlin did not take these rights guarantees seriously at first, but many Soviet and East European citizens did, forming "Helsinki Watch" committees to monitor Soviet compliance with human-rights conventions.

Although Carter's policies achieved notable advances in the field of human rights, his less confrontational stance toward the USSR in the early years of his administration may have led some Soviets to believe that the United States would not oppose the further expansion of Moscow's influence, especially in the Third World. Cuban forces intervened in conflicts in Ethiopia and Angola in order to help solidify Soviet positions in those African countries. Cuban actions could not have been taken without Soviet approval, since the USSR was heavily subsidizing Cuba's international military actions (as well as its domestic economy).

Soviet actions and American reactions in the Third World heightened mutual suspicions and thereby threatened progress on arms control. In spite of mutual agreement on the need for another arms-control accord, the United States and USSR squabbled endlessly over the details of a new treaty. An initial agreement between Brezhnev and Ford had been reached in the Soviet city of Vladivostok in 1974, but the talks dragged on, complicated by criticism from American conservatives and by Soviet deployments of new nuclear missiles. In 1979 Carter and Brezhnev finally signed the SALT II treaty, which set a cap on all offensive strategic weapons. Critics argued, however, that the new treaty left American land-based ICBMs vulnerable to destruction by a Soviet surprise attack, reservations that delayed ratification of the new treaty. (As described in Chapter Fourteen, the U.S. Senate must approve all treaties signed by the United States before they can come into force.)

By the late 1970s it appeared unlikely that the Soviet Union and the United States could reach a modus vivendi even when both sought means of controlling the competition. Domestic influences in each country and unanticipated developments around the world seemed either to thwart attempts at cooperation or to tempt one or both sides to compromise détente. In 1979, for example, the Shah of Iran, one of America's most important and long-standing allies in the Third World, was ousted from power by an Islamic fundamentalist revolution. Many Americans feared that Moscow would capitalize on the revolution to advance its interests in Iran. (In fact, however, the Iranian revolution worried the Soviet Union as well, as many Soviets feared that Islamic radicalism might spread across the border and provoke unrest in the USSR's predominantly Muslim Central Asian republics.)

Also in 1979, in Nicaragua, the forty-year-old dictatorship of the Somoza family was overthrown in a rebellion led by a socialist-oriented alliance, the Sandinista Front. Although Carter attempted to work with the Sandinistas at first, growing consternation over their socialist ideology and support of radical insurgents in neighboring countries increased American opposition to the new government, while the USSR and Cuba extended political and material support to the Sandinista regime.

THE COLD WAR RETURNS, 1979–1985

The Soviet-American disputes arising during the Carter administration might have been resolved in a manner that would have preserved détente, albeit in a diminished form. At the end of 1979, however, the Kremlin took an action that seriously damaged the possibility of a cooperative relationship between Washington and Moscow.

Invasion of Afghanistan

In December 1979 the USSR sent 80,000 troops into Afghanistan to overthrow the existing fledgling Marxist government and replace it with a stronger pro-Soviet regime in that mountainous nation. The invasion marked the first time the USSR had deployed a large number of troops outside of the satellite states of Eastern Europe. The reasons why Soviet leaders felt they could take such a blatantly forceful step without serious international political consequences remain unclear. Perhaps they had become accustomed to the Carter administration's lack of strong resistance to Soviet-sponsored activities in the Third World. Perhaps Moscow believed that the invasion would be quickly successful and forgotten just as rapidly. Or perhaps Brezhnev and other Soviet Communist leaders were hopelessly out of touch with domestic and international political realities and consequently confident that Afghanistan would accept communism without a fight.

The invasion was denounced in the West and much of the Third World as an act of naked aggression. In actuality, the invasion proved disastrous both for Soviet domestic politics and for the morale of Soviet troops. Soviet military resources were seriously depleted when an alliance of Islamic groups established a guerrilla campaign based in neighboring Pakistan that was supported by the United States.

In an effort to coerce the Soviet Union to withdraw, Carter suspended grain sales to the USSR, withdrew the SALT II agreements from consideration by the Senate, increased defense spending, and refused to allow the U.S. Olympic Team to participate in the 1980 Summer Olympics in Moscow. These steps failed to convince Moscow to withdraw its forces, however, and Soviet troops soon became bogged down in a quagmire in Afghanistan just as American troops had become mired in Vietnam fifteen years earlier.

Reagan and the Reagan Doctrine

The war in Afghanistan pushed America toward a revival of Cold War perceptions. The rise of a renewed Cold War in turn contributed to the election of Ronald Reagan as U.S. president in 1980. Although Carter had increased defense spending during the latter part of his term, Reagan expanded defense budgets still further. Through both direct U.S. intervention and indirect support for insurgencies, Reagan abandoned the policy of détente and returned to an assertive form of containment. Like Truman at the outset of the Cold War, Reagan couched his arguments for opposition to Soviet expansion in terms of moral duty, labeling the Soviet Union "the focus of evil in the modern world."[28]

Supporting indigenous anticommunist insurgencies came to be the Reagan administration's specialty. The resulting so-called **Reagan Doctrine** was played out in a variety of locations around the world. Anticommunist insurgents were encouraged in Angola, Cambodia, and, most controversially, in Nicaragua, where assistance was provided to the ***Contra*** rebels even after Congress prohibited direct military aid. Governments threatened by Soviet- or Cuban-supported insurgencies also received substantial assistance, especially those in Central America such as El Salvador and Guatemala. The United States unsuccessfully intervened in Lebanon in 1982 in an attempt to restore the unity of the country in the wake of a long civil war. In 1983 Reagan sent U.S. forces to Grenada to defeat a newly imposed Marxist government supported by Cuban advisors and construction troops. Afghan rebels were supplied with highly effective Stinger missiles that brought down Soviet aircraft in great numbers. The growing successes of the rebels confounded Soviet forces, and the USSR finally abandoned its war effort and withdrew its troops in 1989.

Reagan's policies in the 1980s helped reverse what many had viewed as a decline in U.S. power and influence in the 1970s, but they didn't come cheap. During his presidency, Reagan authorized more than $2 trillion in defense spending, increasing the size and quality of American nuclear and conventional forces. Critics claimed these defense expenditures wasted American resources that were needed to address domestic problems. Reagan's political popularity, however, enabled him to continue his defense policy. Despite protests from peace activists in the United States and Europe, he carried out the deployment of intermediate-range nuclear missiles to Europe, which NATO had agreed upon during the Carter administration to counter a Soviet buildup of missiles designed for use against European targets.

PERESTROIKA AND THE END OF THE COLD WAR, 1985–1991

While the Cold War was being fought with renewed vehemence in the international arena in the early 1980s, the Soviet Union began experiencing a series of domestic political upheavals. Brezhnev died in 1982, and both of his successors died in office within a year of acceding to power in the Kremlin. Consequently, Soviet policy entered a period of inertia as the Reagan Doctrine applied pressure to the USSR and its allies. The shooting down of a Korean Airlines flight bound from New York to Seoul in September 1983 symbolized the stagnation of Soviet policies at home and abroad. While the aircraft had accidentally strayed over Soviet territory, the fact that the Soviets shot down a civilian airliner that was not moving in a suspicious manner indicated either a callous lack of consideration for civilian life, bureaucratic inefficiency, or gross incompetence. By the mid-1980s, many Soviets were convinced that the Communist system in their country was suffering from all three of these ills.

In 1985, when Mikhail Gorbachev assumed leadership of the Soviet Union, Soviet-American relations had reached low ebb, recalling the tense early days of the Cold War, and the Soviet political and economic system was in need of a massive overhaul. Several important changes occurred within the Soviet Union itself as Gorbachev's policies of *glasnost* ("political openness") and *perestroika* ("economic restructuring") promoted democratization and free markets. However, on the whole, the economic reforms did not go far enough to reinvigorate the USSR's economy, while political changes swept forward at a pace that was exhilarating to some and threatening to others. As the 1990s began, the entire Communist system was being challenged and was failing to overcome the obstacles it faced.

The liberalization that began in Soviet society spread to Eastern Europe, culminating in a series of revolutions in 1989. Regimes that had taken decades to establish were overthrown within months or weeks and even, in Czechoslovakia and Romania, in a matter of days. The deterioration of living standards and the perceived illegitimacy of the governments of these Eastern European countries led to mass uprisings that erupted as soon as the Soviet Union abandoned the Brezhnev Doctrine and declined to use its forces to keep Communist governments in power. Popular movements, such as *Solidarity* in Poland, that had been in perilous existence for years were finally able to assume power in their countries. In an ironic domino effect, the governments of Eastern Europe fell one by one, first Poland, followed by Hungary, East Germany, Czechoslovakia, and Romania. What had seemed impossible for more than a generation finally occurred when the Berlin Wall was dismantled in November 1989, and Germany was reunified in 1990. Thus, appropriately, the Cold War ended where it had begun, in Eastern Europe. An abortive coup in Moscow by hard-line Communists attempting to resurrect the old order in August 1991 resulted in the final discrediting of the old regime and the disintegration of the Soviet Union, bringing the era of U.S.–Soviet antagonism to a close.

WHY DID THE COLD WAR END?

The Cold War between the United States and the Soviet Union lasted for more than four decades and at times took on the appearance of a permanent fixture in international politics. It had arisen gradually and predictably, but it ended abruptly and in a manner that caught the entire world by surprise. As with the Cold War's origins, a variety of possible explanations have been advanced for its end, each corresponding to one of the images of world politics and levels of analysis presented in Chapter One.

The Gorbachev Factor

Many analysts who adopt the "great-man" theory of world politics point to Mikhail Gorbachev and argue that the end of the Cold War could have only come about with someone of his character and stature at the helm. Just as an individual like Stalin or Truman might have been a necessary ingredient in causing the Cold War or influencing its nature, this argument contends that it took someone like Gorbachev to bring it to a close. With initial hesitancy but growing energy, Gorbachev worked to reverse the downward trend in superpower relations. Early in his tenure in office, he stated his intention to put the U.S.–Soviet relationship on a new nonconfrontational footing:

> We certainly do not need an "enemy image" of America, neither for domestic nor foreign-policy interests. An imaginary or real enemy is needed only if one is bent on maintaining tension, on confrontation with far-reaching and, I might add, unpredictable consequences. . . . It is a sad, tragic fact that Soviet-American relations have been slipping downhill for a long time. Short periods of improvement gave way to protracted spells of tension and a build-up in hostility. I am convinced that we have every opportunity to rectify the situation, and it appears that things are moving that way.[29]

Things were indeed moving that way. Under Gorbachev's leadership, major agreements were reached in the arms-control arena, beginning with an agreement on the elimination of intermediate-range nuclear forces (the INF Treaty) in 1987, continuing on to the Strategic Arms Reduction Treaty (START I) of 1991 by which Soviet and American strategic forces were to be reduced by approximately one-third, and progressing with further unilateral cuts on both sides announced later in 1991. Gorbachev also ended the USSR's Afghan debacle by ordering the withdrawal of Soviet forces in 1989. Had Soviet leaders with attitudes similar to those of Brezhnev or Stalin been in power during the late 1980s, the Soviet policies that contributed to the lessening of U.S.–Soviet tensions would probably never have been adopted.

The End of History

A second explanation deemphasizes the role of individual leaders and instead claims that the growing similarities in ideologies and ways of life account for the waning of the Cold War. According to this domestic-level argument, internal changes within the USSR precipitated a new foreign policy. The most important changes were Gorbachev's policies of *glasnost* and *perestroika,* which encouraged a gradual process of democratization and the attempt to open the country to free markets and foreign investment. Through these reforms, Soviets sought to embrace private property and individual rights such as freedom of religion, assembly, and speech. In fact, the Soviets sought American and Western help and sought out Western advisors to assist in making the transition from a planned to a market economy. The outcome was that in the West, the talk of reform led many to believe that Soviet society would shortly mirror its own and would no longer be foreign or threatening. Incorporating this perspective, Francis Fukuyama contends in his influential book *The End of History and the Last Man* that the victory of capitalism and democracy over communism will result in the end of global ideological conflict.[30]

End of the Evil Empire

A third explanation for the close of the Cold War holds that it ended because the Soviet Union collapsed. The decline of the Soviet Union demonstrated that the Communist system had failed. The Soviet economy was fraught with inherent inefficiencies and outdated technology, particularly after computers and information technology transformed the world economy in the 1980s. The prolonged dismal Afghan fiasco tarnished the reputation of Communist party elites. Additionally, with Gorbachev, a new generation came to power in the USSR that had experienced the economic deprivation and political stagnation of the Communist system but had not endured the immense suffering of World War II, which had so often been used as an excuse for continued demands for sacrifice to defend the (increasingly dubious) achievements of communism and to control Eastern Europe. With the USSR no longer able to compete, the superpower competition ended.

A variant of this explanation holds that competition with the West was the deciding factor in the political, social, and economic decline of the Soviet system. In part, the laggard nature of the Soviet economy was a result of the huge military expenditures necessary to compete with the United States. It is argued by some that the U.S. defense buildup, especially Reagan's **Strategic Defense Initiative (SDI)** proposals, convinced many in the Soviet elite that the USSR could no longer compete, and thus that the United States had finally won the Cold War. To this way of thinking, George Kennan's original containment doctrine had finally been proven correct, as American political and economic "counterforce" had prevailed without the need for direct military confrontation.

A New World Order

A fourth explanation for the Cold War's end considers the changes in the international system in the decades since World War II and concludes that U.S.–Soviet antagonism was bound to lessen due to the decline of bipolarity. As noted in the discussion of the origins of the Cold War, one explanation for the rise of U.S.–Soviet enmity was the advent of a bipolar distribution of power. To be sure, massive military spending exhausted the Soviet Union, but it is also apparent that the arms race took its toll on the United States. The consequence, from this viewpoint, is that in fact the real "winners" of the Cold War were countries like Japan and Germany, which rode on American coattails, allowing the United States to provide for their security while they invested in their domestic industry. The decline of the Soviet Union therefore meant that Moscow was no longer a threat to American security and that the world was moving in the direction of either unipolarity, with the United States as the sole superpower and facing no immediate challengers, or multipolarity, with Japan and Germany (or perhaps a unified Europe) as the new economic superpowers confronting the United States. (For more on polarity, see Chapters Twelve and Thirteen.)

From this systemic perspective, the Soviet Union posed only a minimal threat even before its final collapse, and a decline in U.S.–Soviet tensions could have been expected even in the absence of ideological change or a reformist leader such as Gorbachev. Many people would dispute this conclusion, but just as the reasons why the Cold War began were argued while U.S.–Soviet competition raged, the reasons why that competition ended are likely to be debated for many years as the structure of world politics assumes a new form.

CONCLUSION: MAJOR "ACHIEVEMENTS" OF THE COLD WAR

A comparison of this chapter with the previous two historical chapters reveals that the Cold War era was a relatively stable one. This is not to say there was no bloodshed during this period or that the respective clients of the two superpowers did not fight, but that in contrast to previous periods, there were no wars among the great powers. Indeed, for most of the Cold War a total war between the United States and USSR was unthinkable, as it would have meant the nuclear destruction of global civilization. As dangerous as it was, the fact that the two superpowers did not go to war despite their many differences and periodic sharp confrontations makes the Cold War a comparatively peaceful interval in the long and bloody annals of international politics.

In order to gain some understanding of the Cold War, it is necessary to wrestle with three deceptively simple questions: Why did it start, why did it end, and why did it not turn hot? The reader will not find any simple answers to these questions here and should be very suspicious of any analysis that attempts to offer them. Instead, this chapter has sought to present the reader with the basic tools necessary to begin answering these questions, including competing explanations for the Cold War's origins and decline and an outline of its most important events. As noted earlier, the explanations are related to the images and levels of analysis of world politics introduced in Chapter One. Subsequent chapters will explore these concepts in more detail, frequently referring to the events of the Cold War era to illustrate the ways in which individual, state-level, and systemic influences affect international relations. The Cold War offers many striking examples of how personalities, ideology, and the structure of the international system can have a major impact on global politics. For this reason, even if no consensus is ever achieved on the basic questions surrounding the Cold War, attempting to answer them will remain outstanding exercises for anyone desiring a better understanding of the forces that shape the contemporary world.

In the final analysis, the Cold War ended neither with a bang nor a whimper, but with a sigh of relief. The fact that Americans and Soviets resolved the dangerous conflict between their two countries without going to war with each other bodes well for the post–Cold War relationship between America and Russia, even as the uncertain political and economic future of the former Soviet republics clouds the prospects for the emergence of a successful new world order.

Perhaps more than any previous period, the Cold War saw the complete globalization of political conflict. In its wake, political fragmentation coexists with economic globalization, but the peaceful end to the once seemingly intractable U.S.–Soviet rivalry offers hope that local disputes can be kept from escalating into global confrontations, and that global conflicts need not be resolved by global war.

PRINCIPAL POINTS OF CHAPTER FOUR

1. With the end of World War II, the United States and the USSR entered into a global political competition that became known as the Cold War.

2. Possible causes of the Cold War include:

   a. Soviet actions.

   b. American actions.

   c. The beliefs and interaction of Stalin and Truman.

   d. The competing ideologies of communism and capitalism.

   e. The fact that the United States and the USSR were the only remaining great powers.

   f. Misperception by each side of the other's actions.

3. The Cold War proceeded through a series of ebbs and flows, in which tensions never escalated into actual warfare between the superpowers, but periods of quiet never resulted in total accommodation.

4. From 1945 to 1953, Moscow and Washington were frequently involved in conflicts on the periphery of the USSR. The sharpest of these were the Berlin blockade in 1948 and the Korean War from 1950 to 1953.

5. In 1953 Stalin died and Eisenhower replaced Truman, but both sides missed or ignored opportunities for reducing tensions.

6. By 1957 the Cold War became globalized as more and more developing states gained independence. The two superpowers began to compete in the Middle East, Africa, Latin America, and Southeast Asia. Hopes for reconciliation were raised at a series of summits, but dashed by the U-2 incident in 1960.

7. U.S.–Soviet rivalry continued at a high level throughout the Kennedy administration, aggravated by a second Berlin crisis. Growing superpower tensions culminated in the Cuban Missile Crisis, the most dangerous confrontation of the Cold War. Afterward, the superpowers adopted a series of limited confidence-building measures.

8. From 1964 to 1969, the Cold War heated up again as U.S. forces fought in Vietnam and the USSR built up its strategic nuclear arsenal to a level roughly equal to that of the United States, while its dispute with China intensified.

9. From 1969 to 1972, a relationship of relaxed tensions called détente developed. Nixon and Brezhnev signed SALT I and other agreements intended to foster cooperation, but these accords were undermined between 1973 and 1979 by differing understandings of the actions allowable under détente and by domestic politics in both countries.

10. In 1979 the Soviet invasion of Afghanistan ushered in a renewed freezing of the Cold War. American policy became more competitive in the 1980s under Ronald Reagan as the USSR faced growing internal political and economic problems.

11. In 1985 Gorbachev came to power in the USSR and presided over a series of reforms collectively known as *glasnost* and *perestroika*, which reduced U.S.–Soviet tensions but were only partially successful in resolving the Soviet domestic crisis.

12. By 1991 continued economic stagnation and social and political upheaval resulted in the collapse of Communist regimes in Eastern Europe and the Soviet Union. The Cold War came to an end with the reunification of Germany and the disintegration of the USSR.

13. Possible explanations for the end of the Cold War include:

    a. Mikhail Gorbachev's policies.

    b. Growing similiarities in ideologies.

    c. Collapse of Soviet power.

    d. Decline of bipolarity as other nations gained in economic and political strength.

Part III

The Legacy of
European Domination

Chapter 5

The Emergence of North-South Relations: Imperialism and Its Legacy

It should be said that the moment one has completed one's trade and loaded the Negroes on the ship, one must set sail. The reason for this is that the slaves have such a great love for their land that they despair to see that they are leaving it forever, and they die from sadness. I have heard merchants who participate in this commerce affirm that more Negroes die before leaving port than during the voyage. Some throw themselves into the sea and others knock their heads against the ship; some hold their breath until they suffocate and others starve themselves.

French author Jacques Savary, writing in 1697, as cited in Robert Louis Stein, *The French Slave Trade in the Eighteenth Century: An Old Regime Business* (Madison, WI: The University of Wisconsin Press, 1979), p. 94.

The slaves were brought in, one at a time, and mounted upon the chair before the bidders, who handled and inspected them with as little concern as if they had been examining cattle at Smithfield market. They turned them about, felt them, viewed their shape and their limbs, looked into their mouths, made them jump and throw out their arms, and subjected them to all the means of trial as if dealing with a horse or any other brute animal.

A local witness named G. Pinkard, as cited in C. M. MacInnes, *Bristol and the Slave Trade,* ed. Patrick McGrath (Bristol, UK: Historial Association, The University of Bristol, 1963), p. 15.

Two stories of slavery—one dealing with the capture of slaves; the other with their sale. Slavery was not necessarily endemic to colonialism; indeed it had largely been abolished by the last quarter of the nineteenth century. It was, however, typical of the imperial mentality. The local natives—whomever they might be—were pawns in the designs of the European powers. The religion, the lives, the economies, the resources, the culture—in sum, the fate of the local peoples—were mere putty in the hands of their colonial masters.

Major Events in Imperialism, Tenth Century to the Present

10th Century: Kievan Rus state emerges, uniting Slavic peoples of what is now Ukraine, Belarus, and western Russia; Grand Duke Vladimir adopts Greek Orthodox Christianity as the Russian state religion.

13th Century: Mongol Empire under Genghis Khan and his sons destroys the Kievan state and conquers most territory between the Black Sea and Pacific Ocean.

1389: Ottomans defeat the Serbs at the Battle of Kosovo, ending the Serb Empire.

1402: Mongol army defeats Ottoman forces at the Battle of Ankara.

1469: The two major Spanish kingdoms are unified through the marriage of Isabella I of Castile and Ferdinand II of Aragon.

1487–1488: Portuguese explorer Bartholomeu Dias leads the first European expedition to round the Cape of Good Hope.

1497–1498: Vasco da Gama rounds the Cape of Good Hope and establishes sea route between Portugal and India.

1492: Sailing for the Spanish crown, Columbus makes the first known European landing in the Western Hemisphere; Isabella I and Ferdinand II attempt to "ethnically cleanse" their kingdom by decreeing that all Jews must convert to Christianity or leave the country.

1494: Spain and Portugal agree to the Treaty of Tordesillas, dividing up the world.

16th Century: Spanish conquistadors topple Aztec and Inca empires in Mexico and Peru.

1529: Ottoman Empire reaches height of imperial expansion, but fails to capture Vienna.

1533–1584: Russian Empire expands during the rule of Ivan the Terrible.

1545: A major silver vein is discovered in what is now Bolivia.

1588: Spanish Armada is defeated by the British; leads to Spanish decline and opens world to English trade and colonization.

1602: Dutch East India Company is founded to expand spice trade in Asia.

1607: First area of English overseas colonization occurs at Jamestown, Virginia, followed by other colonies in North America.

Mid-1600s: Dutch replace Portuguese as naval hegemon in Asian waters.

1652–1674: Sporadic Anglo-Dutch wars occur; one result, Dutch lose New York and Delaware.

1756–1763: Seven Years' War occurs; most of French territory in North America ceded to Great Britain; French defeat also paves way to British domination of Indian sub-continent.

1776: The United States declares independence from Britain; American Revolution begins.

1783: Treaty of Paris between the United States and Britain ends the American Revolution; U.S. independence is recognized by Britain.

1795–1796: British seize Ceylon from the Dutch.

19th Century: British add Burma and Malaya in Asia and parts of Africa to their empire, and colonize Australia and New Zealand; French add colonies in Africa, Indochina, and a number of Pacific Islands.

1803: United States purchases the Louisiana Territory from Napoléon.

1804: Rebellion occurs in Serbia against Ottoman rulers.

1806: British seize the Cape Colony in southern Africa from the Dutch.

1810–1825: War for independence of Spanish colonies occurs.

Not surprisingly, as a result of colonial rule there remains a pronounced geographic dimension to the contemporary global distribution of power and wealth. In general, those countries located north of the Tropic of Cancer—such as the United States, Germany, France, Britain, and Japan—have much higher standards of living than countries situated between the Tropic of Cancer and the Tropic of Capricorn, which include much of Latin America, Africa, and Southeast Asia. (Refer to Map 8.1 in Chapter Eight for a graphic portrayal of wealth.) Thus, the "North" refers to the wealthy, developed countries of North America, Western Europe, and Japan, while the "South" refers to the poor, developing countries of Latin America, Africa, South and Southeast Asia, and the Pacific.

The North-South distinction in world politics is therefore both a relationship and a divide between countries that are profoundly unequal in their relative capabilities. Northern countries generally have prosperous economies, political stability, technical expertise, and military might. By contrast, many Southern countries confront severe economic problems such as hyperinflation and huge foreign debts, risky political problems such as the destabilizing threats of military coups and social rebellions, and daunting social problems including high illiteracy, unsustainable population growth, and minimal public health systems. Not surprisingly, the South

1814–1815: Congress of Vienna occurs to restore European balance of power.

1819: United States acquires Florida from Spain.

1822: Dom Pedro announces formation of the independent Brazilian Empire.

1828–1829: Russia defeats the Ottomans and receives part of what is today Romania.

1830: Serbia gains autonomy; Greek independence occurs; France conquers Algeria.

1839–1842: Opium war opens Chinese market to western states.

1845: Republic of Texas is admitted to the United States.

1846–1848: Mexican-American War occurs; U.S. gains California and American southwest.

1850–1864: China's Taiping Rebellion occurs.

1853–1854: American Commodore Perry travels to Japan; ends Japanese isolation and establishes friendly relations.

1878: Serbia, Montenegro, and Romania become independent states.

1880s: "Scramble for Africa" takes place among European powers.

1898: United States obtains Puerto Rico, Guam, and the Philippines after war against Spain.

1899–1902: Boer War occurs in South Africa.

1903: U.S. supports Panamanian independence from Colombia, and then signs treaty with Panama to build Panama Canal.

1910: Japan annexes Korea.

1917–1922: Bolshevik Revolution occurs in Russia; leads to civil war, expansion of territory, and formation of USSR.

1920: Britain and France assume control of Middle East after defeat of Ottoman Empire.

1921–1922: Britain grants home rule to most of Ireland.

1923: Turkey is declared a republic, replacing the Ottoman Empire.

1941–1945: Japanese "co-prosperity sphere" throughout much of Southeast Asia and parts of China expands and then disappears with the defeat of Tokyo in World War II.

1946: U.S. grants independence to Philippines.

1947: British India is divided into independent states of India and Pakistan.

1948: Afrikaner Nationalist Party in South Africa wins election and creates a legal system of rigid hierarchy, eventually known as apartheid; Burma and Ceylon gain independence from

Britain; Britain forced to depart last Middle East colony, Palestine, completing independence of Arab states and Israel.

1949: Indonesia gains independence from the Netherlands; China regains genuine independence with rise of Mao Zedong's Communist regime and the establishment of the People's Republic of China.

1952: Puerto Rico is granted "commonwealth" status.

1954: Battle of Dien Bien Phu occurs in Vietnam; leads to France's departure from Indochina and the partition of Vietnam along the 17th parallel between a Communist North and a pro-western South..

1962: Independence for most African colonies becomes complete; France leaves Algeria after years of war between Muslims and French.

1971: East Pakistan declares its independence as Bangladesh; Britain leaves Persian Gulf.

1974–1975: Independence occurs for Portugal's colonies in Africa: Guinea-Bissau, Angola, and Mozambique.

1985: Mikhail Gorbachev comes to power in the Soviet Union.

1992: USSR fragments into constituent republics.

looks to the North for economic opportunities and assistance, political support, technical guidance, medical supplies, and military equipment. Much of the debate surrounding the relations between North and South revolves around the terms of trade of these transactions (which are far more critical to the South than the North) as well as what obligations, if any, rich nations have in assisting the development of poorer nations.

Before examining the contemporary North-South relationship, it is essential to appreciate its historical context, especially the critical impact of European imperialism on the Americas, Africa, Asia, and the Pacific. **Imperialism** is a process of extending a nation's authority by territorial acquisition or by the establishment of political and economic hegemony over other nations.[1] Columbus's "discovery" in 1492 initiated a process of European expansion that would eventually lead to European (or European-settled) countries ruling virtually the entire globe by the end of the nineteenth century. As mentioned in Chapter Two, European colonialism resulted from the need to find space for expanding populations, new sources of wealth and raw materials, and outlets for trade and production.

In retrospect, this process of expansion might seem natural or inevitable. Throughout history, empires have risen and fallen. The Egyptians, Persians,

Romans, Chinese, Huns, Aztecs, and Incas all established extensive empires dominating their local regions of the world. However, these empires were isolated from one another by what probably seemed to be insurmountable geographical barriers—vast mountain ranges, oceans, and deserts. European expansion, in contrast, created the first truly global empires extending across oceans and continents; the resulting political and economic globalization was unprecedented. Whether this achievement is viewed as glorious or dubious, though, often depends on the extent to which the viewer benefited from or was victimized by imperialism.

In any case, imperialism, for good or ill, changed the course of history; and awareness of its origins and consequences is necessary for an understanding of world politics. With this in mind, the first half of this chapter will focus on the *causes* of imperialism. It examines the impetus for the rise of European empires and then chronicles the competition among the empires for global predominance. The different economic and political strategies that each empire employed as well as the various decolonization processes are also surveyed. The chapter's second half considers the *effects* of imperialism on the areas of the world that were subjected to or influenced by it. The legacy of imperialism is likely to remain a matter of debate for a very long time, but it is evident that throughout the world many people suffered from it, some greatly gained because of it, and it has left a deep and lasting imprint on global civilization.

The economic, social, and political differences between northern and southern countries have been described in numerous ways. Terms that are most frequently employed are developed, underdeveloped, First World, and Third World. Developed countries are economically advanced, with high levels of per capita GNP, while underdeveloped or **less developed countries (LDCs)** are relatively poor, with low levels of per capita GNP. **First World** was a term coined at the United Nations to refer to a group of the industrial countries, especially the so-called **Group of 7** or **G7**—the United States, Japan, Germany, France, Britain, Italy, and Canada—but also such countries as Sweden, Switzerland, and Belgium. **Third World** typically refers to the agrarian countries of Latin America, Africa, and South Asia. **Second World** referred to the Communist bloc during the Cold War, but this expression was never widely used.

Be aware that these terms can have pejorative overtones, suggesting that some countries are superior to other countries in such noneconomic ways as culture or customs. To extend such terms into this realm is little more than stereotyping on a global scale and, most of all, neglects the potential contributions that all people and societies can make to the betterment of the human condition.

ORIGINS OF IMPERIALISM

At the beginning of the sixteenth century, regions of the world were so isolated from one another that most had little or no knowledge whatsoever of other peoples and civilizations. When Hernán Cortés lead his band of mercenaries into the Aztec Empire in 1519, many Aztecs believed that Cortés and his men were gods. This isolation would soon end. Within three centuries, European states ruled the Americas and large parts of Africa and Asia, controlled all significant world trade from spices to slaves, and increasingly competed against one another for international predominance. In short, European expansion gradually but inexorably globalized world politics. No longer could any country or empire isolate itself from events and processes in the rest of the world, although a few countries, such as Japan, did resist such influences until the mid-nineteenth century.

The expansion of European political and economic dominance, which reached its peak in the first half of the twentieth century, was built on three foundations: first, the search for trade routes to the Orient, source of high-value commodities like spices; second, the expectation that controlling this trade or exploiting resources found in other areas would strengthen the European home country, the **metropole,** in its competition with other European countries; and third, a growing and rapidly accelerating European superiority in technology, including shipbuilding, communications, weaponry, and medicine.

One critical key to European expansion was the result of both a social necessity and a technological revolution in seafaring. By the fifteenth century, western Europe was one of the most densely populated regions of the globe, land was scarce, and natural resources were being exhausted. When population begins to outstrip resources, deep crises can result—this contributed to the collapse of the Mayan Empire in Central America and the cycles of China's dynasties. Yet, instead of turning inward, some European countries directed their endeavors outward to the seas.

Long before the sixteenth century, Europeans came into contact with Asia. For centuries, the European demand for spices and other valuable commodities from the Orient was supplied via a land route across Asia and the Middle East, and then transported through the Mediterranean by Italian, primarily Venetian, merchants. In the mid-fourteenth century Prince Henry the Navigator of Portugal formed a special center to focus the efforts of expert navigators, shipbuilders, and seamen on expanding Portuguese trade and dominion overseas. One advance in navigation—the sextant—enabled sailors to plot direction by use of the stars. This invention allowed explorers to travel farther, to heretofore unknown waters, while still being able to return home with some degree of certainty. Long-distance navigation became feasible.

In an effort to break into the oriental spice trade, both Spain and Portugal commissioned sailors to use the new technology in order to find alternative routes to the Orient (see Map 5.1). The most famous of these explorers was Christopher Columbus. While Columbus did not find an alternative route to the Orient, he stumbled onto the Americas, two continents rich in natural resources and fertile land, but lacking the spices that first generated interest in exploration. The Portuguese explorers Bartholomeu Dias and Vasco da Gama made equally important contributions to the globalization of trade. From 1487 to 1498 they led the first European expeditions to round the Cape of Good Hope at the southern tip of Africa, thereby opening up a new route to India

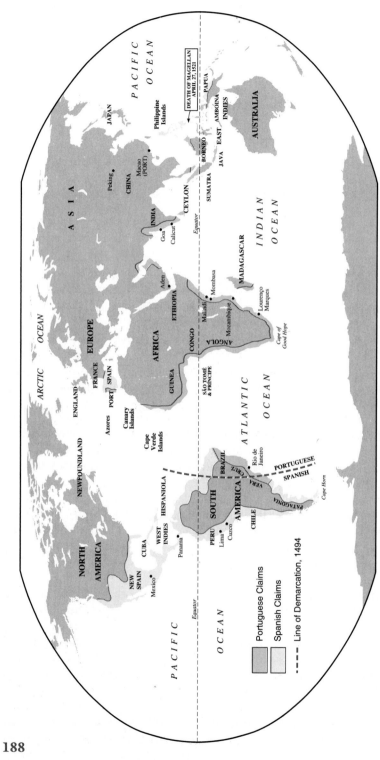

Map 5.1 Empires of Spain and Portugal, 15th and 16th Centuries

and China through the Indian Ocean. The need for fresh water and food led the Portuguese to establish supply stations along the western and eastern coasts of Africa, as well as on the Indian subcontinent and in Southeast Asia.

For the next three centuries, the competition for trade routes to East and South Asia was dominated by the Portuguese, then the Dutch, and finally the British. Controlling extensive tracts of territory was not the prime motive. Rather, it was sufficient to control a port and to provide support to local leaders to ensure the provision of commodities. Local leaders gained in the exchange as well, as the European supply of weapons and other goods strengthened their positions relative to regional opponents. The competition among various local elites eased the ability of the Europeans to make inroads, especially in India and other parts of Asia. This allowed Europeans to bypass the Arab monopoly on trade with Asia.

In the Americas, European competition was equally intense, although it took a different form. The vast land and natural resources of the New World enabled Spain, France, and Britain to acquire important raw materials and ease their population pressures. These attractions increased the rivalry among the contending empires. In short, one of the most fundamental distinctions between European empires was that some emphasized territorial conquest, while others concentrated on control of trade routes. Territorial-based empires, such as the Spanish and Russian, tended to concentrate on the conquest of interior regions where natural resources could be exploited and immigrants settled. By contrast, trade-based empires like the Dutch and Portuguese were typically interested in strategic ports from which the exchange of goods could be carried out in a predictable and secure manner. Both imperial strategies could be used to increase the power of the metropole, and the strategy chosen was often a result of the particular needs at a particular time in the metropole.[2]

Without the application of the advanced seafaring technologies, without the political and economic competition engendered by the fragmented European state system, and without the belief that rich lands and salvageable souls lay just over the horizon, European countries could have turned inward as did China and Japan at the time. Instead, European explorers, conquerors, and settlers ventured out to chart unknown waters and far-off lands. The following sections present a brief history of European imperialism, offering an overview of the rise, decline, extent, and global impact of each major empire.

THE FIRST TRANS-OCEANIC EMPIRES: SPAIN AND PORTUGAL

The year 1492 was pivotal in Spanish history. The country was becoming a unified, cohesive entity. The two major Spanish kingdoms had been unified through the marriage of Isabella I of Castile and Ferdinand II of Aragon in 1469. These two monarchs consolidated their power in 1492 in order to defeat and evict the last of the Moors (North African Muslims) from southern Spain. In the same year, the ardently Catholic king and queen attempted to "ethnically cleanse" their kingdom by decreeing that all Jews were either to convert to Christianity or leave the country. Having completed its military, political, and religious reconquest and unification of its own territory, Spain was ready and eager to focus its energies on the conquest of the new lands that Christopher Columbus encountered in 1492 and claimed in the name of Spain.

Meanwhile, by the end of the fifteenth century, the Portuguese had already been extremely active in oceanic exploration. The area that is now Portugal was wrested from the Moors about 200 years before the final Moorish stronghold, Granada, fell in Spain. Subsequently, the Portuguese worked to maintain their independence from neighboring Spanish kingdoms. However, because of the small and rather inadequate nature of their land, the Portuguese turned to the seas as a means of conquest and survival. At around the same time Columbus was attempting to go west toward the Indies, the Portuguese were heading east toward the same goal.

Colonial Collusion: Dividing the World

In order to avoid conflict over their competing expansion, representatives of Spain and Portugal established in 1494 an imaginary line that ran north to south approximately 300 miles west of the Azores Islands—a Portuguese possession in the Atlantic Ocean (see Map 5.1). The Treaty of Tordesillas thus purported to divide up the world: Spain was granted possession of all lands to the west of this line, Portugal the lands to the east. The treaty thus established the authority of Spain in the New World except for what is now Brazil, which was on the Portuguese side of the line drawn up at Tordesillas (though Europeans would not land on Brazil until 1500). The Portuguese, in turn, gained supremacy over Africa and the Indian Ocean, indeed a lucrative trade route.

At first, it seemed that Spain was left with a less appealing territory, but the vast wealth of what Europeans came to call the New World soon became apparent: first gold and then silver enriched the coffers of the Spanish crown. In particular, the discovery of a major silver vein in Bolivia in 1545 meant fabulous riches that would finance Spain's many military endeavors back in Europe as well as further exploration.[3]

Spanish Colonial Administration

The Spanish Empire in the New World emphasized the acquisition of territory. Considering the advanced level of development of the native civilization that the conquistadors ("conquerors") encountered, Spain's expansion into the New World took a relatively short time. Conquistadors like Hernán Cortés, who defeated the Aztecs in Mexico, and Francisco Pizarro, who vanquished the Incas of Peru, were aided by a number of factors. European use of gunpowder and muskets vastly outclassed the weapons of the Aztecs and Incas. Native Americans had less immunity to the diseases that had ravished Europe and Asia, so the maladies the Europeans carried to the New World devastated the indigenous

This sixteenth-century sketch depicts the lucrative silver mines of the Cerro Rico, the fabulous mountain of silver at Potosi in the Andes Mountains (now Bolivia). Conscripted indian laborers worked the mines under extremely harsh conditions.

Source: © Hulton Deutsch Collection Limited London.

population. Moreover, the political systems of the Aztecs and Incas were so tyrannical that foreign intervention was often welcomed by many subjects over continued rule by the established elites.

The Spanish crown quickly moved to consolidate its control over the territory subdued by the conquistadors. The crown was the ultimate authority on matters in the New World, though a large bureaucracy actually did most of the direct work of governing. The main characteristics of this colonial administration reflected the idea that the role of Spanish possessions was to enrich the mother country. For instance, the crown monopolized the mining of gold and silver and, at the same time, restricted trade in other goods. Spanish possessions were to trade only with Spain, and the formation of industries in the New World was thwarted. Over the centuries, these restrictions would eventually lead to dissatisfaction and then rebellion among many colonial subjects.[4]

Portuguese Colonialism

The colonial situation in Portuguese lands was different than in the Spanish territories. Most of the Portuguese Empire was based on trade. Rather than subduing and occupying territory on a grand scale, the Portuguese were content to establish trading ports.[5] The far-flung but strategically placed Portuguese colonies reflect this approach: outposts included Guinea-Bissau, the Cape Verde Islands, São Tomé and Principe, Angola, and Mozambique along the coast of Africa; Goa in India; and Macao on the coast of China (see Map 5.1).

Even in South America, the Portuguese did not colonize with the same vigor as the Spanish. What was to become modern-day Brazil was sparsely populated and devoid of gold and silver. The Portuguese turned to growing sugar cane in large plantations, primarily on the northeastern coast. African slaves were imported to compensate for the lack of indigenous labor. These slaves were readily available since a large slave trade already existed off the coast of Africa. In southern Brazil, the climate was quite temperate, similar to that of Europe, and many Europeans were attracted to the open land for cattle ranching and farming. The wide influx of various groups into Brazil contributed to its rich ethnic diversity.

Spanish-American Independence

The Spanish monarchy attempted to keep close tabs on its far-flung possessions, prohibiting trade with countries other than Spain and reserving for itself control of the lucrative mines. The proscription on free trade, especially with other colonies and with England, irritated many of the elites in the colonies. Despite festering discontent within the colonies, rebellion did not break out until events in Europe created an opening during the Napoleonic Wars. In 1808 Napoléon continued his quest to dominate Europe by invading Spain (see Chapter Two). The Spanish king was forced to abdicate, and Napoléon's brother, Joseph, was placed on the throne. This move sparked protest and rebellion within Spain itself, and also made refusal to obey Napoleonic rule a patriotic endeavor in the colonies. Elites in the colonies took advantage of the situation to press for independence, even after Napoléon was defeated in 1815 and Ferdinand regained the crown of Spain.

The struggle for independence was encouraged by Great Britain, which was often alone in carrying on the struggle against Napoléon in Europe and therefore welcomed the opportunity to harm Spain, now a French ally, by removing a critical source of its wealth. In addition, England was eager to trade freely with the colonies, and thus preferred to have them be independent countries. Spain was not willing to blithely relinquish its possessions, and the fight for independence lasted roughly from 1810 to 1825. Most of Spain's American colonies (excluding the islands of Puerto Rico and Cuba) achieved political independence under the leadership of the legendary Símon Bolívar, the "Great Liberator" of South America. Bolívar attempted to unify the continent in a United States of South America, but the divisions among the Latin American peoples were too great to overcome.

Independence from Portugal

Portugal's empire was more enduring than Spain's, in part because it was never as extensive. For instance, by the sixteenth century Portugal's trading empire had already been usurped, mainly by the Dutch. Portugal's American colony—Brazil—gained its independence rather painlessly. The catalyst for independence came, as it had with the rest of Latin America, with the Napoleonic Wars in Europe. However, when Portugal was invaded, the Portuguese monarchy was whisked away by British ships to Brazil. Throughout the French occupation, the center of the Portuguese empire resided in its colony, and the Portuguese king, João IV, allowed Brazilians to trade freely with other countries, particularly England. When Dom João returned to Portugal, he left his son Dom Pedro in charge, but the Brazilians chafed at the new trade restrictions the Portuguese wished to impose. In 1822 Dom Pedro bowed to domestic social pressure and peacefully announced the formation of the independent Brazilian Empire. Thus, with relatively little conflict, and certainly without the enormous bloodshed that the rest of the continent experienced, Brazil became an independent country. However, the independence of Portugal's colonies in Africa—Mozambique, Angola, and Guinea-Bissau—would wait until the 1970s, occurring only after decades of bitter colonial and civil war.

DUTCH EMPIRE

The Dutch Empire began with the founding of the Dutch East India Company in 1602. Like the Portuguese, the Dutch were not particularly concerned with controlling extensive continental territory, but rather key strategic trading ports, straits, and coasts (see Map 5.2). In the Indian Ocean, the Dutch established trading stations at the Cape of Good Hope in Southern Africa and at Batavia on the island of Java (now part of Indonesia), effectively giving them control over both ends of Indian Ocean trading. Soon thereafter, the Dutch ruled all of Java, the key island of Ceylon (now Sri Lanka) off the southern coast of India, and most of the coast of South Africa, displacing the Portuguese by the mid-1600s as the naval hegemon in Asian waters. In the New World, the Dutch picked up the Caribbean Islands of Curaçao and St. Eustatius, the South American territory of Guyana, and the North American island of Manhattan, establishing the settlement of New Amsterdam. The Anglo-Dutch Wars of 1652–1674 forced them to cede New Amsterdam to England, and the village was renamed New York. Overall, the Dutch Empire never became a major factor in the colonial struggle in the Americas.

The real wealth of the Dutch colonial empire came from the spices of the Dutch East Indies, and from tea plantations on the island of Ceylon. These precious commodities brought very high profits in European markets. The Dutch were well situated in Europe to take advantage of this trade because, unlike the Spanish and Portuguese, the Dutch had extensive trading networks into Germany, France, the British Isles, Scandinavia, and even Russia. Their navy

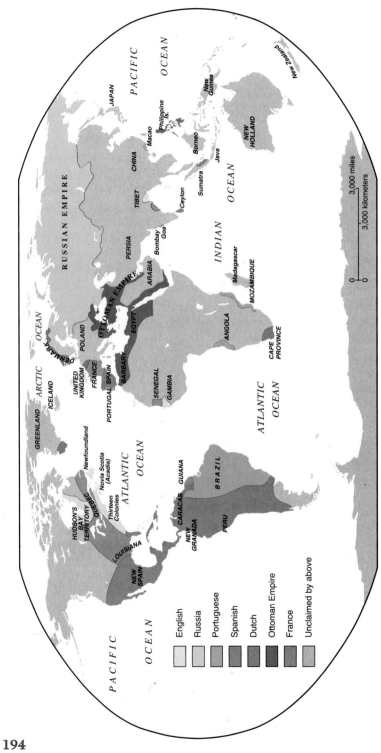

Map 5.2 Worldwide Empires, 17th and 18th Centuries

was large enough to protect the trade from the Indian Ocean, but perhaps of greatest importance, the Dutch cities of Amsterdam, the Hague, and Rotterdam were the financial centers of European trade. Thus, the Dutch bankrolled much of the emerging global trade in the sixteenth and seventeenth centuries. The colonial empire was in essence just one appendage of their growing participation in global commodities and financial markets, and as a result, the colonies' impact in spurring high levels of international trade was far greater than their size, population, or longevity would indicate.

Dutch power waned in the 1700s, but the key event for the Dutch Empire was the Napoleonic Wars. The Netherlands was conquered by Napoléon, and the British responded by seizing Ceylon in 1796 and the Cape Colony in South Africa in 1806, effectively ending major Dutch colonial presence in the Indian Ocean. However, the British did allow the Netherlands to retain Java and the other East Indies islands in the 1815 settlement at the Congress of Vienna. Thereafter, the Dutch East Indies were ruled by the Netherlands until the Japanese invaded and conquered the islands during World War II. After the war, a growing nationalist movement fought for and achieved independence in 1949 as Indonesia, leaving the Netherlands with only a few Caribbean islands as the last vestige of a once impressive trading empire.

ANGLO-FRENCH RIVALRY

After the 1588 defeat of the Spanish Armada by the British, Spanish power rapidly declined. Portugal and Holland did not have the population or resources to defend, let alone extend, their colonial outposts. This left the principal colonial competition to Britain and France for most of the eighteenth and nineteenth centuries. The Anglo-Franco rivalry for colonies was one of the most enduring political contests of modern history, taking place throughout the world and, as we saw in Chapter Two, frequently leading to war.

Britain and France brought different strengths and weaknesses to their struggle. Because the British Isles made foreign invasion unlikely, Britain could focus its energies on the Royal Navy and neglect creating a large standing army. Moreover, although Britain had coal, it had to trade for many raw materials and a significant portion of its food. By contrast, France was a continental power with vulnerable borders and therefore had to devote large amounts of its resources to a standing army. As a result, the French navy was never able to overcome British oceanic hegemony. In addition, French self-sufficiency in food meant that France was consistently more inward-looking in economic matters, while British population pressure encouraged emigration to overseas colonies. The combination of these factors gave Britain consistent advantages over France in their colonial competition. In the eighteenth century, the British-French struggle took place in North America and India, with Britain emerging victorious. In the nineteenth century, Britain and France vied for colonies in Africa, the Middle East, Southeast Asia, and the Pacific, yet after the Napoleonic era the two countries were able to resolve their colonial differences without going to war.[6]

France's Bid for Empire

The first area of overseas colonization by French explorers was along the St. Lawrence River in North America. The French soon established the cities of Quebec and Montreal in New France (today the Canadian province of Quebec), and thereafter established a series of forts along the Great Lakes and down the Mississippi River, including New Orleans. They also seized the western half of Hispaniola (now Haiti) as well as a few other smaller Caribbean islands such as Martinique and Guadeloupe. In the Indian Ocean, they established a number of trading outposts on Mauritius, Madagascar, and the Seychelles, as well as in the Indian coastal cities of Mahe and Pondicherry. These French overseas possessions, however, never attracted great numbers of French settlers. Thus, although the French typically emphasized control of territory, they never fully succeeded in achieving lasting dominion.

This early French Empire collapsed as a result of the Seven Years' War (1756–1763) between Britain and France. Initially, the French utilized their inland fort system along the Appalachian Mountains and Mississippi-Ohio Rivers in alliance with a number of Native Americans to capture some critical British outposts on the North American frontier (as depicted in James Fenimore Cooper's *The Last of the Mohicans* and its several film versions). However, the British navy decisively defeated its French counterpart in 1759, and thereafter French overseas forces wilted for lack of reinforcements and supplies. In 1762–1763 France was forced to cede Quebec to England and Louisiana to Spain, effectively removing the French presence in North America. France regained Louisiana in 1803 as a result of the Napoleonic Wars, only to sell it to the United States the following year. In India, French influence was limited to a few small coastal cities.

After the Napoleonic Wars, France again began to build an overseas empire, this time in Africa, Southeast Asia, and the Pacific. In 1830, motivated in part by the need to stop raids by the Barbary pirates, France conquered Algeria in North Africa. Elsewhere, in West Africa, the French extended their influence inland, coming to dominate a vast region of little economic value due to the arid climate and sparse population. In Asia they were able to colonize Indochina and a number of Pacific islands such as Tahiti. French colonialism of this era has often been characterized as "direct rule," driven by the ideological rationale of a *mission civilatrice*. The French saw their role as bringing culture and civilization to backward peoples and thus attempted to assimilate and colonize them to the French way of life. This French Empire was extensive in its territory, covering large areas of Africa. Moreover, in light of France's protectionism, virtually all trade involving French colonies was conducted with France.[7] After World War I, the French also expanded to the Middle East, adding the territories now know as Syria and Lebanon.

Given the high level of French political commitment to and control of their colonies, decolonization was a particularly difficult ordeal for the French Empire, whose end was precipitated by the French defeat in World War II.

German victories in North Africa and Japanese advances in Asia demonstrated the inherent weakness of the colonial powers. In Indochina, for instance, insurgents led by Vietnam's Ho Chi Minh immediately began to fight for independence at the end of World War II. The decisive battle in a long struggle came at Dien Bien Phu in 1954, when a portion of the French Foreign Legion was defeated and captured. No sooner had France withdrawn from Indochina, when rebellion began in Algeria. That war dragged on for many years as well, until Charles de Gaulle became president, and by 1962 completed the process of granting independence to most of the African colonies. Today, only a few Caribbean and Pacific islands remain "overseas departments" of the French Republic.[8]

BRITISH EMPIRE

It is difficult to overstate the importance of the impact of the British Empire on the peoples of the Americas, Africa, Asia and the Pacific. Today some fifty nations, including Canada, Australia, and New Zealand, are members of the Commonwealth of Nations, and for many, the British monarch remains their official head of state. By 1914 the British Empire had more than 500 million inhabitants; today more than 2 billion people live in areas that were once British colonies. In short, the British Empire was probably one of the most important political entities in the history of humanity and England probably contributed more to the globalization of the modern world than any other country, as evidenced by the primacy of the English language in international trade, diplomacy, and entertainment.

In reality, there were several British empires that can be delineated both by era and by the type of colonialism. In the seventeenth and eighteenth centuries, British colonialism was mostly composed of settler colonies in North America, the Caribbean, and later in the South Pacific; these colonies emphasized territorial expansion and control. In the eighteenth and nineteenth centuries, the British Empire increasingly added territories in Africa and Asia, where British colonial officials ruled over masses of indigenous people, but where there existed relatively few European settlers. In these colonies, the British were content to increase trade and investment (see Map 5.2).

Seventeenth and Eighteenth Centuries

The very first area of English overseas colonization was at Jamestown, Virginia, in 1607. Soon thereafter, other colonies with numerous English settlers were established on the North American coast: Massachusetts, New Hampshire, Connecticut, Pennsylvania, Maryland, the Carolinas, and Georgia. Dutch and Swedish settlements in New York, New Jersey, and Delaware were seized by the British in 1664. Elsewhere in North America, colonies were established in Hudson Bay, Newfoundland, and Nova Scotia; and in the Caribbean, the

BRITISH INDIA

It is a mistake to believe that European imperialism was a precisely executed plan for global domination controlled and ordered directly from Madrid, Lisbon, Paris, or London. Instead, many explorers and conquerors—such as da Gama, Columbus, Magellan, Cortés, Pizzaro, Hudson, Cartier, Cook, and even Lewis and Clark—had only the vaguest notion of what lands and civilizations they might find. Much of European expansion resulted from a combination of initiative by the explorer and collaboration by natives who often detested their native rulers. Some have referred to this kind of expansion as the "turbulent frontier," where new lands were added to empires in the monarchs' names but without their orders and sometimes without even their knowledge. Nowhere was this more evident than in the extension of British rule in India.

The first British citizens to go to India did so under the auspices of the English East India Company, a semiprivate company given a monopoly to trade with India. The company set up trading ports on the Indian coast, but by the mid-eighteenth century, it had gained effective political control over much of eastern India. The East India Company achieved political supremacy mostly through economic superiority, which allowed the company to hire many native "collaborators" to fight for them. In 1757 these troops won the Battle of Plassey in the Bengal region of India, which ensured the company's control of the critical Ganges River valley. Over the next few decades, one kingdom and/or region of India after another fell under rule of the company until virtually all of the subcontinent was effectively subordinated, whether under direct administration or indirectly through "princely states." Typically, these kingdoms or princely states were conquered by Indian mercenary troops under the command of ambitious British officials who only ex post facto informed their superiors in Calcutta, Bombay, or London of the latest addition to the empire.

In 1857, however, many of the native troops mutinied, exposing the thin grip of the East India Company. The British government then intervened, put down the rebellion, and instituted a series of reforms, including replacing the East India Company

British seized Jamaica from Spain. The British victory in the Seven Years' War (1756–1763) added large amounts of North American territory to the British Empire, including Quebec from France and Florida from Spain. This English hegemony in North America lasted only a few years. The American Revolution left England with only Canada, where many loyalists from the thirteen colonies had fled.[9]

The British Empire in Asia lasted longer. In India the British gained footholds in Bengal, Bombay, and Madras in the eighteenth century. Decisive military victories over the French and the Mughal Empire (the Muslim Empire that ruled Central India) during the Seven Years' War paved the way for British domination of the subcontinent. The capture of South Africa, Ceylon, and other Indian Ocean Islands during the Napoleonic Wars ensured that the Indian Ocean would become a "British Lake."[10]

with a colonial regime that became known as the British Raj. Thereafter, the British built an extensive network of railroads and roads throughout the subcontinent that increased trade, helped to unify a huge region, and ensured British economic and political dominance. By the late nineteenth century, India had become the "brightest jewel in the crown" of the British Empire, and Queen Victoria was crowned empress of India. However, few British citizens were even remotely associated with India, as only about 100,000 British ruled over hundreds of millions of native inhabitants. Moreover, the day-to-day administration of India was actually carried out by newly trained Indian civil servants, and the vast majority of the police and the army were Indian as well. Thus, British rule in India was based on the massive collaboration of the indigenous population.

The First and Second World Wars dramatically weakened British authority in South Asia. Limited self-government was extended to India, including some economic policy-making powers after World War I. By the 1930s British rule in India was clearly waning, and the Indian National Congress under Mahatma Gandhi led numerous campaigns and demonstrations demanding that Britain "quit India."

After the Second World War, with British resources depleted and spread precariously thin around the world and a new Labour government in London, the former Raj was spilt into two independent states, India and Pakistan. British rule in India, which had been so haphazardly assembled, was thus quickly removed. The British colonial elite that had conquered and ruled India for almost two centuries was replaced by an emerging Indian elite—many of whom (such as Gandhi and Jawaharlal Nehru) had been educated in England. Waves of ethnic and religious fighting broke out immediately, however, and the threat of communal violence haunts India to the present day. The legacy of British rule in India is therefore a mixed one; while British colonialism fostered economic development and brought India squarely into the global economy, it did little to alleviate the subcontinent's potentially dangerous political fragmentation.

Nineteenth and Twentieth Centuries

During the nineteenth century, the British added Burma and Malaya to their Asian Empire and attempted but failed to conquer Afghanistan. Moreover, Australia and New Zealand were colonized by the British as their indigenous peoples, the Aborigines in Australia and the Maoris in New Zealand, were ruthlessly repressed and the land was converted to sheep and dairy farming.

During the nineteenth century, the British government in London, fearing a repeat of the American Revolution, moved to grant self-government (so called "dominion" status) to the white settler colonies of Canada, Australia, and New Zealand. With Latin America independent and open to British trade, and South Asia under British hegemony, the British generally refrained from adding new territories to their empire. However, the rise of Germany and the renewed push by France for colonies in the early 1880s posed a difficult problem for Britain. If Germany and France gained colonies, Britain would have been essentially locked out of those areas because of the high protectionism that characterized German and French foreign economic policies. Therefore, as the so-called "scramble for Africa" of the 1880s got under way, Britain again became a very active imperialist power.

When the competition for colonies reached a fever pitch in the late 1880s, Britain used its superior naval and strategic resources to secure the proverbial "lion's share," especially in eastern and southern Africa. The most ambitious "man on the spot" in Africa was Cecil Rhodes, an English chauvinist and white supremacist who began his colonial career as an impoverished diamond prospector in South Africa. Rhodes founded the DeBeers company (which still controls most of the world's supply of diamonds), became prime minister of Cape Colony, and dreamed of "painting the map red" (establishing British dominion) from the mouth of the Nile River to the Cape of Good Hope. Rhodes gained most of central Africa for British influence by establishing Northern and Southern Rhodesia, which today are Zambia and Zimbabwe, respectively.[11] Though his career ended in scandal and disgrace, many of his dreams for British control of Africa were fulfilled, as Britain dominated the whole of the Nile Valley, including Egypt, the Sudan, Uganda, and Kenya. (In his will, Rhodes established the Rhodes Scholarships for students from America, Germany, and the British colonies to study at Oxford University, in the hope of strengthening political and cultural ties within the Anglo-Saxon world.)

Britain's most important and costly colonial war, the Boer War, took place in South Africa. Disputes between the Dutch Afrikaners and British in South Africa increased after huge deposits of gold were found in the nominally independent Dutch Boer republic of the Transvaal. Rhodes tried to engineer British control over the Transvaal with a raid in 1895; his attempt to foster a coup failed disastrously and increased the antagonism between Britain and Germany (see Chapter Three). Anglo-Boer tensions finally broke into warfare in 1899. By mid-1900, Britain occupied the capitals of both Boer Republics, the Orange Free State and the Transvaal; the war then became a guerrilla conflict in which the British rounded up Boer families into what were essentially concentration camps. As the war became increasingly unpopular and expensive, Britain reached a compromise peace with the Boers in 1902. Eight years later, the Boer republics were absorbed into the newly created Union of South Africa, which was granted self-governing dominion status (though only whites enjoyed full civil and political rights).

Britain was also able to reserve for itself some of the most fertile areas of the West African coast in the colonies of Nigeria, the Gold Coast (modern Ghana), and Sierra Leone. By the eve of World War I, the "sun never set" on an empire that extended from the South Pacific islands to the hinterlands of Africa to the British Isles and through Canada. With victory in World War I, Britain added the mandates of Palestine, Trans-Jordan, and Iraq from the Ottoman Empire in the Middle East, and Tanganyika (now Tanzania) and Southwest Africa (now Namibia) from Germany in Africa. It was at this apex of expansion and influence that the empire began to unravel.

Twilight of Empire

The first country to break free of the British Empire since the American Revolution was Ireland. In 1922, after eight centuries of British rule, decades of agitation, and six years of civil war, Britain granted home rule to most of Ireland. (The counties of Northern Ireland that remain under British rule continue to present complex political and social problems, aggravated by terrorism and violence). In the Middle East, in the period between World Wars I and II, the Arab states began to gain their independence. By this time, Mahatma Gandhi was leading the Indian National Congress in "non-cooperation campaigns" to get Britain to "quit India." World War II sealed the fate of London's Asian Empire, as an exhausted Britain simply no longer had the resources to hold on to territories halfway around the world. India was granted independence and partitioned into India and Pakistan in 1947. Burma, Ceylon, and Israel gained independence in 1948. In Africa, most colonies were also granted independence between the mid-1950s and the early 1960s, followed by most of the Caribbean and South Pacific island territories over the next decade. Of enormous significance for later developments, Britain left the Persian Gulf in 1971, where its navy had held sway for a century and a half. This created a power vacuum, and the region has been embroiled in conflict ever since, including the Persian Gulf War of 1991.

Perhaps the most remarkable aspect of the decolonization of the British Empire was how generally peaceful it was. When the British saw the sun finally setting on their empire, they got out before they were sucked into any quagmires—a lesson learned from both the American Revolution and the Boer War. Even the violent Mau Mau opposition in Kenya and the communist rebellion in Malaya in the 1950s caused very few British casualties, but often the local population suffered grievously from internal conflicts as in Kenya and Malaya. Similarly, war among the former colonial subjects often followed British departures, as in India and Palestine. British policies were very effective in ruling with little cost, but the withdrawal of British power often left nothing to contain indigenous conflicts. On the whole, however, Britain's assembly and relatively peaceful divestment of its vast empire were both remarkable accomplishments.[12]

TWO GREAT CONTINENTAL EMPIRES—RUSSIA AND THE UNITED STATES

All empires examined thus far have been trans-oceanic empires of the major states of western Europe. However, most empires throughout history have been continental in scope, with expansion based on extending control by land from already conquered territories. During the era of Portuguese, Spanish, Dutch, French, and British overseas colonialism, other empires were pursuing the strategy of contiguous imperialism. Two of these empires—Russia and the United States—deserve particular attention because of their critical role in modern history, especially for their impact on the peoples of Asia, the Middle East,

THE MAHATMA

One of the greatest heroes in the annals of the human spirit is Mohandas Karamchand Gandhi. Born to a Hindu family in Bombay in 1869, Gandhi initially pursued a career in law, studying for the bar in London and practicing in India and South Africa. As a young barrister, he affected the dress and mannerisms of an affluent English gentleman, working within the colonial legal system to fight discrimination against Indians. But as his struggle for political and civil rights continued, he set his sights higher, and devoted himself to the abolition of the colonial system in his home country. He returned to India in 1915, renounced all material possessions, and adopted a life of voluntary poverty, vegetarianism, celibacy, and nonviolent opposition to colonial oppression. (After his vow of poverty,

Gandhi always dressed in simple homespun clothes, usually only a loincloth. When someone commented on his scanty attire during a meeting with King George V at Buckingham Palace in 1931, he replied, "The king was wearing enough for us both.")

Campaigning tirelessly against British rule, Gandhi developed the resistance strategy of *satyāgraha,* "holding to the truth," which sought to expose the immorality of oppression through peaceful civil disobedience. He used personal fasts and hunger strikes as nonviolent weapons against the colonial authorities, and was repeatedly jailed for his protests against the British. Realizing that philosophy alone could not effect political change, he proved to be a brilliant political tactician, organizing strikes, boycotts, and, in 1930, a 200-mile

and the Americas. Both political entities were extremely successful in coming to dominate vast areas that spanned continents.

The Russians

The Russian Empire was the most territorially vast of the European empires and the longest-lived (see Map 5.3). While Russia relentlessly pursued a policy of territorial expansion for more than a millennium, it deliberately remained economically and culturally isolated. As a result, Russia remained the least advanced of the major European powers in terms of technology and economic and political organization, and this backwardness ultimately was the root cause of its collapse. The history of the Russian empire may be roughly divided into three periods. From its earliest days until the late seventeenth century, Russia was essentially a feudal or absolutist monarchy. Between the late seventeenth and early twentieth centuries, the political and social system of Imperial Russia was dominated by the struggle between absolutism and Western political ideas. The victory of one of those ideas, communism, led twentieth-century Soviet Russia to the zenith of its global power and then to the stagnation and collapse of its empire.

march from Ahmadabad to the sea to gather salt crystals in defiance of the government monopoly on the sale of that basic necessity of life. This demonstration electrified India and precipitated a wave a peaceful protests throughout the subcontinent. Gandhi was arrested, as he had been many times before, but knew that his movement had scored a major victory. As he put it, "The honor of India has been symbolized by a fistful of salt in the hand of a man of nonviolence."

Gandhi's methods and infinite patience got results. His "Quit India" campaign persuaded London that British control of India could not be maintained, and in 1947 the colonial Raj was dismantled. The two new nations of India and Pakistan were immediately wracked by bloody fighting between Hindus and Muslims, and in 1948 the aged, frail philosopher fasted until Hindu and Muslim leaders signed a peace agreement. He was not able to enjoy the fruits of his lifelong struggle for independence, however; he was fatally shot by a Hindu extremist that same year.

Throughout his long fight against colonialism, Gandhi displayed a rare combination of enlightened spirituality and political canniness. Journalist William Shirer said of him, "I never knew a more deeply religious man, nor a subtler politician." The most fitting tribute to Gandhi, however, is the sobriquet he was granted by his followers and by which he will be remembered throughout the world as an example of nonviolent resistance: Mahatma, or Great Soul.

Ninth through Eighteenth Centuries

The origins of the Russian Empire lie in Kievan Rus, a feudal state founded in the tenth century that united the Slavic peoples of what is now Ukraine, Belarus, and western Russia. Political and cultural links with Europe were strengthened at the end of the tenth century when Grand Duke Vladimir adopted Greek Orthodox Christianity as the state religion. Russia was drawn away from the European orbit in the thirteenth century, however, when the Mongol Empire under Genghis Khan and his sons destroyed the Kievan state and conquered most of the territory between the Black Sea and the Pacific Ocean.

After the decline of Mongol power, Ivan the Terrible, who ruled from 1533 to 1584, used terror and violence unsparingly to construct a centralized absolute monarchy. Based in Moscow, he simultaneously tried to expand the empire in all directions. Throughout the sixteenth and seventeenth centuries, the Russian Empire expanded relentlessly to the east across Siberia and toward the Baltic Sea. Trade and contact with Europe nevertheless remained limited, and thus Russia was little affected by advances in modern science, capitalism, and democratic government.

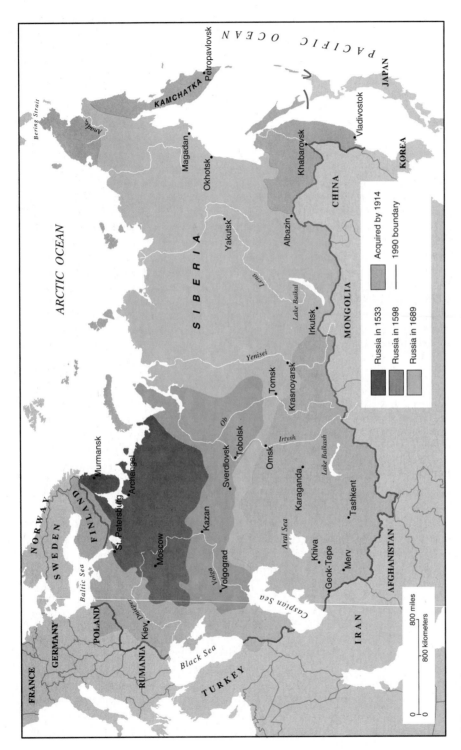

Map 5.3   Growth of Russia, 1533–1914

After Peter the Great ascended to the throne in 1689, Russia's territorial expansion continued unabated, most notably in east-central Europe in the eighteenth century and in the Caucasus, Central Asia, and North America in the nineteenth century. Russian armies conquered most of Poland and made substantial gains against the Ottoman Empire and Persia.

Nineteenth and Twentieth Centuries

Russia became firmly established as a European power during the reign of Alexander I (1801–1825), when Russian forces were instrumental in the defeat of Napoléon and the establishment of the Concert of Europe in 1814–1815. Westernizing forces were strengthened by active participation in European politics, but after an attempted coup by progressive officers in 1825 (the Decembrist Revolt) failed, Russia aligned itself for many years with the conservative European powers that sought to suppress nationalism.

It was clear to even the most conservative leaders that the Industrial Revolution was reforging the economic and strategic environment, but industrialization in nineteenth-century Russia began late and progressed slowly. At the same time, Russian expansionism led to conflicts with other European empires and Japan, and Russian defeats in the Crimean War (1853–1856) and the Russo-Japanese War (1904–1905) spurred economic and political reforms. However, these reforms did not go far enough to enable the Russian regime to meet its internal and external challenges, and though a revolution in 1905 failed to topple the tsar, it demonstrated that the Russian Empire's political structure could not meet the needs of a modern society.[13]

By 1917, under the strains of world war, Russia—which had missed or attempted to suppress the major intellectual and socioeconomic revolutions of its European neighbors—finally had one of its own, led by the visionary communist Vladimir Lenin. The Bolshevik Revolution and the civil war that followed destroyed the centralized, bureaucratic, and repressive Russian Empire, and replaced it with the equally centralized, bureaucratic, and repressive Union of Soviet Socialist Republics. After Lenin's death, Joseph Stalin quickly and ruthlessly consolidated his leadership of the Communist party. Tremendous material and human resources were poured into the Soviet military, especially after the German invasion of 1941 brought the USSR into the Second World War. By the end of the war, Soviet forces had repulsed the invasion, defeated the German army on the eastern front, captured Berlin, and established Moscow's domination over Eastern Europe, at the cost of about 20 million military and civilian deaths.[14]

As discussed in Chapter Four, Russian influence over world politics peaked during the Cold War that followed, as the superpower rivalry between the Soviet Union and the United States was played out in political conflicts and "proxy" wars in Europe, Asia, the Middle East, Africa, and Latin America. The Soviet-American conflict never erupted into a direct military confrontation, but massive military spending and continued inability to compete with Western technology exhausted the USSR nonetheless. By the time Mikhail Gorbachev came to power in 1985, many Soviets regarded their country as economically stagnant and the Communist Party as politically and morally bankrupt. The USSR might have been able to sustain either its status as a superpower or its Communist system, one or the other. Gorbachev tried to preserve both, and failed, but in so doing stimulated the growth of nationalist and democratic forces throughout the Soviet empire. By 1992 the collapse of the empire was complete, the USSR was broken up into its constituent republics, Russia was governed by a fledgling democratic regime, and Moscow controlled less territory than it did in 1689.

Considering the vast territories the Russian Empire once controlled, and its role as a major power in world politics for centuries, its bequest to the contemporary world is remarkably small. Russia's lack of natural defenses and difficulty of communications with far-flung provinces made it vulnerable to invasion, which heightened security consciousness, and prompted political repression at home and "defensive expansion" abroad. Both these policies made its neighbors and other great powers distrustful throughout its history. The collapse of the Russian Empire was rapid and disorderly, though accompanied by little large-scale violence. Russia must now grapple with the dilemma caused by centuries of Russian settlement in neighboring areas, including the Muslim-majority countries of Central Asia, the Baltic States (Latvia, Lithuania, and Estonia), and Ukraine, which Moscow ruled from 1654 until 1991 (see Map 5.3). Russians living in these states may look to Moscow for protection if their rights are violated, and "national-patriotic" forces in Russia, nostalgic for the days of empire, may be eager to respond with force, creating substantial potential for conflict with Russia's newly independent neighbors. Overall, the early 1990s saw Russia struggling to maintain democracy, rebuild a functioning economy, and reclaim its status as a major world power. Its success or failure in these endeavors will have a major impact on the rest of the former Russian Empire and on the world as a whole.

The Americans

Just as Russia expanded eastward through Asia, the United States expanded westward through North America in the nineteenth century. Like Russia, the United States first concentrated on contiguous expansion and territorial absorption. In 1803 it bought the Louisiana Territory from Napoléon and in 1819 acquired Florida from Spain in exchange for $5 million. The admission of the republic of Texas (which had broken away from Mexico) to the United States in 1845 set the stage for the Mexican-American War of 1846–1848, in which the United States seized what is now the American Southwest and California. These conquests made the United States a transcontinental country and immediately raised the question of whether slavery would be permitted in the new territories, setting off the Civil War. After the war, the United States bought Alaska from Russia. The social, economic, and political organization in these territories was transformed to conform to the established American patterns from the eastern seaboard. Thus, the United States ensured its hegemony over North America.

Until the end of the nineteenth century, Americans resisted overseas expansion and instead focused on developing the western "frontier." In 1898, like a coiled spring unleashed, the United States entered the ranks of the overseas imperialist powers. In a brief but decisive war with Spain, the United States obtained Puerto Rico and the Philippines, the remnants of the Spanish Empire. Elsewhere, it seized Hawaii, Guam, and other Pacific islands, making it a major power in the Pacific. Taken together, these acquisitions transformed the United States into a global power. In contrast to the American West, these overseas territories were acquired primarily to expand American economic and political influence and were not used as new realms for settlement, with the partial exception of Hawaii.

The United States did not take official possession of all overseas territories. Like the British in the nineteenth century, it also created an "informal empire" where it controlled political and economic development de facto without direct colonial rule. After the turn of the century, for instance, Washington increasingly dominated the Caribbean region. In 1903 the United States backed a rebellion that detached Panama from Colombia, and then proceeded to build the Panama Canal. In Nicaragua and Haiti, the United States "sent in the Marines" in numerous interventions, making Washington the effective ruler of these countries. In 1917 it bought the Virgin Islands from Denmark. American political and economic influence in Cuba, Guatemala, Honduras, and El Salvador was also considerable. This empire allowed the United States to project naval power throughout the world and thus protect and promote American foreign trade, especially in the Caribbean, South America, and the Pacific.

Since the United States generally avoided direct colonial rule, certain aspects of decolonization never presented the difficult political problems faced by Britain and France. For instance, the Philippines was granted independence after World War II on July 4, 1946, and Puerto Rico was granted "commonwealth" status—internal self-governance—in 1952. (The possibility of statehood or independence remains a major issue in Puerto Rico.) Nevertheless, American attempts to keep "friendly" governments in power in some Third World countries often led to disaster. Probably the furthest outpost of American influence in the post–World War II era was South Vietnam, the best case of the "overextension" of American power in the 1960s. Regimes bent on reducing previous American influence occurred after violent revolutions in China, Cuba, Iran, and Nicaragua. Only in Nicaragua has this process been reversed, when pro-American Violeta Chamorro defeated the Sandinista revolutionary Daniel Ortega in an election in 1989.

In many ways, however, American expansionism was successful. The territorial strategy of the nineteenth century brought about the total and unquestioned absorption of the western half of North America and Alaska. Compared to the dissolution of the Soviet Union or even the decolonization of the British and French Empires, the American assimilation of most territories and peoples into its existing political framework provides a model that few other political units have ever achieved.

The overseas record of the American trading empire is less formidable and more spotty. Hawaii did achieve statehood, other Pacific islands, like Guam and American Samoa, have remained territories of the United States, and the Philippines has remained friendly. However, while the frequency of U.S. intervention in Latin America has been declining in recent decades, there remains a latent (sometimes even blatant) anti-Americanism in the region that is typical of anticolonial movements elsewhere in the Third World. This "Yankee Go Home" attitude reflects the ambiguity of American expansionism, which at times has been extremely territorial and in other periods was concentrated merely on expanding and controlling trade. Overall, though, compared to the Russians, the Americans adjusted to their imperial decline with relatively minimal domestic political upheaval.[15]

OTTOMAN EMPIRE

The one successful non-Christian empire since 1500, the Muslim empire of the Ottoman Turks was a major force in world politics for more than 500 years. Many of the violent conflicts in the world today, including the fighting in the former Yugoslavia, the Arab-Israeli conflict, the Greek-Turkish dispute over Cyprus, and the various troubles in the Persian Gulf, are located in former Ottoman territory and are influenced by developments that occurred during the centuries of Ottoman rule. From the early fourteenth to the beginning of the twentieth century, the Ottoman Empire grew from a small and weak principality in western Turkey to, at its height in the seventeenth century, a mighty empire that controlled the Balkans, the Middle East, North Africa, and parts of what are now southern Russia and Ukraine (see Map 5.4). The empire slowly declined until after World War I, when it ceased to exist and was replaced by the Turkish Republic in 1923. How did this important Islamic entity compete in a period when the great Christian empires were emerging? In order to understand the evolution of the Ottoman Empire, we must look to its origins.[16]

Fourteenth through Eighteenth Centuries

The source of this empire, which would become the most important Islamic political unit in world politics for centuries, hardly seemed auspicious: a small and relatively weak principality in western Turkey, bordered to the east and west by more powerful neighbors. Around 1300, however, Osman, the empire's founder (from whose name "Ottoman" comes) launched successful raids against areas controlled by one of those neighbors. From the very beginning, the Ottomans encountered the fundamental problem of facing foes both to the west and to the east. Their expansion into the Balkans, however, was facilitated by social disorganization and fragmentation there. Eventually this expansion met opposition, led by the Serbs, in an ironic precursor that would have an impact on conflicts within the former Yugoslavia in the 1990s. In 1389 the Ottomans

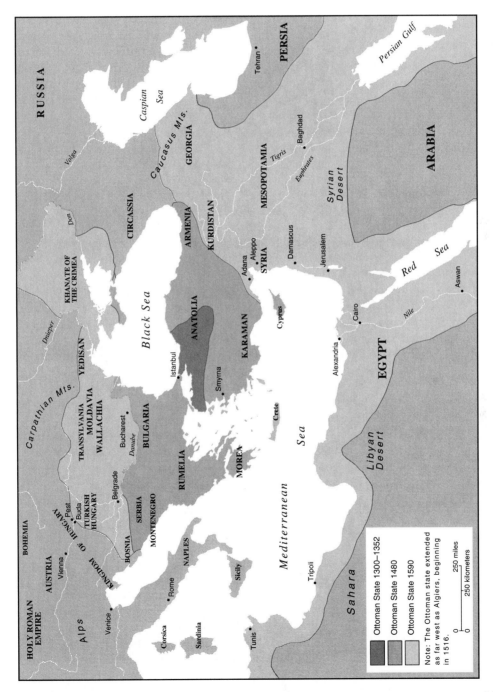

Map 5.4 Growth of Ottoman Empire, 1300–1566

RUSSIA

PERSIA

Tehran

Persian Gulf

Caspian Sea

Volga

Caucasus Mts.

GEORGIA

MESOPOTAMIA

Baghdad

Tigris

Euphrates

Syrian Desert

ARABIA

Don

CIRCASSIA

ARMENIA

KURDISTAN

KHANATE OF THE CRIMEA

Aleppo

Damascus

SYRIA

Adana

Jerusalem

Red Sea

Aswan

Dnieper

YEDISAN

Black Sea

ANATOLIA

KARAMAN

Cyprus

Cairo

Nile

TRANSYLVANIA

MOLDAVIA

WALLACHIA

Istanbul

Smyrna

Alexandria

EGYPT

Carpathian Mts.

Bucharest

BULGARIA

Danube

Crete

Libyan Desert

BOHEMIA

Belgrade

RUMELIA

MOREA

AUSTRIA

Vienna

Pest

Buda

TURKISH HUNGARY

SERBIA

BOSNIA

MONTENEGRO

Mediterranean Sea

Sahara

HOLY ROMAN EMPIRE

KINGDOM OF HUNGARY

NAPLES

Rome

Tripoli

Alps

Venice

Corsica

Sardinia

Sicily

Tunis

Ottoman State 1300–1352

Ottoman State 1480

Ottoman State 1590

Note: The Ottoman state extended as far west as Algiers, beginning in 1516.

0   250 miles

0   250 kilometers

209

defeated the Serbs, who were joined by Bosnian and Bulgarian contingents, at the Battle of Kosovo. The contemporary hostility between the Serbs and the Muslims in Bosnia dates back to this period.

The Ottoman victories generated more serious threats. The Hungarians organized a crusade, joined by the French and Venetians, which the Ottomans defeated in 1392. From the east came the Mongol hordes, which defeated the Ottoman army in the Battle of Ankara in 1402. Later, though, the Ottomans gradually regained power and eventually resumed their conquests. By the end of the fifteenth century, they had conquered Constantinople, the rest of Turkey, Greece, and parts of Albania after defeating the Venetians—and the Balkans after again defeating the Serbs.

By the beginning of the sixteenth century, Ottoman control of the Balkans was secured, but a new struggle developed with the Hapsburg Empire. The Ottomans took Hungary, and in 1529 unsuccessfully besieged Vienna, the fall of which would have left open central Europe. Their advance in the west had been stopped. To the east, the Ottomans neutralized Persia and proceeded to conquer most of what we now know as the Middle East. This included Egypt and the western littoral of the Arabian peninsula, as well as Mecca and Medina, the two holiest cities in Islam, thus consolidating the Ottoman claim to be the protector and benefactor of Islam.

The conquest of the Middle East also brought economic gains, namely control of the important land routes connecting Asia and Europe. But, ironically, the opening of sea routes between Europe and Asia cut into and eventually eliminated profits from the land routes. In fact, the increasing economic, political, and military strength of European states prevented further Ottoman development. No longer able to expand, and with the profits from the land routes dwindling, the Ottoman government was forced to rely solely on internal sources of revenue, such as agriculture. At home, peasants resented the Ottoman tax demands and political control. They often fled or formed rebel bands that created swaths of lawlessness. These conflicts were compounded by the constant problems generated by the frequent changes of Ottoman rulers and their occasional incompetence.

Nineteenth and Twentieth Centuries

In the nineteenth century, the weakened Ottoman Empire increasingly came under attack from Russia and Austria, both of which vied for control over the former Ottoman territories. As the century proceeded, the Ottoman decline accelerated, notwithstanding internal attempts at reform and the efforts of different European countries—especially Britain—to prevent a total collapse. The British saw the Ottoman Empire as a critical counterweight to Russian expansion. The increasingly obvious weakness of the empire only encouraged external intervention on the part of European powers anxious for some of the spoils left by the crumbling Ottoman authority. Yet, because each of the European great powers had interests to protect in Ottoman-controlled areas, all sought to ensure that none would gain the upper hand. They thus tended to counterbalance each other, and all the while the "sick man of Europe" gradually continued to deteriorate.

In 1829 Russia defeated the Ottomans and received parts of what is today Romania. A rebellion broke out in Serbia in 1804, and it gained autonomy in 1830 and independence in 1878. The French invasion of Egypt of 1789–1801 by Napoléon undermined Ottoman control there. The Greeks rebelled in 1821, and when the combined forces of Russia, France, and Britain defeated the Ottoman attempt to subdue Greece, Greek independence, achieved in 1830, was a foregone conclusion.

While the Ottoman Empire progressively sought to adopt Western military technologies, its fate was no longer in its own hands. It had fallen too far behind, and the social, educational, and technical obstructions to modernization were too difficult to overcome. The intensification of nationalism in the Balkans naturally led to rebellions, which the Ottomans attempted to violently repress. Russia, which claimed to be the protector of fellow Slavs, responded with force in 1877, only to be restrained by other great powers. In the four decades before World War I, the Ottomans gradually lost control of the area—to either Austria and Russia, or to newly independent states.

As we have seen, the resulting chaos eventually created the spark that triggered World War I. In that war, the Ottoman Empire joined on the side of Germany and Austria-Hungary, in part because of the influence of German military advisors on the Ottoman army, in part due to the favorable impression the early German successes made, and in part in the hope that revenge could be exacted on Russia for many past defeats. By joining what was to be the losing side, the Ottoman Empire signed its death warrant; at the end of the war it was stripped of its Middle Eastern territories.[17] In 1923 Turkey was declared a republic, and in 1924 the caliphate was abolished and all members of the Ottoman dynasty were expelled.

Although the Ottoman Empire, like its Austro-Hungarian counterpart, dissolved in World War I, its legacy continues to be felt. The territorial claims of successor states remain a bone of contention. Many Arab-Israeli disputes are in part conflicts over the rights to former Ottoman lands. Moreover, Iraq's longstanding claim that Kuwait was part of Iraq when Iraq was in the Ottoman Empire is part of the background to its invasion and occupation of Kuwait in 1990–1991. (Because Iraq itself had no independent existence prior to 1914, this claim is difficult to justify as well as historically inaccurate in that Kuwait was declared autonomous by the Ottoman sultan in the 1890s.) Similarly, the intermingling of Muslims, Serbs, Croats, and other ethnic groups forms the backdrop of the breakup of Yugoslavia and the subsequent fighting that wracked the Balkans in the early 1990s.

TOO LITTLE, TOO LATE: GERMAN AND JAPANESE EMPIRES

Not every country that pursued imperialism succeeded as well as those discussed in the previous sections. Some empires, such as the Chinese, were simply too stagnant to compete with European imperialism and even struggled just to maintain their independence. Others, such as Austria-Hungary and Italy, were too weak and

AT A GLANCE

THE EMPIRES

Spanish
1492–1898

Extent of Empire: North, Central, and South America (except Brazil and the Philippines)

Type of Control: Territorial expansion

Decline: Spanish Armada destroyed by British; rebellion in the colonies; Spanish–American War in 1898

Portuguese
1488–1970s

Extent of Empire: Brazil, Guinea-Bissau, the Cape Verde Islands, São Tomé and Principe, Angola, Mozambique, Goa in India, and Macao in China

Type of Control: Colonies, trading posts

Decline: Bowed to colonial pressures and colonial and civil wars. Navy declined in power. Mother country did not have the population or resources to defend outposts

Dutch
1602–1806

Extent of Empire: Cape of Good Hope, Java, Sri Lanka (Ceylon), certain Caribbean Islands, and Manhattan (New York)

Type of Control: Control key strategic trading ports, straits, coasts

Decline: Defeat at the hands of Napoléon weakened its colonial rule; the British seized Ceylon in 1796 and the Cape Colony in South Africa in 1806; the Japanese invaded Dutch East Indies during World War II

French
Early 1500s–1962

Extent of Empire: Louisiana Territory (now part of the United States), Quebec, Caribbean Islands, Mahe and Pondicherry in India, Indochina, Algeria, Syria, Lebanon, parts of sub-Saharan Africa, Tunisia, and Morocco

Type of Control: Colonies, forts, trading posts

Decline: The Seven Years' War; World War II losses; rebellion in the colonies

British
1603–Present

Extent of Empire: America, India, Egypt, Sudan, Iraq, Jordan, Kuwait, Israel, South Africa, parts of sub-Saharan Africa, Hong Kong, Canada, Australia, New Zealand, Persian Gulf Sheikdoms, and Aden Protectorate

Type of Control: Colonies

Decline: The Boer War; "noncooperation campaigns"; weakened in World War II; peacefully relinquished most colonies

Russian
9th Century–1917

Extent of Empire: Ukraine, Belarus, Siberia, Caucasus, Central Asia, Alaska, and most of Poland

Type of Control: Territorial expansion and absorption

Decline: Internal

---

internally divided to extend their domain overseas with any lasting conviction. Two additional countries attempted to create empires that deserve attention—not because they were very successful in the long term, but because their aspirations and failures had global implications. Those countries are Germany and Japan.

The bids by Berlin and Tokyo for empire produced numerous, bloody wars between 1860 and 1945. In terms of territory actually ruled, neither the Germans

Soviet
1917–1991

Extent of Empire: Former Soviet Union and Eastern Europe

Type of Control: Territorial expansion and absorption. Control over Eastern European pro-Soviet regimes

Decline: Internal

American
1776–Present

Extent of Empire: United States, Philippines, Puerto Rico, Cuba, Guam, and other Pacific islands

Type of Control: Territorial expansion and absorption

Decline: Peacefully relinquished colonies

Ottoman
1500–1917

Extent of Empire: The Balkans, the Middle East, North Africa, and parts of what are now southern Russia and Ukraine

Type of Control: Territorial expansion and absorption

Decline: Rebel bands; internal dissolution and fragmentation; attacked by Russia and Austria; World War I

German
1880–1945

Extent of Empire: Pre-World War I: Togo, Cameroon, Tanzania, Namibia, and islands in the South Pacific; World War II: France, the Netherlands, Luxemburg, Crete, French North Africa, Belgium, Austria, Czechoslovakia, Denmark, Poland, Norway, Yugoslavia, Greece, Latvia, Lithuania, Estonia and western Russia

Type of Control: Territorial expansion and absorption

Decline: World War I defeat, World War II defeat

Japanese
1880–1945

Extent of Empire: Taiwan, parts of China, Korea, Philippines, French Indochina, Burma, Indonesia, Malaysia, Thailand, New Guinea, and many islands in the Pacific

Type of Control: Territorial expansion and absorption

Decline: World War II defeat

nor the Japanese were effective in creating permanent structures, largely because of their defeat by other powers. At the end of the nineteenth century, Berlin was able to secure only a few areas of Africa (present-day Togo, Cameroon, Tanzania—including Zanzibar—and Namibia) and a few islands in the South Pacific. The Japanese conquered Taiwan in 1895 and annexed Korea in 1910. However, for both countries, attempts to seize much larger areas provoked immense

WHAT WOULD YOU DO?

You are the leader of Egypt in July 1956. Since ousting the former king four years earlier, you have wanted to accelerate your country's economic development. A crucial element of your development plan is a new 100-meter-high dam at Aswan, which, with a capacity to store up to two years' flow of the Nile River, would allow you to expand irrigation to 1 million acres of land. Thus far, neither the Soviets nor the Americans have actually agreed to fund this $1.3 billion project. Indeed, the Americans have just insulted you by reneging on the deal proposed by

them with their allies and the World Bank. An advisor has suggested nationalizing the British-controlled Suez Canal Company in response, using its $25 million annual profits toward construction of the dam.

Gaining physical control over the Suez Canal could serve many goals. It would help you acquire funds to construct the dam, which you need as the late summer and fall floodwaters race down the Nile. It would also allow you to control millions of tons of oil that move through the canal every year to Europe; and help you recover some of your damaged prestige at

opposition, particularly from Britain and the United States. These free-trade democracies opposed both Germany and Japan in part because they both were protectionist and authoritarian. Moreover, by the end of the nineteenth century, new colonies would have to be established only by subjugation of previously independent territory or by acquisition of territory previously held by another great power. There were no new, easily gained "open spaces" like those other Europeans had found in Africa in the late nineteenth century. Indeed, after World War I, Germany was stripped of its overseas colonies, which became League of Nations' mandates but were administered by Britain and France. German bitterness over the loss of these territories helped to undermine support for the ill-fated Weimar Republic. In the 1930s the Japanese bid for empire started in China and eventually resulted in war with the United States, which Japan decisively lost. (Chapter Three discusses the conflicts created by German, Italian, and Japanese expansion from 1880 to 1945.)

DECLINE OF IMPERIALISM

As the preceding sections describe, the European empires expanded prodigiously in the eighteenth and nineteenth centuries. The conflicts among the imperial powers in the first half of the twentieth century, however, undermined their collective hold on the area that came to be known as the Third World. The two world wars greatly weakened all the great powers but the United States and the USSR. Particularly in the Middle East and Asia, the two wars strengthened the former colonies that were gaining their independence because the great powers competed home and abroad. By provoking Western opposition, it might also force the Soviets to step up their aid and arms shipments, and solidify the growing support of the Arab masses and their governments for an alliance against Israel.

On the other hand, nationalizing the canal could provoke Britain, which is highly dependent on Middle East oil, to counter-attack. France, which bitterly opposes your support of the Algerian rebels, would certainly participate. The United States might encourage them to attack in order to further thwart your revolutionary aspirations.

And the Soviets might not back your ambitions sufficiently. The Western countries could hamper your efforts to capture Nile water behind a large dam in other ways, too. Britain could fund construction of dams in those upstream African territories that it still dominates, claiming other sites are better locations than Aswan because they would result in less evaporation.

Nationalizing the Suez Canal is a bold move.

What would you do?

for the locals' support against their foes. Finally, the wars demonstrated that the strength of the colonial powers was much weaker than the indigenous peoples had thought. For example, in Indochina the Japanese exposed the weakness of the French when Tokyo was able to defeat them. When the Allies, in turn, defeated the Japanese, they revealed Japan's weakness as well.

In the war's aftermath, native cultures everywhere were emboldened to seek independence; one by one the imperial powers concluded that these territories were not worth keeping at the military, political, and economic costs they would take to maintain. The succeeding system of indirect control, in which the United States and USSR competed for influence in many former colonies of the Third World, also collapsed when neither superpower could afford to maintain the competition, and one—the USSR—collapsed along with the empire it had controlled on its frontiers.

Ultimately, history had imposed a harsh irony on the imperial powers. From Vietnam to Algeria to India to Palestine to Nicaragua to Kenya, European ideas of nationalism and political sovereignty served to undermine the colonial powers' legitimacy throughout the Third World. The age of empire is over. Today, few countries even acknowledge overseas territories as being part of an empire. France calls its South Pacific islands such as Tahiti an "overseas department" of the republic of France, Britain no longer has an empire but rather a Commonwealth of Nations, and the United States has "territories" such as Guam and the Virgin Islands, but meticulously avoids any reference to "empire." Empire has become politically incorrect, as the subjugation of foreign lands is no longer justifiable in terms of "civilizing missions" or "white man's burdens."

These political changes, however, do not mean that the legacy of empire has ended. Indeed, the impact of European imperialism was profound; it changed the struggle for power in Europe, and it profoundly altered the economic, political, and even social organization of the peoples of the Americas, Africa, Asia, and the Pacific. It also created global links that would otherwise have hardly been possible, and established the basis for ethnic fragmentation in many former colonies. In many ways the impact of empire was more important on the colonies than the metropole, and this is where we will now turn our attention, beginning with the changes wrought on the societies subject to varying degrees of colonial domination.

SOCIAL IMPACT OF IMPERIALISM

Today virtually all countries that comprise the South are direct descendants of European empires and colonialism. There were two forms of colonialism that most significantly affected the social organization of the colony: (1) settler colonialism, where immigrants seized land from the indigenous population and became the dominant population and (2) elite colonialism, where the indigenous rulers were replaced by a European political and economic elite but where the native population remained essentially in place and thus much of the culture remained intact.

Probably the most important factor determining whether a territory would be subjected to settler or elite colonialism was geography, and more specifically climate. Settler colonies tended to be located in regions with a temperate climate—North America, the Southern cone of Latin America (Argentina), and Australia and New Zealand. Since Western Europe has a temperate climate, this offered European settlers the least difficult environmental transition in a process that was otherwise very hazardous. By contrast, tropical colonies were far less hospitable for European settlers due to endemic diseases, particularly malaria and yellow fever, against which most Europeans have very little immunity. Therefore, virtually all large-scale European settlement in tropical areas took place in highland regions (such as the Andes and Central Mexico) where tropical pests and ailments were less numerous. As a result, most tropical colonies were characterized by elite colonialism, where Europeans ruled (often ruthlessly) but did not oust the native population. A brief review of the European impact on the Americas, Asia, Africa, and the Pacific will show how the two types of colonialism led to different social consequences.

North America

European conquest of North America is one of the best cases of settler colonialism. Starting in the early seventeenth century on the Atlantic seacoast, settlers, often fleeing religious persecution in Europe, quickly overwhelmed the native population and in essence transplanted their cultural traditions onto North American soil. Typically, the new European settlers established their own family farms, something that was almost impossible to do in most areas of northwest Europe where the landed aristocracy dominated politics and monopolized control of land. These settlements initiated a centuries-long process of driving native Americans into smaller and smaller enclaves while replacing them with mostly European immigrants. Native North American groups have only relatively recently begun to win legal challenges forcing various levels of American government to comply with treaties signed long ago.

The Caribbean

The Caribbean region also experienced large-scale settler colonialism, but most "settlers" were Africans imported as slaves to work on sugar plantations. The indigenous peoples often fell victim to European diseases (especially smallpox and various venereal diseases) and escaped from servile labor on tropical plantations. Because Europeans could not survive tropical diseases, there was an acute labor shortage. The colonial powers needed a labor force for plantation agriculture, and found it in Africa. On the western coast of Africa, a multitude

Colonial plantations of Brazil and the West Indies operated only with the use of slave labor. This late seventeenth-century sketch from Brazil shows slaves engaged in the sugar cane grinding and refining process. Sugar was then exported to European markets.

Source: © Hulton Deutsch Collection Limited London.

ETHNICITY IN MODERN SOUTH AFRICA

Although not densely populated, few countries can compare with the complexity and diversity of the ethnic heritage in modern South Africa. This divergence of cultures forms the basis of much of the conflict in the country. The most obvious cleavage is between whites, who have traditionally monopolized economic and political power, and blacks, who have generally been restricted to menial laborers. However, this obscures many other important differences. Whites in South Africa—15 percent of the total population—are split between the more numerous Afrikaners and the less numerous English. Afrikaners are descendants of the original seventeenth century Dutch settlers (hence the name Boer, the Dutch word for "farmer") but also include some French Huguenots who fled France after their Protestant religion was banned in 1685. The English settled in South Africa in the nineteenth century after Britain seized the Cape Colony for strategic reasons. Generally speaking, the English in South Africa are the wealthiest segment of society, and tend to be more liberal than the Afrikaners.

Among black Africans, there also are very salient ethnic divisions, exacerbated by widespread poverty. The two most numerous black ethnic groups in South Africa are the Zulus (6 to 8 million, about 25 percent of the total population), and the Xhosa (numbering approximately 5 million). The Zulus who live in the southwest province of Natal and have a long history of fighting for their political independence. The next most numerous ethnic group are the Xhosa, who live in the eastern Cape province. Other ethnic groups include the Sotho, Twana, and Swazi. In the 1960s the white South African

of mutually hostile ethnic groups often battled with one another, abducting and selling the defeated or defenseless into slavery as the booty of war. These unfortunates were then transported as slave labor to European colonies in the New World. The net result for most Caribbean countries was a type of settler colonialism where a European elite ruled over African slave laborers. Today most Caribbean countries are either overwhelmingly African in ancestry, as in Jamaica and Haiti, or heavily mulatto (mixed African-European ancestry), as in Cuba.

Latin America

In the early sixteenth century, Spanish conquistadors toppled the despotic Aztec and Inca empires and proceeded to establish an equally tyrannical system of haciendas, where natives were turned into servile laborers and forced to convert to Catholicism and to adopt the Spanish language. Yet, relatively few Spaniards and even fewer Spanish women emigrated to Spain's vast empire in the New World. Instead, many Spanish colonialists took indigenous wives and concubines, resulting in a three-tiered social structure: (1) a small white political and economic elite, (2) a significant population of mestizos (mixed European–native government attempted to keep the blacks divided by establishing "homelands" for each ethnic group. As apartheid broke down in recent years, this policy provoked some intense intra-black rivalries and conflict between those who allegedly collaborated with the whites, such as the Zulu Inkatha movement, and those who sought revolutionary change, such as the multi-ethnic African National Congress (ANC).

Between white and black in South Africa are the so-called coloreds, numbering some 2 to 3 million and living mostly in the western Cape province. They are the descendants of liaisons between the first Dutch settlers, who were mostly males, and native African women. The coloreds share much of the same culture as the Boers, typically speaking Afrikaans (the form of Dutch spoken in South Africa) and even practicing a similar form of Calvinist Christianity. As a result, the imposition of apartheid was in reality a rejection of their own history. Asians, mostly from the Indian subcontinent, constitute the other major ethnic group in South Africa. Like the coloreds, the Asians are generally richer than black Africans but poorer than whites, and thus occupy an intermediate status.

Given the breadth and scope of the divisions, the efforts at reconciliation among representatives of all of these groups in South Africa are likely to be difficult and protracted. Many ethnic and political conflicts regularly turn violent, threatening progress toward a more open, inclusive, and tolerant society. However, after agreement on a new democratic constitution, Nelson Mandela's election in the spring of 1994 promised the possibility of a new era in South Africa.

American ancestry), who played an intermediate role in towns and villages, and (3) a countryside of indigenous workers and peasants.

Thus, Latin America experienced a hybrid mixture of settler and elite colonialism. In some colonies, such as Guatemala, Peru, Ecuador, and Bolivia, native American ethnic groups survived Spanish forced-assimilation attempts. In other colonies, such as Mexico, Colombia, and Venezuela, the Spanish language replaced native languages, even though a large mestizo population ensured the perpetuation of cultural symbols and practices predating the arrival of Columbus. Yet, in the most temperate of Spanish colonies, Argentina, European settlers pushed the natives to the social, economic, political, and geographic fringes of the country.

Africa

Most of Africa was spared European colonization until the late nineteenth century, when medicines for such diseases as malaria and yellow fever permitted Europeans to survive in the tropical parts of the continent for extended lengths of time. Virtually all of European imperialism in Africa was elite colonialism: examples include Nigeria, Ghana, Senegal, Cameroon, Uganda, and Tanzania.

'You have the key, remember?'

Until the end of South Africa's Apartheid policy in the early 1990s, white rule chained peoples black and white in a never-ending cycle of increasing violence and poverty.
Source: © Dennis Renault, *Sacramento Bee.*

While there was some missionary activity that did convert some Africans to Christianity, European colonialism did not result in the wholesale destruction of native cultures or languages. For many Africans who lived far from cities or trade routes, European colonialism only marginally affected their daily existence.

There were, however, a few African colonies that did experience some settler colonialism—most notably, South Africa, Kenya, Rhodesia (now Zimbabwe), Angola, and Algeria. In the latter four cases, European settlers in the late nineteenth and early twentieth centuries confiscated some of the best agricultural land in the territories but did not achieve a large enough population base to sustain their political and economic supremacy once Africans began to mobilize politically after World War II. After bitter anticolonial struggles, the European settlers in Algeria, Kenya, Angola, and Rhodesia surrendered political power to Africans during the 1960s and 1970s and in many cases emigrated elsewhere.

In South Africa, however, European settlers became far more deeply entrenched. Cape Town was established by the Dutch as a strategic trading port in 1652. At first many Boers took native wives and concubines, as few

European women immigrated to the then distant supply and trading outpost. This resulted in the "colored," or mixed-race population that lives in Cape Town and its environs—the western Cape. In 1806 Britain seized the Dutch enclave for its own strategic trading reasons and brought English settlers and political administrators to the colony. After bitter struggles throughout the nineteenth century, including the Great Trek inland by the Boers in the 1830s and the Boer War (1899–1902), the English and Boers agreed to a white dominion government (1910) within the British Empire that attempted to secure white political and economic supremacy. In 1948 the Afrikaner Nationalist Party won an election and soon created a legal system of even more rigid racial hierarchy, eventually known as *apartheid* ("separateness").

For most of the twentieth century, the minority whites ruled over and thus excluded majority black Africans from any meaningful political participation. In South Africa, this hybrid system of elite and settler colonialism persisted even after other African colonies achieved independence in the 1960s. However, by the 1980s, white domination was slowly but surely unraveling as blacks gained in economic power domestically and the white government became ever more isolated internationally. Today in South Africa, difficult steps have been taken by the principal white and black organizations to create a new political system that can accommodate the very diverse mix of ethnicities, languages, and cultures. A major step along this path occurred when Nelson Mandela took office as the first black president in May 1994.

Asia

The northern half of Asia, Siberia, is one of the most sparsely populated regions in the world. This condition allowed Russian settlers and internal exiles of the tsarist regime to range ever eastward in the seventeenth and eighteenth centuries until reaching the Pacific, creating the world's largest country. Siberia thus experienced settler colonialism; it remains part of Russia, and most inhabitants of that region are ethnically Russian. By contrast, the southern half of Asia is among the most densely populated regions of the planet. Yet, nowhere in South Asia did Europeans settle in any significant numbers.

Thus, South Asia is one of the most obvious cases of elite colonialism. The British may have claimed their objective in India was to turn Indians into "brown Englishmen," but the Indian political elite that took control after Britain granted independence in 1948 appealed to India's rural masses using traditional cultural symbols. In fact, the reliance of Europeans on indigenous "collaborators" in Asia was so great that one might say that Europeans reigned but did not really rule.[18] The French colonization of Indochina was also elite colonialism, but it was a particularly intense form of "direct rule." Although very few French actually settled in Indochina and little of the land was alienated, the French sent as many administrators to Indochina as the British sent to India. As a result, the French administration was extremely intrusive into and disruptive of the traditional Vietnamese society.[19] On the other hand, a high level of colonial taxation allowed

SOCIAL IMPACT OF COLONIALISM

North America
Settler colonialism started in the early seventeenth century on the Atlantic seacoast by settlers who were fleeing religious persecution in Europe. They transplanted their culture.

Caribbean
Experienced large-scale settler colonialism, but most "settlers" were Africans imported as slaves to work on sugar plantations. The indigenous peoples often fell victim to European diseases and escaped from servile labor on the plantations.

Latin America
Conquistadors set up a system of haciendas, where natives were turned into servile laborers and forced to convert to Catholicism and adopt the Spanish language. Experienced a hybrid mixture of settler and elite colonialism.

Africa
Africa experienced some settler colonialism, but the native cultures were not wholly destroyed. And in most areas, elite colonialism prevailed. When medicines for malaria and yellow fever were discovered in the late-nineteenth century, Europeans could survive in tropical parts of the continent and settler colonialism increased. In South Africa, settlers became deeply entrenched after they first arrived in the mid-seventeenth century. The

the French authorities to build a relatively elaborate system of modern transportation and communications. These improvements in time reduced the incidence of famine and disease and thus allowed for high population growth rates. Overall, the French introduced radical changes in the social and economic structure of Vietnamese life, but did little to encourage the formation of a native elite with the skills necessary to govern a modern society. Indeed, the contradictions of French rule (depicted in the French film *Indochine*) set the stage for the twentieth century's longest anticolonial revolution.

The Pacific

In the island nations of Indonesia and the Philippines, a European elite ruled from the sixteenth century onward—concentrating on directing the export of tropical spices, but the tropical climate never attracted significant numbers of permanent European settlers. In contrast, British colonialism in Australia led to the near genocide of the Aborigines by British settlers. On the island of Tasmania, south of Australia, Europeans actually hunted the Aborigines virtually into extinction. Similarly, on the mainland, Aborigines survived the European onslaught only in the wilds of the Australian outback. Today Australia is overwhelmingly white in ancestry and thus is one of the most extreme cases of settler colonialism. The Aborigines now constitute only 1 percent of the Australian population. Even though they have received legal and civil rights since the 1960s, their communities remain tiny, poor, and isolated. In New Zealand minority whites ruled over the majority blacks until 1994.

Asia
Siberia experienced settler colonialism. Nowhere in South or Southeast Asia did Europeans settle in any significant numbers, demonstrating a clear case of elite colonialism.

The Pacific
A European elite ruled Indonesia and the Philippines from the sixteenth century onward. The tropical climate never attracted significant numbers of permanent European settlers. However, colonization of Australia and Tasmania resulted in the extermination of many of the Aborigines. In New Zealand the Maoris were overwhelmed by the British, but their culture survived.

China and Japan
Neither country was effectively colonized. Japan was isolationist until 1854, while China allowed very little trade with Europe. Both succumbed to Western pressures in the latter half of the nineteenth century.

the British overwhelmed the Maoris but their culture survived. They still represent 9 percent of the population and play a meaningful role in society.

China and Japan

East Asia was the only part of the world (save for inaccessible mountainous countries like Ethiopia and Nepal) that avoided direct colonial rule by European powers. By the nineteenth century, however, after sustained attempts to remain insulated from Western influence, both China and Japan were in severe economic crises. Meanwhile, European powers were growing ever more powerful and threatening. Large parts of China rebelled against Manchu rule from Beijing in the mid-nineteenth century, including the massive Taiping Rebellion (1850–1864), which left tens of millions dead from war and starvation. In Japan, Western pressure, especially from the United States via Commodore Matthew Perry in 1853 and 1854, ended Japan's isolation, leading to the Meiji Restoration (1868) in which the young emperor Mutsuhito decided that his country should modernize and begin to adopt Western ways. In neither case did European powers ever impose foreign colonial rule, but China was forced to sign "unequal treaties" that gave Western powers control over foreign trade and granted Europeans special legal privileges. (Areas such as parks reserved for Europeans in Shanghai had signs that read, "No dogs or Chinese allowed.")

China was divided into spheres of influence among the great powers in the late nineteenth century only to regain genuine independence in 1949 with the rise of Mao Zedong's Communist regime. By contrast, Japan quickly adopted many Western reforms in government, education, industry, and finance, and thus reestablished its political independence by the late nineteenth century.[20] Japanese emulation of the West included turning to imperialism and expansion. Japan annexed Taiwan (1895) and Korea (1910), placing Tokyo on a collision course with the United States.

Two important factors allowed China and Japan to avoid direct colonial rule. First, East Asia is on the other side of the globe from Europe, and the sheer magnitude of the distance served to insulate both countries from European imperialism until the nineteenth century, when ships were invented that depended on steam, not wind, in order to travel. However, other countries in the region such as Indonesia and the Philippines were colonized earlier, so the second point is particularly significant. Both China and Japan's dense populations and centralized governments made them uniquely capable of resisting and eventually adapting to foreign political pressures without capitulating formal political independence. To summarize, while both China and Japan attempted to isolate themselves from European influences, Japan's isolation was ended by Commodore Perry and China was coerced into unequal treaties before adapting politically and economically to Western pressures in the late nineteenth and early twentieth centuries.

ECONOMIC CONSEQUENCES OF COLONIALISM

The economic effects of European colonialism are, generally speaking, more uniform than the social repercussions. As discussed further in Chapter Eight, colonies, almost by definition, are subordinate economic units to the metropole. Almost invariably, European metropoles initiated economic trading policies that constrained their colonies to be little more than producers of raw materials for export to the mother country and captive markets for manufactured goods from the metropole.

Latin America, Africa, and the Pacific

The North American colonies of Quebec and the thirteen English colonies, for example, initially sent furs, timber, fish, and tobacco back to France and Britain, respectively. In fact, a major impetus for the American Revolution stemmed from the restrictions that Britain placed on American exports—they could be transported only on British ships to British ports—which severely limited the colonists' economic options. From American independence through the mid-nineteenth century, the export of cotton from the American South helped to spur Britain's textile industry and at home created a regional economic and political schism that resulted in the American Civil War.

In South America the Spanish plundered and mined large quantities of gold and silver. They also transplanted two high-quality food sources to Europe from the New World: corn and the potato. After independence in the 1810s and 1820s, many South American countries in the nineteenth century exported coffee, grains, copper, and other minerals to Britain.

The major export from Africa in the sixteenth, seventeenth, and eighteenth centuries was coerced labor in the form of slaves. However, Britain abolished most trans-Atlantic slave trade in the 1830s, and by the late nineteenth century, African colonies turned to such raw material exports as cocoa, coffee, palm oil, tea, cotton, ivory, tropical hardwoods, copper, and gold.

In the Pacific, Britain turned Australia and New Zealand into huge sheep and dairy farms in the late nineteenth century, supplying Britain with wool and food. Thus throughout Latin America, Africa, and the Pacific in this period, natural-resource-poor Britain traded for raw materials in return for railroads, textiles, capital goods, and foreign investment. This has led some observers to characterize the nineteenth century as *Pax Britannica,* in which Britain created a far-flung informal trading empire based on the import of raw materials and the export of manufactured goods and finance capital.[21]

Asia

Trade among India, China, the Dutch East Indies (now Indonesia), and Europe was actually complicated by the era of European domination. Britain, for one, did not gain control of overseas trade routes primarily in order to seize natural resources but rather to gain control over Asian trade. In 1840, for example, China attempted to shut off the import of opium due to the social problem of high rates of drug addiction and the gold drain on the faltering Chinese economy. However, the British navy in the Opium War of 1839–1842 forced China to cede Hong Kong and keep China open to opium and other imports. Only in the rubber plantations of Malaya (now Malaysia) did Britain impose an export crop on its Asian colonies. Yet Britain did use its hegemonic position to ensure that British-manufactured goods received de facto preferential treatment in these captive markets. For instance, British textile export to India undermined India's labor-intensive native weavers in the nineteenth century. The Indian National Congress under Mahatma Gandhi in the first half of the twentieth century used the spinning wheel as a powerful symbol of its opposition to British rule in India.

Economic Consequences: An Assessment

Whatever economic difficulties colonialism may have introduced, there can be no denying that colonialism did create a degree of political and economic predictability that allowed for increased trading opportunities, higher levels of foreign investment, and thus economic growth for the colonies as well as for the metropole. This is particularly true of physical infrastructure. Most of the railroads that now run throughout Asia and Africa were built under European tutelage during the colonial era. European colonialism also created predictable conditions in which ports, electric power plants, roads, schools, hospitals and

DEPENDENCY THEORY

In the 1960s, an intellectual paradigm known as *dependency theory* was promoted to explain why the South was poorer than the North. This perspective asserted that the economic subjugation of the Americas, Africa, Asia, and the Pacific by European states starting in the sixteenth century and culminating in the late nineteenth century created the first truly global economy with a distinct international division of labor. Western European states of the North became the "core" of the international economy by monopolizing and controlling world trading networks for their own advantage. As a result, the "core" specialized in high-value manufacturing (textiles, metals, and chemicals) while Third World countries became an economic "periphery" of servile and dependent suppliers of cheap raw materials, often resulting in many countries becoming precariously dependent on a single export industry. From this perspective, world trade is essentially a zero-sum game; the core's gain was and is the periphery's loss, and the economic development of Europe was predicated on the plunder of the resources of the Americas, Africa, and Asia. The North grew richer as the South grew poorer.

There are, however, some substantial complications with dependency theory.

water systems could be built. Of course, the principal beneficiaries of such infrastructure improvements during the colonial era were mostly European colonial officials. For instance, railroads in the colonial era were typically segregated by race, with the Europeans riding first class, complete with dining cars, while natives had to ride in (or on top of) overcrowded third-class cars.

Colonial rule also significantly increased the building of such "public goods" as roads and extended modern education and health care to areas previously unexposed to the advanced technologies available in Europe. Moreover, the colonial system provided for economic predictability—for instance, by introducing stable currencies, codified laws, and access to the home markets of the metropole. Such stability may seem trivial compared to the excesses of colonialism, but as many Southern countries have discovered since independence, economic development is impossible without political stability and economic predictability.[22]

CULTURAL AND IDEOLOGICAL IMPACT OF COLONIALISM

In the cultural and ideological legacies of European domination, the distinction between settler and elite colonialism again becomes meaningful. Where settler colonialism took root, the transplantation of European political, legal, cultural, and ideological traditions was relatively easy. By contrast, where elite colonialism took root, there were many more difficulties. To explain why, it is necessary

First, those European states (most notably Spain and Portugal) that did little more than pillage their colonial holdings often stunted their own long-term development. The gold and silver that Spain sacked from the Aztec and Incan empires may have enhanced its wealth and power in the sixteenth century, but also led to tremendous inflation and contributed to Spain's long-term economic stagnation in the eighteenth century. Second, it would be difficult to describe British trading policies in the nineteenth century as merely the looting of raw materials, especially in India, where the colonial regime undertook major economic development projects. Third, virtually all countries start their development by exporting raw materials; for instance, the United States initially exported little more than tobacco and cotton, while Canada exported wheat, and Japan rice. These countries only later went on to become industrial powerhouses. Moreover, some raw materials, like oil, are so valuable that they can within a very short period radically change the economic fortunes of a country.

Thus, it is difficult to sustain the argument that the export of raw materials necessarily means that a country is being exploited within the international economy. (Dependency theory will be discussed further in Chapter Eight.)

to consider several examples of colonialism and their impact on culture and ideology in the former colonies.

Colonialism and Culture

For countries that were settled by European immigrants, their colonial era is typically viewed as a necessary step in the development of the nation, like childhood in the growth of a human being. In the United States, Canada, Australia, and New Zealand (the clearest cases of settler colonialism) the legacy of Anglo-Saxon traditions of rule of law, private property, and individual rights has never been seriously questioned as the basis for a legitimate political order. Most debates in these countries have concerned the pace and scope of the extension of political rights to excluded groups, principally ethnic minorities and women. Moreover, due to the compatibility of political interests with Britain in particular, these countries have maintained relatively high levels of trade and foreign investment with Europe, which in turn has helped to secure long-term economic growth and prosperity. With such significant economic resources available, these countries have achieved a high degree of political cohesion and stability.

Where settler colonialism did not take root—where European administrators governed an indigenous population—postcolonial political cohesion and stability has been much more difficult to achieve, for numerous reasons. One element typical of elite colonialism was the strategy of "divide and conquer," coined by the Romans and perfected by the British. European colonial officials often attempted to accentuate ethnic and cultural differences among their colonial subjects in order to make rebellion and resistance to colonial rule more difficult to organize and sustain. For example, in India, Britain used Muslim mercenary troops against Hindus and vice versa, thus contributing to the maintenance of indigenous ethnic conflicts that eventually resulted in the bloody partition of the subcontinent at independence in 1947 into India and Pakistan.

In many other places, colonialism similarly contributed to contemporary political fragmentation. In Africa, European colonial officials often established ethnically based police and army forces that had little in common with other ethnic groups in the colony. After independence, these forces, some of which were little more than mafia cliques, frequently staged military coups d'etat, intensifying political instability. In Uganda, for example, the British established a very tall height standard for enlistment into the colonial army that effectively excluded most Ugandans and created an army of uneducated "Nubians" (southern Sudanese) who had precious little in common with other Ugandans. A few years after independence, the army led by "Field Marshall" Idi Amin seized power and ruthlessly pillaged the country. Similar military coups have occurred in other formerly British territories such as Sudan, Nigeria, and Ghana as well as in the colonies of other Western powers such as the Belgian Congo (now Zaire), and the former French territories of Guinea and the Central African Republic. In these cases, this type of military rule only contributed to economic collapse and social chaos.

Beyond the inheritance of European divide and conquer tactics, European colonialism also created countries in Africa and parts of Asia that made little if any political sense. It often threw together peoples that had little in common, and divided ethnic groups across borders for no better reason than to satisfy European diplomats quarreling over which European country should control a given port, river, or mountain. Somalis in the Horn of Africa were divided between Italian, British, French, and Ethiopian imperialists and are today still fighting among one another as well as with their neighbors over the definition of Greater Somalia. Elsewhere, Nigeria, Africa's most populous country, has three major and dozens of minor ethnic groups all struggling for their share of political power and economic development. In 1966 the Ibo tribe revolted and tried to create the country of Biafra until it was defeated by the central Nigerian government. Most other African states were afraid to back Biafra—despite the relative legitimacy of its claim for independence and its suffering at the hands of the Nigerian armies—for fear a dangerous precedent would be set for their own countries. Indeed, the first successful secession in Africa occurred only in 1993 with the independence of Eritrea from Ethiopia after a thirty-one-year war. In the Middle East, the Kurds are a stateless and restless minority in Iraq, Iran, Turkey, and Syria.

Clearly, most African and Asian countries have numerous ethnic and religious divisions in their societies. If every African ethnic group had its own country, there would be literally thousands of African countries, so it is impossible in practical terms to make every African country a nation-state. Thus, for many developing countries, the lack of a common culture, language, and/or religion has meant that there is no consensus on the fundamental political values of the country.[23] This fragmentation in turn has made the governance of these societies problematic. It is often very difficult to secure stability in institutions and policy, and disaffected groups can and do resort to violence in an attempt to redress their grievances and achieve their aims.

Colonialism and Ideology

The ideological impact of colonialism on political ideals has been a double-edged sword. On the one hand, European notions of liberty and democracy were to some degree diffused to the South over the past two centuries. For instance, some former colonial territories have maintained democratic government in the postcolonial era, especially formerly British-ruled countries such as India, Botswana, Malaysia, and Jamaica. Other former British colonies have often vacillated between democracy and dictatorship, such as Nigeria, Zambia, the Sudan, and Pakistan. In general, the longer the British ruled, the greater the likelihood that democracy would be sustained in the postcolonial era. The world's largest democracy is India and it is inconceivable that contemporary India would be democratic without some two centuries of British colonial rule. In contrast, there are many countries where Britain ruled for a relatively short period (such as Iraq, Kuwait, Sudan, Uganda, Malawi), where democracy has not taken root.

Generally speaking, democracy in formerly French colonies such as Vietnam, Cambodia, Syria, Algeria, Madagascar, Guinea, and Gabon has been more difficult to achieve, and is often absent. In such cases, democratic characteristics such as a free press, elections, and truly representative legislatures typically were only granted as the last step prior to independence—too little and too late for creating stable democratic rule in the postcolonial era. Thus, dictatorships often prevail in many parts of the contemporary South, especially the Middle East, Africa, and Asia.

Finally, there is one ideological movement that virtually all Southern countries have agreed on and that Southern rulers have often appealed to for widespread political support: anticolonialism. One major legacy of elite colonialism in particular has been to make the postcolonial countries exceptionally resentful of foreign domination. Unlike settler colonies, there is no romanticization of the colonial period (exemplified by the classic John Wayne-type "cowboys and Indians" stories and films set in America's Old West). Rather, the former elite colonies often look upon colonialism as an era of profound humiliation in their long and proud cultural history; this in turn can create a backlash in the form of rejection of "Western" influence. Many leaders of newly independent countries in the 1950s and 1960s achieved power by being more anticolonial than any other rival political leaders; Gamal Abdel Nasser in Egypt, Fidel Castro in Cuba, Ho Chi Minh in Vietnam, Kwame Nkrumah in Ghana, and Jomo Kenyatta in Kenya all appealed to the masses by denouncing colonialism and Western foreign domination.

This anticolonialism is easily understandable. European colonial rulers often arrogantly denigrated and offended native cultures and beliefs while claiming that European imperialism was the "white man's burden" to spread civilization. Not surprisingly, colonial subjects often protested against and sometimes violently resisted having their cultural traditions insulted and being ruled by foreigners. When colonial subjects began to organize politically, the "masses" almost spontaneously supported anticolonial nationalist movements for political independence. However, as demonstrated in Chapter Eight, the problem with anticolonialism in its postcolonial form of an anti-Western bias is that it often serves to rationalize economic policies that have very high costs. This tends to hinder the accelerated economic development that independence is expected to bring. The issue of "rising expectations" will be explored in the next chapter.

CONCLUSION: A WORLD OF FORMER EMPIRES

We have seen in this chapter how European empires served to globalize international relations over the last several centuries and how they also contributed to fragmentation, especially in the developing world. Colonialism has ended too recently (indeed, some would argue that it still continues in a modified form) to allow an objective analysis of its net effect on the peoples and societies that were subjected to it. The indignity, cruelty, and brutality inflicted by European imperialism on many people in the developing world is undeniable, and rivals or exceeds the atrocities perpetrated by earlier non-European empires. At the same time, imperialism integrated the South into the world economy in a way that benefited many in developing areas, and set the stage for possible further economic and social progress after the achievement of independence. The legacy of imperialism is thus a mixed one, and it is far from clear that even the metropolitan powers benefited, on balance, from imperial expansion. The era of imperialism is past, but its effects on the world economy and global politics remain, as we will see in several of the chapters to follow.

For now we can conclude that it is clear contemporary world politics has been patterned both by the expansion of the Europeans across oceans and continents and then the collapse of these empires. It is this combination of expansion over the last five hundred years and contraction during the last century which is a fundamental contributor to the tension between globalization and fragmentation in the post–Cold War era. One political legacy of the independence of former colonies has been to create a series of regional relationships among states on the local level. How and whether the tension between globalization and fragmentation will or even can be resolved will be determined on that local level, and it is therefore to these relationships which we now turn.

PRINCIPAL POINTS OF CHAPTER FIVE

1. Five hundred years of colonialism by the European powers had a major impact on the evolution of Third World states—their social, political and economic milieu.

2. The history of imperialism is at the heart of the North-South distinction in world politics.

3. Spain and Portugal, seeking new routes to the Orient for the lucrative spice trade, began the race for colonies in the late fifteenth century.

4. The principal colonial competition was between Britain and France through most of the eighteenth and nineteenth centuries, but it was the British Empire that had a particularly important impact on the peoples of the Americas, Asia, Africa, and the Pacific.

5. In the nineteenth century, both the Russian and American empires expanded across the Asian and North American continents, respectively, so that each was poised to emerge under the proper conditions as a major world power.

6. The complex collapse of the Ottoman Empire by the end of World War I laid the basis for several of today's major crises, including the conflict over the former Yugoslavia, the Arab-Israeli dispute, and the tensions of the Persian Gulf.

7. The Italian, German, and Japanese pursuit of empire emerged too late to have a major impact on framing the development of the Third World.

8. By the end of the Cold War, every empire, with the exception of the United States, had collapsed.

9. In settler colonialism (based especially in North America, Australia, New Zealand, and Argentina), where immigrants seized land from the indigenous population and became dominant, the European culture and political system dominated.

10. By contrast, elite colonialism, where the Europeans replaced the indigenous rulers but the native population and culture remained intact, usually left economic and social chaos and political instability.

Chapter 6

Global and Regional Conflict in the Developing World

In this chapter, we address the dynamics of regional international politics. And so we begin with an excerpt from the account by an Indian prisoner of war of his detention during the Indian-Pakistani war of 1971–1972.

> During my captivity in Pakistan, I discovered that human psychology and nature are essentially the same everywhere. The realities of happiness, sufferings, pain often transcend the barriers of language, creed and colour. Even an enemy is not immune to emotions. Kindness and sympathy are expressed instantaneously when we find another human being in agony. A Muslim is generally thought to be cruel and unkind to non-Muslims, but is not in actual fact. . . .
>
> Since I was a vegetarian, Col. Peerzada, my mentor in Lahore Hospital, had issued strict instructions to the cook to ensure that I was served pure vegetarian dishes.
>
> One day the cook brought my lunch with 'rice-pulao' as part of the menu. As I began eating it I discovered a huge piece of bone in the plate. I summoned the cook and asked him why he had served me such 'pulao.' When I showed him the bone he was scared to his wits' end. He was apologetic for the mistake. He begged me not to report him as it would mean not only loss of his job but even jail.
>
> I assured him that it was all right and I would not report him. He took the dish away and soon returned with a bowl of sweet curds.
>
> I thus discovered that the setup in the Pakistani hospital was no different from ours: the hospital staff were mortally scared of Col. Peerzada, who was reputed to be a strict disciplinarian. No wonder my stay in Lahore hospital was smooth and comfortable.
>
> S. S. Chowdhary, *I Was a Prisoner of War in Pakistan* (New Delhi: Lancer International, 1985), pp. 85–86.

Regions are composed of a variety of ethnic, cultural, racial, and political groups living in close proximity. Such conditions give rise to frequent and intense

Major Events in the Developing World: 1848–1994

1848: United States establishes military dominance in the Western Hemisphere, providing a measure of stability to Latin America.

1885: Decline of the Ottoman Empire leaves a power vacuum that contributes to the first of several Balkan wars.

1917: Britain issues the Balfour Declaration supporting a Jewish homeland in Palestine.

1923: Republic of Turkey is founded to replace the Ottoman Empire.

1947: Independence of India and Pakistan, accompanied by ethnic and nationalist conflict and dispute over Kashmir, leads to war.

1948: British departure from Palestine and the subsequent founding of Israel results in the first Arab-Israeli War.

1950–1953: United States' desire to prevent the spread of communism causes Washington to counter the North Korean invasion of South Korea, thereby entering the Korean War.

1951–1954: United States signs security treaties with the Philippines, Japan, Australia, New Zealand, South Korea, and Nationalist China (Taiwan).

1956: Israel invades Egypt with support of Britain and France following Nasser's nationalization of the Suez Canal.

1965: India and Pakistan clash over continuing dispute surrounding the control of Kashmir.

1965–1973: Fear of South Vietnam falling to the Communists leads the United States to intervene in the Vietnam War.

1967: During the Six-Day War, Israel captures West Bank from Jordan, the Golan Heights from Syria, and the Sinai peninsula and Gaza Strip from Egypt; Association of Southeast Asian Nations (ASEAN) is formed for economic and cultural cooperation.

1969: Soviet and Chinese forces clash along the Ussuri River.

1969–1970: Military confrontations known as the War of Attrition occur between Israel and Egypt along the Suez Canal.

conflicts that spring from very deep and old hatreds, some having existed for centuries. Yet, as this story suggests, toleration and reconciliation can exist in the most unusual of circumstances, revealing something of the unpredictable and complex nature of regional conflict.

In the previous chapter we traced European imperial expansion and its effects on what today is known as the Third World. European control of territory outside Europe reached its peak during the 1920s, but the origins of the continent's impending retreat were already apparent at the end of World War I. World War II exposed Europe's weakness, which combined with increased self-assertion in the Third World and the anti-imperial policies of the United States and the USSR to bring about a rapid retreat of European colonialism. A plethora of new states were formed, which sought to expand their political and economic strength, and consequently new regional balances of power developed. The ebb and flow of East-West conflict during the Cold War influenced these regional balances, while at the same time local conflicts played a major role in the U.S.-Soviet rivalry. The interaction of all these forces—state creation and consolidation, ethnic and religious conflict, and superpower competition—is the focus of this chapter.

We shall explore this interaction by first outlining the major causes of conflict between and within developing nations, including domestic factors and those "imported" from the developed world. Then we will survey regions of the developing world that are relatively free of interstate conflict, analyzing why conflicts in these areas tend to be intra-national rather than international in character. Next, we will examine in some detail three regions where the entry of postcolonial states into the modern international system has been marked by violence and war: the Middle East, South Asia, and East Asia. The chapter's conclusion will reveal how the globalization of conflict during the Cold War exacerbated indigenous conflicts in developing areas, while at the same time the fragmentation of the South spilled over into the political and military rivalries of the North.

1971: East Pakistan declares its independence as Bangladesh; West Pakistani troops invade Bangladesh but are defeated when India intervenes; UN votes to expel Nationalist China (Taiwan) and admit Communist China.

1973: Yom Kippur War between Israel and Egypt leads to confrontation between the U.S. and Soviet Union; Arab oil embargo in response to Western support of Israel precipitates energy crisis in the West.

1975: South Vietnam surrenders to Communist Viet Cong and North Vietnam; Cambodian and Laotian governments fall to Communist insurgents.

1977–1978: Somalia's invasion of the Ogaden region of Ethiopia fails.

1978–1979: Vietnam invades Cambodia and creates a Vietnamese backed Communist government.

1979: Reacting to Vietnam's invasion of Cambodia, China initiates a short border war with Vietnam; Iranian Revolution overthrows the Shah and establishes a fundamentalist Islamic government led by the Ayatollah Khomeini; Egypt and Israel sign peace treaty.

1979–1989: Soviet Union invades and occupies Afghanistan, which leads to war with Muslim rebels.

1980–1988: Iran-Iraq War is triggered by Iraqi invasion of Iran.

1987: *Intifada* in the West Bank and Gaza Strip reflects Palestinian frustration and discontent with Israeli rule.

1990–1991: Persian Gulf War occurs, in which a U.S.-led coalition removes Iraqi invaders from Kuwait and severely impairs Iraq's potential to gain a dominant position in the Persian Gulf.

1991–1994: Slovenia, Croatia, and Bosnia secede from Yugoslavia, resulting in civil war.

1992: U.N. supervises multiparty elections in Angola, but peace eludes the civil war-wracked country.

1993: New government is established in Cambodia after the United Nations carries out elections, although the Khmer Rouge refuse to participate; Israel and PLO sign mutual recognition accord.

1994: Nelson Mandela assumes presidency of South Africa after first election in which all people, regardless of race or color, are allowed to vote; Israel and Jordan sign peace treaty.

LASTING IMPACT OF EMPIRE

The most obvious and direct political consequence of European imperialism was the introduction of the European state system throughout the globe. The European conception of government, involving states with defined borders, capitals, judiciaries, bureaucracies, and sovereignty, is now ubiquitous. Today even the world's most isolated societies (the Amazon basin in Brazil, the Philippine island of Mindanao, and the highlands of Papua New Guinea, for example) are ruled by governments modeled on the state system that emerged in seventeenth-century Europe.

One consequence of this political reality is that the South today looks to the North for models of political and social development, not vice versa. Indeed, most elites that now rule developing countries received their education in the United States (particularly Latin Americans), Western Europe (particularly Africans and Asians), or the Soviet Union (particularly Communist revolutionaries). By contrast, only a small proportion of the political elite of most Northern countries have even studied about, let alone worked in, Southern countries. The major exception here is Britain, which during its imperial period had a tradition of sending many of its best and brightest overseas as colonial administrators.

Asymmetric Interdependence

Occasionally, major events in developing countries have political consequences in the North. The Arab oil embargo of 1973 sent economic shock waves through the North, and the Vietnam War led to domestic unrest in the United States. Likewise, the Iranian revolution dealt a blow to the political fortunes of Jimmy Carter, and Moscow's fruitless intervention in Afghanistan accelerated the disintegration of the USSR. Yet, in none of these cases did the South cause violent upheaval in the North. By contrast, even small fluctuations in the American or European economies can result in serious economic dislocations and even military coups d'etat or rebellions in developing countries. Dips in the prices of commodities such as oil, tin, and coffee can devastate the economies of developing countries that depend heavily on the export of a single product. (When the Coca-Cola Company changed the formula of its "classic" cola beverage in the 1980s, the government of Madagascar complained loudly because the new recipe didn't include vanilla beans, a lucrative source of export revenues for Madagascar.) Moreover, the International Monetary Fund (IMF) often makes its loans to Third World countries conditional on changes in economic policies, and the implementation of these programs has led to riots in such countries as Venezuela, Nigeria, and Zambia.

Thus, the contemporary relationship between North and South is best described as one of **asymmetric interdependence.** Developed and developing countries both need each other; the North needs Southern raw materials and labor, while the South needs Northern capital, export markets, and technology. The economies of developed states are usually more robust and diverse than those of developing nations, however, and are thereby more able to adapt to the changing economic conditions that cause disruptive shocks in the developing world.

To a significant degree, this asymmetric interdependence is another consequence of imperialism. In order to guarantee the supply of specific raw materials that were scarce or unavailable in Europe or North America, many colonial powers concentrated their investments in a few export-oriented commodities in the territories they controlled. When the former colony became independent, one industrial sector (geared to the needs of the former ruler rather than those of the new nation) may have been developed while the rest of the economy suffered from decades of neglect. Moreover, after independence, many developing states continued to specialize in areas where they had a comparative advantage over developed nations, such as tropical agricultural products or low-skill, low-wage manufacturing. This pattern of development did not result from a desire on the part of industrialized states to keep developing countries in a state of permanent inferiority (see the boxed feature on dependency theory in Chapter Five and Chapter Eight). Rather, it was a consequence of the integration of the South into the global economy during the colonial period, which promoted economic specialization for comparative advantage.

Just as the economic development of many Southern nations is heavily influenced by changes in the world economy, the independence of many Third World countries today is more an outgrowth of changing patterns of international relations in the North than any other factor. For example, the Napoleonic Wars in Europe (1803–1815) fatally weakened Spain's grip on Latin America. Britain stepped in and helped colonial rebellions in each of Spanish America's administrative regions achieve independence with financial aid, immediate diplomatic recognition, and control of the seas. Similarly, after World War II, the United States insisted on a number of policy changes (such as the end of the British Imperial Preference System of tariffs) by Britain and France that effectively made direct colonial rule a losing proposition. Not surprisingly, within twenty years after World War II, most European colonial empires had dissolved.

Legacy of Conflict

Just as the creation of empires is often a violent process of conquest, so the breakup of empires is frequently accompanied by violence. Two types of violent situations are probable. First, when metropolitan powers are reluctant to relinquish control, violent wars for independence sometimes result, as in Algeria, Vietnam, and Aden (now part of Yemen). Second, new states often engage in violent conflict over territory and even the very existence of a competing state, as happened with India and the newly created rival state of Pakistan. Long after the colonialists have gone, many areas in the developing world continue to be plagued by recurrent intra- and international conflict and war. The origins of some conflicts can be traced to the imposition of the political structures and military rivalries of the North onto the emerging nations of the South, but other disputes in the Third World are entirely home-grown. The next section will discuss the major contributing factors in the persistent and often intractable conflicts that rage in much of the developing world.

SOURCES OF REGIONAL CONFLICT

The primary causes of conflicts in the developing world may be divided into the two broad categories of "imported" and "domestic" problems. The domestic sources of disputes lie in **indigenous conflicts,** many of which predated the era of European imperialism and would be just as likely to cause dissension and violence if Europeans had never visited the region. **Imported conflicts,** on the other hand, are generally consequences of integration into the global political and economic system, or essentially extensions of Northern ideas and problems into the South. Having made this distinction, note that many conflicts are not purely imported or domestic in character. For example, ancient animosities between ethnic groups may have been exploited to further a colonial power's imperial ambitions, reinforcing a history of hatred that spills over into the present day. On the other hand, religious conflicts that have persisted for centuries may have originated with the introduction of a faith, such as Christianity or Islam, by an imperial power. Nevertheless, the grouping of sources of regional conflicts into imported and domestic varieties is useful for the analysis of contemporary disputes in the developing world.

Domestic Sources of Conflict

Foremost among the domestic sources of regional antagonisms is ethnic conflict. Empires are typically composed of different ethnic groups, usually occupying distinct territories that are all ruled through a center controlled by one of the ethnic groups. The end of empire involves the removal of the center's control and

AT A GLANCE

SOURCES OF REGIONAL CONFLICT

Ethnic Conflict: Domestic Source

Definition: Empires are typically composed of different ethnic groups, usually occupying distinct territories that are all ruled through a center controlled by one of the ethnic groups. The end of an empire involves the removal of the center's control and often the revival of ethnic disputes over territory. These disputes are often complicated because different ethnic groups have intermingled.

Examples: The breakup of the Soviet Empire and the subsequent regional hostilities, along with the Balkan conflict that has resulted from the breakup of Yugoslavia are directly related to ethnic problems.

Religious Conflict: Domestic Source

Definition: Violence in the name of faith persists in many nations where norms and institutions of religious tolerance have not taken root.

Religious disputes were the primary source of bloodshed before the twentieth century.

Examples: The breakup of British India into India and Pakistan allowed religious passions to explode. Religious differences emphasize the ethnic differences in the Middle East, as can be seen between the largely Sunni Muslim Arabs and the mostly Shiite Iranians.

Economic: Domestic Source

Definition: In the developing world, the gap between rich and poor can be very painful, especially when two states representing the two extremes share a common identity. Such material factors can exacerbate political and economic cleavages.

Examples: The United Arab Emirates enjoyed a per capita GNP of $19,800 while Egypt's per capita GNP was $600 in 1990. This disparity

often the revival, usually with renewed intensity, of ethnic disputes over territory. Often, these disputes are complicated by the fact that in certain areas different ethnic groups have intermingled. For example, the decline of the Ottoman and Austro-Hungarian empires left a vacuum in which the new states of the Balkans fought wars that eventually contributed to the outbreak of World War I. Then, for some seventy years the Balkan conflicts remained dormant, as fighting between the different ethnic groups was suppressed by monarchical and Communist regimes in Yugoslavia, and after World War II by Communist regimes in Romania, Hungary, and Bulgaria. The breakup of the Soviet empire and the subsequent violence in this region clearly showed that these ethnic problems were not solved. This sad pattern has been repeated in many instances throughout the developing world.

Another source of conflict is religion. Before the twentieth century, more blood was shed over religious disputes than any other cause, and this history of violence in the name of faith persists in many nations where norms and institutions of religious tolerance have not taken root. For instance, long-standing religious hatreds exploded into violence after British India was divided into independent India (with a Hindu majority) and Pakistan (where most of the population is Muslim). In many cases, the line between ethnic and religious conflict is blurred, because concepts of ethnic or national identity sometimes between rich and poor was one of the reasons that Iraq invaded its wealthy Kuwaiti neighbor.

Legacy of Imperialism: Imported Source

Definition: Borders that were arbitrarily drawn for the convenience of former colonial powers are a primary source of conflict. These borders can separate ethnic groups that would prefer to be united, or they might unite historically antagonistic groups that have no desire to live together.

Examples: Conflict resulting from this problem can be seen in Nigeria, Sudan, Ethiopia, Rwanda, Burundi, and Angola.

Nationalism: Imported Source

Definition: Groups have sought to unify politically fragmented nations. Many times, ethnic groups have tried to break away from existing states and create their own nations. This usually leads to fighting of one form or another.

Examples: Germany and Italy in the nineteenth century and Pan-Arabism in the twentieth century are examples of struggles for political unity. The successful Eritrean battle to separate from Ethiopia exemplifies the effort of many groups to renounce the status in which they find themselves.

Cold War: Imported Source

Definition: The Cold War brought the developing world into the bipolar confrontation between the United States and the Soviet Union. Both states supported insurgencies in developing areas in order to achieve their political and military objectives and to protect their strategic interests.

Examples: The Arab-Israeli conflict was influenced by the Cold War, and rebellions in Afghanistan and Nicaragua were also supported by each of the superpowers at various times.

center on religion. In other instances, religious differences reinforce ethnic antipathy, as shown by the recurrent conflicts between Arabs, most of whom adhere to the Sunni branch of Islam, and Iranians, the majority of whom belong to the Shia Islamic sect.

A third domestic source of conflict is economic, having nothing to do with spiritual values and everything to do with material goods. Economic factors alone rarely result in violence, but they can exacerbate political or economic cleavages. In many parts of the developing world, prosperous states border upon desperately poor neighbors with much larger populations. The gap between rich and poor can be particularly painful when the states involved share a common linguistic, ethnic, and cultural identity. This situation is most pronounced in the Arab world, where in 1990 the oil-rich United Arab Emirates enjoyed a per capita GNP of $19,800, compared with a figure of $600 for the most populous Arab state of Egypt.[1] As in the developed North, economic and class differences can generate conflict within as well as between countries, as shown by the violent disputes over land reform in much of Latin America. Few poor states have the resources necessary to make war on their richer neighbors, though Iraq's invasion of smaller and wealthier Kuwait in 1990 offers a notable exception. Still, in the developing world, as in American cities, the juxtaposition of wealth and poverty can be politically explosive.

Imported Sources of Conflict

Torn as they are by ethnic, religious, and economic conflicts, many developing countries would have more than enough to worry about without any problems brought in from the developed world. But few Third World countries are free of imported sources of conflict. One factor mentioned in the previous chapter is the legacy of **imperialism,** manifested in forms such as arbitrary borders drawn for the convenience of former colonial powers. These borders can separate ethnic groups that would prefer to be united, or unite historically antagonistic groups that have no desire to live together. If one of these groups becomes dominant and carries out policies regarded as unjust (often with very good reason) by the others, violence is the predictable result. This type of conflict has led to bloody struggles in Nigeria, Sudan, Ethiopia, Rwanda, Burundi, and Angola.

As we read in Chapter Two, the notion that each nationality should ideally live in its own sovereign state with defined borders was originally a European idea. Thus, **nationalism** may be counted as one of the imported causes of conflict in the developing world. Several of the conflicts just mentioned resulted from attempts by ethnic groups to break away from existing states and create their own nations. Other groups sought instead to unify politically fragmented nations: in the nineteenth century, it was Italy and Germany; in the twentieth, it was **Pan-Arabism,** an ideology that contends that all Arabs constitute one nation and should be politically united. This chapter's section on the Middle East will say more about Pan-Arabism and another nationalist movement that has had a profound impact on the region, **Zionism** (Jewish nationalism).

While nationalism and the aftereffects of imperialism are likely to persist for some time, one of the greatest external causes of conflict in the Third World has come to an end. This was the Cold War, discussed in Chapter Four, which inexorably brought the developing world into the bipolar confrontation between the United States and the Soviet Union. Both superpowers supported states and insurgencies in developing areas in order to further their political and military objectives and to protect their strategic interests. For example, in Central America in the 1980s, the United States sent generous amounts of military aid and expertise to the government of El Salvador, which was opposed by the Cuban and Soviet-backed Farabundo Marti National Liberation Front (FMLN) movement. Meanwhile, in neighboring Nicaragua, the USSR supported the socialist Sandinista regime in its fight against Contra rebels supplied by the United States. The only instances where the Cold War escalated into actual war occurred when the superpowers intervened in such conflicts in the developing world. Tens of thousands of Americans and their allies were killed fighting against Communist forces in Korea and Vietnam, thousands of Soviets died in the USSR's attempt to bring Afghanistan into the Soviet orbit, and millions of citizens of those three developing countries lost their lives in those "limited" wars. Several leaders of nonaligned nations, most notably Nasser in Egypt and Nehru in India, attempted to play the USSR and United States off against one another in hopes of receiving largesse from both.

During the Cold War, many wondered whether the U.S.-Soviet rivalry was intensifying Third World conflicts, or whether the reverse was true—that disputes in developing areas were heating up the Cold War. Much evidence supports both sides of this argument; many insurgent movements would have had little or no chance of success without U.S. or Soviet support, and so would have "died aborning," but many interstate disputes (particularly the Arab-Israeli conflict) put the interests of both superpowers at risk and so demanded action from Washington or Moscow. This question was the greatest "chicken or egg" controversy of the Cold War: Which came first, the indigenous conflict or superpower involvement?

When the Cold War ended, the debate fizzled out without resolution, but it is worth mentioning because it illustrates an important point regarding conflicts in the developing world. Like the struggles in which the superpowers became entangled, many Third World conflicts have been intensified and perpetuated by a vicious cycle of internal and external causes. An ancient ethnic hatred may have been brought to the fore when a colonial power exited, leaving behind borders with no economic or cultural justification, and guerrilla forces on both sides of the dispute received weapons from the superpowers. Because of the multiplicity of causes and influences that underlie them, subnational conflicts in the developing world often defy simple analyses and solutions. The height of absurdity occurred in Angola, a former Portuguese colony in southern Africa, when troops from Communist Cuba guarded oil fields operated by American companies against attack from UNITA guerrilla forces—which were backed and supplied by the United States!

In a sense, the complexity of conflicts in the developing world reflects the forces at work in the contemporary international system. The external sources of conflict generally derive from the political and economic **globalization** of the South, while the indigenous sources typically result from **fragmentation** within developing nations. While every region of the South (and much of the industrialized North as well) has been affected by intrastate violence as a result of these contending forces, wars between (rather than within) states have been concentrated in a few regions of intense conflict, especially the Middle East, South Asia, and East Asia. These areas are the loci of the most dangerous interstate conflicts in the contemporary developing world. Before turning our attention to them, however, it will be instructive to examine the areas of the developing world where fighting has been comparatively rare between—but common within—nations. The reasons why violence has usually been confined to the subnational level differ for each region.

REGIONS OF INTRA-NATIONAL CONFLICT

This section will explain why three areas of the developing world—Latin America, Africa, and Oceania—have not been embroiled in international wars. Most wars in the industrialized North have occurred *between* sovereign states, often beginning as disputes over which state should have sovereignty over specific territories. In much of the developing South, however, most wars have been fought *within* sovereign states, though other nations have frequently supported one or more of the parties to these conflicts.

In most cases, these intra-national wars are the result of attempts to resolve domestic political conflicts by violent means. Organized political violence is more likely in nations where institutions for peaceful resolution of political disputes, particularly democratic ones, are poorly developed, and the state's authority to govern is questionable or demonstrably ineffective. These conditions apply in much of the developing world, where many states gained independence only recently, and borders and government structures were hastily created by retreating imperial powers. In other Third World countries, governments of long-established states have lost legitimacy because they have excluded much or all of their populations from participation in the democratic process. To paraphrase the nineteenth-century Prussian military theorist Clausewitz, intrastate wars are best characterized as extensions of domestic politics, by violent means. Other nations can and do influence or intervene in such conflicts for their own purposes, but the underlying issues remain domestic rather than international in character.

Africa

Post–World War II Africa has not been a peaceful region, but it has been one where wars between nations are rare. The few attempts at aggressive territorial aggrandizement by African countries have failed completely. Somalia failed to capture the Ogaden region of Ethiopia in 1977–1978, the invasion of Tanzania by Uganda in 1978 led to the overthrow of Ugandan dictator Idi Amin, and Libya's invasion of Chad in the 1980s became an embarrassing debacle for Libya's president, Mu'ammar Gadhafi. Wars within African nations, however, have been depressingly frequent, and many have raged for years or decades without resolution of their underlying conflicts. Angola has been wracked by civil war from the mid-1970s onward; UN-supervised multiparty elections in 1992 failed to bring peace. The civil war in another former Portuguese colony, Mozambique, lapsed into a fragile peace in the late 1980s. In the early 1990s, Liberia was wracked by violent conflict between competing political foes. Ethnic violence has killed hundreds of thousands in Nigeria and Rwanda, and separatist fighting still threatens to tear apart Sudan and did lead to the withdrawal of Eritrea from Ethopia in 1993 (See Map 6.1).

Not all African conflicts have proven interminable, however. The decolonization process was accompanied by fierce fighting in Algeria and by considerable violence in such places as Kenya, Zaire, and Zimbabwe, but the conflicts directly resulting from the retreat of colonial powers in those countries were resolved. A peace plan for Namibia, formerly controlled by South Africa in defiance of international law, was put into operation in 1990 and has so far been successful. A negotiated settlement to the internecine racial and ethnic conflicts in

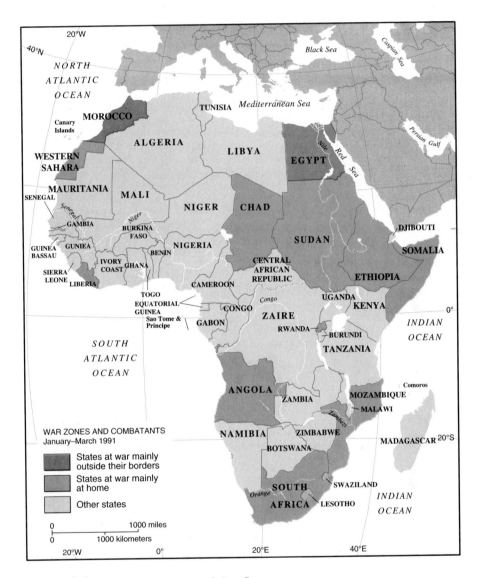

Map 6.1   Africa: Regions of Conflict

South Africa itself has been achieved, but the final outcomes of that nation's many disputes remain uncertain.

   Although most of the warfare in postcolonial Africa has arisen out of domestic conflicts, outside actors have been involved in much of it. French and Belgian forces have intervened repeatedly in Zaire and Rwanda, Cuban troops were deployed to Angola and Ethiopia, and South Africa made extensive use of its armed forces in Namibia before Namibian independence. Many African conflicts

AT A GLANCE

INTRA-NATIONAL CONFLICTS

Africa

Situation: Few African states command enough resources to build effective military forces without extensive outside aid. No African government has been able to use military power to gain a decisive victory over its foreign enemies. Political and military institutions in many African countries are poorly developed and unable to maintain sovereignty over a government's own state, let alone contest sovereignty over a neighbor's territory. Internal and external opponents can carry on insurgencies or guerrilla struggle with relative ease, making territorial conquest in Africa generally a losing proposition. For the majority of African countries, war has been a poor investment, though many ruling regimes have resorted to it to defend against internal enemies.

Superpower Involvement: Many African nations were dragged into the context of the Cold War as the United States, the Soviet Union, China, and France supplied various factions in the numerous civil wars with funds and weapons. Overall, however, the superpowers' competition for influence in Africa had little effect on their global rivalry. Now that the Cold War has ended, there are no vital interests in the region for either of the superpowers.

Conclusion: War solves nothing. Lasting solutions to conflicts have required extensive negotiations and international mediation and supervision.

Latin America

Situation: Few conventional wars are fought in Latin America because of the United States. The United States has dominated the Western Hemisphere militarily since 1848, and has not hesitated to suppress or intervene in any conflict

were dragged into the context of the Cold War as the United States, the Soviet Union, China, and France supplied various factions in the continent's many civil wars with funds, weapons, and other equipment.[2] Overall, the superpowers' competition for influence in Africa had little effect on their global rivalry. African states such as Ghana, Ethiopia, and Somalia changed sides during the Cold War with small loss to their former patron's interests and few gains, if any, to their new ally's objectives. Though it only marginally impacted the global balance of power, the Cold War in Africa generated heated political debate in both the United States and the USSR. (The Soviet Communist system ensured that the controversy in Moscow never became public.) In general, despite many dire warnings in the United States of disastrous consequences if various African countries became dominated by Marxist regimes, the interests of the superpowers in Africa were never great enough to risk international war.

Indeed, the main conclusion one may draw from these African conflicts is that in Africa, war solves nothing. Lasting solutions to conflicts, as were achieved in Zimbabwe and Namibia, have required extensive negotiations and international mediation and supervision. Few African states command enough resources to build effective military forces without extensive outside aid. Even when the superpowers or other donors have obligingly provided troops, arms, and money, no African government has been able to use military power to gain a decisive victory over its enemies, foreign or domestic. Political and military institutions in which has threatened its vital interests. America's military and economic power has enabled it to maintain hegemony over the entire region, preventing wars and incursions by outside powers that might pose a serious threat to its vital interests. Castro's Cuba is the one exception.

Superpower Involvement: Latin America, and specifically Central America, is a region where the United States demonstrably possesses both vital interests and the power to protect them.

Conclusion: American power has not been sufficient to resolve all intra-national conflicts within the region to its liking, but it has been able to maintain a *Pax Americana* that has prevented wars that would threaten key American interests.

Oceania

Situation: The developing island nations could not make war on one another even if they wanted to. Most are separated by large expanses of ocean, and few possess either the resources to build military forces or security problems great enough to justify their construction.

Superpower Involvement: The U.S. Navy, which remains dominant in the region, can quickly put a stop to any conflict that develops between neighboring countries in the region.

Conclusion: As the developing nations of Oceania lack the motive, means, and opportunity for war, the Pacific region has lived up to its name admirably.

many African countries are poorly developed and unable to maintain sovereignty over a government's own state, let alone contest sovereignty over a neighbor's territory. Internal and external opponents can carry on insurgencies or guerrilla struggles with relative ease, making territorial conquest in Africa generally a losing proposition. (Chad, one of the world's poorest countries, was able in the late 1980s to defeat an invasion from oil-rich Libya with a small amount of French assistance.) For the majority of African countries, war has been a poor investment, though many ruling regimes have resorted to it to defend against (or attempt to exterminate) internal enemies. The weakness of most African states and the absence of vital superpower interests have combined to make Africa since 1945 a region of much violence, but little international war.

Latin America

Like Africa, Central and South America have experienced few wars between nations in this century but have been shaken by intra-national fighting, particularly in Central America. But the reasons for the relative lack of international war in the region are quite different. Most Latin American states achieved independence in the nineteenth century, and have well-developed institutions for maintaining their sovereignty and government authority. Argentina and Brazil, in particular, have substantial military forces, and Brazil has become a major exporter of arms, including aircraft, tanks, and missiles. Most states in Latin America are fully capable of making war on one another, but have hardly ever done so since the 1930s.

The main reason why few conventional wars are fought in Latin America may be found to the north. The United States has dominated the Western Hemisphere militarily since 1848, and has not hesitated to suppress or intervene in any conflict that has threatened its vital interests. It has been especially assertive in Central America and the Caribbean, which is crisscrossed by vital American trade routes and lines of communication. In the twentieth century, the United States has sent forces into Mexico (in 1914), Guatemala (1954), Nicaragua (1912–1933), Panama (1903–1918, 1989), Cuba (1921–1923, 1933), Haiti (1915–1934, 1994–), the Dominican Republic (1916–1924, 1965–1966), and Grenada (1983)—not counting the blockade of Cuba during the Cuban Missile Crisis or various covert operations.[3] America's military and economic power has enabled it to maintain hegemony over the entire region, preventing wars and incursions by outside powers that might pose a serious threat to its vital interests. Only two international wars have occurred in Latin America since 1945: the Falklands War of 1982, during which Britain could not have recaptured the disputed islands from Argentina without American consent, and a minor conflict between Honduras and El Salvador in 1969 that originated in riots surrounding a World Cup soccer game.

Thus, unlike Africa, which had no areas of vital interest to either superpower, Latin America is a region where the United States demonstrably possesses both vital interests and the power to protect them. American power has not been sufficient to resolve all intra-national conflicts within the region to its liking, but it has been able to maintain a *Pax Americana* that has prevented wars that would threaten key American interests.

Oceania

The islands of the Central and South Pacific were the scene of bitter fighting in World War II, as Japanese and Allied ground, naval, and air forces struggled for control of the region. Since the war, most of the island groups formerly controlled by Japan, the United States, Britain, and France have become independent states. Decolonization proceeded very smoothly in Oceania (which excludes the Philippines and Indonesia, herein considered part of Southeast Asia), and the legacy of imperialism has generated conflict in only a few areas. Conflict between indigenous inhabitants of Fiji and Fijians descended from Indians who settled in the islands during British rule led to a military coup in 1987, and separatist unrest periodically leads to violence in New Caledonia, which remains a French territory. On the whole, however, the developing island nations could not make war on one another even if they wanted to. Most are separated by large expanses of ocean, and few have either the resources to build military forces or security problems great enough to justify their construction. Should any conflict somehow develop between the island states, the U.S. Navy, which remains dominant in the region, could quickly put a stop to it. As these developing nations of Oceania thus lack the motive, means, and opportunity for war, the Pacific region has lived up to its name admirably.

INTERNATIONAL CONFLICT AND REGIONAL BALANCES OF POWER

This chapter now turns to areas of the developing world that have experienced frequent international conflict and war since 1945. As is the case with other parts of the Third World, the imported and domestic causes of conflict in the Middle East, South Asia, and East Asia are often interrelated. Unlike the areas surveyed in the previous section, however, most of the conflicts in these three regions are not domestic disputes writ large. Although domestic politics naturally plays a role in the ways the involved countries deal with the conflicts in which they are embroiled, the regional conflicts examined here are first and foremost disputes between states rather than within them. Many of the most intractable conflicts in these regions center on whether certain nations should exist as independent states. As we saw with the nationalist conflicts of nineteenth century Europe, when other states (usually those who have lost or would lose territory) oppose nationalist aspirations, nationalist conflicts immediately acquire an international dimension.

A key factor in the resolution or prolongation of many of the conflicts in these areas is the regional balance of power. Recall from Chapter Two that the term balance of power refers to the distribution of capabilities (usually military and economic strength) among the states in the international system. (See Chapters Twelve and Thirteen for detailed discussions of this concept.)

While Chapters Two, Three, and Four are concerned with the global balance of power, the concept of the balance of power may be usefully applied on a less than global scale as well. Many states in East and South Asia, and in the Middle East, possess considerable military forces and economic strength but cannot project their capabilities beyond the regions in which they are located. Since the conflicts in these regions often find one or more states aligned on opposing sides of disputed issues, the relative power of each state is frequently a critical factor in their disputes. States or alliances often attempt to gain enough power to force a resolution of the conflict favorable to them, or at least enough to prevent their opponents from doing so. (Their opponents, of course, are usually doing the same.) The predictable result in these cases is a regional balance of power that shifts according to changes in alliances, economic developments, or acquisition of military capabilities. The efforts of several states to maintain the balance often creates an arms race, usually involving the sale or transfer of arms from developed to developing states, since few Southern states have the capacity to manufacture modern weapons. An imbalance of power that leads one side to believe it has a decisive advantage (or that it must act to prevent its opponents from gaining one) has often led to war. The following sections will illustrate how regional balances of power have at times prompted attempts to resolve interstate conflicts by war and at other times prolonged disputes in an uneasy state of "no war, no peace."

THE MIDDLE EAST

Of the three regions we will examine, the Middle East shows in starkest relief the effects of domestic, regional, and global struggles for power. Within the various Middle Eastern states, domestic struggles for power have often led to states that were unstable, frequently governed by the military and intelligence agencies, and prone to use an exterior enemy in order to stifle internal opposition. The many intertwined conflicts have created not one but three regional balances of power—Arab-Arab, Arab-Israeli, and Arab-Iranian—that are separate but also interact, with conflict in one frequently spilling over into another. On top of this already volatile situation, the Cold War added the struggle between superpowers for allies and clients in the region. The superpowers' provision of economic and, in particular, military assistance to their regional allies helped maintain the regional balances of power but fueled a spiraling regional arms race.[4]

Conflicting nationalist aspirations are the foundation of the three regional balances of power. The conflict between Zionism, or Jewish nationalism, and Arab and Palestinian nationalism forms the core of the Arab-Israel conflict. The Arab world itself has been divided between the tug of Pan-Arab nationalism, which calls for a single Arab state and denies the legitimacy of separate Arab states, and the pull of distinctive statist nationalism (in Egypt, Jordan, Syria, Iraq, and elsewhere), which argues that the independent Arab states are legitimate entities. The ancient rivalry between Arabs and Persians formed one of the bases of tensions between Iraq and Iran, onto which was added the religious conflict between Sunni Islam, dominant in Iraq, and Shia Islam, dominant in Iran.

Thus, although the Middle East is suffused with ancient indigenous hatreds, many of its conflicts are sustained by a concept of nationalism that originated in nineteenth-century Europe (see Chapter Two). Nationalist aspirations in the region draw upon interpretations of history that emphasize periods of national glory but are also to a large extent responses to European events. Zionism was a reaction against the continual persecution of Jews in Europe, culminating in the Holocaust during World War II. It held that Jews would never be safe until they had their own state. Arab nationalism was a reaction to increasing European encroachment on the Middle East; it emphasized the unity and power of the early Arab caliphates. Though Arab-Iranian antagonism has persisted for centuries, Iranian nationalism was partly a response to the indignity of being dominated by Russia and Britain during the nineteenth century and during World War II and to the predominance of American influence after World War II. The shahs who formerly ruled Iran claimed that their dynasties were a continuation of the great Persian empires, while the leaders of the Islamic revolution of 1979 rallied around the struggles and sufferings of Shia Islam.

End of the Ottoman Empire

Prior to 1914 the Middle East was dominated by the Muslim Ottoman Empire for four hundred years. Unlike modern forms of political identification, which are based on nationalism, religion was the most important political basis of the Ottoman Empire. Because the Ottomans controlled most of the Middle East, areas of which were distinguished only for administrative purposes, peoples' identities were based on family, tribe, occupation, and religion. By the end of the nineteenth century, however, distinct nationalism began to form, as the Turks "rediscovered" their distinctive ethnicity and sought to exclude Arabs from administrative posts. In turn, the Arabs increasingly "rediscovered" their own ethnic identity and began to press for autonomy and independence. Turks, Arabs, Persians, and Jews were all influenced by European ideas of nationalism and national identity.

Like the Austro-Hungarian Empire, the Ottoman Empire was on the losing side in World War I and relinquished its imperial possessions; the empire itself ceased to exist upon the declaration of the Republic of Turkey in 1923. What to do with its Middle East holdings became a matter of considerable contention in the peace conferences after World War I, in large part because of the contradictory promises Britain had made to various groups during the war. In return for Jewish support, Britain issued the **Balfour Declaration,** which stated in 1917 that Britain supported the establishment of a Jewish "national home" in Palestine, as long as it did not prejudice the civil and religious rights of non-Jewish residents. This promise appeared to conflict with Britain's promises to support Arab independence in exchange for Arab participation in the war against the Ottoman Empire. Conflicting with both of these promises was the arrangement Britain made with France to divide the Middle East into spheres of influence. (Wits remarked that Palestine was truly the Promised Land, as Britain had promised it to both Arabs and Jews.) Trying to reconcile these conflicting promises amounted to squaring a circle; many of the opposing demands were irreconcilable. As it turned out, because they were the most powerful actors in the region after the war, the British and French adhered to their own arrangements and drew the boundaries of their mandated territories to serve their own interests.[5]

This does not mean that the promises to either the Zionists or the Arabs were ignored. The British control of Palestine, Transjordan, and Iraq, and French control of Lebanon and Syria, were mediated through the League of Nations. The Middle Eastern areas were not colonies but mandates to be held until the local peoples were ready for independence and self-government. Arab claims that they were prepared for independence, based in no small measure on their contribution of troops in the war against the Ottomans, were forcefully suppressed, with particularly bloody results in French-controlled Syria. The British and French drew international borders—none had existed previously—to suit their own interests and to the benefit of ethnic or religious communities to whom they were sympathetic. Thus, to the preexisting Maronite Christian areas of

Lebanon, France added the predominantly Sunni Muslim north and Shiite south. Britain, to fulfill its promises to Arab leaders, separated Jordan from Palestine.

The new states were not yet independent, but they still faced considerable internal problems in their attempts to consolidate their control. During the Ottoman period many groups had maintained considerable autonomy because of the center's weakness, limitations of communications, and geographic boundaries. The new states, and their British and French overlords, sought to increase their control over such communities. Since the Arab elites' pressure for independence conflicted with the desires of the French and British to maintain control, the latter turned to divide-and-conquer policies. For example, in Syria the French turned to the poorer Alawites and Druze, who were discriminated against by the Sunni majority, as the backbone of the military and internal security apparatus. This would have considerable impact on future developments.

Arab-Israeli Conflict Begins

By the end of World War II, several Arab states had finally become independent, but their weakness was one of the main factors that prevented a coherent and forceful response to the Zionist movement in Palestine. After 6 million Jews were murdered by the Nazi regime in World War II, international support for Zionism increased, as did the pressure for emigration of Jews into Palestine. As fighting intensified there between Arabs and Jews, the British were caught in the middle and decided to withdraw and turn the problem over to the UN. For different reasons both the Soviet Union and the United States supported the UN-proposed partition of Palestine and thus the creation of two independent states, one Jewish, the other Arab; Jerusalem was to become an international city. The Jews accepted the plan, but the Arab Palestinians—backed by the other Arab states—insisted that all of Palestine must become an independent Arab state. When the British departed in May 1948, Israel declared its independence and the surrounding Arab states invaded, beginning the first Arab-Israeli war.

After almost a year of fighting, Israeli forces repulsed the invading Arab armies, and some 760,000 Arab refugees fled. Israel conquered lands allotted to the Arab state of Palestine, which never came into being. Territory allocated to the proposed Palestinian Arab state was also conquered by Jordan, whose annexation of the West Bank in 1950 was never internationally recognized as legitimate. Egypt controlled the last portion of Palestine, the Gaza Strip, a small sliver of land onto which were crowded tens of thousands of refugees.

The defeat of the Arab states dealt a considerable blow to the legitimacy and stability of the existing regimes, exacerbating preexisting socioeconomic and political divisions. In 1950 King Abdullah of Jordan was assassinated, and in 1952 King Farouk I of Egypt was overthrown by a nationalist revolution, led by Gamal Abdel Nasser, who soon became the country's president. During the 1950s, Syria experienced several changes of government as military clique replaced military clique, each basing its support on various ethnic groups.

The new Arab regimes in Syria and Egypt were authoritarian. They held the West, including the United States, responsible for Israel's establishment, and

Jewish troops check interiors of Arab houses along a Palestinian village street in June 1948. The fledgling nation of Israel was barely three weeks old at the time.

Source: © UPI/Bettmann.

resented the limitations of arms supplies imposed on the region by Britain, France, and the United States. Egypt's Nasser was especially incensed by the American-British effort to form an alliance against the Soviet Union that would have transformed Egypt's arch-opponent Iraq into the political center of the Middle East. When the United States offered to sell him arms under tight conditions, Nasser rejected the idea and instead approached the Soviet Union for economic and military assistance. The Soviets jumped at the opportunity to play a major role in the Middle East and began to supply Egypt with aid and weapons, thereby destabilizing the delicate balance of power between Egypt and Israel.

Conflicts of the 1950s and 1960s

Nasser was also angered by the American rejection of economic assistance to construct the Aswan High Dam, which was designed to control the Nile River and was seen as crucial to Egypt's economic development. In retaliation, in July 1956 he nationalized the Suez Canal, which was under the jurisdiction of an Anglo-French company. Nasser's moves infuriated the British and French, the latter already angered by his support for the Arab rebellion against French control of Algeria.

Britain and France began to coordinate policy with Israel, which was concerned about Egypt's growing military strength, and the three states agreed on a secret plan to attack Egypt. The plan was set in motion when Israel invaded Egypt's

Sinai Desert in October 1956, and shortly afterwards Britain and France intervened, ostensibly to separate the two sides and protect the Suez Canal. Although Israel gained a military victory, Egypt scored a political knockout when both the United States and the USSR, each for its own reasons, forced Britain, France, and eventually Israel, to withdraw. President Eisenhower, infuriated by the secrecy of the attack, believed that it undermined American efforts to build good relations with the Arab states. The Soviets saw an opportunity to demonstrate their importance in the fight against imperialism, and ostentatiously threatened Britain and France with missile attacks and Israel with destruction. After Britain, France, and Israel backed down, Nasser's prestige in the Arab world rose dramatically.

Nasser's appeal increased the attractiveness of his call for Arab unity, the central goal of Pan-Arabism, and his cries for the overthrow of Arab regimes viewed as puppets of the imperialist West. During the late 1950s there was considerable domestic unrest throughout the Middle East, and 1958 proved to be a fateful year for many Arab countries. Lebanon experienced a civil war, which eventually led to American intervention. (The U.S. forces landed with no opposition; sunbathers on Beirut beaches, surprised by American landing craft, asked the Marines if they had come to start a war and resumed sunbathing when told that the Marines were a peacekeeping force.) King Hussein of Jordan was threatened at home by supporters of Nasser. Meanwhile, in Iraq the monarchy was overthrown by radicals, who were in turn overthrown in 1963 in a coup executed by the Ba'ath (Arab Socialist Renaissance) party. In Syria the internal upheaval was so severe that the ruling clique united the country with Nasser's Egypt, thus forming the United Arab Republic.

The domestic unrest was eventually quelled with the assistance of U.S. intervention in Lebanon and British intervention in Jordan. In 1961 the United Arab Republic dissolved when Syria seceded from Egypt. With his standing in the region now diminished, Nasser increased political propaganda and subversion efforts against the regimes he saw as opponents. In 1962 Egypt intervened in North Yemen on the side of socialist-oriented republicans, who were fighting a civil war against the Saudi-supported monarchists. The Egyptian intervention in Yemen has been called "Nasser's Vietnam," and his economic and political costs, including the antagonism of Saudi Arabia and the United States, were considerable. In 1966 the radical left wing of the Ba'ath Party took control of Syria and supported military and terrorist attacks against Israel. Syria was militarily weak, however, and was consistently defeated in skirmishes with the Jewish state. The government in Damascus, joined by Jordan and Saudi Arabia, accused Nasser's Egypt of failing to confront Israel, which they contended was their primary threat.

Six-Day War (1967) and Its Aftermath

The charge of failing to confront Israel was embarrassing to Nasser, and when Syria and Israel engaged in border clashes during the spring of 1967, his rhetoric against Israel intensified. In May 1967 the Soviets, fearing for the survival of the fragile Syrian regime, falsely told Nasser that Israel was planning to invade Syria. Nasser moved Egyptian troops into the Sinai Peninsula in order to deter Israel from such an attack. If this policy had been successful, it would have brought Egypt considerable prestige. Instead, the move initiated a crisis in which an escalating spiral led inexorably toward war.

The UN next acceded to Nasser's demand that its peacekeeping forces already in Sinai withdraw, thus removing a crucial buffer between Egyptian and Israeli troops. Nasser promptly blockaded the important Israeli port of Eilat. Significantly, Jordan and Syria then placed their armies under Egyptian command; this formation of a unified coalition against Israel represented a dramatic shift in the Arab-Israeli balance of power, alarming the Jewish state. Fearing encirclement and an imminent Arab attack, Israel launched a preemptive war on June 5. In the course of the next six days, Israeli ground and air forces routed the armies of Egypt, Jordan, and Syria. The Soviets, who had contributed to provoking the crisis, were stunned by the rapid Israeli defeat of their Arab allies. Fearing that Israel might drive for total victory, Moscow decided to break diplomatic relations with the Jewish state and to pressure the United States to restrain Israel.

The 1967 war, known as the Six-Day War, was the definitive event in contemporary Middle East history. Israel captured the Sinai Peninsula and the Gaza Strip from Egypt, the West Bank from Jordan, and the Golan Heights from Syria (See Map 6.2). The devastating defeat severely weakened Nasser, and he was forced to rely on economic aid from the oil-producing Gulf states, especially Saudi Arabia (in exchange for Egyptian withdrawal from Yemen). The inability of the superpowers to control events, and the possibility that a Middle East crisis could lead to a superpower confrontation, increased the desire of the United States and the USSR to attain some sort of settlement.[6]

While Washington and Moscow engaged in diplomatic efforts to achieve a negotiated settlement, their positions generally reflected those of their combative allies fairly closely. The early result of the diplomacy was UN Security Council Resolution 242, which enshrined the principle of "land for peace." The resolution called upon Israel to return "territories occupied" in 1967 in exchange for recognition of its right to exist within secure borders. (The resolution was very carefully worded and deliberately ambiguous; it did not explicitly call for Israel to return *all* territories occupied in the war.)

Meanwhile, the superpowers rearmed their regional clients. The result was the 1969–1970 War of Attrition that Egypt initiated in frustration when it did not regain the Sinai. Initially the fighting consisted of artillery duels across the Suez Canal, but it soon escalated as Israel launched deep-penetration air attacks against Egypt. Placed on the defensive, Nasser sought and received direct military support from the Soviets, who sent in advisors and pilots. Because it was preoccupied with events in Vietnam, America's response to this unprecedented Soviet intervention was initially subdued, but Washington's diplomatic efforts brought about a cease-fire in August 1970.

If one of the effects of the 1967 war was to demonstrate the weakness of the Arab states, another was to increase the importance of the Palestinian national movement. Prior to 1967 the Palestine Liberation Organization (PLO) was poorly led and was a tool of various Arab states, especially Nasser's Egypt. After 1967 this organization, an umbrella for various Palestinian groups with different

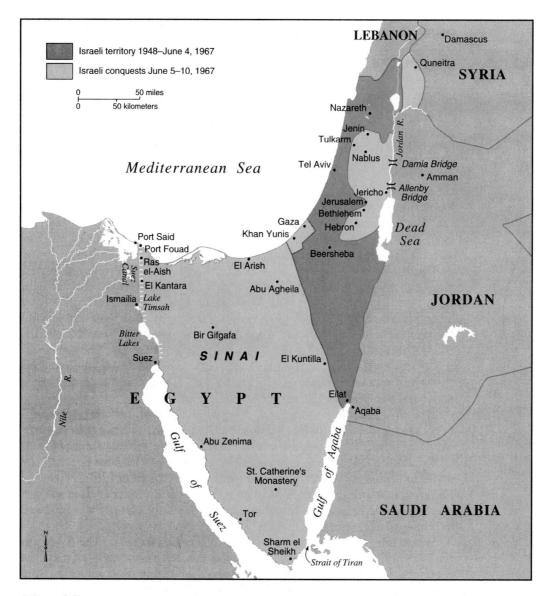

Map 6.2   Israel: Boundaries before and after the 1967 War

ideologies, became more independent under its dominant faction, Yasser Arafat's al-Fatah. As the PLO launched terrorist attacks against Israel, it increasingly came into conflict with the Arab states, which were suffering from Israeli military retaliation. In Jordan the PLO's strength made it resemble a state within a state, and its power was seen as a challenge to King Hussein. After numerous skirmishes, in September 1970 a full-fledged civil war broke out between the PLO and the Jordanian army. Serious Palestinian setbacks led to Syrian intervention. This move initiated an international crisis, in which the United States and Israel put pressure on Syria to withdraw its forces from Jordan. As the Jordanian army drove the Syrians out and routed the PLO forces, Nasser engaged in diplomacy aimed at saving the PLO's position in Jordan. The PLO survived the civil war but was forced to shift its base to Lebanon. Upon completing his mediation efforts, Nasser suffered a heart attack and died, marking the end of an era.

Petroleum, Power, and Politics

The 1950s and 1960s were decades of revolutionary nationalism in the Arab world, but the 1970s was a decade of oil wealth. In the years immediately after Nasser's death, Egypt's new president, Anwar el-Sadat, moderated Cairo's foreign policy by improving relations with the rich oil-producing states. Not surprisingly, Egypt's relations with the Soviet Union grew cooler, and in 1972 Sadat expelled the Soviet military advisors Nasser had invited. In an attempt to improve relations, the Soviets subsequently sold considerable quantities of arms to Egypt, paid for in part with Saudi money. At the same time, the United States and other Western countries became increasingly dependent on Middle Eastern oil, due to the rapid economic growth of the 1960s and the correspondingly rapid depletion of U.S. oil reserves.[7] Unable to gain support for their demands that Israel return the territories it conquered in 1967, Egypt and Syria grew progressively resentful and came to believe that only another war would enable them to create favorable political conditions. The two countries thus began to coordinate their strategies in another attempt to turn the Arab-Israeli balance of power to their advantage. They also received assurances from Saudi Arabia that in the event of war, it would impose an oil embargo against Israel's supporters among Western countries.

Their strategy was implemented in October 1973 when Egypt and Syria launched a surprise attack against Israel known as the October War (or the Yom Kippur War, because the attack began on that Jewish holiday). Israel's forces in the Sinai and Golan Heights were initially thrown on the defensive, but after suffering heavy losses took the offensive. Because of the intensity and length of the fighting, both the USSR and the United States conducted emergency airlifts of weapons and supplies to their allies. After a brief cease-fire arranged by the superpowers, fighting resumed, and Israel was positioned to annihilate the portion of the Egyptian army trapped in the Sinai. Fearing the complete defeat of its ally, the Soviet Union mobilized airborne troops and threatened to intervene directly. In response, the United States put its military forces, including its nuclear weapons, on heightened alert. The risk of a direct superpower confrontation was exaggerated, but American pressure convinced Israel to accept a cease-fire.[8]

During the war, Saudi Arabia and the other Arab oil-producing states imposed an oil embargo on the United States and the Netherlands for their support of Israel. The price of oil, a vital resource for industrial economies, increased dramatically, and the startling rise in the price and disruption of the availability of gasoline sent shock waves throughout the industrialized states. This use of the "oil weapon" prompted the United States to redouble its efforts to bring about a political settlement of the Arab-Israeli conflict.[9]

NASSER

Within the Arab circle there is a role wandering aimlessly in search of a hero. For some reason it seems to me that this role is beckoning to us—to move, to take up its lines, put on its costumes and give it life. Indeed, we are the only ones who can play it. The role is to spark the tremendous latent strengths in the region surrounding us to create a great power, which will then rise up to a level of dignity and undertake a positive part in building the future of mankind.

This statement by Gamal Abdel Nasser in 1958 exemplified the frustration and hope of the Arab world in the 1950s. Newly independent in the 1930s and 1940s, the Arab world underwent a wave of revolutions after its defeat at the hands of Israel in 1948. A decade later, a new optimism had emerged. Many believed the Arabs—united by culture, religion, and history—should unify and become a major economic and military power on the world

scene. Israel would be defeated, prosperity would arrive, the great powers would take the united Arab government seriously, and a major social and intellectual renaissance would occur.

Nasser offered himself as the leader of the Pan-Arab movement. In Egypt, he launched sweeping programs of land reform and economic development, including a project to dam the Nile at Aswan. But the United States and Britain, concerned over Nasser's ties with the Soviet bloc, withdrew funding for the dam in July 1956; five days later, Nasser announced the nationalization of the Suez Canal. A subsequent invasion by Israeli, British, and French forces failed to topple his government, and Nasser emerged from the crisis more popular than ever. His most dramatic step toward unifying the Arab states was the joining of Egypt and Syria in the United Arab Republic in 1958. Another victory for Nasser occurred

Land for Peace

During the 1970s, politics in the Middle East was marked by two contrasting tendencies. On the one hand, there was growing instability within many countries in the region. In one horrendous example, a civil war in Lebanon broke out in 1975 as Maronite Christians opposed attempts by various Muslim groups to change the country's political balance of power. In early 1976 the Muslims, supported by the PLO, seemed to be gaining the upper hand until Syria intervened on the side of the Maronites. Meanwhile, the PLO remained an independent force in southern Lebanon, which it used as a base for terrorist attacks against Israel.

On the other hand, in the midst of the turmoil in Lebanon, the United States continued its diplomatic efforts to resolve the region's seemingly intractable conflicts. Between 1973 and 1976, Secretary of State Kissinger sought to bypass the Soviets to deal directly with the Middle Eastern states. U.S. diplomatic efforts resulted in a disengagement agreement between Israel and Syria and two agreements between Israel and Egypt, in both of which Israel pulled back its forces when the pro-Western Iraqi government he opposed was toppled by the Baghdad regime's radical adversaries.

Yet many of his gains were illusory. While many Arab leaders supported Pan-Arabism, they were not prepared to relinquish their regime or their rule to others. Thus, Nasser soon found that the radical Iraqi regime caused him as much trouble as the old pro-Western rulers. Syria withdrew in disgust from the union with Cairo in 1961. After Nasser ordered Egyptian troops to intervene in the 1962 civil war in Yemen, the Saudi monarchy put a $1 million price on his head.

Facing growing problems at home as his development plans foundered, Nasser tried to rally support by railing against Egypt's main enemy, Israel. His remilitarization of the Sinai and blockade of the Strait of Tiran prompted Israel to strike pre-emptively in 1967, and Egypt suffered another devastating defeat. Although Nasser remained in office, his power was irretrievably diminished. He died of a heart attack in September 1970 after working furiously to bring about a settlement of the civil war in Jordan.

Nasser's dream of a unified, secular Arab state died with him, but his example as a leader who defied colonialism and the superpowers lives on throughout the Arab world. His frustrations and failures symbolize the underlying divisions that remain among Arab countries. A quarter century later, Islamic fundamentalism has replaced secular radicalism as the central threat to Western interests. In the wake of the new divisions in the Arab world created by the Persian Gulf War of 1991, Pan-Arabism is now weaker than ever. An Arab world of individual rulers and regimes has for now won out over the Pan-Arab vision.

in the Sinai. Believing that Kissinger's step-by-step approach had achieved all it could, in 1977 the new Carter administration sought to reengage the Soviets in an effort to achieve a comprehensive peace. Although the operation was a failure, the patient's health improved: fearing that a peace process including the Soviets and the Syrians would go nowhere, Egypt's President Sadat astounded the world in 1977 by visiting Jerusalem, Israel's capital. As the Egyptian-Israeli peace process proceeded with active American involvement, other Arab states vilified Sadat. The next year, with President Carter's mediation, Egypt and Israel agreed to a "framework for peace" outlined in the Camp David Accords and concluded a peace treaty in 1979.[10] The other Arab nations expelled Egypt from the Arab League and stopped providing Cairo with economic aid.

Conflicts of the 1980s

If 1979 was a year of peace, it was also a year of revolution. The repressive shah of Iran, a close American ally who was regarded as a stabilizing influence in the Persian Gulf, was overthrown by a radical Islamic revolution. The new government in Teheran was anti-American to the core, led by the Ayatollah Khomeini (whose own regime was also brutally repressive). In part the revolution was a legacy of the profound social disruption caused by the vast wealth derived from oil exports. The fact that many of the Arab Gulf states, including Iraq, Kuwait, Saudi Arabia, and the United Arab Emirates, were also experiencing considerable social change meant that Khomeini's call for the overthrow of these regimes generated deep concern. While many Arab regimes feared that the spread of Islamic radicalism would lead to further instability, it was clear that the delicate balance of power that had existed in the Gulf region had been disturbed. Worries over instability in the Gulf raised oil prices in developed countries; Americans waited in long lines for gasoline, and industrialized economies slumped into recession.

In 1980 Iraq invaded Iran. The attack was motivated in part to forestall the threat of Khomeini's revolution spreading across the border, in part to take advantage of Iran's preoccupation with its confrontation with the United States over American hostages being held in Teheran, and in part to gain revenge for previous Iranian territorial gains. To the surprise of most, Iran put up a stiff fight, not only halting the Iraqi attack but also going on the offensive. Fearing that Iraq might lose the war and that Iran might subsequently come to dominate the Persian Gulf, the wealthy oil-producing Arab states provided Baghdad with substantial economic aid. As the war bogged down into an eight-year struggle of attrition, the United States progressively backed Iraq, although it secretly attempted to trade arms to Tehran in hopes of securing the release of American hostages. In the mid-1980s Iran appeared to have the upper hand, and even to be on the verge of victory. In response the United States supplied Iraq with military intelligence and intervened in the Persian Gulf. By 1988 both sides were exhausted and agreed to a cease-fire, which was viewed as a victory for Iraq at the time.

The Iran-Iraq war and the Israel-Egypt peace created great unease in the Arab world. Arab countries were not only more divided than ever, but their financial and political fortunes were declining as well. Although the price of oil rose dramatically in the wake of the Iranian revolution, it gradually declined as oil-importing states cut back on their use of oil and developed domestic energy resources. Some Arab oil-producing states, particularly Saudi Arabia, undermined OPEC's efforts to maintain high prices by increasing production in an effort to gain a greater share of the world market for oil.

In 1982 Israel launched a major invasion of Lebanon to eliminate the PLO and in the process dealt a devastating blow to the Syrian forces in Lebanon. The absence of Arab support for either the PLO or Syria during the war was a demonstration of how divided and weakened the Arab world had become. Israel's initial success was soon overshadowed by debilitating guerrilla attacks on its troops, and Lebanon began to be called "Israel's Vietnam." Israel eventually withdrew most of its forces, but maintained a "security zone" in southern Lebanon. The Lebanese civil war dragged on, until after the Iraqi invasion of Kuwait. In the light of Syria's support of the American-sponsored coalition against Saddam, the U.S. looked on quietly as Syria solidified its dominance over most of Lebanon.

New World Order, Old Regional Conflicts

As the 1980s came to a close, three trends developed that would have considerable impact on the balance of power within the region. The first was the gradual decline and then demise of the Soviet Union. In practical terms, Russian weakness meant that it was both less able to provide support to its Arab allies and less willing to back them if such support came at the expense of relations with the United States.[11] The second development was the Palestinian uprising, or *intifada*, in the Israeli-occupied Gaza Strip and West Bank. Beginning with spontaneous riots in late 1987, the uprising grew and spread without the direction of the PLO, reflecting the frustration and despair of Palestinians over the absence of any diplomatic progress that promised to meet their goals. The *intifada* put considerable strains on U.S.–Israeli relations, and contributed to a brief American willingness to talk directly with the PLO in 1989. Talks were broken off soon after they began, however, in the wake of a PLO terrorist attack against Israel.

The third development was a disturbance of the regional balance of power caused by the continued weakness of Iran and the growing strength of Iraq. After the Iran-Iraq war, the Gulf Arab states put pressure on Iraq to repay its debts, which the Baghdad regime resisted. Faced with economic problems and possessing a huge military machine, Iraq invaded Kuwait in 1990, and in so doing threatened to gain a dominant position in the Persian Gulf. (Iraq's move was encouraged by a huge imbalance of power between the two Arab countries, as the size of Iraq's army was roughly equal to that of Kuwait's total population.) This act of naked aggression—the first attempt by one Arab state to conquer another—shocked the world. In an equally unprecedented move, the United States spearheaded an international coalition, diplomatically supported by the Soviet Union, that sent troops to defend Saudi Arabia. The following year, in the face of Iraq's refusal to accept UN demands to withdraw, the coalition launched an offensive to evict Iraqi forces from Kuwait.

The American-led coalition drove Iraq from Kuwait and severely damaged Iraq's military capability, especially its programs to develop nuclear, chemical, and biological weapons. The American-led victory, along with the decline of the USSR, also reinvigorated the Arab-Israeli peace process: In 1991 Israel and its Arab neighbors began direct bilateral negotiations for the first time, supplemented by multilateral talks that included other Arab states. After more than four decades of violence, the possibility of a new order in this war-torn region had finally emerged.

Whether the new order will be more peaceful than the old, however, remains a question. The collapse of the Soviet Union has removed the U.S.-Soviet rivalry that fanned the flames of the region's many conflicts, but the conflicts themselves remain. Despite the overwhelming victory won by the coalition forces in the Gulf War, the terms for a final political settlement have yet to be determined. None of Iraq's neighbors want it to reemerge as the dominant power in the region, but most feel that a counterweight to Iran is still needed to prevent

Teheran from dominating the Persian Gulf. The stability of many Arab governments is illusory—the departure of President Hafez al-Assad of Syria or King Hussein of Jordan from the political scene could easily lead to violent succession struggles within those states.

Yet, there have been encouraging developments. The Arab-Israeli negotiations resulted in a September 1993 breakthrough between the PLO and Israel, which recognized each other's legitimacy for the first time. Dramatic diplomatic progress on the Israeli-Jordanian front leading to a peace treaty followed in 1994. Many fundamental conflicts remain unresolved, but progress is beginning to be made. The regional balances of power in the Middle East offer the primary guarantee against the outbreak of war. The region's violent history shows how often that guarantee has failed in the past. Yet, the new contacts between Arab and Israeli officials since the Persian Gulf War show that progress is possible.

SOUTH ASIA

Like the Middle East, post–World War II South Asia has been a region marked by continual tensions with occasional outbreaks of violence, both within and between states. Instead of three distinct but interacting balances of power, as in the Middle East, the international relations of South Asia have been dominated by the antagonism between India and Pakistan. Here, too, the sources of instability stem from the colonial legacy, the efforts of the regional states to consolidate control, and ethnic and religious hatreds. Both superpowers were actively involved in South Asia, and their involvement exacerbated the indigenous tensions. But the direct involvement of China, through its border disputes with India and its ties with Pakistan, distinguishes South Asia from the Middle East.

As noted in Chapter Five, Britain had imperial control over virtually all of the Indian subcontinent prior to World War II. As pressure for independence became stronger between the two world wars, the Indians themselves increasingly became divided along religious lines—that is, between the Hindu majority and Muslim minority. The bases of these differences were in part theological (Hindus are polytheistic while Muslims are monotheistic), in part historical (Hindus resented the past Muslim domination of India), and in part political. As independence appeared increasingly likely, both sought to ensure that their economic, political, and social interests would be protected. When suitable provisions for their interests could not be agreed to, Muslims demanded independence for the areas in which they constituted a majority. In 1947 these two areas, in the northwest and northeast corners of India, separated by 1000 miles of Indian territory, became the nation of Pakistan (See Map 6.3).

Severely weakened by World War II, Britain sought to eliminate the burden of controlling India as quickly as possible. In the hasty withdrawal, the British tried to draw borders that were generally acceptable; nevertheless, the final demarcation left many Muslims in India and Hindus in Pakistan. Independence thus created a massive refugee problem, as more than 12 million Muslims and

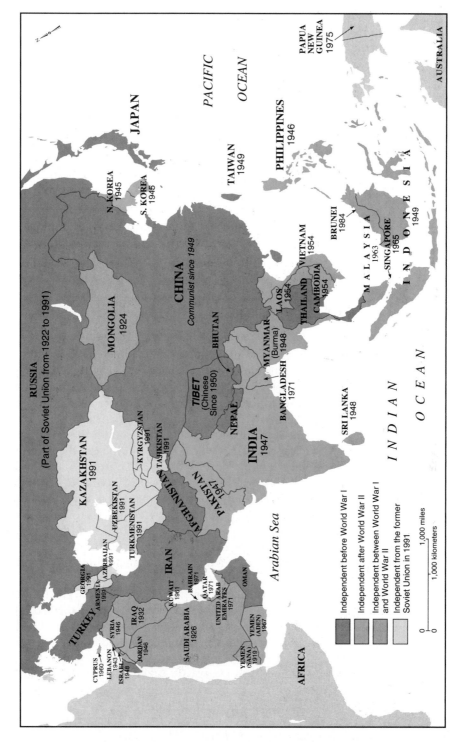

Map 6.3 South and East Asian Independence after 1945

Hindus fled to their new "homelands." The migration of refugees was accompanied by widespread violence; 1 million people died as a result of massacres, other hate crimes, and starvation.

The most contentious area was and is Kashmir, where the population is primarily but not exclusively Muslim. When in 1947 the Hindu prince of Kashmir was given the choice of joining Pakistan or India, he procrastinated, and even contemplated declaring independence, since joining either would mean giving up power, and becoming part of India risked popular rebellion. Since the majority of the population was Muslim, and Pakistan's raison d'etre was to be a Muslim state, Pakistan naturally felt strongly that Kashmir should accede to it. When the prince's temporizing led to revolts among the Muslim population of Kashmir, Pakistani tribesmen infiltrated to give support. Facing a revolution, the prince joined India, which thereupon sent troops to put down the rebellion and repulse the Pakistani tribesmen. In December 1947, India appealed to the United Nations, which called for a cease-fire and a vote to determine the wishes of the people. Instead Pakistani troops intervened in early 1948 and occupied parts of western Kashmir; a cease-fire was finally agreed to in 1949. The vote has yet to be held.[12]

Era of Nonalignment

During the 1950s the Kashmir dispute receded into the background as India and Pakistan sought to address internal demands. Under the leadership of Jawaharlal Nehru, India claimed to base its foreign policy on a set of principles known as *panchsheel*: respect for other countries' sovereignty and territorial integrity; nonaggression; noninterference in the internal affairs of others; equality and mutual benefit; and peaceful coexistence. India sought to remain neutral, stay outside the Cold War alliances then forming, and to keep the superpowers out of South Asia. India's neutral stance and moralistic attitude rankled the United States in particular. Meanwhile, the other, weaker countries of South Asia saw India's neutralism as an attempt to dominate the region and its moralism as pure hypocrisy, given India's sometimes heavy-handed policies toward them.

As the weaker state, and fearing impending Indian domination, Pakistan sought out external allies for help. In 1954 it obtained U.S. military assistance and then joined both the Baghdad Pact and the Southeast Asia Treaty Organization (SEATO), becoming a crucial hinge in the U.S. containment policy. In 1959 the United States pledged to protect Pakistan's independence and territorial integrity, with force if necessary. These developments angered India, which increasingly turned to the Soviet Union for political backing and military assistance. Ironically, both India and Pakistan received economic aid from the two superpowers.

In addition to its border problems with Pakistan, India also had territorial disputes with China. One disputed area was the Aksai Chin, to India's northwest, while the other was in its northeast, bordering Tibet. As China's relations deteriorated with the Soviet Union in the late 1950s, Beijing began to build a road through the Aksai Chin to link Tibet with the western province of Xinjiang, which it feared the Soviets might try to destabilize. At about the same time, China faced internal unrest in Tibet, which it had forcibly occupied in 1950, and greatly resented India's grant of asylum to Tibet's spiritual leader, the Dalai Lama, in 1959. Disgusted by India's recalcitrance in resolving their border disputes and angered at the encroachment of Indian forces in Tibet, China invaded the disputed area in 1962 and dealt India a sharp, though indecisive, blow.

India-Pakistan: Hostilities

The 1962 Sino-Indian war created great concern in the United States and the Soviet Union, both of which saw China as an increasingly aggressive and unpredictable power. New Delhi called for both American and Soviet assistance, and both moved to support India. Pakistan saw these developments as detrimental to its balance of power with India. Superpower support for India thus naturally brought Pakistan and China closer together, and Beijing backed Pakistan's claim to Kashmir. Convinced that India's poor performance in the 1962 war meant that it was for the moment weak, and fearing that the American and Soviet assistance would make India stronger soon, Pakistan began to contemplate launching a war over Kashmir. India in turn increased its own military spending and turned to the Soviet Union for military assistance, having first been rebuffed by the United States.[13]

The Pakistani government came to believe that India was consolidating its control of Kashmir, but that in the short term the balance favored Pakistan. Religious conflict soon created a spark in the region's volatile atmosphere. In 1963 the theft from a Muslim shrine in Kashmir of a holy relic, a hair from the Prophet Mohammed, led to rioting there and in Pakistan. This development strengthened the belief of Pakistani leaders that they could gain the support of Kashmir's Muslims and that they had a short-term advantage—a conclusion reinforced in 1964 by the death of Nehru, India's popular, charismatic leader.

In April 1965 Pakistani tank forces defeated Indian troops at the Rann of Kutch, a sparsely inhabited area of salt flats on the Indian-Pakistani border. After the British and the UN intervened diplomatically, both sides agreed to a cease-fire and a partial withdrawal of forces. The victory emboldened Pakistan, which now believed it had military superiority. Consequently, in August 1965, Pakistan sent agents into Kashmir in the expectation that they would generate a rebellion among Kashmir's Muslims, a rebellion in which Pakistan could intervene in their support. Although the uprising never occurred on a wide scale, Pakistan still invaded, seeking to cut Kashmir off from India. To Pakistan's surprise, India did not counterattack in Kashmir, but instead launched an offensive across the Indian-Pakistani border and drove for the important Pakistani city of Lahore. The United States slapped an arms embargo on both sides and secured a cease-fire. Both India and Pakistan accepted a Soviet invitation to mediate, which led to an agreement to return to the status quo ante bellum (a Latin term in international law meaning "situation before the war").[14]

Neither side gained from the 1965 war; to the contrary, both India and Pakistan suffered economically and politically. Pakistan suffered more, as an economic

WHAT WOULD YOU DO?

You are the leader of Pakistan in early 1965. You have received reports that India is tightening its grip over Kashmir, thus reinforcing its refusal to allow a plebiscite that would surely lead Kashmir's overwhelmingly Muslim population to vote in favor of joining your country. To counter India's move, you are considering a war to expand the part of Kashmir your own troops occupy.

Several conditions favor an attack now. FIrst, India suffered a blow to its hegemonic aspirations during the 1962 war with your ally China, which exploded its first nuclear bomb just last year. Second, delaying attack will only allow India, which is trying to play both sides of the fence, to amass more military support from the Soviet Union and the United States. Third, the blasphemous theft of a hair of the Prophet Mohammed from a holy shrine in Kashmir two years ago still stirs the passions of Kashmiris. They are supported by your fellow countrymen, and the theft presents unscrupulous politicians with another opportunity to question your rule. Thus, a

downturn exacerbated long-standing differences between the western and eastern sections of the country. Although the eastern sector, East Bengal, had the majority of the population, the west was dominant politically and economically. Even before 1965 there had been growing resentment in East Pakistan against West Pakistan, and when elections were held in 1970, the east overwhelmingly elected a party that favored increased autonomy. When negotiations broke down between the Pakistani government and the victorious party, riots erupted in East Pakistan, only to be ruthlessly suppressed by the Pakistani military. The East Pakistani leadership now declared its independence as Bangladesh in March 1971, and a civil war ensued. As up to 10 million refugees flowed into India, New Delhi moved its forces to the border.

Pakistan feared that it was about to lose the eastern half of the country, but it knew that if it tried to restore order in East Pakistan by force, India would inevitably intervene. Faced with the prospect of a war it could not win in the long run, Pakistan thought that if it attempted a preemptive attack against India, it could defeat the larger Indian forces, just as Israel had defeated the Arabs by striking first in 1967. When Pakistan finally declared war on India in December 1971, things did not work out that way. India was ready for the conflict after years of military preparations and rapidly defeated the Pakistani forces. The new state of Bangladesh replaced the old eastern sector of Pakistan. India also retook parts of the Rann of Kutch and a portion of Kashmir, lost in previous Indian-Pakistani clashes in 1947 and 1965.[15]

In the wake of its defeat, Pakistan had little choice but to accept India's de facto control of Kashmir. But the war did not shift the balance of power in the subcontinent decisively in India's favor. In spite of its victory over Pakistan and its closer relations with the USSR, represented by a 1971 Treaty of Mutual popular war would help channel some of this passion.

On the other hand, an attack could backfire. You have not completely secured the entire length of your border with India. A move against Kashmir could provoke the Indian army to counterattack against your weakest point of defense. Also, you never established complete legitimacy in your Eastern Province (East Pakistan), whose language, ethnicity, and economy are quite distinct from those in the Western Provinc (West Pakistan). While the battle in the west distracts your forces, East Pakistani politicians could put plans for secession into motion, using your failure to consult them on the attack as a pretext.

You want to mount a clean, decisive offensive on India's forces in Kashmir without provoking an Indian counterattack on your weakest western points and an East Pakistani secession.

What would you do?

Friendship and Cooperation, India still felt threatened. Ironically, despite India's democratic regime, the United States frequently tilted toward Pakistan during the Cold War because of the close ties between New Delhi and Moscow. Pakistani governments, even though they were usually run by dictators, were often seen in Washington as more compliant with American interests.

India also became concerned in the early 1970s that its security was being threatened by nuclear weapons. During the 1971 war, the United States had dispatched a nuclear-armed aircraft carrier to the Bay of Bengal as a sign of support for Pakistan. China, a previous and potential adversary, was developing its nuclear forces, and the nearby USSR already possessed a huge nuclear arsenal. In response to these perceived threats and in an effort to demonstrate its military and technical potential, India began a program to develop nuclear weapons in 1972. Two years later, India conducted what it called a "peaceful nuclear explosion," thereby declaring to the world that it had nuclear capabilities. Pakistan's fear that India could someday use nuclear threats to blackmail it accelerated efforts to gain the capacity to produce nuclear weapons, and in February 1992 Islamabad admitted that it had the capacity to produce at least five nuclear weapons. Pakistan's efforts to produce nuclear weaponry has strained relations with its neighbors, as well as the United States.

Global Tensions and Internal Conflicts

The 1979 Soviet invasion of Afghanistan proved fortuitous for Pakistan. The United States began to pour large amounts of economic and military aid into Pakistan, which became the bulwark against further Soviet expansion into South Asia. The United States also muted its public concern over Pakistan's nuclear program. Through the 1980s, U.S. relations with Pakistan improved dramatically, as Pakistan provided a crucial base of support to the Afghan rebels fighting against the Soviet occupation. After the Soviet withdrawal from Afghanistan in 1989, U.S. relations with Pakistan cooled, with the nuclear issue returning to the fore. Pakistan's recent tentative return to democracy has done little to improve relations with the United States, as the army still plays too large a role in Pakistani politics to allow democratic institutions to take root. The nuclear issue also remains important.

During the 1970s and 1980s India increasingly came to dominate the international politics of South Asia, but it also experienced heightened domestic turmoil. These domestic problems stemmed from the tensions between various ethnic groups and increased demands for autonomy. In the northeastern state of Assam, the Hindu population increasingly resented the influx of Muslim Bengalis and communal violence began anew. Continued ethnic and religious violence prompted the suspension of the country's democracy and the declaration of a state of emergency in 1975, but the emergency was suspended and democracy restored in 1977. An explosive situation remained in the northwest state of Punjab, where the Sikhs, a slight majority, progressively pressed for increased autonomy and possibly independence. In 1984, after Indian forces assaulted rebels holed up in the Sikhs' holiest shrine, the Golden Temple in Amritsar, Prime Minister Indira Gandhi, who had ruled almost without interruption since 1966, was assassinated by two of her own Sikh guards.

These internal problems have not prevented India from assuming a dominant, even hegemonic, role in the international relations of South Asia. India has been quick to show its displeasure at the attempts of smaller states to conduct foreign policies that are not to its liking, going so far as to blockade Nepal in 1989–1990. In the 1980s, Sri Lanka (formerly Ceylon) was convulsed by a civil war pitting the majority Sinhalese against the minority Tamils. India came to the support of the Tamils, whose ethnic brethren were preeminent in a southern Indian state. In 1987 the Sri Lankan government launched a major attack against Tamil rebels, and in response to domestic demands the Indian government sent relief supplies to Tamil-controlled areas.

Justifiably enraged, but recognizing that India might intervene, the Sri Lankan government reached an agreement with India in which autonomy was given to the Tamil areas in exchange for India's commitment to prevent its territory from being used as a rebel base. More to the point, India also agreed to send a peacekeeping force to disarm the Tamil rebels in Sri Lanka; in effect, Sri Lanka got India to do its dirty work. The Indians were no more successful at this task than Sri Lankan forces had been, however, and in 1990 India's troops withdrew. The following year, Indira Gandhi's son Rajiv Gandhi was assassinated as he campaigned in the southern Indian state of Tamil Nadu to again become prime minister of India; the assassin allegedly was a Sri Lankan Tamil.

Thus, nearly a half century after the British withdrawal, South Asia again has a dominant power, but India faces many serious challenges to this role. It is increasingly torn by internal dissension and opposed by a tacit alliance between

China and Pakistan. The collapse of the Soviet Union has deprived India of its major ally on the international scene and has offered Pakistan new opportunities for influence among the Muslim former Soviet republics of Central Asia. But the end of the Cold War also meant that the United States had less reason to align with Pakistan, and India's recent experimentation with capitalism has opened up the possibility of closer relations between India and the United States. The end of both the colonial era and the Cold War has left South Asia with an imbalance of power in India's favor, but the region's frequently violent indigenous conflicts continue to cast doubt on India's capacity for leadership. Local conflicts have repeatedly pushed international tensions in South Asia to the brink of war and beyond. If this pattern is repeated, the next such confrontation may be between regional powers beset by ancient quarrels, and in possession of modern nuclear weapons.

EAST ASIA

The post–World War II balance of power in East Asia is a complex relationship between global powers (the United States and, before its collapse, the USSR), major regional powers with global aspirations (China, Japan, and now Russia), and smaller regional powers that nonetheless possess significant economic and/or military strength (North and South Korea, Taiwan, Vietnam, and others). Because most states with interests in this region have been weak in one or more of the basic forms of power—military, economic, and political—the history of the region has been one of shifting alliances as the regional powers try to compensate for their weaknesses and protect their interests. Throughout all of the military posturing and diplomatic maneuvering, however, a central goal has usually been the containment of China, which dominated the region before the mid-nineteenth century and could easily do so again. Because of its large number of strong independent actors, East Asia since 1945 has resembled eighteenth- and nineteenth-century Europe in many respects, including the frequent occurrence of limited but nevertheless destructive warfare.

Three main features characterized post–World War II international relations in East Asia: the emergence of a new and powerful Communist China and its support of Communist insurgent activities in its neighboring states, the independence of formerly colonized Asian countries, and the global rivalry between the two superpowers.

Early Cold War Tensions

Although Asia was not the top priority on America's foreign policy agenda, the conflicts between the superpowers in this region did not wait long to surface after 1945. From the advent of the Cold War, the United States and the Soviet Union were at odds over the former Japanese colony of Korea. Their division and occupation of the Korean peninsula in 1945 anticipated the future instability and conflicts of the area. Furthermore, the civil war in China between Nationalist and Communist forces reinforced a widespread perception that conflicts in East Asia could easily kindle a new global conflagration.

After the establishment of the People's Republic of China in 1949 and the conclusion of a Sino-Soviet Treaty of Friendship and Alliance in 1950, the United States adopted its policy of containing China as part of its global strategy. Though some U.S. officials realized that potential fissures in the Sino-Soviet relationship were already apparent, many Americans regarded Moscow and Beijing as part of a monolithic Communist bloc that was bent on world revolution. Fiery rhetoric from the Communist capitals reinforced this perception.

In this atmosphere of suspicion, many regarded the outbreak of the Korean War in 1950 as the first step in a global confrontation. The conflict, which dragged on for three years before it became clear that the United States would never permit Communist forces to gain control of the South, set off a new round of balancing and counterbalancing in Northeast Asia. The fighting between Chinese and American forces in Korea had terrible consequences for the relations between these two countries for the next two decades. Both countries firmly perceived each other as a major threat to their vital interests. The United States viewed the Chinese as desirous of overrunning all of East Asia while China vehemently denounced American "hegemonism" in the region.[16]

The American policy of containing Chinese expansion manifested itself in a series of bilateral treaties with several of China's neighboring countries. The United States–Japanese and United States–Philippine security treaties were signed in 1951. Following the signing of a mutual defense treaty between the United States and South Korea in late 1953, a similar treaty was concluded in 1954 between the United States and the Republic of China on Taiwan, where Nationalist forces had fled after the Communist victory in China. These actions reinforced the Chinese view that the United States was determined to encircle it with hostile forces (which was half correct; the United States was attempting to encircle China, but for defensive—not offensive—purposes). Meanwhile, Beijing's stated determination to capture Taiwan and its continued bellicose posture toward countries aligned with the United States heightened American fears.

The containment of China had become an inseparable part of America's global response to the possibility of Communist expansion. Washington's system of alliances in East Asia succeeded in protecting the areas it regarded as vital to its security and economic interests, namely Japan, South Korea, Taiwan, and the Philippines. To counter the encirclement created by the United States and its Asian allies, China was prompted to develop closer relations with the Soviet Union. Thus, in the 1950s, when East-West tensions were at their height, East Asia was the military focal point of the Cold War.

Sino-Soviet Split

This rigid balance of forces began to change as Sino-Soviet relations deteriorated. The ideological and policy differences between the two Communist giants broke into the open in 1958 over the USSR's weak support for China's attempt to capture Taiwan, an endeavor Moscow regarded as dangerously reckless. Moscow's retraction of its promised support for the Chinese nuclear weapons program was also a point of contention, though this dispute was less publicized. The United States was slow to realize the implications of the Sino-Soviet split. The stalemate of antagonism between China and the United States (and its Asian allies) was reinforced by China's explosion of a nuclear bomb in 1964, by its bellicose support for revolutionary **guerrilla warfare** ("peoples' wars," as Beijing called them), and by its self-imposed isolation during the Great Proletarian Cultural Revolution of 1966–1969. At the same time, the competition between Moscow and Beijing for the leadership of the Communist bloc was strengthened by continued ideological disputes and unrest along their long common border.[17]

Ironically, because of the Sino-Soviet split in the 1960s, Northeast Asia proceeded through a relatively stable period, as neither Communist power wanted a renewed conflict between the Koreas to complicate an already tense situation. In the meantime, the primary focus of U.S. policy shifted to Indochina. After the victory of the Vietminh over French forces and the interim partition of Vietnam in 1954, Southeast Asian nations' fears of Chinese expansion grew. As a result, in the 1950s and 1960s Washington not only contained China in Northeast Asia, but also built military alliances in Southeast Asia, establishing a limited military presence in South Vietnam and Thailand. In an attempt to break out of the U.S. containment along its southern flank, China sought better relations with its neighbors in Southeast Asia, but most remained alienated from Beijing because of its continuing support of Communist insurgencies within their countries. Their suspicions were reinforced by the strong Chinese backing of North Vietnam and Communist forces in South Vietnam fighting against American "imperial aggression." By 1965 the fighting between South Vietnamese government troops and the Vietcong in South Vietnam drove the United States to intervene with substantial ground and air forces, and the Vietnam War began in earnest (see Chapter Four).

Chinese-American Rapprochement

Three events changed the outlines of international politics in East Asia near the end of the 1960s. First, China gradually recovered from its self-imposed diplomatic isolation and began to seek improved relations with the outside world. Second, border clashes between Chinese and Soviet troops in 1969 (during which Moscow hinted that it could employ its nuclear weapons) contributed to the Chinese regime's willingness to consider a closer relationship with the United States. Third, the new American president, Richard Nixon, belied his past record as a fierce anticommunist by being much more receptive than his predecessors to the mending of fences between the United States and China.

During his first term, a series of small steps and signals from both sides suggested a possible improvement in Sino-American relations. (One of these signals was Beijing's granting of permission for a Chinese table tennis team to compete in the United States, which might today look like a trivial gesture but at the time was a startling departure from China's venomous anti-American

AT A GLANCE

INTERNATIONAL CONFLICT

The Middle East

Situation: The three regional balances of power—Arab-Arab, Arab-Israeli, and Arab-Iranian—are separate but also interact with each other. Many of the conflicts are sustained by a concept of nationalism that originated in nineteenth-century Europe.

Superpower Involvement: The Cold War added to the struggle between the superpowers for allies and clients in the region. The superpowers' provision of economic and military assistance to their regional allies helped maintain the regional balance of power, fueling a spiraling regional arms race.

Conclusion: The collapse of the Soviet Union has removed the Cold War rivalry as a force that has fanned the flames of the region's many conflicts. After the defeat of Iraq in the Persian Gulf War, no Arab nation has been able to emerge as the region's dominant power. Government stability is illusory. However, progress has been made with the Israeli and Palestinian recognition of each other and the new moves toward peace between Israel and Jordan. Although many fundamental conflicts remain unresolved, a peacemaking process has finally begun.

South Asia

Situation: Post–World War II South Asia has been a region marked by continual tensions with occasional outbreaks of violence, both within and between states. The region has been dominated by the antagonism between India and Pakistan. The source of instability stems from the colonial legacy, the efforts of the regional states to consolidate control, and their ethnic and religious hatreds and the territorial dispute over Kashmir.

Superpower Involvement: Both superpowers were actively engaged in South Asia, and their involvement exacerbated the indigenous tensions. But the direct involvement of China, through its border disputes with India and

rhetoric and isolation from the outside world. The U.S. government reciprocated by officially referring to China as the People's Republic of China rather than "Red China.") The nervous and halting Sino-American courtship culminated in Nixon's dramatic visit to China in February 1972, which constituted a profound breakthrough in relations. Both China and the United States had gained powerful leverage with respect to the USSR. For Beijing, the opening made it harder for Moscow to threaten to wage war along their common frontier. Washington, for its part, hoped that the rivalry between Moscow and Beijing would increase American leverage and that both Communist powers would help the United States end its long Vietnam nightmare without a total defeat for the South Vietnamese.

The rapprochement between Washington and Beijing revolutionized the balance of power in East Asia. Hostility between China and Japan had reached high levels during the Cultural Revolution, but in the wake of the "Nixon shock" Tokyo quickly readjusted its posture toward Beijing, seizing the opportunity to establish a profitable trade relationship. After twenty-two years of Cold War confrontation, full diplomatic relations between the two most powerful Asian countries was established after Japanese Prime Minister Kakuei Tanaka's visit to through its ties with Pakistan, distinguishes South Asia from the Middle East.

Conclusion: The end of both the colonial era and the Cold War has left South Asia with an imbalance of power in India's favor, but the region's frequently violent indigenous conflicts continue to cast doubt on India's capacity for leadership. Local conflicts have repeatedly pushed international tensions in South Asia to the brink of war and beyond. If this pattern is repeated, the next such confrontation may be between regional powers beset by ancient quarrels, and in possession of modern nuclear weapons.

East Asia

Situation: There is a complex relationship between global powers, major regional powers with global aspirations, and smaller regional powers that nonetheless possess significant economic and/or military strength. The history of the region has been one of shifting alliances, as the regional powers try to compensate for their weaknesses and protect their interests.

Superpower Involvement: The end of the Cold War between the superpowers and rapprochement between the two Communist giants created a favorable environment for a solution to many troublesome regional conflicts. After the fall of the Soviet Union, the United States reoriented its Asian-Pacific policy by reducing its commitments in East Asia.

Conclusion: The ASEAN countries have recognized the necessity of creating new mechanisms to maintain a balance of power. The region resembles a classical multipolar system. The changes in the economic and military strength of East Asian nations will lead to the shifting of alliances.

Beijing in September 1972. China also established diplomatic ties with U.S. allies Australia and New Zealand. Meanwhile, the USSR attempted, clumsily and unsuccessfully, to lure Japan away from China.

The only ally that the Soviets could now rely upon in East Asia was Vietnam, which was brought into closer alignment with Moscow by yet another series of dramatic developments.[18] In 1973 a cease-fire between the warring parties in Vietnam cleared the way for an American withdrawal. However, fighting between the North and South Vietnamese soon resumed, but American disillusionment and disgust with the war eliminated any possibility of U.S. reentry into the conflict. Saigon fell to North Vietnamese forces by April 1975, and by the end of that year Communist forces had gained power in all three Indochina states of Vietnam, Laos, and Cambodia. After its victory in Indochina, Hanoi, the capital of reunified Vietnam, emerged as an important potential regional power, but its war-torn economy urgently needed outside assistance. Because China was still recovering from the disastrous Cultural Revolution, the Soviet Union became the only available contributor to Vietnam's economic reconstruction. The entente that developed between Hanoi and Moscow caused anxiety in both China and the United States. Although it tried hard to maintain the friendly relations with

President Richard Nixon's historic February 1972 visit to Beijing broke more than 30 years of Chinese-American hostility. Here Nixon and Chinese Premier Zhou Enlai toast each other at a banquet hosted by the visiting Americans.
Source: © UPI/Bettmann Newsphotos.

both Moscow and Beijing that existed during the war, Hanoi soon realized that the Sino-Soviet split had made this policy impossible.

New Asian Cold War

By 1978 the antagonism between China and the Soviet Union in the region had acquired the outlines of a regional cold war. The withdrawal of U.S. troops from Indochina in 1973 created a power vacuum that the USSR was happy to fill. As Hanoi began to develop its own regional ambitions and aligned itself closer to Moscow, the Chinese leaders became concerned that Vietnam would become an "Asian Cuba" for Russian expansion into Southeast Asia. The chance of a Sino-Soviet conflict through their proxies in Indochina increased as the tension between the Soviet Union and China over Indochina escalated.

The state of the Sino-Soviet-American triangular relationship illustrated the fluidity of alliances in the East Asian region. In the early stages of the Cold War in Asia, the United States had used its regional allies to contain China, while China and the USSR built friendly relations. By the late 1970s, however, the Soviet Union was endeavoring to contain China with its own regional allies, while U.S.-Chinese ties gradually improved.

Emboldened by an alliance treaty with the USSR, Vietnam invaded Cambodia in 1978 and replaced the pro-Chinese Khmer Rouge regime with a Communist government friendly to Moscow and Hanoi. Though they had no sympathy for the brutal Khmer Rouge, the United States, Japan, and the **Association of South-East Asian Nations (ASEAN)**—Indonesia, Malaysia, Singapore, Thailand, Brunei, and the Philippines—joined China in condemning Vietnam's invasion of Cambodia and demanding the withdrawal of foreign troops from that country. A UN resolution to that effect was vetoed by the Soviet Union, however. Chinese leaders undoubtedly felt uneasy about a possible two-front confrontation with the Soviet Union on their mutual frontier in the north, and with pro-Soviet Vietnam in the south.

To reduce the possibility of a two-front war, Chinese party leader Deng Xiaoping strove to gain the support of the United States and Japan. Although he failed to elicit any explicit backing from these two countries, he was confident that the international community would not oppose his efforts to block Soviet expansion in Southeast Asia. Convinced that Vietnam wanted to increase its power and influence not only in Indochina, but also in the whole of Southeast Asia, Deng was now ready to move. Charging that Vietnam had violated China's borders, he launched a massive "punitive measure," sending his troops into Vietnam for seventeen days in February 1979 to "teach Vietnam a lesson" China's incursion into Vietnam helped to solidify ties between Moscow and Hanoi: Vietnam now needed outside assistance more than ever, since ASEAN nations had refused to help.

Yet Sino-Soviet relations took another plunge after the Soviet invasion of Afghanistan in December 1979. Beijing perceived this development as a serious threat, because a pro-Moscow regime in Afghanistan could become a Soviet surrogate on China's western border, just as Vietnam was on its southern frontier. In response, the Chinese Communist party announced in 1980 that Beijing would not continue the ongoing Sino-Soviet negotiations on the "normalization" of their relations. When the talks between the two countries were finally resumed in 1982, Beijing insisted on three pre-conditions for the normalization of Sino-Soviet relations: (1) the USSR should remove its massive military deployment along the Sino-Soviet border and in outer Mongolia, (2) Moscow should stop aiding Vietnam's aggression in Indochina, and (3) the Soviet Union should withdraw all its troops from Afghanistan.

The shock waves created by the invasion of Afghanistan were also felt in Japan. For most of the postwar era, Japan felt quite secure under the U.S. commitment to Japan's defense, codified originally in the Mutual Security Treaty of 1951. The Soviet invasion of Afghanistan made some Japanese worry about what might also happen to their own country, which had territorial disputes with Moscow over the Kuril Islands that the USSR occupied at the end of World War II. Accordingly, in 1980 the Japanese government explicitly identified the Soviet Union as a major threat to its security for the first time. China, reversing other long-standing Cold War policies, not only endorsed the U.S.–Japan Mutual Security Treaty but also made public pronouncements advocating a Japanese

NGUYEN THE PATRIOT

Few of the marchers who chanted the name of Ho Chi Minh to protest against the Vietnam War knew that the name they shouted was only one of many that the Vietnamese president had used during his career as a Communist leader. Fewer still were aware that he had once collaborated with American intelligence services as part of his revolutionary activities. The man who became world famous as Ho Chi Minh was born Nguyen That Thanh in northern Vietnam (then part of French Indochina) in 1890. He grew up poor, but worked his way through school, became a teacher, and studied at a technical institute before shipping out as a cook on a French steamship in 1911. He was a merchant seaman (under the name of Ba) for several years before he came to Paris during World War I, where he found work as a gardener, waiter, janitor, photo retoucher, and oven stoker. While he changed his name and occupation frequently, his ideological convictions solidified. Now calling himself Nguyen Ai Quoc (Nguyen the Patriot), he became a committed socialist and joined the French Communist party.

Inspired by Lenin and the Russian Revolution, he went to Moscow in 1923 and quickly became a major figure in the Communist International (the world association of Communist parties, closely governed by the Soviet party). The following year, he went to China to form a Vietnamese nationalist association, and helped found the Indochinese Communist party in 1930. By this time, Nguyen was wanted as a subversive by the French colonial authorities in Indochina, and sought refuge in Hong Kong and Moscow, from where he continued to direct revolutionary activities in his home country until the outbreak of World War II.

When France was overrun by German forces in 1940, he saw that Vietnam had a golden opportunity to break free of French colonialism. Now calling himself Ho Chi Minh ("He Who Enlightens"), he slipped back into Indochina and organized the Vietminh (League for the Independence of Vietnam). In 1945, when the Japanese troops occupying Vietnam dismantled the French colonial government, Ho made contact with American intelligence agents and arranged for the Vietminh to cooperate with the U.S. Office of Strategic Services (the precursor of the Central Intelligence Agency) against the Japanese. Vietminh forces entered Hanoi after Japan surrendered to the Allies, and in September 1945 Ho read a proclamation declaring the independence of Vietnam. Ho, who became

military buildup to oppose Soviet hegemonism. In short, Soviet moves in Afghanistan prompted an alignment of Washington, Beijing, and Tokyo against Soviet expansion in Asia. [19]

Anti-Soviet sentiment was also widely shared among the ASEAN countries of Thailand, Singapore, and Malaysia in the wake of the Afghan crisis, which came just one year after the Vietnamese invasion of Cambodia. ASEAN anxiety was further aroused by Vietnam's armed incursion into Thailand in 1980 and by a mini-summit of Soviet, Vietnamese, and Cambodian leaders in Moscow. The new perception of a Soviet threat worked dramatically in favor of China's relations with the ASEAN countries, enabling a new cooperative relationship the new nation's president, hoped that the United States would support Vietnamese independence from France, and some of the language of the proclamation was inspired by the American Declaration of Independence: "All men are born equal; the Creator has given us inviolable rights, life, liberty, and happiness . . ."

When French troops returned to Vietnam, fighting soon erupted between French and Vietminh forces. The United States, needing Paris as an ally in the Cold War, sided with the French. The Vietminh won a decisive victory in 1954, and the peace agreement provided for a temporary division of Vietnam (with the Vietminh controlling the North) until 1956, when elections would be held for a unified government. The elections were postponed in the South, however, and Ho's socialist government in the North became increasingly repressive. By 1959 Hanoi was supporting Communist Vietcong guerrillas in their efforts to destabilize the U.S.–backed regime in the South, and the insurgency soon escalated into full-scale war. In July 1959 the aging and ailing Ho began to take a less active part in the Hanoi government, though he retained his formal position as president and a great deal of influence. He cultivated a public image as the benevolent Uncle Ho who was trying to unite the divided Vietnamese family. His country remained divided when U.S. ground and air forces intervened in the war in 1965.

Ho urged his people to remain steadfast during the bitter conflict until he died in 1969, genuinely beloved by a great many Vietnamese. He never married and had no children, having given his entire life to the struggle for independence and socialism in his own country, and for a worldwide Communist revolution. (Ho saw no contradiction in his beliefs; he was a fighter for nationalism, not democracy, and believed that national independence and world communism were not incompatible.) Had the Cold War not broken out so soon after World War II, Ho Chi Minh might have found considerable common ground with U.S. leaders in their support for decolonization. In the climate of the Cold War, however, Ho and many others in the developing world believed that communism offered hope for national independence, while the United States regarded communism to be a threat to its vital interests. The inevitable enmity between Ho and the United States thus became one of many tragic ironies of the Vietnam War.

between them to gradually take shape. Thus, by the early 1980s the balance of power in East Asia took an essentially bipolar form, as a tacit alliance between the United States, China, Japan, and ASEAN coalesced to contain expansion by the Soviet Union and Vietnam.

Global Confrontation Recedes, Regional Powers Emerge

This new strategic alignment proved to be short-lived. However, it was not broken up by diplomatic maneuvering, but rather by domestic political developments. In March 1985 Mikhail Gorbachev became the new leader of the

USSR and soon began active pursuit of a rapprochement with both China and the United States. As recounted in Chapter Four, the new Soviet leadership hoped to create a favorable international environment for Soviet economic reconstruction. It therefore sought to cut back costly, wasteful, and counterproductive commitments abroad. When foreign leaders became convinced that Gorbachev was intent on carrying out this reform, Moscow's relationship with China, Japan, and the United States improved markedly.

In a 1986 speech in Vladivostok, on the USSR's Pacific coast, Gorbachev outlined the main principles of a new Soviet Asian-Pacific policy. These included the recognition of the Soviet Union as an Asian country, the acknowledgment of the United States as a partner in many Asian-Pacific issues, the improvement of relations with Japan and China, the reduction of Soviet military forces in East Asia, and the call for an Asian-Pacific regional organization similar to the Conference on Security and Cooperation in Europe.

Gorbachev's new policy was not all talk. In 1989 Moscow began to withdraw its troops from Afghanistan and to reduce its military presence in Mongolia. In response, the Chinese government invited Gorbachev to visit Beijing in May 1989. This summit completed the prolonged process of normalizing relations between Moscow and Beijing, and it had a direct impact on relations between Vietnam and the Soviet Union. First, Moscow started to withdraw its military equipment and personnel from Vietnam. Second, in late September 1989, Vietnam withdrew its troops from Cambodia. These actions led to a more receptive attitude toward Moscow on the part of the ASEAN countries. The development of a rapprochement between Moscow and its two regional rivals, Beijing and Washington, facilitated other bilateral interactions among the major powers in East Asia. For example, Japan and Moscow entered into extended discussions over the Kuril Islands after 1988, although the dispute remained unresolved as of 1994.

While the Soviet Union's reputation in the international arena was rising, China's took a dramatic turn downward. China had been liberalizing its economic policies throughout the 1980s but consistently resisted change in its political system. When in 1989 thousands of protesters camped for months in Tiananmen Square in Beijing to demand democratic reforms, the government sent soldiers and tanks to clear the square. The brutal repression, accompanied by live television reports, forcibly demonstrated that Beijing was not interested in political change. As the USSR adopted new policies, shed its socialist empire, and finally began to disintegrate, China's value to the United States as a counterweight to Soviet power diminished, and Sino-American relations cooled once more.[20]

The end of the Cold War between the superpowers and rapprochement between the two Communist giants created a favorable environment for a solution to many troublesome regional conflicts. In January 1991 a peace conference was held in Paris to discuss solutions to Cambodian issues, and by October an agreement was reached among representatives from eighteen nations to end the war in Cambodia and carry out elections under UN supervision. The agreement proved difficult to implement, but a new government was finally established two and one-half years later even though the Khmer Rouge refused to participate. In Northeast Asia, the possibility of another North Korean attack against the South was reduced by the establishment of full diplomatic relations between the USSR and South Korea in 1990 and between China and South Korea in 1992. Direct talks between the two Koreas and their entry into the UN in 1991 as member states further muted tensions on the Korean peninsula, though talk of the possible development of nuclear weapons and missiles by North Korea rekindled tensions. The death of North Korea's leader Kim Il-Sung in the summer of 1994 added further confusion to an already volatile situation.

After the collapse of the Soviet Union, the United States reoriented its Asian-Pacific policy by reducing its commitments in East Asia, including the reduction of military forces in South Korea, the Philippines, Japan, and Thailand. However, the increasing economic ties between the United States and the Asian countries ensures that America will remain actively engaged in the region. Since the mid-1980s bilateral trade between the United States and Asian countries has been exceeding trade between the United States and Europe. While the quality of technological and investment interchange with Europe remains greater, the importance of Asian trade is still growing. The volume of American exports to Asia is the highest in the world and imports from that region account for most of the U.S. trade deficit. Therefore, despite pressure in Washington to further reduce U.S. force levels in order to cut the defense budget, it remains clear that America will continue to maintain a military presence to protect its interests in East Asia.

The reduction of Russian and American military forces in Asia significantly reduced the threat to China posed by the former Cold War antagonists. As the balance of power in the region shifted yet again, China began to perceive Japan as the major potential threat to its security. This was indicated by Beijing's opposition to Japan's 1991 decision to allow the deployment of non-combat troops overseas as part of UN peacekeeping forces. On the other hand, China itself experienced remarkable economic growth in the late 1980s and early 1990s. Its economic power should be enhanced further by its acquisition of Hong Kong, scheduled for 1997. It appears as if China, like Japan, has much potential to emerge as a regional hegemon.

To prevent the emergence of either China, Japan, or India as a regional hegemon in Southeast Asia, the ASEAN countries have recognized the necessity of creating new mechanisms to maintain a balance of power. Many ASEAN nations have actively strengthened their own defenses and some (notably Singapore) have allowed the United States to use military facilities in their territories should a new crisis arise. Finally, in November 1991 ASEAN countries and other major powers in the region initiated wide-ranging discussions on security and cooperation in Southeast Asia.[21] In July 1993, ASEAN members met in Singapore with U.S. Secretary of State Warren Christopher and foreign ministers from the EU, Japan, and South Korea to discuss Southeast Asian regional security. They reconvened in July 1994 to discuss multilateral security issues together with China, Russia, and Vietnam.

With the disappearance of the United States–Soviet Cold War rivalry, East Asia resembles a classical multipolar system. The key relationship in future regional balances of power may well be between Japan and China, with Russia, the Koreas (which may not remain plural), Vietnam, Taiwan, and Indonesia as secondary but nonetheless important regional powers. As long as the United States has vital interests in the region, it will continue to be a major extra-regional actor, but its level of involvement is likely to be determined by economic factors and not ideological considerations. In the less developed parts of the region, particularly Southeast Asia, subnational conflicts retain the possibility to escalate into major international confrontations. On the other hand, since the end of the Vietnam War, intra-national conflict has played less of a role in the politics of East Asia than had previously been the case. If anything can be said about the future balance of power in the region, it is that changes in the economic and military strength of East Asian nations will lead to the shifting of alliances, as it has since the end of World War II and decolonization. The players change, but the game remains the same.

CONCLUSION: IMPERIALISM AND THIRD WORLD CONFLICT—THE CHICKEN OR THE EGG?

Which came first in the developing world, imperialism or conflict? Our examination of hostilities in developing areas has shown how difficult it is to answer that question. The "imported" and "domestic" causes of most Third World conflicts are clearly and closely interrelated. As is the case with many intra- and international conflicts, the root causes of disputes are frequently matters of opinion or perspective rather than historical fact. The legacy of imperialism, as we have seen, often resulted in the drawing of arbitrary borders and the coexistence of historically hostile ethnic groups within the same state. But in many instances ethnic antagonism arguably opened the door to imperialism by presenting would-be colonial powers with ready-made conflicts that could be exploited to establish or strengthen imperial control. If the history of conflict in the developing world after decolonization reveals anything, it shows the difficulty of determining whether imported causes or domestic sources of conflict came first.

That said, it is at least possible to draw some conclusions about the origins and resolution of conflicts in the regions discussed here. First, the withdrawal of the colonial powers from the developing world left a political mess. The retreat from empire retained economic globalization in the Third World but increased political fragmentation. It is clear that imperialism certainly exacerbated local conflicts to some degree, but it is also clear that there are enough indigenous conflicts in the developing world to lead to oppression and war without any outside interference. Regardless, in many cases, European imperialism made matters worse. Whether the developing world as a whole would have been more or less conflictual if imperialism had never existed, however, is impossible to determine and not relevant to solving contemporary problems.

Second, as the Cold War recedes farther into history, some imported factors in regional conflicts will become less important. Foreign meddlers and domestic dictators alike will no longer be able to exploit U.S.–Soviet antagonism to advance their own interests. Other imported sources of conflict, however, will not go away so easily. Postcolonial borders, for example, are unlikely to change except by force or meticulous negotiation. More important, the European concept of nationalism, which has animated some of the most bitter disputes in the developing world, shows no signs of going away and may even be strengthened. Nationalism has clearly taken root.

Third, whatever their origins, regional conflicts have hindered economic and political development. Many developing states have spent huge resources and/or have maintained authoritarian regimes in order to keep from falling behind in regional balances of power. These limited funds could be much better spent on education, health, industrial development, or to prevent depletion of natural resources. However, as long as many regimes in developing countries fear that their internal or external enemies may resort to violence to overthrow them, it is likely that they will spend whatever it takes to keep their nations independent, with themselves in power. Perhaps the spread of democracy can alleviate this problem, but whether democracy can survive and promote stability in deeply divided developing countries remains an open question.

The drain of resources caused by international conflicts may best be alleviated by the strengthening of international institutions. The final conclusion drawn from our overview of conflicts in the developing world is that global and regional organizations offer some hope of overcoming fragmentation. Regional institutions that have played a critical role in the successful resolution of complex conflicts include, for example, the Organization of American States (OAS) in Central America, the Organization of African Unity (OAU) in Namibia, and ASEAN in Cambodia. Such types of organizations can sponsor negotiations and observe the implementation of agreements, although global powers like the United States and global institutions like the UN Security Council are often indispensable as guarantors.

It is only logical that both domestic and international institutions must be involved in the resolution of conflicts that are simultaneously internal and external in origin. Though the active involvement of regional organizations may provide means for tackling the problem of regional conflict, the solutions will never be cheap or easy, and it is not likely that regional powers alone will be able to handle the task. If the end of the Cold War enables the North to let oppression and aggression go unchecked in the South, the resulting legacy of neglect may be worse than the legacy of imperialism.

PRINCIPAL POINTS OF CHAPTER SIX

1. As empires disintegrated, new forms of economic dependence by Third World countries on their former masters developed.

2. The collapse of empire was accompanied by various forms of violence: (a) wars of independence, (b) wars between new states, and (c) wars within these new states.

3. Domestic causes of conflict have included ethnic, religious, and economic hostilities—usually examples of fragmentation.

4. Imported causes of conflict from outside particular regions and as a legacy of imperialism include arbitrary borders, nationalism, and struggles between great powers—the latter typically a consequence of globalization.

5. In some Third World regions, particularly in Latin America, Africa, and Oceania, conflicts within states have dominated.

6. In other Third World regions, particularly the Middle East, South and East Asia, interstate conflict and regional balances of power have been more typical.

7. In the Middle East, three balances of power have dominated: Arab-Arab, Arab-Israeli, and Arab-Iranian.

8. By contrast, South Asia has been dominated by the antagonism between India and Pakistan.

9. The post–World War II balance of power in East Asia is the most complex of these—consisting of global powers (the United States and, before its collapse, the USSR), major regional powers with global aspirations (China, Japan, and now Russia), and smaller regional powers (such as North and South Korea, Taiwan, and Vietnam) that nonetheless possess significant economic and/or military strength.

10. Despite indigenous conflicts, in many cases European imperialism made matters worse.

11. As the Cold War recedes further into history, some areas of tensions projected onto regional conflicts from the global arena will become less important.

12. Whatever their origins, regional conflicts have hindered economic and political development.

13. Global and regional organizations offer some hope of overcoming the fragmentation that typically epitomizes Third World regions.

Part IV

The Economic Dimension in International Politics

Chapter 7

The World Economy

In the early 1990s, a tough recession swept through the industrialized countries. Canada was one country hit hard. In June, 1992, its popular news magazine, *Maclean's,* reported on one unemployed woman fortunate enough to find a new job.

> It took a draining 8 months for Ellen Soyka of St. Catharines, Ont., to find a new job. And when she did, her new position was not as rewarding as her old one as a buyer and store manager for Coy Bros. Ltd. The small, family-owned department store chain went out of business in February, 1991. Now, Soyka, 37, manages the costume jewelry department at a local Birks outlet. She earns less than the $23,000 she earned at Coy, and her new hours leave her less time to spend with her two young children. But she is not complaining.

> "I've had to make concessions," said Soyka, "but I knew I couldn't have what I'd had before." And despite her time without work, she says that with the help of her auto mechanic husband, Thomas, and unemployment insurance, her family has kept their home and still has enough money to enjoy life. "It was hard at times—money comes into everything," she acknowledged. "But it probably has given all of us a better understanding of getting along together."

> Still, Soyka says that this recession has left a lasting impression, unlike the previous one in 1981–1982. "After what I went through in the past year-and-a-half," declared Soyka, "nothing is going to be safe for me anymore."

> Brenda Douglish, "Back to Work at Last: Canadians Grapple with Slow Recovery," (*Maclean's,* June 29, 1992), p. 44.

It may come as a surprise, but part of Sokya's problem was Canada's place in the international economy. If political or industrial leaders make poor economic decisions and/or their country becomes less competitive, individuals like Ellen Sokya suffer. Therefore, it is imperative that we consider how world politics not only affects people's physical survival (in terms of war and peace), but their material wealth as well.

Thus far, the reader may feel that our examination of international relations has emphasized war and conflict. Indeed, most studies of world politics focus on

283

conflict for the same reason that public affairs broadcasts seem to devote most of their time to scandals, crime, earthquakes, and plane crashes: These developments are out-of-the-ordinary, dramatic events—they are "news." But just as most neighbors don't fight one another and most planes don't crash, most states interact with each other peacefully most of the time. Trade and economic exchange have always accompanied the ongoing struggle for national power and security. With this in mind, this chapter presents an overview of the history and operation of the global economy.

Like any other field of human relations, economic exchange can involve conflict as well as cooperation. Many scholars contend that rising economic **interdependence**—the mutual dependence of national economies—has facilitated cooperation among nations. At the same time, however, this interdependence has produced its own set of international and domestic political tensions, especially for the advanced industrialized states. To see why these tensions occur and how they may be resolved, this chapter will first introduce the basic economic concepts required for an understanding of the global economy. Then we will describe how the world economy evolved from a disconnected aggregate of local and regional trade into an integrated system regulated by international political and financial institutions.

PART I: INTRODUCTION TO INTERNATIONAL TRADE AND FINANCE

The first part of this chapter covers the fundamental "building blocks" of international economics. It is divided into three main sections. The first is a basic nation clause; International Monetary Fund (IMF) begins operation to fix exchange rates and provide international loans to war-torn countries.

1957: Treaty of Rome inaugurates the European Economic Community.

1960: First run on the dollar occurs, leading the United States to abandon unilateral management of the monetary system in favor of multilateral management to promote stability.

1971: United States suspends its commitment to convert dollars into gold and resorts to protectionism, indicating the decline of its hegemony.

1973: Bretton Woods regime fails, and currency rates float in financial markets; Arab nations of OPEC impose an oil embargo on the United States, raising oil prices dramatically; G7 leaders attempt to restore international economic stability.

1974–1975: Stagflation occurs in many developed countries as a result of the 1973 oil crisis.

1979: Iranian Revolution causes oil prices to skyrocket again, leading to more stagflation.

1980: United States demands that Japan enact voluntary export restrictions on automobiles to protect domestic auto producers; Federal Reserve Bank raises interest rates to fight inflation.

1981–1982: United States experiences a severe recession that spreads worldwide, causing President Reagan to push for economic deregulation and tax cuts—while increasing spending—leading to large budget deficits.

1985: Single European Act accelerates economic integration of EU members.

1990–1991: America's allies pay much of the cost to protect Middle East oil supplies in the Persian Gulf War; German unification allows the former East Germany to integrate into West Germany's strong economic and political institutions.

1991: Maastricht Treaty among EU states sets basis for monetary union and intensified political cooperation.

1992: ASEAN Free Trade Area reduces tariffs among ASEAN members.

1993: Uruguay Round of GATT is successfully concluded; Treaty of European Union (Maastricht Treaty) is ratified by all member states finalizing their political and monetary union.

1994: North American Free Trade Agreement goes into effect in Canada, Mexico, and the United States, beginning the process of eliminating internal trade barriers.

---

outline of trade theory and the notions of free trade and protectionism. The second is an introduction to international trade and finance, including a simplified explanation of international monetary systems, balance of payments, and how exchange rates affect international trade. The third deals with the political elements of the world economy, presenting three contending perspectives on the interaction between politics and economics, both within nations and in the global economy as a whole. Readers who have a strong background in economics should regard this chapter as a quick review of basic concepts. Readers unfamiliar with economic theory shouldn't worry; the following sections will be quick and painless.[1]

Why Nations Trade

Although some states have tried, none has ever achieved total economic self-sufficiency. Most states need goods and services that other states produce, and most produce goods and services that other states need. Thus, the only way for states to get all the goods and services that they need (short of conquering other countries, which is usually very expensive if not morally repugnant) is to trade for them.

This is especially true for certain natural resources that are unevenly distributed across states. For instance, just a few countries such as Saudi Arabia and Iran produce large quantities of oil, but virtually all countries use oil in their economies for industrial processes, heating, generating electricity, or as fuel for automobiles. This is also true for many agricultural products. For instance, coffee grows best in highland tropical climates, so if Americans want to have a cup of coffee, it has to be imported from countries like Colombia, Brazil, or Kenya (although the United States does produce a small amount of coffee in Hawaii). Similarly, bananas do not grow in the United States (though some farmers have tried), and thus must be traded for with tropical countries like Ecuador or Honduras. This works both ways, of course. If Brazilians want apples or maple syrup, they must trade with temperate agricultural countries like the United States or Canada.

Even when countries can produce the same goods or services, trade may occur because states have different allocations of resources. Trade theory usually identifies three categories of resources: land, labor, and capital. A nation is land-abundant if it has a lot of land (agriculture and resources) relative to its population, while it is labor-abundant if wages are relatively low, usually caused by a large population. Similarly, capital-abundant means that a nation is relatively rich, both in terms of money and industrial plant and equipment.

Because nations have different allocations of resources, each enjoys a **comparative advantage**[2] in producing those goods that utilize its abundant factor. Some specialize in labor-intensive industries like textiles because they are abundant in labor. Others specialize in capital-intensive industries like airplane manufacturing because they are wealthy and can build factories and develop technology. And still others produce agriculture because their land is inexpensive. Comparative advantage is thus an explanation for why countries with different resources and skills engage in trade.

It is logical to expect that a country will produce the goods it can make more efficiently than other countries. When a country is more efficient than others in producing a certain good, it is said to have an **absolute advantage** in that good's production. However, mutual gains from trade are still possible even if one party has an absolute advantage in all goods. David Ricardo (1772–1823), an English economist who contributed to the development of both economics and political economy, proved why this is so. Although his simplified model only took into account how labor productivity differs across nations, it provided a stepping stone for the theoretical developments of a century later.[3]

Ricardo's Model of Trade

Ricardo showed that even if one nation has an absolute advantage in the production of all goods, trade can still be mutually beneficial if the less efficient nation has a comparative advantage in one good over another. To see why this is so, consider two imaginary countries, Fredonia and Sidania. Both countries produce only two goods, wine and cloth. Table 7.1 shows the amount of labor (a cost of production) required to produce one bottle of wine and one bolt of cloth in each country.

The figures indicate that Sidania has an absolute advantage in both wine and cloth; each is more costly to produce in Fredonia. Nevertheless, mutual gains from trade are still possible due to comparative advantage. The ratio of production costs for the two goods differ in the two countries. In Sidania, one bottle of wine will exchange for one-half bolt of cloth (because the ratio of labor costs per unit of output of the two goods is 2:4), while in Fredonia, one bottle of wine

Table 7.1	Comparative Advantage	
Country	*Worker-hours needed to produce one unit of:*	
	Wine	*Cloth*
Fredonia	12	6
Sidania	2	4

will exchange for two bolts of cloth (because the ratio of labor costs for the two goods is 12/6). These ratios reflect the labor input to produce each item. Cloth is *relatively* cheaper in Fredonia than in Sidania; because one bottle of wine earns more cloth (12:6 versus 2:4), Fredonia has a comparative advantage in cloth-making. Wine is relatively cheaper in Sidania; because one bolt of cloth garners more wine (4:2 versus 6:12), it has a comparative advantage in wine-making. Therefore, due to these relative prices, trade between these two countries will be mutually advantageous. Fredonia can sell one bolt for one-half bottle of wine domestically—or it can sell it for two bottles in Sidania. Clearly, Fredonia will choose to trade with Sidania. Sidania can get one-half bolt per bottle of wine domestically, but it can trade with Fredonia for two bolts.

Each country gains by exporting the good in which it has a comparative advantage and by importing the good in which it has a comparative disadvantage. Mutual gains will lead to specialization within each country, making goods less expensive and production more efficient for both. But the gains are not necessarily equal; since Fredonia has higher production costs for both goods, it gains more through trade and specialization. This is because trade and specialization allow nations to concentrate on the production of the goods they produce most efficiently. When goods are produced efficiently, they are produced at minimum cost. As Fredonia's costs decrease, so should the prices charged to consumers for those products. Of course, the same pattern occurs in Sidania, but because it was more efficient to begin with, its gain from trade is less than Fredonia. Nevertheless, consumers in both countries benefit from trade.

Trade Barriers

Given the preceding discussion, it might seem counter-intuitive for states to implement barriers to free trade. Yet, governments often attempt to protect their domestic markets from international competition. Why? The trade theory just presented shows that national welfare improves when consumers purchase goods from the most efficient (least expensive) producer, whether it is foreign or domestic. However, competition may force domestic producers to go out of business if they become less efficient than foreign producers. Often times, governments will not stand idly by while companies or entire industries go bankrupt. This is especially true if those industries employ many workers and/or have tremendous political influence (like the U.S. automotive industry). States may therefore impose trade barriers to protect domestic industries.[4]

Barriers to free trade result from the conflict of two interests: consumers who want inexpensive products versus industries who want to stay in business. Since protection benefits a concentrated group of industrialists and workers and hurts a large group of unorganized consumers, political support for protection can usually penetrate even the most ardent free-trade governments. This section will present various kinds of trade barriers, citing examples of their use in the U.S. economy.

One common form of protection is the **tariff,** a tax imposed on a good entering a country from abroad. This additional cost makes the foreign good more expensive than it was before. If domestic consumers are relatively price conscious, they will curb their consumption of foreign goods in exchange for locally produced goods. Thus, tariffs aid local producers who compete against foreign-produced goods. One negative consequence of a tariff is that consumers pay higher prices because they no longer have access to cheaper foreign products. Also, local firms have less incentive to become more efficient because they are subject to less international competition. Nevertheless, in the short term, the domestic economy might improve because the tariff encourages domestic production, albeit at the cost of higher consumer prices and less efficient production.

One famous example of a tax on imports is the **Smoot-Hawley tariff.** After the stock market crash of 1929 (described later in this chapter), many in the United States feared that foreign competition would destroy even more U.S. jobs than had been lost as a result of the crash. In an attempt to protect remaining jobs, Congress in 1930 raised prices on all imports by 19 percent; by 1932 the average tariff reached 59 percent. Foreign countries responded to the Smoot-Hawley tariff by raising tariffs of their own. Such a course of action is called a **beggar-thy-neighbor policy.** The United States succeeded in raising import prices and making foreign goods less competitive domestically, but once other states responded with tariffs of their own, U.S. exports became more expensive abroad. As a result of these countervailing tariffs, export industries collapsed worldwide because they were increasingly shut out of the international market. Ultimately, this cycle of protection had a devastating impact on the world economy by accelerating and deepening the Great Depression.[5]

In addition to tariffs, there are other impediments to free trade, collectively known as "non-tariff barriers." The first is called an **import quota.** A state can put a limit on the number of imports it receives from the rest of the world. This is an explicitly protectionist barrier. However, sometimes a state will compel another nation to "voluntarily" limit its exports. These are called **voluntary export restrictions (VERs).** The importer might threaten to impose tariffs if the exporter does not comply. A government can demand VERs in order to protect its own industries from being pushed out of its own market. Since 1980 the United States has demanded that the Japanese restrict car exports to the American market in order to protect local automobile producers. Japan has complied, but it is interesting to note that Japanese automakers have responded to VERs by building factories in the United States and exporting higher-value Japanese luxury cars to meet the VER quota. This helped soften the blow of export restrictions.

Finally, governments can use **subsidies** to support domestic industries. These are government payments that allow producers to price their goods below the cost of production without going out of business. While the ostensible purpose of **internal subsidies** (called price supports in the United States) is to allow producers to compete against imports in the home market, and that of **external subsidies** is to allow these producers to compete in the international market, both in effect aid domestic producers. In the international system, it may be very hard to distinguish between external subsidies and **dumping,** where one country sells (or "dumps") its products in a foreign market so far below the costs of production that it causes other producers in that market to go out of business. In the last two decades, U.S. steel producers, for instance, have frequently brought anti-dumping suits against foreign steel producers before the Department of Commerce (to determine whether the products were "dumped" or unfairly subsidized) and the International Trade Commission (ITC) (to determine, if dumping has occurred, whether it resulted in "material harm" to domestic producers). One of the problems with dumping is that after a domestic producer has been driven out of business, the foreign company may then increase the price so both domestic producers and consumers lose.

International Finance

Our simplified discussion of international trade has so far focused on goods and services, but as we all know, almost all trade involves money in some form. Prior to the development of money, trade was conducted by barter, the mutual exchange of goods and services. This system was inefficient because, in the first place, it was difficult to establish rates of exchange between goods and services. Second, in a barter system there must be a coincidence of wants—every party must want exactly what the other has to offer. If you have a cow and want apples, then you need to find someone with apples who wants a cow; otherwise, you need a third person or another commodity to trade. Third, many commodities are perishable and may not last long enough to trade. Money solves all these inconveniences as a medium of exchange, unit of account for contracts, and store of value. Within countries, authorities have been established to ensure the legitimacy and stability of the currency and to deter counterfeiting and fraud; in the United States, for example, the Treasury Department has exclusive authority to issue paper and coin currency and to ensure that no one else does.

Exchange Rates   Of course, each state has its own currency: the U.S. dollar, the German mark, the British pound sterling, the Japanese yen, the French franc, the Italian lira, and so on. A way must always be found to exchange these equitably. As those who have traveled abroad know only too well, rates today change constantly; so, for example, the exchange rate between the dollar and franc may be altered daily. For the individual traveler, this is enormously inconvenient and potentially expensive. Such has not always been the case, however. Between 1870–1914 and 1945–1973, as we will discuss in Part II of this chapter,

AT A GLANCE

TRADE BARRIERS

Tariffs

Definition: A tax imposed on a good entering a country from abroad. This additional cost makes the foreign good more expensive than it was before. If domestic consumers are relatively price conscious, they will curb their consumption of foreign goods in exchange for locally produced goods. Thus, tariffs aid local producers who compete against foreign-produced goods.

Example: The Smoot-Hawley Tariff was passed in Congress in 1930, raising prices on all imports by 19 percent. By 1932, the average tariff reached 59 percent. Many foreign nations responded by raising their own tariffs. This led to a collapse of export industries worldwide and accelerated and deepened the Great Depression.

Import Quotas

Definition: A limit on the number of imports a state receives from the rest of the world. This is an explicit protectionist barrier.

Example: The Japanese government has import quotas on the amount of foreign rice that it will allow into the country. It does this to protect the domestic producers of rice by keeping prices artificially high.

Voluntary Export Restrictions

Definition: A state compels another nation to "voluntarily" limit its exports. The importer might threaten to impose tariffs if the exporter does not comply. A government can demand these restrictions in order to protect its industries from being pushed out of its own market.

countries agreed to fix their currencies' value so that they would not fluctuate on a daily basis. Although this might seem like a worthwhile system, there are benefits and costs to both fixed and floating exchange-rate systems.

Fixed exchange-rate systems arise when nations agree to establish a set of currency rules. Two examples of such a system are the **gold standard** (1870–1914) and the **Bretton Woods system** (1945–1973). During each period, all currencies were valued at fixed rates against one another. Aside from the benefits to travelers (as implied earlier), it also encouraged international trade. Let's examine why this should be so. Suppose an American restaurant owner wants to buy fifty bottles of wine from a French vineyard next month. In order to do so, she must make the purchase in francs. One bottle costs 5 francs, and today's exchange rate is $1/10 francs. If the American makes the purchase today, she pays $25. Under a fixed system, she will also pay $25 next month.

But what if a **floating exchange-rate system** is in effect? If the franc fluctuates during the month so that when she actually purchases the wine, $1 equals 5 francs, she would then owe $50, twice as much as before. Because prices can fluctuate, people might be less likely to trade because of its inherent risks. This problem, of course, is alleviated with fixed exchange rates because everyone is certain about future currency values.

Given this problem, why would countries choose to have floating exchange rates, as the United States does today? There are surprising advantages to floating

Example: Since 1980, the United States has demanded that the Japanese restrict auto exports to the American market in order to protect local domestic manufacturers.

Subsidies

Definition: Government payments that allow producers to price their goods below the cost of production without going out of business. While the ostensible purpose of internal subsidies is to allow producers to compete against imports in the home market, and that of external subsidies is to allow producers to compete in the international market, both in effect aid domestic producers.

Example: Several nations subsidize the European conglomerate Airbus in order to help keep it competitive in the international airplane manufacturing business.

Dumping

Definition: A process in which one country or firm sells (or "dumps") its products in a foreign market so far below the costs of production that it causes other producers in that market to go out of business.

Example: For the past two decades, U.S. steel producers have frequently sought anti-dumping protection against foreign steel producers before the Department of Commerce and the International Trade Commission.

rates. Exchange rates are supposed to reflect the general health of an economy. If a nation goes into a prolonged recession, people expect its currency to weaken as well. In a fixed arrangement, however, exchange-rate values cannot change. If a recession does occur, a government has two choices. First, it can pursue policies, like raising interest rates, that inflate the exchange rate in order to maintain its fixed value. Officials might choose to do this because they have made agreements with other nations to defend their currency. As will be discussed later in this chapter, the United States made this sort of agreement during the Bretton Woods period between 1945 and 1973.

However, artificially inflating a currency can worsen a country's domestic economy. For example, if a government attempts to shore up its exchange rate by raising interest rates, then foreign nationals will increase their demand for domestic investments, like savings accounts and certificates of deposit (CDs), because they will receive a good rate of return on their money. If interest rates are 10 percent in one country and 8 percent in another, money is likely to flow to the country giving a better deal. Citizens of the country with the 10 percent rate will also deposit their money at home. Thus, when domestic investments become more attractive (especially relative to foreign investments), people demand more local currency, increasing its value.

What are the drawbacks of this policy? While high interest rates might help preserve a country's fixed currency rate, this policy decision also makes borrowing money more expensive. To the extent that borrowed funds help us buy goods like homes and cars, higher interest rates reduce the number of these purchases. When people choose to reduce their own spending on goods and services, it hurts the national economy. Therefore, in order to defend its currency's value, a state often has to jeopardize its national economy.

A second option for policy-makers is to stop defending their currency. This action reduces the exchange rate's value, and does not have the same negative consequences on the economy that defending the currency might have. In fact, it might improve economic conditions by making exports less expensive (see the discussion on trade deficit and exchange rates later in this chapter). Under a fixed exchange-rate system, however, if a weakened currency is not bolstered, a country will have to renege on an agreement it made with other countries, potentially harming its reputation. This can become important because states have to interact in the future, on currency issues and others as well. If animosity develops, it can affect trade relations, security arrangements, and other related issues. Floating exchange rates thus have an advantage over fixed rates in that they accurately reflect a state's economic health and allow governments to pursue economic policies independent of exchange-rate requirements.

This explanation of the benefits and costs of fixed and floating exchange rates has revealed two important points. First, fixed exchange rates make the international economy more stable and predictable, but they can also force governments to pursue harmful policies when the currency's value goes in one direction and the economy's health in the other. Second, floating exchange rates accurately reflect an economy's well-being, but they create additional uncertainty in the world economy. This uncertainty can develop into an international crisis if individual governments—especially leaders of powerful economies—try to raise or lower their own currency in relation to their trading partners, most of whom will resist this action if they fear it will adversely affect their own economies. This maneuvering can itself create tensions, as it did between the United States and Japan in the 1980s and 1990s, which can produce bitterness and severe economic problems for one or both countries.

Balance of Payments   Another important concept for understanding international economic relations is the **balance of payments.** Much like companies, states keep "balance sheets" that present its transactions with the rest of the world. These national accounts tell us a country's trade balance (exports of goods and services minus imports of goods and services), how much money locals earned overseas, the amount of foreign currency invested in the domestic economy, the level of official foreign aid given to other countries, as well as the amount of foreign currency held by the central bank (the Federal Reserve in the United States or the Bundesbank in Germany).[6]

The sum total of a nation's imports, exports, foreign aid and other government transactions, and investment income and payments is referred to as the **current-account balance.** This is the figure usually cited in news reports about a country's "balance of trade." If the current-account balance is positive, the country enjoys a **trade surplus**—or a "net profit" from trade. If it is negative, the state is experiencing a "net loss," or **trade deficit**—though consumers in the state may still be better off as a result of trade, because they are able to buy less expensive and/or higher quality imported goods.

Accounting procedures guarantee that the balance of payments always equals zero. This is due to double-entry bookkeeping. For example, if an American purchases a foreign good, the import's value is recorded as a reduction from the balance of payments. However, once that foreign producer obtains U.S. dollars in exchange for his good, he usually deposits it in a bank, the same way most people deposit paychecks. If he does a lot of business in the United States, he might deposit it in an American bank. Once a foreigner decides to deposit his money in the United States, his account's value is added to the plus side of the balance of payments. Even if the foreign producer deposits it in his own bank abroad, that foreign bank must eventually deposit it in a U.S. bank in order to redeem its value—that is, in order to get paid back. This has the effect of an addition to the balance of payments. For accounting purposes, this transaction's net effect is zero. However, as we are about to see, the balance of payments can tell us something about a nation's trade balance, which has important ramifications for the state's economy. While accounting procedures might make the balance of payments appear to be in equilibrium, the potential problems suffered through a trade deficit cannot be overcome by sleight of hand on the accountant's ledger.

Link between Trade Deficit and Exchange Rates   Thus far we have discussed exchange rates and the balance of payments, but no direct link has been established. For our purposes, the most important tie is between the exchange rate and trade deficit. To see how this works, let's go back to our American restauranteur who wants to purchase French wine. In that case, using floating exchange rates, as the dollar depreciated (became less valuable relative to the franc), the wine's price increased. This occurred because, even though the bottle's price remained constant at five francs, it took more dollars to purchase the same number of francs; the price of five francs rose from fifty cents to one dollar. This fluctuation automatically doubled the price of a bottle of wine to a foreign purchaser.

Now, what effect might this price doubling have on the restaurant owner? First, she might decide to purchase the wine anyway, causing her to reduce her spending on other matters or go into debt. Second, she could choose to purchase a California wine whose price (for instance, $30 per bottle) is now cheaper than French wine. In general, we assume that if the California wine is relatively similar to the French wine, then the owner will probably increase her consumption of the local product relative to the foreign one.

This situation can easily be extrapolated to the national economy. If the dollar weakens relative to foreign currencies, foreign goods tend to become more expensive than domestic goods. In most instances, this leads to a relative decline in the consumption of foreign goods and an increase in the consumption of domestic goods. Conversely, the opposite occurs abroad. As the dollar becomes cheaper, American exports become less expensive in foreign countries, increasing consumption of U.S. goods. Both of these effects improve the U.S. trade balance by reducing imports and increasing exports. Of course, the opposite occurs when the dollar strengthens against foreign currencies. Under those circumstances, the U.S. trade balance worsens as Americans consume more imports and export less abroad.

Figure 7.1 shows that this relationship between the exchange rate and trade balance does exist, albeit imperfectly. For example, in both 1980 and 1991, the dollar exchange rates were roughly equal. Why was the American trade deficit so much worse in 1991? As the graphs shows, the dollar strengthened (and the trade deficit worsened) dramatically during this period, only to revert back to its original level. Many reasons can explain why the trade deficit did not improve as much as one would expect after the dollar weakened. For example, consumer behavior might have lagged. If American consumers believed that foreign products were better than domestic ones, they might have been unwilling to change brands, even if their favorite items' prices increased. Second, once importers got a foothold in the U.S. market, they might have been willing to risk profits to maintain their presence. Therefore, even when the exchange rate forced their goods' prices higher, they did not pass this cost along to the consumer so that they could remain competitive.

Finally, Americans' demand for foreign goods might have become **price inelastic,** meaning they bought the good regardless of its price. This could be true for some goods, like oil, that the United States imported in larger amounts in the late 1980s than it did in the 1970s. All three effects played a role in enlarging the trade deficit in 1991 despite the dollar's reversion to 1980 levels. In spite of these deviations, the relationship between the exchange rate and trade balance, as the graph suggests, remains generally intact.

Relationship between Politics and Economics

Our brief discussion of free trade and protectionism reminds us that governments very often make economic decisions for political reasons, and vice versa. The discipline of *international political economy* explores the many ways in which politics and economics interact at the national and global levels. This section outlines three major schools of thought on the complex web of relationships between the world economy and national and international politics. These three perspectives are commonly referred to as liberalism, realism, and Marxism.[7]

Liberalism   In the late eighteenth and early nineteenth centuries, many economists (particularly David Ricardo) who studied international trade concluded that trade barriers were an impediment to economic growth. They theorized that if states allowed the market to function autonomously, trade would evolve to the benefit of all concerned, much as Adam Smith had predicted. As suggested in Chapter 2, Smith was the first major economist to espouse the benefits of free markets. His belief in **laissez faire** (translated as "leave well enough

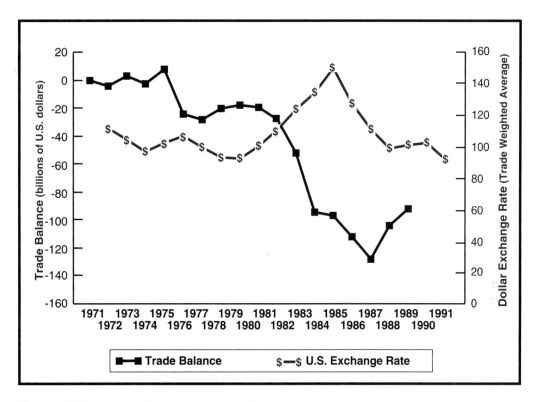

Figure 7.1 U.S. Trade Balance and Exchange Rate

Source: The data are taken from Department of Commerce, *National Trade Data Bank,* October 1991.

alone") inspired governments, especially Britain's, to reduce their intervention in economic activity. His theory ultimately became known as *liberalism.*

Economic liberals make three assumptions: first, that individuals are the principal actors in the political economy. Thus, in order to understand the world economy, we must focus on individuals within society and how they interact with the market. Second, individuals are rational. They have certain preferences that are consistent and stable over time. Finally, individuals maximize their utility by making trade-offs between costs and benefits. Under these assumptions, liberals argue that the market best allocates the world's scarce resources in the most efficient manner possible. They view trade as a positive-sum game, meaning that when nations develop their own comparative advantage, trading benefits every actor involved. According to this theory, governments need not involve themselves with the market mechanism—indeed, government intervention only frustrates the most efficient outcome. Liberals thus conclude that states should practice laissez-faire.[8]

Liberal theory is useful because it helps us understand how economic incentives would guide states if all they were concerned about was maximizing their

AT A GLANCE

THE THREE PERSPECTIVES

Liberalism

States should allow the market to function autonomously.

Assumptions: First, individuals are the principal actors in the political economy. Second, individuals are rational. They have certain preferences that are consistent and stable over time. Third, individuals maximize their utility by making trade-offs between costs and benefits.

Argument: The market best allocates the world's scarce resources in the most efficient manner possible. Trade is a positive-sum, win-win game. Government need not involve itself by interfering with the market mechanism—indeed, government intervention only frustrates the most efficient outcome. Therefore, states should practice laissez-faire.

Usefulness: It helps individuals understand how economic incentives would guide states if all they were concerned about was maximizing their national incomes.

Realism

Because relative levels of power matter in the international system, economics must follow politics. The more powerful one country is relative to another, the more capable it is of coercing other states in trade and economic dealings, as well as on political issues.

Assumptions: First, nation-states—rather than individuals—are the appropriate units of analysis in the international political economy. Second, these nation-states are rational actors. Third, each seeks to maximize power.

national income. However, states are not only wealth maximizers. National policies are implemented by leaders interested as much in the state's survival and security as their own job security. For both purposes, a country's wealth may matter less than its relative strength.

Realism   While liberals argue that economics should be independent of politics, realists look at power relations among nations to determine economic outcomes. They contend that because relative levels of power matter in the international system, economics must follow politics. The more powerful one country is compared with another, the more capable it is of coercing other states in trade and economic dealings as well as political issues.

The three basic assumptions of realists are that nation-states, rather than individuals, are the appropriate units of analysis in the international political economy; that these nation-states are rational actors; and that they seek to maximize power. States act in a manner that they feel will promote their military prominence, even if it means that economic factors are compromised. Realists think states often have no choice but to sacrifice maximum economic growth for national security. Consequently, while classic liberals contend that the search for individual wealth is at the heart of the international economy, for realists the world economy pivots on the quest for national power.

The realist perspective dominated international trade policies prior to the late eighteenth century. Before economists developed theories of the market and

Arguments: States act in a manner that they feel will promote their military prominence, even if it means that economic factors are compromised. States often have no choice but to sacrifice maximum economic growth for national security. The world revolves around the quest for national power.

Usefulness: It helps us to understand how leaders evaluate their nation's military power and their relation to other states in the international arena.

Marxism

Class interests determine economic policy. Adherents believe that the state itself is the expression of the interests of the dominant class.

Assumptions: In industrial states, the dominant class, the bourgeoisie, is the owner of capital.

These capitalists control the means of production while the working class, or proletariat, provides the labor to fuel the capitalist system.

Argument: Marxists foresee alienation on the part of the exploited proletariat. The working classes will unite, both domestically and internationally, to revolt against capitalism. The final result will be communism, where the state—on behalf of all the people—controls the means of production and ensures that everyone benefits equally.

Usefulness: It helps to analyze the role of labor in our increasingly global economy, as well as the plight of the lesser-developed world.

comparative advantage, most states followed policies of **mercantilism,** an economic philosophy that regards trade primarily as an instrument of power politics. As one author describes (during the era of mercantilism):

> The economic realm became the main arena for political conflict. The pursuit of state power was carried out through the pursuit of national economic power and wealth. . . . All international economic transactions were regulated for the purpose of state power.[9]

Mercantilists thus argued that states should exercise strict control over trade, protect domestic industries through tariff barriers and subsidies, and obtain and monopolize trade with overseas colonies. European governments and an emerging class of merchants gained the most from these policies, reaping tremendous profits. During this period, the European powers established colonies in the New World, Asia, and Africa and sought to control trade. Their goal was to expand their own export markets to these new areas, prohibit rival states from doing the same, and import inexpensive commodities at artificially low prices. (These policies, when applied to Britain's colonies in America, were major causes of the American Revolution.)

If trade barriers help states to maximize their power, however, why have there been various periods in history when world trade was relatively free from barriers? Many contemporary realists explain this apparent contradiction with the **hegemonic stability theory,** according to which, from time to time one major

KARL MARX

The thoughts of Karl Marx (1818–1883) have had sweeping effects on the politics, economics, and history of the twentieth century. Dubbed Marxism, his theories of socialism and revolution have been a powerful ideological force in the modern world.

Marx's central work, *The Communist Manifesto* (1848), has become the cornerstone of socialist thought. This pamphlet, written in collaboration with Friedrich Engels, called on the workers of the world to unite against the exploitation inherent in the capitalist system. He argued for revolution as the mechanism to instill communism, a societal framework wherein workers benefit equally from their labor. The main problem with capitalism, Marx argued, is that the workers do not own the means of production and thus do not reap the rewards. Workers toil in factories, which are owned by capitalists.

state becomes the dominant military and economic power in the international system. This dominant power, or hegemon, sets and enforces the rules for the global economy. The United States, for example, was often considered a hegemon from 1945–1973. It assumed the responsibility of guaranteeing the free flow of international goods, providing international security arrangements (such as NATO), and stabilizing world currencies (through the Bretton Woods system, discussed later in this chapter).

During a hegemonic period, the international economic system works well because a dominant state pays the costs of providing these economic stabilizers. Why is it prepared to do that? Because the hegemon, as the world's economic and military giant, furthers its own interests by creating a stable economy and expanding its sphere of influence. By pursuing its interests, it effectively guarantees that many of its smaller allies will be able to take advantage of a stable economic and military environment without paying any of the costs.

But uneasy is the head that wears a crown. There is a problem with hegemony: It is ultimately self-defeating. While in the short run all trading partners gain because the hegemonic influence helps open markets and increases trade, the costs of hegemony tend to grow over time. As the hegemon's trading partners become more competitive relative to the hegemon, the hegemon becomes increasingly less capable of maintaining open markets for its partners' products, policing the open seas, and protecting access to crucial resources (such as oil) without its partners' help. As the hegemon begins to decline relative to its trading partners, it will be more willing to use its residual economic clout in coercive ways to get growing partners to pay for their share of the benefits they receive. For example, beginning in the 1970s, the United States began to demand that its European and Japanese allies help maintain a stable economic system and international security. By the time the Gulf War occurred in 1991, however,

Marx's other significant work, *Das Kapital* (1867), is representative of this position. In it, he writes that misery for the worker will continue until "the knell of capitalist private property sounds. The expropriators are expropriated."

In short, the essential assertion by Marx is that the *proletariat,* or working class, must unite globally and revolt against the *bourgeoisie*—the beneficiaries of the capitalist system, those who own property of any kind—in order for the proletariat to receive the full benefits of its labor. Marx advocated central (government) ownership of the means of production to ensure equal distribution.

America's allies were paying much of the cost of sending U.S. troops into combat in order to protect oil supplies from the Middle East.[10]

But what happens if there is no hegemon? Stability can still emerge if a number of states choose to cooperate. In other words, an alliance of leading economic states can serve the same role as the hegemon. But a multilateral system has lots of problems—like how do you keep the coalition functioning? What do you do if one or more of the parties decide not to abide by their agreements with their allies? This cooperation can be difficult to achieve because in an anarchic world, no state can be punished for breaking an agreement (without going to war, of course). Despite this danger, cooperation can emerge if states acknowledge that they will need one another's help in the long run.[11] If the major trading states do not cooperate, however, realists warn that they are likely to form trade blocs and set up trade barriers to promote their exports and protect their domestic markets from foreign competition. Many analysts thus fear that regional trading areas such as the European Union and North America under the North American Free Trade Agreement (NAFTA) could become "fortresses" closed to imports from outside.

Marxism[12]   While liberals view the international political economy from the level of the individual and realists from the nation-state level, Marxists see it at a class level. Class interests, for Marx and his followers, determine economic policy. Indeed, Marxists believe that the state itself is the expression of the preferences of the dominant class. In industrial democracies, the dominant class, the bourgeoisie, is the owner of capital. These capitalists control the means of production while the working class, or proletariat, provides the labor to fuel the capitalist system. Marxists foresee alienation on the part of the exploited proletariat. The working classes will unite, both domestically and internationally, to revolt against capitalism. The final result will be communism, where the state, on behalf of all the people, controls the means of production and ensures that everyone benefits equally.

Although Marxism might seem out of date today due to the collapse of communism worldwide, it is still a useful tool that some scholars use to analyze the role of labor in our increasingly global economy, as well as the plight of the less developed world. Regarding the role of labor, Marxists believe that multinationalism—the advent of international capital mobility through multinational corporations—has undermined labor's ability to negotiate an equitable division of profit. Researchers spend their time analyzing how labor should respond to this growing division. Second, as we saw in Chapter Five, a branch of Marxist-inspired thought known as **dependency theory** studies how the world system has divided between industrialized "core" countries and underdeveloped "periphery" countries. From this perspective, core countries exploit the periphery for their own ends and stunt industrialization. Dependency theorists thus focus on strategies for ending this dependency. (For much more on dependency theory and the role of developing countries in the global economy, see Chapter Eight.)

International Conditions and the Domestic Political Economy

Regardless of whether one adopts a liberal, realist, or Marxist perspective on international political economy, it is clear that leaders have both economics and politics in mind when making trade policy. How does increased exposure to international trade affect domestic politics? Do domestic actors prefer fixed or floating exchange-rate systems? In order to answer these types of questions, one needs an analytical framework for understanding how conditions in the international economy affect domestic politics. Two methods will be discussed here: one called the factor approach, the other the sector approach. These approaches can help us to better understand the domestic conflicts over international trade that, as national economies become progressively globalized, are becoming increasingly prominent features of the political landscape.

The **factor approach** hypothesizes that every society has three basic interest groups: landholders, capital owners (shareholders in corporations, investors, and so on), and workers.[13] Conflicts arise between those groups that benefit from international conditions and those that are harmed. For example, increased exposure to free trade will benefit those people associated with factors that have a comparative advantage domestically (because they can sell their products abroad); it will hurt those who are associated with scarce factors. This might explain why American organized labor opposed the North American Free Trade Agreement (NAFTA), while factory owners supported it. Unskilled Mexican labor is cheaper than unskilled American labor, giving Mexico a comparative advantage. U.S. workers feared that free trade would encourage United States factories to go south to take advantage of these lower costs. Because the United States has a comparative advantage in capital, capital owners have an incentive to export (this includes exporting factories) if they can earn higher profits overseas. In this case industrialists will make more money if they employ cheaper labor in Mexico than if they use the more expensive workers in the United States. Therefore, in this example, a natural conflict emerges between capital and labor.

The **sector approach** focuses on sectors of the economy rather than factors of production.[14] A sector is a group of related industries within a nation; oil, coal, natural gas, and nuclear power, for example, make up the "energy sector." The sector approach assumes that capital is fixed in a particular industrial sector, at least in the short term. This means that increased foreign competition might hurt some capital owners more than others. Let's say there is an economy in which capital is specific to either the production of clothing or computers. If international trade hurts clothing manufacturers but helps computer manufacturers (because the latter are more competitive internationally), then cloth producers might begin lobbying for protectionism against the wishes of computer makers. This model suggests that a rivalry will develop between these sectors, with one being for and the other against free trade.

The sector approach is useful for understanding why, at any given time, some industries will support free trade while others favor protectionist policies. In the United States, the automobile industry has consistently sought protection from foreign competition, particularly through the use of voluntary export restrictions (VERs), as discussed earlier. On the other hand, pharmaceutical companies, which are very competitive internationally, have lobbied against any protectionist provisions, fearing that foreign reprisals would affect their industry. In this circumstance, sector divisions transcend other divisions between factors that might exist in society.

Do these models necessarily contradict? Not always. Some argue that the sector approach is useful for predicting short-term cleavages while the factor model better explains long-term political divisions. In the short term, it is reasonable to believe that capital is fixed—a computer manufacturer cannot become a cloth producer quickly and cheaply. Yet, in the long term, capital tends to be mobile. Capital owners, like the investors in the clothing industry just mentioned, might find that in the long term they can earn higher profits in other industries or abroad. If this situation materializes, divisions between capital owners and labor could easily become the dominant division, just as they did in the case of NAFTA.

Effect of Domestic Politics on the International Arena

Just as international trade can affect domestic politics, domestic politics can have an impact on the global economy. One approach to the study of international political economy concentrates on the fact that the trade policies of a state are often shaped by the domestic interest groups that exert the most influence nationally. (For more on the role of interest groups in the making of foreign policy, see Chapter Fourteen.) International cooperation can thereby arise when a group of states' domestic coalitions all agree on specific policy goals. For example, some analysts argue that fixed rates succeeded prior to World War I because influential domestic interests in each state supported a cooperative international monetary system. This was due to the fact that export-oriented industries had a tremendous amount of political clout in most of the dominant states at the time.

As we suggested earlier in this chapter, exporters will often prefer fixed rates over floating rates because they reduce the risks involved with international trade. In general, these dominant interests can be represented by landowners, laborers, and capital owners, or various economic sectors. Regardless of which it is, these interests will have to be more powerful than their competitors in order to succeed. The main point of this approach is that preferences for free trade or protection do not rely directly on the relationships among states in the international system, but on the preferences of domestic coalitions. According to this view, coalitions of interest groups within and between the major trading states will be more important than diplomacy in determining the basic conditions of the international economy.

PART II: EVOLUTION OF THE GLOBAL ECONOMY

The concepts and approaches outlined in Part I of this chapter were intended to provide the reader with the basic economic and theoretical tools necessary to analyze the world economy. The goal of Part II is to outline the history of the international political economy. The reader should continue to think about how the tools and theories connect with history, keeping in mind that the prevalent theme throughout is the interconnection between politics and economics.

Origins of the World Economy

Since ancient times, societies have engaged in exchange and trade.[15] Nations have traded for goods, ranging from olive oil to silk, which they do not produce at home. Not until the Industrial Revolution and the concomitant rise of British manufacturing and trade in the late eighteenth century, however, did a truly global economy begin to emerge. Trade and economic relations between nations had existed long before this time, but the growth of world (as opposed to regional) trade, especially in manufactured goods, increased interdependence dramatically and distinguished international economic relations in the industrial era from those of earlier periods. The Industrial Revolution (see Chapter Two) prompted a powerful expansion of trade, capital flows, and population movements unlike any that had come before, the consequence of which was the development of a "truly international economy."[16]

Rise of Britain   As the first industrialized nation, Britain enjoyed the advantages of economic and technological leadership, achieving what many analysts consider to be hegemonic status. In this country, already a highly commercialized one with the largest market in Europe by the late eighteenth century, population growth and rising agricultural productivity laid the basis for rapid industrialization.[17] Britain's long and successful experience with international trade, a relatively unrestricted labor market (facilitating the internal migration of workers from rural to urban areas), and availability of capital paved the way for the development of industry, wool-spinning (later textile-weaving) and iron-making in particular. Within this context, British entrepreneurs developed new, more productive techniques of production (such as the use of fertilizer in agriculture, and the steam engine and coal in manufacturing) to drastically reduce the costs of production. As a result, the country enjoyed a subsequent explosion of exports.

British exports, dominated by cotton products (mainly textiles), increased sharply from the 1780s to 1814, becoming for the first time a powerful engine of growth.[18] By 1801, sales abroad approached 18 percent of national income, with the cotton industry alone representing almost 7 percent of national product.[19] To meet the increasing demand for industrial goods at home and abroad, British entrepreneurs turned to alternative sources of supply outside the British Empire (see Chapter Five). The expanding United States became one such source, providing cheap and abundant cotton to Britain, and in return absorbing a large portion of British exports.[20] This growth of trade between sovereign states, as opposed to that within the British Empire, presented statesmen with tremendous opportunities to capture gains from trade. By the mid-1800s, Britain's industrial capacity, financial strength, political influence, and worldwide network of colonies and military bases made it the first industrialized global superpower.

While British economic and social innovations set the stage for the creation of a truly global economy, the initial spread of industrialization occurred very unevenly across the world. The French Revolution and the Napoleonic Wars (see Chapter Two) delayed economic development and trade on the European continent, and allowed Britain, on the basis of its naval superiority, to extend its imperial reach. Only after British political and economic leaders restored order on the Continent and recognized that mercantilism mitigated further economic growth and development, however, could the leap to an interdependent world economy be made.

Period of British Hegemony

In the wake of the Napoleonic Wars (see Chapter Two), Britain moved away from a protectionist foreign economic policy and actively promoted a more open international economy, one based upon the liberal approach to trade embodied in the writings of such early economists as Adam Smith and David Ricardo (mentioned earlier). Convinced that trade and exchange were "a source of peaceful relations among nations because the mutual benefits of trade and expanding interdependence among national economies tended to foster cooperative relations,"[21] British policy-makers turned towards free trade.

WHAT WOULD YOU DO?

You are the British prime minister in 1846. As head of the parliamentary ruling party, you are aware of the growing support among the Manchester manufacturers and toiling classes for the idea of international free trade, and of the growing discomfort of the landed nobility over such an idea. The debate centers on whether to repeal the Corn Laws, a set of tariffs on grain imports.

Repeal of the Corn Laws would probably result in an influx of cheap grain imports, which would decrease the costs of food for the lower classes. This would have several results. First, it would allow for the lowering of wages at no real cost to the workers. Second, it would allow British manufacturers to reduce the price of their wares on the world market. Third, it might also persuade other countries to repeal

---

The movement toward free trade in Britain, however, was not without political difficulty. After the initial burst of free trade following the Congress of Vienna (refer again to Chapter Two), Britain began to experience a growing urban population and falling export prices, necessitating the search for a means to counter growing unemployment and economic troubles at home while reestablishing competitiveness abroad. Exports no longer acted as "the engine of growth" they had once been, falling from 18 percent of the national income in 1801 to 11 percent in 1841.[22] Initially, Britain experienced a decline in exports of its comparatively disadvantaged agricultural sector, as countries with a comparative advantage in agricultural production, such as Russia and the United States, began to develop this potential more fully, thereby depriving Britain of a large segment of its market.

The loss of export markets for agricultural products, mainly wheat, threatened politically powerful landed interests. In the late eighteenth and early nineteenth centuries, British landowners were accustomed to trade protection through the set of tariffs and other restrictions on agricultural imports collectively known as the **Corn Laws.** Along with the growing working class, British manufacturing and financial interests—based in Manchester and London and imbued with the ideals of economic liberalism—came to regard these agricultural restraints as barriers to solving Britain's problems. Proponents of freer trade hoped that a unilateral reduction in British tariffs would induce other countries to adopt freer trade policies as well, leading to an international division of labor. This division would lead those countries with abundant labor to exploit their comparative advantage in agriculture while other countries (Britain in particular) would specialize in the production of capital-intensive manufactured goods. Britain's landed elites ultimately recognized that they could not defend the Corn Laws any longer. By 1846 these laws were repealed, facilitating a boom in international trade.

their own tariffs and thus open up their markets to British manufactured goods.

On the other hand, repeal of the Corn Laws does not necessarily mean other countries will purchase a greater amount of Britain's exports. Many of these countries tax imported goods in the hope that they too can build a manufacturing economy that will be the envy of the world. Britain could also become dependent on foreign countries for its food supply, leaving it vulnerable to blockades in time of war. Finally, repeal of the grain tariffs might increase social blight by destroying what is left of Britain's farming past, forcing even more people into crowded and squalid city slums and eroding the economic privileges of many members of your party.

Will you choose to support repeal of the Corn Laws?

We see here the operation of several of the trends discussed earlier. On the one hand, Britain was acting as the classic hegemon, using its advantages to promote a free-trade system. Then, too, the system it promoted encouraged competition from others, in this case American agriculture. On the other hand, we also see the influence of domestic pressures and influences, and the reflex reaction of a threatened group to cry out for protection, in this case agricultural interests. Only when these internal conflicts were resolved in favor of free trade could Britain resume its hegemonic role.

Thus, Britain coupled its unilateral move towards openness with persistent diplomatic efforts to promote free trade abroad. Negotiations between Britain and France in the 1850s, culminating in the Cobden-Chevalier Treaty of 1860, were significant in this respect. France, traditionally protectionist under Napoléon III, used trade policy to improve relations with Britain, an ally during the recent Crimean War (see Chapter Two). This treaty removed tariffs on British imports of French goods, such as wine and perfume, and opened the French market to British textiles and other commodities.

An important feature of the treaty was the inclusion of a **most-favored-nation (MFN)** clause. Even today, the MFN principle symbolizes the cordiality of bilateral relations, as the debate in the United States over revoking Communist China's MFN status attests (see Chapter Eight). In the Cobden-Chevalier accord, the MFN clause meant that if Britain (or France) signed a tariff agreement with a third party, the goods of France (or Britain) were entitled to enter British (French) markets on terms "no less favorable" than those of the third party. In other words, both France and Britain promised each other that they would both receive the best deal available in their respective markets. Subsequent British and French trade agreements, all of which contained the MFN clause, helped to hasten the spread of free trade throughout Europe. As one scholar recounts, "For a decade or so, in the 1860s and 1870s, Europe came as close as ever to complete free trade until after World War II."[23]

A number of significant developments between 1850 and 1875 expedited the growth of trade and the world economy. As industrialization proceeded apace on the European continent and in North America, a number of new industrial powers, notably the United States, France, and Germany, rose to challenge Britain's industrial preeminence, the upshot of which was a tremendous expansion of the international economy. Technical innovations in textile and iron production, and later in the manufacturing of steel, machine tools, and chemicals, resulted in a flood of new goods, including railway equipment, steamships, steel and electrical products, machinery of all kinds, and a variety of other manufactured products. In addition, many items already traded on the world market, especially cotton products, became substantially cheaper, resulting in the rapid expansion of foreign trade in manufactures.

While it is difficult to convey the dramatic growth of industry at the close of the 1800s, Tables 7.2 through 7.4 offer some insight into the productive and trading capacities of the great powers at the close of the nineteenth century (see also Table 3.1 on page 83).

Technological developments, especially steam-powered industrial machinery, railroads, and the telegraph, played a vital role in the growth of the world economy. As one author describes it,

> By promoting the exchange of a growing volume of goods; by expanding markets, as well as opening up new sources of supply of many products; by permitting the concentration of certain types of production in fewer centers, thereby encouraging specialization and assisting the realization of economies of scale; and by allowing a greater interregional flow of men and capital, the new forms of transport and communications made possible that growing economic interdependence of the whole world which is so remarkable a feature of nineteenth-century economic development.[24]

Challenges to British Hegemony   The growth of railways, in particular, paved the way for greater German participation in international affairs. Aware of the economic changes in Britain and elsewhere on the continent, the leaders of Prussia (the most powerful German state) enacted reforms resulting in the formation of the ***Zollverein*** (customs union). The *Zollverein* abolished internal tolls and customs barriers between the various German states, in effect creating a German "common market," characterized by a uniform external tariff and creating an economic basis for subsequent German unification (see Chapter Two). This tariff was relatively low, allowing Germany to participate in the world economy.[25] An influx of foreign capital, technology, and enterprise in the 1850s contributed to Germany's development, but railroad construction played the key role in setting the stage for unification and industrial growth.

Ironically, British trade in the Continent, particularly in manufactured goods, facilitated continental industrialization because these exports were necessary for economic development, and they reduced the gap between Britain and other European powers.[26] Britain had played the classic hegemonic role, leading eventually to the creation of its own competitors. In fact, rival industrial states, namely the United States and Germany, had begun to eclipse the once preeminent Britain. While quantitative indicators of power, and the notion of power

Table 7.2 Distribution of World Industrial Production, 1820–1913

Country	Percentage of global industrial production in:					
	1820	*1840*	*1860*	*1881–1885*	*1896–1900*	*1913*
Britain	24	21	21	27	20	14
France	20	18	16	9	7	6
Germany	15	17	15	14	17	16
Russia	–	–	–	3	5	6
Italy	–	–	–	2	3	3
United States	4	5	14	29	30	36

Source: Walt W. Rostow, *The World Economy: History & Prospect* (Austin: University of Texas Press, 1978), p. 52–53.

itself, are often ambiguous (see Chapter Twelve), it is clear that Britain's standing among the great powers had suffered. In particular, the United States and Germany, as Figure 7.2 indicates, emerged as significant economic and potential military rivals. The implications of this change in the international distribution of

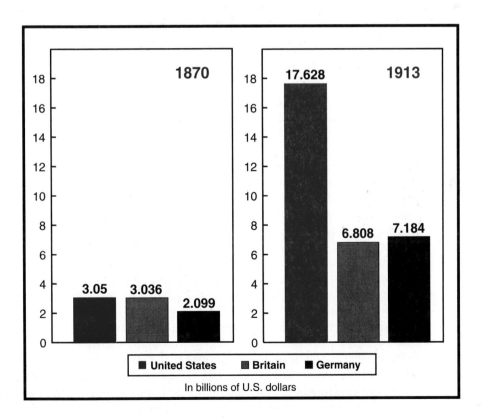

Figure 7.2 GNP of the United States, Great Britain, and Germany: 1870 and 1913

Source: Albert Chandler, *Scale and Scope: The Dynamics of Industrial Capitalism* (Cambridge: Harvard University Press, 1990), p. 52.

Table 7.3   Distribution of World Trade, 1840–1913

Country	Percentage of world trade in:				
	1840	*1860*	*1880*	*1901–1905*	*1913*
Britain	25	25	23	16	16
France	11	11	11	7	7
Germany	8	9	10	12	12
Russia	5	3	4	4	–
Italy	5	3	3	3	3
United States	7	9	10	11	11

Source: Rostow, *The World Economy*, pp. 70–73.

power reverberated throughout the international economy from the 1870s to World War I and beyond.

Protectionism and Discord   The international economy continued to expand in the years from 1873 to 1914. Industrialization even spread to a limited extent to the Third World (see Chapter Eight). The continuing expansion of production promoted a greater degree of interdependence among national economies. At the same time, however, this growing interdependence became increasingly difficult to manage, as manifest in the return to protectionism beginning in the 1880s.

Why did interdependence create problems for various nations? Free trade pressured economies to cease producing goods for which they did not have a comparative advantage. This inevitably hurt many capital owners and laborers who relied on these industries for their livelihood. Many of these sectors were politically powerful and were able to lobby governments for protection from foreign competition. Even in those states that maintained open trading policies, these political cleavages made jobs of policy makers significantly more difficult. Thus, one of the great problems of free trade was operating again—the constant pressure by industries disadvantaged by competition for protection.

The growing dislocations of domestic economies was brought about by two concurring phenomena. First, the increasing volume of world trade intensified competition for international markets. Governments wanted to increase their wealth and stay on the road toward industrial development. Many feared that international competition would hinder their prospects for growth. Their response was to increase protectionism at home in order to help domestic industries develop into world competitors. They felt that protecting industries would reduce the inevitable time lag between industrialization and domestic development.

The second phenomenon associated with protectionism was the revival of nationalism, particularly in Germany and Italy (see Chapter Two). All states were sensitive in this period to the promotion of their industries as a matter of national honor. In some sense, economic power was seen as an achievement worthy of national pride. Taken together, as one scholar argues, "nationalism

Table 7.4   Gross National Products of European Great Powers

Country	GNP (in billions of 1960 U.S. dollars)		
	1840	*1870*	*1890*
Austria/ Hungary	8.3	11.3	15.3
Britain	10.4	19.6	29.4
France	10.3	16.8	19.7
Germany	8.3	16.6	26.4
Italy	5.9	8.2	9.4

Source: Paul Kennedy, *The Rise and Fall of the Great Powers* (New York: Vintage, 1987), p. 171.

and the lag in industrialization made protection inevitable."[27] Related to nationalism was the rise of security concerns stemming from the fears of military aggression that accompanied the changing balance of power in Europe. This also prompted states to employ tariffs (in this period, the direct income tax was not yet known) as a means to raise funds in order to pay for military expenditures (see Chapter Five regarding imperial competition among the great powers in this era).

Through it all, Britain remained the center of world trade and finance, commanding 31 percent of world trade in manufactured goods, with Germany at 27.5 percent and the United States at 13 percent, even as late as 1913.[28] Britain also remained the dominant financial power of the time, possessing 44 percent of the great powers' overseas investment, compared to France's 19.9 percent and Germany's 12.8 percent in 1914. Yet the great powers' ability to manage the increasingly interdependent world economy proved more and more difficult after 1870, beginning with two unforeseen economic developments: the huge influx of cheap U.S. and Russian grain into European markets, and the depression of 1873–1879.

By the 1870s the growth of railroads enabled the United States to export its surplus wheat more rapidly from the fields of the Great Plains states to markets in Europe. As more wheat entered the world market, the price of wheat began to fall. As other commodity producers began to sell their goods internationally, this pattern repeated itself. Regional commodity markets broke down and developed into international markets, increasing world supply and reducing prices. While this was good for consumers, it was bad for many countries that relied on commodity sales for national wealth. In combination with an economic depression during 1873–1879, falling commodity prices resulted in a shuffling of traditional political and economic alignments throughout Europe and the world, especially on the tariff issue, and an intense lobbying effort for protection by those industrial and agricultural producers whose livelihoods were threatened by cheaper imports. Many governments, notably those of Germany and France, accommodated the rising demands for protection. Pressure for protectionism was particularly strong in Germany, where the protectionist coalition of heavy industry and the landed aristocracy—which controlled much of the nation's agriculture—became known as the "marriage of iron and rye."

The Calm before the Storm   By the close of the 1880s, much of the free trade system had begun to collapse. However, these events manifested themselves slowly over time. As we saw in Chapters Two and Three, the period between 1870 and 1914 was still one of relative stability, especially when compared to the period between World War I and World War II. There were storm clouds gathering over Europe, especially in the Balkans, but there were no great totalitarian ideologies or blatantly aggressive moves of one European state against another as would occur in the 1930s.[29]

One reason relative stability prevailed as long as it did before World War I was the existence of a strong international monetary (exchange rate) system. The gold standard, as it was called, lasted between 1870–1914. It was reintroduced again after World War I (see later discussion). In this fixed exchange-rate system, each nation set its currency's value to gold. For example, if one ounce of gold was worth ten U.S. dollars and five British pounds, then the dollar/pound exchange rate would be 2:1, and it remained at the same rate regardless of particular economic developments.

The pre-World War I gold standard's success was due largely to England's devotion to stable exchange rates as well as to France's and Germany's active participation in monitoring the system. These states were able to cooperate because each one of them agreed to pursue economic policies that guaranteed exchange rate stability, even if it caused temporary domestic economic hardship (see the section on fixed and floating exchange rates earlier in this chapter). One example of cooperative behavior occurred during a currency crisis in 1907. England began to experience a severe drain on its gold reserves, which translated into international pressure on its currency to devalue. However, due to England's premier position in the world economy at the time, a devaluation of the pound sterling would have led to an immediate crisis internationally. The crisis was not contained until France and Germany reduced their own gold reserves and transferred some gold to Britain. A reduction in gold reserves affects the economy in the same way that a rise in interest rate does. Although higher interest rates dampened economic activity in Germany and France, their leaders believed that global stability benefited them more in the long run, because it encouraged trade and international investment.

Another reason that these countries chose to emphasize international over domestic concerns was that labor and import-competing firms (domestic firms producing goods that competed with foreign imports) were either underrepresented in legislatures or placated with tariff protection. As noted earlier, different groups benefit and lose from the existence of a fixed exchange-rate system. At the time, labor feared that it would lose jobs as firms were forced to become more competitive by laying off workers. However, its views were usually marginalized, mainly because few workers were organized into labor unions (in many states unions were illegal). Import competitors had a greater voice in government but did not oppose the gold standard as long as other policies, like tariff protection, were implemented on their behalf. Tariff protection for the coalition of iron and rye in Germany is one example of such a policy.

Governments at the time felt that the trade-off between international currency stability and moderate tariff protection was worthwhile. Although tariff protection and international monetary cooperation might seem to contradict each other, the world economy has never been completely free from economic nationalism. Trade-offs always exist, and managing those inherent in free trade and protection is a major task of any national government. Because these trade-offs were successfully managed at the national and international levels, the world economy was relatively stable in the first decade of the twentieth century.

As World War I approached, however, Britain remained staunchly committed to an open international economy, but the failure of France and Germany to follow suit doomed efforts to manage the effects of economic interdependence. Protectionism became more popular as domestic groups who had opposed the gold standard, like labor and import competitors, increased their political power. In fact, the growing tide of protectionism, fed by nationalistic fervor, helped to create the spiral of insecurity that led to World War I (see Chapter Three). The failure of nations to achieve their goals of prosperity and security within the tightening confines of interdependence resulted in four bitter years of military struggle that disrupted the world economy and redistributed international economic power. Thus, the international coalition that had functioned to preserve Britain's hegemony broke down, leaving few vestiges of either hegemony or multilateral cooperation. After World War I, the situation would only get worse.

World War I and Collapse of the World Economy

As did earlier wars, World War I disrupted the international economy. It did, however, prove a boon to previously peripheral states. The United States, in particular, quickly emerged as the chief supplier of war-related materiél to the Allied powers. By war's end, Britain and France had accumulated over $10 billion in war debts to the United States, which became the world's largest creditor as a result. Other states benefited from the war's disruption of traditional export markets and created significant export sectors of their own. Japan, for example, experienced dramatic industrial improvements in the course of meeting the various needs of open markets in Europe and Asia.[30]

The impact of the war on the European participants, however, was not nearly as benign. Besides huge war debts, the victors of World War I inherited a devastated production base (Britain and France, in particular, lost almost an entire generation of young men), inflation, and the loss of traditional export markets. As the vanquished power, Germany faced punitive demands for reparations, which Britain and France forced on that country in order to pay off their debts to the United States. This state of affairs produced a precarious situation for the world economy, a situation exacerbated by the inability of the world's leading industrial economies to cooperate in order to manage the ensuing economic turmoil.

This sequence of events deserves some more attention, largely because the most important diplomatic negotiations throughout the 1920s centered around the issue of war debts and reparations.[31] Two things proved constant over the decade—the United States insisted upon being paid back for its war loans to France and England, and these Allies were determined to extract reparations from Germany, both for punitive reasons and in order to pay back their war debts. By 1924 it became apparent that Germany would be unable to meet its obligations. It was forced to print money in order to pay its debts. Printing money, however, led to the condition known as **hyperinflation,** which made German prices rise as much as 500 percent or more each month.

Hyperinflation was destroying the German economy and making its currency worthless (the U.S./German exchange rate exceeded 1 million marks to the dollar). Clearly, something had to be done to alleviate the pressure caused by reparations. In 1924 the **Dawes Plan** was signed by the Allies, Germany, and the United States. Under the agreement, the United States (primarily American private investors) would lend money to Germany, which it could use to pay its reparations to the Allies. These reparations payments could then be transferred to the U.S. government from the Allies in order to service war loans.

Why would the United States lend money to Germany only to have it return as Allied debt repayment? It is important to note that the American private sector was primarily investing in Germany, not the U.S. government. The German government was willing to pay an attractive interest rate, much like a bank pays interest on a savings account, so American investors invested in Germany out of self-interest, not for humanitarian reasons. When this money was recycled to the U.S. government as debt service, all parties, including the U.S. government and investors, seemed to be made better off by the Dawes Plan. In fact, this system stabilized the international economy for the next few years. Many countries began to experience rapid economic growth, including the United States.

Boom and Bust   By 1928 America's economic expansion was at its peak. One particular manifestation of this was a stock-market boom. Investors continued to pump significant amounts of money into speculative investments, pushing the stock market to record heights. The Federal Reserve (the American institution responsible for guiding U.S. monetary policy) began to fear that this speculation was getting out of control. Its response was to raise U.S. interest rates. Their economists felt that raising interest rates would dampen economic activity just enough to slow down this speculative investment.

Let's try and analyze what the effect of rising U.S. interest rates would have on the international economy. As an analogy, pretend that you have $100 to invest in a savings account. You have a choice between two banks, both of which pay an interest rate. If they pay the same rate, you will be relatively indifferent as to which bank receives your money. But what if one bank decides to raise its interest rate? If you are a smart investor, you will choose to invest your money in the bank with the higher interest rate.

How bad was German inflation in the 1920s? Here a man papers his wall with worthless German marks.
Source: © UPI/Bettmann.

How does this relate to U.S. monetary policy in 1928? When the Federal Reserve raised interest rates in the United States, many investors in Germany decided to switch their investments into U.S. interest-bearing accounts. This essentially broke the cycle of capital that flowed through the international economy. Without foreign capital, Germany was forced to delay its reparations payments, and the Allies ultimately did the same regarding their debts to the United States. Even though U.S. domestic policy instigated this hardship, the United States was unwilling to renegotiate war debts because the American public, isolationist as ever, did not want to acquiesce to European demands. This pushed the Allies into remaining steadfast on reparations payments. As a result, Germany's economy collapsed altogether. (As Chapter Three relates, this collapse occasioned the rise to power of Adolf Hitler's Nazi party.)

The inability to cooperate on debt and reparations led to increased tension and further economic nationalism. The gold standard, which had been reintroduced after World War I, collapsed in 1931 because states were unwilling to cooperate on monetary policy. Additionally, protectionist trade policies, like the Smoot-Hawley tariff (discussed earlier in this chapter), appeared throughout the globe. The Great Depression, initiated by the crash of the overvalued U.S. stock market in 1929, would prove unmanageable until the great powers could agree to pursue cooperative economic policies.

Thus, the interwar period proved to be a model for the disasters that can arise when there is no hegemon (the isolationist United States refused to play this role in the interwar period), the major industrial states do not cooperate, and protection reigns supreme. For the post–1945 generation of leaders after World War II, the nationalism that had led to the global economy's collapse proved to be as important a lesson of what not to do as the appeasement of Hitler that had led to Munich.

Transformation of the World Economy

World War II and the subsequent rise of the United States to global preeminence heralded a new age of global **economic interdependence** and growth. The Second World War fundamentally altered the distribution of power in the international system, ultimately set the stage for Cold War polarization between the communist and capitalistic blocs of nations (see Chapter Four), and brought about great changes in the international political economy.

Foremost among these changes was the emergence of U.S. hegemony. The events of 1939–1945 both revealed and underscored the dominance of the U.S. economy. The United States dominated the world in terms of production. The supply of war matériel and finance, largely through the Lend-Lease program to the Allies during the war, and the vast destruction of European physical and capital stock, ensured a prominent role for U.S. finance following the war. By war's end, the United States was producing 40 percent of the world's armaments, and its productivity (output per unit of input, usually labor) far surpassed that of its nearest competitors. The result was a massive increase in U.S. gross national product (GNP), from $88.6 billion in 1939 to $135.0 billion in 1944.[32]

This rise of American hegemony coincided with a rapid resumption of growth in the world economy as shown in Figure 7.3. Bolstered by the outbreak of the Cold War and the desire to preserve economic stability and peace, international trade and investment grew within the American sphere of influence. The 1950s and 1960s were decades of rapidly rising living standards throughout much of the industrial world. From 1950 to 1973, production of the major industrial countries in Europe rose at an average annual rate of 4.8 percent, while the rate of productivity increased dramatically as well.[33] Economic growth, fueled by accessible Middle Eastern oil, a relatively cheap source of energy, solidified the recovery of Western Europe and Japan.

The Bretton Woods System   Unlike the disarray characteristic of the international economy during the interwar period, the growth of the world economy

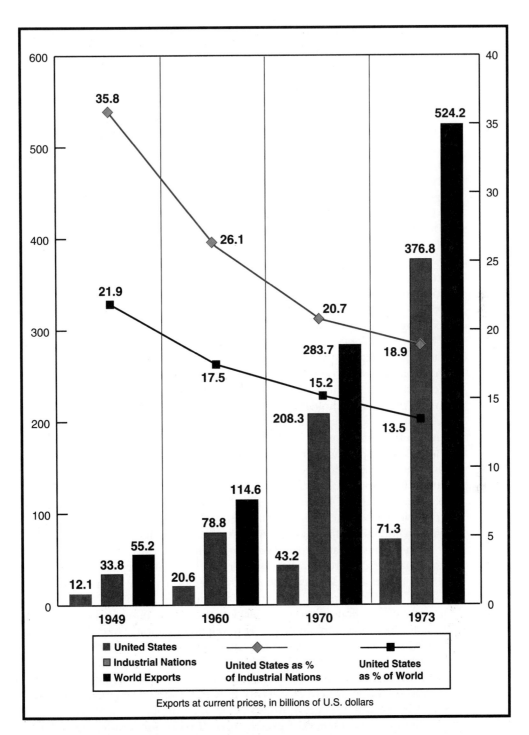

***Figure* 7.3** U.S. and World Trade, 1949–1973

Source: International Monetary Fund, *International Financial Statistics Yearbook, 1979,* pp. 62–67.

after 1945 took place within the context of an institutionalized economic system, known as the Bretton Woods system, led by the United States but premised on cooperation between the major Allied powers. The foundations for the postwar liberal economic system, one designed to avert economic nationalism and the mistakes of the interwar period by fostering free trade and a high level of interdependence, were laid at a 1944 conference held at Bretton Woods, New Hampshire. Here policy-makers attempted to tackle the difficult tasks of creating an international monetary system, a prerequisite for the smooth operation of international economic transactions, and more specifically, an international lending mechanism to help nations get back on a secure economic footing. To realize these ends, the conferees at Bretton Woods established the **International Monetary Fund (IMF)** and the **International Bank for Reconstruction and Development (IBRD,** more commonly known as the **World Bank),** to assist in the recovery effort.[34]

The IMF served to coordinate national currencies by establishing fixed exchange rates and helping to settle international accounts by advancing credit to countries with balance-of-payments deficits. On the basis of rosy recollections of how the nineteenth-century gold standard worked, the IMF established fixed exchange rates in the belief that they would best promote economic stability. The Bretton Woods monetary system fixed the dollar's value in gold at $35 per ounce, and pegged the value of other currencies to that of the dollar (that is, governments were committed to intervene in the currency exchange market to keep the value of their currencies within the permissible bounds of the fixed rate). As the largest holder of the world's gold at the time and the primary contributor of funds to the IMF, the United States exercised a preponderant influence in the institution.

One of the primary purposes of the IMF was to provide short-term loans so that countries could rebuild their war-torn economies (the Marshall Plan, discussed in Chapter Four, was one such vehicle for doing this) and rectify balance-of-payment deficits. In the case of very serious imbalances, the IMF permitted countries to devalue their currency relative to the value of other currencies, with the intention of increasing export revenue and reducing international debts.

Also established at Bretton Woods was the World Bank. Initially created to help finance reconstruction after the war, the World Bank played only a marginal role to that end. As interest grew in developing the newly independent nations of the Third World in the 1950s and 1960s, however, the bank found a new purpose, lending billions of dollars annually to these lesser developed countries. (See Chapter Eight for more on financing development in the Third World.)

Creating institutions designed to manage international trade proved to be somewhat more complicated.[35] The U.S. government originally hoped to create an international organization, the International Trade Organization (ITO), to serve as the equivalent of the IMF in the area of international trade. Opposition in the U.S. Congress, however, derailed the ITO. An alternative arose in 1947 called the **General Agreement on Tariffs and Trade,** or **GATT** (see the boxed feature), which formed one section of the ITO's proposed charter.

GATT's emergence as a practical replacement for the doomed ITO reflected the political consensus that a liberal trading regime containing certain safeguards for disadvantaged domestic social groups would promote both peace and prosperity.

International Economic Relations under American Hegemony

The Bretton Woods institutions, bolstered by U.S. leadership, functioned relatively smoothly throughout the 1950s. By 1949 the formation of the North Atlantic Treaty Organization (NATO), which signaled a clear commitment on the part of the United States to defend its allies and trading partners in Europe, had helped to quell fears of the Communist expansion into western Europe (see Chapter Four). Aid to western Europe, through the Marshall Plan in 1948–1952 and additional military aid, further enshrined the dollar as the key international currency and, together with easy access to vital energy resources such as oil (which the U.S. government's military and political protection of the conservative monarchies of the oil-rich Middle East helped to secure), ensured a rapid European recovery. In short, the system functioned as most policy-makers had hoped. The developed world grew at a dramatic pace, and the United States benefited through its own export promotion.

Yet the Bretton Woods system created its own set of problems for the United States. The role of the dollar as the key international currency gave the United States considerable leeway in managing the international economy—for instance, by granting it the prerogative of printing money to cover its balance-of-payments accounts (other states had to earn money through exporting in order to pay for their debts). But the tremendous outflow of dollars required to finance the postwar recovery eventually undermined foreign confidence in the dollar. The Bretton Woods agreement guaranteed that the United States could convert dollars into gold on demand. As the number of dollars increased faster than the American gold stock, it became very difficult for the United States to cover this obligation. The United States was caught in a catch-22; mitigating this problem would require limiting the number of dollars abroad, but these overseas dollars were necessary in order to maintain a sufficient level of cash flow in the global economy.

By the late 1950s, U.S. policy-makers tried to respond to this dilemma. Although imbalances in countries' balance of payments often occurred during the 1950s and were usually restored by increasing or lowering the exchange value of their currencies, the U.S. government could not employ such an option. Because the United States was committed to defend the Bretton Woods system, whose cornerstone was the convertibility of the dollar to gold at $35 per ounce, dollars held abroad had to be redeemed at that price. As stated earlier, if the amount of dollars held abroad exceeded U.S. gold supplies, all potential claimants could not be paid without raising the dollar price of gold—that is, devaluing the dollar. Devaluing the dollar, however, was politically problematic,

GATT

In 1947, twenty-three of the major trading countries convened under the auspices of the United Nations and agreed upon a set of basic rules and procedures for reducing tariffs. That charter agreement now has more than 100 signatories and is known as the General Agreement on Tariffs and Trade (GATT for short). Central to the GATT is the "most-favored-nation" (MFN) clause, embodying the principle of nondiscrimination, which obligates each signatory to treat all GATT partners equally in terms of tariffs and other restrictions on trade. Codes of conduct, agreed upon by GATT members, outline rules on quotas, subsidies, and other unfair trade practices. Special rules for developing countries allow Third World states to give special protection to their "infant industries."

Since its foundation, several rounds of renegotiation of GATT rules have progressively lowered tariffs and nontariff barriers to trade among member states. The multilateral nature of GATT, however, has allowed many member nations to negotiate exceptions to the GATT rules for some of their export products. Agriculture, in particular, has traditionally received special treatment. In 1955 the United States, supposedly the linchpin of the free-trade system, received a GATT waiver allowing it to limit agricultural (especially cotton-related) imports. This action triggered a chain effect, as many countries resorted to protecting agriculture with nontariff barriers

since it might adversely affect the economies of allies who held large amounts of dollars as a reserve currency and provided political and military support in the struggle against communism. (Devaluing reduced the amount of gold their dollars were worth.)

Furthermore, the possibility of devaluation fueled currency speculation and fears of a "run" on the dollar, meaning that if countries speculated that a currency was about to decline in value, they might try to hedge their bets by reducing the supply of that currency in their overall basket of currency holdings. Since confidence in the dollar, or the belief that the dollar's value was secure, represented the key to international monetary management, U.S. efforts to resolve its balance-of-payments problem dominated international economic relations in the 1960s.

As early as 1960, the amount of foreign-held dollars exceeded the U.S. supply of gold, and U.S. liabilities continued to grow throughout the 1960s and 1970s. After the first run on the dollar in November 1960, the U.S. government abandoned unilateral management of the monetary system and moved towards multilateral management. Together with other Western industrialized countries, the United States developed a number of new institutional arrangements to help resolve problems of monetary coordination and stability. The IMF became more active in lending funds to European countries to help finance and subsidies, making this sector exempt from most GATT regulations.

Many countries, including the United States, now contend that trade-distorting subsidies, especially in the field of agriculture and aircraft production, must end. This represents a relatively recent about-face for the United States government, one that has not been reciprocated in France and Japan, whose powerful farm constituencies make their parliamentary governments more reluctant to liberalize agricultural trade or end farm subsidies.

The most recent round of GATT negotiations, known as the Uruguay Round, was especially difficult and sometimes acrimonious. The talks ground to a halt twice over the failure to come to an agreement on eliminating agricultural subsidies. Finally, in December 1993, the round concluded with a compromise agreement covering agriculture, tariff and nontariff barriers, and intellectual property (copyrights and patents). The accord also establishes a World Trade Organization designed to enforce GATT rules by imposing trade sanctions on violators. The effectiveness of this new organization in regulating world trade will be an important test of the ability of nations to cooperate on economic issues in the absence of a hegemonic power to enforce the rules of free trade.

temporary payment imbalances. Cooperation among central banks (such as the U.S. Federal Reserve Bank and Germany's Bundesbank) emerged as a form of multilateral management. Cooperation was further institutionalized through regular meetings of the finance ministers of the **Group of Seven (G7),** the seven leading member nations of the Organization for Economic Cooperation and Development (OECD).[36]

Yet, despite the efforts of the Western industrialized nations to hold the Bretton Woods system together, economic and political developments in the 1960s and 1970s proved too debilitating to the already unraveling system. The growth of monetary interdependence accompanying the revitalization of Western Europe and Japan complicated efforts to manage the international economy. Multinational banks and corporations arose as vehicles for large international financial flows. By 1974 the assets of foreign branches of U.S. banks totaled over $125 billion, and those of foreign banks operating in the United States totaled roughly $56 billion. **Multinational corporations** (MNCs)—that is, corporations headquartered in one country but with production facilities and assets in more than one country—also became significant players in the world economy. While the overall costs and benefits of these MNCs is controversial (see Chapter Eight), they did show up on the otherwise unfavorable U.S. balance-of-payments ledger in the assets column.

The tremendous growth of international capital markets further complicated the increasingly difficult task of international monetary management. Consequently, multilateral and individual efforts to support international economic practices notwithstanding, international economic relations between the United States and other Western nations continued to worsen. With the economic recovery of Europe and Japan complete by the 1960s, U.S. economic dominance and the prerogatives of unilateral leadership were no longer politically sustainable either at home or abroad.

Decline of U.S. Hegemony   The Bretton Woods system ultimately fostered two concurrent outcomes: the rise of Western European and Japanese economic power and the development of U.S. trade imbalances. These conditions, along with greater fluidity in international financial markets, destabilized the international economic order. In order to understand its eventual demise, however, one must focus on the actual decline of U.S. hegemony. While still the dominant player in the international economy, other industrialized nations, as Table 7.5 reveals, became increasingly important.

Although U.S. export volume increased throughout the 1960s, exports of West Germany, France, and Japan increased much more rapidly. Moreover, these countries, in contrast to the United States, captured an increasingly greater share of the world export market throughout the decade. By 1972 West Germany nearly rivaled the United States in terms of volume and percent of world exports.

Associated with these divergent export growth paths were adverse trends in the U.S. economy. A glance at some data reveals an inflating trade deficit by the early 1970s. In 1960 the United States had a current-account surplus equal to $1.8 billion. By 1972 the balance spiraled into a deficit of over $8.4 billion.[37] In addition to the deteriorating U.S. trade balance, budget deficits were increasing rapidly and the economy was slowing down at home. Fueled in large part by excessive domestic expenditures on new antipoverty and social welfare programs, the rising costs of financing the Vietnam War, and the refusal to either raise taxes or cut spending, budget deficits and inflation on the home front contributed to a crisis in the international economic arena. Another look at Figure 7.3 illustrates the declining U.S. position in world trade by 1973.

In 1971, after several years of seeing its share of the world export market decline, the United States began to register a persistent trade deficit. This deficit added to the costs of the war effort and shortfalls in domestic revenue, ultimately proving detrimental to the international monetary system. Continued "benign neglect" in the area of monetary policy proved untenable in the face of rising foreign pressure, and on August 15, 1971, President Nixon announced that the United States would no longer bear a disproportionate share of the burden of maintaining the international monetary system. The United States suspended its commitment to convert dollars to gold, imposed domestic wage and price controls, demanded dollar depreciation, and imposed a 10 percent tariff on foreign imports. Collectively, these actions amounted to a rejection of the basic rules of

Table 7.5	World Exports, 1960–1972 (billions of U.S. dollars, with percent of world total)							
Country	*1960*	*%*	*1965*	*%*	*1970*	*%*	*1972*	*%*
United States	20.6	18.0	27.5	16.5	43.2	15.2	49.8	13.2
Great Britain	10.6	9.3	13.8	8.2	19.6	6.9	24.7	6.6
West Germany	11.4	9.9	17.9	10.7	34.2	12.1	46.7	12.4
France	6.9	6.0	10.2	6.1	18.1	6.4	26.5	7.0
Japan	4.1	3.6	8.5	5.1	19.3	6.8	29.1	7.7
World Exports	114.6		167.1		283.7		376.8	

Source: Adapted from International Monetary Fund, *International Financial Statistics Yearbook, 1979,* pp. 62–63.

international monetary relations and a demand for greater "burden-sharing" by U.S. military and economic allies.

The "Nixon shock" of 1971 was indicative of the problems inherent in a hegemonic system. For decades the United States had been the preeminent state in the world economy, forging a united front with its allies against the Soviets and augmenting the economic development of those allies. Yet, this process ultimately created a tremendous amount of instability, as disagreements arose between the United States and its now powerful allies over how to fix the international system. The French and the Japanese governments resisted U.S. pressure most strenuously, with France insisting that the United States honor its commitment to convert dollars into gold, and Japan demanding that it fix its domestic economic problems. Negotiations continued for thirteen months over how to salvage the Bretton Woods regime. Ultimately they failed, and the leading industrial powers agreed to eliminate the fixed exchange-rate system. By March 1973 most major currencies floated in financial markets.

The eclipse of U.S. predominance contributed to the decline of international economic order. In the past, the United States had been welcomed as a necessary stabilizer for the international economy. By the 1970s American leadership was viewed more suspiciously, especially as other Western industrial powers grew. Accordingly, efforts to restore order in international economic relations in the wake of the collapse of the Bretton Woods system took on a decidedly more multilateral cast. Just as the United States and Western industrial powers began the arduous task of restoring international monetary order, however, unexpected crises made an already difficult endeavor even more so.

OPEC and the Oil Crisis While negotiations to reform the international monetary system continued, developments in the Middle East threatened the supply of cheap oil upon which the Western industrial nations had come to rely by the early 1970s. The U.S. case exemplifies this growing dependence. Its share of world oil production between 1957–1972 declined from 43.1 percent to 21.1 percent. A concomitant rise in Middle East oil production increased its world share from 19.0 to 41.0 percent. During the same period, U.S. oil imports also

According to this 1972 cartoon, the consequence of floating the dollar was a decline in its value, thereby imperiling a life-jacketed George Washington.
Source: © Jeff MacNelly.

rose dramatically, from 11.0 to 35.5 percent of total U.S. consumption. Other Western industrialized states were similarly dependent upon foreign oil. As demand for oil began to outstrip supply worldwide, the price of oil, historically very moderate, was poised for a substantial increase by the early 1970s.[39]

In October 1973 Egypt and Syria launched an attack on Israel. U.S. support of Israel in the resulting Yom Kippur War prompted several Arab members of the Organization of Petroleum Exporting Countries (OPEC) to impose an oil embargo. This involved reductions in total oil production and a ban on shipments to the United States and the Netherlands (both supporters of Israel). By January 1974 oil prices had risen from $3.01 a barrel at the outset of the crisis to $11.65, a near fourfold increase, confronting the United States with a shift in economic power that, according to Henry Kissinger, "altered irrevocably the world as it had grown up in the postwar period."[40]

Cooperation and Conflict in the Modern Global Economy

With the demise of the Bretton Woods system in 1971 and the oil crisis of 1973, the postwar international economic order lay in partial disarray. Despite the relative decline of the United States, however, international economic activity continued to thrive. Rather than shrinking, trade and finance expanded markedly after 1973. Spurred by the need to recycle the OPEC states' surplus "petrodollars," finance became truly international, with worldwide financial markets inseparably linked. Trade levels, although subject to marked fluctuations, also increased dramatically, fueling spectacular growth in Japan and Southeast Asia. As Figure 7.4 shows, although trade increased worldwide, it increased at a faster rate for industrialized countries.

The expansion of trade and financial flows prompted the advanced industrial states to renew their efforts to manage the international economy in a cooperative manner. Nations developed common interests in managing interdependence to minimize its conflictive aspects. These interests have given rise to many new arrangements, perhaps the most important of which include recurrent efforts to manage floating exchange rates and coordinate macroeconomic policies (which use taxation, spending, and money supply to regulate aggregate national economies). The state of the economy is no longer the province of "low politics" that it once was: Presidents and prime ministers, finance ministers and their staffs, and central bankers have become deeply involved in these matters for national security reasons.

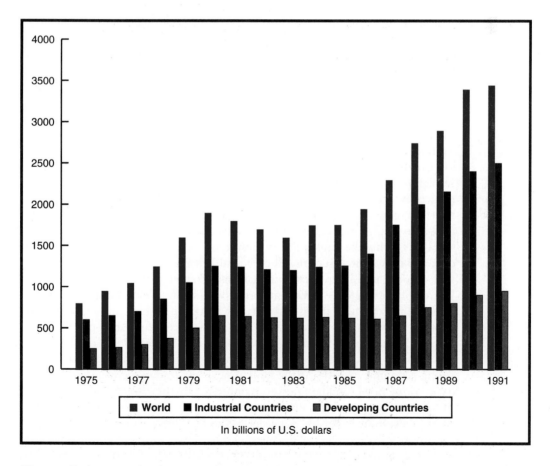

Figure 7.4 World Exports: 1975–1991

Source: International Monetary Fund, *International Financial Statistics Yearbook, 1992,* p. 8.

Despite the cooperative trends, conflict is never far behind. The international economy still generates powerful competitive incentives. Those actors able to set the world economic agenda will benefit, while others will lag behind. Thus, the need for international cooperation is often mitigated by a countervailing need for institutions and national strategies capable of adapting to and prospering in an intensely competitive environment. The growth of world trade, the declining dominance of the United States, and the seemingly extraordinary success of Japan have intensified concerns about competitiveness as markets for goods and services have become increasingly globalized.[41]

From Hegemony to Multilateralism   Cooperation and conflict in the international political economy developed within the tumult of events and policy shifts after 1973. The unprecedented increase in oil prices in 1973–1974 forced dramatic adjustments on industrial nations already highly dependent on oil. Largely unable to lessen their demand for oil despite the dramatic price increase, the developed countries experienced severe economic dislocations, including reduced purchases of many goods, long lines at the gas pumps, and inflation. Throughout 1974 and 1975, many countries in the developed world experienced **stagflation,** a combination of low, or stagnant, economic growth and a high rate of inflation. According to classical economic theory—the history of business cycles up to this time had confirmed this point—unemployment and inflation were thought to correct each other, with unemployment dampening consumer demand and putting downward pressure on prices, and inflation increasing production and employment levels. Economic recovery and relatively stable crude oil prices (at a new level of $11 to $13 per barrel) set in during the mid-1970s, but came to an abrupt end once again in 1979 with the Iranian revolution and overthrow of the shah. Already tight oil supplies were reduced by the loss of production in Iran; as a result, oil prices again skyrocketed. By 1980 oil prices had reached about $35 per barrel, and the world economy, unable to adjust, once again entered the throes of stagflation.

Efforts within the United States to overcome these shocks to the world economy had only limited success. The Federal Reserve, in order to eradicate inflation, chose to raise interest rates dramatically. This led to a severe recession in the United States in 1981–1982 that spread worldwide. The economic doldrums caused the advanced industrial nations to consider radical shock therapy. Brought to power in part to provide this shock treatment, American President Ronald Reagan and British Prime Minister Margaret Thatcher implemented deregulatory policies and tax cuts, which they felt would facilitate a return to strong economic growth. At the same time, these leaders were elected to combat growing Soviet military power, heightened by the 1979 Soviet invasion of Afghanistan (see Chapter Four). The combination of increased defense spending and tax cuts led to record U.S. peacetime budget deficits.

Although U.S. budget deficits increased, the rise in government (defense) spending and reduction in taxes spurred a strong economic recovery in the country. The United States ultimately became the world's engine for growth, as its prosperity filtered worldwide. One consequence of these policies, however, was to push American interest rates above those in other countries. As was discussed in the beginning of this chapter, higher interest rates have two effects on the domestic economy: They appreciate the currency and increase the price of domestic goods abroad. In fact, both phenomena occurred in the United States during the 1980s. The result was a persistent, massive trade deficit. The Reagan administration's effort to revitalize the national and world economy worked in the short term, but this growth came at a severe price. Trade and budget deficits grew out of control, manufacturers of exports and domestic goods could not compete with foreign firms, and U.S. savings and investment rates declined dramatically.

Imbalances in the world economy since the 1970s are shown in Figure 7.5, which details the current-account balances of the three major trading states: the United States, Germany, and Japan. All were basically balanced until the early 1980s, when the U.S. figures began to show a deficit and German and Japanese figures began to show surpluses until Germany began to dip in 1991 with reunification.

Ultimately, interdependence has brought nations closer together, increasing their reliance on one another for economic prosperity. In the postwar era, particularly since the 1970s, trade has increased substantially, capital flows between nations have ballooned, and foreign exchange transactions have reached tremendous proportions. The consequences of these forces have been significant for the world economy and its major participants in many ways. First, multilateralism has increased, as nations are forced to coordinate in order to succeed economically. Unlike the periods of British and American hegemony, today the great powers cannot afford to go it alone. Unilateral pursuit of economic policy often yields tremendous trade imbalances and unwanted exchange-rate fluctuations.

Second, and in direct contrast to the previous point, as the number of powerful states has increased, so has the probability for conflict. With more and more nations vying for market share and profits, competition has become intense, and the failure to keep up with one's competitors often has dire consequences.[42]

Eastern Europe and Russia: From Communism to the Free Market? The collapse of Communist regimes in the former Soviet bloc nations (see Chapter Four) has profoundly affected European economies, and its potential impact on the world economy is much greater.[43] The complete transformation from communism to capitalism in Russia, Eastern Europe, and Central Asia will probably take a generation to occur, require a coordinated effort along many fronts, and take place at different rates among the former Soviet bloc countries. Specifically, economic reform entails ending fiscal deficits and establishing monetary stability, eliminating price controls and state subsidies, creating a convertible currency, and eliminating trade barriers.

These economic reforms will require sweeping institutional changes, including privatization of state firms and the banking system, provisions to protect private property, revamping of the tax system, and establishment of a social safety

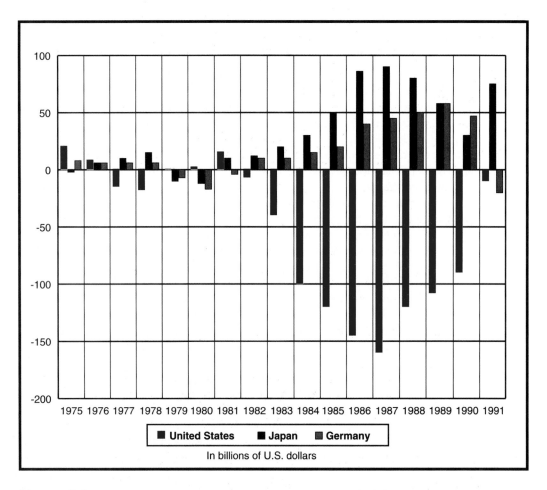

Figure 7.5 Current Account Balances of the United States, Japan, and Germany

Source: International Monetary Fund, *International Financial Statistics Yearbook, 1992,* p. 128.

net for pensioners, the unemployed, and other vulnerable groups. Moreover, in many ex-Communist states, all these reforms must be carried out in a political climate in which many government officials and political parties are reluctant to give up Soviet-style state control of the economy.

Those countries that have been most successful thus far are the ones that pursued economic liberalism most fervently. Poland, the Czech Republic, and Hungary each implemented privatization policies along with democratic reforms that protect and encourage private ownership. The former East Germany was fortunate in this respect, as German unification allowed integration into strong West German economic and political institutions—but the social and financial costs of unification have proven higher than anticipated. Other countries, including Romania and Bulgaria, have been less successful, largely because electorates have been unable or unwilling to remove former Communist bureaucrats.

In many respects, a state's ability to achieve reform depends on the political will to accept economic hardship. This transition requires a tremendous amount of pain, including high inflation, unemployment, and a scarcity of basic goods and services. In some states, particularly Hungary and the Czech Republic, the public was willing to support political parties that sought to liberalize the economy. In other states, including Russia and Ukraine, the hardship has been extremely severe, and the public's support for reformers has waned. Even in East Europe, by 1994 people in several countries were beginning to vote for socialists and ex-Communists in response to the economic pain imposed by new liberal programs. Only the future will tell how successful many of these states will be at integrating into the world economy.

The West has more than an academic interest in the former Soviet bloc's success. Throughout the Cold War, East-West trade was minimal. U.S.–led institutions like GATT and the Bretton Woods system helped integrate the economies of the capitalist world, while Soviet-led institutions, particularly the **Council of Mutual Economic Assistance (CMEA),** solidified trade relations in the East. Now that political tensions have eased and these Communist institutions have collapsed, most capitalist nations see this region as an untapped market. Yet, there are more general reasons why the West hopes reform will continue. Their leaders believe that a capitalist and democratic Russia and Eastern Europe will eliminate the need for massive military budgets. The less money needed for weapons, the more money that can be spent on creating economic wealth.

Despite these concerns, the West has only tentatively helped these states, providing relatively small amounts of economic aid and only partial acceptance into their institutions. The European Union (EU), for example, has thus far refused to establish a free-trade area between itself and Eastern Europe. Why would the United States, Japan, and the EU respond in such a manner? The answer points to the inherent tensions present in an interdependent world. Although no one wants these states to revert to Soviet communism or other forms of authoritarianism, many powerful interest groups are worried about increased economic competition from the East. Economic integration might lead Western firms to relocate in the East, because many former Communist states have cheaper labor and lax environmental laws. The European debate over economic integration with Eastern Europe thus closely resembles the debate in the United States over NAFTA (discussed later).

The West has thus far been unable to solve this puzzle: How can they guarantee that capitalism will take hold within the former Soviet bloc without infringing upon their own economic position? In the short run, the puzzle may be insoluble, but accepting pain now in return for gain later could make both Eastern and Western Europe more secure and prosperous in the long term.[44]

The Need for Cooperation   Increasing interdependence has taught policy-makers that it often pays to cooperate to manage international economic relations. Yet, it is often difficult to predict when cooperation between states will emerge or how it will manifest itself. What we do know is that cooperation results from strategic bargaining between two or more states; it does not connote that states work together in perfect harmony. States often have very different preferences, but situations can arise in which compromise can be very beneficial for all. The goal, of course, is to give up as little as possible, while achieving an outcome that benefits all states involved. This balance between national autonomy and international cooperation is tenuous and suggests why states often cannot agree on a set of policy outcomes.

Since the breakdown of the Bretton Woods system, economic summits among the Group of Seven (G7) have tried to restore a degree of international economic stability. There have been many instances of great success. Four summits were arranged between 1975 and 1978 in order to facilitate a world recovery from recession. An agreement materialized whereby the major powers agreed to coordinate their fiscal policies and reduce their reliance on foreign oil. In 1985 the G7 nations agreed to alter their currencies' values in order to eliminate the tremendous trade imbalances that appeared worldwide. The resulting policy changes had a tremendous effect, with the dollar depreciating 67 percent in three years, just as the states had hoped.

The ad hoc nature of the G7 summits, however, suggests that international cooperation can be muddled if one or more states decide not to cooperate. A prime example of this can be seen by analyzing U.S. economic policy during the early 1980s. Suffering from high inflation rates, the United States decided to raise interest rates in order to squelch inflationary pressure. Because the United States was such an important factor in the world economy, its unilateral policy decision had a momentous impact both within the nation and on its trading partners. Higher interest rates led to a deep global recession in 1981–1982, broadsiding the efforts of other states that were trying to manage their own economies. Additional effects were an appreciated dollar and an enlarged U.S. trade deficit. Even though the recession ended in 1982, the resulting trade imbalances led to a degree of conflict between the United States and its trading partners. Although the 1985 economic summit alleviated some of this diplomatic pressure, this unilateral policy action had a negative impact on international relations.[45]

These examples show that even though most states claim to be in favor of international economic cooperation, domestic considerations can mitigate policy coordination. It is clear that states can successfully collaborate; the prospects for sustained cooperation, however, are far from certain. Domestic considerations can change a state's proclivity for international coordination. In order to counterbalance this uncertainty, states have begun to form additional relationships that parallel global summitry. The formation of economic blocs, such as the European Union and the North American Free Trade Agreement, have simultaneously increased the possibility for free trade and protectionism in the world economy, and will conceivably alter the nature of global economic relations.

ECONOMIC BLOCS: THE SHAPE OF THE FUTURE?

An **economic bloc** is a political or economic organization designed to promote high levels of internal cooperation as well as enhance competitiveness with the rest of the world.[46] The two most common types of economic blocs are **common markets,** which are characterized by common external trade barriers and uniform internal trade barriers, and **free-trade areas,** which are generally characterized by uniform internal trade barriers alone. One of the greatest concerns about economic blocs is that they might promote internal cooperation by increasing trade levels among bloc members but create conflict between different blocs. Also, by discriminating against imports from non-bloc countries, economic blocs may function as protectionist "fortresses" for member countries. In fact, some critics of economic blocs believe that by concentrating more of their regional economic activity, the advanced industrialized states might undo the accomplishments of international institutions such as GATT in reducing global tariff levels and increasing global trade.

In spite of their importance in the contemporary world economy, it is too early to tell what impact trade blocs will have. If the world divided into different blocs, some suggest it might become easier to negotiate international economic agreements. Why? Today, many countries acting individually negotiate agreements like GATT. If they were organized into blocs, there would be fewer actors at the negotiating table, conceivably making it easier to compromise. Others say that regions will never become self-sufficient and that inter-regional trade will increase further. The bottom line is that while no one can be sure what the future holds, regional trade blocs seem likely to become increasingly important.

European Union (EU)

Among economic blocs, the European Union (EU) is the largest (comprising over 380 million people) and the most highly integrated. The foundations of the EU were laid in 1951, when France's foreign minister, Robert Schuman, initiated the European, Coal and Steel Community (ECSC) to create a common market in coal and steel as a means of guaranteeing peace, especially between France and Germany. By 1955 this organization had contributed to a 23 percent increase in coal production and a 150 percent increase in iron and steel production. In the 1957 Treaty of Rome, the six members of the ECSC (France, West Germany, Italy, Belgium, the Netherlands, and Luxembourg) inaugurated the **European Economic Community (EEC).** The members envisaged the EEC to be much more than just a free-trade union: They sought the eventual elimination of internal tariffs, a free flow of capital and labor, and similar wage and social benefits in all the participating countries.[47]

The EEC proved so successful at increasing trade and prosperity levels among its members that in 1973 members of the **European Free Trade Area (EFTA)**—including Britain, Norway, Sweden, Switzerland, Austria, and Portugal, formed in 1959 as a British-dominated counterweight against the French-dominated EEC—entered into a free-trade agreement with the Common Market. Great Britain, Ireland, and Denmark became EEC members in 1973, Greece in 1981, and Spain and Portugal joined in 1986. Five current members of EFTA—Norway, Sweden, Finland, Switzerland, and Austria—have also applied for EU membership. Further applications from former Soviet-bloc countries, such as Poland, Hungary, and the Czech Republic, are being considered as well.

Progress toward the full economic integration of EU members entered a new stage when they signed the Single European Act in December 1985. This act entailed 282 new laws that all members agreed to implement by January 1993, including the elimination of customs checks, the creation of a single banking market among these states, and a uniform value-added tax (the European equivalent of sales taxes). At their meeting in December 1991 at Maastricht in the Netherlands, the EU nations agreed to the Treaty of European Union to finalize their political and monetary union (symbolized in their new collective name, the European Union). They agreed to establish a single currency for most members (Britain and Denmark were allowed to "opt out" of joining) by the year 2000. They also agreed to create an independent European central bank governed by a twelve-person board, with members representing each state. EU nations whose aggregate economic indicators conform to certain standards are expected to join this arrangement by 1998.

Greater economic and political cooperation within Europe is based on a convergence of interests. Germany would like to see its major Continental trading partners follow its own low-inflation policies, and it is willing to relinquish some autonomy over the German economy in return for a powerful European central bank independent of political control and capable of managing European inflation. Other EU states, especially France and Italy, are willing to surrender a measure of sovereignty over inflation rates and budget deficits in return for an additional role in European policy-making.

Despite its steady progress since 1951, European economic integration has been neither smooth nor easy. Referenda in Denmark and France ratified the Maastricht treaty by slim margins, indicating the level of popular apprehension about integration in much of the Union. Disagreements over trade and monetary policy still divide EU members. France would like monetary union, but it fears being dominated by Germany. Other states, in particular Britain, fear losing sovereignty to a Continental institution, and have resisted certain aspects of the plan, in addition to demanding a clause for their departure if they see fit. Germany has also been uncooperative at times. Attempting to cope with unification (see Chapter Four), Germany pursued economic policies that threw the entire continent into a deep recession. Despite these setbacks, it seems that integration is moving forward, albeit slowly and with much trepidation.

North American Free Trade Agreement (NAFTA)

The movement toward European integration, as well as Japan's increasing assertiveness in Asia and the world, led the United States to develop its own regional response. The **North American Free Trade Agreement** between Canada, the United States, and Mexico created a free-trade area within North

America that went into effect January 1, 1994. It does not go nearly as far as the EU regarding integration. NAFTA only eliminates internal trade barriers between these three countries. It does not set barriers with other states, nor does it create supra-national economic or political institutions (except panels to resolve disputes over tariffs and dumping). Nevertheless, it was an important step for the United States in its attempt to remain competitive in the world economy.

The history of NAFTA began in January 1989, when the U.S.–Canadian free-trade agreement took effect. Its objective was to eliminate virtually all tariffs and duties between the United States and Canada by 1999.[48] Incorporating Mexico into this free-trade pact encountered significant political opposition from environmental groups, some industries (mainly low-tech and low-skill), and labor organizations in the United States due to the substantial economic differences between the United States and Mexico. Environmental groups feared that more U.S. industries would set up ***maquiladoras*** (factories that assemble inputs produced in the United States into goods reexported to the U.S. market) in Mexico to take advantage of poorly enforced environmental laws. Labor unions were alarmed by the prospect of job flight to Mexico, where the wage rates for unskilled labor are roughly one-seventh of those in the United States.

Barrels full of chemicals, abandoned by a U.S.-owned business in Juarez, rust in the Mexican desert. Scenes like this inspired many opponents of NAFTA, who believe that U.S. companies take advantage of lower environmental standards across the border.
Source: © Richard Perry/Sygma.

Supporters of the trade accord argued that freer trade would create jobs and lower consumer prices in all three countries, and that as Mexico grew more prosperous, environmental regulations would become more popular and more effectively enforced. After an acrimonious debate (see Chapter Eight), and after the Clinton administration added side agreements to make the transition to freer trade more palatable to labor, farm, and environmental groups, NAFTA was finally ratified by the U.S. Congress in November 1993. Detractors attributed Clinton's success in getting NAFTA passed to the side deals (bribes, to some) given to pressure groups and crucial industries, but it was clear that an important step had been taken toward free trade with America's northern and southern neighbors.

Free-Trade Areas of the Pacific Rim

The movement toward economic integration in Europe and North America accelerated the movement toward a free-trade area or common market in Asia. In 1992 the member states of **ASEAN (Association of Southeast Asian Nations),** concerned that the single European market and NAFTA would divert global investment to Europe and North America, launched the **ASEAN Free-Trade Area (AFTA),** a fifteen-year plan for reducing tariffs on products in fifteen major categories. Asian leaders also formed an **East Asian Economic Caucus (EAEC),** devoted to rapid economic growth. It includes the six ASEAN nations, Japan, China, and other Asian countries, but not the so-called "Anglo-Saxon states" of Australia, New Zealand, Canada, and the United States.

Concerned by an apparent desire to keep these states out of the fastest growing economic region in the world, President Clinton convened the first meeting of the **Asia-Pacific Economic Cooperation (APEC)** organization in 1993. Originally proposed by Australia, APEC is a loose conglomeration of more than a dozen Pacific Rim states (Australia, Brunei, Canada, China, Hong Kong, Indonesia, Japan, Malaysia, New Zealand, the Philippines, Singapore, South Korea, Taiwan, Thailand, and the United States) with a combined GNP of over $14 trillion. Like other economic blocs, APEC embodies a mix of cooperative and conflictive interests. The U.S. government desires APEC to ensure a foothold for the United States in Asian markets, and it sees APEC as a way to pressure European governments to open their markets and make concessions in world trade talks or else be shunned by the United States. On the other hand, the export-oriented Asian states seek to preserve their share of the U.S. market and prevent NAFTA-member Mexico from replacing Asia as the United States' source of electronics and semi-processed goods.

Are Trade Blocs Examples of Cooperation or Conflict?

In many ways, regional integration and trade blocs have arisen in response to the decline of U.S. economic hegemony. Their emergence makes clear two themes that underlie foreign economic relations since 1973. First, the major industrialized states have repeatedly attempted to cooperate in order to manage the world economy. Through G7 meetings, these states have succeeded at avoiding an economic collapse that many feared would materialize without a hegemon at the center of the international system. There has also been an upsurge in regional cooperation, as economic blocs formed in order to deal with intensified global competition.

A parallel trend, however, has been the resurgence of economic conflict and uncertainty. Although G7 meetings were successful forums for discussion, they were no substitute for strong international institutions to regulate trade and finance. The summit meetings often failed to accomplish their goals and left world markets wondering what would happen next. Additionally, the emergence of economic blocs makes it unclear whether regional cooperation will lead to greater global tension. Trade blocs have unquestionably spurred the growth of regional trade and the institutionalization of regional cooperation; whether they will heighten cooperation, or conflict, at the global level remains an open question.

CONCLUSION: THE GLOBAL ECONOMY IN THE NEW ERA

More than any other aspect of international relations, the changing world economy exemplifies the intertwining trends of cooperation and conflict, globalization and fragmentation. The explosive growth of world trade since 1945 has made nations more interdependent than ever, as states have come to depend on one another for markets, capital, natural resources, and financial stability. This interdependence has fostered the growth of international institutions, such as the G7 and GATT, and of regional organizations like the EU and ASEAN. These cooperative institutions have succeeded in making conflicts over trade less intense, but their myriad of rules, regulations, and panels for resolving disputes indicate how economic conflicts have become more frequent as trade has expanded. As economic activity inherently involves both cooperation (between partners in an exchange) and conflict (between buyers and sellers over prices, and between competitors for customers), this should not be too surprising.

What is more surprising is how the world economy has simultaneously become more globalized and more fragmented. Air transportation and satellite communications have given small firms and individuals routine access to global markets; TV commercials for air express services trumpet how easy it now is for a corner store in Moscow, Idaho, to reach customers in Moscow, Russia. At the same time, some economists warn that the world may be dividing into antagonistic trading blocs, as Europe, Japan, and the United States break down barriers to regional trade while setting up barriers to imports from other regions. National leaders demand that their governments "get tough" in pressuring others to lower tariffs and nontariff barriers (conveniently ignoring the barriers that protect their own industries), while regions within nations, from Siberia to Scotland to Chiapas (in Mexico), demand more autonomy and worry about the effects that regional integration may have on their local economies. Overall, the twin processes of globalization and fragmentation are weakening the economic sovereignty of the nation-state and transferring it to supranational institutions and subnational groups. Marx predicted in the nineteenth century that communism would make nation-states obsolete, but the contemporary global economy shows that the triumph of capitalism, rather than communism, is causing the state to wither away.

This chapter has outlined how the structure of the world economic system changed from British hegemony in the mid-nineteenth and early twentieth centuries to conflicting trade blocs between the World Wars, U.S. hegemony after World War II, and cooperative multilateralism since the 1970s. Throughout all these periods, some governments and industries have called for freer trade, while other interests have demanded barriers against international competition. Whatever structure the world economy takes on in the New Era, the struggle between free-traders and protectionists is almost certain to continue, as are the disagreements between liberals, realists, and Marxists over the goals and functioning of world trade. These political conflicts will continue to be played out in the economic sphere, and vice versa.

This chapter was designed to introduce the concepts and historical background that will enable readers to better understand those aspects of international relations that will have the greatest impact on their personal lives and careers. Regardless of what shape the global economy takes, this impact can only increase in the future. Those who doubt that this is so—who think that economic globalization, fragmentation, cooperation, and conflict are of purely academic interest—should turn off their TVs (made in Taiwan, showing news live via satellite from South Africa), put on their running shoes (made in Korea), get in their cars (built at a Japanese-owned factory in Ohio), drive (using gasoline made from Saudi oil) to McDonald's (a multinational corporation), and order a hamburger (made from Brazilian beef) to remind themselves that as the world economy gets bigger, the world gets ever smaller.

PRINCIPAL POINTS OF CHAPTER SEVEN

1. The operation of the global economy has a tremendous political and economic impact on all states. This impact is greater on states that trade more, but international economic relations affect even states that strive for self-sufficiency.

2. States that produce specific goods more efficiently than other states can clearly profit from trade. However, comparative advantage can make mutual gains from trade possible even if one trading partner has an absolute advantage in the production of all goods.

3. Free trade (open access to markets for all goods, regardless of country of origin) maximizes economic efficiency and benefits to consumers. Because domestic industries often find it difficult to compete with more efficient foreign producers, however, governments often impose trade barriers favoring domestically produced goods and services. Because these barriers seek to "protect" domestic producers from foreign competition, their imposition is referred to as protectionism.

4. There are two basic types of trade barriers:

   a. Tariffs, or taxes on imports; and

   b. Nontariff barriers, including

      i. Subsidies for domestic producers, including price supports,

      ii. Quotas, or limits on the quantity of goods that may be imported, and

      iii. Structural barriers, such as discriminatory safety and inspection standards or distribution systems.

5. Unless it is conducted through barter (direct exchange of goods for goods), trade involves money. Because different states have their own currencies, a system of exchange rates must be established to determine the relative value of national currencies.

6. Exchange-rate systems may be fixed, like the gold standard and Bretton Woods system, or floating, in which currencies are allowed to fluctuate. Both systems have advantages and disadvantages.

7. A nation's balance of payments summarizes all of its international trade and financial transactions, including exports, imports, foreign-aid transfers, and investments.

8. The most commonly cited component of the balance of payments is the current-account balance, which is the sum of a country's imports, exports, government payments and receipts, and investment income and payments. If the current-account balance is positive, the state has a trade surplus; if it is negative, it has a trade deficit.

9. There are many links between domestic and international politics and the world economy; international political economy is the study of how these links function.

10. There are three basic schools of thought on the relationship between global politics and economics:

    a. *Liberalism* contends that the purpose of economic activity is to maximize national and individual wealth. According to liberals, free markets allocate scarce resources in the most efficient manner possible, giving maximum benefit to consumers. Therefore, liberals usually argue for free trade and against trade barriers.

    b. *Realism* views the accumulation of state power as the purpose of economic activity. Realists thus often contend that trade barriers can be used to increase a nation's economic, military, and political power.

    c. *Marxism* perceives economic activity as a political class struggle between workers and capital owners and rich and poor nations. Many Marxists contend that developed countries and multinational corporations exploit developing nations in order to exact excessive profits.

11. Theories of hegemonic stability seek to explain why some powerful states have supported free trade. According to this theory, the world economy is most stable when a global dominant power (the hegemon) sets and enforces rules of free trade, but the hegemon will eventually decline as the costs of hegemony grow over time and trade enriches rival powers.

12. Although states have traded for thousands of years, the origins of the modern global economy lie in the Industrial Revolution, which began in the late eighteenth century and led to the explosive growth of world trade.

13. Britain, as the first industrialized nation and the leading naval power, established hegemony in the mid-nineteenth century and encouraged free trade.

14. As the nineteenth century progressed, the economies of other states (especially Germany and the United States) grew rapidly, and Britain faced challengers for hegemonic status. Nevertheless, the world economy remained relatively stable from the establishment of the gold standard in 1870 until World War I.

15. Between the two world wars, the world economy lacked a clear hegemon. After 1929, war debts, German reparations, a stock-market crash in the United States, and a wave of protectionism launched by the Smoot-Hawley tariff created a global depression.

16. After World War II, the United States emerged as the global economy's hegemon. The Bretton Woods system was set up to provide fixed exchange rates and financial stability, and the General Agreement on Tariffs and Trade (GATT) sought to promote free trade and resolve trade disputes.

17. As the economic strength of Europe and Japan grew in the 1950s, 1960s, and 1970s, the United States found it difficult to maintain its hegemonic status. The collapse of the Bretton Woods system in 1971 and the oil crisis of 1973 inaugurated a period of cooperative multilateralism, during which the leading industrial states attempted to cooperate to regulate international trade and finance (not always successfully).

18. In the late twentieth century, many states increasingly integrated their economies into regional trade blocs, such as the European Union and the North American Free Trade Agreement (NAFTA). It remains to be seen, however, whether these blocs will cooperate to promote freer trade and

financial stability or will become protectionist "fortresses" against imports from other regions. In either case, technology, international institutions, and demands for regional and local autonomy are eroding the economic sovereignty of the nation-state.

Chapter 8

North-South Economic Relations: The Challenge of Development

With her feet on the cement rim of the gaping water well, the Kenyan girl balances herself precariously as she lowers a jerrycan at the end of a rope to the water some 10 metres (33 feet) below. Seconds later, the can hits the water with a splash. The girl tugs at the rope several times to get the water flowing into the can, and after a while begins to pull her heavy cargo of 20 litres (4 gallons) up to the surface.

She seems unaware of the danger of her feet slipping as she hauls up her load of water, and the danger of tumbling to her death down the dark pit. She is more concerned about not letting any of the water spill from the can as it sways to and fro on its way up the well. The girl is typical of many other females in Kenya's coastal villages of the Kwale district, who risk their lives each time they go to draw water from the well.

Winnie Ogana, "Kenya: The Water That Brings New Life" in Donatus De Silva, *Against All Odds* (Washington, DC: The Panos Institute, 1989), p. 112.

Daughters [in Kenya] are prized . . . as valuable, since it is the women who do the farming. The groom's father must, therefore, pay for his son's bride, for he is getting, not simply a daughter-in-law, but a farmhand as well. . . . [Heavy loads they carry lead to] a permanent crease in the forehead where the tie holding the water can was bound to the carrier. The women . . . had a permanent headache, though they did not call it such. They regarded it as a normal condition of life, since they begin to carry when they are three or four years old.

Michael Harrington, *The Vast Majority: A Journey to the World's Poor* (New York: Simon and Schuster, 1977), pp. 169, 177.

Young women throughout the underdeveloped world suffer in similar fashion; age-old cultural and economic traditions have entrenched these customs. These and other practices indicate some of the challenges that several parts of the world face in moving toward development.

Major Events in North-South Economic Relations: 1500–1994

1500–1920: European colonization of the Southern Hemisphere creates relationship of Southern subservience to the North.

1839–1842: Attempting to stop the outflow of capital, China seizes chests of British opium; Opium War results.

1890s: American manufacturers begin investing in plants overseas.

1898: Spanish-American War occurs; Spain gives up Cuba and cedes Guam, Puerto Rico, and the Philippines to the United States.

1914–1918: World War I causes collapse of international trading system, which does not fully recover after the conflict concludes.

1939–1945: World War II causes upheaval in the economies of many developing countries worldwide.

1946: World Bank begins operation; primary task eventually becomes lending money to underdeveloped countries.

1947: International Monetary Fund (IMF) is formed, stabilizing international currency exchange rates and providing short-term loans to developing countries.

1947–1991: During the Cold War, the United States and Soviet Union use economic aid to further their geopolitical and strategic interests.

1958: Gamal Abdel Nasser gets the Soviet Union to finance and build the Aswan Dam for Egypt.

1960: Organization of Petroleum Exporting Countries (OPEC) is formed to gain higher prices and greater control over the petroleum production of member states.

1960s–1970s: Many Southern countries nationalize their mineral and agricultural export sectors, wresting control of these industries from multinational corporations.

1973: Retaliating for U.S. support of

THE CONTEMPORARY SOUTH

The reader will recall from Chapter Five that the problems facing the developing countries of the South (chiefly Latin America, South and Southeast Asia, the Middle East, Africa, and the Pacific) are very different from those confronting the industrialized states of the North (North America, Western Europe, and Japan). Many Southern countries are very poor, and large segments of their population have minimal access to education, medical care, and employment opportunities. Economic development is the first priority all governments of the South claim to have on their agenda. Indeed, development is the central topic of negotiation, if not a preoccupation, in contemporary relationships between South and North. It is, however, a nebulous concept subject to radically different interpretations. To the U.S. Agency for International Development (USAID), development may mean increasing agricultural productivity or opening up Southern markets to American exports. Development to the World Health Organization (WHO) may mean expanding rural health clinics to stop babies from dying from dysentery. Development to environmentalists may mean creating a sustainable economy that generates minimal waste and pollution. Development to Iraq's Saddam Hussein may mean producing a nuclear bomb or other weapons of mass destruction. Thus, development is one of the most ambiguous terms in contemporary social science.

One thing clear about development is that it is a constantly moving goal. This is because the "standard" for development is "what developed countries have," and the developed countries are themselves continuing the development process. In the mid-nineteenth century, the "high-tech" industries were textiles and railroads, which were the foundation of Britain's industrial might. By the 1930s one critical standard of development was the capacity to produce steel and heavy machinery; consequently, Joseph Stalin sacrificed enormous human and material resources to construct the Soviet Union's massive metallurgical

Israel in the Yom Kippur War, Arab members of OPEC institute an oil embargo and reduce oil production, which leads to a quadrupling of oil prices.

1974: New International Economic Order movement is started, seeking to end the South's dependency on the North.

1979: The Shah is overthrown in the Iranian Revolution, leading to a worldwide oil crisis.

1979–1984: Global recession exacerbates the debt crisis in developing countries.

1980s: China opens coastal areas for foreign investment for the first time;

several Asian states experience rapid economic growth.

1980: More than 100,000 people are allowed to flee Cuba to other countries by Fidel Castro during the Mariel boat lift; U.S. agrees to accept political prisoners released by Cuba, some of whom are later discovered to be criminals and mental patients.

1980–1988: Political disagreements among OPEC members are exemplified in the Iran-Iraq War.

mid-1980s: Famine throughout the Horn of Africa caused by drought and exacerbated by political and economic crises in local countries leads to massive suffering.

1986: Mexico joins GATT, lowering its tariffs and dramatically increasing trade with the United States.

1994: Despite continuing human rights violations, the U.S. renews China's most-favored nation status; U.S. lifts trade embargo on Vietnam; NAFTA begins eliminating trade barriers between the U.S., Canada, and Mexico; another exodus from Cuba occurs, but the U.S. refuses to accept refugees and a compromise is reached with the Cuban government.

complexes to defend "socialism in one country." Today, of course, textiles and steel are increasingly produced in developing and (newly industrialized) countries, while many factories in the English midlands, where the Industrial Revolution began, and the Ural mountains, where Soviet Russia built the tanks to defeat the Nazi invasion, are obsolete by most international standards. Instead, most developed countries compete against one another in the electronics, computer, and aviation industries, and scramble to develop biotechnology and optical computer systems to gain a competitive edge in the next "industrial revolution."

Since the development standard is a constantly moving target, countries that do not grow economically for a prolonged period, such as Argentina after World War I, are in effect rapidly falling behind. Many Southern countries, particularly in Africa, have not achieved significant economic development in the post-World War II era, meaning that the gap between the "haves" in the North and the "have-nots" in the South has dramatically widened (see Map 8.1). For instance, between 1950 and 1990, the gross national product (GNP) of the United States tripled while its population increased by only two-thirds. America's per capita income therefore more than doubled. For Japan and the countries of Western Europe, which were devastated by World War II but today have standards of living roughly equivalent (if not superior) to that of the United States, the increase in per capita GNP has been even greater. By contrast, some African countries produce less total economic output in the 1990s than they did in the 1960s because of civil wars or political instability, while the population in these countries has been increasing at rapid rates (see boxed feature on "One Planet, Many Worlds"). Imagine a car traveling along a road at 25 mph while a jet aircraft soars overhead at the speed of sound and you begin to get the picture. Only in the East Asian "Tigers" of South Korea, Taiwan, Hong Kong, and Singapore have per capita incomes risen quickly enough to begin catching up with the advanced industrial countries.

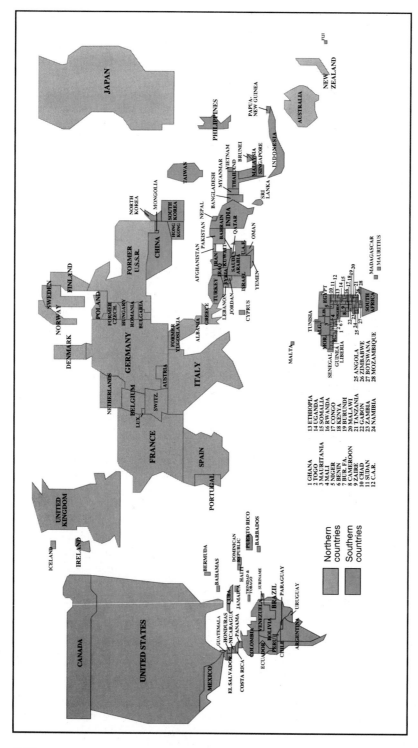

Map 8.1   Status Depicted by National Wealth on the Basis of Gross National Product, 1991

Some believe that the increasing disparity between North and South makes the development process much more difficult for late developers by demanding ever larger inputs of capital to make the leap from underdeveloped to developed. This is, of course, disputed by others.[1] Development may be more like a learning process, in which all countries have to begin with low-technology industries and then gradually acquire the skills and capital to expand and upgrade their international competitiveness. What is clear, however, is that in the age of instantaneous global communications that reach the most remote areas of the planet, even the poorest rural residents of Asia and Africa know that they live far below the standard of living achieved by the average American, European, or Japanese. Thus, a "revolution of rising expectations" is likely to increase the demand for faster economic development.

Development in Theory and Practice

While it is difficult to predict the precise development path of any country, development in all countries is similar in some important respects. Virtually all countries start the development process as rural societies where the vast majority of the population engages in **subsistence agriculture** (hand-to-mouth farming for the direct consumption of one's own family). As development occurs, fewer and fewer people work in the agricultural sector and more people find employment in the manufacturing and service industries that are typically located in urban areas. Development has therefore meant a huge migration of labor from farms to cities. With fewer farmers to grow food (and other agricultural products like cotton) and with more urban dwellers to feed, the productivity of agriculture must increase (as it has, exponentially, in the United States and Western Europe) if food shortages and widespread hunger are to be avoided.

Moreover, when people first enter the urban labor market, they usually lack skills and must take low-wage jobs. As a large percentage of their wages must be spent on food, the price of food typically becomes a major political problem in countries just beginning to industrialize. If food prices are too high, urban unrest and riots become likely. If food prices are kept artificially low (through subsidies), however, farmers will not produce enough to supply urbanites, and the impoverished countryside may become fertile ground for rebellion. The initial stages of development thus often generate intense **rural-urban cleavages** as the economy shifts away from subsistence agriculture and toward industry.

Clearly, raising both agricultural and industrial productivity is as critical to development in the South today as it was in the North over the past two centuries. The major question facing Southern governments is, therefore, not whether to modernize their traditional agricultural economies, but how to do so. The main challenge they face is determining the economic development strategy that will best redeploy their human resources into more productive endeavors. In making this determination, Southern countries must keep in mind two sets of variables that will influence their chances for successful development: domestic political and social factors and the international environment in

ONE PLANET, MANY WORLDS

In discussions of economic development, states have typically been categorized into a tripartite classification: the First, Second, and Third Worlds. The **First World** was the industrialized West, the **Second World** was the Communist East, and the **Third World** was the developing South. However, with the rapid industrialization of several Southern states and the end of the Cold War, this rough classification of states has become outdated, and the World Bank now uses several classifications for developing countries, as shown in the following table.

Category	Total Population (millions)	GNP per Capita	Life Expectancy at Birth	Adult Illiteracy (%)
Low income	3,127.3	350	62	40
Lower Middle	773.8	1,590	67	26
Oil Exporters	262.8	1,990	60	44
Upper Middle	627.0	3,530	69	14
OECD	783.1	21,530	77	4

Source: World Bank, *World Development Report 1993* (Oxford: Oxford University Press, 1993), pp. 238–239.

First World

The First World consists of the industrialized countries and includes the states of Western Europe, North America, and Japan (see Chapter Seven). While comprising only a quarter of the world's population, the First World accounts for over four-fifths of the world's GNP. In 1991 the aggregate GNP per capita of the nineteen high-income countries belonging to the Organization for Economic Cooperation and Development (OECD) was $21,530.* Topping the list were Switzerland at $33,610, Japan at $26,930, Sweden at $25,110, Norway at $24,220, and Finland at $23,980. (The United States ranked eighth at $22,240.) Besides a high per capita GNP, the First World is characterized by the export of services and manufactured goods. Other important characteristics include a low infant mortality rate, low illiteracy rate, long life span, and low population-growth levels (0.7 percent from 1980 to 1990).

Second World

The Second World consists of the former Communist nations of the USSR and Eastern Europe. Although economic data on these states have been scarce and unreliable, the Second World has roughly matched the First in some indicators of development, such as physicians per capita, literacy, and life expectancy. In other respects, however, such as percent of workers in agriculture and per-capita GNP, Second World countries have mirrored the level of development characterized by the wealthier Third World countries. Even though these states no longer have centrally planned economies, most now share serious problems associated with the transition from communism to a market-oriented economic system, often including high under- or unemployment and rapid inflation coupled with declining real wages.

Third World

Finally, the Third World includes over 160 underdeveloped and developing nations in the Middle East, Asia, Africa, and Latin America. The Third World accounts for three-fourths of the world's population but less than one-fifth of the world's production of goods and services. In contrast to industrialized countries, which usually have a diversified economic base, many Third World countries depend heavily on the export of a single commodity or raw material, such as cocoa, coffee, copper, timber, and petroleum. Most Third World states also have a high percentage of workers in agriculture (often in subsistence farming), a highly skewed distribution of wealth between the rich and poor, low levels of literacy, short life spans, a high level of infant mortality, and a high rate of population growth. However, the Third World is far from uniform in its level of economic development, and several additional classifications have evolved to more precisely categorize Southern states.

The *low income countries* are the poorest of the poor. These states have a much lower standard of living in comparison to other states in the Third World. Their per-capita income averaged $350. (The poorest states in 1991 for which reliable data are available include Mozambique, with a per-capita GNP of $80; Tanzania, with $100; Ethiopia, with $120; Uganda, with $170; and Bhutan, with $180.)[†] Two-fifths of the adult population is illiterate, life expectancy is only fifty years, and many farmers are subsistence farmers, producing only enough for their family's consumption.[‡] India is included in this group of countries, as is China, which despite its rapid industrial growth had a per capita GNP of only $370 in 1991. In between the low income and developed countries are *lower-middle-income* economies, such as Ecuador and Turkey, with per-capita GNPs averaging $1,590 in 1991, and *upper-middle-income* countries, such as Mexico and Lithuania, with an average per capita GNP of $3,530.[§]

A group of Third World states consisting of *oil-exporting countries,* including the member states of OPEC (Organization of Petroleum Exporting Countries), stands out from other developing nations. While sharing many similarities with low income countries, such as the reliance on the export of a single product, the most notable difference is their comparatively high average per capita income—over $1,990 in 1991. Some smaller members of this group have per-capita GNPs that are quite high; in 1991 that of the United Arab Emirates was $20,140 and Qatar's was $14,770. However, like all states that rely on the production of a single good, these countries are very vulnerable to fluctuations in the price of their primary export. The oil exporters often resemble other developing states in other aspects, such as adult illiteracy.

The **newly industrialized countries (NICs)** comprise another group of developing states. NICs are generally characterized by rapid growth in the export of manufactured goods. They include such states as Mexico, Brazil, and the four Asian "Tigers" (Hong Kong, Singapore, South Korea, and Taiwan). The Asian NICs share a number of features, including great success at promoting the export of manufactured goods (which will be discussed later in this chapter), a Confucian cultural heritage, strong regimes that have made economic development their highest priority, and finally, a high level of foreign investment, particularly from Japan. With a relatively high GNP per capita ($7,165 in 1991), low mortality, and high literacy levels, the Asian NICs come closest to bridging the gap between the First and Third Worlds.

Problems with Classification

While it provides a convenient verbal shorthand, the division of states into First, Second, and Third World categories based on their income levels has a number of problems. As noted, a number of NICs traditionally classified as Third World states now have little in common with their less developed neighbors. With a high GNP per capita, rapid industrialization, low illiteracy levels, and long life spans, they share many of the characteristics of the industrialized North. By contrast, the oil exporters have high per-capita incomes, but lack a diversified industrial base, and their prospects for sustained growth are problematical at best. Any attempt to divide the countries of the North and South into convenient categories shows how difficult it is to come up with a single standard of "development" that all states can aspire to, given their differing strengths and problems.

[*]World Bank, *World Development Report 1993.* (Oxford: Oxford University Press, 1993), p. 239.
[†]Ibid., p. 238.
[‡]*Human Development Report 1991* (New York: Oxford University Press, 1991), pp. 122–123, 174.
[§]World Bank, *World Development Report 1993,* p. 239.

which development must occur. With this in mind, the first part of this chapter presents two contending schools of thought, modernization theory and dependency theory. These theories hold differing views on the ways in which domestic and international factors create opportunities and challenges to development. In a nutshell, **modernization theory** contends that the global trading system can be a great help to development, while dependency theory argues that it has been a great hindrance. The second part of this chapter examines the successes and failures of some development strategies that Southern countries have followed in their quest for economic growth and social progress. The chapter's final section uses the debates over extension of most-favored-nation status (see Chapter Seven) to China and the North American Free Trade Act (NAFTA) as examples to consider how trade between North and South presents dilemmas and opportunities to both developing and developed countries.

PART I: CONTENDING THEORIES OF DEVELOPMENT

Modernization Theory

Modernization theory contends that the most important factors contributing to development, and the primary causes of underdevelopment, can be found within the Southern states themselves.[2] In reaching this conclusion, the founders of modernization theory studied the experience of both long-established developing states, such as Iran and Turkey, and the newly independent nations of Asia and Africa, including India, Pakistan, Côte d'Ivoire (Ivory Coast), Myanmar (Burma), Ghana, and many others.

Modernization theory draws a sharp distinction between "traditional" and "modern" societies. A traditional society is usually depicted as a peasant village where generations pass on their customs, rituals, and folkways to each new generation. Modern societies, in contrast, are more urban, dynamic, flexible, and innovative, and ready and willing to adapt. To develop, modernization theorists contend, Southern societies must undergo the same process of transition from traditionalism to modernity previously experienced by the states of the North.

From this perspective, the fundamental obstacle to development is traditional culture that blocks the societal transformations necessary for rapid economic growth. Traditional societies are dominated by religious or aristocratic authority, are based on rural life, and are characterized by rigid social structures, such as the Indian caste system. While replacing traditional customs with a more modern outlook is essential to development, traditional culture is very resistant to change. Thus, getting from traditional to modern values can take generations, as well as produce enormous social tensions.

Guided by the Western experience of development, modernization theorists contend that less developed states will develop only by shedding their traditional social, political, and economic institutions. Socially, this requires the ability to achieve status through merit or success (rather than birth or caste) and tolerance of social and intellectual diversity. Politically, this translates into the emergence of democracy, the rule of law, political opposition, human rights, and basic freedoms. Economically, development means the creation of a market-based economy, though some level of state intervention for social reasons (to relieve poverty, care for the elderly, or cushion the shock of unemployment, for example) is possible and desirable. From the modernization perspective, therefore, economic growth and democratization form a virtuous circle, each strengthening the other as both progress. Industrialization, increased incomes, education, and urbanization all increase the likelihood of political democracy—which, in turn, protects and reinforces the market economy that is necessary for continued economic development.

For many modernization theorists, trade is the engine of economic growth. Accordingly, they call for free trade and open markets. In this relationship, Northern multinational corporations and international investment play an important role in disseminating capital, managerial and technical skills, and technology necessary for the emergence of a modern industrial sector. Aid from the developed countries will help fill the resource gaps in underdeveloped states. At the same time, developing countries can "pull themselves up by their own bootstraps" by saving to accumulate financial capital, buying equipment and improving infrastructure to increase physical capital, and investing in education and training to improve human capital. One U.S. program for economic development in Puerto Rico was even called "Operation Bootstrap."

Growing Pains: The Social Impact of Modernization   At first glance, the path to development as prescribed by modernization theory may appear straightforward. In practice, however, modernization creates wrenching changes in a society. These changes lead to political, social, and economic problems that must be addressed in order for development to continue. The opportunities and challenges presented by development are illustrated by two trends characteristic of modernization: demographic transition and urbanization. (These trends occur in all developing societies, not just those where development is guided by modernization theory. They are discussed here because modernization theory regards them as "growing pains" that societies must deal with in the modernization process.)

Underdeveloped, traditional societies generally have very high birth and death rates, whereas in modern societies these rates are much lower. This change is termed demographic transition. In many underdeveloped countries, the number of children who die prior to reaching one year of age—the **infant mortality rate**—exceeds 100 per 1000 live births. In OECD countries (those which are members of the Organization for Economic Cooperation and Development), by contrast, infant mortality averaged 9 per 1000 live births in 1992.[3] High infant mortality, poor sanitation, and inadequate medical care combine to make life expectancy shorter in most preindustrial societies—an average of fifty-six years for most low-income countries, compared to an average of seventy-seven years in the developed world.[4]

In most traditional societies, a high death rate leads to a high birthrate. In order to ensure that enough children will survive to help with the back-breaking labor of subsistence agriculture, women in many underdeveloped areas are compelled by social conventions to marry young (often at age fourteen or fifteen, or as soon as puberty is reached) and bear as many children as possible. Children are also expected to support their parents in their old age, serving as a kind of social security system. Consequently, the fertility rate (the average number of children born per woman) is very high in most low-income countries; in 1992 the average woman in Ethiopia, Mali, Niger, Uganda, and Yemen could expect to bear more than seven children in her lifetime.[5] (See Map 8.2.)

A real dilemma, then, arises when the introduction of modern drugs causes the death rate to fall dramatically. Infant mortality may fall from more than 200 to less than forty within twenty or thirty years in even the most impoverished of traditional societies, and life expectancy may rise from forty to sixty-five years or more in the same period. The traditional emphasis on having many children often persists long after the death rates fall, resulting in a population explosion. As countries industrialize, however, fertility rates tend to decline as more women go to work, death rates tend to decline as nutrition and medical care improve, and population growth slows markedly. Table 8.1 compares annual rates of population growth in representative countries of the North and South. Many sub-Saharan African countries experience annual population growth of over 3 percent, meaning that the country's population could double in twenty years. Accordingly, the OECD countries have the lowest population-growth rates, followed by the rapidly industrializing East Asian "Tigers."

In Southern countries, with so many new mouths to feed, clothe, shelter, and educate, the economy and society are put under enormous strain, and there is little left over for investment. In order to keep population growth from overwhelming the resources of the country, the birthrate must be brought down, which means that overall health standards must be improved so that infant mortality is lessened. However, traditional social values concerning the necessity to marry young and have many children are often very difficult to change. Additionally, some Northern development agencies such as the Population Council that do promote family planning and contraception are often accused of racial or ethnic discrimination in their attempts to reduce population growth, despite the fact that they spend the vast majority of their resources on maternal and infant healthcare in order to reduce infant morality and thus save lives.

The net result of rapid population growth in the early stages of demographic transition is that about one-half of the population consists of children who require significant long-term investments in education and training if they are going to gain the skills necessary for the further development of the country. However, poor countries typically do not have the means to educate all their children, and so, a cycle of grinding poverty perpetuating high birthrates and resulting in more poverty is established. Few economies can generate jobs fast enough to employ all the workers available when population is growing at 3 percent or greater per year. Consequently, very rapid population growth can

Table 8.1   Population-Growth Rates in Selected Countries

Country	Annual Average Population-Growth Rate (%)		Population (millions)	
	1970–1980	*1980–1991*	*1950*	*1990*
Tanzania	3.0	3.0	7.89	27.32
Zimbabwe	2.9	3.4	2.7	39.71
Egypt	2.1	2.5	20.33	52.43
Cameroon	3.0	2.8	4.47	11.83
Ecuador	3.0	2.6	3.31	10.59
Mexico	2.9	2.0	28.01	88.60
South Korea	1.8	1.1	20.36	42.79
Denmark	0.4	0.1	4.27	5.14

Source: World Development Report 1993, pp. 288–289; World Resources Institute, *World Resources 1992–1993* (New York: Oxford University Press, 1992) pp. 246–247.

overwhelm the capacity of an economy to prosper and a society to develop, and it is one of the principal reasons why several African and Asian countries have failed to raise their per-capita incomes since their independence in the 1960s. Conversely, the success of East Asian NICs and China in reducing their population growth and managing demographic transition has been an important feature of their relative economic success.

A major consequence of demographic transition and industrialization is **urbanization.** One way that many families in traditional societies attempt to cope with the pressure of chronic overpopulation and the resulting unemployment is to send some children to urban areas to find cash employment. If work can be found, the proceeds can then be sent back to the family in the rural home to be used to educate younger siblings or support parents in their old age. There is no social security for the elderly in most Southern countries, so parents often rely on their children for support. However, in many cases, work cannot be found, yet rural migrants nevertheless settle in urban areas, becoming part of the vast shantytowns that have grown up around virtually all cities of the contemporary South, such as São Paulo, Calcutta, Soweto, Cairo, and Jakarta.

The rate of urban population growth in the South during the 1960s and the 1970s was typically between 3.5 and 5 percent, and in some countries even higher, sometimes reaching twice the rate of population growth. Obviously, these newly burgeoning cities do not have the resources to provide services such as fire, police, and sanitation that residents in Northern cities take for granted. Whatever services that were provided by Europeans in the colonial era in the way of sanitation, electricity, and water have been quickly overwhelmed in postcolonial in Asia and Africa. Therefore, urban shantytowns are often overcrowded, acutely poor, and persistently crime-prone.

Despite these hardships, the modernization perspective generally views urbanization as an essential step in the development process away from subsistence

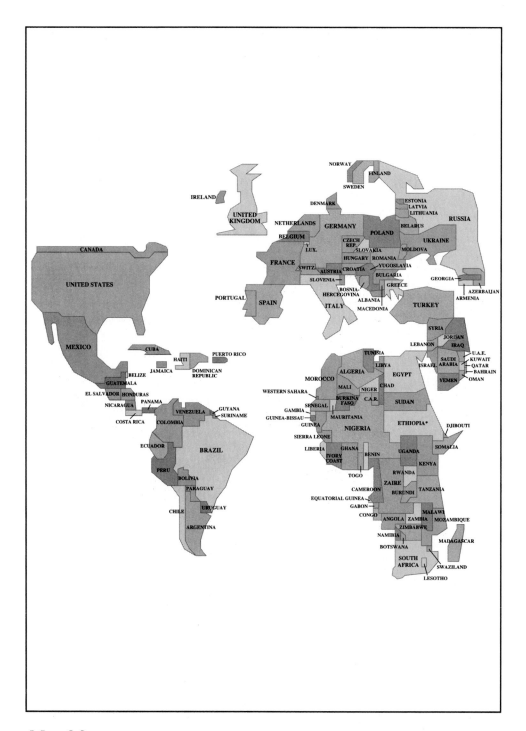

Map 8.2   Population of States, 1991

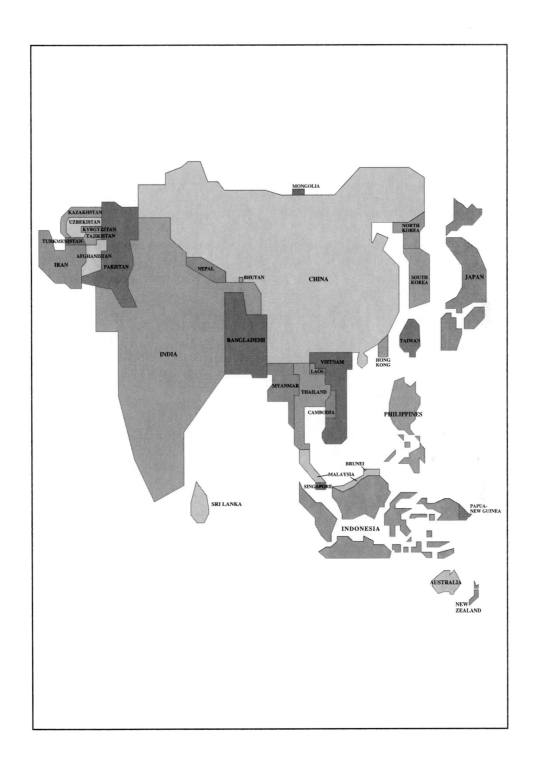

351

agriculture and toward a modern economy. The newly urbanized migrant is undergoing a difficult but necessary shift away from traditional superstitions and beliefs and toward a more flexible and adaptive view of the world. This process of urbanization is never easy, but it may be a necessary stage in creating a modern society—the Industrial Revolution produced vast urban slums in nineteenth-century Britain. Additionally, from the perspective of modernization theory, the city becomes the focus of the diffusion of new ideas, of science and technology, of social mobility based on merit and the rise of a professional and middle class, the development of a division of labor within society, and perhaps most importantly, the center of an industrial manufacturing and service-based economy.

Critiques of Modernization Theory   Modernization theory has been criticized on a number of fronts. First, its critics question whether the North's path of development can be duplicated by the South.[6] Countries modernizing in the late twentieth century, they contend, are likely to face different kinds of problems (such as global environmental degradation and resource shortages—see Chapter Ten) from those faced by the Northern countries that developed in the nineteenth century. In addition, while in the nineteenth century countries like Britain, the United States, and Japan were able to develop autonomously, the Third World today is dependent on industrialized nations for markets and capital.[7] Finally, industrializing countries in Europe faced little competition from already developed rivals, while today Southern countries must compete with industrialized states with well-developed manufacturing sectors.

Second, critics of modernization theory stress that traditional social and political institutions are often very difficult to change. As one author notes, "We have learned that in much of the Third World, so-called traditional institutions have, first of all, proved remarkably resilient, persistent, and long-lasting; rather than fading, crushed under the impact of change, they have instead proved flexible, accommodative, and adaptive, blending to the currents of modernization but not being replaced by them."[8] The survival of these traditional institutions can force Southern societies into paths of development very different from those taken by Northern industrialized states.

Third, many theorists and policy-makers contend that modernization theory is Eurocentric. That is, this pattern of development is grounded essentially on the singular experience of Western Europe. Similarly, some contend that modernization theory is a product of the Cold War mentality that seeks to keep the Third World out of the Soviet sphere by tying Third World nations into a Western and liberal development pattern.

Finally, some political economists and many Third World states contend that the structure of the international trading system is biased against the South, and that, historically, wealth has not flowed from the rich states to the poor states through trade and aid, but in fact the opposite has occurred. This perspective on trade and development contends that, at first through colonialism and later through multinational corporations and foreign lending, Northern countries have kept the South in a perpetual state of underdevelopment. This criticism is the heart of the alternate school of thought on development known as dependency theory.

Dependency Theory

Dependency theory rejects the modernization theory premise that the source of Third World problems is domestic in nature.[9] Instead, it emphasizes the international context, contending that international institutions, multinational corporations, and the states of the First World have deliberately kept the Third World in a dependent condition. In contrast to modernization theory, which has its roots in classical economics and the liberal perspective on world trade (refer to Chapter Seven), dependency theory draws many of its insights on the relations between the North and South from a branch of Marxist thought.

Dependency theorists argue that the existing international economic system is inherently biased against the South. The roots of this unequal relationship between the periphery (the Third World) and the core (the First World) can be traced to the sixteenth century, when European countries began to colonize the Southern Hemisphere.[10] In this relationship, the periphery exported raw materials to the industrializing states in Europe (and later to the

Bolivian miners in the early 1980s were out of work because their country was in the midst of a terrible economic and political crisis. Often the only industry in remote locations, such mines pay low wages and employees endure harsh working conditions.
Source: © Alain Keler/Sygma.

AT A GLANCE

CONTENDING THEORIES OF DEVELOPMENT

Modernization Theory

Definition: Contends that the most important factors contributing to development, and the primary causes of underdevelopment, can be found within the Southern states themselves. A traditional society is depicted as a peasant village where generations pass on their customs, rituals, and folkways to each new generation. Modern societies, in contrast, are more urban, dynamic, flexible, and innovative, and ready and willing to adapt. To develop, Southern societies must undergo the same process of transition from traditionalism to modernity previously experienced by the states of the North.

Obstacles: The fundamental obstacle to development is traditional culture, which can block the societal transformations necessary for rapid economic growth. Religion, aristocratic authority, and the rural lifestyle are more prominent in traditional societies and are very difficult to change due to their resistance to change itself.

Necessary Changes: Politically, the emergence of democracy, the rule of law, political opposition, human rights, and basic freedoms are vital. Socially, this requires the ability to achieve status through merit or success (rather than birth or caste) and the tolerance of social and intellectual diversity. Economically, development means the creation of a market-based economy, in which some degree of state intervention for social reasons is possible and desirable. Trade is vital for economic growth.

Problems: A high death rate leads to a high birth rate. Women in many underdeveloped areas are compelled by social conventions to marry young and bear as many children as possible to help with the labor of farming. These children are also expected to care for their elderly parents. When new drugs are introduced that reduce infant mortality, a population explosion results. With so many new mouths to feed, clothe, shelter, and educate, the economy and society are put under enormous strain, with little left over for investment. Many children are sent to the urban area to find work, which leads to urbanization. As a result, the cities are overwhelmed and overcrowded; and acutely poor and persistently crime-prone shantytowns evolve. Although difficult, this process is seen as necessary.

Critiques: Its critics question whether the North's path of development can be duplicated by the South. Also, critics suggest that since traditional social and political institutions are so difficult to change, perhaps the attempt to change them is misguided. Others contend that modernization theory is Eurocentric. Finally, some believe that the structure of the international trading system is biased against the South, and that historically, wealth has not flowed from the rich states to the poor states through trade and aid, but in fact the opposite has occurred.

United States and Japan), and in turn the North exported manufactured goods to the periphery. More recently, multinational corporations based in the North have replaced the colonial powers in sustaining this relationship. According to *dependencistas* (adherents of dependency theory), this unequal relationship has ensured that Third World states remain the global economy's "hewers of wood and drawers of water." This fundamental inequality of the economic relationship between North and South, dependency theorists contend, fueled development in the North and stifled it in the South.

Dependency Theory

Definition: It emphasizes the international context, contending that international institutions, multinational corporations, and the states of the First World have deliberately kept the Third World in a dependent condition. Dependency theory draws many of its insights on the relations between the North and South from a branch of Marxist thought.

Obstacles: It argues that the existing international economic system is inherently biased against the South. This fundamental inequality of the economic relationship between the North and South fueled development in the North and stifled it in the South.

Necessary Changes: Southern nations need to diversify their product lines. While some products are booming on the international market, others are not. As a result, those nations that produce a primary product that is not in high demand are facing difficult times. Theorists believe that the nations of the South need to produce manufactured goods and diversify their export products. The unequal terms of trade will thus be altered and must continue to change. Governments must limit the amount of exploitation that multinational corporations commit.

Problems: The disadvantaged position of the South stems from the fact that most Southern countries' economies depend heavily on the export of primary products. These include raw materials such as timber, oil, and metals, and

agricultural goods such as coffee and bananas. Dependency theorists view this as the **international division of labor** where the South does the "dirty work." Furthermore, the economies of many of these primary-product producers are dominated by a single commodity. Thus, they lack diversity in the goods and services that they can export. These economies can easily go through periods of booms and busts. Theorists also argue that the terms of trade are against the South—the value of the products that they import is greater than the value of the products that they export. Consequently, they will lose money. These situations must be changed. Dependency theorists believe that multinational corporations exploit the South, hinder its development, and contribute to the widening of the gap between rich and poor.

Critiques: Critics of dependency theory argue that a number of Southern states have managed to industrialize, and have done so with the help of Northern investment and trade with developed states. Furthermore, it is unclear whether a number of dependency theory's assumptions can be substantiated. Specifically, while dependency theory contends that the terms of trade are declining for the South, the data do not clearly support this contention. Critics also believe that dependency theorists lay the blame for the South's poverty squarely on the North, with little if any discussion of factors within the developing world itself that contribute to economic stagnation and poverty.

Primary-Product Exports   In dependency theory, the disadvantaged position of the South stems from the fact that most Southern countries' economies depend heavily on the export of **primary products**—that is, raw materials such as timber, oil, and metals, and agricultural goods such as coffee and bananas. Beginning in the sixteenth century, the "periphery" supplied the raw materials and foods for the economies of Europe, and then for the Industrial Revolution in Europe and later the United States. In turn the periphery imported manufactured goods from the industrialized countries. Capitalist economists view this relationship as the operation of comparative advantage (see Chapter Seven), but dependency theorists view it as an international division of labor wherein the South does the "dirty work" of producing raw materials while the North gets the "good jobs" in manufacturing and services. They contend that this division of labor encourages the Third World to remain exporters of primary goods and discourages the development of a modern manufacturing sector.

Table 8.2 compares the exports of typical less developed, developing, and industrialized countries. Primary products make up a very high percentage of the exports of developing countries like Nigeria, which exports oil, and Côte d'Ivoire, which produces cocoa. Middle-income countries like Malaysia and Brazil have much more diversified economies, and therefore export a higher percentage of manufactured goods, while exports from more developed states like Singapore and Japan consist primarily of manufactures. Note how Malaysia, Brazil, and Singapore increased the share of manufactured goods in their exports as their development strategies succeeded over the two decades from 1970 to 1991.

To make matters worse, the exports of many Southern countries are dominated by a single commodity. These countries lack the diversity of goods and services that most Northern countries have achieved in their exports and are thus very vulnerable to fluctuations in the demand for or price of their main export. Perhaps the best examples of one-commodity countries are the oil-exporting states. Petroleum in its various forms accounts for virtually all of the exports of Saudi Arabia, Kuwait, Iraq, Iran, the Persian Gulf states, Libya, Nigeria, Gabon, Angola, and Brunei, and is the most important export of Venezuela, Mexico, and Indonesia. When the world price for oil is high, these countries reap large rewards, but a drop in the oil price can lead to economic disaster for them. Many other developing countries are dependent on exports of a single commodity. Sugar dominates the exports of Cuba, Fiji, Mauritius, and, to a lesser degree, the Philippines. Coffee is the principal export of Colombia, El Salvador, Burundi, Rwanda, Uganda, Costa Rica, Kenya, and Ethiopia. Elsewhere, copper is the major export of Zaire, Zambia, and Chile. Jamaica, Guinea, and Surinam export bauxite, Honduras produces bananas, Niger mines uranium ore, Liberia exports iron ore, and Peru's main export is an illegal drug—cocaine.

Dependency theorists argue that this international division of labor—primary products in the South, manufactured goods in the North—perpetuates the Third World's backward position. As long as the South remains the exporter of primary products for the world, they contend, Southern countries will not develop their own indigenous industries and will remain dependent upon the North for manufactured goods and technology.

According to the dependency school, fluctuations in the prices of primary goods perpetuate the dependency of Southern countries. Countries that depend heavily on primary product exports are very sensitive to sudden changes in the world prices for those commodities. Fluctuations in price can create externally induced boom-and-bust cycles. Random events may allow the producers of a specific commodity to enjoy a short period of excellent prices—such as when a freeze ravaged Brazilian coffee production in the mid-1970s and sent coffee

Table 8.2   Percentage Share of Merchandise Exports by Product Category, 1970–1991

	Fuels, Minerals, Metals		Other Primary Goods		Machinery and Transport Equipment		Other Manufactured Goods		Textiles and Clothing	
	1970	1991	1970	1991	1970	1991	1970	1991	1970	1991
Nigeria	62	96	36	3	n/a	0	1	1	0	0
Côte d'Ivoire	2	11	92	79	1	2	5	9	1	2
Malaysia	30	17	63	22	2	38	6	23	1	6
Brazil	11	16	75	28	4	18	11	38	1	4
Singapore	25	18	45	8	11	48	20	26	5	5
Japan	2	1	5	1	41	66	53	31	11	2

Source: *World Development Report 1993*, pp. 268–269.

prices to all-time highs. Though the Brazilian industry took a loss, all other coffee producers reaped great profits. This boom lured growers to switch to coffee, and the next year, when Brazilian coffee returned to the global marketplace, the glutted market led to a bust as prices—and profits—plummeted.

Commodity industries may also enjoy a period of boom that prompts the development of substitutes or replacements, or of compensatory measures leading to a collapse in prices. The rubber boom of the 1920s (which resulted from the rise of the automobile) fell apart when synthetic rubber was introduced during World War II. Similarly, the oil-price boom of the 1970s was followed by the oil glut of the 1980s as new oil fields were tapped, alternative energy sources were developed, and consumers began using less oil.

Boom times typically result in overinvestment in speculative ventures that, when they go bust, create disastrous ripples throughout the economy and cause a depression. Moreover, boom-and-bust cycles make long-term planning difficult, especially for government expenditures in such areas as education, health, and infrastructure. Price fluctuations hit especially hard in countries that rely extensively on the export of a single commodity, such as oil, coffee, or rubber, and are at the mercy of the world market. In contrast, in industrialized states with large and diversified economies, fluctuations in the price of a few primary or finished products usually have little impact on the economy as a whole.

Unequal Terms of Trade   Dependency theory also argues that disadvantageous **terms of trade**—that is, the ratio of export prices to import prices—further impoverish the Third World.[11] If the prices of a country's exports are rising faster than the prices of the goods it imports, its terms of trade are increasing; conversely, if import prices are increasing faster than export prices, its terms of trade are declining. For most developing countries, this means that if the prices of primary products decline while the prices of manufactured goods from the North increase, the Southern nation's terms of trade will worsen. Dependency theorists contend that prices of primary goods tend to decline over the long run relative to the price of manufactured goods. (Whether or not this is actually occurring will be discussed later.)

At the same time, many *dependencistas* contend that in the global market, since there are often many sellers of raw materials and few buyers (a condition known as **monopsony**), it is easier for the buyers to impose artificially low prices. According to dependency theory, this "monopsony power" creates a buyers' market in which Northern buyers can hold down the prices of Southern primary goods. To give one example, sales of bananas in the United States, Western Europe, and Japan are dominated by three corporations. When banana-producing countries formed the Union of Banana Exporting Countries (UBEC) and tried to impose an export tax in 1974, the buyers refused to purchase bananas from participating countries, stopped production at their plantations, and destroyed crates of bananas at the ports. Eventually, the banana-exporting countries backed down and the taxes were withdrawn.[12]

Multinational Corporations   Typically, **multinational corporations (MNCs),** large corporations that have branches in many countries (see Chapter Nine), have their headquarters in the North, but many invest in, own, and/or operate factories and subsidiaries in the South as well. MNCs and foreign investment are nothing new. European firms made huge investments in the developing United States in the nineteenth century, and by the early 1890s several American manufacturers, such as Singer, American Bell, and Standard Oil, had manufacturing investments and plants overseas.[13] Some MNCs, such as General Motors, IBM, Toyota, British Petroleum, and Siemens, are massive corporate giants, with total sales rivaling or surpassing the GNP of many countries. In 1988, forty-one of the world's one-hundred largest economic units were MNCs, and General Motors' sales amounted to more than the GNPs of such countries as Finland, Denmark, Indonesia, Argentina, or South Africa.[14] MNCs also wield a tremendous amount of power within developing countries, particularly due to their control over manufacturing in the Third World. For example, MNCs control 70 percent of the manufacturing industry in Nigeria, 50 percent in Ghana, and 44 percent in Malaysia.[15]

Modernization theorists contend that MNCs promote development in the South, providing capital, technology, training, and managerial know-how to Southern states. Dependency theorists, however, challenge this benevolent view of MNCs. They contend that MNCs exploit the South, hinder its development, and contribute to the widening of the gap between rich and poor. According to dependency theory, MNCs have replaced the colonial system as the primary means of penetrating the South and extracting wealth from the Third World. Three primary complaints are as follows:

1. MNCs avoid paying their share of taxes by bookkeeping and accounting tricks devised to increase profits and minimize tax burdens. Because they have subsidiaries throughout the world, MNCs are able to use **transfer-pricing mechanisms** to transfer profits to countries where taxes are lower. Here is one author's description of a transfer-pricing scheme:

A U.S. manufacturer, for instance, might produce parts in a factory located in Texas but ship these parts to a plant in Mexico for assembly. In turn, the assembled product is transported back to the United States for final sale. The price that the home firm charges the Mexican subsidiary for the parts or that the subsidiary charges the home firm for the assembled product is essentially arbitrary since these transactions take place within the same company and are not exposed to market forces. If, let us say, Mexico imposes a higher tax on corporate profits than does the United States, then the MNC can lower its overall tax bill by overpricing the parts shipped to Mexico while underpricing the assembled products that are "sold" back to the home firm in the United States. By manipulating the prices on intra-firm trade in this way, the Mexican subsidiary will show little profit on its books, thus avoiding the high Mexican tax rate, while the profit of the home firm will be artificially boosted—allowing it to be taxed at the low U.S. rate.[16]

Of course, MNCs use transfer pricing to avoid taxes in industrialized countries as well. In addition, dependency theorists claim, MNCs remove scarce capital from the South by charging royalties and licensing fees for manufacturing products on which they hold copyrights and patents (as they do in the North). Finally, through bribery and lobbying, MNCs prevail upon Third World legislators to give them special tax breaks. For instance, when Honduras imposed a tax on the export of bananas, United Brands (formerly United Fruit) bribed a government official to reduce the tax.[17] In short, *dependencistas* claim that many business practices—legal and illegal—carried out by MNCs all over the globe cause more harm when they are applied in the resource-poor developing world.

2. The technology that MNCs transfer to the South is often not appropriate for the region. In many instances, it is **capital-intensive technology,** which relies on expensive equipment and highly skilled workers and therefore does little to lower the often very high Southern unemployment rates. In addition, imported technology may stunt the development of local technology, discourage local research and development, and drive out local entrepreneurs. Developing areas, according to the dependency school, often don't need high technology—instead, they need low technology that can be produced locally, run and maintained by local workers, and adapted to Third World conditions.

3. MNCs do not bring capital into the Third World, but instead often set up businesses that use up the limited supply of local capital. Bank loans to MNCs mean less money is available for local entrepreneurs to borrow. By using local capital, MNCs crowd out local entrepreneurs, and competition from MNCs often destroys existing domestic industries.[18] In addition, top managers of MNC operations are often brought from the parent country, not recruited in the host country.

In general, dependency theorists allege that MNCs can control and manipulate the production of primary commodities in developing countries; in so doing, they act as the North's instruments of control and subjugation over the South. This "neocolonial" exploitation of the developing world is actually more efficient and more profitable than the colonial system under which the United States and the European powers dominated most of Asia, Africa, and Latin America before World War II. Dependency theory concludes that while Third

In the post–Cold War era, investment has replaced aid and military intervention as the prime source of great-power interest in the Third World.
Source: Efeu/Nebelspalter/Rorschach, Switzerland.

World states may have achieved political independence, they cannot achieve economic sovereignty because they are kept in a dependent state by the capitalist world economy.

Critiques of Dependency Theory   Dependency theory has been criticized on a number of fronts.[19] The first and foremost criticism is that it has been proven false by the fact that a number of Southern states have managed to industrialize, and have done so with the help of Northern investment and trade with developed states. These NICs, particularly the East Asian "Tigers," have large, vibrant, and diversified industrial sectors and improving standards of living. By pursuing a strategy promoting the export of manufactured goods instead of isolating themselves from the global economic system, they have embraced international trade as a means of growth. (For more on their strategy, see the discussion on export-led growth in the next section.)

Second, the plight of primary product exporters may not be as bad as dependency theorists claim. While world prices for primary commodities (except oil) have tended to decline since 1973, many developing countries that have improved productivity in their primary product industries have achieved substantial economic growth. Commodity producers that boosted agricultural productivity and lowered barriers to foreign trade and investment, such as Malaysia, Thailand, and Chile, have used primary product exports as a springboard to diver-

Table 8.3   Average Annual Percentage Change in Terms of Trade, 1965–1986

Country Group	1965–1973	1973–1980	1980–1986
Low- and middle-income countries by region:			
Sub-Saharan Africa	–8.5	4.8	–4.0
East Asia	–0.6	1.2	–1.3
South Asia	3.7	–3.4	1.5
Latin America	3.8	2.3	–3.3
Oil exporters	0.3	11.5	–7.3
OECD members	–1.0	–3.3	1.1

Source: World Bank, *World Development Report 1990* (New York: Oxford University Press, 1990), p. 165.

sified economic development. By contrast, countries that raised barriers to imports of agricultural machinery and imposed export taxes on farm products (as have many in Africa) have remained dependent on primary products and lost market share to more efficient producers.[20]

Moreover, while dependency theory contends that the terms of trade are declining for the South, the data do not clearly support this contention. Table 8.3 shows the changes in the terms of trade for low- and middle-income countries in developing regions, oil-exporting countries, and the developed OECD states from 1965 to 1986. While some regions or categories of countries have gone through periods of sharp declines in terms of trade (such as sub-Saharan Africa in 1965–1973 and the oil exporters in 1980–1986), the table shows that both developing and developed countries have experienced periods of declining terms of trade.

The table does indicate, however, that the terms of trade for developing countries generally tend to fluctuate more than those of the developed North. (Notice the sharp drop in the terms of trade of oil exporters between 1973–1980 and 1980–1986, reflecting the global oil boom of the 1970s and bust of the 1980s.) Once more, this may be attributed to greater reliance on primary products (with prices often subject to change without notice) in the South, while most industrialized Northern countries have diversified economies less vulnerable to sudden changes in prices. Apparently, economic downturns and business cycles hurt both industrializing and developed states alike, though underdeveloped Southern countries may be hurt more.

Third, dependency theory lays the blame for the South's poverty squarely on the North, with little if any discussion of factors within the developing world itself that contribute to economic stagnation and poverty. There can be little doubt that domestic factors such as rapid population growth, high rates of illiteracy, and corruption are partly responsible for persistent poverty and underdevelopment.

Critics of the dependency school do not seek to "blame the victims" for underdevelopment. They recognize the disadvantages of heavy dependence on primary-product exports and realize the extent of poverty and suffering in the developing world. They also offer a ready solution to the problems of underdevelopment:

develop! As we have seen, however, this is far more easily said than done. The next part of this chapter discusses how Southern countries have tried to tackle the problem of development, with varying degrees of success.

PART II: DEVELOPMENT STRATEGIES

Our discussion of theories of development has highlighted the daunting internal and external obstacles Southern states must overcome in order to achieve their development goals. Given the geographic, ethnic, and political diversity of developing countries, it should come as no surprise that they have adopted a variety of development strategies. The sources of ideas for development have been numerous. Many developed countries, such as the United States, Britain, France, Sweden, and Japan, have offered examples, recommendations, and aid for various development programs. China and the now defunct Soviet Union also extended advice and assistance to the South, particularly in the 1950s, 1960s, and 1970s. There has thus been no lack of ideas or experimentation in the field of development.

This section describes and evaluates how development strategies have fared in practice. First, we will examine the types of international aid that developed countries have provided to developing nations. Afterward, we will survey the trading strategies that developing countries have adopted to find and increase their roles in the global economy.

International Development Assistance

In the late 1940s the United States recognized the need to jump-start the reconstruction of war-torn Europe in order to forestall political extremism. The Marshall Plan provided billions in much-needed assistance, and by the 1950s Western Europe was enjoying an "economic miracle." The success of the Marshall Plan led many in and out of government around the world to believe that international aid might be a critical means by which development could be initiated or accelerated in many Southern countries. Since World War II, international aid has been provided in essentially three forms: bilateral, multilateral, and private.

In the 1950s, 1960s, and 1970s, the United States, as well as many other countries in the North, extended significant economic assistance directly to many developing countries—a process called **bilateral aid.** Moreover, the United Nations agencies that were set up to facilitate the rebuilding of Europe—the International Bank of Reconstruction and Development (the World Bank) and the International Monetary Fund (IMF)—gradually but steadily turned their focus from war reconstruction to the problems of development in the South and thus have become the principal distributors of **multilateral aid.** Finally, outside official government channels, **private aid** has been provided by nongovernmental organizations (NGOs) such as the Red Cross, Save the Children, Oxfam, and CARE. In short, an entire infrastructure of international development assistance sprang up after World War II. Each form of assistance, however, has its own agenda and problems.

Bilateral Aid   In the case of bilateral aid, direct aid in the form of grants or loans from a single developed country is provided to a specific developing state, especially when it is a victim of natural disaster or it suffers from severe defense burdens. Today the importance of bilateral aid to development has been down-graded, primarily because the success of the Marshall Plan has not been repli-cated in developing countries despite the transfer of billions of dollars of resources. Indeed, foreign aid is often harshly criticized for becoming something like an international form of welfare that inhibits economic initiative and encour-ages corruption within the South. Often, it seems that the more aid a country receives, the worse it does.

For many low-income countries, aid has become a very significant percentage of GNP. A glance at some data shows that in extreme cases, foreign-aid receipts can account for more than one-half of a poor nation's GNP. Some of the most extreme cases are Mozambique, Guinea-Bissau, and Tanzania, where official development assistance as a percentage of GNP equals 69.2, 43.4, and 33.8, respectively.[21] In the long run, such huge infusions of aid are unhealthy for a country's economy, as recipient states come to depend on foreign assistance and lack incentives to develop local production. Too much aid can also allow countries to delay necessary reforms (such as breaking up huge plantations into smaller farmer-owned plots, selling state-owned enterprises to private investors—**privatization**—and allowing prices to reflect supply and demand) by subsidizing bureaucracies or elites who look after their own narrow inter-ests. By contrast, the end of significant direct American aid to South Korea in the late 1950s induced the government to initiate economic reforms that became the basis for South Korea's spectacular economic success.

Bilateral aid has other drawbacks from the points of view of both donors and recipients. Many citizens of developed countries question whether devel-opment assistance is a worthwhile use of tax money. Most opinion polls in the United States indicate that foreign aid is the least popular of the federal gov-ernment's expenditures, and consequently, American aid in terms of a percent-age of GNP has steadily decreased. In 1965, for instance, the United States spent .26 percent of its GNP on development assistance to low-income countries, while in 1990 it spent only .05 percent of GNP on such endeavors. But since its economy is so big, the United States is still one of the largest donors. By com-parison, in 1990 Britain also spent only .05 percent of GNP on development aid and Italy .09 percent, but France spent .13, Sweden, Denmark, and the Nether-lands spent about .25 percent, and Norway .40 percent.[22] The end of the Cold War may increase demands to redirect American resources from foreign-aid pro-grams, but some European countries, though smaller, are more active.

Multilateral Aid   The drawbacks of bilateral aid have led to a rise in multilat-eral aid, in which aid is channeled to many countries through international orga-nizations. Multilateral aid is still official, or public, assistance because the providing agencies are funded and supervised by two or more governments pooling their resources.

Two UN agencies in particular, the World Bank and the International Monetary Fund (IMF), have become the chief sources of development assistance and technical economic advice for most Southern countries, as well as for Eastern Europe and the former Soviet Union. (See Chapter Nine for more on the World Bank and IMF.) These organizations provide billions of dollars worth of financial assistance (mostly long-term loans at very favorable interest rates) every year, but that is only one aspect of their influence. The financial contributions of their member states determine voting rights, and given that virtually all the capital is provided by the United States, Western Europe, and Japan, these two agencies generally reflect the economic policy preferences of the industrialized North. However, since they are independent of any single government and are affiliated with the UN, they are perceived as being more politically neutral by many Southern states, and they also provide a forum for Southern concerns. Importantly, the World Bank and the IMF do not lend money directly for military purposes, but instead focus exclusively on economic development. (Of course, providing funds for economic projects frees up resources for other purposes.)

Multilateral Aid and the Debt Crisis   By working with Northern lenders and Southern borrowers, the IMF and the World Bank helped prevent the debt crisis of the 1980s from turning into a global financial disaster. In the early 1970s, multinational banks were awash with huge sums of "petrodollars" deposited by the newly rich nations of OPEC. The banks "recycled" the petrodollars by making loans to developing countries on generous terms, thereby providing Third World states with badly needed capital while earning substantial profits for themselves. When oil prices soared again after 1979, however, the resulting worldwide recession prompted banks to tighten up their terms for loans to developing states and, simultaneously, reduced the demand for many exports from the developing world.

By the 1980s, therefore, many Third World countries found themselves with an enormous debt burden piled up during the "easy money" years of the petrodollar period. In many of these states, foreign debt totaled 400 to 3000 percent of annual export earnings, and a large proportion of their foreign exchange earnings went for the repayment of old loans.[23] As private investment began to dry up, heavily indebted nations were caught in a ruinous financial trap. They were faced with three basic options, all of them bad: squeeze domestic consumption and investment to pay their foreign creditors, borrow new money to pay off old debts, or default on their loans. In a sense, their "credit cards" were "maxed out"—they had reached the limits of their allowable debt, and needed to borrow more money just to make the payments. The situation was precarious for lenders as well, because if big Third World debtors such as Mexico, Argentina, and Brazil had defaulted on their loans, multinational banks could have lost billions of dollars, which might have precipitated a global financial panic.[24]

The IMF and World Bank stepped in by providing short- and long-term loans to developing countries to get them out of their debt fix. However, debt relief came with strings attached, in an arrangement referred to as **conditionality.** As a condition of receiving financial assistance, the debtor countries had to undertake **structural-adjustment** policies approved by the lending institutions. Usually, these policies included the opening of markets to imports, devaluation of overvalued currencies, cutting government spending, reducing price controls and subsidies, and reducing direct state ownership of industries. These free-market-oriented reforms are often very unpopular when they are first instituted, as they frequently require cutting government jobs and reducing the subsidies on food that keep the prices of staple foods low for urban consumers.

In 1989, the IMF began brokering packages of payment rescheduling and partial debt forgiveness for countries that agreed to carry out programs of structural adjustment. This arrangement, known as the Brady Plan, was named after its chief proponent, then—U.S. Treasury Secretary Nicholas Brady. Five years later, roughly 80 percent of the money lent by commercial banks to developing countries had been restructured.

The IMF and World Bank recognize the hardships that structural adjustment often entails, but they see them as necessary changes to make it possible for debtor countries to pay back the loans, attract private investment in the future, and reorient economies for long-term growth. However, many debtor governments resent these policies and view conditionality as foreign meddling. In some cases, structural-adjustment policies have led to violent protests, as in Venezuela in 1989 when rising food prices sparked off riots that killed 300 people and injured over 1000. Some countries attempt to unilaterally "cap" payments, or simply default on their loans, but when Peru tried this in the 1980s, it quickly ran out of foreign exchange and was forced to borrow more money under even more restrictive conditions to pay for essential imports.

Like it or not, many debt-strapped countries have little recourse but to accede to conditionality because of their great need for foreign capital. Private investment often shuns Southern countries that do not meet IMF- and World Bank–conditioned targets on policy reform. Moreover, the World Bank in particular has specialized in the analysis of development, carrying out studies and collecting economic information that few countries would have provided to any single other country or private concern. (That is why so much of the data used in this chapter comes from World Bank development reports.) Technical expertise coupled with financial resources have given the World Bank and IMF enormous political clout in their own right; most contemporary development debates, for instance, are centered on how swiftly and how far "structural adjustment" should go, not on whether the changes are essential. Of course, many Southern countries would prefer to set their own development agendas and avoid borrowing from the IMF and the World Bank. As they are often essentially bankrupt, however, they must negotiate with the North for assistance, and that job has been taken on by these agencies.

Private Aid   There is one other major means by which development assistance is transferred to the South: private organizations and other nongovernmental organizations (NGOs) (see Chapter Nine for more on NGOs). This type of assistance is not tied to any particular government directly and thus is considered private. Unlike governments or the IMF or World Bank, which usually seek to promote economic development with their major development projects and loans, NGOs typically emphasize humanitarian aid. Moreover, unlike official assistance, which generally comes in the form of loans, private assistance usually is given as grants that need not be paid back directly.

Private aid is hardly a new idea. Throughout the era of European imperialism, religious missionaries often provided what now would be considered development assistance, particularly in the fields of health and education by building schools and hospitals. Since World War II, a wide variety of humanitarian private organizations have established international aid programs. Some organizations, like *Medecins sans Frontiers* ("Doctors without Borders") and the Red Cross, move from one crisis area to another, attempting to distribute food and medical supplies to victims and refugees of famine, floods, and wars, while others, like CARE and Save the Children, attempt to alleviate chronic problems in many countries.

NGOs rely mostly on private donations from individual citizens in the North and distribute their aid directly to individuals in the South, thus bypassing official channels at both ends. With the rising global concern about overpopulation, the global environment, and the spread of diseases like AIDS, these humanitarian, health, and environmental organizations translate the concerns of their memberships and donors into pragmatic action. In many cases, they are seeking to fill voids left by lack of official action by governments in both the North and South. Their efforts are largely stop-gap in nature, although some would argue that this is all that ever can be expected of international aid.

Evaluating Aid   Developing countries often complain that the single largest problem with bilateral aid is that it is almost always driven more by political concerns than by any humanitarian or economic criteria. Typically, military assistance forms a major aspect of bilateral aid. During the Cold War, the United States and the USSR both used development assistance to further their geopolitical and strategic interests. Though some of its interests have changed, the United States continues this practice in the post-Cold War era, sending large amounts of aid to Egypt and Israel for the sake of political and strategic stability in the Middle East. Other big recipients of American aid in the 1980s included the following:

1. Pakistan, largely because of its permission to use Pakistani bases to funnel U.S. military supplies to the Afghan guerrillas—the *Moujahadeen*—in their struggle against the Soviet Union (see Chapter Four). (After the Soviets withdrew, aid to Pakistan was suspended because of the country's nuclear program.)

2. Turkey, because of its close proximity to the Soviet Union at a critical strategic crossroads.

3. The Philippines, mostly because of the huge naval and air bases that the United States established there during its period of colonial rule and

A father of three listens as a nurse from the Thailand Planning Association explains its free vasectomy program in 1986. He and 195 others underwent the procedure on the same day in the ballroom of a luxury hotel in Bangkok.
Source: © Reuters/Bettmann.

maintained as a means of projecting American military might toward East Asia. (These bases were shut down in late 1992, in part because the U.S. and Philippine governments could not agree on the amount of aid the United States would provide in exchange for permission to continue using the bases.)

Other developed countries have displayed similar political objectives in their aid programs. Virtually all French development assistance goes to former French colonies in West and Central Africa in what some have referred to as a neocolonial relationship. Britain sends most of its development aid to poorer countries in the Commonwealth of Nations, which is composed of most of the countries that once made up the British Empire. Of course, when political and strategic objectives override any economic concern, such assistance is not likely to spur economic growth.

A second complaint by the Third World is that bilateral aid is often tied to the purchase of products from the donor country, even in instances where aid takes the form of a loan. This requirement forces Third World countries to purchase goods that might not be the most appropriate or the cheapest available. This policy benefits manufacturers in the donor country and promotes future orders for spare parts and other equipment. One source calculates that over two-thirds of bilateral aid is tied.[25] Of Germany's $1.4 billion in bilateral aid in 1986, for instance, 86 percent was earmarked for the purchase of German goods, and 80 percent of Japanese aid was tied in this way.[26] Strings can be tied to bilateral aid in other ways. Many Japanese-funded road-building projects in Latin America, for example, are designed to open forest areas to logging in order to ensure a steady supply of logs to Japanese industries.

A third problem in foreign aid has been the North's preference for big projects over smaller ones.[27] Large, visible projects such as dams or port facilities often win over less visible projects such as health care, schools, and agricultural programs, because they are more easily identified with the donor, and the donor therefore receives more credit and publicity. In many cases, the unfortunate result has been the construction of huge "white elephants" of dubious value. Perhaps the biggest white elephant of all was the Aswan Dam on the Nile in southern Egypt. Egyptian President Nasser (see Chapter Six) played the Soviet Union and the United States off against each other in attempting to finance the dam. In so doing, Egypt got the dam financed and built by the Soviets, but along the way the project increased U.S.–Soviet competition, setting the stage for the Suez Crisis of 1956. And, the dam itself may be doing more long-term harm than good to Egypt's economy and environment, as it has reduced the productivity of downstream farms and accelerated the erosion of scarce arable land.[28]

As the 1990s have progressed, the white-elephant syndrome has lessened as environmental concerns have been raised about big projects like dams and highways being constructed through sensitive rain forests (see Chapter Ten). Indeed, there now seems to be growing coordination among aid donors as bilateral and UN donors increasingly channel aid through NGOs and local development groups in Southern countries. The watchword for development aid in the next century may be "small is beautiful" as Southern governments, private donors, and international organizations work with communities in the developing world on projects designed to fulfill local needs rather than national ambitions. Official and private aid to developing countries will clearly continue to play a vital role, but disenchanting experiences with aid in both the North and South seem likely to prompt the exploration of other alternatives.

Development through Trade—Alternative Strategies

The deficiencies of and stigma associated with the various forms of aid have led many in developed and developing countries alike to call for greater reliance on "trade, not aid" to promote development. There are three general trading strategies that Third World states have used to pursue their development goals: import-substitution industrialization, collective bargaining among Southern states, and export-led industrialization. **Import-substitution industrialization (ISI),** a strategy followed by numerous developing states after World War II, seeks to promote domestic industries by reducing imports from the North. Some of the states that initially adopted this strategy later turned toward **export-led industrialization (ELI),** which promotes growth through trade in the global market. Finally, during the 1970s a number of Third World states sought to coordinate their efforts to change the international trading system and improve the terms of trade for primary product exporters through collective bargaining. This section will survey the positive and negative aspects of all three of these strategies.

Import-Substitution Industrialization (ISI)   The global market is highly competitive, and industries struggling to get off the ground in the developing world often find it very difficult to compete with established industries in the industrialized North. For this reason, many developing countries have at various times chosen to protect their infant industries from foreign competition and promote domestic production of goods that had formerly been imported. This import-substitution industrialization (ISI) strategy aims at greater economic self-sufficiency. To a large extent, the young United States pursued this policy throughout the nineteenth century; the high tariffs that protected Northern manufacturers were a major source of the antagonism between North and South that led to the Civil War. Many Latin American states were pressed to adopt de facto import substitution because of the collapse of international trade between the beginning of World War I and the end of World War II (see Chapters Three and Seven). Many of these countries continued to pursue such policies in the 1950s and 1960s.

ISI is a strategy of economic isolation intended to encourage domestic entrepreneurs to manufacture products otherwise imported from abroad. First, the exchange rate is overvalued, meaning that the rate at which currencies are exchanged makes imported goods relatively cheaper and exported goods relatively more expensive. Second, high tariff barriers are erected on consumer goods to block foreign competition. The intention is to make imports of capital goods (such as manufacturing equipment and spare parts) cheap while making imported consumer goods (such as automobiles and appliances) expensive, so that consumers will buy from domestic producers.

The trouble with ISI is that it typically requires a great deal of foreign capital to create and subsidize domestic industries. Since ISI undermines the profitable export sector, it tends to lead to a balance-of-payments deficit (that is, the nation's economy cannot earn enough through exports to pay for the imports it needs). (See Chapter Seven.) This makes it very difficult to purchase capital goods from industrialized countries, which may defeat the whole purpose of the strategy.

Most countries pursuing an ISI strategy initially experience growth in domestic industries that produce consumer goods, just as planned. The next stage of the strategy, sometimes called "deepening," is the development of manufacturing capabilities in intermediate industries such as steel. However, investments in these industries require more capital and more sophisticated technology from the North, and an overvalued exchange rate hurts exports, which are necessary to earn foreign capital. Consequently, in practice ISI has very often led to massive borrowing from foreign banks and growing external debt, resulting in even greater dependence upon Northern states for capital.

AT A GLANCE

STRATEGIES OF DEVELOPMENT

Import Substitution

Definition: Many developing countries at various times choose to protect their "infant industries" from foreign competition and promote domestic production of goods that are imported. This strategy aims at greater economic self-sufficiency.

Process: First, high tariff barriers are erected on some goods to block foreign competition. Second, the exchange rate is overvalued, meaning that the rate at which currencies are exchanged make imports cheap and exports expensive. Tariffs are manipulated so that foreign consumer goods become expensive and capital goods become cheap. The next stage is the development of manufacturing capabilities in intermediate industries such as steel. The following stage calls for the development of capital goods, but as noted above these goods require substantial foreign investment and technical know-how.

Evaluation: In short, import substitution has not been very successful at either emancipating the South from economic dependence or in providing a basis for long-term economic development.

In most instances, ISI has resulted in greater dependence upon capital and imports from the Northern industrialized states without raising the general standard of living in Southern countries.

Collective Bargaining

Definition: Using this process, many Southern countries tried to pool their resources in order to press for changes in the international economic system in the early 1970s. It was hoped that the developing states could gain higher prices for primary product exports and greater access to Northern markets.

Process: Proposals for solidarity among Southern nations culminated in the call for a New International Economic Order (NIEO), issued by a group of developing states (the Group of 77) at a special session of the United Nations in 1974. The NIEO movement was inspired by dependency theory, which contends that declining terms of trade for primary product exporters—and control of industries in developing countries by multinational corporations—keep the developing South subordinate to and dependent upon the industrialized North. NIEO advocates sought

Latin America offers the best examples of the successes and limitations of the ISI strategy.[29] The rapid decline in world trade that was a cause and effect of the Great Depression prompted Argentina, Brazil, and Chile to pursue de facto strategies of import substitution. In the years following World War II, ISI was formally adopted as a strategy of economic development and a way to reduce economic and political dependence. High tariffs were established to protect infant industries, and currencies were overvalued. The short-run impact was a shortage of foreign capital and a steep decline in the profitable export-oriented sector. Around 1960, through import and exchange controls, the initial, easy stage of industrialization characterized by the substitution of locally produced for imported consumer goods was successfully completed. In some cases, notably in Brazil, great strides were made in the domestic production of more durable consumer goods and some intermediate goods, including transportation and electronic equipment, metal fabrication, and chemicals.

The next stage of industrialization called for the development of capital goods, but as noted previously, these goods require substantial foreign investment and technical know-how. Because their export-oriented industries had declined as a result of the to exploit industrialized countries' dependence upon primary goods from the South and thus "turn the tables" on the North.

Evaluation: By the end of the 1980s, repeated failures to improve primary product exporters' terms of trade prompted most countries to conclude that collective bargaining was no substitute for the development of a diversified economy. The problem of exactly how to achieve economic growth, however, remained.

Export-Led Growth

Definition: Development is promoted by working within, rather than against, the global economic agenda. This strategy's advice to developing countries on their relationship to the industrialized North is simple: "If you can't beat 'em, join 'em."

Process: In the 1960s and 1970s, several developing countries adopted an export promotion strategy by giving substantial economic incentives to firms to export their products, particularly by undervaluing their foreign exchange rates, which made their exports cheap and their imports expensive. The results of this strategy

are especially impressive in the East Asian "Tigers" (Hong Kong, Singapore, South Korea, and Taiwan). In less than two generations, these countries have been transformed into industrialized nations poised to produce the high-tech products of the twenty-first century. Their tremendous growth rates have been accomplished through intensive state intervention in the economy and society, borrowing of technology from the industrialized North, and the promotion of research and development.

Evaluation: Some theorists have argued that the success of the NICs cannot be duplicated elsewhere in the South, as East Asian NICs have saturated trading opportunities with the North to such an extent that other Southern countries have been squeezed out. But global demand for most products is not static—as economies grow, they typically generate more demand for raw materials, consumer and capital goods, and services. Opportunities are likely to exist as long as markets remain open.

ISI strategy, Latin American countries lacked the foreign exchange necessary for the import of the appropriate technology from the North. This led to heavy foreign borrowing and severe indebtedness, which contributed to the "stalling out" of their industrial development.

In Africa, one country very closely associated with import substitution was Tanzania, whose policies of *ujamaa* ("unity") and *kujitegamea* ("self-reliance") received great attention in the late 1960s. However, by the early 1980s Tanzania's economy was in severe crisis. Many of its state-owned industries were operating at roughly 10 percent capacity, and because farmers were taxed so heavily to pay for critical imports, agricultural exports fell. Essentially, after a period of initial success, ISI had stalled and failed once again.

In short, ISI has not been very successful at either emancipating the South from economic dependence or providing a basis for long-term economic development. In most instances, it has resulted in greater dependence upon capital and imports from the Northern industrialized states without raising the general standard of living in Southern countries.[30]

WHAT WOULD YOU DO?

You are the king of Saudi Arabia in mid-October 1973. You desire a leading role in the Arab states' collective effort to punish the backers of Israel after the current war ends. Your energy minister has suggested a plan whereby the Arab members of the Organization of Petroleum Exporting Countries could impose an embargo on the shipment of oil to Israel's Western supporters (especially the United States and the Netherlands) to drive up the "true" costs of their support for Israel.

Collectively, OPEC controls 50 percent of the world's oil reserves. An oil embargo would dramatically increase the short-run price of oil, leading to higher energy costs and inflation in the Western industrialized economies (especially in Japan and in most of the European countries), and forcing the most vulnerable Western states to distance themselves from Israel, further isolating it. By raising the price of oil, the embargo could increase your own prosperity, and allow you to demonstrate the international magnanimity of your royal

Collective Bargaining   In the early 1970s many Southern countries tried to pool their resources in order to press for changes in the international economic system. It was hoped that through collective bargaining, developing states could gain higher prices for primary-product exports and greater access to Northern markets. Proposals for solidarity among Southern nations culminated in the call for a **New International Economic Order (NIEO)** issued by a group of developing states (the Group of 77) at a special session of the United Nations in 1974.[31] The NIEO movement was inspired by dependency theory, which (as we saw earlier in this chapter) contends that declining terms of trade for primary-product exporters and control of industries in developing countries by multinational corporations keeps the developing South subordinate to and dependent upon the industrialized North. NIEO advocates sought to exploit industrialized countries' dependence upon primary goods from the South and thus turn the tables on the North.

During the 1960s and 1970s, many Southern countries nationalized their mineral and agricultural export sectors, wresting control of these industries from multinational corporations. Although no single Third World country controlled enough of any primary commodity to restrict supplies, many Southern countries hoped to increase their collective-bargaining power by forming **commodity cartels.** The members of these cartels hoped to duplicate the success of the Organization of Petroleum Exporting Countries (OPEC) in raising the price of oil and achieving control over their own natural resources by reducing the power of multinational oil companies (see the boxed feature on OPEC). If collective action by oil exporters could be effective, why not try collective action by exporters of coffee, copper, bauxite, or bananas?

house toward poorer Third World countries. This would augment the political influence of your conservative regime within the more radical nonaligned movement.

Conversely, by leading the oil embargo, your government would have to act as a "swing producer" (adjusting your own oil production levels to accommodate the desire of the more desperate OPEC nations for larger production quotas). In the short run, a desperate United States might decide to take military action if the pinch becomes too painful. In the long run, as your Western-educated economic advisers have also warned, an oil embargo could lead Western countries to develop their own sources of oil or other substitute energy sources. This would depress the price of oil and lead OPEC members to cheat by exceeding their production quotas. Still, Saudi Arabia would have to decrease its own production quota to maintain the ceiling on overall OPEC supply.

You want to balance these short-run and long-run considerations.

What would you do?

However, many would-be cartelizers soon found that other primary materials did not lend themselves to similar results. OPEC's success was due to the pivotal role petroleum plays in the world economy and the geographic accident of the distribution of oil reserves. By the late twentieth century, the supply of oil was concentrated in the hands of a few states. In 1970, for example, OPEC members accounted for 90 percent of world oil exports.[32] Oil also was, and remains, a resource of critical importance to industrialized nations. Coffee, sugar, rubber, and so forth, are not as critical as oil, and alternative sources or substitutes are more easily found. Also, controlling production and coordinating policy are much more difficult when there are many producers. Therefore, the commodity cartels' bargaining position was far weaker than OPEC's.

The Group of 77 (which never changed its name, though it grew to over 120 members) called for other measures, including **buffer stocks** and compensatory pricing mechanisms, to stabilize commodity prices.[33] By the end of the 1980s, however, repeated failures to improve primary-product exporters' terms of trade prompted most countries to conclude that collective bargaining was no substitute for the development of a diversified economy. The problem of exactly how to achieve economic growth, however, remained.

Export-Led Industrialization (ELI)   The third principal strategy of growth promotes industrialization through trade. Export-led industrialization (ELI) seeks to promote development by working within, rather than against, the global economic system. Its advice to developing countries on their relationship to the industrialized North is simple: "If you can't beat 'em, join 'em."

RISE AND FALL OF OPEC

OPEC, the Organization of Petroleum Exporting Countries, was formed in August 1960 with the purpose of gaining higher prices and greater control over production of member states' petroleum resources. OPEC's thirteen members have been Algeria, Ecuador, Gabon, Indonesia, Iran, Iraq, Kuwait, Libya, Nigeria, Qatar, Saudi Arabia, the United Arab Emirates, and Venezuela. (However, in 1992 Ecuador withdrew from the organization.) The potency of the OPEC cartel was demonstrated to the world in 1973 when, in response to the Yom Kippur War, the Arab members of OPEC reduced production and embargoed oil to the United States and the Netherlands, countries considered pro-Israeli; then OPEC raised prices fourfold. OPEC's success encouraged other developing states to believe that they, too, could achieve control over their natural resources by forming similar cartels.

OPEC's pride, in many ways, led to its fall. In response to skyrocketing oil prices in the 1970s and the possibility of another embargo, industrialized countries reduced their demand for OPEC oil. This was accomplished by a combination of energy

In the 1960s and 1970s, several developing countries, particularly Brazil and the newly industrialized countries (NICs) of East Asia, adopted an ELI strategy by giving substantial economic incentives to firms to export their products, particularly by undervaluing their foreign exchange rates, which made their exports cheap and their imports expensive.[34] For Japan, South Korea, Taiwan, Hong Kong, and Singapore, export promotion has proven to be a major impetus for exceptionally rapid economic development. The results of this strategy are especially impressive in the East Asian "Tigers" (Hong Kong, Singapore, South Korea, and Taiwan). In the course of less than two generations, these countries have been transformed into industrialized nations poised to produce the high-tech products of the twenty-first century. Their tremendous growth rates have been accomplished through intensive state intervention in the economy and society, borrowing of technology from the industrialized North, and the promotion of research and development.

Figure 8.1 summarizes the results of this development strategy in economic terms, showing the high growth of trade and GNP in the Four Tigers since 1970. Although some average growth rates appear to dip during the 1980s, they remained higher than average OECD growth rates, let alone most other developing countries. The standards of living, life expectancy, health, literacy, and educational levels in these countries have shown equally impressive improvement.[35]

Some theorists have argued that the success of the NICs cannot be duplicated elsewhere in the South, as those East Asian nations have saturated trading opportunities with the North to such an extent that other Southern countries have been squeezed out.[36] In essence, this perspective argues that trading opportunities with the North are a fixed sum, and thus the gain in trade by conservation efforts, the discovery of other sources of oil (in the North Sea and Mexico, for example) and the switch to alternative sources of energy (France, in particular, increased its reliance on nuclear power). In large part, these conditions were of OPEC's own making, as the price increases arranged by the cartel made the development of remote oil fields and alternative energy techniques more economically viable. Disagreements among OPEC members themselves also undermined OPEC's influence. Difficulties intensified over questions of pricing and production levels between states that had immense reserves (Saudi Arabia) and those with fewer reserves, and between those with larger and smaller populations. Political disagreements, as well, led to tensions, and in some cases open hostilities, most dramatically exemplified by the Iran-Iraq War of the 1980s and the long-term dispute between Iraq and Kuwait over oil fields that contributed to the Persian Gulf War in 1991. While still a potentially powerful actor because of the continued importance of oil, OPEC has lost the prominent position it enjoyed in the mid-1970s.

one developing country forecloses openings for other developing countries. This view has some merit; as prices rise, international primary-product markets can become glutted from increased production in other Southern countries. But global demand for most products is not static—as economies grow, they typically generate more demand for raw materials, consumer and capital goods, and services. It must also be noted that industrial development in the Four Tigers has had significant social and environmental costs, just as it has everywhere else.[37] (Chapter Ten discusses these problems in more detail.) The ELI strategy is therefore not a panacea for development by any means. Nevertheless, while the striking success of the Asian NICs may be difficult to duplicate, as long as markets remain open, opportunities for export-led growth are likely to exist for Southern countries seeking to expand and diversify their economies.

PART III: DEVELOPMENT DEBATES OF THE 1990s AND BEYOND

It has been said that "success has many fathers, while failure is an orphan." In the field of development, success typically generates many imitators in a kind of trendy bandwagon effect. The East Asian NICs, who have pursued an ELI strategy, have been the most successful developers. In the late 1980s and early 1990s, many diverse developing countries adopted trading policies remarkably similar to the policies of the Four Tigers in the 1960s and 1970s. China eased its dogmatic Maoist opposition to capitalism and opened up many areas to foreign investment. India, formerly committed to economic self-sufficiency, reduced its

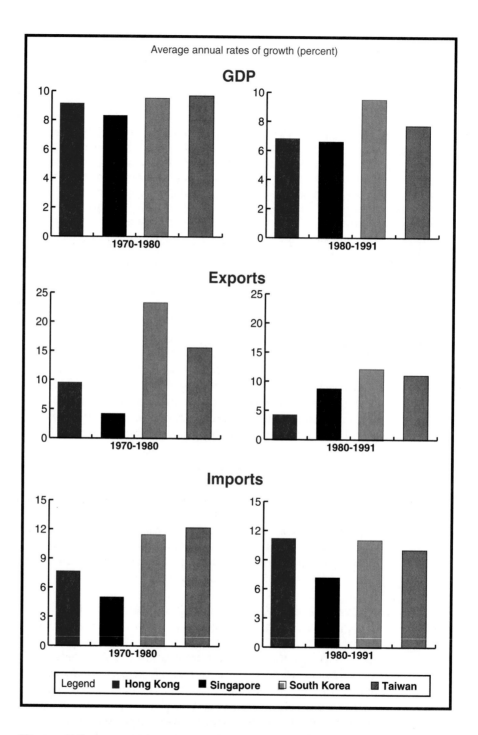

Figure 8.1 The Four Tigers

Source: *World Development Report 1993,* pp. 264–265; Republic of China, Council for Economic Planning and Development, *Taiwan Statistical Data Book,* 1993, pp. 26–27.

legendary bureaucratic barriers to imports and exports. Turkey sought membership in the EU hoping that this would expand its trading opportunities. South Africa abandoned its policies of apartheid (see Chapter Five) and began a major effort to attract foreign investment.

Though many countries thus agreed that ELI offers good prospects for development, many developing states face serious problems of market access. Without open markets, particularly in developed states, exports cannot flourish. Indeed, one of the arguments for ISI in the interwar period was rampant protectionism in many of the major trading states (see Chapter Seven). Getting some countries, especially Japan and the members of the EU, to open their domestic markets to the exports of developing states has been far from easy. To date, only the United States has allowed truly open access to the exports of many developing nations. Consequently, the success of Taiwan, South Korea, Singapore, and Hong Kong was based in large part on their ability to export to the American market.

One of the critical reasons why the United States allowed the East Asian NICs access to its huge domestic market was that they were perceived as "bulwarks against communism" in Asia. With the end of the Cold War, this political rationale for open markets is no longer pertinent. Instead, the debate in the United States has shifted to the domestic consequences of free trade, which effectively integrates First World economies with Third World economies. Recent controversies over the U.S. extension of most-favored-nation status (see Chapter Seven) to China and the North American Free Trade Agreement (NAFTA) highlight the problems and opportunities of North-South trade. In both cases, the debate has centered on whether the economic benefits of increased trade outweigh the social costs and political dilemmas.

China: Should Free Trade Require Freedom?

During the 1980s the People's Republic of China, for the first time since the Communists seized power in 1949, opened many of its coastal regions to significant foreign investment. In the process, many profitable trading relationships were established, and the United States extended most-favored-nation (MFN) tariff rates to Chinese exports. It looked as if China and the United States had turned the corner on what had been a very hostile relationship (see Chapters Four and Six).

However, in May 1989 many Chinese students demonstrated in Tiananmen Square, in the heart of Beijing, for greater democratization in China's political system. The Chinese government responded by sending in soldiers and tanks to massacre hundreds of peaceful demonstrators. After the massacre, many in the United States called for the end of MFN status for China because of the Tiananmen incident and other human rights abuses. It was further pointed out that some Chinese exports were made by prison labor, and thus could not be legally imported into the United States. China's repression of ethnic Tibetans was also offered as proof of Chinese political intransigence. Why, many Americans asked, should the United States extend the benefits of free trade to a nation governed by a repressive Communist regime?

The Bush administration, however, opposed the end of MFN status for China and resisted congressional efforts to revoke it. Many U.S. interest groups also favored continued extension of MFN to China. The Boeing corporation, for example, sells dozens of airplanes worth hundreds of millions of dollars to China's growing airline industry. In 1994 the Clinton administration separated MFN from human rights, but declared it would still try to convince China to improve its human rights record.

China's authoritarianism almost ensures that some level of political conflict over MFN will continue for the foreseeable future. Its rapidly expanding economy, however, is likely to attract foreign investment and increase demand for imports. Balancing the benefits of increased trade with China's abysmal human rights record will be far from easy for the United States, especially because many countries are prepared to simply ignore human rights violations in favor of profits.

Controversy over NAFTA

Like many other developing countries, Mexico in the 1980s radically changed the direction of its economic policies from heavy protectionism to more open economic links with the developed world—especially the United States. Mexico joined the General Agreement on Tariffs and Trade (GATT) in 1986 (see Chapter Seven), and since then has lowered tariffs and dramatically increased trade with its northern neighbor. By the early 1990s the United States, Canada, and Mexico were negotiating the sweeping free trade pact known as the North American Free Trade Agreement (NAFTA). This agreement is an ambitious and unprecedented experiment in integrating First and Third World economies.

The debate in the U.S. Congress and among the American people over NAFTA highlighted the difficulties of the agreement. Detractors pointed out that Mexican labor unions are controlled by the government, that Mexican wages are much lower than American wages, and Mexican health, safety, and environmental standards, while similar on paper to those in the United States, are sparsely enforced. In the United States, labor and environmental groups lobbied strenuously to defeat NAFTA, fearing that American jobs, wages, and environmental standards would "go South." However, advocates of free trade argued that in the long run, the pact would create more American jobs (through increased trade) and improve Mexican environmental standards (because as countries become richer, they tend to be more concerned about environmental quality).[38] After impassioned speeches, media blitzes, and political pressure and logrolling from both sides, Congress voted to ratify the agreement in November 1993.

Whatever costs and/or benefits NAFTA will have for the United States and Canada, the agreement will almost certainly have a much greater impact on Mexico. NAFTA guarantees Mexico a huge market for its ELI strategy, but it also is likely to bring Mexico much greater scrutiny from the United States. Mexico's government is dominated by a single party, the Institutional Revolutionary Party (PRI), which has often held onto power by voter fraud and intimidation of political opponents. With NAFTA, the United States is likely to look at anti-democratic practices and abuses of power much more closely than in the past, and Mexico is likely to resent the resultant criticism and potential interference in its sovereignty. On balance, Mexico's form of "soft" authoritarianism is not as objectionable to the United States as China's Communist system, and many NAFTA supporters argue that the free-trade agreement will create pressure and incentives for more real democracy. This may in turn allay the fears of labor unions and environmentalist groups that NAFTA will be a means by which American corporations will be able to avoid labor and environmental standards by moving their plants and facilities to Mexico.

Political Aspects of Economic Interdependence

Considering that ELI is now the preferred development strategy for many Southern countries, the debates over NAFTA and MFN for China are likely to be repeated many times over. As trade between the North and South grows, greater economic interdependence between developed and developing countries will pose many questions with both political and economic implications. Will increased trade between the First and Third Worlds undermine employment and wages for low-skilled workers in developed countries? Will multinational corporations take advantage of lax environmental laws in developing nations to avoid pollution-control measures? Will increased trade help entrenched authoritarian regimes hold on to power, or will it instead give impetus to the spread of democracy and human rights?

At the core of all these questions is an enduring political dilemma: As the global economy leads to greater interdependence among all nations, what standards should be adopted to govern the disputes that inevitably arise from higher levels of trade—the minimal standards of many developing countries, or the exacting standards of developed countries? It is far too early to speculate on how this question or any of the other dilemmas of interdependence (see Chapter Ten) will be resolved. All that can be said with any confidence at the present time is that parts of the developed and developing worlds are becoming more closely linked economically, that growing trade and interdependence will create greater prosperity for many but will pose some challenges to all, and that solutions to the dilemmas of economic globalization will not be found quickly or easily.

CONCLUSION: THE DEVELOPMENT IMPERATIVE

Throughout this chapter, we have referred to the relationship between the "First World" and the "Third World," or the "developed world" and the "developing world," almost as if industrialized and nonindustrialized states were located on different planets. In reality, of course, developed and developing states share the same small world, which is being made smaller every day by the globalization of trade and communications. At the same time, however, a process of fragmentation is also occurring, as rapidly growing NICs pull farther and farther ahead of the low income countries and primary-product exporters struggle to achieve the stability and prosperity enjoyed by developed states with diversified economies.

The concurrent processes of globalization and fragmentation lead some authors to conclude that in the near future, the contrasts between the "zones of turmoil" in developing areas and the "zones of peace" in industrialized regions will become even greater, but the two zones will nevertheless become increasingly interdependent.[39] As trade flows increase, the channels through which the problems of one zone spread into the other will widen (see Chapters Six, Ten, and Sixteen). As nations become more closely tied together, and thus more affected by one another's problems, demands for development can only increase, because diversified economies become less vulnerable to both domestic crises and external shocks.

While modernization theorists and adherents of the dependency school disagree on the causes of underdevelopment, both agree that industrialization, with all its attendant drawbacks, is the only cure for the poverty and misery that billions of people in the developing world experience every day. This cure does not come without costs; as this chapter has noted, industrialization creates social and environmental problems as developing states "graduate" from the dilemmas of poverty, through the dilemmas of transition, to the dilemmas of affluence. (See Chapter Ten for more details.) The environmental costs of development, in particular, have led some to contend that curbing population growth and reducing consumption of resources, rather than expanding production, are the only long-term solutions to the economic, health, and environmental problems that affect both industrialized and nonindustrialized countries. These environmentalists therefore counsel programs of development that are ecologically sustainable—but they still call for development, recognizing that people who lack food, shelter, and safe water can't afford to worry too much about the ozone layer.

For Southern countries, therefore, development is not an option, but an imperative. Disagreements exist not over the need for development, but over the means to that end. Each of the development strategies discussed in this chapter has been tried by a number of developing states. Each has succeeded in some cases and failed in others. The varied track records of ISI, collective-bargaining, and ELI strategies have led many development theorists to contend that no single strategy offers all Southern states the best chance to achieve their development goals. Rather, developing states must consider many factors, including their resources and the conditions prevailing in the global marketplace, when they formulate their development programs.[40]

In many ways, a country's choice of a development strategy is very similar to an individual's career. Just as most people must either get a job or go on welfare, most states must either adopt a strategy for development or resign themselves to the fact that the vast majority of their citizens will continue to live in miserable poverty. Also, like a student trying to decide what career or course of study to pursue, a nation attempting to develop its economy must take into account its own strengths, weaknesses, and values, and must make a careful survey of the global "job market." Success is never assured for either individuals or nations, but in both cases industriousness, a positive attitude, innovation, flexibility, and perseverance all increase one's chances.

PRINCIPAL POINTS OF CHAPTER EIGHT

1. It is difficult to derive a precise definition for development, as the international standard for development is a constantly moving target. By any definition, however, development includes economic diversification; transition away from subsistence agriculture toward manufacturing, services, and modern farming; and improvements in health and in standards of living.

2. Development in any form typically results in social changes that can cause serious political problems in developing states. Two of the most important changes brought about by development are demographic transition and urbanization.

    a. Demographic transition refers to the change from the high birth and death rates characteristic of traditional societies to the low birth and death rates usually found in industrialized countries. It is typically accompanied by rapid population growth until the decline in the birthrate matches the decline in the death rate.

    b. Urbanization, or the rapid growth of cities, is often accompanied by overcrowding, unemployment, and crime.

3. There are two major schools of thought on the root causes of development and underdevelopment: modernization theory and dependency theory.

4. Modernization theory holds that domestic social and political structures are the key factors for development. Grounded in the liberal perspective on international political economy (see Chapter Seven), modernization theory views development as a transition from a "traditional" agrarian economy to a "modern" capitalist economy. This school contends that development may be achieved through open markets and investment in physical, financial, and human capital.

5. Dependency theory, based on Marxist ideas, focuses on a country's assigned role in the global economic system. Dependency theorists contend that the global economy operates to keep primary-product exporters (countries that produce commodities such as copper, petroleum, and bananas) dependent on industrialized countries and multinational corporations for manufactured goods, thereby hindering their development. From this perspective, development can be achieved only if primary-product exporters improve their terms of trade (the ratio of export prices to import prices) so that capital will flow from developed to developing countries rather than vice versa.

6. Developing countries may attempt to achieve development through aid, trade, or some combination of both. The course a country adopts in its pursuit of development is termed its development strategy.

7. Three types of development aid, each with its own advantages and disadvantages, may be extended to developing countries:

   a. Bilateral aid is direct aid from one developed state to one developing state, typically handled by the donor's and recipient's governments.

   b. Multilateral aid is aid channeled through international organizations, most often the World Bank and the IMF. This type of aid usually (but not always) comes in the form of loans from the international organization to the recipient government.

   c. Private aid is donated by individuals and groups through nongovernmental organizations (NGOs). This type of aid usually bypasses the recipient's government and goes directly for humanitarian purposes or economic-development projects.

8. In the 1970s, many developing countries borrowed heavily from multinational banks to raise capital for development. This led to a debt crisis in the 1980s when many Third World states became unable to repay their loans. The IMF arranged for debt relief and rescheduling for many debtor nations, but made debt relief conditional upon the adoption of free-market economic reforms, or structural adjustment. Some governments regard conditionality as foreign interference, however, and contend that structural adjustment imposes unnecessary economic hardships.

9. Three basic trading strategies are available to developing countries, each having its own record of success and failure:

   a. Import-substitution industrialization (ISI) attempts to replace imports from developed countries with domestically produced goods.

   b. Collective bargaining attempts to change primary-product exporters' terms of trade through commodity cartels (such as OPEC).

   c. Export-led industrialization (ELI) promotes production of goods for the global market. The newly industrialized countries (NICs) of East Asia (Hong Kong, South Korea, Singapore, and Taiwan) have achieved spectacular growth with this strategy.

10. The experiences of various developing countries prove that there is no single strategy for development that works best in every situation. Countries must carefully assess their own resources and respond to conditions in the global market in order to achieve their development goals.

11. The increasingly close economic relationships between developed and developing countries have lead to political dilemmas. For example, labor unions often complain that trade with Third World states destroys lower-skilled jobs in industrialized states, human rights advocates oppose trade with Southern states ruled by authoritarian regimes, and environmentalists worry that multinational corporations will set up operations in developing areas to circumvent environmental standards in industrial states.

12. While development has drawbacks, often including social upheaval and environmental pollution, there is no real alternative to development if global standards of living are to be improved. (Some of these drawbacks may be alleviated or avoided by sustainable development, which stresses the need to conserve natural resources over the long term; see Chapter Ten.)

13. Increased trade and communications are likely to continue to make developed and developing countries more interdependent—and therefore more susceptible to one another's problems.

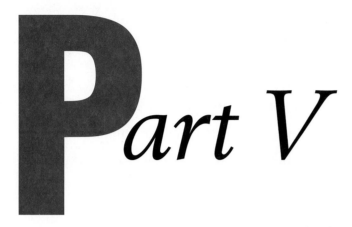

Issues and Institutions in World Politics

Chapter 9

International Law and Organization

CHARTER OF THE UNITED NATIONS SIGNED AT SAN FRANCISCO ON JUNE 26TH, 1945

We, the Peoples of the United Nations, Determined

- to save succeeding generations from the scourge of war, which twice in our life-time has brought untold sorrow to mankind, and
- to reaffirm faith in fundamental human rights, in the dignity and worth of the human person, in the equal rights of men and women and of nations large and small, and
- to establish conditions under which justice and respect for the obligations aris-ing from treaties and other sources of international law can be maintained, and
- to promote social progress and better standards of life in larger freedom,

And for These Ends

- to practice tolerance and live together in peace with one another as good neighbors, and
- to unite our strength to maintain international peace and security, and
- to ensure, by the acceptance of principles and the institution of methods, that armed force shall not be used, save in the common interest, and
- to employ international machinery for the promotion of the economic and social advancement of all peoples,

Have Resolved to Combine Our Efforts to Accomplish These Aims.

Edmund Osmăczyk, *Encyclopedia of the United Nations and International Agreements,* 2nd ed. (New York: Taylor and Francis, 1990), p. 946.

These are great words, accompanied by great promise: the promise of a new era when the rule of law would govern the relations between states, and a new international organization would resolve disputes peacefully. A half century later,

Major Events in International Law and Organizations: 1789–1994

1789: American Bill of Rights and French Declaration of the Rights of Man provide a legal framework for fundamental rights and freedoms.

1856: Declaration of Paris clarifies the rights of neutral vessels, an early agreement on the conduct of warfare.

1884: Delegates from fourteen nations at the Berlin Conference on African affairs agree to work for the suppression of slavery and the slave trade.

1889: Hague Convention outlaws the use of poisonous gases, expanding bullets, and explosives discharged from balloons.

1919: League of Nations is created by the Treaty of Versailles; when the U.S. Senate rejects membership, the League's ability to facilitate cooperation and prevent war is immediately inhibited.

1923: International Criminal Police Organization (Interpol) is created to promote international cooperation between police authorities.

1925: Geneva Protocol outlaws the use of chemical weapons.

1926: League of Nations Slavery Convention seeks an end to slavery around the world.

1945: United Nations is created to safeguard the independence and integrity of member states and to promote international law.

1946: Nazi leaders are prosecuted for "crimes against humanity" at the Nuremberg Trials.

1948: Convention on the Prevention and Punishment of the Crime of Genocide is agreed to by UN General Assembly; Universal Declaration on Human Rights is signed.

1950–1953: Korean War occurs, providing the first opportunity for UN Security Council-sponsored military action.

1957: European Economic Community (the Common Market) is established by the Treaty of Rome to facilitate European economic cooperation.

1959: Antarctic Treaty is signed, banning military activity and setting guidelines for scientific research in Antarctica.

1966: The International Covenant on Civil and Political Rights; The International Covenant of Economic, Social, and Cultural Rights; and the Optional Protocol strengthen provisions of the Universal Declaration of Human Rights.

1967: Outer Space Treaty bans territorial claims in space and space-based weapons of mass destruction.

these promises still have not been fulfilled, but they have proceeded further than most believe. Now in the wake of the end of the Cold War, these promises have new potential.

The New Era has been characterized by the simultaneous, yet contradictory trends of globalization and fragmentation. Two contemporary events illustrate the uncertainty as to whether international law and organizations will be able to bring about increased global cooperation and at the same time reduce the fragmentation that has marred the "new world order" since the end of the Cold War. In 1991, for instance, the global community showed that it was capable of exerting its collective might to oust the forces of Iraqi leader Saddam Hussein from neighboring Kuwait. Because of the favorable battlefield terrain, high economic stakes, clearly defined objectives, and an agreed upon division of the war's costs, enough countries believed that fulfilling their collective obligation under the United Nations (UN) to defend a fellow UN member from outside aggression would be a worthwhile endeavor. On the other hand, the international community's defense of UN member Bosnia-Herzegovina's territorial integrity and Muslim population has proved to be generally ineffective. In this case, unfavorable battlefield terrain, low economic stakes, and uncertainty and disagreements over the objectives of any UN armed intervention in Bosnia have made it difficult for the great powers to seriously stem the unfortunate course of that country's fragmentation and disintegration.

These two different international responses to the aforementioned crises illustrate the fundamental difference between international and domestic politics introduced in Chapter One: that while domestic politics functions under a system of authority, global politics is anarchic. There is no central authority to

1972: UN Conference on the Human Environment in Stockholm approves Declaration on the Human Environment.

1974: UN Declaration on a New Economic Order (NIEO) aims at reducing economic inequalities between the North and the South.

1975: Conference on Security and Cooperation in Europe is finalized.

1982: UN Convention on the Law of the Sea regulates the finite resources of the ocean.

1984: Nicaragua wins 15–0 decision from the International Court of Justice against the U.S. for mining of the Managua harbor, blockading of its ports, and supporting counterrevolutionary activities (Contras); UN General Assembly adopts the Convention Against Torture and Other Cruel, Inhuman, or Degrading Treatment or Punishment.

1985: Vienna Convention establishes framework of worldwide cooperation for pollution control.

1987: Montreal Protocol builds on the Vienna Convention by calling for a phase-out of CFCs by the end of 1995.

1989: President Bush sends approximately 24,000 troops into Panama to oust and arrest Manuel Noriega; China cracks down on student demonstrators in Tiananmen Square; Helsinki declaration proposes halting production and use of CFCs by the year 2000.

1990: Iraq occupies Kuwait; UN Security Council approves military action to restore Kuwait's sovereignty; UN World Summit for Children is held in New York.

1991: U.S.-led coalition frees Kuwait from Iraqi occupation; United States and Soviet Union sign START treaty; UN begins peacekeeping in Cambodia.

1992: Bosnia secedes from Yugoslavia; Serbs begin "ethnic cleansing" of Bosnia; UN imposes sanctions and initiates peace-keeping operation in attempt to stop bloodshed in Yugoslavia; UN Conference on Environment and Development convenes (the "Earth Summit") in Rio de Janeiro.

1993: More than 120 nations sign the Chemical Weapons Convention to ban production, stockpiling, and use of chemical weapons.

1994: UN Conference on Population and Development is held in Cairo; nearly 180 nations adopt plan to prevent the world population from exceeding 7.2 billion people over the following two decades.

---

determine how nations should act toward one another and unilaterally enforce rules for such interactions. Chapter One likened domestic politics to a football field and international politics to a jungle: Both are competitive environments, but on the gridiron there are rules and referees, while the "law of the jungle" is "every creature for itself." Not surprisingly, in this environment, states often follow the principles of "kill or be killed" and "do unto others before they can do unto you," and the result has been frequent, violent conflict and war.

Throughout history, many people have been profoundly disturbed by this state of affairs, and it is easy to understand why. The death, destruction, and suffering caused by war over the centuries are powerful arguments for making the international system less anarchic. From the seventeenth century onward, systematic efforts have been made to establish some form of authority in the international system in the hope that doing so might facilitate peace and cooperation among nations. International law and organizations are manifestations of this hope, and this chapter looks at how they attempt to make the international system less anarchic.

The chapter begins with a definition of international law, an overview of how it is established, and an assessment of how effective it is in the absence of a global authority to ensure compliance with it. Special attention will be given to global conventions on human rights, which are among the most worthwhile and admirable components of international law, but are also the most frequently violated and difficult to enforce. Following this, the chapter turns to international organizations, especially those that have attempted to replace international anarchy with systems of collective security. The most recent of these is the United Nations, whose structure, function, successes, and failures will all be discussed in detail. Finally, the chapter looks at how other international groups, from the Organization for Economic Cooperation and Development (OECD) to Amnesty International, attempt to exert varying degrees of influence on international politics.

Not all groups covered in this chapter seek to promote international cooperation. Some, such as the Hezbollah and the Provisional Wing of the Irish Republican Army, carry on acts of violence to pursue their objectives. But all of the organizations and agreements examined here have one thing in common. In one way or another, intentionally or not, they are all forces for **globalization.** Humanitarian relief agencies and terrorist groups alike attempt to mobilize opinion and gather resources for solving problems across state boundaries. Some treaties and organizations try to solve global problems at the global level, while other groups strive to globalize a local conflict in the hope that other nations will intervene. It is clear, therefore, that while the successes attained by international law and organizations in making the world less anarchic are debatable, the increasing ability of various groups to voice their concerns on the world stage must be acknowledged. Though many have been slow to take hold, international institutions have become an integral part of global politics.

INTERNATIONAL LAW

International law, also referred to as the *law of nations*, may be defined as "a body of rules which binds states and other agents in world politics in their relations with one another."[1] International law has evolved in tandem with the nation-state system, from the Peace of Westphalia (see Chapter Two) to the present. It conforms to the decentralized nature of the international system, and differs from domestic law in two fundamental ways. First, the law of nations reflects the lack of an international **sovereign,** or single institution possessing a monopoly on coercive force. Because the international system lacks such a central authority, international law can only be enforced through **reciprocity** (doing unto other states as you would have them do unto you), individual or collective sanctions (such as freezing assets or imposing trade embargoes), or, when all else fails, reprisals (retaliation or response in kind). Second, international law differs from domestic law in that there is no global legislature, or lawmaking body, to set down laws for all nations. International law is therefore ultimately based on consent—states must accept its provisions, explicitly or implicitly, in order to be bound by them.[2]

The array of issues addressed by international law are diverse and wide-ranging. These areas include, but are not limited to, rules regarding human rights, warfare and aggression, the law of the sea, outer space, Antarctica, the environment, and the new international economic order. (Chapter Ten addresses several of these global issues in more detail). Before looking at how international law attempts to promote cooperative solutions to these problems, it is necessary to examine the origins of international law, and why states bother to obey it at all.

Violation and Adherence

Considering that there is no world legislature to make international law and no global authority to enforce it, one may wonder if states ever observe international law at all. Indeed, many states regularly flout international law when it runs counter to their national interests. In 1984, for instance, the government of Nicaragua (then ruled by the Soviet-backed Sandinista regime) won a unanimous decision from the International Court of Justice supporting its contention that the U.S. government's support of anti-Sandinista *contra* rebels and mining of Nicaraguan harbors violated international law. But the United States simply ignored the ruling. When Nicaragua took its claim to the UN Security Council, the United States vetoed its consideration.[3] Such flagrant violations of international law reinforce the widespread notion that it rarely works.

As with domestic law, however, violations regularly make the headlines, whereas adherence to the law is much more common—and therefore isn't news. A wide variety of actors, including governments, private companies, and individuals, adhere to international law on a regular basis. For example, freedom of the seas is observed as a customary principle of international law. Thousands of ships with millions of dollars worth of goods sail to hundreds of ports every day, unaccosted by pirates of other governments, and kidnapping or abuse of embassy personnel by host-country governments is rare. While international law may not always work as well as it is intended, it works better than is often realized.

Today, most governments justify what they do in terms of international law, even when their actions are questionable. For instance, when the Bush administration sent 24,000 U.S. soldiers to Panama in December 1989 to oust and arrest Panamanian dictator Manuel Noriega (who refused to relinquish the presidency of Panama despite having been defeated in an earlier election), the deployment was justified as "an exercise of the right of self-defense recognized in Article 51 of the United Nations charter" and "to fulfill our responsibilities under the Panama Canal Treaties."[4] Noriega, however, disputed the legality of this action, and claimed to be a prisoner of war rather than a common criminal. The incident serves to illustrate how the legality of an action under international law often depends on one's point of view—another effect of the lack of an internationally sovereign authority.

There are a number of reasons other than moral principle why states obey international law. First, international law provides a framework for the orderly conduct of international affairs. If norms of behavior such as the granting of diplomatic immunity were not followed, states would quickly find themselves unable to do business with one another. Nations adhere to international law because it is in their interest to preserve international order, just as most automobile drivers probably follow the convention of driving on the right side of the road for the sake of their own safety, even without a highway patrol to enforce regulations.

Second, states may adhere to the law of nations for fear of sanction or reprisal. For example, the use of chemical weapons in war was outlawed by the Geneva

THE FIRST INTERNATIONAL LAWYER

Dutch jurist Hugo Grotius (1583–1645) is considered the "father" of international law. Grotius began life as a very gifted child—he wrote poetry in Latin at age eight, and enrolled at Leiden University at eleven. Grotius gained firsthand experience in what would now be called human rights law when he was sentenced to life imprisonment for his political activities in 1618. He escaped to Paris in 1621, however, hidden in a box of books. In Paris, during the calamitous Thirty Years' War, he published *De Jure Belli ac Pacis (On the Law of War and Peace),* an ambitious study of the rules of conduct applying to nations. This work publicized many of the emerging practices of customary law, especially attempts to humanize the conduct of war.

Protocol of 1925. Although both Germany and Britain possessed stockpiles of chemical weapons during World War II, both elected not to use poison gas against each other because both feared retaliation in kind, with potentially dire consequences to civilian populations and industry. (Hitler had no qualms, however, about using poison gas to exterminate concentration camp inmates, who lacked the capability to respond in kind.)

Third, international law may be enforced by reciprocity. In many cases, the long-term benefits of observing international law outweigh the short-term advantages of violating it. If states expect that they will be interacting with each other in the future, and value their future relations highly enough, they will be more likely to follow laws and conventions as long as other states respond in good faith. This behavior is referred to as **tit for tat,** or doing as the other side does as long as the other side keeps doing it.[5] Many trade agreements are conducted on a tit-for-tat basis; the General Agreement on Tariffs and Trade (GATT), for example, specifies that if a country raises discriminatory tariffs on goods coming in from another, the second country has the right to respond with "countervailing" tariffs.

Reciprocity in adhering to international law promotes an international environment in which, in the long run, "cheaters never prosper." If a state routinely violates international norms, it may acquire a general reputation for lawbreaking that could result in international ignominy and erode opportunities for trade and cooperation with other nations. States that consistently prove they cannot be trusted at their word may become **"pariah states"** and be ostracized. Although North Korea initially signed the Nuclear Nonproliferation Treaty (see Chapter Six), it withdrew from the agreement in early 1993 and has repeatedly refused to allow international inspections of its nuclear facilities, despite mounting evidence of attempts to develop nuclear weapons. This reinforces the North Korean government's reputation for untrustworthiness and unpredictability, which continues despite the 1994 agreement with the U.S.

In his further writings, Grotius also formulated the legal basis for the principle of national sovereignty, which would later be codified in the Peace of Westphalia. When not devoting his energy to legal scholarship, he wrote works on history, linguistics, and theology as well as a prodigious amount of poetry. He served as the Swedish ambassador to France from 1634 until his death in a shipwreck in 1645, three years before the treaty ending the Thirty Years' War incorporated into its terms many of the concepts he developed. Though he achieved little fame during his lifetime, many of the ideas he espoused later became the guiding principles of the Concert of Europe and the United Nations.

Sources of International Law

Without a world legislature, who puts international law "on the books"? There are two primary sources of international law: treaties and customary practices. Essentially, signing a treaty constitutes explicit consent to be bound by international law, while customary practices establish international law through implied consent. (Similar principles apply in some aspects of domestic law: A person who signs a contract explicitly agrees to its provisions, while anyone who applies for a driver's license gives implied consent for a police officer to pull over a motorist suspected of driving while intoxicated.) In addition to treaties and customary practices, the writings of legal scholars, rulings of courts such as the International Court of Justice, and decisions of international organizations such as the UN help to refine, enrich, and expand upon international law.

Customary Practices   International custom, or **customary practices,** refers to established and consistent practices of states in international relations. The notion of custom as a source of law has its origins in the ancient Roman concept of *jus gentium*, the "law of the tribes," which were the common features Roman jurists identified among the subject peoples of their empire. Later, when states' adherence to unwritten rules of conduct or multilateral declarations became commonplace and widespread—that is to say, customary—they were regarded as binding on all states, even those that never expressly consented to them. The most prominent aspects of customary international law include diplomatic immunity and many provisions of human rights law, including the prohibition of slavery (later codified in the 1926 Slavery Convention), genocide (codified in the 1948 Genocide Convention), racial discrimination, and torture.[6]

The concept of **diplomatic immunity** illustrates how international law develops from customary practice. For centuries in Europe, diplomats representing foreign states were accorded freedom of movement without fear of molestation from the governments they were sent to negotiate with. UN Resolution 43/167 and the Vienna Convention on Diplomatic Relations codified what had by the nineteenth century become the practice of diplomatic immunity, or extending freedom from arrest and prosecution to accredited diplomats. This practice has become crucial to the stability of interstate relations, as negotiators must be able to conduct diplomatic business without worrying about being harassed, or arrested on trumped-up charges. (Members of Congress enjoy similar freedom from arrest in the United States.)

States violating this custom usually receive immediate international condemnation and political sanctions, as Iran did in 1979 when U.S. embassy personnel were kidnapped and held hostage. Controversy over this custom arises when embassy personnel fail to adhere to the provision of the 1961 Vienna Convention, which states that diplomats must abide by the laws of the host country. The inability of host countries to prosecute protected diplomats accused of serious crimes raises the question of how far the protection afforded by this custom should extend. Some countries, notably Libya, have been accused of sending terrorists abroad under cover of diplomatic passports. If a foreign diplomat is suspected of committing an offense, all a nation may do according to customary law is declare that individual *persona non grata* (an "unwelcome person") and expel him or her. To curb abuse of this practice, it is customary for the home country of the expelled diplomats to make a similar declaration regarding an equal number of the other country's envoys and order them out as well.

Treaties   Also known as charters, pacts, conventions, or covenants, **treaties** represent the second main source of international law. Forming a large part of modern international law, treaties are similar to written contracts in that they impose obligations only on the parties that sign them. However, if the provisions of a particular treaty become customary practice, it can be argued that it has become a general law binding on all states. International law takes treaties very seriously; in practice it is assumed that agreements must be kept (*pacta sunt servanda*) and performed in good faith (*bona fide*). Also, a state's internal laws cannot exempt it from compliance with international laws.

Some treaties become part of international law in a process quite similar to that of domestic legislation. UN conventions, for instance, become law in a three-stage process. Delegates from a member state must sign the treaty, the state's national legislature must then ratify it, and domestic legislation must finally be enacted to bring the nation into compliance. Article 18 of the 1969 Convention on the Law of Treaties stipulates that a state that has signed a treaty subject to ratification must refrain from acts that would defeat the object and purpose of the treaty.

Not all treaties are enacted through the United Nations, of course. Some are *bilateral,* or agreed upon by two countries. Unless it later entered into that agreement between those two countries, a third country would not be bound by its provisions. For example, when the United States and the Soviet Union signed the bilateral START arms reduction agreement in 1991, it was binding on these two countries only. Problems arose when the Soviet Union broke up at the end of the same year, leaving four Soviet successor states with nuclear weapons deployed on their territory—Russia, Ukraine, Belarus, and Kazakhstan.

As the volume of international transactions increases through the growth of global trade and communications, treaty-making has tended to become **multi-lateral**, or conducted between more than two parties at the same time. Many multilateral treaties are now hammered out in common forums, such as special conferences, such as the 1992 UN Conference on Environment and Development (the Earth Summit), or in intergovernmental organizations, such as the UN or Organization of American States (OAS).

The "New Era" promises an accelerating trend towards multilateral treaty-making, as global issues such as population growth, environmental degradation, resource depletion, and migration come to dominate the attention of governments. Treaty negotiations can strengthen already existent customary practices by creating new organizational venues to disseminate new information and foster international cooperation. Or, like the ill-starred **Mutual and Balanced Force Reductions (MBFR)** talks, which strove fruitlessly for over twenty years to reduce the North Atlantic Treaty Organization (NATO) and Warsaw Pact conventional forces, they can produce mountains of verbiage with no appreciable effect. (This constitutes another similarity between domestic and international lawmaking.) Overall, it appears that the trend toward globalization and greater cooperation among nations will become more pronounced as global issues continue to dominate domestic agendas.

AREAS OF INTERNATIONAL LAW

The Principle of Sovereignty

One of the fundamental principles of international law is national sovereignty. Set forth in the Peace of Westphalia in 1648 (see Chapter Two), this principle holds that individual states are the ultimate authorities within their own countries. (Before, under the feudal system, two or more rulers often held joint jurisdiction over various territories, which predictably caused frequent conflict.) A sovereign state has complete freedom of action in international law to deal with its own nationals ("personal sovereignty") and its own territory ("territorial sovereignty"), to make use of the public domain (the high seas, the atmosphere, and outer space), to enter into legal relationships with other sovereign states, to become a member of international organizations, to fight wars in self-defense, and to remain neutral when others are at war. Sovereignty also implies that, in all matters falling within the domestic jurisdiction of any state, any interference by another state is outside the scope of international law.[7]

Even though national sovereignty makes only one country sovereign over a given territory, other countries may claim the right to rule over that territory. In the 1930s Japan conquered Manchuria, Italy invaded Ethiopia, and Germany stormed into Austria and Czechoslovakia; in the 1970s Vietnam occupied Cambodia, and Soviet tanks rolled into Afghanistan; in the 1980s Israel and Syria invaded parts of Lebanon, and Argentina attempted to seize the Falkland Islands (Malvinas); and in 1990 Iraq occupied Kuwait. While few such transgressions against the rule of sovereignty go unprotested, many go unpunished. The League of Nations applied sanctions against Italy for attacking Ethiopia, protests were lodged at the UN against the Vietnamese invasion of Cambodia, and the United States placed a grain embargo against the USSR for its invasion of Afghanistan, but none of these measures convinced the invaders to pull out even though each departed years later through a combination of diplomatic and military pressure. Similarly, efforts to resolve the Falklands/Malvinas conflict by diplomatic means failed, and Britain fought a war with Argentina to secure the return of the islands. The UN applied economic sanctions against the Iraqi invasion of Kuwait, but stronger measures were needed to restore Kuwait's sovereignty: military force applied by a UN-sponsored and U.S.–led multinational coalition.

While armed intervention to redress transgressions of sovereignty can be effective, its legality is often subjective. Invaders frequently claim that failure to intervene in the transgressed territory would have lead to threats to their own or another country's sovereignty. For instance, in the years since civil war broke out in Lebanon in 1975, the United States, France, Israel, Syria, and the UN stationed troops in that country at various times, ostensibly to restore internal order. While U.S. troops withdrew after a terrorist's car bomb killed 241 U.S. Marines in 1983, Israeli and Syrian troops still occupy territory inside Lebanon to protect what both countries define as their vital interests. The Vietnamese and Soviet governments used similar justifications for invading and occupying Cambodia and Afghanistan, respectively. Detractors argue that such military interventions are really opportunistic seizures of territory or attempts to set up regimes friendly to the invaders.

Another problem with national sovereignty is that some countries believe that it allows them to flout their international commitments. Though North Korea signed the Nuclear Nonproliferation treaty and an additional pact obligating its plants to inspection by the UN International Atomic Energy Agency (IAEA), it has not always permitted the inspections to take place. One North Korean newspaper warned that forcing inspections "on us and the inviolable soil of our country . . . would result in plunging the whole land of the north and south into the holocaust of war."[8] Then North Korea simply withdrew from the treaty and later indefinitely suspended its withdrawal. These actions have raised international concerns over its nuclear program to even higher levels.

The thorniest issue pertaining to national sovereignty is the notion of "personal sovereignty," which implies that since a sovereign government has exclusive control over its subjects, individuals cannot be the targets of international law or claim any rights under that system for themselves.[9] This aspect of national sovereignty has allowed governments that do not face democratic constraints on their power to run roughshod over human rights. Dictators such as Hitler in Germany and Pol Pot in Cambodia committed unspeakable crimes against humanity while they were in power; Hitler committed suicide before he could be brought to justice, and Pol Pot remains a leader of the Khmer Rouge insurgent faction at the time of this writing. Globalization, however, has been able to bring recent human rights abuses to the world's attention; while Hitler and Pol Pot carried out their extermination programs in secret, China's 1989 crackdown on the student demonstrations at Tiananmen Square was broadcast throughout the world on television.

Human Rights under International Law

The idea that sovereign governments should be subject to some form of international legal constraints to prevent them from abusing the rights of their citizens is a relatively new phenomenon, although the idea that human beings have certain inalienable rights is not new. In eleventh- and twelfth-century Europe, Christian canon lawyers debated the legal maxim that "an unjust law is not a law," which implies that even though a law has been enacted through due process, it may not be in accordance with accepted standards of justice. This developed from Roman and Greek philosophical principles that human beings have inherent rights regardless of the laws enacted by governments. After the Protestant Reformation, writers, including John Locke and Jean Jacques Rousseau, promoted the idea of a social contract that conferred rights as well as obligations on citizens and their rulers. The English Bill of Rights (1689), the American Declaration of Independence (1776) and Bill of Rights (1789), and the French Declaration of the Rights of Man (1789) offered lists of fundamental rights and freedoms regarded as both inherent in all human individuals, by the sole virtue of their humanity, and as inalienable, not capable of being taken away or given up.

In the 1800s international law began to develop a doctrine of humanitarian intervention in cases where states committed shocking atrocities against their own subjects. For example, international collaboration pushed for the abolition of the slave trade (at the 1884 Berlin Conference on Africa) and then slavery (at the 1926 League of Nations' Slavery Convention), set regulations for the conduct of war and treatment of prisoners (at the Hague and Geneva Conventions in the years before World War I), and offered protection from gross exploitation of workers (through the League of Nations' International Labor Organization, founded in 1919).

Efforts to extend international law to cover human rights were hindered, however, by the doctrine of **positive law,** which held that rights could not derive from a higher law—divine or secular—above men and women, but instead human action was the foundation of law. Therefore, according to positivists, international law stems from the tacit or specific actions of people, and any law is meaningless without a sovereign authority to enforce it. (The opposite doctrine, **natural law,** holds that certain human rights derive from just such a "higher law," divine or secular, above people, and thus cannot justly be taken away by governments.) Many positivists even denied the very existence of international law, contending that states could act however they wished in domestic affairs. The doctrine of positive law was taken to its cruel extreme in the National Socialist laws, enacted by the German Nazi government in 1936 at

Nuremberg, which legalized first the persecution and then the wholesale murder of Germany's Jews.

Nuremberg Trials

During World War II, the Allies served notice on the Axis that trials for violations of international law would be held after the war. The St. James's Palace Declaration of 1942 stated, "There will be punishment of those guilty or responsible for the crimes, whether they have ordered them, perpetrated them or participated in them." After the Allied victory, Nuremberg was chosen in 1946 as the site of trials for Nazi officials accused of "crimes against humanity" in the Holocaust and other atrocities (see Chapter Three). The Charter of the International Military Tribunal of Nuremberg was endorsed by the fledgling UN in 1946. The charter defines crimes against humanity as "murder, extermination, enslavement, deportation, and other inhuman acts committed against any civilian population before or during the war, or prosecutions on political, racial or religious grounds . . . whether or not violation of the domestic law of the country were perpetrated." The document thus asserts the superiority of international law over national law in questions of the grievous violation of human rights.

Twenty-one of the top Nazi leaders were convicted and sentenced to death or to life imprisonment, and ninety-eight lower-ranking defendants were also convicted. (The proceedings and many issues surrounding them are dramatized in the classic courtroom drama film *Judgment at Nuremberg*.) Analogous trials were held in Tokyo for Japanese officials arraigned on similar charges. Two legal and moral principles became part of international law at Nuremberg: Orders given by one's superiors do not justify transgressions against human rights, and individuals as well as governments may be held accountable for war crimes.

After the Holocaust and Nuremberg Trials of 1946, the UN took the lead in codifying principles of human rights into international law. An early result was the 1948 Universal Declaration of Human Rights, a comprehensive statement of principles not binding on UN member states, but generally recognized as customary law. In 1966 the UN General Assembly strengthened the declaration's provisions with three covenants: the International Covenant on Civil and Political Rights; the International Covenant on Economic, Social, and Cultural Rights; and the Optional Protocol, which allows citizens to sue governments for redress of human rights violations. The covenants received the required number of ratifications (thirty-five nations) and went into effect in 1976.

The UN has refined some of the basic principles through recent, more specific agreements. These include an agreement outlawing racial discrimination (1969), a convention on eliminating discrimination against women (1981), an accord forbidding torture (1984), and a convention on children's rights (1990). Not surprisingly, these and other agreements have not escaped controversy: Western, industrial countries have tended to focus on individual civil rights and freedoms (reflecting Lockean tradition), while non-Western countries frequently stress collective economic rights (consistent with Marxist thought). These differences have led to questions over how to enforce human rights around the world.

Nazi war criminals listen during the third day of document presentation at the Nuremberg Trials. Each was prosecuted for crimes against humanity committed during World War II.

Source: © Bettmann Archive.

Can Human Rights Decrees Be Enforced?

Historically, when principles of human rights have clashed with the principle of state sovereignty, sovereignty has usually won out. Torture, imprisonment for political activity, and other abuses of human rights are practiced by governments in many parts of the world, despite protests from the UN and human rights organizations like Amnesty International (the latter being dedicated to the release of all political prisoners).

During the Cold War, the issue of human rights became politicized along East-West lines, as UN member states disagreed fiercely over who was in violation of human rights law. When the United States accused Communist and non-aligned regimes of human right abuses, those regimes countered that such charges masked an "imperialistic" desire to interfere in their internal affairs and cited examples of human rights abuses in the West. In the late 1970s, for instance, the United States repeatedly accused the USSR of violating the human rights provisions of the 1975 Helsinki Accords, citing Soviet restraints on Jewish emigration and imprisonment of dissidents in psychiatric hospitals. In response, the Soviet Union maintained for years that Leonard Peltier, a Native American rights activist convicted in the deaths of two FBI agents in a June 1975 shootout at Wounded Knee, South Dakota, was a political prisoner. Peltier's attorney even visited the Soviet Union in 1988 to seek aid on behalf of the jailed militant.[10] Recent controversies over alleged U.S. violations of human rights include the 1991 police beating of Los Angeles motorist Rodney King and Amnesty International's condemnations of U.S. death penalty policies. China and several African countries charged the United States with hypocrisy in citing other countries for human rights violations given its own problems at home.

With the demise of the Cold War, countries have been more willing to consider enforcing human rights guarantees with multilateral intervention, at least in principle. In practice, however, the UN has been very reluctant to commit troops to potential combat situations in order to safeguard human rights. The peacekeeping mission in the former Yugoslavia illustrates the difficulties inherent in preventing human rights violations or bringing their perpetrators to justice. Since fighting broke out over the secession of Croatia in 1991 and Bosnia in 1992, more than two hundred thousand people have lost their lives, and over 2 million have been driven from their homes in the resulting conflicts.[11] Serbian forces have carried out a policy of "ethnic cleansing," entailing the imprisonment, torture, rape, and murder of Muslim Bosnians, as well as their expulsion from Serb-controlled territory. Croatian and Muslim forces have committed similar atrocities. Although the UN Security Council authorized the formation of an international court to investigate and punish war crimes committed in the war-ravished ex-Yugoslav republics, little could be done to stop the massive human rights abuses or apprehend those accused of ordering them without the use of military intervention, a step the UN has been very reluctant to take because of the risk of high military and civilian casualties. Therefore the UN peacekeepers have not been able to enforce international law, but rather have been reduced to the dual roles of observers and providers of humanitarian assistance.

Warfare and Aggression

Another important area of international law concerns states' conduct during periods of warfare and aggression. Efforts to regulate the conduct of warfare have evolved from the task of articulating the legal obligations of belligerents to the relatively more difficult one of securing protection for individual noncombatants during wartime. An early agreement on the conduct of warfare was the 1856 Declaration of Paris, which clarified the rights of neutral vessels. However, it is the 1945 UN charter that contains the most universally accepted rules of conventional warfare. The charter allows states to use force or other coercive methods (including economic sanctions) against other states in self-defense or as part of an organized peacekeeping organization. In an anarchic environment though, aggression is still too often justified as self-defense when it is perceived as furthering a state's national interests.

Another set of conventions sets limits on the methods of warfare. The 1899 Hague Convention and 1925 Geneva Protocol, in particular, prohibit the use of poisonous or asphyxiating gases. As of 1986, 105 nations had signed the 1925

This cartoon suggests that Americans monitor human rights violations in Third World countries without always ascertaining the true picture.

Source: © Clay Bennett, *St. Petersburg Times.*

accord, although the U.S. Senate did not ratify it until December 1974. In January 1993, 125 nations signed the Chemical Weapons Convention, which is much stronger—banning the possession, acquisition, production, stockpiling, transfer, and use of chemical weapons. There is also an accord banning the use of biological weapons. Saddam Hussein violated the accord on poisonous gas use during the 1980s in his war with Iran and against his own Kurdish residents, but the world community was slow to respond.

A third set of agreements seeks to protect human rights during warfare. Rules to protect sick and wounded combatants are laid out in the 1864 Geneva Convention. The rights of prisoners of conventional war were refined most recently in 1977, which extended protection to those involved in guerilla warfare.

As can be surmised by the violations mentioned in the preceding paragraphs, efforts to regulate the conduct of warfare, protect combatants and noncombatants alike, and punish those who violate the rules have been only partially successful. The reasons for this limited success stem not only from the enforcement

THE 1992 RIO EARTH SUMMIT

Few events have captured the world's imagination as the 1992 Earth Summit in Rio de Janerio did, but few have also given rise to as many misunderstandings and false hopes. The two years of preparation for the conference were marked by conflict, especially between the industrialized Northern states and the developing South, and between the United States and other states in the North. The conference did produce a weak treaty on global warming and a stronger treaty intended to preserve the world's biodiversity. However, it remains to be seen whether these actions will lead to the kind of detailed environmental action plan that conference organizers desired.

The conference had its roots in the 1972 UN Stockholm Conference on the Human Environment, which elevated environmental issues to the international level by urging states to cooperate in their resolution. Then, in 1983, the UN-created World Commission on Environment and Development warned that patterns of contemporary economic growth were not environmentally sustainable. Although states at the regional level had united in solving environmental problems, the world was still becoming a dirtier, noisier, and poorer place. The 1990s brought additional international environmental concerns, such as global warming (caused by the buildup of carbon dioxide and methane in the atmosphere) and rapid loss of plant and animal species (a result of industrialization).

The central question at the Earth Summit was how to protect the environment and still maintain development. This question pitted North against South with respect to financial aid and transfers of technology. Industrialized states feared that issues of

of international law in an anarchic environment, but also from the inherent contradiction of trying to establish rules of "conduct" for violent, aggressive, and often desperate acts. Such rules work only when both sides fear retaliation should they violate them.

New International Economic Order

Inspired by the work of the 1964 and 1972 UN Conferences on Trade and Development (UNCTAD), the UN General Assembly adopted the Declaration on the Establishment of a New International Economic Order (NIEO) in late 1974. The measures in the declaration consist of proposals advanced by the South (the **less developed countries,** or **LDCs**) for eliminating the economic inequities between them and the advanced industrial nations of the North. (See Chapter Eight.)

The NIEO advocates permanent sovereignty of developing states over their natural resources, promotion of technology transfer, regulation of multinational corporations, debt reform (in 1974, debt servicing constituted about 20 to 25 aid and debt relief would simply take on an environmental label, which would make it more difficult for Northern nations to negotiate foreign-aid agreements, since domestic environmental groups also would want their concerns accounted for. Developing states argued that although they supported protection of the environment, they would be unable to implement programs without financial and technical assistance.

How to balance environmental and economic concerns was also the basis for a more specific dispute at Rio: whether or not to include reductions of carbon dioxide in the World Climate Convention. Western European states, most of which had already agreed as members of the European Union to limits on emissions of carbon dioxide and other pollutants, called for stringent international reductions. As the state with the highest levels of carbon dioxide emissions, the United States charged that these demands were too costly to undertake, especially when the effects of global warming remained uncertain. Indeed, the economic costs associated with air-pollution regulations had already led to "environmental" conflict within the United States. Environmentalists and industry, for instance, disagreed over the implementation of a 1990 Clean Air Act rule that allows businesses to increase polluting emissions without public notice. And automobile companies attacked the Environmental Protection Agency for proposed changes in smog-testing rules that would increase transportation costs. All in all, the contentious Earth Summit offered a vivid illustration of the difficulty of reconciling specific needs and interests with the overweening objective of safeguarding the global environment.

percent of the South's foreign exchange earnings), and elimination of some developed countries' tariff barriers.

Many NIEO advocates believed that Third World poverty is an inherent by-product of world capitalism. This belief, along with the economic strains caused by the Arab oil embargo and OPEC price rises of 1973, heightened fears in the industrialized North that the LDCs would attempt to restructure the world economic system to the North's disadvantage. So far, these fears have proven largely unfounded. NIEO has produced divisions between the poorest of the poor countries' demand for preferential treatment of Third World exports and the demands of the less disadvantaged countries (for example, the newly industrialized countries of Taiwan, Malaysia, and Indonesia) over the lifting of trade barriers in the industrialized world. Furthermore, the large number of commodity and raw-materials producer cartels (such as the International Coffee Organization) set up to maintain and raise price levels have not avoided the difficulties that also hurt the Organization of Petroleum Exporting Countries (OPEC) in the 1980s: overproduction, the growth of substitutes, and falling world demand. Overall, then, the growth of international law into areas of economic concern symbolize the ever increasing globalization and interdependence of the world's economies.

The Environment

We turn now to another set of concerns that also know no national border: concerns about the environment. Protection of the environment has become a focal point on several continents for international cooperation *and* conflict, especially between the economically advanced and less developed countries.

In 1972 delegates at the Stockholm Conference on the Human Environment issued and approved the Declaration of the Human Environment, which stresses that poor countries cannot and should not bear the largest burden of cleaning up the environment, and that countries should cooperate in establishing rules for reducing pollution that crosses political borders. The Stockholm Declaration's twenty-six principles have formed the basis for further cooperative effort in areas such as marine and air pollution, depletion of the ozone layer, and global warming and the so-called greenhouse effect. Recently established, the UN Commission on Sustainable Development has been charged with monitoring progress in implementing "Agenda 21," an environmental action program adopted at the 1992 Rio Summit that covers these various issue areas in a comprehensive and systematic manner.

Meanwhile, several other agreements that relate to the environment have been enacted. Many of the conventions pertaining to marine pollution have been formulated under the auspices of a UN subsidiary organization, the International Maritime Organization. These agreements include the 1975 Convention that held liable ships from which polluting oil escaped for any pollution damage caused. Specific accords on air pollution include the 1979 Convention and Resolution on Long-range Transboundary Air Pollution and a 1985 protocol (signed by Canada, but not by the United Kingdom or the United States) to this agreement on reducing sulphur emissions and their transboundary movement. In 1986 Canada and the United States agreed on a plan to combat the effect of "acid rain," which occurs in Canada but is caused by pollution from power plants and factories in the United States. However, the plan stalled in the U.S. Congressional legislative process until the passage of the Clean Air Act in 1990.

Another set of important environmental treaties pertains to preservation of the ozone layer (the belt of rarified gas above the earth's surface which protects us from the sun's harmful rays). Building on the 1985 Vienna convention on the ozone layer, the 1987 Montreal protocol called for a freeze in the production of **chlorofluorocarbons,** or **CFCs** (a primary agent of ozone depletion found in aerosols and refrigerants), and a nonbinding 1989 Helsinki declaration (signed by seventy-nine countries) that proposed halting production and use of CFCs completely by the year 2000. This set of treaties has divided the advanced and developing countries. The European Union countries, Canada, the United States, and Australia all announced dramatic unilateral cuts, but several developing countries, including China and India, have protested the enormous cost of adapting to environmentally friendly technologies. The arguments of those developing nations that have opposed international environmental law is quite controversial, but also interesting: Since the industrialized nations took over 100 years to develop their economies, contaminating much of the world's environment along the way and depleting the natural resources of their colonies, shouldn't the newly independent, developing countries have an equal opportunity to modernize their economies without costly environmental regulations imposed on them by the already developed nations?

Antarctica

An issue related to the environment that has produced more cooperation than conflict is the use of Antarctica. Since the late 1950s, the uses of the resources of the South Pole, especially for scientific purposes, have become increasingly subject to international regulation. In 1959 twelve nations signed the thirty-year Antarctic Treaty, which declared that Antarctica shall be used for peaceful purposes only. The treaty also prohibited new territorial claims to the continent, and outlawed nuclear explosions and the storage of radioactive waste there. Later, twenty additional states had become parties to the treaty, as well as states from the former Soviet Union.

Other efforts to impose international regulations on that icy land mass to the south have not escaped controversy, however. In 1989 France and Australia, backed by Belgium, Italy, and a coalition of 200 environmental organizations in thirty-five countries, launched a proposal to ban all mining on the South Pole and establish a nature reserve there. The United States, Great Britain, Japan, New Zealand, and Chile opposed the ban, contending that it would be too detrimental to business and economic development. So, another agreement was drafted and signed in 1991 by representatives from twenty-four nations. It banned mining and oil exploration in Antarctica for a period of fifty years and extended the original treaty's ban on use of the continent for military purposes as well.[12]

Law of the Sea

The Law of the Sea is an international treaty that governs uses of the oceans. Initially drafted by the UN in 1958, a comprehensive **UN Convention on the Law of the Sea (UNCLOS)** was not approved until April 1982, following years of protracted and often volatile multilateral negotiations. In simple terms, the convention divides the world's oceans into public (free-access) and private (regulated-access) property zones for the purpose of regulating competition over the finite resources of the world's oceans. For example, the area of water extending twelve miles from a state's coastline is defined as that state's "territorial waters." Each state is also permitted exclusive rights to exploit natural resources lying within 200 miles of its shorelines.

What to do with the remaining, undivided part of the ocean has proven to be more controversial. Lacking the sophisticated mining technology of the major industrial states, the less developed countries suggested that an International Seabed Authority (ISA) be established to manage ocean resources beyond the 200-mile limit, including the mining of ocean-floor materials. The advanced, industrialized countries, however, want to enjoy continued free access. Such concerns over business interests prevented the United States and Great Britain, among others, from signing the 1982 UNCLOS Treaty. The Reagan administration complained that the treaty's regulation of deep-seabed mining was in opposition to the economic interests of U.S. companies, although the administration did agree to abide by other provisions in UNCLOS.

Clearly, the issues surrounding UNCLOS illustrate the obstacles in formulating international law. What appears to be in accordance with most nations' interest might run counter to those of a few, and if the few are powerful, they may count for more than the majority. It usually takes at least minimal support by key states to sign and successfully implement an agreement in international law. As is the case with many other multilateral treaties, further negotiation will be necessary to bring about an agreement on the Law of the Sea that all interested parties will be willing to sign. Meanwhile, however, the required minimum of sixty states ratified or acceded to the treaty and it came into force in November 1994.

Outer Space

It is appropriate to conclude our discussion of international law with a look to the future. Most treaties pertaining to outer space are analogous to the Law of the Sea, because they address an area equally accessible (or inaccessible) to all of humankind, regardless of artificially imposed political boundaries. However, since space exploration has been generally limited to the advanced industrial nations, with a few exceptions, laws regulating outer space have not been subject to intense North-South disagreements. In this area there has been a lack of pronounced international conflict, even during the Cold War, although the comparative quiet might have ended if the Soviet-American conflict had continued and America's "Star Wars" program had been implemented.

Among its sixteen articles, the 1967 Outer Space Treaty recognizes a common interest for all humankind in space exploration and use, prohibits territorial claims in space, and extends the provisions of the 1963 Test-Ban Treaty (which prohibited nuclear testing in outer space) by forbidding states to orbit weapons of mass destruction or place them on celestial bodies. The 1984 Moon Treaty, which no state with any space capability has ratified and incorporated into its national law, declares that the Moon and all its natural resources, green cheese or otherwise, are the "common heritage of mankind."

States have not devised any legal mechanisms for resolving other problems. One of these relates to space "junk." It has been estimated that 85,000 fragments larger than one centimeter, ranging from burnt-out rockets to flying bolts, are cluttering space and threatening to collide with operational spacecraft. Another problem pertains to the location of the boundary between air space and outer space. Just where should the earth's atmosphere legally end and outer space begin? This question is important, because it affects the jurisdiction covered by space treaties and the applicable area to which environmental agreements on the atmosphere apply.

The Verdict on International Law

The successes and failures of international law over the centuries suggest that the same attitudes toward law that prevail among individuals are shared by states. Some persons obey the law because they believe it is their moral duty to do so; others disregard it whenever possible, and still others are swayed by circumstances. Similarly, some governments have taken great pains to abide by international law; others have repeatedly and flagrantly ignored it; while still others weigh the advantages of breaking the law against the risk and costs of enforcement sanctions in a given situation before deciding whether or not to obey. The vital role that effective enforcement plays in keeping honest people honest and making dishonest ones think twice before breaking the law thus has implications for international law. Generally speaking, elements of international law that have been readily enforced, such as diplomatic immunity, the prohibition of slavery, and the General Agreement on Tariffs and Trade, are less frequently violated than those provisions that nations have been unwilling or unable to enforce, such as the Kellogg-Briand Pact (which outlawed war except in self-defense) or conventions against torture.

As this section has shown, the international system is not a totally anarchic environment. The world may perhaps best be likened to a town in the American Old West that lacks a competent sheriff or marshall. Laws are on the books, and there may even be a courthouse and jail, but catching suspected criminals and bringing them to trial is a chancy business. Because the authorities cannot keep order, many citizens carry guns, and violent and sometimes deadly fights break out all too often. Persons who are wronged may resort to vigilante justice, taking the law into their own hands, often without regard for the rights of the accused. Even the most dangerous criminals can be brought to justice, however, when a posse is organized and sets out to catch the desperados.

The "Wild West" analogy suggests that good organization is the key to effective law enforcement in a society without a sovereign authority. This thought occurred to international jurists generations ago, prompting many to give first priority to the establishment and strengthening of international organizations. The next section will examine how well their efforts have succeeded.

INTERNATIONAL ORGANIZATIONS

While states may be the most important actors in the international system, they are not the most numerous. The *Yearbook of International Organizations* lists over 24,000 entries, as compared to about 200 nation-states[13]. Despite the proliferation of international organizations (IOs) in the last few decades, a debate continues over whether they are in fact manipulated and controlled by governments. In either case, it is clear that international organizations try to make the world a less anarchic place by assuming tasks states cannot or will not undertake themselves, from humanitarian efforts to peacekeeping. They are

AT A GLANCE

INTERNATIONAL ORGANIZATIONS: INTERGOVERNMENTAL (IGOs) AND NONGOVERNMENTAL (NGOs)

Specialized IGOs with Global Membership

Promote international mutual assistance between members of a specific field (for example, Interpol provides assistance to law enforcement)

Examples: Interpol, World Health Organization, International Civil Aviation Organization, International Atomic Energy Commission

Notes: Sometimes become involved in political controversies related to where they are situated (for example, Interpol, in 1938, moved to Berlin and came under Nazi control)

General-Purpose Regional IGOs

Promote regional security and provide forum for resolving regional disputes

Examples: League of Arab States (Arab League), Organization of American States, Commonwealth of Independent States, European Union, and Association of South-East Asian Nations

Notes: The European Union is the most successful general-purpose regional IGO. It began in 1957 as primarily an economic union.

Specialized Regional or Limited-Membership IGOs

Promote collective defense, human rights, or political issues

Examples: North Atlantic Treaty Organization, Conference on Security and Cooperation in Europe

Notes: Limited-membership. IGOs are not always effective in promoting local security (for example, NATO was unable to take effective action in Yugoslavia).

Other Specialized IGOs

Oversee primarily economic matters

Examples: Organization for Economic Cooperation and Development, European Free Trade Area, and Organization of Petroleum-Exporting Countries

---

both a cause and an effect of globalization in the contemporary era, and they are called upon to deal with an increasingly wide array of political, social, and economic issues.

IOs may be divided into two broad categories, intergovernmental organizations and nongovernmental organizations. **Intergovernmental organizations (IGOs)** are associations of sovereign states that are established through formal agreements. IGOs include the United Nations (UN), the North Atlantic Treaty Organization (NATO), and the European Union (EU). **Nongovernmental organizations (NGOs)** are groups of institutions and individuals established through more informal means. Greenpeace, Amnesty International, and the International Olympic Committee are familiar examples. Even though NGOs do not include states in their membership, and so lie outside the structure of traditional international politics, many have exerted a significant impact on world affairs. Groups such as Amnesty International have influenced governments' policies through public pressure and lobbying, while organizations

Notes: OPEC was created in 1960 by oil producers to increase their profits from oil exports.

Humanitarian Organizations (NGOs)
Work toward ameliorating pain and suffering or otherwise forwarding the welfare of humanity

Examples: International Red Cross, Amnesty International, Doctors without Borders, International Child Care USA, Save the Children, International Community for the Relief of Starving and Suffering

Notes: Many of the most famous NGOs are humanitarian organizations.

Terrorist Organizations (NGOs)
Use violence or terror for political aims

Examples: Abu Nidal terrorist group, provisional wing of the Irish Republican Army, Hezbollah, Red Brigade

Notes: Although terror and murder are easy to recognize, the categorization of an organization as a terrorist group is often politically charged. One side's "terrorist" may be the other side's "freedom fighter."

Multinational Corporations (MNCs)
Exist for financial reasons: seek worldwide profits, promote needs of the home country

Examples: Sanwa Bank, General Motors, AT&T, IBM, Mitsubishi, and Toshiba

Notes: MNCs are seen by some as having inhibited Third World development and by others as having promoted it. They are also NGOs.

like *Medicin sans Frontiers* ("Doctors without Borders") have acted directly to provide humanitarian relief.

IOs can be further categorized by their membership base and intended purpose. Some, such as the International Red Cross, seek members throughout the world, while others are oriented towards a particular region, like the Economic Community of West African States. Multipurpose organizations such as the Organization of American States (OAS) handle a broad range of tasks, while specialized organizations like the **International Criminal Police Organization (Interpol)** perform more specific functions. The charts in the "At a Glance" box indicate the wide range and diversity of contemporary IOs. The sections that follow are intended to give the reader an idea of the roles IOs play in global politics and economics, thus illustrating the impact IOs have on the international system. The survey of international organizations will begin with a discussion of those IOs historically most prominent on the world stage: intergovernmental organizations designed to foster collective security.

INTERGOVERNMENTAL ORGANIZATIONS

The primary reason why IGOs have taken on increasingly important roles in the nineteenth and twentieth centuries is that sovereign nation-states gradually came to the realization that they could not address all problems that plague the international system by themselves. They came to acknowledge that institutions promoting and facilitating international cooperation are required in order to deal more effectively with problems that affect them all.

By now, the reader has become familiar with IGOs that address a variety of issues. For example, the UN is the premier global organization, addressing a range of issues, while the EU is a regional organization focused mainly on economic issues. Both were established with the primary purpose of promoting cooperation in day-to-day matters, as well as resolving acute conflicts. Although various IGOs frequently propose solutions for problems that confront states, states often ignore or fail to abide by the IGOs' recommendations and decisions for fear of losing their sovereign powers. Because one of the most vital sovereign rights of a nation-state is that of self-defense, organizations formed to promote collective security as an improvement over the anarchic "every state for itself" security environment have found it very difficult to achieve their objectives despite centuries of effort. The sections that follow reveal the constant tension that exists between sovereignty and cooperation within IGOs designed to provide collective security.

GENEALOGY OF THE UNITED NATIONS

Concert of Europe

As discussed in Chapter Two, the Treaty of Paris (1814–1815) and the Congress of Vienna (1814–1815) established the Concert of Europe to restore the European balance of power after the Napoleonic Wars. As the Quadruple Alliance (Austria, Britain, Prussia, and Russia), the concert fulfilled its immediate purpose by defeating Napoléon once and for all at Waterloo in 1815. The Congress of Vienna revealed, however, that the concert was not an autonomous organization that could make rules for sovereign nation-states in a disinterested manner. The Congress disposed of much European territory in a way that reflected the existing power relationships among the European great powers. Once the monarchy under Louis XVIII had been restored, France was confined to its somewhat expanded 1792 borders. As for the rest of Europe, to the victors went the spoils: Austria gained parts of Italy, Prussia gained parts of Austria, Russia gained most of Poland and Finland, Britain gained overseas territories seized from France and the Dutch, and the Netherlands regained its independence. The world's first collective-security organization did not start life in an unselfish spirit of international cooperation.

While the concert system at first dampened nationalist and liberal aspirations of many European peoples (including those of Belgium, Greece, Italy, and the German Confederation, among others), it did keep the peace among ideologically opposed great powers. Nevertheless, the excessively elitist orientation of the concert's concept of balance power made it incapable of responding to the desire on the part of many subject people in Europe for national self-determination, and this elitism proved to be its Achilles' heel. As Chapter Three recounts, the concert deteriorated in the latter part of the nineteenth century, and the unstable peace it kept collapsed with the outbreak of World War I.

The League of Nations

The successor of the Concert of Europe was the League of Nations, created by the Treaty of Versailles at the end of World War I in order to prevent another catastrophic global war (see Chapters Two and Three).[14] The Geneva-based organization lasted from 1919 until 1946, although for all practical purposes it was moribund by 1939. Many would argue that the League was in fact stillborn, because the isolationist United States did not ratify the Versailles Treaty, which incorporated the League's charter. Without the support of the most powerful country, the organization could do little to prevent the instances of military aggression that led to World War II.

Unlike the Concert of Europe, which operated informally, the League was specifically chartered as a formal international organization dedicated to arbitration of international disputes, disarmament, and open diplomacy. Its founders were convinced that the nineteenth-century doctrine of the "balance of power," loosely maintained by the concert, failed to prevent World War I because that doctrine was in disharmony with the ideals of national self-determination. As a result, a more active form of collective security, an "international police force," was deemed necessary for preventing future war. Collective security is an attempt to replace the "every state for itself" of the anarchic international system with a "one for all, and all for one" mentality; in other words, "the organizing principle of collective security is the respect for the moral and legal obligation to consider an attack by any nation upon a member of the alliance as an attack upon all members of the alliance."[15] By ostensibly guaranteeing the security of all states in the international system regardless of their size or power, it was hoped that collective security would be a mechanism to pull states away from the brink of war in the nick of time.

In reality, collective security proved very difficult to organize. To begin with, states such as Britain and France continued to practice balance-of-power politics, as demonstrated by the way they handled the Italian invasion of Ethiopia in 1935 (see Chapter Three for details). Additionally, the League did not include key global players in its membership. Original members Japan and Italy quit in 1933 and 1937, respectively. After having failed to gain a reversal of the provisions of the Versailles Treaty, Germany also withdrew from the League in 1933. A few months after the Soviets signed the Nazi-Soviet Pact and Hitler invaded Poland in 1939, a League council resolution revoked the USSR's five-year old membership. And, as mentioned before, the United States never joined the League and thus missed many opportunities to exert its influence to avert the events that escalated into World War II.

The League of Nations' decision-making structure also hampered the organization's political power. There were three main components to the League: the Assembly, composed of representatives from all member states; the Council, consisting of permanent seats held by the most powerful states as well as rotating members chosen by the Assembly; and the Secretariat, a primarily administrative organ. For example, the Council, which during the history of the League ranged from eight to fourteen members, handled mainly political matters. These included major disputes likely to lead to war, as well as minor problems such as frontier adjustments. All decisions of substance required a unanimous vote of all Council members, except for those directly involved in the dispute in question (whose votes did not count). However, any members of the League Assembly whose interests were concerned in the decision's outcome also had the right to veto League action.

Thus, the League was doubly constrained in taking action against belligerents. In the first place, the negative vote of any member (including one in the Assembly, not just the Council) sufficed to block any decision to authorize sanctions. Few of the Council's decisions were vetoed, if only because they tended to be watered down to near-meaninglessness. Second, even when the Council could manage to get a unanimous decision to use force, the League found it almost impossible to enforce the sanctions available to it, which ranged from trade embargoes to air and naval strikes against offending nations. The League's deficiencies rendered it powerless to stop Italy from invading Corfu (a Greek island) in 1923 and Ethiopia in 1935, to stop Bolivia and Paraguay from fighting over possession of the Chaco region in a war that claimed 200,000 lives (1932–1935), to stop Japan from invading Manchuria in 1931, to stop Germany from its host of treaty violations and aggressive acts in the years before World War II, or to stop the Spanish Civil War.

In many respects, the structure of the League was an overreaction to the great-power politics that plagued the Concert of Europe. The feebleness of the League's collective-security provisions reflected a forlorn hope that these measures could work through moral force alone, without the backing of the most powerful states. But without the tangible support and concerted effort of the great powers, the organization's vacillations and meek declarations merely aggravated expansionist dictators, inviting further aggression. After such aggression led to a war even more horrible than the First World War, world leaders attempted to construct an organization that could ensure the widest possible respect for and adherence to its decisions.

United Nations

President Franklin D. Roosevelt and Secretary of State Cordell Hull coined the name of the League of Nations' successor organization in the 1942 Declaration of the United Nations. (British Prime Minister Churchill liked Roosevelt's proposed name "United Nations" better than his own suggestion of "Associated Powers.") The new organization was officially established in June 1945 when fifty-one founding members signed the charter of the United Nations (UN), which came into effect that October, after the surrender of Germany and Japan ended World War II. The League of Nations quietly voted itself out of existence and transferred its assets to the new UN in April 1946.

Thus, the UN supplanted the League of Nations as the preeminent collective-security organization in the international system. Its primary purpose was and still is to maintain international peace and security. It is also dedicated to developing friendly relations between peoples, cooperating internationally in solving international economic, social, cultural, and humanitarian problems, and promoting respect for human rights. The UN charter established six primary organs of the United Nations, headquartered in New York City. These six organs are the General Assembly, the Security Council, the Economic and Social Council, the Secretariat, the Trusteeship Council, and the International Court of Justice (ICJ), or World Court. While these organs and their auxiliary and subsidiary bodies are supposed to promote the widest possible cooperation among member states in the areas of collective security and peacekeeping, in practice states have traditionally hewn to narrow definitions of their national interests in determining the desirability of international cooperation. This has often transformed the UN into an arena for political grandstanding and competition. The next section will assess the effectiveness of each of the six bodies, looking at the effect of politics on decision making, and at the nature of the political and economic difficulties that each body faces. The focus will be on the two organs that deal most directly with issues of international security, the Security Council and the General Assembly.

UNITED NATIONS' ORGANS: STRUCTURE, FUNCTIONS, AND POLITICS

General Assembly

From 51 original members, the UN General Assembly (GA) has expanded to include 181 nation-states as of 1993. Figure 9.1 shows its organization and scope. All UN members have a seat in the GA, and almost all independent nations are members of the UN. Those that are not include Switzerland, because of its longstanding tradition of strict neutrality, and Taiwan because Beijing will veto its claims to be the rightful government of all of mainland China. A few states have not been permitted to join: Previously, North and South Korea were denied membership; today, Monaco is denied membership, as its foreign policy is controlled by France.

The GA is the UN's primary forum for the discussion of global issues. Operating according to the "one state, one vote" principle, it embodies the idea that the United Nations is based on the sovereign equality of all its members. Dominance of the GA, defined as the ability to get one's resolutions passed by the required two-thirds vote, was first held by the United States, whose supremacy continued up until the 1960s, at which point the United States found itself at odds with the assembly majority on a number of issues involving decolonization

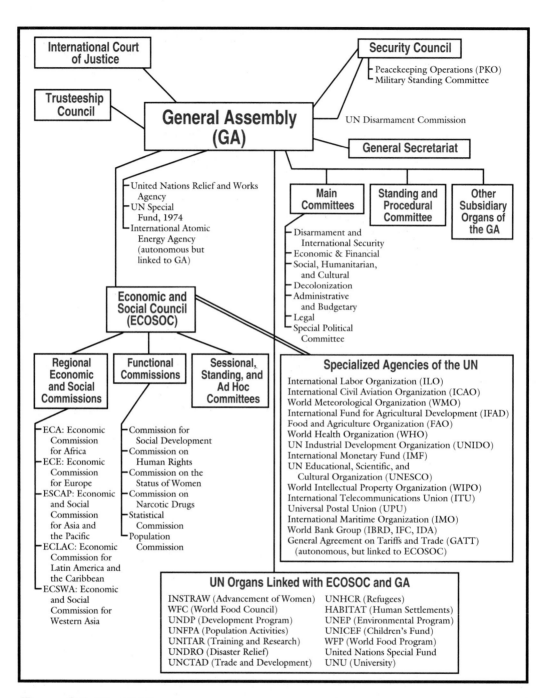

Figure 9.1 The UN System

and development. (The USSR exploited this rupture to its advantage by taking the opposite stance.) The decline in U.S. influence began in 1960, when seventeen new nations joined the GA, largely all African. Many of these states identified the United States as the prime patron of their colonial oppression, because of its alliance with all of the former colonial European powers.

By the 1980s well over half of the 160 members of GA were either Asian or African, and these developing countries continued to use the UN as a forum to espouse their preferences and aims. For many smaller countries of the developing world, the GA remains their most important channel to international diplomacy. However, since the breakup of the Soviet Union and the Persian Gulf War, there has been a marked increase in the American success rate, mirroring the end of the Cold War and a new cooperative industrial environment.

While East-West and North-South disagreements have inhibited the effectiveness of the General Assembly, budget disputes have been even more detrimental. Members are often delinquent in their payments; in 1992 over 80 percent of member nations owed money. At other times, nations have threatened to withhold money because of developments within the UN itself. In 1980, for example, the United States withheld over $100 million in contributions, primarily because of its frustration with a preemptive anti-Western bias and repeated incidents of wasteful spending. By 1994, the United States, the largest UN debtor, owed $531 million for the regular budget and $1.2 billion for peacekeeping operations, although Congress had approved payment of most of this sum by the end of that year.

Still another concern affecting GA effectiveness is the overloading of the assembly agenda when it convenes every September. Some feel that the GA is losing its focus: In a recent year, the GA agenda contained over 140 items, some of which are also on the agenda of the Security Council (which, by the charter, has precedence). Some proposals to limit the bloating of the GA agenda and thereby enhance its effectiveness include creating a specific "steering group" that would set and refine agenda items; a cessation of annual discussions of intractable questions, discussing them instead at greater intervals, like every couple of years; a time limit on speakers whose windy ramblings distort the proceedings; and more meetings between the support staffs of major powers before GA sessions, in order to become aware of their key positions earlier on and thus save time.[16]

Security Council

The Security Council (SC) is the might behind the UN's olive branch. It is charged with organizing collective-security operations and dispatching observer missions and peacekeeping troops around the world at the request of one or more of the combatants involved. This body has the right to investigate any dispute or situation that might lead to international friction, and to recommend methods of settlement. On all resolutions and proposals for action the rule of **great-power unanimity** holds: a veto by any one of its five permanent members (China, France, the United Kingdom, Russia, and the United States) will kill any proposal. Every permanent SC member has used its veto power to protect what it

CONFLICT IN THE SECURITY COUNCIL

In hindsight, it appears that the UN Security Council (SC) was not designed with a bipolar world in mind. Throughout the Cold War, the SC served as a forum in which the Soviet Union and the United States fought to influence world opinion in favor of their respective positions.

For nearly the first two decades of the UN's existence, the USSR had no allies in the SC and few in the General Assembly (GA). As a result, the Soviet Union had to lean heavily on its veto power to kill recommendations on peace and security matters with which it did not agree. In the first five years of the SC's existence, the USSR used the veto forty-seven times; the United States, zero. In fact, the United States did not veto a single SC resolution until 1970.

In the 1960s and 1970s, however, many newly independent African and Asian countries leaned toward the Communist bloc or Non-aligned Movement because they resented the West for its colonial past. They began to pack the GA and fill some of the two-year seats in the SC. As a result, fortunes began to reverse themselves in favor of the Soviet Union. By the mid-1980s, the votes of the GA and the Soviet delegation were in agreement 79 percent of the time; during the same period, the U.S. figure had plummeted to 14 percent. In the early 1980s, the USSR used its veto power

has seen as its vital interests. An example was Moscow's veto of the SC resolution condemning the Soviet downing of a Korean passenger jet in September 1983. Another example from that same year was the U.S. veto of the SC vote against the American intervention on the Caribbean island of Grenada.

Over the past five decades, the SC has employed a wide variety of ways to maintain international peace. These have ranged from resolutions condemning violence to the establishment of peacekeeping forces and the implementation of sanctions.

Through its debates, the SC has reflected the sentiment of the international community. Simply by allowing grievances to be aired, debates have often diffused tension. On the other hand, bitter debates in public view sometimes intensify disputes, to the detriment of private negotiation. If such disputes result in resolutions that are perceived by member nations as biased, the status of the Council is undermined, along with its ability to act (see the boxed feature, "Conflict in the Security Council").

The SC also serves as a forum for negotiation. By arranging cease-fires or disengagements, and by setting up fact-finding missions, the SC can "buy time" in crucial situations to allow participants in a given conflict to reconsider their positions. Even more so, resolutions passed by the SC can provide the framework for dispute settlement. The "land for peace" provisions in UN Resolutions 242 and 338 have served as a basis for settling the Arab-Israeli conflict.

If peaceful means fail, the SC also can impose harsh sanctions on a nation or even launch military actions. Prior to the UN's authorization of the U.S.–led intervention to forcibly expel the Iraqi army from Kuwait in 1990, the only significant only twice, while the United States resorted to it twenty-eight times.[*]

With the collapse of the Soviet Union, debate over whether the membership composition of the SC reflects the current global power structure (see Chapter 12) has been renewed. Serious consideration has been given recently to whether the SC should be expanded to include Japan and reunited Germany, especially since other countries have become increasingly dependent on them to fund expanded UN programs. Reluctance to give Japan and Germany permanent seats both within and outside those countries is a reaction to their legacies of aggression, their postwar constitutional prohibitions against fielding large standing military organizations, and a general feeling that both nations are not (or should not be) wholeheartedly committed to active participation in international politics. Additionally, the United States has anticipated that new admissions to the SC would reduce U.S. leverage, renew Third World countries' demands for an end to the permanent members' veto power, and invite other large Third World nations such as India and Brazil to seek permanent SC membership.[†]

[*]Robert E. Riggs and Jack C. Plano, *The United Nations: International Organization and World Politics* (Chicago: Dorsey, 1988).

[†]For discussions of these issues, see James Weish, "The Partnership to Remember," *Time,* March 11, 1991, pp. 49–50; and *The New York Times,* September 27, 1992, and January 12, 1993.

military action on which the SC was able to achieve a consensus was intervention in the Korean War. The United Nations intervened in Korea because the Soviet Union had been boycotting SC meetings as a protest against the continuing presence of nationalist China (Taiwan) as a permanent member, rather than the Communist People's Republic of China (PRC), which controlled the mainland. With the USSR out of the picture, the pro-Western SC was easily persuaded by the United States to authorize the Korean "police action" under its leadership. The assembled military forces were dispatched by President Truman to drive North Korean forces back across the Thirty-eighth Parallel. After a three-year struggle, the conflict ended in a stalemate and frustration for both sides (see Chapter Four). However, because it was a successful collective effort to block aggression and limit its consequences, the Korean War was the first instance where the UN acted as a "world police officer," just as its founders intended. U.S.–Soviet antagonism during the Cold War ensured that it would not do so again until the Persian Gulf War, forty years later (again, see the boxed feature, "Conflict in the Security Council" for more on superpower conflict).

Secretariat and Secretary-General

Headed by the secretary-general, who serves a five-year term and reports to the GA, the Secretariat is the UN's chief administrative body. The secretary-general is thus the "chief executive" of the UN, but he or she has little power to act independently of the SC or GA. However, the secretary-general can bring any

WHAT WOULD YOU DO?

You are the president of the United States of America in the 1990s. You had been trying to get Kim Il-Sung, the totalitarian dictator of North Korea throughout the post–World War II period until his death in 1994, to allow full inspection of that nation's declared nuclear facilities. Kim had agreed to inspection of seven out of nine of its plants, but the International Atomic Energy Agency (IAEA) had been pressing Kim to open up two additional sites. You fear that North Korea is building nuclear weapons and may try to sell some of them to states with records of regional aggression and support for terrorism and use the others to blackmail South Korea into unification under Communist rule.

North Korea has balked at opening up the two additional plants, threatening to withdraw from the 1968 Nuclear Nonproliferation Treaty regime. However, you also know that in 1991 Kim agreed in principle to create a denuclearized peninsula and to account for all North Korea's plutonium, and you suspect it may be willing to fulfill this agreement if you reciprocate by lifting your trade embargo.

If these two plants are the ones producing any nuclear weapons, you want North Korea to submit to inspections on demand. Even though you are committed to decreasing your country's troop presence in South Korea as part of overall military budget reductions, you do not want to

matter that threatens world peace to the SC's attention and can call special sessions of the GA. In keeping with the tradition established by the League of Nations covenant, the UN Charter pledges the secretaries-general to strict impartiality in the discharge of their responsibilities.

The Secretariat contains a 16,000-member international civil service staff, 11,000 of whom are located throughout the world, with 5,000 remaining at UN headquarters in New York City. Despite the large size of the staff, this administrative body has been hindered in the past by the limited resources available. The secretary-general is not authorized to engage in certain types of activities that might be perceived as violations of national sovereignty. One such example is that the secretary-general cannot order intelligence-gathering activities. If member states are not willing to provide sufficient information when a crisis erupts, the danger increases that the secretary-general's effectiveness as an impartial arbitrator will suffer. Some analysts suggest ways to get around these types of restrictions. For example, to accomplish intelligence-gathering the Secretariat could push for the development of special UN satellite-gathering equipment capabilities, or perhaps just send special UN ambassadors to global capitals on a regular basis to gather information for the secretary-general.

These proposals would improve the resources available to the secretary-general but would not necessarily safeguard the desired impartiality of the office itself. Indeed, the process of selecting the security-general can be an especially political undertaking. Starting in 1956, the UN undertook an obligation to demobilize too rapidly. This might leave South Korea and Japan, valuable allies and trading partners, with the following options: 1) appease North Korea; 2) seek closer military ties with China; or 3) build or purchase their own nuclear arsenals.

On the other hand, if you step up your demands on North Korea, it may either threaten war with South Korea or Japan or seek a closer rapprochement with the People's Republic of China. The first scenario could drag the United States into Korean War II. The second could result in the collapse of the U.S. security regime in east Asia, leading to a bandwagon effect as less powerful Asian states rush to kowtow to a new Asian Communist alliance, and ruining the credibility of U.S. security commitments elsewhere.

You face a dilemma: You want to take all necessary measures to reassure other Asian countries that North Korea is not producing nuclear weapons, but not in such a way that provokes the very result— North Korean aggression or North Korean–Chinese rapprochement—that you are trying to avoid. It is also possible that North Korea is just using its nuclear program to gain trading and other economic concessions from you.

What would you do?

---

consider geographic origins when selecting a secretary-general. This was to ensure that no one particular region of the world was more "represented" than others, although geographic distribution was still supposed to remain subordinate to questions of merit when selecting the most desirable candidate.

Of the six individuals who have served as secretary-general since the UN's inception, all have made significant contributions to the peaceful resolution of conflicts in many parts of the world. Some have been more activist than others in terms of leadership style, some more controversial than others, but all have been political figures dependent upon the cooperation (and influence) of member nations (especially the five permanent SC members) and all have sought to wield influence over the membership as well as over the UN bureaucracy.

Norway's Trygve Lie (1946–1953) called the then-raw position of secretary-general "the most impossible job in the world." Despite a broadly recognized talent for negotiating, he was forced to leave office in April 1953, a political victim of the Cold War. Communist countries accused Lie of serving Western imperialism and boycotted him after he recommended UN intervention in the Korean War, causing him to depend more on the West. At the time of his resignation, however, he was having problems with the FBI over questions of staff loyalty; sixty American citizens employed under Lie were being investigated for alleged Communist subversion.

Sweden's Dag Hammarskjöld (1953–1961) lost his life in the line of duty, as he was killed in a plane crash in the Congo (now Zaire) while directing UN attempts to end fighting there. He was posthumously awarded the 1961 Nobel Peace Prize for his efforts.

Hammarskjöld believed that the chief executive of a body that represents so many nations must play a large role, and he did. He established the precedent of inserting the UN into troubled areas and made the secretary-general the leading political officer of the organization. In his first years, he restored confidence in the SG, and turned his role into chief negotiator of the UN, often in the face of vague and unhelpful directives from the SC and the GA. He also clashed with Nikita Khrushchev repeatedly; the Soviet premier first demanded Hammarskjöld's ouster in 1960 because he was perceived to be a Western puppet.

U Thant (1961–1972) was a Burmese diplomat and civil servant before taking the position of secretary-general. He believed that the secretary-general "must be impartial, but not necessarily neutral." In other words, he believed that the SG must make decisions on his own in moments of crisis. He was nonaligned in every sense of the word, so that he maintained the support of both Moscow and Washington, which helped him to be unanimously reelected for a second term.

Kurt Waldheim's (1972–1982) polished, nonideological style was acceptable to both superpowers, making him a desirable candidate for secretary-general. He faced the difficult task of reconciling the superpowers and also the developing states at a time when the latter were increasing their power as a voting bloc. His strategy was to lead by consensus. While Waldheim's tenure was relatively uncontroversial, the Austrian-born secretary-general became embroiled in a bitter controversy over his World War II service during his successful 1986 bid for the Austrian Presidency. Accused of being a former Nazi, Waldheim claimed that he had served in the Balkans with the German Army but not in any decision-making capacity. Nevertheless, the World Jewish Congress revealed that he had served as an intelligence officer and alleged that he had a direct role in Nazi activities. Overall, the controversy tarnished his reputation as well as that of Austria, which elected him to office despite international condemnation.

Like his immediate predecessors, Javier Perez de Cuellar (1982–1992) showed little in the way of activism as secretary-general. The former Peruvian diplomat was elected to the position as a dark-horse, compromise candidate. He was acceptable to many states because he was perceived as a man of caution who would not upset the status quo.

The current, activist secretary-general, Boutros Boutros-Ghali (1992–present), is the first African and the first Arab to head the UN. An Egyptian, Boutros-Ghali assumed office shortly after the end of the Cold War. The UN was therefore expected by many to play a more dominant role in global politics, and he responded to the challenge with a vigorous administration, attempting to revitalize the UN, overseeing the expansion of peacekeeping, and pushing for democratization of the international community.

International Court of Justice

Headquartered in the Hague, Netherlands, and permanently in session, the International Court of Justice (also known as the World Court, previously a League of Nations institution) is the principal judicial organ of the UN. Its fifteen judges are elected by the GA and SC for nine-year terms. All questions brought before the court are decided by majority vote.

The court hears cases brought to it by the state involved. It also provides advisory opinions to the GA and SC at their request. While its decisions are formally binding between the parties concerned, there are no formal mechanisms to enforce its rulings. However, the UN charter provides that if a party fails to perform its obligations under a judgment, the other party may go to the SC, which may apply more pressure on the offending party to enforce the ruling.

The notion of state sovereignty also limits the effectiveness of court decisions. Since there is no formal obligation to accept the rulings, those that are perceived as violating state sovereignty are often brushed aside. Iran, for example, ignored the court's order to release the hostages held after the takeover of the U.S. embassy in Teheran in 1979, and the United States similarly dismissed an order to halt the mining of Nicaraguan harbors in the 1980s.

The election of the fifteen judges to the International Court is one of individuals, not of states. Individuals are chosen on the basis of their high moral character and their expert legal qualifications. No two judges are to be from the same nation, in order to ensure that most of the world's principal judicial and legal systems are represented on the court. The implication, though, is that the membership of the court will be drawn from leading states—those whose legal systems and institutions are well-established, legitimate, and stable. Today's court has six justices from European nations, three each from Asia and Africa, one from North America, and two from South America.

Economic and Social Council

The UN's six main organs are large bureaucratic structures that consist of a cornucopia of subsidiary agencies and offices, many of which are based all over the world. The **Economic and Social Council (ECOSOC)** is responsible for coordinating the work of the UN "family" of more specialized agencies and organizations.

The general objectives that some of the organizations work toward are supported by virtually all UN member states. Least controversial is the work performed by several humanitarian organizations falling under the ECOSOC umbrella, such as the Universal Postal Union (UPU), **International Children's Emergency Fund (UNICEF),** the World Meteorological Organization (WMO), and the **World Health Organization (WHO).**

As examples of how these organizations function, we can examine the **Food and Agriculture Organization (FAO)** and the International Labor Organization (ILO). Established October 16, 1945, the FAO is the oldest permanent specialized agency of the United Nations. The principal functions of the FAO include raising nutrition levels of the world's population, securing efficiency improvements in the production and distribution of all agricultural products, and bettering conditions for the world's rural population.

To obtain these objectives, the FAO undertakes various agricultural-related research, subsidizes technical assistance to individual nations, distributes

AT A GLANCE

UN BODIES: STRUCTURE AND FUNCTION

General Assembly (GA)

Contents: 181 members

Qualifications for Membership: All UN members are part of the GA

Voting Requirements for Resolutions: Two-thirds majority on "important issues"; simple majority on "ordinary issues"

Activities: UN's primary forum for discussion of global issues; makes recommendations on all matters within scope of the UN charter; determines membership of other UN organs; approves UN budget

Security Council (SC)

Contents: five permanent members (China, France, Russia, United Kingdom, United States), ten non-permanent members

Qualifications for Membership: GA elects non-permanent members to two-year terms

Voting Requirements for Resolutions: nine members for "procedural" matters and nine, including unanimity of permanent members, for "substantive" issues

Activities: Organizing collective-security operations; dispatching observer missions and peace-keeping troops; investigating disputes that might cause international friction. Every permanent member has used veto power to protect what it views as its national interest.

Economic and Social Council (ECOSOC)

Contents: UN specialized agencies and GATT

Qualifications for Membership: GA elects ECOSOC's 54 members to three-year terms

Voting Requirements for Resolutions: Not applicable

Activities: Coordinates work for the "UN family" of organizations. Many organizations under

information through educational projects, and publishes a variety of periodicals and yearbooks about the production, trade, and consumption of agricultural commodities.

Headquartered in Rome, the FAO is governed by the biennial FAO Conference, in which each member nation is represented and has one vote. The Council, which supervises the work of the FAO, is composed of representatives of twenty-four member governments and is elected by the Conference.

By comparison, the ILO was established in 1919 by the Treaty of Versailles, and transferred its affiliation from the League of Nations to the UN after World War II. To achieve its principal aim of enhancing living standards and conditions of labor throughout the world, the ILO promotes international standards for working conditions and wages, provides assistance in social policy and administration, fosters cooperation between workers and employers, and compiles labor statistics.

During its affiliation with the League of Nations, the ILO was principally concerned with the economic development of its European members. Since 1945, the ILO gradually shifted its attention to the states of the Third World. Because of its far-flung and constructive activities in these states, the ILO was awarded the Nobel Peace Prize in 1969.

ECOSOC umbrella are humanitarian; GATT, while linked to ECOSOC by agreement, is an autonomous organization

Secretariat
Contents: Secretary-general, his or her aides and other officials

Qualifications for Membership: Officials appointed by secretary-general, who is elected to a five-year term

Voting Requirements for Resolutions: Not applicable

Activities: Chief administrative body; can bring any matter threatening world peace to SC's attention; can call special GA sessions

International Court of Justice
Contents: Fifteen judges

Qualifications for Membership: Elected by the GA and SC for nine-year terms

Voting Requirements for Resolutions: Majority vote

Activities: Principal judicial organ of the UN. State sovereignty limits effectiveness of court's decisions

Trusteeship Council
Contents: five members (China, France, Russia, United Kingdom, United States)

Qualifications for Membership: No formal requirements

Voting Requirements for Resolutions: Not applicable

Activities: Administration of trust territories or non-self-governing areas. Has the least to do; supervises only Palau, a tiny island in the South Pacific

The executive authority of the ILO, the Governing Body, is elected during the annual International Labor Conference, which has representatives from trade unions, employers, and national governments. Daily ILO operation is handled by the International Labor Office in Geneva, which is under the direction of an appointed director general.

In contrast, the specific tasks that other specialized agencies have sought to accomplish have drawn widespread criticism. Again, disputes between member states and ECOSOC specialized agencies seem to erupt most often when the question of state sovereignty becomes prominent. In 1992, for example, inspectors from the Vienna-based International Atomic Energy Agency (IAEA) endured verbal and physical harassment when trying to inspect alleged nuclear weapons production facilities inside Iraq. Inspectors were to determine whether Saddam Hussein was complying with UN prohibitions against such facilities there. Hussein opposed the holding of inspections, claiming they violated Iraqi sovereignty. In response, President Bush, in August 1992, threatened to bomb the Iraqi Ministry of Military Industrialization, largely responsible for Baghdad's nuclear programs, if inspections were not permitted. The confrontation fizzled as the IAEA team was allowed to complete its inspection without attempting to enter the national security ministry itself.

A second set of controversies surrounding an ECOSOC agency has its roots in the Cold War. The Paris-based **UN Educational, Scientific, and Cultural Organization (UNESCO)** is responsible for promoting international collaboration among states in those fields. In 1984 the Reagan administration withdrew the United States from UNESCO, charging it with anti-Western bias and economic mismanagement. Lack of American funding greatly reduced the effectiveness of the organization, although the recent end of the Cold War has led to renewed calls for the United States to rejoin UNESCO. Britain, which dropped out along with the United States, already has taken steps to rejoin the organization. Meanwhile, the United States has expressed its approval of a set of Japanese proposals to streamline and reform UNESCO's bureaucratic apparatus. Overall, much like their primary organs, UN specialized agencies have not always lived up to the lofty goals proclaimed by their founders.

Trusteeship Council

The UN primary organ with the least to do today is the Trusteeship Council. This body was set up to supervise the administration of trust territories, or non-self-governing areas assigned to other states for temporary administration before graduating to full independence. (These areas were known as mandates under the League of Nations, and comprised many former European colonies.) Once responsible for eleven trust territories covering most of the Pacific Islands, the Council for the moment oversees only Palau, a tiny island in the South Pacific once administered by the United States.

Compared to the other organs discussed here, scant attention is paid to the Trusteeship Council. Political maneuvering today occurs far less often than in the other five more important arms of the UN. During the Cold War, one way in which politics affected the SC was in the interpretation of Trusteeship Agreements. The United States interpreted them to mean that the United States was the sole power over its own trust territories, while the USSR insisted that the agreements were under the approval of the SC. This dispute ended with the independence of all but one former trust territory and the demise of the USSR.

UN MISSIONS: EXPECTATION, EXPERIENCE, AND THE FUTURE

When UN collective-security operations involve the use of force against a belligerent, UN peacekeeping and truce-supervision forces serve as armed sentries. Known as the "Blue Berets" and **"Blue Helmets"** because they retain their national uniforms but wear UN headgear, they are dispatched only at the invitation of parties to a local conflict (sometimes with great-power prodding), with their primary mission to separate armed combatants in order to make violation of a peace agreement more difficult. Peacekeeping forces are assigned to the UN by member states; the UN does not maintain a standing army, although this has been suggested. Since 1948 the SC has authorized thirty-three peacekeeping

People wait in line to receive humanitarian aid as a UN armored personnel carrier rolls through war-torn Sarajevo, Bosnia-Herzegovina in 1991.
Source: © Reuters/Bettmann.

operations, as well as a number of observer missions, involving over 500,000 troops, 800 of which have died in the line of duty. The Blue Helmets collectively received a Nobel Peace Prize in 1988 in recognition of their efforts.

There are three types of missions that the UN undertakes: observer, peace-keeping, and peace enforcement. The **observer missions** are those international forces that are present to observe a cease-fire that has been organized by the two opposing sides of a dispute. These forces are not usually large enough to make the cease-fire effective. **Peacekeeping missions** not only observe the cease-fire but also act as a buffer between the two sides of a conflict. **Peace-enforcement missions** observe, act as a buffer, and, as a last resort, are allowed to use military force to keep the peace. Thus, peacekeeping operations differ from peace-enforcement actions in that peacekeepers are dispatched to prevent combat, not take part in it. UN-approved military operations in Korea and the Persian Gulf were classified as "peace-enforcement" according to the UN charter, and did not require the permission of the countries where UN forces operated. (It would have been difficult to imagine Iraq's President Saddam Hussein giving "permission" for UN forces to enter Kuwait to reverse the gains made by the Iraqi invasion of that country.) Like the Wild West, these military actions represent cases where a "sheriff's posse" was successfully organized to act against blatant aggression that violated the law of nations.

The end of the Cold War has allowed ethnic conflicts to resurface in various regions of the world, just as the decline of Cold War politics within the UN has encouraged the wider use of UN missions to mitigate these conflicts. However, expectations of what peacekeepers can now accomplish in a post–Cold War world frequently outpace what they can in fact achieve. The mixed success of UN missions in the former Yugoslavia, Cambodia, and Somalia provide illuminating examples.

Ethnic tensions in Yugoslavia between Serbs, Croats, and the Bosnia Muslims were unleashed following the collapse of that Communist state. The UN has set up a mission in Bosnia and Croatia to help ease, if not prevent, civilian illnesses, lack of supplies, and in some cases, starvation. While the UN has for the most part been successful in distributing and ensuring access to humanitarian relief supplies, it has not been able to serve as a buffer between the warring factions. More fundamentally, it has been unable to find a solution to the root problem of ethnic hatred in that region. Despite higher expectations, its 45,000 troops in the former Yugoslavia have been limited to assisting civilians whenever possible, even though it faces blockades, inspections, and snipers from every side of the war.

Another ambitious UN project was the peacekeeping operation in Cambodia, initiated in 1991. Costing $2.6 billion in a single year and involving over 22,000 troops and civilian officials, the mission achieved noteworthy successes, but did not prove fully adequate to the huge task demanded of it. It managed to register 4.64 million voters (96 percent of the population) and supervise elections for a constituent assembly. Yet the peacekeepers were not able to convince the forces of the Khmer Rouge (the deadliest of four major guerrilla factions) to demobilize and disarm, and reports persist of both government- and rebel-sponsored political murders.[17]

The UN intervention in Somalia was even more painful. It began initially as a humanitarian mission in late 1992 to alleviate mass starvation and widespread suffering. By mid-1993 it deteriorated as UN peacekeepers were gradually drawn into local politics. Fighting and casualties began affecting both local militias and UN forces. For a time UN troops, led by the United States, sought to arrest faction leader Mohammed Farah Aidid for his guerrillas' attacks on UN soldiers, and to assist in the organization of a viable government. In the end, however, Aidid was not captured, and the United States completed the withdrawal of its troops at the end of March 1994. The remaining UN mission was left understrength and over-committed. Meanwhile, the UN attempted to come to terms with the requirements for continued humanitarian assistance and the need to confront local political factions—including Aidid's.

Perhaps the biggest challenge facing UN peacekeeping missions in the future rests not on the field of battle, but rather in the pocketbooks of member states. An independent advisory group conceived by the Ford Foundation concluded that the UN still lacks the funding necessary for most effective peacekeeping and enforcement operations. According to that group, in no area have international demands on the UN grown as quickly as they have in peacekeeping; in 1991 about

15,000 UN peacekeepers were deployed around the world; in early 1994 the number had increased to 72,000 in fourteen different countries.[18]

Three recommendations have been made by the Ford Foundation for resolving the funding dilemma. First, create a united peacekeeping budget to replace the current system, in which each mission is financed separately. Second, assess governments an annual amount to support the budget. As a result, they would have to consider financing future peacekeeping costs from their own annual defense budgets. Third, to ensure reliable funding in the crucial startup stage of peacekeeping missions, establish a $400 million revolving fund for peacekeeping, to be financed by all member states in three annual payments.[19]

Overall, despite the ongoing problem of inadequate funding, UN missions have played a vital role in bringing many conflicts to an end, especially in Africa, Central America, and the Middle East. Since the end of the Cold War has led to a proliferation of regional and ethnic conflicts all over the world, it is clear that UN forces will continue to be called upon to play a major role in the resolution of these conflicts. The question remains whether UN forces should help settle conflicts, build new governments, or just separate the combatants. Currently, their specific tasks often remain unclear (consider the cases of Yugoslavia and Somalia), and the extent to which UN member states are willing to commit troops and funds for their efforts is even more in doubt.[20]

United Nations' Effectiveness as an International Organization

Like the Concert of Europe, the basic idea for the UN was forged by the "Big Three" allies (Great Britain, the United States, and the Soviet Union) in the crucible of war. The wartime participants met in San Francisco (April–June 1945) to create an organization whose primary purpose, like the League of Nations, would be maintaining collective security against military aggression. To this effect, they established a Security Council (SC), whose permanent members were recognized and expected to act as the "world's policemen."

Mindful, however, of how the lofty expectations for the League of Nations had quickly been dashed, the founders of the UN sought to dampen expectations about what the new organization could accomplish. They believed that only the concerted will and strength of the great powers, reflected in agreement between the five permanent SC members, could rebuff aggression. While it would seem that the veto power exercised by any permanent SC member could prevent the United Nations from taking any action and thus limit its effectiveness, the veto was intended to ensure that the UN would undertake only those actions that all the great powers would support.

It was hoped that this "great power government" would be adequate to meet any challenge presented to the postwar international system. In recognizing that the power of all nations was not created equal, the UN's founders demonstrated a more realistic grasp of global power politics than the idealistic founders of the League of Nations.

Thus far, the UN appears to be the only existing organization with a chance of countering aggression in a legitimate and impartial manner. As we will see in the next chapter, its activities transcend those of the collective-security organizations that preceded it, as its various agencies deal with a wide array of global issues. The power and effectiveness of the UN is still hamstrung, however, by its inability to claim sovereign authority over all nations engaged in international affairs. Action by the UN usually requires consent of the countries involved.

This need for consent creates an obstacle to UN resolution of conflicts, especially in the developing world. It is not surprising that the developing states are reluctant to give up even a modicum of sovereignty to an international organization, since most have gained independence recently and are thus extremely sensitive to interference in their internal affairs. Just as individuals usually resent searches of their persons and property by the police, so countries regard intervention by outside agencies, however well-intentioned, as an unwelcome intrusion.

As was the case with the League of Nations, the UN cannot force any state to comply with its resolutions if the major powers are not committed to enforcing those resolutions with military might when necessary. Many argue that UN sanctions per se against Iraq for its invasion of Kuwait in 1990 would not have sufficed to compel Iraq to withdraw. Rather, a coalition of great powers (especially Britain, France, and the United States) was necessary to achieve that goal in the Persian Gulf, and would similarly have been required to put an end to the fighting in Bosnia in an expeditious manner. Might may not make right, but right is often impotent without might.

Lack of sovereign authority does not mean that UN sanctions are condemned to futility. In some cases, a UN sanctions resolution alone can inflict considerable costs on a state that is transgressing international law if the resolution's goals are shared by other states. Although many states find ways around sanctions, a state facing a UN-sanctioned embargo carries the stigma of being an international troublemaker, and few states wish their good standing tarnished by being associated with a stigmatized state. Arguably, for example, the governments of Rhodesia (now Zimbabwe) and South Africa were pressured to change their racist domestic policies by UN-sponsored sanctions.[21]

Overall, the UN's nearly five decades of existence have proven that the objectives and expectations of the organization's founders were essentially correct. The UN was not designed to be all things to all nations. It was created as a forum for the discussion of global issues, as a coordinating body for development aid and humanitarian relief, and as a means to facilitate collective security when the world's major powers agreed on what should be done to meet specific threats. It has performed these functions rather well, though it has been a target of justifiable criticism as mentioned in this section. It has not brought about world peace; it cannot do so, and it was never intended to.

The UN is capable of doing more if its member states provide it with more resources, but its efforts will always be subject to the limitations imposed by national sovereignty as long as sovereignty remains a fundamental principle of international relations. Sovereignty constrains international organizations just as civil rights constrain national governments. In both cases, the governed cannot be blamed for thinking very carefully before conceding more power to the government, even in the interest of law and order.

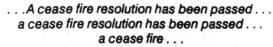

Like a parrot, the UN often proclaims the words "cease fire, cease fire." But at times, mere utterances seem to be the limit of its capabilities.

Source: © Kenneth Mahood, Punch, London.

INTERGOVERNMENTAL ORGANIZATIONS OTHER THAN THE UNITED NATIONS

The last section examined the structure, operations, and effectiveness of the UN, a multipurpose intergovernmental organization (IGO) with a global membership base. This section will briefly discuss other kinds of IGOs. Some of these organizations operate worldwide, but confine their activities to a few specific functions; others undertake a wide range of activities in a particular geographic region; still others are specialized both in membership and in purpose. Regardless of their objectives or scope of membership, most of these IGOs are affiliated with the

UN in one way or another. And like the UN, most are constrained or limited by the will and resources of their members.

General-Purpose IGOs

One of the most famous specialized IGOs with a global membership base is the International Criminal Police Organization (Interpol), based in Lyons, France. Created in 1923 and now composed of more than 150 members, Interpol's purpose is to promote the widest possible mutual assistance between all police authorities within the limits of the law existing in the different countries and in the spirit of the universal Declaration of Human Rights. Perhaps because of its limited objective—it is forbidden to undertake any intervention or activities of a political, military, religious, or racial character—Interpol serves as an example of how IGOs can effectively foster cooperation between states. Once focused on terrorism, almost half of Interpol's activities are now dedicated to countering drug trafficking and money laundering.

General-purpose regional IGOs include many associations of states that promote regional security and act as forums for resolving regional disputes. The League of Arab States (commonly called the Arab League) includes among its membership twenty-one Arab states, as well as the Palestinian Liberation Organization (PLO). It was created in 1945 to "safeguard the independence and integrity" of the member states and unsuccessfully tried to mediate in the dispute which led to the Iraqi invasion of Kuwait in 1990.[22] The **Organization of American States (OAS),** which includes most of the nations of the Western Hemisphere, is another example of an organization that attempts to address a number of regional concerns.

Other general-purpose regional IGOs include the **Organization of African Unity (OAU),** which promoted decolonization and now focuses on regional development and cooperation, and the Association of South-East Asian Nations (ASEAN), which encourages peaceful cooperation and economic development among its members (Brunei, Indonesia, Malaysia, the Philippines, Singapore, and Thailand). The **Commonwealth of Independent States (CIS),** the organization of successor states to the former Soviet Union, could also be considered a general regional IGO, although its primary goals and the extent of its authority remain unclear. The most successful general-purpose regional IGO is the European Union (EU), which began life in 1957 as a primarily economic organization but has made halting progress in the direction of becoming a regional "superstate" with a common European citizenship, currency, and other features associated with sovereign states.

Overall, the record of general-purpose regional IGOs in fostering international cooperation and reducing anarchy is mixed. They have by no means stopped or prevented all regional conflicts, but what is more certain is that such organizations at the very least serve as effective forums for debate among member nations. Because debate and public discussion in themselves increase the likelihood for peaceful dispute resolutions, these IGOs have at times made important contributions to regional cooperation.

Specialized IGOs

Specialized regional or limited-membership organizations include several groups of states designed to promote collective defense. Prominent among these is the North Atlantic Treaty Organization (NATO), comprising fourteen European states as well as the United States and Canada. NATO was created in 1949 to promote defense cooperation in Western European and repel any armed aggression directed against a member state. The main threat that led to NATO's creation came from the Soviet Union (and later the Soviet bloc countered with a military alliance of its own, the Warsaw Treaty Organization). While the demise of the USSR and the Warsaw Pact has left many of NATO's members wondering what, if anything, the alliance should do in the future, NATO was a definite success in bringing a sense of order, purpose, and focus to Western defense efforts during the Cold War.

Collective security throughout post–Cold War Europe is the province of the **Conference on Security and Cooperation in Europe (CSCE).** Created in 1975 as part of the Helsinki negotiations, the CSCE is composed of most NATO and ex–Warsaw Pact nations, the United States, Canada, and Russia included. The end of the Cold War has given the CSCE the opportunity to come into its own as a new Concert of Europe designed to manage regional crises, but so far its record in this area has not been promising, as it, like NATO, proved unable to take effective action against the fighting following the breakup of Yugoslavia.[23]

Other specialized IGOs are concerned with economic matters. The twenty-four–member Organization of Economic Cooperation and Development (OECD), composed of mostly advanced industrial states, was formed in 1961 to promote economic and social welfare in member countries and to stimulate and harmonize efforts on behalf of developing nations. As we saw in Chapter Seven, a smaller subset of the OECD countries, the Group of Seven (G-7), comprising Canada, France, Germany, Italy, Japan, the United Kingdom, and the United States, is an organization of the world's major industrial countries whose leaders meet periodically to discuss global economic issues. Common markets and free-trade areas have been established in many regions with varying degrees of success. These include the Economic Community of West African States (ECOWAS), the Caribbean Community and Common Market (Caricom), the Latin American Free Trade Association (LAFTA), and the European Free Trade Area (EFTA), although none come close to the achievements of the European Union (EU). Whatever their focus or accomplishments, economic IGOs strive to bring order to the global or regional economy for common benefit, thus making the world a less anarchic place.

NONGOVERNMENTAL ORGANIZATIONS

Not all organizations taking an active part in international politics are directly affiliated with governments. These nongovernmental organizations (NGOs) operate across national boundaries independent of governments. Like IGOs,

A HERO OF PEACE

A few years after the founding of the International Committee of the Red Cross, the international businessman and philanthropist who set up the organization was living in poverty in his native Switzerland. Jean-Henri Dunant (1828–1910) was introduced to the horrors of war in 1859 as a neutral observer at the Battle of Solferino, which resulted in 40,000 French and Austrian casualties. Dunant organized emergency medical attention for the wounded on both sides, and a few years later proposed the formation of voluntary societies in all countries dedicated to humanitarian relief, regardless of nationality, religion, or ethnicity. His vision for an international humanitarian organization became a reality in 1864, when Dunant founded the International Red Cross in Geneva. That same year, the first Geneva Convention on the conduct of war and the treatment of prisoners of war was convened at his initiative.

they can be widely or narrowly focused, with either more broadly based or narrowly restricted memberships. The Roman Catholic Church, the International Red Cross, Amnesty International, Greenpeace, and many multinational corporations (MNCs) are examples of NGOs with broad-based memberships (the Roman Catholic Church has over 800 million members). Because most NGOs cannot command resources as easily as states or IGOs, they tend to focus their efforts on specific projects in order to maximize their effectiveness. Through these projects or through global public support, they can exercise a profound influence on the conduct of states.

Humanitarian NGOs

NGOs vary widely in terms of their stated purpose. Many of the most famous NGOs engage in humanitarian activities. The **International Red Cross** (called the Red Crescent in Muslim countries) acts as an international relief agency and maintains strict neutrality in order to alleviate suffering without becoming involved in politics. Its many activities include disaster and famine relief, immunization and public health programs, and efforts to ensure humane treatment of prisoners of war. **Amnesty International (AI)** works on the behalf of prisoners of conscience around the world. It seeks the release of political prisoners and the abolition of torture, investigating abuses of human rights and organizing campaigns for the release of persons jailed for political activity.

Terrorist NGOs

Terrorist NGOs, which use violence and terror to further their political aims, have been a feature of international politics for many years but became prominent on the world scene in the 1960s and the 1970s. The growth of air transport

Dunant soon went on to become one of the promoters of another well-known charitable organization, the World Alliance of Young Men's Christian Associations (YMCA). By 1867, though, he was bankrupt, having spent most of his time on charity work rather than on his business. Dunant left Geneva for an austere life in the Swiss countryside, but he continued to promote disarmament, settlement of international disputes by arbitration, the foundation of a Jewish homeland, and the abolition of slavery. He was not destined to end his life as an unsung hero, however. After a chance encounter with a newspaper reporter in 1895, Dunant was finally brought out of seclusion and awarded many honors. In 1901 he was the co-recipient of the first Nobel Peace Prize.

and developments in small arms and explosives since World War II have enabled many terrorist groups to strike at targets all over the world. The Abu Nidal terrorist organization, for instance, which split from the Palestinian Liberation Organization in 1974, has carried out more than 900 terrorist attacks in twenty countries, killing almost 1000 people.[24] The Provisional Wing of the Irish Republican Army, which initially focused on British targets in England and Northern Ireland, has extended its attacks to Belgium, the Netherlands, and Germany, and a number of IRA operatives have been apprehended in the United States. Though terror and murder are easy to recognize, the categorization of an organization as a terrorist group is often politically charged. One side's "terrorists" may be the other's "freedom fighters."

MNCs as NGOs

Some NGOs are just in it for the money. **Multinational corporations (MNCs),** based in a specific home country, have branches that conduct business all over the world. Banks such as Japan's Sanwa and industrial giants such as General Motors tend to be the largest MNCs in terms of capitalization and sales, but the most familiar and pervasive multinational corporation is McDonald's. The Golden Arches can be found in almost every country in the world, and when the huge Moscow franchise opened in 1990, it was not only the most popular restaurant in the city for several months, but also the only place in Moscow to find fresh lettuce! While MNCs seek profits worldwide, many promote the interests of their home countries directly or indirectly, and a few have even developed reputations for meddling in the politics of developing countries. (The role of MNCs in the global economy is discussed in Chapter Eight; for their political activities during the Cold War, see Chapter Four.)

Other NGOs

A wide variety of NGOs that do not fit in any of the preceding categories seek to promote global cooperation on specific global issues. These groups will be discussed along with the issues they address in the following chapter, so only a few will be mentioned here. Greenpeace and the World Wide Fund for Nature (WWF) focus on environmental issues, and the International Olympic Organizing Committee (IOOC) stages the winter and summer Olympic Games in the hope of enhancing ties between nations through sport. Finally, persons who believe that these undertakings should be pursued by a global government can join the World Federalist Association.

CONCLUSION: A LESS ANARCHIC WORLD?

In this chapter, we have seen how international law and organizations constitute both a source of conflict and cooperation in the international system. While usually designed to promote cooperation or end conflict on some set of issues, international law and organizations sometimes generate new controversies. These unintended effects of attempts to reduce anarchy, coupled with the failures of international security organizations to prevent conflict and war, lead many to question the whole enterprise of international law and organizations. It cannot be said that international law has worked perfectly or that the functioning of the UN and other global organizations has been above reproach. Still, these drawbacks are often apparent in domestic law and government as well, and few reasonable people would conclude that laws and governments in general should be abandoned. Sometimes both domestic and international institutions fail because they are poorly designed; at other times the laws and organizations are not themselves faulty, but failures result from weaknesses in the ethics or leadership of the individuals charged with running them. Many efforts to make the world less anarchic have failed for either reason, and sometimes both, but much good has come from their efforts nonetheless. If nothing else, international law sets ethical standards for the conduct of nations, and facilitates the coordinating of action on various matters.

Like domestic law and government, international law and organizations tell us how we *should* act, and why. Sovereign authority can give us powerful incentives to comply, but the decision to obey or disobey is ultimately ours, as is the responsibility for paying the penalty if we choose to break the law. Constrained as they are by national sovereignty, international law and organizations have weak enforcement mechanisms, but they can still give nations and leaders incentives to behave in ways that benefit the global community without sacrificing vital national interests.

In his pivotal book *Leviathan*, the seventeenth-century philosopher Thomas Hobbes argues that all-powerful sovereign authority is the only possible way to raise society above its "natural" state of "war of every one against every one."[25] As long as international relations are based on national sovereignty, the effectiveness of international law and organizations will be inherently limited. Nevertheless, through example and the threat of sanctions, international institutions have helped to advance the world a few steps beyond the near-anarchy that prevailed before the Peace of Westphalia set the foundations for the modern international system.

PRINCIPAL POINTS OF CHAPTER NINE

1. International law and organizations are efforts to make the international system less anarchic.

2. International law attempts to set rules for interactions among nations and to safeguard human rights. Its fundamental principle is that of national sovereignty, set forth in the Peace of Westphalia in 1638. There is no global legislature to make laws that are binding on all nations. Instead, international law is established through formal treaties (bilateral, multilateral, or negotiated through international organizations) or through customary practice (such as diplomatic immunity).

3. In the absence of a global sovereign authority or police force, international law may be enforced through reciprocity (mutual adherence), sanctions (such as trade embargoes), or responses in kind to transgressions (such as retaliation for aggression).

4. International organizations are of two kinds: intergovernmental organizations (IGOs) and nongovernmental organizations (NGOs). Both have multiplied in recent years as groups of states and individuals have come to regard these organizations as the best forums for coordinating action on various issues.

5. The world's most important IGO is the United Nations (UN), established after World War II by the victorious Allies to further collective security, sponsor cooperation to address global problems, and promote human rights. (Previous collective-security institutions, the Concert of Europe and the League of Nations, had failed to prevent destructive global wars.)

6. The UN's central organizations are the General Assembly (in which all UN members are represented), the Security Council (which has five permanent members with veto power—the United States, the United Kingdom, Russia, France, and China—and ten other rotating members), and the Secretariat, headed by the secretary-general.

7. In addition, the "UN family" of IGOs (including WHO, IAEA, and UNICEF) promote cooperation on a wide variety of global issues.

8. Other IGOs include specialized global institutions (such as Interpol), general-purpose regional organizations (such as the Arab League and ASEAN), and specialized organizations with limited or restricted memberships (such as CSCE and OPEC).

9. Groups that operate across national boundaries independent of governments are nongovernmental organizations (NGOs). These may be narrowly or widely focused, contain broad-based or narrowly restricted membership, and pursue peaceful or violent means to their ends. Examples include the Roman Catholic Church, MNCs, and terrorist organizations.

Chapter 10

Global Issues

The rain forest is perhaps more truly a silent world than the sea. The wind scarcely penetrates; it is not only silent, it is still. All sound then gains a curiously enhanced mystery. A sudden crack—what could have made it? An inexplicable gurgle. A single clear peal—that was a bird, probably a trogon. A whistle, impossible to identify. But mostly silence. The silence sometimes becomes infectious; I remember sometimes trying to blend into this world by moving along a trail without rustling a leaf with my feet or popping a twig. But more often I purposely scuffled, broke noisily through this forest where I didn't belong, tried to advertise my presence both to reassure myself and to warn the creatures of the forest that a stranger was there.

Naturalist Marston Bates, quoted in Kermit Smith, *Changing Attitudes Towards the Tropical Forest* (Los Angeles: University of California at Los Angeles, 1963), p. 308.

This excerpt describes the response of one naturalist to the mystery, beauty, and power of the Brazilian rain forest. Today, few global issues are more poignant than the possible disappearance of the rain forest. Not only are aesthetic issues at stake, but many scientists believe that the global environment itself is at risk. It is well worth remembering, though, that despite clearly defined aesthetic and scientific issues, practical solutions for managing the rain forest are rather murky. In this, as in most global issues, many difficulties exist for cooperative international relations.

WHAT MAKES AN ISSUE GLOBAL?

"No man is an island, entire of itself; every man is a piece of the continent, a part of the main," the English poet John Donne wrote in 1623. What Donne said about individuals applies even more to states in the New Era. Nations are becoming tied together ever more closely, through communications, trade, population movements, changes in the environment, and other manifestations of globalization. In an era when news is transmitted by satellite, nuclear bombs can

Major Events Affecting Global Issues: 1798–1994

1798: Thomas Malthus publishes *Essay on the Principle of Population.*

1892: The Sierra Club is founded in the United States to protect America's natural environment.

1924: The United States passes the Immigration Act, which establishes a national origins quota system.

1927: The Second Report of the Malarial Commission of the League of Nations reveals difficulties in its anti-malarial campaign.

1948: The International Union for the Protection of Nature, now the World Conservation Union, is created to work toward global environmental goals; the World Health Organization is organized to control the spread of disease.

1949: The United Nations hosts the Scientific Conference on the Conservation and Utilization of Resources to discuss problems relating to natural resources.

1955–1975: As a result of the Vietnam War, 2.5 million acres of forest are leveled and at least 5 million acres rendered unproductive due to Agent Orange and other chemical pollutants.

1959: A water-sharing agreement between Egypt and Sudan regulates the use of the Nile.

1967: The United Nations High Commissioner of Refugees defines refugee status.

1968: The Club of Rome, a multinational group of economists and other specialists, is formed to warn of the dangers of continued population growth and pollution.

1970s: United Nations-sponsored African census program illustrates the full dimensions of the population problem.

1972: The United Nations Conference on the Human Environment in Stockholm pledges continued worldwide discussion and cooperation on environmental issues, establishes an action plan, and approves the Declaration on the Human Environment.

1973: Arab oil producers institute an oil embargo, causing an energy crisis.

1974: The Abu Nidal Organization, a terrorist group, is founded; the United Nations Environmental Program and the United Nations Conference on Trade and Development meet in Mexico to discuss environmental problems and the distribution of the world's resources; the International Energy Agency is created among major industrial states to develop an emergency system for sharing oil.

1975–1992: The United States admits 1.7 million political refugees, most from east Asia and the USSR.

1979: The Iranian Revolution results in the cessation of Iranian oil exports, causing another energy crisis.

1980: The United States imposes a grain embargo on the Soviet Union in

---

be delivered by missile, and narcotics are smuggled in the stomachs of airline passengers, no country can remain isolated from the world beyond its borders.

As nations have become more interconnected, however, they have not become noticeably less argumentative. Indeed, as the ties that bind countries become more numerous and stronger, countries seem to have found more to disagree about, not less. In many ways, although **interdependence** has become the defining factor of the New Era, it has led to as much conflict as cooperation. The need to rely on other states for markets and resources, and to cooperate to solve common problems, has created friction and frustration. Like high school friends who become college roommates, nations must learn to share their living space, and all too often their friendship breaks under the accumulated weight of disputes and quarrels.

This chapter will survey some problems and controversies that cross national boundaries and figure prominently on the agendas of decision makers around the world. Global issues that will be covered include the world's increasing population, population movements (migration), food and hunger, energy and natural resources, concerns about the environment, health issues, drug traffic, and terrorism. It is impossible to examine any one of these issues in depth in a single chapter, and this book does not attempt to do so. Instead, it introduces the reader to the most salient issues in the community of nations and offers an overview of how the community is attempting to address them. In many cases, these problems are closely interrelated; an increase in population, for example, frequently leads to migration and environmental degradation.

retaliation for its invasion of Afghanistan; World Health Organization announces that it has reached its goal of eradicating smallpox; another oil crisis occurs as a result of the Iran-Iraq War.

1981: The U.S. grain embargo against the Soviet Union is lifted.

1984: Ronald Reagan orders a cutoff of funding for all international organizations, including the United Nations Population fund, which support abortion as a birth control means of last resort.

1985: Live Aid benefit concert raises funds for short-term relief of famine in Africa.

1986: The world's worst nuclear reactor accident occurs at Chernobyl in the former USSR; large amounts of radioactive material are released into the atmosphere.

1987: The Montreal Protocol requires signatory states to phase out the use and importation of chlorofluorocar-

bons; the World Health Organization establishes the Global Program on AIDS to unify national and international efforts against the disease; Turkey imposes a water embargo on Syria in retaliation for its support of Kurdish terrorists in Turkey.

1988: The U.S.-sponsored International Drug Enforcement Conference (IDEC) is put into operation.

1989: The United Nations sponsors the International Conference on Central American Refugees, obtaining pledges for aid and resettlement.

1990: UN General Assembly convention seeks to protect the human rights of migrant workers; General Assembly proclaims a United Nations Decade against Drugs (1991–2000).

1991–1992: Somalia suffers a famine that threatens over four million people with starvation.

1992: U.S. troops arrive in Somalia to augment the United Nations relief effort; Rio Earth Summit occurs; UN

imposes sanctions against Libya for refusing to hand over suspects in the 1988 bombing of a Pan American airlines jumbo jet.

1993: Several Central American countries issue the Declaration of Belize, promising cooperation with the United States in addressing the drug problem; Israel and PLO sign mutual recognition accord.

1994: "Carlos the Jackal," a celebrated international terrorist, is arrested in Sudan and extradited to France; IRA calls for a cease-fire in the twenty-five year struggle to end British rule in Northern Ireland; UN Conference on Population and Development succeeds in approving a plan to limit the world's population, despite reservations by Catholic and Islamic representatives.

Before examining each issue, it is necessary to identify what makes a common problem a global issue. There are a number of serious problems that affect millions of people worldwide but do not become international political issues. The simple fact that a problem is widespread does not qualify it as a global issue, since it does not automatically demand the attention of all nations, though persons and governments throughout the world may care about the problem and try to alleviate it. Issues become global only when there is transnationality of cause and effect—a fancy way of describing a problem that originates in one country but is felt in others. Muggings in New York's Central Park do not lead to increased crime in Toronto, but pollution from American factories does kill Canadian trees. The international links between causes and effects may be either unintentional (as they are in the spread of tuberculosis) or deliberate (as in the case of terrorism), while other problems (such as global warming) arise in and affect all countries simultaneously. This chapter will not examine every problem that each nation faces, but will show how pressing problems that cross national boundaries affect international politics, and vice versa.

POPULATION EXPLOSION

The rapid growth of the world's population is the root cause of many global problems. It took two centuries (1650–1850) for world population to double from 550 million to 1.18 billion, but a second doubling took only 100 years

(1850–1950, from 1.18 billion to 2.56 billion) and a third doubling occurred in only 41 years (1950–1991, from 2.56 to 5.42 billion). The 1991 world population of 5.42 billion people is projected to double by the year 2155 (see Figure 10.1).[1]

Why is the world's population increasing so fast? Chapter Eight discussed the phenomenon of the **demographic transition** that accompanies technological and economic development. To review, once a population gains access to rudimentary sanitation and medical services, the fertility (birth) rate quickly overtakes the mortality (death) rate, life expectancy increases, and the size of the population begins to increase steadily. In industrialized nations, population growth then levels off; the developed regions of Europe, the former USSR, and North America are growing very slowly or not at all. In these areas, increased life expectancy and participation in the workplace has led many couples to postpone marriage and have fewer children.[2] In the less developed countries of Asia, Africa, and Latin America, by contrast, medical advances such as vaccination have reduced death rates, but families often remain large and birth rates remain high, mainly because children are needed to provide labor and income for the family. As a result, developed countries generally have older and stable, slowly growing, or declining populations, while the populations of many Third World states remain younger and faster-growing. In 1950 the less developed countries (LDCs) had double the population of the more developed countries (MDCs); at the present time, they have about three times as many people, and by 2020 they are expected to have more than four and one-half times as many.[3]

Alarmingly, by the time you finish reading this paragraph about fifty people will have been born around the world (a rate of three people per second, or a quarter of a million people a day). The world's fastest growing regions continue to be its poorest, and most of the growth is occurring in already overburdened, heavily polluted urban regions. Mexico City and São Paulo, Brazil, already the world's most populous metropolitan areas, are expected to be home to about 30 million and 25 million inhabitants, respectively, by the year 2000.[4] The crowding in many cities is made even worse by the huge population density per square mile: enormous numbers of people squeezed into comparatively small places. Several Chinese and Indian cities fall into this category as well as Lagos, Nigeria; Dahka, Bangladesh; and Jakarta, Indonesia. The people of Lagos, for example, live in thirteen times as densely populated a city as New York.[5] The emergence of such "mega cities" has exacerbated already acute difficulties in providing basic services in developing countries. Affordable housing is difficult to find, crime rates are on the rise, transportation and communication infrastructures are increasingly strained, and social tensions are more pronounced. How long can this go on?

International Responses to Overpopulation

Reducing overall population growth is linked to achieving the international goal of "replacement-level fertility," where two parents are replaced by two children. Even though the results of their efforts will not be evident for a few

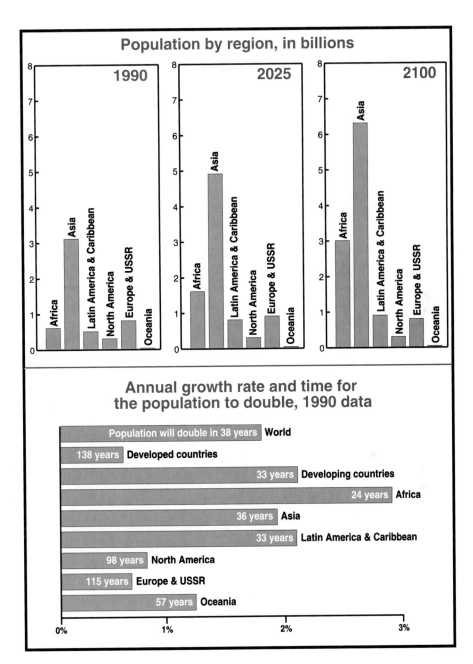

Figure 10.1   Projected Population by Regions over Time

generations, international organizations, such as the United Nations Population Fund (UNFPA) and International Planned Parenthood (IPP), have concentrated on trying to create the social, economic, and political conditions necessary

THE MALTHUSIAN SCENARIO

The vision of doomsday promulgated by English clergyman Thomas Malthus (1766–1834) has had a profound impact on the way scholars evaluate the effects of population growth. Though a churchman, Malthus did not draw his dire predictions from the Bible, but from mathematics. In 1798 Malthus wrote his *Essay on the Principle of Population*, in which he contended that population grows at an exponential rate, while the food supply expands only arithmetically. These divergent growth paths inevitably mean that a chronic growing population would be faced with increased food shortage over time.

Overpopulation, according to the utopian writers of the day, was a problem for the very far future, but Malthus argued that this problem had always plagued humankind. Technical advances that increased the food supply would actually result in greater numbers of births and more people. Population growth would bring about greater despair and poverty, until the ravages of famine, disease, and war brought the food supply and population back into balance.

for reducing the birthrate. The challenges are daunting. Achieving "replacement-level fertility" where it is most urgently needed—the LDCs—will require an increase in investments in human resource developments, such as improvements in women's status and access to education on health, and the means of family planning. This section will focus on the latter.

According to a UN estimate, the world's population is projected to be as high as 14 billion by the year 2025 without an increase in the use of family-planning measures. To prevent this from happening, women in developing countries would have to steadily reduce the average number of children they bear from a high of 4.2 (1980–1985) to a low of 1.9 by the year 2025. In response to estimates like these, in 1994 the UN Conference on Population and Development succeeded in reaching an agreement by nearly 180 nations to limit the world's population to 7.2 billion over the following two decades. The plan passed despite reservations about abortion and other similar issues by many Islamic and Catholic representatives.

The level of fertility is strongly related to contraceptive use. According to most estimates, a 10 percent rise in contraceptive use results in roughly a 70 percent drop in the fertility rate. To keep the world's population at a more acceptable level of 8.5 billion in 2025, the proportion of couples using contraception must rise from today's 45 percent to at least 56 percent by the year 2000, an increase from 326 to 535 million.[6] Thus, the mission of international organizations such as the UN's IPP is clear: design and implement effective family-planning programs throughout the world.

Family-planning programs have succeeded in fits and starts. Information provided by programs such as the UN-sponsored African Census Program in the 1970s illustrated to many governments the full dimensions of the population

While many have recognized that advances in medical and food production technology (see this chapter's section on food and agriculture) have made Malthus's doomsday scenario increasingly less plausible, others are not as willing to discount it.* It has been argued, for example, that a continued high rate of population growth will result in catastrophic environmental degradation, which through pollution and exhaustion of the soil, will still result in a reduced food supply.

Malthus was one of the earliest and most influential contributors to the field of economics. Although his pessimistic vision is not likely to come true, his somber economic predictions certainly helped set the tone for the field of economics, which became known as "the dismal science."

*See, for example, R. Paul Shaw, "Population Growth: Is it Ruining the Environment?" *Populi* 16, no. 2 (1989), p. 22. A cogent defense of some of Malthus's conclusions can be found in Paul Harrison, "Beyond the Blame Game: Population-Environment Links," *Populi* 17, no. 3 (1990), pp. 14–21.

problem, and thus won their support for population programs. However, government support does not automatically lead to successful program implementation. Between 1982 and 1986, for example, the UN was unable to stop the Mexican government from cutting its national health budget by two-thirds, resulting in slowed rates of growth in the number of modern birth-control users.[7] And in Africa, an average of only 14 percent of women use contraceptive devices, a figure that needs to be more than doubled if desired projections are to be met. Overall, because many developing countries are chronically strapped for funds, they often have difficulty in fully staffing and funding family-planning programs. Thus far, the international community has been unable (and perhaps unwilling) to foot a large enough portion of the bill for curbing population growth.

Clearly, continued population growth will only result in increased strains on the world economy and the global ecosystem. Huge increases in Third World populations have led and will continue to lead to increased numbers of emigrants to the hard-pressed developed countries of the world, more demand on the world's available supplies of food and energy resources, and greater stresses on the environment. While the developing countries of the South are currently affected most by the population explosion, the industrialized North must either cooperate in solving the problem now or join in suffering its effects later.

The Abortion Debate and Family-Planning Assistance

Although they have their detractors, government family-planning programs do reduce the rate of population growth. One widely quoted study found that at any level of social development, the stronger the family-planning effort, the greater the decline in the birthrate. In developed countries, for example, the birthrate decline between 1965 and 1980 in countries with a strong family-planning program was three times faster than those with a very weak or nonexistent program.[8]

Most people support the goals of family planning—to reduce poverty, overcrowding, and other harmful effects of unrestrained population growth—but many object to some of the means employed. Religious objections to contraception restrict or prohibit the use of birth control in many countries. The most controversial aspect of family-planning programs, however, is abortion. China's draconian (but effective) family-planning laws, for example, restrict couples to a single child, and officials pressure or compel many women to have abortions in observance of this requirement.

President Ronald Reagan, a staunch supporter of the American right-to-life movement, in 1984 ordered a cutoff of funding for all international organizations, including the United Nations Population Fund (UNFPA), that supported abortion as a birth control means of last resort. Since no U.S. funds had gone to the support of abortion in other countries, Reagan's decision did not have much direct impact on the provision of abortion services abroad. Criticism of family-planning programs by opponents of abortion, however, may have led to decreased levels of overall funding. While the net impact of the U.S. abortion debate on population control in developing countries is difficult to assess, the controversy illustrates how domestic political disputes can affect international efforts to address global issues.

MIGRATION

An imbalance between population and economic resources often leads to movements of population, or migration. In general, migration brings people from regions that suffer from a dearth of land or capital resources, such as Central America or Eastern Europe, to those which are richer, like the United States and the European Union. In recent years, however, many developed countries have gone through cycles of economic recession and thus are becoming more reluctant to accept more immigrants. Additionally, migration is not a purely economic phenomenon, but emerges out of a complex mix of economic scarcity, warfare, ethnic conflict, religious persecution, and political repression. Migration has always played a major role in the history of the human species (and, indeed, that of its hominid ancestors). This section will focus on patterns and problems of migration at the end of the twentieth century.

Economic Migration

With rare exceptions (such as the African slaves brought to the Americas), most people who have immigrated to the richer countries of the world have done so in search of a higher standard of living. This is hardly surprising, as higher birthrates in the developing world have produced an enormous population that has sought work in the industrialized world, with its comparative wealth, low birthrates, and aging citizenry. It is estimated that 70 million people now work legally or illegally in countries other than those in which they were born, a number increasing by almost 2 million annually. Three countries—the United States, Canada, and Australia—admitted more than 8 million settlers during the late 1980s, including an average of 603,000 per year in the United States. This influx of immigrants is surpassed only by the two surges of European immigration into the United States during the first two decades of the twentieth century, when there were almost no immigration restrictions. Recently, Asia has supplanted Europe as the main source of documented U.S. immigrants.[9] Large numbers of immigrants also enter the United States illegally, mostly from Latin America.

Refugees from War and Persecution

In addition to those seeking economic opportunity, migrants today also flee from war and oppressive dictatorships. These persons are collectively referred to as **refugees,** because they are forced to flee their home countries for reasons not related to their economic standard of living. The UN High Commissioner of Refugees (UNHCR) defines a refugee in its 1967 protocol as a person who, "owing to well-founded fear of persecution for reasons of race, religion, nationality, membership of a particular social group or political opinion, is outside of the country of his nationality and is unable or, owing to such fear, is unwilling to avail himself of the protection of that country."[10] However, many countries suspect that new arrivals may be claiming some sort of persecution in order to enter a country for the purpose of securing a better job. These countries, including the United States, tend to accept refugees who are fleeing persecution but refuse to admit economic migrants.

Most refugees are displaced within their own countries, or flee to neighboring states or regions. As an indication of the dimension of the problem, there were 2.5 million refugees in 1970; 8 million in 1980; and more than 18 million in late 1993—with the number growing by 10,000 a day. Not surprisingly, refugees tend to be from poorer parts of the world. Iran alone has more than 4 million refugees, Pakistan 1.6 million, and Malawi, where more than 10 percent of the population are refugees (more than 1 million). As indicated in the first part of Table 10.1, most of these people fled from horrid conflicts within countries, especially Afghanistan and Mozambique, a nation in southeast Africa torn by decades of civil war and economic hardship. Conflict in recent years in the former Yugoslavia, Burundi, Liberia, Somalia, and Eritrea—among others— have added to refugee statistics.

In addition to these large sources of refugees, the world is beset by old problems (such as Palestinian unrest), recurring troubles (in Sudan, Ethiopia, Somalia, and Rwanda), and constantly emerging tragedies (such as strife in the former Yugoslavia and parts of the former USSR). There are approximately 20 million refugees out of their home countries, but the UN also estimates that there are more than 25 million people who are displaced within their own states. In the early 1990s, African countries were particularly prominent as sources of internal refugees (South Africa, Sudan, Mozambique, Angola, and Liberia). The former Yugoslavia, Iraq, Burma (Myanmar), the Philippines, and parts of the former

Table 10.1   Refugees

**Principal Sources of World's Refugees and Asylum Seekers
(as of December 31, 1993)**

Countries That Have Generated the Greatest Number of the World's Refugees

Afghanistan	3,429,800 *	Armenia	200,000 *
Palestinians	2,801,300	Tajikistan	153,000 *
Mozambique	1,332,000 *	Georgia	143,000 *
Former Yugoslavia	1,319,650 *	Iraq	134,700
Burundi	780,000	China (Tibet)	133,000
Liberia	701,000 *	Sri Lanka	106,650 *
Somalia	491,000 *	Bhutan	105,800 *
Eritrea	421,000 *	Mali	87,000
Sudan	373,000	Western Sahara	80,000 *
Angola	335,000	Zaire	79,000
Vietnam	303,000	Mauritania	79,000
Azerbaijan	290,000 *	Bangladesh	53,500
Burma	289,000 *	Uzbekistan	51,000
Rwanda	275,000 *	Guatemala	49,200
Sierra Leone	260,000 *	Iran	39,000
Togo	240,000	Cambodia	35,500
Ethiopia	232,000	Chad	33,400

*Indicates that sources vary widely in number reported.
Source: World Refugee Survey, 1994.

Soviet Union were also identified as places where those who left or lost their homes remained, voluntarily or not, within their own country. The refugee problem is therefore growing at an alarming rate both within and between states.

One estimate suggested that the total number of uprooted people in the world in 1991 may actually have been as high as 53 million.[11] Clearly, the New Era is a period characterized by increased movement and, disturbingly, increased uprootedness.

Consequences of Migration

The influx of immigrants, whatever their reasons for coming, have periodically provoked backlashes by the host-country population. Reactions are often racially motivated; **nativist** movements (political movements favoring the native-born and discriminating against immigrants) arise and gain strength during economic downturns, when immigrants are often blamed for unemployment and rising crime rates. Nativist pressure in the United States prompted the passage of the Immigration Act of 1924, for example, which installed strict quotas on the number of immigrants who could enter the country each year. This act discriminated particularly against potential immigrants from Southern and Eastern European countries and tightened already existing restrictions against Asians.

Selected List of Significant Population of Internally Displaced Civilians (as of Decenber 31, 1993)

Persons Displaced within Their Own Countries;
Relocation Is Due to Internal Conflict or Forced Removal

Sudan	4,000,000	Sierra Leone	400,000
South Africa	4,000,000	Croatia	350,000
Mozambique	2,000,000	Colombia	300,000–600,000
Angola	2,000,000	Kenya	300,000
Bosnia	1,300,000	Rwanda	300,000
Liberia	1,000,000	Haiti	300,000
Iraq	1,000,000	Cyprus	265,000
Lebanon	700,000	Iran	260,000
Somalia	700,000	Georgia	250,000
Zaire	700,000	India	250,000
Azerbaijan	600,000	Philippines	200,000–4,000,000
Sri Lanka	600,000	Eritrea	200,000
Peru	500,000	Guatemala	200,000
Burma	500,000–3,000,000	Togo	150,000
Burundi	500,000	Djibouti	140,000
Ethiopia	500,000	Cambodia	95,000

Source: World Refugee Survey, 1994.

The economic recession of the early 1990s in Europe and North America was similar in this regard, with calls for limiting foreign immigration.

Negative reactions to immigrants have spread throughout the European Union (EU), which has declared that citizens of EU member states should be able to move freely from one country to another. However, faced with waves of immigrants from Eastern Europe and North Africa, EU member states have begun to close their national borders, at least symbolically. In France, increasingly strict controls on immigration have been enacted since Algeria became independent in 1962, partly as a result of the belief that immigrants from North Africa were not being assimilated into French society. More recently in France, nativist forces such as Jean-Marie Le Pen's National Front have used the immigration issue as a means of gaining political power, creating pressure on the French government to take further action against immigration.

The welcome mat has been pulled back elsewhere in Europe, too. In the spring of 1991 about 24,000 Albanians fled to Italy, which responded with an ineffective naval blockade; when the Albanians defied the blockade and continued to come ashore, Italian authorities shipped them back.[12]

Germany's situation is becoming similar. With some of the most liberal asylum provisions in the world, the German government's review of an individual's request for asylum may take years, during which time each asylum-seeker is given housing, food, clothing, and medical expenses. Even though only 5 percent ultimately qualify, about 438,000 people sought asylum in Germany in 1992. With unemployment hovering around 7 percent in West Germany and 35 percent in the formerly Communist East, the climate is conducive to racist violence against foreigners. Incidents of anti-foreigner and anti-Semitic violence by neo-Nazi extremists (who number about 42,500) climbed to 2285 and resulted in seventeen deaths in 1992.[13] Frequent targets of ethnic hate crimes were Turkish "guest workers" and their families, residing legally in Germany but not possessing full German citizenship. Although this violence has aroused protest at home and abroad, it has had its effect: German politicians have passed revisions in Germany's asylum law, previously perceived as excessively generous.

EU member states are particularly worried about the possibility of a flood tide of immigration resulting from the collapse of the Soviet Union and the Communist regimes in Eastern Europe, but so far non-EU countries have absorbed the greatest numbers of immigrants from the former Soviet-bloc states. In 1990 Hungary's relatively stable economy and liberal immigration policy attracted 90,000 asylum- or work-seekers, resulting in a tightening of immigration restrictions in 1991.[14] Another small European state faced with large numbers of asylum requests, Austria, has considered sending 150,000 persons believed to be living illegally within its borders back to their home countries.[15]

Even in the United States, where the Statue of Liberty beckons to immigrants, political pressure to restrict immigration is rising. It is not so much political refugees that Americans mind, as the United States has historically granted asylum to people fleeing countries with which the United States has less than friendly relations. Between 1975 and 1992, the United States admitted about 1.7 million political refugees, most from East Asia (particularly Vietnam) and the Soviet Union.[16] The United States has not extended the same welcome, however, to people fleeing from noncommunist countries. While almost 97 percent of Soviet and ex-Soviet asylum-seekers and 95 percent of Vietnamese refugees were admitted from 1975 to 1992, only 1.2 percent of persons attempting to flee from impoverished, politically repressed Haiti were granted asylum. In 1992 hundreds of Haitian refugees attempting to sail to Florida in homemade crafts were detained at sea and sent to the U.S. naval station at Guantanamo Bay, Cuba.[17] In contrast, virtually all those fleeing the Communist island of Cuba interdicted at sea en route to Florida were granted asylum in the United States as political refugees. This policy changed, however, in 1994 when the United States refused to grant asylum to Cubans attempting to flee, instead sending them to safe havens in Guantanamo Bay and Panama. This exodus led to an agreement between Washington and Havanna for controlled immigration from Cuba.

Many U.S. citizens, like their counterparts in other industrialized countries, are becoming less receptive to economic migrants, fearing that immigrants are taking jobs away from native-born Americans (even though great numbers of immigrants accept low-paying jobs that few native-born citizens are willing to take). Particularly in California, long a favored destination for immigrants to America, nativists claim that new immigrants are consuming government services (such as Medicare and welfare) in excess of what they contribute in taxes. (The fact that many native lower-income Americans also benefit from more services than they pay in taxes is frequently ignored by anti-immigration activists.) Fear and resentment of immigrants and the inevitable friction caused by cultural diversity have spawned a variety of nativistic reactions, ranging from "English Only" ballot initiatives in many areas to the 1992 presidential candidacy of David Duke, a reactionary former Grand Wizard of the Ku Klux Klan.

International Solutions to Problems of Migration

Several international organizations have attempted to address the issues and problems surrounding economic migration. For instance, an international convention approved by the UN's General Assembly in December 1990 seeks to protect the human rights of migrant workers. The convention recognizes that migration results in the scattering of the family; illegal, often secret movements; trafficking in human cargo (such as the smuggling of Mexican and Chinese people into the United States for exorbitant fees); and the exploitive employment of undocumented workers. More importantly, it also codifies a series of rights to which migrant workers and their families are entitled. Countries such as Morocco and Mexico, both of which have many citizens who work abroad, have supported the convention, while many richer countries such as Oman, Japan, and Australia, worried about an influx of economic migrants, have expressed reservations about adopting it.[18]

The UN High Commissioner for Refugees has carried out a number of programs designed to protect, resettle, and repatriate political refugees. The UN-sponsored 1989 International Conference on Central American Refugees (CIREFCA), for example, obtained pledges of $156 million for aid and resettlement of over 440,000 persons displaced in that region.[19] In recent years, many states have cooperated to promote efforts for voluntary repatriation of political refugees, and these attempts have been successful at times. For example, after the Iraqi invasion of Kuwait in August 1990 displaced some 5 million people from several countries of origin, an April 1991 Memorandum of Understanding between the UN and Iraq initiated a mass voluntary repatriation effort involving some 1.5 million refugees. Most of these were Iraqi Kurds who had been displaced to squalid camps along the border with Turkey and Iran. While there, up to 800 people reportedly fell victim to disease and malnutrition every day.[20]

Another international voluntary repatriation effort, the 1989 Comprehensive Plan of Action (CPA) for Indochinese refugees, has aided in repatriating thousands to their homelands in Cambodia, Laos, and Vietnam. As a result of the CPA, the number of Vietnamese asylum-seekers in the region dropped from about 73,000 in 1989 to 31,000 in 1990, and over 11,000 Vietnamese returned voluntarily in the program's early stages. More than half of the 300,000 Cambodians living in camps along the Thai border have also been repatriated.[21]

Recent international efforts have made substantial progress in assisting refugees. In many other cases, however, displaced persons find themselves with no place to go. While many Kurdish and Vietnamese refugees returned voluntarily to their homelands in 1991, the United States sent almost 2000 Haitians

Having fled the chaos in their country, Albanian refugees are detained in October 1991 by Italian authorities at the port city of Bari.

Source: © P. Durand/Sygma.

back to Haiti, Italy returned 17,000 Albanians, and Turkey expelled almost 450,000 Kurds.[22] Indeed, long-term refugees continue to pose major problems for their host countries and the international community. Although many economic migrants achieve the prosperity for which they came to their new homelands, thousands of others face discrimination and anti-immigrant violence. Until democracy and economic progress catch up with population growth in the developing world, great numbers of people will continue to leave developing countries in search of political freedom and economic opportunity in the developed world. Industrialized nations can choose between turning away immigrants or welcoming them, and can decide how and how much to promote economic development abroad, but they cannot ignore the crowds outside their gates forever.

FOOD AND HUNGER

Population increases have resulted in more than just migration. A second, perhaps more fundamental challenge is that of adequately feeding the more than 5.4 billion mouths that inhabit the planet. The problem, interestingly, is not a lack of food worldwide, but rather of getting the food to those who need it most, before hunger, malnutrition, and ultimately death result. The rest of this section will show that distribution generally differs from developed to developing countries. While developed countries are easily able to feed their populations, many developing states are not.

Daily per capita caloric intake (that is, how many calories each person, on average, consumes every day) serves as a rough indicator of the adequacy of a nation's food supply. Great disparities exist between developed and developing regions in terms of daily calorie intake. During the 1980s, average calorie consumption in the developed countries (3404 calories) was roughly 25 percent greater than the world average (2617 calories), and more than a third greater than caloric intake per person in developing countries (2473 calories). These worldwide figures conceal great variations in calorie supply in the developing world. On average, calorie consumption per person in Africa (2204 calories) was 81 percent of the world average, 64 percent of the average for the developed countries, 64 percent of the average for Europe (3452 calories), and only 61 percent of the average for North America (3603 calories).[23]

These figures do not consider quality of diet; many people in Third World countries have inadequate supplies of protein and other nutritional necessities. It will come as no surprise that the richer nations consume diets vastly superior in quantity and quality from those of the developing nations. It has been estimated that the average North American consumes five times as many agricultural resources as the average person in India, and that average American consumption exceeds by two to four times the quantity of protein that the human body can utilize.[24]

Despite these differences in average consumption, food supplies in just the developing world as a whole are adequate—few people will starve on an average of 2000 calories per day. Nevertheless, the grave consequences of inadequate nutrition are readily apparent. It is currently estimated that more than 500 million people suffer from chronic malnutrition, and that each year hundreds of thousands die from hunger-related diseases. Again, this happens despite the fact that developing countries produce about 150 percent of their daily per capita calorie requirements (1988 figures).[25]

Why are people suffering in the midst of such plenty? The answer is that while quantity of food produced is generally adequate, its distribution is not; poverty, natural disasters, and war limit or prevent access to food supplies. Areas prone to drought, for example, can suffer drastic temporary shortages of food. If drought-stricken regions have poorly developed transportation systems and lack the cash to buy food from nearby sources, the result can be mass starvation. This is what occurred during the famines in the Sahel (the semiarid region of Africa just south of the Sahara Desert) in the late 1960s and mid-1980s. In other cases, hunger results from man-made disasters, such as political chaos and intra-national warfare. During the civil wars in Ethiopia in the 1980s, government forces often blocked food supplies to rebellious regions and hampered international relief efforts, in effect using famine as a weapon against separatist uprisings.

The situation in Somalia prior to the arrival of U.S. troops in 1992 to augment the UN relief effort there provides another example of tragically inadequate food distribution. In 1991 and 1992 Somalia suffered a famine that threatened over 4 million people with starvation. The cause was not only a severe drought, but also the factional fighting and violent disputes over farmland that followed the collapse of the Somali government. Consequently, less food was grown, and much of the food that had been produced was hoarded by people afraid that they would not have enough to eat in the future and by those eager to get a higher price for their foodstuffs in the short term. A tragic irony for Somalia was that there was food in the markets, but the prices were prohibitive for most people. Local strongmen and armed gangs took what they needed by force, while children, the aged, and those who couldn't steal succumbed to hunger. At the start of 1993 Somalia relied on foreign aid for its food supply, and, despite the efforts of U.S. forces and the UN, more than one-sixth of the country's population still faced starvation. By the time that the last of the U.S. troops departed in March 1994, leaving a weaker UN presence, these conditions had improved but the country was suffering from a huge cholera outbreak.

International Food Aid and Famine-Relief Efforts

Efforts to get food to countries that cannot feed themselves have been relatively successful, even though donating governments sometimes resort to using food as a weapon to try to get recipient countries to change their policies. Many states have acted independently to redress the balance between food production and consumption. The United States, rich in agricultural resources, has been active in fighting hunger and starvation on its own, as well as through contributions to UN relief agencies and other international relief efforts. However, the United States has also tried to use food as a political tool, most obviously in the grain embargo directed against the Soviet Union in 1980 as punishment for its invasion of Afghanistan. This attempt to use food for political purposes failed, chiefly because the Soviet Union was able to purchase grain from other countries such as Canada and Argentina, and the embargo was lifted in 1981 after fifteen months (much to the relief of American farmers, who had profited from the sale of grain to the USSR throughout the Cold War).

International organizations have taken a number of approaches to alleviate the problems of hunger and malnutrition. Several **nongovernmental organizations (NGOs)** such as Oxfam (Britain's largest overseas charity) and the United Support of Artists for Africa (best known for its recording of the song "We Are the World" in 1985) concentrate on short-term relief of acute food shortages. Other groups, such as the UN **Food and Agriculture Organization (FAO),** work toward long-term solutions to problems of food production and distribution, providing technical and financial assistance for agricultural projects in developing countries.

Though all are well-intentioned, some famine relief and agricultural development efforts generate a great deal of controversy. The UN's relief effort in Somalia, for example, has been widely criticized for failing to create the necessary infrastructure for food distribution, primarily because of its difficulties in persuading Somalia's fractious warlords to cooperate. Other famine-relief efforts

life with robinson

Controversy swirled around the 1979 U.S. grain embargo. Americans may have despised the Soviets during the Cold War, but U.S. farmers loved selling them grain.
Source: © Jerry Robinson, © Cartoonists & Writers Syndicate.

have been criticized for their shortsighted solutions. Often, because debt-ridden developing countries do not have adequate export earnings to pay for food imports, they are encouraged by international organizations to increase domestic food production. Bringing more land under cultivation, however, often entails clearing ecologically valuable forests for farming and ranching. The use of traditional farming and ranching methods on these lands leads to further deforestation or gradually turns arable lands into desert, thus paradoxically leaving countries more vulnerable to drought and famine. The ecological balance of the Brazilian Amazon, for example, has been upset by clear-cutting and the introduction of agricultural techniques to farm the land. Such land is unable to sustain itself for food-growing over time, leaving the country more vulnerable than ever in the long term, with even less usable land.

Despite the many difficulties relief efforts have encountered, the problem of world hunger appears to be the least contentious and most easily soluble global issue. However, the longer that states and international organizations wait to adopt solutions, the more urgent the problem becomes, since the world's population continues to expand. In the long term, economic development is the best solution to hunger and malnutrition, but as noted earlier, economic development must proceed in such a way as to minimize environmental costs. In the short term, the best solution to the food and hunger problem is to improve distribution networks and the type of aid given. Developed countries produce more than enough food to feed themselves and their less developed neighbors, and usually prefer to donate surplus food—bulky, difficult to transport, and quick to spoil—instead of money—easy to transport, but often subject to theft by corrupt officials or speculators. At the same time, free distribution of food aid to famine-ravaged areas undercuts the efforts of local farmers to increase production and improve long-term food security.[26] Both short- and long-term solutions to world hunger are relatively straightforward, but each has its costs.

THE ENVIRONMENT

Environmental issues vividly demonstrate the reality of global interdependence. In 1986 the world witnessed a striking example of how environmental problems can cross national boundaries when an accident at a nuclear reactor at Chernobyl, then in the Soviet Union and now in Ukraine, spread radioactive fallout throughout Europe and parts of the Middle East and North Africa. The most severe effects of the radiation were felt in Ukraine, in the form of radiation sickness and cancers, but eventually traces of fallout from the partial meltdown could be detected all over the globe.[27] Although this incident and others illustrate the international scope of environmental hazards, individual states have historically addressed environmental concerns mainly through domestic laws and regulations. Only recently have nations begun to use international forums to address global environmental issues and promote collective solutions. We will examine these solutions after addressing the environmental issues that presently concern most states.

Representative Environmental Problems: Deforestation and Pollution

The contemporary joke that a developer is someone who wants to build a house in the woods, while an environmentalist is someone who already has a house in the woods, illuminates one of the reasons why environmental problems can be difficult to solve: Few people pollute deliberately, but most cause some form of environmental damage in the pursuit of their material needs. This section will briefly examine two ways in which economic activity causes environmental degradation, namely through deforestation and industrial pollution.

Deforestation occurs when people cut down trees without planting enough new ones to replace them. Contrary to popular belief, which often holds that greedy lumber companies are responsible for denuding the earth of trees for wood profits, commercial logging is not the primary cause of deforestation. The real culprit has been the clearing of forests for human settlement, cattle pasture, and farmland, which resulted in the loss of two acres of forest for every one acre of arable farmland between 1971 and 1986. By the early 1990s, rain forests were being destroyed at a pace of almost 40 million acres a year, close to a 50 percent higher rate than a decade earlier. More than one-third of the area originally forested globally had no trees.[28]

The traditional slash-and-burn technique for clearing land for crop rotation can also contribute to deforestation and **desertification,** as well as a host of additional environmental concerns, including topsoil erosion and increased emissions of nitrous oxide, methane, and carbon dioxide.[29] War and other unnatural disasters can also result in deforestation. It has been estimated that between 1955 and 1975, the Vietnam War leveled 2.5 million acres of forest and rendered at least 5 million acres unproductive due to the defoliant Agent Orange and other chemical pollutants.[30]

Deforestation does not just mean the loss of trees. It also contributes to a loss of wildlife. Over 34,000 plant species and at least 700,000 animal species live on only 3.5 percent of the earth's remaining primary forests. Loss of the forest cover in these wooded areas, occupying a mere 0.2 percent of the earth's surface, would mean the extinction of almost 7 percent of all plant and animal species on land. At present, between 1000 and 2000 species become extinct every year, resulting in a severe decline in biological diversity and the ability of nature to adapt to change.[31] Additionally, the burning of forests produces carbon dioxide, which many ecologists fear is causing the earth to become gradually warmer (see the boxed feature, "Is the Earth Getting Warmer?"). Some studies suggest that halting deforestation could cut worldwide emissions of carbon dioxide by 25 percent.[32]

While deforestation has become an increasing global concern in recent years, most people traditionally associate environmental damage with **industrial pollution.** After all, urbanization and industrialization create such familiar and readily noticeable environmental ills as smog, acid rain, and elevated levels of

Brazilian homesteaders clear burned rain forest debris to ready the soil for cultivation. This family has cleared 50 of their 123 acres in such a manner.
Source: © AP/Wide World Photos.

IS THE EARTH GETTING WARMER?

A well-publicized, and controversial, global environmental concern is the emission of gases such as carbon dioxide and methane, which can trap heat in the earth's atmosphere. The source of carbon dioxide that has attracted the greatest environmental concern is the burning of fossil fuels (including coal, oil, and gasoline) for energy. It is estimated that annual carbon-dioxide emission from man-made sources rose globally from 2.3 billion tons in 1950 to around 6.7 billion tons in 1985, a growth rate of 3.1 percent a year.*

This statistic has many people worried. Many scientists have argued that continued emission of greenhouse gases has increased the earth's average temperature, a phenomenon known as the **greenhouse effect.** Some studies predict that if production of greenhouse gases is not slowed, by the middle of the twenty-first century average world temperatures will rise by 1.5 to 2.8 degrees centigrade, making the world hotter than at any time during the last 120,000 years. This may not sound like much, but it might cause enough melting of the polar ice caps to raise the world's sea level by as much as 70 centimeters, causing serious flooding in low-lying areas.[†] Climate change could hurt more than real estate values; for example, an average warming of just 2 degrees Fahrenheit could melt enough Hudson Bay ice to wipe out the local polar bear population, since they need ice as a platform for hunting seals, a main source of food.

carbon dioxide and **chlorofluorocarbons (CFCs).** This air pollution is glaringly evident in smog-blanketed cities all over the world, from Mexico City to Los Angeles to Moscow to Bangkok. The six countries emitting the most carbon dioxide in order of largest to smallest are the United States, the former Soviet Union, China, Japan, Germany, and India. Moreover, all seven members of the G7 are among the top eleven nations in CO_2 emissions.[33] Such pollution not only worsens the problems of global warming and the depletion of the ozone layer (which shields the earth from harmful ultraviolet radiation), but creates other health problems as well. Seventy percent of urban dwellers breathe unhealthy air, and another 10 percent breathe air of questionable quality.[34]

Airborne pollutants can affect areas far from the cities and factories where they are emitted. For example, the burning of **fossil fuels** (coal, oil, and gasoline) spew sulphur oxides into the air, which eventually fall back to earth in the form of "acid rain." This combination of toxic chemicals and atmospheric moisture kills trees, erodes the surfaces of buildings, and acidifies bodies of water, making them inhospitable to the life therein and even creating a threat to safe drinking supplies. Tension between the Canadian and U.S. governments over acid rain flares up periodically. The Canadian government insists that American industries, which produce most of the acid rain that falls on both sides of the U.S.–Canadian border, clean up their manufacturing processes. Attempts at doing so have run into political obstacles, however, as companies ordered to

There is convincing evidence of recent global warming. The part of the Northern Hemisphere covered by snow has been shrinking, sea ice in the Arctic Ocean is receding toward the North Pole, huge expanses of the sea ice north of Greenland have thinned by about 15 percent, and the Canadian and Alaskan permafrost has warmed by about 3.7 percent over the past 100 years.

Some experts, however, remain skeptical that a greenhouse effect even exists, or that, if it does, it is dangerous. While scientists agree that levels of carbon dioxide in the atmosphere have increased by about 25 percent over the last century, some point out that the earth has gone through other warm spells, none of them brought on by human activity. A single volcanic eruption, for example, can spew forth billions of tons of greenhouse gases, and variations in solar radiation have a much greater effect on global temperatures than that exerted by industrial emissions. As reliable records of temperatures have existed for little more than 100 years, proving whether or not a greenhouse effect exists and poses a threat is likely to be a difficult but controversial task for quite some time.

*Harrison, "Beyond the Blame Game," *World Monitor*, (January 1990), p. 17.

†Estimates cited in Mary Williams Walsh, "An Early Warning of Warming," *Las Angeles Times*, Feb. 8, 1993, pp. A1, A19–A20.

reduce sulfur-dioxide emissions contend that the increased costs would result in the elimination of many jobs.

An Increasingly Global Problem

Efforts by the developed nations to get the issue of atmospheric pollution on the agenda have not always been accepted by the developing nations, whose concern for preserving forests, wetlands, and the ozone layer pales in comparison to their desire to industrialize. As a whole, the major industrialized countries account for most of the emissions of greenhouse gases in the world and burn 75 percent of the fossil fuel used each year. Developing countries, however, are closing the pollution gap. The annual carbon-dioxide output in Third World nations grew almost 2.4 percent per year between 1960 and 1990 (with emissions from industrial sources increasing almost sixteen-fold from 1950 to 1985), and energy consumption grew at 4 percent per year between 1980 and 1986, ten times faster than in industrialized countries. If past trends continue, by 2025 developing countries will be emitting over four times as much as developed countries today, leading to a total world output per year of three times the present level.[35] Much of the rapid rise in pollution in developing countries is attributable to the fact that industries in poorer states often tend to use dirtier fuels. China, for instance, relies on cheap, abundant high-sulfur coal, which is among the most polluting energy sources known.

Development that produces more pollution will in the long run damage the global ecosystem, with potentially severe repercussions for international politics. For example, if significant changes in the climate were to occur, creating increased precipitation in some areas and desertification in others, the ability of many states to produce enough food for their people could be drastically reduced. In turn, this could cause huge population movements with potentially disruptive consequences, as discussed in the previous section.[36]

International Cooperation for Saving the Environment

International organizations began to focus their attention on environmental issues in the mid-twentieth century. The objectives of the Council of Europe (1949) included preservation of the environment and responsible uses of natural resources, goals the EU continues to advocate today. In 1949 the UN hosted the Scientific Conference on the Conservation and Utilization of Resources to discuss problems relating to natural resources. This was the first international forum convened to address the problem of resource conservation, although no major recommendations were issued.

During the late 1960s and early 1970s, the issue of the environment moved closer to the top of the UN's agenda. In 1968 the **UN Economic and Social Council (ECOSOC)** approved an initiative by Sweden calling for legislation to address the "human environment." The first result of this initiative was the Founex Report of 1971, which recognized the important relationship between development and the environment in the Third World. The report suggested that the poverty found in the developing world was directly related to environmental degradation. The 1972 Stockholm Conference helped to establish the UN Environmental Program (UNEP), whose main purpose was to promote international environmental cooperation. In 1974 UNEP, along with the UN Conference on Trade and Development (UNCTAD), held a symposium in Mexico to discuss further the links between environmental problems and the distribution of the world's resources. The symposium found that the international community needed to take the necessary steps to ensure that the world's people were provided with "basic human needs." That same year, the third UN Conference on the Law of the Sea (UNCLOS) established a new law for protecting the marine environment. (See Chapter Nine for more on UNCLOS.) Overall, these international reports and conferences did much to raise awareness of environmental concerns, although very little progress was made in terms of finding implementable solutions to the problems at hand.

International efforts in the 1980s and 1990s continued to link environmental concerns to issues of trade and economic development. As in the 1960s and 1970s, these cooperative endeavors have greatly increased awareness of these issues, but their attempts at practical problem solving have yielded mixed results. A typical example is the 1987 Montreal Protocol, which required signatory states to phase out the use of CFCs (ozone-depleting chemicals) over a period of time and obligated them to prohibit importation of all products containing the offending chemicals. The protocol contained a loophole, however, which permitted developing countries to increase their per capita use of CFCs, which could allow a 70 percent rise in CFC emissions by the year 2040.[37] (For more on the failures and successes of **intergovernmental organizations [IGOs]** to address environmental issues, see Chapter Nine and the box on the 1992 Earth Summit in that chapter.)

Some of the most effective efforts to preserve the environment have been carried out by nongovernmental organizations (NGOs), through independent projects and through the pressure they apply on states and IGOs. In the United States, one of the earliest environmental organizations, the American Forestry Association (founded in 1875), is still active in trying to preserve and manage natural resources. Another well-known environmental organization, the Sierra Club, was founded in 1892 to promote the conservation of public lands in the form of national parks. Environmental concerns took a back seat during the Great Depression, but after World War II a renewed interest in the environment emerged because of pollution resulting from industrialization and a perceived serious reduction in available natural resources.

The year 1948 saw the creation of the International Union for the Protection of Nature (IUPN), now the World Conservation Union. This organization consists of both governmental and nongovernmental actors and focuses on the use of science to work toward environmental goals, including the preservation of biodiversity, the creation of national parks, and the promotion of environmentally safe economic development. Other environmental NGOs emerged in the 1960s, including the World Wildlife Fund (WWF), now called the World Wide Fund for Nature, which is primarily concerned with the conservation of biodiversity.

Growing awareness of environmental problems and related global issues prompted the 1968 formation of the Club of Rome, a multinational group of economists and other specialists. The organization produced a report, *Limits to Growth*, warning that if population growth, food consumption, and pollution continued at their current rates, the planet's potential to support growth would cease after a hundred years. Interestingly, when this report was issued, the main concern of the environmental organizations was that depletion of natural resources would eventually reduce production and consumption. By the 1990s, however, their primary worry was that continued increases in production and consumption would result in severe environmental damage.

Today NGOs and other private actors are engaged in efforts to save all sorts of natural treasures, especially tropical rain forests. Rock musicians such as Sting, REM, and the Grateful Dead have lent their names to campaigns to preserve the Brazilian rain forest and halt deforestation. Businesses like Ben & Jerry's Ice Cream and The Body Shop have purchased products grown in rain forests to show that these areas do not have to be converted to farmland in order to have economic value. By using trade, rather than aid, to promote conservation of biological resources, these companies try to convince governments that the long-term economic benefits of environmental protection can exceed the short-run profits from environmentally destructive activities.

A Green and Pleasant Globe?

NGOs concerned with environmental issues may have shown states and IGOs that economic incentives are the best way to address the problems of pollution and deforestation. Few incentives are great enough, however, to convince poorer countries to cease environmentally harmful development efforts, and a strategy of relying on the social consciousness of governments, private companies, and individuals is questionable at best. At the same time, developed countries have a long way to go to put their own environmental houses in order, as shown by the problems with acid rain and carbon emissions.

The world's track record on the environment illustrates how awareness of a global problem does not necessarily lead to global changes in behavior. The costs of environmental damage usually accumulate over the long term, while the benefits from production and consumption can be enjoyed quickly. Adoption of the long-term perspective on the ecosystem is the only way that environmental movements within states have been able to make their countries cleaner and greener. Global environmental preservation efforts cannot succeed unless they instill this outlook in governments. In countries overwhelmed by the immediate concerns of poverty and overpopulation, however, the argument that the long-term benefits of conservation outweigh the short-term gains from deforestation and industrialization is a difficult case to make.

HEALTH AND DISEASE

The Global Health Picture

Previous sections have touched on some of the consequences of overpopulation, environmental degradation, and malnutrition on human health. This section takes a closer look at global health issues, examining some of the problems and prospects for improving health and eradicating epidemics across international boundaries.

At almost every stage of life, people in developing countries are more susceptible to health problems than those in richer nations, because poverty, malnutrition, and poor sanitation contribute to the spread of disease. One broad measure of general health, life expectancy, is now about sixty-two years for the world as a whole, but on average, people in developed regions can expect to live fourteen years longer than those in poorer nations.[38] In 1990, 96 percent of child and infant deaths occurred in the Third World.[39] While the rate of death from complications during pregnancy is only 5 out of 100,000 live births in some parts of Europe, the rate soars to 1000 per 100,000 live births in parts of Africa and Asia.[40]

The prevalence of certain diseases illustrates the distressing condition of health in the developing world. Every year 8 million children in developing countries either die or are disabled from six vaccine-preventable diseases:

measles, poliomyelitis, tuberculosis, diphtheria, whooping cough, and tetanus. Without immunization, virtually 100 percent of the children in developing countries would contract measles between the ages of six months to three years.[41] It has also been estimated that 300 million people, almost 80 percent of them in Asia, are infected with Hepatitis B, which can develop into serious liver disease and cancer in persons forty years of age and up.

Many developing countries face serious problems with tropical diseases. In 1990, for example, the UN Population Division produced data showing significant increases in the rate of infection of malaria. Ninety percent of people infected by the malaria parasite (which is carried by anopheles mosquitos) and over 80 percent of the approximately 120,000 cases treated annually are located in African countries.[42] The risk of infection with malaria is high where anti-malaria programs are weak or nonexistent, such as in "frontier areas" of economic development, farming and mining projects in newly cleared jungle, and areas suffering the effects of warfare, smuggling, and refugee migration.

Cholera also claims a significant number of casualties. This disease results mostly from contaminated water used for drinking or cooking. Of the almost 600,000 recorded cholera cases worldwide in 1992, two-thirds were located in the Americas following an epidemic that started in Peru and spread throughout the hemisphere, even up to Los Angeles in one case. Although 150,000 cases were in Africa, a much higher percentage of the African cases resulted in death.[43] Besides malaria and cholera, other tropical diseases claim a substantial number of victims: leprosy, schistosomiasis, river blindness, Chagas' disease, and African sleeping sickness.[44]

While it has thus far claimed far fewer victims than these tropical diseases, acquired immune deficiency syndrome (AIDS) has become one of the world's most serious health problems. Caused by the human immunodeficiency virus (HIV), it is actually a complex interaction between impairment of the immune system and opportunistic infections such as pneumonia, tuberculosis, syphilis, or other conditions. It is transmitted through blood (via intravenous drug use or, rarely, transfusion of infected blood), sexual contact, and from pregnant women to the fetuses they carry. While intravenous drug use is said to carry the highest risk of HIV transmission, most recorded cases of AIDS are the result of unprotected sexual contact. The global AIDS epidemic began in the early 1980s; by mid–1994 an estimated 17 million people had become infected with HIV, of whom 4 million had AIDS. In addition, by this time more than 2.5 million people had died.[45]

As with the diseases just discussed, patterns of HIV infection differ between developed and developing countries. In the United States in 1992, over 80 percent of AIDS cases were concentrated in urban areas, and two-thirds of all AIDS cases involved either homosexuals or bisexuals.[46] In developing regions, by contrast, the primary means of HIV transmission is through heterosexual contact. In Zaire, for example, an estimated 1 percent of the sexually active population in the countryside and 8 percent of the population in towns may suffer from AIDS.[47] According to 1990 estimates, in some developing countries as

AT A GLANCE

GLOBAL ISSUES

Population

Reasons: Once a population gains access to rudimentary sanitation and medical services, the fertility rate overtakes the mortality rate, life expectancy increases, and population steadily grows. In industrialized nations, population growth levels off, but in less developed countries, the birthrate remains high.

Problems/Consequences: World population grows at the rate of three people per second. Most growth takes place in Third World urban areas (such as Mexico City and São Paulo.)

International Response: International goal of the UNFPA is "replacement-level fertility."

Solutions: Consider contraception, abortion, family-planning assistance. Improve women's status and provide access to education on health and the means of family planning.

Migration

Reasons: People move from regions that suffer from a shortage of land or capital resources to those that are richer. Many do so in search of a higher living standard. Many flee from war and oppressive dictators. Most refugees are displaced within their own countries or flee to neighboring states. Several populations in "refugee-like situations" are not recognized as asylum-seekers.

Problems/Consequences: Periodically provokes backlashes in host countries, often racially motivated. Nativist movements arise and gain strength during economic downturns, when immigrants are scapegoats for unemployment.

International Response: International Labor Organization convention approved by the General Assembly recognizes that migration results in the scattering of the family, clandestine movements, trafficking in human cargo, and the exploitative employment of undocumented workers. The UN Commissioner for Refugees has carried out a number of programs designed to protect, resettle, and repatriate refugees.

Solutions: Democracy and economic progress need to catch up with population growth in the developing world.

Food and Hunger

Reasons: There is more than enough food worldwide, but the problem is uneven distribution and consumption. Hunger is often the result of poverty, natural disasters, war, and poorly developed transportation systems.

Problems/Consequences: About 500 million people suffer from chronic malnutrition. Each year, 40 million people, half of them children, die from hunger and hunger-related diseases.

International Response: Contributions are made by UN relief agencies and other international relief efforts. Some NGOs concentrate on short-term relief of acute food shortages. Others work toward long-term solutions.

Solutions: Improve food production and distribution, provide technical and financial assistance for agricultural projects in developing countries.

Environment

Reasons: Few people pollute deliberately, but most cause some form of environmental damage in the pursuit of their material needs (such as deforestation and industrial pollution.)

Problems/Consequences: Deforestation results from the slash-and-burn technique for clearing land. Results in a loss of trees and animal life. The burning of forests produces carbon dioxide. Industrial pollution creates smog, acid rain, elevated levels of carbon dioxide and chlorofluorocarbons. Creates health problems.

International Response: International forums link environmental problems to the distribution of the world's resources and environmental concerns to issues of trade and economic development. The UN Conference on the Law of the Sea established a new law for protecting the marine environment in 1974. The 1987 Montreal Protocol requires signatories to phase out the use of chlorofluorocarbons over a period of time. The 1992 Rio Summit resulted in the establishment of the UN Commission on Sustainable Development. This organization was given the task of implementing "Agenda 21," an environmental action program.

Solutions: Higher usage of nonpolluting technologies and sustainable development.

Health and Disease

Reasons: Poverty, malnutrition, and poor sanitation.

Problems/Consequences: Every year, 4 million children in developing countries die and an equal number are mentally or physically disabled from six vaccine-preventable diseases: measles, poliomyelitis, tuberculosis, diphtheria, whooping cough, and tetanus. In addition, 300 million people are today infected with Hepatitis B, and by mid-1994, an estimated 17 million people were infected with HIV, of whom 4 million had AIDS.

International Response: The WHO Expanded Program on Immunization has sponsored the immunization of over 70 percent of the world's children. WHO also concentrates on promoting awareness of high-risk behavior relating to AIDS.

Solutions: Provide education and promote vaccinations and awareness of high-risk behavior for certain diseases.

Drug Traffic

Reasons: Many Third World nations charge that their legal products do not make enough money. Drugs, however, are very profitable. Drug production is sustained in many regions by insurgencies, civil war, and other violent internal conflicts.

Problems/Consequences: Drug trafficking is a major international criminal enterprise. The largest consumer of illegal drugs is the United States. Within drug-producing nations, violence and intimidation of political and judicial authorities have stalled crop-eradication efforts. Domestic resistance to what is perceived as

Yankee imperialism has been exploited by drug traffickers to undermine joint U.S.–South American anti-drug action. Destruction of the environment has occurred through slash-and-burn techniques.

International Response: The International Drug Enforcement Program is a multilateral program designed to stop drug trafficking. The 1990 Cartagena Declaration committed the United States to financially support alternative development strategies in the Andean countries of South America. The Central American Declaration of Belize promised cooperation with the United States in introducing drug-abuse programs, drug eradication, development of alternative crops and relieving foreign debt. The period 1991–2000 has been declared the UN Decade against Drug Abuse, and the UN has adopted a thirty-point Political Declaration and Global Program of Action against illegal drugs. The 1990 London Declaration calls for drug-abuse education, prevention, and treatment programs, improved living conditions for those affected by drug abuse, and alternatives to prison for drug-abuse offenders who wish to undertake treatment. The U.S.–led Chemical Action Task Force is dedicated to ensuring "that precursor and essential chemicals are not diverted to manufacture illicit drugs."

Solutions: Reduce the supply and the demand through interdiction and eradication. Provide support for drug-producing countries to offset the earnings lost by going to legal substitutes. Provide education.

Terrorism

Reasons: Terrorists use violence, directed at an audience, as an extension of politics. Nationalist groups aspire to statehood. Domestic opposition groups seek a radical transformation of a political regime. Official and unofficial groups are sometimes an extension of the state.

Problems/Consequences: Death squads and attacks against individuals and groups of people continue. Terrorists claim their violence is committed for a reason.

continued

CONTINUED FROM PAGE 463

International Response: Governments devote resources and their intelligence agencies cooperate with other countries to locate, capture, and imprison terrorists. INTERPOL has an antiterrorist division.

Solutions: Do not give the terrorists the audience that they seek. Search out, infiltrate, and destroy terrorist networks.

Energy and Natural Resources

Reasons: Societies need energy to survive. Between 1973 and 1980, there were three major oil crises. Natural gas, coal, nuclear, and renewable energy sources are important. Water is vital.

Problems/Consequences: Fluctuating oil and fossil fuel supplies directly affect the people and the economies of nations around the world.

Eighty percent of all cases of disease in the Third World are linked to contaminated water. Nations fight over water and fossil fuel rights.

International Response: One example, the International Energy Agency, was created in 1974 among industrialized states to develop an emergency system for sharing oil, establishing an information system to monitor the oil market, facilitating long-term measures to reduce net demand for oil on world markets, and setting up joint energy research and development activities.

Solutions: The supply of all resources is limited, and therefore must be allocated to all parties. This occurs either politically or economically.

many as one woman in forty may be carrying HIV.[48] The central African countries of Congo, Zaire, Rwanda, Kenya, Uganda, and the Central African Republic have been the worst affected by the disease, but the spread of AIDS is increasing in Asia as well. Accurate figures for rates of HIV infection in Asian countries are said to be less reliable, but it is estimated that upwards of 500,000 people in Thailand and over a million people in India are infected by HIV.[49]

Currently, the prospects for curing AIDS or even curbing its spread appear grim, especially in some developing regions. The World Health Organization (WHO) has projected that by the year 2000, 30 to 40 million people may be infected with the HIV virus, and there may be an additional 12 to 18 million cases of full-blown AIDS.[50] According to even more pessimistic estimates, as many as 30 percent of the overall population of sub-Saharan Africa, and 40 percent of urban populations there, may become HIV carriers.[51] For sexually active adults in this region's urban areas, the figure could become as high as 70 percent.[52]

Responses to Global Health Problems

Most global responses to international problems depend upon the individual reactions of single states, many of whom are constrained by domestic financial considerations. Global health problems present no exceptions. AIDS is only the most recent of many deadly diseases to which the world community has tried to formulate a unified response. The ways in which the international community has dealt with these problems, ranging from immunization to attempts at eradication, illustrate the difficulties in securing international cooperation, even on the most deadly issues.

Immunization is one of the most cost-effective weapons for disease prevention in developing countries. Since its foundation in 1948, the UN-affiliated World Health Organization (WHO) has done much to control diseases through immunization. In 1980, for example, WHO announced that it had reached its 1965 goal of eradicating smallpox, a malady that killed millions worldwide for centuries.[53] WHO's Expanded Program on Immunization (EPI) has achieved great success in expanding its immunization coverage of the world's children. In 1989, the EPI was credited with preventing the deaths of 2.2 million children. As of mid-1990, EPI sponsored the immunization of over 70 percent of the world's children less than one year of age against the six vaccine-preventable diseases mentioned previously.[54]

Other diseases, such as malaria and AIDS, have been more resistant to eradication. The malaria virus, for instance, has proven very resistant to a variety of treatments. One observer believes that the statement of the second Report of the Malarial Commission of the League of Nations in 1927 is still substantially valid today: "The history of special antimalarial campaigns is chiefly a record of exaggerated expectations followed sooner or later by disappointment and the abandonment of work."[55] For example, WHO has already abandoned its goal of eradicating malaria by the year 2000.[56]

Since no vaccine or cure has yet been discovered for AIDS, WHO has concentrated on promoting awareness of the high-risk behaviors associated with HIV infection (namely, unprotected sex with multiple partners and shared use of needles among intravenous drug users). In 1987 WHO established the Global Program on AIDS, whose goals include the prevention of HIV transmission, care for HIV-infected people, and unification of national and international efforts against AIDS. Together with its scientific advisory body, the Global Commission on AIDS, the program supports national AIDS-control plans, which use education and information to try to curb the spread of the disease. The concerted international drive for AIDS awareness has spurred most UN member states to create and develop national AIDS-control programs.

As with most global issues, the problem of AIDS has exacerbated international conflict as often as it has contributed to cooperation. Many national governments have reacted to the spread of AIDS in their countries by denying it is "their" problem. In the United States, AIDS was initially perceived as a Haitian and gay disease. In Europe, it was first considered a disease of African and Caribbean people, while in developing countries AIDS was commonly regarded as a disease primarily afflicting "foreigners." As a result of these perceptions, governments have enacted more stringent travel restrictions and screening procedures. The United States, for example, has a law prohibiting entry to people with a "deadly, infectious or contagious disease," a prohibition that was extended to cover HIV in 1987 and upheld in 1993.

An additional problem is that the huge potential profits in an AIDS cure have reinforced competition among nations and pharmaceutical companies, leading to duplication and waste in research endeavors.[57] It may be hoped that the stigma associated with AIDS will fade over time, but the initial difficulties in securing international cooperation to fight this devastating disease show how governments remain reluctant to combat diseases that they perceive to be somebody else's problem.

DRUGS

Many Third World nations charge that their terms of trade with the developed world are unfair, because the prices industrialized nations pay for their exports of commodities (such as cooper and coffee) are too low (see Chapter Eight). There is one category of products from the developing world that has made fabulous fortunes for their producers, though few citizens of developing nations share in these profits: narcotics and other illegal drugs. As with population, health, and environmental concerns, the problem of drugs at times has fostered admirable international cooperation. In other instances, disputes over the method employed to combat the movement of drugs across international boundaries has severely strained relations between states.

Historically, efforts to reduce or stop the drug trade have focused on curbing the supply of illegal drugs moving from developing regions to richer countries, where the bulk of demand for drugs has always been located. Only since the late 1980s have international efforts begun to focus on curbing demand for drugs. This section examines the roots of the drug problem, the effectiveness of supply-side programs, and the emergence of more comprehensive measures in the war on drugs.

Drug Production

World narcotics production is concentrated in four areas: Southeast Asia, the Middle East, Central America, and South America. Each region has its own specialty product, with Southeast Asia concentrating on opium and its derivatives (including heroin), the Middle East on hashish, Central America on marijuana, and South America on cocaine. In many cases, drug production in these regions is sustained or encouraged by insurgencies, civil war, and other violent internal conflicts.

The world's main source of opium is the three-nation region of Myanmar (formerly Burma), Laos, and Thailand, known collectively as the Golden Triangle. These nations accounted for almost 85 percent of total world opium production in 1991, with Myanmar alone producing and supplying 70 percent of the world's heroin.[58] The lack of international influence over the isolationist regime in Myanmar is demonstrated by the continued increases in opium production and the acreage devoted to growing the opium poppy there. Those increases can be attributed to the fact that the government in Rangoon, the capital, has allied with major traffickers and permitted trafficker-affiliated insurgent groups to produce narcotics, and even to exercise security and police functions in the areas under their control.[59]

The Levant, an area of the Middle East centered in Lebanon, is the hub of the world's production of hashish, a drug made from a cannabis-like plant related to marijuana. Before its civil war began in 1975, Lebanon was one of the principal trading states of the Middle East, and also was a leading center of the drug trade. In the 1960s Lebanon's Maronite Christian community became involved in shipping hashish from Lebanon's Bekaa Valley and Asian heroin from ports run and protected by Christian militias. In the early 1980s Turkish poppy-growers introduced opium and heroin to the Bekaa valley, which also became home to cocaine refiners who obtained their coca paste from Lebanese merchant communities in South America. During its civil war, Lebanon's hostile factions, including elements of the Palestine Liberation Organization (PLO) and the Popular Front for the Liberation of Palestine (PFLP), exported hashish, opium, heroin, and cocaine to Europe and the United States in return for cash and armaments. There is substantial evidence that the Syrian government, as well, has become engaged in the Lebanese drug trade.[60]

In 1991 Mexico cultivated nearly 86 percent of the world's 21,000 net hectares of the marijuana plant and accounted for nearly 58 percent of marijuana production. This nevertheless represented a substantial decrease from previous cultivation levels, as Mexico's marijuana eradication programs had nearly halved the amount of land devoted to growing the crop the year before. During this same period, Mexico also reduced its opium cultivation and production by nearly one-third of its 1990 levels, even though opium production and land devoted to opium cultivation in Guatemala, the other significant Central American opium-grower, each increased by over 30 percent. Mexico serves as not only a major producer of the world's marijuana crop, but also as a key transporter of a more deadly drug, cocaine. It has been estimated, for example, that Mexico transports about 70 percent of the Colombian cocaine consumed in the United States.[61]

Four South American countries, Peru, Bolivia, Colombia, and Ecuador, grow the bulk of the world's coca leaf, from which cocaine is derived. Peru's Upper Huallaga Valley accounts for almost 58 percent of total world cultivation. Over half of the cocaine used in the United States comes from Peruvian coca.[62] The cocaine trade brings in much of these countries' export revenues. In recent years Colombian cocaine producers earned between $800 million to $1 billion a year. Peru's drug trade brings in $500 to $700 million annually, equivalent to about 20 to 25 percent of the country's legal exports. Bolivian cocaine earns roughly $250 million per year, one-fourth of that country's total foreign exchange earnings and 60 to 90 percent of its exports, and employs about 4.3 percent of its 7 million people.[63]

Growth of International Drug Trafficking

Because cocaine, heroin, marijuana, and other drugs are illegal in most countries, drug trafficking, the transportation of drugs from producers to consumers, has become a major international criminal enterprise. As official efforts to curb drug supply and abuse have attained moderate success, many traffickers have responded by expanding the geographical scope of their production and distribution channels. The complex operations mounted by drug cartels to purvey their illicit goods rival major multinational corporations in scope and sales volume (see Figure 10.2).

Colombian traffickers headquartered in the cities of Medellín and Cali, for instance, have skillfully forged some of the most widely spanning international production and distribution networks. When the Colombian government began cracking down on domestic drug operations, the drug rings moved some of their operational centers to Brazil, where they could more easily obtain chemical processors, and some of their coca processing laboratories to Ecuador. As cocaine abuse has stabilized somewhat in the United States but expanded in Europe and elsewhere, the Colombian cartels have offered cocaine-smuggling networks into the United States to the heroin traffickers of West and Southwest Asia in return for access to more of the world's illegal drug-distribution avenues. After the 1992 arrest of Colombian drug lord José Duran in Rome, Italian investigators found that the Colombians were working out a deal to grant to the Sicilian Mafia the entire cocaine-dealing franchise for all of Europe, in return for a share of the Mafia's global heroin market as well as assistance in laundering profits through legitimate businesses.[64]

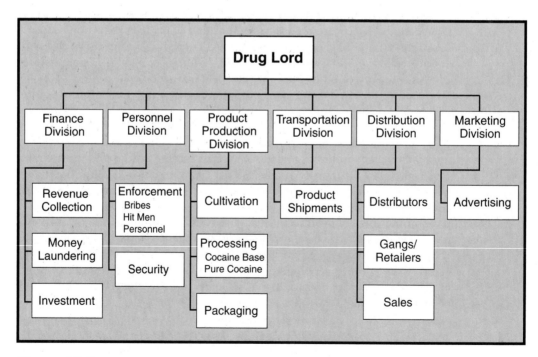

Figure 10.2   The Drug Cartel as a Corporation

Africa has also become a major locus of drug traffic. Transshipment of South American cocaine through Africa has soared, and cocaine has been seized in almost every region in Africa.[65] While South American traffickers initially had used these countries as springboards for smuggling cocaine into Western Europe, they have expanded into local cocaine sales in the major cities of Morocco, Nigeria, and Kenya. Africa now has its own cocaine producers and distributors, which emulate Colombian operations. Nigeria and Cameroon grow coca crops, and increasing amounts of heroin are being shipped through Ghana and Nigeria to Europe and the United States.[66] Nigerian drug traffickers have recently begun hiring Polish and other Eastern European nationals to conduct illegal trade in Europe and elsewhere.[67]

Middle Eastern drug rings have also expanded their worldwide operations, primarily to purchase more weapons. Lebanese drug rings operating in Brazil have begun moving cocaine into the Middle East.[68] European criminal networks have assisted Middle Eastern drug traffickers and terrorist groups. In a complex arrangement, Palestinian drug traffickers traded hashish, heroin, and morphine (another opiate) produced by Palestinian and Syrian-controlled labs in Syria or Lebanon's Bekaa Valley to Bulgarian connections in return for light infantry weapons. The Bulgarian smugglers then sold the heroin to the Sicilian Mafia for hard currency. Italian law enforcement authorities also believed at one time that a member of a ranking Italian crime family administered Syrian drug-running operations worldwide.[69]

Asian traffickers have also expanded or shifted their distribution networks in response to changing patterns of demand and enforcement. In 1990 and 1991 Russian authorities seized tons of Afghan hashish, along with marijuana and opium grown in Central Asia. Some Southeast Asian heroin producers have begun routing their goods through China, contributing to new addiction problems and the spread of AIDS through the use of contaminated hypodermic needles.[70]

Bilateral and Multilateral Drug-Control Efforts

The world's largest consumer of illegal drugs is the United States, and by a wide margin. Figures for 1990 estimate the number of habitual cocaine users in the United States at 16 million, regular users of marijuana at 18 million, and users of heroin at 500,000. (A substantial amount of the marijuana consumed in the United States is domestically produced, whereas cocaine, opium, and their derivatives are imported.) Even though casual cocaine consumption was down in the early 1990s, heroin-use surged. Authorities estimate that users in the United States spent up to $51 billion on illegal drugs annually between 1988 and 1991.[71]

This staggering total of drug money provides U.S. officials with a large incentive to take the initiative in combatting the international drug trade. Common American rhetoric, both within and outside of Washington, holds that primary responsibility for the drug problem lies with pushers and criminal gangs who prey upon vulnerable citizens. (This was the same line taken during the

Prohibition in the 1920s and the marijuana scare of the 1930s, depicted in the films *The Untouchables* and *Reefer Madness*.) Accordingly, the United States has traditionally concentrated on restricting the supply of drugs rather than reducing demand for them. This may be done through **interdiction** (stopping drugs from coming into the country, primarily through customs inspection) or **eradication** (destruction of the crops that are processed into illegal drugs).

Dissatisfied with the inability of interdiction alone to prevent importation of drugs, the United States has recently shifted the focus of its drug-control efforts to eradication of crops. Many U.S.–led eradication programs involve attempts to use military means to crack down on the drug trade. Most of these projects have been controversial bilateral programs over which the United States can generally exercise more operational control. The United States has also organized multilateral programs, such as the thirty-nation International Drug Enforcement Conference (IDEC) put into operation in 1988.[72] The Bush administration's $2.2 billion Andean Initiative, launched in 1990, was designed to foster cooperation between the United States and South American nations to disrupt drug production at the processing stage.[73]

Attempts by the United States to try to reduce drug production in cooperation with South American countries have frequently been stymied, however, by four factors: the need on the part of these debt-saddled countries for the revenue that the drug trade brings, the inability to find equally lucrative legitimate crops for those who grow drug crops, the corruption and violence that the drug trade produces, and historical resentment of U.S. imperialism.

First, as noted earlier, the drug trade is a major source of employment and export revenues in many Latin American countries. Their governments have attempted to impress upon the United States that one of the ultimate solutions to the drug trade is for the United States to import more of the legal goods of their countries. At a meeting with George Bush in Washington in September 1989, President Virgilio Barco of Colombia implicitly reminded Bush that the Colombian drug economy flourished because Colombia could not earn the foreign exchange it needed through legitimate exports. He obtained a pledge from Bush to restore the International Coffee Agreement, whose collapse in July 1989, partly because of U.S. objection, threatened the Colombian economy with an annual loss of $400 to $500 million.[74]

Second, efforts at drug eradication that do not provide for a transition to legal alternative employment for coca and marijuana growers, or balance-of-payments support for drug-producing countries, encounter a great deal of resistance. The United States, with a dwindling pool of dollars to spend on international aid, has been reluctant to commit funds for agricultural and industrial development designed to supplant drug cultivation. While the 1990 Cartagena Declaration committed the United States to financially support alternative development strategies in the Andean countries of South America, the U.S. government has been slow to fulfill those commitments. In early 1993 a group of Central American countries issued the Declaration of Belize, which promised cooperation with the United States in introducing drug-abuse programs, drug eradication, development of alternative crops, and relieving foreign debt. Again, the United States has offered words of encouragement, but has been reluctant to pledge further financial assistance.[75]

Third, within drug-producing nations, violence and intimidation of political and judicial authorities have stalled crop-eradication efforts. In Peru's Upper Huallaga Valley, for example, the government has limited its crop-eradication efforts for fear of increasing support for the Sendero Luminoso (Shining Path) or Tupac Amaru guerrilla movements.[76] In Colombia, powerful kingpins rarely hesitate to use kidnapping and assassination to undermine government attempts to curb their activities. By the late 1980s the drug war in Colombia had claimed the lives of thousands of public officials, including three presidential candidates, an attorney-general, twelve supreme court justices, over forty judges, more than 170 other judicial employees, dozens of journalists, and more than 3000 police and soldiers.[77]

Finally, domestic resistance to what is perceived as Yankee imperialism has been exploited by drug traffickers to undermine joint U.S.–South American antidrug action. In Bolivia and Peru, coca-growing families are organized into associations that can be mobilized to shut down eradication efforts. As is the case with many Latin American governments, U.S. pressure on the Mexican government to stamp out drug-related corruption has often offended anti-imperialistic sensitivities in Mexico. U.S.–Mexican tension came to a head in 1985, when U.S. drug enforcement agent Enrique Camarena was tortured and murdered, reputedly by associates of a Mexican drug lord. A diplomatic furor subsequently erupted over the DEA-arranged abduction, for trial in the United States, of a Mexican doctor who was suspected of keeping Camarena alive during torture. The doctor was subsequently acquitted, but Mexican authorities warned their American counterparts that such infringements on Mexican sovereignty would not be permitted in the future.[78]

Toward More Comprehensive Solutions to the Worldwide Drug Problem

In the past few years, an international consensus about how to deal with the drug problem has begun to emerge. The advanced industrial nations, especially the United States, have slowly come to realize that as long as their demand for illegal drugs does not drop appreciably, their crop-eradication and antismuggling programs merely prompt traffickers to move their operations to areas outside the programs' geographic compass. (In other words, until there is a substantial change of strategy, the industrial nations will continue to lose the "war on drugs.") The industrialized nations have started to approach the problem of curtailing demand in a variety of ways, ranging from mandating tougher penalties for convicted drug kingpins to expanded education and treatment programs to decriminalization and legalization of some drugs.[79]

On the other hand, the expansion of drug production has brought the concomitant ills of addiction to more developing nations. In Colombia, for

WHAT WOULD YOU DO?

You are the president of the United States in the 1990s. Even though past drug-interdiction and demand-reduction efforts have achieved some successes in reducing illegal drug availability and abuse in the United States, these successes have been modest. Shipments of drugs into the United States continue unabated, and drug abuse remains stubbornly high in many inner cities. Because the federal budget for fighting the drug war is shrinking, you must decide whether to concentrate these limited dollars on attempts to reduce demand through education and treatment programs, or on efforts to reduce supply through drug-interdiction efforts. These interdiction efforts include the sending of U.S. troops to the source countries, an action that has proved very unpopular in countries where it has been tried.

Suppose you invest drug-fighting dollars in education and treatment programs. Because drugs go to where the demand is located, this strategy could have numerous benefits. It would reduce demand at home, thus convincing drug producers and traffickers to get out of the business or move their operations elsewhere. It would also be more effective than border-control efforts (for example, stationing radar balloons and AWACS surveillance planes at the border, or beefing up customs personnel), and less intrusive than sending U.S. troops to source countries. But demand-reduction programs work slowly and uncertainly (no one can be positive that these programs are getting to the hard-core addicts who commit much of the drug-related crime). Meanwhile, drug shipments continue to come into the country,

example, about 400,000 people, mostly coca harvesters, smoke *basuco,* a highly addictive residue of inferior coca base.[80] The Central American countries have also had to deal with the money laundering, drug abuse, and corruption associated with the drug trade.[81] Thai authorities calculate that the 1 percent of the population that is addicted to heroin has greatly contributed to the spread of AIDS in that country.[82] Of the estimated 2.5 million drug users in Pakistan, more than 1 million were reported to be heroin abusers, and heroin use is on the rise in many Indian cities.[83] In the Middle East, heroin abuse is spreading in conjunction with hashish abuse.[84]

The drug trade has also had unforeseen effects on the environment. Drug producers, using slash-and-burn techniques, are responsible for significant destruction of forests and the erosion of topsoil, as well as the pollution of waterways through the dumping of chemicals used to process cocaine and heroin.[85]

UN-coordinated efforts to fight drug abuse and trafficking intensified in the early 1990s. At a special session of the General Assembly held in February 1990, the United Nations, as mentioned earlier, proclaimed a UN Decade against Drug Abuse (1991–2000) and unanimously adopted a thirty-point Political Declaration and Global Program of Action against illegal drugs. The declaration recognized that the drug problem in all its dimensions is linked to economic, social, increasing the pressure on you to produce quicker and more visible results.

Suppose you put drug-fighting dollars in continued efforts to interdict supply, either at the border or to work on the source countries. Interdiction efforts give the politically popular impression that you are actually doing something (shipments halted, traffickers arrested), and sometimes they produce real results in terms of curbing availability. However, if demand remains high, drug traffickers usually find a way of designing their routes around these barriers, often by transshipping the drugs through third countries.

Sending U.S. troops to source countries is risky. Although it can give the impression that you are tackling the source of the problem, it can also antagonize the populations of the source countries, who then accuse the United States of imperialism. And it can harm the legitimacy of source-country governments, many of which are already facing severe political difficulties. These governments often wink at drug production because it provides employment and income for many poor peasants, employment that otherwise would not exist, in part because of the failure of the wealthier drug-consuming nations to purchase the legitimate products of the source countries.

You face a dilemma: You need to decide which strategy will be most effective in solving the drug problem.

What would you do?

and cultural conditions in affected countries and acknowledges links between drug abuse and the spread of AIDS, as well as the connection between drug trafficking and terrorism. Among its main recommendations, the Global Program suggested giving higher priority to drug-abuse prevention programs, especially those directed at children.[86]

Concluded later that same year, the UN-sponsored London Declaration called for drug-abuse education, prevention, and treatment programs, improved living conditions for those affected by drug abuse, and alternatives to prison for drug-abuse offenders who wish to undertake treatment. Also at the London summit, then-UN Secretary-General Perez de Cuellar suggested mobilizing support from young environmentalists against drug abuse by emphasizing the link between drug cultivation and environmental degradation.[87]

Only some of the recommendations made by less developed countries on the supply side of the drug equation have been carried out. For example, while the London Declaration was successful in devising strategies to reduce demand for drugs in the industrial nations, the drug-producing developing nations failed to win more than a general pledge of help in supporting crop-substitution programs.[88] On the other hand, a number of developed countries have joined the Financial Action Task Force (FATF), which will study measures to cooperatively prevent laundering of drug money through financial institutions. Additionally, over twenty countries now belong to the U.S.–led Chemical Action Task Force (CATF), an organization dedicated to ensuring that certain chemicals are not used to manufacture illicit drugs.[89]

In contrast to supply-side programs, which have been largely ineffectual overall, the demand-side provisions of the UN programs have met with mixed success. The U.S. Bureau of International Narcotics Matters (BINM), for instance, has provided demand-reduction training and technical assistance to over 1500 private and public officials in twenty-eight countries, and has pursued joint training activities with the Colombo Plan in Southeast Asia and the Organization of American States (OAS) in Latin America. Furthermore, in response to the UN Summit for Children, BINM has developed pilot drug-prevention programs for "street kids" in Lima, Peru, and São Paulo, Brazil.[90]

What they give with one hand, however, states sometimes take away with the other when they cannot control the details and direction of drug-control programs. In 1992 President Bush announced that the United States would slash its contribution to the UN drug-control program's budget by about 40 percent, even though the United States—the world leader in drug consumption—was providing only about 7 percent ($4.5 million) of the program's total budget, almost half of which went to activities in Latin America and the Caribbean.[91] This action was taken despite suggestions that the United States shift funds from its own programs to the UN's multilateral programs, since multilateral, UN-sponsored programs were less likely to offend nations' perceptions of their own sovereignty than was unilateral U.S. pressure or conditions on aid.[92] Others argue that the post–Cold War international economy makes multilateral cooperation more important than ever because it relies heavily on the free exchange of goods, services, labor, and capital across sovereign borders. One author puts it starkly enough. He claims that no unilateral customs effort in the world "could conduct detailed inspections of the 430 million people, 120 million automobiles, 8 million containers, 720,000 jets and small planes, and 290,000 ships and small boats that cross U.S. borders in a single year. But somewhere amidst that traffic is all the cocaine needed to satisfy the American coke habit for a year—enough to fill 13 tractor trailer trucks."[93]

Disagreements between the United States and Latin American countries over drug-control strategy show how the drug trade exerts different effects on drug-producing and drug-consuming nations. Rich, drug-importing countries experience the health problems, crime, and economic harm attributable to addiction, while corruption and narco-terrorism become endemic in the poorer states that produce the narcotics. Because no nation is immune to some of the ills created by drug abuse and trafficking, almost all states now regard the international war on drugs as an important and urgent cause. But unlike hunger or disease, the drug trade is a hugely lucrative business, and traffickers have a strong motivation to match supply to demand. Unless individual states and the international community take further steps to reduce both the supply and demand sides of the drug equation, the global narcotics industry will continue to find ways to turn coca, hemp, and poppies into gold.

TERRORISM

The previous section described the frightening impact of narco-terrorism on countries with well-established drug cartels. Terrorism, however, is carried out in a wide variety of places for an equally wide variety of reasons. It can be defined as the use of violence by an individual or group, designed to create extreme anxiety in a target group larger than the immediate victims, with the purpose of coercing that group into meeting certain political demands.[94] Thus, unlike war or simple murder, terrorism is violence directed at an audience, not just at those who are directly victimized. Such extension of politics by other means can be effective; through the use of systematic and prolonged campaigns of violence, some terrorists have succeeded in making their voices heard in the international community.

Although terrorist activity in recent years appears to be on the wane, the increasing trend toward globalization in the New Era presents challenges to those who have combatted terrorism during the 1970s and 1980s. Faster transportation, improved communication technologies, and easier access to weapons of mass destruction exemplify the increasingly sophisticated and dangerous array of tools that are available to potential terrorists. In the New Era, the stakes of the terrorist game are more serious than ever before.

The distinction between terrorism and "legitimate" violence in support of a political cause or national goal is subjective, however. One group's heroic revolutionaries are often another's murderous thugs. The Contra insurgents who fought against the socialist Sandinista regime in Nicaragua in the 1980s illustrate this difference in perspective. To the Sandinistas, the Contras were criminal terrorists bent on the violent overthrow of a legitimate government. To President Ronald Reagan, who supported them, the Contras were Nicaraguan "freedom fighters"—"the moral equivalent of our Founding Fathers."

Terrorism around the World

Terrorism in its various forms is hardly a modern phenomenon. Secret police agencies in Russia used terror from the days of Ivan the Terrible in the fifteenth century to the Soviet-era KGB and MVD. The Fenian Society of Irish nationalists assassinated British politicians in the nineteenth century, and Gavrilo Princip, whose assassination of Austria's Archduke Franz Ferdinand sparked World War I in 1914, had ties to Serbian nationalist groups. Modern transportation (especially airlines) and communications (especially television), however, have given terrorists new targets and new ways of reaching and even expanding their audiences. As a result, terrorist organizations now strike directly and indirectly at targets all over the globe, far from their bases of operation.

According to counter-terrorism specialists in the U.S. State Department, there were 11,269 international terrorist acts between 1968 and 1992. During these years, the lowest single number was in 1968 (124); the highest number was in 1987 (672). Afterward, there was a downward trend (except in 1991), with the figure for 1992 (362) serving as the lowest number since 1975. While the end of the Cold War may indicate decline, unfortunately it is still too early to declare the terrorist plague under control.

Groups that perpetrate terrorism may be divided into three categories: nationalist groups that aspire to statehood, domestic opposition groups seeking a radical transformation of a political regime, and official or unofficial groups that act as extensions of the state.[95] Examples of nationalist groups that have sponsored terrorism include the Irish Republican Army (IRA), which aims at unification of Northern Ireland with the Irish Republic, and the Palestine Liberation Organization (PLO), which employed terrorism in its search for Palestinian independence. Not everyone belonging to these organizations is necessarily a terrorist; such groups are often umbrellas for movements that include units that support nationalist causes by peaceful means.

Domestic opposition groups that practice terrorism include Italy's Red Brigades, the French group Action Directe, and the Japanese Red Army. These types of groups usually seek to paralyze, delegitimize, or even overthrow the existing governments ruling those countries in which they operate.

Groups that carry out terrorism on the orders or on behalf of the state include independent state-sponsored or tolerated organizations, such as the "death squads" of El Salvador in the 1970s and 1980s, and agencies of the state that use terror in their own or other countries as part of government policy, like the now-dismantled security organizations of BOSS in South Africa, SAVAK in Iran, and the KGB in the former USSR. Terrorism carried out by a government or government-backed groups against their own citizens can be characterized as **enforcement terror,** while the terrorist activities of nationalist or opposition groups would be referred to as **agitational terror.**[96] Both enforcement terror and agitational terror are typically carried out within a single state by organizations based in that state. Nationalist groups, on the other hand, often have terrorist cells in several countries, and some have demonstrated the ability to strike far beyond the regions they claim as their national territory. Because of the broad geographic scope of their activities, nationalist groups are widely known practitioners of international terrorism.

Terrorism in Europe

Terrorism in Europe reached its peak in the 1970s, but many European-based terrorist organizations remain active. Among the most feared of nationalist terrorists are the Provisional Irish Republican Army (PIRA) and the Irish National Liberation Army (INLA), the Catholic-dominated terrorist factions of the seventy-year old Irish Republican Army. The goal of these groups is the withdrawal of the British military from Northern Ireland and the unification of all Ireland, even against the wishes of the Protestant majority in the north. Militant Protestant groups in Northern Ireland also carry out terror campaigns, illustrating how terror often begets terror in nationalist conflicts. However, with its 1994 cease-fire declaration, the IRA may well have moved in a new direction.

Radical opposition groups still use terror in much of Western Europe. The German-based Red Army Faction (RAF), also known as the Baader-Meinhoff Gang, carries out terrorist attacks all over Europe, sometimes in collaboration with other radical socialist groups. NATO personnel and installations have been favored targets in recent years, but the RAF was responsible for a wave of car bombings and assassinations in protest of German unification in 1990 and the transformation of the former East German Communist economy to capitalism. A frequent RAF collaborator is the left-wing French anarchist group Actión Directe, which has struck at police stations, courts, businesses, and individuals since its formation in the late 1970s in order to destroy the French state. The leading Italian terrorist organization, the Brigate Rosse (Red Brigades), won special notoriety in the 1970s and 1980s through bombings and kidnappings. The most infamous kidnappings perpetrated by the Red Brigades were those of Italy's ex–prime minister, Aldo Moro, and American general, James Dozier. (Dozier was released alive; Moro was killed.) The goals of the brigade were to make possible a coup that would then lead to a Communist revolution.

Terrorism in the Middle East

Terrorism is endemic in the Middle East, almost to the point of being synonymous with that geographic region in the popular imagination. The PLO forswore the use of terrorism against Israel in its 1993 agreement with the Jewish state, but its renegade units have included terrorist groups such as the Popular Front for the Liberation of Palestine (PFLP) and the Democratic Front for the Liberation of Palestine (DFLP), and some of the world's most vicious terrorists, including "Carlos the Jackal," Abu Nidal, and Ahmed Jabril.

Domestic opposition groups, as well, engage in terrorism in the Middle East. Many of these have a radical Islamic orientation, such as the Muslim Brotherhood in Egypt and Hezbollah ("the party of God") in Lebanon. Lebanese groups, in particular, became notorious in the 1980s by taking American and European nationals as hostages and holding them captive for years in an attempt to punish the United States for its past military presence in Lebanon and its support of Israel. State-sponsored terrorism is also rife in the region, as agents of the Syrian, Iranian, Iraqi, and Libyan governments have carried out bombings, kidnappings, and assassinations throughout the Middle East and in Europe. In one of the deadliest incidents of international terrorism in recent years, Libyan agents were accused of planting a bomb that blew up a Pan American airliner over Scotland in 1988 with more than 250 people aboard.

Terrorism in Latin America

State-sponsored terrorism is also common practice in much of Latin America. One analyst contends that political and social structures in many Latin American

AT A GLANCE

SELECTED TERRORIST ORGANIZATIONS

Abu Nidal Organization (ANO)

- Split from PLO in 1974
- International terrorist organization led by Sabri al-Banna (better known as Abu Nidal)
- Several hundred-plus "militia" in Lebanon and overseas support structure
- Believed to be based in the Bekaa Valley and in several Palestinian refugee camps in Lebanon. Operates in the Middle East, Asia, and Europe

Activities: Has carried out more than 90 terrorist attacks in 20 countries since 1974, killing or injuring almost 900 people. Targets vary depending on who is sponsoring them. Major attacks include Rome and Vienna airports in December 1985 and the September 1986 Pam Am Flight 73 hijacking in Karachi

External Aid: Received aid from Iraq (1973–1974) and Syria (1983–1987). Supported by Libya afterward

Basque Fatherland and Liberty (ETA)

- Founded in 1959
- Has the aim of creating an independent homeland in Spain's Basque region. Divided into two factions in 1974—ETA-Political-Military and ETA-Military. The former has been inactive since receiving limited home rule. The latter has continued to conduct lethal attacks.
- Strength unknown. Could be in the hundreds
- Operates primarily in Spain and France and to a limited degree in Italy and Germany

Activities: Carries out bombing and assassinations of Spanish government targets, especially security forces. More than 40 people were killed and 200 injured in ETA attacks in 1991

External Aid: Has received training from Libya, Lebanon, and Sandinista-controlled Nicaragua. Has close ties to PIRA

Farabundo Marti National Liberation Front (FMLN)

- Formed in 1980 with Cuban backing

- The guerrilla umbrella organization is composed of five leftist groups. The group reached a peace agreement with the government of El Salvador on December 31, 1991.
- Numbers 7500 combatants
- While headquartered near Managua, Nicaragua, it maintains political-diplomatic offices in Panama, Mexico, and Europe.

Activities: Before agreement with El Salvador government, conducted bombings, assassinations, economic sabotage, and arson. After 1988, it increased urban terrorism in the capital.

External Aid: Supported by Cuba and the Sandinistas in Nicaragua, along with sympathetic organizations in the United States and Europe. Also believed to have received support from the Soviet Union and Vietnam, along with some radical Middle Eastern states.

Hezbollah ("Party of God")

- Radical Shia group formed in Lebanon under the guidance of the Ayatollah Khomeini in 1982. Dedicated to the creation of an Iranian-style Islamic republic in Lebanon and the removal of all non-Islamic influences from the area. Strongly anti-West and anti-Israel
- Numbers 700 to 4000
- Operates in Lebanon and has established cells in Europe, Africa, and South America
- Linked to Islamic Jihad

Activities: Known or suspected to have been involved in numerous anti-U.S. and anti-Israel terrorist attacks, including the October 1988 suicide attack on Israeli security forces that killed eight Israeli soldiers and the July 1994 bombings of Jewish community centers in Buenos Aires and London and of the Israeli Embassy in the U.K. Also, largely responsible for the taking of Western hostages in Lebanon in the 1980s.

External Aid: Receives financial support, weapons, explosives, political, diplomatic, and organizational aid and training from Iran

Japanese Red Army (JRA)

- An international terrorist organization formed in 1971
- Stated goals are to overthrow the Japanese government and monarchy and to help foment world revolution. Is closely associated with the PFLP and is heavily dependent upon that organization for financial support
- Includes about 25 core members with 100 sympathizers
- Based in Lebanon

Activities: Before 1977, JRA carried out a series of brutal attacks, including the massacre of passengers at Lod airport in Israel in 1972. Since the mid-1980s, the JRA has carried out several crude rocket and mortar attacks against a number of U.S. embassies.

External Aid: Receives aid from radical Palestinian terrorists and possibly from Libya

Kurdistan Workers Party (PKK)

- The PKK was established in the mid-1970s
- Seeks to set up a Marxist state in southeastern Turkey, which has a large population of Kurds
- Includes 3000 main members with 2000 to 5000 supporters
- Operates in Turkey and Western Europe with training grounds in Lebanon and strongholds in Iraq and Syria

Activities: Primary targets include the Turkish government and civilians in southeastern Turkey but it is becoming increasingly active in Western Europe against Turkish targets and rival Kurdish groups

External Aid: Thought to receive Syrian support

Mozambican National Resistance (RENAMO)

- Established in 1976 by the Rhodesian security services before the minority white-governed Rhodesia became Zimbabwe
- Numbers 20,000 guerrillas
- Based in Mozambique

Activities: Operates as a guerrilla insurgency against Mozambican government and civilian targets; frequently and increasingly runs cross-border operations into Zimbabwe, Malawi, and Zambia

External Aid: Previously received aid from South Africa, as well as from private individuals in Europe and elsewhere

Islamic Jihad (IJ)

- Formed in 1983
- May be a series of loosely affiliated factions rather than a cohesive group. It is committed to the creation of an Islamic Palestinian state and the destruction of Israel through holy war. The United States has been identified as an enemy because of its support for Israel.
- Strength unknown
- Based in Lebanon
- Linked to Hezbollah

Activities: Carries out cross-border raids against Israeli targets. Responsible for the 1983 attack on the U.S. Marine barracks at Beirut Airport which killed 241. Also carried out several other bombings of French, U.S., and Israeli installations in Lebanon and the downing of a French airliner in September 1989

External Aid: Receives aid from Iran, and possibly Syria

Popular Front for the Liberation of Palestine—Special Command (PFLP—SC)

- Founded in 1979
- A Marxist-Leninist group formed by Abu Salim after breaking away from the now-defunct PFLP—Special Operations Group
- Strength is 50 members
- Based in southern Lebanon, it operates in the Middle East and Western Europe

Activities: It has claimed responsibility for several notorious international terrorist attacks in

continued

AT A GLANCE

SELECTED TERRORIST ORGANIZATIONS *continued from page 479*

Western Europe, including the bombing of a restaurant frequented by U.S. servicemen in Torrejon, Spain, in April 1985.

External Aid: Probable sources of aid include Syria and Libya. Believed to have ties to terrorist groups focused on Armenia and Colombia as well as the Abu Nidal Organization

Provisional Irish Republic Army (PIRA)
- A radical terrorist group formed in 1969
- It is the clandestine armed wing of Sinn Fein, a legal political movement dedicated to removing British forces from Northern Ireland and then to unify Ireland. It is Marxist in orientation.
- Includes several hundred members, plus thousands of sympathizers
- Based in Northern Ireland, Irish Republic, Great Britain, and Western Europe

Activities: Carried out bombings, assassinations, kidnappings, extortion, and robberies. Targeted British government and private-sector interests along with Northern Irish Protestant paramilitary organizations. In the autumn of 1992, PIRA launched a major bombing campaign in London against train stations, hotels, and shopping areas, resulting in casualties and major property damage. Such activities were suspended when a cease-fire was called in 1994.

External Aid: Has received aid from a variety of countries and sympathizers, including Libya, and private U.S. citizens. Linked to the Basque ETA.

Red Army Faction (RAF)
- Originated in the student protest movement of the 1960s
- Also known as the Baader-Meinhof Gang
- An obscure mix of Marxism and Maoism, it is committed to armed struggle. Has survived despite numerous arrests of top leaders over the years
- Numbers twenty to thirty, plus several hundred supporters
- Based in Germany

Activities: Conducts bombings, assassinations, kidnappings, and robberies. Targets the German government, the private sector, and U.S. interests

External Aid: Self-sustaining

Revolutionary Armed Forces of Colombia (FARC)
- Established in 1966
- The military wing of the Colombian Communist Party, it is the largest guerrilla group in the country. Goal is to overthrow the government and ruling class. It is anti-United States
- 5000 armed combatants with 10,000 supporters
- Based in Colombia

Activities: Carries out armed attacks against Colombian targets, bombings of U.S. businesses, kidnappings of Colombians and foreigners for ransom, and assassinations. Traffics in drugs

External Aid: FARC has ties to Cuba

Sendero Luminoso ("Shining Path," SL)
- Formed in 1970
- Peru's largest subversive organization, it is among the world's most dangerous and ruthless terrorist groups. Its goal is to destroy existing Peruvian institutions and replace them with a peasant revolutionary regime as well as to rid Peru of foreign influences.
- Includes 4000 to 5000 combatants, and receives strong rural support
- Rival of MRTA
- Based in Peru

Activities: Engages in particularly brutal forms of terrorism. It has attacked diplomatic missions of nearly every country represented in Peru, foreign businesses, and humanitarian aid projects in addition to Peruvian government and private-sector targets. Its leader, Abimael Guzman, was arrested in 1992, inhibiting its effectiveness. Specializes in the assassination of government officials

External Aid: It has no known foreign sponsors, although it receives money from Colombian narcotics traffickers.

Sikh Terrorism

- Aim is to carve out an independent Sikh state called Khalistan from Indian territory
- Strength is unknown
- Based in India, Western Europe, and North America

Activities: Regular and bloody attacks are mounted frequently in India against Hindus and against Indian officials and facilities, particularly in Punjab. They include assassinations, bombings, and kidnappings. Sikh terrorists bombed the Air India 747 jetliner downed over the Irish Sea in June 1985, which killed 329 passengers and crew.

External Aid: Supporters within and outside of India contribute to these organizations

Terra Lliure (TL)

- Formed in the 1970s
- A left-wing Catalonian separatist terrorist group, it has the goal of establishing an independent Marxist state in the Spanish Provinces of Catalonia and Valencia. Its leadership announced in July 1991 that the group had ceased terrorist operations, but hard-core members may remain active.
- Strength is unknown
- Based in Spain

Activities: TL carries out mainly small-scale bombing attacks against property in northeastern Spain. Targets include foreign banks and travel agencies

External Aid: It has no known sponsors

Tupac Amaru Revolutionary Movement (MRTA)

- Formed in 1982
- A traditional Marxist-Leninist revolutionary movement in Peru, its objective is to rid Peru of "imperialist" influence and establish a Marxist regime.
- Numbers approximately 500 to 1500 combatants
- Based in Peru and Bolivia

Activities: MRTA is responsible for more anti-U.S. attacks than any other group in Latin America. Acts include the burning of several KFC restaurants in 1985 and a car bombing outside the U.S. Ambassador's residence in Lima.

External Aid: It has received training from Cuba and possibly from Libya

Sources: U.S. Department of State, *Patterns of Global Terrorism, 1992;* released April, 1993; Stephen E. Atkins, *Terrorism: A Reference Handbook,* (Santa Barbara, CA: Contemporary World Issues, 1992); Jay M. Shafritz, E.F. Gibbons, Jr., and Gregory E.J. Scott, *Almanac of Modern Terrorism,* (New York: Facts on File, 1991).

nations encourage violent means for the resolution of political conflicts, for a number of reasons. First, authoritarian dictators in Latin America tend to be extremely suspicious of those who oppose their policies. Meanwhile, Latin American populations are perceived by the state to be increasingly restive,

PROFILE OF A TERRORIST

Abu Nidal is the assumed name of Sabri Khalil al-Banna, and also the name of his group—the Abu Nidal Organization (ANO). Known at times as the Fatah Revolutionary Council, the Arab Revolutionary Council, the Arab Revolutionary Brigade, Black September, and the Revolutionary Organization of Socialist Muslims, the ANO opposes all efforts toward political reconciliation of the Arab-Israeli conflict. It believes that both inter-Arab and intra-Palestinian terrorism is needed to lead to an all-embracing Arab revolution that will liberate occupied Palestine, or, in other words, destroy Israel. Abu Nidal began his independent efforts after the October 1973 Arab-Israeli War, when Yasir Arafat decided to restrict PLO's terrorism to Israeli targets in Israel and the occupied territories. He broke with Arafat and decided to fight all moderates, committing terrorist acts against Israeli targets, pro-Arafat Palestinians, moderate Arab states, and countries (usually European) that had imprisoned ANO members, as well as other Western nations like the United States, United Kingdom, and France.

The Arafat–Abu Nidal rift intensified in the mid-1970s, when the PLO chairman sentenced the renegade Nidal to death. In response, in 1978 the ANO assassinated three prominent PLO officials allied with

angry over income inequalities and corruption in the police and in the government. These conditions, when considered alongside calls by university students for the overthrow of the state, lead to a lack of state tolerance for those perceived to be in opposition to it.[97]

The atrocities perpetrated by right-wing "death squads" in El Salvador in the 1970s and 1980s and the "dirty war" conducted against opponents of the state in 1970s Argentina exemplify the use or tolerance of terrorism by Latin American governments. More recently, however, the progress of democratization in the region led to a decrease in state-sponsored terrorism in many countries, especially in Argentina.

Latin American opposition groups frequently employ terrorism as well. The Argentine-born Ernesto "Che" Guevara, a leading proponent and practitioner of guerilla warfare in Latin America until he was killed in 1967 while fighting in Bolivia, acknowledged the advantages and disadvantages of using terrorist tactics. Guevara believed that terrorism did not always lead to the desired result, that it turned people against a revolutionary movement, and that it often resulted in loss of life disproportionate to what it produced. Nevertheless, he also thought terror was "a valuable tactic when it is used to put to death some noted leader of the oppressing forces."[98] One of the most persistent and violent opposition terrorist groups in Latin America has been the Sendero Luminoso ("Shining Path"), a Maoist guerilla group based in Peru. Operating primarily in the mountainous terrain of the Andes region but also effective in shutting off electric power in Lima, the Shining Path has attempted to cultivate the support of

Arafat, yet this act was followed by a temporary rapprochement between the two adversaries.

Abu Nidal's vicious attacks have been felt worldwide. In over ninety terrorist incidents in twenty countries, more than 900 people have been killed or injured. The most infamous attacks were the 1985 shootings of civilians at the Rome and Vienna airports, the 1986 bombing of the Neve Shalom synagogue in Istanbul, the 1986 hijacking of a Pan Am jet in Karachi, and a July 1988 attack on an excursion ship off the coast of Greece.

The ANO maintains its own political agenda, despite the government aid it has received. Nidal headquarters were in Iraq from 1974 to 1983, in Syria from 1983 to 1987, and in Libya since then. It is possibly the most economically stable terrorist group in the world: One-third of its income comes from patron states; one-third is from graft and blackmail; and one-third is from its network of business companies and front organizations. Reports have circulated that Abu Nidal is ill or even dead; however, the ANO is said to be so strong that his demise would affect the group's operations minimally, if at all.*

*Compiled from *Patterns of Global Terrorism 1992*, U.S. Department of State, released April 1993; and *Terrorist Group Profiles*, U.S. Department of Defense, miscellaneous publications, 1989.

peasant farmers for its antigovernment insurgency. However, following the 1992 capture and imprisonment of its leader, Abimael Guzman (alias, Comrade Gonzalo), the resiliency of Sendero Luminoso seems to have eroded.

Terrorism in Africa, South Asia, and North America

Africa   Although the incidence of terrorism is comparatively low in sub-Saharan Africa, terrorist tactics have been used by African states and rebels alike. As noted in Chapter Six, many African states are deeply riven by religious and ethnic conflict, and this factionalism has contributed to terror campaigns waged by and against governments in Nigeria, Chad, Sudan, Ethiopia, Zaire, Angola, Rwanda, Mozambique, South Africa, and elsewhere.[99]

South Asia   Very few regions of the world have yet to experience terrorism. The increased frequency of terrorist activities has been especially alarming in South Asia, where Hindu, Muslim, Sikh, and Tamil extremist groups have carried out bombings and assassinations, primarily on the Indian subcontinent. For the most part, these groups are fighting for their own separate national homeland.

North America   Though the causes for which terrorists fight often arise out of local conflicts, the effects of terrorism are felt all around the world. The bombing of New York's World Trade Center in 1993 by Islamic radicals demonstrated that not even the United States is immune to terrorism, although North America has been the region of the world least victimized by terrorist activities.

Global Responses to Terrorism

There have been few efforts to organize an effective global mechanism to combat terrorism, partly because so many governments either support terrorism or engage in it themselves. It has been suggested that the collapse of the Soviet Union is likely to lead to a decline in the overall incidence of terrorism, since the USSR was a prime supplier of military, financial, and moral support to many Marxist terrorist groups.[100] There is only limited evidence of such a decline, however, as too many other nations have shown their willingness to support terrorism, especially when it promises to further their policy goals. Furthermore, many nationalist and opposition groups that once received Soviet aid have turned to drug trafficking and extortion as alternative sources of funding for their activities.

Despite these obstacles, the United States, the EU countries, and other nations have attempted to foster international cooperation to locate and apprehend terrorists. In 1992, for example, the UN imposed economic sanctions against Libya when it refused to hand over two suspects in the 1989 Pan American airliner bombing. Moreover, some other countries, Cuba and Syria in particular, are notorious terrorist havens, as East Germany and the USSR were before the demise of Communist government in those states. The efforts of some law enforcement and intelligence agencies to nab terrorists, therefore, often raise serious questions of national sovereignty. Because so many states offer freedom from **extradition** (surrender of a suspect to another country for trial), the techniques used to apprehend suspected terrorists have sometimes been tantamount to kidnapping.

Yet all states, whether they recognize it or not, have an interest in curbing terrorism. National, ethnic and religious conflicts spill across state boundaries so easily that no state can consider itself immune from the contagion of political violence. The thought that killers armed with machine guns or plastic explosives could strike in any country is worrisome enough, but the prospect that terrorist groups may someday buy, steal, or otherwise acquire nuclear weapons is especially frightening. Many of the mechanisms for cooperation against terrorism by police and security agencies are already in place—the International Criminal Police Organization (Interpol) has existed for decades, and Moscow and Washington began joint counterterrorist initiatives even before the collapse of the USSR. However, in order to take full advantage of existing avenues for cooperation against terrorism, or to build new ones, states will have to abandon the support of terrorism as a component of their foreign policies. Nations cannot completely prevent the victimization of innocent civilians by those who want to publicize their causes. But governments can come together to seek better ways of preventing terrorist attacks, apprehending suspected terrorists, and denying modern weapons to fanatics willing to kill and die for ancient and recent hatreds.

ENERGY AND NATURAL RESOURCES

As populations grow and economies industrialize, the world's available supplies of nonrenewable energy and natural resources become increasingly scarce. International forums such as the 1992 Earth Summit have sought, with varying degrees of success, to promote widespread commitment to economic development that is sustainable in the long run; that is, development that can be implemented without depleting valuable resources of energy. In the absence of an international agency to enforce accords that deal with energy use, states do not face many incentives to use resources in a manner that takes into account the needs of other countries and future generations.

This chapter has already noted the inherent tension between conservation and utilization of resources in its discussions of conflicts over farmland (in the section on food) and rain forests (in the environment section). As with all the global problems considered in this book, it would be impossible to explain fully the complexity and urgency of natural-resource issues in the space available here. This section, therefore, will present "snapshots" of the conflicts over two vital resources that have sparked conflicts in the past and may cause more in the future: energy and water.

Need for Energy

Societies need energy to survive just as human beings do. In a sense, the course of technological progress is the story of the discovery, utilization, and conservation of new sources of energy. All societies consume energy in some form; before the Industrial Revolution, demand for wood fuel was a major reason for deforestation on every continent. As states attain higher levels of economic and technological development, they "graduate" to dependence on different sources of energy—from animal power, to wood, to coal, to oil, to nuclear power, and so on. While a significant amount of the energy used by the developed world comes from nuclear fission and hydroelectricity (electricity generated by water power in dams), the main sources of energy for developed and developing countries alike are fossil fuels (oil, coal, and natural gas).

There is a close relationship between economic growth and consumption of energy resources. While total fuel consumption in the developed countries grew an average of approximately 2 percent a year between 1985 and 1989, it grew by less than one-tenth of 1 percent between 1989 and 1990, reflecting a slowdown in rates of economic growth.[101] Much of the increased demand for energy resources in recent years has come from the developing countries. In fact, half of the world's energy consumption now occurs in countries outside of the Organization of Economic Cooperation and Development (OECD), which includes most of the developed countries of the world. While the 1973 OPEC oil crisis and the 1990 Persian Gulf War reinforced the importance of securing energy supplies in the developed world, economic growth in the developing world poses the possibility of a new struggle over supplies, especially among those countries that rely heavily on imports to meet their energy requirements.

Oil's Critical Role

Since the invention of the automobile, oil has been the Western world's most important source of energy, especially after the post–World War II boom. However, the greater the reliance on oil to fuel the developed countries' economic (and automotive) engines, the greater is the danger they face to their economies if the oil stops flowing. This was illustrated by the long lines at gas stations following the energy crises of 1973 and 1979. After the OPEC oil embargo of 1973, the OECD countries progressively reduced their dependence on oil (as will be discussed further in the following section). This decreased reliance on petroleum, combined with the glut on the world market, has lessened OPEC's power over the price of global oil supplies since the early 1980s (see Chapters Six and Eight). In 1973 oil accounted for almost 55 percent of total primary energy supplies (TPES), while in 1990 it accounted for only 43 percent.

There is considerable variation in demand for oil across regions. The pattern has been set in the advanced industrial areas such as North America and Europe, where oil demands follow economic activity. Thus, the recession of the early 1990s led to decreased demand (by 2 percent in 1990–1991 in North America). As soon as economic activity increased, so too did demand (by 1.5 percent in 1992 in North America). In Eastern Europe and the former Soviet Union, by contrast, the convulsions caused by the collapse of the Soviet Union and the Communist system have led to a precipitous decline in oil use. In the developing countries, especially in Asia, oil demand is rising (including increases of 20 percent in Thailand and 24 percent in South Korea in 1990), reflecting their economic growth. Therefore, between 1986 and 1992, there was an overall increase among the industrialized economies of 10.2 percent in oil demand. In Eastern Europe and the former Soviet Union there was a 32.7 percent decrease. The developing countries exhibited a 32.9 percent increase in oil demand, ranging from 19.1 percent in Latin America to 78.9 percent in South and East Asia.[102]

Energy Crises and Global Responses: The International Energy Agency (IEA)

Since the early 1970s, there have been three major oil crises—in 1973, 1979, and 1980. The first involved an approximately 7 percent reduction in world oil supplies following the decision of the Arab members of OPEC to impose embargoes on the United States and Netherlands for their support of Israel during the 1973 Arab-Israeli war. The response of oil-consuming countries to the embargo was uncoordinated and competitive. Many countries sought to position themselves favorably, by issuing pro-Arab pronouncements (a case of "bandwagoning" or "appeasement," terms discussed elsewhere in the book), giving their oil companies preferential treatment, and imposing restrictions on petroleum exports. This "anarchy" of national responses contributed to the quadrupling of official prices (from $3 to almost $12 per barrel) between the beginning of October 1973 and January 1974.

The energy crisis of the early 1970s produced ironic changes in international relations. Industrial powers found their well-being dependent on the will of Arab sheiks.

Source: © John Collins, *The Gazette*, Montreal.

Concerned with the effects of the embargo on its economy, the United States led an initiative to establish the International Energy Agency (IEA) in 1974. The initial objectives of this agency were to develop an emergency system for sharing oil, establish an information system to monitor the oil market, facilitate long-term measures to reduce net demand for oil on world markets, and set up multinational energy research and development activities. The IEA Program is designed to protect member states from the economic difficulties that would result if their access to oil was significantly reduced. For example, if any member of the IEA suffers an oil-supply shortfall exceeding 7 percent, it can request the IEA secretariat to put into effect the emergency sharing system.

NUCLEAR POWER AND CHERNOBYL

Nuclear power is another way to generate electric power. The oil crises of the 1970s led states to diversify their approaches to electric power generation and resulted in increased funding for nuclear power research. Compared to its fossil-fuel counterparts, nuclear power uses less "fuel" per unit of power and thus has the potential to lead to a lower cost of electricity overall. It also compares favorably to traditional fossil fuels in that nuclear power does not spew noxious smoke into the air.

For many years, there were suspicions about the potential environmental side effects of nuclear power. The nuclear accident at Three Mile Island, Pennsylvania, in 1979—and especially the one at Chernobyl, in the former Soviet Union, in 1986—changed worldwide opinion about nuclear power plants.

In the latter case, at the Chernobyl nuclear power plant, north of Kiev in what is now Ukraine, the world's worst nuclear reactor disaster occurred. Three explosions occurred on April 26, 1986, in the plant's number-four reactor. The first two explosions blew the lid off the reactor, and the third scattered fragments that caused local fires. This reactor was entombed in concrete to prevent further radiation contamination, while the three remaining reactors continued in operation. (Reactor No. 2 was closed in 1991 following a turbine fire.)

Thirty-two fatalities were immediately reported and approximately 500 people were hospitalized. Most of those killed were firefighters and plant emergency personnel. Within a few days, 135,000 people were evacuated from an area of nineteen miles surrounding the plant. Within this contaminated area, there have been excessively high cancer rates, especially thyroid cancer, leukemia, and other radiation-related diseases. Radioactivity from the force of the explosion was spread across the Northern Hemisphere, with the heaviest radioactive fallout in the western Soviet Union and parts of Europe. The Byelorussian, Ukrainian, and Russian

---

The IEA was put to its first test in 1979, when the Iranian revolution resulted in a virtual cessation of Iranian oil exports. Oil-consuming nations responded by scrambling to ensure supplies (usually by stockpiling) for themselves at whatever price had to be paid, and as a result, prices doubled, even though production outmatched consumption for 1979 as a whole. When Sweden, suffering from an oil-supply shortfall of more than 7 percent, requested that the emergency sharing system be activated in the winter of 1979, the IEA's governing board declined the request. In this case the IEA did not come through when it was needed.

The third oil crisis resulted from the onset of the Iran-Iraq war in September 1980. This time, prices did not rise precipitously. In July 1981 they were only 5 percent higher than prewar levels. Oil prices remained stable, due mostly to weakness in demand and to the Saudis' willingness to increase production, and also to the IEA's efforts to persuade oil companies to sell oil inventories rather than stockpile them.[103]

republics experienced the worst plumes of contaminated air.

The contamination affected buildings, transportation facilities, roads, water, forests, and other vegetation. Radioactive material entered the food chain, particularly in milk, vegetables, and fruit. In Ukraine, panic resulted. Orders were issued not to swim in reservoirs or eat leafy vegetables. Radiation checks on people leaving the contaminated areas were mandatory. The sale of ice cream, cakes, and drinks on the street were banned.*

By early 1994, Ukrainian authorities had listed up to 8000 deaths from illnesses caused by the explosion. The number-four reactor was leaking and deteriorating rapidly and was in danger of collapsing. The International Atomic Energy Agency, in a report filed in March 1994, also listed "numerous safety deficiencies at the plant." Meanwhile, the United States was negotiating with Ukraine to facilitate a shutdown of the two remaining operational reactors "at the earliest possible date."†

The Chernobyl experience and resulting fear of a possible nuclear meltdown led to protests worldwide over the continued construction of nuclear power reactors. Nevertheless, nuclear power generators remain fairly numerous today. As late as 1992, over 400 reactors were operating in 27 countries with 72 additional reactors under construction. The nations that currently use nuclear power the most are the United States, France, Japan, Great Britain, Russia, Canada, Germany, Ukraine, and Sweden. Of these countries, the United States and France are the largest users. As of 1992 the United States had 109 reactors in operation, with the capacity to supply over one-fifth of national energy needs. France had fifty-six reactors. By the end of the 1990s, U.S. dependence on nuclear energy is expected to increase to about 25 percent.

*Richard F. Mould, *Chernobyl: The Real Story* (Oxford: Pergamon Press, 1988).

†Compiled from the *Los Angeles Times,* April 10, 1994 and the *Washington Post,* April 10, 1994.

Coal and Natural Gas

While petroleum is the energy resource that receives the most attention, other fossil fuels are also extremely important. Natural gas, for example, is used for cooking, and for the heating of homes and offices. North America accounts for two-thirds of total OECD gas consumption, but the politically unstable territory of the former Soviet Union holds 40 percent of the world's natural gas reserves. Exports from the former Soviet territories constitute one-third of all internationally traded volumes. Overall, natural gas is difficult to transport over long distances, especially by sea, and as a result, internationally traded gas still accounts for only 15 percent of total global gas consumption.[104] But because of its important and widespread uses, natural gas will continue to remain a significant source of energy.

Another primary energy source is coal, especially for generating electricity. (In 1990 coal contributed 40 percent of electricity generation in the OECD, while nuclear power and oil contributed only 24 and 9 percent, respectively.[105]) Coal is also the dirtiest fossil fuel, and the fact that a large percentage of electric power is generated by burning coal has caused some environmentalists to question the wisdom of encouraging the development of electric cars. If the batteries on electric vehicles are charged with coal-generated electric power, the overall pollution produced by each car could well be higher than that produced by gasoline.

Renewable Energy

Not all sources of energy pollute the environment as much as fossil fuel does, but more environmentally friendly alternative energy sources remain a small part of global energy consumption. Renewable energy sources contributed only 6 percent of total OECD energy supply in 1991, with **hydroelectric** (water-generated) power accounting for 5.9 percent and other sources (wind, solar, and so on) only 0.1 percent.[106] Currently, North America is the leader in the development and use of alternative energy sources.

Every alternative to fossil fuels has drawbacks, however. Most of the time, nuclear power is relatively clean and safe, but nuclear plants are expensive to build, and the possibility of spectacular accidents such as those that occurred at Three Mile Island in Pennsylvania in 1979 and Chernobyl in Ukraine in 1986 makes many people nervous about reliance on nuclear energy. Solar and wind power are unreliable and very expensive. Hydroelectric power is available only near major rivers and has severe environmental side effects, such as killing the aquatic wildlife of the rivers on which plants are located, and rendering the land surrounding the power plant useless. Almost all energy sources apart from fossil fuels are prohibitively expensive for developing countries, making coal and oil the most affordable energy options in most of the South.

In the long run, states will have to learn to do more with less energy in order to sustain economic growth without dangerously depleting world energy resources. In the short term, however, states have no choice but to use all means to conserve and safeguard their supplies of energy. For some, this has meant shedding blood for oil.[107]

Water

Though oil is a crucial and valuable commodity in the modern world, only one fluid is vital: without water, life itself is impossible. A growing global population places strains on available fresh-water supplies, for industrial and agricultural use as well as for basic household consumption. An estimated 1.2 billion people lack clean and safe water, and almost 1.8 billion live without adequate sanitation. Nearly 80 percent of all cases of disease in developing countries have been linked to contaminated water.[108] In areas where fresh water is plentiful, disputes over water are usually limited to arguments between farmers over water

| *Table 10.2* | Middle East Water Availability | |
Country	*1990 Per-Capita Water Availability*	*2025 Projected Per-Capita Water Availability*
Algeria	750	380
Egypt	1,070	620
Iran	2,080	960
Israel	470	310
Jordan	260	80
Kuwait	<10	<10
Lebanon	1,600	860
Libya	160	60
Morocco	1200	680
Oman	1,330	470
Qatar	50	20
Saudi Arabia	160	50
Tunisia	530	330
United Arab Emirates	190	110
Yemen	240	80

Note: Some hydrologists have identified 1000 cubic meters per person per year as a minimum water requirement for an efficient, moderately industrialized nation. The countries of the Middle East listed here are those that either in 1990 or in 2025 will fail to meet this level of fresh water availability. The change between 1990 and 2025 is due solely to increases in population.

Sources: Computed from United Nations population data and estimates. Population and water availability data come from World Resources Institute, *World Resources 1991–92* (New York: Oxford University Press, 1991). Adapted from Peter H. Gleick, "Water and Conflict: Fresh Water Resources and International Security," *International Security* (Summer 1993), vol. 18, no. 1, p. 101.

rights. In many dry regions, however, water is a scarce resource, lending more than a ring of truth to Mark Twain's adage, "Whiskey is for drinking, water is for fighting."

In the mostly arid Middle East, serious concerns over water supplies add to the potential for international conflict. With population growth of 3 percent per year, inadequate rainfall, and boundaries of important water resources (rivers, lakes, aquifers, subterranean canals) shared by more than one state, many believe that the next war in the Middle East will be fought not for land, but for water.[109] Table 10.2 indicates how rapid population increases have put serious strains on the region's water resources. Indeed, it shows that according to current projections every country cited will have less per capita water available in 2025 than it had in 1990.

Three Middle Eastern river basins, the Jordan, the Tigris-Euphrates, and the Nile, have been scenes of recurring conflict over water among neighboring states for thousands of years. In recent decades, cooperation among states in the Jordan river basin has been rare. Although the Johnston Plan for assigning Jordan River water rights has played a constructive role in providing a basis for "equitable water sharing" between Israel and its Arab adversaries, that 1950s-era plan has not stopped the various states, especially Israel and Jordan, from bitterly arguing over transboundary water resources.[110] Access to important water sources reinforces Israel's reluctance to relinquish the Golan Heights captured from Syria in 1967. The 1993 PLO-Israel agreement will also force the Palestinians and Israelis to confront more directly their differences over water resources, but the 1994 Jordan–Israel peace treaty may lead to new technical solutions that may help resolve differences over water issues between the two countries.

Equally complex has been recurring conflict over the resources of the Tigris and Euphrates, which rise in Turkey and flow through Iraq and Syria before converging at the Shatt-al-Arab, where Iraq borders Iran. Turkey's goal of developing its southeastern Anatolian region (near its border with Syria) has brought it into conflict with its downstream neighbors. In the mid-1970s, the lakes behind the newly completed Keban Dam in Turkey and Ath-Thawrah Dam in Syria began filling at the same time, reducing the flow of water running through Iraq by about 75 percent. This brought Syria and Iraq to the brink of war, which was averted by Saudi intervention.[111]

The upstream position of Turkey provides it with a lever of power in the Tigris-Euphrates basin. In 1987 Turkey imposed a water embargo on Syria over the latter's support for Kurdish terrorists in Turkey. In late 1989 the Turkish president announced that his country would temporarily block the flow of the Euphrates to both Syria and Iraq in order to fill Turkey's just completed Ataturk Dam, a mammoth project designed to turn the country into a food exporter.[112] Turkish "water pressure" is particularly feared by Syria, which has few water resources under its own control. In turn, Damascus has successfully pressured the World Bank to make the release of development funds for Turkey's vast $23 billion, thirteen-part southeastern Anatolia project contingent on Turkish agreement to share water.[113]

Conflict over water among the Nilotic countries (the states of the Nile river basin), especially Sudan and Egypt, has stimulated efforts to achieve lasting cooperation. Ever since Sudan and Egypt squared off over Egypt's plans to build the Aswan High Dam in 1958, use of the Nile has been loosely regulated by a 1959 Sudanese-Egyptian water-sharing agreement.[114] Presently under discussion by a consultative group comprising all the Nile countries is an Egyptian proposal to tap the Nile to generate massive electric power for export to other regions (including Syria, Turkey, Jordan and the EU) in exchange for hard currency, which would be used in turn for water and irrigation projects in the Nile countries.[115]

Conflict and Cooperation on Resource Issues

The supply of all resources is limited, and therefore must be allocated in some manner among all the parties that require them. The mechanisms for allocation may be economic (like the global market for oil) or political (like the agreements governing the use of water from the Rhine to the Rio Grande). When the means of allocation are regarded as fair, states have been able to cooperate in sharing resources equitably. When they are not, governments in some cases have gone to the brink of war and beyond to protect their access to crucial resources.

Since the end of World War II, states have gained a great deal of experience in resolving resource issues peacefully. Perhaps the best example is the European Coal and Steel Community, which originally coordinated the use of energy resources but gradually evolved into a supra-national political entity, the EU. Indeed, the international system has come a long way from the days of the War of the Pacific, 1879–1883, when Chile, Bolivia, and Peru fought one another over nitrate deposits (in other words, petrified bird droppings), which were used to make explosives. But scarcity still has great potential to provoke conflict, and if markets and negotiations fail to provide countries with adequate access to vital resources, nations will still find conflict preferable to freezing, starvation, or thirst.

CONCLUSION: GLOBAL ISSUES—SOURCE OF COOPERATION; SCENE OF CONFLICT

In the New Era, pressing global issues are the source of both cooperation *and* conflict among nations. All states have common interests in each of the issue areas discussed in this chapter; all countries want to control the spread of AIDS, for example, and no state wants terrorism to occur on its own territory. At the same time, interests between and within states can conflict sharply. Farmers in the Peruvian highlands may view the cultivation of the coca leaf as the only feasible means of earning money to feed their families, while the Peruvian government may agree with drug-enforcement agencies in Europe and the United States that cocaine traffic must be curtailed.

Like hawkers and shoppers in a street bazaar, countries attempting to address global issues have objectives that are simultaneously complementary (buyers and sellers both want to strike a bargain) and competing (buyers want low prices while sellers want high ones). Unlike the street vendors and shoppers, however, nations have no global police force to call upon when brawls break out because of heated arguments and accusations of cheating. Instead, they must work out agreements among themselves to enforce rules and strive for fairness in their transactions. In regard to some global issues, such as the eradication of smallpox, international organizations have formed to facilitate cooperation, and many have performed remarkably well. In regard to other issues, like combating drug traffic, they have failed dismally. Despite this mixed record, the growing urgency of the problems discussed in this chapter makes it imperative for the international community to continue its coordinated efforts to tackle the related problems of population, migration, environmental protection, food, health, drugs, terrorism, and resource conservation.

Many specific issues appear to place developed and developing countries in opposing camps. Rich countries tend to support restrictions on the use of chlorofluorocarbons (CFCs) and the preservation of tropical rain forests, for example, while many developing countries regard CFC use and clearing rain forests for farmland as economic necessities. In part, these differences suggest that while world politics in the mid-twentieth century was dominated by the conflict between the democratic West and Communist East, global affairs in the New Era may see increasing contentiousness between the developed North and the developing South. Conflict may not be limited to the North-South divide, however, because there are as many opposing interests and perspectives on global issues *within* both North and South as there are differences of opinion between them.

Despite (or because of) this conflict potential, industrial and developing countries alike are increasingly coming to the realization that collaborative efforts between them will be necessary, and unavoidable, in order to control problems that cross national and regional boundaries. In the New Era, as North-South conflicts become more frequent, they will likely be balanced by attempts at cooperation.

In the final analysis, there is only one world, and it appears to be shrinking. More people, faster transportation, new technologies, and heightened awareness of transnational problems all promise to make interdependence a defining characteristic of world politics. But, as repeatedly shown in this chapter, interdependence does not guarantee cooperation. Leaders and citizens will be faced with difficult decisions as nations are drawn closer together and interact more frequently (and on more levels) than previous generations would have thought possible, or even desirable. It is far too early to tell whether such globalization will make world politics more or less conflictual. What is abundantly clear, however, is that successful resolution of global issues requires states to recognize their responsibilities toward their neighbors. To deal successfully with the problems that confront them all, the nations of an increasingly interdependent world must develop and practice a code of global citizenship. Donne described interdependence in the language of the seventeenth century, but the international community would do well to recall his words in the New Era: "Any man's death diminishes me, for I am involved in mankind; and therefore never send to know for whom the bell tolls; it tolls for thee."

PRINCIPAL POINTS OF CHAPTER TEN

1. The world's nations are becoming increasingly interdependent. As a result, transnational problems—those with origins in one state but affecting others—are becoming issues of growing salience and urgency in world politics.

2. While population growth has tapered off in the developed countries, it continues strong in the developing states. This growth has severe consequences for immigration into the developed countries; the world's supply of food, energy, and natural resources; and the health of the world's people and environment.

3. The number of migrants and refugees throughout the world is at an all-time high. Because many economic migrants are attracted to countries with higher standards of living, many developed countries have received more immigrants than they can absorb. As a result, pressures to close borders and tighten requirements for political asylum have increased, particularly in North America and Western Europe.

4. The world overall has an abundance of food. Food is especially plentiful in the developed world, but often scarce elsewhere. This is because food distribution is not only uneven across regions, but uneven within many developing nations as a result of government policies, poor planning, or war.

5. Economic pressures in both developed and developing countries lead to actions that harm the global environment, such as deforestation and industrial pollution. Sustainable, environmentally sound economic growth is possible, but efforts to control and repair environmental damage must take into account economic necessity as well as environmental factors.

6. Even though more of the world is immunized than ever before, many old diseases have proven quite resilient in the face of changing population and environmental conditions, especially in the developing world. New diseases, such as AIDS, have taken their toll in both the North and South.

7. The war on drugs is a relatively new phenomenon. While drugs are produced mostly in the developing world, which initially prompted developed countries to focus their drug-control efforts there, they are consumed in greater quantities in industrialized states. A consensus has begun to emerge as the developed countries realize that they cannot begin to stop the supply of drugs unless they do more to help the economies of the developing countries and curb demand at home.

8. All countries are vulnerable to terrorism, though many nations support terrorist organizations as part of their foreign policies. International cooperation to stop terrorism is relatively undeveloped, but has been given a boost by the collapse of the Communist regimes in Eastern Europe and the former USSR.

9. The access of all nations to important natural resources, such as petroleum and water, is threatened by the increased demand resulting from population growth and industrialization. Market mechanisms and political agreements have proven to be fair and efficient systems of allocating scarce resources in many cases, but war often results from conflicts over resources or attempts to cut off supplies of critical resources for political purposes.

10. Interdependence fosters both cooperation and conflict. Experience has shown that international cooperation to resolve global issues is possible, but states must recognize their responsibilities toward one another if they are to live together peacefully in a world where states interact more frequently and closely.

Part VI

The Security Dimension in World Politics

Chapter 11

Security

There was just too damned much fear in the missile crisis. If you just keep piling it on, well, people may crack. You do not want to reduce your leaders to quivering, panicky, irrational people, do you? Look, we've been piling it on ever since the missile crisis, and even before. That's my point: piling up weapons, reducing flight times, creeping toward a functional launch-on-warning posture—all of these were much less troubling in the missile crisis than now and there was, I assure you, plenty of fear to go around in October 1962.

Robert McNamara, as quoted in James G. Blight and David A. Welch, *On the Brink: Americans and Soviets Reexamine the Cuban Missile Crisis* (New York: Hill and Wang, 1989), p. 198.

How much security is ever enough? This is a troubling question to anyone who has wrestled with providing his or her country just the right amount of defense—enough so that one is protected against adversaries and yet not too much so that one creates enemies. According to Goldilocks' principle, "just right," is no easy task. As much was admitted by John F. Kennedy's secretary of defense, Robert McNamara, in ruminating about this issue a quarter of a century after the Cuban missile crisis. Given the dilemmas of mutual security in the nuclear age, McNamara's comment is worth remembering.

For better or for worse, nations have always been preoccupied with security. In many periods of history national security was such an important value that people were expected to lay down their lives for it without question. This attitude was manifested in the ancient Roman expression, *dulce et decorum est pro patria mori* ("how sweet and beautiful it is to die for the fatherland"). In many parts of the world, this old principle continues to be strongly felt; states threatened by conflicts often have little choice but to devote vast resources to protecting their sovereignty and independence.

Although most of us have never personally experienced war in all its cruelty, violent interstate conflict continues to be a fact of life in the New Era, as best exemplified by the bloody conflict that broke out between the remnants of the former Yugoslavia, including Bosnia, Croatia, and Serbia. Indeed, as long as the international system remains predominantly anarchic, the provision of national security will remain a fundamental duty of national leaders, and they will continue to ask or compel their citizens to make sacrifices to provide for the common defense.

This chapter examines how the pursuit of security affects international politics: In other words, it looks at how states attempt to protect themselves and how their efforts at self-protection affect their relations with other states. There will be little here about war or battles, which are the province of military history, and not much about defense budgets, which are intimately connected with domestic politics.

Chapter One introduced the concept of the **security dilemma:** Measures that states take to make themselves feel more secure will inevitably make other states feel less secure, so other states respond with their own security measures, which in turn make the first state feel less secure, and so on. Chapter Nine discussed how states attempt to escape from the security dilemma by making the international system less anarchic. This chapter will consider how nations try to manage the security dilemma by adopting unilateral strategies of self-protection and by trying to limit arms or prevent arms races from erupting into war. Before looking at how states attempt to achieve security, however, it is necessary to understand what it is they are trying to achieve; in other words, what is "national security"?

THE MANY FACES OF SECURITY

The term "security" is used much more frequently than it is precisely defined. In the absence of a generally agreed upon definition, virtually anybody can invoke the slogan of "national security" for any purpose. As one analyst wrote,

1964: Nuclear proliferation occurs as China gains nuclear capability, prompting India and Pakistan to follow suit in subsequent years.

1967: Six Day War demonstrates Israeli military prowess, but prior crisis represents failure of Israeli deterrent; flexible response strategy gives credibility to NATO's deterrent capability.

1968: Nonproliferation Treaty prohibits states possessing nuclear weapons from helping others to acquire them, and forbids nonnuclear states that adhere to the treaty from manufacturing or otherwise obtaining nuclear arms.

1970: Israel practices nonnuclear deterrence by threatening Syria with retaliation should it attack Jordan.

1972: United States and Soviet Union sign SALT I, limiting the deployment of offensive strategic weapons, such as ICBMs and SLBMs; ABM treaty limits U.S. and USSR to not more than two ABM sites each.

1979: United States and Soviet Union sign SALT II, limiting launchers and numbers of warheads; a ceiling is placed on missiles that can be MIRVed.

1987: Intermediate-range Nuclear Forces Treaty signed, for the first time banning an entire class of nuclear weapons.

1990: NATO and Warsaw Pact countries sign the Conventional Forces in Europe Treaty, limiting conventional forces in Europe and removing the threat of a blitzkrieg-type Soviet invasion of Western Europe.

1991: Persian Gulf War occurs as U.S.-led coalition expels Iraq from Kuwait; Yugoslavia breaks up, leading to wars between states of the former republic; United States and Soviet Union sign START I, reducing for the first time the number of nuclear arms; breakup of the Soviet Union causes uncertainty about nuclear arms agreements.

1993: United States and Russia sign START II, further reducing strategic nuclear arsenals and eliminating MIRVed ICBMs.

1994: United States and Russia stop aiming their nuclear missiles at each other; also agree to speed up dismantling of nuclear weapons ahead of START II schedule. U.S. reaches 10-year pact with North Korea trading improved ties and assistance for North Korea gradually relinquishing nuclear weapons option.

National security is a modern incantation. As in any incantation the words have both power and mystery. In the name of national security, all things can be threatened. All risks can be taken. All sacrifices can be demanded. . . . The ultimate catch-all term, it can mean anything the user chooses it to mean.[1]

Unfortunately, it is easier to point out why we need a precise definition of security than to actually offer one. One of the main reasons why this is so is that the concept of security has many different aspects and is constantly changing. This can easily be understood if we ask what security means to us as individual human beings. Immediately, it becomes apparent that security means very different things to different people in different environments. What security means to a *!Kung* hunter in the Kalahari Desert might differ from the idea held by a college student in the United States. Even in similar environments, security can be interpreted differently by different individuals. For some students, security will mean assuring one's financing for the next academic year (economic well-being), for others it may have medical connotations (physical health), and for still others it may refer to personal safety in a crime-infested neighborhood (protection from violence).

When we return our analysis to the level of the nation-state, the multidimensional nature of security becomes even more apparent. Like humans, states also differ in the nature of their security predicaments. Poor nations may count provision of adequate food and clean water among their primary security necessities, while more advanced, developing countries may simultaneously face ethnic separatism and foreign military threats, and industrialized countries may fear pollution and the loss of manufacturing jobs to other countries. During the Cold War, the military aspects of security received the most attention, largely because of the ever-present risk of nuclear war. Now that the Cold War is history, decision makers are under more pressure to address the economic, environmental, and even cultural aspects of security. (Cultural security may seem a strange concept to Americans, but American rock music and fast-food chains have "invaded" far more countries than have American troops.)

External and Internal Threats

Even when considering the military aspects of security, most states face both external and internal security threats. External threats come from beyond a nation's borders and differ according to geopolitical factors. A country such as Israel, which occupies a thin piece of hotly contested real estate along the Mediterranean Sea and is surrounded by adversaries, finds itself in a profoundly different security predicament than a country like Malta, an isolated island in the Mediterranean with few coveted resources. Internal threats are found within national boundaries, and also vary greatly among states. Countries such as India and Egypt face serious problems with domestic terrorism, while Denmark and Canada experience almost no political violence within their boundaries.

External and internal threats to security are often interrelated. Ironically, an obsession with one can increase the risks from the other. The former Soviet Union serves as a powerful example. Throughout the Cold War, Moscow expended enormous resources on national defense, allegedly to ensure the continued survival of the country and to protect it from foreign aggression. Ultimately, the demise of the USSR had little or nothing to do with foreign intervention but occurred almost spontaneously from within, caused in part by economic tensions exacerbated by defense expenditures. Most analysts now agree that the Soviet Union's huge military budget, rather than strengthening its security, actually contributed to its downfall.

Now that the end of the Cold War has focused the world's attention on common global problems, more attention is being given to dimensions of security that transcend its traditional military-territorial aspects. Transnational threats to the community of nations and the global ecosystem include the issues addressed in Chapter Ten: population pressures, environmental pollution, AIDS, drug trafficking, and terrorism. As one analyst wrote, security means a lot more than just military threat:

> It means an informed electorate, healthy environment, a strong economy, and a just society. We are endangered not just by nuclear weapons, but also by pollution of our air, rivers, lakes, and oceans, by leaking nuclear waste dumps, by the hole in the ozone layer and by the greenhouse effect. We are endangered not just by foreign economic competition, but also by drugs, illiteracy, and disease, by unregulated corporate greed, and by the wasting of our technical talent in the weapons industry.[2]

It is important to recognize, however, that there are dangers in expanding the concept of security to include every problem faced by a nation or the world. Powerful bureaucratic players in many countries have a vested interest in broadening the definition of national security to include any activity that falls under their responsibility. Many ministers and cabinet secretaries responsible for health, education, the environment, or trade policy have been quick to claim that the issues they deal with are matters of national security in order to obtain more resources from the state. A more insidious potential danger in expanding the concept is that national security has traditionally been a favored excuse for governments to suspend or ignore civil rights. While states may be wise to give more attention to aspects of security outside of military threats, citizens should not allow expanding definitions of national security to erode personal, political, and economic freedom.

Subjective versus Objective Aspects of Security

Another factor complicating the task of defining security is that security and insecurity frequently have a strong subjective dimension. In other words, security is in large part a perception or feeling. At the level of the individual, some residents of New York may feel perfectly safe walking after dark, whereas others might feel constantly threatened. In the international system, some states (such as Stalin's Soviet Union or Kaiser Wilhelm II's Germany) have at times behaved as if they were under an imminent threat for reasons that outsiders could not understand. Conversely, some countries have felt unjustifiably safe in periods where they should have taken the threats that confronted them more seriously, and as a result suffered surprise attacks (such as the United States in 1941).

Subjective perceptions of security show up in nations' defense budgets. Defense spending may be thought of as an insurance policy against the vagaries of the international system. Just as people can take out different types of insurance policies for their cars, states also vary in their approach to risk: They can underestimate danger and not take out sufficient insurance, or they can be paranoid and overinsure. This relationship between objective threat and subjective perceptions of security may be represented as a matrix as shown in Figure 11.1

In this matrix, the right-hand column represents cases of high objective threat, such as the presence of well-armed expansionist neighbors. Within this column, the top right corner of "underinsurance" (quadrant I) represents a dangerous situation where a country is objectively in danger but believes itself to be secure. A country that fails to correctly evaluate the threats to its security is far less likely to invest sufficient resources into its defense, and could therefore easily become a victim of aggression. For example, before World War II many European countries believed Hitler could be appeased and thus were not adequately prepared to resist when he attacked. France was especially unprepared; after Hitler invaded Belgium, he was able to bypass France's much heralded defensive fortification, the Maginot Line.

The lower right corner (quadrant II) depicts a state that is objectively in danger, and at the same time, is aware of its insecurity. Israel, for instance, has been surrounded by well-armed adversaries. However, because it remains acutely aware of its situation, for over four decades it has been able to safeguard its security through a mixture of political and military means, which has finally begun to pay off with moves toward peace in the area.

The left-hand column of the matrix represents countries that face few actual threats to their security. States that exist in low-threat conditions and perceive

Figure 11.1   Matrix of Objective versus Subjective Aspects of Security

Subjective Perception of Security	*Objective (Real) Threat to Security*	
	Low Threat	*High Threat*
Secure	**Pacifism III** (Malta, 1993)	**Underinsurance I** (France, 1940)
Insecure	**Overinsurance IV** (USSR, 1980)	**Prudence II** (Israel, 1948–)

themselves to be secure have small defense budgets (quadrant III). In contrast, however, those states that are not objectively threatened but believe danger is imminent tend to plan on the basis of worst-case assumptions. This often results in "overinsurance" (quadrant IV). Such a country is likely to waste large amounts of resources against an illusory threat. The most salient example of security overinsurance is the Soviet Union after World War II. Despite its possession of nuclear stockpiles, friendly neighboring states, and a huge conventional army, Moscow continued to spend enormous sums of money on security, much to the detriment of its economic system.

The psychological mechanisms behind a country's perception of its security do not readily lend themselves to rational analysis. Intuitively, one might expect that as a country becomes more powerful, it would start to feel more secure. Historically, this proposition has been violated with astonishing regularity. Political scientist Karl Deutsch called this anomaly Parkinson's Law of National Security: "A nation's feeling of *insecurity* expands directly with its power" (italics added).[3] As most nations become more powerful, they acquire more interests that need defending, and more potential adversaries. The United States, for example, had few interests outside the Western Hemisphere when it was an isolationist power before World War I, and accordingly spent little on defense. After World War II, however, the United States made commitments to defend its allies all over the globe. Its defense budgets then rose to unprecedented levels, though few Americans felt any more secure than they had before World War II.

Working Definition of Security

Now that we understand how national security is a partly objective, partly subjective condition, the rest of this chapter will examine the measures states take to survive as independent entities within the international system. A country's security will be defined herein as a condition in which the sovereignty and the territorial integrity of a country are guaranteed.

Given the anarchic nature of the international system, this condition has been difficult for states to achieve. It is an unfortunate but inescapable reality that the history of international relations has been punctuated by innumerable military conflicts, many of which resulted in massive bloodshed. Even in the New Era, many states face threats against their sovereignty or territorial integrity, and as a result have little choice but to try to protect themselves through various means.

Will the world ever reach a condition in which no country's independence or integrity is threatened? Possibly, but not likely. The international system is composed of states whose internal situations constantly fluctuate. Just as a young family with new children will look for larger living accommodations, states with growing populations and economic needs have looked for more territory, more resources, and so forth. Since most of these resources are scarce commodities, there is always potential for conflict. As a state's internal pressures increase, conflicts are bound to multiply, and if states cannot or will not resolve them by political means, armed aggression might become a temptation for one of the parties and thus a danger to the others. Hence, as pressure mounts, security threats are created, and states must respond to them if they hope to preserve their independence, territory, resources, or values. (These issues will be discussed further in Chapters Thirteen and Fourteen.)

SECURITY DILEMMA REVISITED

When threatened, the instinctive reaction of states will be to try to protect their sovereignty and territorial integrity against the pressures created by internal factors, such as uneven development and social upheavals, and external conditions, like armed threats from neighboring countries. For many states, responses to these conditions mean arming themselves against the possibility of aggression, or allying with other states that were facing similar dangers. The Romans summarized this idea with the adage, *si vis pacem, para bellum* ("if you want peace, prepare for war"). One of the tragic traits of the international system is the uncertainty of the effects of these defensive efforts—sometimes they work and deter a potential aggressor, other times they backfire and decrease the defender's security (as their neighbors arm themselves in response, and so on). Countries thus face the painful security dilemma discussed in Chapter One: The measures a state takes to increase its own security are likely to decrease the security of other states. If all states then take steps to increase their own security, the net effect may be that the security of all is actually diminished.

Here again, the concept is not exclusively restricted to the international system. Our own individual "security policies" may be useful in explaining the basic idea. Consider a person (let's call him Steve) living in an unsafe neighborhood where many muggings and burglaries take place. In the absence of gun-control laws, Steve may decide to purchase a firearm for self-defense, "just to play it safe." Upon hearing that Steve has bought a gun, his neighbor Beth may well do the same, again "just in case." After a period of time, most of the neighborhood's residents are now armed. Even if no one in the neighborhood has aggressive intentions, it's not very likely that the residents feel much safer than before, because there are far more guns now floating around. The existence of so many firearms increases the likelihood that someone will use one of them, either deliberately (in a domestic quarrel, perhaps), as a result of poor information (mistaking a roommate entering the house through a window because he lost his keys for a prowler), or accidentally (by a small child or intoxicated person). Thus, even though Steve, Beth, and everybody else bought guns to increase their personal safety, the whole neighborhood has become objectively and subjectively less safe.

A similar situation to this neighborhood arms race occurs in the international system, where all countries face the security dilemma. On the one hand, all nations understandably want to counteract the threat of an expanding neighbor, either by building up their own military strength internally, or by allying with third powers who feel equally threatened by the rising state. But, on the other hand, by resorting to these techniques, they may give the ascendant power an incentive (or excuse) to beef up its military strength, which in turn decreases the first country's security. As a result, states continuously get trapped in this vicious action-reaction spiral. (This dilemma aside, some states will follow a deliberate policy of aggression or coercion, which makes matters even worse. As the old saying goes, even paranoids have real enemies.)

One of the best examples of this lethal logic was the start of World War I. No country seemed to really want to start a war, yet an apparently inconsequential act (the assassination of the Austro-Hungarian archduke by a Serbian terrorist) led to a chain reaction of military mobilizations that ultimately led to what was at that point the world's largest war (see Chapter Three). No one country could afford not to mobilize, and when it did, it made mobilization by the other countries even more imperative, thus leading to a rapid escalation of the crisis into full-blown war.

Why can't all these countries just act rationally? The point is, they *are* acting rationally. In an anarchic environment where the possibility of conflict is ever present, it makes sense for each state to arm itself, because the risk of preparing for armed conflict seems less than the risks incurred by remaining defenseless. It is therefore extremely difficult to escape from the security dilemma in an anarchic system, and as a result, all states have to adopt a security strategy of one kind or another. (If this section makes you wish for a world government or global police force, see Chapter Nine for a discussion of the problems with international law and organizations.)

STRATEGIES FOR SECURITY: DETERRENCE, DEFENSE, AND COMPELLENCE

There are essentially three types of strategies states use to protect their sovereignty and territorial integrity from external challengers: deterrence, defense, and compellence. While not mutually exclusive, these strategies are based on different assumptions and seek to protect the state through different means.

Deterrence

Deterrence attempts to prevent war by discouraging a potential aggressor from attacking. The primary goal for the defender is to convince the challenger that the probable cost of attacking will far exceed any anticipated gain. This is usually accomplished by threatening to militarily retaliate or punish the initiator if it commits the undesired action. More precisely, the defender must signal its **commitment** to punish or retaliate and its **capability** to do so in order to demonstrate the **credibility** of the deterrent threat. If the defender succeeds, the challenger will back down without a shot being fired; if it fails, the challenger will attack.

The concept of deterrence is commonly associated with nuclear weapons, but its application extends to any situation where one side seeks to prevent another from taking some action that has not already been taken. When a five-year-old boy accosted by bullies attempts to warn them off by threatening, "You better leave me alone or my big brother will beat you up," he is using a strategy of deterrence to deal with a security problem.

Deterrence can also be used by the strong to prevent the weak from trying to overthrow the established order. Its use dates back thousands of years. In 70 A.D., for example, a Jewish rebellion against Roman rule in Palestine was crushed, but a few managed to escape to the mountain fortress of Masada. Although it could easily have chosen to ignore the remaining rebels, Rome painstakingly and expensively assaulted Masada to demonstrate that it "would pursue rebellion even to mountain tops in remote deserts to destroy its last vestiges, regardless of the cost."[4] Rome's purpose was to deter any other groups in the empire from rebelling. In more recent times, the same argument could be made about the Soviet Union's strongarm tactics in putting down the 1956 Hungarian revolt; Moscow's harsh action was intended to send a strong and clear message to neighboring Soviet satellites in Eastern Europe.

Strategists identify four basic types of deterrence. Two kinds, general and immediate, have to do with the time frame of the strategy. **General deterrence** is a long-term strategy intended to "discourage serious consideration of any challenge to one's core interests by an adversary."[5] General deterrence operates all the time, attempting to prevent an adversary from attempting any kind of military challenge because of its expected consequences. **Immediate deterrence,** by contrast, is a response to a specific and explicit challenge to a state's interests. Once an aggressor has begun an attack, general deterrence has failed, but immediate deterrence may still convince it to stop what it is doing and go no further.

As an illustration of the difference between general and immediate deterrence, consider the marshal of a town in the Old West. When he walks around town with his six-guns strapped on, he is exercising general deterrence, tacitly reminding potential lawbreakers that they will have to answer to him if they try to make any trouble. When he sees a desperado about to draw a gun and warns, "Ya better not try it, varmint," he is exercising immediate deterrence, attempting to dissuade the outlaw from taking a specific action.

Two additional types of deterrence deal with the geographic scope of the intended strategy. **Primary deterrence** is intended to dissuade a challenger from attacking a state's own territory, while the objective of **extended deterrence** is to discourage a challenger from attacking an ally or partner. Through its commitments to NATO and Japan, the United States has used extended nuclear deterrence to protect its major allies. As one might guess, extended deterrence often fails because challengers are more likely to doubt the willingness of one state to risk war (especially nuclear war) over its partner. For this reason, France developed its own nuclear arsenal during the 1960s, as French President Charles de Gaulle argued that France could never be sure that in a confrontation with the Soviet Union, the United States would be willing to "trade New York for Paris" and risk nuclear war to defend France.[6]

An example of extended nonnuclear deterrence was Israel's response to a Syrian threat in 1970. Israel believed that Syria would soon intervene in neighboring Jordan's civil war. (Israel did not want Syrian troops so close to major Israeli cities.) To dissuade Damascus from attacking Jordan and overthrowing King Hussein's government, Israel threatened direct retaliation against Syrian forces. Israel, in effect, made it clear that any attack on Jordan would be treated the same as an attack on Israel. Syrian forces, which had previously started to intrude, withdrew, and the Syrian air force did not attack—an example of successful extended deterrence.[7]

Defense

A strategy of **defense,** by contrast to deterrence, attempts to reduce an enemy's capability to damage or take something away from the defender.[8] The purpose of defense is to resist an attack in order to minimize losses after deterrence has failed. It minimizes the damage to the defender and denies its territory, raw materials, or other valued resources to the aggressor. While a strategy of deterrence aims to provide security by raising the prospective costs of aggression to unacceptable levels, a strategy of defense attempts to thwart the aggressor's aims even if the aggressor decides to attack. In particular, deterrence is primarily psychological and intends to influence the challenger's decision process, while defense is physical and intends to rebuff the challenger.

This distinction can be illustrated by a simple example. Someone who wants to protect an expensive car from theft can seek to discourage potential thieves by installing a car alarm and placing a warning sticker in the window. On the other hand, the owner can put the car in a locked garage where it is physically impossible for someone to steal it. The difference between these strategies of protecting the car is that in the first case, the owner seeks to dissuade the thief by influencing the thief's mental calculations, whereas in the second instance the owner physically tries to deny the thief the valued goods. Both of these strategies are potentially effective, but both have drawbacks. In order for deterrence to be effective, the owner must pay for an alarm, the thief must be convinced that someone will come if the alarm goes off, and if the thief decides to attempt to steal the car anyway, the alarm must actually go off and the thief must either run away or be apprehended before he can make off with the car. In order for defense to work, a garage must be available (the owner may have to add one on to his house), and the owner must remember to lock the garage door—and even then, the thief might still pick the lock.

These strategies for protection against theft can be combined, of course: The owner can set an alarm and lock the car in a garage. But in this case the owner must pay the costs of both strategies, which may be more than he can afford. States, too, have finite resources to devote to security, and so must choose the mix of deterrence and defense that makes the best use of the resources available.

To take nuclear war as an example, while the provision of strategic nuclear weapons such as ICBMs and SLBMs provides a powerful deterrent capability, they cannot shoot down incoming missiles or stop enemy armies from marching across borders. Once war has broken out, deterrence has failed (and nuclear weapons are more or less useless) and defensive resources must be used.

The nuclear exception aside, almost any weapon or type of military unit can be used for defense. Equally important, though, is the fact that most forces usable for defense have some expansive capability as well, which is the very heart of the security dilemma. As long as a nation's soldiers, ships, tanks, artillery, and aircraft are capable of being used to attack as well as defend, its neighbors are likely to find it hard to believe that these forces are intended for purely defensive purposes.

This caveat even applies to seemingly defensive concrete bunkers and trench lines. Rather than make one's neighbors less suspicious, they often increase suspicion by indicating to neighboring states that an attack on them is imminent. Additionally, fortifying territory that another state claims as its own (such as the Golan Heights, annexed by Israel but claimed by Syria) may well be regarded as a warlike act.

Overall, as shown by the car thief example, the two strategies of deterrence and defense are not mutually exclusive—a state's security is a function of both. Defensive measures typically also have some deterrent value; a would-be car thief who sees a well-built garage will probably be deterred from trying to break into it. To guarantee security, countries must pursue a mix of these strategies, and not pursue only one at the expense of the other. What constitutes a proper mix is often a major point of debate among policy-makers and military planners.

Compellence

While deterrence attempts to dissuade an adversary from a damaging action, and defense attempts to reduce an enemy's capability to inflict damage, **compellence** attempts to force an adversary to reverse or undo some damaging action that has already been taken. If both deterrence and defense fail to prevent or halt an invasion, then the defender's next step is to convince or force the initial aggressor to withdraw from the territory it has occupied. Compellence is almost always more difficult than deterrence.[9]

There are several well-known cases of successful compellence in American foreign policy. Although often coined as a case of deterrence success, the Cuban missile crisis can more accurately be described as a case of compellence success (and also deterrence failure). In 1962 President Kennedy communicated a commitment to the Soviet Union that the United States would never allow offensive weapons to be stationed on Cuba.[10] However, Premier Khrushchev decided to challenge Kennedy's commitment and proceeded to deploy ballistic missiles

CLAUSEWITZ ON WAR AND POLITICS

A number of strategists and military theorists have expounded their views on the conduct of war through the centuries. For example, the writings of the ancient Chinese General Sun Tzu on the art of war are still studied for their strategic insights. Most of these military thinkers have viewed the conduct of war as a specialized activity, outside the sphere of "normal" activities of a state or society. In the early nineteenth century, the Prussian soldier Carl von Clausewitz (1780–1831) realized that holding this attitude was a good way to lose wars.

Born to a lower-middle-class family, Clausewitz studied literature and philosophy and attended the War College in Berlin, but his experience of war was more than academic. He served in the field during the French Revolutionary and Napoleonic Wars, became a prisoner of war after the crushing Prussian defeat by Napoléon at Jena in 1806, and joined the Russian army to fight against Napoléon's invasion of Russia in 1812. After Napoléon's final defeat inaugurated what became a century of relative peace in Europe, Clausewitz concentrated on the theoretical study of military affairs as a War College professor.

Unlike most other strategists, Clausewitz did not produce a system of guidelines for the conduct of battles or campaigns. Instead, his major work, *On War,* emphasized that mechanistic principles are of little value in carrying out military operations, because war is inherently a risky and uncertain business. Chance, psychological factors, and the "fog of war" (the inability of commanders to have precise information

in any case. This is a case of deterrence failure, because despite U.S. warnings, the Soviets still put missiles on Cuba; some part of the initial commitment was unclear or lacked credibility. After thirteen days of negotiations, threats, and military jousting by both sides, the United States was able to persuade the Soviets to withdraw the missiles, successfully executing a strategy of compellence.

More recently, the United States and its allies resorted to force in order to compel Iraqi forces to leave Kuwait in 1991. This example also illustrates how difficult compellence can be. The transport of U.S. forces to Saudi Arabia was not enough to encourage Iraqi President Saddam Hussein to back down. Instead, it took a strategic bombing campaign and a ground war to expel Iraqi troops from Kuwait.

REQUIREMENTS FOR DETERRENCE

As shown in the previous section, deterrence can be a difficult strategy to successfully implement. It was mentioned that three conditions must be met in order for it to work. First, the defending state must define behavior that is unacceptable and communicate its commitment to punish the challenger. Second, the defender must possess the capability to punish an attacker. Finally, the defending state must demonstrate that it is willing to carry out its commitment to retaliate against the attacker; that is, the deterrent threat must have credibility.[11]

about their own forces, let alone those of the enemy) make war a chaotic enterprise. To be successful, he argued, commanders must adapt to constantly changing conditions (on the battlefield and off) without losing sight of their strategic objectives.

Moreover, Clausewitz wrote, war is fought not just by armies, but by nations. In order to defend itself, a state must mobilize not only its military forces, but its resources and will to fight as well, and must seek to reduce the enemy's army, industry, and national morale. His famous dictum, "War is nothing but the extension of politics by other means," reminds soldiers and statesmen alike that wars are fought for political objectives, and that defeat is far more likely if the nation does not support the underlying goals of a military campaign.

Clausewitz's studies of war had a major impact on strategic thinking throughout the world, and many of his writings are still read at military academies and war colleges. Modern strategists, such as those on the American side in Vietnam, were foolish to ignore his conclusions that the political goals of war must be expressed and maintained. Though he wrote before the era of "total war," Clausewitz warned civilian and military leaders that national security is an activity to which the whole nation must contribute. Clausewitz thus anticipated, and may well have inspired, the well-known remark made by French Prime Minister Georges Clemenceau during the First World War: "War is too important to be left to the generals."

Before we discuss these "three Cs" of successful deterrence, it must be made clear that the concept of deterrence assumes that decision makers are essentially rational. Rational decision making means choosing to act in a way that best enables you to maximize your own position, based on calculations of potential gains and losses, and of probabilities of enemy actions.[12] It does not mean that decisions are made without emotion; obviously, human beings are often influenced by their emotions. But it does assume that the leader of the challenging nation is capable of weighing the potential benefits of attacking against the costs of the defending nation's probable response, and that the decision to attack or not will be made on the basis of this calculation. (The question of whether this is an accurate depiction of the way in which decisions to attack are made will be considered later.)

Commitment

As the first step in successful deterrence, the defending state must make a commitment to punish the challenger if the challenger takes a specified action. In other words, the defender must "draw a line in the sand" and warn the challenger that it will suffer if it crosses it. This commitment must be stated clearly, unambiguously, and before the challenger commits the act of aggression. For example, Israel repeatedly stated that a blockade of the Strait of Tiran, the only waterway passage to its southern port of Eilat, would be regarded as an act of war, and Egyptian attempts to blockade the strait in 1955 and 1967 were contributing factors in both the 1956 and 1967 Arab-Israeli wars.

It is important that deterrence commitments be definite and specific, as ambiguity may elicit probes by challengers interested in testing a defender's resolve. In 1950 the United States omitted South Korea from its announced defense perimeter in the Pacific, and this may have encouraged North Korea to believe that the United States would not respond if it attacked its southern neighbor (see Chapter Four). Likewise, prior to the outbreak of World War I, Britain wavered on its commitment to support the Entente (France and Russia) in the event of war against the Triple Alliance (Germany, Austria-Hungary, and Italy). Had Britain clearly voiced its position, Germany might have been dissuaded from attacking France in 1914.

Deterrence often fails because a defender does not properly signal a commitment to punish or fails to specify the precise retaliatory actions to be undertaken in case of aggression. Prior to Argentina's invasion of the Falkland Islands in 1982, for example, Britain failed to issue any verbal warning or to start any military preparations as a deterrent signal.[13] As a result, the ruling Argentine junta probably doubted Britain's interest in defending a small colony left over from its imperial past, and thus was not deterred from seizing the islands. More recently, there has been considerable debate over the mixed signals that the United States sent Saddam Hussein prior to his decision to invade Kuwait, specifically regarding the alleged comments that U.S. Ambassador April Glaspie made to Hussein shortly before Iraq's invasion of Kuwait. She reportedly stated that the United States had "no opinion" on Iraq's border dispute with Kuwait and did not warn Saddam Hussein of the consequences of using force against Kuwait.[14] In this case, deterrence appears to have failed because a defender did not state its commitment to punish, or was ambiguous about its position.

Capability

The clearest commitment is useless if a state does not have the means to carry it out. Since deterrence revolves around convincing a challenger that the cost of a certain action is not worth the benefit, the challenger must be convinced (or at least strongly suspect) that the defender has the capability to retaliate. Even if a state's deterrent capability is weak, it may try to convince a challenger that its power to punish is greater than it actually is, just as a homeowner might hope to dissuade trespassers by posting a "Beware of Dog" sign even though she doesn't own a dog. This is one reason why some countries (for example, Israel and pre-1993 South Africa) refuse to reveal their suspected nuclear capabilities; the very possibility that a defender might respond to an attack with nuclear weapons may be sufficient to deter an aggressor.

Deterrence with conventional weapons is considerably more difficult, because aggressors can better estimate their capability to inflict punishment. Even though Britain and France had more tanks than Germany in 1940, because Hitler knew he could compensate with a lightning campaign against France, he was not deterred

Three U.S. tanks maneuver en route to an engagement with Iraqi troops in the Gulf War. The poor showing of Saddam Hussein's vaunted military machine against U.S.-led coalition forces suggests the unpredictability of warfare.

Source: © A. Tannenbaum/Sygma.

from attacking and decisively defeated Allied forces there. Similarly, America's naval strength in the Pacific in 1941 did not deter the Japanese attack on Pearl Harbor, and the combined armed forces of Egypt and Syria did not deter the Israeli attack in 1967, because Israel and Japan gambled that they could each score a knockout blow with preemptive strikes. (Israel's gamble paid off; Japan's didn't.)

Credibility

Third, a state must convince the aggressor of its resolve and willingness to carry out its commitment to punish. Even if a defender has clearly stated its commitment to punish and has the capability to do so, deterrence can still fail if the challenger doubts the willingness of the defender to risk war. As a result, this commitment to punish must be persuasive to keep from sounding like a bluff. In part, the defender's success will depend upon its reputation, past behavior, and image. With this in mind, Israel has consistently pursued a policy of harsh retaliation in order to foster its credibility, although its failure to respond to Iraqi SCUD missile attacks during the Persian Gulf War was disturbing to many Israeli decision makers, who feared future deterrence would be eroded. Forty years earlier, many believed that the United States had little strategic interest in Korea, but that it had to respond to North Korea's attack to signal American willingness to protect its Pacific and Western European allies from Soviet aggression.

Ironically, the fearsome destructive power of nuclear weapons that makes their retaliatory capability unquestioned also leads to a credibility problem. Would the defender really be willing to sacrifice millions of people in a nuclear war? For example, in June 1948, one year before the Soviet Union exploded its first nuclear bomb, the American nuclear monopoly was still not able to prevent the Soviets from blockading Berlin. Similarly, in both the 1973 Arab-Israeli and the 1982 Falklands wars nonnuclear challengers (Egypt and Syria, and Argentina) doubted the defenders' resolve to retaliate with their nuclear weapons. (As it turned out, neither Britain nor Israel had to resort to nuclear arms to turn back the aggressors.)

In many ways, crises where nuclear weapons are involved often resemble the game of "chicken." In the classic film *Rebel without a Cause*, James Dean and a rival play this game by racing their cars toward the edge of a cliff; the first to "chicken out" and swerve is the loser, but if neither swerves, both will go over the cliff. In this game, each player wants the other to swerve before he does, but both players prefer swerving away from the edge and letting the other side win to going over the cliff. The object of the game, like the object of deterrence in a confrontation between two nuclear powers, is to prevail by convincing the opposing player of your willingness to risk destruction.

The Cuban missile crisis is often presented as a game of chicken, where the Soviets were the first to blink. If neither side was willing to retreat or "swerve," the outcome would have been war between the nuclear-armed superpowers. This might have occurred if the Soviets had attempted to proceed with their plan of placing more missiles on Cuba and the United States had launched an air strike on Cuba or invaded the island.

To summarize, deterrence can fail because a challenger doubts the defender's commitment, capability, or credibility to punish the aggressor. However, deterrence theory recognizes instances in which the defender clearly signals its commitment to credibly defend its interests, but the challenger then calculates that the benefit or prize exceeds the punishment. In such a case, it is still rational for the challenger to choose to attack. In 1914 Austria-Hungary probably knew that an attack on Serbia would mean war with Russia, but it declared war on Serbia anyway because it believed it would win. If the government in Vienna had known that its empire would be destroyed as a result, it would not have attacked. Deterrence always involves risk and uncertainty. Like Clint Eastwood in the film *Dirty Harry*, defenders point their weapons and ask, "Do you feel lucky?" If the aggressor feels lucky despite the defender's commitment, capability, and credibility, deterrence will fail.

CRITICISMS OF DETERRENCE

The risks and uncertainties inherent in deterrence have prompted a number of scholars and policy-makers to challenge the assumptions of deterrence theory and question its usefulness as a strategy for national security. Similarly, the history of the Cold War indicates to some that deterrence was of limited

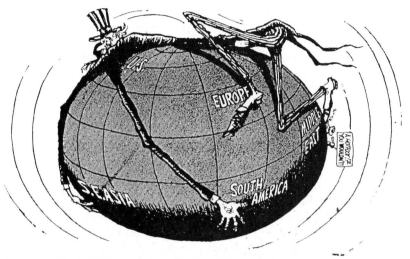

At the height of the Cold War, many saw the United States as world policeman. Uncle Sam was stretched out on nearly all continents and often vulnerable to local animosity.

Source: Copyright Los Angeles Times Syndicate.

utility. Even when the United States held a nuclear monopoly, it could not prevent the USSR from taking control of Eastern Europe, nor could it deter nonnuclear powers such as Vietnam or China from taking undesirable actions. For these reasons, a number of criticisms have been leveled at both the theory and practice of deterrence, such as its inability to clearly distinguish successes from failures, its neglect of the possibility of misperception, and its overemphasis on rational decision making. Let's look at each of these criticisms individually.

Assessing Results of Deterrence

One bone of contention between proponents and opponents of deterrence is how to determine whether it has succeeded or failed. Proponents often point to the absence of war as proof of deterrence success, but the absence could be attributable to other factors. Does the fact that the Soviet Union never attacked Western Europe or the United States during the Cold War demonstrate the effectiveness of a deterrence strategy? Not necessarily. It may be that despite all of NATO's military hardware, the Soviets never intended to attack Western Europe or the United States in the first place. Instead, all they might have wanted was a secure buffer zone in Eastern Europe. It is difficult to determine whether deterrence worked without knowing the objectives of potential aggressor states. Until researchers have access to Soviet records, Moscow's true intentions will not be known.

To determine a deterrence success, it is necessary to demonstrate that (1) the challenger intended to commit the action and (2) the challenger backed down because of the defender's threat of punishment. The difficulty of proving the second point can be illustrated by an analogy. Return to the example of the marshal trying to deter crime in his western town. If his jailhouse is empty, it indicates one of two things: Either the marshal is doing a good job and people are obeying the laws, or the marshal is doing a lousy job and no one has been caught. The point is that the challenger might back down for reasons that have nothing to do with the actions of the defender.

Misperception of Deterrence

Opponents in international conflicts rarely understand one another perfectly. (If they did, they might not be in conflict in the first place.) Thus, a second criticism of deterrence is that even if the defender does everything right, the message the defender is trying to send may be misinterpreted by the challenger. To convince a challenger that you have the commitment, capability, and credibility to carry out a threat, you must at each stage send signals to the challenger, but these signals can be misinterpreted.

First, it is particularly easy to misperceive the resolve of the defender if the challenger is strongly intent on taking a particular course of action. For example, prior to Iraq's invasion of Kuwait, the United Arab Emirates (UAE) and the United States held an air-refueling exercise to indicate American support for the security of the Gulf sheikdoms (of which Kuwait is one). However, because Saddam Hussein was bent on invading Kuwait, he may have interpreted the exercise as a signal of limited American interest in that it included only one tanker aircraft.

Similarly, a challenger might underestimate the defender's intentions and believe the defender is bluffing when it actually intends to fulfill its threat. During the Korean War, the United States misperceived China's signals prior to the UN troop advance toward the Chinese-North Korean border. As UN troops pushed the North Korean army back and began to approach China, Chinese officials repeatedly issued warnings that Beijing would enter the conflict if the UN continued north. Discounting the likelihood of Chinese intervention, MacArthur ordered the advance to continue. China then entered the conflict and sent UN troops into full retreat. Thus, American failure to give full consideration to the negative Chinese signals led to a major setback.

Third, aggressors can underestimate their adversaries' military capabilities and therefore expect an easier fight than actually occurs. This happened at least twice during World War II. When the USSR attacked Finland in 1939, Moscow expected that its 1 million soldiers would easily defeat the 200,000 Finnish troops but was stunned when Finnish forces dealt several heavy blows and held out for almost four months before being forced to meet Soviet demands. Similarly, in 1941, Italy expected a rapid victory in its attack on Greece, but instead underestimated the capabilities of Greek forces, which were able to drive the Italians back into Albania until German forces joined the offensive.

Deterrence thus depends on clarity of communication and accuracy of perception, either or both of which are often absent in the confusion and uncertainty

A typical conventional war involves calculated tactics to overcome enemy strength. Here U.S. infantry-men dash across a Korean field under enemy fire as they attempt to cut off retreating Chinese Communist forces in 1951.

Source: © UPI/Bettmann.

of crisis situations. It is worth noting, however, that misperception does not always lead to fighting, and in fact it is possible for a challenger to misinterpret the defender's resolve or capability and still avoid war.[15] When the Berlin Wall was erected in 1961, for example, the Western Allies never considered knocking down the wall by force, believing that Allied-Soviet fighting would result. In reality, Soviet and East German troops were under orders to simply retreat and set up a new barricade some distance behind if Allied troops attempted to break down the first barrier.[16] In this case the West overestimated Soviet willingness to fight, which served to preserve stability. To put it in other terms, Western misperception facilitated Soviet deterrence.

Rationality and Deterrence

A third criticism of deterrence questions the assumed rationality of leaders and their ability to make all the necessary calculations. According to deterrence advocates, rationality requires the ability of a decision maker to make comparisons among the possible options and rank them. Successful deterrence also requires that each party have sufficient, accurate, and up-to-date information about the situation at hand. Thus, to take the Cuban missile crisis as an example, President

Kennedy and his advisors needed to compare and contrast their alternatives and be able to put them into order of preference. They, and their Soviet adversaries, also needed reliable information on each other's moves as each stage of the crisis unfolded.

Critics of deterrence argue that policy-makers are not the perfectly rational beings that deterrence theory makes them out to be. The problem is that humans have limited capacity to obtain, receive, process, and assimilate information about a situation and to evaluate all the policy options in the most thorough and accurate way. In short, critics question the ability of humans to make all the necessary cost-benefit analyses and calculations that deterrence requires.

The psychological factors that might adversely affect rational decision making are numerous. Decision makers' biases and beliefs, for example, can often lead to perceptual errors. More specifically, an individual's preconceptions can limit his or her examination of the entire range of policy options. Playing "Monday morning quarterback," many scholars and policy-makers have wondered how Israel's intelligence agency failed to anticipate Egypt's intention to attack in 1973. Many decision makers believed that Israel's preemptive strike against Egypt that began the 1967 war was so devastating that the Egyptians would not dare to attack since they would suffer certain defeat. As a result, when the Egyptians once again mobilized their troops along the Suez Canal in 1973, Israel was reluctant to strike first, and start a war unnecessarily, even though this time Cairo did intend to attack. Egypt deliberately deceived Israel about its intentions, seeking (successfully) to gain the advantage of surprise. In this case, Israeli preconceptions (and overconfidence) prevented the most thorough examination available of all policy options. The possibility that Egypt did intend to attack was not given adequate attention.

To Deter or Not to Deter?

There is no final verdict on the controversies surrounding deterrence. The debate on whether deterrence was responsible for the "long peace" of the Cold War will probably last far into the future. Just as deterrence itself depended on the unknowable (the consequences of attack and retaliation) to prevent the unthinkable (a nuclear war that would have destroyed civilization), the precise reasons why the United States and USSR never went to war between 1945 and 1991 may never be known for certain. Proponents of deterrence will contend that the strategy was successful despite all of its flaws and contradictions (that is, nations which upheld peace, prosperity, and human rights as their highest goals could guarantee their security only by threatening their adversaries with the destruction of millions of people). Deterrence detractors will argue that the strategy was similar to an "elephant repellent" that a con artist might sell to a Midwestern farmer; if the farmer later complains that he never saw any elephants that needed repelling, the con man replies, "Then it must be working." Regardless of the outcome of the deterrence debate, nuclear war did not break out during the Cold War; and we can only hope that whatever prevented nuclear destruction in the past will continue to operate in the future.

MILITARY TECHNOLOGY AND THE SECURITY DILEMMA

Most textbooks on international relations, if they cover any military history at all, confine their discussion of the subject to the Cold War security system and often just to the development of the nuclear balance between the North Atlantic Treaty Organization (NATO) and the now-defunct Warsaw Treaty Organization (WTO, or Warsaw Pact). The New Era forces us to take a novel and broader look at military developments. The euphoria of the Cold War's demise has been replaced by the sobering realization that war has not become obsolete but instead remains an everyday fact of life for millions of people. Because wars are fought with the weapons of the time, the history of international security has been inextricably linked to the history of military technology. Changing military technology has made territorial acquisition and war more likely at certain points in time and less likely at others. This section will examine how the introduction of new military technologies (such as gunpowder and the machine gun) affected the intensity of the security dilemma. It will be shown that when weapons that enable a state to go on the offensive become predominant, war is more likely, and thus the security dilemma becomes more acute. Conversely, when defensive weapons come to dominate a specific era, war is less likely, and the nature of the security dilemma changes. Hence, the main point is that the intensity of the security dilemma has historically been affected by technological developments. Although it will not be possible here to examine the developments of military history in much detail, some general examples may illustrate the point.[17]

The Offense/Defense Balance

The history of military technology can be interpreted as a struggle between offense and defense referred to as the offense/defense balance. The argument is that certain periods in history can be characterized by a technological dominance of either the offense or the defense. Whenever the offense is dominant, wars are more likely to occur and can be expected to be shorter in duration and less costly. When the defense is dominant, wars are less likely to occur, but if they do break out, they can be expected to last longer and to be more destructive. At the same time, territorial aggrandizement is unlikely to occur, although internal security challenges may arise.[18]

In the heyday of medieval feudalism, for instance, defensive technology reigned. Strongly fortified castles were extremely difficult to capture with existing offensive technology (swords, bows, and catapults) even if the attacker could afford to lay siege to the castle for months or years. This allowed petty overlords to maintain their domains for years without being absorbed by larger states. By the mid-fifteenth century, however, the introduction of gunpowder and cannons shifted the offense/defense balance back toward the offense. Castles and fortified towns could be captured more easily, which led to more frequent and shorter wars that allowed for the forceful absorption of local fiefdoms

THE FATHER OF THE ATOMIC BOMB

The Manhattan Project—the huge research and development effort that the United States carried out in 1941–1945 to create the atomic bomb—was not only a major military, industrial, and engineering enterprise but was a cutting-edge experiment in nuclear physics as well. Accordingly, many of the leading physicists in the United States participated in the project for scientific reasons as well as patriotic ones. The eminent researchers who were involved included Ernest Lawrence, Edward Teller, Leo Szilard, Hans Bethe, and Enrico Fermi (all except Lawrence had fled to America to escape Nazi persecution). Even the pacifist Albert Einstein had a hand in the bomb's development when he was persuaded by Szilard to sign a letter to President Roosevelt in 1939 saying that nuclear fission would produce a bomb of tremendous explosive power. (Einstein later confided, "I made one great mistake in my life, when I signed the letter to President Roosevelt.")

The scientist who was in charge of the actual design and construction of the first atomic bomb was J. Robert Oppenheimer (1904–1967). Oppenheimer earned accolades through his research in England, the Netherlands, Germany, and Switzerland before holding academic posts at the California Institute of Technology and the University of California at Berkeley. In 1942 he was asked by the Manhattan Project's director, General Leslie Groves, to set up a laboratory for making the bomb. Oppenheimer chose a site that he had stumbled upon while vacationing in the mountains of New Mexico. Thus, the Los Alamos Ranch School was taken over by the U.S.

into new and larger kingdoms and, eventually, nation-states. In this case, the offense/defense balance played an important role not only in the dynamics of military conflict, but in the size and character of geopolitical units as well.

A similar technological shift also occurred in the late nineteenth century with the introduction of the breech-loading rifle and the machine gun. Prior to these developments, it was possible (albeit at an often staggering cost in human lives) to break through defensive lines with a well-organized large-scale offensive, as had been demonstrated many times during the wars of the eighteenth century and the Napoleonic Wars. However, with these new defensive weapons, frontal assaults became tantamount to mass suicide. This became painfully obvious during the American Civil War, but this lesson was ignored by the European powers until the massive carnage of the First World War drove the point home. By World War II, however, defensive dominance was again overturned by the introduction of the tank and aircraft onto the battlefield. These new weapons allowed aggressors once more to quickly break through defensive lines and thus conduct rapid, short wars, most dramatically demonstrated by the German **blitzkrieg** attacks on Poland and France.

Although certain technological developments seem to make territorial conquest and empire-building easier or harder, it is not always simple to classify a given historical period as offense- or defense-dominant—particularly during government and converted to a national laboratory.

Under Oppenheimer's direction, the top-secret laboratory complex became a scientific city of over 5000, where many of the nation's brightest minds labored to create the most formidable and powerful weapon the world had ever known. Throughout the project, Oppenheimer was well aware of the destructive potential (and moral implications) of the forces his team was working to unleash. When he witnessed the first test of the atomic bomb in the desert near Alamogordo, New Mexico, on July 16, 1945, he quoted the words of the Hindu god Shiva: "I am become death, the shatterer of worlds."

After the war, Oppenheimer helped draft the proposals for the international control of atomic energy, which were rejected by the USSR (discussed later in this chapter). Subsequently, as chairman of the Scientific Advisory Committee of the U.S. Atomic Energy Commission, Oppenheimer recommended against the development of the hydrogen bomb. When the United States went ahead with the project, Oppenheimer was accused of being a Communist traitor during the "witch hunts" of the McCarthy era (see Chapter Four). He was then investigated, denied access to classified information, and removed from his advisory post. He was later cleared and remained a physics professor for the rest of his life. The fact that the scientist who directed the development of the first atomic weapon became a victim of the atomic spy hysteria, prevalent in the United States in the early 1950s, was one of the many ironies of the Cold War.

the period itself. Although the lessons to be drawn from the defensive wars of the end of the nineteenth century may seem fairly straightforward from hindsight, they were generally unappreciated at the time. In fact, most countries flatly ignored them and continued to believe in the possibility of offensive breakthroughs. It has been argued that this erroneous perception of the offense/defense balance (the "cult of the offensive") was one of the important factors leading to World War I, as Chapter Three points out. While the Persian Gulf War of 1991 may hold some lessons for tacticians and strategists, it may well take a new war to show how technologies such as navigation and reconnaissance satellites, "stealth" aircraft, and precision-guided "smart bombs" will affect the contemporary balance between offense and defense.

The Nuclear Revolution

The most dramatic example of the impact of military technology on international relations was the nuclear revolution in military affairs after the Second World War. For many analysts, nuclear missiles represented the ultimate weapon, so powerful that it would make war unthinkable. Gradually this idea spread throughout the international community, and most existing military doctrines changed to place the nuclear weapon at the center of the military universe.

Now that the Cold War is over, some historians and political scientists are claiming that nuclear weapons were responsible for the absence of a major war between the two key geopolitical alliances during this period.[19] The domination of nuclear weapons in military strategy changed the focus of the security dilemma; first, the incredible destruction wrought by the use of these weapons raised the stakes of an arms race. Second, the startling offensive potential of these weapons made a long, drawn-out nuclear war (characteristic of eras in which defense dominates) practically impossible. In particular, though, the emphasis on nuclear weapons produced some peculiar concepts of strategy that deserve more detailed explanation.

A state is said to possess first-strike capability if it can launch an attack that destroys the defender's retaliatory capability and prevents the defender from inflicting major damage in return.[20] A situation in which any nation has a first-strike capability would be highly unstable, because that side might feel able to do whatever it wanted, believing that it was invulnerable to nuclear retaliation. The other side would then have an incentive to preempt such a situation by attacking with a **preemptive strike** in the hope of knocking out the adversary's nuclear arsenal while it still could. The most likely outcome of such a situation is thus a short and catastrophic war.

Nuclear weapons that are vulnerable to attack encourage a first-strike mentality, because in a crisis a nation might feel the need to "use them or lose them." For example, during the Cold War, if the United States had placed all of its nuclear missiles on trucks in open view in the middle of cornfields in Iowa, and the Soviets had done the same in the middle of the tundra in Siberia, each side might have been tempted during a confrontation such as the Cuban missile crisis to try to attack the other in the hope of destroying its rival's arsenal. U.S. strategists became concerned with this possibility in the late 1950s. At that time, even though the American strategic nuclear arsenal was much larger than that of the USSR, slow, highly visible bombers were the only means available to deliver **atomic weapons** to their targets. Washington recognized the incentive for the Soviets to launch an all-out surprise attack on the vulnerable American bombers.

The solution to this dilemma was to develop and deploy a nuclear force that could be nearly impossible to destroy. Known as a second-strike capability, the purpose of such a force is to ensure that enough weapons would survive an initial attack to launch a retaliatory second strike that would inflict unacceptable damage on the enemy. For stable mutual deterrence, each side must have the ability to inflict massive damage on the other even if the other side strikes first. This situation would nullify any advantage or incentive for launching a first strike, since destroying a part of an adversary's strategic forces would still invite devastating retaliation.

The acquisition of an assured second-strike capability by both the United States and the USSR meant that either would be able to retaliate massively if the other attacked. The existence of such a condition was termed mutual assured destruction, referred to by its acronym, MAD. Mutual assured destruction, the highest stage of the nuclear balance (or balance of terror, as Winston Churchill called it) is a stable situation because there is no incentive or temptation for either side to strike first or even launch a surprise attack. To do so would mean that both the defender and the initiator would suffer devastating casualties. In the 1960s Secretary of Defense Robert McNamara realized that with 400 warheads the United States had the ability to destroy 30 percent of the Soviet population and 76 percent of its industrial capacity. By that time, the United States already had over 10,000 warheads.[21] At the end of the Cold War, both sides had considerably larger and more powerful nuclear arsenals.

A second-strike capability was achieved in the United States through the development of the **nuclear triad**. This consists of the ability to "deliver" (a euphemism for "attack with") nuclear weapons by bombers, intercontinental ballistic missiles (ICBMs), and submarine-launched ballistic missiles (SLBMs). In this way, even if the Soviets launched an all-out attack on the United States, and even if this attack destroyed the entire land-based missile force, the other two "legs" of the triad would survive and be able to deliver a devastating blow.

Each leg of the nuclear triad has certain advantages and drawbacks. Submarines are difficult to destroy and the least vulnerable of the three, so they have the best second-strike capability. Even with present-day technology, it is hard to detect their exact location far beneath the surface of the world's oceans. Their drawbacks include their lack of pinpoint accuracy because they are constantly in motion, although improvements have been made in the last twenty years.

Bombers can carry heavy payloads and can be recalled until a couple of hours before they reach their destination, so they can be launched during a crisis without irrevocably committing a nation to carrying out a nuclear attack. However, they have limited ability to penetrate air defenses. **ICBMs** (intercontinental ballistic missiles), or land-based missiles, are the most accurate of the three in hitting their targets, but they remain vulnerable to attack because their locations can be pinpointed fairly accurately. Although missiles are generally easy to launch, as unmanned crafts they are impossible to recall; once they are launched, the nation is committed to a nuclear attack.

The two superpowers emphasized different legs of the strategic triad for geopolitical and technological reasons. The United States always placed more emphasis on its sea- and air-based forces, whereas the Soviet Union favored its land-based leg. However, in both cases the triad served the same purpose—by spreading its ability to retaliate over land, sea, and air, each side could guarantee that enough of its nuclear arsenal would survive a first strike to be able to retaliate with massive and deadly force.

The Importance of Being Invulnerable

Although it may seem illogical, there is a high level of interdependence among adversaries under nuclear deterrence. In fact, changes in one side will have an impact on how secure both actors feel. Just as in the "cult of the offensive," vulnerability leads to instability. A state's nuclear arsenal is vulnerable if it can be destroyed in a first strike by another nuclear power. **Invulnerability** is the ability of a significant portion of a state's arsenal to survive an attack, thus guaranteeing

NUKESPEAK

Can't tell the difference between an ICBM and an SLBM? Don't know your GLCMs from your SLCMs? Need to impress your classmates and relatives? Here's a quick reference guide to nuclear weapons terminology used in this and subsequent chapters.*

ABM: Antiballistic missile; a missile designed to destroy incoming missiles or their warheads before they hit the designated targets.

ALCM: Air-launched cruise missile; a cruise missile launched from an airplane. *See* Cruise missile.

Atomic weapon: Explosive device that derives its power from nuclear fission, or the "splitting" of atoms (uranium or plutonium).

Ballistic Missile: A missile that "coasts" to its target on a free-falling trajectory following a period of powered flight.

Biological weapon: Germ or bacteria based weapon, also known as a "living weapon," which spreads disease, infection, or toxins.

Chemical weapon: A weapon that uses a chemical agent to kill or disable military personnel and civilians. These weapons consist of poisoned gas, mists, and powders, and can only be effective when they come into contact with people.

Conventional weapon: Nonnuclear weapon such as a tank, artillery piece, or tactical aircraft (troops that operate these weapons are referred to as conventional forces).

Cruise missile: A missile that resembles a pilotless aircraft and flies on a horizontal trajectory. This missile operates completely within the earth's atmosphere and may be launched from the air, the ground, or from the sea, and can carry conventional, chemical, or nuclear warheads.

First strike: Ability to destroy or decisively weaken an opponent's strategic weapons, or prevent retaliation with an initial attack.

GLCM: Ground-launched cruise missile; a cruise missile launched from land.

Hydrogen bomb: A thermonuclear weapon that uses a hydrogen or fusion reaction in which atoms are fused together to produce an energy release. These weapons require a fission reaction that uses uranium or plutonium in order to get the temperature high enough to have the hydrogen atoms react.

a second strike. In one of the many paradoxes of the nuclear age, invulnerability does not include the protection of population centers. In fact, according to the logic of MAD, the cities of both sides should be vulnerable to attack, so that each party in effect takes the other side's population hostage.

What is important is that strategic weapons be invulnerable; both sides must have a secure second strike for MAD to be stable. Mutual invulnerability of forces is stabilizing because neither side can hope to destroy the other's warheads with a first strike. However, vulnerability of the nuclear weapons of both sides, or even of just one side, is dangerously destabilizing. Under this condition, the

ICBM: Intercontinental ballistic missile; a land-based missile able to deliver a nuclear payload to a target over 3400 miles away (in practical terms, capable of going directly from the United States to Russia, or vice versa).

IRBM: Intermediate-range ballistic missile; a land-based missile with a range of 1700 to 3400 miles.

MAD: Mutual assured destruction; a condition that exists when both sides are able to survive a first strike with sufficient forces to retaliate in a second strike and inflict unacceptable damage on their opponent. Thus both would be destroyed regardless of who struck first, and therefore neither has an incentive to initiate a nuclear war.

MIRV: Multiple independently-targeted reentry vehicle; a single ballistic missile with several warheads that can each hit a separate target.

Second strike: Ability to retaliate even after a nuclear attack, and thus punish the initiator of a nuclear war.

SLBM: Submarine-launched ballistic missile; a long-range ballistic missile carried in and launched from a submarine. Examples include the U.S. Poseidon and Trident missiles.

SLCM: Sea-launched cruise missile; a cruise missile launched from a ship or submarine.

Strategic weapon: Weapon that strikes directly at a nation's home territory and the industry, resources, population, or military forces located there.

Tactical weapon: Weapon designed for use on the battlefield, often in support of ground troops.

Thermonuclear weapon: Explosive device that derives its power from nuclear fusion, or the coming together of atoms (usually hydrogen or helium; this is the same process that gives the sun its energy).

Warhead: The bomb that a missile delivers to its target.

*For the technical definitions of this subject, see Norman Polamr, *Strategic Weapons: An Introduction* (New York: National Strategy Information Center, 1982); Lawrence Freedman, *The Evolution of Nuclear Strategy* (London: St. Martin's Press, 1983); Sheila Tobias, et al., *The People's Guide to National Defense* (New York: Morrow, 1982), or Sheikh R. Ali, *The Peace and Nuclear War Dictionary* (Santa Barbara, CA: ABC-CLI0, 1989).

invulnerable side will be able to attack with little fear of the defender's retaliatory capability. The vulnerable side will then feel highly insecure and might seek to take advantage of any opportunity to destroy the adversary's weapons or, if desperate enough, target its adversary's population. Likewise, if both sides feel vulnerable, both have an incentive to strike first in the hope of eliminating the other's weapons. The consequences of vulnerability mean that MAD, the ability of both sides to survive a first strike and retaliate with a massive second strike, is the most stable condition for both actors, and the key to strategic stability in the nuclear age.

Defensive Weapons Systems

As stressed earlier, a key aspect of deterrence is credibility, and anything that weakens credibility is destabilizing. For this reason, defensive weapons systems that shoot down incoming missiles are potentially destabilizing because they reduce the effectiveness of mutual deterrence and increase a state's vulnerability. For example, an attacker might think it could deliver a first strike and then it could protect its population by shooting down the defender's second-strike retaliatory missiles—thereby destroying mutual deterrence and increasing the defense's vulnerability. Two prominent examples are **antiballistic missiles (ABM)** systems proposed in the 1960s and the **Strategic Defense Initiative** (SDI, or "Star Wars") of the 1980s.

Both systems were designed to destroy incoming missiles. Not all ABM systems, however, are destabilizing. For instance, ABMs can be placed around missile sites, which would decrease their vulnerability to an attempted first strike. SDI, however, was first intended to create a "peace shield" or "nuclear Astrodome" over the United States. The danger of these systems is that, if they are fully effective (that is, if nothing can get through them), a country could initiate a first strike with little fear of retaliation if it was the only nuclear adversary that possessed the system. In this sense, they are destabilizing because they reduce the credibility of a retaliatory second strike. Some critics of SDI, in fact, argued that deploying the system would encourage the Soviet Union to attack before it became completely operational, since once it was operational, the USSR would be unable to retaliate. More recently, some decision makers have called for the renewed use of a limited SDI-type system, known as Global Protection Against Limited Strikes (GPALS), to defend against missiles launched by terrorists or irrational or suicidal leaders who feel they have nothing to lose (see Chapter Nine). Such a defense system could not completely guard against nuclear terrorism, however, as there are other ways to deliver a nuclear bomb to a target. Terrorists could detonate one in a ship docked in a harbor, for example, or assemble one in the target city if they are able to smuggle in the required nuclear material.

Because of the security interdependence of nuclear states, it is to the advantage of all states to reduce or eliminate any systems that weaken a second-strike capability. So, even the offensive-minded technology of **multiple independently targeted reentry vehicles (MIRVs),** which have several warheads per missile, and the increased accuracy of ICBMs threaten to undermine an opponent's second-strike capability because of their potential ability to destroy all of an opponent's arsenal on the first strike. In this case, it is offensive, rather than defensive, weapons that weaken an opponent's second-strike capability, thereby destabilizing the balance. (For this reason, one of the main goals of the START I negotiations begun in 1985 was a ban on land-based MIRVed ICBMs.)

Nuclear Weapons and Conventional Defense

Nuclear weapons are not useful for meeting all the military challenges a state or alliance faces. Responding to a conventional attack with strategic nuclear weapons would be like using a machine gun to kill houseflies—it might take care of the problem, but it creates a bigger one. For this reason, the superpowers and their allies all maintained substantial conventional forces, and developed strategies for using them, throughout the Cold War.

When the euphoria of the end of the Second World War was replaced with superpower rivalry, NATO was organized and adopted a defense plan that called for a large conventional force in Europe, backed up by U.S. strategic nuclear bombers, to counterbalance Soviet geopolitical and military advantages in Communist-controlled Central and Eastern Europe. It quickly became clear that the goal of conventional parity with the Soviets and their European satellites was unrealistic (primarily for financial reasons), and so in 1957 NATO adopted a new strategy known as **massive retaliation.** This strategy acknowledged NATO's conventional inferiority and sought to offset it by relying on massive nuclear escalation as the principal deterrent to possible Soviet conventional aggression. A heated debate took place on both sides of the Atlantic as to whether this strategy was too inflexible to be credible. Why would the United States launch a nuclear strike and risk Soviet nuclear retaliation if the Soviets were to take over Berlin by conventional means? Western strategists thus began to worry that the Soviet bloc would make gains in Europe by using "salami-tactics," cutting off small "slices" of territory in order to circumvent nuclear retaliation.

After a long debate within NATO, the strategy of massive retaliation was replaced in 1967 with the strategy of **flexible response.** According to this revised strategy, NATO needed enough conventional capabilities to counter Soviet

NATO tanks take part in 1986 maneuvers involving U.S., French, and German troops in Bavaria. During the Cold War, exercises on both sides were integral to the East-West military confrontation in Europe.
Source: © Regis Bossu/Sygma.

offensives at each step of the escalation ladder: at the conventional level, the battlefield nuclear level, and the strategic nuclear level. A conventional attack would be met by NATO conventional forces along the former border between East and West Germany. Should that fail, NATO would have various nuclear options at its disposal to respond with "controlled escalation." If all of these escalatory measures were still unable to stop a Soviet offensive, the last option remained a massive strategic nuclear strike against the Soviet homeland. Flexible response was thus intended to meet a variety of threats with a variety of responses, but its capability (and thus credibility) was more expensive to maintain than massive retaliation, since it required larger and more varied forces. Throughout the 1970s and 1980s, the range of options for conventional defense was continuously expanded by new technological and doctrinal innovations (that is, new weapons and new ways of using them in combat). Overall, from the mid-1960s onward, the military balance between NATO and the Warsaw Pact witnessed an almost continuous deemphasizing of nuclear weapons toward a more credible conventional posture.

Soviet military thinking underwent similar changes over the years. Although the Red Army demobilized after the Second World War, it increased its manpower to 5.7 million during the Korean War. The Soviets detonated their first atomic device in 1949, but the real impact of this new weapon was not incorporated into Soviet military strategy until after Stalin's death. Under Khrushchev, Soviet conventional capabilities were cut back significantly, and Soviet military doctrine was reduced to a "single-variant war" scenario: Any military conflict between the superpowers (unleashed only by the "imperialist" Western countries, of course) would invariably lead to a massive nuclear exchange. The Soviet strategy was thus very similar to the U.S. doctrine of massive retaliation.

The evolution of Soviet military thinking after the early 1960s represented a gradual transition from this single nuclear option to a more balanced nuclear and conventional mix in the 1960s and 1970s, and finally to a pronounced preference for conventional war in the mid-1970s to early 1980s. This new doctrine, along with its corresponding buildup of Soviet conventional forces, alarmed NATO, which responded with force enhancements of its own. The later stages of the Cold War saw the security dilemma in action, as the measures taken by each side to make itself more secure made the other side feel more threatened, resulting in a conventional arms race in Europe.

The trend away from exclusive reliance on nuclear weapons continued after the revolutions in Eastern Europe and the subsequent disintegration of the Warsaw Treaty Organization and the Soviet Union itself. With the reemergence of fully independent countries in Central and Eastern Europe, a de facto buffer zone has been created between two major historical antagonists in the region: Germany and Western Europe on the one hand and Russia on the other. Although these developments have created many new security problems in Europe (as exemplified by the conflict in the former Yugoslavia), these new post–Cold War issues seem to be less threatening than the nuclear and conventional confrontation between the Warsaw Pact and NATO during the Cold War. In sum, the geopolitical configuration of the New Era seems less likely to provoke a nuclear war, although, as some theorists suggest, the lessening of the danger of nuclear war may make limited conventional wars more likely.[22]

REMAINING NUCLEAR CHALLENGES

A strategy of mutual assured destruction (MAD) does not sound very reassuring, and, as one might expect, neither superpower felt very comfortable relying solely on MAD for its security. Before the end of the Cold War, therefore, both the United States and the USSR started to move away from national security strategies based on MAD and nuclear weapons. The end of the Cold War accelerated this process. Recent arms-control developments reflect this trend: Whole classes of nuclear weapons are being abolished (various categories of tactical nuclear weapons, intermediate-range nuclear forces, and MIRVs) and the total number of strategic nuclear weapons is being drastically cut. American and Russian military strategies also reflect the downplaying of nuclear weapons.

All of this is not to say that there are no more nuclear threats. It is important to remember that the nuclear arms race did not start with the Cold War, but with the discovery of nuclear technology. In a sense, there was already a "nuclear arms race" between Germany and the United States in the early 1940s, as both countries strove to be the first to develop the atomic bomb. Since the world cannot disinvent nuclear weapons, and these weapons remain a cost-effective solution to many countries' security predicaments, it would be wrong to think that nuclear weapons will pose no dangers in the New Era. More specifically, two important sets of "nuclear" issues remain: problems of nuclear proliferation and problems of reliable command and control for the existing nuclear stockpiles.

Nuclear Proliferation

There are currently eight acknowledged nuclear powers: the United States, the United Kingdom, France, China, and the four former Soviet republics of Russia, Belarus, Ukraine, and Kazakhstan. The last three have all made commitments to transfer their nuclear weapons to Russia and to sign the nonproliferation treaty as nuclear-free states by 1999, which would bring the number of nuclear weapon states back down to five. Three other countries are strongly believed to have some nuclear capability, either possessing operational weapons or being capable of assembling them in a short period of time: Israel, India, and Pakistan. (In 1993 South Africa announced that it had possessed a small number of nuclear weapons since the mid-1970s, but that it had since destroyed all of them.) On top of that, there are a number of countries that are known to have programs to develop nuclear weapons, including North Korea (which may be very close to acquiring operational weapons), Iraq, Iran, Libya, and, formerly,

Brazil and Argentina. As the security dilemma would lead us to expect, many more countries would like to acquire nuclear weapons, especially if some of their neighbors were to achieve nuclear capabilities. The pattern has existed in the past: Once China developed nuclear weapons, for example, India pursued a nuclear capability, which then prompted Pakistan to follow suit. Table 11.1 displays both declared and undeclared nuclear power capabilities.

Two schools of thought exist on the issue of **nuclear proliferation.** On the one hand, we have already noted that numerous scholars and policy-makers attribute the relative stability of the Cold War era (that is, the absence of major war between the great powers) to the presence of nuclear weapons—in particular, a secure second-strike capability for both sides. Thus, nuclear proliferation can be seen as a strategy for peace, or nuclear deterrence.

Proponents of nuclear deterrence believe it to be more stabilizing than conventional deterrence because a challenger is less likely to miscalculate an adversary's strength or the cost of punishment. With conventional weapons, a decision maker might expect war at an "affordable" price, which means that countries are more likely to run the risks of war when defeat is expected to bring only limited damage. As we have seen, prior to World War I, it was widely believed that war would be quick and decisive, based on Prussia's rapid defeats of Austria in 1866 and France in 1870–1871 in a matter of weeks. The belief in the possibility of a quick and cheap triumph encouraged the outbreak of the First World War, which turned out to be the most destructive war in history to that point.

Hostilities become less likely as the cost of war increases relative to the possible gains. With nuclear weapons, states are less likely to expect victory at an affordable price. The consequence is that nuclear weapons lead countries to act more carefully. During the Cuban missile crisis, for instance, both the United States and the USSR behaved very cautiously, fearing that the conflict could escalate into a nuclear war. In particular, the option of a surgical air strike against the Soviet missile sites on Cuba was eliminated because there were no guarantees that all the Soviet missiles would be destroyed and that the USSR would not respond aggressively to the strike. Furthermore, the downing of an American U-2 spy plane over Cuba by surface-to-air missiles, an incident that could easily have led to war before the nuclear era, did not result in escalation of the crisis.

This leads one to ask, "If nuclear weapons induced caution in the U.S.–Soviet rivalry, wouldn't they work on a worldwide scale?" If nuclear weapons enhance peace, shouldn't their proliferation be encouraged? Perhaps the possession of nuclear weapons by Third World states would make war less likely. But is nuclear proliferation the only way to have "peace in our time"?

Opponents of proliferation—the second school of thought—ask us to imagine what individuals such as Kim Jong Il, Mu'ammar Gadhafi, or Saddam Hussein might do with a few nuclear bombs. It is often argued that national leaders who do not attain power as a result of a democratic process can be irrational and juvenile, or worse yet, irresponsible, radical, fanatical, or reckless. Since they have the least to lose, they may be the most willing to risk using nuclear weapons. Finally, any nuclear country—developing or otherwise—that

Table 11.1   Mass Destruction Weaponry

Nation	Longest Range for Ballistic Missiles (in miles)	Total Number of Warheads	Chemical or Biological Weapons
Declared Nuclear Weapons States			
Britain[*][†]	2,900	200	No
China[*]	8,100	435	Yes
France[*]	3,750	480	Yes
Russia[*][†]	8,100	6,737	Yes
Belarus[#]	6,500	81	No
Kazakhstan[#]	6,800	1,410	No
Ukraine[#]	6,200	1,240	No
United States[*][†]	9,250	9,000	Yes
Undeclared Nuclear Weapons States			
India	1,550	50	Yes
Israel[*]	930	200	Probably
Pakistan	190	15	Probably
Working on Obtaining Nuclear Weapons			
Algeria	40	None yet	No
Iran	300	None yet	Yes
Iraq	190	None yet	Yes
Libya	190	None yet	Yes
North Korea	300	Enough plutonium for 1 to 2 bombs	Yes
Syria	300	None yet	Yes
Ceased Developing Nuclear Weapons			
Argentina	60	Renounced nuclear weapons	No
Brazil	190	Renounced nuclear weapons	No
South Africa	930	Renounced nuclear weapons and has destroyed its stockpile	Yes
South Korea	160	Renounced nuclear weapons	No
Taiwan	60	Renounced nuclear weapons	Yes

[*]Confirmed capability to deliver nuclear weapons by aircraft and/or missiles.

[†]Confirmed capability to deliver nuclear weapons by submarine.

[#]Committed to becoming nonnuclear states but currently possessing nuclear weapons under Russian control stationed in their territory.

Note: Figures for this table are for the early 1990s.

Sources: *Time,* June 21, 1993; *Los Angeles Times,* May 10, 1994, p. A1, A16; *Arms Control Today,* May 1993, pp. 28–29; *The Defense Monitor,* 1992. I.S.S.N. #0195-6450; *Los Angeles Times,* May 8, 1994, pp. A1, A18; *Los Angeles Times,* May 9, 1994, pp. A1, A16; *The Military Balance, 1993–1994; SIPRI Handbook 1993; Defense & Foreign Affairs Handbook, 1994.*

experiences domestic political instability also faces the constant danger that "undesirable" actors, such as renegade or terrorist groups, will get their fingers on the nuclear button.

In addition to this view of "irrational" leaders, there are other arguments against nuclear proliferation. Most developing countries lack the resources needed to establish a credible and secure second-strike capability. Developing nuclear and missile technology and keeping abreast of constant changes require a large portion of scarce resources. This would leave fewer resources to develop a nuclear triad and produce warheads in numbers sufficient to guarantee a second-strike capability. Failure to do these things would lead to dangerous instability; remember that vulnerable nuclear weapons are destabilizing because they give a challenger an incentive to strike first or launch a surprise attack in the hope of destroying all the defender's nuclear weapons. Thus, if a state cannot afford a secure second strike, acquiring a few nuclear weapons might actually increase the likelihood of a preemptive war. For these reasons, most states actively oppose the spread of nuclear weapons, although many private firms have inadvertently or deliberately exported nuclear-related technology to nations that wish to develop them.

Command and Control

As if nuclear proliferation were not enough to worry about, the reliable command and control of existing nuclear stockpiles is by no means certain. Nuclear forces require both positive control (the capability to launch weapons when ordered by national leaders) and negative control (safeguards to prevent them from being launched when leaders do not order it). The problem of reliable control is especially acute in states that experience political instability.

The nuclear stockpile of the former Soviet Union is most worrisome because of the political instability of the four states that now have the weapons. Only the president of the Russian Federation has the technical capability of both positive and negative control, whereas the presidents of the other republics have the right "to be consulted" before the Russian president makes any decision. However, this arrangement will likely be questioned by local actors in one or more of the nuclear republics. The result could be the increase of weapons throughout the region, because of both the security dilemma facing the former Soviet states and the fact that central control over the use of weapons could further weaken. Another danger is that weapons could eventually be sold to other countries or to terrorists.

ARMS CONTROL AND DISARMAMENT

Just as nations have invested their resources in building up adequate defensive capabilities against real or perceived threats, they also have tried to control the dangerous and wasteful arms race. The most obvious way to do so has been through negotiations on arms control and disarmament.

Arms Control

Arms control can be defined as "measures, directly related to military forces, adopted by governments to contain the costs and harmful consequences of the continued existence of arms (their own and others), within the overall objective of sustaining or enhancing their security."[23] In other words, the main ambition of arms control is to manage an arms race in such a way as to minimize the most dangerous consequences of the unavoidable security dilemma. Theoretically, this aim could be accomplished without any real decrease in the overall levels of armaments, and in this way arms control differs from **disarmament,** where states actually reduce their overall arms levels. Even though disarmament seems to be the more desirable strategy, certain types of injudicious disarmament would actually increase the danger of international conflict. Highly asymmetrical disarmament initiatives imposed on a weakened opponent, for instance, could increase the latter's feeling of subjective insecurity, leading to a renewed cycle of arms races. This is precisely what happened to Germany in the immediate aftermath of World War I.

To avoid such paradoxical effects of arms reductions, the primary aim of arms control is strategic stability, meaning a situation in which neither side has an incentive to launch an attack on an opponent or to increase its armaments because of the particular configuration of armed forces. This concept was the basis for the CFE (Conventional Forces in Europe) talks and the U.S.–Soviet START negotiations during the 1980s.

Early Efforts at Disarmament

At the turn of the twentieth century, there was already a widespread feeling in the international community that the existing level of armaments was excessive. Two international peace conferences were convened in The Hague in an attempt to restrict or prohibit the use of certain weapons systems in war. The outbreak of war in 1914 ended this first effort at international disarmament, but the movement was revitalized through several disarmament initiatives following four years of World War I's unprecedented carnage and brutality. The most grandiose of these efforts was the Kellogg-Briand Pact (1928), in which almost all the nations of the world agreed to renounce war as an instrument of national policy and instead settle all international disputes by peaceful means. In reality, however, various countries interpreted the obligations of the treaty differently (particularly the one that safeguarded a nation's right to self-defense). Because there were no effective means to ensure compliance, the treaty was a dead letter.

A somewhat more successful set of arms-control agreements was that of the naval treaties of the 1920s and 1930s, in which the world's most prominent seafaring nations (the United States, Britain, Japan, Italy, and France) agreed to quantitative and qualitative restrictions on certain types of warships. These agreements, too, were beset by problems. First, the signatories complied with the letter of the treaty but redirected their efforts into nonregulated areas of warship construction (especially aircraft carriers, which were not covered in the treaties).

AT A GLANCE

MAJOR NUCLEAR WEAPONS TREATIES

Limited Test Ban Treaty, 1963
Nations: United Kingdom, United States, USSR, and over 100 states (excluding China and France)

Commitments: Outlawed nuclear explosions in the air, under water, and in outer space. Underground testing is still allowed.

Nonproliferation Treaty (NPT), 1968
Nations: More than 100 states

Commitments: Prohibited "nuclear weapon states" from helping other states to acquire nuclear weapons. "Nonnuclear weapon states" were forbidden to manufacture or otherwise obtain nuclear arms and required to submit their nuclear programs to monitoring by the International Atomic Energy Agency (IAEA).

Threshold Test Ban Treaty, 1974
Nations: United States, USSR

Commitments: Confined their underground explosions within an upper limit of 150 kilotons.

Strategic Arms Limitation Treaty (SALT I), 1972
Nations: United States, USSR

Commitments: Interim Agreement put a ceiling on the number of land- and sea-based strategic nuclear delivery vehicles the two sides were allowed to have while they were negotiating a more substantive agreement to be signed at some future date. No sacrifices were required by either side because it did not prohibit qualitative improvements such as MIRV. Instead, it froze the number of offensive strategic missiles deployed or under construction for five years as of the date of the signing.

Anti-Ballistic Missile (ABM) Treaty: Restricted both parties to having not more than two ABM sites, with not more than 100 interceptor missiles each. An additional protocol in 1974 further

Second, two major powers were not sufficiently involved: Germany was left out of the negotiations, and Japan withdrew from the treaties in 1934.

The end of World War II saw renewed attempts to achieve far-reaching arms control agreements. One of the most important efforts was the **Baruch Plan,** in which the United States proposed that all atomic-energy activities fall under the control of an international atomic-development authority. The Soviet Union rejected this plan primarily because it would have made permanent the existing U.S. monopoly over nuclear weapons.

The enthusiasm for far-reaching arms control agreements waned during the Cold War, although efforts to regulate the arms race were not abandoned altogether. Negotiations continued over two principal areas: control of weapons of mass destruction (including strategic nuclear weapons, intermediate and tactical nuclear weapons, nuclear proliferation, and chemical and biological weapons), and conventional arms control.

Strategic Nuclear Weapons

The most important efforts to limit weapons of mass destruction have been made in the area of nuclear weapons. The accompanying "At a Glance" box restricted the deployment of a ballistic missile defense system to a single area designated by each country.

SALT II, 1979

Nations: United States, USSR. Never ratified by the U.S. Senate due to the Soviet invasion of Afghanistan.

Commitments: Although not ratified, both sides adhered to the broad guidelines of the treaty, which were an aggregate ceiling of 2400 launch vehicles for each superpower until the end of 1981 and 2250 launch vehicles from the end of 1981 until the treaty expired in 1985. A number of subceilings were designed to put a cap on MIRVs.

Intermediate-Range Nuclear Forces (INF) Treaty, 1987

Nations: United States, USSR

Commitments: Totally eliminated all nuclear missiles with a range of 310 through 3400 miles.

Strategic Arms Reduction Talks (START I), 1991

Nations: United States, USSR

Commitments: First arms-control treaty mandating genuine reductions in strategic weapons. Main parameters were set at 1600 launch vehicles and 6000 warheads for each side.

START II, 1993

Nations: United States, Russia

Commitments: Reduced strategic nuclear arsenals to between 3000 and 3500 warheads by the year 2003. Eliminated MIRVed ICBMs completely and, as a sub-ceiling, limited SLBM warheads to 1750.

presents the relevant treaties. The first significant achievement was the Limited (or Partial) Test Ban Treaty of 1963, which was inspired by the dangerous nuclear face-off during the Cuban missile crisis. In this treaty, the United Kingdom, the United States, and the USSR committed to refrain from nuclear testing except in underground explosion sites. Since 1963 the treaty has been signed by more than 100 states, but two nuclear powers, France and China, have refused to adhere to it. The Limited Test Ban Treaty was supplemented in 1974 by the Threshold Test Ban Treaty, which confined the superpowers' underground explosions to an upper limit of 150 kilotons. Pressures on all sides to formally conclude a Comprehensive Test Ban Treaty are increasing, especially following recent revelations about the environmental consequences of nuclear tests. Nevertheless, there remains considerable resistance in the defense communities of the nuclear states, which contend that continued testing is necessary to maintain the safety and reliability of existing weapons.

In the late 1960s the strategic nuclear arsenals of the two Cold War superpowers became symmetrical enough to allow for talks on strategic nuclear arms control. The principal negotiations of the process, the Strategic Arms Limitation Talks (SALT), took place in two slow and protracted stages. The

GAS, GERMS, AND MISSILES

Terrible as nuclear weapons are, they are neither the first nor the only weapons of mass destruction in evidence today. *Chemical weapons,* poisons designed to incapacitate or kill people after touching the skin or being inhaled, were first used as a weapon in World War I and have been employed in several wars since, such as in Yemen in the 1960s and in the Iran-Iraq war of the 1980s. In 1925 the Geneva Protocol prohibited the use but not the possession of chemical weapons, allowing many countries to build large stockpiles and continue their research and production programs. In 1980 the UN Conference on Disarmament began work on a treaty that would ban chemical weapons. In January 1993, 130 nations signed the Chemical Weapons Convention, which bans their possession, acquisition, production, stockpiling, transfer, and use. Signatory states must dispose of these weapons over the ensuing ten years.

As if chemical weapons weren't bad enough, *biological weapons* use viruses or bacteria to infect an enemy's population or territory through "germ warfare." These weapons are covered by the 1925 Geneva Protocol and the 1972 Biological Weapons Convention (BWC), which 134 states had signed by 1993. Each signatory is formally committed to not develop, produce, stockpile, acquire, or transfer biological agents. Although many experts claim that biological weapons have never been successfully used as a military weapon, many countries

first stage culminated in the signing of the Strategic Arms Limitation Treaty (SALT I) in Moscow in 1972.

SALT I consisted of the Interim Agreement and the Anti-Ballistic Missile (ABM) Treaty.[24] The Interim Agreement put a ceiling on the number of land- and sea-based strategic nuclear missiles the two sides were allowed to retain while they were negotiating a more substantive agreement, which was to be signed at a future date. This ceiling froze the number of offensive strategic missiles at their 1972 levels of 2568 for the USSR and 1764 for the United States. The disparity was justified by the exclusion of long-range bombers, of which the United States had many more.

Overall, the Interim Agreement did not require any sacrifices by either side; it simply froze the arsenals at their existing levels and left many loopholes for both superpowers to exploit. The most important of these was the failure to limit the number of warheads per launcher, which allowed for the creation of multiple-warhead missiles (MIRVs) throughout the 1970s. These loopholes aside, the Interim Agreement at least provided ways to verify arms limitations (that is, to make sure the other side didn't cheat) through the use of orbital reconnaissance, or "spy satellites." (Because neither side wanted to officially admit that such satellites existed, they were referred to in the treaty as "national technical means" of verification.)

continue to fund biological-weapons programs, including Iraq, Iran, Libya, Syria, and until its breakup, the Soviet Union.

Chemical and biological weapons, like nuclear weapons, can be delivered by ballistic missiles. Throughout the 1980s concerns rose about the proliferation of ballistic missiles in many regions of the world. In 1983 seven Western nations began negotiations to limit the export of ballistic missile technology. Although they could not agree on a treaty, they did agree on the creation of a *Missile Technology Control Regime (MTCR)* that restricted the export of ballistic missiles capable of carrying more than 500 kilograms (considered to be the minimum payload required for a nuclear warhead) over a distance of 300 kilometers or more. This agreement was subsequently strengthened by the inclusion of several key suppliers, including Russia, Israel, Argentina, Brazil, and China.

The missile agreement has not yet succeeded in eliminating missile deployment programs already existing in several countries. It does, however, offer the prospect of significantly restraining exports if its members adhere to their agreements and accept limitations that restrict potential sales. The involvement of a growing number of countries in efforts to control missiles and weapons of mass destruction shows how the spread of military technology has become a global problem curable only through global cooperation.

The ABM treaty of SALT I proved to be of greater long-term significance. Both parties were limited to not more than two ABM sites (one for the protection of the national capital, another to protect an ICBM complex), with not more than 100 interceptor missiles each. These restrictions did not result in any significant strategic adjustments by either side, because both had become disappointed in the utility of ABMs. However, the ABM treaty did prohibit the deployment of any space-based ABM system, which was an important element in the debate surrounding the Strategic Defense Initiative (See Chapter Four for more on SDI, or "Star Wars").

The follow-up agreement to SALT I, creatively termed SALT II, was signed in 1979 but was never ratified by the U.S. Senate following the Soviet invasion of Afghanistan (see Chapter Four again). Even so, each side adhered to the guidelines of the treaty, while often accusing the other of noncompliance, sometimes justifiably and sometimes not. The provisions of the treaty were complex, but its central points were an aggregate ceiling of 2250 launchers (including ICBMs, SLBMs, and heavy bombers) for both superpowers, as well as other limits on MIRVs. MIRVs are viewed as extremely destabilizing because they may either tempt an aggressor to strike first or conversely represent extremely valuable targets for a first strike. (If it is possible to knock out a larger percentage of the opponent's arsenal with fewer missiles, this increases the temptation to strike first.)

Unfortunately, the ceiling for MIRVed ICBMs still permitted both sides to increase their warheads by more than 40 percent from the initial signing of the treaty.

Indeed, a serious shortcoming of SALT II as a whole was that all of its aggregate limits were significantly higher than the levels existing at the time, thus allowing the superpowers to expand their arsenals to the treaty limits. Although it may have provided more predictability in the nuclear arms race, the SALT process was not particularly successful in curbing it; both qualitative improvements and quantitative increases in the superpower nuclear arsenals were permitted.

When Ronald Reagan assumed the presidency in 1981, the name of the negotiations was changed to the Strategic Arms Reduction Talks (START), to reflect his insistence on mutual and balanced reductions in strategic nuclear forces. The intellectual seeds of the START treaties were planted during the 1986 Reykjavík summit meeting between Reagan and Soviet President Mikhail Gorbachev, but it took negotiators over four years to work out the final provisions of the January 1991 START I treaty. For the first time, an arms-control treaty mandated genuine reductions in strategic arms, also addressing some of the weapons systems that are widely perceived to be destabilizing. The main parameters were set at 1600 launchers and 6000 warheads for each side.

On the negative side, the treaty suffered from several significant problems. It excluded certain weapons systems, had very permissive counting rules for some of the systems that were included, and placed far too few restrictions on modernization of existing systems. In a general sense, although strategic stability was one of the declared goals of the negotiations, the final result was somewhat disappointing because major steps like eliminating MIRVed ICBMs were not taken.

Significant as it was, START I was soon overshadowed by the collapse of the Soviet Union. Indeed, as the Cold War gave way to the New Era, the arms race appeared to turn into an arms-control race. Instead of trying to stay a step ahead of the adversary by developing new weapons systems, both the United States and Russia tried to outdo each other by advancing new proposals for nuclear arms reductions and even by unilaterally implementing cuts. This process led to the signing of START II in January 1993, whereby both sides pledged to reduce their strategic nuclear arsenals to between 3000 and 3500 warheads. In addition, START II "rectified" some of the problems with START I; for example, some of the permissive counting rules were tightened, and potentially destabilizing MIRVed ICBMs were to be totally eliminated. Thus, through many disappointments and detours, the SALT and START negotiations finally achieved significant agreements on the reduction of the two largest nuclear powers' strategic arsenals.

Intermediate-Range and Tactical Nuclear Weapons

In December 1987, after seven years of negotiations, the United States and the USSR signed the Intermediate-Range Nuclear Forces (INF) Treaty, which eliminated all nuclear missiles with a range of 310 through 3400 miles. Although these weapons represented a relatively small portion of both superpowers' nuclear arsenals, the INF treaty marked the first time that an entire class of nuclear weapons had been banned. By June 1991, all such weapons had been destroyed by both sides. In hindsight, this treaty became especially important following the breakup of the Soviet Union. Imagine the potential dangers if the successor states to the USSR still possessed intermediate-range nuclear weapons, particularly those which have experienced domestic political upheaval. Without the INF Treaty, the risks of nuclear proliferation and possible nuclear conflict within the former Soviet Union would have been immeasurably greater.

Another class of nuclear weapons lost much of their military significance after the disintegration of the Warsaw Pact and the reunification of Germany in 1990. **Tactical nuclear weapons,** with ranges between 95 and 310 miles, and battlefield nuclear weapons, with ranges of less than 125 miles, were no longer of any military importance in Europe. It was no great surprise, then, that both the Soviet Union (and subsequently Russia) and the United States announced unilateral steps to remove many of these weapons as the Cold War wound down to a close. After the August 1991 coup attempt in the Soviet Union, President Bush declared that the United States would unilaterally reduce its short-range nuclear forces. In response, Soviet President Gorbachev also announced similar steps. After the final demise of the Soviet Union, the successor states agreed to transfer all of the tactical nuclear weapons on former Soviet territory to storage depots in Russia. By July 1992, the United States and former Soviet states had completed these steps, and in the end, thousands of nuclear weapons were destroyed without any type of formal arms-control agreement.

Nuclear Proliferation

In addition to strategic nuclear weapons and intermediate-range and tactical nuclear weapons, a third major area of arms control after World War II concerned the proliferation of nuclear weapons. After the development of the atomic bomb and its use by the United States on Hiroshima and Nagasaki in 1945, nuclear weapons were developed by the USSR, United Kingdom, France, and China. Many more countries embarked upon research programs that gave them the potential to construct their own nuclear weapons.

To stem the danger of proliferation, the UN General Assembly adopted a resolution in 1961 calling on all states to sign a treaty prohibiting the transfer and acquisition of nuclear weapons. The 1968 **Nonproliferation Treaty** (NPT) prohibited states already in possession of nuclear weapons from helping other states to acquire them. Furthermore, nonnuclear weapon states were forbidden to manufacture or otherwise obtain nuclear arms and were to submit their nuclear programs to monitoring by the International Atomic Energy Agency (IAEA). Nuclear weapon states were allowed to facilitate the exchange of equipment, materials, and scientific and technical information on the peaceful uses of nuclear energy, and were encouraged to pursue further negotiations on arms control and disarmament.

Most of the countries signing the NPT treaty had no intention of acquiring nuclear weapons in the first place. Several states with nuclear ambitions at the time

WHAT WOULD YOU DO?

As the collective leadership of the UN Security Council, you represent the world's club of great powers—*nuclear* powers. You have been informed that several Third World countries have developed nuclear weapons. You are trying to decide whether to force them to conform to the inspection mandates of the Nuclear Nonproliferation Treaty (NPT) of 1968 or, in a novel endeavor, try to channel their development of these capabilities in such a way that these weapons promote regional versions of Mutual Assured Destruction (MAD).

As some of your advisors have pointed out, the NPT guidelines provide the only clear-cut sanctions against the development of nuclear weapons in areas of the world where too many leaders might be willing to use them. These guidelines also limit the feasible size of weapons R&D programs by forcing them underground (literally and figuratively). They have also argued that unless the international community is financially willing to ensure that the weapons program of every country in a nuclearized region promotes MAD, then even the most rational Third World leader will have no inducement to refrain from using these weapons for purposes of extortion, thereby increasing tensions and instability.

(including India, Pakistan, South Africa, and Israel) refused to sign the treaty. Other countries, including Iran, Iraq, and North Korea, signed it but still continued their nuclear weapons programs. To prevent these countries from acquiring the weapons, the major nuclear suppliers began to meet in London in 1975 to develop a common approach to limit their nuclear exports. The "London Club" eventually was able to produce a set of guidelines for the transfer of peaceful nuclear technology. However, as the recent examples of Iraq and North Korea indicate, transfer guidelines remain insufficient to prevent nuclear proliferation.

The fragmentation of the New Era may lead many developed states to rethink their policies toward nuclear proliferation. This has already happened with France and China, both of whom finally signed the NPT after holding out for more than two decades. On the other hand, the dangers of new states gaining nuclear weapons in a more fragmented international arena has increased. A new round of negotiations aimed at revising the NPT is due to begin in 1995, suggesting that proliferation will become a key problem of the New Era.

Conventional Arms Control

The control of conventional arms has remained one of the most difficult areas for arms limitation. Throughout the Cold War, the Warsaw Pact maintained an overwhelming quantitative conventional superiority that led to corresponding NATO buildups. This resulted in a situation where two enormous armies of over 1 million troops each, equipped with the most sophisticated weapons, confronted each other for more than forty years along the East German–West German border. NATO's

Others argue that forcing Third World countries to conform to the NPT provisos (for example, IAEA inspections) has proven to be highly unpopular, leading to charges of meddling in countries' sovereign affairs. Forcing countries to develop their weapons programs surreptitiously only increases regional insecurities, as other countries, which cannot be certain whether the first group of countries has weapons or not, consider developing their own programs as insurance against attack or blackmail. Instead of banning these weapons, as the Americans once did with alcohol, the nuclear club should promote the development of secure second-strike capabilities: Assuming that Third World leaders would treat nuclear weapons any less rationally than those of the nuclear club smacks of Western ethnocentrism.

As a member of the Security Council, would you be willing to promote nuclear responsibility in the Third World by aiding in the development of secure second strike capabilities for all Third World states that possess nuclear weapons?

worst military nightmare was a Soviet surprise attack across this line with the vast Warsaw Pact army already in Eastern Europe.[25] From 1973 until 1986 both alliances negotiated to little avail over reductions of conventional forces in the **Mutual and Balanced Force Reduction (MBFR)** talks.

As with the nuclear arms race, the end of the Cold War proved to be a major catalyst for change. In November 1990 NATO and the Warsaw Pact countries signed the Conventional Forces in Europe (CFE) Treaty, one of the most intricate arms-control agreements ever reached. The treaty called for the destruction or removal from Europe of over 125,000 tanks, artillery, armored vehicles, aircraft, and helicopters. In sharp contrast to the protracted MBFR negotiations, it took the twenty-two signatory states only twenty months to complete the treaty. The Soviet Union in particular made large concessions that removed the threat of a blitzkrieg-type Soviet invasion of Western Europe even before the final collapse of the USSR. The demise of the Communist superpower, ironically, created new difficulties in implementing the CFE Treaty as the USSR's successor states have argued amongst themselves over the allocation of the remaining weapons permitted under the agreement.

CONCLUSION: TO ARM OR NOT TO ARM?

All nations face a security dilemma that they must manage, either through international negotiations, unilateral measures, or both. Regardless of their choice, the pursuit of the various goals that states include in their definition of "national security" consumes a significant portion of their available resources. This is understandable, since one of the primary responsibilities of a state is the provision of security for its citizens. Beyond a certain point, however, the pursuit of security begins to have detrimental effects on a state's relations with its neighbors and the international community, and on the state itself. Determining the point where the proportion of a nation's material and human resources devoted to security becomes self-defeating is a difficult task for its leaders, but an essential one.

Because many aspects of international security are fraught with uncertainty, there is no way to precisely determine how much security is enough. The threats a nation faces and the measures it should adopt in response depend heavily on perceptions. Former President George Bush, an advocate of prudence in security policy, views the resources earmarked for national security as money well spent:

> Throughout our history, our national security has pursued broad, consistent goals. We have always sought to protect the safety of the nation, its citizens, and its way of life. We have also worked to advance the welfare of our people, by contributing to an international environment of peace, freedom, and progress within which our democracy—and other free nations—can flourish.[26]

A proponent of disarmament has a quite different view of security:

> Security has become a god, and a cruel and demanding one. Our tribute to fear now runs at around $1 trillion a year. But the real cost is the diversion of resources needed elsewhere. And our insecurity increases. We live under the shadow of nuclear war, of famine, violence, and human and environmental tragedy.[27]

These views can be difficult to reconcile. Recall the images of world politics introduced in Chapter One. A person who holds the "Star Wars" image of international relations, who is worried about the threat presented by "evil empires" and undemocratic leaders, is more likely to be concerned with national security than someone who believes that all conflicts are simple misunderstandings, because "it's a small world after all." Events may temporarily incline a nation's government or citizenry towards one view or the other, but are not likely to cause a shift in the underlying difference in perspective. For this reason, debates over how much security a nation should "purchase" for itself are among the most persistent and contentious controversies in democratic societies, and are difficult to resolve even in undemocratic ones.

Ultimately, if national security is defined as the preservation of sovereignty, the resources a state spends on national security are part of the price of independence. Just as an individual must decide how much health or accident insurance to purchase depending on his or her specific needs, nations must consider the threats confronting them and the strategies and resources available when they purchase their "sovereignty insurance." If they spend too little, they risk catastrophic losses from aggression not covered by their defense effort; if they spend too much, their other goals or values may suffer.

No matter how much attention a nation gives to these matters, absolute security is impossible to attain. Every security strategy involves risks of one sort or another, even for the most powerful nation. Consequently, states must choose armament or disarmament, deterrence or defense, and multilateral cooperation or unilateral action to meet their security needs, and each option has its own inherent drawbacks. As long as the possibility of conflict exists—and it always will—all nations must size up the threats they face, decide how best to safeguard their land and people, pay their money, and make their choice.

PRINCIPAL POINTS OF CHAPTER ELEVEN

1. The concept of national security can include many elements, such as territorial integrity, economic prosperity, maintenance of basic values, and preservation of the natural environment. For the purposes of this text, security is defined as a condition in which the sovereignty and the territorial integrity of a country are guaranteed.

2. In the anarchic international system, every state faces the security dilemma: The actions a state takes to increase its own security may decrease the security of other states, which may respond by taking actions that decrease the security of the original state.

3. A variety of strategies for protecting national security are available to states:

   a. States may unilaterally build up their armed forces, join with other states in military alliances (such as NATO), or rely on collective-security organizations (such as the UN) to protect them from aggression.

   b. Each nation must also determine the mix of deterrence (persuading opponents not to attack by threatening them with punishment) and defense (resisting or stopping an attack) upon which it will rely. Compellence attempts to force an adversary to reverse or undo some damaging action that has already been taken.

4. There are two main types of deterrence. General deterrence attempts to dissuade adversaries from attempting any type of challenge to a state's interests, while immediate deterrence is a response to a specific, imminent threat.

5. A distinction may also be drawn between direct deterrence, which threatens punishment for attacks on a nation's own territory, and extended deterrence, which threatens sanctions against attacks on a state's allies.

6. Successful deterrence requires the "three Cs": commitment, capability, and credibility. In addition, the opponent must be rational enough to weigh the likely costs and benefits of attacking.

7. Critics of deterrence contend that deterrence often fails because challengers do not accurately perceive the defender's capabilities or commitment, or have limited ability to make cost-benefit calculations when considering an attack.

8. Military technology can have a great impact on the success or failure of security strategies, particularly if it alters the offense/defense balance.

9. The development of nuclear weapons radically changed military strategy in the following ways:

   a. If a state possesses the ability to destroy all of an adversary's nuclear forces with its initial attack, it is said to have a first-strike capability. This is a very dangerous situation, as the state may be tempted to launch a nuclear attack during a crisis.

   b. To preserve the strategic balance and ensure that neither side has an incentive to launch a nuclear attack, states must maintain a second-strike capability by ensuring that enough of their nuclear arsenal will survive a nuclear attack to inflict unacceptable damage on the enemy. The preferred way of doing this is to deploy a nuclear triad of land-based missiles (ICBMs), submarine-based missiles (SLBMs), and bombers.

   c. If both states possess a secure second-strike capability, a condition of mutual assured destruction (MAD) exists, and neither side has an incentive to attack first (as it would be destroyed by the opponent's retaliatory strike).

10. Even though the end of the Cold War has halted the arms race between the United States and Russia, problems with the command and control of nuclear weapons possessed by unstable states and the spread of nuclear weapons, or nuclear proliferation, still remain.

11. States may attempt to enhance their mutual security through arms control or disarmament.

   a. Disarmament seeks to reduce existing levels of weapons as a goal in itself.

   b. Arms control seeks to limit and manage an arms race; this may or may not entail reductions in weapons.

12. Major arms control treaties since 1945 include the following:

   a. The Limited Test Ban Treaty (1963) and the Threshold Test Ban Treaty (1974), which restrict testing of nuclear weapons.

   b. The multilateral Nonproliferation Treaty (1968), designed to control the spread of nuclear weapons.

   c. The first U.S.–Soviet Strategic Arms Limitation Treaty (SALT I) (1972), consisting of the Interim Agreement, which put temporary limits (different for each state) on strategic offensive weapons, and the Anti-Ballistic Missile (ABM) Treaty, which severely restricted the development and deployment of anti-missile systems.

   d. SALT II (1979), signed by the United States and USSR but not ratified by the United States (though both superpowers generally complied with it), which set equal overall ceilings on strategic weapons.

   e. The INF Treaty (1987), in which the United States and USSR eliminated intermediate-range nuclear forces.

f. The first Strategic Arms Reduction Treaty (START I) (1991), which committed the United States and USSR to reduce their strategic nuclear forces to equal lower levels.

g. START II (1993), which codified further reductions in U.S. and Russian nuclear weapons and banned land-based missiles with MIRVs (multiple warheads).

h. The agreement on Conventional Forces in Europe (CFE) (1990), limiting conventional (nonnuclear) weapons and forces in Europe and the successor states to the USSR.

i. The multilateral Biological Weapons Convention (1972), which bans germ-warfare weapons.

j. The Chemical Weapons Convention (1993), which bans poison gas and other chemical-warfare agents.

k. Although it is not a formal multilateral treaty, the Missile Technology Control Regime, or MTCR, engages key suppliers in the effort to seek limitations on the export of ballistic missile technology.

Chapter 12

Power

The overriding goals remained to effect a withdrawal of the United States from South Vietnam and to bring about negotiations between the Front and its adversaries, in order to form a new Southern government. To achieve these political objectives we would pursue the struggle on three fronts: political, military, and diplomatic. We would simultaneously confront our enemy in the field, mobilize our domestic support while undermining Diem's, and gather allies internationally—not forgetting the American people themselves.

This three-pronged strategy was to characterize our approach throughout the war. Every military clash, every demonstration, every propaganda appeal was seen as part of an integrated whole; each had consequences far beyond its immediately apparent results. It was a framework that allowed us to view battles as psychological events and to undertake negotiations in order to strengthen our military position. The Americans seemed never to appreciate fully this strategic perspective, which among ourselves we most often simply called *Danh va dam, dam va danh* ("fighting and talking, talking and fighting"). It was, after all, a traditional Vietnamese approach to warfare, a technique refined over centuries of confrontation with invaders more powerful than ourselves.

Truong Nhu Tang, *A Vietcong Memoir* (New York: Harcourt Brace Jovanovich, 1985), pp. 86–87.

Was the United States defeated in Vietnam by a superior power? It absolutely was not, according to one Vietcong soldier, Truong Nhu Tang; instead, he maintains, the United States was defeated by a superior strategy. In addressing issues of power in international politics, Tang's account of how Vietnam won the war should remind us of the inadequacy of determining a country's strength by simply counting the numbers of its soldiers and weapons.

Power is central to both the theory and practice of world politics, but power in international relations is a complex and sometimes nebulous concept. Some basic aspects of power are straightforward and may be precisely calculated; others, however, are similar to a commonly held idea of obscenity—you cannot exhaustively define it, but you know it when you see it. Despite the ambiguities inherent in defining and measuring power, actors in the international system frequently make decisions based on their assessments of their own power relative to that of their allies and adversaries. Because the components that constitute power are numerous and often intangible, these assessments are frequently wrong, and decisions founded on them can lead to disaster. Conversely, miscalculations of power may cause states to miss important opportunities for gain or cooperation. Although more discriminating evaluations of power do not guarantee successful or even prudent policies, they at least provide a clearer view of the international scene. Regardless of how one defines power, attempts to assess strengths and weaknesses will be an integral part of international affairs in the New Era.

Traditional attempts to rank states and other actors in the international system have tended to emphasize military capability. History has shown time and again, however, that the ability to destroy does not necessarily translate into the ability to dictate, and military power alone rarely enables a state to achieve its goals. With the end of the Cold War, many analysts believe that economic considerations are replacing military factors as the most important determinants of power. Proponents of this argument point to the growing influence of Japan and Germany, which have limited capability to project military force beyond their borders but whose economic reach equals and may even surpass that of the remaining military superpower, the United States. Even China is gaining more attention in the 1990s because of its growth in economic—not military—capability.

Mindful of these changes in the nature and possession of power, this chapter first will identify and discuss the ingredients of power, as policy-makers perceive them, that make up the distribution of capabilities in the international system. The attributes of a state that determine its power relative to that of other states may be divided into four categories: material power, military power, motivational

1973: Oil crisis causes Japan to focus on a steady supply of oil from the Middle East.

1973–present: American failure in Vietnam dampens U.S. motivation for military intervention.

1978: Vietnam's invasion of Cambodia shows how a brutal regime like that of the Khmer Rouge finds enemies even among ideologically similar states.

1979: Ayatollah Khomeini's harsh anti-Western ideology following the Iranian Revolution impairs Iran's relations with the West.

1979–1981: Soviet invasion of Afghanistan prompts a grain embargo from the United States; embargo fails because the Soviet Union is able to buy grain from other sources.

1979–1989: Soviet Union's occupation of Afghanistan fails despite superior economic and military power.

1980s: High cost of new technologies like the B-1, the B-2, and Star Wars threatens the future of such advanced projects in the United States; Libyan leader Gadhafi's willingness to sponsor terrorism does not lead to international influence.

1982: Britain's weak reputation prompts Argentinian invasion of the Falkland Islands; war ensues.

Mid-1980s–present: Japanese-American disputes over their respective economic policies lead to continued feuding between Tokyo and Washington over such matters as trade practices and financial issues.

1990: President Bush seeks public support before committing forces to expel Iraqi troops from Kuwait.

1990–1991: Economic sanctions fail to encourage Iraq to withdraw from Kuwait.

1991: With the end of the Cold War, state power is defined more by economic and less by military factors; easy victory over Iraqi army in Kuwait shows how highly trained professional forces can be much more effective than a larger army of draftees; breakup of Yugoslavia and aggression by Serbia shows how nationalism can be used as an excuse for expansionism and demonstrates weakness of great power ability to control local conflicts.

power, and reputation. After examining each of these four basic elements, the chapter will analyze the differences between actualized and potential power, and then discuss the so-called great powers, the manner in which they are identified, and the impact they have on international politics.

WHAT IS POWER AND WHY DOES IT MATTER?

At this point it is appropriate to step back for a moment and ask what states and leaders really mean by power, and why they seem so preoccupied with it. Is the struggle for power actually worth anything? Like Olympic athletes, perhaps states meekly vie with one another for honor and glory, or compete simply for the sake of competing. The concept of power in international politics does not mean merely status or ranking, it also means **capability. Power** is conventionally defined as the ability of one actor to get another to do what the other would not otherwise have done. (This includes preventing an actor from doing something that it otherwise would have done.) More broadly, power may be understood as the actual and potential ability and willingness of one government to influence the decisions that other governments make. If two governments were in perfect agreement, the use of power to influence decisions would not be necessary, as both would act in their own as well as each other's best interests (assuming they knew what those were). If states never disagreed, power would never be useful or necessary. History shows, however, that the international system is rife with disputes and conflict, and the most utopian of theories nevertheless recognizes that conflicts of interests and values would exist even under a world government. Power therefore matters a great deal in international politics, because it defines a state's probable ability to resolve disputes in its favor, and to achieve its goals in a world of scarce resources and conflicting ideas.

Though the basic definition of power is constant, power itself is not. An important source of power today might become less significant tomorrow, while what was not important a century ago might be vital in the future. In his book *Bound to Lead: The Changing Nature of American Power,* from which Table 12.1 was adapted, Joseph Nye points out that different factors have played critical roles in different historical periods.

Given that the sources and applications of power change continuously, how can power be identified and measured? Some aspects are clearly more measurable than others. **Material power** is generally the easiest to quantify, followed by **military power, motivational power,** and, lastly, **reputation.** The difficulty of measurement is compounded by the interaction between the quantitative and qualitative aspects of power. A state's effectiveness in directly and indirectly using its military forces, for instance, can be influenced by the determination of its leaders, as well as by its reputation for success in military conflicts.

The manner in which decision makers use the capabilities of their own states to affect other states' decisions is perhaps the most interesting and critical feature of international relations. To a large extent, the successful conversion of capacities and potential into influence is what the study of international politics is all about. Since the distribution of power influences how states act toward one another, changes in the power of one state will have an impact on other states, and for this reason we will focus on **relative power** rather than **absolute power.**

Although the indicators of material and military power may be measured in absolute terms (such as dollars or numbers of warheads), their ability to become influential depends on how they compare with those of other states. Motivational power, furthermore, is difficult to measure absolutely, and reputation has practically no meaning at all without comparison to that of other actors in the system.

With this in mind, our survey of the four elements of power will begin by considering the most quantifiable elements first. The material components of power form the basic fabric of a nation's might. These include geographic location, natural resources, population, economic development, industrial capacity, and technology. Military elements of power comprise a nation's ability to wage war, expressed in terms of size and quality of military forces, weapons, and equipment, and mobility and logistical capability. The motivational elements of power are less empirical; they center on a nation's quest for prestige and status in the international system and the willingness of its leaders and citizens to make the sacrifices needed to build material and military power.[1] Motivation is affected by such variables as ideology, national traits and morale, the personalities and abilities of particular statesmen, nationalism, social and political unity, diplomatic skill and experience, and administrative efficiency. Calculations of material, military, and motivational power are essential for estimating the basic capability of states to achieve their goals in international politics, but they do not tell the complete story. To round out the picture, it is necessary to also consider a nation's reputation as an actor in the international system, which includes its "track record" in disputes and conflicts, the ideology and values it espouses, and its status as an example to other states or as a leader in the community of nations.

Table 12.1	The Changing Nature of Power	
Period	*Leading State*	*Major Resources*
16th Century	Spain	Gold bullion, colonial trade, mercenary armies, dynastic ties
17th Century	Netherlands	Trade, capital markets, navy
18th Century	France	Population, rural industry, public administration, army
19th Century	Britain	Industry, political cohesion, finance and credit, navy, liberal norms, island location
20th Century	United States	Economic scale, scientific and technological leadership, universalistic culture, military forces and alliances, strategic forces, liberal international regimes, hub of transnational communication

Source: Adapted from Joseph S. Nye, Jr., *Bound to Lead: The Changing Nature of American Power* (New York: Basic Books, 1991).

The following sections will provide a basis for analyzing the complexities and changing nature of the factors that comprise power. Data and statistics that suggest the willingness and ability of governments to take an active part in international affairs will be presented. These indices are not causes or determinants of the strength of states; they merely reflect how that strength may be measured and the way in which it is perceived. As an example, compare the basic indicators of material and military power among the three contenders for global leadership in Table 12.2. The table reveals that the United States remains the leading power in the world, but has been overtaken by its rivals in some areas. Japan, while weak in terms of military power and natural resources, has encroached on the United States' leading economic position. The European Union (EU) has already surpassed Japan and the United States in the categories of population, size of armed forces, and share of world exports, but remains far behind in strategic weapons.

These simple numerical comparisons can be misleading, since they do not take motivational power and reputation into account. For example, when a crisis erupts, many nations still look to the United States for leadership because of its willingness to intervene militarily. In contrast, Japan's constitution prohibits it from employing military force as a political instrument, and the EU has often proven unable to produce a coherent foreign policy among its member states.

Other states in the international system that rank lower in all of these categories still possess a tremendous potential for power. China is considerably weaker than the United States, the EU, or Japan in many aspects of military and economic power, but its potential for economic growth is immense, and it appears likely to narrow several gaps that separate it from the advanced industrialized states over the next several decades. In 1993, for example, China had one of the world's five largest economies, having surpassed several EU countries in the previous two

Table 12.2   Basic, Economic, and Military Resources of the EU, Japan, and the
United States, 1991

	EU	Japan	United States
Basic Resources			
Land area, percent of world total	1.7%	0.3%	7.0%
Population, in millions	345.9	124	252.5
Economic Resources			
Gross national product (GNP)	$6.2 trillion	$3.4 trillion	$5.7 trillion
Share of world exports	40%	9%	12%
Military Resources			
Strategic Nuclear warheads	594	0	9,745
Personnel in armed forces, in millions	2.6	0.25	2.1
Military expenditures, percent of world total	17%	3%	27%

Source: Adapted from Nye, *Bound to Lead*, p. 144. Updated from IMF, *Direction of Trade Statistics Yearbook*, p. 3, and U.S. Arms Control and Disarmament Agency, *World Military Expenditures and Arms Transfers, 1991–1992*, pp. 36–43.

years. Likewise, America's former global adversary, Russia, has vast natural resources, agricultural potential, abundant scientific talent, and a well-educated workforce, which might allow it to regain its status as a major player in world politics.

Before examining the four components of power separately, we should note that while each is a useful tool for assessing the positions of states, none exists independently of another. For example, sophisticated weapons such as precision-guided missiles require a highly developed industrial sector and great wealth, and for this reason the most economically developed states have tended to be the most militarily powerful ones. At the same time, the American experience in Vietnam and the Soviet experience in Afghanistan showed that greater economic and military power does not always enable a state to get what it wants. Few predicted North Vietnam's tenacity in fighting the United States and its allies or Iraq's refusal to back down in the face of superior force during the 1990–1991 Persian Gulf crisis. Hence, the power of a state consists of a range of interrelated factors, none of which is in itself sufficient to indicate its capabilities or standing in the international system. Even though some aspects of power may be readily quantified, there is no way to add them to produce an aggregate sum of a nation's power. In the New Era, international politics remains an art of the possible rather than an exact science.

MATERIAL POWER

Material power is first and foremost economic power. Some elements of economic strength, such as gross national product (GNP), oil reserves, and balance of trade, are relatively easy to calculate to allow comparison with other states.

Other components of material power, such as the skills of a nation's labor force and the creative potential of its research and development establishment, are equally important but more difficult to quantify. In all its aspects, material power forms the physical basis of a nation's political strength. For our survey of the sources of power it is convenient to divide material power into the three subcategories of territory, population, and trade and industry. As with other components of power, these facets are closely related, if not interdependent.

Territory: Geography and Natural Resources

A nation's most important territorial assets include its geography (size, location, climate, and physical features), and its natural resources. A glance at the globe shows how geography benefits the United States and Russia. The United States is separated from both Europe and Asia by oceans, which provide convenient trade routes but make invasion more difficult. Russia's vast land area straddling these two continents gives it a strong strategic position in both. The territorial expanse of Russia and the United States (the world's first and fourth largest nations in terms of land area, at 6.59 and 3.68 million square miles, respectively) gives them control over abundant natural resources, an advantage shared by other large nations such as Canada (second largest at 3.85 million square miles), China (third, at 3.69 million square miles), Brazil (fifth, at 3.29 million square miles), and Australia (sixth, at 2.97 million square miles).

Size is not all that matters, however. In geopolitics, as in real estate, the three most important factors are location, location, and location. While the areas of Japan and the United Kingdom do not even rank in the top thirty, both countries are island powers whose positions provide them with a strong buffer against invasion (Britain has not been successfully invaded since the year 1066), as well as a strong orientation toward maritime trade. Since neither nation has needed a large army since World War II, both have concentrated on building strong navies for the twin purposes of defense and protection of trade. Location on an island is no guarantee of safety or political influence, though; island nations such as Madagascar, Sri Lanka, Indonesia, and the Philippines have been colonized or occupied by more powerful states at various times.

Just as being surrounded by water has influenced some nations' policies, partial and total landlock have also played a significant role in shaping the viewpoints of many states. Located in the heart of Europe, surrounded by sometimes unfriendly neighbors and lacking formidable natural barriers, Germany has traditionally found it necessary to field large armies to protect its frontier, a need not fully alleviated until the end of the Cold War. Israel's strategic geography is even more unfavorable, because it occupies a small, narrow strip of land, which some of its Arab neighbors claim as their own. Surrounded by adversaries, Israel has relied upon strong, mobile armed forces and a "hair-trigger" strategy of prompt retaliation or preemptive strikes to defend itself. In contrast, countries completely surrounded by land and dependent on their neighbors for access to trade routes, such as Afghanistan, Bolivia, the Czech Republic, Laos, and Chad have rarely adopted assertive foreign policies.

AT A GLANCE

TYPES OF POWER

Material Power

Function: Forms the basic fabric of a nation's might

Components: Geographic location, natural resources, population, economic development, industrial capacity, and technology

Military Power

Function: Comprises a nation's ability to wage war

Components: Size and quality of military forces, weapons, equipment, and mobility and logistical capability

Motivational Power

Function: Centers on a nation's quest for prestige and status in the international system and the willingness of its leaders and citizens to make the sacrifices needed to build material and military power

Components: Ideology, national traits and morale, the personalities and abilities of particular statesmen, nationalism, social and political unity, diplomatic skill and experience, and administrative efficiency

Reputation

Function: A state's perceived ability to accomplish the goals it sets for itself. Reputation reflects the operation of chance

Components: "Track record" in disputes and conflicts, the ideology and values a regime espouses, and its status as an example to other states or as a leader in the community of nations.

A second and equally important set of territorial assets are natural resources, such as iron, coal, oil, timber, and arable land (land usable for agriculture). In considering the short-term value of a nation's natural resources, both production and reserves must be taken into account; in the long term, renewability and sustainability must be considered as well.

Since the Industrial Revolution, the most important natural resources have been metals and fossil fuels, and many wars have been fought over the possession of both. In the years following World War I, oil became the source of energy most important to the world economy, and to the world's military forces. Petroleum remains critically important, providing the classic example of how resources affect power in international politics.

Figure 12.1 shows that among the world's leading oil producers, only the United States, the former Soviet Union, China, and the United Kingdom are among the world's leading economic powers. They also have large proven reserves, which mean they have clear advantages over other major economic powers. Russia, having inherited most of the former USSR's oil reserves, should find its energy resources to be a major advantage in its economic development. Japan, on the other hand, is poor in oil reserves, and must rely heavily on oil imports to meet its energy needs. A consequence of Japan's dependency on imported oil is its economic vulnerability to any threat against its energy supply. The oil price rises of 1973–1974 and 1979 dealt sharp jolts to Japan's economy; to avoid such shocks in the future, a main objective of Tokyo's foreign policy is to ensure a steady flow of oil from the Middle East. Although Britain, with its relatively large North Sea reserves, enjoys a good measure of energy security, the other leading industrial nations of the EU (Germany, France, and Italy) have inadequate oil reserves and depend heavily on Middle Eastern oil to satisfy their energy requirements. This dependence has often affected European policies toward Middle Eastern nations, especially in times of conflict.[2]

While the protection of energy supplies has been a salient issue in recent decades, the supply of food is even more important. As with oil, any state self-sufficient in its basic food requirements enjoys significantly greater flexibility in economic and foreign policies than those states unable to feed their people from domestic agricultural production. Japan and the United Kingdom, both lacking in **arable land,** have traditionally had to rely on imports of food. This caused serious problems for both countries during World War II, when their import lifelines were attacked by enemy submarines. In recent times, Tokyo has continued to heavily subsidize its politically powerful but highly inefficient rice farmers in order to prevent Japanese dependence on other states for this dietary staple. The United States, by contrast, has been called the "breadbasket" of the

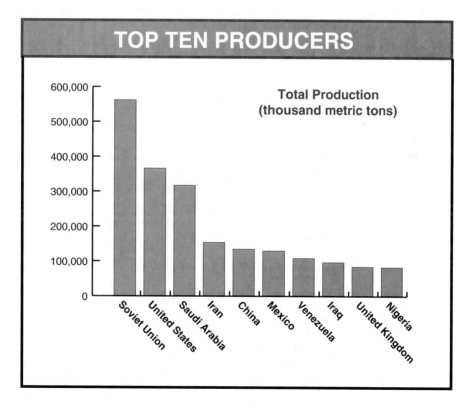

Figure 12.1   Crude Oil Production, 1990
Source: *UN Monthly Bulletin of Statistics,* May 1992, pp. 39–40.

BLOOD FOR OIL?

Neither modern industrial economies nor modern armies, navies, and air forces can operate without oil. "My men can eat their belts," U.S. General George Patton once growled, "but my tanks have gotta have gas." The status of petroleum as a key strategic resource has led some countries to guard their oil supplies jealously and tempted others to use oil as a political weapon. In an attempt to halt Tokyo's expansionist designs in China, the United States imposed an oil embargo on Japan in 1941. When the United States and the Netherlands supported Israel in the 1973 Arab-Israeli War, oil-exporting Arab states slapped Israel's allies with an embargo. Although gas prices skyrocketed and the U.S. economy slumped, Washington did not alter its policy of backing Israel with military and economic aid, but Secretary of State Henry Kissinger did initiate a dizzying round of shuttle diplomacy to help ameliorate Arab-Israeli tensions.

world because of its abundant arable land and continues to be a major exporter of agricultural products. Although the Soviet Union possessed vast expanses of rich farmland, the inherent inefficiencies of its overcentralized planned economy created chronic grain shortages that had to be made up with imports.[3] (Soviet farms consistently produced more than enough food for the USSR's population, but an inadequate transportation network was often unable to deliver food supplies in time to prevent spoilage.)

Again, as with oil, dependence on imported food makes states vulnerable to interruption of supplies. Following the Soviet invasion of Afghanistan in 1979, the United States halted all grain sales to the Soviets in the hope that the embargo would press them to withdraw their forces. However, as Washington soon discovered, economic sanctions are effective only when the embargoed good is unavailable elsewhere; the USSR simply bought grain from other suppliers and did not alter its policy toward Afghanistan. (The United States canceled the embargo in 1981.)

Population

In determining the extent to which population will be a factor in material power, what matters most is size, demographic structure, and the educational and skill levels of the labor force. A sufficiently large population is a prerequisite for great-power status, but not sufficient in itself. Too large a population might create a drain on resources while one too small might prevent economic growth and limit military capabilities.

As shown in Table 12.3, in 1970 the ten most populous countries included six major economic powers—China, the Soviet Union, the United States, Japan, West Germany, and the United Kingdom. By 1990 Indonesia and

Concern over a threat to the world's oil supply was one of the main motivations for the United States' forceful response to Iraq's occupation of Kuwait in 1990. Referring to President Bush's noted dislike of a certain green vegetable, U.S. critics of the Persian Gulf War quipped that there would have been no war if Kuwait's main export were broccoli. Military force was not the UN's first response to the Iraqi invasion. The Security Council initially ordered economic sanctions (an embargo on all trade, including food) in order to persuade Baghdad to withdraw, but Iraqi President Saddam Hussein ignored the sanctions' effects and refused to back down.

The embargoes against Japan in 1941, the United States in 1973, and Iraq in 1990 all failed to bring about the desired changes in those states' foreign policies. Economic sanctions, even when they cause severe hardships, are not guaranteed to provoke the intended response from the targeted states.

Bangladesh had supplanted united Germany and the United Kingdom on the list of the world's top ten countries in terms of population. Despite their size, China, Bangladesh, India, Indonesia, and Nigeria are developing countries that must devote large shares of their resources to basic food production, often at the expense of industrial development. On the other hand, Israel's population of about 5 million is so small that it cannot become a major power, despite its military and economic strength. Similarly, the highly industrialized countries of Finland and Switzerland have been prevented from becoming major economic powers by their small populations.

In addition to size of population, the demographic structure of a state's population can have a major impact on its ability to exert power. A nation that has a relatively large proportion of children and teenagers, typically due to high birthrates and short life expectancies, will face greater challenges in developing a highly skilled labor force and must devote substantial resources to child education and welfare. On the other hand, states fortunate enough to have a low birthrate and long life expectancies will face the problem of caring for senior citizens, especially if a pronounced "baby boom" is followed by a "baby bust," as is the case with Japan and the United States. Both these conditions can constrain the resources available to conduct an activist foreign policy.

The size and quality of a nation's labor force is crucial to its economic strength. The overall skill level of a country's working population is difficult to measure, but some indices offer a rough idea of the education and skills possessed by a nation's workers. The percentage of the labor force employed in agriculture is a useful indicator of economic advancement; as a rule, as industrialization increases, the percentage of workers engaged in farming drops. This is because of two factors: (1) the increased availability of jobs in manufacturing and services and (2) the greater agricultural productivity made possible by scientific and technological development. In 1990, China had 67.5 percent of its labor force in agriculture, Brazil, 24.3 percent, and the Soviet Union, 13 percent—a sign of continuing weaknesses in the economies of all three countries. By contrast, the United States had only 2.3 percent of its population engaged in agriculture, despite its position as one of the world's major agricultural producers—an indication of enduring strength for the American economy.[4]

A country's literacy rate roughly indicates the educational and skill level of its labor force. For example, more developed nations, such as EU members Italy (97 percent) and Greece (93 percent), tend to have a higher rate of adult literacy than developing countries such as India (48 percent) and Nigeria (51 percent). China's literacy rate of 73 percent reflects a potential for enhancement of its workers' productivity, while countries such as Nigeria and India face a more difficult task in developing a well-educated, skilled labor force; Somalia's (24 percent) challenge is enormous.[5]

Overall, population has a significant impact on a nation's potential for making war as well as for producing goods and services. Until the twentieth century, a large population was an absolute prerequisite for military power because war required the mobilization of large numbers of men into the army. With the explosive development of military technology in this cen-

Japanese farmers plant seedlings by hand in a rice paddy. This ancient, labor-intensive agricultural method is still widely employed despite Japan's myriad other modern industrial advances.

Source: © AP/Wide World Photos.

Table 12.3   Ten Most Populous Countries, 1970 and 1990

Top Ten Countries	Population (millions)
1970	
China	759.62
India	550.38
Soviet Union	242.77
United States	205.40
Pakistan	126.74 *
Japan	103.54
Brazil	95.31
West Germany	59.55
United Kingdom	55.71
Nigeria	55.07
1990	
China	1139.06
India	827.05
Soviet Union	288.60
United States	249.98
Indonesia	179.30
Brazil	150.36
Japan	123.54
Bangladesh	115.59 *
Nigeria	108.54
Pakistan	102.05 *

*While it might appear from these tables that the population of Pakistan declined between 1970 and 1990, it did not; rather, East Pakistan became the independent nation of Bangladesh in 1971.

Note: According to the World Bank (*World Development Report, 1993*), in 1991 united Germany had a population of 80 million and Russia, after the breakup of the Soviet Union, was now reduced to 149 million.

Source: *UN Demographic Yearbook 1970*, pp. 126–133; and *UN Demographic Yearbook 1990*, pp. 165–169.

tury, weapons, equipment, communications, and logistics have become much more important to military strength, and smaller but better-equipped armies have beaten larger but less technologically advanced armed forces on many occasions; two recent examples are Israel's 1967 victory over Egypt, Syria, and Jordan, and the Allied Coalition victory over the Iraqi army, then the fourth largest in the world.[6] The advent of nuclear weapons in 1945 made technology still more important relative to mobilized manpower. Today, only in conventional "wars of attrition" (those decided by sustained combat rather than lightning campaigns) does a large population give a state an advantage, since populous countries can absorb higher losses than their smaller enemies. In the Iran-Iraq War of 1980–1988, for example, Iran's larger population enabled it to fight Iraq to a standstill despite Teheran's inferiority in weapons technology.

Trade and Industry: Economic Indicators

A nation's material power is also determined by its success in utilizing its human and natural resources through domestic production and foreign trade. Economic strength is readily quantifiable through such measures as **gross national product (GNP),** per capita income, growth rate, and trade balance, although such numbers do not tell the whole story. A state's industrial capacity also depends on important unquantifiable measures like technology.

GNP serves as a crude but convenient means of comparing the economic strength of various countries. GNP measures the market value of goods and services produced during a particular time period (usually a year) and provides an estimate of a nation's total agricultural, industrial, and commercial output. GNP differs from **gross domestic product (GDP)** in that the latter does not take into account income earned by a nation's citizens and corporations that operate outside its borders. GNP also is a useful way to compare the growth rates of states in both absolute and relative terms. For example, during the 1980s, while the U.S. economy was growing larger in terms of total output, its share of world production was declining relative to both Japan and Germany. Since power in international politics is relative, the relative size of national economies has more political significance than their absolute size. Table 12.4 lists the ten nations with highest GNPs in 1970, 1980, and 1990 in order to give an indication of the changes in the balance of economic power over that twenty-year period.

The GNP tables show that while the United States has remained the world's principal economic power throughout the period, the relative margin between it and its economic rivals has been steadily narrowing. If Japan and Germany increase their economic strength, they could continue to improve their economic positions, perhaps even enough to challenge the United States for political leadership. However, in the early 1990s they both suffered from recessions, exacerbated for Germany by the difficulties encountered in the absorption of the former Communist East. Meanwhile, the American economy improved and it began to move ahead again.

The Soviet Union's decline in relative economic strength, which contributed to its political collapse, is also apparent from this rough comparison of total output. The USSR's economy remained about half the size of the United States' from 1970 to 1990, but other nations' economies grew faster, and by the end of this period Moscow had been eclipsed by Japan as the second-ranked economic power. Since the breakup of the USSR at the end of 1991, Russia has fallen even farther behind because of reduced size and economic performance, and now requires heavy doses of economic aid from its former adversaries. At the same time, China has grown by about 9 percent a year since 1978 and now ranks as one of the world's five largest economies.

Another measure of economic wealth is per capita income (GNP divided by population). Although the most economically advanced states will generally have the highest per capita incomes, the statistic does not provide a measure of a state's total economic capability, nor does it show how equally income is shared throughout a society. Nations with high per capita incomes have an advantage in

Table 12.4   Gross National Product of Top Ten Countries, 1970–1990

Top Ten Countries	GNP *(billions of dollars)*
1970	
United States	$976.8
Soviet Union	497.0
Japan	197.2
West Germany	185.5
France	145.9
United Kingdom	121.0
China	120.0
Italy	91.8
Canada	78.1
India	52.9
1980	
United States	$4,025.0
Soviet Union	2,257.0
Japan	1,956.0
West Germany	1,010.0
France	790.0
Italy	705.7
United Kingdom	652.5
Canada	398.0
Brazil	384.0
Spain	289.1
1990	
United States	$5,543.0
Japan	3,117.0
Soviet Union	2,660.0
West Germany	1,472.0 *
China	1,369.0
France	1,136.0
Italy	1,078.0
United Kingdom	985.4
Canada	549.0
Spain	490.8

*Estimated 1991 German GNP for the united country is $1586.0 billion.

Note: Figures are in current dollars.

Source: *World Military Expenditures and Arms Transfers,* 1971, p. 50; 1981, p. 43; and 1991–1992, pp. 38, 47–88.

that a higher percentage of their national income is likely to be available for investment in further growth, for spending on military forces, or for increasing the state's political influence worldwide through channels such as foreign aid. Table 12.5 lists the top ten nations in terms of per capita income in 1970, 1980, and 1990. Comparison with the tables for GNP shows immediately that the nations with the greatest total production do not necessarily have the highest standards of living.

The figures for 1980 illustrate the impact of the energy crises of the 1970s on the world economy as OPEC's cutbacks in petroleum production caused oil prices to quadruple in the 1970s. As a result, per capita incomes of oil-exporting countries soared. In the 1980s, however, oil prices declined, as oil-importing states substituted other energy sources (such as coal, hydroelectric power, and nuclear energy) for oil, took steps to conserve energy, and developed previously unexploited oil fields (like those in Alaska and the North Sea). Table 12.5 reflects the impact of the rise and fall of oil prices on the fortunes of OPEC. While only Kuwait appears in the top ten in 1970, the per capita GNPs of OPEC member countries Qatar, the United Arab Emirates (UAE), Kuwait, and Libya ranked first, second, third, and ninth, respectively in 1980, but none made the top ten in 1990.

The figures on per capita income show the relative economic positions of the superpowers as well. While the United States' 1970 per capita GNP of $4,758 topped the list of the ten largest, its 1980 per capita GNP had slipped to seventh, only one-third that of oil-rich Qatar's. By 1990 the United States' per capita income of $23,020 trailed Japan's and West Germany's before unification. Meanwhile, though the Soviet Union's total GNP was among the world's largest, its per capita GNP consistently fell below all the developed Western states. (Note that it never appears in the top ten per capita income rankings.) This meant that Moscow had few resources to spare to enhance its military power or political status; by spending massively in these categories nonetheless, Soviet leaders hastened their nation's economic decline and political disintegration.

To measure how fast a nation's relative economic power rises or declines, it is helpful to look at rates of growth. A state that maintains higher annual growth rates than its partners or adversaries is gaining on its rivals; a state with comparatively lower growth rates is falling behind. For example, while the American economy grew faster in 1980–1990 than it did in the previous fifteen years, Japan's economic growth outstripped that of the United States in both periods. West Germany's GDP growth slowed in the 1980s, and the output of the united Germany may further slacken if the costs of German reunification continue to mount.[7] In the early 1990s, America's ability to emerge from recession earlier than Japan or Europe gave the United States a relative boost, high growth rates accelerated China's emergence, and an actually declining economy reinforced Russia's woes.

While total output, per capita income, and growth rates are important indicators of economic strength, so is a nation's ability to trade effectively with other states. With the disappearance of the ideological and military threat posed by the former Soviet Union, competition for global markets is likely to become even more important. Accordingly, a nation's trade balance (see Chapter Seven) is likely to become an increasingly useful indicator of its relative economic power. A positive current-account balance indicates a trade surplus; a negative balance shows a trade deficit. Between 1970 and 1990, the shifts from trade surplus to deficit (experienced by the United States and the United Kingdom) and from trade deficit to surplus (Japan and Germany) indicate a dramatic change in the flow of world trade during the twenty-year period.[8]

Table 12.5   Gross National Product per Capita of Top Ten Countries, 1970–1990

Top Ten Countries	Per Capita Income (dollars)
1970	
United States	$4,758
Kuwait	3,929
Sweden	3,872
Canada	3,651
Switzerland	3,256
Luxembourg	3,237
Denmark	3,146
West Germany	3,006
France	2,872
Norway	2,864
1980	
Qatar	$53,720
United Arab Emirates	46,150
Kuwait	33,140
Switzerland	23,930
Sweden	18,790
Iceland	18,100
United States	17,670
Finland	17,490
Libya	17,060
Japan	16,750
1990	
Switzerland	$35,920
Luxembourg	32,170
Sweden	27,490
Japan	26,240
Finland	25,970
West Germany	24,260
Iceland	24,090
Denmark	24,000
Norway	23,810
United States	23,020

Note: Because Germany included the poorer Eastern sector in 1991, it dropped to thirteenth in that year's statistics. All figures are in constant dollars.

Source: *World Military Expenditures and Arms Transfers,* 1971, p. 50; 1980, p. 43; and 1991–1992, pp. 43, 47–88.

In 1970 most of the G7 countries, the leading economic powers, enjoyed a trade surplus, while in 1990 most experienced a trade deficit. The glaring exceptions are Germany and Japan. Both nations emerged from the rubble of World War II to eventually become trade powerhouses. For numerous reasons, Japan often has been singled out for special criticism of its trade policies. Even before

U.S.–Soviet tensions diminished, many Americans began to complain that "unfair" Japanese trading practices were helping to fuel Japan's economic growth while hurting the welfare of the United States, and by implication, the viability of the liberal trading order. They called for establishment of a "level playing field" through equalization of trade barriers—either by lowering those around Japan or raising those around the United States. Today many Americans are concerned that Europe as well as Japan might soon wrest economic leadership from the United States. The question of what to do about trade barriers is an issue of growing prominence. Map 12.1 is a cartogram showing relative trade power for selected countries.

Trade and Industry: Technology

Another factor that plays a major role in the creation and utilization of a nation's economic power is technology. However, because a state's overall level of technology is made up of a plethora of products, techniques, and ideas, a nation's relative technological capability is difficult to measure. A rough approximation of scientific and technical capacity may be arrived at by examining a nation's spending on technological research and development (R&D). Such a figure will not reveal how well a nation is succeeding at advancing its military and civilian technology, but it will at least provide an idea of how hard it is trying.

A comparison of R&D spending from 1986 to 1989 among the three largest Western industrial countries suggests the strengths and weaknesses of each party at the end of the Cold War. On the surface, the United States appears to have the clear lead. While it spent $100 billion on R&D, Japan spent $39 billion, and West Germany $19 billion. America has a similar lead in terms of numbers of scientists and engineers.[9] On the other hand, in terms of percentages of GNP spent on R&D, the three were nearly identical (2.6 percent for the United States, 2.9 percent for Japan, and 2.8 percent for West Germany). Moreover, the United States spends a greater percentage of its total scientific and technical resources on the defense industry than either Japan or Germany, as suggested by their comparative defense burdens. In 1987 the United States spent 6.3 percent of its GNP on defense; the West Germans 3.1 percent; and the Japanese, 1 percent. Targeting a higher percentage of R&D expenditures directly at civilian industry gives Germany and Japan an advantage in developing industrial technology. With the end of the Cold War, the ability of the United States to convert its concentration on defense R&D to civilian pursuits will help determine its future competitiveness relative to Japan and Germany.

Technology, trade balance, growth rates, and total production may all be used as indicators of a state's economic power. Taken together, they provide a picture of a nation's capabilities in trade and industry, which can be examined alongside a state's territory and population in order to determine its material power. This chapter has devoted a great deal of space to material power because it provides the potential for the other elements of power. For example, material power can be used to enhance a state's reputation in the world community and

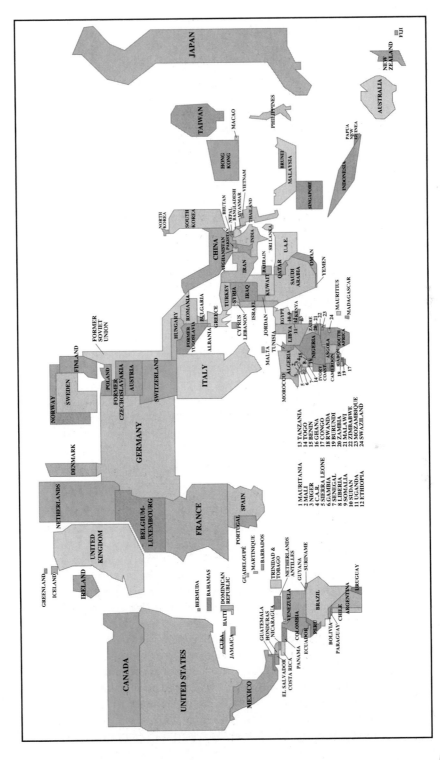

Map 12.1 World Export Trade, 1991

WHAT WOULD YOU DO?

You are the prime minister of Japan in the 1990s. You have reached a point where you face the decision whether to continue concentrating your resources primarily on increasing economic security or devoting a greater share to building your military power projection capabilities (long-range aircraft, ships, nuclear weapons, long-range missiles, and so on). You may not be able to continue using your record of economic successes to increase your overall global influence forever.

Devoting more resources to enhancing military power projection capabilities would not be too economically difficult and would help you to reverse your reputation for international political passivity. No longer would you feel prone to fear the bullying of a North Korean despot such as Kim Jong Il, pressure by the United States government to

to build military arsenals; without material power to provide the wherewithal, a state's motivation to accomplish its goals means little. Material strength does not provide a complete picture of a nation's capabilities and vulnerabilities, however; without the will to use it, it will remain mere potential, and without military force to defend it, it can be seized or destroyed by enemies. Material power is thus only the first element necessary for a state to accomplish its objectives in the international arena. Though it provides the foundation on which the other elements of power must be built, it is but a prerequisite for the second element, military power.

MILITARY POWER

When Stalin was once told that the pope disapproved of one of his policies, he reportedly dismissed the criticism with the question, "How many divisions has the pope?" Not all leaders share Stalin's enthusiasm for military power, but its importance to world politics cannot be denied. Military power refers to the size of a state's armed forces, to their quality and quantity of weaponry, and to their training, morale, organization, and leadership. It thus consists both of "hardware" (weapons and equipment) and "software" (personnel and their direction), and both must be of high quality in order for a state's armed forces to perform their missions. Because of the importance of the "hardware," it is impossible to divorce military from material power; throughout history the most developed states often have been the most militarily powerful ones. It is rarely possible to know beforehand, however, whether the numbers or the quality of forces engaged in combat will prove to be adequate to the task. One of the world's greatest military geniuses, Napoléon Bonaparte, once claimed that in war, "the moral is as to the physical as three is to one," but he also said that "victory goes dictate your foreign policy, or future threats by some other great power to disrupt your precious trading routes. A militarily more powerful Japan would also boost your chances of getting a permanent seat on the UN Security Council.

On the other hand, increasing your military power is fraught with risk. It could actually increase the sense of insecurity on the part of other East Asian states, provoking them to form a counterbalancing coalition. This would force you to spend even more on your military, thus risking the erosion of your economic base, the trap into which you claim the United States has fallen.

You want to increase your overall political influence without damaging the economic base that makes efforts to increase political influence possible.

What would you do?

to the bigger battalions." In attempting to develop military power, states must pay their money and take their chances.

Although military power depends greatly on material power, traditionally it alone has been one of the main measurements of a state's capability to directly or indirectly influence world politics. Chinese leader Mao Zedong best expressed this view in his famous aphorism, "Political power grows out of the barrel of a gun." The role of military power in the New Era, however, has been brought into question by the emergence of China as a major economic player, as well as by the resurgence of Germany and Japan, both of which after World War II concentrated on economic development and did not expend massive amounts of scarce resources on defense spending. (The defense of these two states was guaranteed by reliable alliances with the United States and its allies; without them, Germany and Japan would not have been able to forsake guns for butter.)

Military power, like material power, has a number of distinct but related components. In the modern era, strategic nuclear forces have been the most dramatic measure of a state's military strength. Just as it is unwise to use machine guns to kill houseflies, nuclear weapons are not useful for all applications of military force, so the size of conventional armies remains a vital part of military capability. As the largest armies are not necessarily the most effective, military expenditure is another means for gauging military power. These aspects of military power are relatively easy to quantify, but as with material power, other components are not so easy to express but remain important to consider. These factors include training and morale, power projection, and technology.

Strategic Nuclear Forces

Since 1945 nuclear weapons have dominated military affairs, and a modern state cannot be considered a global military power if it lacks **strategic nuclear**

forces (designed to attack long-range targets, including cities). The number of strategic nuclear warheads is a convenient indicator of the size of a state's nuclear arsenal. At the end of the Cold War, the world's top five nuclear powers deployed the following number of strategic nuclear warheads:[10]

Soviet Union	11,159
United States	9,745
France	402
China	320
United Kingdom	192

Of these nations, the United States and the Soviet Union obviously had by far the largest nuclear inventories; the nuclear balance between the two superpowers was in a very real sense *the* strategic balance of the Cold War era. (In addition to strategic forces, most of the nuclear powers possess a number of **tactical nuclear weapons,** which are short- or medium-range weapons designed to be used primarily against conventional military forces.)

Shortly before the collapse of the Soviet Union, Moscow and Washington concluded the START I treaty on the reduction of their strategic nuclear forces; accordingly, both sides were allowed 1600 launchers and 6000 warheads. Then in January 1993 the United States and Russia signed START II, which provided for further cuts in their nuclear weapons arsenals. If these agreements are fully implemented, the strategic arsenals of Russia and the United States will be reduced to between 3000 and 3500 each.[11] The reductions mandated in START II are scheduled to be completed by the year 2003.

Defense Expenditures

Few states have nuclear weapons, however, and strategic nuclear forces constitute a relatively small fraction of the total defense expenditures of the states that do deploy them. By comparing defense expenditures, it is possible to see how much material power a state is attempting to convert into military might. Table 12.6 gives the top ten military spenders in 1970 and 1990.

The figures in the table indicate the massive efforts of the two superpowers to maintain military parity. Figures from disparate sources and societies are difficult to compare, but to put it in perspective, U.S. 1970 military expenditures equaled approximately two-thirds of China's GNP and a little over half that of France. That same year, Soviet military expenditures totaled 54 percent of the Chinese or British GNPs and 45 percent of France's. Twenty years later, the figures were not quite so stark, but both U.S. and USSR military spending was still equivalent to more than 20 percent of China's GNP and more than 25 percent of France's. Surprisingly, even though Japan has continued to spend only about 1 percent of its GNP on the military since World War II, and has refrained from building nuclear weapons, its military expenditures of approximately $30 billion in 1990 made it the world's seventh largest military spender.

Table 12.6   Military Expenditures, 1970 and 1990

Top Ten Countries	Total Military Spending (billions of dollars)
1970	
United States	$77.80
Soviet Union	65.00
China	10.00
West Germany	6.20
France	6.00
United Kingdom	5.90
Italy	2.50
Poland	2.20
East Germany	2.20
Canada	1.90
1990	
United States	$306.20
Soviet Union	292.00
China	50.31
West Germany	41.28
France	40.82
United Kingdom	40.66
Japan	30.25
Italy	23.29
Saudi Arabia	23.16
Kuwait	13.82

Source: *World Military Expenditures and Arms Transfers*, 1971, p. 50; and 1991–1992, pp. 36, 47–88.

Note: Figures are in current dollars.

Total military spending indicates the absolute size of a state's military efforts, but a different measure is needed to show how much of a state's total resources are being spent on arms: military expenditure as a percentage of GNP. Figure 12.2 shows the ten nations that spent the highest percentage of their total economic output on military forces in 1970 and 1990, and presents figures for the leading economic powers.

In examining this figure, note the disproportionate appearance of nations from the Middle East. Of the top ten spenders in terms of percentage of GNP in 1970, four were located in the Middle East, and four others were located in war-torn Southeast Asia. In 1990 eight of the top ten spenders were from the Middle East. These figures show that living in a "tough neighborhood" prone to violent conflict forces states to devote more resources to defense.

Numbers of Military Personnel

How much bang are these states getting for their bucks? The overall number of military personnel is another important measure of military power. It indicates

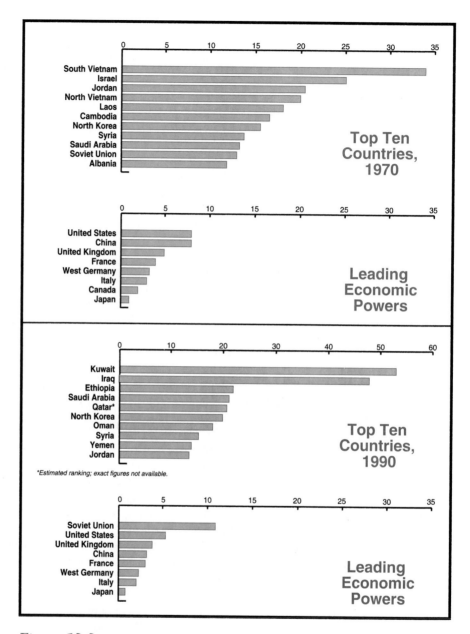

Figure 12.2   Defense Spending as Percentage of GNP, 1970 and 1990

Note: In 1970, the Soviet Union was in the top ten countries worldwide, and therefore does not appear with the other leading economic powers.

Source: *World Military Expenditures and Arms Transfers*, 1971, pp. 26–29; 1991–1992, pp. 39, 47–88.

the total strength of a nation's ground, naval, and air forces, although it does not take into account the often vital factors of quality of equipment, technology, training, morale, command and control, and leadership.

In 1990, China, the Soviet Union, and the United States maintained the largest number of armed forces—consistent with their roles as leading military powers. Nations such as Japan and Canada that depend on friendly neighbors or alliances for their security spend large amounts of money on relatively small forces, relying on quality rather than quantity of weapons and personnel to provide defense capability. Iraq, a developing country much poorer than other top military spenders, instead chose to field a large military force, and it turned out to be of dubious quality. The breakup of the Soviet Union and the downsizing of the U.S. armed forces will reduce their respective rankings, leaving China as the largest army in the world. Not surprisingly, given current world conflicts, other countries maintaining large armed forces include India and Pakistan, as well as North and South Korea.[12]

All in all, troop strength can be a poor predictor of a war's outcome. For example, in its four major wars, Israel's opponents had more troops and weapons, but Jerusalem's better trained, equipped, and organized forces consistently prevailed. In addition, common estimates of troop strength usually do not include ready reserves, which play a vital role in the defense plans of countries such as Sweden, Switzerland, and Israel. In 1991 Switzerland had only 3500 troops in its regular army, but could mobilize 625,000 soldiers within forty-eight hours.[13]

The size of nuclear and conventional forces and the amount of money spent on defense are useful numerical indicators of military power. Nevertheless, there are qualitative components of these indicators that are equally important to consider. Aggregate numbers fail to reveal the accuracy, lethality, or reliability of weapons, for example, or the skills and morale of the troops who use them. Does one Israeli tank equal one Syrian tank? Does a twenty-five-year-old plane equal one that is only five years old? How many Iraqi tanks equal an American helicopter? The same problem arises in attempts to compare nuclear weapons. During the Cold War it was hard to determine which side was ahead in nuclear capability because of the numerous ways possible of measuring the utility of nuclear warheads. Should comparisons be based on the numbers of launchers (missiles and aircraft), numbers of warheads, the yield (explosive power) of weapons, or their accuracy? Not surprisingly, by carefully choosing the indicators to examine, it was possible to argue throughout the latter years of the Cold War that either the United States or the USSR had the superior nuclear arsenal.

Training and Morale

Even if the preceding problems of measurement could be overcome, numbers could not adequately reflect some of the most important aspects of military power. The training and morale of armed forces have proven crucial to the outcome of many conflicts. In the opening campaign of the battle for North Africa during World War II, for example, 30,000 British Commonwealth troops rapidly defeated 80,000 ill-trained and poorly motivated Italian soldiers; in December 1940 the British were able to capture 39,000 prisoners in *three days*. Similarly, Allied Coalition forces in the Persian Gulf War of 1991 found that demoralized Iraqi troops surrendered almost faster than they could be captured. Small, professional forces that receive intensive training are usually far more capable than large numbers of draftees who are looking for the first opportunity to desert or surrender once combat has begun. Leadership at every level plays a critical role in the effectiveness of training and the maintenance of morale under the sometimes debilitating stress of combat. No matter how plentiful or sophisticated its weaponry, any military force is useless without adequate training for those who use the weapons, and without competent leadership from the people who direct them in battle.

Power Projection

Though they are vital to the success of any military organization, leadership and morale are notoriously difficult to measure at an aggregate level. A somewhat more tangible characteristic is **power projection.** Like police forces or fire brigades, to be successful, military forces must arrive where they are needed in time; wars are won, as one Civil War logistician put it, by the side that "gets there firstest with the mostest." States that can mobilize, supply, and transport sizable forces far from their own borders are in a position to better use military power than states that cannot. When considering power projection, then, geography becomes a major factor. States with ports and free access to sea-lanes, such as the United States or Britain, can more easily make their power felt all over the globe. Conversely, large nations with restricted access to the sea, such as Russia and China, often have difficulty getting their forces where they are needed to stop an invasion, and so must compensate by maintaining larger forces at home (which, in turn, make their neighbors nervous). The United States demonstrated the value of mobility and power projection during the Persian Gulf War of 1991, when it was the nation most capable of rapidly deploying and supplying the forces used in Operation Desert Storm.

Technology

The rapid pace of development of both nuclear and conventional weapons since World War II underscores the importance of technology to military power. During the Cold War, frequent innovations in Soviet and American strategic weaponry produced a rough technological parity between the two superpowers but at the same time broadened the gap between them and the smaller nuclear powers. The successful use of high-tech weapons and information technology in the Persian Gulf War suggests that advanced technology is likely to become increasingly important in conventional military operations as well. While the pace of technological advance has been quite dramatic since World War II, especially in aerospace and electronics, technical developments have revolutionized warfare many times over since the first time a primitive hominid picked up a rock. Historically, three aspects of technological advance have proven particularly important: breakthroughs, lead times, and cost.

Technological breakthroughs refer to the introduction of new weapons with potential capabilities so great that they require a new calculation of military strength; in such cases, if other states do not keep up with the innovator, they are quickly left behind in the competition for military power. The introduction of the machine gun in the late nineteenth and early twentieth centuries was such a breakthrough, as was the development of nuclear weapons by the United States at the end of World War II. Technological revolutions can have unpredictable effects, however. In 1906 Britain introduced the dreadnought, a new type of battleship with high-caliber guns and steam turbine engines. Dreadnoughts were so fast and powerful that older battleships quickly became obsolete. This ultimately worked to Britain's disadvantage, however, because it led to intense German efforts to achieve parity with the Royal Navy. A new naval arms race ensued, and Germany proved better able to compete in the construction of the new warships. Ultimately, the expense of conducting a naval arms race damaged the British economy almost as much as the German submarines that were eventually produced.

Although new weapons may initially seem impressive, the effect of a technological breakthrough on warfare is often not realized until a dramatic event or military disaster occurs. European armies did not realize how the machine gun would change the nature of war until the opening months of World War I, when the new weapons caused horrendous casualties and led military planners to abandon hopes for a short war. Although tactical missiles had existed for decades, the 1982 Falklands War demonstrated for the first time their devastating effect in naval combat. Argentina was able to effectively use a French-made air-launched Exocet missile (costing $200,000) to disable a British destroyer (costing $50 million). Britain eventually won the war, but the use of advanced missile technology demonstrated the vulnerability of its naval surface forces to missile attack.

Lead time is the time required between the initial decision to produce a weapon and its operational deployment. The production of weapons systems with long lead times may allow an innovator to widen (or narrow) the gap with its nearest competition, but the whole process carries with it considerable risk. For instance, it may allow a nation's closest competitor to neutralize that weapons system with an innovation of its own, or at least improve its already existing weapons. During World War II, Germany devoted substantial technological and material resources to the development of jet fighter aircraft. When the aircraft were developed and deployed, they were clearly superior to anything the Allies could put in the air. While Germany was developing the new weapons, however, the Allies concentrated on the refinement and mass production of tried-and-true designs. By the time the German jet fighters became operational, Allied superiority in numbers made the air war no contest, and Germany's advanced weapons had little impact.

A third important aspect of technological development is cost. High technology usually requires big money, and political and military leaders often face difficult decisions as to whether the new weapons will justify their increased costs. Throughout the 1980s, the increasing costs of the United States' "Star Wars" ballistic missile defense system (see Chapters Four and Eleven) threatened that program's budgetary future in Congress, especially because it was not known

Pride of the British navy, the missile-launching destroyer Sheffield *sits dead in the water with severe damage during the Falklands War. The ship was hit by a single Exocet missile fired from an Argentine air force jet.*
Source: © Sygma.

whether the system would work. Similarly, cost overruns on the B-1 and B-2 bombers led to successive controversies over whether to scale back or cancel production plans, and the United States is unlikely to ever deploy these advanced aircraft in the numbers initially proposed.

Technology is only one of several qualitative aspects that must be taken into account when evaluating a state's military power. Because quality is difficult to quantify, the military balance between states can be only a rough guide to action, and there will always be some doubt as to whether an attack or defense will succeed or fail. This uncertainty is not necessarily detrimental; arguably, the great uncertainties inherent in the U.S.–Soviet strategic balance was one of the factors that helped prevent the Cold War from erupting into nuclear war. A leading historian of the Cold War, John Lewis Gaddis, has observed that military force has lost much of its former utility in international relations.[14] He may be right, but the continued prevalence of violent conflict in the New Era suggests that force will continue to be a major factor in world politics.

MOTIVATIONAL POWER

Motivational power refers to the willingness of a government to take an active part in world affairs and its determination to see that conflicts are resolved in its favor. In the broadest sense, it is the ability to translate goals and resources into concrete actions. A state may have considerable material assets, but if it cannot successfully convert them into armed might, foreign aid, cultural programs, foreign investment and trade, effective propaganda, or any other instrument of foreign policy, then its ability to act in foreign affairs is limited. For example, in the tumultuous 1920s and 1930s, the materially powerful United States could have had a far greater say in world politics if it had chosen to participate more actively, but the Senate refused to allow the United States to join the League of Nations and end its isolationist course. On the other hand, as China and Israel have demonstrated in the past, a lower level of material power can be offset in part by a strong willingness to act assertively in foreign affairs. But it can be offset only in part. Neither Italy under Mussolini nor Indonesia under Sukarno's 1949–1967 rule was able to surmount material and military deficiencies to accomplish foreign policy goals. In the 1980s Libyan leader Gadhafi's fiery rhetoric and willingness to support acts of terrorism did not prevent the United States from downing Libyan fighter planes and bombing Libyan territory in retaliation. Libya had oil and forceful leadership, but little else; in this case, strong motivation plus limited means did not equal major influence in international politics.

In analyzing motivational power, it is useful to distinguish between its passive and active elements. The passive components consist of circumstances, vulnerabilities, notions of national identity, and the "burden of history" that can act to "pull" nations onto or off the international scene, even when, from a national perspective, this activity might be contrary to the state's best interests. Such passive elements of motivational power include historical experience, internal divisions, and political culture. The active elements, on the other hand, may be thought of as the initiative, determination, and energy that can be mobilized to "push" a state into the global political arena. These aspects of motivational power include regime type, leadership, government efficiency, ideology, and public opinion.

Passive Elements of Motivational Power

The first passive element to be considered is the history of a state, which can have an impact on its foreign policy regardless of the nature of the regime or the leaders in power. For instance, a former empire or recently unified state might have a different outlook on its role in the world than a state that has suffered through a history of partition or persecution. Many recently unified states, like China after 1949, Germany in 1870, and Vietnam after 1975, have demonstrated greater willingness to assert themselves in the affairs of other countries. China intervened in the Korean War in 1950, Germany invaded and occupied adjacent states in the world wars, and Vietnam invaded Cambodia in 1978. On the other hand, countries once unified but then truncated or partitioned, like Poland from the late eighteenth century to 1918, China before 1949, and Germany before 1870 and from 1945 to 1990, have concerned themselves first and foremost with survival or reunification.

In addition to history, underlying internal divisions may be a factor in determining what a particular regime seeks to accomplish. These divisions may be either political, as in El Salvador or Peru; ethnic-linguistic, as in Canada, Belgium,

Malaysia, and Yugoslavia; religious, as in Lebanon; or a combination of all three, as in Northern Ireland and India.

Serious internal cleavages need not prevent a state from taking an active part in world politics, however. India's various ethnic and religious divisions have embroiled its leaders in various internal and external conflicts and have periodically erupted into violence, but India remained a leader in the nonaligned movement throughout the Cold War, and has become the dominant regional power in South Asia. The stable parliamentary systems of Canada and Belgium have accommodated ethnic-linguistic divisions peacefully, although Canada now faces a separatist movement from predominantly French-speaking Quebec and pressure for autonomy from Native American groups. As in India, the Canadian and Belgian divisions have not been so self-absorbing as to prevent those two countries from playing active roles in international economic and political institutions such as in the G7 and EU, respectively.

A state's political culture can also influence foreign policy. The notions of a Russian fatherland, Arab unity, or special ties between members of the British Commonwealth or the French Community may motivate states to strengthen political ties. The dialectic between intervention and isolation in American political culture, and what the great nineteenth century French analyst, Alexis de Tocqueville identified as a "pronounced streak of self-righteousness" have frequently set the terms for debate over American foreign policy. Similar traits include the Japanese assertion of their unique society, a Russian tradition of grandiose gestures or actions, and an Arab penchant for equating the desired with the achieved. The net effect—and even identification—of these characteristics remains controversial and difficult to measure. Nonetheless, factors of political culture undoubtedly shape assumptions of national interest, the domestic environment in which foreign policy is formulated, and perceptions of other countries' motives.

Active Elements of Motivational Power

The active elements in motivational power are often easier to observe. The changes in a state's foreign policy brought about by a change in **regime type** illustrate the importance of the goals and ambitions of national leadership. Authoritarian states that become democratic, or vice versa, often alter their foreign policy goals and switch alliances with bewildering speed. For example, in the 1920s the Weimar Republic (the ill-fated democratic regime set up in Germany after World War I) frequently cooperated with the Soviet Union on economic and security issues, but when the Nazi Party came to power in Germany in 1933, Berlin and Moscow became instant enemies (see Chapter Three). Similarly, when Poland, Hungary, and Czechoslovakia replaced their Communist regimes in 1989, they quickly pushed for the dissolution of the Warsaw Pact and expressed a desire to join the EU.

Regime type can affect foreign policy even when dramatic changes in government type do not occur. As will be discussed in Chapter Fourteen, the world's democracies rarely fight wars amongst themselves, while nondemocratic states fight both with democracies and with one another.

Even if the type of government remains the same, individual leaders can have a profound effect on the ability of a state to transform resources into power. Chapter Fifteen will have much more to say about this; for now, it is sufficient to note that the personalities and beliefs of leading statesmen can profoundly influence foreign policy decisions and the ability of states to achieve their goals in the international system. Charismatic nationalists such as Bolívar, Ataturk, Nehru, and Nasser became symbols of national unity. As a result, they were able to create the political and social unity that allowed their nations to engage in activist foreign policies, at least while they were alive. Napoléon, Bismarck, and Stalin all combined ideology, concepts of national identity, and individual idiosyncrasies and experiences to help shape the international system in their lifetimes. Such leaders are the individual embodiment of motivational power.

The impulse to take an active role in world affairs is not confined only to the highest levels of government, however; even the most charismatic leaders can do little if the administrative apparatus backing them up is uncooperative or inefficient. Administrative efficiency and effectiveness is an overlooked but important element of motivational power. The ability to convert potential strengths into real power also depends upon the capability, energy, and loyalty of the numerous individuals who staff government bureaucracies, and the structure and functioning of those organizations responsible for international affairs. The methods by which a government coordinates its physical and human resources may not be as "glamorous" as a state's political leadership or armed forces, but they remain important to the success or failure of a nation in the international arena. In a similar context, the members of the EU have found it difficult to play an activist role in the world because EU policy must be both coordinated and implemented by a large, slow-moving army of "Eurocrats" who often favor the interests of their native countries.

While leadership might be the most important single factor in determining motivational power, and while administrative efficiency can make a major difference as well, public support for foreign policy objectives is also an important factor to consider. In both democratic and nondemocratic societies, motivational power can be affected as much by the willingness of individuals to bear the costs of foreign involvement as by the skill of political leaders and bureaucrats in making and implementing good decisions. In looking at the United States' ability to conduct activist policies, one can see that the American public has a low "pain index," meaning a low tolerance for policies that might lead to many American casualties. The failure of U.S. policy in Vietnam is often cited as an example by those who argue that America could not win the Vietnam War because Hanoi was more willing to sacrifice Vietnamese than Washington was to lose American lives.

In general, a nation's citizens are usually willing to make greater sacrifices to repel an aggressor than to expand a state's power and influence. Also, ambiguous, controversial, or poorly articulated goals are less likely to persuade citizens that pain is necessary for gain. In 1990 the governments of those states opposed to the Iraqi occupation of Kuwait were careful to mobilize public support for the use of force to expel Iraqi forces before actually doing so. Even then, because the U.S. government feared that the American public would not support the war if it caused many American casualties, its subsequent strategy relied heavily on high-tech weaponry and a short, rapid ground offensive after massive aerial bombardment. It should be noted that for the last several decades presidents have tended to avoid public debate before committing American troops to combat; the Congressional debate on whether to go to war with Iraq was the first of its kind since the United States entered World War I in 1917.

The final active element of motivational power is **ideology.** The type of ideology a state espouses is usually linked to the type of regime that governs it. For example, Communist states generally promulgate some form of Marxism, while theocratic Iran dedicated itself to the promotion of Islamic fundamentalism. Ideology helps to shape (and sometimes limit) a government's worldview, goals, and policy options. After World War II Stalin's adherence to the tenets of Soviet socialism led to a lopsided concentration on military-related industries, which made many outside observers suspicious and exacerbated the U.S.–Soviet security dilemma (see Chapters Four and Eleven).

In another example, the Iranian revolution that overthrew the Shah and brought the Ayatollah Khomeini to power in 1979 also resulted in the dramatic reversal of decades of Iranian partnership with the United States, denounced by Khomeini as "the Great Satan." The seizure and 444-day occupation of the U.S. Embassy in Teheran (with American hostages inside), poisoned Iran's relations with most of the West and created an image of the Iranian regime as a threat to political stability in the Middle East that had to be contained. Iran's subsequent difficult relations with much of the world is just one example of how governments that attempt to wield the power of ideas often find them to be a double-edged sword.

Measuring Motivational Power

Clearly, because numerical values cannot be assigned to intangible factors such as charisma, determination, legitimacy, or revolutionary zeal, it is difficult to use quantitative means for measuring motivational power. Still, there are other quantitative indices that may give an impression of a state's motivation in translating resources into influence. One such indicator is the percentage of GNP spent on defense, discussed in the previous section on military power and illustrated in Figure 12.2 on page 570. A state that appears willing to devote a large percentage of its economic output to enhance military strength signals to other states its determination and ability to play a significant role (if necessary) in influencing others.

Just as military spending is a signal that a state is willing to coerce adversaries, economic aid is a sign that a state is willing to win friends and influence people. A state persuades another state to do something that it would not otherwise do through either the threat of punishment or the offer of reward, and nations willing to spend big money on international affairs can offer big rewards. States offer aid for economic development in hopes of persuading the recipient to cooperate with the donor's policies, or they extend security assistance or military aid to promote cooperation against a common enemy. Aid is used to influence the attitudes and policies of adversaries as well as neutrals or allies. One

Iranians reach out to touch the Ayatollah Khomeini in February 1979. Returning from exile two days earlier, Khomeini took control of the new revolutionary government in Teheran to rule Iran according to fundamentalist Islamic principles.

Source: © UPI/Bettmann.

NATIONAL DREAMS AND NATIONALIST NIGHTMARES

Nationalism has proven to be one of the strongest elements of motivational power. Chapter Two described how German and Italian political leaders in the nineteenth century harnessed the ideological force of nationalism to bring about the unification of their respective nations despite vehement opposition by other European powers. After independence, the presence of minorities of a state's own nationality in neighboring states can be a powerful influence on foreign policy if leaders feel a responsibility to safeguard the rights of their ethnic brothers and sisters. The governments of Greece and Turkey both feel the need to protect their kinsmen in nearby Cyprus, as does the Republic of Ireland (Erie) in Northern Ireland and India in Sri Lanka. Russia feels the same about the former republics of the Soviet Union. The perceived duty to protect one's own nationals in foreign countries has contributed to ethnic conflicts in all of these areas.

Nationalism can also be used as an excuse for expansionism. Hitler used German nationalism to justify the forcible

of the United States' objectives in establishing détente with the Soviet Union was to create economic and cultural ties between the United States and the USSR in order to lessen the incentives for conflict; another was to open channels for influence over Soviet policy by threatening to cut off access to Western capital and technology.

During the Cold War, both superpowers sought to gain the cooperation of strategically important countries by providing generous donations of arms and other military aid as well as economic assistance. However, there were other, more subtle forms of competition. To understand these attempts to gain greater influence in international affairs, we can compare the assistance provided by OECD and OPEC countries in 1965 and 1990.

While the United States was unquestionably the largest aid donor in 1965 among these countries, France and Japan came close to surpassing it in 1990. This reflects a change in the balance of economic power: While the United States was clearly the world's economic leader in 1965, the EU and Japan were better able to capitalize on their increased economic strength twenty-five years later. In an even more dramatic development, Saudi Arabia emerged as a major aid donor, ranking first among these countries in the percentage of GNP it was prepared to devote to economic assistance. The high levels of effort by Saudi Arabia, the United Arab Emirates, and Norway—countries whose economies are nowhere near the G7 states—reflect their determination to play a role in world politics by promoting economic growth in the developing world. An examination of the percentage of GNP spent on economic aid from 1965 to 1991 also shows that the United States, the United Kingdom, and Japan had fallen out of the top ten, replaced by several smaller European and Middle Eastern nations. (Increasingly preoccupied with domestic problems, the United States devoted incorporation of Austria and the Sudeten-land of Czechoslovakia into Germany in 1938. Similarly, after the breakup of Yugoslavia in 1991, many Serbian leaders pushed for the creation of a "Greater Serbia" at the expense of Bosnia and other former Yugoslav republics.

There is marked disagreement over whether nationalism is a primordial force that pushes states into wars of national unification, or merely a convenient sentiment that ambitious leaders can manipulate in order to mobilize public support for their goals, peaceful or otherwise. The use of nationalism for aggressive ends has repeatedly confirmed English author Samuel Johnson's observation that "patriotism is the last refuge of the scoundrel." On the other hand, while nationalist ideologies have helped to fan the flames of many of the world's bloodiest conflicts, it is also clear that nationalism can be a positive force for political, economic, and social development. Because of its wide range of consequences, nationalism is a force that should not be ignored.

0.20 percent of its GNP to development assistance in 1991, behind all OECD countries except Ireland.)[15]

Imprecise as they are, numerical indices of motivational power provide an inkling of the relative determination of countries to exercise influence in the international system. Other, lesser used indicators to measure motivational power include visits abroad by leading officials, hours of government-sponsored radio and television broadcasting beamed across borders, and numbers of military or economic advisors stationed abroad. As with military spending, however, all of these measures are better indicators of effort than results, as aid recipients may simply accept assistance and ignore attempts by donors to influence their policies. The net effect of the "pull" of historical, cultural, and ethnic ties and the "push" exerted by leaders determined to carve out a place in history for their nations is hard to measure with any degree of precision; nevertheless, it is undeniable that these factors affect and help shape international relations. Regardless of its source, motivational power in international politics is in essence a measure of the will to win. In politics, just as in athletics, ability is useless without determination. And as in many other areas, competitors for leadership in world politics soon discover that nothing succeeds like success.

REPUTATION

"Reputation of power, is power; because it draweth with it the adherence of those who need protection . . . good success is power; because it maketh reputation of wisdom, or good fortune; which makes men either fear him, or rely on him."[16] Thomas Hobbes came to this conclusion over three centuries ago,

THE ROUGH RIDER

Though material power often translates into political influence, a state that becomes economically strong does not automatically achieve the influence and status commensurate with its economic might. Often, visionary leadership is necessary in order for a nation to realize its potential for global power.

Though America was by some indices the strongest country in the world at the start of the twentieth century, it took the vision and drive of Theodore Roosevelt (1858–1919) to make it a truly global power. Teddy Roosevelt (second cousin to later U.S. President Franklin D. Roosevelt) made up for a frail and sickly childhood by adopting a competitive outlook and aggressive personality. He wanted to be involved in everything and to take charge of as much as he could; one friend remarked that Roosevelt felt compelled to be "the center of every stage, the bride at every wedding, the corpse at every funeral." His hard-charging manner earned him rapid success in law and politics, and as secretary of the navy under President William McKinley, he argued for war with Spain over Cuba. When the Spanish-American War broke out in 1898, Roosevelt resigned his cabinet post to form a regiment of volunteer cavalry that became known as the "Rough Riders." He became a national hero with his impulsive leadership of the unit in Cuba.

After the war, Roosevelt was elected McKinley's vice president in 1900 and took over as president in 1901 after McKinley was assassinated. In his two terms, Roosevelt was an activist leader both at home and abroad. He championed the regulation of railroads and other powerful industrial interests, enforced antitrust legislation, and vastly expanded the system of National Parks and National Forests to protect America's environment and natural resources.

but it remains a valid description of the role of reputation in international politics. Reputation refers to a nation's track record in world affairs—its perceived ability to accomplish the goals it sets for itself. More than any other single component of power, reputation is determined by factors outside the control of a particular government. As a result, reputation sometimes reflects the operation of chance; where in a few instances events turn out favorably, a state is able to build the impression of momentum and use it to its own advantage.

Success must be assessed in relation to a government's resources and objectives. Countries like Brazil, Sweden, and Switzerland have limited aims in international affairs relative to their material and military power, and thus can point with pride to a string of modest foreign policy achievements. On the other hand, nations such as Iraq and Libya, whose objectives have been much more ambitious, have greater difficulty in establishing a reputation for success. As long as a nation's reach exceeds its grasp, that nation's reputation will not be one of success. This in itself is not necessarily bad, as many objectives are worth striving for even if they are not completely attained, but the audience to which leaders must play is often an unforgiving one—at

It was through his foreign policy, however, that Roosevelt led America to make its greatest impact on the world to that point. During his presidency, the United States followed an interventionist policy in Central and South America, breaking Panama off from Colombia and building the Panama Canal. He initiated a peace conference at Portsmouth, New Hampshire in 1905, which successfully ended the Russo-Japanese War. Roosevelt's critical mediation between the two sides earned him the 1906 Nobel Peace Prize, gained America new respect worldwide, and asserted an important U.S. role in Asia. By participating in the Algeciras conference called to resolve the Moroccan Crisis in 1906, the United States took its first steps toward involvement in European affairs. In keeping with his oft-quoted aphorism, "Speak softly, but carry a big stick," Roosevelt maintained an official policy of neutrality toward the major European powers but ordered a contingent of U.S. Navy ships, called the "Great White Fleet," to sail around the world to demonstrate American military prowess and technology.

Roosevelt's heavy-handed policy in Latin America established a pattern of American military hegemony in the Western Hemisphere that continues to the present day. Despite the controversy over his policies, Theodore Roosevelt will be remembered as the president who made the United States a major world power. He will also be remembered in a gentler manner: The small toy bears he handed out to guests at a White House dinner became an instant hit with children. The rough-and-ready statesman, big-game hunter, and conservationist thus lent his name to the teddy bear.

home and abroad. There are three main avenues by which states derive power from reputation: military victory, economic achievement, and ideology or moral example.

A reputation for military success or failure powerfully influences the future willingness of decision makers to act in foreign affairs. While American foreign policy in the 1950s and 1960s was influenced by America's leading role in World War II, America's more reluctant outlook on global affairs since the 1970s has been shaped by the Vietnam debacle. The "no more Vietnams" imperative limited American options in the Lebanese Civil War (1982), the Gulf War (1991), Somalia (1992–1994), and the war following the breakup of Yugoslavia (after 1991).

States need not fight wars to benefit from their military reputations. A most useful aspect of reputation is a demonstrated willingness to employ force. In many cases, this credibility alone will be sufficient to accomplish the intended results. Particularly for a state pursuing a strategy of deterrence, success will be a product not only of tangible capability, but also of its past behavior and its image. These factors will influence an adversary's calculus on the expected utility of an attack. With this in mind, Israel has deliberately pursued a policy of harsh retaliation in order to foster a reputation for toughness and determination in the eyes of its adversaries. It has gained a reputation for success by prevailing over its enemies more often than expected, given its deficiencies in material and military power. Conversely, a widespread belief that a state is unwilling to use force frequently leads to the necessity of doing so. Argentina's belief that Britain would not be willing to fight for the Falklands in 1982 was proven wrong when London decided to recapture the island chain. If Britain's reputation had been stronger beforehand, however, Argentina would have been less likely to invade the Falklands in the first place. In this case, London's use of force resulted from a perception of weakness.

Clearly, it is most advantageous to actually succeed in order to gain the reputation for success. But since no regime accomplishes all its aims, those that are skillful in creating the appearance of success are more likely to achieve future objectives than those who fail to put a positive "spin" on events. Two examples are Egypt's Gamal Abdel Nasser, who was able to enhance his reputation and influence by surviving through Egypt's losses in the 1956 Suez War and the 1967 Six-Day War, and Iraq's Saddam Hussein, whose very survival of the Persian Gulf War allowed him to claim victory, given that his regime was not destroyed by the coalition's superior military force.

States can gain reputations through peaceful efforts as well as war. Economic success can be as important as military victories, if not more so. The prestige of South Korea, Singapore, and Taiwan have risen enormously because of their economic advances and ability to assist other states. Capitalist South Korea, although starting with a smaller industrial base than its Communist northern counterpart, now serves as a major model for other developing countries because of its rapid economic growth, while North Korea appears increasingly backward. For many years, Taiwan's economic accomplishments created a favorable reputation relative to its main adversary, the People's Republic of China. Today, China's vast population, resources, and economic reforms challenge Taiwan's achievements. Although a small city-state, Singapore's economic accomplishments have created an aura of success disproportionate to its material and military resources.

A state's reputation may be based on ideology or moral standing as well as material and military achievements. Countries that promote ideologies found objectionable by others make it difficult to build a reputation for credibility and trust. In many cases, of course, a state's reputation for immorality or unpredictability is well-deserved. Notoriously brutal regimes, such as that of the Khmer Rouge in Cambodia in the 1970s, may win few friends even among ideologically like-minded states, as Cambodia discovered when Communist Vietnam invaded it in 1978. Few states can claim to be paragons of moral virtue, but nations such as Switzerland, which has remained neutral since 1815, Sweden, which devotes a comparatively large percentage of its GNP to development aid, and Norway, which played a crucial role in mediating the Palestinian-Israeli breakthrough in 1993, create reputations for generosity and impartiality that are then used to further their international aims.

At one point in his presidency, Lyndon Johnson underwent a surgical procedure and later displayed his scar to the news media. Here, the scar is shaped like Vietnam, suggesting the war's devastating impact on 1960s America.

Source: © Drawing by David Levine. Reprinted with permission from *The New York Review of Books.* Copyright © 1967 Nyrev, Inc.

Regardless of how achieved, a nation's reputation can do much to enhance or reduce the power provided by material resources, military force, and motivation. Reputations are relatively often short-lived, however. In the 1950s many Third World leaders looked to the USSR as a model for their own development, an attitude that began to change in the mid-1960s and was gone by the time the

Soviet Union collapsed in 1991. Because fame is so fleeting, reputation is the most perishable element of power. Nations that repeatedly accomplish their goals can capitalize on their reputations to ride a wave of success that their material, military, and motivational strength might not have been able to generate. States that encounter setbacks, however, are likely to discover that their former glory counts for little, especially when their enemies begin to doubt their credibility and their allies ask, "What have you done for me lately?"

POTENTIAL FOR POWER

All elements of a state's power exist in both potential and actual forms. The calculations of governments concerning their own strength and that of other states must always take into account what elements of power a government has at its disposal and what elements it can expect to have in the foreseeable and distant future. Often states are treated with respect or disdain not out of regard for their present strengths, but rather because of their potential for power. Potential has figured largely, for example, in appraisals of resource-rich states like Russia, Brazil, China, and India. Of course, potential is not always realized, and significant effort is required to turn potential into capability. Nevertheless, the potential for each of the four basic elements of power—material, military, motivational, and reputation—must be included in any estimate of a country's strengths and of that of its rivals.

Material Potential: Growth versus Decline

An analysis of material potential requires identifying and projecting economic trends within a nation, especially regarding access to goods, resources, and capital. An evaluation of a nation's potential material power is therefore an estimate of its ability to take advantage of the territorial, technological, and human resources available to it.

Developing countries like Brazil might improve their future standing in world affairs by means of internal developments in material power, reflected in indicators such as increased labor productivity, growth of GNP, and exploitation and conservation of resources. Potential for material strength is an especially important factor in calculations of power within regional systems where most of the main players are newly industrialized or developing countries. In the Arab-Israeli context, for example, frequent arguments concerning the likelihood of stability in the area revolve around the ability of Arab states to realize their economic potential in time to overcome handicaps such as overpopulation and scarcity of water. Similarly in Southeast Asia, Thailand, Vietnam, and Indonesia keep watchful eyes on one another's success in developing their considerable human and territorial resources.

Economic growth may bring political problems, however, which can hamper a state's ability to achieve its international goals. The early stages of industrialization have historically led to greater economic inequality, which sometimes creates social dislocation and even political instability. At the same time, rapid industrialization frequently means accelerated depletion of natural resources and increased environmental degradation, both of which may reduce a state's material power or its quality of life in the long run.

The potential for growth is not the only factor in calculating material power; the potential for decline is an equally important consideration, especially among industrialized countries. As with growth, material decline may be measured in absolute or relative terms. A state may continue to increase its total output while its rate of growth is less than that of its rivals (as was generally the case with the United States from 1970 to 1990). Occasionally, material power may decline absolutely; most industrialized countries suffered a net decline during the global depression of the 1930s, which decreased political stability and heightened the potential for military conflict throughout the world. The Soviet Union also experienced an absolute decline in the three years prior to its 1991 collapse.

Military: Active versus Reserve

Potential military power refers to the ability to mobilize personnel and equipment. Calculation of maximum military potential must include a nation's ability to convert its economy to a war footing, and to increase troop strength through conscription (the draft). Because of the time needed to organize military industry and put military forces into action, military potential must be considered over three time scales. The first, termed rapid-reaction strength, measures the ability to mobilize and transport forces within a matter of days, hours, or minutes if they are required in an acute crisis or are needed to repel a surprise attack. Standing armies, rapid-deployment forces, and nuclear forces maintained at a high degree of readiness fall into this category of military potential. The second time scale is called ready reserves and refers to forces that have been trained and can be put into action in a matter of weeks. Finally, sustained mobilized strength refers to the ability to be prepared for both anticipated and unexpected conflicts over a longer, extended period of time. The maintenance of sustained military potential was a critical factor in the conventional arms facet of the Cold War, and it continues to be of importance in the Middle East and South Asia. Overall, then, potential military power must be assessed in the light of a state's ability to mobilize its strength immediately, within a short time span, or over a prolonged period of war or peace.

Potential military strength, especially in terms of sustained mobilized strength, is a reflection of a nation's potential material power. The United States' great industrial potential was a decisive factor in winning World War II, for example. Production figures for aircraft illustrate how the United States was able to mobilize its potential military power. In 1939 the United States was producing 5856 fighter planes a year; in 1941, the year the United States entered the war, it was producing 26,000. By 1944, the year of the Allied invasion of Europe, American production reached 96,000, or one aircraft every five minutes.[17]

As the Second World War also demonstrated, the gap between potential and actual military power can be significant and mobilization of strategic assets to full capacity can take years. In a long war, military potential may prove more important than the strength of military forces at the start of the conflict, a fact that careless or overconfident aggressors have discovered to their chagrin many times.

Motivational: Dynamism versus Stagnation

Motivational potential involves the potential for change in policy, or in the interests that shape it. Passive elements such as the burden of history, national identity, or ethnic affinity tend to change very slowly, and even dramatic developments often change culture or the perception of history only gradually. Many argue that ever since Vietnam, the United States has lost its desire for large-scale military interventions in international conflicts, even after America's lopsided victory in Desert Storm.

The active elements of motivational power can change in a relatively brief period. The extent of bureaucratic or leadership change, for example, influences whether or not a change in regime alters the will to act in foreign affairs. Changes in the top echelon of leadership usually leads to a radically new foreign policy only when new government institutions are created or the balance of power between existing ones is changed. Revolutions, on the other hand, almost always lead to dramatic changes in motivational power; the best examples are France after 1789 and Russia after 1917.

Unforeseen events outside a state can alter the motivational direction of a particular government in less dramatic fashion. The Suez Crisis of 1956 spurred French efforts to seek a role in world affairs independent of the United States, and dampened the will of the British government to remain actively involved in the region. The crisis of 1958 between China and Taiwan, which was focused on the islands of Quemoy and Matsu, increased Chinese efforts to pursue goals independent of the USSR. On the other hand, the brief Sino-Indian war of 1962 led India to concentrate on self-defense at the expense of efforts to become a global political force.

Any assessment of potential change in motivational power must include an analysis of internal political and social cohesion. Truman's advocacy of Communist containment as a moral crusade equivalent to the war against Nazi Germany helped forge an interventionist, anticommunist consensus in U.S. foreign policy. Defeat in the Vietnam conflict, however, dissolved the American consensus in favor of activist intervention abroad. The disintegration of the Soviet Union and the threat of further fragmentation of Russia has forced Moscow to scale back its international commitments drastically. Similarly, regimes that have appeared overdue for revolution or radical change, such as those of Kim Jong Il in North Korea and Fidel Castro in Cuba, lose the potential for motivational power through internal stagnation or the expectation that an upcoming change in government might result in a fundamental change in the state's interests and objectives.

Reputation: Success versus Failure

Because success and failure in international affairs often hinges on short-term developments and on the actions of other actors in the international system, as well as luck, the potential for reputation is inherently difficult to assess. Potential reputation also depends on context (that is, whether a state's role in global or regional affairs is under consideration). For example, if a strong state is perceived to have become too powerful, other states may turn to other sources of support or band together to resist domination. One of the reasons the Arab Gulf states aligned with Iraq during the Iran-Iraq war (1981–1988) was that they feared Iran, but after Iraq invaded Kuwait in 1990, they turned to the United States out of fear of their former ally. Hence, changes in political alignments can significantly alter expectations of gains and losses.

A state's potential for continued success is often assessed, fairly or unfairly, through historical analogy to other states. Since Britain lost its status as the world's leading economic power, both its influence on world affairs and its growth rate compared to its major rivals have continued to decline. Will the United States suffer a similar fate now that Japan and the EU challenge it for economic leadership? Will China follow the same path of democratization, and consequently disintegration, as the USSR? Or will it become a new economic superstar like Japan? Will Argentina and Brazil preserve their democratic systems, or will national emergencies lead to a backslide into authoritarianism, as in Peru? Will Thailand become the next South Korea? All of these nations might prefer to be judged on their own merits, but comparisons with other states, past and present, will inevitably arise. The perceived potential for a state to achieve or maintain a reputation for getting its way in world politics depends not only on its own successes and failures, but on the triumphs and tragedies experienced by other nations long ago and far away.

THE GREAT POWERS

Throughout most of history, observers of the international system have identified a certain group of states to be in a "class by themselves." These states are commonly referred to as the great powers because they compete with one another for power and influence at a level that non–great powers cannot match. While attainment of great-power status has traditionally been acknowledged by mutual recognition (that is, a state is recognized as a great power because the other great powers agree that it is), there are more precise definitions to consider. Some of these overlap, but most emphasize different aspects of power.

One characteristic that defines the great powers is global reach. As mentioned earlier, not all states have significant interests in all parts of the world, and fewer still have the capacity to protect those interests when they are threatened. One possible definition of a **great power,** therefore, is a state that possesses, exercises, and defends interests throughout the globe. A second characteristic is power level. The level of power used to determine great-power status may be quantitative, such as a certain size of GNP or armed forces, or qualitative, such as industrialization or demonstration of the capability to make and use nuclear weapons.

A third way to define the great powers is by institutional recognition. International organizations like the League of Nations and United Nations have recognized certain states as having special powers and responsibilities for maintaining international peace and security by giving these nations particular positions of authority (for example, there are five permanent members of the UN Security Council). While this method allows the great powers to be identified with legalistic precision and emphasizes the positive contribution each can make to world peace, there have been other states that were perhaps just as powerful but did not receive special recognition. The United States refused to join the League of Nations, for example, and the People's Republic of China was left off the UN Security Council for three decades.

Regardless of how one defines the great powers, the same set of states will usually fit each definition at any given time. As the sources of power change over time, however, some nations will acquire great-power status while others will lose it. This process is the subject of Paul Kennedy's *The Rise and Fall of the Great Powers*, and Kenneth Waltz's *Theory of International Politics*, both of which should be required reading for any serious student of world politics. In Waltz's list of the great powers from 1700 to 1979 (see Table 12.7), several interesting trends can be seen. First, while several states have been able to maintain great-power status over a period of centuries, the membership roster of the great-power club has constantly changed. Second, until the twentieth century, club membership was exclusively European and since 1900 it has become increasingly less so. Third, although China, France, and Britain also became permanent members of the UN Security Council in 1945, only the United States and Soviet Union were considered great powers after World War II.

The reader is invited to develop his or her own list of the great powers in the New Era. Should the permanent member states of the UN Security Council be included? What about Germany and Japan, who have become leading economic powers since the end of World War II? Will the EU develop as a future superpower, despite its current internal travails? Does recent Chinese economic growth suggest it is no longer a "sleeping giant"? Does Russia, the world's largest geographic nation and nuclear great power, deserve to belong to the club, even in its current state of political and economic disorganization? Or should its place be taken by Third World nations with future economic potential, like India and Brazil? Perhaps only the United States, as the "one remaining superpower," deserves the title of world leader. How you answer these questions and resolve the ambiguities they present will reveal a great deal about your perception of power in the New Era.

CONCLUSION: THE SEARCH FOR INFLUENCE IN THE SOURCES OF POWER

Influence in global politics may be gained through material power, military power, motivational power, or reputation. States possessing these elements of power usually rise to positions of leadership in world affairs, and any state's likelihood of resolving conflicts in its favor is largely dependent on the level of power it can bring to bear. However, since the Peace of Westphalia established the concept of sovereignty under international law (see Chapter Nine), the world has not been governed by

Table 12.7   The Great Powers, 1700–1979

Nation or empire	Ranked among great powers in year:					
	1700	*1800*	*1875*	*1910*	*1935*	*1945*
Turkey/Ottoman Empire	X					
Sweden	X					
Netherlands	X					
Spain	X					
Austria/Austria-Hungary	X	X	X	X		
France	X	X	X	X	X	
England/Britain	X	X	X	X	X	
Prussia/Germany		X	X	X	X	
Russia/USSR		X	X	X	X	X
Italy			X	X	X	
Japan				X	X	
United States				X	X	X

Source: Kenneth Waltz, *Theory of International Politics* (New York: Random House, 1979), p. 162.

naked power alone. As we have seen repeatedly throughout this book, the great powers have failed many times to prevail over less powerful states in times of conflict. Indeed, you could take the position that great-power status is a relic of a Eurocentric and violent past, an anachronism in the New Era, especially if international law will be able to resolve disputes by right rather than might.

If this is true, it would indicate that power is losing its relevance to international politics. Before jumping to this conclusion, however, look at domestic politics within democratic states. Although these political systems usually operate according to well-developed legal codes and institutions, by the laws in their statute books rather than the law of the jungle, power in various forms still matters a great deal within them. In fact, power remains vitally necessary for achieving any societal goal and preserving it once attained. For better or worse, power is an integral part of politics at any level. Insofar as politics is the art of the possible, in international politics nothing is possible without power.

PRINCIPAL POINTS OF CHAPTER TWELVE

1. In international politics, power may be defined as the ability of one actor to influence another to do what the other would not otherwise have done.

2. The four basic elements of power in the international system are material power, military power, motivational power, and reputation.

3. Material power includes the following:

   a. Territory, comprising geography (including defensive terrain and proximity to trade routes) and natural resources (arable land, minerals, oil, and so on).

    b. Population—preferably neither too large nor too small—including educational level and skilled labor force.

    c. Trade and industry (measured by GNP) per capita income, growth rate, and industrial technology).

4. Military power encompasses strategic nuclear forces, power-projection capabilities, size of conventional armed forces, weapons technology, and training and morale of military personnel.

5. Motivational power is divisible into active and passive elements:

    a. Passive elements include historical experience, internal cohesion or division, ethnic and linguistic diversity or conflict, and nationalism.

    b. Active elements of motivational power include leadership, regime type, public support for foreign policy goals, and ideology.

6. A state's reputation for success in global politics is enhanced by its demonstrated military prowess, moral standing, initiative and leadership on global issues, and willingness to take risks or make sacrifices in support of national goals.

7. Each element of power exists in potential as well as actualized form:

    a. Economic growth potential, reserve military capabilities, political dynamism, and leadership potential can add to a state's power in the international system.

    b. Conversely, expectations that a nation's material or military power will decline, that its political system will stagnate, and that it will ignore or bungle opportunities to take a leading role will all reduce its status and influence in world politics.

8. Great-power status indicates that a state is widely regarded as a leader in global politics—roughly equivalent to other great powers and more powerful than other states.

9. Different states have been recognized as great powers at different points in time. Historically, great-power status has usually been acknowledged by mutual recognition, but several characteristics may be used as qualifying criteria:

    a. Global reach (possession of interests all over the world and the ability to protect them).

    b. Power level, either quantitative (ranking by GNP or size of armed forces) or qualitative (such as industrialization or development of nuclear weapons).

    c. Institutional recognition (such as a permanent seat on the UN Security Council).

Levels of Analysis

Chapter 13

The International Systemic Level of Analysis

It is true that a union among sovereign bodies is a very difficult thing to accomplish. If you take fourteen grains of sand on the seashore and put them in your hand and attempt to make a ball of them, you would not be trying anything more difficult than to get fourteen independent nations working together for a common purpose.

But we do know that we can go to another part of the countryside, get a bit of rock, make some cement from it, and then—out of those fourteen grains of sand—create something that is practically indestructible.

Dwight D. Eisenhower, quoted in "Eisenhower: Rekindling the Spirit of the West" by Stephen E. Ambrose with Morris Honick in Robert S. Jordan, ed., *Generals in International Politics* (Lexington, KY: University Press of Kentucky, 1987), p. 9.

How can we describe an international system? States compete and they cooperate; they go to war and they enter into alliances. In theory, at least, states can do whatever they want because they are sovereign and because there is no world government. And yet, states do find it in their interests to cooperate. Few analysts or participants have described these phenomena more graphically than the first Allied Commander of NATO and later president of the United States, Dwight D. Eisenhower, whose words are cited above.

A group of psychologists recently met at a Fantasy University conference to explain the behavior of an individual human being, a political science undergraduate major, specifically. Some psychologists put forth the argument that the undergraduate's mental state is primarily controlled by the chemical balance of the brain. Their explanations for the person's behavior were said to derive from the "biochemical" level of analysis. Others emphasized the person's childhood experiences, emotional traumas, and personality traits; these doctors stressed the "personal" level of analysis to explain specific actions. Finally, some of the psychologists concentrated on outside influences such as family, workplace, community, or even the

Major Events in the International Systemic Level of Analysis: 1513–1994

1513: Niccolò Machiavelli's *The Prince* argues that security is possible only when government is strong and that man's innate selfish and aggressive nature motivates state behavior.

1648: Peace of Westphalia ends the Thirty Years' War and inaugurates modern international system whose basic unit is the nation-state.

1648–1945: International relations are characterized by a multipolar system.

1702–1713: A counterbalancing coalition defeats France in the War of the Spanish Succession.

1789–1815: French Revolution initiates period of European instability that ends with final defeat of Napoléon in 1815.

1815: The Concert of Europe is formed after the Napoleonic Wars, replacing the balance of power with a collective security arrangement.

1868: Japan begins practice of internal balancing through rapid modernization during the Meiji Restoration.

1895–1914: A naval arms race between Britain and Germany mimics the Prisoner's Dilemma.

1904: Fearing potential German hegemony, Great Britain and France put aside their historical rivalry in the Anglo-French entente.

1914: Multipolar instability and miscalculations of rival states' intentions lead to World War I.

1919–1939: Hegemonic stability theory attributes the instability during the interwar period to Britain's decline and the United States' return to isolationism.

1931: The problem of collective action in collective security systems is illustrated by the League of Nations' failure to respond to Japan's invasion of Manchuria.

1938: Problems with alliances are illustrated when France cooperates with Britain to allow Hitler to take the Sudetenland from Czechoslovakia at the Munich Conference, despite a French treaty commitment to help protect Czechoslovakia.

1939: Stalin and Hitler's ideological differences are set aside in the signing of the Nazi–Soviet Nonaggression Pact.

---

television programs watched. These specialists examined the "environmental" level of analysis to try to understand the person's behavior. The doctors at the conference could only reach agreement that the food was bad. The psychologists could not agree on the level at which the most powerful influences were to be found, and as a result their recommendations for modifying the person's behavior still differed. One prescribed drugs, a second advised helping the person work through an emotional problem, and a third suggested doing something to reduce stress "on the job" or in the family. (No one suggested switching majors.)

This story is not intended to suggest that international politics resembles mental illness. (The reader should draw his or her own conclusion in this regard.) Rather, it is designed to show that when behavior can be influenced by many factors, it must be examined at a number of levels in order to be explained fully. We can apply this principle to international politics this way: The fact that there is a significant number of possible influences on the actions of states means that there will inevitably be disagreement over which factors exert the greatest impact. This chapter and the two that follow will discuss various theories, derived from one of the three levels of analysis that seek to explain why states do what they do.

The three levels of analysis were first introduced in Chapter One; as you will recall, analysts of global politics find it useful to categorize the many factors that affect international relations according to the level at which they exert their influence. Factors arising from the nature and structure of the world political system (such as the number and relative strength of major powers) fall under the **systemic level of analysis.** These influences are essentially external to the individual states within the international system in that they are attributes of

1941: Following a U.S. oil embargo in response to its territorial expansion, Japan attacks Pearl Harbor.

1941–1945: Ideological differences are put aside when the United States, Great Britain, and the Soviet Union ally against Nazi Germany; U.S. development of the atomic bomb pressures the Soviet Union to pursue its own nuclear program.

1944: Bretton Woods system is adopted as an international regime to help stabilize the world economy after World War II.

1945–1991: A bipolar system with nuclear weapons prevents direct military confrontation between the United States and the Soviet Union.

1955: Austrian State Treaty, making Austria neutral, results from a suc-cessful strategy of gradual and recip-rocal reduction in tensions.

1957: Soviet launch of Sputnik fuels the arms race.

1961: Sino-Soviet split is finalized.

1965–1973: American involvement in the Vietnam War illustrates limitations on a superpower and opportunities for weaker states in a bipolar system.

1973: Extensive bipolar superpower involvement in the Third World nearly escalates into military confrontation during the Yom Kippur War when U.S. forces are placed on nuclear alert in response to a Soviet threat of direct intervention.

1974: Egypt defects from Soviet camp to the West after realizing that the United States could offer superior long-term diplomatic and economic assistance.

1990–1991: Collective security suc-ceeds when the United States leads the international community in freeing Kuwait from Iraqi occupation during the Persian Gulf War.

1991: Collapse of USSR brings the Cold War to an end and creates transition in the international system.

1992–present: Difficulties of collective security are exemplified by unwillingness of Western nations to form a coalition against Serbian aggression in Bosnia-Herzegovina.

1993: Ratification of the Treaty of European Union (Maastricht Treaty) demonstrates cooperation between EU member states for mutual benefit.

the system itself rather than of the units (the states) within the system. The unique characteristics of nation-states that shape their foreign polices (such as form of government, historical experience, and ideology) fall into the domestic level of analysis, which will be examined in Chapter Fourteen. The skills, beliefs, personalities, and idiosyncrasies of leaders come into play at the individual level of analysis, considered in Chapter Fifteen. Thus, these three chapters together comprise a "top-down" survey of the various theories that attempt to explain the workings of world politics. As we will see, many of these theories appear to compete with one another, although ultimately they are complementary: They help us comprehend the "big picture" of world politics by identifying its component parts and explaining how they interact.

This chapter looks at explanations for state behavior from the systemic level of analysis. As mentioned earlier, systemic arguments contend that factors external to the state will encourage certain actions and discourage others.[1] Accordingly, changes in the structure of the international system will lead to changes in the behavior of states within the system. To examine these ideas in greater detail, the chapter is divided into six sections, each focusing on how systemic factors lead to conflict or facilitate cooperation between states. The first section outlines the realist paradigm, which holds that the distribution of capabilities within the international system (that is, the relative power of states) has a profound effect on how nations act and on the overall stability of the system. The second and third sections examine the debate within the realist school over what leads to the most stable international system. The fourth section considers a rival to the realist paradigm, collective security, an alternative way to maintain peace within the global system. The fifth section examines neoliberal institutionalist theories, which focus on the barriers to cooperation among

AT A GLANCE

SCHOOLS OF THOUGHT

Classical Realism

Theory: The world is governed by the "law of the jungle" in which each state must protect its vital interests, political independence, and territorial sovereignty at any cost. Individuals are considered evil and must therefore be controlled by the state. The same holds true for the international community. However, there currently is no effective international organization to control individual states.

The System: It is a "dog-eat-dog" world. If a state becomes militarily weaker vis-à-vis other states, its survival might be jeopardized; in this way, the process of the rise and fall of states resembles Charles Darwin's theory of natural selection. Hobbes believed that, in the absence of a civil society, man would be living in a world of "every man for himself." The solution to this chaotic and destructive situation is the creation of the "mortal god" of the sovereign state. This will protect people from each other. The international system does not have any supranational organization to control it.

states. The concluding section explores how strategies, international regimes, and international law can help overcome these barriers and increase the likelihood that states will cooperate with each other in the New Era.

REALISM

The realist school of thought is one of the central paradigms in international relations theory. Its roots can be traced back hundreds of years to Kautilya (around 300 B.C.), a Hindu statesman and philospher, to the Greek historian Thucydides' *Peloponnesian War* (431–404 B.C.), and to Sun Tzu (500 B.C.), the author of the great Chinese classic, *The Art of War*. It also borrows from political theorists such as Niccolò Machiavelli and Thomas Hobbes and academic disciplines such as microeconomics and biology. Modern realist theory is a response to the failure of idealistic attempts during the interwar period (1919–1939) to prevent a new world war (Chapter Nine discusses these noble measures and their disappointing results). In rejecting the "naive" and utopian orientation of idealism, scholars and policy-makers such as Hans Morgenthau, Reinhold Niebuhr, George Kennan, Henry Kissinger, and John Foster Dulles emphasized the logic of **realpolitik** (literally the "politics of realism"), power politics, and the evil—or at least amoral and wicked—nature of humans in shaping interstate relations.[2]

At the core of the realist paradigm is a belief in the primacy of national security issues (referred to as **high politics**) over economic and other domestic issues

Structural Realism

Theory: The system is anarchic. All states are unitary, rational actors. Their primary concern is survival. Although the international system refers to all states in the world, structural realists are primarily concerned only with the most powerful states or great powers.

The System: The system is described in terms of polarity: unipolarity, bipolarity, or multipolarity. Some contend that movement toward an equal distribution of power is most conducive to international stability, while others argue that movement toward dominance of the system by a single state is the best guarantor of stability.

Neoliberalism

Theory: The world is not always consumed by warfare. There have been more instances of international cooperation than conflict. If nations were not willing to cooperate with one another regarding their foreign policies, the world would be much more chaotic and dangerous than it is at present.

The System: States do not exist in a "dog-eat-dog" environment. The inherent anarchy and violence of the international system can be overcome through carefully designed institutions for international cooperation.

(low politics). **Classical realists,** such as Hans Morgenthau and Henry Kissinger, view the world as governed only by the "law of the jungle," wherein each state must protect its own vital interests, political independence, and territorial sovereignty at any cost. In the "dog-eat-dog" world described by the realist paradigm, military power is often a necessary ingredient for national survival. If a state becomes militarily weaker vis-a-vis other states, its survival might be jeopardized; in this way, the process of the rise and fall of states resembles Charles Darwin's theory of natural selection (that is, the survival of the fittest).

In contrast to classical realists, who emphasize the fearful and conflictual nature of humankind, **structural realists** (also known as **neorealists**) such as Kenneth Waltz and Joseph Grieco focus on the structure of the international system rather than on human nature to account for the behavior of states.[3] Although the **international system** refers to all states in the world, structural realists are primarily concerned only with the most powerful states, or **great powers** (see Chapter Twelve). For these theorists, the **structure of the international system** is defined by the distribution of power among the great powers—or in other words, the number of great powers in the system and their relative capabilities.

The structure of the international system is typically described in terms of **polarity,** with each major power representing a "pole" of the system. A **unipolar** system is one in which a single dominant power exists, a **bipolar** structure is one with two great powers, and a **multipolar** structure is one with three or more. Structural realists are intensely interested in the shifts in power among the major states and the impact these will have on the stability of the international system. Some contend that movement toward an equal distribution of power (**parity**) is most conducive to international stability, while others argue that movement toward dominance of the system by a single state (**preponderance**) is the best guarantor of stability. We will return to this question later; for now, we will examine in more detail the basic premises and arguments of structural realism, a leading school of thought in the study of international relations.

Principles of Structural Realism

Any school of thought is based on central assumptions or axioms. The three central assumptions of structural realism are:

1. The international system is anarchic.
2. All states within the system are unitary, rational actors whose authority is supreme.
3. The primary concern of all states is survival.

An anarchic system is one that lacks a legitimate authority to "make and enforce laws, adjudicate disputes, and regulate behavior among states."[4] The international system is thus likened to Thomas Hobbes's "state of nature," where no "world policeman" exists to protect states from one another. (See Chapters Nine and Eleven for more on the effects of anarchy in the international system.)

The second assumption is that the political authority of nation-states is supreme and not subject to any higher political authority. As noted in Chapters Two and Nine, the **Peace of Westphalia** (1648) ushered in the modern international system by legitimating the state as the ultimate sovereign authority over people and geographic territory. Although we tend to identify a state as something that signs treaties and makes war, states exist only as legal, or juridical, entities. A state's legal status is associated with its monopoly over the legitimate use of force within its territorial confines, as well as its authority to wage war against other states. No supranational organization is authorized to maintain order within state boundaries. The United Nations has been constrained in both peacekeeping and peacemaking efforts by an inability to muster and maintain troops without the permission of its sovereign member states.

In conceptualizing the state as a unitary and rational actor, realists recognize that states are sovereign and deemphasize the role of actors within the state (such as political parties or leaders) in shaping the state's actions in the international system. States are often likened to billiard balls on a pool table. Just as players don't care what's inside the balls, so too systems analysts have little concern for domestic factors. In short, structural realists contend that domestic politics do not matter, since states act as though they are rational individuals by making cost-benefit calculations in determining which policy to pursue. According to this line of reasoning, then, U.S. military intervention in Korea and Vietnam, for example, was neither a result of domestic politics such as congressional or public-opinion preferences, nor a product of Pentagon or State Department maneuvering, nor a product of the individual preferences of American presidents Truman, Kennedy, or Johnson; rather, it was a rational, logical result of the international system of the time. U.S. involvement was necessary to contain Communist expansion, regardless of the wishes of other nations. After all, the very survival of the United States could have been at stake.

The third assumption of structural realism is that the primary objective of all states is survival. Since the international system is an anarchic, self-help system, each state is left alone to guarantee its own survival, because no other state will do so.[5] As a result of this assumption, the "hierarchy" of state interests is dominated by security issues. Realism contends that in an anarchic world, power is the means to security, and therefore states seek to maximize their own power. Realists are not interested in a state's absolute power, but instead they are concerned about changes in its relative power or position with regard to other states (see Chapter Twelve). States must always prepare themselves for war or face the risk of annihilation as a sovereign entity. The inherent danger of this situation, of course, is that the heavy emphasis on security issues compels other states in the system to take counter-measures that might ultimately weaken the state's relative position. (For more on the "security dilemma" and its implications, see Chapter Eleven.)

Shifts in System Structure

The primary contention of structural realism is that shifts in the distribution of power among states will pressure them to respond in a uniform and predictable pattern. According to this argument, a decline in a state's relative position will lead it to try to improve its standing relative to that of the dominant power. In a bipolar system where two superpowers vie for leadership, this is usually accomplished through **internal balancing** (building up a state's own capabilities), as during the Cold War. In a multipolar system (1648–1945), balancing is accomplished through the formation of alliances and coalitions. In both cases, all states wish to survive, and this desire will lead them to balance by forming a counter-coalition against the dominant power. States will act similarly despite differences between them in political and economic institutions, historical backgrounds, and individual leaders. Hypothetically, realism would predict that had Britain, and not the Soviet Union, emerged as the other superpower after World War II, then the U.S. would have perceived England as the primary threat to its security. In this view, the Cold War was inevitable, no matter who the contenders.

A second argument of structural realism is that states rarely cooperate, especially on security-related issues. Concerned about any possible changes in their international ranking, states may hesitate to collaborate out of fear that their partner might get a larger share of the benefits than themselves. Although both may gain in absolute terms, both fear that cooperation may strengthen the other, as today's ally might be tomorrow's enemy. During the Vietnam War, for example, China and North Vietnam cooperated to frustrate U.S. objectives and later even set up a "fraternal" Communist regime in Cambodia. After the United

States withdrew its forces in 1973 and Vietnam reunified in 1975, however, conflicts between Beijing and Hanoi quickly resurfaced. Vietnamese forces invaded Cambodia in 1978, and Vietnam and China fought a brief border war in 1979 (see Chapter Six).

Polarity and the Balance of Power

Although they agree that all states seek security through maintenance of a balance of power, realists disagree on the type of international system structure that best promotes stability. One debate centers on whether a balance or an imbalance of power is preferable. The **parity school** argues that an equal distribution of capability among states, or a **balance of power,** creates stability and that war is more likely to occur when one state is the dominant power. On the other hand, the **preponderance school** contends that stability is more likely if there is an **imbalance of power,** where one state dominates the system, than with an equal distribution of power, where war is more likely. (See the boxed feature in Chapter Two for more on the controversy over the balance of power.) The second debate in the realist school exists within the parity version of realism: namely whether a bipolar or multipolar distribution of power is more stable.

However, neither of these debates can be resolved without first defining stability within the international system. A narrow definition of stability is the absence of any war, the continued political independence and territorial integrity of all states in the system, and the maintenance of the status quo, or existing international order. A looser definition would be the absence of war between the great powers, where the system would still be considered stable even if limited wars occurred (that is, war between a great power and a lesser power, or between lesser powers). Using this definition, the Cold War era was relatively stable, despite its numerous regional conflicts, since there was no war between the superpowers (see Chapter Six). Because the realists define the global system by the number of great powers, under the broadest of definitions a particular system is not stable if it ceases to exist when one of the great powers declines, collapses, or is divided or destroyed. Not surprisingly, proponents of different perspectives on the parity/preponderance and bipolarity/multipolarity debates base their arguments on different definitions of stability.

REALISM: THE CASE FOR PARITY

Balance-of-power theory argues that an equal distribution of power is more stable than a hegemonic distribution, where one state dominates. Balance-of-power theory is an equilibrium model, intended to prevent the dominance of the system by any single state. According to this argument when an imbalance does occur, the system is likely to return to an equilibrium; if one state becomes too powerful, other states will form a counterbalancing coalition to restore the original balance.

The reason why dominance of the system by a single state is seen as destabilizing is clear. When one state or bloc becomes preponderant, it is tempted to dominate the system and impose its will on the other states by the threat or use of military force. Perhaps the most prominent twentieth-century example was Nazi Germany, from the mid-1930s up until its defeat in 1945. Even if the hegemon (dominant power) is initially benevolent, there is an ever-present danger that it will become dictatorial; as the noted nineteenth-century English historian Lord Acton wisely noted, "Power tends to corrupt and absolute power corrupts absolutely."[6]

By forming a counterbalancing coalition, states seek to prevent war by deterring the aggressor state. If deterrence fails, however, the members of the counterbalancing coalition must be willing to use military force to restore the balance of power. Remember that states balance not for moral reasons, but for self-preservation. Personal differences among leaders, ideological competition, or historical antagonisms play no role in a state's decision to join a counterbalancing coalition. The mid–twentieth century is full of such cases: the 1939 nonaggression pact between fascist Germany and communist Russia, and the World War II alliance between the Soviet Union and the United States against Germany are two prime examples. When Britain and the USSR became allies, early in the war, Winston Churchill was recognizing the necessity of allying with an ideological adversary to counter even more pressing threats. The British prime minister remarked, "If Hitler invaded Hell, I would at least make a favorable reference to the Devil in the House of Commons."[7]

Going It Alone: Internal Balancing

There are two basic ways that states can balance against a potentially dominant power. The first is through internal balancing. This strategy calls for the domestic mobilization of economic and industrial resources and their conversion into military power in order to match up against the preponderant power's capabilities. Here industrial strength must be converted into military power, which demonstrates the relationship between material power and military power (see Chapter Twelve). As a result, it is not by chance that the most powerful states have often been the most developed ones.

One example of internal balancing is Japan's rapid modernization following Commodore Matthew Perry's forced opening of Japan in 1853–1854. Fearing further Western encroachment, Japan sought to strengthen itself through internal reforms directed by the emperor (the Meiji Restoration of 1868–1912).[8] In another example, after suffering defeats in 1806 at the hands of Napoléon, the Prussian Hohenzollern regime implemented modernization reforms during the Prussian Reform Movement of 1807–1814. In both instances, the international system forced the state to mobilize resources to guarantee its continued survival.

During the Cold War, the only way for the two superpowers to balance against each other was through internal buildup. Alliances were insufficient because both the United States and the USSR overshadowed other powers to

On March 8, 1854, Commodore Matthew Perry and U.S. troops landed in Japan to meet with imperial commissioners at Yokohama. The meeting marked the end of self-imposed Japanese isolation.
Source: © Bettmann Archive.

the extent that even the "loss" of China to the Soviets in 1949 or the "loss" of China by the Soviets in the 1960s did not substantially alter the balance of power. In this system, if the USSR became militarily more powerful, the United States matched it by mobilizing domestic resources. This internal balancing and counterbalancing process is illustrated by the development of military technology. The United States developed an atomic bomb; the Soviets followed shortly. The United States developed a hydrogen bomb; the Soviets responded in kind. The Soviets launched Sputnik; the United States began launching satellites not long afterward. This pattern spread into other areas of competition. For example, the United States viewed the Soviet launch of Sputnik as evidence of Soviet superiority in mathematics and sciences. U.S. schools were then urged to increase their focus on these subjects in order to "catch up." Americans feared that if the Soviets got too far ahead, U.S. security might be endangered. Table 13.1 summarizes this competition.

With Friends Like These: External Balancing

If one cannot go it alone, the second strategy of balancing entails the formation of a **counterbalancing coalition.** Under this strategy, if one state becomes too powerful, the remaining states will balance against it by forming an alliance.

Table 13.1 Internal Balancing: U.S.–Soviet Technological Developments, 1945–1975

Technological Advance	Date of Acquisition	
	United States	Soviet Union
Atomic bomb	1945	1949
Intercontinental bomber	1948	1955
Hydrogen bomb*	1952	1953
ICBM	1958	1957
SLBM	1960	1968
MIRV	1970	1975
ABM	1972	1968

Source: Adapted from David P. Barash, *The Arms Race and Nuclear War* (Belmont, CA: Wadsworth, 1987), p. 195; and George H. Quester, *Nuclear Diplomacy* (New York: Dunellen, 1970), pp. 91–92.

*The United States tested a hydrogen device in 1952, but did not possess a plausibly deliverable bomb until 1954. The Soviets did both in 1953.

The purpose of an alliance is to quickly aggregate capability in order to deter the preponderant power, and if this fails, to prepare for war in order to restore the balance of power. Examples of balancing through alliances against the preponderant power include the countercoalitions that formed against Spain during the Spanish–Dutch Wars and during the Thirty Years' War, against France during the War of the Spanish Succession and the Napoleonic Wars, and against Germany in World War I and World War II (see Chapters Two and Three). Table 13.2 summarizes these major alliances and wars.

Historically, Britain has played the role of continental "balancer," throwing its weight on the side opposing the ascending power. For centuries Britain was concerned that one "continental" power would come to dominate Europe, threaten British commercial links with the continent, and perhaps launch an attack across the English Channel. As balance-of-power theory predicts, Britain's policy was to align with the weaker state or coalition, with little consideration of its political or ideological orientation. Accordingly, Britain balanced against Spain in the seventeenth century, France in the eighteenth and nineteenth century, and Germany in the first half of the twentieth century. As Churchill noted,

> For four hundred years the foreign policy of England has been to oppose the strongest, most aggressive, most dominating power on the Continent. . . . [I]t would have been easy ... and tempting to join with the stronger and share the fruits of conquest. However, we always took the harder course, joined with the less strong powers ... and thus defeated the Continental tyrant whoever he was.[9]

Most balance-of-power theorists envision the formation of fluid and shifting alliances that quickly dissipate after they have served their purpose, only to form again at some future point against another preponderant state. Political scientist Morton Kaplan's "rules" of balancing imply that a balance-of-power system encourages moderation and restraint in international relations. In this system, since today's enemy might be tomorrow's ally, there is an incentive to

Table 13.2   External Balancing: Alliances and Major Wars, 1580–1945

State Seeking Hegemony	Balancing Powers	War against Potential Hegemon
Spain	Britain, France	Spanish-Dutch Wars (1580–1609)
Holy Roman Empire (Spain, Austria)	France, Britain, Sweden, Netherlands	Thirty Years' War (1618–1648)
France	Britain, Netherlands	War of the Spanish Succession (1701–1714)
France	Britain, Austria	War of the Austrian Succession (1740–1748)
France	Britain, Prussia, Austria, Russia	French Revolution and Napoleonic Wars (1792–1815)
Germany	Britain, France, Russia, United States	World War I (1914–1918)
Germany, Japan	Britain, France, USSR, United States	World War II (1939–1945)

Source: Table based on Paul Kennedy, *The Rise and Fall of the Great Powers: Economic Change and Military Conflict from 1500 to 2000* (New York: Vintage Books, 1987).

refrain from treating defeated states too harshly, and therefore wars are unlikely to be total. Kaplan's rules are as follows:

1. Increase capabilities, but negotiate rather than fight.

2. Fight rather than pass up a chance to increase capabilities.

3. Stop fighting rather than eliminate an important power.

4. Oppose any coalition or single state that tends to assume a predominant position within the system.

5. Oppose any nation that subscribes to supranational organizing principles (that is, one promoting an ideology of subordinating the nation-state to some higher body).

6. Treat all major powers as acceptable partners. Permit a defeated state to reenter the system as an acceptable partner, or replace it by strengthening some previously weak state.[10]

These rules also imply that for this system to properly function, states must be able and willing to ally with each other on the basis of short-run interest—their mutual survival. As a result, common ideology, past friendship, enmity, morality, or any other factors should play no role in a state's decision to balance against a preponderant power. These were the guiding principles behind British Prime Minister Palmerston's formulation, "We [Britain] have no eternal allies and we have no perpetual enemies. Our interests are eternal and perpetual, and these interests it is our duty to follow."[11] For much of the eighteenth and nineteenth centuries, Britain and France were intense rivals. However, as Germany began to emerge during the nineteenth century as the continental hegemon, posing a threat to both France and England's position, the two states mended their differences and entered into an entente in 1904 (see Chapter Two). If France had been destroyed after the Napoleonic Wars or not allowed to rejoin the system of states, Britain might have had to confront Germany alone.

During the seventeenth and eighteenth centuries, often referred to as the "golden age of the balance of power," ideology was not a barrier to this process. As a result, as Chapter Two demonstrated, states freely switched back and forth between alliances with little concern. Even with the rise of the twentieth-century rivalry between the United States and the ideologically rigid USSR, ideological incompatibility was still overcome when a greater danger loomed. During World Wars I and II the United States allied with Russia and the Soviet Union, respectively, to face a common and more threatening enemy, Germany. More recently, in the 1991 Persian Gulf War, the United States allied with Syria against Iraq. Saudi Arabia would not align with Israel even though they both were hit by Saddam's SCUDs (Soviet missiles used by Iraq). Would Israel and the Arab states unite against Iran if it threatened both? Would India and Pakistan mend their significant differences if China posed a common threat to their security? According to balance-of-power theory, the answer should be a resounding "yes."

Problems with Alliances: Balancing

There are a number of problems associated with balancing against a preponderant power through alliances. The first is the matter of reliability: allies may not fulfill their commitments to aid their partners.[12] In an anarchic system, a state that is "jilted at the altar" will have little recourse against its partner. In the aftermath of World War I, for instance, France made commitments to defend Czechoslovakia if Germany attacked. However, in 1938, when Hitler demanded the return of the Czechoslovak Sudetenland to Germany, France abandoned Czechoslovakia. This is an example of why realists contend that states should be suspicious of alliances and other cooperative-security arrangements.

Second, counterbalancing alliances are often slow to form. Knowing that an effective countercoalition will take time to come together, a preponderant power might be tempted to attack while the window of opportunity still exists. By March 1939, Hitler had taken Austria and Czechoslovakia, and many believed Poland was next. Both Britain and France responded by guaranteeing Poland's survival. However, from the German perspective, it was unclear what the British or French were willing to do to assist Poland; they were unprepared for an offensive on the Continent, and did not even have plans for any type of offensive action.[13] Thus, Germany decided to attack before Britain and France could prepare for war, and it conquered Poland in September 1939.

AT A GLANCE

PROBLEMS WITH ALLIANCES

Reliability
Allies may not fulfill their commitments to aid their partners.

Example: France made an agreement after World War I to defend Czechoslovakia if Germany attacked. However, in 1938, when Hitler demanded the transfer of the Sudetenland to Germany, France abandoned Czechoslovakia.

Slow to Form
Knowing that an effective countercoalition will take time to come together, a preponderant power might be tempted to attack while the window of opportunity still exists.

Example: After Hitler took the rest of Czechoslovakia in March 1939, both Britain and France responded by guaranteeing Poland's survival. Germany, however, decided to attack Poland before Britain and France could prepare for war, conquering Poland in September 1939.

Buck-passing
The temptation of all parties to "pass the buck" and let other states confront the threatening

Two additional problems with alliances are the twin dangers of buck-passing and chain-ganging.[14] **Buck-passing** refers to the temptation of all parties to "pass the buck" and let other states confront the threatening state. States are tempted to do this because no state wants to bear the high cost, in terms of lives and equipment, of fighting the dominant power. For example, prior to World War II, Britain, France, and the Soviet Union could not negotiate an alliance against Germany. Instead, each elected to pursue a policy of appeasement and passed the "hot potato" of balancing against Germany back and forth. More recently, after Bosnia declared independence from Yugoslavia, the EU nations avoided trying to curb first Serb and then Croat aggressions in Bosnia, preferring instead that the United States take care of the problem. Not willing to bear the high costs of a military intervention, the United States did not take steps believed to be necessary to halt the fighting, either characterizing the situation as a European problem or leaving it for the United Nations to try to resolve.

Chain-ganging describes the danger that a state might get dragged into a war it has no interest in fighting. Picture the prisoners of a chain gang, shackled together at the feet. If the first prisoner falls over a cliff, all of the others will be dragged over, too. In the case of alliances, if an ally goes to war, the other(s) must follow or risk facing the rival alone at some future point. In the case of World War I, it can be argued that once Austria-Hungary went to war, Germany had to follow its partner into war or face the possibility of fighting Britain, France, and Russia alone at some future date. Another example is Jordan's decision to follow Egypt into the 1967 Arab-Israeli war. Jordan feared that a loss by Egypt would leave it isolated, vulnerable, and perhaps a future target either of Israel or of its own Arab adversaries.

state. States do not want to bear the high cost of fighting the dominant power.

Example: Prior to World War II, Britain, France, and the Soviet Union could not negotiate an alliance against Germany. Instead, each elected to pursue a policy of appeasement and passed the "hot potato" of balancing against Germany back and forth.

Chain-ganging
The danger that a state might get dragged into a war which it has no interest in fighting.

Example: In World War I, when Austria-Hungary went to war, Germany had to follow its alliance partner into war or face the possibility of fighting other regional powers on its own at some future date. As explained in Chapter Two, Germany had no choice by August 1914 even though its own actions had contributed to the crisis.

Problems with Alliances: Bandwagoning

Instead of balancing against the dominant state, states may determine that their interests are better served by **bandwagoning** with it.[15] Whereas balancing means that a state aligns with the weaker power or bloc against the stronger one, bandwagoning means that a state jumps on the "bandwagon" and joins the stronger state or coalition. A state will be tempted to do so in order to share in the spoils of victory, or because no other state is willing to form a counteralliance against the preponderant state. During World War II, for example, Italy, Hungary, Finland, Bulgaria, and Romania initially bandwagoned with Germany, but later joined the Allies when it became apparent that they would prevail. In the early stages of the Cold War, Egypt became a client state of Moscow. However, after realizing that the Soviet Union could not offer the diplomatic or economic assistance available from the United States in the long term, Egypt moved into the Western camp. Overall, like balancing, counterbalancing, buck-passing, and chain-ganging, bandwagoning is just another manifestation of the root of realpolitik—using pragmatic means to guarantee state sovereignty and national survival in an anarchic international system.

REALISM: THE CASE FOR PREPONDERANCE

The arguments presented thus far have been based on the assumption that the key to international stability is to achieve a balance of power between the leading states. Considering all the problems encountered in maintaining a balance of power and the many wars that have occurred when coalitions have attempted to block a powerful state's bid for hegemony, it should come as no surprise that some realists believe that an imbalance of power is more conducive to stability. Thucydides, an early realist, wrote in the fifth century B.C. that what made the Peloponnesian War inevitable was the growth of Athenian power and the fear this caused in Sparta, the other great power. Thucydides was arguing that war is most likely to occur in a system with two great powers of relatively equal strength or when two states are approaching parity. To take this theory one step further, it can be argued that international stability is more likely when one hegemonic state dominates the rest, the rationale being that as long as there is one hegemonic power, no state will challenge it because any challenger is likely to lose.

Power-transition theory explores Thucydides' initial assumption that the existence of two powerful states leads to instability. Because states grow at different rates, an emerging state will inevitably encroach upon a dominant state's position. As the gap in power between the rival states narrows and they become more equal in strength, war is likely to occur, since both the challenger and the hegemon believe that they are likely to prevail.

Power-transition theory recognizes that the responsibilities of acting as a hegemon eventually places a strain on a state that then allows other states to mount an effective challenge. A hegemon is the dominant military and economic power among the states in the international system and often has extensive global commitments. It establishes and enforces a set of rules that govern the international system, and it provides a number of global services to its allies (for example, economic and military aid). Often, and especially in the industrial age, the rising costs of armaments, maintaining the global system, and excessive defense spending weaken the hegemon's position and divert resources from investment. The burden of maintaining an empire eventually drags the hegemon down to a level where rival powers can mount a challenge to it.

From this perspective, international relations resembles a game of "king of the hill." Since a challenger is likely to restructure the international order (that is, the existing territorial, political, and economic arrangements), a declining hegemon will not peacefully relinquish its position to a challenger, and a rising challenger is unlikely to back down. The outcome is often a total (or hegemonic) war over succession between the declining hegemon and the emerging challenger, at the point where their relative power is equal.

Long-cycle theory shares many assumptions with the power-transition model. The theory attempts to explain the curiously regular cycles of world leadership and global war, each of which lasts about 100 years. According to George Modelski and William R. Thompson, the theory's primary proponents, every cycle consists of four phases. Out of a global war, a new dominant world power emerges from the struggle for global leadership and maintains its position through naval power. However, the costs associated with global leadership contribute to the world power's decline, giving way to two new stages: **delegitimation** (decline in relative power) and **deconcentration** (challenge by

Table 13.3 Long-Cycle Theory: The Struggle For Global Leadership, 1494–1994

Phase	Hegemon	Years	War	Challenger
Global war		1494–1516	Italian/Indian Ocean Wars	
World power	Portugal	1516–1539		
Delegitimation		1540–1560		
Deconcentration		1560–1580		Spain
Global war		1580–1609	Spanish–Dutch War	
World power	Netherlands	1609–1639		
Delegitimation		1640–1660		
Deconcentration		1660–1688		France
Global war		1688–1713	Wars of Louis XIV	
World power	Britain	1714–1740		
Delegitimation		1740–1763		
Deconcentration		1764–1792		France
Global war		1792–1815	French Revolution and Napoleonic Wars	
World power	Britain	1815–1849		
Delegitimation		1850–1873		
Deconcentration		1874–1914		Germany
Global war		1914–1945	World Wars I and II	
World power	United States	1945–1973		
Delegitimation		1973–		

Source: Adapted from George Modelski, *Long Cycles in World Politics* (Seattle: University of Washington Press, 1987), p. 40.

emerging rivals). Deconcentration proceeds until the new contenders for world leadership attempt to push the declining leader out of its hegemonic position. Overall, periods of hegemony are associated with peace, and periods of hegemonic decline are associated with war. Table 13.3 depicts the five most recent cycles of leadership in world history. According to long-cycle theorists, four states—Portugal, the Netherlands, Britain, and currently the United States—have successively played the role of hegemon, with each cycle of dominance ending in a hegemonic war.

As American economic strength continues to decline relative to that of Japan and the European Union, power-transition theory and long-cycle theory offer a bleak prediction for the stability of the international system. Based on the length of the phases in a cycle, around the year 2000 the United States can expect to enter the deconcentration phase when it will be challenged by another power, with the global-war phase following about thirty years later.

Bleak assessments aside, it is important to note that several factors might mitigate this outcome. First, the impact of nuclear weapons and nuclear deterrence on this cycle is unclear. (Recall that deterrence and balance-of-power theorists attributed the "long peace" of the Cold War era to the stabilizing role of nuclear weapons.) Second, it is uncertain as to what role regime type (that is, whether a state is democratic, authoritarian, communist, and so forth) will play in influencing a nation's behavior toward other states (see Chapter Fourteen). In particular, many theorists contend that democratic states do not fight one another, and with the proliferation of democratic states, one might expect a peaceful transition to the next long cycle.[16] Finally, not all transitions have resulted in a global war. Power-transition theorist A. F. K. Organski writes that while in decline Britain was willing to peacefully accommodate an emerging United States because it had willingly accepted the established Anglo-French international order.[17] In particular, Organski argues, London believed that the United States would maintain the existing international order and that Britain would continue to benefit by it, even if it was no longer the dominant power. The reader is encouraged to draw his or her own conclusions about the utility of power transition and long-cycle theory.

PARITY AND PREPONDERANCE COMPARED

How can one reconcile the parity and preponderance versions of realist theory? Both seem plausible, yet they draw contradictory conclusions concerning which distribution of power is more stable. Furthermore, historical examples contradict both arguments. The Napoleonic Wars and the world wars demonstrate the weakness of the balance-of-power argument. Likewise, hegemonic wars have occurred during periods that long-cycle theorists contend should be stable and orderly. For example, the Thirty Years' War (1618–1648) occurred during the Netherlands' world power phase.

One solution to this dilemma is to define the midway point between parity and preponderance as the most stable.[18] Parity destabilizes because it tempts aggression, leading each state to believe that it will prevail. Preponderance destabilizes because states fear that the dominant state will impose its will on the others, leading them to form a countercoalition. A midway point between parity and preponderance is stabilizing because it deters aggression from both sides. The slightly larger state can defeat any challenger to its power, yet it cannot effectively impose its will on the other states without heavy costs to itself. If this is the situation today, and if this theory is accurate, we can anticipate at least a short period of international stability, since the United States is the slightly larger state in the system.

POLARITY IN REALISM

A second debate within realist theory centers on the distribution of power and asks whether a bipolar or a multipolar distribution is more stable. The period from 1648 until 1945 is characterized as multipolar (with three or more great powers), while the period from 1945 to 1991 is bipolar (with two superpowers contending for world leadership). One can also distinguish between a tight bipolar system where there are only two superpowers, and a loose bipolar system where there are two superpowers and several great powers as well. The period immediately after World War II would be closer to a tight bipolar period, while the 1960s onward represents a loose bipolar structure because rebuilt Europe, Japan, and China emerged as centers of power.

As mentioned earlier, a unipolar, or hegemonic, international system is dominated by a single powerful state, such as the United States ever since the dissolution of the Soviet Union in 1991. Some might consider the Roman Empire an example, even though it predates the formation of the modern international system of states in 1648 and—unlike contemporary America—was in complete control of its system.

How one defines power will determine the polarity of the system. If one focuses on economic factors, the current system is characterized by tripolarity, consisting of three great powers: Japan, Germany, and the United States. Germany soon be encompassed by the European Union, and China is rapidly emerging as a fourth pole. If one focuses primarily on military factors and the ability of a state to project its force over long distance, the current system is unipolar. If one focuses solely on nuclear weapons, it is still bipolar, still engaging the United States and Russia.

The Case for Bipolarity

There are major disagreements within the realist school of thought over which form of polarity is most stable. The absence of war during the Cold War bipolar period and the numerous wars during the multipolar period between 1648 and 1945 are used to support the contention that a bipolar distribution is more stable. (Of course, as Chapter Eleven noted, some theorists contend that the relative stability of the post–World War II period was the result of the massive destructive capability of nuclear weapons and the advent of a secure second strike, having little to do with the bipolar distribution of power.)

In his controversial article, "Back to the Future: Instability in Europe after the Cold War," political scientist John Mearsheimer concludes that the world will soon miss the stability of the bipolar Cold War era.[19] Mearsheimer and international relations theorist Kenneth Waltz contend that a bipolar system is more stable for several reasons: It is simple, since there are only two large states, and small states cannot influence either's policies; it is more efficient, since the two powers do not have to rely on allies; and it is more competitive, since through constant jockeying, imbalances of power are less likely to occur.

To elaborate, in a bipolar distribution of power the two dominant states in the system concentrate solely on each other. This distribution is clear, since there is little doubt who is a friend and who is a foe, and it is easy, since each state need only monitor the actions of the other. Hence, by concentrating solely on a single major adversary, two superpowers are less likely to miscalculate each other's capabilities or intentions.

In a multipolar system, by contrast, it is difficult to devote adequate attention to all of the great powers, and it is often not clear which state poses the greatest threat to the rest—in other words, who is a danger to whom. The task of monitoring interactions between states quickly becomes complicated as the number of great powers rises from only two to six or seven. According to advocates of bipolarity, this poses several dangers. First, since states cannot fully monitor the behavior of every major actor, undetected imbalances of power can easily occur. Second, there is greater likelihood of miscalculating a rival's strength and intentions. Third, as the number of coalitions and alliances between states increases, there is a greater chance of friction and antagonism, which can ignite a conflict. Supporters of bipolarity frequently point to the complex and unreliable European alliance systems that failed to prevent World Wars I and II as evidence of multipolar instability.

This third point is worthy of further comment. In a bipolar system, both superpowers tend to balance through internal means, instead of through alliances, in order to avoid having to satisfy the demands and wishes of third states. By contrast, in a multipolar system, a great power risks being dragged into a conflict by any one of several partners. In World War I, for example, Germany was afraid to confront Russia alone, which would have happened if Germany's ally Austria was defeated. Therefore Berlin had no choice but to support its ally. The same held for Russia in its alliance with Serbia and for France in its alliance with Russia. With so many alliances in existence, it took only one spark to ignite a world war. Such dangers do not exist in a bipolar system, where great powers can pay only minimal attention to the demands of lesser allies. For instance, in 1956, when Britain, France, and Israel launched an attack against Egypt, a Soviet ally, the United States was not dragged into the war. The United States was able to discipline its allies with little fear that they would defect; staying out of the fray would not endanger American security.

Fourth, and related to the point just made, preserving the balance of power in a multipolar system requires careful coordination among several states. There is always the danger that a partner will not fulfill its obligation, as France failed to support Czechoslovakia as it had promised prior to World War II. Alliances take time to form, granting an adversary a temporary window of opportunity to attack with little fear of retaliation. The ever-present dangers of buck-passing and chain-ganging exist.

The final argument against multipolarity is that in a bipolar system, the loss or gain of an ally will have only a marginal impact on the balance of power. For example, the United States' "loss" of China in 1949 to the Soviets added only a minimal amount to the Soviets' overall capability, just as the Soviet "loss" of China following the final Sino-Soviet split in 1961 subtracted only a little from Moscow's immense capability.

The Case for Multipolarity

The multipolar approach refutes a number of these arguments. First, it holds that the uncertainty of a multipolar distribution is stabilizing, not destabilizing.

We know that as the number of states in the system rises, the number of bilateral relationships between them increases at an exponential rate. Political scientists Karl Deutsch and J. David Singer argue that a high number of relationships severely limits the amount of attention a state can focus on any single state in the system. The inability of a state to monitor the behavior of others encourages it to behave more cautiously, further reinforcing deterrence.[20]

Second, multipolar proponents contend that the increased number of inter-action opportunities in a multipolar system leads to cross-cutting concerns, which in turn moderate behavior and reduce the likelihood of war. In other words, a member of one alliance might have interests in common with members of the opposing coalition, as well as interests conflicting with those of its own coalition. This condition, it is argued, moderates the behavior of states. In a bipolar configuration, on the other hand, if all the members of one coalition have common interests, none of which are shared by the other coalition, antagonism between blocs is reinforced and exacerbated, further fueling rivalry. For instance, if members of different ethnic groups have little contact with one another, living in segregated neighborhoods and attending segregated schools and social clubs, differences between the factions are reinforced. Accordingly, permanent alliances are seen as destabilizing because they reduce the potential for the formation of cross-cutting concerns. In a multipolar system, though, uncommitted states encourage the formation of cross pressures, which moderate conflict.

Finally, a multipolar system slows arms races and restrains the security dilemma. A multipolar world is not a **zero-sum game.** If one state initiates an arms buildup, other states do not have to match it equally, since they can balance against it through an alliance. As Deutsch and Singer note, a state can "survive as a second-class power as safely or precariously as it did as a first-class one, provided only that it joins in time the appropriate new alliance or alignment."[21] A multipolar distribution will moderate behavior, too: Since today's enemy might be tomorrow's ally, there is little incentive to impose harsh penalties on a defeated state.

Multipolar proponents criticize bipolarity on several grounds. First, they contend that the notion of "peace through crisis," as occurred during the Cold War, exacerbates antagonism. A bipolar distribution is characterized as a zero-sum situation in which one state's gain is another state's loss; the result is two superpowers who compete over everything. During the Cold War, for example, small, strategically insignificant countries such as Angola, Mozambique, and Laos were highly contested, although they did not alter the balance of power between the two poles. For all their struggle, the United States was able to lose South Vietnam and the Soviets were able to lose Egypt with hardly any impact on the global balance of power.

Second, in a bipolar system, critics contend, the tail (the client state) wags the dog (the great power), instead of the other way around. Bipolarity grants clients significant influence over their patrons, since they can threaten to defect to the other side. While this led to almost comical situations such as when the United States and USSR traded their clients, Somalia and Ethiopia, it also led to proxy

AT A GLANCE

POLARITY

Unipolar/Hegemonic

The international system is dominated by a single powerful state.

Benefits: One great power can produce stability by definition: no conflict between great powers. There is a need for global goods and the hegemon supplies them with little or no assistance from other states. Since the hegemon has the largest economy, is has the most to gain from free trade. For example, after the hegemonic leadership of Britain declined, the consequence was increased protectionism, economic chaos, and the accentuation of the Great Depression.

Drawbacks: One great power may dominate and ultimately oppress other states. If the hegemon cannot provide economic and political services alone, then the international system will decline into disorder. The hegemon has the most to lose if all other states erect tariffs. Hegemons cannot last forever. Therefore, decline will follow in this system and it must ultimately collapse.

Bipolar

Two great powers.

Benefits: Since there are only two large states and small states cannot influence either's policies, the two powers do not have to rely on allies. The system is also more self-contained, since through constant jockeying, imbalances of power are unlikely to occur. These two powers

wars, which almost escalated into superpower conflict. During the 1973 Arab-Israeli war, for example, U.S. forces were placed on an advanced nuclear alert in response to Soviet threats of direct intervention. Thus, in a bipolar system, both superpowers become extensively involved in all regions of the globe, even though in the end, the positioning of small client states does not significantly alter the balance of power.

Can the Polarity Debate Be Resolved?

In the bipolar-multipolar debate, there is a clear trade-off in the virtues and vices of both systems.[22] In a bipolar world, wars between the superpowers are less likely to occur, but because of the intense competition and antagonism that exist in that system, wars are likely to be more violent and costly when they do occur. In a multipolar system, great-power wars are more likely to occur, but will usually be less violent. In other words, there will be more "brush-fire" wars, but they will be less likely to burn out of control. States will have an incentive to moderate their behavior and not treat defeated states too harshly, since today's enemy might be tomorrow's ally.

Role of Nuclear Weapons

One branch of the realist school of thought argues that the existence of nuclear weapons renders the bipolar versus multipolar debate a moot point. Stability is dominate the system. Each power is less likely to miscalculate the other's intentions or capabilities.

Drawbacks: The zero-sum game results in two superpowers competing over everything. In this system, the tail (client state) wags the dog (the great power), instead of the other way around. Bipolarity grants clients significant influence over their patrons, since they can threaten to defect to the other side.

Multipolar
Three or more great powers.

Benefits: Each great power finds it difficult to monitor the behavior of others, which encourages it to behave more cautiously. The increased number of interactions leads to the cross-cutting concerns that moderate behavior. This system also slows the arms race. A multipolar world is not a zero-sum game.

Drawbacks: Since states cannot fully monitor the behavior of every major actor, undetected imbalances of power can easily occur. There is a greater likelihood of miscalculating a rival's strength and intentions. As the number of coalitions and alliances between states increases, there is a greater chance of friction and antagonism, which can ignite a conflict.

fostered by the potential destructiveness of a nuclear war, not by the number of great powers. Consequently, a change in the distribution of power would probably have little if any independent impact on the stability of the system. Judging the costs of nuclear war to be intolerable, post–World War II decision makers, particularly U.S. and Soviet leaders, consistently moderated their behavior, according to this theory. If this is true, then the nuclear age presents an ironic implication: Weapons of mass destruction could be the basis for a lasting international peace. Because the use of nuclear weapons would make any war aim irrelevant, rational decision makers would always choose to behave moderately.

Other realists argue that the bipolar system has a number of special properties that greatly facilitate nuclear stability. Among these is the presence of only two main actors, making it easier for one side to deter the other. There is less likelihood of misperceiving the actions of a rival state, and there are fewer "fingers" on the nuclear button. In a multipolar world, events rapidly become more complicated and changes are harder to predict. It is often not clear which country is the main threat, and uncertainty plays a larger role. In a multipolar system, it is possible for several actors to gang up on a victim and thus nullify the possibility of a second-strike capability. It might therefore be impossible for any single state to ensure that it possesses enough nuclear weapons to survive a first strike and still have the capability to retaliate with a massive second strike against several states (see Chapter Eleven). In this way, nuclear weapons may reverse the traditional strengths and weaknesses of bipolar and multipolar systems.[23]

Clutching an AK-47 assault rifle, a UNITA guerrilla stands beside an artillery piece during a 1984 parade at the pro-Western movement's JAMBA base in southern Angola. The weapons were captured from Soviet-backed MPLA government troops.
Source: © UPI/Bettmann.

BEYOND THE BALANCE OF POWER: COLLECTIVE SECURITY

As we have seen, balance of power has been one historic strategy of managing interstate behavior in the international system. However, after long and destructive conflicts such as the Napoleonic Wars and the world wars, attempts were made by the world's leading nations to replace the balance of power with collective-security arrangements. (Chapters Two, Three, and Nine recount the successes and failures of collective-security organizations such as the Concert of Europe, the League of Nations, and the United Nations.) This section will examine the concept of collective security, and compare and contrast it to balance-of-power theory as an alternative method for managing the international system. In doing so, we will discuss some of the strengths and shortcomings of collective-security arrangements.

The concept of **collective security** is often used as a catchall for any form of multilateral defense arrangement. Collective security describes a system where states join together, usually by signing a treaty, to renounce the use of force to settle disputes with one another, and to promise to use force against any participant who uses force against another member.[24] Accordingly, a collective-security treaty identifies legal obligations and conditions under which signatories are bound. In its most complete form, it involves a legally binding and codified commitment on the part of all members to counter aggression. For example, Article 16 in the League of Nations covenant stated, "Should any member of the League resort to war in disregard of its covenants . . . it shall, *ipso facto*, be deemed to have committed an act of war against other Members of the League."

Collective-defense arrangements such as NATO and the Warsaw Pact share many of these characteristics (such as obligations to consult or act if any member is attacked). The main distinction between these and collective-security arrangements is that the latter applies as well to threats to members that come from *within* the coalition. They are intended to keep peace among the members, in addition to protecting them from outside aggressors. In contrast, collective-defense arrangements are intended only to protect members from external challengers. For example, the Gulf Cooperation Council (GCC), consisting of Saudi Arabia, Kuwait, Bahrain, Qatar, Oman, and the United Arab Emirates (UAE), was formed to guard against threats from Iran and Iraq.[25] To be an effective regional collective-security arrangement, it would have to be expanded to include all potential threats within the organization encompassing Iran, Turkey, other Arab states including Iraq, and Israel.[26]

Collective-security arrangements incorporate the characteristics of deterrence, defense, and compellence (see Chapter Eleven). They are based on the idea of "all against one"—all members are obligated to participate in the countercoalition against an aggressor—and such knowledge should be sufficient to deter any participant from challenging another member. The treaty obligation is intended to increase the certainty that an effective countercoalition will form; a "legal" obligation for all members to participate increases the credibility of the threat to punish any aggressor. Collective security thus argues that a preponderance of power is more stable than a balance of power. It expects that the combined strength of the collective security partners will deter aggression and prevail against an aggressor if deterrence fails.

Not surprisingly, collective-security arrangements encounter some of the same problems as deterrence. The costs of having to effectively demonstrate

WHAT WOULD YOU DO?

You are given the responsibility for designing the best international system for maintaining the balance of power. You can choose between a bipolar or multipolar system. A unipolar system—one great power—would by definition reduce the chances of great-power war, but would also threaten the independence of the other states. You reject this option as it contradicts the heart of the balance-of-power principle.

Some theorists argue that war among major powers results from the inability to identify sources of threat. Accordingly, because a bipolar system—two great powers—allows for easy identification of allies and adversaries, it would be less prone to war than, say, a multipolar system. Also, this easy identification would encourage the two major powers to negotiate individually with one another, without relying on their allies' contributions to the balance of power. The great danger of a bipolar system, though, is that competition between the two major powers may escalate and,

the group's willingness to counter acts of aggression can be significant. And if the threat to punish does not appear to be convincing, it increases the danger that members might be dragged into an unwanted war. Furthermore, any doubt on an aggressor's part about the willingness of all members to fulfill their commitment might lead the aggressor to challenge a member of the coalition.

Once deterrence fails, and a member is attacked, in most cases the collective-security agreement calls for the other members to come to the defense of the victim. In the United Nations, however, this decision is left to the Security Council. The five permanent members must decide unanimously to intervene, either through economic sanctions or through military action. In order to ensure that the UN does not initiate force against the supporter of a great power (and hence possibly involve itself in a war with a great power), each permanent member has a veto, an instrument that was used often in the Security Council during the Cold War. (See Chapter Nine.)

The main benefit of a collective-security system is that if deterrence fails, the member states should be able to respond rapidly and prepare for war, since support is already in place. In the New Era, collective security has not yet fulfilled its vast potential. In the 1990–1991 Persian Gulf conflict, it essentially worked; the international community rushed to the aid of tiny Kuwait after it was invaded by Iraq. In the Bosnian conflict, which began in 1992, collective security failed; Western nations were as a whole unwilling and unable to mount a coalition to turn back Serbian and Croatian aggression in the Muslim-dominated former Yugoslav republic. Thus, the precise role of collective security in the New Era remains to be determined.

It is important to note that collective security can infringe on the traditional rights of nation-states. In one form of collective security, for example, national thus, increase the chances that each great power will try to take advantage of the other at every opportunity.

On the other hand, some theorists argue that war among major powers results from the ability to identify sources of threat. Accordingly, because a multipolar system—three or more great powers—does not allow for easy identification of allies and adversaries, it would be less prone to war than, say, a bipolar system. Thus, unable to distinguish between allies and adversaries, great powers would avoid antagonizing a potential future ally. The great drawback of a multipolar system is that great powers rely heavily on their allies to maintain the balance of power. This prevents great powers from responding promptly to imbalances of power and provides opposing alliances an opportunity to seize the advantage through aggression.

Which system would you implement?

decision makers would grant the decision to use force to a supranational body. By requiring all states to participate in sanctions against an aggressor, decisions would no longer be made at the national level. The Security Council would take over the national-security decision-making role usually reserved for national executives and legislatures—and jealously guarded by nation-states. To what extent would this threaten state sovereignty (see Chapter Nine)?

Collective Security Dynamics

Although intended as an alternative means of managing the interstate system, collective security and balance of power share many of the same dynamics. First, both systems seek to maintain the status quo, or to preserve the existing power hierarchy. As a result, they favor those who benefit by the current system and hinder those whose interests are not served by it. As one would expect, the main challengers to this system come from the ranks of the dissatisfied. It becomes apparent, then, that collective security is more likely to succeed if its members have compatible views of what constitutes a stable international order, and at the same time are satisfied with their position in the international hierarchy.

Second, both systems seek to maintain stability through the threat of a counterbalancing coalition. In both systems there is a distrust of any state so powerful that it can transgress with impunity upon the basic interests of the other states. The result in both systems is the threat, or actual formation, of a counter-coalition, in order to deter any potential aggressors. In the balance of power this is accomplished either through the formation of alliances or through internal mobilization and buildup; in collective security it is accomplished through the fulfillment of formal obligations.

AT A GLANCE

PREPONDERANCE VERSUS BALANCE OF POWER VERSUS COLLECTIVE SECURITY

Argument

Preponderance: War is less likely when one hegemonic state dominates the rest, the rationale being that as long as there is one hegemonic power, no state will challenge it because any challenger is likely to lose. Because states grow at different rates, an emerging state will inevitably encroach upon a dominant state's position. As the gap in power between the rival states narrows and they become more equal in strength, war is likely to occur, since both the challenger and the hegemon believe that they are likely to prevail.

Balance of Power: An equal distribution of power is more stable than a *hegemonic* distribution, where one state dominates. If one state or bloc becomes too preponderant, it would be tempted to dominate the system and impose its will on the other states by the threat or use of military force. The attempt to prevent hegemony may result in alliances as states seek to strengthen their position against possible dominating powers.

Collective Security: Describes a system where states join together, usually by signing a treaty, to renounce the use of force to settle disputes with one another, and to promise to use force against any participant who uses force against another member. The treaty identifies legal obligations and conditions under which signatories are bound.

Balancing

Preponderance: A hegemon is the dominant military and economic power among the states in the international system and often has extensive global commitments. It establishes and enforces a set of rules that govern the international system, and it provides a number of global services to its allies. However, eventually the costs of maintaining its superiority causes the hegemon to decline, therefore allowing an emerging state to challenge its superiority.

Balance of Power: Under a counterbalancing coalition, if one state becomes too powerful, the remaining states should balance against it by forming an alliance. The purpose of an alliance is to quickly aggregate capability in order to deter a potential hegemon, and if this fails, to prepare for war in order to restore the balance of power. Internal balancing calls for the domestic mobilization of economic and industrial resources and their conversion into military power, in order to match up against a potential hegemon's capabilities.

Collective Security: Based on the idea of "all against one"—all members are obligated to participate in the countercoalition against an aggressor, and such knowledge should be sufficient to deter any actor from challenging another member. The theory thus argues that a preponderance of power is more stable than a balance of power.

Problems

Preponderance:

1. Although periods of hegemony are associated with peace, periods of hegemonic decline that have always followed are associated with war.

2. A declining hegemon will not peacefully relinquish its position to a challenger, and a rising challenger is unlikely to back down.

3. War, not peaceful succession, is the usual outcome.

Balance of Power:

1. Allies may not fulfill their commitments to aid their partners. For this reason, states are suspicious of alliances and other cooperative security arrangements.

2. Counterbalancing alliances are often slow to form.

3. The problem of buck-passing, in which "there is a temptation of all of the parties to let other states confront the threatening state," is present.

4. Another problem is chain-ganging. This is the danger that a state might get dragged into a war that it has no interest in fighting.

Collective Security:

1. The costs of having to effectively demonstrate the group's willingness and resolve to counter acts of aggression can be significant. If the threat to punish does not appear to be convincing, it increases the danger that members might be dragged into an unwanted war. Any doubt on the aggressor's part of the willingness of the other members to fulfill their commitments might lead it to challenge another member.

2. The next problem is that of collective action. There is a temptation here to free-ride or pass the buck. Cohesion among members might also be difficult to achieve, especially if member states have competing expectations, outlooks, and positions in the international hierarchy.

3. The difficulty of identifying and defining instances of aggression creates a continuing impediment to success.

4. Some theorists believe that the very cooperative nature of collective security arrangements represents a deficit, not an advantage.

Benefits

Preponderance: The hegemon is able to provide a number of global services that include economic and military aid. During periods of hegemonic superiority, challengers are weak and usually do not face off with the global leader, thereby resulting in a more peaceful international arena.

Balance of Power: Theorists envision the formation of fluid and shifting alliances that form when necessary and quickly dissipate after they have served their purpose, only to form again at some future point against another preponderant state.

Collective Security: If deterrence fails, the member states should be able to rapidly respond and prepare for war, since support is already in place.

Types
Preponderance: Hegemony

Balance of Power: Bipolarity, multipolarity

Collective Security: Collective security treaties (for example, the UN, League of Nations)

Shared Dynamics
All of these systems seek to maintain the status quo or to preserve the existing power hierarchy.

Key Differences
In the balance-of-power and collective security scenarios, the systems seek to maintain stability through the threat of a counterbalancing coalition. The balance-of-power world is one of constant jockeying and rivalry among the great powers to ensure that no one state becomes preponderant. Every state acts only in its own best interest, ignoring some challenges and plotting against others. In contrast, collective security offers a system of general cooperation to hold conflict in check. Formal collective security arrangements offer greater certainty than the balance of power because they increase the chance that an aggressor will be punished. A collective security arrangement has the advantage of simplicity and greater reliability. Advocates of preponderance and collective security both believe a dominant state or coalition is stabilizing because a potential aggressor is unlikely to attack a dominant power because it will almost certainly lose.

The main difference between these two methods of stabilizing the international system is the degree of "managerial centralization." The balance-of-power world is one of constant jockeying and rivalry among the great powers to ensure that no one state becomes preponderant. Each state acts only in its own best interests, balancing against particular challenges but ignoring some and welcoming others. In this sense, balance of power works through an ad-hoc calculation of what state leaders think the national interests require rather than through a formal or legal mechanism like a treaty. Successful deterrence becomes more problematic as a result; the potential aggressor is less sure of the defender's capabilities and less certain about whether some, if any, states will join a counteralliance, and, if they do, how long it will take to form. Thus, a potential aggressor might doubt the willingness of states to join a counteralliance.

In contrast to balance of power, collective security offers a system of general cooperation to hold conflict in check. In this sense, collective security is really just a more managed system of balance of power. First, formal collective-security arrangements offer greater certainty than balance of power because they increase the chance that an aggressor will be punished—a challenger is less likely to think that it can get away with an aggressive act if states are more formally aligned. Collective security is intended to increase the likelihood and credibility that a countercoalition will form; in theory, the fact that all members have signed a treaty should eliminate doubt about what will happen to any one member that challenges another. Of course, it is never guaranteed that a counter-coalition will form.

Second, a collective-security arrangement has the advantage of simplicity. If a treaty has been signed, there should be no need to calculate who will respond and under what conditions a reaction will occur. And because all members are supposed to act against the one that first resorts to force, collective security protects small and weak states. As political scientist Inis Claude notes, in the balance-of-power system, "small states might be protected or they might be chopped to bits; for their fate was dependent upon the convenience, the calculations of self-interest, of the main participants."[27]

Thus, collective security also offers greater reliability. Under balance of power, the formation of a countervailing coalition often takes a lot of time to form, if it forms at all. This system thus provides a challenger with a "window of opportunity"—a period in which it can attack before the defender can marshal a preponderant counterforce. However, collective-security arrangements are designed to expedite the time of response. Since there is already an agreement at hand and an organization to supervise it, the defenders do not need to form an alliance—it is already in existence.

Balance of power is also based on an equal distribution of power, whereas collective security is based on preponderance, or an unbalanced distribution of power. Balance-of-power theory views an equal distribution of power as most stabilizing, since no one state has an overwhelming amount of power to tempt it to impose its will on other states. In contrast, collective security depends not upon an equilibrium of power, but rather upon a preponderance of power.

Advocates of collective security contend that this form of preponderance is more stabilizing, because no state would dare take hostile action against a collective that is clearly superior in power, thereby risking almost certain defeat. In this way, they agree with those realists who believe stability requires clear preponderance, but they seek to accomplish that preponderance through an organized coalition of states that includes a treaty setting out rules and agreements for action in case one of the members is attacked.

Problems with Collective Security

On paper, collective security might seem to be a sure bet. However, the failure of both the League of Nations and the UN to prevent wars clearly demonstrates that collective-security organizations have not lived up to expectations that they would promote peaceful coexistence among states. As history has demonstrated, there are several problems with collective-security arrangements.

The first is the **collective action problem.** In any large organization or group, there is a temptation on the part of each member to pass the buck or free-ride, believing that the other members will fulfill their commitment.[28] Although all members might want the aggressor to be stopped, none is willing to bear the cost of doing so. Unfortunately, if all members act in this fashion, the aggressor will go unchallenged. This is one reason that the League of Nations failed to respond to Japan's invasion of Manchuria, a part of China, in 1931. The League of Nations passed resolutions calling for Japan's withdrawal, but no member was willing to assume the costs of enforcing them, and the Japanese government simply went on with its business (see Chapters Three and Nine).

Second, cohesion among members might be difficult to achieve, especially if member states have competing expectations, outlooks, and positions in the international hierarchy. Perhaps the best example has been the UN Security Council (SC). As we know, the SC became paralyzed by the Cold War split between the United States and the Soviet Union, both of whom had the power to veto resolutions. Unable to mobilize a majority, the United States or Soviet Union would exercise their veto power to block action on matters with which they disagreed, thus preventing the SC from working as an effective collective-security organization. In 1950, after Communist North Korea's invasion of South Korea, the only reason the United States obtained a UN endorsement of action to protect the South was because the Soviet Union was boycotting meetings of the SC.

Not only is cohesion difficult to achieve, but failure to include all the major regional or great-power actors further undermines collective-security arrangements. If major actors are excluded, it is also necessary to form a defensive-security arrangement to defend against states outside of the original organization. For example, at various times in its history, the League of Nations did not include important actors such as the United States, Japan, the Soviet Union, and Germany. A system designed to be based on collective security had retreated back to the classic balance-of-power arrangement.

"We Told You It Wouldn't Work!"

When the U.S. Senate refused to ratify American membership in the League of Nations, it doomed the post–World War I experiment in collective security initiated by President Woodrow Wilson.

Source: © 1994 Des Moines Register and Tribune Company. Reprinted with permission.

A third problem with collective security is the difficulty of identifying and defining instances of aggression. The traditional definition of aggression is "violation of territorial integrity and political independence," but there is often ambiguity in determining what constitutes aggression and even who is the aggressor. For example, many Arab states have argued that the existence of Israel in itself is a form of aggression, because even pre-1967 Israel was perceived as occupying Arab land. In cases where aggression occurs over a long period and in waves, it is difficult or impossible to determine when aggressive action began and who was the initiator. The decades-old India-Pakistan rivalry serves as an example.

Finally, some realists believe that the very cooperative nature of collective-security arrangements represents a problem, not an advantage. Their argument is that states are unlikely to cooperate, out of fear that others will gain more from cooperation.[29] In a dog-eat-dog world, states fear that others will exploit their cooperative behavior, or that others will not carry out their part of the bargain, and thus they distrust the arrangement. Not wanting to be unprepared if abandoned by the other members, states will still seek to maintain their own credible deterrence and defensive force. Not wanting to become entrapped in unwanted wars, states "are not prepared to do, or convinced that they should do, the things that an operative system of collective security would require them to do."[30] In short, states rarely place all of their trust in collective-security arrangements.

Despite these problems, it appears as if the idea of collective security is once again a relevant security topic for diplomatic discussion, at least for the defense of Europe. Recently, there has been discussion of converting the CSCE (Conference for Security and Cooperation in Europe) into a legally binding collective-security arrangement. There are several reasons why it might have a greater chance of success than its predecessors. First, most of its members share compatible views of a stable international order. Second, as developed industrial states, most are satisfied with their position in the international system and interested in maintaining the status quo. Third, as democratic states, they have a similar outlook and a natural compatibility. Finally, they have a common belief that war between them is of little use. These advantages aside, European inability to stop the fighting in the former Yugoslavia remains an important and powerful reminder of the weaknesses of European collective-security arrangements before World War II.

NEOLIBERAL INSTITUTIONALISM: BEYOND THE NATION-STATE?

Not all scholars believe that states exist in a dog-eat-dog environment. As we know, the world is not always consumed by warfare. There have been many instances of interstate cooperation, and relatively few great powers have been destroyed by war. Indeed, if interactions between states were counted, there would be far more cooperation than conflict. The New Era is a period of state creation and rebirth. If nations were unwilling to coordinate their foreign policies, the multiplicity of interactions between states would be far more chaotic and dangerous than has been the case in the past.

The very existence of international cooperation raises the fundamental question, what makes it possible? The school of thought known as **neoliberal institutionalism** argues that the inherent anarchy and violence of the international system can be overcome through carefully designed institutions for international cooperation.[31] This section will examine the premises of this approach in order to identify the barriers to international cooperation, as well as the conditions under which cooperation becomes possible.

Can Nations Cooperate?

Neoliberal institutionalism accepts many of the assumptions of realism, such as the supremacy of the nation-state and the anarchic character of the international system, yet contends that cooperation among states is possible. Neoliberals argue that the world is not a zero-sum game in which one state's gain translates into another's loss (both actors cannot mutually benefit), but that it is a variable-sum game—that is, through cooperation, all states simultaneously and mutually benefit. Cooperation and collaboration allow states to benefit because the pie is not fixed; it continues to grow.

Cooperation is defined as "the voluntary adjustment by states of their policies so that they manage their differences and reach some mutually beneficial outcome."[32] Realists and neoliberals differ over what constitutes barriers to cooperation among states in the international system. According to realists, there are two barriers: First, because states seek to maximize their power to ensure their chances of survival, they are sensitive to any decline or loss in their relative capabilities. When also guided by the assumption that today's ally may well be tomorrow's enemy, states become reluctant to cooperate because they fear that they might be helping to strengthen a potential rival. The barrier, then, is that states are more concerned about any loss in their relative ranking in the international system of states. The question is not "will both of us gain," but "who will gain more" from cooperation. The implication is that in some instances, even when both states will obtain absolute gains, they will still fail to cooperate because one state fears that the other might disproportionately benefit from collaboration. Accordingly, states may give up increases in their absolute gains if doing so prevents others from achieving even greater gains. This has been the case, for example, within the European Union during negotiations over the Maastricht Treaty, and also with India and Pakistan during negotiations to reduce nuclear arsenals.

The second barrier to cooperation has its root in states' natural distrust of one another. Since there is no supranational body to guarantee that agreements are honored, states are reluctant to cooperate, because they fear getting duped by a partner who defects from an agreement.

Neoliberals counter that it is possible to achieve cooperation, even in an anarchic system where there is no supranational body to enforce compliance. Factors besides state interests and power can foster cooperation, they contend, namely the mediation role of international institutions and international law, and economic interdependence. Realists respond that those factors are conducive to cooperation and are likely to be ignored whenever the cooperative action involved is inconvenient or costly. Thus, cooperative behavior will reflect only a state's temporary interest. Primary issues of state survival or security will take precedence, say the realists, over any incentives to cooperate.[33] As evidence, they cite the failures of the Kellogg-Briand Pact, the League of Nations, and the United Nations to restrain states from acting aggressively (see Chapters Three, Four, and Nine).

Barriers to Cooperation: The Problem of Collective Goods

Recall that the main barrier to cooperation in the international system is the temptation for states to cheat, or "defect," by not fulfilling their share of an agreement. This temptation arises because security, like law, order, and environmental cleanliness, is a public, or collective, good.

Public goods have two defining characteristics: They are nonexcludable and indivisible.[34] **Nonexcludability** means that once enough contributors are available to finance any one of these amenities, all others can also enjoy the benefits of the public good without contributing to its provision—and, in fact, cannot be prevented from doing so.[35] A familiar example of a nonexcludable good is public television; anyone can watch it without having to subscribe or contribute to a public broadcasting system (PBS) station. (This explains why PBS constantly asks viewers to donate money.) In contrast, cable television is not a public good, since the only people who can obtain it are paying members; nonpaying members are excluded.

Public goods are also indivisible, in that one person's consumption of the good does not reduce the amount available to others. Any ship entering a harbor can benefit from a lighthouse, for example, without reducing the navigational aid the lighthouse gives to any other boat. Most public goods, however, are not completely indivisible. Public highways and beaches, for example, can suffer from overcrowding, which reduces the level of benefits to all users.

The consequence of nonexcludability and **indivisibility** is that public goods are often underprovided or not provided at all, even though people want them. This occurs because noncontributors are able to obtain them without making any contribution toward their provision. What often happens is that most people do not contribute to the provision of the public good, but instead select to **free-ride;** meaning they use the public good without paying as much as they should or even paying nothing whatsoever. Free-riding is a temptation for everyone, but if everyone succumbs to it, the good will not be provided. That is why it is so difficult to clean up polluted rivers or get states to cooperate regarding other environmental concerns—like watching PBS, everyone wants others to assume the burden.

Some theorists argue that defense within an alliance is an example of an international public good.[36] Admittedly, all states benefit from deterring an aggressive state, even if they do not directly contribute to the deterrence effort. It is not surprising, then, that alliances often acquire two characteristics: (1) there is a tendency for larger and wealthier members to pay a disproportionate share of the costs of the public good; and (2) alliances often fail to meet the overall goals that they set for defense spending. Among alliance members there are often debates over burden-sharing and free-rider problems. In the case of NATO, for example, the United States has historically contributed the largest share for Europe's defense and has frequently complained that certain members within the alliance have not carried their weight.

Providing for Collective Goods: Hegemonic-Stability Theory

Hegemonic-stability theory, discussed in Chapter Seven, is based on the concept of public goods. It holds that there is a link between the provision of certain public goods or "services" and the degree of openness and stability of the

IS THE UNITED STATES A HEGEMON IN DECLINE?

Despite the challenge of the Soviet Union, for the three decades following World War II, the United States was the hegemonic leader according to both hegemonic-stability and long-cycle theorists. As hegemon, the United States assumed many global responsibilities and established and enforced the "rules of the game." It created a number of international organizations such as the World Bank, the Bretton Woods system, the IMF, and GATT to maintain economic and political stability. It implemented programs such as the Truman Doctrine and created numerous defense organizations to contain communism. It rebuilt Europe through the Marshall Plan and Japan during U.S. occupation. And, like the British pound in the previous century, the American dollar became the means of exchange, and the United States became the primary global lender.

Yet, beginning in the 1970s, U.S. hegemony began to wane. In terms of economic trends, in 1971, President Richard Nixon abandoned the gold-exchange created by the United States under the the Bretton Woods system for a floating exchange rate system. The United States began to run a trade deficit, importing more than it was exporting. It moved from a net lender of capital to a net debtor and began to run a huge federal deficit, relying on foreigners to finance its debt. Other indicators of decline included falling student test scores, a smaller number of scientists produced, and declining research and development expenditures. One consequence was that American per capita GNP, once the world's highest, began to decline. The United States also experienced a number of foreign policy failures, including defeat in Vietnam, the OPEC oil embargo, and the taking of American hostages in Iran.

Paul Kennedy, in *The Rise and Fall of the Great Powers,* attributes U.S. decline to "imperial overstretch." Like Spain, the Netherlands, France, and Britain before, the United States gathered extensive global commitments during its ascendancy. However, military spending required to defend international commitments diverted resources from domestic investment in research and development, education, the infrastructure, and the like. In contrast, emerging powers such as Japan and Germany, with few global

international trading system.[37] These global services are provided by the hegemon, with little or no assistance from other states. They include making loans to countries in need, providing markets for various commodities, and defending the seas to make them safe for international trade. Neoliberal institutionalists would argue that since these global services are public goods, other states are tempted to free-ride, hoping that the hegemon alone will provide the service. However, if no state provides them, or if the hegemon cannot do it alone, then the international system will decline into disorder.

Proponents of this theory contend that Britain provided hegemonic leadership in the nineteenth century and that the United States played a similar role following World War II. During the interwar period, Britain, exhausted after commitments, could allocate a much larger share of their wealth toward domestic investment. Thus, claims Kennedy, the cost of global leadership contributed to the uneven rates of growth experienced by the United States, Japan, and Germany. His prescription to slow the U.S. decline calls for American retrenchment from some global commitments and earmarking the savings for greater domestic investment.

As this chapter has emphasized, there are both economic and military dangers associated with a possible American decline. First, based on the findings of hegemonic-stability theory, hegemony is often associated with periods of economic stability and openness, and hegemonic decline is associated with periods of economic chaos. Second, power transition and long-cycle theorists contend that war among the great powers is most likely to occur around the intersection of the trajectories of rising and declining states.

Yet, there remains considerable debate whether the United States is truly a declining power. While there is no doubt that Europe and Japan have encroached on the position of the United States, this can be attributed, in part, to the recovery of their economies damaged by World War II. In absolute terms, the U.S. economy remains nearly twice the size of that of the next largest, Japan's ($5.96 trillion versus $3.51 trillion in 1992). The United States remains the technological leader and innovator in key sectors such as aircraft, computers and software, and chemicals. While one indicator of economic strength, relative share of world production, does demonstrate that the U.S. percent of production declined from under 45 percent in 1950 to about 25 percent by 1974, it has stabilized at roughly this level for the past twenty years and recently began to rise.

While power transition and long cycle theorists forecast a rise in global conflict because of the decline of the United States, other scholars question the significance of the relative American decline. They note that in contrast to the emerging challengers that previous hegemons confronted, the rising powers the United States faces are trading states and democracies. According to this perspective, the United States has a lot to gain by the emergence of Japan and Germany.

World War I, was unable to provide these services. The United States, adhering to an isolationist strategy, was also unwilling to provide them. The consequence was increased protectionism, economic chaos, an accentuation of the Great Depression, and ultimately political and military upheaval.[38]

According to hegemonic-stability theory, the hegemon's rationale for unilaterally providing the public good is that since it has the largest economy, it has the most to gain from free trade, even if the other states elect to free-ride. Likewise, it also has the most to lose if all other states impose tariffs and other trade barriers (see Chapter Seven). The consequence is that periods of free trade tend to correspond with periods of hegemony, while economic protectionism and chaos often correspond with periods of hegemonic decline. In the

"PRISONERS' DILEMMA" GAME

Prosecutors believe that two suspects have collaborated in a major crime. Once captured, they are kept in separate rooms for interrogation. If neither prisoner talks to the police, the authorities have only enough circumstantial evidence to convict the prisoners of a minor offense. The district attorney thus offers both suspects a deal: If one prisoner turns state's evidence and testifies against the other, he or she will be released. The other will receive a life sentence.

The choices the prisoners face are modeled in the matrix. If both prisoners cooperate with each other (tell the police nothing), they each achieve their second-best payoff, spending only six months in jail apiece.* This outcome is represented by the upper left (C,C) cell of the matrix. However, if one turns state's witness against the other (that is, defects), the prisoner who squeals will be set free, and thus gain his/her best possible payoff, while the partner in crime gets his/her worst penalty,

life imprisonment. If A cooperates and B defects, the outcome is found in the upper right cell; if A defects and B cooperates, the situation in the lower left quadrant applies. If both defect, then there is no trial because both have confessed, and the

| | | Prisoner B | |
		Cooperate	Defect
Prisoner A	**Cooperate**	A jailed for 6 months C, C B jailed for 6 months	A imprisoned for life C, D B goes free
	Defect	A goes free D, C B imprisoned for life	A jailed for 10 years D, D B jailed for 10 years

New Era, then, American economic decline is a preview of global instability, unless a substitute hegemon is found soon.

"Prisoners' Dilemma" as a Metaphor for World Politics

The game of **"Prisoners' Dilemma"** serves as a metaphor for the difficulty of providing collective goods like international cooperation in an anarchical system.[39] In this game, two suspects face prosecution for a crime they are accused of jointly committing. Each is offered a lighter sentence by the police in return for testifying against the other. As explained in the boxed feature on this subject, the game shows how two players acting to maximize individual interests can bring about an outcome that neither desires.

In world politics, states are often confronted with situations resembling the Prisoners' Dilemma. In arms-control negotiations, for example, both sides would become more secure if they could agree not to deploy a destabilizing prosecutor gives them a medium sentence—ten years.

The game predicts that if both prisoners act in their own self-interest, each will defect—in other words, each prisoner will rat on the other. The consequence is that both end up with their second worst outcome, spending ten years in jail, as indicated in the lower right cell. The irony of the game is that if both had cooperated with each other (exercising their right to remain silent), each would spend only six months in jail, clearly a better outcome than life imprisonment. However, individually, both prisoners can do better by defecting or cheating than by cooperating because neither can be sure of the other's actions. The consequence is that both end up with a worse outcome than they would have secured if they had cooperated.

In the "Prisoners' Dilemma" game, the structure of the situation shapes and influences the moves of each player. The prisoners defect not because they are immoral or dislike their partner, but because the structure of the game offers an incentive for each to defect or cheat; any rational, self-interested person would defect under these circumstances. The "Prisoners' Dilemma" model is an attempt to explain why sovereign states, each acting in their own self-interest, will often fail to cooperate even though cooperation offers the potential for substantial gains.

*The payoffs of the "Prisoners' Dilemma" as presented here are based on punishments. In other "Prisoners' Dilemma" games, payoffs can—and often do—reflect rewards.

weapons system. However, as a result of the higher payoff for defection over cooperation, both have an incentive to cheat on the agreement or not to agree in the first place because they might be able to gain a quick or temporary advantage over the other. In the end, though, if each state acts in this manner, both will suffer.

The years between 1895 and 1914 saw an intense naval arms race between Britain, the established naval power, and Germany, its emerging challenger.[40] In 1912 both states demonstrated an interest in cooling down the naval race, since the domestic economic costs were becoming more difficult to manage. As the Prisoners' Dilemma model would predict, however, both sides attempted to circumvent the potential restrictions placed on arms control in order to gain the upper hand.[41] Each feared the other would cheat, so they both did. Instead of ending up with a controlled arms race (the second best outcome for both), the naval race continued, resulting in the second worst outcome for both. (The worst outcome for either, of course, was having the other side attain a decisive advantage.)

TRUE GRIT

GRIT (Graduated and Reciprocated Initiatives in Tension-reduction) is a strategy that is similar to tit-for-tat, except that it does not require cooperation after the first move. In GRIT, the state desiring to foster cooperation makes an opening cooperative move that involves some moderate risk, but displays the state's good intentions. GRIT does not assume that the other side will immediately reciprocate, and accordingly counsels patience. Although not willing to be exploited, the initiator will continue incremental concessions over a period of time to convince the other side of its good will.

Political scientist Deborah Welch Larson points to the Austrian State Treaty of 1955, which led to the neutralization of Austria, as a successful example of GRIT in action.* Like Germany and Korea following World War II, Austria was divided by American and Soviet occupation. After the death of Stalin in 1953, Larson contends that Soviet

OVERCOMING BARRIERS TO COOPERATION

The Prisoners' Dilemma illustrates the problems states face when trying to cooperate without any supranational guarantee that agreements will be enforced. Is it possible to overcome the incentive to cheat and instead obtain an outcome mutually beneficial to both states? The previous section used neoliberalist theory to identify various barriers to interstate cooperation, all of which revolve around the problem of free-riding. This section will explore ways to surmount those barriers and thereby facilitate international cooperation. Four possible strategies will be discussed; tit-for-tat, international "regimes," international law, and economic interdependence. Each demonstrates that cooperation is possible among states through self-enforcing strategies and international institutions. It is up to the reader to decide which particular strategy (or combination thereof) represents the best possible solution to the problems of free-riding.

Tit-for-Tat

If a game of Prisoners' Dilemma is played for only one round, it is expected that both players will defect. However, if the game is played over and over again with the same players, and if they value future gains from cooperation, it is possible to achieve a mutually beneficial outcome by employing a **tit-for-tat strategy.** This is accomplished by cooperating on the first round, no matter what the other party does, and then mimicking that party's moves on subsequent rounds—cooperating when it cooperates, defecting when it defects. The purpose of this strategy is to convince the other side that you are willing to cooperate if it does. You show your willingness to take a chance premiers Malenkov and Khrushchev pursued a strategy of GRIT by making numerous incremental conciliatory gestures designed to gain American confidence in the Soviet desire to reach an agreement concerning Austria. Even after U.S. Secretary of State John Foster Dulles rebuked several attempts, the Soviets persisted in making unilateral concessions to the United States. The result was the Austrian State Treaty, in which both superpowers (as well as Britain and France) agreed to withdraw their troops from Austria so that it could reunify as a neutral state. The United States reciprocated by agreeing to a summit meeting that was held in Geneva in July 1955. In this case, a GRIT strategy led to a favorable outcome for all sides.

*Deborah Welch Larson, "Crisis Prevention and the Austrian State Treaty," *International Organization* 41, no. 1 (Winter 1987), p. 32. Charles Osgood defines GRIT in "The GRIT Strategy," *Bulletin of Atomic Scientists* (May 1980), pp. 58–60.

on the first round by cooperating unconditionally, but you also demonstrate that you will not be taken for a "sucker." This strategy shows that cooperation is possible, even in a decentralized and anarchic system, through a self-enforcing strategy.

The pricing of oil on the world market illustrates both the barriers to achieving cooperation and how tit-for-tat can be used to overcome them. The price of a barrel of oil is determined by the amount of oil in the market; a lot of oil means low prices, a little oil means high prices (assuming the same level of demand). If oil-producing states are able to cooperate and reduce their production, then, in effect, they are able to increase the price of a barrel. Production is held down by setting a quota, whereby members agree to sell less than the maximum amount each can produce. However, as the Prisoners' Dilemma suggests, each oil producer is tempted to cheat and sell additional oil beyond the limit. After all, if one country can get away with cheating while the others comply, it will make a large profit. Once other oil producers catch on and begin producing at full capacity, there will be an oil glut. Prices will decline, and no producers will benefit.

The problem that oil-producing states face is to ensure that member states will not cheat and sell their excess reserves. Hypothetically, within the Organization of Petroleum Exporting Countries (OPEC), Saudi Arabia, the biggest producer, could use the strategy of tit-for-tat to induce other members to cooperate. Saudi Arabia could initiate the strategy by unconditional cooperation (producing at its quota level), and then mimic the subsequent actions of other OPEC members. If Iran cheated (overproducing), then Saudi Arabia would in turn defect and continue to do so until Iran decided to cooperate, at which time Saudi Arabia would also cooperate. As long as both players continued to cheat and overproduce, prices would continue to drop, due to overproduction. Saudi Arabia would have the upper hand in this game, however, because even as prices fell, it would have a lesser need for revenue than Iran because of larger financial reserves and a smaller population. In the real world, Iran cannot afford to let prices drop because of its larger population and higher demand for resources. As a result, at some point Iran will curb its overproduction and cooperate (that is, produce at its quota level) in order to boost its oil revenues. When this happens, Saudi Arabia will also cooperate by fulfilling its quota, driving supply down and in turn prices up. Riyadh will continue to cooperate as long as Teheran fulfills its quota. In this case, then, cooperation is achieved without any supranational authority.

One problem with tit-for-tat is that it becomes almost impossible to effectively pursue as the game expands from two actors to several. The difficulties arise from any one actor's inability to discriminate between the target and non-target states. In the case of OPEC, it is impossible to cooperate with some states and defect against others, since defecting against only one is in effect the same as defecting against all; overproduction will bring prices down for everyone, not just Iran. As a result, tit-for-tat is a more useful strategy for obtaining cooperation between two actors, or two blocs of states, as in bilateral or arms-reduction negotiations. Usually, though, it is a far less effective way to ensure cooperation in larger groups, such as OPEC. This explains in part the difficulties these states have experienced in collaborating on oil pricing policy.

International Regimes

A second solution to the Prisoners' Dilemma resembles Hobbes's prescription of creating Leviathan (the state) to allow human beings to escape from the anarchic "state of nature." Many theorists advocate the creation of strong international institutions to help states work together in an otherwise anarchic world.[42] As discussed in Chapter Nine, these institutions, more broadly termed **regimes,** can range from informal customs to negotiated agreements to long-term organizations like GATT. Neoliberal institutionalists contend that regimes influence and change the costs and benefits of individual state actions. More specifically, they alter states' interests or preferences by reducing the attractiveness of cheating, thereby allowing states to cooperate without fear of being taken advantage of. In exchange, states become willing to relinquish at least some independent decision making and instead agree to act according to a certain established international norm.

International regimes establish the general rules and principles, or **norms,** of state behavior that facilitate cooperation. These norms are usually formalized in treaties, which in turn establish institutions and/or organizations to provide states with opportunities to meet and discuss their common problems. In the international system, institutions can emerge as a result of traditional international customs, such as freedom of the seas, or through a more specific process of bargaining and negotiation over a set of issues. Regardless of why, most theorists contend that regimes are created by the hegemon who then enforces the rules to make them work. Soon after the United States established its hegemony in the wake of World War II, Washington created regimes such as the Bretton Woods system, the World Bank, and the International Monetary Fund (IMF). Some theorists contend that the continued existence of international regimes, even after a hegemon has declined, will prevent the world economy from descending into economic chaos.[43] Regimes are not limited to formal institutions, but may include informal cooperative programs by which governments abide, such as arms control agreements or arrangements regarding rivers, seabeds, or outer space.

In contrast to a national, state, or local government, however, international regimes often lack any mechanism to enforce compliance. As a result, states seem unlikely to comply with regimes when they find it particularly inconvenient or costly.[44] Many theorists argue that this lack of enforcement power means that regimes reflect only a state's temporary interest and are thus unable to constrain national behavior. OPEC, lacking any enforcement mechanism, is frequently unable to force overproducers (that is, cheaters) to comply with their set quotas. Iraq's invasion of Kuwait in 1990 was in part caused by Kuwait's continued overproduction, which kept international oil prices down and thereby hurt Iraq, which needed prices to remain high to earn income. In this case, the failure of an international regime to enforce its agreements prevented it from overcoming the barriers to cooperation.

International Law

International law is a third strategy to overcome the Prisoners' Dilemma. As discussed in Chapter Nine, international law is defined as "a body of rules which binds states and other agents in world politics in their relations with one another."[45] As with international regimes, the basis of international law is that it discourages states from unilaterally trying to maximize their individual gains, which of course leads to a suboptimal outcome for all involved. In particular, international law encourages all states to forgo short-term advantages gained by cheating and instead concentrate on the long-term benefits gained from compliance.

In the aftermath of World War I, for example, a number of European states signed the Geneva Protocol of 1925, which outlawed the use of chemical weapons. During World War II, all parties abided by the protocol as far as each other's military forces were concerned, even though any one state could have benefited by cheating and using poison gas in battle. The combatants realized that not using poison gas in the short term had greater long-term benefits, especially when the other side could easily retaliate in the next battle. As Chapter Nine noted, however, there is no international sovereign authority to enforce international law. Thus, international law could not stop Saddam Hussein from using chemical weapons against Iran and the Kurds in northern Iraq, even though doing so violated the 1925 Geneva Protocol. The overall result, many realists argue, is that international law has the same advantages and disadvantages of international regimes as a strategy for facilitating cooperation; both establish rules or norms of desirable state behavior, but neither provides an adequate enforcement mechanism to maximize effective compliance.

Interdependence

Finally, neoliberals argue that interdependence among states overcomes the Prisoners' Dilemma by reducing a state's ability to pursue a unilateral strategy of defection. Interdependence links together the fate of states, primarily through the flow of money, goods, people, and information across international boundaries. The result is a true "global village."

At its most basic level, **interdependence** is defined as "a relationship of interests such that if one nation's position changes, other states will be affected by that change."[46] Thus, what happens to one state will have a ripple effect across the others. (See Chapter Ten for examples of how interdependence affects global issues.) For our purposes here, interdependence characterizes any relationship between states that would be costly to break.[47]

Interdependence varies along two dimensions: sensitivity and vulnerability.[48] **Sensitivity** refers to the speed and extent with which changes in one country bring about changes in another. Changes in German interest rates, for example, usually have an immediate economic impact in the other members of the European Union, but not in the nations of Central America. The other dimension, **vulnerability,** measures the degree to which a state can suffer costs imposed by external events even after policies have been altered in response to them. For instance, in the case of the 1973 oil embargo and subsequent price increase, the United States was less sensitive than Japan to the external event because a smaller proportion of the U.S. economy was dependent upon foreign imports. However, the United States was also more vulnerable, since domestic constraints made it more difficult to adjust to changes in oil prices.

While the flow of people and information across state lines is an important aspect of economic interdependence, the flow of money and goods (trade) is even more important components for facilitating interstate cooperation. The eighteenth-century French philosopher Montesquieu remarked that "peace is the natural effect of trade." A strand of interdependence theory, commercial liberalism, focuses on the pacific effects of trade between states. It is widely believed that war among interdependent states is now obsolete because a state would only be destroying a trading partner. Author Norman Angell tried to demonstrate this as early as 1910 in *The Great Illusion,* which argued that war was unlikely among modern, industrial societies. (In 1914, of course, Angell was proven wrong.)

More recently, political scientist Richard Rosecrance draws distinctions between territorial states and trading states.[49] Territorial states, he argues, are those that amass power through expansion and geographic conquest;

examples include most of the European great powers prior to the end of the nineteenth century, or Serbia and Iraq in the early 1990s. Such states attempt to strengthen themselves by capturing an adversary's population and natural resources.

However, since the rise of Britain in the nineteenth century as the first trading state, territorial conquest has become a less important aspect of increasing national power. Instead, using the concept of comparative advantage explained in Chapter Seven, we can say that trading states specialize in certain products and trade for what they don't produce. As long as states can get what they want through trade, there is no incentive to wage war, since it will only disrupt trade and destroy markets. Rosecrance argues that trying to capture new territory through military invasion became more risky for states, especially with advances in weapons technology; meanwhile, the alternative of development through trade provided greater incentives for a peaceful strategy.[50]

One would expect a world of only trading states to be relatively stable and peaceful. But the world consists of both territorial and trading states, and so clashes are likely to occur, as happened during the Gulf War. Moreover, when states restrict trade and erect isolationist barriers, the breakdown of the global trading system often forces those reliant on trade to revert to the old territorial strategy to get what they need. This is one possible explanation for Japan's decision to attack Pearl Harbor in 1941. When Japan continued its aggressive policies in China, the United States imposed an oil embargo to compel Tokyo to withdraw. Highly dependent on U.S. oil, Japan could no longer get the resources it needed through trade, so it attempted instead to grab oil reserves in Southeast Asia. The Japanese attack on the U.S. Pacific Fleet at Pearl Harbor, some argue, was simply a way to prevent Washington from reversing this territorial expansion.

Does interdependence foster cooperation? Not necessarily. In fact, interdependence sometimes creates tension and even conflict between states. Just as close and continuous contact between family members or roommates often illuminates differences of opinions, frequent and long-term interaction between states often creates or exacerbates hostility.

Realists recognize other dangers associated with interdependence, which can mean economic vulnerability, insecurity, and dependence in a power relationship with another state. It can leave the dependent state vulnerable to blackmail. Increased dependence also means less government control over domestic affairs, and less flexibility in addressing domestic problems.

Finally, in cases where interdependence leads to conflict between two states, other nations often feel a ripple effect as well. Heightened competition and recent economic hostility between the United States and Japan serves as a powerful illustration. Despite their interdependence, Japan has been concerned about the U.S. debt and its impact on the world economy, while the United States has focused on the imbalance of American-Japanese trade tilted in Tokyo's favor. The deterioration in this relationship in turn has sent chills through the world economy. Over the long term, U.S.–Japanese interdependence has paradoxically fostered international cooperation while at the same time creating new sources of conflict.

Our discussion of these four strategies illustrates that cooperation is possible, even in an anarchic system. For neoliberals, as we know, the main barrier to cooperation is the temptation of states to cheat in order to maximize their individual gains. Tit-for-tat, international regimes, international law, and interdependence are intervening strategies and institutions that at times shape and encourage interstate cooperation, thereby helping to resolve the Prisoners' Dilemma. A weighing of their strengths and weaknesses suggests that these self-enforcing methods probably do reduce the attractiveness of cheating, thus increasing the likelihood that states will elect to cooperate. To what extent do you agree?

CONCLUSION: STRENGTHS AND LIMITS OF SYSTEMIC ANALYSIS

Whether it is being used to explain cooperation or conflict, one of the main strengths of the international systemic level of analysis is that it is extremely parsimonious (that is, brief). Systemic theory rarely requires extensive studies of a particular country, its political or economic system, or its leaders and decision makers in order to predict how a state will behave in the international system. Instead, to draw their conclusions, systems theorists need only study about changes in a state's position or ranking in the international system and the existing distribution of power—that is, the nature of the system itself. The predictions of systemic theory are also often compelling and powerful. Structural realists, for example, are able to make broad and accurate generalizations about state behavior, predictions which are borne out in the real world of global politics.

Systemic theories cannot forecast everything, of course. They are often crude, and their time frames are often vague and broad. Balance-of-power theory, for example, cannot predict which states will balance against a preponderant power, let alone when a given state will do so. Likewise, systemic arguments are better at explaining consistency than change; they can explain why different states respond to a similar situation in a similar fashion, but not why states in a similar situation respond in a different manner. Systemic predictions of state behavior are not unbreakable laws of nature, but only generalizations of how the international system creates pressures that drive the behavior of individual states. As the next two chapters will discuss, there are numerous subsystemic factors that can impede the "invisible hand" of the international system from determining the actions of large and small powers alike.

Many observers of world politics contend that systemic arguments, despite their weaknesses, still explain a great deal about state behavior. Systemic arguments can tell us how states will respond to changes in the distribution of power. They can help us explain why cooperation is possible in an anarchic system. In a broader sense, they explain the general patterns of interaction among states, even if they cannot explain the specific policies of a particular state. The dean of structural realists, Kenneth Waltz, makes a comparison to the theory of gravitation, which, though it predicts that objects will fall downward, cannot predict the "wayward path of a falling leaf."[51] Similarly, in order to more accurately account for the specific aspects of a state's behavior in the international system, it is necessary to consider the domestic and individual levels of analysis. Let us turn to these subjects now.

PRINCIPAL POINTS OF CHAPTER THIRTEEN

1. The systemic level of analysis looks at how features of the international system external to individual nations influence the behavior of states.

2. Classical realists such as Henry Kissinger, Hans Morgenthau, Reinhold Niebuhr, and John Foster Dulles emphasize the logic of realpolitik, power politics, and the evil nature of humans in shaping interstate behavior.

3. Structural realists, or neorealists, focus on changes or shifts in the distribution of power among states in the international system. The following are the major tenets of structural realism:

    a. Anarchy—the absence of any central authority to enforce laws or agreements among states.

    b. The sovereign nation-state acts as a unitary and rational actor—a single, independent unit capable of cost-benefit analysis.

    c. A state's hierarchy of interests is dominated by survival and security-related issues.

4. Balance-of-power theory argues that an equal distribution of power is stable, and that if the balance is upset by one state becoming too powerful, there is a tendency for the other great powers to form a counterbalancing coalition to restore the balance. Balancing is accomplished either through internal buildup or through alliance formation.

5. Preponderance theory contend that a hegemonic distribution of power (dominated by a single state) is more stable. The rationale is that as long as there is one hegemonic power, no state will challenge it, since any challenger is most likely to be defeated. However, as two states become roughly equal in power, war is likely to occur, since both the challenger and the hegemon believe that they are likely to prevail.

6. Many theorists contend that a bipolar distribution of power (where two superpowers dominate the international system) is more stable than a multipolar distribution (where there are three or more great powers). Arguments for bipolarity include the notion that it is simple, that there is little doubt who is the adversary, that third states have little influence on great power

behavior, and that great powers do not need to rely on other states for their survival.

7. Other theorists, however, conclude that a multipolar system is more stable. Arguments for the stability of multipolarity are that the complexity of the system breeds caution, that members within and between alliances interact, which creates cross-cutting concerns and encourages moderation, and that the system dampens arms races.

8. Collective security is based on the notion of "all for one and one for all." As in the balance of power, if one state acts in a threatening fashion, the other members agree to balance against it. However, in contrast to a balance-of-power system, collective security is a formal (or managed system) of balancing against aggression in which all members agree that they will rally to counter any of their number that commits aggression. As in the case of the proponents of preponderance, the advocates of collective security believe that no state would dare take hostile action against a coalition that is clearly superior in power, therby risking almost certain defeat.

9. Neoliberal institutionalism contends that cooperation is possible among states, even in the absence of a centralized global organization. For neoliberals, the main barrier to cooperation is the temptation of each state to maximize its individual gains, which results in an outcome that no state desires. (This situation is modeled in the Prisoners' Dilemma.) However, neoliberals contend that it is possible to resolve the Prisoners' Dilemma in a number of ways that alter states' interests and preferences and reduce the attractiveness of cheating:

   a. A tit-for-tat strategy prescribes that a state initially cooperates and thereafter mimics another state's moves—cooperating when it cooperates, defecting when it defects. Over time, the other state will become convinced that the first state will cooperate if it does.

   b. As international institutions, or informal arrangements, regimes reduce the temptation to cheat by providing an agreed upon set of rules of behavior and conduct, reliable information about the behavior of other states, and a procedure for arbitration and consultation to settle disputes.

   c. International law discourages states from unilaterally seeking to maximize individual gains by encouraging them to forgo short-term advantages gained by violating agreements or established procedures of international interaction.

   d. Interdependence fosters cooperation by linking states together across economic, political, and social dimensions. Trading states, which seek power through economic gains from free trade, are more likely to cooperate and avoid war than are territorial states, which seek to strengthen themselves by capturing land and resources from other countries.

10. Some realists counter neoliberal arguments by contending that these strategies and institutions are likely to be ignored when it is costly to comply with them. They point to failed attempts to restrain states, ranging from the Kellogg-Briand Pact (1928), to the League of Nations, to the United Nations.

11. While systemic-level arguments are parsimonious and powerful in their ability to predict state behavior, they have their limitations. As discussed in the next two chapters, numerous subsystemic factors impede the "invisible hand" of systemic-level influences.

Chapter 14

The Domestic Level of Analysis

In 1964, President Lyndon Johnson's campaign wanted a message that would reinforce his image as the candidate of peace, and cement in viewers' minds the picture of his opponent, Barry Goldwater, as the candidate of war. . . . The result was "Daisy"—a little girl whose image ran only once, but who has earned a permanent place in the annals of American campaign history.

Video: Camera up on little girl in field, picking petals off a daisy.

Audio: Little girl: "One, two, three, four, five, seven, six, six, eight, nine, nine—"

Video: Girl looks up startled; freeze frame on girl; move into extreme close-up of her eye, until screen is black.

Audio: Man's voice, very loud as if heard over a loud-speaker at a test site: "Ten, nine, eight, seven, six, five, four, three, two, one—"

Video: Cut to atom bomb exploding. Move into close-up of explosion.

Audio: Sound of explosion. Johnson voice over: "These are the stakes—to make a world in which all of God's children can live, or to go into the dark. We must either love each other, or we must die."

Video: Cut to white letters on black background: "Vote for President Johnson on November 3."

Audio: Announcer: "Vote for President Johnson on November 3. The stakes are too high for you to stay home."

William Lasser, *Perspectives on American Government* (Lexington, MA: D.C. Heath, 1992), p. 274.

Although the ad cited above ran only once, it was devastating to Goldwater's prospects, and it demonstrates the importance of domestic interests and values in determining foreign policy. Just how important various domestic factors are and under what conditions they become important in shaping foreign policy is the subject of this chapter.

Major Events in the Domestic Level of Analysis: 1795–1994

1795: Philosopher Immanuel Kant, in *Perpetual Peace,* hypothesizes that democratic regimes are unlikely to go to war with one another.

1789–1815: French Revolution and subsequent Napoleonic Wars spread the ideological concepts of liberalism, egalitarianism, and nationalism throughout Europe.

1848: Revolutions in central and western Europe, fueled by nationalism, popularize Marxism.

1871–1890: Domestic opposition inhibits Bismarck's policies after German unification.

1914: Organizational standard operating procedures (SOPs) of Europe's military bureaucracy propel it into World War I.

1917: Bolshevik Revolution in Russia leads to the formation of the Soviet Union, which seeks to foment Communist revolutions around the world.

1919–1920: Division of responsibility in U.S. government results in the Senate obstructing the president's foreign policy by failing to ratify the Treaty of Versailles.

1930s: Frustration with economic chaos and harsh terms of the Treaty of Versailles helps bring Hitler to power in Germany; under his leadership, the Nazi Party rules unchecked by any effective parliamentary authority; public revulsion at the use of military force inhibits democratic states' reactions to fascist aggression.

1934: Publication of Engelbrecht and Hanighen's *The Merchants of Death* leads to congressional committee hearings to investigate charges that

banks and arms manufacturers led the United States into World War I.

1939–1941: Constraints in democracies are illustrated by public hostility toward intervention in international affairs, delaying the U.S. entrance into World War II until the bombing of Pearl Harbor.

1945: American belief in peace through a legal framework is instrumental in the creation of the United Nations.

1947: Breakup of the British Empire leads to the partition of India into a secular India and an Islamic Pakistan, resulting in violent mass migrations of Hindus and Muslims.

1952–1953: Senator Joseph McCarthy undertakes a campaign based on accusation and innuendo intended to root out alleged Communists within the U.S. government, which

---

The systemic-level theories discussed in the last chapter describe how external factors shape and constrain a state's behavior in the international system. These theories are "outside-in" arguments because they contend that the primary source of a state's foreign policy is found in shifts in the distribution of power among states, rather than domestic political forces or the personal characteristics of leaders (considered in Chapter Fifteen). As compelling as their arguments may be, there is much that systemic theories cannot explain about state behavior in any given situation. To better understand a state's role in the international system, it is also necessary to look at domestic politics and decision making. This chapter examines theories of decision and action in foreign policy of the "inside-out" variety; that is, they describe how domestic political, economic, and social factors affect the choice of options for a state's foreign policy.

The domestic level of analysis considers not only a state's interests, resources, and objectives, but the process by which national leaders make foreign-policy decisions. In theory, a perfectly rational decision maker would gather all the relevant facts, carefully weigh all the available evidence, and select the course of action that offers the greatest benefits in relation to costs. This approach is called the **rational actor model,** and it is consistent with many of the systemic approaches to international relations discussed in Chapter Thirteen. In practice, however, it is difficult for both individuals and organizations to make decisions in this ideal manner.

For example, consider what a student would have to do to choose a type of transportation to and from school each day. The student would have to weigh the importance of school attendance relative to other daily activities and the relative merits and drawbacks of foot, skateboard, bicycle, bus, car, and train

leads to widespread anticommunist hysteria throughout the country.

1961: In his farewell address, President Eisenhower warns that the military-industrial complex is gaining too much influence; Bay of Pigs fiasco results from defective decision-making process characterized by groupthink.

1962: During the Cuban Missile Crisis, President Kennedy and the Executive Committee of the National Security Council conduct extensive deliberations in choosing to blockade Cuba.

1965–1973: Bureaucratic inefficiencies cause the United States to make poor decisions based on limited information, escalating the Vietnam War.

1967: President Johnson's decision to allow the deployment of a limited antiballistic missile system is heavily influenced by rival forces within the adminstration and pressures of domestic politics, illustrating that decisions are not always made on pure foreign-policy grounds.

1973: War Powers Act is adopted by Congress, restricting flexibility of the president in committing U.S. forces to long-term, large-scale operations.

1979: Iranian revolution results in the formation of a fundamentalist Islamic theocracy in which political and religious law are fused into one.

1985: As part of *glasnost*, Soviet analysts admit that the Soviet Union's policy in Afghanistan following the 1979 invasion was constrained by public disapproval.

1986–1993: Farmer's lobbies in the EU, particularly France, and Japan pressure governments to continue nontariff barriers in the form of subsidies on agricultural products entering their countries, thereby delaying the Uruguay round of GATT negotiations.

1989: Mass media coverage makes it difficult for the Bush administration to resume business as usual with China after the Tiananmen Square massacre.

1990: Iraq's authoritarian ruler Saddam Hussein invades Kuwait without having to consult a legislature.

1992: Initial rejection of the Maastricht treaty by Denmark, and its narrow passage in France, leads EU member states to reconsider the pace and depth of European union.

1993: Interest groups in the U.S. heavily pressure congress to vote for or against the North American Free Trade Agreement, proponents *win;* rare peaceful separation occurs when Czechoslovakia becomes the Czech Republic and Slovakia; Treaty of EU (Maastricht Treaty) is ratified.

travel. Perhaps a dozen questions would have to be considered, among them: Should I buy a commuter bus ticket or a car parking pass, or should I invest in a bicycle? Is the increased efficiency of train travel worth the higher cost? Finally, after responding to all such questions, the student would have to make the best possible, or optimal, choice. According to this model of decision making, policymakers must order national objectives from most to least important, determine all the possible ways to achieve those objectives, evaluate the consequences of each possibility, and then select the best policy.

The problem with characterizing a foreign-policy decision as the outcome of a rational, value-maximizing calculation is that decision makers rarely have enough time or information to make an ideally rational choice. Relying on rational calculation to solve our student's transportation problem might be sensible, but the complexity and uncertainty inherent in foreign-policy issues render such calculations impractical. A more streamlined decision-making process is necessary. (Indeed, how often do individuals make personal decisions using this rational actor model?) Additionally, in practice, decision makers frequently make choices based on factors other than cost-benefit analysis. The commuter student in our example might, for instance, choose a particular mode of transportation for social or stylistic reasons rather than cost-effectiveness.

It is possible to study any foreign-policy decision using the rational-actor model. During the Cuban missile crisis, President Kennedy and his advisors decided to impose a blockade on Cuba in order to compel the USSR to remove the nuclear missiles deployed on the island. (See Chapter Four for more details on the crisis.) Throughout the crisis, top Kennedy advisors and other U.S. officials met as the Executive Committee of the National Security Council, or ExComm;

the functioning of this committee has been held up as an excellent example of a rational decison-making unit.[1] But in considering the momentous decisions that resulted from ExComm's meetings, one can't help but wonder whether a different group might have taken a different course of action. What if Richard Nixon, the famously anticommunist Republican, had been elected president in 1960? What if ExComm had not included individuals who had no official responsiblity for foreign policy, such as former Secretary of State Dean Acheson and the attorney general, JFK's brother, Robert Kennedy? What if a similar group of French or Japanese decision makers were faced with the same situation? In order to answer these "what ifs," one must consider how policy decisions can be affected by influences operating at the domestic level of analysis.

Analysis on the domestic level views a state's foreign-policy decisions as the results of internal political processes that in turn shape a state's relations with other states. Central to these processes are political institutions (executives, bureaucracies, and legislatures), and societal forces (public opinion, interest groups, political culture, and ethnic tension) that can push states toward conflict or cooperation. We have already seen a variety of cases in which domestic politics played a primary role in the evolution of major events. For example, Bismarck was inhibited after 1871 because of significant domestic opposition to his policies. The decision by European governments to go to war was facilitated in 1914 because of public enthusiasm, but the course of World War I was in large measure determined by the strategies of the competing military bureaucracies. Then, widespread public revulsion to the use of military force inhibited the democracies' reactions to fascist aggression in the 1930s. By contrast, the frustration with economic chaos and the adverse result of World War I helped bring Hitler to power. In all of these cases government institutions or nongovernmental groups and pressures significantly influenced or facilitated the decisions made by key policy-makers. Similarly, public opposition to the Vietnam War was an important aspect of American policy-making in the 1960s and early 1970s, and public skepticism about the Afghan war in the 1980s helped bring down the Communists in Russia.

It is sometimes said that when two leaders or foreign ministers meet, they are really negotiating about how each can help the other with his or her problems at home. For example, in a meeting between the American president and the Japanese prime minister over trade disputes, both will be concerned about how the outcome will be interpreted by the media, by corporate leaders, by key bureaucratic figures (especially in Japan), and by consumer and labor groups (especially in the United States). Whether or not the president and prime minister reach an agreement will be determined at least as much by whether they can figure out a way to satisfy their domestic constituencies as by their ability to reach a "rational" or "fair" compromise. This domestic-centered calculus is as true of adversaries as of allies, of security as of economic issues. When negotiators from the Israeli government and the PLO met in 1993–1994 to discuss the future status of the West Bank and Gaza (see Chapter Six), both sides had to consider how they and their opposite numbers would have to "sell" any proposed agreements to the publics they represented.

STATIST AND SOCIETAL EXPLANATIONS

This chapter will not attempt the impossible task of describing and explaining every possible domestic influence on states' actions in the international arena. Instead, it will present an overview of the most important factors operating on the domestic level. Analytic approaches that emphasize these domestic determinants of foreign policies may be grouped into three broad categories: statist explanations, societal interpretations, and arguments that look at state institutions and social structures as an integrated whole.

Statist theories focus on the foreign-policy implications of a state's institutional and government structures. Some of these theories contend that a state's overall form of government (democratic, authoritarian, socialist, and so on) has a major impact on how that state carries on its dealings with other states. Other theories examine how particular political institutions and procedures, including elections, specialized bureaucracies, the legislature, and constitutional division of power and responsibility, shape the interests and behavior of states. These institutional structures vary among states in important ways. In the United States, for instance, the Constitution divides foreign policy-making power between the legislative and executive branches of government. This division of responsibility means that Congress can obstruct the president's foreign-policy agenda, as the Senate did after World War I when it refused to ratify U.S. participation in the League of Nations. Such conflicts between branches of government are less important in nations where legislative and executive powers are combined, as in Britain and Japan—but in these two states, powerful bureaucracies responsible for various aspects of foreign policy often conflict with cabinet members and legislators. The statist argument, then, is that institutions and organizations profoundly affect foreign policy.

But what about the impact of nongovernmental structures, such as interest groups, and influences such as national style and culture? **Societal theories** counter that a state's national interest merely reflects the strengths of organized domestic interests. From this viewpoint, a state's definition of its national interest is determined by the success of domestic interest groups in promoting their particular needs, concerns, and objectives. For instance, policy-makers might subsidize agricultural products in response to farmers' demands for protection from foreign competition. Support for the international legitimacy of such subsidies may then become the objective of those foreign policy-makers in international economic relations. This chapter's survey of societal influences on foreign policy includes active participants in the policy-making process, such as the lobbyists of the military-industrial complex, passive influences such as political culture, and public opinion, which can exert influence both actively and passively.

Many influences operating at the domestic level encompass both government institutions and cultural attributes. To give one example, political parties are integral parts of the political systems and government institutions of many states, but they also act as two-way channels of communication between the state and society. Similarly, in states inhabited by several ethnic groups, ethnic diversity may have both an institutional and a cultural impact on foreign relations.

APPROACHES TO DOMESTIC LEVELS OF ANALYSIS

STATIST

Theory: Domestic political institutions shape the form and substance of a state's foreign policy and can enhance or constrain the state's ability to achieve its objectives in the international system. Government agencies with responsibilities for international affairs attempt to define national interests and evaluate, choose, and carry out strategies for pursuing those interests.

Sample arguments: A state's overall form of government (democratic, authoritarian, socialist, and so on) has a major impact on how that state

carries out its dealings with others. Particular political institutions and procedures, including elections, specialized bureaucracies, the legislature, the nature of the executive, and the constitutional division of power and responsibility, shape the interests and behavior of states.

SOCIETAL

Theory: State institutions are not autonomous and disinterested, but instead reflect the interests of the most powerful forces in society. Foreign policy reflects the objectives of whichever

Because state institutions affect society and vice versa, it is impossible to fit many domestic influences on foreign policy into neat categories. Indeed, because a state's political institutions implicitly or explicitly reflect its social structure and cultural norms, all of the explanations for foreign-policy decisions discussed in this chapter combine elements of state and society to some extent. Nevertheless, dividing domestic-level approaches to the study of international relations into statist, societal, and combination approaches can make it easier to grasp how both state institutions and social structures can shape a state's role in international affairs. Many of the systemic approaches discussed in the previous chapter consider the process by which states determine their international actions as a "black box," with state interests (input) going into one end and state actions (output) coming out the other. Our task in this chapter is to open up this "black box" and take a look at its inner workings. The first things we should take out and examine are a number of smaller boxes—all securely wrapped in red tape, of course—which contain the government institutions that do the actual work of formulating a state's foreign policy.

STATIST APPROACHES

Domestic political institutions shape the form and substance of a state's foreign policy in a number of ways and can enhance or constrain the state's ability to achieve its objectives in the international system. The "three branches of government" (executive, legislative, and judicial) all have roles to play in international relations just as they do in domestic politics and policy-making. Even in states where the legislature and courts have little independence from a strong executive, groups or forces in society exert the most influence over policy-making.

Sample arguments: A state's definition of its national interest is determined by the success of domestic interest groups in promoting their particular needs, concerns, and objectives. In pluralist societies, politics is a wide-open game, and those groups expecting to gain from a specific foreign policy will come into conflict with those most likely to lose.

State/Society as an Integrated Whole

Theory: Many influences that operate at the domestic level encompass both government institutions and social/cultural attributes. Because state institutions affect society and vice versa, it is impossible to fit many domestic influences on foreign policy into neat categories.

Sample Arguments: Parties and ideologies often serve as links between state and society. The ability of constituent ethnic groups within a country to coexist has a major impact on a state's foreign policy.

bureaucracies and government officials at many levels can influence the making and implementation of foreign-policy decisions. Statist approaches to the study of international relations consider how the form and functioning of state institutions influence a state's interests and actions in the international arena.

At the very least, government agencies with statutory responsibilities for international affairs (such as foreign ministries and congressional or parliamentary committees on foreign relations) attempt to define national interests and evaluate, choose, and carry out strategies for pursuing those interests. At the same time, however, many state agencies pursue their own interests and objectives, and the influence of bureaucracies or legislators can lead to the adoption of foreign policies that do not necessarily reflect the interests of the nation as a whole. For example, many congressional representatives from U.S. states that depend heavily on the automobile industry consistently push for restrictions on imports of autos, which would result in price increases for American consumers. Thus, policy-makers can use government institutions to carry out objectives that do not have widespread public support and may actually be detrimental to the interests of the nation as a whole. The following sections will examine in greater detail how a state's basic form of government, or regime type, and specific structures of government, such as legislatures and bureaucracies, influence a state's behavior in the international system.

Regime Types

One school of thought within the statist approach focuses on the general structure and underlying philosophy of a state's political system. **Regime type** refers to a state's basic form of government, whether democratic or authoritarian, liberal or Communist. Proponents of the regime-based approach argue that the type of regime governing a state can exert a powerful influence on the nature of that state's foreign policy. This section examines several ways that regime type is alleged to affect foreign policy, for both democratic and authoritarian governments.

Authoritarian versus Democratic Foreign Policy-Making   It is often argued that in states governed by authoritarian regimes, where democratic controls on the state are weak or absent, the state has a freer hand to pursue costly or aggressive foreign policies. Because they are not accountable to the electorate, authoritarian governments with aggressive intentions are less constrained than democratic states from initiating international conflict. Mussolini's fascist government was impervious to any public opinion that might have discouraged it from seizing Ethiopia in 1935, and Japanese expansion in Manchuria and China in the 1930s was made easier by the lack of any need to mobilize popular support. Similarly, in 1990 Iraq's autocratic ruler Saddam Hussein did not have to seek legislative approval before ordering the invasion of Kuwait, and the Iraqi regime believed it would be difficult if not impossible for the countries of the U.S.–led coalition to gain public support to reverse the invasion. The Iraqi gamble did not pay off, however, as leaders of the coalition states were able to convince their citizens that driving Iraqi forces out of Kuwait would be worth the economic and human cost.

The absence of the deterrent effect of public opinion can give dictators additional bargaining power in crisis situations, as it enables them to risk war with greater credibility. Hitler exploited this advantage at the Munich Conference in 1938, when widespread aversion to war among the British and French populations was a major factor in their governments' decisions to make concessions rather than threaten to fight. In the United States, meanwhile, President Franklin Roosevelt pushed for greater American support for Britain's war effort against Germany. Lack of public support and opposition from isolationist groups such as the "America First" committee forced him to delay intervention until the U.S. naval base at Pearl Harbor was bombed by the Japanese.

The same general rule for military intervention holds true for questions of economic policy. Because authoritarian states are rarely open to influence by industrial, consumer, or labor organizations, trade policy becomes an extension of the state's overall foreign or security policy line. In the former Soviet Union, for example, oil and agricultural export policies were often determined by Moscow's political and military competition with the West rather than by economic rationality. Thus, in order to subsidize the fragile Cuban economy to strengthen Castro's regime, the USSR would export oil to Cuba at prices far below world market levels and import Cuban sugar at inflated prices. From an economic perspective, Moscow's policies were disadvantageous to many citizens in the country. Unfortunately for them, domestic interest groups in the Soviet Union had no way of bringing about change in policy; what the Kremlin said, went. In contrast, individuals and interest groups in democratic governments can influence foreign economic policy because government officials are politically accountable to the electorate. Constitutional guarantees of political and civil rights enable groups outside government to voice their perspectives on and interests in foreign policy.

Regime type also determines how much access domestic interest groups have to the foreign-policy process. In democratic regimes, domestic conflicts of interest are more likely to "spill over" into a state's foreign relations. For example, the access of agricultural interest groups to the foreign policy-making process in the United States and the European Union (EU) countries has been a continuing source of trade friction, as farmers lobby for protection against imports of farm products. In contrast, farmers in closed authoritarian states such as Syria and Myanmar (Burma) have little say in the food import or export policies of their respective governments.

Additionally, regime type has a major effect on the origin and scope of domestic interest-group support for a foreign-policy initiative. In authoritarian states, the impetus for organizing a regional trade bloc is more likely to originate in a bureaucracy, such as the foreign or industrial ministry, than in an association of economic enterprises. While industries related to national defense or agriculture often have some influence over foreign policy regardless of political system, the influence of other important industries frequently depends on the relative openness of the government. In monarchist Saudi Arabia the State Oil Ministry exercises tight control over decisions on petroleum production, export, and pricing, while in the United States and Great Britain, private oil companies have much more influence over energy export policies. In states where the major export industries have been nationalized, the ruling regime can dictate trade and production policies because the government *is* the company; that is, it owns almost everything having to do with production.

Peace among Democracies   The idea that it is more difficult for a state to engage in war when its leaders are accountable to the public forms the basis of a theory with far-reaching implications. In his essay *Perpetual Peace*, the eighteenth-century philosopher Immanuel Kant wrote that democracies are much less likely than other types of states to go to war with each other. According to Kant, "If the consent of the citizens is required to decide whether or not war is to be declared, it is very natural that they will have great hesitation in embarking on so dangerous an enterprise."[2]

Since the time of Kant's writing, democracies have participated in war about as often as authoritarian states, but they have gone to war *against one another* only very rarely (or never, some argue). Freely elected high-level policy-makers are accountable to society and constrained by a public that demands justification for war; when both states in a conflict are democratic, political constraints are doubled, making war even less likely.

Contemporary theorists have concluded that the power of independent domestic interest groups and political institutions contributes only one part of what restrains democracies from rushing headlong into battle. **Normative influences** constitute the other source of restraint. Democratic polities operate under norms of peaceful conflict resolution, through debate, elections, and judicial judgments. Thus, all democratic states share a common democratic political culture, and all expect to apply its method of resolving conflict at home to resolving international disputes amicably, without recourse to war. Democracies therefore try to externalize their norms of political competition, compromise, and peaceful transfer of power. When two democracies confront each other, the argument goes, they are able to draw upon democratic norms to prevent international conflicts from escalating into war.[3]

Political scientist Michael Doyle's exhaustive study of wars occurring since 1815 supports the argument that democracies do not go to war against one another.[4] Overall, though, there is no clear consensus that democratic countries are inherently more peace-loving than authoritarian or other types of states.[5] (On the contrary, one theorist contends that military regimes are peaceful only because their armed forces are preoccupied with repressing dissent at home.[6]) Regardless, history has repeatedly demonstrated that democracies are willing to engage in wars with non-democratic states. One consequence of the need to garner public support for military action is that leaders of democratic states frequently attempt to justify wars by "overselling" them, making it difficult to stop short of complete victory. Thus, although it appears that democracies are at peace with one another, it is difficult to conclude confidently that democratic regimes are inherently more peaceful.

Norms of political behavior and democracy take time to develop institutional and cultural roots, and the world may experience a period of violent conflict before a lasting peace among democratic states emerges. It is still too early to tell, but the argument that democracies do not go to war with one another may not hold for fledgling democracies without a democratic tradition within their societies. If the argument does hold true for even these newly democratic states, then the recent democratization of the former Soviet republics and Eastern European states bodes well for international stability.

Executive-Legislative Relations

The executive (for example, the president, prime minister, or cabinet) is usually at the center of a state's foreign-policy apparatus. Most countries have some sort of legislature or parliament, but these bodies vary enormously in the degree to which they genuinely represent the wishes of the public and act as a check against executive power. Under most one-party dictatorial regimes, parliamentary bodies do little more than "rubber stamp," or legitimatize for foreign-relations purposes, the decisions made by party leaders. Adolf Hitler, leader of the Nazi party, was able to rule unchecked by any effective parliamentary authority; in fact, he ruthlessly used the security apparatus and military arm of the German state to attack, subdue, and destroy his domestic enemies at will. The former USSR's legislative body, the Supreme Soviet, had the power to ratify treaties in theory, but in practice it slavishly followed the instructions of the ruling Politburo of the Communist Party of the Soviet Union. A similar system operates today in many countries where parliaments, elected or otherwise, have no authority independent of the executive or ruling party leadership.

Legislative constraints on executive authority, by contrast, are prominent features of domestic political institutions in democratic societies. In most democratic states, legislatures can actively participate in foreign-policy decisions or oversee the government's conduct of foreign affairs. In Germany, Israel, and Italy, for example, leaders of ruling parties or coalitions are severely constrained in their foreign-policy actions by the need to maintain the confidence (support) of their parliament, which if lost could lead to the fall of the government. Israeli governments, in particular, must take into account the various positions of that nation's multiplicity of parties when negotiating peace with neighboring Arab states, and when formulating policy on the occupied territories (see Chapter Six). The more fractious parliaments can make the foreign policy-making process particularly contentious. In the early 1990s, the many parties of the Russian parliament disagreed on whether that nation's foreign policy should be primarily oriented toward the industrialized West, toward Eastern Europe, toward China and India, or toward the developing countries of the South. Though Russian President Boris Yeltsin usually agreed with those deputies who favored a Western orientation, he was frequently required to make policy compromises in order to quell parliamentary rebellions and stave off constitutional crises.

In the United States, the Constitutional separation of powers allows the U.S. Congress to compel or constrain executive action, depending on its collective view of national interests. For instance, in 1930, the Senate attached 1253 amendments to the Smoot-Hawley Tariff Act to ensure that few industrial and agricultural interests were excluded from tariff protection. Tariff rates rose to their highest level ever, and the president was prohibited from entering into bilateral agreements that could have made possible free trade with European states. Not coincidentally, the Smoot-Hawley Tariff was one of the main reasons why the stock-market crash of 1929 turned into the global depression of the 1930s (see Chapters Three and Seven).

The legislature's authority to ratify treaties is perhaps its greatest constraint on the executive's foreign-policy behavior, both in the United States and elsewhere. Many international agreements do not go into effect until a specified number of signatory states ratify them; when ratification authority is lodged in the legislature, it thus has the power to impede international cooperation. The best-known historical example was the U.S. Senate's refusal to approve the original version of the League of Nations charter. The League was significantly weakened without U.S. membership, and subsequently failed to resolve the international conflicts that preceded the outbreak of World War II. Similarly, the legislatures of several European and North American states have often been reluctant to endorse the lowering of trade barriers provided for in GATT trade agreements painstakingly negotiated by their countries' leaders and diplomats. Thus, according to a statist approach to the study of world politics, executive-legislative relations and the nature of their institutions hold a key to understanding why states act as they do in foreign affairs.

Electoral Politics and Foreign Policy   A state's electoral system has a major impact on executive-legislative relations, and this in turn affects the foreign-policy process. In the United States, where both the executive and legislators are elected for fixed terms, the president often schedules foreign-policy initiatives around

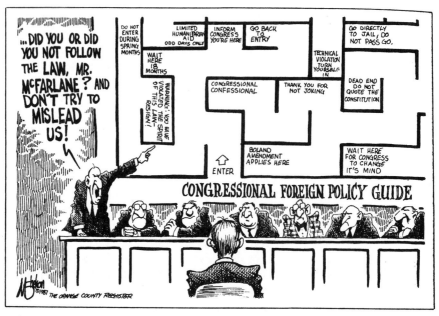

Relations between the executive and legislative branches of U.S. government can become complicated at times. Former National Security Advisor Robert McFarlane was the object of congressional scrutiny for his role in the Iran-Contra affair.

Source: © King Features.

the electoral calendar. Debates over contentious issues, including free-trade agreements (such as NAFTA) or economic relations with countries where human rights abuses are endemic (such as the former Soviet Union, China, and South Africa under the apartheid regime) are usually scheduled for years when there are no presidential or congressional elections, in the hope that unpopular decisions will be less fresh in the minds of the voters when they go to the polls. In election years, presidents tend to avoid risky foreign-policy initiatives that could be criticized by political challengers or opponents in Congress, and instead travel around the globe to summit meetings, which they hope will generate cheering crowds and lots of photo opportunities making them look like respected world leaders. Of course, events can force a president to make difficult decisions in election years. Richard Nixon's triumphant meetings in Beijing and Moscow in 1972 were one factor in his landslide victory in that year's election, but Jimmy Carter's need (and failure) to handle the Iranian hostage crisis successfully in 1979–1980 dealt a crippling blow to his campaign in 1980.

In most parliamentary systems, by contrast, legislators do not serve for fixed terms, though the government must hold elections within a specified time limit. On the one hand, this enables the party in power to call elections at politically opportune moments in order to make the most of a major foreign-policy triumph or military success. When Margaret Thatcher called elections shortly after Britain's victory in the Falkland Islands War in 1982, her party won handily, but

George Bush was unable to capitalize on the U.S.–led coalition's victory in the Gulf War in 1991, because by the time of the 1992 presidential election, domestic economic problems had become the electorate's primary concern. On the other hand, parliamentary governments can be brought down at any time because of a vote of no confidence. This can make it very difficult for prime ministers who govern with small majorities or in a coalition government to stay in power while pursuing controversial foreign policies. During the delicate negotiations between Israel and the PLO in 1993–1994, Israeli Prime Minister Yitzhak Rabin often had to tread carefully to avoid alienating any of his government's coalition partners, who might have defected to the opposition if they had believed the outcome of the talks would harm their values or constituencies.

The uncertainty of a government's term in office in parliamentary systems often enhances the role of the foreign-policy bureaucracy, as prime ministers come and go while bureaucrats remain in office. This can encourage continuity and stability in a state's foreign policy, because the impact of the electoral calendar and changes of government are diminished, but it can also result in stubbornness and inflexibility if powerful bureaucrats feel able to ignore or delay the policies of elected leaders. As anyone who deals with government on any level knows all too well, bureaucrats can have an enormous impact on the formation and implementation of policy. As the next section discusses, however, exactly how bureaucratic influence operates is not that clear-cut.

Bureaucracies

Government bureaucracies are designed to expedite the process by which government officials identify foreign policy objectives, formulate specific policy options, and choose and evaluate policies. Unfortunately, entrenched organizational routines (sometimes formalized as **standard operating procedures,** or **SOPs**) and the competitive politicking that occurs within bureaucracies often result in policy outcomes that fail to maximize a nation's goals.

Organizational Process   Bureaucratic organizations can facilitate the evaluation of foreign-policy options by acting as information processors for decision makers. Ideally, these agencies can channel timely, unbiased information enabling calculations of costs and benefits of various policy options. Unfortunately, studies of bureaucratic organizations suggest that the way various departments are organized and interrelated is not always conducive to the making of policy decisions that maximize a nation's goals; in other words, the rational-actor model often gives way to standard operating procedures (SOPs). When confronted with a foreign-policy problem, large organizations tend to follow a set of decision-making guidelines and make routine recommendations without calculating the advantages and drawbacks of all available options (see box on page 658).

According to this **organizational-process model,** an almost mechanical process governs the formulation and implementation of foreign policy within the purview of a given government department. As long as an agency has developed an SOP for every foreseeable contingency, all goes according to plan. But

ORGANIZATIONAL PROCESS IN 1914

The rigid mobilization plans that helped draw the European powers into war in 1914 (see Chapter Three) are tragic examples of bureaucratic rigidity and inertia. The German Schlieffen Plan, in particular, called for an attack on France through Belgium in order to capture the strategic railroad juncture at Liege. After rapidly defeating France, the German army would attack Russia. The basis of this plan was that it would take Russia six weeks to fully mobilize. As a consequence, in order to ensure that Germany did not fight a two-front war (Russia and France were allies),

Germany would have to defeat France during this six-week window.

The commitment of the German military bureaucracy to the Schlieffen Plan was so steadfast that the General Staff offered the kaiser the stark choice between its immediate implementation and no action at all. At the same time, Tsar Nicholas of Russia did not realize that partial mobilization of his troops could not be carried out in response to Austria-Hungary's ultimatum to Serbia, as the Russian army had plans only for full mobilization. When the tsar ordered partial mobilization, he was

foreign-policy situations are usually unanticipated, and organizational performance rarely approaches the standards of omniscience. Even so, organizations still tend to follow preset guidelines, or SOPs, in dealing with events for which no programmatic response is available. This often makes organizational behavior appear rigid, inflexible, and unimaginative. Indeed, the biggest problem with organizational routines is that they contribute to inertia. Once an SOP is triggered, it is often difficult to reverse it.

Bureaucratic Politics   The organizational-process model just described sees foreign-policy decisions as the product of SOPs. A related model of bureaucratic politics argues that decision-making outcomes represent neither a rational value-maximizing calculation of the state's interest nor the simple output of an organizational SOP. Rather, the foreign-policy outcome, according to this model, is a result of political competition among government agencies.[7]

Bureaucracies can be seen not as smaller parts of a larger unit (the state), but instead as independent organizations that compete with one another to forward their own parochial interests. A **bureaucratic-politics model** makes a number of assumptions about how a government's policy choices are formulated and selected. According to this argument, a bureaucrat's policy stance will reflect his or her organizational affiliation. Organizational interests shape and constrain an official's preferences and range of policy recommendations. An old Washington proverb is, "Where you stand [on an issue] depends on where you sit [within the federal bureaucracy]." If a bureaucrat moves to a new agency, it is expected that his or her position on various issues will change to reflect the new agency's interests. The consequence is that bureaucratic chiefs will advocate informed mobilization would have to be total, thereby triggering a set of organizational processes that had disastrous consequences. The German General Staff believed that once Russia mobilized, Germany would have to mobilize immediately in order to carry out its plan to avoid the dreaded two-front war.

Because European armies of the period believed that the first side to initiate an effective large-scale offensive operation would win the war, the armies of the great powers would not respond to mobilization without attacking. The necessity of a response to Russia's mobilization prompted Germany to implement its offensive plan against France and Belgium, which drew Britain into the conflict in order to back up its guarantee of Belgian neutrality and independence. Thus, when the crisis came to a head in July 1914, organizational SOPs did not allow for intermediate options; mobilization meant war.*

*For more on the influence of offensive doctrine on the outbreak of World War I, see Stephen Van Evera, "The Cult of the Offensive and the Origins of the First World War," *International Security* 9, no. 1 (Summer 1984), pp. 58–107.

policy options that advance their organization's interests, no matter which organization they head, and regardless of a rational calculation of the national interest.

It is easy to observe how this plays out in real life. Military organizations develop defense plans, diplomatic staffs try to manage political relations between countries, intelligence agencies create information-gathering networks, and economic departments make trade and investment recommendations. In the United States, managing U.S.–Japanese economic relations, for example, requires involvement of, at a minimum, the Department of State, the Department of Commerce, the Office of the U.S. Trade Representative (USTR), and sometimes the Departments of the Treasury, Labor, and Agriculture, and the Office of Technology Assessment (OTA). Bureaucrats in these different agencies often view trans-Pacific relations from different perspectives; the Defense Department worries that trade friction could damage the U.S.–Japanese strategic alliance, while the Labor Department fears that imports of Japanese products will destroy American jobs.[8] On the other side of the Pacific, bureaucrats from the Japanese Ministry of International Trade and Industry (MITI) and the Ministry of Finance are the key players in trade negotiations.

Bureaucratic chiefs not only seek to protect the agency's interests, but they also strive to maintain and even improve its position in the government. Bureaucrats are concerned about ensuring their organization's political autonomy, role, and mission, and maintaining or increasing its budget. They do not like other organizations trespassing in their domain and are often unwilling to share any of their responsibilities with other agencies. Bureaucrats have several avenues for promoting their objectives: They acquire and supply information designed to protect their organization's interests; they try to develop a menu of options that supports their organization's position; and they actively challenge any policy recommendation contrary to their agency's objectives.[9]

Bureaucratic politics breed vigorous turf battles and policy advocacy among agencies. On any issue, each agency will advance a menu of options favoring its position, even if in opposition to other organizations in the same government. The costs of not influencing the final outcome, and the benefits of successful influence, further fuel inter-agency competition. The result of these tendencies, according to the bureaucratic-politics model, is that policy is made through "pulling and hauling" among bureaucratic chiefs. In contrast to the rational-actor model, then, the final decision rarely reflects the preferred choice of the nation as a whole. In contrast to the organizational-process model, the final outcome rarely reflects the preference of any single organization. Rather, the outcome is a policy resulting from conflict and compromise among government agencies.

One danger of bureaucratic politics is that such policies sometimes send mixed and contradictory messages to other states. In 1989 the U.S. Department of Agriculture extended credits to Iraq for the purchase of U.S. agricultural exports. The Bush administration approved these credits, which allowed Iraq to use other funds to purchase weapons prior to its 1990 invasion of Kuwait. A major controversy broke out in 1992 when it was revealed that the credits were approved even after the CIA had reported that Iraq had organized a secret network to buy components for ballistic missiles and nuclear, chemical, and biological weapons. Congressional critics of the Bush administration charged that one U.S. government agency was thereby indirectly financing Iraqi aggression at the same time that other agencies were trying to deter it. The White House contended that it was trying to use U.S. aid to persuade Iraq to pursue less aggressive policies.[10] This explanation could not hide the contradictory results of the "pulling and hauling" among government agencies.

Policy Implementation   Bureaucratic interests and SOPs have an even greater impact on the implementation of policy than they do on its formulation. Leaders rarely have the time or energy to ensure that every detail of their policies are carried out according to instructions and intentions. As Franklin Roosevelt's aide, Jonathan Daniels, put it,

> Half of a President's suggestions, which theoretically carry the weight of orders, can be safely forgotten by a Cabinet member. And if the President asks about a suggestion a second time, he can be told that it is being investigated. If he asks a third time, a wise Cabinet officer will give him at least part of what he suggests. But only occasionally, except about the most important matters, do Presidents ever get around to asking three times.[11]

During crises, leaders have even less time to attend to details. During the Cuban Missile Crisis (see Chapter Four), heeding Kennedy's preference for giving Soviet leaders more time to halt further shipments of supplies to Cuba, Defense Secretary Robert McNamara ordered the U.S. Navy to draw its line of blockade about 300 miles closer to the Cuban coast. Subsequent events revealed that the Navy failed to follow this order. With Kennedy expressing concern that the Navy might blunder into a confrontation that it was unprepared to handle, McNamara grilled the chief of naval operations on his plans for making the first interception of Soviet submarines that were expected to try to break through the blockade:

> "Who would make the first interception? Were Russian-speaking officers on board? How would submarines be dealt with?" At one point McNamara asked Anderson [the chief of naval operations] what he would do if a Soviet ship's captain refused to answer questions about his cargo. Picking up the *Manual of Regulations,* the Navy man waved it in McNamara's face and shouted, "It's all in there!" To which McNamara replied, "I don't give a damn what John Paul Jones would have done; I want to know what you are going to do, now." The encounter ended on Anderson's remark: "Now, Mr. Secretary, if you and your Deputy will go back to your offices, the Navy will run the blockade."[12]

Other government departments also implemented Kennedy's orders in a manner more consistent with their own interests than the president's objectives. Beginning in 1961, Kennedy had ordered U.S. missiles to be removed from Turkey several times, but because the Turkish government wanted them to stay, various U.S. government agencies delayed removal of the missiles, so they were still in Turkey at the time of the Cuban Missile Crisis. Because Khrushchev had demanded the removal of the missiles from Turkey in return for withdrawing Soviet missiles from Cuba, many felt that a Soviet strike against the Turkey-based missiles would be seen as legitimate retaliation for any U.S. strike against the Cuban-based rockets. The continued presence of U.S. missiles in Turkey in spite of his repeated orders to remove them caused Kennedy to lose his temper at one point in the crisis: "Get those frigging missiles off the board!" he reportedly shouted (though his original expletive was probably different).[13]

Don't Presidents Matter? A Critique of Bureaucratic Politics

Decision making does not necessarily follow the procedure outlined in the bureaucratic-politics or organizational-process models. Critics of these approaches contend that the greatest determinants of important policy outcomes are the president's values and his own calculations of political risk.[14] (Their arguments will be examined in Chapter Fifteen, which considers the individual level of analysis.) The bureaucratic-politics approach, in particular, has had a number of criticisms leveled against it. First, heads of organizations often do not "stand" where they "sit." One might expect, for example, that the head of the State Department would tend to support negotiated solutions to foreign policy problems, while the Defense Secretary would be more likely to support the use of armed force. During the Reagan administration, however, Secretary of State George Shultz supported military action in Lebanon and military support for the Contras in Nicaragua while Defense Secretary Caspar Weinberger argued against these policies. Second, bureaucratic chiefs do not always defend their turf at the expense of the national interest. During the Cuban Missile Crisis, some ExComm advisors such as Dean Acheson had no bureaucratic turf to defend, and others,

VIETNAM: THE INFORMATION GAP

Parochialism has been identified as one of the major causes of repeated U.S. policy blunders in Vietnam. After officials in Washington began to realize by the summer of 1965 that Operation Rolling Thunder, the massive bombing campaign against North Vietnam, was not succeeding in deterring the Vietcong from infiltrating South Vietnam, President Johnson approved a huge increase in ground troops requested by General William Westmoreland, the U.S. military commander in Vietnam.*

The U.S. presence in Vietnam was dominated by a military organization, the Military Assistance Command Vietnam

(MACV), which controlled much of the information that decision makers received on the effectiveness of U.S. policies. Many analysts concluded that LBJ and many of his policy advisers shared a monolithic conception of the Communist bloc and feared that the loss of Vietnam to communism would inexorably lead to the loss of all of southeast Asia (the **domino theory**). The result was that the decision makers relied exclusively on military solutions and repeatedly caved into military pressures to enlarge the scope of the war effort.†

To further compound the information problem, the State Department suffered from a shortage of expertise on Asian

including Robert Kennedy and Theodore Sorensen, were primarily motivated by their personal loyalty to President Kennedy. In general, say its critics, the bureaucratic-politics approach puts too much emphasis on the roles and interests of presidential advisors and the agencies they represent, and not enough on the president, who must take ultimate responsibility for foreign-policy decisions. Remember, too, that senior bureaucratic officials are nominated by the president. In most instances they are likely to hold similar views and be long-standing supporters of the president's policies.

Taking into account these criticisms in the context of the Cuban Missile Crisis, it is not difficult to argue that the choice of a blockade in 1962 resulted not from some organizational procedure, or from a hard-fought game of bargaining among independent and equally powerful bureaucratic fiefdoms, but rather from JFK's personal values, political objectives, and leadership style. Kennedy's support for a blockade was illustrated by his later statements on the dangers of crises in the nuclear era:

> Above all, while defending our own vital interests, nuclear powers must avert those confrontations which bring an adversary to a choice of either a humiliating retreat or a nuclear war. To adopt that kind of course in the nuclear age would be evidence only of the bankruptcy of our policy—of a collective death wish for the world.[15]

The influence of Kennedy's leadership style is revealed by transcripts of ExComm meetings. Consultations during the crisis were usually characterized by open exchanges of information and ideas that produced a genuine consensus countries after the department's Bureau of East Asian Affairs had been purged of many of its experts during the "red scare" of the late 1940s and early 1950s. In addition, U.S. diplomats in Vietnam remained primarily in the company of Vietnam's French-speaking urban elites, which sharply narrowed the range of Vietnamese opinion to which they were exposed.‡ In this case, then, the military was the organization that dominated the flow of crucial information regarding policy and battlefield developments to top decision makers in the White House. The State Department was so weakened that it played a less significant role in policy formulation. What are

the dangers of such overreliance on one bureaucratic agency for decision making?

*Irving Janis offers an innovative critique of U.S. decision making during several foreign-policy fiascos, including the Vietnam War, in *Groupthink* (Boston: Houghton Mifflin Company, 1982). According to Janis, groupthink refers "to a mode of thinking that people engage in when they are deeply involved in a cohesive in-group, when the members' striving for unanimity override their motivation to realistically appraise alternative courses of action" (p. 9).

†For an example of this argument, see James C. Thomson, "How Could Vietnam Happen? An Autopsy," in Morton Halperin and Arnold Kanter, eds., *Readings in American Foreign Policy: A Bureaucratic Perspective* (Boston: Little, Brown and Company, 1973), pp. 100–101.

‡Ibid., pp. 99, 101.

around a position. This free-wheeling, open approach, which Kennedy encouraged, served U.S. interests well during this confrontation.[16]

SOCIETAL APPROACHES

So far, this chapter has considered international relations to be more or less synonymous with interstate relations, but world politics also involves interactions between a wide variety of groups other than national governments. While the statist approach treats the state as the dominant institution in the decision-making process, the societal approach suggests that foreign policy reflects the objectives of whichever groups or forces in society exert the most influence over policy-making. Interest groups, for example, try to "capture" the political institutions of the state responsible for making decisions that most affect the interests of those groups. In pluralist societies, politics is a wide-open game, and those groups expecting to gain from a specific foreign policy will come into conflict with those most likely to lose. In this view, state institutions are not autonomous and disinterested, but instead reflect the interests of the most powerful forces in society. Public opinion also reflects and is influenced by ongoing policy debates and controversies involving the media, policy elites, government officials, and major interest groups. Throughout the policy-making process, a state's political culture can shape policy by defining the values and goals that governments are expected to pursue and policy-makers are expected to uphold.

Interest Groups

Interest groups in the largest sense of the word include business groups, military organizations, veterans groups, environmental lobbies, labor unions, agricultural interests, issue-specific groups, groups organized around ethnic interests, and the media. Groups in society may be concerned with foreign affairs directly, or their involvement in foreign policy may originate in their domestic economic or political interests. Examples of interest groups in the United States that are directly interested in world politics include the Arms Control Association, the World Federalist Association, the American Israel Public Affairs Committee (AIPAC), and the Japan Society. What do these types of groups do? AIPAC, for example, supports efforts to increase U.S. aid to meet Israel's economic and security needs and presents arguments for the compatibility of American and Israeli interests. To achieve these ends, it organizes letter-writing campaigns, encourages its members to support candidates for Congress and the presidency who are believed to be sympathetic to Israel, and lobbies Congress to support its preferred policies. Sometimes AIPAC gets its way; other times the Arab lobby is more successful. U.S. sales of military equipment to Saudi Arabia, for example, please the companies selling weapons, or oil companies with interests there, while American guarantees of loans for housing and economic development in Israel further AIPAC's objectives.

Thus, while AIPAC's goals are primarily political, other interest groups become involved in international politics for economic reasons. Defense firms in many countries seek to promote the sales of their equipment to foreign governments. These products are often exported to nations that then use the weapons in a way that threatens the security of the defense contractor's home nation; Western exports to Iraq before the Gulf War are a recent example. The motives of textile manufactures are also economic. They often try to restrict imports of foreign-made garments even when their policies lead to higher prices for consumers. Labor unions pressure governments to cut back on foreign aid for industrial development abroad, fearing that it could result in the "export of jobs." Many labor groups in the United States and Canada opposed the North American Free Trade Agreement (NAFTA) in the early 1990s for this reason. Some labor groups also lobby for tighter restrictions on immigration so that immigrant labor will not undercut union wages.

Group Interests versus the National Interest   The diversity and frequent conflicts between interest groups lend support to the notion that national interests are determined not by a state's position in the international system, nor by government institutions, but rather by whichever particular interest has effectively "captured" the relevant policy-making apparatus. Proponents of this perspective would argue, then, that the United States' "national interest" in the Middle East, as defined by influential oil companies, is to secure the supply of imported oil, because it is most important to powerful industrial interests such as automobile manufacturers, oil companies, and industrialists. In international trade, higher incomes for farmers, even if it comes at the expense of international cooperation to reduce agricultural export subsidies, would be in the "national interest" not because of any national calculation, but because of effective lobbying by an influential domestic interest group, in this case agricultural interests. Throughout the 1980s and early 1990s, farmers' lobbies in the United States, the EU, and Japan consistently pressured governments to slap tariffs on agricultural products coming into their countries. At the same time, the office of the U.S. Trade Representative and its European counterparts worked to break down the trade barriers faced by their own agricultural exports. The predictable result was a series of domestic political conflicts over tariffs and subsidies on beef, citrus, fruit, wine, soybeans, and other farm products. Overall, it is up to the reader to decide when interest groups really represent the "national interest," or whether the "national interest" is nothing more than the sum total of winning interest groups, as some societalists would have you believe.

To increase their influence, some interest groups develop an institutional presence within governments. For example, in the 1980s in Germany, environmental "citizen action groups" evolved into the Green Movement, which at first behaved like a domestic interest lobby. The Greens' solicitation of government support for specific policies, such as a prohibition against building additional airport runways and opposition to nuclear proliferation, created the organizational nucleus for a new political party, and in 1983 the Greens won 27 seats in the Bundestag, the lower and more important house of the German parliament. They immediately stated their opposition to NATO's development of theater nuclear missiles on German territory. While that opposition failed to produce results, other Green efforts have been instrumental in German leadership on international environmental issues. With the Green party in the vanguard, Germany initiated EU legislation to reduce vehicle and industrial plant emissions during the 1980s, and also urged international restrictions on carbon dioxide emissions at the 1992 UN Conference on Environment and Development (UNCED).

While the impact of interest groups on foreign policy in open societies is undeniable, this does not necessarily mean that the national interest can be defined as the outcome of political competition between specific interests. For one thing, it is difficult to separate the national interest, however defined, from the interests of individual citizens and social groups, or even to identify factors constituting individual, group, and national interests. For example, while all Americans benefit from lower automobile prices, competition from foreign auto makers may force U.S. companies to close plants and lay off workers, who would not be able to benefit from lower new car prices if unemployed. Higher unemployment would be detrimental to the U.S. economy, but higher automobile prices would harm U.S. consumers. And consider the complexities of energy policy. Imports of oil from the Middle East help keep U.S. gasoline prices down, but dependence on foreign oil may oblige the United States to intervene militarily to protect oil-exporting nations, despite their undemocratic governments. Furthermore, the availability of cheap imported oil reduces the incentive to develop alternative energy sources, which would pollute the environment less. The varied and conflicting interests involved in foreign policy can be as difficult to untangle as the complex international conflicts that characterize the New Era.

Members of the Green Movement protest at a German factory believed to be violating environmental standards. The action was timed to attract attention prior to the opening session of the Bundestag, the German legislature, in March 1983.

Source: © Regis Bossu/Sigma.

Interest Group Power: The Military-Industrial Complex   In many representative democracies, powerful interest groups are able to exert influence over foreign policy through close ties with the government agencies that regulate their operation and consume their products. The relationship between private interests and public institutions is particularly strong in the defense sector, and as a result many observers have questioned what they consider to be an excessive level of influence exercised by the military-industrial complex in the foreign relations of industrial societies.[17] In his farewell address, for example, President (and former army general) Dwight D. Eisenhower warned against "the acquisition of unwarranted influence, whether sought or unsought, by the military-industrial complex."

Military organizations have close working relationships with the industries that produce military hardware in most nations, but charges that these relationships result in undue influence over foreign and defense policy arise most frequently in the liberal democracies, especially Britain and the United States. According to critics, the danger is that the military-industrial complex will support an active and aggressive military posture, since both the military and industry will benefit. In some instances, it has even been blamed for inciting warfare.[18]

An early opponent of the military-industrial relationship was the mid-nineteenth-century British statesman Richard Cobden. In his 1861 book, *Three Panics, An Historical Episode,* Cobden noted that each of the British "invasion scares" of the preceding twenty years had been provoked by sensational stories in newspapers, and mysteriously subsided after the government allocated generous shares of the national budget to the Royal Navy. This pattern continued throughout the nineteenth century, and by 1900, many Britons were concerned with the power exerted by the nation's well-established defense industries and the nature of their relationship with the national government. Meanwhile, across the Atlantic, the military-industrial complex was coming under increasing criticism, particularly after the outbreak of World War I led to huge profits for manufacturers of war matériel. The American public remained focused on the arms industry in the interwar period, and in 1934 H. C. Engelbrecht and F. C. Hanighen's *The Merchants of Death* sought to build support for arms control and disarmament by exposing the cozy relationship between the military and heavy industry.

> There is an international munitions industry whose various parts conspire together to control Government officials and, through them, the destinies of nations in such a way as to maximize profits at the expense of human lives.[19]

War profiteers were satirized in American culture as well. Military industrialists who enjoyed rich rewards while soldiers died on the battlefields were the inspiration for Daddy Warbucks, the archetypal "fat cat" character in the popular comic strip *Little Orphan Annie*.

The role of the defense sector in federal budgets and the U.S. economy burgeoned enormously after the Korean War. By 1960 even President Eisenhower, who had been the Supreme Commander of Allied Forces in the European theater during World War II, was concerned at the growth of military spending. Responding to Democratic charges that the United States was not spending enough on conventional armed forces and had allowed a strategic missile gap to occur, Eisenhower criticized large military expenditures as "just negative stuff adding nothing to the earning capability of the country" and denounced the "almost hysterical fear among some elements of the country" that prevented reductions in the defense budget.[20]

The Cold War continued to drive U.S. defense budgets upward, and America's defense industries continued to grow. By 1980, according to one author's estimates, the jobs of 18 million people in the armed forces, government, and industry depended on the level of defense spending for that year. During the Vietnam War, defense spending accounted for as much as 40 percent of annual federal spending, and the figure remained at least at 20 percent or above from 1970 to 1990.[21]

Though public debate over arms spending is most intense in democratic states, the influence of the military-industrial complex is not limited to democratic societies. A powerful alliance of military officers, Communist Party officials, and *apparatchiks* (party-appointed bureaucrats) operated in the USSR to keep military expenditures booming. Indeed, many explanations for the dissolution of the Soviet Union contend that excessive military spending helped to precipitate the USSR's collapse. The military-industrial sector dominated the USSR's economy, political system, and culture; Western wags quipped that while the United States has a military-industrial complex, the USSR *is* a military-industrial complex.

ECOPOLITICS

The so-called military-industrial complex is often raised as an example of why domestic politics can lead to international conflict, but another approach suggests a way in which domestic developments might lead to increased cooperation among nations in the New Era. **Ecopolitics** emerged as a new paradigm in international relations in the 1970s. With the realization of the limitations on the world's natural resources, the rapid growth in population, and the related problem of increasing consumption of energy (all discussed in Chapter Ten), various scholars observed that the dynamics of the existing international system had begun to change. The growing influence of Third World states and their demands for a new international economic order could not be ignored; for example, OPEC's impact on the economies of oil-importing states illustrated the increasing shift in focus from military power to economic power in world politics. According to one of its advocates, ecopolitics is an impending revolution in world affairs that could lead to new interests and rules in the New Era: "Global ecopolitics involves the use of environmental issues, control over natural resources, scarcity arguments, and related concerns of social justice to overturn the international political hierarchy and related system of rules established during the period of industrial expansion."*

Ecopolitics encompasses many issues that have become more salient in recent decades and are changing the way in which international relations is understood. The increasingly interdependent world and the growing focus on North-South relations, rather than on the Cold War–era East-West conflict, have given priority to new issues. Issues of economic equality, environmental protection, and more equitable distribution of resources between the wealthier and the poorer states have become important items on the agenda of the United Nations and of the relations between states. In essence, then, ecopolitics argues that human needs are displacing the competition for power

The end of the Cold War calls the continued influence of the military-industrial complex into question. First, whatever political power arms manufacturers had was not enough to block U.S.–Soviet agreements on arms limitation. Second, as the Soviet-American competition for global political influence gives way to the economic, political, and social challenges of the New Era, the share of human and material resources solely devoted to defense purposes in the West is declining. Nevertheless, defense-related industries and their corresponding government organizations are likely to continue to be important factors in the formulation of foreign policy. The issue of whether and how to keep defense production lines running or undertake expensive "defense conversion" programs to protect high-skilled, high-wage jobs remains an important one in both the United States and Russia. The influence that defense industry groups will be able to exercise in the New Era remains as uncertain as the political structure of the post–Cold War world.

among governments as the central concern of world politics. The interdependence of disparate groups both within and between nations, the model contends, will eventually force conflicting domestic groups to cooperate in the interest of mutual survival. For instance, the industrialized world is beginning to recognize that a rapidly rising Third World population will diminish the amount of resources available for all states.

If the predictions of ecopolitics advocates are realized, ethnic conflicts will fade and economic classes will view one another not as antagonists, but as allies in the struggle to preserve and improve the world's natural and social environment. Interdependence, of course, can prompt conflict as well as cooperation, and it is far from guaranteed that issues of resource depletion and environmental protection will be resolved in favor of the common good rather than parochial interests. Perceptions of economic and environmental interests can vary considerably; labor, business, and

environmental groups may clash over New Era policy issues. In the NAFTA debate in the United States, for example, many environmental and organized labor groups were in opposition; most business interests were supportive. On another dimension, Western nations consider rain forests in Brazil and Malaysia to be global treasures that must be preserved, but many residents of those states view the logging and clearing of the forests to be a necessary avenue for badly needed economic development.

The possibility of conflict aside, the ecopolitics paradigm does offer at least some hope that domestic concerns for economic equality, sustainability of resources, and protection of the global environment can provide the impetus for states to act cooperatively to solve pressing global problems.

*Dennis Pirages, *Global Ecopolitics* (Belmont, CA: Wadsworth, 1978), p. 5.

Public Opinion

Despite the influence that industrial, labor, or environmental lobbies can exert on foreign policy, participation in politics and policy-making is not limited to powerful special interests, especially in democratic states. **Public opinion** plays a role in shaping foreign relations not only in pluralist states, where it may be expressed openly, but even in dictatorial regimes. Since the nineteenth century, public opinion has been an important part of the foreign-policy process in advanced industrial states, and even more so since the extension of the franchise to larger proportions of the population. Perhaps the most obvious way in which the public affects a democratic state's foreign policy is through the election of policy-makers, including the chief executive. Politicians in democracies take great pains to stay apprised of public opinion and frequently commission and consult polls on foreign-policy issues. (President Johnson was known to carry the results of public opinion polls in his pajama pockets.) While politicians do not necessarily allow public opinion to dictate their policies, they certainly consider it before selecting a particular policy from among a menu of options. Generally, democratic leaders tend to eliminate the options least palatable to the voting public. Thus, public opinion often constrains the set of options open to selection.[22] On the other hand, government officials often try to persuade or even manipulate public opinion. Some argue that such government influence can be genuinely beneficial, as when presidents use the executive office as a "bully pulpit" (a term coined by President Theodore Roosevelt) to educate the public on the merits of untried, untested, and probably initially unpopular policies.

Another way in which the electorate can participate in formulating foreign policy is through referenda, which governments may call to obtain a popular mandate for major changes in policy or constitutional structure. The initial rejection of the Maastricht treaty on closer unification within the European Union by Danish voters in 1992, and that treaty's narrow approval in France later that year, led EU member states to reconsider the pace and depth of European union. Many European governments had regarded closer unification as a foregone conclusion until the general public voiced its concerns over the issue. This is a case, then, of public opinion constraining the set of options open to policy-makers, and affecting the pace and nature of policy implementation. Public opinion slowed European integration.

In more authoritarian states, public opinion may be expressed through work slowdowns—many Soviet workers, protected by the government's guarantee of full employment, came to work drunk or drank on the job or expressed their dissatisfaction more directly by clandestine dissidence, protest demonstrations, and riots. During the Persian Gulf War, for example, citizens of authoritarian regimes in the Middle East, North Africa, and South Asia took to the streets to demonstrate against their governments' support for the Allied coalition. Beginning with the era of *glasnost* (see Chapter 4) in the USSR, Soviet analysts admitted that Moscow's policy in Afghanistan was constrained by the public's overwhelming disapproval of the 1979 invasion and decade-long intervention in that country.

The example of Afghanistan, which has striking parallels to the U.S. war in Vietnam, illustrates that public support is most important when a government decides to initiate or join a war. War requires mobilization of a nation's troops and material, war-related industries and resources, and sometimes even society itself. Complete national mobilization may be less of a problem for governments when the state in question is attacked, or when the war is anticipated to be brief. Following the Japanese attack on Pearl Harbor in 1941, for instance, the American public immediately supported U.S. entry into World War II, despite the strength of isolationist sentiments before December 7. In another example, initial support for World War I in several countries derived in part from the popular belief that the war would be over quickly and was even "necessary for human progress."

This kind of mass support for war is often described as a "rally-around-the-flag effect"; it is simply a consensus among members of diverse social and political groups to stand behind a tough foreign-policy decision and present a united front against a foreign enemy, whether the adversary represents a real threat or just a convenient scapegoat. Although this rallying effect may initially be an asset to politicians, it is difficult to sustain. In the long run, wars are almost always a political burden because of the human and economic costs that they entail. The protracted Vietnam War destroyed Lyndon Johnson's presidency, and several British and French governments fell as their successive military plans failed to stop the senseless slaughter of World War I.

In most countries, the media also plays a progressively critical role in mobilizing public opinion on a host of key issues. People are influenced by the pictures they see. The British and Israeli publics, for example, have been deeply influenced by news reports of IRA, Palestinian, or Islamic fundamentalist terrorism. It was difficult for Western governments—especially the Bush administration—to resume business as usual with China after the televised massacre at Tiananmen Square in 1989. The United Nations might never have intervened in Somalia in 1992 except for the pictures of starving men, women, and children on international television. Yet people can also become accustomed to violence, as suggested by Western inaction during the crises in Bosnia, Rwanda, and Haiti. Despite these cases, certainly the media today frames public debates and discussions of foreign policy in distant lands that might otherwise be barely recognized—even by elite opinion.

Political Culture

Political culture fuses a nation's historical traditions to its cultural institutions and values to form a national style of politics and policy-making. One aspect of a nation's culture that can shape its foreign policy is its cultural vision of its proper role in the world. In the fifteenth and sixteenth centuries, for example, Spain viewed itself as champion and defender of the Roman Catholic Church. In response, Spain sent out explorers and conquistadors, including Columbus, Cortés, and Pizarro, in an effort not only to open new trade routes and settle new territory, but also to win souls for the church and thereby gain glory for the Spanish Crown. Three centuries later, England tried to bring liberal democratic ideals to the indigenous populations of present-day Africa and Asia in fulfillment of what English author Rudyard Kipling (born in British India) called "the white man's burden." France, too, established colonies and imposed its language and form of government on Africans and Asians as part of carrying out *la mission civilistrice*—the "civilizing mission."

Other states' foreign policies have been similarly affected by historical and cultural traditions. Islamic fundamentalism has inspired efforts (heroic or fanatical, depending on one's point of view) to rid the Middle East of American influence, drive Soviet forces out of Afghanistan, and combat or destroy the state of Israel. To consider another example, some observers have argued that Japanese traditions of deference to authority, avoidance of direct confrontation, and preoccupation with achieving group consensus have had an impact on Tokyo's recent foreign policy, which has been relatively unassertive despite Japan's great economic strength. As discussed earlier, the norms of nonviolent conflict resolution inherent in the political culture of many democratic states may have contributed to the maintenance of peace among democracies, even

The political culture of many European nations was imbued with a "civilizing mission" toward their colonies in the late nineteenth century. In this 1895 illustration, a Belgian official settles a tribal dispute in the Congo.

Source: © Hulton Deutsch Collection Limited London.

though some democratic states have been willing to take military action against nondemocratic enemies.

Many scholars perceive the American style of foreign policy as characterized by a conflict between a crusading idealism to change the world in America's image and an isolationist impulse to disengage from international politics altogether.[23] The interventionist spirit may be traced to the Puritan ideals of many English settlers in colonial America and to the nineteenth-century concept of America's "manifest destiny" to dominate North America and transform the world for the better:

> [The American claim] is by the right of manifest destiny to overspread and to possess the whole of the Continent which Providence has given us for the development of the great experiment of liberty and federative self government entrusted to us.[24]

Interestingly, one author finds that America's "colossal liberal absolutism . . . is inspired either to withdraw from 'alien' things or to transform them: it cannot live in comfort constantly by their side."[25] Another author suggests that the American style of foreign relations exhibits the irresolvable dualistic tendency to speak two languages simultaneously: one of power and the other of community and harmony. "Only a symbolic eagle can hold both the arrows and the olive branch easily at the same time . . . the impulse of violence and the thrust toward harmony are both escapes from the unbearable reality of inevitable conflict."[26]

Another tension in American foreign policy—that between the desire for change and the desire for order—gives U.S. policy a bias toward intervention to preserve stability even if it has meant supporting nondemocratic governments abroad. This tendency reflects America's 200-year-old experience of constitutional continuity that has instilled in the United States a "nostalgia for tranquillity [and a] faith in the highly debatable assumption that a stable polity is a healthy one. . . ."[27] Those who see the United States as isolationist contend that America has a low pain index, thus decreasing its willingness to become involved in foreign affairs and war. Pointing to the relatively small number of American deaths in Vietnam (58,000) and Lebanon (258), and the degree of domestic controversies those interventions entailed, foreign leaders might think that if they can inflict enough casualties, the American public will become restive enough to force its leaders to retreat. The notion of a low "pain index" can be seen today in America's reliance on weapons of high technology to reduce casualty levels.

Over the years, the tension between trying to transform international relations into a harmonious whole through intervention and then retreating into isolationism when other countries do not want to conform to the U.S. vision has made American foreign policy appear inconsistent, if not schizophrenic. Arguably, it also has undermined rational calculations of military strategy, diplomacy, and international economics.

Another American cultural trait that has influenced its foreign policy is legalism. During and after World War I, for example, President Wilson tirelessly insisted that a new international order based on his "Fourteen Points" of collective security and national self-determination would be the best way to secure peace in postwar Europe. American faith in the power of legal institutions to restrain conflict and aggression has been regarded by many foreign diplomats as naive; one European diplomat remarked that it was grandiose of Wilson to insist on fourteen points when God was content with only ten. American beliefs in peace through the framework of a legal system were instrumental in the creation of the League of Nations (which the U.S. Senate ironically prevented America from joining), and the United Nations (for which the United States has been a guiding force since its inception).

The end of the Cold War has energized efforts by U.S.–based groups such as the World Federalist Association to continue to preserve peace through international law. How successful these efforts will be in the New Era remains to be seen. American-style legalism may not be the cultural norm with the greatest impact on global politics. Political scientist Samuel Huntington has argued that future world politics may become a "clash of civilizations." While he does not contend that the nation-state will disappear, Huntington believes that global politics will increasingly be divided along cultural lines:

> [C]onflict between civilizations will supplant ideological and other forms of conflict as the dominant global form of conflict; international relations, historically a game played out within Western civilization, will increasingly be de-Westernized and become a

WHAT WOULD YOU DO?

You are a philosopher-king with the responsibility for designing a political and economic system for a new country. You want to set up political institutions conducive to international peace. You have concluded that liberal democracy would accomplish this.

You want a system that requires the government to obtain popular approval before going to war; this would ensure that participation in a war had the support of those most likely to risk their lives. You also want a system that allows for individual freedom to engage in commercial pursuits. You believe that citizens who are engaged in commerce and producing wealth have more to lose in supporting a war and, therefore, will not take war lightly.

On the other hand, in the debates at the philosophers' collegium, your critics have

game in which non-Western civilizations are actors and not simply objects. . . . [A] central focus of conflict for the immediate future will be between the West and several Islamic-Confucian states.[28]

If Huntington's thesis turns out to be correct, culture may become an even more important factor in both foreign policy and international politics in the New Era.

LINKS BETWEEN STATE AND SOCIETY

We have thus far discussed two views of the influence of domestic politics: one stressing government institutions (the statist approach) and the other stressing groups, culture, and the public (the societal approach). In the rest of this chapter we will examine three factors that operate both within government institutions and in the broader context of society as a whole. Political parties, ideology, and ethnic conflict all affect how both the state and society are organized to interact with the outside world.

Political Parties

On the one hand, political parties are the epitome of the societal approach. In democratic states they represent the ultimate influence of public groups in the political arena. In essence, parties are coalitions of groups seeking control over the political process. They formulate and advocate their foreign-policy positions to maintain or attract support from voters or interest groups. Consequently, parties often make a major difference in a state's foreign policy. In Israel, the Labor party is prepared to relinquish at least a part of the occupied territories; the Likud party is not. In Britain, the Conservative party has been more cautious than the Labour party in integrating Britain's economy into the EU. In pointed out that a liberal democracy will not necessarily prevent belligerency. They argue that in a liberal democracy, leaders may galvanize public support for war (and themselves) if rival leaders are against war. Also, in a liberal democracy, once a leader initiates war through public approval, he or she may not be able to stop that war short of total victory. Furthermore, these critics point out that the popular consultation process in a liberal democracy is so time-consuming and distracting that war-prone despots have an opportunity to gain the advantage.

How would you promote a liberal democracy capable of protecting the territorial integrity of your country?

Russia, reformist parties argue for the development of trade and political links with Europe and the United States, while nationalist parties contend that Moscow must be prepared to use military and political muscle to protect the rights of Russians living in the "near abroad" (the former republics of the USSR). U.S. parties are strongly influenced by interest groups; most labor unions supply strong support to the Democrats, while Christian fundamentalists (who oppose foreign-aid programs that fund abortions) back the Republicans—but both parties get massive campaign contributions from agricultural and manufacturing interests.

Yet there is another view of parties that conforms more closely to the statist approach. Often particular groups seek influence across the political spectrum so they can win no matter who gets elected, which accounts in part for the oft-noted similarities between supposedly competing parties in democracies. In the United States, for example, both Democrats and Republicans support continued military spending—as long as the money continues to be spent in their districts. The major parties in Germany and France have consistently supported full integration into the EU even though public opinion on the subject has often been divided. Moreover, parties may themselves represent a national consensus on particular issues or they may reflect a national style, such as the Japanese reliance on leading bureaucrats no matter who is in power or the vaunted influence of the British civil service.

Parties also reflect the institutional characteristics of a state's political system. In multiparty states such as Israel and Russia, the need to maintain a governing coalition of parties complicates the process of making foreign policy. In Russia's case, this has led to conflicting signals from Moscow and sudden, worrisome shifts in Russia's general policy toward Europe, NATO, and the former Soviet republics. By contrast, in states where one party has dominated for an extended period (as the Liberal Democratic party did in Japan from the 1950s to the early 1990s), a consistent foreign-policy line is easier to achieve—but the lack

AT A GLANCE

FACTORS AFFECTING THE DOMESTIC LEVEL OF ANALYSIS

Statist Approaches

Regime Type

Definition: Regime type is a state's basic form of government, whether democratic or authoritarian. In states governed by authoritarian regimes, where controls on the state are weak or absent, the state has a freer hand to pursue any policy that it chooses. The government of a democracy is held responsible for its actions by the electorate, which often constrains foreign policy flexibility.

Effect: Authoritarian regimes often have aggressive and expensive foreign policies and economic policy, in many cases, becomes an extension of foreign policy. In democratic nations, norms of harmony and stability tend to prevail, and popular support is necessary in making the decision to go to war. Therefore, democracies rarely, if ever, fight each other. However, if democracies go to war against authoritarian states, the effort is often oversold by leaders in order to gain popular backing.

Executive-Legislative Relations

Definition: The executive is at the center of a state's foreign-policy apparatus. Most countries have some sort of legislative body, but these bodies vary enormously in the degree to which they genuinely represent the wishes of the public and act as a check against executive power. In most dictatorial regimes, the legislative branch is nothing more than a "rubber stamp." However, in democratic societies legislative constraints on executive authority are prominent features of domestic political institutions.

Effect: In democratic countries, the legislature's authority to ratify treaties is frequently its greatest constraint on the executive's foreign-policy behavior.

Bureaucracies

Definition: Bureaucracies are domestic political institutions designed to expedite the process by which government officials identify foreign-policy objectives, formulate specific policy options, and choose and evaluate policies.

Effect: Bureaucrats follow a set of decision-making guidelines and make routine recommendations. This mechanical process is often slow. Each bureaucracy promotes policies that are in its own best interest.

Societal Approaches

Interest Groups

Definition: Interest groups are powerful groups that can exert influence over foreign policy through close ties with the government agencies that regulate their operation and utilize their services and products.

Effect: Interest groups organize letter-writing campaigns, lobby members of Congress, publish materials that propound their arguments, and educate their constituencies on the importance of providing campaign funds to sympathetic candidates.

Public Opinion

Definition: Views and attitudes on national issues held by the people of a nation, with particular emphasis placed on elite views and media influence.

of partisan debate over foreign-policy issues may strengthen the power of unelected bureaucrats. In authoritarian and would-be totalitarian societies, the party captures the state. The Nazi and Communist parties became the state, in practice meshing the two and destroying the difference between state and society—the essence of totalitarianism. The Chinese Communist Party has relaxed

Effect: In democracies, voters influence the government by having the power to elect the decision makers. They can participate in referenda. In more authoritarian states, public opinion can be expressed through work slowdowns, clandestine dissidence, protest demonstrations, and riots.

Political Culture
Definition: Political culture fuses a nation's historical traditions to its cultural institutions and values to form a national style of politics and policy making. One aspect of a nation's culture that can shape its foreign policy is its cultural vision of its proper role in the world.

Effect: A nation's past influences its current policies and activities.

Links Between State and Society

Political Parties
Definition: Coalitions of groups that either seek or maintain control over their country's political process.

Effect: Parties formulate and advocate their foreign policy positions to maintain or attract support from voters or interest groups. They often make a major difference in a state's foreign policy. Often particular groups seek influence across the political spectrum so they can win no matter who gets elected, which accounts in part for the oft-noted similarities between supposedly competing parties in democracies. In authoritarian states, parties often control the state, and foreign policy reflects party preferences.

Ideology
Definition: Ideology refers to the belief systems on which states and groups within states base their actions—in other words, the grand ideals that provide a system of values for a state's institutions and foreign policy-making process. Ideological influence on foreign policy can have very deep roots.

Effect: Ideology shapes a state's political institutions and provides a context within which social forces and public opinion exert influence over foreign policy.

Ethnic Conflict
Definition: The culture of a state is the product of the cultures of the various ethnic groups to which its citizens belong. A single ethnic group constitutes a large majority of the population in very few states; usually a number of different religious, linguistic, and racial groups inhabit the same state, and many ethnic groups are split between two or more states. Ethnic tension, with accompanying international implications, sporadic violence, and even war, is rampant throughout the globe.

Effect: Because relations between ethnic groups within a state can create complex problems and stir powerful emotions, it is not surprising that ethnic conflict is another societal force that can have a major impact on a state's foreign policy institutions, its relations with its neighbors, and its international behavior.

its control over the economy but reacts violently to suggestions that domestic interest groups should have more influence over foreign policy.

The specific features of a nation's political system thus have a strong effect on its relations with other states. In all states, whether democratic or authoritarian, capitalist or socialist, political parties develop links between state and society. In authoritarian states, however, these links are not as strong because generally the party, through the state, imposes its will on society. Therefore, the foreign policy process is far less constrained by domestic politics. In democratic states these links act as two-way channels of influence between society and the foreign-policy process.

Ideology

Ideology refers to the belief systems on which states and groups within states base their actions—in other words, the grand ideals that provide a system of values for a state's institutions and foreign policy-making process. Ideology provides a context within which social forces and public opinion exert influence over foreign policy. (In Chapter Fifteen, we will discuss the related concept of operational code, which refers to the belief systems that guide individual leaders.)

Ideological influence on foreign policy can have very deep roots. In England and the United States, the origins of democracy and individual liberty in political institutions can be traced from the Magna Carta (a written agreement between King John and his feudal barons signed in 1215) to the American Declaration of Independence and the U.S. Constitution, and right down to the present. Consequently, these nations often frame their foreign policy (forthrightly or otherwise) in an ideological context, such as the need to protect democracy throughout the world. As we saw in Chapter Two, similar ideals grounded in the eighteenth-century Enlightenment inspired the French Revolution in 1789, which smashed the monarchical *ancien régime;* and during the subsequent Napoleonic Wars, French arms and diplomacy spread the new concepts of liberalism, egalitarianism, and nationalism throughout Europe.

After the Napoleonic Wars, the European great powers established the Concert of Europe as an institution dedicated to maintaining peace by moderating nationalism. Worker revolts in Western and Central Europe in 1848, however, popularized Marx's thoughts and were further animated by socialist ideas and the nationalist spirit sweeping Europe at the time. The year 1848 also saw the publication of Karl Marx's *Communist Manifesto,* which further inspired unrest in many countries. Russia, acting as the "gendarme of Europe," suppressed many of the revolts but failed to stamp out either Marxism or these new nationalist ways of thinking. Russia itself was transformed by Marxist ideas in the Bolshevik Revolution in 1917, after which its successor, the Soviet Union, sought to foment Communist revolutions in the belief that overthrowing the capitalist system would lead to world peace and social justice.

Soviet and American foreign policy went on to have an especially strong ideological cast. Some argue that post–World War II American foreign policy represented an attempt to extend to the rest of the world the ideas of John Locke (who argued that people have a natural right to own and use property for individual enrichment) and Adam Smith (who contended that the free market is the most efficient, and therefore the most just, system for distributing rewards). In order to do so, the United States had to prevent the encroachment of the ideas of Marx and Lenin. To this end the United States used its political, economic, and military strength to stop Communist movements from taking over Western Europe, and to assist other countries in strengthening their domestic economies. The United States acted even when this effort meant erecting trade barriers against American products, which ran counter to the more open trade system sought by the GATT accords.

Soviet postwar foreign policy, on the other hand, was ostensibly driven by the belief that a powerful Soviet Union was required to protect the achievements of socialism and hasten the collapse of the exploitative capitalist system. Accordingly, this led the USSR to install compliant Communist regimes in Eastern Europe, form the Warsaw Pact, build up its industrial and military infrastructure, and support "wars of national liberation" in Cuba, Vietnam, Angola, Nicaragua, and elsewhere. Regardless of the degree to which Soviet and American policies were influenced by their respective ideologies, their ideological conflict certainly reinforced mutual perceptions of threat, served their security interests, and intensified the global political competition during the Cold War.[29]

In another context, the theocracy established after the Iranian revolution of 1979 represented a conscious repudiation of Western Enlightenment ideology. The 1979 revolution ushered in a fundamentalist Islamic theocracy in which political and religious law were to be merged into one. In terms of foreign policy, Iran's new government led by religious *mullahs* justified violence when it declared that the United States was the "Great Satan," intent on destroying Islam and denying basic human rights to the people of developing nations. (The officially atheistic USSR was awarded the title of "Little Satan" as a second prize.) Therefore, terrorism against Americans was not only justified but would ensure a martyr's place in heaven. This ideology is practiced through Iranian support of terrorist organizations throughout the Middle East and the backing of radical Islamic parties in Central Asia and North Africa. Thus, ideologies developed within states or adapted from ideas originating elsewhere often become the source of—or at least justification for—actions a particular regime pursues in its foreign policy.

Ethnic Conflict

In a sense, the culture of a state is the product of the cultures of the various ethnic groups to which its citizens belong. Because relations between ethnic groups within a state can create complex problems and stir powerful emotions, it is not surprising that ethnic conflict is another societal force that can have a major impact on a state's foreign-policy institutions, its relations with its neighbors, and its international behavior. A single ethnic group constitutes a large majority of the population in very few states; usually a number of different religious, linguistic, and racial groups inhabit the same state, and many ethnic groups are split between two or more states. Both of these conditions frequently lead to conflict, within and between states.

Ethnic tension, with accompanying international implications and sporadic violence, is rampant throughout the globe. Often, attempts to assert ethnic identity take the form of separatist movements that seek at least a measure of autonomy—if not outright independence—from the central government. For example, many in French-speaking Quebec seek to secede from Canada. Basques and Catalans see themselves as separate from Spain. Some Sikhs want to leave India. Some Scots want to separate from the United Kingdom. Russia is plagued by several movements that seek at least autonomy from Moscow. In the most peaceful, but also starkest case of separatism of the early 1990s, the Czech Republic and Slovakia decided on a peaceful divorce into two distinct states carved out of Czechoslovakia, which had existed since the end of World War I.

Ethnic divisions can contribute to several types of violent conflict.[30] Ethnic strife within the territory of a single state can lead to civil wars. Though they may spring from other sources, civil wars are often caused by the competition between two or more national groups for control of the state. When disagreements are so profound and intractable that one or more groups deny the very legitimacy of the state, they may try to break away from it and form a new state, leading to a **war of secession.** Conflicts between states also can be caused by one state claiming territory which is controlled by another state, whether for historical reasons or because the population of that territory shares the nationality of the aggrieved state; this is **irredentism.** Finally, nationalist leaders who promote the rights, or supremacy, of a particular nation may attempt to wage a **war of unification,** in order to create a single nation-state for an ethnic group previously divided among several different states.[31] Figure 14.1 summarizes these four types of war.

All of these phenomena have been frequent throughout history and remain so in the New Era. The frequency of these conflicts is hardly surprising given the proliferation of states after World War II and, more recently, after the breakup of the Soviet Union. In many cases, state borders were drawn by imperial authorities for their own purposes, often in complete disregard of the ethnic groups that were forced together or split apart. The result was to exacerbate tensions between ethnic groups, sometimes leading to violent conflict.

Certainly, ethnic conflict has often led to civil wars, some of which have turned into wars of secession and some of which have provoked foreign intervention. In the Middle East, the country of Lebanon epitomizes how ethnic conflict can spiral out of control. From 1943 onward, as a result of a national pact, the president was a Maronite Christian, the premier a Sunni Muslim, and the speaker of the National Assembly a Shiite Muslim. With this delicate balancing act, it is perhaps not surprising that the country has twice in recent decades experienced civil wars in which various factions fought over the distribution of power, in both instances with external engagement. The 1958 civil war was quickly quelled by American intervention; the civil war that started in 1975, however, lasted sixteen years and was sustained in part by the active involvement of Syria, Israel, the United States, France, Iraq, Iran, and the Palestinians. The complexity of the conflict in Lebanon, exacerbated by foreign power intervention in pursuit of their own objectives, shows why many ethnic conflicts are so stubbornly difficult to disentangle and resolve.

The decline and disintegration of empires often leads to extensive conflict as ethnic groups attempt to stake and enforce their claims over a given territory that

TYPE	CAUSE
Civil War	Violent competition between two or more national groups for control of the state.
War of Secession	When disagreements are so profound and intractable that one or more groups deny the legitimacy of the state, they may try to break away from it and form another state or join with another state.
Irredentist War	Conflicts between states caused by one state claiming territory that is controlled by another state, either for historical reasons or because the population of that territory shares the nationality of the aggrieved state.
War of Unification	Leaders attempt to wage a war in order to create a single nation-state for an ethnic group divided among several different states.

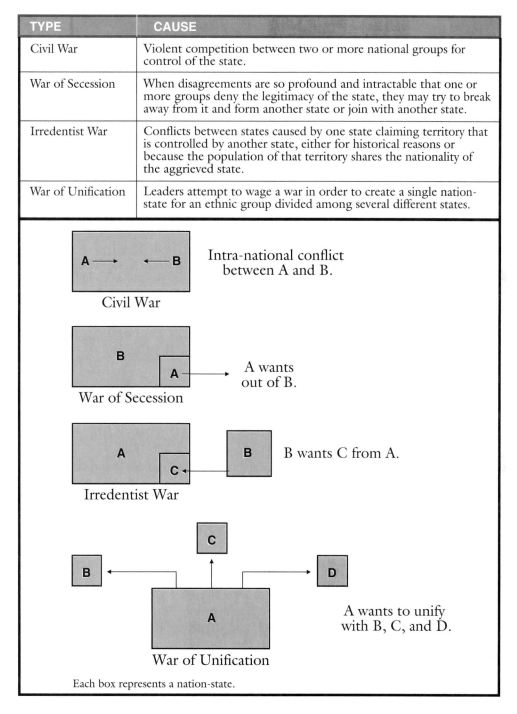

Civil War — Intra-national conflict between A and B.

War of Secession — A wants out of B.

Irredentist War — B wants C from A.

War of Unification — A wants to unify with B, C, and D.

Each box represents a nation-state.

Figure 14.1   Types of Ethnic Wars

YUGOSLAVIA: A MODERN TRAGEDY

"My apologies to Attila," French Premier Georges Clemenceau once said, "but the art of arranging how men are to live is even more complex than the art of massacring them." Both Attila and Clemenceau would find the tragic events surrounding the dissolution of Yugoslavia all too familiar. During the Cold War, the neutral Communist state of Yugoslavia was often held up as an example of how ethnic groups with long histories of violent conflict could live together peacefully in the same state. However, warning signs of the multiethnic state's impending collapse began to appear shortly after the death in 1980 of Josip Broz (Marshall) Tito, the Communist leader and former anti-Nazi partisan fighter whose legendary reputation and skillful leadership helped hold the country together.

After World War II, Yugoslavia was organized as a federation of ethnically based republics. In the late 1980s, the country became increasingly divided politically, as conflicts appeared between the Belgrade government, dominated by Serbs, and Yugoslavia's other nationalities, including Croats, Slovenes, Albanians, and Muslim Slavs. Following flare-ups of violence in the southern region of Kosovo in 1990, the republics of Slovenia and Croatia seceded from the federation in 1991. Intervention by the federal army did not prevent Slovenian and Croatian independence, but thousands of casualities resulted from the fighting, which ended in an uneasy truce in 1992. The republics of Bosnia and Macedonia seceded shortly afterwards.

The most violent act in the tragedy opened in 1992 when a three-sided civil war broke out in Bosnia, between Serbian nationalist forces backed by the federal army, Croatian militias receiving support from Croatia, and predominantly Muslim

is occupied by other ethnic groups as well (see Maps 14.1 and 14.2). For example, as both the Ottoman and Austro-Hungarian empires began to disintegrate in the late nineteenth and early twentieth centuries, fighting broke out between Serbs, Bulgarians, Romanians, and other ethnic groups in the region over the forming of new states (a historical antecedent to the more recent fighting in the Balkans). As we saw in Chapter Three, Serbian support for a secessionist movement in the Austro-Hungarian Empire was the trigger for the beginning of the First World War.

The dismantling of the British Empire after World War II also led to fighting among various ethnic groups. For example, conflict between Hindus and Muslims led to the creation of Islamic Pakistan and secular India, where the Hindus are in the majority. In the turmoil of independence, approximately 7 million Muslims fled to Pakistan and 6 million Hindus to India, and about 1 million people were killed in communal violence. Similarly, fighting erupted between Arabs and Jews in British-controlled Palestine and escalated in 1948 when the surrounding Arab states declared war on the new, Jewish state of Israel. More recently, the disintegration of the Soviet Union led to many conflicting claims

Bosnian forces. The war was fought with a savagery that most modern Europeans would have liked to believe was a thing of the past on their continent. Bosnian Muslims in particular were terrorized by unspeakably brutal policies of "ethnic cleansing," wherein civilians were systematically driven from their homes, put into concentration camps, tortured, raped, or simply slaughtered. An accurate account of casualties from the war may never be made, but estimates of the numbers killed run into the tens or hundreds of thousands.[*]

The United Nations, the Council on Security and Cooperation in Europe (CSCE), the European Union, and NATO were slow to coordinate an effective response to the bloodshed. UN peace-keeping forces and relief convoys were deployed early in the conflict, but it was not until 1994 that NATO organized sporadic military action to enforce the UN-ordered cease-fire. By that time, well over 70 percent of Bosnia had been carved up by Serbian and Croatian forces, and hopes of reuniting Bosnia looked increasingly dim.

The possibility of continued peace among the former Yugoslav republics appeared even more uncertain, as ethnic conflicts still smoldered in several areas. The halting response of the international community to the war in Bosnia augured poorly for the ability of international institutions to maintain peace, and the human tragedy of the breakup of Yugoslavia proved that ethnic and nationalist conflicts in the New Era could be every bit as bloody as they were in the past.

[*]For more on the many conflicts in the former Yugoslavia, see James Gow, "Deconstructing Yugoslavia," *Survival* 33, no. 4 (July/August 1991), pp. 299–311; Misha Glenny, *The Fall of Yugoslavia* (New York: Penguin, 1992); and Robert Kaplan, *Balkan Ghosts* (New York: St. Martin's, 1993).

over land among ethnic groups both in Russia and in several other former Soviet republics. For example, ethnic warfare has occurred in Moldova, Georgia, Armenia, and Azerbaijan. In South Africa, the legacy of British imperialism and the policy of apartheid intensified ethnic strife and violence throughout the second half of the twentieth century.

Irredentist claims have frequently created tensions and violence between states. After the Franco-Prussian War in 1870–1871, for example, France lost Alsace-Lorraine; and the desire for revenge poisoned relations between France and Germany (Prussia's successor) and eventually contributed to World War I. In the late 1930s, Hitler's claim that all Germans should live in one German state led him to annex Austria and then claim the Sudetenland from Czechoslovakia, which was forced by Britain and France to accede to Hitler's demands at the now infamous 1938 Munich Conference. More recently, Iraq cited irredentist claims against parts of southwestern Iran, inhabited primarily by Arab Sunni Muslims, as justification for its war with Iran in 1980–1988. In the 1990s, Russian claims to the Crimea, which is currently part of Ukraine, offer another example of political irredentism.

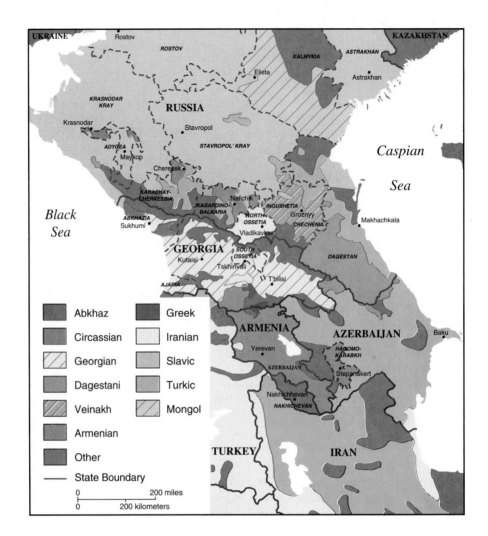

Map 14.1 Ethnic Groups in the Caucasus Region

Wars of national unity have also created considerable international conflicts. Perhaps the most prominent example was a series of three wars during the mid-nineteenth century. First, Prussia fought Denmark, then Austria, and finally France, all in order to unify and dominate Germany. Italy was also unified during the mid-nineteenth century, with the Italian state of Piedmont taking the lead and fighting a war with Austria in the process. The Kurds were promised a state by the great powers after World War I. Instead, they were divided into areas that are now in Turkey, Iraq, Syria, and Iran—leading to violent conflicts that have lasted decades and have involved efforts both to secede from some or all of these countries and to achieve unification. Recently, the collapse of the Soviet Union left millions of Russians living in independent former Soviet republics

Map 14.2   Ethnic Groups in Eastern Europe

with non-Russian majorities. Many new states have subsequently been rocked by ethnic violence; Russians in Moldova, many hoping to eventually reunify with Russia, created their own secessionist republic amidst bitter fighting in 1992. On the other hand, the Abkhazians and the South Ossetians tried to secede from Georgia after the collapse of the USSR. Extremist "national-patriotic" movements in Russia have called for the reunification of the great Russian state, and many leaders in Moscow have asserted their country's right to protect the rights of ethnic Russians residing in neighboring states.

It is readily apparent from these examples that ethnic conflict is an ancient curse that continues to plague contemporary international relations. Disturbingly, it appears that ethnic conflict could become a defining characteristic of the New Era. It is one of the key factors producing fragmentation in current world politics. Table 14.1 summarizes the forms of ethnic strife that have erupted into violent conflict since 1945 and gives representative examples of each type. Many of the conflicts listed here could be classified in more than one category; this should come as no surprise, as clear distinctions are rare in many aspects of ethnic conflict.

The long list of violent ethnic conflicts in the post–World War II period should not prompt the conclusion that ethnic divisions always lead to violence. In many European countries, notably Switzerland, Belgium, and Finland, ethnic groups with long histories of warfare live together peacefully, with the rights of all groups protected by law and constitutional arrangements.[32] It is also not easy to conclude whether some Asian states which have experienced communal conflict, such as Malaysia, Indonesia, and India, represent successes or failures of their regimes in controlling ethnic violence, as the long history of conflict between the ethnic groups in these states might have led one to expect a great deal *more* violence than has actually occurred. Nationalism, which has often been derided by world leaders since the nineteenth century, can be a force that unites as well as divides people, especially if the nationalism is civic rather than ethnic in character.[33] Thus, while ethnic conflict may very well be a major factor in international relations in the New Era, there are a number of hopeful examples indicating governments and international organizations can find ways to moderate ethnic tensions.

CONCLUSIONS—OR CAN THERE BE ANY?

This chapter has examined the ways in which the unique attributes of states and societies can influence how states behave in the international system. It has shown how states differ and why their differences matter. The previous chapter on the systemic level of analysis, on the other hand, focused on how states were alike in their power, security, and prosperity, and outlined how these similarities lead states to act in similar ways. The question that arises is, which are more important, the similarities or the differences? Are the actions of states in the international system affected more by the distribution of capabilities among them or by the character of their individual political, economic, and social systems? And if countries' unique attributes are the driving forces behind their foreign policies, which of the many attributes exert the greatest influence?

Perhaps the best way to answer this question is by drawing an analogy between states and persons. The physiological structure of every human being is essentially similar, and humans share many common needs, wants, desires, and fears. At the same time, each individual is unique in many important respects,

Table 14.1 Ethnic Conflict in the International System, 1945–1994

Type of Conflict	*Selected Examples*
Civil war	India, 1947
	Malaysia, 1948–1960
	Kenya, 1952–1956
	Rwanda, 1962–1965; 1993–
	Yemen, 1962–1969
	Sudan, 1963–
	Cyprus, 1974
	Lebanon, 1975–1991
	Angola, 1975–
	Afghanistan, 1989–
	Sri Lanka, 1983–
War of secession	Zaire, 1960–1965
	Ethiopia, 1961–1993
	Nigeria, 1967–1970
	Bangladesh, 1971
	Georgia, 1991–
	Moldova, 1992
	Croatia, 1992
Irredentism	Israel-Egypt-Jordan-Syria, 1948, 1967, 1973
	India-Pakistan, 1965, 1971
	Armenia-Azerbaijan, 1991–
	Bosnia, 1992–
	Iraq-Kuwait, 1990–1991
War of unification	Korea, 1950–1953
	Vietnam, 1956–1975
	Northern Ireland, 1969–
	Kurds, 1961–

as each has a unique combination of special concerns, hopes, and dreams. The similarities among people lead to common patterns of behavior (any person who is hungry will attempt to get food), but differences in capabilities, resources, values, and attitudes prompt individuals to pursue commonly held goals in distinctive ways (a variety of factors will determine whether a hungry person goes to a restaurant or goes out hunting). Thus, while knowledge of human behavior makes it possible to offer statistical predictions of what people are likely to do in a given situation, the factors that cause a person to act in a specific manner in a specific situation may be difficult, if not impossible, to ascertain.

If this sounds like a refusal to answer the question of whether systemic or domestic factors exert greater influence on a state's foreign policy, it is. The study of world politics involves many controversies, and the relative impact of the international system and domestic concerns is one unlikely to be resolved anytime soon. Nevertheless, the examples of peace among democracies and the ability of ideology to intensify disputes show that it is possible to identify specific features of states and societies that can be expected to promote cooperation or exacerbate conflict. And just as the inability to predict the actions of individuals with absolute certainty does not make the study of human behavior a useless enterprise, the existence of contending theories on why states act as they do does not mean that the study of international relations is pointless. Any knowledge of how to avoid the mistakes of the past can help governments make more effective policy—or at least leave them free to make new mistakes.

The parallels drawn here between international relations and human behavior remind us that although the language of global politics often refers to abstract entities—states, regimes, forces, and so forth—political decisions are always made and carried out by individuals. With this in mind, the next chapter will consider how individual leaders can affect foreign policy and world politics in the New Era.

PRINCIPAL POINTS OF CHAPTER FOURTEEN

1. This chapter examines the domestic level of analysis. Analyses on this level contend that it is not always useful to treat states as unitary rational actors that are essentially similar to all other states. Instead, they focus on how attributes of individual states affect their actions in the international system.

2. The statist approach to the study of domestic-level factors contends that political institutions and state structures shape the content and substance of a state's foreign policy.

3. In contrast, a societal approach argues that a state's national interest merely reflects domestic interest groups, political forces, and cultural attributes.

4. The statist approach focuses on domestic political institutions that shape the preferences and behavior of states, which include the following:

   a. Regime type, or basic form of government—authoritarian, democratic, or communist. Illustrating one effect of regime type, a large body of research suggests that democratic states rarely, if ever, go to war against one another.

   b. Executive-legislative relations, usually determined by a state's constitutional structure, which sets out the legislature's role in the foreign policy–making process. In democratic states, the system and schedule (or lack thereof) of elections can have a major impact on the timing and content of foreign-policy initiatives.

   c. Bureaucracies, which pursue their own interests through their responsibility for many of the routine aspects of foreign policy–making as well as the implementation of policy. Bureaucracies can affect policies in practice through standard operating procedures (SOPs) or may pursue their own institutional agendas and goals, which can lead to confusing and contradictory policies.

5. Societal approaches examine how groups, social structures, and cultural features outside government can affect a state's international relations.

   a. Interest groups seek to influence foreign policy to favor their specific objectives. In democratic states, organized interest groups attempt to shape policy through campaign contributions, lobbying, and mobilizing public opinion.

   b. Close ties between the defense industry, government agencies responsible for national security, and legislators from districts heavily dependent on defense-related jobs—collectively referred to as the military-industrial complex—often operate to increase military spending and may promote an active and aggressive military posture.

   c. Politicians in democratic states pay close attention to public opinion. However, it is not clear whether policy-makers base their decisions on public opinion or whether they manipulate public opinion to support their decisions.

   d. Political culture, a combination of historical traditions and the cultural norms of a society, can shape a state's values, goals, and style in its interaction with other states.

6. Some domestic influences on foreign policy directly combine aspects of both state institutions and social norms and structures:

   a. Political parties maintain links between state and society. In democratic states, parties use foreign policy as an arena of political competition, and the need to retain the loyalty of party supporters can constrain policy. In authoritarian states, the ruling regimes use parties as instruments of the state, but must still take the need to maintain the effectiveness of these instruments into account when making foreign policy.

   b. Ideology can constrain policy, especially if a ruling group's policies takes an extreme form.

   c. Ethnic conflict can shape a state's foreign policy through the need to maintain support from domestic ethnic groups. Ethnic consciousness and nationalism can lead to irredentism (the pressing of territorial claims against other states on the basis that the disputed land is part of a nation's historic territory), wars of secession (when one group attempts to leave a state), or wars of unification (when a state tries to incorporate all members of an ethnic group). While there are a number of examples of peaceful resolution or moderation of ethnic conflicts, violent ethnic conflicts within states can explode into civil war, spread to neighboring states, or prompt military intervention by outside powers or international organizations.

Chapter 15

The Individual Level of Analysis

In 1947 Stalin chanced to remark at a meeting of the Council of Ministers that "the Russian people had long dreamed of having a safe outlet to the Arctic Ocean." The result was what is now called in Russia "the Railway of Death." For more than four years, in subfreezing temperatures in winter, and swamps and mosquitoes in summer, scores of thousands of forced labourers worked at a railway to Igarka. There were more than eighty campsites, along a 1300-kilometre stretch of tundra. It was even planned to extend the whole project into an Arctic Trans-Siberian railway, right across the north. In the end 850 kilometres of rail were constructed, at enormous cost of money as well as lives. After Stalin's death the whole thing was abandoned, and the line and its equipment were left to rust in the snow—until the glasnost era, when photographs of this vast wastage, including derelict locomotives, appeared in the Russian press. There were photographs, too, of the endless cemeteries of those who, in the words of the organ of the Soviet government, died of "intolerable toil, cold and starvation, unheard-of degradation and humiliation."

Robert Conquest, *Stalin: Breaker of Nations* (New York: Viking Penguin, 1991), pp. 242–243, 294.

Many analysts believe that leaders have a major impact on foreign and domestic policy-making. This impact is most vivid in the actions of all-powerful dictators in totalitarian states. Joseph Stalin, for instance, almost single-handedly changed the political, military, and economic landscape of his country. Furthermore, he did so by acting erratically and brutally, as illustrated in the excerpt above. The impact of democratic leaders may not seem as dramatic as that of dictators, but many analysts agree that they do exert a significant influence over policy-making. Assessing the impact of leaders is difficult, for it entails a close look at the behavioral makeup of the individual and of the conditions within which he or she must act.

Theories that approach international politics from the systemic and domestic levels of analysis hold that a decision maker's foreign-policy choices are shaped either by the nature of the international system or by forces in state and society. Proponents of these approaches do not claim that their theories can predict the decisions that will be made, but they do contend that factors operating "over the heads" of individual leaders—the balance of power and anarchic nature of the international system for systemic-level theorists, and the nation's political institutions and social forces for domestic-level theorists—create the context for decisions on foreign policy and determine the range of options available to policy-makers. Even the most ardent systemic or domestic theorist will concede, of course, that individuals have at least some influence on the foreign policy ultimately chosen. But just how important is the individual? This is the issue so fervently debated. This chapter will consider theories of global politics and foreign policy that reckon the characteristics of and relationships between individual leaders to be of primary importance in shaping their nations' course in world affairs.

No one claims that individuals are able to ignore the constraints imposed by the international system or domestic political institutions. The prime minister of Belgium, no matter how motivated or capable he or she may be, cannot raise Belgium's GDP to the size of Germany's by fiat, or erase the influence of ethnic ties with France and the Netherlands. Even so, that doesn't reduce the Belgian premier's role in foreign policy-making to a mere figurehead. It is clear that individuals have some leeway in interpreting the stringency of systemic and domestic constraints and in deciding how to act within those boundaries. In fact, in most states, the final decision on major issues is ultimately made by one person, the president, prime minister, monarch, dictator, and so forth. It is the personal characteristics and traits of this individual that will shape the policy choice and quality of the nation's foreign policy.[1]

1956: Egypt's military defeat in the Suez Canal crisis results in an Egyptian political victory which elevates Egyptian President Gamal Abdel Nasser's status in the Arab World.

1958: Soviet Premier Nikita Khrushchev's personal conflict with Chinese Communist Party Chairman Mao Zedong contributes to the Sino–Soviet split.

1959: Khrushchev's strong Communist ideology does not prevent him from developing a respectful friendship with Eisenhower during his visit to the United States.

1960: Eisenhower and Khrushchev's relationship is ruined by the U-2 incident, and U.S.–Soviet relations deteriorate.

1965: President Lyndon Johnson, by ordering a military intervention in the Dominican Republic, demonstrates cognitive dissonance in failing to recognize the differences between the Dominican Communists and Cuban Communists under Castro.

1972: Soviet Premier Leonid Brezhnev and President Richard Nixon establish a relationship of trust during détente, which facilitates the signing of SALT I.

1973: Egypt enjoys initial successes against Israel during the Yom Kippur War, which permits Egyptian President Anwar el-Sadat to reverse his policy and become the first Arab leader to begin public negotiations with Israel.

1978: President Jimmy Carter's "hands-on" leadership style helps him mediate Camp David accords between Israel and Egypt, which leads to a stable relationship between the two countries.

1985: Mikhail Gorbachev, whose generational experience leads him to attempt to safeguard Soviet security by peaceful political means in addition to traditional Russian military methods, comes to power in the Soviet Union.

1989–1994: During the tenure of F. W. de Klerk, South Africa's system of apartheid is dismantled, culminating in the election of Nelson Mandela as president in 1994.

1990: Use of heuristics leads President George Bush to equate Iraq's invasion of Kuwait to Germany's expansion following the 1938 Munich Conference; Bush is able to secure the approval of the United Nations Security Council for the use of military force against Iraq, following its invasion of Kuwait.

Consider President Ronald Reagan's 1983 remark that the Soviet Union was "the focus of evil in the modern world."[2] How should this remark be interpreted? Was Reagan merely couching the bipolar global rivalry between the United States and the USSR in moral terms in order to mobilize public support for his defense policy? Was he prompted by the crusading spirit in American political culture? Was he expressing a heartfelt personal conviction? In theory, factors operating at the systemic, state, and individual levels each exert identifiable influences on a nation's actions in the world arena, but in practice the three levels of analysis can be difficult to separate when a state's foreign policy is expressed through a leader's words and actions. Individual-level perspectives on world politics cannot present an infallible means of determining *how much* individuals matter relative to the international system and domestic politics, but they can offer organized means of looking at *how* human factors affect international relations. They examine how human nature, psychology, emotional temperament, attitudes, perceptions, and beliefs direct decision makers to choose one foreign-policy option from the available repertoire.

The two questions that dominate controversies over the relationship between human nature and world politics concern the "nature of human nature": first, whether human nature is essentially good or bad, and second, whether it is fixed or changeable. Moral pessimists believe that humans are greedy, jealous, and violent by nature, and are thus predisposed to settle their differences through conflict and war. Moral optimists, on the other hand, believe that the innate goodness of human nature is potentially boundless, but that ignorance keeps individuals at war with one another. When confronted with the prevalence of violent conflict throughout history, many moral optimists hold that human nature is malleable, and through education, enlightenment, and the exercise of reason, humans can learn to cooperate. The pessimists regard the possibility of obtaining peace through the reform of human nature as an impossible, utopian dream; they see human nature as fixed.

Few scholars who concentrate their studies on individual politicians are utopians, but not all are pessimists. To determine the role of the individual, though, human nature (to the extent that such a concept has any meaning) is less important to individual-level theorists than personal attributes, such as personality, temperament, background, beliefs, and goals. In considering these attributes, there is disagreement over the relative influence of those that remain fairly constant, such as generational experiences or fundamental psychological makeup, and those that can change with specific situations, such as energy, morale, and physical and mental health. Decision makers are frequently subjected to severe stress, and the intense pressure of an international crisis can push leaders beyond their breaking point—or lead them to discover new strengths and abilities.

The fact that crucial foreign-policy decisions are often made rapidly by a limited number of policy-makers leads many scholars to focus their studies on members of the political elite. Indeed, many individual-level theories of international relations are fundamentally theories of elites in politics, specifically concerned with analyzing the backgrounds, beliefs, and leadership styles of those individuals who occupy the highest positions in a nation-state's foreign policy-making apparatus. In other words, while elites in general may guide public opinion, only certain members of the elite (such as presidents or foreign and defense ministers) make decisions that directly affect a state's foreign relations.

This chapter begins with a discussion of human nature, whether it is inherently good, evil, immutable, or redeemable, and whether it predestines humanity to constant warfare or holds out the prospect for perpetual peace. We then move away from the moral and philosophical dimensions of the debate over human nature to look at the behavior of political leaders. Theories that concentrate on psychological aspects of decision making, personality traits, leadership style, and personal disposition will be examined to show how the characteristics of individual leaders can affect the nature of their decisions and policies. By discussing the capabilities and fallibilities of people in general and persons in particular, this chapter will provide a basis for understanding how and why foreign policy-makers can overcome or be overcome by the limitations imposed by domestic politics and the international system.

HUMAN NATURE

World politics has entered a New Era, but human nature has remained the same for thousands of years. Or has it? What is the essence of human nature, anyway? This section will explore the "nature of human nature" by focusing on three related debates: (1) the characteristics of human beings, (2) the malleability of human nature, and (3) the overall utility of the concept itself. Criticisms of human-nature arguments will be considered, along with new alternatives to the model.

The Pessimistic View

The undertones of avarice, duplicity, and violence dominating much of human history have led many observers to conclude that human beings are fundamentally flawed—that is, aggressive and warlike by nature.[3] Various forms of this pessimistic conclusion have been advanced for thousands of years. The Christian doctrine of original sin holds that ever since Adam and Eve tasted the forbidden fruit in the Garden of Eden, humans have been irredeemably sinful, wicked, full of pride, and power-hungry. Theologians such as Saint Augustine, John Milton, and more recently Reinhold Niebuhr use this belief to argue that war is a product of an inherent, fixed human moral weakness that enables passion to overwhelm reason and sin to conquer love. As Milton once wrote,

> For though it were granted us by divine indulgence to be exempt from all that can be harmful to us from without, yet the perverseness of our folly is so bent, that we should never cease hammering out of our own hearts, as it were out of flint, the seeds and sparkles of new misery to ourselves, till all were in a blaze again.[4]

Political philosophers Niccolò Macchiavelli and Thomas Hobbes also used the pessimistic view of human nature as the basis for their theories of domestic and international politics. Hobbes wrote that the defining characteristic of the human condition was "a perpetual and restless desire of power after power, that ceaseth only in death," and that without some greater power to keep this desire in check, the natural state of mankind was a "war of every one against every one" wherein human life was "solitary, poor, nasty, brutish, and short."[5] A similar moral pessimism appears in the writings of twentieth-century classical realists such as Hans Morgenthau, who believed that conflict and evil were not tied to a struggle over scarce resources, but rather to a desire for power for power's sake.[6] For these moral pessimists, theologians, and classical realists, the visions of universal peace advanced by idealists such as Mahatma Gandhi and Martin Luther King, Jr., are condemned by the inherent baseness of humankind to remain dreams or utopian fantasies. Most pessimists believe that the source of peace among humans, if attainable, lies in the coercive power of political institutions. According to Niebuhr, for instance, the "sinful character of man," which cannot be changed, requires political strategies that involve the "balancing of power with power."[7]

Not all pessimistic views of human nature are rooted in theology; many scientists contend that the evils inherent in humankind are a result of evolution, not creation. Some biologists and anthropologists theorize that war stems from an aggressive instinct inherited by human beings from their animal ancestors. Konrad Lorenz, an ethologist (one who studies animal behavior), finds that many animal species use aggression for self-defense, protection of the young, selection of mates, and to maintain territorial spacing within a habitat to prevent depletion of food supplies in one location. Lorenz further writes that an instinct against violence in those same species keeps aggression from destroying them altogether. This instinct is triggered whenever the victim of an attack gives an appropriate signal of submission. The strength of the inhibition against violence in each species is proportional to the "lethality" of the species' weapons—the more dangerous the natural weapons (teeth, claws, poison, and so on), the firmer the inhibition against violence.[8]

To illustrate, consider the difference in behavior between "harmless little" doves and "big bad" wolves, ruthless predators equipped with deadly fangs. When wolves fight, one wolf signals submission by exposing a vulnerable portion of its neck, and the winner will cease its attack. On the other hand, doves, traditional symbols of gentleness and peace, lacking fangs, claws, or venom, have little natural inhibition against aggression. They have been known to occasionally kill one another by plucking an opponent apart over a two-day period. Humans, who lack formidable natural weapons of aggression, also lack any mechanism to inhibit aggression, as any spectator at a hockey game knows. However, humans have used their brains to build artificial weapons to augment the lethality of the species. According to Lorenz, by doing so, humans have upset nature's balanced design, and their aggressive instinct threatens to make them extinct.

The Optimistic View

In contrast to these pessimistic views, moral optimists hold that human beings are not inherently aggressive or evil, that it is possible to turn wicked into good, and that the violent conflicts of the past can be overcome through education and the fostering of moral values. This optimism manifests itself in pacifist movements, which assert that wars will not end "until men in one way or another become better."[9] American poet Henry Wadsworth Longfellow, after visiting an arms factory, captured the sentiment of the optimists elegantly:

> Were half the power that fills the world with terror,
> Were half the wealth bestowed on camps and courts,
> Given to redeem the human mind from error,
> There were no need for arsenals or forts.[10]

Essentially, then, moral optimists believe that in spite of its predilection for war and conflict, humankind can be saved from itself. This may be accomplished by first acculturating the world's population to the norms of peace, then curing the social ills that cause violent conflict, and finally by influencing the moral and social behavior of individual decision makers. Changing individual behavior can be done through moral refinement, education, and sensitivity training, and by preventing "bad" individuals from assuming power in the first place.

Is Human Nature Changeable?   The horrors of modern warfare have not destroyed hopes that the refinement of global standards and norms of morality

AT A GLANCE

HUMAN NATURE

Viewpoint

Pessimistic: Human beings in general are fundamentally flawed—that is, aggressive and warlike by nature. Evils inherent in humankind are seen as either a result of evolution or creation. There is a "perpetual and restless desire of power after power, that ceaseth only in death." Without some greater power to keep this desire in check, the natural state of mankind is a "war of every one against every one" wherein human life is "solitary, poor, nasty, brutish, and short."

Optimistic: Human beings are not inherently aggressive or evil. It is possible to turn wicked into good. The violent conflicts that have plagued society are essentially superficial and can be overcome through education and the fostering of moral values. Changing the views and behavior of political leaders and seeking to mute aggressive instincts through reeducation and knowledge would solve the problem.

Feminist: Conclusions on "human" behavior are frequently based only on observations of men. Since women are inherently nurturing and cooperative, arms races and war would be less frequent if more women played leading roles in foreign-policy decisions and politics in general.

Supporters

Pessimistic: St. Augustine, John Milton, Niccolò Machiavelli, Thomas Hobbes, Hans Morgenthau, and Reinhold Niebuhr.

Optimistic: Henry Wadsworth Longfellow, Norman Angell, Margaret Mead, Bertrand Russell, Beverly Nichols, Gordon Allport.

Feminist: Mary Daly, Carol Gilligan, Nel Noddings, Sara Ruddick, and Birgit Brock-Utne.

can contribute to peace, cooperation, and harmony. During World War I, English philosopher Bertrand Russell wrote that perpetual peace was not impossible, but would require a gradual decline in the acquisitive instincts of humankind.[11] Similarly, in the 1920s, a conference of the Society of Friends (popularly known as Quakers) appealed to the world's population to replace self-seeking behavior with the spirit of sacrifice, cooperation, and trust. American anthropologist Margaret Mead was convinced that greater knowledge of cultural diversity would make war obsolete:

> If we wish to build a world which will use all men's diverse gifts, we must go to school to other cultures, analyze them and rationalize our findings. We must find models and patterns which, orchestrated together on a world scale, will make the world as different from the old as the machine world was from the craft industries of the Middle Ages. . . . We must know what the Chinese mothers say to their babies and how they hold them, to develop their special virtues; and what the Russian mothers say to their babies and how they hold them, to develop theirs.[12]

Mead's sentiments were echoed by President Eisenhower when he remarked in 1954, "If the mothers in every land could teach their children to understand the homes and hopes of children in every other land—in America, in Europe, in the Near East, in Asia—the cause of peace in the world would indeed be nobly served."[13]

The school of pacifist thought that concentrates on changing the views and behavior of political leaders also seeks to mute aggressive instincts through reeducation and knowledge. Some believe that improving the moral and intellectual caliber of individual heads of state would suffice to bring about international peace. The pacifist Beverly Nichols wrote in 1933 that if Norman Angell—whose book *The Great Illusion* predicted on the eve of World War I that war between the great powers would be so foolish that it could never occur— "could be made the educational dictator of the world, war would vanish like the morning mist, in a single generation."[14] Similarly minded moral optimists focus on increasing leaders' sensitivities to the suffering that their decisions inflict. The suggestion was once made that either a hideously maimed soldier or child, or a sculpture of one, should be placed in the center of disarmament conference tables. Peace activist Gordon Allport, a sociologist/psychologist, even advocated arranging the entrance to the General Assembly and Security Council of the United Nations building so that the delegates would have to pass through the playground of a nursery school on the way to their meetings.[15] The idea behind proposals of the above sort is that sensitizing world leaders to the consequences of war and peace might keep them from rushing into war.

Other optimists place an emphasis on preventing "bad" individuals from ever assuming positions of decision-making authority. According to this viewpoint, the collective expertise of psychiatrists and other mental health professionals should be used to weed out those mentally or psychologically unfit for office. One advocate of this approach, former Danish delegate to the United Nations William Borberg, writes that such experts would "recognize the leader who says 'my ideology or my death' as an obsessed, domineering, unintegrated personality. . . . In other words, he is a patient—but he is armed. Your human duty and duty as scientists is by all means at your disposal to prevent him from remaining in power."[16] (Proponents of this argument, however, need to recognize that much good has been accomplished by persons who were willing to die for their convictions and were therefore regarded by many as obsessive or fanatical.)

The argument here is that aggression, or belligerence, is not necessarily rooted in ignorance or moral insensitivity, but rather in psychological factors. This assumption has led many behavioral scientists to focus on the psychological motivations behind the decisions involved in domestic and foreign policy-making. The belief is that war is the result of correctable failings of individuals, rather than of inherent imperfections in humanity, and thus not caused by fixed characteristics of human nature as the pessimistic-view theories hold.

Criticisms of Human Nature Arguments

Many counterarguments have been raised against the proposition that original sin or biological necessity makes human beings warlike by nature, and also against the proposition that the uplifting or sensitizing of people will eradicate the primary cause of warfare. The most convincing criticism of the theory that innate human aggressiveness leads to war is that it cannot explain periods of relative peace. If humans who share the same fixed nature can be alternatively warlike and pacific, then the causes of war and peace must be found in something other than humanity's unchanging basic nature. Critics still acknowledge, however, that pessimists such as Morgenthau and Niebuhr at least provide a valuable warning against expecting too much from the application of reason and logic to social and political problems.

Critics of the optimistic view of human nature, on the other hand, point out that in most cases sensitivity, education, and mutual understanding are neither necessary nor sufficient for resolution of a dispute. Searching for understanding, they add, sometimes distracts attention from efforts to find practical solutions to concrete problems. Political scientist Karl Deutsch pointed out that one problem with the optimists' emphasis on eradicating war through greater understanding is that the connection between greater understanding and greater tolerance is far from certain. Deutsch observed that "many emotionally, culturally, and politically sensitive individuals react to a sojourn abroad . . . with a far stronger assertion of nationalism and of allegiance to their own language, culture, and people."[17] There is always the possibility that as people come to understand other countries' cultures better, their newfound knowledge may lead them to conclude that their own countries' cultures are genuinely superior.

Sensitivity training of the world's leaders may not work, either. For example, the symbolic placement of a children's sandbox at the UN's front entrance might make an initial impact on delegates arriving for work. Over time, however, the power of a symbol (or a situation) can weaken to the point of irrelevancy. Just as civilians in war-torn areas adjust to conditions others would find intolerable, so the UN delegates might become accustomed to the sight of a children's sandbox or a sculpture of a maimed soldier.

In addition to the problems with symbols, additional questions arise over the content of the advice to be given leaders, and the mechanisms for ensuring that they follow it. As for ensuring peace by preventing unstable leaders from taking power, standards of sanity, or "normal" behavior, are culturally conditioned, and what some observers regard as dangerous fanaticism, others may view as admirable persistence and determination. Where you stand on such issues may well depend on where you sit; your side's heroic freedom fighter may be your opponent's murderous terrorist.

A final problem with the notion that "knowledge ensures peace" has to do with implementation and timing. In the most ideal case, even if the knowledge of how to end war could be discovered, it would have to be simultaneously applied across all nation-states to be effective. And in real life, there is no consensus on how to end war. People disagree over the utility and desirability of various methods. Some even wish to reserve the option of using violence to fight what they see as intolerable injustice—thereby creating the exception of a "just war." Finding a solution to end warfare that everyone agrees on would be the first impossible hurdle, and implementing it successfully would be still another challenge.

An Alternative Conception of Human Nature: Feminist Theory

Feminist theorists offer yet another criticism of human-nature theories by arguing that conceptions of "human" behavior are frequently based only on observations of men. Because societies are male-dominated, they contend, the international system that accepts war as a legitimate means of resolving conflict is a product of the male values of aggression and dominance. Assuming that women are less violent and aggressive than men, feminist theorists argue that arms races and war would be less frequent if more women played leading roles in foreign-policy decision making, and in politics in general.[18]

The record of women involved in defense and foreign-policy decisions provides little support for this argument. Historically, female leaders have not proven less aggressive or warlike than their male counterparts, as the careers of Elizabeth I of England, Catherine the Great of Russia, Maria Theresa of Austria, Golda Meir, Indira Gandhi, and Margaret Thatcher attest. Feminist theorists would respond that these women were corrupted by male-dominated social and political systems and that their behavior was a reflection of male domination rather than of an intrinsic female nature.

Margaret Thatcher, the "Iron Lady," was the British prime minister during the 1980s. Through sheer force of will and commitment, she set the political agenda in her own country and was a formidable foe or ally of other world leaders.

Source: © Reuters/Bettmann.

In a more egalitarian society, they argue, women's more natural concerns would become part of the social and political milieu. Relationships based on caring, collaboration, cooperation, and consensus-building would replace those that rest on domination and subordination. As women's oppression became unacceptable, so too would the subjugation of all other less-powerful groups, including racial or ethnic minorities or the economically disadvantaged. The world would no longer be seen in terms of haves and have-nots, rulers and subjects, or aggressors and victims. With these changes in relationships, the entire international arena would be transformed. Preoccupation with power and conflict would be replaced by cooperation and collaboration, and by a more ecological orientation, epitomized by the effort to save Mother Earth.

Human Nature in Perspective

In the final analysis, it seems that the only sustainable conclusion about the relationship between human nature and war is that human nature does not (or cannot) stop war from occurring. War is possible because there is nothing in human nature to prevent it; likewise, peace is possible because human nature does not demand continued violent conflict. The inability of human nature to definitively explain either war or peace gives pessimists reason to worry and optimists reason to hope. It also encourages analysts and policy-makers to look elsewhere for explanations of conflict and cooperation in international affairs. As with much else in world politics, how you view the role of human nature depends heavily on your attitudes, experiences, and beliefs. With this in mind, the chapter now turns from the general nature of humankind to the more specific attributes of the all-too-human individuals who make decisions for peace or war.

PSYCHOLOGICAL ASPECTS OF DECISION MAKING

Approaches to international politics that focus on individual leaders are not concerned with the goodness or evil inherent in the human heart en masse, but rather with what goes on in the particular human minds of each decision maker involved in a situation. The ability of these key individuals to gather and process information, particularly under stress or time constraints, is important to consider, especially because it falls far short of the requirements for perfect **rationality** as depicted in the rational-actor model of decision making (see Chapter Fourteen). Individual policy-makers, like groups and organizations, must handle the problems associated with uncertainty, **value complexity** (where a decision brings two or more conflicting values into the decision), contradictory data, and the availability of too much or too little information.[19] While some analysts examine how organizations and groups deal with these problems, this chapter will discuss studies of how individuals' capabilities, attitudes, biases, reactions to stress, and miscellaneous idiosyncrasies influence how they process information and, equally important, the ramifications these characteristics can have on policy choices. The reader will discover that even when various decision makers receive the same information, different policies result. Thus, personal traits are likely to lead each to adopt a divergent solution (see Figure 15.1).

Belief Systems: The Operational Code

Some psychologists believe that people develop their own mental "flowcharts," which contain sets of rules enabling them to more easily process information, invent and appraise options, and choose the action that seems best in the face of uncertainty. Based on an intensive study of Bolshevik and later Soviet leaders, Nathan Leites concludes that policy-makers subconsciously use these "flowcharts," termed **operational codes,** as a way to translate their fundamental moral and political beliefs into policy decisions.[20] According to Leites and other scholars, an individual leader's operational code contains his or her fundamental beliefs about the nature of international politics and conflict, perceptions of the extent to which future developments can be shaped by intelligent or misguided action, and maxims regarding correct strategy and tactics for dealing with political adversaries and allies.[21] The operational code thus has both a philosophical and an instrumental content; it is both a **belief system** and a guide to action.

To illustrate these concepts, it is useful to briefly compare the operational codes of Soviet and American leaders during the Cold War. Western studies found that the operational codes of the original Communist leaders of the Soviet Union closely resembled one another and appeared to be heavily influenced by Marx's ideas on dialectical materialism and class struggle.[22] These leaders believed, for instance, that the political universe was one of acute conflict, with a capitalist opponent inherently hostile toward and determined to destroy the Soviet Union. Thus, capitalism itself must be decimated if the Soviet Union was to escape destruction. Distrust of opponents aside, the Bolshevik code was basically optimistic, because it was predicated on a belief in the inevitability of the eventual global triumph of communism. This optimism was balanced by an awareness of the possibility of catastrophe—the idea that miscalculation by Bolshevik leaders could lead to disaster. Intelligent action would be important, in the short term to reduce the likelihood of miscalculations, and in the long term as a means of expediting the historical process from capitalism to communism. In accordance with these beliefs, the Communist Party was obliged to seize any opportunity to advance history in the right direction.

Marxism also influenced the instrumental beliefs of the early Soviet leaders, specifically by affecting their views on strategy and tactics, and their attitudes toward risk. The makers and guardians of the Russian Revolution were risk-takers; they were willing to pursue the most ambitious objectives obtainable, even though the probability of a successful outcome might be difficult to calculate. They wanted to avoid approaching political action too conservatively and were afraid of missing opportunities to further their cause. Still, they did not neglect calculations of risks and benefits; they recommended against embarking on "adventures" where the only possible outcomes were either spectacular victory or disastrous defeat. Scholarly analyses of Soviet leaders' operational codes during

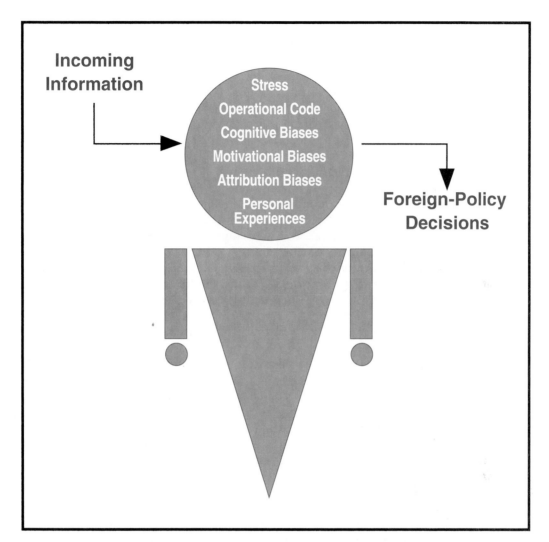

Figure 15.1   Personal Characteristics and Foreign-Policy Decision Making: Garbage In, Garbage Out?

Source: Diagram patterned after Deborah Welch Larson, "Research Note: Problems of Content Analysis in Foreign Policy Research: Notes from the Study of the Origins of Cold War Belief Systems," *International Studies Quarterly* 32 (1988), pp. 241–255.

the Cold War found that the Bolsheviks' successors were more averse to risks. Risks were to be contained, not by pursuing limited objectives, but rather by restricting the means employed to pursue ambitious objectives. As a result, some analysts contend, Soviet leaders thought that the risks associated with the Berlin blockade in 1948–1949, the construction of the Berlin Wall in 1961, or the placement of missiles in Cuba in 1962 could be limited and controlled, while Western leaders saw such actions as escalating steps that could lead to nuclear war.[23]

American leaders, in contrast, tended to feel that the best way to minimize the risks of escalation was to limit the objectives of a conflict.[24] This belief was the basis for the American concept of **limited war,** fought by limited means for limited objectives, which was developed after the failed attempt to forcibly unify Korea during the Korean War. During subsequent conflicts, U.S. policy-makers sought to communicate to their opponents that American objectives were limited, and that they were not intent on their adversaries' total destruction. In the Vietnam War, for example, U.S. aircraft were ordered to avoid striking targets in "bombing sanctuaries" around Hanoi in order to demonstrate that the United States did not want to destroy North Vietnam completely. In the Persian Gulf War, President Bush limited American objectives to driving Iraqi forces out of Kuwait; he stopped allied military operations without advancing on Baghdad or totally destroying the Iraqi army. Bush also avoided announcing that coalition forces would attempt to remove Saddam Hussein from power, instead calling on Hussein's opponents to do this themselves. Bush's operational code, it would seem, contained maxims that the use of force is justified only if the opponent is evil, but even then, unity among allies should not be jeopardized by opportunistic attempts to exceed agreed upon objectives.

Effects of Stress

The risks and uncertainties inherent in important decisions often create stress for the people who make them. Of all the challenges faced by foreign-policy decision makers, international crises are the most formidable because they create the highest degree of tension and stress. Crises have a number of stress-inducing characteristics: usually they come as a surprise, they threaten important values and interests, they require quick decisions, and therefore they impose emotional and physical fatigue on top decision makers.[25] In their memoirs of the Cuban Missile Crisis, participants Robert Kennedy and Theodore Sorensen both claimed that pressure to decide what to do about the Soviet missiles in Cuba was intense. For Kennedy, "that kind of [crisis-induced] pressure does strange things to a human being, even to brilliant, self-confident, mature, experienced men. For some it brings out characteristics and strengths that perhaps they never knew they had, and for others the pressure is too overwhelming."[26] Sorensen reports that during the week-long crisis, he witnessed "how brutally physical and mental fatigue can numb the good sense as well as the senses of normally articulate men."[27]

Stress does not always reduce a decision maker's ability to evaluate information and options; if the situation demands a relatively uncomplicated response, mild levels of stress sometimes facilitate decision-making performance. Still, increasingly higher levels of stress can push decision makers over a threshold where performance begins to suffer. This threshold level varies across individuals, so that in any foreign-policy decision-making group, some individuals may continue to function effectively as others begin to crack under the strain.[28]

Dissociative Reactions   When events push decision makers beyond their level of tolerance, stress can lead to wildly erratic behavior or temporary incapacitation. Sometimes the result is a **dissociative reaction,** whereby a person's thoughts, feelings, or actions are not associated or integrated with relevant information. The clinical symptoms of a dissociative reaction can include withdrawal into a trance-like state, paramnesia (where individuals are detached or disengaged from persons, places, situations, and concepts), fugue (sudden mental flight, accompanied by amnesia and lack of care for one's person or surroundings), frenzied behavior, delirium, and hallucinations.[29]

Throughout history, various leaders have suffered these symptoms under the intense pressure of international crises. There is evidence that British Prime Minister Anthony Eden during the 1956 Suez crisis, Indian leader Jawaharlal Nehru in the 1962 Sino-Indian war, and both Israeli Chief of Staff Yitzhak Rabin and Egyptian President Nasser during the 1967 Arab-Israeli conflict all became temporarily incapacitated, mentally and physically, as a result of tremendous crisis-induced stress.[30] But perhaps a more illuminating example is the behavior of Soviet Premier Joseph Stalin at a key turning point in World War II.

In June 1941 Stalin broke down and became temporarily paralyzed after hearing about Germany's invasion of the Soviet Union, an action he had thoroughly believed Hitler would never risk. Marshal Georgii Zhukov remembered that when he telephoned Stalin and told him of the German attack, a long silence followed, punctuated only by the Soviet leader's loud breathing.[31] Another Stalin aide reported that "from the moment of the attack by Germany, Stalin locked himself in his study, would not see anybody, and did not take any part in state decisions."[32] At a meeting of the Politburo convened to discuss Soviet options, Stalin sat silent, cradling his unlit pipe, his mind apparently somewhere else. This indecision allowed the German advance to continue and exact a heavy toll in Soviet lives and territory. Even after he knew of Germany's formal declaration of war, Stalin clung to his belief that the German generals had initiated the invasion without Hitler's approval. Stalin's initial orders reflected this belief: The Soviet Air Force was not to penetrate more than ninety miles beyond the frontier, the radio link with the German foreign ministry was kept open, and Japan was asked by the Soviets to mediate the conflict in the hope that Hitler would reconsider and call off the attack.[33]

Integrative Complexity   Stress in crises can also affect a leader's decision-making ability in less dramatic ways. It can reduce what psychologists call the **integrative complexity** of information processing.[34] When decision makers' integrative complexity is high, they can make subtle distinctions among multiple dimensions of a message, respond more flexibly to new situations, and consider large amounts of diverse information in order to make coherent judgments. When decision makers' integrative complexity is low, they tend to make grosser, less nuanced distinctions, respond less flexibly to information, and rely on a narrower range of information to choose policy options. In other words, leaders exhibiting low integrative complexity tend to think in black-and-white, or all-or-nothing terms, leaving them less open to the possibility of compromise with an opponent.

One study found that the integrative complexity of leaders' messages was significantly lower in crises that ended in war than in crises that were resolved peacefully. In the July 1914 crisis preceding World War I, for example, integrative complexity declined as war approached. In other words, as the crisis appeared to become more severe, the actors involved tended to think more in black-and-white terms. On the other hand, the integrative complexity of leaders' messages during the 1962 Cuban Missile Crisis (which was resolved peacefully) increased as the crisis neared its resolution.[35]

Cognitive and Motivational Biases

Crisis-induced stress is not the only factor that can lead policy-makers to make bad decisions, of course; sometimes, they make mistakes in the ordinary day-to-day formulation of foreign policy. Some of these errors can be attributed to conscious or unconscious psychological biases. **Cognitive bias** (related to cognition or reasoning processes) and **motivational bias** (related to basic motives such as fear or desire) enter into decision-making processes because individual decision makers rarely meet the stringent requirements of rational decision making (see Chapter Fourteen). In the ideal model of rational decision making, the problems of value complexity, uncertainty, incomplete information, and information overload never arise to bedevil an omniscient policy-maker. In the real world of policy-making, however, no one is likely to escape difficulties. Thus, policy makers adopt a variety of coping mechanisms to alleviate the difficult job of reaching complex and consequential decisions. These methods include cognitive consistency and dissonance, defensive avoidance, and bolstering. Let us now look at how these psychological aspects of decision making affect real-life policy outcomes.

Cognitive Consistency and Dissonance   Some theorists contend that people often try to simplify difficult decisions by seeking **cognitive consistency.** That is, they tend to see what they expect to see and thus assimilate incoming information according to the beliefs and images that they have already formed—they make the facts fit their theories. **Cognitive-dissonance** theory tells us that "inconsistencies [dissonance] within the cognitive system cause an uncomfortable state of tension that people are then motivated to reduce or eliminate."[36] Individuals often try to resolve the tension between their deeply held beliefs and contradictory information by discrediting or ignoring the source of the information, reinterpreting the information, or replacing it with other information more consistent with their beliefs.

Excessive consistency seeking can lead to serious policy miscalculations. Prior to the Nazi invasion of the Soviet Union in 1941, Stalin had sufficient information about Hitler's military disposition and plans, but he still refused to believe that Hitler would launch an attack. Stalin's image of Hitler, possibly derived from their negotiations over the 1939 Nazi–Soviet Pact, supported the Soviet leader's belief that Hitler would almost certainly engage in a bargaining game before deciding on the need to use force.[37] Stalin seriously miscalculated the Fuhrer's intentions, and the result was a near-disaster for the USSR. Similarly, when Egypt nationalized the Suez Canal in 1956, British leaders believed that the Egyptians would not be able to operate the canal. The pilots who navigated ships through the waterway were European, and they were expected to quit if nationalization took place. As a result of these assumptions, the British cabinet mistakenly concluded that the canal would have to shut down; they overlooked the fact that it took minimal training to produce competent pilots.[38]

Some argue that cognitive consistency seeking on the part of U.S. leaders also exacerbated the Cold War, especially in the face of acute domestic political pressure. Political scientist Deborah Larson asserts that cognitive-dissonance theory could account for abrupt changes in the attitudes of American policy-makers toward the USSR after World War II:

> Washington officials changed their estimate of Soviet foreign policy intentions in February 1946, a few months after the Truman administration had decided to adopt a "tougher" stance toward the Soviets in response to Republican criticism of the so-called "appeasement" policy. American policy-makers would have been reluctant to admit to themselves that, for illegitimate political motives, they had diminished the chances for Soviet-American cooperation and increased the risks of war. Accordingly, they would have been motivated to change their attitudes toward the Soviet Union, to make them more consistent with the public "hard-line" policy.[39]

Several other occasions can be identified where U.S. officials may have interpreted Soviet actions to fit their view of the Soviet Union as a hostile power.[40] When the Soviets rejected the Baruch Plan for international control of nuclear weapons in the late 1940s, U.S. officials discounted the legitimate reasons why the Soviets might find the plan unacceptable, instead interpreting Moscow's rejection as evidence that the USSR harbored aggressive and expansionist intentions. After Stalin's death in 1953, Secretary of State John Foster Dulles discounted the conciliatory gestures of the triumvirate of Soviet leaders (Malenkov, Molotov, and Khrushchev) that succeeded Stalin, believing there was no change in the inherent "rottenness" of communism. As Eisenhower's chief foreign relations officer, Dulles dismissed the signing of the 1953 Korean armistice, the Soviet acceptance of the Berlin Foreign Ministers Conference in 1954, the 1955 signing of the Austrian State Treaty (neutralizing Austria), and the Geneva Summit Conference as indicators of Soviet weakness, not lack of hostility. In ordering the 1965 U.S. military intervention in the Dominican Republic, President Lyndon Johnson focused only on information suggesting that the Dominican crisis was a "second coming" of Cuba, even though the Dominican Communists lacked a charismatic leader like Castro, a strong popular base, and internal unity, all elements that contributed to the Cuban Communists' rise to power.

Generally, decision makers who engage in consistency seeking are responding to some sort of difficult value trade-off inherent in domestic or international politics. In other words, when decision makers realize that two or more values will come into direct conflict with one another, they tend to react by downplaying or ignoring some of the values in order to avoid the psychological discomfort that

REINFORCING BAD DECISIONS: EXAMPLES OF BOLSTERING

- The German General Staff engaged in wishful thinking in the July 1914 crisis by discounting the possibility that Britain would intervene if Germany went to war with France and invaded Belgium, and again in 1917 when it concluded that unrestricted submarine warfare would force Britain to surrender before the United States entered the war. Britain intervened in 1914 and did not surrender in 1917.

- During the planning stages of the Bay of Pigs invasion, JFK and his advisors convinced themselves that the U.S. role in the invasion would not become known. Castro found out. So did the American public.

- During the Korean War, President Truman and Secretary of State Acheson bolstered their decision to allow MacArthur to occupy North Korea by

occurs when important interests or morals seem to be sacrificed. Decision makers may engage in a process of **cognitive restructuring** by turning aside information that calls attention to or aggravates a value conflict. Thus, they may "discount, deny, forget, or unintentionally misinterpret information about some of the competing values."[41] In their own minds, they may also "devalue" one of the interests that they or others close to them hold dear. As a result of restructuring their values, decision-makers may refuse to consult with advisors who they suspect hold the devalued interests, fail to credit their information, or even belittle them in front of others.

Defensive Avoidance   Individual decision makers also attempt to eliminate the psychological tension that accompanies the need to make choices in the face of uncertainty by attempting to avoid making a decision. This coping mechanism is known as **defensive avoidance.**[42] One of the most popular means of defensive avoidance is procrastination. This occurs when policy-makers feel that they do not need to immediately resolve the conflict at hand. For instance, when the Taiwan Straits crisis erupted in March 1955 and made a war between the United States and China seem likely, President Eisenhower sent a high-level delegation to Taiwan (then called Formosa) to persuade Taiwan's Chiang Kai-shek to thin out his forces on the offshore islands, which lie between the main island of Taiwan and the Communist Chinese mainland. When Chiang complied, Eisenhower's interest in the problem quickly waned, even though U.S. officials had every reason to anticipate a resurgence in tensions, since Chiang was expected to redeploy troops on the islands. He proceeded to do this without objection from Washington, and when tension in the strait flared up in 1958, the Eisenhower administration had even less room to maneuver than in 1955. When the crisis again died down, the president turned his attention to more salient issues.[43]

assuming that they could reverse the decision or mitigate its undesirable consequences if the Russians or Chinese intervened. When the Chinese became involved, the United States could not reverse its decision.

- In the Vietnam War, LBJ and his advisors bolstered their decision to use air power against North Vietnam with the falsely optimistic expectation that Ho

Chi Minh's government would quickly accept U.S. terms in order to get the United States to stop the bombing. When American terms were not accepted, the United States had no clear alternatives.

Source: Alexander L. George, *Presidential Decision-Making in Foreign Policy: The Effective Use of Information and Advice* (Boulder, CO: Westview, 1980), p. 39.

When decision makers cannot string a decision out over a long period of time, they may engage in **bolstering,** another form of defensive avoidance. When pressured to meet a short deadline, the bolstering decision maker will respond by increasing the attractiveness of a preferred option, magnifying its expected gains and minimizing its expected costs and risks. Simultaneously, the potential gains of less preferred options are discounted and their drawbacks exaggerated, a practice known as **spreading the alternatives.**[44] Decision makers who bolster favored options under time constraints seem to engage in wishful thinking, convincing themselves that the selected options will meet with success even if the odds against them are high.

Attribution Theory: The Decision Maker as "Naive Scientist"

Another way to examine the role of psychological factors in decision making is provided by **attribution theory,** which considers decision makers to be "problem solvers" or "naive scientists." According to this approach, decision makers attempt to discern the attributes of other actors, to infer the causes of salient events, and to predict historical trends and the behavior of other persons, all in order to understand and exercise more control over the environment and, specifically, the outcomes of particular situations. In contrast to the "consistency seeker," the "naive scientist" is "relatively open-minded in the search for truth, untrammeled by the need to maintain a favorable self-image or preserve a favored belief."[45]

Even though this model at first glance seems to view decision makers in a more positive (and perhaps unrealistic) light, it does acknowledge that particular aspects of the decision-making process are subject to certain biases. For example, attributional biases occur when decision makers must infer, or guess, the motivations of other actors. One of the most common attributional biases is known as **fundamental attribution error,** which consists of applying a double standard in which one's own inappropriate behavior is attributed to situational variables (related to circumstances beyond one's control), while an adversary's are attributed to dispositional variables (related to character and fundamental goals). Similarly, one's own positive behavior is attributed to strong moral character but an opponent's to outside pressures.[46]

George Kennan, the author of America's Cold War containment strategy, warned against allowing fundamental attribution error to guide U.S. policy toward the Soviet Union: "Now is it our view that we should take account only of their [Soviets'] capabilities, disregarding their intentions, but we should expect them to take account only of our supposed intentions, disregarding our capabilities?"[47] U.S. policy-makers frequently ignored Kennan's warning. In the early postwar period, many State Department officials viewed Soviet attempts to establish an exclusive sphere of influence in Eastern Europe as evidence of Soviet expansionist aims, refusing to consider that the USSR might have had valid concerns for its own security. At the same time, these officials maintained that Central and South America—an area far larger than Eastern Europe—remained off-limits for the new UN Security Council.[48]

To consider another example, both sides in the Arab-Israeli conflict have tended to make fundamental attribution errors. A summary of one author's analysis of the double-standard behavior of the Arabs and Israelis follows:

View of Self

1. The explanation for one's own "good" behavior, by both Arabs and Israelis, is usually dispositional. Good actions are seen as proof of inherent good character.

2. However, when explaining actions of which the opponent disapproves, situational terms predominate. Circumstances are used to excuse one's own poor behavior.

View of Opponent

1. When the opponent behaves well in a particular instance, the tendency of both Arabs and Israelis is to explain it in situational terms. Neither would concede that the opponent may have positive dispositional elements.

2. When the opponent is found behaving badly, it is offered as evidence of inferior disposition. Situational factors are discounted as a possible explanation.[49]

A second attributional bias related to fundamental attribution error is the tendency of policy-makers to attribute decisive importance to their own role in bringing about a favorable outcome while blaming circumstances beyond their control for unfavorable outcomes.[50] Many supporters of the American policy of "peace through strength" claimed that it was the U.S. defense buildup rather than the Soviet Union's reevaluation of its priorities under

Gorbachev that finally convinced Moscow to make serious concessions at nuclear arms control talks. Similarly, advocates of détente in the 1970s claimed that improvements in U.S.–Soviet relations were the result of giving the USSR a "stake in the system" through increased trade and extending Western credit. These same advocates suffered a rude shock when Moscow continued its attempts to expand its influence in the Third World at the expense of American interests even after implementation of détente.

A third type of attribution bias is the tendency for policy-makers to assume that opponents act as unitary rational actors, free from the constraints of domestic political processes and bureaucratic routines, which are factors they see as influencing only their own policy.[51] One analyst counted a dozen instances of this sort of misperception between the British and American governments during the 1956 Suez Crisis and 1962 Skybolt airborne missile system controversy.[52] The assumption on the part of some U.S. policy-makers that the Soviet destruction of Korean Airlines Flight 007 in 1983 represented a deliberate decision to murder civilian passengers rather than the result of an intelligence failure or bureaucratic snafu also illustrates this bias, as does Iran's misinterpretation of the 1988 downing of an Iranian civilian airliner by the U.S. Navy cruiser *Vincennes* as a deliberate act of state-sanctioned murder.

An attributional bias different from those discussed thus far is the tendency, when making inferences about other people or when explaining their behavior, to ignore or discount nonoccurrences or nonevents—things that did not happen.[53] One diplomatic historian argues that President Truman and his advisors might not have concluded that Soviet expansion into Eastern Europe was comparable to Hitler's policies had they considered several actions which Stalin did *not* take. In Finland, for example, Soviet authorities did not object to the existence of a non-hostile noncommunist regime. In Hungary, Soviet occupation authorities did not interfere with elections that produced an overwhelmingly noncommunist parliament and cabinet until after the announcement of the Truman Doctrine. In Czechoslovakia, Moscow did not initially suppress a coalition government in which Communists were not the dominant faction, even though it later sponsored a coup that brought a Communist government to power. The Truman administration instead emphasized the hardline position that Stalin took in Poland, Romania, and Bulgaria, concluding that Soviet behavior was uniformly aggressive.[54]

Heuristics and Schemas

Another bias stems from the overuse of **heuristics** (which are defined as rules of thumb or mental shortcuts) in processing large flows of information and assessing the likelihood that certain policy options will be successful.[55] One such rule of thumb is the availability heuristic, which suggests that policy-makers are prone to expect a situational outcome that is most easily remembered or imagined on the basis of past experience. A second is the representativeness heuristic, which refers to the proclivity to expect an outcome that is most consistent with or most

WHAT WOULD YOU DO?

You are the head of a large industrialized country with many international interests. Puzzled by the aggressive and apparently irrational behavior of a Third-World dictator, you have invited a team of renowned mental-health professionals to interpret his behavior. After some private discussion, the team issues a limited-circulation report suggesting that the root of his behavior stems from the dictator's mental instability. The team's findings point to the need to organize the overthrow of this leader.

The conclusion that this leader is irrational and possibly psychotic sounds plausible—after all, why would any leader risk war in an era of nuclear weapons? At any rate, these specialists have tried to convince you of the futility of applying a deterrent strategy, because this dictator cannot make the calculation that war may lead to his overthrow, environmental destruction,

resembles the salient features of the situation in question. After the Iraqi invasion of Kuwait in 1990, for example, many American policy-makers believed that the situation in the Persian Gulf closely resembled that which existed in Europe before the 1938 Munich Conference (the availability heuristic). Believing that Hussein resembled Hitler in methods and motivation, they expected that unless the occupation of Kuwait was reversed, Hussein would make ever increasing demands on neighboring countries (the representativeness heuristic).

Both of these cognitive shortcuts reflect a tendency to recall concrete historical analogies—the "lessons" of history—in diagnosing a new situation and surveying the options for dealing with it. These analogies are termed **schemas,** generic concepts stored in an individual's memory that refer to objects, situations, events, or people.[56] Schemas allow a decision maker to select what is important out of a large flow of data, thus providing an economical means of storing memories of objects and events. They enable an individual to go beyond the information given and, using the lessons drawn from a similar previous experience, make useful inferences about an object or situation. Finally, they even permit a decision maker to envision and carry out a sequence of actions to achieve a particular goal.

It is worth noting that important bits of data can be lost in this process, leading to misperceptions and sometimes inappropriate behavior. The experience of war, for instance, is often burned deeply into the memory of those who live through it. Consequently, there is a tendency for strategists and policy-makers to assume that the next war will closely resemble the last one, and to make plans accordingly. The events of the late nineteenth and early twentieth centuries are illustrative. Because of the rapid defeat of France in the Franco-Prussian War of 1870–1871, European military planners assumed that the next war would be won by the side that mobilized first. The race to mobilization went on to become a the collapse of his industrial base, or massive loss of life. Eliminating aggression requires elimination of the aggressor's political and military power.

However, members of your regular foreign policy staff who have seen the report threaten to leak it to the media, citing its tenuous assumptions. Some of them argue that dictators are rational actors, regardless of their intentions. These staff members recommend signalling a credible commitment to use force in retaliation for any aggressive actions. Other staff members hold that this aggressive behavior does not lie in mental imbalance—or balance for that matter—but in the nature of the dictatorship. They recommend using aid or sanctions to promote a different set of political and economic values and encourage a change in calculations by the dictator and his aides.

How will you act on these competing counsels?

decisive factor in the outbreak of World War I. This assumption proved wrong, however, as the Great War dragged on for years of grinding trench warfare—the previous schema for war did not apply. The situation repeated itself before the outbreak of the next war: Most strategists of the 1920s and 1930s expected the next war would be fought in the trenches, like the last one. When World War II erupted, their analogies again proved inappropriate, and in 1940 France was defeated more rapidly and thoroughly than it had been in 1871.[57]

PERSONAL EXPERIENCE AND LEADERSHIP STYLE

The frequency with which historical analogies are used to make inferences about current problems underscores the importance of leaders' backgrounds and experiences in affecting foreign policy decisions.[58] Those who can remember the past are not necessarily condemned to repeat it, but everyone relies to some degree on powerful or relevant life experiences in interpreting complex situations and making difficult choices. Consequently, it is often argued that the beliefs and leadership styles of national leaders are shaped in important ways by their previous perceptions of, and experiences in, personal relationships, politics, executive or other management roles, and foreign policy-making.

This section will examine the leadership style of several important individuals, their strengths and weaknesses, their skills and deficits. Leadership style consists of the individual's considerations of ends (for example, one's desired role in the foreign policy-making process; one's country's role in global affairs) and means (for example, the methods one uses to define and play out those roles; one's approach and organization—whether one delegates authority or not). To illustrate how experiences affect beliefs and decisions, the following pages will compare and contrast leaders from Western, Communist, and Third World societies. What should become apparent is that even within the same political system, leadership style will vary widely across individuals, often with important policy implications. This approach to ends and means is combined with the particular idiosyncratic background and personal traits an individual brings to specific decisions to produce a powerful influence over the fate of a particular nation and often even over other states with which it interacts.

American Presidents

Woodrow Wilson, Idealist   Wilson's leadership style contained an intriguing mix of traits that paradoxically prevented him from achieving his major foreign-policy objectives. Idealistic, moralistic, and self-righteous, Wilson was also an activist, a genuine product of the Progressive Era in America. The influence infused him with a desire to take part energetically in various problem areas of policy in order to come up with the best possible remedy. Unfortunately, this essentially optimistic desire to "fix" problems was counterbalanced by a negative "inflexibility"—a lack of willingness to reach a bargain or compromise solution with one's political opponents. A political scientist by profession and former president of Princeton University, Woodrow Wilson was elected president of the United States in 1912 on a platform emphasizing the reform of American domestic politics. Shortly after his election, he remarked to a close friend, "It would be an irony of fate if my administration had to deal chiefly with foreign affairs." Fate wasted little time in handing him an irony. After campaigning for reelection in 1916 with the slogan, "He kept us out of war," Wilson reluctantly decided to take the United States into World War I within a few months of the start of his second term.

After the war, President Wilson took a leading position at the Paris Peace Conference. "To make the world safe for democracy," he proposed a new world system in which states "all act in the common interest and are free to live their own lives under a common protection."[59] Wilson's vision of a collective-security community was the League of Nations, intended to maintain peace by ensuring justice and self-determination for all peoples and envisioned in his "Fourteen Points."

Many Americans criticized Wilson for his decision to personally go to Versailles to participate in the peace settlement (he was the first American president to cross the Atlantic while in office). He also had to reassure Congress that he was not trying to usurp its role in international politics, but was going to secure a just and lasting peace.

The peace conference became in effect a battle between Wilson and representatives of the other Allied powers, led by French Premier Georges Clemenceau, who favored the maintenance of a balance-of-power system (see Chapter Thirteen). Wilson, considered by his fellow peacemakers to be an upstart American with little practical experience in world affairs, was never able to convince his colleagues to agree to a system of collective security. When he returned to the United States in February 1919, he remained confident that he would be able to secure Senate support for the Versailles Treaty. Yet, Republicans in the Senate, led by Henry Cabot Lodge, argued that the League would lead the United States back into war, give Britain too much influence and, most importantly, threaten the nation's isolationist tradition. They would not accept the treaty without an overhaul of the League of Nations Covenant, which Wilson had just helped author.

In an effort to gain Republican support, Wilson returned to Paris in March 1919 and secured amendments to the League's Covenant. But Republican opposition remained steadfast and public sentiment grew increasingly negative. Failing to garner public support for the treaty upon his return to the United States, Wilson refused to compromise with the Republicans and asked Senate Democrats to vote against the Senate's proposed version of an amended League of Nations Covenant because it did not incorporate the strong provisions for collective action against aggression that he insisted upon. His lack of flexibility, no doubt tied to his strong sense of self-righteousness, prevented the United States from signing the treaty and joining the League, which became ineffective without U.S. involvement (see Chapter Three). Wilson also refused to recognize the American public's weariness with its involvement in Europe's affairs and lack of enthusiasm for any role as global policeman. As a result, the United States retreated into its prewar isolationist mode and played a relatively minor role in world politics during the tumultuous 1920s and 1930s.

Harry Truman, Pragmatist   Truman was far less rigid than Wilson in leadership style, but still adhered to a strong code of ethics and morality in making foreign-policy decisions. He had an essentially positive view of human nature, and this led him to trust foreign leaders—sometimes too much. When this trust was broken, however, Truman would not raise his hands in frustration, but rather would search for pragmatic solutions to the problems he faced.

Truman became president upon the death of Franklin Delano Roosevelt in 1945, after having had no prior experience in foreign affairs. As vice president, he had been kept "out of the loop" on many strategic decisions during World War II; indeed, he was told about the existence of the atomic bomb only after being sworn in as president after Roosevelt's death. Consequently, Truman formed his ideas about international relations through his experience in domestic politics. For instance, because Soviet Premier Stalin reminded him of Boss Thomas Pendergast, his Democratic-Party mentor in Missouri politics, Truman initially assumed that, like the Missouri machine politician, the Russian dictator could be trusted to keep his word.[60] Later, he was bitterly disappointed by Stalin's behavior after World War II, such as when the Kremlin leader reneged on his promise to withdraw Soviet troops from Iran within six months of the end of the war. This disappointment led Truman to conclude that Communists could not be trusted, a belief that influenced the types of solutions he sought to Cold War crises. As in his response to the Berlin blockade and in the establishment of NATO, he tried to create faits accompli without relying on the word of the Soviets, which he had concluded they would break anyway.

Truman was a "hands-on" decision maker, but he also took pride in his ability to delegate responsibility, and he backed up those he trusted. Accordingly, he was willing to take the political fallout from ending aid to the Chinese Nationalists in 1949 and from the refusal to escalate the Korean War after the Chinese

Communist intervention. He also established the National Security Council (NSC) in 1947, thus creating a more formal and bureaucratic framework for the making of U.S. foreign and defense policy.

Dwight Eisenhower, Soldier   Dwight David Eisenhower was not a politician; he had never held elective office before becoming president. He gained considerable political and diplomatic experience during World War II, however, when he proved able to get many contentious and stubborn Allied commanders to cooperate, and he could be tactful or profane as circumstances demanded to get his point across.

Ike's desire not to become involved in the less savory aspects of politics may have contributed to a more formal style of leadership, characterized by a clear chain of command between him as president and his advisors. For example, he differed from Truman in that he established a "chief of staff" position as a buffer between himself and cabinet secretaries (a position filled through most of his tenure in office by Sherman Adams, who became known as the "abominable noman" for restricting access to the president). In foreign policy, Secretary of State Dulles played a similar role, creating a widespread impression (which Dulles gladly cultivated) that he was making Ike's foreign policy.

Another manifestation of Eisenhower's disdain for politics was his reluctance to become embroiled in the highly political matters of the day. Eisenhower refused to stand up to radical cold warrior Joseph McCarthy and as a result allowed Congress to blacklist hundreds of innocent people. Such reluctance has led many analysts to characterize Eisenhower as one of the most "passive" of American presidents. However, recently declassified government documents have revealed a more active role on the part of Ike in formulating foreign policy. In contrast to Truman, Eisenhower wielded his influence over his secretary of state entirely behind the scenes.

JFK, First among Equals   John Fitzgerald Kennedy employed a far less rigid, less hierarchial style of formulating American foreign policy. Born into a political family, Kennedy learned early on to engage in and enjoy politics. He worked with lawmakers of both parties while serving in the House and the Senate, and he developed a collegial style of leadership, which included a high level of tolerance for hearing each advisor out during foreign policy-making sessions.

Whereas Ike's decision-making system resembled that of a pyramid, JFK's resembled a spoked wheel. In other words, for Eisenhower information on foreign policy-making had to travel up a successively narrow bureaucratic "ladder" in order to reach the "top." In contrast, Kennedy placed himself at the center of a wheel with easy access to almost any piece of relevant information. Kennedy's less formal style had its advantages and drawbacks: On the negative side, it increased the dangers of "information overload" and chaos; on the positive side, it may have contributed to the relative thoroughness with which the Kennedy team considered its foreign-policy options. This was especially true during the Cuban Missile Crisis (see Chapter Fourteen).

LBJ, Good Old Boy   Kennedy was a consensus politician, but Lyndon Johnson would do anything to get his way: haranguing, chastising, cajoling, or pleading with other political leaders for hours until they came around to his point of view. LBJ demanded unswerving loyalty from his aides, and tended to disregard the advice of those whose loyalty he questioned. Like Truman, LBJ had little experience with foreign policy, and even less interest in it. Rather than relying on the advice of his aides or on information about the specific situation, he was prone to thinking in stereotypical terms about the expansive threat of world communism.

Even more than Truman, Johnson was an active president with an ambitious agenda, both at home and abroad. Johnson's "Great Society" domestic agenda was difficult to achieve but a success overall. Yet, his insistence and Wilson-esque inflexibility in pursuing an unpopular foreign policy (the Vietnam War) in the face of severe setbacks left him and the nation physically exhausted. Frustrated, unpopular, discredited, and facing probable defeat, Johnson stunned the country with his March 1968 announcement that he would not run for reelection. His administration's policy failures in Vietnam had ultimately destroyed his presidency.

Richard Nixon, Man Alone   In spite of political experience as a member of Congress and Eisenhower's vice president, President Nixon's heightened desire for privacy and extreme distrust of the media and the federal bureaucracy led him to develop a style of leadership that minimized interpersonal contact with his advisers. Nixon had long had an active interest in foreign policy, but, much like Eisenhower, he used his special assistant for national security affairs, in this case Henry Kissinger, as a "gatekeeper" who would filter most information about foreign policy and national security developments before it reached the top. This type of system allowed Nixon to preserve his sense of control over foreign policy as in his stunning breakthrough in relations with China. However, Kissinger, and not the president, often appeared to be in control. This was an impression which Kissinger, like Dulles before him, reinforced whenever possible.

Nixon would often detach himself from the process of foreign-policy decision making; some reports indicate that while his advisors met in some crises, he would retreat to the upstairs White House quarters. During the crisis created by the Jordanian Civil War in 1970, Kissinger found him bowling alone in the White House basement, and during the Yom Kippur War of 1973, Nixon was so distraught over the Watergate scandal that Kissinger chaired the special action group meeting that decided to place U.S. nuclear forces on alert.[61] Kissinger became even more central to the making of U.S. foreign policy as secretary of state under Gerald Ford, who became president after Nixon's resignation, since Ford's congressional career had not provided him with extensive engagement of international affairs.

Jimmy Carter, Activist   His engineering background gave Jimmy Carter confidence in his ability to solve difficult problems. Carter had scant direct experience in foreign affairs, but he pursued an activist foreign policy and wanted to imbue America's international relations with a renewed sense of moral purpose. To this end, he launched a series of initiatives on human rights. He adopted a hands-on leadership style that worked well when he helped mediate the Camp David Accords between Israel and Egypt.

Unlike Eisenhower or Nixon, Carter did not elevate any one advisor to the position of "gatekeeper" and did not circumscribe the role of the State Department in favor of the national security advisor as Nixon did in his first term. Instead, he put both offices on an equal footing, which led to a different set of problems. In many instances, his secretary of state, Cyrus Vance, and his national security advisor, Zbigniew Brzezinski, would clash on policy matters. This resulted in no small amount of confusion, both at home and abroad, on the substance and objectives of U.S. foreign policy. In developing a set of options and implementing a decision, the Carter administration's actions sometimes appeared to contradict themselves. Such tendencies were accentuated during the botched mission in April 1980 to rescue the American Embassy hostages in Iran.

However, historical hindsight has lent prestige to some of the Carter administration's foreign-policy accomplishments, such as the small number of American casualties from 1977 to 1981. As with Truman, Carter did not let low public-approval ratings constrain his activist tendencies while he occupied the Oval Office.

Ronald Reagan, Hands-off Leader

In contrast to Carter, Ronald Reagan adopted a hands-off style of decision making in foreign policy, preferring to delegate authority to his advisors. It would have been difficult for him to convince other government officials to defer to his expertise in foreign affairs (he had none), but they had to respect his ability to mobilize public support for the policy options he favored. This method of policy-making worked well in the areas of arms control and mediation of regional conflicts, since experts were left to complete their tasks without the specter of presidential micromanagement. In Reagan's second term, however, the dangers of a hands-off approach were brought to light. Lack of adequate oversight led to the embarrassing Iran-Contra scandal, in which funds from secret weapons sales to Iran (a sworn enemy) were illegally diverted to fund the Nicaraguan Contras, whom Congress had previously barred from receiving aid.

In general, Reagan was an ideologue rather than a policy analyst; he set the general direction of U.S. foreign policy, maintained a vehement opposition to communism, believed that increased defense spending would force Soviet compromise, thought the U.S. should go on the offensive as in Afghanistan and Nicaragua, and mobilized public support for his policies masterfully. For better or worse, he let others fill in the details.

George Bush, Diplomat

Despite George Bush's experience with the give and take of congressional politics, or perhaps because of it, he displayed a great distaste for cutting deals, an innate sense of caution, a distrust of grand ideas, and a great loyalty to friends. Thus, he preferred to surround himself with a close group of trusted aides, like Secretary of State James Baker and National Security Advisor Brent Scowcroft. Bush had gained diplomatic experience as U.S. representative to the UN and to China, but unlike Reagan, he did not promote a sweeping vision of America's role in the world, concentrating instead on managing the practical problems of adjusting America's foreign policy to the end of the Cold War. Bush acted decisively during the Persian Gulf crisis and war of 1990–1991, and was effective at securing the approval of the UN Security Council for the use of military force against Iraq, but was unable to translate the allied victory into future foreign-policy successes as America entered the New Era.

Like FDR, Bush was born a patrician. He felt comfortable dealing with other world leaders on an informal, personal basis, frequently calling friendly heads of governments for spontaneous discussions over the phone. Bush's policies were much more successful abroad than they were at home, and he much preferred the genteel world of diplomacy to the rough-and-tumble bargaining of domestic politics. He summarized succinctly one reason why many presidents have found foreign policy more absorbing and satisfying than domestic politics:

> Some people say, why can't you bring the same kind of purpose and success to the domestic scene as you did in Desert Shield and Desert Storm? And the answer is, I didn't have to get permission from some old goat in the United States Congress to kick Saddam Hussein out of Kuwait. That's the reason.[62]

Like all leaders, the U.S. presidents discussed in this section did not make decisions in a vacuum. Their policies were influenced by domestic politics and by factors operating at the level of the international system. Nevertheless, their own beliefs, goals, and style of leadership mattered. Each made decisions that their opponents would probably have made differently had they been elected instead. Each president, in his own way, had an impact on U.S. foreign policy that cannot be attributed to the American political system or America's role in the world at the time. As Bush's remark points out, U.S. presidents have a great deal of independent authority over U.S. foreign policy. The leaders of other countries may enjoy more or less autonomy in conducting international affairs than American presidents, but as the following examples of Egyptian and Soviet leaders will show, their unique personalities and perspectives can also have a major impact on their nation's policies.

Third World Leaders: Egypt as a Test Case

Gamal Abdel Nasser, Pan-Arabist   On July 23, 1952, a group of young military officers, part of the clandestine Free Officers Society, overthrew King Farouk of Egypt. Among this group was Egypt's first long-term president, Gamal Abdel Nasser, in office from 1954 to 1970, and his successor Anwar el-Sadat, who served between 1971 and 1981. Nasser, the son of an Alexandria postal clerk, got his break in 1937 when the Royal Military Academy allowed young men without palace or aristocratic connections to enter the officer corps. For many from lower-class families, the academy was an opportunity to rise to

AT A GLANCE

LEADERSHIP STYLES

Woodrow Wilson
Leadership Type/Image: Idealist

Style: Wilson was an idealistic, moralistic, and self-righteous activist molded by the ideals of the Progressive Era in America. He would not accept anything short of the best possible solutions to problematic areas of policy. This altruistic goal was outweighed by a negative "inflexibility," illustrated by his battle over the League of Nations.

Harry Truman
Leadership Type/Image: Pragmatist

Style: Truman was a "hands-on" decision maker, but he also took pride in his ability to delegate responsibility, and he backed up those he trusted. The origins of his approach to international relations can be found in his experiences in domestic politics.

Dwight Eisenhower
Leadership Type/Image: Soldier

Style: Eisenhower had never held elective office before becoming president. He had a formal style of leadership characterized by a clear chain of command. He established a "chief of staff" position as a buffer between himself and his cabinet secretaries.

John F. Kennedy
Leadership Type/Image: First among equals

Style: Born into a political family, Kennedy learned at an early age how to engage in and enjoy politics. He developed a collegial style of leadership that included a high level of tolerance

for hearing each advisor out during foreign policy-making sessions.

Lyndon B. Johnson
Leadership Type/Image: Good old boy

Style: Johnson would do anything to get his way. He demanded unswerving loyalty from his aides and tended to disregard the advice of those whose loyalty he questioned. He had little experience with foreign policy and even less interest in it. Although largely successful with his domestic policy, he was a clear failure in his Vietnam War policy.

Richard Nixon
Leadership Type/Image: Man alone

Style: Nixon had a keen distrust of the media and the bureaucracy. His leadership style led to minimal interpersonal contact with his advisors. He used his special assistant for national security affairs to communicate with many subordinates and to conduct secret diplomacy.

Jimmy Carter
Leadership Type/Image: Activist

Style: Carter felt confident of his ability to solve difficult problems. He had very little experience in foreign affairs, but he followed an activist, moralistic policy. He launched a series of initiatives on human rights.

Ronald Reagan
Leadership Type/Image: Hands-off leader

Style: Reagan had no experience in foreign policy. He preferred to delegate authority to his advisors, and as a result, he was seen as an

a modest rank based on merit. Yet, dissatisfaction among the junior officers with their superiors and the unsuccessful attempt to prevent the establishment of Israel in 1948 created a hotbed of political activism.

Although Nasser rose from the ranks of the lower middle class and instituted many programs that benefited them, there is evidence of dualism in his ideologue rather than a policy analyst. He set the general direction of U.S. foreign policy, maintained a vehement opposition to communism, and mobilized public support for his policies masterfully, but let others fill in the details.

George Bush
Leadership Type/Image: Diplomat

Style: Bush displayed a great distaste for politics, an innate sense of caution, a distrust of grand ideas, and a great loyalty to friends. He surrounded himself with a close group of trusted aides. He preferred the genteel world of foreign diplomacy to the rough-and-tumble bargaining of domestic politics.

Gamal Abdel Nasser
Leadership Type/Image: Charismatic dualism

Style: Nasser rose in the ranks of the military from a lower-class family. He had a dualist leadership style. While appealing to the masses, he also distrusted them. His conspiratorial style led him to be suspicious of potential opponents at home and abroad. Nasser stood for defiance of the West that resulted in Nasserism, a personality cult that made the Egyptian leader seem bigger than life.

Anwar el-Sadat
Leadership Type/Image: Dramatic reversals

Style: Sadat reversed many of Nasser's policies. He believed in "Egypt for the Egyptians." He had a penchant for dramatic, unilateral actions as in his historic and astonishing trip to Jerusalem in 1977.

Hosni Mubarak
Leadership Type/Image: Moderate

Style: Mubarak carefully prepared and implemented his policies with an emphasis on gradual, rather than sudden, change. Although more pragmatic in terms of policy, and moderate in terms of rhetoric, he was no more successful in dealing with Egypt's domestic problems than his predecessors. Hosni Mubarak is an example of how leaders can make a substantial difference in the policy courses that their countries pursue, especially in foreign affairs. However, they can rarely devise means for overcoming fundamental domestic problems.

Nikita Khrushchev
Leadership Type/Image: Bluff and bluster

Style: Khrushchev was outgoing, demonstrative, and confrontational. He rarely shied away from risks, either in domestic politics or foreign policy, and loved a good argument. He was prone to making dramatic gestures and enjoyed "photo opportunities." The Soviet leader pursued a combative stance vis-à-vis the West. While he could be pushy, rude, boorish, and cruel, he was never boring.

Leonid Brezhnev
Leadership Type/Image: Consolidation and stagnation

Style: Brezhnev stood for stability and predictability. He was a deliberate, cautious leader, who was careful to consult with other Politburo members before making important decisions in an effort to build consensus for his policies. He avoided risks and was able to establish a good relationship with Richard Nixon. The 1979 Soviet invasion of Afghanistan is the great exception to his circumspect and calculating style.

personal beliefs. While appealing to the masses, he also distrusted them, destroying all political parties except the state party, and severely curtailing freedom of the press. While supporting the notion of a democratic Egypt, Nasser believed that Egypt was still in a pre-democratic stage and required authoritarian rule. He therefore employed a large corps of domestic spies to monitor the behavior of

Egyptian President Gamal Abdel Nasser waves to the crowd at a sporting event in December 1961. One of Nasser's greatest leadership qualities was an ability to inspire his countrymen.
Source: © UPI/Bettmann.

both friend and foe. As one author notes, Nasser could be "dictatorial or deferential, charismatic or suspicious, ingenuous or crafty."[63]

For many in the Arab world, Nasser stood for defiance of the West. In 1954 he forced the British to withdraw their army of 80,000 from the Suez Canal Zone; in 1955 he acquired Soviet arms; in 1956 he recognized Communist China and in the same year nationalized the British-controlled Suez Canal Company. Nasser was able to convert the military defeat that Egypt suffered as a result of the Suez Crisis (see Chapter Six) into a political victory, because the United States joined the USSR in condemning the British-French-Israeli attack on Egypt. This victory further elevated Nasser's status in the Arab world, and in the Nonaligned movement. Even when he attempted to resign after the disastrous Arab defeat in the Six-Day War of 1967, massive street demonstrations by his supporters and a vote of confidence by the National Assembly allowed Nassser to remain in power.

Nasser's successes—or more accurately, his survival—contributed to the emergence of **Nasserism,** a personality cult that made the Egyptian leader seem bigger than life. He became identified with a new revolutionary nationalism and effectively promoted **Pan-Arabism,** a movement to unify the Arab world into a single state. Toward this end, from 1958 to 1961, Egypt and Syria unified to form the United Arab Republic, with Nasser at the helm. Yet, while many viewed Nasser as a champion of the Arab cause, Western states and conservative Arab monarchies in Jordan and the Gulf region perceived Nasser's bullying as an ambitious attempt to extend Egyptian influence throughout the region.[64]

When Nasser died of a heart attack in 1970 shortly after mediating an end to a civil war in Jordan, his country faced a host of economic, social, and diplomatic problems. He was widely praised as a hero, though his dream of Pan-Arabism had fallen far short of its goal. Regardless of the final verdict on Nasser, it is clear that he played the critical role in shaping Egyptian foreign policy during nearly twenty tumultuous years.

Anwar el-Sadat, Independent Peacemaker   Nasser's particular policies were not inevitable, as was soon demonstrated when he was succeeded as president of Egypt by Anwar el-Sadat. Although following on the heels of a revered hero, Sadat reversed many of Nasser's policies and at the same time revived Egypt's sagging fortunes. While Nasser spoke of "Egypt for the Arabs," Sadat's actions reflected his belief in "Egypt for the Egyptians," often with little concern for outside Arab opinion. An example is the way Sadat dealt with the strong political pressure to reverse the defeat Egypt had suffered in the 1967 war with Israel. Although he named 1971 the "Year of Decision," meaning the year the lost territory would be recovered by political means if possible, and by military instruments if necessary, he was unwilling to be cajoled into action before Egypt was prepared for war. Moreover, when Egypt and its ally Syria finally attacked Israel in 1973, Sadat did not attempt to achieve a complete defeat of the Jewish state, but instead wanted to demonstrate that Jerusalem could never be secure without making peace with Cairo. He accomplished this goal by successfully ordering Egyptian troops to cross the Suez Canal and maintain a beachhead in the Sinai.

The surprise attack in October 1973 was typical of Sadat's decision-making pattern: procrastination followed by a sudden and dramatic turnabout in policy. After the war, he switched superpower allies from the Soviet Union to the United States, and began to move his country away from Nasser's authoritarian version of "Arab socialism." In 1977, seeking to break the impasse with Israel, Sadat made a historic visit to Jerusalem and appeared before the Israeli Knesset. A number of Arab leaders criticized his unilateral action, but he was not swayed by their stance. Shortly thereafter, Sadat made an even more historic decision to "go it alone" and sign with Israel the Camp David Accords, which led to the return of the Sinai Peninsula to Egypt in exchange for a peace treaty with Jerusalem. While Sadat established a basis for a stable relationship between Egypt and Israel and for closer ties between his country and the United States, many in the Arab world never forgave him for signing a separate peace with the "Zionist enemy." Egypt was expelled from active participation in the Arab League, and Sadat himself paid the ultimate price for peace: He was assassinated in 1981. Despite Sadat's controversial legacy, few Third World leaders have made as much of an impact on foreign affairs.

Hosni Mubarak, Moderate   Nasser was beloved by the masses, but he was unable to transform his Pan-Arab vision into practical policies. Despite regaining the Sinai Peninsula, by the end of his life, Sadat was less popular. His treaty with Israel had brought an end to the threat of constant war, but it had not translated into the major economic gains he had promised, and he appeared closer to the Western elite than the Egyptian street. Sadat's successor, Hosni Mubarak, entered office in 1981 and brought with him an entirely different leadership style and set of policies. Mubarak exhibited none of Nasser's overt ambition or Sadat's penchant for dramatic policy shifts. His policies were carefully prepared and implemented with an emphasis on gradual change, not sudden switches. After a dozen years in office, he had upheld the peace agreement with Israel, but little of the excitement and promise created by Sadat's dramatic signing of the treaty remained. Slowly and gradually, however, Mubarak inched Egypt back to a position of leadership within the Arab world.

Although more pragmatic in terms of policy and moderate in terms of rhetoric, Mubarak was no more successful than his predecessors in dealing with Egypt's domestic problems, particularly rapid population growth. Indeed, his major problem at the start of the New Era was the threat to Egypt's political stability posed by an upsurge of Islamic fundamentalism at home. Thus, the Egyptian case suggests that while leaders can make a substantial difference in the policy courses that their countries pursue, especially in foreign affairs, they can rarely devise means for overcoming fundamental domestic problems. In Egypt's case an exploding population and deepening domestic crisis occupied Mubarak's attention and limited his flexibility, thereby constraining his ability to act dynamically in regional politics.

Soviet Leaders

Nikita Khrushchev and the Politics of Bombast   The leadership styles of the two Soviet premiers who successively held power in the Kremlin through almost three decades of the Cold War are a study in contrasts. Nikita Sergeyevich Khrushchev, Ukrainian by birth, was outgoing, demonstrative, and confrontational. During his tenure from 1958 to 1964, he rarely shied away from taking risks, either in domestic politics or foreign policy. Khrushchev loved a good argument and was fond of making dramatic gestures. Under his leadership, the USSR temporarily took the lead in the "space race" by orbiting Sputnik and launching the first human voyagers into space.

Khrushchev's bombastic pronouncements, grandiose claims, and bluffs often caused alarm in the Western world. He once boasted, for example, that communism would "bury" the West with superior production, and during the Suez Crisis in 1956 his government threatened Britain and France with nuclear devastation. Khrushchev delighted in what politicians in later years would call "photo opportunities." He took full advantage of public appearances to unleash barrages of Cold War rhetoric (accenting a speech at the UN by banging his shoe on the rostrum) or to promote an image of himself as a warm personality who empathized with the man and woman on the street (as when he extolled the progressive Soviet attitude toward women to visiting U.S. Vice President Nixon in the so-called "Kitchen Debate").

Khrushchev's combative stance with respect to the West was reflected in the frequent East-West crises that erupted during his tenure in office. His bombastic

Soviet Premier Nikita Khrushchev listens to debate at the UN General Assembly in October 1960. Moments before, he had dramatically pounded the desktop with his shoe (still visible) while driving home a point against the United States.
Source: © New York Times Pictures.

pronouncements during the Suez, Taiwan Straits, Berlin, and Cuban crises (see Chapter Four) symbolized the sharpness of the Cold War's ideological conflict. Yet, his passionate speeches did not prevent him from developing a respectful relationship with Eisenhower during his 1959 visit to the United States. Reflecting Khrushchev's mercurial style, the new relationship with Eisenhower was in turn ruined by the U-2 crisis the following year. At the same time, Khrushchev's conflict with a fellow Communist, China's Mao Zedong, was often played out on a personal level, and the poor relationship between Khrushchev and Mao certainly did nothing to lessen the growing rift between Moscow and Beijing in the late 1950s and early 1960s. Ultimately, Khrushchev's risky moves at home and abroad (such as cutting the Soviet conventional defense budget in favor of nuclear weapons, pumping resources into the "virgin lands" agricultural development fiasco, and precipitating a frightening nuclear crisis by attempting to place missiles in Cuba) alienated too many of his colleagues in the Soviet Communist Party, and he was removed from power in 1964.[65]

Leonid Brezhnev, Party Man   While Khrushchev could be pushy, rude, boorish, and cruel, he was never dull. Boring, however, is the adjective that best describes the leadership style of the next Soviet ruler, Leonid Ilyich Brezhnev, who served from 1964 to 1982. In appointing Brezhnev, the Soviet party leaders hoped for stability and predictability, and they got plenty of both. Brezhnev was a deliberate, cautious leader, who was careful to consult with other Politburo members before making important decisions in an effort to build consensus for his policies. He avoided risks whenever possible, and cautiously made preparations for every contingency before taking actions that could alarm the West, such as the invasion of Czechoslovakia in 1968, or the deployment of Soviet air defense personnel, pilots, planes, and surface-to-air missiles to Egypt in 1970.

While Brezhnev's monotonous constancy and aversion to risk and change prevented him from reversing the economic and social stagnation of the USSR in the 1970s and early 1980s, they were arguably assets to Soviet foreign policy in the decade of détente, the 1970s. Many in the West who were suspicious of the USSR conceded that under Brezhnev, the Communist superpower was at least predictable, and would be unlikely to make risky moves that could provoke crises such as those which dominated the Cold War of the 1950s and early 1960s. Brezhnev and U.S. President Nixon, who had once been fervent ideological opponents, were able to establish a working relationship. Although not without its problems, their personal connection helped facilitate the signing of SALT I in 1972 and the movement toward East-West economic and cultural exchange that followed.

In retrospect, it is ironic that one of Moscow's most startling foreign-policy actions occurred under Brezhnev's leadership. Because the USSR's foreign policy had been as staid and predictable as its leader in the mid-1970's, the Soviet invasion of Afghanistan in 1979 came as a rude shock. Some Soviet analysts later pointed to the decision to send troops into Afghanistan as the one hasty and incautious decision that Brezhnev ever made. By the time of his death in 1982, Brezhnev had become the embodiment of a moribund Communist system that would disintegrate within ten years.[66]

GENERATIONAL EXPERIENCE

Sometimes the experiences that shape leaders' attitudes on the nature of world politics are those that have affected the entire generation to which the leader belonged.[67] In other words, events that have a powerful impact on a generation's consciousness may be uppermost in the minds of its members who rise to political power and gain the responsibility for making foreign policy. This kind of **generational experience** sometimes leads to misguided policies. Let's travel back in time to Europe to look at several examples. As explained in Chapters

Two and Three, the stunning results of Bismarck's wars of German unification against Austria (1866) and France (1870–1871) led European leaders (and much of the European public) to enter the 1914 crisis with a shared image of war as glorious, short, and beneficial.[68] When war broke out that August, many leaders believed that their soldiers would be "home before the leaves fell," and military plans were predicated on the idea that if mobilization could be accomplished quickly enough, an offensive would quickly overwhelm defensive forces.[69] The European leaders, however, could not foresee the implications of new technologies, and the resulting war turned into a bloody four-year conflagration. Demonstrating how generations as a whole can get caught up in an error, leaders focused on Bismarck's rapid and relatively cost-free victories and ignored other available lessons from conflicts that were dismissed as peripheral, such as the American Civil War, the Russo-Japanese War of 1904–1905, and the Boer War (1899–1902) between Britain and the Afrikaner republics of South Africa. All of these experiences showed that war could be quite prolonged and costly.

The tragedy of World War I left no European untouched and imbued a generation of leaders with the moral imperative to prevent such a disaster from ever happening again. This imperative helped sway British and French leaders to adopt the policy of appeasement in dealing with the German and Italian aggression of the 1930s. When British Prime Minister Neville Chamberlain returned to London after the Munich Conference in 1938, his declaration that the Munich Agreement had secured "peace in our time" at the cost of concessions to Hitler reflected the hope that appeasement could stave off another catastrophic war. This wish was shared by the majority of British and French citizens at the time; their leaders may have suspected that the hope was a forlorn one, but their generation's experience of conflict made it difficult to maintain peace by preparing for war.

Appeasement, of course, failed miserably (see Chapter Three). After World War II, the Munich analogy became the lesson of choice for a succession of leaders who had fought in or otherwise experienced the war. British Prime Minister Anthony Eden used the analogy in advocating the use of force against Egypt when Nasser ordered the nationalization of the Suez Canal in 1956. Recalling Chamberlain's experience with Axis leaders at Munich, Eden argued that anything short of an armed response would constitute appeasement and called Nasser the "Mussolini of the Nile." President Bush likened Iraqi leader Saddam Hussein to Hitler and incorporated his own experiences as a young pilot during World War II into his admonitions to avoid another Munich. By contrast, the experience of the Vietnam War taught a more recent generation of Americans that the use of force can easily cause more problems than it solves. American fears of "another Vietnam" were reflected in the country's reluctance to become involved in the conflicts following the breakup of Yugoslavia in the early 1990s, as well as the turmoil in Rwanda, Somalia, and Haiti.

The generation of Soviet leaders from Joseph Stalin to Konstantin Chernenko (Gorbachev's immediate predecessor) vividly recalled another "lesson" from the appeasement of Hitler: The Soviet Union must maintain a buffer zone of states it controlled around its periphery, especially its European border, to prevent invasion. With this lesson in mind, the USSR occupied Eastern Europe and the Kuril Islands off Japan, secured the neutrality of Austria and Finland, suppressed worker demonstrations in East Germany in 1953, engineered the Warsaw Pact's invasions of Hungary in 1956 and Czechoslovakia in 1968, maintained a huge force on the border with China after the Sino-Soviet split, and invaded Afghanistan in 1979. On the other hand, Mikhail Gorbachev was unconvinced of the correctness of these policies; he was old enough to remember World War II, but too young to have fought in it. The positive effects of the "thaw" in U.S.–Soviet relations during the Khrushchev era (when many of Stalin's draconian measures were muted or reversed), and of détente under Brezhnev, may have taught Gorbachev that Soviet security could be safeguarded by political as well as by military means, and that the USSR's huge military arsenal made other nations fear and distrust it. These impressions may have made it more palatable for the new generation of Soviet leaders to negotiate the arms reductions provided for in the INF, CFE, and START treaties, to withdraw Soviet troops from Afghanistan, to abandon the Soviet empire in Eastern Europe, and to improve the USSR's image in world public opinion shortly before its final collapse.

RELATIONS BETWEEN LEADERS

This chapter has considered the impact that relations between leaders and their advisors can have on foreign policy. Decision makers must deal not only with officials in their own governments, but also with leaders of other nations, friendly and otherwise. The need for leaders to interact with one another during negotiations or confrontations makes their relationship important for the achievement and implementation of international agreements. For example, in a book entitled *The Presidents and the Prime Ministers,* Lawrence Martin correlates the fluctuations in U.S.–Canadian relations directly with the personal relationships between the leaders of the two countries. He points out that Roosevelt and Mackenzie King established a close and amicable personal relationship, leading to a major enhancement of the cooperation between the two countries. In the 1950s the relations between Prime Minister John Diefenbaker and President Eisenhower were cordial and respectful, but the same prime minister detested Kennedy—an attitude resulting in a subtle but rapid deterioration in relations between the two countries. Matters were not improved by the cool relationship between Lester Pearson and Lyndon Johnson later in the 1960s.[70]

As another example of the effect that personal relationships can have, consider the ties that bound the leaders of the major Allied nations in World War II. Roosevelt, Churchill, and Stalin, the "Big Three," had developed out of necessity a close working relationship, in spite of American and British distrust of the Soviet premier. The serious threat posed by the Axis Powers increased the importance of such a relationship, for if the Allies were significantly divided in terms of their objectives and strategies, they would be weakened severely. That the Allied leaders were able to forge a consensus on most issues of strategy and tactics was an invaluable factor contributing to their eventual victory.

The nature of the Allied leaders' relationships remained important even as Germany and Japan neared surrender. The war resulted not only in an unprecedented level of death and destruction, but also in the creation of atomic weaponry that threatened incomprehensible devastation in the case of a future worldwide conflict. Allied leaders thus became convinced that another global war must not occur. In 1941, before the United States even entered the war, Roosevelt and Churchill agreed to the establishment of a "permanent international body" to provide "a wider and permanent system of general security" at the war's end.[71] Inspired by Wilson's vision of international peace, and aware of the League of Nations' failure to guarantee it, President Roosevelt committed himself to a more realistic plan for collective security. In fact, Roosevelt devised his "Great Design" for the postwar international system as an antidote for the ailing League of Nations, basing it on a continuation of the wartime alliance among the United States, Britain, and the Soviet Union, rather than on ideals (see Chapters Three and Nine). A necessary part of the plan, however, was a continuation of a working relationship, like that which Roosevelt, Churchill, and Stalin had developed, into the postwar period.

The key component of Roosevelt's global security plan was a basic agreement among the leaders of the great powers to oppose aggression. His concept of an Anglo-American international police force was expanded to include the Soviet Union and eventually China, a state he believed would become a major power and in any case would play a pivotal role in the future security of Asia. These "four policemen" would become permanent members of the Security Council of the United Nations, a forum which, not unlike the nineteenth-century Concert of Europe, would provide an institutional framework for those powers to cooperate in maintaining world peace (France was added to the Security Council after the war). The United States, Britain, France, and the Soviet Union would collectively decide territorial and political issues in postwar Europe, preventing further conflict in that region. All other states would be prohibited from establishing military forces large enough to threaten their neighbors. Though Roosevelt's plan may look antiquated and Eurocentric in the New Era, Churchill, Stalin, and China's President Chiang (who were, after all, leaders of states that had governed great empires in previous centuries) responded favorably to the plan in principle.

The devil, of course, was in the details. Stalin maintained that the USSR had special security requirements, which called for a zone of Soviet-controlled states on the Russian frontier as a buffer against future invasions. This requirement was the basis for an earlier informal agreement between Churchill and Stalin on the principle of "spheres of influence" for each of the major powers in an updated balance-of-power system. While Roosevelt understood Stalin's concerns, he felt that the American public would not support U.S. participation in a system of European-style "entangling alliances," especially one premised on the blatant

GEORGE BUSH, THE UN COALITION, AND THE GULF WAR

On August 2, 1990, Iraq invaded the tiny oil-rich emirate of Kuwait. In response, instead of taking unilateral action, U.S. President George Bush undertook to organize an unprecedented coalition of states, acting with the authority of the United Nations, to compel Saddam Hussein's forces to leave Kuwait. This coalition included Arab states such as Egypt, Saudi Arabia, Morocco, and Syria; NATO allies such as Britain, France, Turkey, and Belgium; and Asian states such as Pakistan and Bangladesh. Holding little hope that economic sanctions alone would persuade Hussein to withdraw Iraqi forces from Kuwait, Bush lobbied for a UN Security Council resolution authorizing the use of military force if Iraq refused to pull out of Kuwait by January 15, 1991. This resolution provided the international legal authority for Operation Desert Storm.

Because the coalition partners had different notions of the appropriate response to the Iraqi invasion, however, the creation and maintenance of the international partnership to expel Iraq from Kuwait required constant interaction with numerous political leaders and considerable behind-the-scenes diplomacy to gain their cooperation. Bush, a tactful negotiator who was willing to make compromises to keep allies "on board," proved well-suited to the role of "first among equals" in assembling and maintaining the alliance.

The ever-present danger in any coalition is that it will unravel because of differences among its members. Not surprisingly, therefore, keeping the coalition together during the Persian Gulf crisis proved no easy task. In order to maintain the support of Israel, Egypt, and Turkey, the United States promised additional foreign aid. Many states willing to commit military forces, such as France, had to be cajoled to participate in the attack on Iraq, and not merely play a supporting role or help to defend Saudi territory. In one instance, to maintain French support, Bush reached a compromise with the French President Francois Mitterrand on a UN resolution critical of Israel's treatment of the Palestinians. An eleventh-hour Soviet truce proposal

denial of national self-determination in Europe. Thus Stalin's insistence on pro-Soviet regimes in Eastern Europe was doubly problematic. By imposing a form of government dictated from Moscow, it ran counter both to the concept of an international body intended to preserve the sovereignty of independent states and to American ideals; thus, it jeopardized U.S. membership in the anticipated United Nations (UN).

Finally persuaded by Roosevelt of the material and political value of cooperating with the United States in establishing the UN, Stalin pledged to hold "free" elections in Poland and other Eastern European states. The February 1945 Yalta Declaration on Liberated Europe was true in principle to the Atlantic Charter and the basic idea behind the United Nations, though it merely delayed Communist takeovers in Eastern Europe. The Soviets' violation of the Yalta threatened to split the coalition, between states willing to halt the fighting and states seeking to greatly reduce Saddam Hussein's military forces. Furthermore, the marginal military contributions made by Germany and Japan, two prosperous economic powerhouses, angered some states in the coalition.

Seeing that his invasion of Kuwait had met with international opposition, Saddam Hussein sought to provoke a split in the coalition by linking any retreat from Kuwait to settlement of the Palestinian problem and Israeli withdrawal from the occupied territories. Once the fighting began, Hussein attempted to goad Israel into taking military action by launching SCUD missiles at Israeli targets. He hoped that if Israel joined the fighting, the Arab coalition partners would denounce the military operation and leave the coalition. These efforts failed, however, and the coalition remained together until the war's end. This was due in no small measure to Bush's ability to formulate countermeasures to Hussein's moves at each turn, such as providing assistance and assurances to Israel to encourage its forbearance.

The relatively few allied casualties and the speed with which Iraq was defeated greatly reduced the potential for discord among the allied leaders over the war. Nevertheless, the need to maintain the coalition's cohesion entailed many political and strategic compromises. Most notably, it hampered the possibility of overthrowing Saddam Hussein because many allied leaders feared that his ouster would lead to a dangerous power vacuum in the crucial and unstable Persian Gulf region.

The coalition that Bush forged thus achieved a spectacular military success, but had to moderate its war aims in order to keep itself together long enough to reach its minimum objectives. It is doubtful that the coalition would have performed as well as it did, or would have come together in the first place, had it not been for Bush's ability to manage relations among key coalition leaders.

agreements confirmed Western suspicions about Stalin's lack of commitment to Western political ideals. Yet, the "Big Three" leaders had overcome deep differences in order to cooperate against the Axis during the war, and these veterans of global politics might have been able to work out a compromise that would have allowed the UN to function as Roosevelt envisioned. But by the end of the war, Churchill had been voted out of office, Roosevelt was dead, and his successor Truman was inexperienced, unknown, and therefore not widely respected. The UN was eventually established in a much weaker form than had been originally conceived. Roosevelt's vision of collective security based on great-power agreement might have been difficult to implement, but the end of the working relationship between the "Big Three" wartime leaders ensured that it would never get the chance to prove itself.

CONCLUSION: WHAT DOES THE INDIVIDUAL LEVEL OF ANALYSIS EXPLAIN?

The "great man" theory of history contends that individuals are the driving force behind momentous events. This idea contrasts with the concept of history expressed in the writings of Russian novelist Leo Tolstoy, who believed that the relentless ebb and flow of events swept up both the weak and powerful, and heroes and leaders were merely individuals fortunate enough to be in the right place at the right time. Clearly, the truth about the role of individuals in world politics lies somewhere in between these extremes. But where? How much impact do the decisions and characteristics of individuals have, relative to the larger structures of the international system or domestic institutions? For example, Nixon opened new relations with China, causing a major change in the patterns of international politics at the time. Was he only recognizing the reality of the system—that anyone else as president of the United States would have similarly identified—or was he acting as a figure uniquely capable of altering the policy because of his past opposition to China? Similar questions can be asked about French President Charles de Gaulle's decision to leave Algeria; Gorbachev's policies of *glasnost* and *perestroika;* de Klerk's abolishment of apartheid in South Africa. Were these unique figures whose vision and personality changed history, or were they simply accepting the inevitable imposed by the international system or domestic conditions as most other leaders of their country would have done at about the same time?

These questions, like all major questions in the study of international relations, are far from easy to answer. The careers of leaders such as Napoléon or Bismarck clearly changed not only the course of world politics, but its essential nature as well. On the other hand, leaders like Neville Chamberlain and Lyndon Johnson had their otherwise distinguished careers ended by failure to overcome the constraints that international and domestic politics placed on their policies. Systemic and state-level factors have an undeniably powerful influence on the foreign policies adopted by decision makers. Their impact is rarely absolute, however, as leaders usually have some freedom of action to make policy choices, even when they publicly claim that the situation gives them "no choice." There are many instances when uncertainty or ambiguity requires leaders to make judgment calls on the risks, benefits, or morality of specific policies. In order to understand how individual decision makers are likely to use what freedom of action they have, it is necessary to consider what they are like as human beings—their mental and physical limitations, and their unique beliefs, goals, and character.

The degree of maneuverability possessed by individual leaders is rarely obvious. For a variety of reasons, leaders may perceive constraints on their options that do not actually exist, or they may fail to recognize ones that in fact are there. Either way, personal characteristics such as imagination and courage, or the lack thereof, can create new obstacles, or perhaps lead to ways of overcoming old ones. Our discussion thus finds itself back at its original question: How much can be explained by the individual, state, and systemic levels of analysis? Let's look back at the causes of World War I as an example. Systemic-level theories argue that World War I represents the outcome of a classic security dilemma that led to an arms race. Domestic-level theories contend that factors such as the *cult of the offensive* (discussed in Chapter 3) fueled the security dilemma by biasing each state's military planning in favor of all-out mobilization. The individual level of analysis argues that it was the idiosyncrasies and incompetence of many European leaders that caused them to horribly mismanage the crisis that broke out in July 1914, initiating a chain of events leading to the bloodiest war the world had yet experienced.

Now let's look at the Cold War. At the most general, international level, one could argue that bipolarity created the U.S.–Soviet rivalry and that the collapse of Soviet power ended it. Or, at the state level, that the Russian Revolution ushered in a Marxist system fundamentally opposed to capitalism and democracy and that only the liberalization of Russia brought about the Cold War's demise. Or, at the individual level, that Stalin's and Truman's misperception and distrust of each other's intentions set into motion a competitive spiral that deescalated only after Mikhail Gorbachev and Ronald Reagan developed a cooperative relationship that turned their countries' relations in a more positive direction. The interpretation you believe to be most correct may depend, like many other political questions, on your own beliefs and assumptions. Thus, the answers to questions on international relations depends to a great extent upon the views and goals of the observer, as well as of the participants. In this manner, political science is not too different from the other social and natural sciences—that is, it has its element of subjectivity—as much as practitioners of those disciplines may be loath to admit it.

In any field of inquiry, it is usually easier to identify patterns of causal relationships than it is to explain an event fully. "What is the effect of X on Y?" is a relatively straightforward question that lends itself to classification according to level of analysis. (In international politics, this question may take forms such as, "How does polarity affect stability?" "What role has the War Powers Act played in decisions to commit American troops to combat?" or "Did Eden's illness during the Suez Crisis affect his judgment?") Questions of the form, "Why did X happen rather than Y?" are inherently more complex and controversial. They involve more variables, not all of which may be identifiable, and they require the analyst to consider counterfactuals (a fancy term for things that might have been: what might have happened if Chamberlain had called Hitler's bluff at Munich, for example). Both types of questions are nevertheless useful, and in fact both must be asked in order to attempt a better understanding of world politics; after all, a good question for scientific inquiry is not one producing a definitive answer, but one which, when answered, produces more good questions.

PRINCIPAL POINTS OF CHAPTER FIFTEEN

1. Simply put, the individual level of analysis examines how people can make a difference in world politics. It considers how traits shared by all human

beings, and traits unique to individuals, shape the decisions and actions taken by leaders and citizens.

2. Many arguments attributing the existence and persistence of war to human nature have been advanced. There are several contending perspectives:

   a. The pessimistic view considers aggression and violence natural consequences of human nature, which cannot be avoided;

   b. Optimists do not accept the inevitability of evil human behavior, but think that negative traits can be eliminated through global education;

   c. Feminists contend that the notion of "human nature" is an artificial construct because it is based exclusively on observations of male behavior and masculine characteristics; if societies allowed authentic female values and practices to develop, many problems in international politics would be resolved.

3. A number of psychological factors can have profound effects on the decisions made by national leaders:

   a. Operational codes, including belief systems, basic values (morals, religious beliefs, and so on) and concepts of the nature of the international system;

   b. The effects of stress, which are especially prevalent in crisis situations;

   c. Cognitive biases (attempts to make new information fit into an individuals' preexisting knowledge and beliefs) and motivational biases (ignoring or distorting information that indicates that a preferred course of action may not succeed);

   d. Attributional errors, such as applying a double standard to one's self versus one's adversaries, and believing that an opponent has complete freedom of choice while one's own side is constrained by circumstances; and

   e. Heuristics and schemas, or "shortcuts" and simplifications used to assimilate new information.

4. The personal style, background, and experience of leaders often color their perceptions and affect the decisions they make. Different persons, confronted with the same facts and acting within the same political system, can interpret a given situation in diverse ways producing markedly different results.

5. Certain formative experiences, such as wars, economic depressions, or political upheaval, can be shared by a generation of leaders, and may give rise to distinct generational perceptions and attitudes.

6. Relationships between individual leaders can make a significant difference in the ability of states to cooperate or the tendency of states to conflict.

Conclusion

Chapter 16

The Future of International Politics

On each landing, opposite the lift shaft, the poster with the enormous face gazed from the wall. It was one of those pictures which are so contrived that the eyes follow you about when you move. BIG BROTHER IS WATCHING YOU, the caption beneath it ran.

Inside the flat a fruity voice was reading out a list of figures which had something to do with the production of pig iron. The voice came from an oblong metal plaque like a dulled mirror which formed part of the surface of the right-hand wall. Winston turned a switch and the voice sank somewhat, though the words were still distinguishable. The instrument (the telescreen, it was called) could be dimmed, but there was no way of shutting it off completely. He moved over to the window: a smallish, frail figure, the meagerness of his body merely emphasized by the uniform of the Party. . . . The Ministry of Truth—Minitrue, in Newspeak—was startlingly different from any other object in sight. It was an enormous pyramidal structure of glittering white concrete, soaring up, terrace after terrace, three hundred metres into the air. From where Winston stood it was just possible to read, picked out on its white face in elegant lettering, the three slogans of the Party:

WAR IS PEACE
FREEDOM IS SLAVERY
IGNORANCE IS STRENGTH

George Orwell, *1984* (New York: The New American Library, 1949), pp. 5–7.

In his book *1984,* George Orwell provided us with a frightening, but extreme, vision of the future. Although the world described in his book has not come to pass, the book continues to inspire debate, and it does raise an essential question: What kind of world are we heading into? This final chapter seeks a realistic answer to that question by applying international relations history, issues, concepts, and theories to the problems of the future.

Our examination of world politics past and present has revealed a constant tension between increased interdependence and cooperation among states on the one hand and continuing fragmentation and conflict on the other. As has been shown, these processes are not mutually exclusive; several contradictory trends exist in the world simultaneously. It is clear, however, that these trends do not move at the same rate in all parts of the globe. Some parts seem mired in intractable and violent conflict, while others appear to be absolutely rushing toward economic and political integration.

The historical chapters of this text have described how the international system has changed over the centuries. Whenever one turns on a television, however, the stark contrasts observable in the contemporary world make it appear as if different international systems were coexisting in the present day. Do not adjust your set; as this chapter will show, that is precisely what is going on.

THREE TIERS OF THE INTERNATIONAL SYSTEM

The New Era is enormously complicated by the coexistence of three different kinds of states: high-technology, nationalistic, and transitional. Each type has its own particular international objectives and problems, social structures, and levels of political and economic development. With their unique characteristics and common concerns, these three tiers interact to create a world that differs from our past experiences.[1] This new world, brave and otherwise, offers abundant opportunities and benefits to those who wish to cooperate, but costly policy errors may result from attempts to apply old perspectives to contemporary problems without considering the features of each tier of states.

High-Technology States: The Twenty-First-Century Style

The most advanced participants in international relations are the **high-technology states,** characterized by a "twenty-first-century style" defined by the politics of the microchip, the computer, the communications satellite, bioengineering, robotics, microelectronics, telecommunications, and information and semiconductor technology. Economic instead of military competition is emphasized; states gain power through trade and internal sources of development rather than through territorial acquisition.[2] Research and development, scientific advancement, and the conversion of high-technology breakthroughs into practical applications become the measures of status, influence, and power for high-technology states.

The United States, Canada, Western Europe, Japan, Australia, and the newly industrialized countries of Asia (South Korea, Taiwan, and Singapore) are all rapidly moving into this twenty-first-century style of international behavior. Here capitalism, technological innovation, and, in most cases, democracy create a powerful combination that increasingly dominates international relations within this tier. Relations between such states are more likely to deteriorate from trade wars than military combat. For instance, the eighth round of GATT negotiations, finally completed in late 1993, temporarily stalled over the refusal of the United States

Representative of high-technology capability is the Very Large Array radio receiving dishes in use near Socorro, New Mexico.

Source: Roger Ressmeyer-Starlight © 1990. All Rights Reserved.

and the EU to compromise on the issue of European agricultural subsidies. At times, the United States and Japan have clashed over the subject of Japan's wide variety of tariff and non-tariff barriers. Any additional trade restrictions created by the formation of the North American Free Trade Area, a unified Europe, or an Asian trading bloc promise to be contentious.

Perhaps most promising for high-technology states is that their disputes (involving, for example, management of international trade, protectionism, foreign investment in the United States, and the level of European economic cooperation) are not resolvable by military force, and their interests (research and development, scientific advancement, and increased trade) are not served by territorial acquisition. People are simply unwilling to die for tariffs or Toyotas. Potentially most dangerous, though, is that the new scientific achievements of these states could lead to military spinoffs with lethal impact. This is especially true, as we shall see in this chapter, when twenty-first-century states engage in the arms trade: Many of these weapons wind up in the hands of highly nationalistic states, such as Iraq, which are only too willing to use them against neighboring states and even against their own citizens.

Nationalistic States: The Nineteenth-Century Style

While twenty-first-century states experiment with new technologies and new cooperative arrangements in their international relations, the opposite form of political behavior is occurring elsewhere in the world. Many developing countries still adhere to a "nineteenth-century style," or nationalistic practice of politics. Here, religious, ideological, and racial hostility have dominated one region or another for centuries. For these states, nationalism remains the central motivation of political activity; nothing has changed to ameliorate historical enmities. Dominated by nationalist hostilities, both within and outside state boundaries, and culturally, politically, and economically unable to adapt to changing world conditions, many of these countries are ruled by corrupt regimes or governments organized around outdated models of social and economic development.

The challenges faced by these states are evident upon a visit to their major cities, or a check of their economic statistics. In these states, deprivation and poverty are often paramount. Famine, ideological divisions, ethnic tensions, territorial disputes, ideological rivalries, corruption, debt, and political, social, and economic chaos add to the unhappy and unhealthy stew. Where an impressive degree of wealth has been achieved, as in Kuwait or Saudi Arabia, the possibility of regional or internal instability has remained. **Nationalistic states** are plagued by classic balance-of-power considerations, and within many countries feuding parties, factions, or alliances jockey for position and influence. Capitalism is infrequent and democracy is even less likely. Even when these regimes occasionally experiment with democratic methods, they rarely last.

In many cases the difficult situation faced by nationalistic countries has external causes. Most sub-Saharan African states, for instance, contain ethnic and tribal rivalries stemming from the way in which their borders were drawn by the colonial powers. These internal divisions have in turn hampered social stability and economic growth and have thus contributed to high levels of government corruption and debt. In a few cases, these divisions have even led to widespread famine, as in Ethiopia, Somalia, and Rwanda.

In the Middle East, nationalist rivalries stem not only from the drawing of contemporary territorial boundaries, but also from ancient ethnic hatreds and religious disputes. At various times, Israel has been attacked by its Arab neighbors, who have expressed resentment towards Israel's existence as a state. Ethnic divisions and sectarian tensions among the Sunni and Shia sects of Islam spilled over into a bloody war between Iran and Iraq from 1980 to 1988. In part, resentment over the oil riches of the Kuwaiti royal family led Saddam Hussein to invade Kuwait and seize its oil fields, sparking the second Persian Gulf conflict. For sixteen years after 1975, Lebanon experienced perpetual civil war among its various ethnic groups, nationalities, and religious sects. Despite moves toward an Arab–Israeli settlement in the early 1990s, many of the countries in the area have a long way to go before they will enter into a more advanced category of nation-state.

Transitional States: The Twentieth-Century Style

The future of **transitional states** is the most uncertain of the three types. These governments are caught in a tense and constant vise between their impressive, even surprising, technical and scientific achievements in certain areas, and their

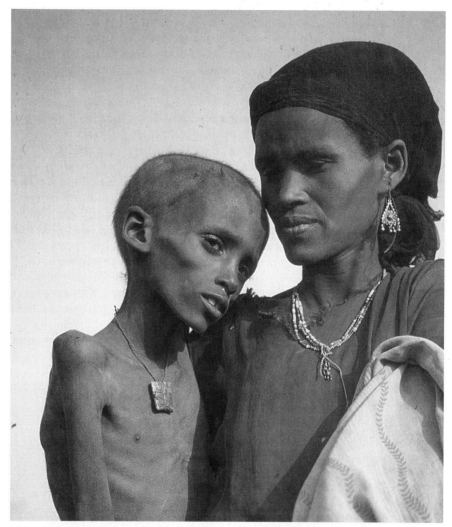

Effects of starvation symbolize the horrid conditions of life in some nationalistic states. This Ethiopian woman and child suffered from a famine in 1991 caused partly by political and military factors.
Source: © Les Stone/Sygma.

economic crises and social tensions, which often lead to political instability, even upheaval. Democracy is present or incipient for many of these states, even when it is suppressed, as in China. Still, most transitional states have had a poor political record regarding rights and liberties, and quite often socialism or communism dominated in the past and stifled growth and economic efficiency.

Today the governments of these states are trying to reverse past practices and economic philosophies to take advantage of new globalized trade patterns and interdependence. Products of the twentieth century, and deeply affected by the Cold War, most are emerging either from Communist dictatorship or right-wing authoritarianism, and are trying desperately to change politically and economically. "We want to be like you" has replaced Khrushchev's old boast, "We will bury you," as the dominant refrain. Caught tensely between a future of either progress or backwardness, they seek to move from autarky to reliance on trade, as China has, but instead could move at any time from autarky to anarchy, as Yugoslavia has done.

Indeed, examples of states in transition span the globe. The Chinese leadership is trying to achieve economic advances without democratization, although its prospects of retaining an antiquated political system remain questionable. The upheaval in the former Soviet republics has alarmed the Chinese leadership, whose country could still disintegrate as a result of internal conflict. But in contrast to today's China, the former USSR was a failure on every index except military power, as shown by its outdated economic organization, its abysmal social structure, and its internal ethnic turmoil, all of which led to its dissolution. When the history of this century is written, no country will epitomize the tragedy, the suffering, and the disappointment of the era more than the former USSR.

The former Communist regimes of Eastern Europe represent a mixed bag. The Czech Republic, Hungary, and Poland appear to have been successful in establishing democratic systems, and have a reasonable chance of developing their economies to the level of twenty-first-century states. On the other hand,

The future of transitional states depends on their ability to upgrade manufacturing systems. This outdated automobile assembly line in the Czech Republic must be modernized; otherwise its products will fail in the marketplace.

Source: © G. Giansanti/Sygma.

the ethnic tensions throughout the Balkan peninsula are more reminiscent of the highly destructive nationalism of nineteenth-century Europe.

The transitional states in Latin America, such as Brazil and Mexico, have emerging democratic states that belong to GATT and are highly engaged in trade. However, widening income gaps between the richest and poorest strata of each country's population constrain efforts to reach the level of general prosperity enjoyed by such countries as the United States, Japan, and the EU states. The growing numbers of the poor in Latin America result in increased immigration across the U.S.–Mexican border, greater movement into the overcrowded slums of national capitals in search of a better life, and the proliferation of shantytowns outside large cities, especially in Brazil. Recent accounts of poor Brazilian teenagers mobbing resort beaches en masse to rob sunbathing tourists provides a dramatic illustration of this phenomenon.

Asian countries such as India, Indonesia, Malaysia, and Thailand are transitional states that also have made dramatic economic and technological advances. While India is riven by many different types of internal divisions, it does have a large population of scientists and a strong parliamentary democracy. In the last two and one-half decades, Indonesia has developed a sizable middle class, even if democracy remains virtually nonexistent under President Suharto. In spite of repeated military coups d'etat and lingering rural poverty, Thailand has developed a burgeoning middle class as well. To the south, Malaysia, despite ethnic tension between native Muslim Malays and the Chinese and Indian minorities, has profited from large infusions of Japanese investment, especially in the areas of automotive and electronic goods assembly. All of these examples are states in transition, current bastions of hope and despair, yet places whose future is loaded with promise—and often high expectations.

The Role of Military Power in the New Era

War remains a fact of life for each tier of states in the New Era. Although states fight over territory, the development of military technology has extended the arena of warfare to the oceans, air, and space. For high-technology, militarily advanced countries, geographic expansion is of limited value and will usually have serious costs, even when states voluntarily unify (as in the German unification). The education of the populace and the transfer of funds into research and development will go further toward the accretion of power than the addition of population or territory, especially when the conquered population is hostile to a takeover. Some observers even argue that in advanced industrial states, attitudes have changed, and people no longer see war as a useful activity.[3] For twenty-first-century states, combat is an instrument for destroying economic and political competitiveness. The fear of losing power this way becomes a deterrent, however imperfect, to entry into battle. Therefore, high-technology states rarely if ever go to war.

Nationalistic states take the opposite approach. In these areas, eighteenth- and nineteenth-century attitudes prevail. The potential gain of territory becomes a vehicle for advancing objectives, as spatial politics—either through

AT A GLANCE

THREE TIERS OF FUTURE STATES

Style

High-technology: Politics of the microchip, the computer, the communications satellite, bioengineering, robotics, microelectronics, telecommunications generally, and information and semiconductor technology.

Nationalistic: Dominated by national hostilities within and without; culturally, politically, and economically unable to adapt to changing world conditions. Many of these countries are ruled by corrupt regimes or regimes that are organized around outdated models of social and economic development.

Transitional: A constant tension between their impressive, even surprising, technical and scientific achievements in certain areas mixed with economic crises and divisive tendencies that may lead to social and political dissolution or disintegration.

Emphasis

High-technology: Economic in preference to military competition.

Nationalistic: Religious, ideological, ethnic, and racial hostility dominate both within states and in their foreign policies. Many are fiercely antagonistic toward neighboring nations.

Transitional: Trying to reverse past practices and economic philosophies.

Century of Origin

High-technology: 21st century

Nationalistic: 19th century

Transitional: 20th century

Government

High-technology: Mostly democratic

Nationalistic: Democracy is rare. Although these regimes occasionally experiment with democratic methods, they usually do not continue with them.

Transitional: Democracy is present or incipient for many of these states, but remains fragile.

overthrowing a regime or attacking a neighbor—continues to be an organizing principle and a means of increasing power. Whatever the ideological, racial or religious rationale offered for territorial acquisition, territory provides resources, prestige, expanded influence, and a larger population. Even civil war or guerilla violence is spatially oriented—the overthrow of a regime that controls territory. Iraq's invasion of Kuwait was a classic example of nineteenth-century politics, as are the bitter conflicts in Somalia, Bosnia, and Rwanda.

For transitional states, territory plays an anomalous role. On the one hand, it is not an object of policy in the sense that states neither aim to acquire neighbors' land nor desire to use military force against them. On the other hand, the threats of geographic splintering or internal secessionist movements are frequent problems that transitional state regimes must confront, as in the former USSR, India, and China. In such instances, military force may be used to consolidate existing borders or subjugate peoples within a regime's frontiers.

In sum, then, military force is not ordinarily used between states on the high-technology level. States on the transitional level, where violence is frequent,

Path to Power

High-technology: Primarily through internal sources of development rather than through territorial acquisition.

Nationalistic: Military forces are used for stability because of the lack of political unity.

Transitional: These are countries that seek to take advantage of the newly globalized trade patterns and interdependence, but can easily sink into civil war or cross-border military involvement.

Role of Military

High-technology: Combat is an obvious instrument for destroying their economic and political competitiveness.

Nationalistic: The potential gain of territory becomes a vehicle for advancing objectives.

Transitional: Territory plays an anomalous role. On the one hand, territory is not an object of policy in the sense that states do not aim to acquire neighbors' land and do not typically use military force against them. On the other hand, the threat of the breakup of countries or internal secessionist movements are frequent problems transitional state regimes must confront, and they often lead to violence.

Countries

High-technology: United States, Canada, Western Europe, Japan, Australia, Hong Kong, South Korea, Taiwan, and Singapore

Nationalistic: Most Third World nations

Transitional: Former USSR, Eastern Europe, China, India, Indonesia, Brazil, Mexico, Argentina, Thailand, Malaysia, and Chile

do use force within their territories. We have seen these conflicts manifest in the former Soviet republics, such as Moldova, Georgia, Armenia, and Azerbaijan. Overall, however, the great majority of military force used today occurs on the nationalistic level.

THREE TIERS IN COEXISTENCE

If each tier of states existed in isolation, the three types of politics would be played out in their own way and by their own rules. But, as this book has demonstrated, economic globalization and interdependence makes such isolation an impossibility. Each sector interacts with the other two—producing a new world where the three tiers coexist and the three types of politics balance one another in a cauldron of chaos and order, globalization and fragmentation.

In this interaction of tiers, one type of state affects the others. For example, by the nature of their technological advances, economic achievements, and diluted borders, twenty-first-century states have become extremely vulnerable to disruption by such problems as illegal immigration, terrorism, and drugs. Transitional states are subject to secessionist influence by nationalistic neighbors or independence movements, as exemplified by the impact of Islamic fundamentalism on the Muslim populations of the former Soviet republics, by the Indian–Pakistani dispute over Kashmir, and by the Tibetan movement for independence from China. Resolution of internal or border disputes is often a prerequisite to achieve high-tech status for transitional states. In this way, nationalistic states or movements can succeed in bringing transitional states down to their level, especially if these twentieth-century regimes become bogged down in nineteenth-century politics. On the other hand, through arms sales and interference, high-tech or transitional states can poison relations between or within nationalistic states, which often pursue the politics of the nineteenth century with the military instruments of the twentieth and twenty-first. No one tier is isolated from the other.

Thus, history did not end with the resolution of the Cold War: It moved into a New Era, one potentially as dangerous as its predecessor. The old East-West global struggle has been replaced by a new instability. Those who believe that the United States will be able to retreat to domestic concerns with diminished international responsibility in the 1990s may be deeply disappointed. The role of conflict in international politics has not been terminated; it has been displaced and diffused.

We see the reasons for this changed role of international tensions in the interactions of the three tiers, which are like the layers of a marble cake—the brown fudge running through from the top to the bottom, zigging and zagging throughout the cake. Not only do the countries within each tier affect one another, but states in the three tiers affect politics and conditions up and down this new international hierarchy. The three types of states are more conceptual devices to illustrate the complexity of the New Era than descriptions of actual relations between particular entities. Yet, they demonstrate how we have come full circle from the pre-1945 period. Previously the great powers were in conflict and competition with one another while they controlled their colonial empires, thereby providing a degree of international stability in the Third World. The major international conflicts were on the higher "tier" of states. Today the process is reversed. The great powers, most of them twenty-first-century states, are preoccupied with trade, consumer benefits, and scientific advancements. It is on the lowest tier of international politics—the former colonies—where the major tensions, hostilities, and conflicts now occur. We have thus embarked on a New Era that is more complex than a simple return to politics before the Cold War.

BEYOND THE NEW ERA: SCENARIOS FOR THE FUTURE

But where do these interdependent yet competing tiers lead us? Any number of different world orders might evolve in the future—each a combination of varying amounts of twentieth-century, nineteenth-century, or twenty-first-century politics. The sections that follow group various possible scenarios into three broad categories. It is up to the reader to decide which outcome would be most desirable, and which is most likely to occur.

Same Game, New Players: Twentieth-Century Scenarios

Among some possible twentieth-century worlds might be a new pentagonal, multipolar international system. This development has long been predicted by a number of analysts, including the late President Richard Nixon.[4] In this conception, world politics would revolve around five competing foci, somewhat analogous to pre-1914 Europe except for the actors involved: the United States, Russia, Japan, China, and a United Europe. Most of these actors face certain challenges that may prevent them from becoming great powers. Russia, for one, is presently weak and divided. Its ability to engage in an active foreign policy remains questionable. China is growing economically, but a leadership crisis in the near future is likely as its octogenarian rulers die off. Japan enjoys the benefits of superior status without the burdens, but its history of aggressions before and during World War II might undermine its effectiveness should it try to expand its role in foreign affairs. Europe is not a united sovereign state, and the adjustment to the breakup of the Soviet empire has exacerbated rather than ameliorated its divisions, making European unity less likely than before. Only the United States, despite its uncertain economy and setbacks abroad, still acts like a classic great power.

The number of changes that would have to occur in all these countries to recreate a pentagonal balance of power makes such a scenario unlikely. Furthermore, this scenario fails to account for increasingly powerful transitional states that might seek great-power status; India and Brazil are but two examples. Thus, at least seven, not five, countries are potentially great powers of the future.

Perhaps an even larger multipolar system will emerge in the New Era, in which each of several major states compete for influence in weaker polities. These new great powers could involve all or some of the countries just cited, and several others not mentioned. If such a development occurred, the competing powers would likely have nuclear weapons; if more than two such powers emerged, alliances would be formed as a result. If the theory of bipolar stability is accepted, then this large multipolar system would constitute a more dangerous international arena than in the past. Although the situation prior to World War I would lead us to predict much instability, it has already been stated that the nature of twenty-first-century foreign policy is to emphasize technology and economics; thus, there is a net disincentive to pursue classic great-power competition for these states. The new kind of great-power competition, if it emerged, might be one of intense balancing on the nuclear level, or it might incorporate the new norms of greater emphasis on trade, science, and technology and thereby concentrate on peaceful, economic forms of competition.

As an alternative, it is possible to argue that we are about to return to a World War II pattern, with the United States and Russia aligned against Japan and Germany. Internal instability in Germany, caused by problems associated with German reunification, and continuing American-Japanese tensions over trade are just two reasons why the United States might consider these countries to be future threats. Furthermore, Germany certainly seems destined to play a dominant role in Europe once its own house is in order, whether or not a United Europe emerges. And Japan is likely to play a greater role throughout Asia, given its position as an economic powerhouse.

All things considered, however, this formulation seems highly unlikely. First, the Japan and Germany of the 1930s are not the same as the Japan and Germany of the New Era. In the 1930s, these two nations succumbed to a peculiar combination of virulent nationalism and fascism. Today they may have difficulties adjusting to their enhanced roles in international affairs, but there is no evidence to substantiate the claim that their democratic institutions and high-tech capitalism will be transformed into some new hostile global force. Second, instead of competing with the United States, and perhaps Russia, on a global level, both countries are likely to be preoccupied with their regional environs for the foreseeable future. A growing China is likely to divert Japanese attention from any concerns raised by economic competition with the United States. Similarly, Germany is overwhelmed with its own internal problems, the struggle over the delineation of the future Europe, and instability in Eastern Europe. Third, because of the foregoing reasons, neither Japan nor Germany has any incentive to confront the United States or Russia. It seems unlikely that this situation will significantly change over the next several decades.

The potential Japanese-Chinese competition is just one aspect of what might become an Asiacentric world. Indeed, it has been argued that the growing economic and political power of the Pacific Rim will make the twenty-first century the "Asian century." There are at least two formulations: perhaps Japan, China, or even India will emerge as the world's great powers, with various other non-Asian powers aligning with one or the other. Also possible is a racially based conflict between Asia and the rest of the world, with Russia split apart in the process between its European and Asian sectors. No matter what form it takes, proponents of an Asiacentric world tend to focus on the region's scientific achievement and growing economic prowess, not on its immediate ability to exert military influence worldwide.

As an organizing principle of world politics, however, an Asian-centered balance of power seems unlikely to happen, given the continued strength of the United States, Europe, and a potentially rejuvenated Russia. Furthermore, a global race war seems incompatible with the twenty-first-century style of world politics and its emphasis on economic, not military or ethnic, relations. Instability on the peripheries of the industrial centers of the Far East is a greater possibility and may distract nations such as China, India, and Japan from extending their foreign policies to more distant parts of the globe. Political difficulties in North Korea, Sri Lanka, Myanmar, and Kashmir are just a few possible distractions. Central Asian violence in Tajikistan matched by potential instability in other former republics of the USSR, such as Uzbekistan and Kyrgyzstan, represent further possible examples.

Yet, even the potential global dominance of Asian economics on a worldwide scale is doubtful. Certainly, several Asian states have demonstrated their

AT A GLANCE

TWENTIETH-CENTURY SCENARIOS

Multipolar International System

Foci: Several possible major states, including the United States, Russia, Japan, China, Brazil, India, and a United Europe

Concept: A great-power dominated international system is possible, in which each of the major states is competing for influence with weaker polities and with one another.

World War II Pattern

Foci: United States and Russia against Germany and Japan

Concept: Germany and Japan return to expansionist foreign policies that force the United States and Russia to form a countercoalition. Highly unlikely given contemporary moderate Japanese and German governments.

Asiacentric World

Foci: Japan, China, India

Concept: One prediction holds that the economic and political power of Asia will dominate the twenty-first century.

Rejuvenated Europe

Focus: Europe

Concept: If the nations of Europe unite, then they will be a formidable factor in the international politics of the future. Local nationalism in most major countries suggests that a loose confederation is far more likely than a Europe modeled after the United States.

Return to the Cold War

Foci: United States, Russia

Concept: If Russia is revitalized under a Communist or fascist government, a bipolar situation could evolve again. Russia still has an impressive scientific base as suggested by its nuclear missiles and past achievements in space.

ability to adjust to new technological innovations. However, other twenty-first-century regions, primarily North America and Europe, are hardly likely to fail to adapt to scientific and high-tech breakthroughs, despite their current economic problems. Proponents of an Asiacentric world cannot be disputed on their prediction that Asia will become more important in the future than it has been in the past, but they have to acknowledge that Asia cannot be an exclusive domain for the control of world politics in the way that Europe was in past centuries.

Still another possibility is a rejuvenated Europe dominating world politics. As shown in Chapter Twelve, a United Europe would represent an imposing political and economic giant according to any index of power. If European political and economic unity is achieved, then it will be a formidable factor in the international politics of the future. However, the difficulties engaged thus far in producing such an entity, demonstrated by the reluctance of citizens in Denmark, France, and Britain to unite, suggests that a loose confederation is far more likely than a Europe modeled after the United States of America. This conclusion that European unification will be difficult to achieve is reinforced by the uncertainties and counterpressures generated by the collapse of Soviet domination of Eastern Europe.

We should not rule out a return to the Cold War if a revitalized Russia were to emerge as a Communist or fascist superpower. After all, Russia, with all its problems, still has an impressive scientific and economic base, as suggested by its nuclear arsenal, its achievements in space, and its relatively large GNP. To Russia, the New Era has meant a new, weaker, and confused present, but given its potential, the possibility of its revival as a Cold War adversary should not be ignored.

Everything Old Is New Again: Nineteenth-Century Scenarios

The various twentieth-century scenarios just described are all at least conceivable, whereas the nineteenth-century scenarios that follow seem improbable. The history of international politics is one in which the strong states dominate the weak, whatever measure of power is used. In the New Era, strong states are located on the transitional or high-tech tiers, as discussed in the previous section. Those that practice the nineteenth-century style of politics are the weaker ones. It is difficult to visualize a system in which these relatively poor, nationalistic states could come to dominate the high-tech powerhouses of Asia, Western Europe, and North America. What would have to happen for such a system to emerge?

Conceivably, the postmodern world could be dominated by ancient hatreds; those who cannot forget the past may be condemned to repeat it. Nineteenth-century style movements like ethnic nationalism or Islamic fundamentalism might gain strength. These are problems that led to the breakup of Yugoslavia and the emergence of new intense relations between and within the former Soviet republics, and they could continue to cause trouble.

But a new nineteenth-century world need not be as conflictual and violent as the historical nineteenth century. The dominance of nationalism or fundamentalism could begin to divert the attention of the advanced states to the lower-income countries of the world. Perhaps as part of their own competition, the more advanced states could begin to cater to the political, economic, financial, and social needs of the world's impoverished, leading to an ironic triumph of nineteenth-century problems on a global scale.

Still, as suggested previously, this result seems improbable. It can be argued that during the Cold War, just such a scenario as this existed, with no discernible change in the international system. For example, the superpower rivalry provided the advanced states with greater incentive to be solicitous of Third World needs, yet in no way did the nineteenth-century values or political style of the developing states come to dominate world politics. The idea that the lowest rung of world politics could end up dominating the other two and cause stronger states to give top priority to Third World development and growth stretches the imagination. A global system in which the North puts the South above all else would represent a rejection of all established patterns in international politics. The "At a Glance" box on the next page summarizes the possible, though not probable, nineteenth-century scenarios. Note there are fewer of them than twentieth-century examples.

AT A GLANCE

NINETEENTH-CENTURY SCENARIOS

Pessimistic Version

The postmodern era could be dominated by ancient hatreds that would lead to widespread instability in the Third World.

World politics would then be dominated by such issues as the Middle East, South Asia, Islamic fundamentalism, the types of problems

represented by the breakup of Yugoslavia, and internal upheavals as have occurred in the 1990s in Rwanda, Somalia, and Haiti.

Optimistic Version

The twenty-first-century states could begin catering to the economic, financial, and social needs of the world's impoverished.

The Revolution Will Be Televised: Twenty-First-Century Scenarios

Our last set of scenarios are those in which twenty-first-century politics control the other two types of states. At first glance, this appears to be the most logical outcome, since high-tech politics as defined here are the most orderly and technologically and economically advanced. But the world is not always a logical place. Since the diminished use of military power, twenty-first-century states rarely encourage physical control of other states. This style of politics, however cosmopolitan its scope and global its reach, is still inward-looking, as twenty-first-century states are concerned first and foremost with their own internal economies.

Therefore, we can identify three conceivable twenty-first-century world orders, although none seems especially realistic, given the self-absorption of these states. First, the level of cooperation exhibited by high-tech, scientific states might lead to a grand **world federalism,** in which the countries of the world would unite in a huge, global state. According to this dreamlike scenario, there would be no international politics, and thus international conflict would not exist. As the events of the New Era have demonstrated, the major amount of conflict and violence in the world today is within states, not necessarily between them, which calls into question the correlation between political boundaries and conflict per se. Moreover, since even the cooperative European states seem reluctant to relinquish sovereignty, it is inconceivable that all countries of the world will ever unite in the first place. Even more questionable is the desirability of world federalism. Such a huge government would place enormous control in one domineering institution. Cultural identity would be threatened, not to mention many of the world's languages. Furthermore, how would the edicts of a world government be enforced? (For more on this problem, see Chapter Nine.)

And now a second scenario: The worldwide emphasis on the environment and the emerging superiority of scientific states might result in a kind of planetary politics, where environmental issues reign supreme. In this context, the high-tech

AT A GLANCE

TWENTY-FIRST-CENTURY SCENARIOS

World Federalism
Benefits: Countries of the world would unite in a huge, global state.

Problems: States are reluctant to relinquish sovereignty. No force currently exists to impose world federalism. May not eliminate conflict and violence.

Planetary Politics
Benefits: The high-tech states would concentrate on the environment as their major goal. The stronger states would have to be more generous to weaker countries in order for environmentalism to be pursued with a global impact.

Problems: Southern states believe that they are at a disadvantage. They argue that the industrialized states now seek to limit their development. To them, the North's environmental preoccupation is a ruse to limit their ability to catch up. Besides, the industrialized states' commitment to environmentalism is uneven.

Three Trade Blocs (North America, Asia, Europe)
Benefits: The preoccupation of the major powers with economics would lead to the centrality of economic as opposed to military rivalry.

Problems: It is possible that trade disputes could deteriorate into military confrontation.

states would prioritize environmental protection as their major goal. The stronger countries would have to exhibit a high degree of generosity toward the weaker states in order for environmentalism to be pursued with a global impact; such solicitousness, of course, is unlikely. Indeed, many countries of the South argue that the industrialized states seek to limit their development, claiming that the environmental preoccupation of the North is a ruse to limit the South's ability to catch up (since any country's industrialization results in pollution and environmental degradation). Therefore, while there is no question that environmentalism is likely to be a major issue in the new era, and that high-tech states will push the issue most strongly, it is unlikely that environmentalism will be the primary force to shape world politics. It will be one of many to be discussed in international meetings but hardly priority number one.

To understand a third scenario, remember that anarchy is the central feature of world politics. If anarchy produces conflict, and if the major powers today continue to be preoccupied with economics, then economic rivalry and conflict should dominate the international system. Indeed, current world politics are falling into three trade blocs: the North American Free Trade Area, the European Union, and an Asian economic sphere dominated by Japan and possibly China.

Despite the economic tensions that accompany a world dominated by trade blocs, there is no indication that such competition will degenerate into military conflict. Remember, the very nature of high-technology politics is to stress economic—and, therefore, politically controlled competition—not military power. Were rival blocs to resort to military confrontation, economics would become less important and world politics would begin to resemble a classic balance-of-power system as described in our nineteenth-century scenarios. In the future, although a high degree of economic rivalry may continue and even increase among these powerful states, it is unlikely that it will explode into armed warfare.

HAVE I SEEN THE FUTURE? EMERGING GLOBAL PROBLEMS AND POSSIBLE SOLUTIONS

If no one scenario within a given category will dominate, and if none of the three types of states will dominate, where does that leave us? On a road to nowhere? Don't worry, be happy; it is a small world after all—or is it? Toward what sort of New Era are we headed?

In a world where the three levels coexist, the three types of politics will be constantly balancing between interdependence and tension; turmoil and tranquility; cooperation and conflict. It will be a problem world rather than a polar world, a world of instability, cold war, and hot war.

On the nineteenth-century level, the proliferation of dangerous weapons will continue. We already see the emergence of chemical and long-range ballistic missiles as threats in the Middle East, and their production and use will spread if unchecked. Nuclear (and to a much lesser extent, biological) proliferation are also continuing problems. Regional crises may explode—as in the continuing dispute between India and Pakistan over Kashmir, the Arab-Iranian confrontation over the Persian Gulf, the Kurdistan problem, the Arab-Israeli conflict, and the turmoil in the Balkans, to name just a few examples.

These problems will be exacerbated by the fact that each level of states has the ability to worsen the problems that the other levels confront, such as when twenty-first-century states sell arms to the Third World. In a deteriorating twentieth-century arena, the republics of the former Soviet Union and China have an incentive to sell advanced weaponry to terrorist groups and rogue states.

Problems of the developing world can easily be exported to high-technology states in the form of drugs, terrorism, immigration, and health issues, such as AIDS. Instability in resource areas, especially oil, can similarly lead to devastating problems for advanced industrial states, even requiring military action, as in the case of the Persian Gulf War. Finally, twentieth-century states, particularly the former Soviet Union and Eastern Europe, are affected adversely when the high-tech states refuse to assist them. Thus, the coexistence of the three tiers means that, like spreading viruses, each is able to pollute the politics of the other: a small world indeed.

A New International Concert?

These problems require immediate international attention. Fortunately, a reemergence of cooperation, analogous to the Concert of Europe after the Napoleonic Wars, seems already to have taken place, as suggested by cooperation among the permanent members of the UN Security Council in a variety of crises, especially the Persian Gulf War. However, the laggard response to civilian suffering in Haiti, Somalia, Rwanda, and what was Yugoslavia suggests that the major powers will act only when they see their vital economic and security interests at stake.

The international reaction to the Iraqi invasion of Kuwait points to a central element of the emerging post–Cold War system: the dominance of the United States as the only remaining superpower. America is not in a position to assume the role of a Rome, dominating the known world. Rather, it is first among equals, especially in the political-military sphere. Preoccupied with domestic problems, it cannot provide order, but must work closely with other advanced states, especially the Europeans and Japanese. If the United States is able to organize a new international concert, it will contribute to muting the continuing conflicts, which will proceed in any case. If it does not succeed, then deterioration across the three levels is more likely.

While the United States cannot alone determine the future of international politics, it is the country that has the most to contribute to future stability or chaos. It is likely that Americans, accustomed to alternating cycles of isolationism and internationalism, will have trouble accepting a role of permanent interventionism in world politics. Americans typically support interventionist policies when they are associated with an adversary who can be identified and personalized (Hitler, Tojo, Ho Chi Minh, Saddam Hussein). In a new international concert, the foe is disorder—chaos that can destroy the hope of building a new world order, chaos that can bring instability and dangerous new ideologies to prominence, chaos that can reverse the benefits of the end of the Cold War, chaos that can destroy fledgling democracies, and, finally, chaos that can undermine the stability that high-tech states crave. If the United States is to organize a new international concert and simultaneously rehabilitate its own economic structure, it will have to pursue several objectives at once. But first, to be successful in creating a new system, American leaders and citizens will have to recognize several important conditions that have emerged in the New Era:

1. In the post–Cold War world, America is no hegemon. Washington cannot deal with all these issues alone, nor can it realistically engage in every problem on every level. To an unprecedented degree, effective policy will require identification and utilization of cooperative partners for dealing with issues worldwide. Coordination with these partners (who will vary depending on the issue) will be critical if a modicum of international stability is to be maintained.

2. Franklin Roosevelt's dream at the end of World War II of a collective-security mechanism for dealing with world problems has become feasible. In Central America, Namibia, the Persian Gulf, Cambodia, and in the unification of Germany, conflict management has been possible even when there was tenuous agreement between great powers. In many areas of the world (the Middle East, South Asia, Central Asia, and so forth), significant problems will remain, but their intensity, explosiveness, and potential for escalation will be restrained somewhat if a new U.S.–led concert successfully emerges.[5] The reversal of Iraq's invasion

of Kuwait is an example of what might happen if the United States effectively leads; Yugoslavia is an example of what does happen when it fails to lead.

3. Despite instances of successful collective security, the nature of both twentieth- and nineteenth-century problems promises continued turmoil and instability, and the means available for dealing with these issues will be limited. In particular, the option of military intervention will be exceptionally expensive to implement, especially as most major states decrease defense expenditures in their adjustment to the economic dictates of the New Era.

States that engage in expansive military expenditures will lose their competitiveness on the twenty-first-century level, and those that aim to reach this level, yet still spend, will see their aspirations doomed. The nature of the new high-technology competition means that states cannot afford to "take time out" while they build huge armies and march off to war. If they do so, they will lose important ground in the "science race" of the twenty-first century. Their ability to spend funds on research, development, infrastructure, education, and high technology will be diminished. They will not be able to compete.

4. In the New Era, then, political and economic strategies are more important than ever before, and the utility of military solutions is diminished—but not erased. Given the unstable nature of world conditions, twenty-first-century states will still need to maintain a substantial military force, but as part of the new concert there will need to be coordination among the great powers, perhaps by creating a UN Rapid Deployment Force, by using NATO in new ways, by attempting to create ad hoc institutions when crises occur in particular areas, or by developing innovative defense structures among allied countries.

5. The events that brought about the New Era are likely to accentuate the importance of the peripheries of the former USSR—in Eastern Europe and Germany to Russia's west, in the Islamic areas to Russia's south, and in Asia to Russia's east. In devising a new international concert, it is important to realize that the attention of many countries is likely to be riveted on these regions thrust into significance by the collapse of the Soviet empire. At least in the short run, it is in these areas that the major crises of the New Era are most likely to emerge.

6. The importance of twenty-first-century politics means that Asia will join Europe and North America as major players. The globalized economy will be matched by a globalized political stage, even if only Washington emerges as the leader of a new international concert. The Pacific Rim will be a center of power, but not *the* center.

Perhaps the most critical determinant in shaping the future international system is the ability of the United States, Europe, and Japan to adjust to the New Era. America for now is the only superpower, but the economic influence of Japan, Europe, and perhaps even China will become increasingly important. These countries' adjustment to new conditions will require a revolution in how they regard the world. Americans are prone to view international affairs in nineteenth- and twentieth-century terms, as a morality play in which conflicts between good and evil, totalitarianism and freedom are played out. The Europeans and Japanese became accustomed during the Cold War to domestic policies oriented to economic advancement and foreign dependence on American military responsibility. Until recently, the Chinese have remained inward-looking and suspicious of any foreign involvement that might adversely affect the state's control over Chinese society.

7. Where will Russia fit into this picture? Its future remains the great enigma of the New Era. Will it explode into chaos and civil war, reemerge as a strong, democratic, vibrant participant in great-power politics, or descend into nationalism and fascism or a revitalized communism and become a new adversary of the West? The future of Russia will have a major impact on how the great powers organize themselves in the New Era.

8. All parties will have to alter their perspectives, for the old East-West global struggle has been replaced by a generalized instability covering most of the planet. On the whole, the new world politics will be distinguished by a proliferation of problems, replacing the lethal, but less complex superpower Cold War. The current panoply of horrors includes drugs, debt, terrorism, nuclear and missile proliferation, religious fundamentalism, economic competition, environmental deterioration, crumbling state structures, separatism, and irredentism. The ability of the leading industrial states to organize a concert to deal with these conditions will be one of the critical factors in determining the success of the future system, whatever form it takes.

This new system will be made more complex because of the dialectic between globalization and fragmentation, cooperation and conflict, and expansion and contraction of state institutions. The twenty-first-century style of international politics will require coordination on trade, environmental issues, and high technology. If state institutions prove inadequate to cope with growing economic interdependence and interconnectedness, then expect institutions such as the multinational corporation and the media to become even more prominent.

At the same time, the growing globalization brought on by the end of the Cold War has resulted in a proliferation of attempts by smaller communities to establish their own identities through self-determination. This process has led to peaceful separations of states, as in the case of Czechoslovakia, or to violent bloodshed, as in Yugoslavia. These contrasting patterns are likely to remain distinctive of the New Era in world politics.

The Cold War imposed a simplicity on world politics. That simplicity is gone. Instead, the emergence of three tiers consisting of different types of states diffuses international politics, and increases the complexity of many problems. This creates a new world that not only demands careful attention to its economic, political, and military dimensions, but also encourages the creation of new types of international institutions to solve a diverse array of problems. Every student of world politics should leave the classroom with a new appreciation of the issues we confront, especially the problems that need to be addressed if we are to make the New Era a better era.

Notes

Chapter 1

1. Lyrics from "It's a Small World" (Sherman).
2. Lyrics from "Russians" (Sting).
3. Lyrics from "Imagine" (Lennon).
4. For a more detailed discussion of the role of natural resources in world politics, see Chapter 7 of Richard Rosencrance, *The Rise of the Trading State* (New York: Basic Books, 1986), or Daniel Yergin, *The Prize: The Epic Quest for Oil* (New York: Simon & Schuster, 1991).
5. Russell B. Scholl, Raymond J. Mataloni, Jr., and Steve D. Bezirganian, "The International Investment Position of the United States in 1991," *Survey of Current Business* 17 (June 1992): 47.
6. The data cited in this section is adapted from *The Information Please Almanac, Atlas and Yearbook 1993*, 46th ed. (Boston: Houghton Mifflin, 1993), and *World Military Expenditures and Arms Transfers, 1991–1992*, U.S. Arms Control and Disarmament Agency.
7. This breakdown follows that presented by Kenneth Waltz in *Man, the State, and War: A Theoretical Analysis* (New York: Columbia University Press, 1959).

Chapter 2

1. For analyses of political and economic trends during this period, see W.H. McNeill, *The Rise of the West* (Chicago: University of Chicago Press, 1967); *The Pursuit of Power: Technology, Armed Forces and Society Since 1000 AD* (Chicago: University of Chicago Press, 1983); Albert Hirschmann, *The Passions and the Interests: Political Arguments for Capitalism Before Its Triumph* (Princeton, NJ: Princeton University Press, 1977); and E.L. Jones, *The European Miracle: Environments, Economics, and Geopolitics in the History of Europe and Asia* (Cambridge: Cambridge University Press, 1981).
2. For more on social and political conditions in eighteenth-century Europe, see J.C.D. Clark, *English Society 1688–1832: Ideology, Social Structure, and Political Practice in the Ancien Régime* (Cambridge: Cambridge University Press, 1985); and C.B.A. Behrens, *Society, Government, and the Enlightenment* (New York: Harper & Row, 1985).
3. On the causes and nature of wars in the eighteenth century, see Kalevi J. Holsti, *Peace and War: Armed Conflicts and International Order 1648–1989* (Cambridge: Cambridge University Press, 1991); and Geoffrey Parker, *The Military Revolution: Military Innovation and the Rise of the West, 1500–1800* (Cambridge: Cambridge University Press, 1988).
4. The relative strengths and weaknesses of the eighteenth-century European powers are discussed in Paul Kennedy, *The Rise and Fall of the Great Powers* (New York: Random House, 1987), pp. 73–142.
5. For an overview of the major wars in eighteenth-century Europe, see Michael Howard, *War in European History* (New York: Oxford University Press, 1976).
6. Gordon A. Craig and Alexander L. George, *Force and Statecraft* (New York: Oxford University Press, 1983), pp. 19–20.
7. Quoted in Derek McKay and H.M. Scott, *The Rise of the Great Powers, 1648–1815* (London: Longman, 1983), p. 164.
8. For more on the development of the idea of nationalism and its role in the French Revolution, see E.J. Hobsbawm, *Nations and Nationalism since 1780: Programme, Myth, Reality* (Cambridge: Cambridge University Press, 1990.)
9. Quoted in Gunther Rothenberg, "The Origins, Causes, and Extension of the Wars of the French Revolution and Napoleon," in *Journal of Interdisciplinary History* 28, no. 4 (Spring 1988), p. 780.
10. There are more books on Napoléon than any other real person, with the possible exception of Jesus Christ. Some of the most useful works on the man and his time are Louis Bergeron, *France Under Napoleon*, trans. by R. R. Palmer (Princeton, NJ: Princeton University Press, 1981); J.M. Thompson, *Napoleon Bonaparte: His Rise and Fall* (Cambridge, MA: Blackwell, 1990); and Owen Connely, *Blundering to Glory: Napoleon's Military Campaigns* (Wilmington, DE: Scholarly Resources, 1987).
11. Gordon Craig, *Europe Since 1815* (New York: Holt, Rinehart and Winston, 1974), pp. 12–13.
12. Ibid., p. 13.
13. For more on the changes wrought by the Industrial Revolution, see W.O. Henderson, *The Industrial Revolution in Europe, 1815–1914* (Chicago: Quadrangle, 1961); David Landes, *The Unbound Prometheus: Technological Change and Industrial Development in Western Europe from 1750 to the Present* (Cambridge: Cambridge University Press, 1969); and Sidney Pollard, *Peaceful Conquest: The Industrialization of Europe, 1760–1970* (Oxford University Press, 1981).
14. Geoffrey Best, *War and Society in Revolutionary Europe, 1770–1870* (New York: St. Martin's Press, 1982) discusses the wide-ranging impact of the industrialization of warfare.
15. This pivotal period in the history of France is explored in Maurice Agulhon, *The Republican Experiment, 1848–1852*, trans. by Janet Lloyd (New York: Cambridge University Press, 1983).
16. For comprehensive appraisals of the events of 1848 and their aftermath, see Priscilla Robertson, *Revolutions of 1848: A Social History* (New York: Harper Torchbooks, 1960); and L.B. Namier, *1848: The*

Revolution of the Intellectuals (London: Oxford University Press, 1962).

17. Napoléon I's son, also called Napoléon, lived out most of his short life as a pampered prisoner in Vienna. No Napoléon II every ruled France.

18. Carl von Clausewitz, *On War*, rev. ed., ed. and trans. by Michael Howard and Peter Paret (Princeton, NJ: Princeton University Press, 1984), p. 69.

19. Quoted in Henry W. Littlefield, *History of Europe Since 1815* (New York: Barnes and Noble, 1963), p. 48. The life and career of the Iron Chancellor are presented in Edward Crankshaw, *Bismarck* (New York: Viking, 1981); and Otto Pflanze, *Bismarck and the Development of Germany: The Period of Unification, 1815–1871* (Princeton, NJ: Princeton University Press, 1973).

20. Michael Howard describes how and why Prussia won the war in *The Franco-Prussian War: The German Invasion of France, 1870–1871* (New York: Macmillian, 1961).

21. L.L. Farrar assesses the effectiveness of Bismarck's policies and the system of European alliances in general in *Arrogance and Anxiety: The Ambivalence of German Power, 1848–1914* (Iowa City, IA: University of Iowa Press, 1981).

Chapter 3

1. René Albrecht-Carrié, *A Diplomatic History of Europe Since the Congress of Vienna* (New York: Harper & Row, 1973), p. 295.

2. For contending perspectives on the expansion of German power before the First World War, see Fritz Fischer, *War of Illusions: German Policies from 1911 to 1914,* trans. by Marian Jackson (New York: Norton, 1975), and John A. Moses, *The Politics of Illusion: The Fischer Controversy in German Historiography* (New York: Barnes & Noble, 1975).

3. Albrecht-Carrié, *A Diplomatic History of Europe*, p. 212–214.

4. A.J.P. Taylor, *The Struggle for Mastery in Europe,* (Oxford: Clarion Press, 1957), p. 427; and Paul Kennedy, *The Rise and Fall of the Great Powers* (New York: Vintage, 1987), pp. 215–219.

5. James L. Stokesbury, *A Short History of World War I* (New York: Morrow, 1981), p. 11.

6. Taylor, *The Struggle for Mastery in Europe,* pp. xxix–xxxi.

7. These trends are discussed in Kennedy, *The Rise and Fall of the Great Powers*, pp. 194–249.

8. European colonialism is discussed in more detail in Chapters Five and Six; for more on this subject, the reader is referred to J. Gallagher and Ronald Robinson, *Africa and the Victorians: The Climax of Imperialism in the Dark Continent* (New York: St. Martin's, 1961); and Wilfred Baumgart, *Imperialism: The Idea and Reality of British and French Colonial Expansion* (New York: Oxford, 1982).

9. Quoted in Gordon A. Craig, *Germany, 1866–1945* (Oxford: Clarendon Press, 1978), p. 246.

10. For more on this belief and its origins see Stephen Van Evera, "The Cult of the Offensive and the Origins of the First World War," *International Security* 9 (Summer 1984), pp. 58–107.

11. Cited by J.M.K. Vyvyn in "The Approach of the War of 1914," in *The New Cambridge Modern History*, vol. 12 (Cambridge: Cambridge University Press, 1968), p. 160.

12. Richard Lebow, *Between Peace and War: The Nature of International Crisis* (Baltimore: Johns Hopkins University Press, 1981), pp. 232–233.

13. Charles F. Horne, ed., *Source Records of the Great War* (U.S.A.: National Alumni, 1923), p. 348.

14. Stokesbury, *A Short History of World War I*, p. 29.

15. For more on the outbreak and initial stages of World War I, see Lafore, *The Long Fuse;* Joll, *The Origins of the First World War;* and Barbara Tuchman, *The Guns of August* (New York: Macmillan, 1962).

16. An outstanding comprehensive account of World War I is B.H. Liddel Hart's *History of the First World War, 1914–1918* (London: Faber & Faber, 1938). John Keegan presents a gripping ground-level description of trench warfare in *The Face of Battle* (New York: Penguin, 1976).

17. John Keegan, *The Face of Battle* (New York: Viking, 1986), p. 255, 280.

18. Brian Bond, "The First World War," in *The New Cambridge Modern History*, vol. 12 (Cambridge: Cambridge University Press, 1968), p. 194.

19. Kennedy, *The Rise and Fall of the Great Powers,* pp. 271–274.

20. Estimates taken from D.H. Aldcroft, *From Versailles to Wall Street: The International Economy in the 1920s* (Berkeley, CA: University of California Press, 1977), pp. 13–14.

21. For a firsthand account of the squabbling, see Harold Nicolson, *Peacemaking 1919* (London: Constable, 1933).

22. For more on the Versailles settlement's impact on the Middle East and Eastern Mediterranean, see David Fromkin, *A Peace to End All Peace: The Fall of the Ottoman Empire and the Creation of the Modern Middle East* (New York: Avon, 1989).

23. The Versailles treaty is analyzed in detail from a number of perspectives in Ivo J. Lederer, *The Versailles Settlement: Was It Doomed to Failure?* (Boston: Heath, 1960).

24. Mussolini, his party, and his fascist philosophy are described by James Gregor in *Italian Fascism and Developmental Dictatorship* (Princeton: Princeton University Press, 1979); and *Young Mussolini and the Intellectual Origins of Fascism* (Berkeley, CA: University of California Press, 1979).

25. Germany's difficulties during this period are outlined in S.W. Halperin, *Germany Tried Democracy: A Political History of the Reich from 1918 to 1933* (New York: Norton, 1965).

26. For more on the causes and effects of the Great Depression, see C.P. Kindelberger, *The World in Depression, 1929–1939*, rev. ed. (Berkeley, CA: University of California Press, 1986).

27. This division follows that of William Manchester in *The Caged Lion,* (London: Michael Joseph, 1988), pp. 52–53.

28. There are a great many works on Hitler and on Germany during the Nazi period. Among the most interesting are William Shirer, *The Rise and Fall of the Third Reich* (New York: Simon & Schuster, 1960); Alan Bullock, *Hitler: A Study in Tyranny,* rev. ed. (New York: Harper & Row, 1964); John Toland, *Adolf Hitler* (Garden City, NJ: Doubleday, 1976); Walter Laqueur, ed., *Fascism: A Reader's Guide* (Berkeley, CA: University of California Press, 1976); and Hanna Arendt, *The Origins of Totalitarianism,* 2nd ed. (Cleveland: World, 1958).

29. Kennedy, *The Rise and Fall of the Great Powers,* p. 332.

30. Kennedy, *The Rise and Fall,* p. 296.

31. The Munich agreement and its implications are discussed in A.J.P. Taylor, *The Origins of the Second World War* (New York: Atheneum, 1965); Henri Nogueres, *Munich,* trans. by Patrick O'Brien (New York: McGraw-Hill, 1965); and P.M.H. Bell, *The Origins of the Second World War in Europe* (London: Longman, 1986). Churchill is quoted from his speech to the House of Commons, October 5, 1938.

32. World War II is arguably the most important event in world history. It is certainly the most recounted, documented, and analyzed. Outstanding among the many books devoted to it are Gordon Wright, *The Ordeal of Total War, 1939–1945* (New York: Langer, 1968); J.F.C. Fuller, *The Second World War* (New York: Meredith, 1968); and B.H. Liddel Hart, *History of the Second World War* (New York: Putnam, 1971).

33. The fall of France is analyzed in detail in Alistair Horne, *To Lose a Battle: France 1940* (Boston: Little, Brown, 1969).

34. Basil Collier, *The Battle of Britain* (New York: Macmillan, 1962) is a classic study of the air war over England.

35. For the planning and execution of the attack on Pearl Harbor, see Walter Lord, *Day of Infamy* (New York: Holt, Rinehart & Winston, 1967).

36. Estimated in Kennedy, *The Rise and Fall of the Great Powers,* p. 332.

37. For analysis of Japan's entry into the war, see Ike Nobutake, ed., *Japan's Decision for War* (Stanford: Stanford University Press, 1967). Axis and Allied campaigns in the Pacific are described in John Toland, *The Rising Sun* (New York: Random House, 1970); and Samuel Eliot Morrison, *Rising Sun in the Pacific* (Boston: Little, Brown, 1975).

38. For a compilation of figures, see Kennedy, *The Rise and Fall of the Great Powers,* pp. 352–357.

39. The strained relations between the Soviet Union and the Western Allies are discussed from different perspectives in John Lewis Gaddis, *Strategies of Containment* (New York: Oxford, 1982), pp. 3–24; and Walter LaFeber, *America, Russia and the Cold War 1975–1990* (New York: McGraw-Hill, 1991), pp. 8–28.

40. For a superb account of the development of the first atomic weapons, see Richard Rhodes, *The Making of the Atomic Bomb* (New York: Simon & Schuster, 1988).

41. For alternative views on the decision to use the atomic bombs, see Barton M. Bernstein, "Roosevelt, Truman, and the Atomic Bomb, 1941–1945: A Reinterpretation," *Political Science Quarterly,* no. 3 (Spring 1975), pp. 23–69; and Martin J. Sherwin, *A World Destroyed: The Atomic Bomb and the Grand Alliance* (New York: Random House, 1987).

42. These approximate figures, estimated by Soviet and Western sources, are cited in Kennedy, *The Rise and Fall of the Great Powers,* p. 362.

Chapter 4

1. Quoted in David Holloway, *The Soviet Union and the Arms Race* (New Haven: Yale, 1983), p. 20.

2. Quoted in Joseph Nogee and Robert Donaldson, *Soviet Foreign Policy Since World War II* (New York: Macmillan, 1992), p. 96.

3. Deborah Welch Larson, *Origins of Containment: A Psychological Explanation* (Princeton, NJ: Princeton University Press, 1985), p. 76.

4. Adam B. Ulam, *Expansion and Coexistence: Soviet Foreign Policy 1917–1973* (New York: Holt, Rinehart, and Winston, 1974), p. 428.

5. Winston Churchill, "The Sinews of Peace," March 5, 1946, in *Vital Speeches of the Day,* vol. 12, March 15, 1946, p. 332.

6. William Fox exemplifies this perspective in *The Super-Powers: The United States, Britain, and the Soviet Union—And Their Responsibility for Peace* (New York: Harcourt Brace, 1944.)

7. Adapted from Dean Acheson, *Present at the Creation* (New York: Norton, 1969), p. 196.

8. William A. Williams, *The Tragedy of American Diplomacy,* rev. ed. (New York: Delta, 1962), pp. 269–270.

9. "Text of President Truman's Speech on New Foreign Policy," *New York Times,* March 13, 1947, p. 2.

10. Harold F. Gosnell, *Truman's Crises: A Political Biography of Harry S. Truman* (London: Greenwood, 1980), p. 351.

11. *Department of State Bulletin,* June 15, 1947, pp. 1159–1160.

12. Quoted in telegram from U.S. Embassy Moscow to Secretary of State Marshall, May 26, 1947, papers of Joseph Jones, Truman Library.

13. Joan Spero, *The Politics of International Economic Relations* (New York: St. Martin's Press, 1985).

14. U.S. Senate, Committee on Foreign Relations and Committee on Armed Services, *Hearings: Military Situation in the Far East* (Washington: Government Printing Office, 1951), p. 10; and John W. Spanier, *The Truman-MacArthur Controversy and the Korean War* (Cambridge, MA: Belknap, 1959), p. 67.

15. Dwight David Eisenhower, *Mandate for Change* (New York: Doubleday, 1963), p. 181.

16. Ulam, *Expansion and Coexistence,* p. 540.

17. Quoted in William Zimmerman, "Russia and the International Order," *Survey* 58 (January 1966), pp. 209–213.

18. Tom Gervasi, *The Myth of Soviet Military Supremacy* (New York: Harper & Row, 1986), pp. 411–412.

19. Walter LaFeber, *America, Russia, and the Cold War: 1945–1990* (New York, McGraw-Hill, 1991), p. 205.

20. See Malcom Kerr, *The Arab Cold War: Gamal Abdel Nasser and His Rivals* (London: Oxford University Press, 1971).

21. Quoted in Arthur Schlesinger, Jr., *A Thousand Days* (Boston: Houghton Mifflin, 1965), p. 769.

22. For more on the Cuban Missile Crisis, see Graham T. Allison, *Essence of Decision: Explaining the Cuban Missile Crisis* (Boston: Little, Brown, 1971); and James G. Blight and David A. Welch, *On the Brink* (New York: Hill & Wang, 1989).

23. Robert Dallek, *The American Style of Foreign Policy: Cultural Politics and Foreign Affairs* (New York: Oxford University Press, 1983), p. 231.

24. Dallek, *The American Style of Foreign Policy*, p. 241.

25. R. Ernest Dupuy and Trevor N. Dupuy, *The Encyclopedia of Military History, from 3500 B.C. to the Present*, rev. ed. (New York: Harper & Row, 1977), p. 1221.

26. John Lewis Gaddis, *The United States and the End of the Cold War* (New York: Oxford University Press, 1993), p. 231.

27. Address at the commencement exercises of Notre Dame University, May 22, 1977, in *Department of State Bulletin*, June 13, 1977, pp. 621–625.

28. Ronald Reagan, remarks to the National Association of Evangelicals, March 8, 1983, in Strobe Talbott, *The Russians and Reagan* (New York: Vintage, 1984), p. 116.

29. Mikhail Gorbachev, *Perestroika: New Thinking for Our Country and the World* (New York: Harper & Row, 1987), pp. 216–218.

30. Francis Fukuyama, *The End of History and the Last Man* (New York: Free Press, 1992).

Chapter 5

1. *Webster's Ninth New Collegiate Dictionary* (Springfield, MA: Merriam-Webster, 1989).

2. For an overview of imperial motives and strategies, see Carlo Cipolla, *Guns and Sails in the Early Phase of European Expansion* (London: Pantheon, 1965); D.K. Fieldhouse, *Economics and Empire, 1830–1914* (Ithaca, NY: Cornell University Press, 1973), and *Colonialism, 1870–1945: An Introduction* (New York: St. Martin's Press, 1981); Bernard Semmel, *The Rise of Free Trade Imperialism* (Cambridge: Cambridge University Press, 1970); and Immanuel Wallerstein, *The Modern World-System, Part I: Capitalist Agriculture and the Origins of the European World-Economy in the Sixteenth Century* (Orlando, FL: Academic Press, 1974).

3. The Spanish Empire is described in C. Gibson, *Spain in America* (New York: Harper & Row, 1966); and J.H. Parry, *The Spanish Seaborne Empire* (London: Hutchinson, 1966).

4. For a discussion of different classes in the colonies, see J. Lockhart, *Early Latin America* (New York: Cambridge University Press, 1983).

5. For more on the establishment of the Portuguese Empire, see B.W. Diffie and C.D. Winius, *Foundations of the Portuguese Empire 1415–1580* (Minneapolis: University of Minneapolis Press, 1977).

6. For the story of the Anglo-French imperial rivalry, see J.H. Parry, *Trade and Dominion: The European Overseas Empire in the Eighteenth Century* (London: Weidenfeld & Nicolson, 1971); and C.G. Reynolds, *Command of the Sea: The History and Strategy of Maritime Powers* (New York: Morrow, 1974).

7. France's colonial policies are discussed in Winfried Baumgart, *Imperialism: The Idea and Reality of French Colonial Expansion* (New York: St. Martin's Press, 1961).

8. For an analysis of the political problems that decolonization posed for France, see R. von Albertini, *Decolonization* (New York: Doubleday, 1971); and Jean-Pierre Rioux, *The Fourth Republic, 1944–1958*, trans. Godfrey Rogers (Cambridge: Cambridge University Press, 1989); for more on the case of Algeria, see Alastair Horne, *A Savage War of Peace* (New York: Viking Press, 1978); and for Indochina, see Bernard Fall, *Street without Joy* (Harrisburg, PA: Stackpole, 1964).

9. British colonialism in North America up to the time of the American Revolution is described in Ian K. Steele, *The English Atlantic, 1675–1740* (New York: Oxford University Press, 1986); and Lawrence H. Gipson, *The Coming of the Revolution, 1763–1789* (New York: Harper, 1954).

10. The establishment of British rule in India is outlined in Henry H. Dodwell, ed., *British India, 1497–1858* (Cambridge: Cambridge University Press, 1929).

11. J. Gallagher and Ronald Robinson examine this phase of British imperialism in *Africa and the Victorians: The Climax of Imperialism in the Dark Continent* (New York: St. Martin's Press, 1961), as does Bernard Porter in *The Lion's Share: A Short History of British Imperialism 1850–1970* (London: Longman, 1976).

12. C. Barnett, *The Collapse of British Power* (London: Eyre Methven Ltd., 1972) is a noteworthy study of Britain's retreat from its empire.

13. For more on the history of the pre-revolutionary Russian Empire, see Nicholas V. Riasanovsky, *A History of Russia*, 4th ed. (New York: Oxford University Press, 1984).

14. The achievements and repressions of Soviet communism are discussed in Basil Dmytryshin, *USSR: A Concise History*, 4th ed. (New York: Charles Scribner's Sons, 1984). Both Lenin and Stalin became famous under their revolutionary *noms de guerre*; Lenin was born Vladimir Ulyanov and Stalin was originally called Iosif Dzhugashvili.

15. Outstanding among the many works on American imperialism in the late-nineteenth and early-twentieth centuries are Walter LaFeber, *The New Empire: An Interpretation of American Expansion 1860–1898* (Ithaca, NY: Cornell University Press, 1963); Ernest R. May, *American Imperialism: A Speculative Essay*

(New York: Atheneum, 1968); W.A. Williams, *The Roots of the Modern American Empire* (New York: Random House, 1969); and Robert Dallek, *The American Style of Foreign Policy* (New York: Mento, 1983).

16. The rise and decline of the Ottoman Empire is covered in M.A. Cook, ed., *A History of the Ottoman Empire to 1730* (Cambridge: Cambridge University Press, 1976).

17. For the impact of the collapse of Ottoman power on Middle Eastern politics, see David Fromkin, *A Peace to End All Peace: The Fall of the Ottoman Empire and the Creation of the Modern Middle East* (New York: Avon, 1989).

18. Ronald Robinson, "The Non-European Foundations of European Imperialism: Sketch for a Theory of Collaboration," in E.R.J. Owen and R. Sutcliffe, eds., *Studies in the Theory of Imperialism* (London: Longman, 1972).

19. Samuel Popkin, *The Rational Peasant: The Political Economy of Rural Society in Vietnam* (Berkeley: University of California Press, 1979).

20. The wrenching events that led up to these reforms are recounted in W.G. Beasley, *The Meiji Restoration* (Stanford: Stanford University Press, 1972).

21. See Ronald Robinson and John Gallagher, "The Imperialism of Free Trade," *Economic History Review* (2nd series) 6, no. 1 (1953).

22. For differing views on the economic impact of imperialism on the developing world, see William Woodruff, *Impact of Western Man: A Study of Europe's Role in the World Economy, 1750–1960* (New York: St. Martin's Press, 1967); W. Mommsen and J. Osterhammel, eds., *Imperialism and After: Continuities and Discontinuities* (London: Allen & Unwin, 1986); and Daniel Headrick, *The Tentacles of Progress: Technology Transfer in the Age of Imperialism, 1850–1940* (New York: Oxford, 1988).

23. See Crawford Young, *The Politics of Cultural Pluralism* (Madison, WI: University of Wisconsin Press, 1976), for an excellent survey of the cultural diversity of the South.

Chapter 6

1. Figures from World Bank, *World Development Report 1992,* pp. 218–219.

2. For an overview of superpower involvement in African conflicts, see Gerald Bender, James Coleman, and Richard Sklar, eds., *African Crisis Areas and U.S. Foreign Policy* (Berkeley & Los Angeles: University of California Press, 1985); and Jerry F. Hough, *The Struggle for the Third World: Soviet Debates and American Options* (Washington: Brookings, 1986).

3. Discussions of U.S. policy in Latin America and the USSR's efforts to extend its influence in the region may be found in Robert S. Leiken and Barry Rubin, eds., *The Central American Crisis Reader* (New York: Simon & Schuster, 1987); Abraham F. Lowenthal, *Partners in Conflict* (Baltimore: John Hopkins University Press, 1987); and Cole Blasier, *The Giant's Rival: The USSR and Latin America* (Pittsburgh: University of Pittsburgh Press, 1988)

4. For more on the interrelated balances of power in the Middle East, see L. Carl Brown, *International Politics and the Middle East* (Princeton: Princeton University Press, 1984); Malcom Kerr, *The Arab Cold War*, 3d ed. (London: Oxford, 1971); and Alan Taylor, *The Arab Balance of Power* (Ithaca, NY: Syracuse University Press, 1982).

5. David Fromkin provides an excellent study of the machinations over the Middle East during and after the First World War in *A Peace to End All Peace: The Fall of the Ottoman Empire and the Creation of the Modern Middle East* (New York: Avon, 1989).

6. The story of the Six-Day War and its aftermath is told in David Kimche and Dan Bawly, *The Sandstorm: The Arab-Israeli War of June 1967* (New York: Stein and Day, 1968); Nadav Safran, *From War to War: The Arab-Israeli Confrontation, 1948–1967* (New York: Pegasus, 1969); and Edgar O'Ballance, *The Third Arab-Israeli War* (London: Faber & Faber, 1972).

7. For more on the economic, political, and strategic importance of oil and the efforts of many countries to gain and wield the power it provides, see Daniel Yergin, *The Prize* (New York: Simon & Schuster, 1991).

8. The events surrounding the 1973 war are detailed in Chaim Herzog, *The War of Atonement: October, 1973* (Boston: Little, Brown, 1975); and Edgar O'Ballance, *No Victor, No Vanquished: The Yom Kippur War* (San Rafael, CA: Presidio Press, 1978).

9. The complex relationships between the United States, the USSR, and Middle Eastern states in the 1970s and 1980s are explored in Moshe Efrat and Jacob Bercovitch, eds., *Superpowers and Client States in the Middle East* (London: Routledge, 1991); and Steven L. Spiegel, *The Other Arab-Israeli Conflict* (Chicago: University of Chicago Press, 1985).

10. For the inside story of the negotiations at Camp David, see William B. Quandt, *Camp David: Peacemaking and Politics* (Washington, DC: Brookings, 1986).

11. For discussions of the implications of the end of the Cold War on the Middle East from different perspectives, see John Lewis Gaddis, "Toward the Post-Cold War World," *Foreign Affairs* 70, no. 2 (Summer 1991), pp. 102–122; Michael Hudson, "The Middle East Under Pax Americana: How New, How Orderly?" *Third World Quarterly* 13 (1992), pp. 301–316; and Nikkie Keddie, "The End of the Cold War in the Middle East," *Diplomatic History* 16 (1992), pp. 95–103.

12. For more on the conflict over Kashmir, see Lorne J. Kavic, *India's Quest for Security* (Berkeley & Los Angeles: University of California Press, 1967); and J. Bandyopadhaya, *The Making of India's Foreign Policy* (New Delhi: Allied, 1970).

13. The origins and aftermath of the Sino-Indian conflict are discussed in John S. Dalvi, *Himalayan Blunder* (Bombay: Thacker, 1969); and Neville Maxwell, *India's China War* (Garden City, NY: Doubleday, 1972).

14. For more on international relations in South Asia during this period, see Gunnar Myrdal, *Asian Dilemma* (New York: Pantheon, 1968); and Karunaka Gupta, *India in World Politics: A Period of Transition* (Calcutta: Scientific Books, 1969).

15. Details on the Indian-Pakistani war may be found in Robert Jackson, *South Asian Crisis: India, Pakistan, and Bangladesh* (Boulder, CO: Praeger, 1975).

16. See Chapter Four for more on the Korean War. For an in-depth analysis of the events leading up to the war and of Sino-American antagonism after 1949, see Tsou Tang, *America's Failure in China, 1941–1950,* 2 vols. (Chicago: Phoenix, 1963); and Bruce Cummings, *The Origins of the Korean War* (Princeton: Princeton University Press, 1981).

17. Classic studies of the falling out between Moscow and Beijing include O. Edmund Clubb, *China and Russia* (New York: Columbia University Press, 1971); and Donald Zagoria, *The Sino-Soviet Conflict, 1956–1961* (Princeton: Princeton University Press, 1962).

18. Robert Sutter, *Chinese Foreign Policy After the Cultural Revolution* (Boulder, CO: Westview, 1978), outlines the developments in the region's politics during this period.

19. For more on how this alignment came about, see Raymond L. Garthoff, *Détente and Confrontation* (Washington, DC: Brookings, 1985); and Warren I. Cohen, *America's Response to China,* 3d ed. (New York: Columbia University Press, 1989).

20. Two useful essays on the relationship between China and the other major powers in East Asia after 1989 are Robert Gilpin, "International Politics in the Pacific Rim Area," in Steven L. Spiegel, ed., *At Issue: Politics in the World Arena,* 6th ed. (New York: St. Martin's, 1991), pp. 130–143; and Marie Gottschalk, "China After Tiananmen: The Failure of American Policy," in the same volume, pp. 173–188.

21. For more on post–Cold War developments in Southeast Asia, see Jason D. Lewis, "Southeast Asia—Preparing for a New World Order," *Washington Quarterly* 16, no. 1 (Winter 1993), pp. 187–200.

Chapter 7

1. For a more detailed introduction, see Thomas D. Lairson and David Skidmore, *International Political Economy: The Struggle for Power and Wealth* (Fort Worth, TX: Harcourt Brace, 1993), pp. 11–34. For more advanced discussions, see Robert Gilpin, *The Political Economy of International Relations* (Princeton: Princeton University Press, 1987); and Joan Edelman Spero, *The Politics of International Economic Relations,* 4th ed. (New York: St. Martin's Press, 1990).

2. This is the standard definition of comparative advantage using the Heckscher-Ohlin model. For an in-depth analysis of comparative advantage and other variants of the concept, see Paul Krugman and Maurice Obstfeld, *International Economics: Theory and Policy* (New York: HarperCollins, 1991), p. 9–118.

3. David Ricardo, *The Works and Correspondence of David Ricardo,* Piero Sraffa, ed. (Cambridge: University Press for the Royal Economic Society, 1951).

4. Hundreds of books and thousands of articles have been written from both sides of the free trade vs. protectionism debate. For a strong presentation of the case for free trade, see Jagdish Bhagwati, *The World Trading System at Risk* (Princeton: Princeton University Press, 1991); for arguments critical of free trade, see Paul Krugman, Rethinking International Trade (Cambridge, MA: MIT Press, 1990).

5. For more on the Great Depression's effect on the world economy, see Charles Kindelberger, *The World in Depression, 1929–1939* (Berkeley, CA: University of California Press, 1973).

6. There is also a statistical discrepancy due to some inaccuracy in measuring this data. For more on the balance of payments, see Lairson and Skidmore, *International Political Economy,* pp. 15–20.

7. For more detailed analyses of these three schools of thought, see Gilpin, *The Political Economy of International Relations,* pp. 25–41.

8. Do not confuse this "classical" liberalism with "liberal" thought as it is used in contemporary American politics. Many advocates of government intervention to mitigate the ill effects of market failure or to redistribute wealth are called "liberals" today, but these ideas are not liberalism as the term is used in discussion of international political economy.

9. Spero, *The Politics of International Economic Relations,* p. 5–6.

10. Stephen Krasner, *World Politics—"State Power and the Structure of Foreign Trade,"* (April 1976), pp. 317–347.

11. Duncan Snidal, "Limits of Hegemonic Stability Theory," *International Organization* 39 (Autumn 1985), pp. 579–614.

12. Karl Marx, *Capital.* Edited by Friedrich Engels. *Manifesto of the Communist Party,* by Karl Marx and Friedrich Engels, 2d ed. (Chicago: *Encyclopedia Britannica,* 1990).

13. For a political argument, see Ronald Rogowski, *Commerce and Coalitions: How Trade Affects Domestic Political Alignments* (Princeton, New Jersey: Princeton University Press, 1989). For the economic underpinnings, see Wolfgang F. Stolper and Paul Samuelson, "Protection and Real Wages," *The Review of Economic Studies* 9, no. 1 (1941), pp. 58–73.

14. Jeffrey A. Frieden, "Invested Interests: The Politics of National Economic Politics in a World of Global Finance," *International Organization* 45, no. 4 (Autumn 1991), pp. 425–451.

15. See Rondo Cameron, *A Concise Economic History of the World from Paleolithic Times to the Present,* 2d

ed., (Oxford: Oxford University Press, 1993) for a comprehensive survey.

16. A.G. Kenwood and A.I. Lougheed, *The Growth of the International Economy 1820–1990,* 3d ed. (London: Routledge, 1992).

17. For more details, See *A Concise Economic History,* pp. 163–190; and David S. Landes, *The Unbound Prometheus: Technological Change and Industrial Development in Western Europe from 1750 to the Present* (Cambridge: Cambridge University Press, 1969), pp. 41–123.

18. P.J. Cain and A.G. Hopkins, "The Political Economy of British Expansion Overseas, 1750–1914," *Economic History Review* 33, no. 4 (November 1980), p. 472.

19. McCloskey, "The Industrial Revolution," p. 112.

20. See Cain and Hopkins, "The Political Economy of British Expansion Overseas," pp. 474–475. In fact, the Americas (the United States plus Latin America) accounted for roughly 60 percent of the cumulative increase in British exports between 1783 and 1812.

21. Gilpin, *The Political Economy of International Relations,* p. 31.

22. Cain and Hopkins, "The Political Economy of British Expansion Overseas," p. 475.

23. Cameron, *A Concise Economic History,* p. 279.

24. See Kenwood and Lougheed, *The Growth of the International Economy,* pp. 12–13.

25. Cameron, *A Concise Economic History,* pp. 242–248.

26. For more background, see Sidney Pollard, *The Industrialization of Europe, 1760–1970* (Oxford: Oxford University Press, 1982), pp. 172–183.

27. Kenwood and Lougheed, *Growth of the International Economy,* pp. 70–73.

28. Aaron Friedberg, *The Weary Titan: Britain and the Experience of Relative Decline* (Princeton: Princeton University Press, 1988).

29. For more on this period, see Peter Gourevitch, *Politics in Hard Times: Comparative Responses to International Economic Crises* (Ithaca, NY: Cornell University Press, 1986).

30. Lairson and Skidmore, *International Political Economy,* p. 52.

31. Barry J. Eichengreen, *Golden Fetters: the Gold Standard and the Great Depression, 1919–1939* (New York: Oxford University Press, 1992).

32. See Alan Milward, *War, Economy and Society, 1939–1945* (Berkeley, CA: University of California Press, 1977), p. 67.

33. Kenwood and Lougheed, *Growth of the International Economy,* p. 245.

34. For more on the establishment of the Bretton Woods institutions, see Lairson and Skidmore, *International Political Economy,* pp. 65–66; and Spero, *The Politics of International Economic Relations,* pp. 21–27.

35. See Spero, *The Politics of International Economic Relations,* pp. 68–73, for details.

36. The G7 includes Britain, Canada, France, Germany, Italy, Japan, and the United States.

37. John Odell, *U.S. International Monetary Policy* (Princeton: Princeton University Press, 1982), pp. 203–205.

38. For an in-depth discussion of the oil crisis in the early 1970s, see Daniel Yergin, *The Prize: The Quest for Oil, Money, and Power* (New York: Simon & Schuster, 1991), pp. 563–652.

39. Joel Darmstadter and Hans H. Landsberg, "The Crisis," in *The Oil Crisis,* edited by Raymond Vernon (New York: Norton, 1976), pp. 20–33. See also Simon Bromley, *American Hegemony and World Oil* (University Park, PA: Pennsylvania State University Press, 1991).

40. Yergin, *The Prize,* p. 588.

41. Noteworthy analyses of the competitiveness of nations and firms in the modern world economy include Michael Porter, *The Competitive Advantage of Nations* (New York: Free Press, 1990); Jean Claude Derain, *America's Struggle for Leadership in Technology* (Cambridge: MIT Press, 1990); and William J. Baumol, *Productivity and American Leadership: The Long View* (Cambridge: MIT Press, 1991).

42. Lairson and Skidmore, *International Political Economy,* p. 101.

43. For detailed explanations of the economic failure of socialism in Eastern Europe and the former USSR, see Charles Gati, *The Bloc That Failed* (Bloomington: Indiana University Press, 1990); and Bartlomiej Kaminski, *The Collapse of State Socialism* (Princeton: Princeton University Press, 1991).

44. John Pinder discusses the economic links between Eastern and Western Europe in *The European Community and Eastern Europe* (London: Pinter, 1991).

45. For more on the successes and failures of G7 summits, see Robert Putnam and Nicholas Bayne, *Hanging Together: Cooperation and Conflict in the Seven-Power Summits* (Cambridge: Harvard University Press, 1987); Martin Feldstein, *International Economic Cooperation* (Chicago: University of Chicago Press, 1988); and Richard N. Cooper et al., *Can Nations Agree? Issues in International Economic Cooperation* (Washington, DC: Brookings, 1989).

46. Lairson and Skidmore, p. 113.

47. For more on the development and organization of the European Community, see Nicholas Colchester and David Buchan, *Europower* (New York: Times Books, 1990); and John Pinder, *European Community* (Oxford: Oxford University Press, 1991).

48. This agreement is discussed in Jeffrey Schott, ed., *Free Trade Areas and U.S. Trade Policy* (Washington:, DC: Institute for International Economics, 1989).

Chapter 8

1. For a discussion of this issue, see Robert Gilpin, *The Political Economy of International Relations* (Princeton: Princeton University Press, 1987), pp. 263–305.

2. Classic works of modernization theory include Gabriel Almond and James Coleman, eds, *The*

Politics of the Developing Areas (Princeton: Princeton University Press, 1960); W.W. Rostow, *Stages of Economic Growth: A Non-Communist Manifesto* (Cambridge: Cambridge University Press, 1960); David Apter, *The Politics of Modernization* (Chicago: University of Chicago Press, 1965); Samuel Huntington, *Political Order in Changing Societies* (New Haven: Yale University Press, 1968); Lucian Pye, *Communications and Political Development* (Princeton: Princeton University Press, 1963); and Dankwart Rostow, *A World of Nations: Problems of Political Modernization* (Washington, D.C.: Brookings, 1967).

3. World Bank, *World Development Report 1994*, pp. 214–215.

4. Ibid., pp. 162–163.

5. Ibid., p. 212.

6. Leading critiques of modernization theory are offered in Gunnar Myrdal, *Economic Theory and Underdeveloped Regions* (New York: Harper & Row, 1971); Ragnar Nurske, *Problems of Capital Formation in Underdeveloped Countries* (New York: Blackwell, 1953); and Raul Prebisch, "Commercial Policy in the Underdeveloped Countries," *American Economic Review* 49 (May 1959), pp. 251–273.

7. This criticism is advanced in Arrighi Emmanuel, *Unequal Exchange: A Study of the Imperialism of Trade* (New York: Monthly Review Press, 1972), rebutted in Paul Samuelson, "Illogic of Neo-Marxist Doctrine of Unequal Exchange," *Inflation, Trade, and Taxes*, edited by David Belsey et al. (Columbus, OH: Ohio State University Press, 1976), pp. 96–107; and discussed in Sven Grassman and Erik Lundberg, eds., *The World Economic Order—Past and Prospects* (London: Macmillan, 1981).

8. Howard Wiarda, "Toward a Nonethnocentric Theory of Development: Alternative Conceptions from the Third World," *Journal of Developing Areas* 17, no. 4 (July 1983), p. 437.

9. Outstanding works on dependency theory include Henrique Cardoso and Enzo Faletto, *Dependency and Development in Latin America* (Berkeley: University of California Press, 1979); David Collier, *The New Authoritarianism in Latin America* (Princeton: Princeton University Press, 1979); Theotonio Dos Santos, "The Structure of Dependence," *American Economic Review* 60 (1970), pp. 235–246; Peter Evans, *Dependent Development: The Alliance of Multinational, State, and Local Capital in Brazil* (Princeton: Princeton University Press, 1979); Andre Gunder Frank, *Latin America: Underdevelopment or Revolution* (New York: Monthly Review Press, 1969), and Osvaldo Sunkel and Pedro Paz, *El subdesarrollo latinoamericano y la teoria del desarrollo* (Mexico City: Siglo Veintiuno, 1970).

10. See Immanuel Wallerstein, *The Modern World-System: Capitalist Agriculture and the Origins of the European World-Economy in the Sixteenth Century* (New York: Academic Press, 1976).

11. This argument is set forth in Joseph L Love, "Raul Prebisch and the Origins of the Doctrine of Unequal Exchange," *Latin American Research Review* 15, no. 3 (1980); and Joan Robinson, "Trade in Primary Commodities" in *International Political Economy: Perspectives on Global Power and Wealth*, 2d. ed., edited by Jeffrey A. Freiden and David Lake (New York: St. Martin's, 1991), pp. 376–385.

12. Robinson, "Trade in Primary Commodities," pp. 378–379.

13. Joan Spero, *The Politics of International Economic Relations*, 4th ed. (New York: St. Martin's, 1990), p. 131.

14. Thomas D. Lairson and David Skidmore, *International Political Economy: The Struggle for Power and Wealth* (Fort Worth, TX: Harcourt Brace, 1993), p. 252.

15. Rhys Jenkins, *Transnational Corporations and Uneven Development* (New York: Meuthen, 1987), p. 10.

16. Lairson and Skidmore, *International Political Economy*, p. 260.

17. Spero, *The Politics of International Economic Relations*, p. 287.

18. See Volker Bornschier and Christopher Chase-Dunn, *Transnational Corporations and Underdevelopment* (New York: Praeger, 1985).

19. For critical reviews of dependency theory, see David Ray, "The Dependency Model of Latin American Underdevelopment: Three Basic Fallacies," *Journal of Interamerican Studies and World Affairs* 15, no. 1 (February 1973); Sanjaya Lall, "Is Dependence a Useful Concept in Analyzing Underdevelopment?" *World Development* 3, no. 11 (November 1975); and Tony Smith, "The Underdevelopment of the Development Literature: The Case of Dependency Theory," *World Politics* 32, no. 2 (January 1979).

20. See *World Bank, Global Economic Prospects and the Developing Countries 1994* (Washington: World Bank, 1994) and "Poor Relations: Are Third-World Commodity Producers Condemned to Eternal Poverty?" *The Economist*, April 16, 1994, p. 76.

21. World Bank, *World Development Report*, 1994, p. 198.

22. Ibid., p. 129.

23. World Bank figures quoted in *The Economist*, September 25, 1993, special section on *Third World Finance*, p. 12.

24. For analysis of the debt crisis from a variety of perspectives, see Miles Kahler, ed., *The Politics of International Debt* (Ithaca, NY: Cornell University Press, 1985); Vinod Aggarwal, "International Debt Threat: Bargaining Among Creditors and Debtors in the 1980s," *Policy Papers in International Affairs*, no. 79 (Berkeley, CA: University of California Press, 1987); Barbara Stallings and Robert Kaufman, eds., *Debt and Democracy in Latin America* (Boulder, CO: Westview, 1989); and Gianni Vaggi, ed., *From the Debt Crisis to Sustainable Development: Changing Perspectives on North-South Relations* (New York: St. Martin's, 1993).

25. Clyde Farnsworth, "U.S. Will Tie Aid to Exports in Bid to Curb the Practice," *New York Times,* May 14, 1990.

26. "Playing the Aid Game," *World Press Review,* February 1989, p. 51.

27. Judith Tendler discusses this problem in *Inside Foreign Aid* (Baltimore: Johns Hopkins University Press, 1975).

28. Natasha Bechorner, "Water and Instability in the Middle East," *Adelphi Paper 273,* presented at International Institute for Strategic Studies, London, (Winter 1992–1993), p. 49.

29. See Guillermo O'Donnell, *Modernization and Bureaucratic-Authoritarianism* (Berkeley, CA: University of California Press, 1979).

30. Robert Alexander offers an evaluation of import-substitution industrialization in "Import Substitution in Latin America in Retrospect" in *Progress Toward Development in Latin America: From Prebisch to Technological Autonomy,* edited by James L. Dietz and Dilmus D. James (Boulder, CO: Lynne Rienner, 1991).

31. For more on the NIEO, see Robert Mortimer, *The Third World Coalition in International Politics,* 2d. ed. (Boulder, CO: Westview, 1984); Jeffrey Hart, *The New International Economic Order* (New York: St. Martin's Press, 1983); Stephen Krasner, *Structural Conflict: The Third World Against Global Liberalism* (Berkeley: University of California Press, 1985); and Robert Tucker, *The Inequality of Nations* (New York: Basic Books, 1977).

32. Mortimer, *The Third World Coalition in International Politics,* p. 44. For more on OPEC, see Ian Skeets, *OPEC: Twenty-Five Years of Prices and Politics* (Cambridge: Cambridge University Press, 1988); and Daniel Yergin, *The Prize* (New York: Simon & Schuster, 1991).

33. See Krasner, *Structural Conflict,* for a discussion of the Group of 77's efforts.

34. John Macomber discusses this strategy in "East Asia's Lessons for Latin American Resurgence," *World Economy* 10, no. 4 (December 1987).

35. For more details, see Lairson and Skidmore, *International Political Economy,* pp. 204–205.

36. Robin Broad and John Cavanagh "No More NICs," *Foreign Policy* 72, no. 1 (Fall 1988).

37. See World Resources 1992–93, pp. 41–56; and World Bank, *World Development Report 1992* (which focuses on the environmental costs and benefits of development), for discussions of this issue. More details will also be found in Chapter Eleven.

38. For summaries of the pros and cons of NAFTA, see D.K. Brown, A.V. Deardorff, and R.M. Stern, "A North American Free Trade Agreement—Analytical Issues and Computational Assessment," *World Economy* 15, no. 1 (January 1992), pp. 11–29; and the debates in *Foreign Affairs* 72, no. 5 (November–December 1993), and *Foreign Policy* 93 (Winter 1993–1994).

39. Max Singer and Aaron Wildavsky, *The Real World Order: Zones of Peace, Zones of Turmoil* (Chatham, NJ: Chatham House, 1993).

40. See Stephan Haggard, *Pathways from the Periphery: The Politics of Growth in the Industrializing Countries* (Ithaca, NY: Cornell University Press, 1990); and Lawrence H. Summers and Vinod Thomas, "Recent Lessons of Development," *World Bank Research Observer* 8, no. 2 (July 1993), pp. 241–254.

Chapter 9

1. This definition comes from Hedley Bull, *The Anarchical Society* (New York: Columbia University Press, 1977), p. 127.

2. For a more detailed introduction to these principles of international law, see Paul Sieghart, *The International Law of Human Rights* (Oxford: Clarendon, 1983), p. 10ff.

3. Robert F. Drinan, *Cry of the Oppressed: The History and Hope of the Human Rights Revolution* (San Francisco: Harper & Row, 1987).

4. *A Report on the Development Concerning the Deployment of United States Forces to Panama on December 20, 1989* (Washington, DC: U.S. Government Printing Office, 1990), p. 1.

5. For more on the use of the tit-for-tat (or TFT) strategy in international relations, see Robert Axelrod, *The Evolution of Cooperation* (New York: Basic Books, 1984).

6. These aspects of customary law are discussed in Paul Sieghart, *The Lawful Rights of Mankind* (Oxford: Oxford University Press, 1985), pp. 48–62.

7. Sieghart, *The International Law of Human Rights,* p. 11.

8. Quoted in *Los Angeles Times,* February 23, 1993, p. A9.

9. Sieghart, *The Lawful Rights of Mankind,* p. 32.

10. For more on the Peltier case, see *New York Times,* April 3, 1988, p. 6A.

11. For estimates of the casualties caused by the fighting in the former Yugoslavia, see Milan Andreevich, "Bosnia & Herzegovina: In Search of Peace," *Radio Free Europe/Radio Liberty Research Report,* June 5, 1992, pp. 5–9; and Patrick Moore, "Ethnic Cleansing in Bosnia: Outrage but Little Action," *Radio Free Europe/Radio Liberty Research Report,* (August 28, 1992, pp. 11–15.

12. Nicholas Rengger, *Treaties and Alliances of the World,* 5th ed. (Detroit: Gale Research, 1990). Also see *UN Chronicle* 30, no. 1 (March 1993), p. 93.

13. Union of International Associations, ed., *Yearbook of International Organization 1992/1993* (Munich: Saur, 1992).

14. For more on the objectives and formation of the League, see Edward Hellet Carr, *The Twenty Years' Crisis* (New York: Harper & Row, 1964).

15. Hans Morgenthau, *Politics among Nations,* 5th ed. (New York: Knopf, 1978), p. 200.

16. "On the Lines: The UN Role in Preventing and Containing Conflict," *United Nations Association of*

United States of America News, 1985; and "Report of the 18 UN Issues Conference," 1987, Stanley Foundation.

17. For views on the UN's success in Cambodia, see *Los Angeles Times,* February 23, 1993, pp. H1–2; William Branigin, "UN Performance at Issue as Cambodian Vote Nears," *Washington Post,* May 20, 1993, A25, and William Branigin, "Tarnishing UN's Image in Cambodia," *Washington Post,* October 29, 1993, A33.

18. *UN Chronicle,* June 1993, p. 73.

19. Ibid.

20. The possibilities and problems with UN peacekeeping are debated in William Durch and Barry Blechman, "Keeping the Peace: The United Nations in the Emerging World Order" (Washington: Henry L. Stimson Center, March 1992); John Blodgett, "The Future of UN Peacekeeping," *Washington Quarterly* 14, no. 3 (Winter 1991); and a special issue of *Survival* 32, no. 3 (May–June 1990), which includes contributions from Brian Urqhardt, Aleksandr Belonogov, and Augustus Norton and Thomas Weiss among others.

21. See David Baldwin, *Economic Statecraft* (Princeton: Princeton University Press, 1985).

22. For more on the Arab League, see *Yearbook of International Organizations 1992/1993,* p. 1166ff.

23. CSCE's role in the Yugoslav crisis is discussed in James E. Goodby, "Peacekeeping in the New Europe," *The Limited Parnership: Buillding a Russian-U.S. Security Community* (Oxford: University Press, 1993).

24. Figures from U.S. Department of State, "Patterns of Global Terrorism: 1990," *Terrorism* 14 (1991), pp. 253–254.

25. Thomas Hobbes, *Leviathan,* ed. Michael Oakeshott (New York: Collier, 1962), p. 100.

Chapter 10

1. *World Bank Population Projections,* World Bank, 1985.

2. Council of Europe, Directorate of Economic and Social Affairs, "The Changing Age Structure of the Population and Future," *Population Studies* 18 (1985).

3. Nathan Keyfitz, "Population Growth Can Prevent the Development That Would Slow Population Growth," in Jessica Tuchman Matthews, ed., *Preserving the Global Environment* (New York: Norton, 1991), p. 50.

4. "Mexico City, Sao Paulo Likely to Rank as World's Largest Cities Soon," *UN Observer & International Report* 13, no. 2 (February 1991), p. 3.

5. Mark S. Hoffman, ed. *The World Almanac & Book of Facts* (New York: World Almanac, 1994).

6. Sadik, "The 1990s: The Decade of Decision," *Populi* 17, no. 2 (1990), pp. 10–19.

7. Sadik, "The 1990s: The Decade of Decision," pp. 17, 22.

8. See McGeorge Bundy, "Population: An Inescapable Problem," *Populi* 17, no. 1 (1990), pp. 20–24.

9. Stanley Meisler, "Rising Wind of Migration

Foreseen," *Los Angeles Times,* April 30, 1992, p. A9. For more on economic migration in Europe, see the annual report, *Trends in International Migration,* published by the Organization on Economic Cooperation and Development.

10. Anne-Christine D'Adesky, "UNHCR: Facing the Refugee Challenge," *UN Chronicle* 28, no. 3 (September 1991), p. 43.

11. Refugee section based on *Ibid* and Alain Louyot, "A World in Exodus," *World Press Review,* November 1993, Vol. 40, p. 47; "The World's Shame" *The Economist,* November 13, 1993, Vol. 329, p. 45; *World Refugee Survey,* 1994.

12. "Albanian Exodus Replays Debate Over Vietnamese Boat People," *UN Observer & International Report* 13, no. 9 (September 1991), p. 4.

13. Figures cited in Tamara Jones, "Germany's Troubles," *Los Angeles Times Magazine,* March 7, 1993, pp. 14–20.

14. Eve Koudri Kuhn, "East-to-East Migrant Flow Worries 3 Former Soviet-bloc Countries," *UN Observer & International Report* 13, no. 9 (September 1991), p. 4.

15. "Refuge in Austria a Distant Dream for Bulgarians, Romanians, Turks," *UN Observer & International Report* 15, no. 1 (January 1993), p. 6.

16. U.S. Committee for Refugees, *Refugee Reports,* December 31, 1992, pp. 9–13.

17. *Refugee Reports,* pp. 9–13.

18. "Convention on Migrant Worker Rights Adopted," *UN Chronicle* 28, no. 1 (March 1991), pp. 80–81.

19. D'Alesky, "UNHCR: Facing the Refugee Challenge," p. 46.

20. "Iraqi Refugee Tragedy Steers UN on New Path to Humanitarian Aid," *UN Observer & International Report* 13, no. 6 (August 1991), p. 4.

21. D'Alesky, "UNHCR: Facing the Refugee Challenge," p. 53–54.

22. U.S. Committee for Refugees, *World Refugee Survey 1992,* p. 35.

23. UN Food and Agriculture, *FAO Yearbook,* 1991 (Rome: FAO, 1992), pp. 237–238.

24. Robert C. Johansen, "A Human World Community," in Robert J. Art and Robert Jervis, eds., *International Politics* (Glenview, IL: Scott, Foresman, 1985), p. 76.

25. Bread for the World Institute on Hunger & Development, *Hunger 1993: Uprooted People* (Washington, DC: Bread for the World, 1993), pp. 172–173.

26. For a detailed explanation of why this occurs, see "Somalia, Operation Restore Hope: A Preliminary Assessment" (London: African Rights, May 1993); and Peter Madden, "Brussels Beef Carve-up: EC Beef Dumping in West Africa" (London: Christian Aid, April 1993).

27. Kidron and Segal, *The New State of the World Atlas,* 4th ed., (New York: Simon & Schuster, 1991), pp. 106–107.

28. Paul Harrison, "Beyond the Blame-Game:

Population-Environment Links," *Populi* 17, no. 3 (1990), pp. 14–21.

29. Harrison, "Beyond the Blame-Game: Population-Environment Links," pp. 19–20.

30. R. Paul Shaw, "Population Growth: Is It Ruining the Environment?" *Populi* 16, no. 2 (1989), p. 22.

31. Estimates cited in H.R.H. the Duke of Edinburgh, "People and Nature," *Populi* 17, no. 2 (1990), p. 30.

32. Sadik, "The 1990s: The Decade of Decision," pp. 8–9.

33. World Resources 1994–1995. *A Guide to the Global Environment: People and the Environment.* World Resources Institute with UN Environmental Programme and UN Development Programme (London: Oxford University Press, 1994), p. 201.

34. Estimate quoted in Kidron and Segal, *The New State of the World Atlas,* 4th ed., p. 107.

35. Sadik, "The 1990s: The Decade of Decision," pp. 8–9.

36. George W. Rathjens, "Energy and Climate Change," *Preserving the Global Environment,* edited by Jessica T. Matthews (New York: Norton, 1990), p. 169.

37. See Harrison, "Beyond the Blame-Game," p. 17; and Bruce Babbit, "Earth Summit," *World Monitor* (January 1990,) p. 30.

38. Hiroshima Nakajima, "Epidemiology and the Future of World Health," *Epidemiological Bulletin* 12, no. 4 (1990), p. 4.

39. Barry R. Bloom, "Vaccines for the Third World," *World Health* (June–July–August 1990), p. 13.

40. William H. Foege, "International Health Developments after the Elimination of Smallpox," *World Medical Journal* 38, no. 1 (January–February 1991).

41. Foege, "International Health Developments after the Elimination of Smallpox."

42. "Malaria in the Americas," *Epidemiological Bulletin* 13, no. 4 (December 1992), p. 1.

43. World Health Organization, *World Health Organization,* Weekly Epidemiological Record, August 21, 1992, pp. 258–259.

44. Sharyl Stolberg, "Afflictions Expected to Kill 4 Million Annually by 2010," *Los Angeles Times* March 30, 1990, p. A30.

45. Associated Press, "Full-Blown AIDS Cases Estimated at 4 million (Worldwide Total)," *New York Times,* July 2, 1994, p. 8.

46. James Slack, "Responding to the Global Epidemic of AIDS," *Policy Studies Journal* 20, no. 1 (1992), pp. 125–126.

47. Ivan Gillibrand, "AIDS in Africa," *World Medical Journal* 35, no. 2, (March–April 1988), p. 18.

48. Thomas Netter, "World AIDS Day," *World Health* (November–December 1990), pp. 27–29.

49. Ann Marie Kimball, "AIDS: The Global Epidemic; The Numbers Soar, While Prevention Staggers," *Christianity and Crisis* 52, no. 13 (September 21,1992), p. 300. For a discussion of the possible extent of HIV infection in China, see

50. Slack, "Responding to the Global Epidemic of AIDS," pp. 125–126.

50. Alan Whiteside and David Fitsimmons, *The AIDS Epidemic: Economic, Political, and Security Implications* (Conflict Series, no. 251) (London: Research Institute for the Study of Conflict and Terrorism, 1992), p. 6.

51. Kimball, "AIDS: The Global Epidemic," p. 299.

52. Ivan Gillibrand, "AIDS in Africa," *World Medical Journal* 35, no. 2 (March–April 1988), p. 18.

53. Nakajima, p. 2.

54. Foege, "International Health Developments after the Elimination of Smallpox," p. 7.

55. Jose Antonia Najera-Morrondo, "Malaria Control: History Shows It's Possible," *World Health* (September–October 1991), p. 32.

56. Stolberg, "Afflictions Expected to Kill" (September–October 1991), p. A30.

57. Whiteside and Fitzsimmons, "The AIDS Epidemic," pp. 26–29.

58. "First Lady of Bangladesh Vows to Support War on Illicit Narcotics," *UN Observer & International Report* 12, no. 1 (January 1990), p. 9.

59. See William H. Overbolt, "Dateline Drug Wars: Burma—the Wrong Enemy," *Foreign Policy* 77 (Winter 1989–1990), pp. 72–191.

60. Rachel Ehrenfeld, *Narco-Terrorism* (New York: Basic Books, 1990), pp. 63–64.

61. Marjorie Miller, "New Bosses Taking Over Cocaine Traffic," *Los Angeles Times,* February 20, 1993, pp. A10–A11.

62. Ehrenfeld, *Narco-Terrorism,* pp. 52–73.

63. Rensselaer W. Lee III, "The Political Economy of the Andean Cocaine Industry" in *At Issue: Politics in the World Arena,* edited by Steven L. Spiegel (New York: St. Martin's, 1991), p. 272.

64. William Drozdiak, "World Crime Groups Expand Cooperation, Spheres of Influence," *New York Times,* October 5, 1992, pp. A12, A16.

65. Eve Kouidri Kuhn, "Grim Assessment Greets Arrival of the UN's New Narcotics 'Czar,'" *UN Observer & International Report* 13, no. 3 (March 1991), p. 10.

66. Joseph Treaster, "Smuggling and Use of Illicit Drugs Are Growing, UN Survey Finds," *New York Times,* January 13, 1992, p. A6.

67. Eve Koudri Kuhn, "East Europeans Hired to Push Drugs for Nigerian Traffickers," *UN Observer & International Report* 14, no. 1 (January 1992), pp. 4, 16.

68. Kuhn, "Grim Assessment," p. 10.

69. Ehrenfeld, *Narco-Terrorism,* pp. 1–19.

70. Carey Goldberg, "Russian Police Warn of Cocaine Blizzard," *Los Angeles Times,* February 27, 1993, p. A7.

71. *National Household Survey on Drug Abuse,* Rockville, MD, 1990 and *The Economist,* May 15, 1993, pp. A31.

72. Michael Isikoff, "30 Nations Join in Attacks on Drug Cartels," *Washington Post,* August 31, 1988, p. A4.

73. "What America's Users Spend on Illegal Drugs, 1988–1991." U.S. Office of National Drug Control Policy, August 1993.

74. Bruce Michael Bagley, "Dateline Drug Wars: Columbia—The Wrong Strategy," *Foreign Policy* 77 (Winter 1989–1990), pp. 159–160.

75. Tracy Wilkinson, "Central Americans Vow War on Drugs at Belize Summit," *Los Angeles Times*, February 20, 1993, p. A11.

76. Lee, "The Political Economy of the Andean Cocaine Industry," pp. 277–278.

77. Ehrenfeld, *Narco-Terrorism*, pp. 86–87.

78. For details on this case, see David Lauter, "Mexico Leader Scolds Quayle Over Abduction," *Los Angeles Times*, April 27, 1990, pp. A1, A13.

79. See Lucia Mouat, "War on Drugs Becomes More Cooperative, Global," *Christian Science Monitor*, January 29, 1992, p. 9; and "The Enemy Within: Drug's Policy," *The Economist*, May 15, 1993, p. A31.

80. Ehrenfeld, *Narco-Terrorism*, pp. 101–102.

81. Wilkinson, p. A11.

82. "War on Illicit Narcotics," *UN Chronicle* 27, no. 2 (June 1990), p. 54.

83. "Stronger International Response to Drug Problem Needed, UN Board States," *UN Chronicle* 28, no. 3 (September 1991), p. 62.

84. "Drugs Know No Boundaries," *UN Chronicle* 27, no. 2 (June 1990), p. 54.

85. Michael Isikoff, "World Drug Problem Worsening, UN Reports," *Washington Post*, January 11, 1990, p. A24.

86. "General Assembly Message to World: Reduce Drug Demand," *UN Chronicle* 27, no. 2 (June 1990), pp. 53–60.

87. "Developed Nations Promised Aid to Curtail Drug Demand," *UN Chronicle* 27, no. 3 (September 1990), pp. 60–64.

88. Dan Fisher, "Drug Conference Calls for Global Effort Against Traffickers," *Los Angeles Times*, April 12, 1990, p. A6.

89. U.S. Department of State Bureau of International Narcotics Matters (BINM), *International Narcotics Strategy Report* (Washington, DC: U.S. Government Printing Office, 1992), pp. 22–25.

90. *International Narcotics Strategy Report*, p. 26.

91. Jeffrey Laurenti, "The U.S. Retreats in the War on Drugs," *Christian Science Monitor*, April 30, 1992, p. 19.

92. "Intrusive Role for UN Proposed in Tough New War on Illicit Drugs," *UN Observer & International Report* 14, no. 1 (January 1992), p. 4.

93. Stephen Flynn, "Worldwide Drug Scourge: The Response," Part II, *Brookings Review* (Spring 1993).

94. Paraphrased from George Rosie, *The Directory of International Terrorism* (Edinburgh: Mainstream Publishing, 1986), p. 18.

95. Typology after David Ziegler, *War, Peace, and International Politics* (Glenview, IL: Scott, Foresman, 1990), pp. 494–496.

96. This distinction is made by John W. Sloan in "Political Terrorism in Latin America," *The Politics of Terrorism*, edited by Michael Stohl (New York: Dekker, 1983), p. 368.

97. John W. Sloan, "Political Terrorism in Latin America," in Michael Stohl, ed., *The Politics of Terrorism in Latin America*, p. 377.

98. Ibid., pp. 379–380.

99. For more on terrorism in Africa, see Robert A. Denemark and Mary B. Welfling, "Terrorism in Sub-Sahara Africa" in *The Politics of Terrorism*, edited by Michael Stohl (New York: Dekker, 1983), pp. 357–365.

100. This argument is considered by A. Peter Burleigh in "Terrorism: Efforts Toward International Solutions," *U.S. Department of State Dispatch*, July 6, 1992.

101. International Energy Agency, *Energy Policy of IEA Countries: 1991 Review*, p. 6.

102. *Energy Policy of IEA Countries: 1991 Review*, pp. 8, 66; International Energy Agency, *Energy Policy of IEA Countries: 1992 Review*, pp. 5, 30; and *UN, World Economic Survey*, 1993, p. 257.

103. For more on the IEA, see Robert O. Keohane, *After Hegemony: Cooperation and Discord in the World Political Economy* (Princeton: Princeton University Press, 1984) pp. 217–237.

104. *Energy Policy of IEA Countries: 1991 Review*, pp. 9, 70.

105. *Energy Policy of IEA Countries: 1991 Review*, pp. 9–10.

106. *Energy Policy of IEA Countries: 1991 Review*, p. 10.

107. Daniel Yergin explores the role of oil and energy in international politics in *The Prize: The Epic Quest for Oil* (New York: Simon & Schuster, 1991).

108. Figures from "The Earth Summit," *UN Chronicle* (June 1992), p. 60.

109. See Ewan W. Anderson, "Water: The Next Strategic Resource" in *The Politics of Scarcity: Water in the Middle East* edited by Joyce R. Starr and Daniel C. Stoll (Boulder, CO: Westview Press, 1988); and Joyce R. Starr, "Water Wars," *Foreign Policy* 82, no. 2 (Spring 1991).

110. For more on the plan and its reception by the Arab League, see David Wishart, "The Breakdown of the Johnston Negotiations over the Jordan Waters," *Middle Eastern Studies* 26, no. 4 (October 1991), pp. 536, 546, and Selig A. Taubenblatt, "Jordan River Basin Water: A Challenge in the 1990s," in Starr and Stoll, *The Politics of Scarcity*, p. 46.

111. Taubenblatt, "Jordan River Basin Water: A Challenge in the 1990s," p.13.

112. Starr, "Water Wars," pp. 28–31.

113. John Murray Brown, "Turkey, Syria Set Talks on Euphrates," *Washington Post*, January 22, 1993, p. A27.

114. Raj Krishna, "The Legal Regime of the Nile River Basin" in *The Politics of Scarcity*, edited by Joyce R. Starr and Daniel C. Stoll (Boulder, CO: Westview Press, 1988), pp. 28–30.

115. Starr, "Water Wars," pp. 22–23.

Chapter 11

1. Richard J. Barnet, "Challenging the Myths of National Security," *New York Times Magazine*, April 1, 1979, p. 25.
2. Robert M. Bowman, "Bush Era Begins," *Space and Security News*, January 1989, p. 1.
3. Karl W. Deutsch, *The Analysis of International Relations* (Englewood Cliffs, NJ: Prentice-Hall, 1968), p. 88. "Parkinson's Law" was formulated by British historian Cyril Parkinson, who observed that work expands to fill the time available for its completion.
4. Edward Luttwak, *The Grand Strategy of the Roman Empire* (Baltimore: Johns Hopkins University Press, 1976), p. 4.
5. Patrick Morgan, *Deterrence: A Conceptual Analysis* (Beverly Hills: Sage Publications, 1977), pp. 27–47.
6. An outstanding work on primary and extended deterrence and the policies designed to achieve both is Alexander L. George and Richard Smoke, *Deterrence in American Foreign Policy: Theory and Practice* (New York: Columbia University Press, 1974).
7. Paul Huth, *Extended Deterrence and the Prevention of War* (New Haven: Yale University Press, 1988), pp. 86–97. Although technically a limited number of Syrian tanks and troops had already intervened, the Israelis clearly deterred a full-scale invasion.
8. Glenn H. Snyder, *Deterrence and Defense: Toward a Theory of National Security* (Princeton: Princeton University Press, 1961), p. 3.
9. For more on the differences between deterrence and compellence, see Thomas C. Schelling, *The Strategy of Conflict* (Cambridge, MA: Harvard University Press, 1960); and Thomas C. Schelling, *Arms and Influence* (New York, CT: Yale University Press, 1966).
10. Richard Ned Lebow and Janice Gross Stein, "When Does Deterrence Succeed and How Do We Know?" (Toronto: Canadian Institute for International Peace and Security Occasional Paper, 1990), p. 16.
11. For more on these requirements, see Lebow and Stein, "When Does Deterrence Succeed and How Do We Know?"
12. Snyder, *Deterrence and Defense*, p. 25.
13. Richard Ned Lebow, and Janice Gross Stein, *Psychology and Deterrence* (Baltimore: Johns Hopkins University Press, 1985).
14. See "Missed Signals in the Middle East," *Washington Post Magazine*, March 17, 1991, pp. 19–41. Glaspie challenges the accuracy of the Iraqi transcript and contends that it excluded her warnings that the "United States would protect its vital interests in the area."
15. Arthur Stein notes this possibility in "When Misperception Matters," *World Politics* 34, no. 2 (January 1982), pp. 505–526.
16. See the account of the crisis in Hannes Adomeit, *Soviet Risk-Taking and Crisis Behavior: A Theoretical and Empirical Analysis* (London: Allen & Unwin, 1982).

17. For more thorough treatments of this subject, see Michael Howard, *War in European History* (New York: Oxford, 1976); Paul Kennedy, *The Rise and Fall of the Great Powers* (New York: Random House, 1987); and Geoffrey Parker, *The Military Revolution: Military and the Rise of the West, 1500–1800* (Cambridge University Press, 1988).
18. For an overview of this concept, see Jack S. Levy, "The Offensive/Defensive Balance of Military Technology: A Theoretical and Historical Analysis," *International Studies Quarterly* 28, no. 2 (June 1984), pp. 219–238.
19. See, for example, John Mearsheimer, "Back to the Future: Instability in Europe After the Cold War" in *The Cold War and After: Prospects for Peace,* edited by Sean M. Lynn-Jones (Cambridge, MA: MIT Press, 1991), pp. 141–192.
20. For more on this and other concepts of nuclear strategy, see Freedman, *The Evolution of Nuclear Strategy.*
21. David Ziegler, *War, Peace and International Politics* (Glenview, IL: Scott, Foresman 1990), p. 271.
22. See Mearsheimer, "Back to the Future: Instability in Europe after the Cold War."
23. Patrick Morgan, "Elements of a General Theory of Arms Control" in *Conflict and Arms Control: An Uncertain Agenda,* edited by Paul Viotti (Boulder, CO: Westview Press, 1986), p. 285.
24. For details on the SALT I agreement and the negotiations which led up to it, see John Newhouse, *Cold Dawn: The Story of SALT* (New York: Holt, Rinehart & Winston, 1973).
25. Not all Western analysts agree that Warsaw Pact conventional forces held the upper hand throughout this period. For a contrary argument, see Tom Gervasi, *The Myth of Soviet Military Supremacy* (New York: Harper & Row, 1986).
26. George Bush, *National Security of the United States: 1990–1991* (Washington, DC: Brassey's, 1990), p. 3.
27. Frank Barnaby, ed., *The Gaia Peace Atlas: Survival into the Third Millennium* (New York: Doubleday, 1988), p. 14.

Chapter 12

1. Jacob Viner, "Power Versus Plenty as Objectives of Foreign Policy," in *International Political Economy: Perspectives on Global Power and Wealth,* edited by Jeffrey Frieden and David A. Lake (New York: St. Martin's Press, 1987), p. 72.
2. Data on estimated proved oil reserves drawn from *International Petroleum Encyclopedia* (Tulsa, Oklahoma: Pennwell Publishing Company, 1992), pp. 270–271.
3. For data on amount of arable land available to individual countries, see *UN Food and Agriculture Organization Yearbook,* 1990, pp. 6–34.
4. Ibid., pp. 22–34
5. World Bank, *World Development Report 1992,* pp. 218–219.
6. Of course, while the United States had a larger army than Iraq, its global responsibilities reduced

the number of troops it could deploy in the immediate area of conflict.

7. World Bank, *World Development Report 1992,* p. 221.
8. Ibid., p. 253.
9. In the late 1980s, the United States had 1.4 million scientists, the Japanese 400,000, and the West Germans 100,000. The United States had 2.2 million engineers, the Japanese 1.1 million, and the West Germans 500,000. Comparisons of U.S., Japanese, and West German R&D efforts, 1986–1989, from Joseph S. Nye, Jr., *Bound to Lead: The Changing Nature of American Power* (New York: Basic Books, 1991), p. 166.
10. International Institute for Strategic Studies, *The Military Balance 1991–1992* (London: Brassey's, 1991), p. 95.
11. *Stockholm International Peace Research Institute Yearbook, 1992,* p. 69; Bulletin on START II, *Arms Control Reporter,* January 1993.
12. *World Military Expenditures and Arms Transfers 1970–1979,* pp. 52–81, and *1991–1992,* pp. 47–88.
13. *The Military Balance 1991–1992,* p. 95.
14. John Lewis Gaddis, *The United States and the End of the Cold War* (New York: Oxford, 1992).
15. World Bank, *World Development Report 1994,* pp. 196–197.
16. Thomas Hobbes, *Leviathan,* edited by Michael Oakeshott (New York: Macmillan, 1964), pp. 72–73.
17. Paul Kennedy, *The Rise and Fall of the Great Powers: Economic Change and Military Conflict from 1500–2000.* (New York: Vintage Books, 1987), p. 354.

Chapter 13

1. Robert Keohane, "Theory of World Politics: Structural Realism and Beyond," in Robert Keohane, ed., *Neorealism and Its Critics* (New York: Columbia University Press, 1986), p. 166.
2. Modern classics of the realist paradigm include Edward Hallett Carr, *The Twenty Years' Crisis: 1919–1939* (New York: Harper & Row, 1964); and Hans J. Morgenthau, *Politics among Nations* (New York: Knopf, 1973).
3. See Kenneth Waltz, *Theory of International Politics* (New York: Random House, 1979); and Joseph Grieco, *Cooperation among Nations: Europe, America, and Non-Tariff Barriers to Trade* (Ithaca, NY: Cornell University Press, 1990).
4. Jack Levy, "The Causes of War: A Review of Theories and Evidence" in *Behavior, Society and Nuclear War,* Volume 1 (New York: Oxford University Press, 1989), p. 224.
5. John Mearsheimer, "Back to the Future: Instability in Europe after the Cold War," *International Security* 15, no. 1 (Summer 1990), p. 12.
6. Letter to Bishop Mandell Creighton, April 5, 1887.
7. Quoted in Winston S. Churchill, *The Second World War: The Grand Alliance,* vol. 3 (Boston: Little, Brown, 1950), p. 370. Compare this statement with

a remark by then-Senator Harry Truman before the United States entered World War II: "If we see that Germany is winning the war, we ought to help Russia, and if Russia is winning the war, we ought to help Germany, and that way let them kill as many as possible."

8. Theda Skocpol, *States and Social Revolution: A Comparative Analysis of France, Russia, and China* (New York: Cambridge University Press, 1979).
9. Quoted in Stephan Walt, *The Origins of Alliances* (Ithaca, NY: Cornell University Press, 1987), p. 18.
10. From Morton Kaplan, *System and Process in International Politics* (New York: Wiley, 1967), ch. 2.
11. Speech on the Polish question in the House of Commons, 1848.
12. This difficulty is discussed in Alan Ned Sabrosky, "Interstate Alliances: Their Reliability and the Expansion of War" in *The Correlates of War,* edited by J. David Singer (New York: Free Press, 1980), pp. 161–198.
13. Quoted in Edward Whiting Fox, *The Emergence of the Modern European World* (Cambridge, MA: Oxford University Press, 1991), p. 329.
14. Thomas J. Christensen and Jack Snyder, "Chain Gangs and Passed Bucks: Predicting Alliance Patterns in Multipolarity," *International Organization* 44, no. 2 (Spring 1990), pp. 137–168.
15. Bandwagoning is discussed in Walt, *The Origins of Alliances.*
16. See, for example, Randall Schweller, "Domestic Structure and Preventive War: Are Democracies more Pacific?" *World Politics* (1992), pp. 235–269.
17. A.F.K. Organski, *World Politics,* 2d. ed. (New York, Knopf, 1968) p. 362.
18. Jack Levy, "The Causes of War: A Review of Theories and Evidence," in *Behavior, Society, and Nuclear War,* vol. 1 (New York: Oxford University Press, 1989), p. 233.
19. John Mearsheimer, "Back to the Future: Instability in Europe after the Cold War," *International Security* 15, no. 1 (Summer, 1990), p. 5–56.
20. Karl Deutsch and J. David Singer "Multipolar Power Systems and International Stability," *World Politics* 16, no. 3 (April 1964), pp. 390–406.
21. Deutsch and Singer, "Multipolar Power Systems and International Stability," p. 393.
22. Richard Rosecrance, "Bipolarity, Multipolarity and the Future," *Journal of Conflict Resolution* 10, no. 3 (September 1966), pp. 314–327.
23. This position is discussed in Mearsheimer, "Back to the Future: Instability in Europe after the Cold War," and John Lewis Gaddis, "The Long Peace: Elements of Stability in the Postwar International System, *International Security* 11, no. 4 (Spring 1988), pp. 99–142.
24. For more on the definition and operation of collective security, see Inis Claude, *Power and International Relations* (New York: Random House, 1962); and Charles Kupchan and Clifford Kupchan, "Concerts, Collective Security and the Future of Europe," *International Security* 16, no. 1 (Summer 1991), p. 168.

25. Mahnza Zehra Ispahani, "Alone Together: Regional Security Arrangements in Southern Africa and the Arabian Gulf," *International Security* 8, no. 4 (Spring 1984), p. 152.

26. See, for example, Bernard Avishai, "Shadow of Terror, Hope for Peace," *New York Times*, November 13, 1990, p. A21.

27. Claude, *Power and International Relations*, p. 112.

28. This problem is discussed in Mancur Olson's classic work, *The Logic of Collective Action: Public Goods and the Theory of Groups* (Cambridge, MA: Harvard University Press, 1977).

29. See Grieco, *Cooperation among Nations.*

30. Claude, *Power and International Relations*, p. 204.

31. See, for example, Robert Keohane, *After Hegemony: Cooperation and Discord in the World Political Economy* (Princeton: Princeton University Press, 1984); Robert Axelrod, *The Evolution of Cooperation* (New York: Basic Books, 1984); Axelrod and Keohane, "Achieving Cooperation Under Anarchy: Strategies and Institutions," *World Politics* 38, no. 1 (October 1985), pp. 226–54; and Charles Lipson, "International Cooperation in Economic and Security Affairs," *World Politics* 37, no. 1 (October 1984), pp. 1–23.

32. Grieco, *Cooperation among Nations*, p. 22.

33. Susan Strange, "Cave! Hic Dragones: A Critique of Regime Theory" in *International Regimes,* edited by Stephen D. Krasner (Ithaca, NY: Cornell University Press, 1983), pp. 337–354.

34. For discussions of collective goods, see John Conybeare, "Public Goods, Prisoners' Dilemmas and the International Political Economy," *International Studies Quarterly* 28, (1984), p. 5–22; and Russell Hardin, *Collective Action* (Baltimore: Johns Hopkins University Press, 1982).

35. Olson discusses nonexcludability in *The Logic of Collective Action.*

36. Mancur Olson and Richard Zeckhauser, "An Economic Theory of Alliances," *Review of Economics and Statistics* 48, no. 3 (August 1966), p. 266–279.

37. Duncan Snidal, "The Limits of Hegemonic Stability Theory," *International Organization* 39, no. 4 (Autumn 1985), pp. 579–614.

38. See Charles Kindleberger, *The World in Depression, 1929–1939* (Berkeley, CA: University of California Press, 1973).

39. The "Prisoners' Dilemma" game and its applicability to various aspects of international relations is discussed in Axelrod, *The Evolution of Cooperation.*

40. J.H. Maurer, "The Anglo-German Naval Rivalry and Informal Arms Control, 1912–1914," *Journal of Conflict Resolution* 36, no. 2 (June 1992), p. 285.

41. Deborah Welch Larson, "Crisis Prevention and the Austrian State Treaty," *International Organization* 41, no. 1 (Winter 1987), p. 32.

42. See Keohane, *After Hegemony;* or Stephen Krasner, ed., *International Regimes* (Ithaca, NY: Cornell University Press, 1983).

43. See Arthur Stein, "Coordination and Collaboration: Regimes in an Anarchic World," in *International Regimes*, edited by Stephen Krasner, pp. 115–140; and Jock A. Finlayson and Mark W. Zacher, "The GATT and the Regulation of Trade Barriers: Regime Dynamics and Functions," in the same volume, pp. 273–314.

44. Strange, "Cave! Hic Dragones: A Critique of Regime Theory."

45. Hedley Bull, *The Anarchical Society* (New York: Columbia University Press, 1977), p. 127.

46. Richard Rosecrance and Arthur Stein, "Interdependence: Myth or Reality?" *World Politics* 25, no. 3 (October 1973), pp. 1–27.

47. Waltz uses this definition in *Theory of International Politics.*

48. Both dimensions of interdependence are taken from Robert Keohane and Joseph Nye, *Power and Interdependence* (Boston: Scott, Foresman, 1989), p. 12–13.

49. Richard Rosecrance, *The Rise of the Trading State: Commerce and Conquest in the Modern World* (New York: Basic Books, 1986).

50. Rosecrance, *The Rise of the Trading State*, p. x.

51. Waltz, *Theory of International Politics*, p. 121.

Chapter 14

1. For an example of how the Cuban Missile Crisis decisions may be represented by a rational-actor model, see Graham Allison, *Essence of Decision* (Chicago: Scott Foresman, 1971). For details on what was said during ExComm meetings, see Marc Trachtenberg, ed., "White House Tapes and Minutes of the Cuban Missile Crisis," *International Security* 10, no. 1 (Summer 1985), pp. 164–203; and "October 27, 1962: Transcripts of the Meetings of the ExComm," *International Security* 12, no. 3 (Winter 1987/1988), pp. 30–92. For other perspectives on the crisis, see James G. Blight and David Welch, *On the Brink: Americans and Soviets Reexamine the Cuban Missile Crisis* (New York: Hill and Wang, 1989); and Bruce J. Allyn, James G. Blight, and David A. Welch, "Essence of Revision," *International Security* 14, no. 3 (Winter 1989–1990), pp. 136–172.

2. Quoted in *Kant's Political Writings*, ed. Hans Reiss (Cambridge, MA: Cambridge University Press, 1970), p. 100.

3. For examples of this argument, see Zeev Maoz and Nasrin Abdolali, "Regime Types and International Conflict," *Journal of Conflict Resolution* 33, no. 1 (March 1989), pp. 3–36; Harvey Starr, "Why Don't Democracies Fight One Another?" *Jerusalem Journal of International Relations* 14, no. 4 (December 1992), pp. 41–59; and Bruce M. Russett, *Grasping the Democratic Peace* (Princeton: Princeton University Press, 1993).

4. Michael Doyle, "Liberalism and World Politics," *American Political Science Review* 80, no. 4 (December 1986), pp. 1151–1169.

5. Steven Chan, "Mirror Mirror on the Wall: Are the

Freer Countries more Pacific?" *Journal of Conflict Resolution* 28, no. 4 (December 1984).

6. Stanislav Andreski, "On the Peaceful Disposition of Military Dictatorships," *Journal of Strategic Studies* 13, no. 3 (December 1980), pp. 3–10.

7. Allison presents the bureaucratic politics model in *Essence of Decision*, pp. 144–184. Not all analysts agree with the premises of the bureaucratic politics paradigm; for a contrary view, see Steven D. Krasner, "Are Bureaucracies Important? (Or Allison Wonderland)," *Foreign Policy* 7 (Summer 1972), pp. 159–179.

8. See for example, "China Computer Sale Causes Split," *Los Angeles Times*, December 5, 1992, A16. The State and Commerce Departments favored the proposed sale of a U.S. high-speed supercomputer to China, while the Defense Department sought to block it, warning of the computer's potential military uses.

9. Morton Halperin, "Why Bureaucrats Play Games," *Foreign Policy* 2 (Spring 1971), pp. 70–90.

10. For more on the Iraqi loan controversy, see U.S. House of Representatives, "Need for an Independent Counsel to Investigate U.S. Government Assistance to Iraq: Hearings before the Committee on the Judiciary" (Washington, DC: U.S. Government Printing Office, 1992); and Kenneth I. Juster, "The Myth of Iraqgate," *Foreign Policy* 94 (Spring 1994), pp. 105–119.

11. Quoted in Allison, *Essence of Decision*, p. 172.

12. Ibid., pp. 131–132.

13. Ibid., pp. 141–142.

14. This argument is advanced in Robert J. Art, "Bureaucratic Politics and American Foreign Policy: A Critique," *Policy Sciences* 4 (1973), pp. 467–490.

15. Quoted in Allison, *Essence of Decision*, p. 61.

16. See Trachtenberg, ed., "October 27, 1962."

17. See, for example, Anne Trotter, "Development of the 'Merchants of Death' Theory" in *War, Business, and American Society*, edited by Benjamin Franklin Cooling (New York: Kennikat Press, 1977), pp. 93–104; and Earl A. Molander, "Historical Antecedents of Military-Industrial Criticism" in the same book, pp. 171–187.

18. This charge is raised in C. Wright Mills, *The Power Elite* (New York: Oxford, 1956).

19. Cited in Trotter, pp. 93–94.

20. Walter LaFeber, *America, Russia, and the Cold War 1945–1990* (New York: McGraw-Hill, 1991), p. 198.

21. Tom Kemp, *The Climax of Capitalism: The U.S. Economy in the Twentieth Century* (London: Longman, 1990), pp. 163–164.

22. See John H. Aldrich, John Sullivan, Eugene Borgida, "Foreign Affairs and Issue Voting: Do Presidential Candidates 'Waltz Before a Blind Audience?'" *American Political Science Review* 83, no. 1 (March 1989), pp. 123–141; K. T. Gaubatz, "Election Cycles and War," *Journal of Conflict Resolution* 35 (1991), pp. 212–244; and Barry Hughes,

The Domestic Contents of American Foreign Policy (San Francisco: Freeman, 1978).

23. This theme is developed in Louis Hartz, *The Liberal Tradition in America* (New York: Harcourt Brace Jovanovich, 1991); and Stanley Hoffmann, *Gulliver's Troubles, or the Setting of American Foreign Policy* (New York: McGraw-Hill, 1968).

24. John O'Sullivan, cited in Frederick Merk, *Manifest Destiny and Mission in American History* (New York: Vintage, 1963), p. 259.

25. Hartz, *The Liberal Tradition in America*, pp. 285–286.

26. Hoffmann, *Gulliver's Troubles*, pp. 178–181.

27. Ibid., p. 201.

28. Samuel P. Huntington, "The Clash of Civilizations?" *Foreign Affairs* 72, no. 3 (Summer 1993), p. 48.

29. For more on the role of ideology in the origins of the Cold War, see Chapter Four.

30. For a selection of views on the role of ethnic conflict in world politics, see Michael E. Brown, ed., *Ethnic Conflict and International Security* (Princeton, NJ: Princeton University Press, 1993).

31. Ethnic warfare is discussed further in Manus A. Midlarsky, ed., *The Internationalization of Communal Strife* (New York: Routledge, 1993); and Roy Licklider, ed., *Stopping the Killing: How Civil Wars End* (New York: NYU Press, 1993).

32. For examples of the viability of multiethnic democracies, see Arend Lijphart, *Democracy in Plural Societies* (New Haven, CT: Yale University Press, 1977).

33. Jack Snyder discusses the difference between civic and ethnic nationalism in "Nationalism and the Crisis of the Post-Soviet State" in *Ethnic Conflict and International Security*, pp. 79–101.

Chapter 15

1. George Herek, Irving Janis, and Paul Huth, "Decision Making During International Crises: Is Quality of Process Related to Outcome?" *Journal of Conflict Resolution* 31, no. 2 (June 1987), pp. 203–226.

2. From a speech by Ronald Reagan to the National Association of Evangelicals, March 8, 1983, in Strobe Talbott, *The Russians and Reagan* (New York: Vintage, 1984), p. 116.

3. Miriam Steiner, "Human Nature and Trust as World Order Issues," *International Organization* 34, no. 3 (Summer 1980), pp. 335–353.

4. "The Doctrine and Discipline of Divorce," in *The Works of John Milton*, vol. III, part II (New York: Columbia University Press, 1931), p. 381.

5. Thomas Hobbes, *Leviathan*, edited Michael Oakeshott (New York: Macmillan, 1962), pp. 80, 100.

6. Hans J. Morgenthau, *Scientific Man vs. Power Politics* (Chicago: University of Chicago Press, 1946), pp. 192–200.

7. Reinhold Niebuhr, *Christianity and Power Politics* (New York: Charles Scribner's Sons, 1940), p. 4.

8. Konrad Lorenz, *On Aggression* (New York: Harcourt Brace Jovanovich, 1966), p. 129.

9. Waltz, *Man, the State, and War*, p. 42.

10. Longfellow, cited in Waltz, *Man, the State, and War*, p. 16.

11. Bertrand Russell, *Political Ideals* (New York: Century, 1917), p. 42.

12. Margaret Mead, *And Keep Your Powder Dry* (New York: Morrow, 1942), pp. 235–259ff.

13. Dwight D. Eisenhower, address to the National Council of Catholic Women, *New York Times*, November 9, 1954.

14. Beverly Nichols, *Cry Havoc!* (New York: Doubleday, 1933).

15. Waltz, *Man, the State, and War*, p. 46.

16. William Borberg, "On Active Service for Peace," *Bulletin of the World Federation for Mental Health* 2 (1950), pp. 6–9.

17. Karl Deutsch, "The Growth of Nations: Some Recurrent Patterns of Political and Social Integration," *World Politics* 5 (1953), p. 185.

18. Examples of feminist perspectives on international relations may be found in Helen Caldicott, *Missile Envy: The Arms Race and Nuclear War*, 2d ed. (New York: Bantam, 1986); Rebecca Grant and Kathleen Newland, eds., *Gender and International Relations* (London: Open University Press, 1991); and V. Spike Peterson, ed., *Gendered States: Feminist (Re)visions of International Relations Theory* (Boulder, CO: Lynne Rienner, 1992). For a discussion of the impact of male domination on women's behavior, see Mary Daly, *Gyn/Ecology: The Metaethics of Radical Feminism* (Boston, Beacon Press, 1978).

19. On the impact of uncertainty and information overload, see Irving Janis and Leon Mann, *Decision Making: A Psychological Analysis of Conflict, Choice, and Commitment* (Boston: Houghton Mifflin, 1983); and Ole R. Holsti, "Models of International Relations and Foreign Policy," *Diplomatic History* 13, no. 1 (Winter 1989), p. 36ff. For more on the effects of value complexity, see Alexander L. George, *Presidential Decisionmaking in Foreign Policy: The Effective Use of Information and Advice* (Boulder, CO: Westview, 1980); and Fred Wehling, "The Dilemma of Superpower: Soviet Decision Making in the Six-Day War" in *Conflict Management in the Middle East*, edited by Steven L. Spiegel (Boulder, CO: Westview, 1992), pp. 175–216.

20. Nathan Leites, *The Operational Code of the Politburo* (New York: McGraw-Hill, 1951).

21. See Leites, *The Operational Code;* and Alexander George, "The 'Operational Code': A Neglected Approach to the Study of Political Leaders and Decision-Making," *International Studies Quarterly* 13, no. 2 (June 1969), p. 197.

22. This chapter's outline of the belief systems of Bolshevik leaders are based on George, "The 'Operational Code': A Neglected Approach"; and Leites, *The Operational Code.*

23. For more on Soviet perceptions of risk in crises, see Hannes Adomeit, *Soviet Risk-Taking and Crisis Behavior* (London: Allen & Unwin, 1982).

24. For example, see Stephen Walker, "The Interface between Beliefs and Behavior: Henry Kissinger's Operational Code and the Vietnam War," *Journal of Conflict Resolution* 21, no. 1 (March 1977), pp. 129–161; Ole Holsti, "The Operational Code Approach to the Study of Political Leaders: John Foster Dulles' Philosophical and Instrumental Beliefs," *Canadian Journal of Political Science* 3 (1970), pp. 123–157.

25. See George, *Presidential Decisionmaking*, pp. 42–48; and Michael Brecher with Benjamin Geist, *Decisions in Crisis* (Berkeley, CA: University of California Press, 1980).

26. Robert F. Kennedy, *Thirteen Days* (New York: Norton, 1969), p. 22.

27. Theodore Sorensen, *Decision Making in the White House* (New York: Columbia University Press, 1964), p. 76.

28. George, *Presidential Decisionmaking*, p. 48.

29. Richard Ned Lebow, *Nuclear Crisis Management: A Dangerous Illusion* (Ithaca, NY: Cornell University Press, 1987), p. 144.

30. Ibid., pp. 144–145.

31. Georgii Zhukov, *The Memoirs of Marshal Zhukov* (New York: Delacorte, 1971), pp. 234–238.

32. Ivan Maisky, cited in Adam Ulam, *Expansion and Coexistence* (New York: Praeger, 1968), p. 315.

33. Voitech Mastny, "Stalin and the Prospects of a Separate Peace in World War II," *American Historical Review* 77 (December 1972), pp. 1365–1388.

34. Peter Suedfeld and Philip Tetlock, "Integrative Complexity of Communications in International Crises," *Journal of Conflict Resolution* 21 (March 1977), pp. 169–184. See also Holsti, "Models of International Relations," p. 39.

35. Suedfeld and Tetlock, "Integrative Complexity."

36. See Leon Festinger, *A Theory of Cognitive Dissonance* (Stanford, CA: Stanford University Press, 1957); and Deborah Welch Larson, *Origins of Containment: A Psychological Explanation* (Princeton: Princeton University Press, 1985), p. 29ff.

37. George, *Presidential Decisionmaking*, p. 68.

38. Ibid., p. 64.

39. Larson, *Origins of Containment*, p. 32.

40. These and others are mentioned in George, *Presidential Decisionmaking*, pp. 64–66.

41. Ibid., pp. 32–33.

42. Janis and Mann, *Decision Making*, pp. 88–133.

43. George, *Presidential Decisionmaking*, pp. 36–37; and Richard K. Betts, *Nuclear Blackmail and Nuclear Balance* (Washington, DC: Brookings, 1987), pp. 54–62, 68–79.

44. Janis and Mann, *Decision Making*, pp. 82–95.

45. Larson, *Origins of Containment*, p. 35.

46. George, *Presidential Decisionmaking*, p. 58; and Larson, *Origins of Containment*, pp. 37–38.

47. Quoted in Holsti, "Models of International Relations," p. 37.

48. Larson, *Origins of Containment*, p. 38.

49. Adapted from Daniel Heradstveit, *The Arab-Israeli Conflict: Psychological Obstacles to Peace* (Oslo: Universitetsforlaget, 1979), pp. 48–75.

50. Robert Jervis, *Perception and Misperception in International Politics* (Princeton: Princeton University Press, 1976), pp. 343–355.
51. George, *Presidential Decisionmaking*, p. 66. See also Holsti, "Models of International Relations," pp. 37–38.
52. Richard Neustadt, *Alliance Politics* (New York: Columbia University Press, 1970), p. 115.
53. George, *Presidential Decisionmaking*, pp. 59–60; and Larson, *Origins of Containment*, pp. 39–40.
54. Ernest R. May, *"Lessons" of the Past: The Use and Misuse of History in American Foreign Policy* (New York: Oxford University Press, 1973), pp. 44–45.
55. George, *Decisionmaking*, pp. 60–61.
56. Larson, *Origins of Containment*, pp. 50–57.
57. Jervis, *Perception and Misperception*, pp. 266–270.
58. For more on the use of historical analogies to inform and misinform decision making, see Richard E Neustadt and Ernest R. May, *Thinking in Time: The Uses of History for Decision-Makers* (New York: Free Press, 1986).
59. Quoted in Gordon A. Craig and Alexander L. George, *Force and Statecraft: Diplomatic Problems of Our Time* (New York: Oxford University Press, 1983), p. 52.
60. Larson, *Origins of Containment*, p. 56.
61. Henry Kissinger, *White House Years* (Boston: Little, Brown, 1979), p. 622; and *Years of Upheaval* (Boston: Little, Brown, 1982), pp. 583–588.
62. Quoted in Douglas Jehl and James Gerstenzang, "The Mind of the President," *Los Angeles Times Magazine*, October 11, 1992, p. 62.
63. Arthur Goldschmidt, Jr., *A Concise History of the Middle East* (Boulder, CO: Westview, 1979), p. 281.
64. Carl Brown, *International Politics and the Middle East: Old Rules, Dangerous Game* (Princeton: Princeton University Press, 1984), p. 164.
65. Khrushchev tells his own story in three volumes of memoirs, *Khrushchev Remembers* (Boston: Little, Brown, 1970), *Khrushchev Remembers: The Last Testament* (Boston: Little, Brown, 1974), and *Khrushchev Remembers: The Glasnost Tapes* (Boston: Little, Brown, 1990). A more balanced appraisal of his years in power may be found in Roy A. Medvedev, *Khrushchev* (Garden City, NY: Anchor, 1983).
66. For an assessment of Brezhnev's leadership at the height of his power, see John Dornberg, *Brezhnev: The Masks of Power* (New York: Basic Books, 1974). George Breslauer compares the styles of the two Soviet premiers in *Khrushchev and Brezhnev as Leaders* (London: Allen & Unwin, 1982).
67. Michael Roskin, "From Pearl Harbor to Vietnam: Shifting Generational Paradigms and Foreign Policy," *Political Science Quarterly* 89, no. 3, (Fall 1974), pp. 563–587.
68. Lebow, *Between Peace and War*, pp. 247–254.
69. Stephen Van Evera, "The Cult of the Offensive and the Origins of the First World War," *International Security* 9 (Summer 1984), pp. 58–107.
70. Lawrence Martin, *The Presidents and the Prime Ministers* (New York: Doubleday, 1982).
71. Robert Dallek, *The American Style of Foreign Policy: Cultural Politics and Foreign Affairs* (New York: Oxford University Press, 1983), p. 284.

Chapter 16

1. The ancient and modern challenges faced by all states in the contemporary world are discussed in Paul Kennedy, *Preparing for the Twenty-First Century* (New York: Random House, 1993).
2. This chapter's discussion of high-technology states follows Richard Rosecrance, *The Rise of the Trading State* (New York: Basic Books, 1986).
3. John Mueller takes this position in *Retreat from Doomsday: The Obsolescence of Major War* (New York: Basic Books, 1989).
4. See, for example, Christopher Layne, "The Unipolar Illusion: Why New Great Powers Will Rise," *International Security* 17, no. 4 (Spring 1993), pp. 5–51.
5. Richard Rosecrance discusses this possibility in "A New Concert of Powers," *Foreign Affairs* 71, no. 2 (Spring 1992), pp. 64–82.

Glossary

Absolute advantage
A situation in which one country is more efficient than others in producing a certain good. One party can have an absolute advantage in all goods.

Absolute power
In contrast to relative power, the amount of power a state possesses without regard to other states in the international system.

Agitational terror
Terrorist activities of nationalist or opposition groups against a general audience.

Air-launched cruise missile
A cruise missile launched from an airplane. *See* cruise missile.

Amnesty International (AI)
A humanitarian NGO that works on behalf of prisoners of conscience around the world. It seeks the release of political prisoners and the abolition of torture, investigates abuses of human rights, and organizes campaigns for the release of persons jailed for political activity.

Anarchy
A concept of systems theory contending that the international system is chaotic and unpredictable, with no legitimate international law-enforcement mechanism.

Anti-ballistic missile (ABM)
A missile designed to destroy incoming missiles or their warheads before they hit the designated targets.

Appeasement
One-sided concessions to a potential opponent.

Arable land
Land usable for agriculture.

Arms control
Agreements between two or more states or unilateral actions to regulate the research, manufacture, or deployment of weapons or troops on the basis of number, type, and/or location.

ASEAN Free Trade Area (AFTA)
A fifteen-year plan launched by the members of the Association of Southeast Asian Nations (ASEAN) in 1992 in response to fears that NAFTA and the EU would divert global investment to Europe and North America. This plan calls for reducing tariffs among members on products in 15 categories.

Asia-Pacific Economic Cooperation (APEC)
A loose conglomeration of more than a 12 Pacific Rim countries, including the United States, China, Japan, and Australia, that concentrates on improving economic ties and cooperation.

Association of Southeast Asian Nations (ASEAN)
A general purpose IGO founded in 1967 that encourages peaceful cooperation and economic development among its members (Brunei, Indonesia, Malaysia, the Philippines, Singapore, and Thailand).

Asymmetric interdependence
A description of the economic relationship between the North and the South, in which the South is less able to adapt to changing economic conditions than the North.

Atomic weapon
An explosive device that derives its power from nuclear fission, or the "splitting" of atoms (uranium or plutonium).

Attribution theory
A theory whereby decision makers attempt to discern the attributes of other actors, to infer the

causes of salient events, and to predict historical trends and the behavior of other people, all to understand and exercise more control over the outcomes of particular situations; decision makers are seen to be "problem solvers" or "naive scientists."

Balance of payments
The "balance sheet" of a nation's transactions with the rest of the world. These national accounts tell us a country's trade balance (exports of goods and services minus imports of goods and services), how much money locals earned overseas, the amount of foreign currency invested in the domestic economy, the level of official foreign aid given to other countries, and the amount of foreign currency held by the central bank.

Balance of power
A system of international relations in which states seek security through internal buildup of power or alliances with other states. Used to prevent one state (or group of states) from accumulating too much power. An equilibrium, or at least a rough equivalent used specifically in reference to the relative economic and military strength of nations, by which stability can be achieved. According to some analysts, a condition of equilibrium reduces the likelihood of war or domination.

Balfour Declaration
A statement issued by Great Britain in 1917 promising support of a Jewish homeland in Palestine as long as the "civil and religious rights" of existing non-Jewish communities there were not prejudiced.

Ballistic missile
A missile that "coasts" to its target on a free-falling trajectory following a period of powered flight.

Bandwagoning
An alliance in which a state, instead of joining a counter-balancing coalition, joins the stronger state or coalition.

Baruch Plan
A post–World War II proposal that would have placed all atomic energy activities under the control of an international atomic development authority. This proposal was rejected by the USSR primarily because it would have made permanent the existing U.S. monopoly over nuclear weapons.

Beggar-thy-neighbor policy
A situation where Country B raises tariffs on Country A's goods in retaliation for Country A raising its tariffs on Country B's exports. These countervailing tariffs can eventually lead to declining international trade.

Belief systems
A conviction that certain ideas are true, including basic values like morals, religious beliefs, and the fundamental philosophies by which policy makers operate.

Bilateral aid
Direct aid in the form of grants or loans from a single developed country to a specific developing state, typically handled by governments of the donor and the recipient.

Biological weapon
A germ or bacteria-based weapon, also known as a "living weapon," that spreads disease, infection, or toxins.

Bipolar system (Bipolarity)
An international system dominated by two actors of relatively equal power that overshadow all of the rest.

Bismarckian system
A succession of alliances sought by Otto von Bismarck in the twenty years after his defeat of France in 1871; these were pursued to moderate the demands of Germany's allies, prevent the formation of opposing coalitions, and prevent local conflicts from escalating into general war.

Blitzkrieg
Literally translated as "lightning war." The Nazi employment of this strategy included armor and air attacks that were directed at overwhelming the intended target in a quick victory.

Blue Helmets
UN peacekeeping and truce supervision forces dispatched at the invitation of parties to a local conflict. Their primary mission is to serve as armed sentries, separating combatants in order to make violation of a peace agreement more difficult. Also known as "Blue Berets," they wear UN headgear but retain their respective national uniforms.

Bolstering
A form of defensive avoidance that sometimes occurs when decision makers cannot extend a decision over a lengthy period of time; they increase the attractiveness of a preferred option, despite possible costs.

Bretton Woods system
See International Bank for Reconstruction and Development, and International Monetary Fund.

Buck-passing
The temptation by members of an alliance to avoid the high cost in lives and equipment of fighting an opposing power by letting other members confront the threatening state.

Buffer stocks
Funds provided to countries that participate in international commodity agreements and experience balance of payment difficulties due to fluctuations in the price of primary goods.

Bureaucratic politics model
A model of decision making which sees foreign policy outcomes as a result of political competition (turf battles) among government agencies, not the rational value-maximizing calculation of the state's interest or the simple output of an organizational SOP. Therefore, a bureaucrat's policy stance depends on his organizational affiliation and a desire to protect agency interests as he strives to maintain and improve its position in the government. This results in policy made through "pulling and hauling" among bureaucratic chiefs.

Capability
The aspect of deterrence that refers to the ability to do great harm to an aggressor. A state's ability to retaliate against a challenger should the defending nation deem the challenger's actions to be unacceptable. Also used more broadly as the capacity to act in world politics.

Capital-intensive technology
Highly advanced equipment that lessens the need for manual labor. Frequently brought by MNCs to developing countries.

Capitalism
A belief that the means of production of goods and services should be owned privately, so that the desire for profit will lead to greater efficiency and thus benefit both consumers and producers.

Casualties
Members of the armed forces who have been killed, wounded, captured, are interned, sick or missing, and, therefore, no longer a part of active duty.

Chain-ganging
The danger that a state, by virtue of its membership in an alliance, might be dragged into a war which it has no interest in fighting.

Chemical weapon
A weapon that uses a chemical agent to kill or disable military personnel and civilians. These weapons consist of poisoned gases, mists, and powders, and can only be effective when they come into contact with people.

Chlorofluorocarbons (CFCs)
A primary agent of ozone depletion found mostly in aerosols and refrigerants.

Classical realism
A philosophy that the international system is anarchic, and that each state must protect its own vital interests, political independence, and territorial sovereignty at any cost.

Cognitive bias
A psychological bias related to the cognition, or reasoning, processes that attempt to make new information fit into an individual's preexisting knowledge and beliefs.

Cognitive consistency
An attempt by people to simplify difficult decisions by changing the facts to fit their theories.

Cognitive dissonance
A situation in which consistency seekers attempt to maintain their beliefs in the face of discordant information.

Cognitive restructuring
A situation in which decision makers set aside information that calls attention to or aggravates a value conflict.

Collective action problem
A complication with collective arrangements which refers to the problem that all member states might pass responsibility to other members of the coalition rather than abide by their commitments.

Collective defense
Coalitions of states that band together to protect member states from outside aggression.

Collective security
A system of mutual action to ensure global security in which an agreement is reached between a group of states that provides for unified opposition to any member state that illegally violates the peace.

Colonialism
A policy by which a nation maintains or extends its control over foreign dependencies. The two main types of colonialism are (1) movement of people from the mother country to form a new political institution in the designated distant land, and (2) ruling of the less-developed indigenous peoples by outside powers.

Commitment
The first step in deterrence that must be stated clearly and unambiguously before a challenger carries out an act of aggression. The defending state must make clear its determination to punish a challenger if the challenger takes a specified action that the defender considers unacceptable (such as drawing a line in the sand).

Commodity cartels
Southern nations producing a particular product that have banded together in the hope of increasing their collective bargaining power, the most famous being OPEC (Organization of Petroleum-Exporting Countries).

Common markets
Political or economic organizations characterized by common external trade barriers and uniform internal trade barriers.

Commonwealth of Independent States (CIS)
The organization of successor states to the former Soviet Union.

Communism
In theory, the organization of society—based on collective ownership of the means of production—that assumes an equitable distribution of goods, services, and wealth. In practice, the organization of both the society and polity based on a centralized and totalitarian state which owns all property. A privileged elite controls the state in the name of the workers.

Comparative advantage
A situation where even when one country has an absolute advantage over all goods produced abroad, that country benefits from trade by specializing in its most efficiently produced domestic goods and purchasing other goods abroad.

Compellence
A strategy that attempts to force an adversary to reverse some action that has already been undertaken. Compellence is almost always more difficult than deterrence because the defender must convince or force an adversary to retreat.

Concert of Europe
A special system of consultation utilized by the great powers of Europe after the Napoleonic Wars. A great power could initiate international conferences when it believed that the security and peace of Europe were compromised.

Conditionality
Requirements, in the form of economic reforms, attached to loans from international lending institutions to developing countries.

Conference on Security and Cooperation in Europe (CSCE)
Created in 1975 as part of the Helsinki negotiations, CSCE is composed of most NATO and ex-Warsaw Pact nations, including the United States, Canada, and Russia. Its purpose is to guarantee European security and human rights.

Containment
U.S. foreign policy during the Cold War aimed at halting Soviet expansion through American military and economic power.

Contras
Anticommunist rebels and counter-revolutionary opponents of the 1980s Nicaraguan Sandinistas, organized and armed by the CIA, that were supported by the Reagan administration even after Congress prohibited direct military aid.

Conventional weapon
A non-nuclear weapon such as a tank, artillery piece, or tactical aircraft (troops that operate these weapons are referred to as conventional forces).

Corn Laws
A set of tariffs and other restrictions on agricultural imports that protected British landowners in the late 1700s and early 1800s. Repeal of these laws in 1846 helped facilitate a boom in international trade.

Council of Mutual Economic Assistance (CMEA)
A Soviet-led institution that solidified trade relations in the East during the Cold War.

Counter-balancing coalition
A way to balance a potentially dominant power by which all or most of the remaining states form an alliance to quickly aggregate capability to deter the preponderant power or, upon failure, to prepare for war in order to restore the balance of power.

Credibility
The resolve and willingness of the defending state to carry out its commitment to punish the unacceptable actions of the aggressor state. One aspect of deterrence, credibility is necessary to convince an adversary that its capabilities will be used if the adversary attacks.

Cruise missile
A missile that resembles a pilotless aircraft and that flies on a horizontal trajectory. This missile operates completely within the earth's atmosphere and may be launched from the air, the ground, or the sea and can carry either a conventional, chemical, or nuclear warhead.

Cult of the Offensive
A belief of strategic analysts before World War I that the party which attacked first would win, encouraging immediate mobilization and attack in case of a crisis.

Current account balance
The sum total of a nation's imports, exports, foreign aid, and other government transactions, and investment income and payments.

Customary practices
International customs represent the established and consistent practices of states in international relations; one of the main sources of international law.

Dawes Plan
A plan to alleviate the economic pressure on Germany caused by reparations imposed after World War I. Under this agreement, American banks would lend money to Germany for its reparations payments to the Allies. These payments could then be transferred to the U.S. government from the Allies in order to service war loans.

De facto recognition
Provisional and indefinite recognition by the government of one state that the government or regime in control of a second state has authoritative power.

De jure recognition
Complete and unquestioned recognition of one government by another as the legal government.

Deconcentration
A stage in long-cycle theory in which a dominant power is challenged by emerging rivals.

Defense
A strategy that attempts to reduce an enemy's capability to damage or take something away from the defender. The purpose is to resist an attack and minimize losses after deterrence has failed. Defense is physical and intended to rebuff the challenger.

Defensive avoidance
A situation in which individual decision makers try to eliminate psychological tension that accompanies a need to make choices in the face of uncertainty by attempting to avoid making a decision.

Delegitimitation
A stage in long-cycle theory in which the costs associated with global leadership contribute to a dominant power's relative decline.

Demographic transition
A change from the high birth and death rates characteristic of traditional societies to the low rates associated with industrialized nations; typically occurs until birth and death rates stabilize at lower levels.

Dependency theory
A theory of international economics, following upon the works of Karl Marx, that views the world as divided between industrialized "core" countries and underdeveloped "periphery" countries. It focuses on a country's assigned role in the global economic system, where the core exploits the periphery and stunts industrialization.

Dependicistas
Supporters of dependency theory.

Desertification
The process by which an area becomes a desert. The rapid depletion of plant life and topsoil at desert boundaries and in semiarid regions, usually caused by a combination of drought and overexploitation by humans of grasses and other vegetation. Also called desertization.

Détente
French for "relaxation of tensions," the reduction of tensions between two or more countries. During the Cold War, détente between the United States and Soviet Union referred to cooperation on areas such as arms control, trade, and technology.

Deterrence
The attempt to prevent war by discouraging a potential aggressor. The primary goal of the defender is to convince the challenger that the probable cost of attacking will far exceed any anticipated gain. For deterrence to function effectively, the defender must signal its commitment to punish or retaliate and possess the capability to do so in order to demonstrate the credibility of the deterrent threat. Deterrence is psychological and intended to influence the challenger's decision-making process.

Diplomatic immunity
Freedom from arrest and prosecution for accredited diplomats.

Disarmament
The reduction or elimination of a state's overall arms levels.

Dissociative reaction
A reaction to extreme stress where a person's thoughts, feelings, or actions are not associated or integrated with relevant information.

Domestic level of analysis
A method of analyzing international relations according to the unique characteristics of specific nation-states, including government institutions, society, and the links between them.

Domino theory
A belief that if one country is taken over by the enemy, that country's neighbors will also be taken over one after another, thus upsetting the local balance of power.

Dumping
A situation in which one country sells (dumps) its products on a foreign market at a price below the cost of production, thereby harming another country's domestic producers.

East Asian Economic Caucus (EAEC)
A group of newly industrialized East Asian nations, the activities of which are devoted to rapid economic growth in their region.

Economic and Social Council (ECOSOC)
A UN organ responsible for coordinating the work of the UN "family" of more specialized agencies and organizations.

Economic bloc
An economic arrangement between states designed to promote high levels of internal cooperation and to enhance competitiveness with the rest of the world.

Economic interdependence
The mutual dependence of national economies.

Ecopolitics
A new paradigm in international relations that emerged in the 1970s which argues that human needs, such as the environment and control over natural resources, are displacing the competition for power among governments as the central concern of world politics.

Empire
A situation where a single state dominates other states in the international system to the extent that they are legally subordinate to the dominant state.

Enforcement terror
Terrorism carried out by a government or a government-backed agency against its own citizens.

Eradication
A method for restricting the supply of illegal drugs. It consists of destroying crops that are eventually processed into illegal drugs.

European Community
See European Union.

European Free Trade Area (EFTA)
Originally founded in 1959 by the British as a counterweight to the French-dominated EEC. Most members are now members of the EU or have applied for membership.

European Union
The world's most highly integrated economic bloc. Originally known as the European Economic Community (EEC) and later as the European Community (EC), it was organized in the 1957 Treaty of Rome.

Export-led industrialization
The promotion of development by working within, rather than against, the global economic system through emphasizing export production as an engine for economic growth.

Extended deterrence
A policy that seeks to discourage a challenger from attacking an ally or a partner.

External subsidies
Government payments that allow producers to compete in the international market.

Extradition
A process wherein a country surrenders an individual accused of a crime to another country for trial.

Factor approach
An analytical framework for understanding how conditions in the international economy affect domestic politics. Factor approach hypothesizes that every society has three basic interest groups: landholders, capital owners, and workers. Conflicts arise between those groups that benefit from international conditions and those that are harmed.

Fascism
A doctrine promoted by the far right seeking an authoritarian society built around the rule of an elite led by a dictator or supreme leader. Fascists usually gain power through a coup d'état during a period of revolution, or as a consequence of economic crises.

First strike
Ability to destroy or decisively weaken an opponent's strategic weapons, or prevent retaliation with an initial attack.

First World
Industrialized countries of North America, Western Europe, and Japan that account for four-fifths of global GNP (with one-fifth of the world's population), characterized by export of services and manufactured goods and by high standards of living.

Fixed exchange rate system
A regime in which nations agree to establish a set of currency rules. All currencies in this system are valued at fixed rates against each other. Two examples of this system are the Gold Standard (1870–1914) and the Bretton Woods system (1945–1973). This regime makes the international economy more stable and predictable, but it can also force governments to pursue harmful policies when the currency's value goes in one direction and the economy's health in the other.

Flexible Response
A Kennedy administration strategy that replaced the Massive Retaliation doctrine of the Eisenhower administration. This revised strategy called for sufficient NATO military capability to counter Soviet offensives at each step of the escalation ladder: the conventional level, the battlefield nuclear level, and the strategic nuclear level.

Floating exchange rate system
The value (price) of a currency is allowed to fluctuate in relation to other currencies. This regime accurately reflects an economy's well-being but it also creates additional uncertainty in the world economy.

Food and Agriculture Organization (FAO)
A UN humanitarian organization under the ECOSOC umbrella.

Foreign policy
The actions and positions on key issues taken by an individual state regarding other states or groups outside its boundaries.

Fossil fuels
Forms of energy—oil, coal, and natural gas—that are derived from the remains of living organisms.

Fragmentation
Breakup of a country or other governing body.

Free trade areas
Economic arrangements that are generally characterized by uniform internal trade barriers among members states.

Free trade
International movement of goods based on supply and demand without government intervention.

Free ride
The use of a public good without making any contribution to its upkeep.

Fundamental attribution error
Explaining one's own inappropriate behavior with situational variables (related to circumstance beyond one's control) while attributing an adversary's undesirable actions to dispositional variables (related to one's character or fundamental goals). On the other hand, one's own appropriate behavior is explained using dispositional variables while the opponent's good behavior is seen in situational terms.

General Agreement on Tariffs and Trade (GATT)
An agreement established in 1947 to encourage freer trade. Several rounds of GATT rules negotiations since its founding have progressively lowered tariffs and nontariff barriers to trade among member states.

General deterrence
This long-term strategy operates at all times and attempts to prevent an adversary from attempting any kind of military challenge because of its expected consequences.

Generational experience
A phenomenon in which a group of political leaders are influenced by the events and experiences of the generation to which they belong.

Glasnost
Russian for "openness," referring to the political policies that followed Mikhail Gorbachev's 1985 rise to power in the USSR. Gorbachev increased political freedom dramatically, freed a number of political prisoners, and loosened state control of the news media.

Globalization
A process by which increasing interdependence and communication between states and varying parts of the world lead to shared experiences and common identification of global issues.

Gold Standard
A fixed exchange rate system where each nation's currency value is set to gold. The periods between 1870–1914 and 1945–1971 were at least partial examples of Gold Standard systems.

Great power
A state that possesses, exercises, and defends interests throughout the world. Great-power status may be quantitative, such as a certain level of GNP or the size of its armed forces. It may instead be qualitative, demonstrated by a high level of industrialization or the capability to make and use nuclear weapons. Great powers may also be distinguished by institutional recognition, such as that accorded by the League of Nations or by the UN.

Great power unanimity
A concept which holds that on all resolutions and proposals before the UN Security Council, a veto by any one of the five permanent members (China, France, the United Kingdom, Russia, and the United States) will kill any proposal.

Greenhouse effect
An increase in the earth's average temperature caused by the emission of "greenhouse gases" (especially carbon dioxide and methane), that trap and retain the sun's heat in the atmosphere.

Gross Domestic Product (GDP)
The total sum of goods and services produced by a nation, not including goods and services produced abroad by domestic individuals or firms.

Gross National Product (GNP)
The total sum of all goods and services produced by a nation.

Ground-launched cruise missile
A cruise missile launched from land. *See* cruise missile.

Group of Seven (G7)
The seven leading industrialized member nations of the Organization for Economic Cooperation and Development (OECD). Members include the United States, the United Kingdom, France, Germany, Italy, Canada, and Japan. The leaders and economic ministers of member nations meet regularly to discuss economic policy and resolve their differences.

Guerrilla warfare
An irregular style of warfare fought by small groups against a larger invading army or an established government.

Hegemonic stability theory
A theory stating that a global hegemon, in an international system, allows for more stability than a system based on several great powers. Acting in its own interests, this dominant "hegemon" sets and enforces rules for the global economy. In a hegemonic period the international economic system works because a dominant state pays the costs of providing economic stabilizers (free flow of international goods, providing international security arrangements, and stabilizing world currencies).

Hegemony/Hegemon/Hegemonic theory
The dominant military and economic power among states within a regional or global system.

Heuristics
Rules-of-thumb, or mental shortcuts, used in processing large flows of information to assess the likelihood that certain policy options will be successful.

High politics
Part of the realist paradigm of the systemic level of analysis that places emphasis on national security issues over economic and other domestic issues.

High technology states (21st-century style)
The most advanced participants in international relations. These states emphasize economic instead of military competition; states gain power through trade and internal sources of development rather than through territorial acquisition.

Hydroelectricity
Electricity generated by water power, a frequently touted alternate energy source.

Hydrogen bomb
A thermonuclear weapon that uses hydrogen atoms in a fusion reaction to produce an energy release. These weapons require a fission reaction to achieve a temperature high enough to have the hydrogen atoms react.

Hyperinflation
A situation with an extreme, rapid, and uncontrolled rise in prices. Also, an uncontrollable decline in the value of a currency.

Idealism
A set of beliefs rooted in the assumption that cooperation is possible in the international system. The game of international relations may not always be zero-sum; interdependence may make it necessary and possible for countries to collaborate in order to solve common problems. If the structure of the international system or human nature leads to recurrent conflict, perhaps either or both can be improved in order to create an environment more favorable to cooperation.

Ideology
The set of beliefs on which states and groups within states base their actions. It shapes a state's political institutions and its political, social, and economic relations.

Imbalance of power
An unequal distribution of capability between states in which one state or coalition dominates the international system.

Immediate deterrence
A strategy of response to specific and explicit challenges to a state's interests.

Imperialism
A superior–inferior relationship in which one state controls the people and territory of another area.

Import quotas
Trade barriers erected by a state to limit the number of imports from the rest of the world.

Import substitution industrialization
An attempt to industrialize by protecting domestic industries from foreign imports via price protection, thereby mitigating competition.

Imported conflicts
Conflicts that are extensions of Northern ideas and problems that affect conditions in the South.

Indigenous conflicts
Conflicts that have long histories in a society, predating the era of European imperialism.

Individual level of analysis
A method of analyzing international relations that focuses on the skills, beliefs, personalities, and unique characteristics of the leaders who make decisions within each state. It considers what role, if any, "human nature" plays in world affairs and whether or not it can be changed to make the world a less conflictual and violent place.

Indivisibility
A characteristic of public goods in which one member's consumption of a good does not reduce the amount available to others.

Industrial pollution
Environmental ills such as smog, acid rain, and high levels of carbon dioxide and chlorofluorocarbons (CFCs) caused by urbanization and industrialization.

Infant mortality rate
The ratio of infants who die before reaching their first birthday versus those who survive; usually higher in developing countries.

Influence
A political actor's ability to impact the behavior of others in a direction it favors.

Integrative complexity
When one's integrative complexity is high, one can make subtle distinctions, respond more flexibly, and consider large amounts of information. When one's integrative complexity is low, one tends to think in all-or-nothing terms and is less open to compromise; a reaction to stress.

Intercontinental ballistic missile (ICBM)
A land-based missile able to deliver a nuclear payload to a target more than 3400 miles away (in practical terms, capable of going directly from the United States to Russia or vice versa).

Interdependence
As nations modernize and society becomes more complex, states begin to interact more frequently with other states for a variety of reasons and in a variety of ways, such as trade and diplomacy. Economies become linked to those of other states, creating an interrelatedness of the societies of the world in relation to socioeconomic and technological issues. The nations of the world are mutually sensitive and vulnerable, thus they will behave to attain cooperation rather than conflict over security issues.

Interdiction
A method for restricting the supply of drugs, it entails stopping shipments, usually via customs inspections, before they enter the country.

Interest groups
A group of people who share a common belief and seek government support. These groups operate through lobbying activities with the help of paid professionals.

Intergovernmental organizations (IGOs)
Groups of states or governments created through treaties and organized for a common purpose. Examples include OPEC, OECD, and NATO.

Intermediate-range ballistic missile (IRBM)
A land-based missile with a range of 1700 to 3400 miles.

Internal balancing
A method for states to balance a potential competitor power through the mobilization of domestic, economic, and industrial resources—and their conversion to military power.

Internal subsides (price supports)
Government payments that allow producers to compete against imports in the home market.

International Atomic Energy Agency (IAEA)
A specialized UN agency that monitors nuclear weapons proliferation, safety of nuclear power plants, use of nuclear fuels, and disposal of nuclear waste.

International Bank for Reconstruction and Development (IBRD, or World Bank)
Established as part of the Bretton Woods system, the World Bank was initially created to help finance reconstruction after World War II. Since the 1950s and 1960s, it has lent money to lesser developed countries to finance development projects and humanitarian needs.

International Children's Emergency Fund (UNICEF)
A UN humanitarian organization under the umbrella of ECOSOC.

International division of labor
An economic theory proposed by *dependencistas,* where the South does the "dirty work" of producing raw materials while the North gets the "good jobs" in manufacturing and services; it is believed to encourage developing countries to continue exporting primary goods and discourage development of a modern manufacturing sector in Third World countries.

International law
The law of nations; a body of rules that binds states and other agents in world politics in their relations with one another.

International Monetary Fund (IMF)
Established as part of the Bretton Woods system, IMF is a global lending agency which originally was to aid industrialized nations in stabilizing their economies after the shocks of the Great Depression and World War II. Its goals today are promotion of market economies, free trade, and high growth rates.

International Red Cross
A humanitarian NGO that acts as an international relief agency and maintains strict neutrality in order to alleviate suffering without being involved in politics. Its main activities include disaster and famine relief and efforts to ensure humane treatment of prisoners of war.

International Relations
The totality of interactions, both political and non-political, among states and nonstate actors.

International system
All the states of the world—including the international organizations to which they belong; the general setting of politically relevant relations between nation-states.

Internationalism
A belief that states have no choice but to participate actively in world politics to pursue their basic interests. Problems in one part of the globe, if left unchecked, can eventually spread to every corner, so states ignore the outside world at their own peril. Nations must open their doors and minds to the world whether they like it or not.

Interpol
The International Criminal Police Organization (Interpol) created in 1923 and based in Lyons, France. Its purpose is to promote mutual assistance between all police authorities, within the limits of existing law in each country, and in the spirit of the Universal Declaration of Human Rights.

Intifada
The Palestinian uprising in the Israeli-occupied West Bank and Gaza Strip, beginning in 1987.

Invulnerability
The ability of a significant portion of a state's arsenal to survive an attack, thus guaranteeing a second strike. In the nuclear arena, both sides must have a secure second strike capability for Mutual Assured Destruction to be effective.

Irredentism
Conflicts between states caused by one state claiming territory that is controlled by another state, whether for historical reasons or because the population of that territory shares the nationality of the aggrieved state.

Isolationism
A belief that engagement with other nations is an inherently risky enterprise that affords more dangers than opportunities. Because the world is such a complex and unpredictable place, and each state's resources are limited, it is better to concentrate on solving problems at home and improving the welfare of one's own citizens. Isolationism promotes noninvolvement in the international system and the "live and let live" idea in foreign policy.

Junker
Wealthy landowners, especially in East Prussia, descended from medieval German knights who held a monopoly of civilian and military offices during the reign of Frederick the Great. A conservative group, Junkers led the unification of Germany in 1871, contributed to the rise of Adolf Hitler, and helped the Nazis undermine and overthrow the Weimar Republic in 1933.

Laissez-faire
French for "leave well enough alone," Adam Smith's economic theory that a market free from government interference produces the most benefits for all.

Lend-Lease
A plan designed by the United States early in World War II to assist those countries fighting against the Axis powers. According to this act, which became law on March 11, 1941, the president of the United States could transfer weapons, food, or equipment to any nation whose fighting against the Axis powers aided U.S. defense.

Less developed country (LDC)
A country with a per capita income of less than $3700 and one with low standards of living. Also referred to as the Third World, "developing countries," underdeveloped countries, and the South.

Levels of analysis
Categories of variables that can help decide where to begin the search for answers to questions relating to world affairs.

Limited war

A conflict fought for limited goals by limited means (that is, a war fought for less than total destruction of the enemy and less than unconditional surrender). Limited war was practiced during the Cold War as even though the superpowers possessed nuclear weapons, they did not use them in conflicts, and conflicts were kept isolated to specific locations.

Long-cycle theory

A power transition theory that attempts to explain the regular cycles of world leadership and global war, each of which lasts for approximately 100 years.

Low politics

Politics dealing with economic and domestic issues rather than national security.

Maginot Line

An extensive system of defensive fortifications established by France in 1930 along its border with Germany.

Maquiladoras

Factories located in Mexico that assemble components produced in the United States into goods that are reexported to the U.S. market.

Massive retaliation

The Eisenhower administration's strategic doctrine that Soviet-sponsored aggression would be countered with large-scale nuclear retaliation.

Material power

A state's basic material assets, covering such fundamental factors as location, geographic size, climate, natural resources, size and skills of population, and success in utilizing human and natural resources through domestic production and foreign trade.

McCarthyism

A panic over perceived Communist infiltration of the U.S. government, especially the State Department. It was started by Senator Joseph McCarthy in February 1950, following the Soviet Union's acquisition of the atomic bomb and the victory of the Chinese Communists in 1949.

Mercantilism

An economic theory that trade is a zero-sum game with the objective to gain profits at the expense of one's trading partners. Protective tariffs and other economic measures are undertaken to enhance a nation's power.

Metropole

A European home country in relation to its colonies.

Military power

The factor of power relating to the size of a state's armed forces, its quality and quantity of weaponry, training, morale, organization, and leadership.

Modernization theory

A theory that domestic, social, and political structures are key factors in national development. Supporters of this theory examine the transition from a traditional agrarian economy to a modern capitalist economy, and contend that it can be achieved via open markets and investment in physical, financial, and human capital.

Monopsony

A condition where only one buyer exists for a product, which therefore effectively sets the price.

Most-favored nation status (MFN)

A principle of granting equal treatment to all signatories participating in a trade agreement. The countries involved in such an agreement promise each other that both countries' goods will receive the best terms available in their respective markets.

Motivational bias

A psychological bias related to basic motives, such as fear or desire, that causes the policy maker to distort or ignore information.

Motivational power

The willingness of a government and its population to take an active part in world affairs. A state's determination to see that conflicts are resolved in its favor, and its ability to translate goals and resources into concrete actions.

Multilateral aid
Aid channeled to countries through international organizations, specifically the World Bank and the International Monetary Fund (IMF), usually in the form of loans from the international organization to the recipient government.

Multilateral
Involving more than two parties.

Multinational corporations (MNCs)
Large corporations with branches in many countries, headquarters in the North, and huge investments throughout the world. Examples include General Motors, Pepsi Co., IBM, Sony, and Shell Oil.

Multiple independently-targeted reentry vehicle (MIRV)
A single ballistic missile with several warheads that can each hit a separate target.

Multipolar system (Multipolarity)
A structure of the international system in which more than two states, roughly equal in power, dominate.

Mutual and Balanced Force Reductions (MBFR)
Talks which strove fruitlessly from 1973 to 1986 to reduce NATO and Warsaw Pact conventional forces.

Mutual assured destruction (MAD)
A condition that exists when both sides are able to survive a first strike with sufficient nuclear forces to retaliate in a second strike and inflict unacceptable damage on their opponent. Thus, both would be destroyed regardless of which struck first, and therefore neither has an incentive to initiate a nuclear war.

Nasserism
A cult of personality that made Egyptian President Gamal Abdel Nasser appear to be the leader of all Arabs in the 1950s and 1960s; it became identified with a new revolutionary nationalism and promoted Pan-Arabism.

Nation
A group of people that views itself as having a common heritage, destiny, and sense of mutual identification based on language, history, and culture.

Nation-state
A state structure in which a nation resides and exists (ideally) to protect and promote the interests of that nation. Examples include France, Turkey, Japan, and Brazil.

Nationalism
The belief that all nations should have their own state.

Nationalistic states (19th-century style)
For these states, nationalism remains the central motivation of political activity; nothing has changed to ameliorate historical enmities. They are dominated by nationalist hostilities both within and outside of state boundaries and are culturally, politically, and economically unable to adapt to changing world conditions. Many of these countries are ruled by corrupt regimes or governments organized around outdated models of social and economic development.

Natural law
The approach to international law which claims that universal principles can be derived from human nature or "the mind of God" through the use of human reason. This notion of unchangeable laws as eternal verities leads to an emphasis on human rights.

Neoliberal institutionalism
A school of thought contending that the anarchy of the international system can be overcome through carefully designed institutions for international cooperation.

Neorealism
See Structural realism.

New International Economic Order (NIEO)
A 1974 declaration on the establishment of a New International Economic Order adopted by the UN General Assembly. The proposals were originally

advanced by countries of the South for eliminating the economic inequities between them and the advanced industrial nations of the North.

Newly industrialized countries (NICs)

Developing countries that are characterized by rapid growth of manufactured goods; includes states such as Brazil, Mexico, and the Four Tigers (Hong Kong, Singapore, Taiwan, and South Korea); Asian NICs come closest to bridging the gap between the First and Third Worlds.

Nongovernmental organizations (NGOs)

Groups not directly related to governments but that are organized to take an active part in international affairs. Examples include terrorist, religious, and humanitarian organizations.

Nonproliferation Treaty

Signed in 1968, the treaty provides that signatory nations without nuclear weapons will not seek to build them and will accept safeguards to prevent diversion of nuclear material and technology from peaceful uses to weapons programs. Nations in possession of nuclear weapons at the signing of the treaty agreed not to help non-nuclear states gain access to nuclear weapons, but to offer access to peaceful nuclear technology.

Nonaligned movement

During the Cold War, a movement through which leaders of some states did not pursue a formal alliance with one superpower, but rather found it beneficial to play off one against the other in the hope of gaining aid from both. Leaders of the Nonaligned Movement included Jawaharlal Nehru of India, Gamal Abdel Nasser of Egypt, and Marshall Tito of Yugoslavia.

Nonexcludability

A characteristic of public goods in which once enough contributors have financed the good, others can enjoy the benefits of the public good without contributing to its maintenance.

Normative influences

A source of restraint that prevents democracies from rushing into conflict. Proponents argue that democratic states share a common democratic political culture, and all expect to apply its method of resolving conflict at home to resolving international disputes amicably, without resorting to war. Therefore, the argument holds that democratic nations draw upon their democratic norms (elections, compromise, debates, and judicial judgment) to prevent international conflicts from escalating into war, at least between them.

Norms

General rules and principles established by international regimes to facilitate cooperation between states. Norms are frequently formalized in treaties, which in turn often create institutions and/or organizations to provide states with opportunities to meet and discuss their common problems.

North American Free Trade Agreement (NAFTA)

An agreement between Canada, the United States, and Mexico that created a free-trade area within North America and which went into effect January 1, 1994.

North Atlantic Treaty Organization (NATO)

A formal security agreement between the United States, Canada, and the nations of Western Europe, established in April 1949 to deter Soviet aggression.

NSC-68

A document prepared by the U.S. National Security Council in early 1950 to address the issue of what should be done to counter the spread of international communism. NSC-68 called for expansion of America's armed forces, adding an important military dimension to the economic and political means of containment.

Nuclear proliferation

States acquiring nuclear weapons that did not formerly possess them.

Nuclear triad

Three-pronged capability to deliver nuclear weapons using manned bombers, ICBMs, and SLBMs. This defense posture seeks to preserve a capability to answer a First Strike; should one leg of the triad be attacked and destroyed, the other two legs would survive.

Observer mission
One of the three types of UN missions; international forces that are present to observe a cease-fire organized by or for the opposing forces in a dispute.

Operational codes
Both a system of beliefs and a guide to action utilized by policy makers as a way to translate their fundamental moral and political beliefs into policy decisions.

Organization for Economic Cooperation and Development (OECD)
Composed of advanced industrial states, OECD was formed in 1961 to promote economic and social welfare in member countries and to stimulate and harmonize efforts on behalf of developing nations.

Organization of African Unity (OAU)
A general purpose IGO that promoted decolonization in Africa and which now focuses on regional development and the settlement of regional disputes.

Organization of American States (OAS)
An organization that includes most nations of the Western Hemisphere, it addresses a number of regional concerns.

Organization of Petroleum Exporting Countries (OPEC)
An intergovernmental cartel of oil exporting countries whose goal is to collectively raise the price of crude oil on the world market.

Organizational process model (OPM)
When confronted with a foreign policy problem, organizations follow a prescribed set of decision-making guidelines, or standard operating procedures (SOPs). This almost mechanical process for formulating routine recommendations does not necessarily calculate the advantages or disadvantages of available options. Indeed, it can contribute to policy inertia and behavior that appears rigid, inflexible, and unimaginitive.

Ostpolitik
West German Chancellor Willy Brandt's eastern policy, begun in 1969, that signaled Western aspirations for more contact with, and more independence for, Eastern Europe through conciliation rather than confrontation. Part of *Ostpolitik* involved reversing previous policy by accepting the existence of East Germany and Germany's post–1945 borders.

Pan-Arabism
The idea that all Arabs should belong to a single state.

Panchsheel
Jawaharlal Nehru's set of foreign policy principles, which included respect for other countries' sovereignty and territorial integrity, nonaggression, noninterference in the internal affairs of others, equality and mutual benefit, and peaceful coexistence.

Pariah states
States that consistently prove they cannot be trusted at their word and thereby become ostracized by the world community.

Parity
An equal distribution of power among a group of states in the international system.

Parity school
A division of realism contending that an equal distribution of capability among states creates stability and that war is much more likely to occur when one state is the dominant power.

Peace-enforcement mission
One of the three types of UN missions; these troops observe, act as a buffer, and as a last resort, are allowed to use military force to keep the peace in a particular locale.

Peace of Westphalia
The 1648 treaty that ended the 30 Years' War and marked the beginning of the modern international system by legitimizing the state as the ultimate sovereign authority over people and geographic territory.

Peacekeeping mission
One of the three types of UN missions; these troops not only observe a cease-fire, but also act as a buffer between the two sides of a conflict.

Perestroika
Mikhail Gorbachev's policy for restructuring the economy of the Soviet Union, it promoted democratization, increased privatization of the economy, and created free markets.

Plebiscite
A vote used to determine the desire of a population concerning an area of great public interest.

Polarity
A term referring to the number of major powers, or "poles," in the international system.

Political culture
The fusing of a nation's historical traditions to its cultural institutions and values to form a national style of politics and policy making.

Positive law
A belief that international law exists only through those rules to which states have consented in writing, usually in treaties, or otherwise clearly recognized.

Power
The ability to convince another state do what it would not normally do.

Power projection
The ability of a state to deploy its military forces to distant locations.

Power transition theory
A theory arguing that as the gap in power between rival states narrows and they become more equal in strength, war is likely to occur, since both the challenger and the dominant state believe they are likely to prevail in a conflict.

Preemptive strike
A defensive attack carried out when a fundamental threat to vital interests is identified or when an attack by an opponent is believed to be imminent.

The underlying motivation holds that "the best defense is a good offense."

Preponderance
Dominance of the international system by a single state.

Preponderance school
A division of realism contending that stability is more likely when one state dominates the system, rather than when there is an equal distribution of power.

Price inelasticity
An economic principle that people purchase goods regardless of price.

Primary deterrence
A strategy intended to dissuade a challenger from attacking a state's own territory. It is synonymous with deterrence.

Primary products
Raw materials and agricultural goods upon which most developing nations' economies depend for foreign hard currency through exports.

Prisoners' Dilemma
A model derived from game theory designed to explain the difficulties states experience cooperating in the international system. If both actors in the Prisoners' Dilemma act in their self-interest, each will defect, leading to an unfavorable outcome.

Private aid
International aid donated by individuals and groups through nongovernmental organizations so as to bypass the government, usually for humanitarian purposes or economic development projects.

Privatization
The sale of firms owned by the government to the private sector.

Protectionism
An economic theory pertaining to a system of trade barriers erected to protect domestic industries from foreign competition. Also known as "managed trade," proponents believe barriers should be

erected to protect important industries and high-paying jobs, even if consumers must pay higher prices for goods or pay subsidies through increased taxes.

Public opinion
Views and attitudes on national issues held by the people of a nation, with particular emphasis placed on elite views and media influence. The role of the public in shaping foreign relations can take the form of elections, referenda, or work slowdowns.

Rational actor model
A model of decision making that sees a perfectly rational decision maker who gathers all relevant facts, carefully weighs all available evidence, and selects a course of action offering the greatest benefits in relation to costs.

Rationality
The ability of a decision maker to make and rank cost-benefit comparisons among possible options.

Reagan Doctrine
The Reagan administration's abandonment of détente and return to an assertive form of containment. This was characterized by both direct U.S. intervention and especially by indirect support of anticommunist insurgencies.

Realism
A theory contending that distribution of relative power within the international system has a profound effect on how nations act and on overall stability of the system. A view of world politics which states that in the anarchic international system, states have no choice but to preserve their vital interests through whatever means are available.

Realpolitik
Literally, the "policy of realism" or power politics, a promotion of policies that seek to maximize a nation's security and power in a cold, cruel world in which all other states have no choice but to do the same.

Reciprocity
A response in kind. A mutual exchange, particularly involving privileges between two countries.

Regime type
The general structure and underlying philosophy of a state's political system (democratic, authoritarian, liberal, Communist, and so on). Many domestic level theorists argue that the type of regime that governs a state can exert a powerful influence on the nature of that state's foreign policy.

Regime
A neoliberal institution in which rules or practices are generally accepted by a group of states to help them work together in an otherwise anarchic world.

Relative power
A state's power in comparison to other states in the international system.

Reputation
A nation's track record in world affairs and its perceived ability to accomplish the goals it sets for itself. Reputation can be based upon military success or failure, demonstrated willingness to employ force, economic success, ideology, or moral standing.

Revanchism
The desire for revenge, especially after a loss in war.

Rural–urban cleavages
Often generated in initial stages of development, a rift between urban and rural groups that occurs when an economy first shifts away from subsistence agriculture toward industry.

Schemas
Generic concepts stored in an individual's memory that help process information more quickly and efficiently. They refer to objects, situations, events, or people.

Sea-launched cruise missile
A cruise missile launched from a ship or submarine. *See* cruise missile.

Second strike
Ability to retaliate, even after a nuclear attack, and thus punish the initiator of a nuclear war.

Second World

A term used especially during the Cold War to apply to the bloc of countries consisting of Communist nations of the former Soviet Union and Eastern Europe. The Second World has varying standard-of-living levels and is currently dealing with problems in the transition from communism to a market-oriented economic system.

Sector approach

An analytical framework for understanding how conditions in the international economy affect domestic politics. This approach focuses on sectors of the economy (that is, groups of related industries). It assumes that capital is fixed in a particular industrial sector, meaning that increased foreign competition might hurt some capital owners more than others.

Security Council

The principal organ of the United Nations, responsible for the preservation of peace and security. It is charged with organizing collective security operations and dispatching observer missions and peacekeeping troops around the world. This body has the right to investigate any dispute or situation that might lead to international friction, and to recommend methods of settlement.

Security dilemma

The situation which rises when a state feels insecure and decides that its best policy in the anarchic context of world politics is to increase its military strength. As its potential adversary does the same, an unintended spiral occurs where every nation grows more and more insecure and seeks to stay equal to its neighbors in military strength.

Sensitivity

A dimension of interdependence referring to the speed and extent with which changes in one country can bring about changes in another.

Smoot-Hawley Tariff Act

A tariff passed by Congress in 1930 in an attempt to protect U.S. jobs. This act raised prices on all imports by 19 percent; some reached as high as 55 percent. Foreign countries responded by raising tariffs of their own, thereby spreading and deepening the Great Depression. Such a course of action is called a "beggar-thy-neighbor policy."

Socialism

A belief that productive assets should be owned collectively (which in practice means by the state) in order to maximize the benefits to society.

Societal theories

Arguments contending that the state's national interest is reflected by the strength of organized domestic interests (agricultural, industrial, environmental, and so on). Therefore, the state's national interest is determined by the success of domestic interest groups in promoting their needs, concerns, and objectives.

Solidarity

A popular labor union begun in the 1970s in Poland led by Lech Walesa. Solidarity made political and economic demands on the Communist government for many years before winning elections and assuming power under a new constitution in 1989.

Sovereign

Independent of all others; possessing supreme political authority.

Spheres of influence

A region influenced by one great power. In a sphere of influence, the dominant power does not have sovereignty but imposes its will over several neighboring states, restricting the maneuverability of local territorial leaders.

Spreading the alternatives

A part of bolstering whereby decision makers magnify expected gains from a preferred option, while discounting expected gains and exaggerating expected drawbacks of rejected options.

Stagflation

A combination of low or stagnant economic growth, coupled with high rates of inflation.

Standard operating procedures (SOPs)
Entrenched routines used by organizations (bureaucracies) to evaluate specific policies and their options. When making these evaluations, organizations follows set guidelines that can lead to inertia, or inflexible and rigid solutions. Once triggered, SOPs can be difficult to reverse.

State
An independent political entity with institutions and authority in a specific territory.

Statist theories
Theories that focus on the foreign policy implications of a state's institutional and governmental structures. The statist theory contends that the state's form of government (democratic, socialist, authoritarian, and so on) and/or political institutions (electoral process, specialized bureaucracies, legislature, character of its executive, and constitutional division of power and responsibility) shape the interests and behavior of states in the international arena.

Strategic Defense Initiative (SDI)
A 1980s U.S. program that proposed the creation of a highly ambitious ballistic missile defense system that would produce a total defense against strategic nuclear weapons and missile systems. Also known as "Star Wars," SDI threatened to upset the nuclear balance of power by giving the United States an ability to launch a first strike without fear of a Soviet counterattack. Its potential effectiveness was controversial.

Strategic nuclear forces
Nuclear forces designed to attack long-range targets, including cities.

Strategic weapon
A weapon that strikes directly at a nation's home territory and the industry, resources, population, or military forces located there.

Structural adjustment programs
Policies undertaken to meet the conditions placed on loans from international lending institutions. These include opening markets to imports, devaluating overvalued currencies, and reducing government spending, price controls and subsidies, and direct state ownership of industries.

Structural realism
A philosophy that contends the structure of the international system, rather than innate human aggressiveness, accounts for the behavior of states. Also known as Neorealism, structural realism places emphasis on the actions of the most powerful states, the "great powers."

Structure of the international system
The distribution of power among the major actors in the international system, characterized by the number of great powers in the system and their relative capabilities.

Submarine-launched ballistic missile (SLBM)
A long-range ballistic missile carried in and launched from a submarine.

Subsidies
Government payments to domestic industries that allow producers to price their goods below the cost of production without going out of business.

Subsistence agriculture
Hand-to-mouth farming for direct consumption by one's family.

Systemic level of analysis
A method for analyzing international relations according to factors that arise from the nature and structure of the world political system. The factors that influence individual states are external to the states, coming from the attributes of the system itself.

Tactical nuclear weapons
Weapons designed to attack short- or medium-range (between 95 and 310 miles) targets, primarily conventional military assets.

Tactical weapon
A weapon designed for use on the battlefield, often in support of ground troops.

Tariff
A tax imposed on an imported good.

Terms of trade

The ratio of export prices to import prices. If a country's export prices are rising faster than prices of the goods it imports, its terms of trade are increasing; if import prices are increasing faster than export prices, its terms of trade are declining.

Thermonuclear weapon

An explosive device that derives its power from nuclear fusion, or the coming together of atoms (usually hydrogen or helium; this is the same process that gives the sun its energy). Also called a hydrogen bomb.

Third World

More than 160 underdeveloped/developing non-western nations in Africa, Asia, Latin America, and the Middle East, accounting for three-fourths of the global population. Third World nations frequently depend on the export of a single commodity or raw material.

Tit-for-tat

A neoliberal institutional practice of cooperating with another actor on the first round, and then mimicking its moves on all subsequent rounds to convince it that you will cooperate when it does—as well as cheat when it does. These practices are designed to encourage cooperation.

Total war

War fought to obtain the political objective of complete victory over the enemy. In order to achieve this goal, full mobilization of a country's military, economic, and social resources is undertaken (as in World War II).

Trade deficit

A balance of trade in which imports exceed exports.

Trade surplus

A balance of trade in which exports exceed imports.

Transfer pricing mechanisms

Schemes pursued by MNCs to transfer profits to countries where taxes are lower.

Transitional states (twentieth-century style)

Governments that are caught in a tense and constant vise between their impressive, even surprising, technical and scientific achievements in certain areas and their economic crises and social tensions, which often lead to political instability, even upheaval. Democracy is present or incipient for many of these states; however, most transitional states have had a poor political record regarding rights and liberties. Quite often, socialism or communism dominated in the past and stifled growth and economic efficiency.

Treaties

Documents similar to written contracts in that they impose obligations only on the parties that sign them. Also known as charters, pacts, conventions, or covenants, they are some of the main sources of international law.

Treaty of Versailles

The agreement signed in 1919 at Versailles, France, which formally ended World War I.

Truman Doctrine

A strategy outlined in a speech given before Congress by President Harry Truman on March 12, 1947. The Truman Doctrine pledged U.S. military and economic aid to countries (initially Greece and Turkey) to resist communism. This doctrine is regarded by many as a U.S. "declaration of the Cold War."

Unipolarity

A structure of the international state system in which a single state dominates the system.

United Nations (UN)

A worldwide IGO established in 1945 as the successor to the defunct League of Nations for the purpose of promoting international peace, security, and cooperation in a variety of diplomatic, economic, and social fields.

United Nations Convention on the Law of the Sea (UNCLOS)

A 1982 agreement that divides the world's oceans into public (free access) and private (regulated access) property zones for the purpose of regulating competition over the finite resources of the world's oceans.

United Nations Educational, Scientific, and Cultural Organization (UNESCO)
A specialized agency of the United Nations that attempts to improve literacy rates in the Third World, promote scientific and cultural exchange, and facilitate the distribution of information.

Urbanization
Rapid growth of cities that is frequently accompanied by overcrowding, unemployment, and crime; a major consequence of demographic transition and industrialization.

Value complexity
A situation that brings two or more conflicting values into a decision.

Voluntary export restrictions (VERs)
A situation in which a state sometimes compels another nation to "voluntarily" limit its exports in order to protect the domestic economy.

Vulnerability
The degree to which a state can suffer costs imposed by external events even after policies have been altered in response to them.

War of attrition
A strategy that aims to defeat the opposition by wearing it out. Attrition can be costly in terms of men and matériel. World War I is a classic example.

War of secession
A situation in which disagreements are so profound and intractable that one or more competing national groups deny the very legitimacy of the state and attempt to break away from it and form a new state, or join another state.

War of unification
A war waged to create a single nation-state for an ethnic group previously divided among several different states.

Warhead
The explosive device that a missile delivers to a target.

World Bank
See International Bank for Reconstruction and Development.

World federalism
A possible world order in which all countries unite in a huge, global state.

World Health Organization (WHO)
A humanitarian organization established in 1948 under the ECOSOC umbrella of the UN. WHO aids in the development of national health administrations and provides advisory services.

World politics
The competition for, and exercise of, power and authority in the international system.

Zero-sum game
A situation in which one state's gain is seen as another's loss, encouraging intense competition between the two powers.

Zionism
A political, religious, and social movement that called for the establishment of a national homeland for the Jewish people in the region of the Middle East known as Palestine. Today, Zionists promote political, economic, financial and military support for Israel, and the resettlement of Jews in Israel.

Zollverein
A German customs union that abolished tariffs between German states. Established January 1, 1834, the *Zollverein* resulted in increased industrial prosperity, German economic unity, and beginning in 1867, a common German parliament for economic matters. It marked a significant step in the process of political unification, which was completed with the proclamation of the German empire in 1871.

Index